Culture and Leadership Across the World:
The GLOBE Book of In-Depth Studies of 25 Societies

T0304237

Edited by

Jagdeep S. Chhokar
Felix C. Brodbeck
Robert J. House

Culture and Leadership Across the World:
The GLOBE Book of In-Depth Studies of 25 Societies

Edited by

Jagdeep S. Chhokar
Indian Institute of Management, Ahmedabad
Felix C. Brodbeck
Aston Business School, Aston University
Robert J. House
Wharton School of Management, University of Pennsylvania

Routledge
Taylor & Francis Group

LONDON AND NEW YORK

First published 2008 by Lawrence Erlbaum Associates
2 Park Square, Milton Park, Abingdon, Oxon OX14 4RN
605 Third Avenue, New York, NY 10017

Routledge is an imprint of the Taylor & Francis Group, an informa business

First issued in paperback 2019

ISBN-13: 978-0-8058-5997-3 (hbk)
ISBN-13: 978-0-367-86666-2 (pbk)

Contents

Series Foreword

Our series is intended to be very much about theoretical and methodological innovations in the study of management and organizations. In terms of such innovations, the Global Leadership and Organizational Behavior Effectiveness (GLOBE) Research Project is a monumental winner. GLOBE's hundred plus investigators studied, across 61 countries, the interplay between culture and organizational form to address the conditions under which leaders matter in terms of both economic and social outcomes. We are pleased to become affiliated with the GLOBE enterprise by including this volume: *Culture and Leadership Across the World: The GLOBE Book of 25 Societies* in our series. The volume contains in-depth analyses of culture and leadership in 25 countries. Readers, for example, will travel from Finland to Austria, from Australia to France, from Argentina to Greece, and from Turkey to China, learning all the way about these countries—their cultures and leadership climates. We hope you enjoy it.

—*Arthur P. Brief, University of Utah*
—*James P. Walsh, University of Michigan*

To my parents, Ma and Bhaiji,
and my wife, Kiran
—Jagdeep S. Chhokar

To my partner Mechthild,
and our sons Moritz and Noah
—Felix C. Brodbeck

To Daniel Ken House, Timothy Martin House
and Mary Kathleen Goldman
—Robert J. House

Foreword

It is obvious that globalization is the name of the game in business, and no large firms can afford to ignore their overseas markets. Toyota has 39 overseas production centers in 24 countries, Microsoft has offices in over 60 countries, and Nestlé operates in over 80 countries. Even firms from emerging economies are keen to globalize. Haier, a Chinese firm that sells household appliances, conducts business in over 160 nations and operates manufacturing facilities in many countries, including the United States, Italy, Iran, Jordan, Malaysia, and Vietnam.

Our research enterprise lags embarrassingly behind the multinationals in its international reach. A business executive who takes a cursory look at the leading journals in management would no doubt notice that management research is conducted mostly in one place, the United States, and occasionally in a Western European country. One exception is the surge in the number of papers on China, perhaps because China has recently led the world in terms of direct foreign investments (Leung & White, 2004). In any event, our current literature probably reminds this executive of a bygone era some 40 years ago, when most large organizations were based in the West and their primary focus was the Western markets. The international department in these firms was small and peripheral, and typically people on the way down or out were sent overseas.

GLOBALIZING OUR RESEARCH EFFORTS

The GLOBE project is a rare exception to the parochialism of the management literature. With the participation of approximately 17,300 middle managers from 950 organizations in 62 countries, the scale of this project rivals a large multinational corporation. Aside from its theoretical contributions, this project is ground-breaking in demonstrating how management research can be globalized on a scale that is comparable to the best multinationals. The GLOBE project is perhaps the most large-scale international management research project that has ever been undertaken, involving some 170 coinvestigators from 62 participating countries.

Although how the GLOBE team has been operating may be worth the while of a scientific exploration, we know for sure that the complexity of this enterprise has not jeopardized its effectiveness. Peterson (2001) has provided an astute analysis of international research collaborations and a framework for classifying such collaborations based on a taxonomy of multinational corporations. The GLOBE project is classified into the global category, with the logic for collaboration being "collaborative, common research design," and its utility being "design globally comprehensive theory learning from prior work plus experiences of colleagues" (p. 70). More important to my analysis is that the potential risks and stresses of this type of collaborations include "easy to romanticize. Hard, perhaps sometimes impractical to manage. Easily devolves into international due to varying resource control and available time" (p. 70). "International" in this quote refers to the research goal of evaluating the generalizability of some domestic research in other cultural settings, which lacks originality as compared to global research. In addition, Peterson has provided some examples of dysfunctional dynamics that may threaten a global project, including horse trading (nonsynergistic exchanges), manipulating (uncooperative behaviors that range from passive to aggressive), and expropriating (dominance by those who are resourceful). To overcome such negative dynamics, Peterson has proposed four strategies: a social contract, fostering trust, self-development of collaborators, and an influential leadership and a clear hierarchy. Peterson used the GLOBE project to illustrate the last strategy, and regarded Bob House, the founder and key driver of the project, as an influential, resourceful leader, which is pivotal to the success of the project.

I would add that the GLOBE project also scores high on the first three strategies. The project team assumes a network structure, with Bob House and his key team playing the leading and organizing role. Participants are clear about their roles and obligations as a result of intense face- to-face and written communications. The successful completion of such a colossal project and the consistency displayed by the 25 country-specific chapters in this volume testify to the effectiveness of the social contract that has guided this geographically dispersed, loosely connected team of coinvestigators. Trust among the coinvestigators is evident as they freely exchange ideas and receive credit for their contributions in terms of publications and conference presentations. I was in the audience of a couple of GLOBE symposia, and I was struck by the sincere effort to put all the presenters in the limelight, regardless of whether they were part of the core team or just coinvestigators. I also participated in a couple of informal meetings of the project team to share some ideas on methodological issues, and I witnessed firsthand the free and open exchange among the coinvestigators. Finally, with regard to self-development opportunities, the chapters in this volume make it clear that there is a structured mechanism for individual team members to contribute their local and general knowledge to the project through a variety of physical as well as cyber means. In fact, local knowledge was given a critical role in the planning stage of this project, and the publication of this volume on culture-specific results is a continuous echo of this emphasis. I am sure that the coinvestigators of this project benefit not only from the publications and conference presentations arising from the project, but also from the formal and informal exchange of ideas and expertise.

In summary, the GLOBE project provides a compelling demonstration that with passion, dedication, trust, and ample research funds, an enormous project spanning across many national borders is not only possible, but fruitful. The logistics problems are harsh and trying, but they can be overcome by zeal and curiosity.

CULTURAL DECENTERING AS A STRATEGY FOR GLOBAL RESEARCH

Van de Vijver and Leung (1997) have proposed that an effective way to design a culturally balanced study is to adopt the decentered approach, which involves input from diverse cultural backgrounds to the development of conceptual frameworks and the design of empirical work. The GLOBE project exemplifies this approach. The definition and content of culture and leadership dimensions were the result of collective wisdom gleaned from the first GLOBE research conference in 1994, with the participation of 54 researchers from 38 countries. Furthermore, coinvestigators contributed items to the instruments used, sharpened and reworded items to render them culturally appropriate, assisted in the translation of the instruments, and aided in the interpretation of the results based on indigenous research and unique cultural knowledge. The chapters in this volume document the extensive effort to avoid the dominance of American notions of leadership, and how diverse cultural inputs shaped the final constructs, dimensions, and frameworks emerged from the project.

In globalizing our research effort, diversity in our theorizing is crucial, and I may even go so far as to say that this is a primary reason why we want to go global. Darwin has shown us the supreme value of diversity to the survival and adaptation of species. In the business world, although some people have argued for an inevitable consequence of globalization, isomorphism, the evidence for diversity is mounting (for a recent study documenting divergence in a very global industry, the computer industry, see Duysters & Hagedoorn, 2001). Firms have not become more alike as a result of operating and competing in a global market. Diversity in ideas, constructs, and instruments sprung from global research will ultimately lead to richer, more complete, and more general management theories.

GENERALITY VERSUS RICHNESS

A major strength of the GLOBE project is the deployment of diverse methodologies, both quantitative and qualitative, to enhance the robustness and richness of the findings. The catch from this odyssey is impressive. Nine culture dimensions were identified: Assertiveness, Future Orientation, Gender Egalitarianism, Humane Orientation, Institutional Collectivism, In-Group Collectivism, Performance Orientation, Power Distance, and Uncertainty Avoidance. Six of them correspond to the well-known culture dimensions of Hofstede (1980, 1997), and the remaining three dimensions are also grounded in previous literature. Future Orientation is related to the Past, Present, Future Orientation dimension of Kluckhohn and Strodtbeck (1961); Performance Orientation corresponds to need for achievement (McClelland, 1961); and Humane Orientation is related to the Human Nature Is Good vs. Human Nature Is Bad dimension of Kluckhohn and Strodtbeck, Putnam's (1993) work on the Civic Society, and McClelland's (1985) conceptualization of the affiliative motive.

With regard to leadership behaviors, a total of 21 leadership dimensions were identified, which were found to constitute six factors: Team-Oriented Leadership, Charismatic/Value-Based Leadership, Autonomous Leadership, Humane Leadership, Participative leadership, and Self- Protective Leadership.

A major criticism of this type of etic (culture-general) research for identifying pan-cultural constructs and dimensions is their high level of abstraction and its neglect of subtle, but important local variations and nuances (Morris, Leung, Ames, & Lickel, 1999). An obvious, but hard-to-do, remedy is to augment these etic constructs and frameworks with the richness of emic (culture-specific) concepts and findings (Yang, 2000). This volume, with its richness of culture-specific findings and insights, constitutes an important step of the GLOBE project in giving the etic skeleton flesh and blood. Combining qualitative and quantitative results, and drawing on the extant cultural knowledge and indigenous research on leadership, each of the 25 country-specific chapters describes how leadership is conceptualized and enacted in its cultural milieu, and explores how emic dynamics are related to the etic constructs and frameworks derived from the GLOBE project. It is exactly this type of synergistic integration of culture-general and culture-specific knowledge that is able to address the respective deficiencies of pan-cultural and indigenous research.

IS THE EFFORT WORTH IT?

I would like to end by addressing the bottom-line question. Firms go global not because they love the global village, but because global business is good business. So one may raise the issue of return on investment: Is the new knowledge garnered worth the resources that have gone into the GLOBE project? Only time will tell whether a project actually pays off, and it will perhaps be 10 years from now before we will know for sure. However, all the earlier signals are good, and the pan-cultural dimensions identified and the culture-specific findings obtained will definitely become a major driving force of leadership research in the coming decade.

Although the substantive findings of the GLOBE project are important and valuable in their own right, I want to point out three very important side products that I alluded to earlier. First, this project has leapfrogged management research into the global era by demonstrating how a truly global effort can be sustained and achieved successfully. I hope that the GLOBE project will inspire many others to undertake similarly ambitious global research projects.

Second, the GLOBE project has highlighted many of the theoretical and methodological pitfalls that we encounter in our endeavor to develop universal management theories. I hope this project will bring such conceptual and methodological problems that plague global research to the forefront. It is regrettable that there has not been much progress in solving these problems in the last decade, and more intense research effort into these barriers will hopefully make global research less perplexing and more enlightening and gratifying.

Finally, the GLOBE project has demonstrated a balance of generality and richness as well as a laudable attempt to address cross-level issues. The call for multimethod, multilevel research has been around for decades, but genuine responses to this call are rare. The GLOBE project reminds us of the different limitations of different conceptual and methodological orientations, and of the need to be integrative and pluralistic in our research enterprises. The GLOBE project will go down in the history of management research as a hallmark for diversity, inclusiveness, richness, and multilateralism.

—Kwok Leung
City University of Hong Kong

REFERENCES

Duysters, G., & Hagedoorn, J. (2001). Do company strategies and structures converge in global markets? Evidence from the computer industry. *Journal of International Business Studies, 32,* 347–356.

Hofstede, G. (1980). *Culture's consequences: International differences in work-related values.* Beverly Hills, CA: Sage.

Hofstede, G. (1997). *Cultures and organizations: The software of the mind.* New York: McGraw-Hill.

Kluckhohn, F., & Strodtbeck, F. L. (1961). *Variations in value orientations.* Evanston, IL: Row, Peterson.

Leung, K., & White, S. (Eds.). (2004). *Handbook of Asian Management.* New York: Kluwer.

McClelland, D. C. (1961). *The achieving society.* Princeton, NJ: Van Nostrand.

McClelland, D. C. (1985). *Human motivation.* Glenview, IL: Scott, Foresman.

Morris, M. W., Leung, K., Ames, D., & Lickel, B. (1999). Incorporating perspectives from inside and outside: Synergy between *emic* and *etic* research on culture and justice. *Academy of Management Review, 24,* 781–796.

Peterson, M. F. (2001). International collaboration in organizational behavior research. *Journal of Organizational Behavior, 22,* 59–81.

Putnam, R. D. (1993). *Making democracy work.* Princeton, NJ: Princeton University Press.

Van de Vijver, F., & Leung, K. (1997). *Methods and data analysis for cross-cultural research.* Thousand Oaks, CA: Sage.

Yang, K. S. (2000). Monocultural and cross-cultural indigenous approaches: The royal road to the development of a balanced global psychology. *Asian Journal of Social Psychology, 4,* 241–263.

About the Authors

Staffan Åkerblom is a program director and head of the International Management Program at the Swedish Institute of Management. He is also a doctoral candidate (Ph.Lic) at the Stockholm School of Economics. His research interests and previous publications are focused around conceptions of managerial leadership in various industrial and social contexts.

Carlos Altschul teaches international negotiation at FLACSO/Universidad de San Andrés; negotiation in School of Economics at Buenos Aires University; and organization change at Buenos Aires University and Universidad Siglo XXI, Córdoba. He has directed major consulting projects for AngloGold, DaimlerChrysler, EXXON, Scotiabank, Goodyear, and directed training for Novartis, American Express, Cargill, Bayer, Shell, and Scania. He studied chemical engineering at Buenos Aires University and was awarded MS and PhD degrees from Iowa State University. He recently published *Estar de Paso: Consultant roles and Responsibilities* (Granica) and *Transformando: Prácticas de Cambio en Empresas Argentinas* (University of Buenos Aires Press). Address: Urquiza 1835, (1602) Florida, PBA, Argentina. Telephone: 54 011 4 797 8737. Fax: 54 011 4 797 8745. E-mail: altschul@satlink.com.

Marina Altschul is assistant professor in organization development at the Universidad de Buenos Aires, and is a consultant on group dynamics, coaching, and leadership issues. She designs and coordinates multiyear training projects for leading national and international corporations, such as American Express, Bayer, BankBoston, Banco de Galicia, Cerro Vanguardia, OSDE, Telecom Personal, and Unilever. She graduated from the School of Agronomics, University of Buenos Aires. Address: General Lavalle 2035, (1602) Florida, PBA, Argentina. Telephone: 54 011 4 718 0595. E-mail: marinaaltschul@fibertel.com.

Neal Ashkanasy is professor of management in the UQ Business School, University of Queensland. He came into academic life after an 18-year career in professional engineering and management, and has since worked in the schools of psychology, commerce, engineering, management, and business. He has a PhD (1989) in social and organizational psychology from the University of Queensland, and has research interests in leadership, organizational culture, and business ethics. In recent years, however, his research has focused on the role of emotions in organizational life. He has published his work in journals such as the *Academy of Management Review*, the *Academy of Management Executive*, *Accounting, Organizations and Society*, the *Journal of Management*, the *Journal of Organizational Behavior*, the *Journal of Personality and Social Psychology* and *Organizational Behavior and Human Decision Processes*. He is coeditor of three books: *The Handbook of Organizational Culture and Climate* (Sage), *Emotions in the Workplace; Theory, Research, and Practice* (Quorum), and *Managing Emotions in the Workplace* (M. E. Sharpe), with a fourth under contract with Lawrence Erlbaum Associates. In addition, he administers two e-mail discussion lists: *Orgcult*, the Organizational Culture Caucus list; and *Emonet*, the Emotions in the Workplace list. He has organized three gatherings of the *International Conference on Emotions in Organizational Life* and planned the fourth conference that was held in England in July 2004.

Professor Ashkanasy is also on the editorial boards of the *Academy of Management Journal,* the *Journal of Organizational Behavior, Applied Psychology: An International Review,* and the *Journal of Management.* He is a past chair of the Managerial and Organizational Cognition Division of the Academy of Management.

J. Arnoldo Bautista has an Engineering Interdisciplinary PhD (civil engineering, industrial engineering, crop and soil sciences) from New Mexico State University and a Master of Science, Industrial Engineering from New Mexico State University. His work experience includes *director,* Research and Technology Development National Center (*CENIDET*), 2000–present; *academic dean,* Research and Technology Development National Center (*CENIDET*), 1998–2000; *executive director,* Solar Energy National Association (ANES), 1998–2000; *vice-minister,* Ministry of Agriculture Development, Chihuahua state government, 1996–1998; *office head,* Office of Agriculture Marketing, Ministry of Agriculture Development, Chihuahua state government, 1993–1996; *general coordinator,* Campus Nuevo Casas Grandes of Ciudad Juarez Institute of Technology, 1990–1993, strategic planning, financial and computer systems advisor, 1990–2002; *associate professor,* New Mexico State University, 1989–1990; *assistant professor,* New Mexico State University, 1987–1989; *manufacturing superintendent,* Automatic Insertion Department, R.C.A., 1978–1980; *industrial engineer,* Time and Standards Department, R.C.A., 1977–1978; and *manufacturing supervisor,* Manufacturing and Testing Department, R.C.A., 1975–1977. He is the author of several international and local publications. Contact information: J. Arnoldo Bautista, Director, Centro Nacional de Investigación y Desarrollo Tecnológico, Interior Internado Palmira S/N–Complejo CENIDET, Col. Palmira, Cuernavaca, Morelos CP 62490 México. Phones: 011 52 777 318 7741 & 011 52 777 326 3842. Fax: 011 52 73 12 2434. E-mail: abautista@cenidet. edu.mx or A45L44@cableonline.com.mx.

Muzaffer Bodur is a professor of marketing at Management Department of Bogaziçi University in Istanbul, Turkey. She received her DBA from Indiana University in 1977 and acted as a visiting assistant professor at George Mason University upon graduation. In 1979, she joined Bogaziçi University faculty where she teaches global marketing management course to MBA students and research methods courses to doctoral students. She has organized training programs and seminars for executives and had served as the department head.

She is a member of Academy of International Business (AIB) and Consortium for International Marketing Research (CIMAR). Currently, she is the editor of the *Bogaziçi Journal: Review of Social, Economic and Administrative Studies* and serves on the editorial board of the *Journal of International Marketing.* She has visited Uppsala University of Sweden and Odense University of Denmark to teach international marketing courses and conducted cross-cultural research on the implications of business culture for internationalization of firms. Her publications focus on marketing strategies of multinational firms in emerging markets, export marketing management, expatriate managers, and consumer satisfaction, dissatisfaction, and complaining behavior with services and intangible product.

Simon Booth is a senior lecturer in the Department of Management, University of Reading Business School. He is the author of *Crisis Management Strategy,* and coauthor of *Managing Competition* and more than 30 research articles on strategy. His main research interests currently concern business sustainability, leadership behavior, and organizational change. Full address: Department of Management, University of Reading Business School, PO Box 218, Whiteknights, Reading RG6 6AA, Berkshire, UK.

Lize Booysen is a professor of Leadership at the Graduate School of Business Leadership, University of South Africa. She holds a masters degree in clinical psychology *cum laude* (Rand Afrikaans University), a masters degree in research psychology *cum laude,* and a masters degree in criminology *cum laude* (University of Pretoria). She completed her doctorate in business leadership at UNISA in 1999 on the influence of race and gender in leadership in South Africa.

She participated in the GLOBE study, and is involved in the Leadership Across Differences (LAD) study steered by the Center for Creative Leadership, Greensboro, North Carolina.

Felix C. Brodbeck (born 1960) is professor of organizational and social psychology and director of the Aston Centre for Leadership Excellence (ACLE) at Aston Business School, Aston University, UK, and a member of the GLOBE Coordination Team. He conducted applied research in more than 50 organizations in several countries. He has published eight books and more than 100 scholarly articles in national and international journals, such as *Academy of Management Review, Academy of Management Executive/Perspectives, Applied Psychology: An Introduction Review, European Journal of Social Psychology, European Journal of Work and Organizational Psychology, Journal of World Business, Journal of Cross Cultural Psychology, Journal of Experimental Psychology: Applied, Journal of Experimental Social Psychology, Journal of Personality and Social Psychology, Journal of Occupational and Organizational Psychology, Leadership Quarterly*, in areas such as leadership, cross-cultural psychology, diversity, HRM, team effectiveness, human–computer interaction, innovation, decision making, and applied research methods. His repertoire of experience and practice comprises experimental, applied, and field research, development of theory and practical tools, as well as training, coaching, and consulting in the aforementioned domains.

Philippe Castel is a full professor at the University of Burgundy where he teaches and coordinates courses in social psychology, and recently launched a master's degree in work psychology. He is the codirector of a Clinic and Social Psychology Laboratory (LPCS), whose work focuses on social categorization, social representations, and their linguistic markers. His main publications concern discrimination in the workplace in intercultural situations.

Jagdeep S. Chhokar is a professor at the Indian Institute of Management, Ahmedabad, where he has also been Dean and Director In-charge. He earned his PhD in management and organizational behavior from Louisiana State University. He is also a graduate in mechanical engineering and in law. He is also a citizen-activist for improving democracy and governance in the country; a bird watcher and conservationist. Before becoming an academic, he worked actively with the Indian Railways for 13 years.

He has taught in several countries including Australia, France, Japan, and the United States. His professional interests are eclectic, covering all aspects of organizational functioning such as behavior, structure, design, and effectiveness of organizations, and of people in organizations. The main thrust of his work in the last few years has been cross-cultural management.

His research has appeared in several international journals such as the *Journal of Applied Psychology, Columbia Journal of World Business* (now called the *Journal of World Business*), *International Labor Review, Industrial Relations, Journal of Safety Research, International Journal of Psychology, Applied Psychology: An International Review, International Journal of Management, Management International Review, Educational and Psychological Measurement, American Business Review,* and *American Journal of Small Business.* He has also contributed chapters to edited books and has written several teaching cases. He is on the editorial boards of *The Journal of Management* and of *Insight,* a publication of the Academy of International Business. His writings have also appeared in the Indian business and popular press such as *The Economic Times, The Times of India, The Hindu, The Indian Express, The Financial Express,* and *The Tribune.* His writings on political and electoral issues have appeared in journals in India such as the *Economic and Political Weekly* and *Seminar.* As conservationist, he has published in the *National Geographic Birdwatcher,* among other journals. He has been a member of the GLOBE Coordination Team.

Irene Hau-Siu Chow (MBA and PhD, Georgia State University) is a professor in the Department of Management, The Chinese University of Hong-Kong. Her academic experience includes appointments in Hong Kong, Singapore, and the United States. She published widely in international journals. Her current research interests include gender and cultural issues in Chinese societies, Chinese networks, and comparative human resources management practices.

Jose DelaCerda is a consultant and researcher of business and public organizations. He is currently the chief administrator of Zapopan county, Mexico. He has held executive positions related to organizational development and human resources in government, education, and consulting firms in Mexico. Mr. DelaCerda has an MA in industrial relations and labor sciences (Michigan State University) and a diploma in economics and business (The Economics Institute, University of Colorado, 1980). He has taught in several MBA programs, mainly at ITESO University. His professional projects have dealt with business process reengineering, work redesign and organizational downsizing, ISO 9000 quality management systems, managerial development, human resources management systems, and, more recently, whole-systems change interventions for strategic planning, participative work and organization redesign, and supply chain integration. His work as consultant has included firms in construction and urban development, public services, logistics and warehousing, manufacturing, and universities. As a researcher he has published several books and articles. Contact information: Jose DelaCerda, Compositores 4667, Fraccionamiento Los Pinos, Zapopan, Jalisco 45120, MEXICO. Phone: (33) 3684-2278 (33) 3944-2459. E-mail: josedlac@iteso.mx.

Deanne N. den Hartog is full professor of Organizational Behavior at the University of Amsterdam Business School in the Netherlands. She is director of the Business Studies bachelor and master's programs at the Business School and teaches OB and leadership. Her research interests focus on cross-cultural and inspirational leadership and also include team processes and human resource management issues. Among other things, she studies leadership among cultures, leader personality, and the impact of leadership on employees' learning, affect, cooperation, and innovative work behaviors.

Marc Deneire holds a PhD in second-language acquisition from the University of Illinois— Urbana-Champaign. He's been an associate professor of English linguistics at the University of Nancy 2 since 1998 where he teaches linguistics, discourse analysis, and intercultural communication. His research focuses on sociolinguistics and intercultural relations.

Peter W. Dorfman is a full professor and the department head of the Department of Management, New Mexico State University. His master's and PhD degrees are from the University of Maryland. His articles on leadership, cross-cultural management, and employee discrimination have appeared in the *Journal of Applied Psychology, Academy of Management Journal, Academy of Management Review, Journal of Management, Advances in International Comparative Management,* and *Advances in Global Leadership,* among others. Dr. Dorfman's current research involves investigating the impact of cultural influences on managerial behavior and leadership styles. He has been a coprincipal investigator of the decade-long Global Leadership and Organizational Behavioral Effectiveness (GLOBE) Research Project. As part of GLOBE, he has been a cocountry investigator for Mexico, a member of the GLOBE coordinating team for overall coordination of the project, and is now an executive committee member. Contact information: Peter W. Dorfman, Department of Management, College of Business Administration and Economics, PO Box 30001, MSC 3DJ, New Mexico State University, Las Cruces, NM 88003-8001. Voice: 505.646.1201. Fax: 505.646.1372. E-mail: pdorfman@nmsu.edu.

Michael Frese (born 1949) is professor at the University of Giessen and Visiting Professor at London Business School. He also lectured in the United States, the Netherlands, Finland, Sweden, Zimbabwe, China, and elsewhere. He was editor of *Applied Psychology: An International Review* and is on the editorial board of several journals. He is the author of approximately 200 articles and editor/author of more than 20 books and special issues. His research has been on the effects of unemployment, impact of stress at work, shiftwork, training, errors and mistakes, predictors of personal initiative in East and West Germany, psychological success factors in small-scale entrepreneurs (particularly in developing countries), and cross- cultural factors.

Ping Ping Fu, associate professor of management in the School of Business of the Chinese University of Hong Kong, has been a member of the Global Leadership research project team since 1997. Her current research includes studies of top-management teams, Chinese CEOs, citizenship behaviors, as well as cross-cultural influence tactics. Her work has been published in the *Journal of Organizational Behavior, Leadership Quarterly, Organizational Dynamics, Journal of International Business Studies, Advances in Global Leadership, Journal of Asian Businesses, International Journal of Cross-Cultural Psychology, European Review of Applied Psychology, International Journal of Human Resources Management,* and *Asian Pacific Journal of Management.*

Mikhail V. Grachev (PhD) is associate professor of management at Western Illinois University.

He served as university faculty in the United States, France, Japan, Hungary, the Czech Republic, and Russia. His research is focused on strategy and international human resource management.

Mikhail V. Gratchev served as International Leadership Association (ILA) board member. Contact information: Mikhail V. Grachev, Associate Professor of Management, Western Illinois University, 3561 60th Street, Moline, Il 61265. Tel: (309) 762-9481. Fax: (309) 762-6989. E-mail: mv-grachev@wiu.edu.

Dr. Celia Gutierrez has a varied background and training experience. Currently she is corporate manager of a Spanish business group dedicated to the formation of professionals in many sectors, including computer technology, chemical laboratories, food processing, and the development of leisure-time activities.

As an applied psychologist, she has coordinated the activities for extended culture programs and counseled students at the University of Alcala, Alcala de Henares. As a corporate psychologist, she has created an internship program for students from Syracuse for practicums in the fields of international finance, applied psychology, corporate strategy, organization behavior, and cross-cultural administration and management. As a business administrator, Dr. Gutierrez has coordinated the housing department for exchange programs for American universities and for the Bilbao-Viscaya Bank in Madrid. She has also been visiting professor in various Madrid universities, business schools, and corporations for courses on organizational behavior, global leadership, and cross-cultural management.

Specifically Dr. Gutierrez has published and coauthored in the fields of applied psychology and organization behavior. Also, she has created the first CD-ROM in Spain with the GLOBE (Phases 1 and 2) data.

Ingalill Holmberg is associate professor in organization and management and director of the Centre for Advanced Studies in Leadership at the Stockholm School of Economics. She received her PhD on a study of managerial succession in large corporations. Her current research focuses on managerial leadership in different organizational contexts, the ideology of leadership in the network society, and brands, identity, and leadership. She has published various books and articles on these subjects. She is an adviser to the Swedish Foundation for Strategic Research and the chief editor of the Swedish leadership journal *Ledmotiv.* She has also been an adviser to the Swedish Ministry of Industry.

Michael H. Hoppe*,* PhD, is a senior program and research associate at the Center for Creative Leadership in Greensboro, North Carolina. He conducts leadership development programs worldwide and researches and designs modules on effective leadership in a "global" world.

Dr. Hoppe, born and raised in Germany, also lived and worked in Austria, Greece, Italy, and the Netherlands. He holds an MS in clinical psychology from the University of Munich, Germany, an MS in educational psychology and statistics from State University of New York–Albany, and a PhD in adult education and institutional studies from University of North Carolina—Chapel Hill.

Robert J. House received his PhD degree in management from the Ohio State University, June 1960. He was appointed the Joseph Frank Bernstein Professor Endowed Chair of Organization Studies at the Wharton School of the University of Pennsylvania in 1988. He has published 130 journal articles. In total, his articles have been reprinted in approximately 50 anthologies of reading in management and organizational behavior.

He recevied the Award for Distinguished Scholarly Contribution to Management, and four awards for outstanding publications. The awards were conferred by the Academy of Management and the Canadian Association of Administrative Sciences. He has also authored two papers that are Scientific Citations Classics.

He is a Fellow of the Academy of Management, American Psychological Association, and Society for Industrial/Organizational Psychology. He has served as chairperson of the Academy of Management Division of Organizational Behavior (1972-1973) and President of the Administrative Science Association of Canada (1985-1986).

He was the Principal Investigator of the Global Leadership and Organizational Behavior Effectiveness Research Program (GLOBE) from 1993 through 2003. In this capacity he visited universities in 38 countries. He has also been a visiting scholar or visiting professor at 14 universities, most of which are in Europe or Asia. He is the senior editor of the following book *Culture, Leadership and Organizations,* edited by Robert J. House, Paul J. Hanges, Mansour Javidan, Peter W. Dorman and Vipin Gupta, Sage Publications, 2004. This book reports the result of the first two phases of GLOBE.

His major research interests are the role of personality traits and motives as they relate to effective leadership and organizational performance, power, and personality in organizations, leadership, and the implications of cross-cultural variation for effective leadership and organizational performance.

Jon P. Howell is professor of management and organizational behavior in the College of Business Administration and Economics at New Mexico State University. His MBA is from the University of Chicago and his PhD from the University of California at Irvine. Professor Howell has published book chapters as well as research articles in the *Academy of Management Journal, Academy of Management Review, Leadership Quarterly, Journal of Management, Organizational Dynamics,* and other management journals. His primary research interests are leadership, substitutes for leadership, and international management. He is currently working on the second edition of his book *Understanding Behaviors for Effective Leadership* (Prentice Hall). Contact information: Jon P. Howell, Department of Management, College of Business Administration and Economics, PO Box 30001, MSC 3DJ, New Mexico State University, Las Cruces, NM 88003-8001. Voice: 505.646.4900. Fax: 505.646.1372. E-mail: jhowell@nmsu.edu.

Jorge Correia Jesuino holds a PhD in sociology from the Technical University of Lisbon. He is professor emeritus at Instituto Superior de Ciências do Trabalho e da Empresa (ISCTE) in Lisbon, Portugal. His teaching and research activities focus on organizational behavior and social representations. He has published a number of texts on leadership and group processes. He joined the GLOBE project from its inception as CCI for Portugal.

Hayat Kabasakal is professor of management and organization studies at the Management Department of Bogaziçi University, Istanbul, Turkey. She received her PhD in 1984 in strategic management and organizational behavior from the University of Minnesota. In 1984, she joined Bogaziçi University faculty where she teaches management and organizational behavior courses to undergraduate, MBA, executive MBA, and doctoral students. She has served as the associate dean of the Faculty of Administrative Sciences and department head of the Management Department. She is currently the co-director of the Center for Disaster Management.

Her research interests center on organizational behavior, with a focus on leadership, culture, and gender in organizations. She has published in the *Journal of Strategic Management, Organizational Behavior Teaching Review, Journal of Applied Psychology: An International Journal, Journal of World Business, International Journal of Social Economics,* and *Bogaziçi Journal: Review of Social, Economic and Administrative Studies.*

She is a member of the Academy of Management, Turkish Faculty Members' Association, and GLOBE Foundation. She has served as the editor of *Bogaziçi Journal: Review of Social, Economic and Administrative Studies* and on the editorial boards of several international and national journals focusing on management and organizational studies.

Mary A. Keating lectures in human resource management in Trinity College, Dublin, where she is director of undergraduate studies at the School of Business Studies. She is a research associate in the Institute of International Integration Studies (TCD), a fellow of the Salzburg Seminar, and a member of the worldwide research network GLOBE (Global Leadership and Organizational Behavior Effectiveness) program. She previously lectured at University College, Dublin. She has published and contributed to national policy in the area of human resource management. Her research interests include international human resource management, strategies, and practices, and cross-cultural management and leadership. She is involved in executive education at the Irish Management Institute and has extensive consulting experience.

Jeff Kennedy teaches organizational behavior and international human resource management at both the undergraduate and MBA levels. His research on cross-cultural leadership and management has been published in a variety of journals, including the *Journal of International Business Studies, Academy of Management Executive, Asia Pacific Journal of Management,* and *Organizational Dynamics.* Prior to joining the Nanyang Business School in Singapore, he worked as an industrial/organizational psychologist for the Royal New Zealand Navy, a senior HR consultant for Ernst & Young (specializing in executive recruitment and management development), and a senior lecturer at Lincoln University, New Zealand.

Paul Koopman (1946) is professor of the psychology of management and organization at the Vrije Universiteit Amsterdam, the Netherlands. In 1980, he finished his PhD study on decision making in organizations. Since then, he studied different types of processes of management and decision making on the organizational level (industrial democracy, reorganization, turnaround management, privatization in Eastern Europe) and the departmental level (leadership and motivation, quality circles, teamwork, ICT, innovation management). At this moment, he is interested and actively involved in cross-cultural research, in particular in relation to issues of HRM, leadership, trust, and organizational culture.

Alexandre Kurc is an associate professor in social psychology at the University of Nancy 2 where he created an advanced professional degree in cross-cultural psychology. As a member of the communication and social psychology research team (GRC), his research focuses on intercultural situations, and, more recently, on sanitary and social problems. He has been a member of the ARIC Board (Association for Cross-Cultural Research) since 2001.

Marie-Françoise Lacassagne is a full professor of social psychology at the University of Burgundy where she created a university degree in coaching and mental performance. She is the director of the ISOS (Social Interaction and Sports Organisation) laboratory. Her current research is in sports management with a special focus on social interaction in sport marketing and in sports coaching. She is also interested in fans' behavior.

Christopher Leeds is a member of the council of Conflict Research & Society, London, a visiting research fellow at the University of Kent at Canterbury, and a researcher at the University of Nancy 2 where he taught British studies and humor studies as an associate professor until 2002.

Ji Li, PhD, University of Toronto, 1993, is currently an associate professor in the Department of Management, School of Business, Hong Kong Baptist University. His research interests include the effects of culture or other institutional factors on firm behavior and firm performance.

Martin Lindell is professor in the Department of Management and Organization at the Swedish School of Economics and Business Administration. His main research interests are innovation, leader behavior, strategy development, and acquisitions. He has written articles in journals such as *Technovation, Leadership Quarterly, Scandinavian Journal of Management, International Strategic Management and Organization, Journal of Small Business Management,* and *Business Strategy and the Environment.* He has recently chaired the Scandinavian Academy of Management. Contact information: Martin Lindell, Professor, Swedish School of Economics and Business Administration, P.O.Box 479, FIN-00101 Helsinki, Finland. Phone: 358 9 43133274. Fax: 358 9 43133275. E-mail: Mlindell@hanken.fi.

Mercedes López teaches and researches in the School of Psychology at Buenos Aires University. She consults on qualitative research and directs research and training on interpersonal behavior in organizations for leading national and international organizations: Burke, Business Bureau, "a & c" for Metrogas, Alico, BNP, Cinzano-BAMSA, Coca Cola, Liberty, Jumbo, BankBoston, Psyma, Sky, Guby, Telecom. ASECOM for Travelpass, Aquafresh, St. Ives, Boomerang, ABN AMRO, and Princeton Gallup for Toyota. Holds a master of science degree in Sociology (FLACSO) and her doctorate is in psychology, Buenos Aires University. She has published several academic papers. Address: Pje. Pedro López Anaut 4072, (1228) Capital federal, Bs. As., Argentina. Telephone: 54 011 4 931 4770. E-mail: mlopez@psi.uba.ar.

Gillian S. Martin lectures in business German in Trinity College, Dublin. She holds a PhD in applied linguistics, is a fellow of Trinity College, Dublin, and a research associate at the Institute of International Integration Studies (TCD). She previously lectured in the University of Limerick. Her research interests include cross-cultural negotiation and leadership, organizational communication, and doctor–patient interaction. She is a member of the worldwide research network GLOBE (Global Leadership and Organizational Behavior Effectiveness) program. She has been a guest lecturer at universities in Düsseldorf, Linz, Universität Erlangen-Nürnberg, and Bonn.

Sandra M. Martínez is an assistant professor of management at the Widener University School of Business Administration. She formerly held positions as an adjunct instructor at the Wharton School of the University of Pennsylvania and the Fox School of Business at Temple University. As a recipient of the National Security Education Program Doctoral Fellowship, she conducted an ethnographic study of elite Mexican managers from 1995 through 1998, which became her dissertation. She is a member of the GLOBE Mexican team. Her research is guided by an interest in the impact of cultural and institutional forces on leadership and managerial processes, such as strategic planning. She is a senior consultant with Decision Strategies International, Inc., where she works with nonprofit organizations. Contact information: Sandra Martínez, 274 Hathaway Lane, Wynnewood, PA 19096. Phone: 610-649-9652. E-mail: sanmarti@fast.net.

Phyllisis M. Ngin, PhD, University of Michigan, 1994, taught organizational behavior at the National University of Singapore Faculty of Business Administration, Singapore, and the Melbourne Business School, Melbourne, Australia. Her research interests are in managing technical professionals and sociology of work. She has taken a temporary leave of absence from academe and currently resides in Rochester Hills, Michigan.

Dr. Jeremiah J. O'Connell is emeritus professor of management at Bentley College where he earlier spent 10 years as the dean of the Graduate School and 12 years as professor of management. His career began at the Wharton School where he earned his tenure. He spent the 1970s at an institute of the University of Geneva, Switzerland. In the last quarter of the 21st century he worked in 20 countries, often spending a month or more per year in Spain. His publications have been in the fields of corporate governance, corporate strategy, organization change, and cross-cultural management.

Enrique Ogliastri is a professor in the INCAE Business School (Costa Rica). A PhD in organization theory from Northwestern University, he teaches negotiations, strategy, social enterprise, and organizations. He has published 15 books, the last one coauthored with Austin et al. *Social Partnering in Latin America,* Cambridge, MA: Harvard University Press, 2004. He was a professor at University of the Andes (Bogotá) for 25 years and was visiting faculty at Harvard (1980–1984), Ajiken (Tokyo, 1989), Toulousse ESC, and Nancy University (France, 1997, 1999) and Instituto de Empresa (IE, Spain). He is presently completing books about intercultural negotiations, leadership, and social enterprise.

Nancy Papalexandris is professor of human resources management and vice-rector of academic affairs and personnel at the Athens University of Economics and Business. She also is director of the MSc in Human Resource Management of her university. She has studied business administration and obtained her MA from New York University and her PhD from the University of Bath in the UK. She teaches management theory, human resources management, organizational behavior, public relations, and business communications. She has also taught in various EU universities and in post-training and management development seminars in Greece and abroad.

Her research interests include human resource management, organizational behavior and culture, leadership, small to medium enterprises, issues in public administration, public relations, corporate communications, and women in management. She has published various books and articles in international journals and has participated in a number of international conferences. She is member of the editorial team of *Employee Relations.* She represents Greece in CRANET, a research network on comparative European human resource management, and GLOBE, an international research network on organizational culture and leadership. She is vice president of the Institute of Human Resource Management of the Greek Management Association.

Maria Marta Preziosa teaches business ethics at the Argentine Catholic University Business School. She has a graduate degree in philosophy and an MBA, and is a PhD candidate (philosophy) at Navarra University (IESE Business School). She conducts long-term training projects in business ethics and social responsibility for Novartis, Shell, and DirecTV. She is a member of ALENE and ISBEE (Latin American, and International Society for Business Ethics and Economics). Address: F. J. S. M. de Oro 3065, 1°6, (C1425FOU) Buenos Aires, Argentina. Telephone: 54011-4773-3807. E-mail: mmpreziosa@yahoo.com.ar.

Dr. Jose M. Prieto is senior professor of personnel psychology at the Universidad Complutense of Madrid. His areas of expertise are personnel assessment and training, as well as information and communication technologies in applied psychology. His present focus is the psychological basis for trust among employees as well as in online communication and Web-based training. He is secretary general of the International Association of Applied Psychology, and a member of the European Network of Organizational Psychology. He is also a member of the editorial board of international journals such as *Applied Psychology: An International Review, British Journal of Occupational and Organizational Psychology, European Psychologist,* and *Psycothema.* He has written about 150 articles and chapters in English, French, Italian, and Spanish and is an invited lecturer using these languages in universities around the world.

Leonel Prieto obtained his BS in agricultural engineering from the Universidad Autonoma Chapingo, Mexico; his MS and PhD in production systems from the University of Reading, United Kingdom; and his MBA from the University of Texas at El Paso. His work experience includes the Research Center for Demographic and Urban Studies, El Colegio de Mexico, Mexico; and research scholar, International Institute for Applied Systems Analysis, Laxenburg, Austria. He is currently a graduate student in the Department of Management at New Mexico State University. His research interests include cross-cultural leadership and strategy. Contact information: Leonel Prieto, Department of Management, College of Business Administration and Economics, PO Box 30001, MSC 3DJ, New Mexico State University, Las Cruces, NM 88003- 8001. Voice: 505.646.1201. Fax: 505.646.1372. E-mail: lprieto@nmsu.edu.

Boris V. Rakitski (PhD) is the leading Russian social scholar with exemplary academic contribution to philosophy, sociology, labor economics, and political science. He is acting member of the Russian Academy of Natural Science. Rakitski served as member of the Russian President's Council on Social Policy, as director of the Russian Academy of Sciences' Institute of Labor and Institute of Employment and as vice-president of the USSR Sociology Association. He is the founder of the Institute of Perspectives and Problems of the Country and the School of Worker Democracy. Rakitski is professor of the Academy of Public Policy under the President of the Russian Federation. Contact information: Boris V. Rakitski, 113 Vernadskogo Prospekt Suite 244, Moscow 119571, Russia. Tel: (7-095) 931-4260. Tel: (309) 931-4260. E-mail: schlwd@orc.ru

Gerhard Reber's teaching and research area is organizational behavior. He pursued his academic career in Austria and has taught in various countries and institutions, such as the University of Dallas, the University of Toronto and York University (Toronto), Emory University (Atlanta), Turku School of Business and Economics (Finland), and numerous universities in German-speaking countries (St. Gallen, Heidelberg, Regensburg, Leipzig, Vienna). Currently he is department head of the Institute for International Management Studies and the Institute for Business Languages at Johannes Kepler University–Linz. His academic career has been accompanied by more than 100 publications, intensive consulting, and in-company as well as executive training activities. He has been coeditor of the journal *Die Betriebswirtschaft* since 1977 and a member of the Editorial Board of the *International Journal of Human Resource Management.* Contact information: Institute for International

Management Studies, Johannes Kepler University, Altenbergerstr. 69, A-4040 Linz / Austria, tel. +43 70 2468 9469, fax. +43 70 2468 8418, e-mail: gerhard.reber@jku.at.

Nikolai G. Rogovsky (PhD) is senior specialist at International Labor Organization in Switzerland. His research focus is on international human resource management and social aspect of business. Rogovsky contributed to the GLOBE chapter when he served on the faculty of California State University–Hayward. Contact information: Nikolai G. Rogovsky, Senior Specialist, International Labor Office, 4, route des Morillons, CH-1211 Geneva 22, Switzerland. Tel: (41-22) 799-6116. E-mail: rogovsky@ilo.org.

Flavio Ruffolo is adjunct professor of economic & business history in the School of Economics at Buenos Aires University. He completed coursework at the University of Bari, Italy, and at the University of Wisconsin. He has a master's degree in human resources from Buenos Aires University. He is a consultant for SMBs, public agencies, and educational institutions. He is a researcher and author of papers on public administration and program implementation, Argentine Institute for Public Administration. Address: Industria 3136, 1653 - Villa Ballester, Pdo. San Martín, Buenos Aires, Argentina, Telephone: 54 011 4 768 – 7310, E-mail: flavio@dacas.com.ar.

Camilla Sigfrids is partner and managing director for the Center for Leading Competence. Up until cofounding the company in late 2000, she was a member of the faculty and director of MBA programs at the Department of Management and Organisation at the Swedish School of Economics and Business Administration, Helsinki. Her current research focuses on applying approaches of problem-based learning to corporate leadership development needs. Contact information: Camilla Sigfrids, Chief Sense Maker, Managing Director, CLC Center for Leading Competence Oy, Fredrikinkatu 34 A 12, FIN- 00100 HELSINKI. Phone: +358 9 5657 6262. Fax: +358 9 5657 6260. Mobile: +358 5 0530 8327. E-mail: Camilla Sigfrids@clchelsinki.

Erna Szabo is Assistant Professor of Social and Economic Sciences at the Institute for International Management Studies at Johannes Kepler University–Linz in Austria. She received her doctorate from Johannes Kepler University and her MBA from the University of Toronto. Her current research interest includes cross-cultural leadership and the combined use of qualitative and quantitative methods to study participation in managerial decision making. She teaches organizational behavior and cross-cultural management at Johannes Kepler University and cultural awareness at the Ecole Supérieure de Commerce de Rouen in France and at the Turku School of Economics and Business Administration in Finland. She is the proud mother of a little girl, Lea Johanna. Contact information: Institute for International Management Studies, Johannes Kepler University, Altenbergerstr. 69, A-4040 Linz/Austria, tel. +43 70 2468 9126, fax. +43 70 2468 8418, e-mail: erna.szabo@jku.at.

Albert C. Y. Teo, PhD, University of California–Berkeley, 1993, is currently an associate professor in the Department of Management & Organization, NUS Business School, National University of Singapore. He concurrently holds a joint appointment in the University Scholars Program, National University of Singapore.

Prof. Dr. Henk Thierry (1938) is professor emeritus in work and organizational psychology. He got his degree in psychology at the Free University in Amsterdam. In 1971, he joined the University of Amsterdam in a new chair in work and organizational psychology. In 1993, he joined the Human Resource Science Department at Tilburg University and in 2000 he became full professor in work and organizational psychology at that university.

His current research interests cover compensation at work, work motivation, and strategic human resource management. He coauthored and coedited two editions of the *Handbook of Work and Organizational Psychology*. His most recent publications stem from 2002 and 2005.

Juan Antonio Ortiz Valdés, PhD, is a professor and researcher in organizational behavior in the Economic, Business and Finances Department at Instituto Tecnológico y de Estudios Superiores de Occidente, Guadalajara, Jalisco, México. He obtained his MS and PhD degrees at Vanderbilt University. His current academic activities involve organizational change, quality of work life and stress management and their relationship with job satisfaction, organizational commitment, team building, leadership, and organizational culture in Mexican business. Contact information: Juan Antonio Ortiz Valdés, Jardín de los Tulipanes Sur # 36, Frc. Jardín Real, Condominio (6), Zapopan, Jal. CP 45019 Mexico. E-mail: ao tiz@iteso.mx.

Jürgen Weibler, PhD, is full professor of business administration, leadership, and organization at the University of Hagen (FernUniversität in Hagen), Germany. He received his doctoral degree from the University of Cologne with a specialization in organizational behavior. For many years he was the research director of the Institute for Leadership and Human Resource Management at the University of St. Gallen, Switzerland, and was professor for management at the University of Constance, Germany. Dr. Weibler has extensive research experience in the areas of leadership, human resource management, and organizational change. He has developed an approach for theorizing leadership at a distance. Dr. Weibler has been co-editor of the journal *Zeitschrift für Personalforschung* (German *Journal of Human Resource Research*), and served on the review boards or as an advisory reviewer of the *MIR* (*Management International Review*) and the *Encyclopedia of Leadership* (editorial board) among others. He is the (co-)author of three books and over 80 (inter)national articles or book chapters. Dr. Weibler has broad experiences in teaching and served as a consultant to numerous organizations.

Celeste P. M. Wilderom (1956) is a full professor in management and organizational behavior (University of Twente, the Netherlands). She obtained a PhD from the State University of New York (Buffalo) in 1987. Her main research focus is on effective organizational change, including leadership and culture. She is one of the three editors of the award-winning *Handbook of Organizational Culture & Climate* (2000 & 2004, Sage). She is publishing in a variety of outlets and serves as an associate editor of the *Academy of Management Executive, British Journal of Management,* and *International Journal of Service Industry Management.*

Rongxian Wu is an associate professor of psychology in the Psychology Department of Suzhou University, China. His main research interests include industrial/organizational psychology, Chinese indigenous psychology, and cross-cultural psychology. He was a visiting scholar at the Wharton School of Business and worked with Professor Robert House between July 1997 and August 1998, and again, between July 2002 and July 2003. He is also a consultant for multiple firms, including Unilever. Contact: Wu Rongxian, Psychology Department, East Campus Box 537, Suzhou University, Suzhou, Jiangsu 215021, China. E-mail: wurx@suda.edu.cn.

Rolf Wunderer, PhD, is emeritus professor of business administration, leadership, and HRM at the University of St. Gallen, Switzerland, where he served as a full professor of business administration from 1983 to 2001. He was founder and until 2001 director of the Institute for Leadership and Human Resource Management at the same university. Prior to that, he was a full professor of business administration, entrepreneurship, and leadership at the University of Essen (Germany) and an appointed lecturer at the German Military University of Munich and at the University of Munich, where he received his doctoral degree in management. He was a visiting professor at the University of California (Los Angeles and Berkeley), Hitotsubashi University (Tokyo), and Ludwigs-Maximilian-Universität München.

Dr. Wunderer is coeditor of the *Zeitschrift für Personalforschung* (German *Journal of Human Resource Research*), the *Handwörterbuch der Führung* (*Handbook of Leadership*), member of the editorial board of the *Zeitschrift für Personalpsychologie* (*Personnel Psychology*), and reviewer of numerous journals. He is the author of more than 200 articles and book chapters. He published 43 books as (co-)author or (co-)editor—a lot of them in high editions. Dr. Wunderer has experiences in teaching for 40 years. He served as a consultant to governments and global companies, and was president or board member of various institutions. His main emphasis in research, teaching, and consulting has been personnel management, promoting cointrapreneurs, cooperation between organizational units (lateral cooperation), development of human resources, personnel controlling, and quality management.

Yongkang Yang is a professor of management and director of the Training Department in the School of Business in Fudan University. For the past 25 years, he has been teaching and doing research in the organizational behavior area, and has completed many research projects supported by the Chinese National Science Foundation, Ministry of Education or various business organizations. He has published more than 30 papers in the area.

Jun Ye has a PhD in history from Fudan University. She is currently serving as a commentator for "Daily Economic News" in Shanghai, mostly on economics. She has written over a hundred commentaries, which appeared in various newspapers in Shanghai.

Preface

This is the second book being published by the Global Leadership and Organizational Behavior Effectiveness (GLOBE) research program. The purpose of this book is to report the results of Phase 3 of GLOBE, which is the most recent phase of GLOBE. Phases 1 and 2 are described in *Culture, Leadership, and Organization: The GLOBE Study of 62 Societies,* edited by Robert J. House, Paul J. Hanges, Mansour Javidan, Peter W. Dorfman, and Vipin Gupta, Sage Publications, 2004.

The evolution and research design of GLOBE are described in that book. The objectives of GLOBE are to answer the following questions:

1. Are there leader behaviors, attributes, and organizational practices that are universally accepted and effective across cultures?
2. Are there leader behaviors, attributes, and organizational practices that are accepted and effective in only some cultures?
3. How do attributes of societal and organizational cultures influence whether specific leader behaviors will be accepted and effective?
4. How do attributes of societal and organizational cultures affect selected organizational practices?
5. How do attributes of societal cultures affect the economic, physical, and psychological welfare of members of the societies studies?
6. What is the relationship between societal cultural variables and international competitiveness of the societies studied?

Following is a brief description of Phases 1 and 2.

Phase 1 was concerned with the development and validation of data collection methods including questionnaires and guides for collection of information from interview, focus groups, and media as well as unobtrusive measures of attributes of cultures. Phase 2 was concerned with capturing the major cultural attributes of 62 societies. Phase 2 was also concerned with identifying the leadership attributes that contribute to outstanding leadership in each society. The results of Phases 1 and 2 are reported in the book mentioned earlier edited by House et al.

Results of Phase 3 are reported in the present book. Phase 3 consisted of intensive qualitative and quantitative research in each of 25 societal cultures relevant to the enactment of highly effective leadership. The results of this intensive study of each of the 25 societies are reported in a separate chapter for each society. The final chapter describes the major conclusions that can be drawn from this research.

Phase 3 overlapped with Phase 2. All of the country coinvestigators who participated in Phases 1 and 2 were invited to write a chapter for the present book. Research teams in 25 societies accepted this invitation. The earliest drafts for country chapters came in 1997 and latest in 2001.

The first four chapters that came in, from India, Colombia, Ireland, and the Netherlands, were edited by me. This took place concurrently with the final editing of the book by House et al. (2004). The editing process consisted of having each chapter reviewed and evaluated by independent scholars who were knowledgeable about the cultures described in the present book. These review were summarized and a summary as well as the original reviews were sent to the authors of each of the chapters. The summary included several suggestions for revision of the chapters based on the independent reviews. All of the four chapters required moderate to substantial revision. Upon revision, additional changes were requested of the authors in order to make each chapter as complete and readable as they possibly could be. This process required as many as two or three revisions for each chapter.

On completion of the editing of the first four chapters received, I realized that editing this book would be a substantially larger and more challenging task than originally anticipated. On this realization, I decided to invite Professor Jagdeep Chhokar to be coeditor for the remaining chapters. This required me to prepare explicit guidelines for the entire review process. As Professor Chhokar and I proceeded with the editing of the remaining chapters, we became even more acutely aware of the complexity of the process of coordinating the effort of chapter authors from highly diverse cultural backgrounds. About this time, Felix Brodbeck offered to participate and help us out in the editing process, an offer that Professor Chhokar and I gratefully accepted. Thereafter, Professors Chhokar and Brodbeck jointly edited the remaining chapters. As with the first four chapters, the remaining chapters also required moderate to substantial revisions as suggested by the reviewers. The outcome of this process is the present book. This book consists of the introductory chapter and the chapter on methodology written by Professor Chhokar and the conclusion chapter written by Professor Brodbeck. Professors Chhokar and Brodbeck did an excellent job of editing the chapters of this book, and putting together the entire manuscript. Felix also undertook the major task of final editing of all the chapters. I was happy to let Professors Chhokar and Brodbeck do all that needed to be done to bring this book to completion.

This book is a product of collective efforts of about 60 scholars from the 25 countries it includes. Most of them have firsthand experience with the GLOBE data-collection process and have participated in many discussions among GLOBE members about development of concepts and methods, and about how to interpret the results found in Phases 1 and 2 of GLOBE.

This book is addressed to both university teachers and researchers, and practicing managers. It provides in-depth understanding of 25 cultures from multiple perspectives and suggestions for further research in each of these cultures. Reading all the chapters together will provide a detailed understanding of the similarities and differences of cultural and leadership practices and values in a broad range of countries across major regions of the world. Managers who are planning to work, or who are already working, in cross-cultural environments (which we believe more and more managers will have to do in the coming years) will find each country chapter to be a source for developing a thorough understanding of the culture and leadership practices of that country. In addition, they will find practical suggestions, based on rigorous research and experience rooted in that country, about how to deal with managers of and situations in that country.

Information contained in this book will also be a valuable resource for senior managers planning to do business with other countries or to set up offices or operations in other countries. Taken together, the comparative study of 62 countries presented in House et al. (2004) and the in-depth reports about each of a sample of 25 countries from the present book, constitute a rich source of information for anyone interested in understanding the culture and leadership of countries and organizations across the world.

Such an undertaking is obviously not possible without the help, cooperation, and contributions of several individuals. I would therefore like to thank everyone who was involved in the preparation of this book. Foremost, I thank all the country chapter authors for the unstinted support and patience in the long process of bringing this book to completion. I also acknowledge the generous support of their institutions for providing the resources and facilities to complete various tasks associated with completing their respective chapters. Kwok Leung very willingly agreed to write the Foreword and we are grateful to him. The reviewers of the various chapters made an invaluable contribution in ensuring the high quality of scholarship and accuracy in the country chapters, and I am grateful to all of them. Contributions of all the participants in the GLOBE program involved in the processes of data collection, analysis, and writing are reflected in this book in several ways and I thank them for all their efforts. On the final stretch, it was Anne Duffy of Lawrence Erlbaum Associates who ensured that every detail came together for publishing the book in its present form, and therefore her contribution is acknowledged with gratitude.

—Robert J. House

REFERENCE

House, R. J., Hanges, P. J., Javidan, M., Dorfman, P. J., Gupta, V. (Eds.), & GLOBE Associates. (2004). *Culture, leadership, and organizations: The GLOBE study of 62 societies.* Thousand Oaks, CA: Sage.

1
▼▼▼▼▼▼▼

Introduction

Jagdeep S. Chhokar
Indian Institute of Management, Ahmedabad

Felix C. Brodbeck
Aston Business School, Aston University, Birmingham, England

Robert J. House
Wharton School of Management, University of Pennsylvania

Culture and leadership are probably among the most written about and the least understood topics in the social sciences. This is not only because social scientists find these two topics very challenging, even seductive, but also because these two seem necessary for satisfying human existence. The **G**lobal **L**eadership and **O**rganizational **B**ehavior **E**ffectiveness (GLOBE) Research Project has studied these popular topics afresh and in a simultaneous breadth and depth that has never before been attempted. The comprehensive quantitative findings of all the 61 countries studied are described in an earlier volume (House, Hanges, Javidan, Dorfman, Gupta, & GLOBE Associates, 2004). This book reports the results of the in-depth analyses of culture and leadership in 25 of the 61 countries, each of which is presented by scholars and researchers from those countries, who integrated the quantitative and qualitative GLOBE findings.

This book is addressed to both university teachers and researchers on the one side and practicing managers on the other side. For the former, it provides in-depth understanding of 25 cultures from multiple perspectives and suggestions for further research in each of these cultures. Reading all the chapters, together with the last chapter of this volume ("Integration, Conclusions, and Future Directions"), will provide a detailed understanding of the similarities and differences of cultural and leadership practices and values in a broad range of countries across major regions of the world. For the latter, for example, managers who are planning to work, or who are already working, in cross-cultural environments (which we believe, more and more managers will have to do in the coming years) will find each country chapter to be a source for developing a thorough understanding of the culture and leadership practices of that country. In addition, they will find practical suggestions, based on rigorous research and experience rooted in that country, about how to deal with managers of and situations in that country. Information contained in this book will also be a valuable resource for senior managers planning to do business with other countries or to set up offices or operations in other countries. Taken together, the comparative study of 61 countries presented in House et al. (2004) and the in-depth reports about each of a sample of 25 countries from the present book, constitute a rich source of information for anyone interested in understanding the culture and leadership of countries and organizations across the world.

This chapter starts by explaining the need for country-specific understanding of culture and leadership, goes on to define the constructs used in the research, and is followed by an overview of the history and a description of the GLOBE project. The general structure of country chapters is then described, followed by the plan of the book itself. It closes with a brief comment on the unique contribution the content of this book makes to the domain.

1.   COUNTRY-SPECIFIC UNDERSTANDING

This book focuses on detailed and specific understanding of culture and leadership in the 25 countries represented here. Although there is a need for theories about leadership and organization that transcend cultural boundaries because the goal of science is to discover and construct universally valid theories, laws, and principles, there are however inherent limitations in transferring theories across widely varying cultures. What works in one culture may not work in another culture. As Triandis (1993) suggests, leadership researchers will be able to "fine-tune" theories by investigating cultural variations as parameters of those theories. In addition, a focus on cross-cultural issues can help researchers discover new relationships by suggesting that investigators include a much more encompassing range of variables usually not considered in contemporary theories, such as the prominence of religion, language, ethnicity, history, and political systems (Dorfman, 1996).

Although the quantitative data of the GLOBE research program allow comparisons and contrasts among cultures, they do not allow for culture-specific descriptions of the societies studied. That is why the authors of the 25 country chapters represented here have described selected culture-specific attributes and entities of the national setting in which the middle-management informants are embedded. The attributes and entities are those that the authors have judged as having nontrivial influences on the interpretation and practice of leadership and organizational practices of the cultures studied. Although the authors were given a suggested overall structure for country chapters, they were also free to decide how best to present the specific information pertaining to the country about which they were writing. On the one hand, this gave them the freedom to deviate from the set structure in order to represent cultural and leadership peculiarities more adequately. On the other side, this freedom resulted in chapters where the structure and presentation style differs to some extent. The structure suggested to the authors and that has generally been followed in several, but not all, chapters is described in a later section of this chapter.

2.   DEFINITIONS OF CONSTRUCTS

The three major constructs of interest in GLOBE are culture, organizational practices and values, and leadership. Definitions of these, as used in GLOBE, are given in the next subsections, along with those of the dimensions that form or contribute to these constructs. These are described here in this chapter to avoid the need for repeatedly defining them in every country chapter. It is recommended that readers refer to this section as they come across these constructs in the country chapters.

Culture

There is no universally agreed-upon definition of culture among social scientists. Social scientists generally use the term to refer to a set of parameters of collectivities that differentiate the collectivities from each other in meaningful ways. The focus is on the "sharedness" of cultural indicators among members of the collectivity. The specific criteria used to differentiate cultures usually depend on the preferences of the investigator and the issues under investigation, and tend to reflect the discipline of the investigator. It was also decided to develop a GLOBE definition of culture.

In August 1994, the first GLOBE research conference was held at the University of Calgary in Canada. The participants consisted of 54 researchers from 38 countries. They met to develop a collective understanding of the project and to initiate its implementation. Time was spent generating definitions of *leadership* that reflected the diverse viewpoints held by GLOBE researchers; time was also spent defining and describing culture. Culture was defined as *"shared motives, values, beliefs, identities, and interpretations or meanings of significant events that result from common experiences of members of collectives and are transmitted across age generations"* (House & Javidan, 2004, p. 15). It is worth noting that these are *psychological* attributes and that the definition can be applied at both the societal and organizational levels of analysis.

GLOBE Dimensions of Societal Culture. Culture, being one of the major phenomena of interest in GLOBE, was operationalized at multiple levels. First, cultures were operationalized in terms of quantitative dimensions: (a) Assertiveness, (b) Future Orientation, (c) Gender Egalitarianism, (d) Humane Orientation, (e) Institutional Collectivism (Collectivism I), (f) In-Group Collectivism (Collectivism II), (g) Performance Orientation, (h) Power Distance, and (i) Uncertainty Avoidance. These dimensions were selected on the basis of a review of the literature relevant to the measurement of culture in prior large-sample studies and on the basis of existing cross-culture theory, such as the works of Hofstede (1980), Hofstede and Bond (1988), Kluckhohn and Strodtbeck (1961), McClelland (1961, 1985), and Putman (1993) among others. The definitions of these dimensions adopted by GLOBE are as follows:

1. *Assertiveness* is the degree to which individuals in organizations or societies are assertive, confrontational, and aggressive in social relationships.
2. *Future Orientation* is the degree to which individuals in organizations or societies engage in future-oriented behaviors such as planning, investing in the future, and delaying individual or collective gratification.
3. *Gender Egalitarianism* is the extent to which an organization or a society minimizes gender role differences while promoting gender equity and the equality of genders.
4. *Humane Orientation* is the degree to which individuals in organizations or societies encourage and reward individuals for being fair, altruistic, friendly, generous, caring, kind to others, and exhibiting and promoting altruistic ideals.
5. *Institutional Collectivism* (Collectivism I) reflects the degree to which organizational and societal institutional practices encourage and reward collective distribution of resources and collective action.
6. *In-Group Collectivism* (Collectivism II) reflects the degree to which individuals express pride, loyalty, and cohesiveness in their organizations, families, circle of close friends, or other such small groups.

7. *Performance Orientation* refers to the extent to which high level members of organizations and societies encourage and reward group members for performance improvement and excellence.
8. *Power Distance* is the degree to which members of an organization and society encourage and reward unequal distribution of power with greater power at higher levels.
9. *Uncertainty Avoidance* is the extent to which members of an organization or society strive to avoid uncertainty by relying on established social norms, rituals, and bureaucratic practices to decrease the probability of unpredictable future events that could adversely affect the operation of an organization or society, and also to remedy the potential adverse effects of such unpredictable future events.

Six of the culture dimensions had their origins in the dimensions of culture identified by Hofstede (1980). Power Distance and Uncertainty Avoidance reflect the same constructs as Hofstede's dimensions labeled Power Distance and Uncertainty Avoidance. Collectivism has been broken into two dimensions: the *Institutional Collectivism* (Collectivism I) dimension measures *societal* emphasis on collectivism, with low scores reflecting individualistic emphasis and high scores reflecting collectivistic emphasis; and the *In-Group Collectivism* (Collectivism II) scale measures pride in and loyalty to smaller groups such as family, organization, circle of close friends, and organizational cohesiveness. In lieu of Hofstede's Masculinity dimension, it was decided to develop two dimensions labeled Gender Egalitarianism and Assertiveness, because these attributes are stressed in Hofstede's discussion of his Masculinity dimension. These two dimensions represent the theoretical construct of masculinity better, and avoid the confusion and interpretation difficulties of Hofstede's measure. Future Orientation is derived from Kluckhohn and Strodtbeck's (1961) Past, Present, Future Orientation dimension, which focuses on the temporal mode of a society. Performance Orientation was derived from McClelland's work on need for achievement (McClelland, 1961, 1985).

Humane Orientation has its roots in Kluckhohn and Strodtbeck's (1961) work on the Human Nature Is Good vs. Human Nature Is Bad dimension, as well as Putnam's (1993) work on the Civic Society, and McClelland's (1985) conceptualization of the affiliative motive.

Culture "As Is" and Culture "Should Be."   Culture is often manifested in two distinct ways. The first is as values, beliefs, schemas, and implicit theories commonly held among members of a collectivity (society or organization), and these are variously called the *attributes* of culture. Culture is also commonly observed and reported as *practices* of entities such as families, schools, work organizations, economic and legal systems, political institutions, and the like. The GLOBE program measured all of the nine dimensions of culture in both these manifestations. The former are expressed as response to questionnaire items in the form of judgments of what *should be,* and the latter as assessments of what *is* with regard to common behaviors, institutional practices, prescriptions, and proscriptions.

Societal and Organizational Culture.   The third and final level of operationalization focused on the unit of analysis. Because the GLOBE project was designed to assess the impact of societal culture *and* organizational culture on perceptions of effective leadership, society and organizations within society were considered as separate units of analysis. Therefore, culture has been measured in GLOBE at *both* these levels.

The preceding approach to culture is illustrated in Fig. 1.1.

The intention with the design of Fig. 1.1 was to take into account varying perspectives on culture and its measurement. McClelland (1985) distinguished between the implicit (unconscious)

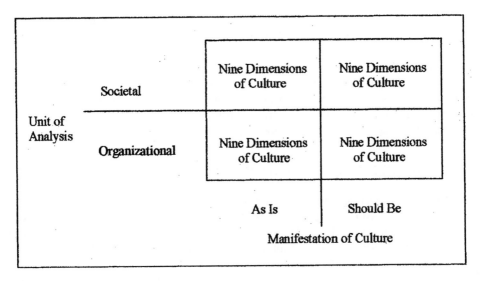

Figure 1.1 GLOBE's multilevel approach to measuring culture

and explicit (conscious) motives. Implicit motives reflect learned emotional and pleasurable association with a select set of stimuli as well as possible genetic disposition. Explicit motives reflect conscious values. Because the GLOBE societal culture dimensions are based on questionnaire responses, at the individual level they are likely to reflect explicit values and motives. When aggregated to the level of the society or organization, the aggregated scores reflect norms of society, which serve to motivate, direct, and constrain behavior of members of cultures. In this manner, aggregated implicit questionnaire responses may reflect powerful incentives, much like implicit motives. The fact that they measured cultural practices ("As Is" measures), and these practices correlated quite highly (>0.60) with unobtrusive measures suggests that aggregated individual responses are analogous to individual implicit motives, at the organizational and societal levels of analysis (Hanges & Dickson, 2004, in press).

Leadership

Leadership has been a topic of study for social scientists for much of the 20th century (Yukl, 2006), yet there is no universally agreed-upon definition of leadership (Bass, 1990). A large number of definitions have been advanced by scholars. The core concept of almost all such definitions concerns influence—leaders influence others to help accomplish group or organizational objectives. The variety of definitions is appropriate, as the degree of specificity of the definition of leadership should be driven by the intentions of the research. Smith and Bond (1993) specifically note: "If we wish to make statements about universal or *etic* aspects of social behavior, they need to be phrased in highly abstract ways. Conversely, if we wish to highlight the meaning of these generalizations in specific or *emic* ways, then we need to refer to more precisely specified events or behaviors" (p. 58). The GLOBE goals are concerned with both aspects of leadership and organizational practices that are comparable across cultures and culture-specific differences in leadership and organizational practices and their effectiveness. It was clear in the Calgary meeting that the evaluative and semantic interpretation of the term *leadership,* and the ways in which leadership and organizational processes are enacted, vary across cultures, and that some aspects of leadership are universally valid.

The commonly agreed-upon definition of organizational leadership that emerged at the Calgary meeting and that was adopted by GLOBE is *"the ability of an individual to influence, motivate, and enable others to contribute toward the effectiveness and success of the organizations of which they are members"* (House & Javidan, 2004, p. 15). The focus was on *organizational* leadership, not leadership in general. Simonton (1994), speaking of leadership in general, defines a leader as a "group member whose influence on group attitudes, performance, or decision making greatly exceeds that of the average member of the group" (p. 411). Project GLOBE concerns the phenomenon of organizational leadership and not leadership in general.

3. BACKGROUND OF THE GLOBE RESEARCH PROJECT

GLOBE as a research program concerned with leadership, organizational practices, and national culture was conceived in the summer of 1991 and initially designed by the third editor of this book as the Principal Investigator. He was later joined by Michael Agar, Marcus Dickson, Paul Hanges, and S. Antonio Ruiz-Quintanilla as Co-Principal Investigators. In the spring of 1993, a grant proposal was written that followed a substantial literature review and development of a pool of 753 questionnaire items. GLOBE was funded in October 1993. Because cross-cultural research requires substantially detailed knowledge of all the cultures being studied, a network of approximately 175 Country Co-Investigators (CCIs) was developed. These are social scientists or management researchers and scholars from the 61 participating countries.

The CCIs, recruited through an extending network of personal contacts and referrals, were responsible for leadership of the project in a specific culture in which they had expertise. Their activities included collecting quantitative and qualitative data, ensuring the accuracy of questionnaire translations, writing country-specific descriptions of their cultures in which they interpreted the results of the quantitative data analyses in their own cultural context, and contributing insights from their unique cultural perspectives to the ongoing GLOBE research. In most cases, CCIs are natives of the cultures from which they were to collect data, and they also resided in those specific cultures. Some of the CCIs are people with extensive experience in more than one culture. Most cultures have a research team of between two and five CCIs working on the project. An initial goal of Project GLOBE was to develop societal and organizational measures of culture and leader attributes that would be appropriate to employ across all cultures. The CCIs played a critical role in enhancing the generalizability of the GLOBE instruments, and also in their development. The major criterion for the selection of GLOBE members was that they were active researchers concerned with cross-cultural issues, leadership, and organizational functioning. The CCIs, together with the Principal Investigators and Research Associates, comprise the members of the GLOBE community. The activities of the project as a whole are coordinated by the GLOBE Coordinating Team (GCT), which was founded in 1996. Its members—in addition to the principal investigators named earlier who were also part of the GCT—reflect a multinational body of scholars (in alphabetical order): Staffan Akerblom (Sweden), Felix C. Brodbeck (Germany at the time, now United Kingdom), Jagdeep S. Chhokar (India), Peter W. Dorfman (United States), Mansour Javidan (Canada at the time, now United States), Enrique Ogliastri (Colombia), Antonio-Ruiz Quintanilla (United States), and Marius van Wyk (South Africa).[1]

---

[1]A more detailed account about how GLOBE operated and developed over time as an organizational and social entity is given in the preface to House et al. (2004).

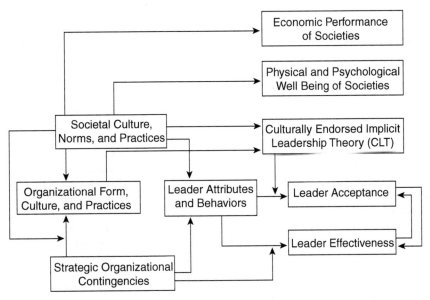

Figure 1.2   Theoretical model of GLOBE

The GCT has been responsible for designing quantitative measures and qualitative methods, performing cross-cultural statistical analyses, and coordinating efforts to present results of the project to the scholarly community.

GLOBE has been a multiphase, multimethod, multicountry project in which researchers spanning the world examined the interrelationships between societal culture, organizational culture, and organizational leadership. Table 1.1 lists the countries that are part of the GLOBE research. The list includes at least three countries in each of the following geographic regions that are represented in the GLOBE sample: Africa, Asia, Europe (Eastern, Central, and Northern), Latin America, North America, North Africa, the Middle East, and the Pacific Rim. The 25 countries covered in the present book are marked with an asterisk.

4.   THE GLOBE RESEARCH PROJECT

The GLOBE Research Project investigated the relationships between societal cultures, organizational cultures, and leadership practices in the participating countries, as well as numerous indicators of the economic competitiveness of the societies studied and the psychological well-being of their members (for details, see Javidan & Hauser, 2004). The independent variables were nine attributes of culture, identified during the program, which when quantified are referred to as core cultural dimensions (for details, see Gupta, de Luque, & House, 2004; Hanges & Dickson, 2004). An overall model guiding the program is shown in Fig. 1.2.

The core of Fig. 1.2 is the relationship between societal culture, norms, and practices, with organizational form, culture, and practices as well as with leadership. Societal culture both affects the other core concepts, and also influences the economic performance of societies, the physical and psychological well-being of the members of societies, and the culturally endorsed implicit leadership theories. Strategic contingencies of organizations also affect organizational form, culture, and practices; leader behavior and attributes; and leader effectiveness.

TABLE 1.1
List of Countries participating in the GLOBE Research Program

Albania	*Hong Kong	Qatar
*Argentina	Hungary	
*Australia		*Russian Federation
*Austria	*India	
	Indonesia	*Singapore
Bolivia	@Iran	Slovenia
Brazil	*Ireland	South Africa (Black sample)
	Israel	*South Africa (While sample)
Canada (English speaking)	Italy	*Spain
*China		*Sweden
*Colombia	Japan	*Switzerland
Costa Rica		
@Czech Republic	Kazakhstan	Taiwan
	Korea, Republic of (South)	Thailand
Denmark	Kuwait	*Turkey
Ecuador	Malaysia	*United States of America
Egypt, Arab Republic of	*Mexico	
*England	Morocco	Venezuela
El Salvador		
	Namibia	Zambia
*Finland	*Netherlands	Zimbabwe
*France	*New Zealand	
	Nicaragua	
Georgia	Nigeria	
Germany (Former East)		
*Germany (Former West)	Philippines	
*Greece	Poland	
Guatemala	*Portugal	

*Countries represented in this book.
@Due to special data-collection issues with the data from Iran and the Czech Republic, one or both of these countries could not be included in some of the comparative analyses. This is why in some of the country chapters in this book the total number of countries is shown as 61.

Globe Objectives

The meta-goal of GLOBE is to develop an empirically based theory to describe, understand, and predict the impact of specific cultural variables on leadership and organizational processes and the effectiveness of these processes. Specific objectives include answering the following fundamental questions:

- Are there leader behaviors, attributes, and organizational practices that are universally accepted and effective across cultures?
- Are there leader behaviors, attributes, and organizational practices that are accepted and effective in only some cultures?

- How do attributes of societal and organizational cultures influence the varieties of leader behaviors and organizational practices that are accepted and effective?
- What is the effect of violating cultural norms relevant to leadership and organizational practices?
- What is the relative standing of each of the cultures studied on each of the nine core dimensions of culture?
- Can the universal and culture-specific aspects of leader behaviors, attributes, and organizational practices be explained in terms of an underlying theory that accounts for systematic differences across cultures?

The preceding questions are dealt with in detail and answered in the first GLOBE book (House et al., 2004). In the present book, each country chapter describes the country-specific leader behaviors and attributes and the societal cultural and organizational cultural practices and values. Moreover, for each country, its relative standing on each of these variables is reflected, on the one side, in relation to the worldwide distribution of country scores, and on the other side, in relation to what these actually mean in relation to the cultural background of the country, its history, its religions, its socioeconomical development, and further relevant characteristics.

Four Phases of GLOBE

To achieve the aforementioned objectives, the GLOBE research program was designed with four planned phases. The first phase consisted of two major tasks. The first task was the specification of a preliminary theory of causal processes and relationships among societal cultural dimensions and various other variables, to guide the research to be conducted. The second task of Phase 1 was the development and validation of questionnaires for data collection purposes as well as standardized guides for qualitative research to be conducted in the societies studied. The questionnaires developed in the second task of Phase 1 have sound psychometric properties such as high within-culture respondent agreement, high between-culture differences in aggregated means of individual responses, and high interitem consistency within scales. The generalizability coefficient (interclass correlation ICC-KK), which jointly measures the psychometric properties, exceeds 0.85 for all of the scales developed in this task (Hanges & Dickson, 2004, in press). Further details are described in Chapter 2 of this book.

The objectives of Phase 2 were to study the participating cultures on the nine core societal culture dimensions, and to test various hypotheses concerning relationships between the core societal culture dimensions on the one hand and dimensions of culturally endorsed implicit leadership theories, organizational cultures, and independently collected measures of the psychological, physical, and economic well-being of the members of the culture studied on the other.

In this phase, data were collected from approximately 17,300 managers in 951 organizations in 61 countries, and exhaustive statistical analyses were done. The results of Phase 2 are described in House et al. (2004).

In the third phase (currently under way), the impact and effectiveness of specific leader behaviors and styles of CEOs on subordinates' attitudes and job performance, and on leader and organizational effectiveness to analyze the longitudinal effects of leadership and organizational practices and organizational form on organizational effectiveness is being investigated. A tentative fourth phase will employ field and laboratory experiments to confirm, establish causality, and extend previous findings.

Generalizability Across Cultures

The cross-cultural literature often struggles in dealing with culturally specific and culturally generalizable aspects. Culturally generalizable phenomena are experienced by all cultures to some extent. A phenomenon can be so categorized if all cultures can be assessed in terms of a common metric relating to the phenomenon. Cultures can be compared in terms of such phenomena. In contrast, culturally specific phenomena occur in only a subset of cultures. Each of the country chapters in this book describes and discusses, on the one side, the culturally generalizable phenomena by comparing the findings of that particular country with the 61 GLOBE countries and relevant subsets of countries, and on the other side, describes and discusses country-specific aspects in detail. Overall the objective of each country chapter is to integrate quantitative-comparative with qualitative-in-depth results about their country into a coherent picture.

The industries studied were food processing, financial services, and telecommunication service because these are provided within all nations. The more than 17,300 respondents were middle managers from more than 950 mainly domestic organizations in the respective industries. Thus, the sampling strategy for the collection of questionnaire data accounted for nation (from major cultural regions in the world, see Table 1.1) and industry (food, finance, telecom) and controlled for occupation (managers) and organizational level (middle management).

Sampling from middle managers permitted us to generalize the subcultures of middle managers in the three industries studied and the cultures studied. This sampling strategy increased the internal validity of the study by ensuring that the units of analysis were well defined and internally homogeneous. This is reinforced by the triangulation of the quantitative results with a variety of other world data sources (Gupta et al., 2004; Javidan & Hauser, 2004) and with the findings of the various qualitative methods followed (for details, see the next chapter, "Methodology") in each country that is represented in this book. The correlation of the aggregate middle-managers responses with those of unobtrusive measures, which reflect the broader aspects of the society with respect to each dimension studied, indicate that the middle managers reflect the broader culture in which they are embedded rather than the culture of middle managers alone. Furthermore, cross-industry analysis permitted us to gauge the relative impact of strategic imperatives imposed by industry regulations as well as contributing cultural influences.

Project GLOBE employs a variety of methods to make comparisons across cultures for culturally generalizable phenomena. The primary method is questionnaire responses of managers in three selected industries. Responses to the questionnaire, when aggregated to the culture level of analysis, provide measurement of the nine core GLOBE culture dimensions. The validity of the middle-manager descriptions of the practices in their cultures (*As Is* responses) was checked using independently collected unobtrusive measures of the dimensions.

5.   BROAD PLAN OF COUNTRY CHAPTERS

The opening section of each country chapter provides a broad and general introduction to the country and also a brief backdrop and context for, and a lead-in to the GLOBE study in the country. This is followed by the historical context of the society indicating the major influences that the societal culture has been through over the years. This usually culminates in a description of the culture in its current state. This is followed by a survey of literature focusing on leadership as it is understood and practiced in the country. In some cases, the authors have also given descriptions of some individuals considered to be outstanding leaders of the country.

The aforementioned is usually followed by a presentation of the quantitative and qualitative findings of societal culture and leadership in the country. The quantitative findings usually consist of the country's scores on "Society *As Is*" and "Society *Should Be*" for all the nine dimensions of societal culture described earlier. These are often presented in reference to the maximum and minimum score of these dimensions among all the countries participating in GLOBE, and the rank of the country on each of these dimensions. These quantitative data are interpreted in the societal and cultural context of the country. The interpretations involve integration of the quantitative results, and participant observations and unobtrusive measurements of the societal culture done by the CCIs. This integration of quantitative and qualitative findings also brings out some country-specific manifestations of societal culture. The outcome is a combined, overall profile of societal culture of the country. The authors also provide their own participant observations and unobtrusive measurements of the nine dimensions of societal culture used in GLOBE. Some of the country chapters present a discussion of the findings of organizational practices and culture following this.

The presentation of the findings on leadership usually follows. This often opens with a review of literature on leadership in the country, which is followed by a presentation of the country's scores on the 21 subscales of leadership that emerged from the GLOBE data and the six-second order leadership factors. These quantitative indicators of leadership are also discussed in the context of the society and culture of the country. The presentation of the qualitative findings on leadership usually follows. This consists of the findings of focus groups, in-depth ethnographic interviews, media analysis, and participant observation and unobtrusive measurement. An integration of all these findings results in a combined, overall profile of leadership in the country. Each chapter usually closes with recommendations of the author(s) for foreign managers who may have to deal with managers from the country that has been written about or who may have to work in that country. Several country chapters also include sections on the limitations of the research on which the chapter is based and possible directions for future research.

CCIs have collected unobtrusive measures of the nine GLOBE *"As Is"* and *"Should Be"* dimensions. These dimensions reflect the practices and values in the culture. CCIs have also conducted participant observations of ongoing activities relevant to the interpretation of the culture, not only with specific reference to the nine GLOBE dimensions but also with respect to specific attributes and practices unique to the cultures studied. They have also collected and content-analyzed transcripts based on the predominant printed media (newspapers and magazines) as well as interviews and focus groups conducted with managers in the industries studied. With these data, CCIs were able to describe and interpret selected unique characteristics of their cultures. Such interpretations have given recognition to gender, ethnic, and religious diversity, generational differences, and other possible issues permeating the studied cultures. Thus the complexity and variability of complex cultures with two or more subcultures have also been described. In essence, these CCIs have written a qualitative analysis of major variables relevant to leadership and organizational practices in the countries studied. The attempt has been to ensure at least a moderate level of uniformity and quality of the qualitative research, while maintaining the uniqueness of each culture studied. The completed chapters are based on the combination of the quantitative survey data of the country in focus in comparison with the data collected in all the countries included in the GLOBE Research Program, and the qualitative research findings produced by CCIs. An interpretive analysis of all of the findings is also included. It is hoped that the quantitative-comparative results reported in GLOBE Book 1 (House et al., 2004) and the more qualitative and in-depth analysis of each of the 25 countries included in this book will provide appropriate conceptual frameworks and sufficient data for the development of a cross-cultural theory of leadership and organizational practices.

Project GLOBE employs both quantitative and qualitative methods to provide richly descriptive, yet scientifically valid, accounts of cultural influences on leadership and organizational processes. Whereas House et al. (2004) provides a comparative understanding of all the GLOBE participating countries on all the nine societal culture dimensions, 21 leadership scales, and their relationship with several socioeconomic indicators of these countries, this book provides much more detailed and comprehensive understanding of the 25 countries represented here.

6. PLAN OF THIS BOOK

This introduction is followed next by a chapter describing the methodology of the GLOBE Research Project as a whole and the country-specific methodology followed by most of the country chapter authors. Then follow the 25 country chapters arranged in 10 clusters based on combinations of several characteristics of the societies and cultures (see Gupta & Hanges, 2004, for details of clustering). The clusters in the order presented in the following chapters, with the countries comprising them, are: *Nordic Europe* (Sweden, Finland), *Germanic Europe* (Austria, Germany, Netherlands, Switzerland), *Anglo* (Australia, England, Ireland, New Zealand, South Africa/w, United States), *Latin Europe* (France, Portugal, Spain), *Latin America* (Argentina, Colombia, Mexico), *Eastern Europe* (Greece, Russia), *Middle East* (Turkey), *Confucian Asia* (China, Hong-Kong, Singapore), *Southern Asia* (India), and Sub-Saharan Africa. Although there is no separate country chapter for the Sub-Saharan cluster, the country chapter on South Africa (included in the Anglo cluster due to its primary focus being on the White population of South Africa) contains some information about South Africa (Black sample), which belongs to this cluster. The complete clusters of all the cultures that participated in GLOBE are shown in Table 1.2. The country chapters of each cluster are preceded by a short introduction to the cluster that follows. This cluster introduction provides a very brief description of the cluster and the countries comprising it. Unavoidably, the introductions are brief and sketchy, and readers are advised to refer to the following country chapters and the last chapter of this volume ("Integration, Conclusions, and Future Directions") for specifics and details.

The concluding chapter provides summary of some of the more interesting findings of the country chapters and attempts to integrate some of the common findings. It also focuses on what is common across all the 25 societies represented in this volume and among the countries comprising each cluster. It also describes the reasons for differences wherever differences are found. It does that for both culture and leadership separately, and then also integrates them. It also discusses emerging theoretical and methodological issues, and derives questions for future research and practical implications that will be of use to researchers, students, and practitioners. It takes an integrative view of societal culture, leadership, and the link between culture and leadership from a within-country and also a between-country perspective.

7. CONTRIBUTIONS OF THIS BOOK

Practitioners involved in cross-cultural management will find chapters in this book particularly useful as they prepare for negotiations with managers of a country with which they

TABLE 1.2

GLOBE Society/Culture Clusters

Anglo	**Latin Europe**	**Nordic Europe**	**Germanic Europe**
*Australia	*France	Denmark	*Austria
Canada	Israel	*Finland	*Germany
*England	Italy	*Sweden	(Former East)
*Ireland	*Portugal		Germany
*New Zealand	*Spain		(Former West)
*South Africa	Switzerland		*Netherlands
(White sample)	(French-speaking)		*Switzerland
*United States			(German speaking)

Eastern Europe	**Latin America**	**Sub-Saharan Africa**	**Middle East**
Albania	*Argentina	Namibia	Egypt
Georgia	Bolivia	Nigeria	Kuwait
*Greece	Brazil	South Africa	Morocco
Hungary	*Colombia	(Black sample)	Qatar
Kazakhstan	Costa Rica	Zambia	*Turkey
Poland	Ecuador	Zimbabwe	
*Russia	El Salvador		
Slovenia	Guatemala		
	*Mexico		
	Venezuela		

Southern Asia	**Confucian Asia**
*India	*China
Indonesia	*Hong Kong
Iran	Japan
Malaysia	*Singapore
Philippines	South Korea
Thailand	Taiwan

* Countries included in this book.

are not familiar, in planning for joint ventures, mergers and acquisitions, and collaborations. It will also be useful in comparing the finer nuances of countries belonging to the same cultural region in order to understand the subtle differences in countries that appear to be similar on the surface. Such comparisons can be done with several countries in a cluster to get a better understanding of the country one is interested in. An interesting analysis of country clusters is contained in the special issue of the *Journal of World Business* (2002) devoted to the GLOBE project. More details are presented in the conclusions chapter of this book.

This book makes a significant contribution to the field as it contains rich descriptions of the culture and leadership practices of the represented countries (a) by researchers and scholars who have lived in this country for quite some time and are therefore highly knowledgeable about these countries (b) based, in part, on data collected through rigorous methodologies used across a large number of countries employing instruments with proven high levels of reliability and validity. The chapters in this book combine the strength of the overall GLOBE study (e.g., by positioning the culture of each country within all the countries studied in the GLOBE program) with the strength of detailed qualitative and quantitative accounts of the country being reported on. The rigor of data collection applies equally to qualitative methods employed. This data collection, supplemented by participant observation and unobtrusive measurement by the authors themselves, provides a uniquely rich perspective on the countries being written about. The specific contribution of this volume therefore is to provide descriptions that are rich and thick while being rigorous and standardized at the same time.

REFERENCES

Bass, B. M. (1990). *Bass & Stogdill's handbook of leadership: Theory, research, and managerial applications* (3rd ed.). New York: The Free Press.

Dorfman, P. W. (1996). International and cross-cultural leadership research. In B. J. Punnett & O. Shenkar (Eds.), *Handbook for international management research* (pp. 267–349). Oxford, England: Blackwell.

Gupta, V., de Luque, M. S., & House, R. J. (2004). *Multisource construct validity of GLOBE scales.* In R. J. House, P. I. Hanges, M. Javidan, P. J. Dorfman, V. Gupta (Eds.), & GLOBE Associates, *Culture, leadership, and organizations: The GLOBE study of 62 societies* (pp. 152–177). Thousand Oaks, CA: Sage.

Gupta, V., & Hanges, P. J. (2004). *Regional and climate clustering of societal cultures.* In R. J. House, P. J. Hanges, M. Javidan, P. J. Dorfman, V. Gupta (Eds.), & GLOBE Associates, *Culture, leadership, and organizations: The GLOBE study of 62 societies* (pp. 178–218). Thousand Oaks, CA: Sage.

Hanges, P. J., & Dickson, M. W. (2004). *The development and validation of scales to measure societal and organizational culture.* In R. J. House, P. J. Hanges, M. Javidan, P. J. Dorfman, V. Gupta (Eds.), & GLOBE Associates, *Culture, leadership, and organizations: The GLOBE study of 62 societies* (pp. 122–151). Thousand Oaks, CA: Sage.

Hanges, P. J., & Dickson, M. W. (in press). Agitation over aggregation: Clarifying the development of and the nature of the GLOBE scales. *Leadership Quarterly.*

Hofstede, G. (1980). *Culture's consequences: International differences in work-related values.* London: Sage.

Hofstede, G., & Bond, M. H. (1988). The Confucius connection: From cultural roots to economic growth. *Organizational Dynamics, 16,* 4–21.

House, R. J., Hanges, P. J., Javidan, M., Dorfman, P. J., Gupta, V. (Eds.) & GLOBE Associates. (2004). *Culture, leadership, and organizations: The GLOBE study of 62 societies.* Thousand Oaks, CA: Sage.

House, R. J., & Javidan, M. (2004). Overview of GLOBE. In R. J. House, P. J. Hanges, M. Javidan, P. Dorfman, V. Gupta (Eds.), & GLOBE Associates, *Leadership, culture, and organizations: The GLOBE study of 62 societies* (pp. 9–28). Thousand Oaks, CA: Sage.

Javidan, M., & Hauser, M. (2004). *The linkage between GLOBE findings and other cross-cultural information.* In R. J. House, P. J. Hanges, M. Javidan, P. J. Dorfman, V. Gupta (Eds.), & GLOBE Associates, *Culture, leadership, and organizations: The GLOBE study of 62 societies* (pp. 102–121). Thousand Oaks, CA: Sage.

Journal of World Business. (2002). Volume 37, Issue 1. Special issue devoted to the GLOBE project. Elsevier Science Inc.

Kluckhohn, F. R., & Strodtbeck, F. L. (1961). *Variations in value orientations.* New York: HarperCollins.

McClelland, D. C. (1961). *The achieving society.* Princeton, NJ: Van Nostrand.

McClelland, D. C. (1985). *Human motivation.* Glenview, IL: Scott, Foresman.

Putnam, R. D. (1993). *Making democracy work.* Princeton, NJ: Princeton University Press.

Simonton, D. K. (1994). *Greatness: Who makes history and why?* New York: Guilford.

Smith, P. B., & Bond, M. H. (1993). *Social psychology across cultures: Analysis and perspectives.* London: Harvester Wheatsheaf.

Triandis, H. C. (1993). The contingency model in cross-cultural perspective. In M. M. Chemers & R. Ayman (Eds.), *Leadership theory and research: Perspectives and directions* (pp. 167–188). San Diego, CA: Academic Press.

Yukl, G. A. (2006). *Leadership in organizations* (6th ed.). Englewood Cliffs, NJ: Prentice-Hall.

2

▼▼▼▼▼▼▼

Methodology

Jagdeep S. Chhokar
Indian Institute of Management, Ahmedabad

Felix C. Brodbeck
Aston Business School, Aston University, Birmingham, England

Robert J. House
Wharton School of Management, University of Pennsylvania

"Cross-cultural research is tricky and difficult" (Triandis, 2004, p. xv), in part because measuring concepts such as culture and leadership is a complex and demanding process. "The logistics problems are harsh and trying" (Leung, Foreword, this volume, p. xiv). The GLOBE project took a multipronged approach to this issue, starting with the fundamentals such as defining the concepts and developing the measuring instruments for them, and deploying "diverse methodologies, both quantitative and qualitative, to enhance the robustness and richness of the findings" (Leung, Foreword, this volume, p. xv). This chapter describes first the methodology of the GLOBE project as a whole and then the country-general and country-specific methodology followed by the country chapter authors.

1. OVERALL METHODOLOGY OF GLOBE[1]

One of the major and unique strengths of GLOBE is the combination of quantitative and qualitative methodologies. The quantitative methodology consisted of starting without any preexisting definitions of concepts. All definitions including those of culture and leadership were developed *ab initio*. All the instruments for measuring these concepts were also developed from first principles starting with item generation and item analysis (across the participating cultures, e.g., by collaborative development of dimensions and respective Q-sorting of items)

---

[1] The methodology is described here in brief due to space constraints. For full details of methodology, please see Hanges and Dickson (2004, in press).

followed by comprehensive and rigorous psychometric analyses to establish properties such as reliability, validity, and so forth. Generalizability of the instruments across various cultures and countries was ensured through two pilot studies. The quantitative data were collected through the administration of the standardized questionnaires to middle managers in at least two of three industries per country, food processing, financial services, and telecommunication services. The specification of middle managers and specific industries was done to ensure comparability of the data across countries. The data thus collected from all the participating 61 countries were analyzed through a variety of statistical techniques to test various hypotheses.

The qualitative methodology consisted of focus groups, in-depth ethnographic interviews, media analysis, participant observation, and unobtrusive measurement within each country. The findings of the focus groups and ethnographic interviews were used to ensure that various items and instruments were applicable in all the countries, and that the concepts and definitions developed were understandable, not culturally offensive, in and relevant to respondents in all the participating countries. Media analysis, participant observation, and unobtrusive measurement were done along with the data collection for Phase 2.

The following section describes the quantitative methodology of GLOBE as a whole, which is followed by the more specific quantitative and qualitative methodologies that are also used in the country chapters included in this book.

Quantitative Methodology for GLOBE

Phase 1 of GLOBE concerned the development and validation of the GLOBE questionnaire scales designed to measure societal and organizational culture variables as well as Culturally Endorsed Implicit Theories of Leadership (CLTs). The original item pool contained 753 items, of which 382 were leadership items and 371 were societal and organizational culture items. The initial scales were refined through several techniques, such as double-blind translation-back translation, item evaluation reports, Q-sorts, and were also tested in two pilot studies. The final GLOBE scales possess sound psychometric properties, and the findings indicate justification for the use of the scales as aggregate measures of cultural phenomena. All 54 GLOBE scales demonstrate significant and nontrivial within-culture response agreement, between-culture differences, and respectable reliability of response consistency. Generalizability coefficients, which are joint measures of these psychometric properties, exceed 0.85 for all the scales. These coefficients indicate that the scales can be meaningfully applied to measure culture differentiation in terms of societal, organizational, and leadership phenomena. Details of the analytic procedures and results are available in Hanges and Dickson (2004, in press).

Organizational and societal culture items were written for the nine core GLOBE dimensions, described in the previous chapter at both the societal and the organizational levels. Items were written to capture two culture manifestations: institutional *practices* reported *"As Is"* and values reported in terms of what *"Should Be."* This schema is shown in Fig. 2.1.

Accordingly, items were written for all the nine dimensions of culture, as "quartets" having isomorphic structures across two units of analysis (societal and organizational) and across two manifestations of culture (*"As Is"* and *"Should Be"*), as shown in Fig. 2.1. Though the four items in a quartet are similar in terms of their structure, what is different is the frame of reference that the respondent is cued to use while responding to each item. The frame of reference is changed according to the particular manifestation of culture and the unit of analysis. An example of such a quartet is shown in Fig. 2.2, which contains

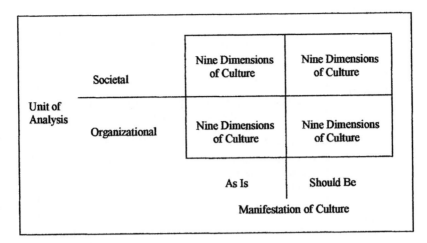

Figure 2.1   GLOBE's multilevel approach to measuring culture

essentially the same statement in the following four forms: Society *"As Is,"* Society *"Should Be,"* Organization *"As Is,"* and Organization *"Should Be."* Items representing the nine dimensions of culture were derived from (a) a review of literature on societal and organizational culture, and (b) interviews and focus groups conducted in several of the participating countries. Appropriate psychometric analyses showed that grouping the items into nine scales each corresponding to one of the dimensions of culture was amply justified (Hanges & Dickson, 2004, in press).

In generating leadership items, focus was on developing a comprehensive list of leader attributes and behaviors rather than on developing a priori leadership scales. The initial pool of leadership items was based on leader behaviors and attributes described in several extant leadership theories. The theories are described in House and Aditya (1997) and in House et al. (2004). These leadership items consisted of behavioral and attribute descriptors. Items were rated on a 7-point scale that ranged from a low of "This behavior or characteristic greatly inhibits a person from being an outstanding leader" to a high of "This behavior or characteristic contributes greatly to a person being an outstanding leader."

Country Co-Investigators (CCIs) made significant contributions in the development of the quantitative methodology. Starting with Q-sorting of the items, they provided Item Evaluation Reports, in which they noted any items containing words or phrases that were ambiguous or could not be properly translated in the target country's native language. CCIs also identified questions and items that might be culturally inappropriate. Most of the items that proved to be potentially problematic were dropped from further consideration. In a few cases, it was possible to rewrite items to eliminate potential problems yet still retain the original item's core intent and dimensionality.

In order to avoid any inherent systematic bias that may be present when respondents complete a survey not in their native language (Brislin, 1986), CCIs were responsible for translating the survey from English into the respondents' native language. This was done by the CCI, by another person fluent in both languages, or by a professional translator. The translation was then independently retranslated, from the specified culture's native language, into English. This back-translation was then submitted to the GLOBE Research Assistants, who compared the translated survey to the original English-language survey to verify the translation's accuracy.

	The economic system in this society is designed to maximize:	The economic system in this society *should* be designed to maximize:
Society	1 2 3 4 5 6 7 Individual Collective Interests Interests (Societal Practices)	1 2 3 4 5 6 7 Individual Collective Interests Interests (Societal Values)
Organization	The pay and bonus system in this organization is designed to maximize: 1 2 3 4 5 6 7 Individual Collective Interests Interests (Organizational Practices)	In this organization, the pay and bonus system *should* be designed to maximize: 1 2 3 4 5 6 7 Individual Collective Interests Interests (Organizational Values)

Figure 2.2   Example of a GLOBE item quartet addressing societal and organizational culture

Through a process of elimination based on sorting, item evaluation, and translation, the item pool was reduced and also made more relevant and appropriate for the project. CCIs also conducted two pilot studies, the first in 28 countries and the second in 15 countries (different from the 28 in the first pilot study), which contributed immensely to the refinement of the scales. Eight hundred and seventy-seven individuals participated in the first pilot study and 1,066 participated in the second.

The process just described resulted in nine scales to measure the nine culture *"As Is"* (cultural practices), and nine *"Should Be"* (cultural values) dimensions for each culture.

The questionnaire data collected in GLOBE Phase 2 consisted of (a) responses to approximately 17,300 questionnaires from middle managers of approximately 950 organizations in 61 countries, relevant to societal and organizational dimensions of culture, (b) unobtrusive measures of the societal culture dimensions, and (c) factors facilitating or inhibiting effective leadership.

Measurement of Organizational Practices and Values.   In each organization where the questionnaires were administered, the respondents were divided into two groups. One group responded to questions designed to capture the societal-level dimensions described previously and the other group responded to questions designed to capture the same dimensions, but at the organizational rather than the societal level.

Samples.   Because numerous countries have large and varied subcultures within their sovereign borders, demarcating cultural boundaries according to sovereign borders may prove inadequate. It is impossible to obtain representative samples of such multicultural nations as China, India, or the United States. Nonetheless, the samples drawn from such countries need to be comparable with respect to the dominant forces that shape cultures, such as ecological factors, history, language, politics, and religion. The country samples also needed to be relatively homogeneous within cultures. For multicultural countries, whenever possible, that subculture was sampled in which there was the greatest amount of commercial activity. More than one subculture was sampled whenever possible, such as indigenous and White subcultures in South Africa, French and German subcultures in Switzerland, and East and West subcultures in Germany.

The units of analysis for the GLOBE project consisted of cultural-level aggregated responses of samples of typical middle managers in at least two of three industries: food processing, financial services, and telecommunications services. The food-processing industry is a relatively stable industry. The telecommunications and financial industries may be stable or unstable, depending on the country and its economic conditions. By including these industries, we have obtained a fair number of dynamic industries and high-technology industries in the overall sample. These three industries were chosen as they are expected to exist in most countries regardless of their level of economic development. This requirement of existing in all participating countries precluded the use of industries such as automobile manufacturing or large chemical refineries as they exist in only a very small subset of the countries in the world.

Respondents were all middle managers. A middle manager was defined as one who had at least two levels above and at least two levels below him or her in an organization. In the case of very small organizations, a middle manager was defined as one who reported directly to the CEO of the organization or had at least one level below him or her in their organization.

Respondents were asked to use a 7-point scale to describe leader attributes and behaviors that they believed either enhanced or impeded exceptional leadership. They were also asked to critique their resident society's practices and values (in the form of *"As Is"* and *"Should Be"* responses, respectively), and the practices and values of the organizations in which they were employed, using 7-point scales as illustrated in Figure 2.2. Independent samples of middle managers completed one of two questionnaires. Half of the respondents in each culture completed the societal culture questionnaire (Sample 1), and the other half completed organizational culture questionnaire (Sample 2). All respondents completed the Leadership Attributes Questionnaire. Thus, the societal culture and the organizational culture questionnaires were completed by independent samples of respondents, thus ensuring no common-source variance.

Through employing a strategy of obtaining responses of middle managers in two of the three target industries in each country studied, samples were taken from approximately 40 countries in each of the target industries.

Our research design also permitted an assessment of whether common source response bias affected our results. Specifically, within each culture, different samples of middle managers completed the two versions of the survey. We were able to compare the responses to the leadership items for these two samples because the identical leadership items were contained on both versions of the survey. The means of the leadership item responses of Sample 1 and Sample 2 within each country were not significantly different. Thus, because separate samples from each society provided responses about organizational culture (Version A of the survey) and societal culture (Version B of the survey), and because the mean CLT responses across the two survey versions in each culture were not different, common-source response bias was not a factor in the quantitative GLOBE study. Given this result, we averaged the individual leadership scale scores for the two samples to produce means on the leadership scales for all cultures.

Phase 2 CLT Scales.   One of the objectives of GLOBE is to determine whether there are dimensions of CLTs that are universally endorsed and dimensions that are differentially endorsed across cultures. Recall that CLTs are culturally endorsed profiles of perceived effective or ineffective leader attributes or behaviors about which members within each culture agree. Profiles of CLT dimensions reflect what is commonly referred to as "leadership styles" in the leadership literature.

Shaw (1990) suggests that much of the cross-cultural literature indicating differences in managerial beliefs, values, and styles is parallel to leader prototypes influenced by cultural differences, which are analogous to CLTs as conceptualized for Project GLOBE. A study by O'Connell, Lord, and O'Connell (1990) supports the argument that culture plays a significant role in determining leader attributes and behaviors that are perceived as desirable and effective. Their study specifically examined Japanese and American CLT similarities and differences. For the Japanese, the traits of being fair, flexible, a good listener, outgoing, and responsible were highly rated in many domains, such as business, media, and education. For Americans, traits of intelligence, honesty, understanding, verbal skills, and determination to succeed were strongly endorsed as facilitating leader effectiveness in numerous domains. A study by Gerstner and Day (1994) also provides additional evidence that cross-cultural variances affect ratings of leadership attributes and behaviors. These investigators identified three dimensions relevant to distinct CLTs expressed by university students from eight nations. These dimensions had rank order correlations with Hofstede's (1980) measures of power distance, uncertainty avoidance, and individualism of 0.81, 1.00, and 0.70, respectively. The GLOBE Research Project follows in the tradition of these studies.

The data from Phase 2 were used to reconfirm the 21 subscales of the Leader Attribute Questionnaire. A multilevel confirmatory factor analysis was performed to test for the dimensionality of these scales at the society and organizational level of analysis. The multilevel CFA has been found to provide unbiased estimates of group-level (e.g., society, organizational) factor structures because it statistically controls for the biasing influence of the within-group factor structure (Hanges & Dickson, 2004, in press). During the Calgary meeting, held after Pilot Study 1 and before Pilot Study 2, it was realized that some leadership dimensions may have been left out. New items were developed during the meeting and the new factors were tested in Pilot Study 2. These additional items reflected the findings from ongoing interview and focus group research. The factor analyses in both the pilot studies were conducted on societal-item responses. Using the societal-level means of these additional items, a societal-level maximum likelihood exploratory factor analysis with a varimax rotation was conducted of these CLT items. This analysis resulted in five additional CLT subscales that displayed sound psychometric properties. Thus, Phase 2 resulted in a total of 21 leadership subscales, which can be seen in Table 2.1.

The discovery of significant interrelationships among the 21 leadership subscales resulted in the need to conduct a second-order factor analysis. The second-order factor analysis of the 21 subscales produced four factors: (a) Charismatic/Value-Based Leadership that is Team-Oriented, (b) Autonomous Leadership, (c) Humane Leadership, and (d) Nonparticipative Self-Protective Leadership. Assisted by prevailing theory, Factor 1 was divided into Charismatic/Value-Based Leadership and Team-Oriented Leadership to create two dimensions. Factor 4 was also divided into two dimensions: Self-Protective Leadership and Participative Leadership (the scores of the nonparticipative subscales were reversed to reflect participative leadership). Empirically derived from the second-order factors, these divisions preserved conceptual clarity while possessing dimensions related to current leadership theory and prior empirical studies.

TABLE 2.1
Leadership Second-Order Factors and Their Component Subscales

1. *Charismatic/Value-Based*	**2. *Team-Oriented***
Charismatic 1: Visionary	Team 1: Collaborative team
Charismatic 2: Inspirational	orientation
Charismatic 3: Self-sacrifice	Team 2: Team integrator
Integrity	Diplomatic
Decisive	Malevolent (reverse scored)
Performance oriented	Administratively competent
3. *Self-Protective*	**4. *Participative***
Self-centered	Autocratic (reverse scored)
Status-conscious	Nonparticipative (reverse scored)
Conflict inducer	
Face saver	
Procedural	
5. *Humane-Oriented*	**6. *Autonomous***
Modesty	Autonomous
Humane oriented	

The *21 subscales* were grouped into *six higher order leader behavior/attribute dimensions,* which are also shown in Table 2.1. The higher order dimensions are referred to as *global* CLT dimensions because they represent *classes* of leader behavior rather than specific leader behaviors. The 21 first-order factors are referred to as CLT subscales. These subscales measure more specific leader attributes and behaviors. Composite profiles of the six CLT dimensions represent what is generally referred to as leadership styles. Several studies using subsamples of the GLOBE data have supported the CLT profiles. Brodbeck et al. (2000), for example, present convincing evidence that clusters of European cultures sharing similar cultural values also share similar CLT profiles. den Hartog et al. (1999) show that attributes of charismatic-transformational leadership are universally endorsed as contributing to outstanding leadership.

2. SPECIFIC METHODOLOGY FOR COUNTRY CHAPTERS

Quantitative Methodology

The quantitative methodology for country chapters was the same as described previously for the overall GLOBE project. CCIs of individual countries contributed to scale development through item evaluation, Q-sorting, and pilot studies. Several of the CCIs also participated in the first GLOBE conference at Calgary in 1994 where the operational definitions of culture and leadership were agreed on. Subsequently, CCIs collected the Phase 2 data in their respective countries through administration of GLOBE questionnaires.

Although the overall statistical analyses of the quantitative data for all the participating 61 countries were done centrally at the University of Maryland, the data for each country, particularly of those that are included in this volume, were also analyzed at the country level and in the country by the CCI teams. This included, in some cases, factor analysis, exploratory or confirmatory or both, or cluster analysis and similar methods. The results of these analyses are reported in some of the chapters of this volume whereas in some these have been omitted for a variety of reasons. The decision whether to include these analyses or not has generally been made by the authors of these chapters primarily depending on what they considered to be the most appropriate for presenting their country data.

A word of caution is necessary here about the within-society factor analysis of the data included in several chapters of this book. As discussed in Hanges and Dickson (2004), the GLOBE scales were designed to measure organizational- or societal-level variability. The scales were never intended to meaningfully differentiate among individuals within a particular society. However, even though the scales were not constructed to provide such information, it may be interesting to assess whether similar factors differentiate individuals within a society. It should be noted, however, that we expect that the loadings of the GLOBE scales' items on within-society factors should be lower than reported in Hanges and Dickson (2004) (i.e., because the GLOBE scales' true-score variability was based on between-society differences and there is probably restriction of variability within society). Further, one should not interpret these within-society factor analyses as replications of the GLOBE factor structure. This analysis is intended as an exploration of the themes captured by GLOBE in a new domain (individual differences within a society). Finally, the absence of a GLOBE factor within a society should not be automatically interpreted as the factor being irrelevant to the people in that country. Rather, a factor may fail to emerge within a society even when that theme is extremely critical because there was no variability in how the individuals from a single society rated the items (e.g., they all rated the items a 7). Factor analysis requires variability and so a factor could fail to emerge because it is extremely critical or completely irrelevant to the people within a society.

Qualitative Methodology

The qualitative methodology consisted, in the main, of focus groups, in-depth ethnographic interviews, media analysis, participant observation, and unobtrusive measurement. Although the CCI teams of all the 61 countries participating in GLOBE collected quantitative data to some extent or the other, not all of them were able to implement the qualitative methodology to the same intensity and depth. And though the CCI teams in all the 25 countries represented in this volume conducted qualitative research in considerable depth, there is a variation in the extent of using them even amongst the 25 countries represented in this volume. The general process followed for each component of qualitative methodology is described in the following subsections. The specifics of the use of these methods are described in more detail in subsequent chapters.

Focus Groups.   The purpose of focus groups was to learn what the middle managers in each culture thought about outstanding leadership. The focus groups provided participants with an opportunity to reflect on and formally discuss effective, above-average, and outstanding managers. It was hoped that at the end of the focus group the participants would have greater insights into various behaviors generally employed by managers when leading organizational work units. The standard material and process for conducting focus groups was provided to the CCIs by the GLOBE Coordinating Team. This is summarized in Boxes 2.1 and 2.2.

BOX 2.1

Focus Group Exercise

(Given to participants a couple of days before the focus group was actually conducted)
To begin, think of a person whom you know, or have observed several times, who you judge to be an outstanding leader. If you do not know such an individual personally, select a prominent leader about whom you have read or one whom you have observed in the media, whom you judge to be an outstanding leader.

Now visualize an important incident in which the leader has interacted with one or more of her or his subordinates or followers. Spend a few minutes recalling the incident in detail, and visualizing the behavior of both the leader and the subordinates/followers.

Please write a short story about the incident using the following questions as guides. Devote one or two paragraphs to each of the questions. The total story should take no more than about 15 minutes to write.

1. What were the background circumstances which lead up to the event?
2. Who were the people involved? What were their formal positions, relationships to each other?
3. What was said during the incident? Did the leader do anything that was particularly effective? Ineffective? Please describe.
4. What feelings were experienced by each party?
5. What was the outcome? Was it a successful incident? Did the manager achieve his or her objective?

Now think of a person whom you know, or have observed several times, whom you judge to be a competent manager but not an outstanding leader. Visualize an important incident in which the manager has interacted with one or more of her or his subordinates or followers. Spend a few minutes recalling the incident in detail, and visualizing the behavior of both the manager and the subordinates/followers.

Now please write a short story in which you address the earlier questions.

Now please develop a list of attributes (skills, abilities, personality traits, values, behaviors) that you believe distinguish outstanding leaders from competent managers in general.

BOX 2.2

Process of the Focus Group

At the start of the focus group, inform participants that they are participating in a cross-cultural research project in which large number of nations is participating. Also inform them that the purpose of the focus group is to understand the meaning of the terms *leadership* and *management* in different cultures, and to gather information concerning the attributes of individuals that are characteristic of effective leaders and managers. Also inform them that this is the beginning step of the research, and that the information obtained will help ensure that the terms *leadership* and

---

(Continued)

management will be defined for each nation in terms of the culturally appropriate meaning for each nation.

Subsequently, request the participants to define the term *leadership*. List their contributions and attempt to come to a consensus concerning the definition of the term *leadership*. Record the majority definition and also any minority opinions.

Now, conduct the same exercise for the term *management*.

Then request the participants to share their thoughts concerning the attributes that distinguish outstanding leaders, above-average managers, and normally effective managers. Follow it up by a discussion of distinguishing behaviors of each class of managers.

After this, request the participants to describe how managers in their culture differ from managers in another country that is one of their major trading partners. After clearly specifying the country chosen for comparison, list the differences pointed out by the participants between managers of the two countries. Further request the participants to mention how managers of their county should behave in order to be effective when dealing with managers of the trading partner.

In-Depth Ethnographic Interviews. The purpose of the interviews was to explore, in some depth, how managers in each culture defined leadership, explicitly or implicitly. It was recommended to the CCI teams that interviews should be conducted with at least five to seven middle managers, till some clear and unambiguous patterns emerged. It was also suggested that the interviews be tape-recorded for subsequent content analysis. Guidelines for the in-depth ethnographic interviews are summarized in Box 2.3.

BOX 2.3

Guidelines for In-Depth Ethnographic Interview

Begin the interview with a brief explanation of GLOBE. Advise the interviewees of the broad purpose of the interview and that it is part of a multination study.

- Clarify to the interviewees that there are no correct, incorrect, or desirable or undesirable responses.
- Stress that their responses would contribute to an understanding of leadership and management in their culture.
- While the interview should be generally free-flowing and exploratory, following are some guiding and suggested questions to broadly guide your exploration:

1. What is your personal definition of outstanding leadership?
2. What is the difference between a competent manager and an outstanding leader?
3. What is your perception of the opposite of outstanding leadership? If the person is in the position of leadership and does not exercise outstanding leadership, what would be the kinds of behaviors in which he or she is likely to engage?

(Continued)

4. Please describe a couple of critical incidents that illustrate outstanding leadership.
5. Were there any obstacles or constraints faced by the leaders in these incidents? Any opposition, resistance, bureaucratic red tape, or lack of resources, for example?
6. Please name two or three well-known individuals who, you think, are or have been outstanding leaders.
7. Is there anything that these leaders have in common that makes them outstanding and differentiates them from others who have been in similar positions? How are the behaviors of these leaders similar?
8. Please describe a specific behavior, something each leader did, that illustrates his or her leadership.
9. Is there something a leader did that resulted in your strong acceptance of or support for the leader or resulted in significantly increased motivation on your part, or willingness to go above and beyond the call of duty in the interest of the leader's vision, objective, or mission? Please describe that in some detail.

CCI teams were informed that the guidelines in Box 2.3 were broad and were likely to enrich the interview and provide more meaningful data about implicit definitions of the leadership used by the interviewees.

Media Analysis.   The purpose of the media analysis was to get yet another interpretation of leadership as it is perceived by members of the society and culture. This was because the portrayal of leadership by the media is expected to reflect what the society thinks of its leaders and the phenomenon of leadership. The analysis of media portrayal and reporting was also expected to provide insights into the process concerning *how* do the members of the society think about leadership. In order to do this, CCIs were advised to analyze media coverage and reports of leadership for arriving at the essence of leadership as reflected in the media. The general process recommended to the CCIs is described in Box 2.4.

BOX 2.4

Guidelines for Media Analysis

Choose some representative publications from different sections of the media, such as one of the most well-respected major national daily newspapers focusing on general issues and broad audience; one of the most well-respected major daily newspapers focusing on business, industrial, and financial audiences; a major national weekly news magazine reporting general news; a major weekly or fortnightly news magazine targeted at the business community. In countries with multiple languages, it is recommended that the focus be on the dominant language used by the larger managerial population.

1. Choose two time periods (anywhere from 2 to 4 weeks each) with a gap of 1 month between the two time periods. The time periods should be such when no large, regularly scheduled event was to happen such as a major public or religious celebration, an important anniversary

(*Continued*)

   of a public event, a major political election, or a major political convention. The reason for avoiding such periods is to get as "normal" representation of the portrayal of leadership in the media as possible.
2. Select all articles and stories related to or referring to leadership in any way whatsoever, appearing in the chosen publications during the chosen time periods. Content-analyze these stories and articles to develop the concepts of leadership relevant to that society, as portrayed in the media.

Though it was left to the CCIs to do the content analyses in the way most appropriate and suitable for them, using the guidelines provided in Agar (n.d.) and Thomas (n.d.), a basic process suggested to the CCIs was to (a) transcribe the extracts of the stories and articles, highlighting the important phrases containing any verbs, adjectives, and nouns relevant to leadership, (b) gather all the phrases together and typify the phrases with one word that best described the event, and (c) sort the phrases by typification categories, leading to a description of how leadership was portrayed in the media.

Subsequently, this portrayal of leadership was related to the countries' profiles on the core GLOBE dimensions. The results of the media analyses also helped provide insights on the various ways in which the GLOBE dimensions get enacted in the culture, and to elaborate and explain the findings of the in-depth ethnographic interviews. In addition, the large amount of information gathered during the media analyses also helped in understanding the findings of the quantitative analyses.

Some countries performed a specific media analysis, such that job advertisements for leaders were analyzed (e.g., the characteristics that were required); for example, see the chapter about Sweden or Germany. Some did extensive analyses of the ethnographic interviews, for example, the chapter on Colombia.

Unobtrusive Measurement and Participant Observations.   Given that most of the CCIs were residing in the cultures that they were to study, they were requested to collect data relevant to unobtrusive measurement of the theoretical dimensions of culture. Unobtrusive measures and participant observations of the researchers were used in conjunction with other qualitative data and questionnaire measures to triangulate measurement of culture dimensions.

Power stratification may be reflected by the number of hierarchical levels in a particular kind of organization, such as in a sample of organizations included in the quantitative data collection. The number of titles and hierarchical levels of domestic help hired by wealthy individuals in the society might also reflect power stratification. It could be expected that there would be more such titles in highly power-stratified society and fewer in societies characterized by low power stratification. The number of status-relevant occupational titles (or other relevant samples) found in the industries in which quantitative data were to be collected could also reflect the power stratification of the society.

The average age of top executive officers in industry might be an unobtrusive measure of tolerance of uncertainty. The higher average age of high-level managers was expected to reflect low tolerance of uncertainty. Some of the sample unobtrusive measurement items are presented in Table 2.2.

TABLE 2.2
Sample Unobtrusive Measurement Items

Uncertainty Avoidance: Existence of laws concerning minimum age for marriage

Power Stratification: Prevalence of conspicuous use of symbols of authority

Collective Orientation: Prevalence of extended families

Gender Differentiation: Proportion of women in top two levels of organizations studied

Humane Orientation: Existence of laws to ensure safe employment conditions

Future Orientation: R & D expenditures in the three GLOBE target industries (controlling for GNP)

Achievement Orientation: Frequency of awards for outstanding student performance at universities

CCIs were also requested to look for unique rituals, myths, and ceremonies in their culture that may have relevance to various societal culture dimensions. History of the society including the political and social history, history of leaders, of the economy, of the industries studied, and of the organizations from which the quantitative data were obtained, could also be a very rich source of information about the culture being studied. The CCIs were requested to develop a description of each of the societal culture dimensions based on their unobtrusive measurements and participant observations. Given the experience and skill of the CCIs in social sciences research, this was expected, and indeed turned out, to be a rich source of developing insights into the cultures studied.

3. RESPONSE BIAS

Triandis (1995) has noted that the various cultures have conflicting response patterns when responding to questionnaires. The presence of these different response patterns can potentially compromise cross-cultural comparisons. Thus several different statistical techniques have been developed to eliminate the contamination of survey responses.

The intercorrelations of the unobtrusive measures and the core *"Should Be"* scale scores for each dimension range from .38 to .88 (all significant, $p < .05$ and less). The intercorrelations of the unobtrusive measures and the core *"As Is"* scale scores for each dimension range from .51 to .65 (all significant, $p < .05$ and less) (Gupta, de Luque, & House, 2004, pp. 153, 171). These intercorrelations indicate validity of the GLOBE societal questionnaire measures. The middle-manager responses to the societal questionnaire also demonstrate that these intercorrelations reflect the society at large in which the managers also exist and not just the specifically defined culture of middle managers. Statistical analyses were also performed for response bias (for details, see Appendix B of House et al., 2004).

4. INTEGRATION OF QUANTITATIVE AND QUALITATIVE FINDINGS

Authors of the country chapters included in this book were requested to develop culture specific interpretations of local behaviors, norms, and practices based on the qualitative research methods listed earlier in this chapter, and integrate those interpretations with the findings derived from the quantitative analyses comparing the results of that particular country with all the countries participating in GLOBE. This integration of the findings of quantitative and qualitative research methods is one of the unique features of this book, and provides a rich and in-depth understanding of the culture of the 25 countries represented in this book.

The integration of the quantitative and qualitative findings of each country is followed by an overall integration in the concluding chapter of this volume which takes an integrative view to point out particularly interesting findings, to identify commonalities among culture-specific findings, and to discuss emerging theoretical and methodological issues. It also derives questions for future research and practical implications, from which researchers, students and practitioners can benefit; for societal culture, leadership, and the link between culture and leadership from between-country and multiple within-country perspectives.

REFERENCES

Agar, M. (n.d.). *Qualitative research manual, I* and *II*. GLOBE Research Project.

Brislin, R. W. (1986). The wording and translation of research instruments. In W. J. Lohner & J. W. Berry (Eds.), *Field methods in cross-cultural research* (pp. 137–164). Beverly Hills, CA: Sage.

Brodbeck, F. C., Frese, M., Akerblom, S., Audia, G., Bakacsi, G., Bendova, H., et al. (2000). Cultural variation of leadership prototypes across 22 European countries. *Journal of Occupational and Organizational Psychology, 73*, 1–29.

den Hartog, D., House, R. J., Hanges, P. J., Ruiz-Quintanilla, S. A., Dorfman, P. J., & GLOBE Associates. (1999). Culture specific and cross culturally generalizable implicit leadership theories: Are attributes of charismatic/transformational leadership universally endorsed? *Leadership Quarterly, 10*(12), 219–256.

Gerstner, C. R., & Day, D. V. (1994). Cross-cultural comparison of leadership prototypes. *Leadership Quarterly, 5*(2), 121–134.

Gupta, V., de Luque, M. S., & House, R. J. (2004). *Multisource construct validity of GLOBE scales*. In R. J. House, P. J. Hanges, M. Javidan, P. J. Dorfman, V. Gupta, & GLOBE Associates (Eds.), *Culture, leadership, and organizations: The GLOBE study of 62 societies* (pp.152–177). Thousand Oaks, CA: Sage.

Hanges, P. J., & Dickson, M. W. (2004). *The development and validation of scales to measure societal and organizational culture*. In R. J. House, P. J. Hanges, M. Javidan, P. J. Dorfman, V. Gupta, & GLOBE Associates (Eds.), *Culture, leadership, and organizations: The GLOBE study of 62 societies* (pp.122–151). Thousand Oaks, CA: Sage.

Hanges, P. J., & Dickson, M. W. (in press). Agitation over Aggregation: Clarifying the development of and the nature of the GLOBE scales. *Leadership Quarterly* (forthcoming).

Hofstede, G. (1980). *Culture's consequences: International differences in work-related values*. London: Sage.

House, R. J., & Aditya, R. N. (1997). The social scientific study of leadership: Quo vadis? *Journal of Management, 23*(3), 409–473.

House, R. J., Hanges, P. J., Javidan, M., Dorfman, P. J., Gupta, V., & GLOBE Associates. (Eds.). (2004). *Culture, leadership, and organizations: The GLOBE study of 62 societies*. Thousand Oaks, CA: Sage.

O'Connell, M. S., Lord, R. G., & O'Connell, M. K. (1990, August). *Differences in Japanese and American leadership prototypes: Implications for cross-cultural training*. Paper presented at the meeting of the Academy of Management, San Francisco.

Shaw, J. B. (1990). A cognitive categorization model for the study of intercultural management. *Academy of Management Review, 15*(4), 616–645.

Thomas, J. (n.d.). *The effective leader as portrayed in the US popular media*. GLOBE Research Project.

Triandis, H. C. (1995). *Individualism and collectivism*. Boulder, CO: Westview Press.

Triandis, H. C. (2004). Foreword. In R. J. House, P. J. Hanges, M. Javidan, P. Dorfman, & V. Gupta (Eds.), *Leadership, culture, and organizations: The GLOBE study of 62 societies* (pp. xv–xix). Thousand Oaks, CA: Sage.

I

NORDIC EUROPE CLUSTER

The Nordic Europe cluster in the GLOBE Research Program consisted of Denmark, Ireland, and Sweden. In this volume, the cluster is represented by Finland and Sweden. This region is generally considered to consist of the Nordic countries: Denmark, Finland, Iceland, Norway, and Sweden. These countries are called Nordic because the word *Nord* means "North" in several languages. Therefore these countries are also referred to as Northern European countries.

In terms of cultural dimensions, this cluster is high on Future Orientation, Gender Egalitarianism, Institutional Collectivism, and Uncertainty Avoidance. This cluster falls in the middle range of scores on Humane Orientation and Performance Orientation. Its scores on Assertiveness, In-Group Collectivism, and Power Distance are low (House et al., 2004).

In terms of Leadership, the Nordic European cluster endorses a blend of high Charismatic/Value-Based and high Team-Oriented leadership with considerable elements of Participative leadership. Although Self-Protective leadership is strongly rejected, there is tolerance of Autonomous leadership.

Although the Scandinavian or Nordic countries are often referred to as a region of culturally similar countries, there are significant variances among these countries. For example, Finland and Sweden, the two countries represented in this volume, differ on how Humane Oriented leadership is enacted. Whereas personal sensitivity and development support are the main means of achieving Humane Oriented leadership in Finland, it is the egalitarian approach in Sweden that grants individual autonomy and hence enables enactment of Humane Oriented leadership.

REFERENCES

House, R. J., Hanges, P. J., Javidan, M., Dorfman, P. W., Gupta, V., & GLOBE Associates. (2004). *Culture, leadership, and organizations: The GLOBE study of 62 societies.* Thousand Oaks, CA: Sage.

3

▼▼▼▼▼▼▼

"Primus Inter Pares": Leadership and Culture in Sweden

Ingalill Holmberg & Staffan Åkerblom
Centre for Advanced Studies in Leadership, Stockholm School of Economics

> *Swedish leadership is vague and imprecise … in giving an order a Swede will typically say "See what you can do about it!" What does this mean? It is obviously connected with the extensive delegation of authority. Managers who say "See what you can do about it!" are demonstrating trust in their co-workers. It is also a question of exercising control through a common understanding of the problem, rather than through giving direct orders. This must be regarded as one of the strengths of Sweden's egalitarian society.*
>
> —Edström & Jönsson (1998, p. 167)

The opening quotation provides a significant image of the enactment of leadership in Sweden: Vagueness, equality, and consensus are three of the notions that are crucial to (an understanding of) established leadership in the Swedish context. They are all rooted in an ideology that evolved over a period of many years between the late 1930s and the 1990s, permeating most, if not all, aspects of life in Sweden, and to a large extent in the other Nordic countries. This ideology, with its strong emphasis on the notion of the collective, emerged from attempts to combine economic growth with democracy and extensive programs for social development. During the 1990s a conviction arose in many quarters that this ideology no longer had a part to play in the increasingly globalized context of the day. In business management, for instance, traditional stakeholder perspectives were often being replaced by a focus on shareholder values, whereas in the management discourse organizations now take second place to the individuals who populate them. This shift is perhaps most clearly expressed in the economic vocabulary subsumed under the label of the "New Economy," a phenomenon that has attracted enormous attention in the public space in recent years (Holmberg & Strannegård, 2002). As Sweden entered the new millennium, the ideological dissonance between the old and the new was reaching its peak. The implications of this ideological shift from the perception, enactment, and evaluation of leadership, is one of the several themes that is examined in this chapter.

The aim of the present chapter is to explore leadership and culture in Sweden, and to see how they are interrelated. The exploration is based on a number of empirical studies carried out between 1994 and 1998 within the framework of the GLOBE project. We start with some general facts about Sweden, its history, and its development as a modern welfare state, after which these studies are presented in separate sections.

General Facts About Sweden

Sweden has an area of 450,000 square kilometeres, which makes it slightly larger than the state of California, USA. The relatively small population of 9 million (Statistics Sweden, 2005) is by no means evenly distributed: About 85% live in the southern half of the country. One in every four Swedes lives in one of the 10 biggest cities, of which the capital Stockholm, Göteborg (Gothenburg), and Malmö are the largest.

Sweden's economy is highly international, albeit heavily dependent on a limited number of very large international corporations. Swedish companies were quick to recognize the importance of being represented in foreign markets, and global free trade has been extremely important to the growth of Swedish industry and prosperity. Sweden's main trading partners are the other Nordic countries and the major countries in the rest of Europe. Sweden joined the European Union (EU) on January 1, 1995, and more than half of Swedish exports are to other EU members. In 2003, exports accounted for 44% of the gross domestic product (GDP; Swedish Institute, 2004b).

Sweden is becoming a postindustrial service-oriented society, but manufacturing still dominates foreign trade. The engineering industry accounts for some 40% of all Swedish exports, the main products being machinery, telecommunications, electrical equipment, and motor vehicles. Other important exports are pulp, paper, paper and wood products, chemical products, and pharmaceuticals (Swedish Institute, 2003a).

The Swedish service sector is dominated by public organizations. Services such as child care, health care, and education are all supplied under public auspices in order to guarantee equally high standards for every citizen.[1] In 2003, nearly a third of the total labor force were employed in central and local[2] public agencies, including the social insurance sector (Swedish Institute, 2004b).

Sweden is a constitutional monarchy with a parliamentary form of government. The King, Carl XVI Gustaf, has ceremonial functions only as head of state. Parliament consists of a single chamber, whose members are directly elected by proportional representation for a 4-year term. Sweden has universal suffrage and the voting age is 18. Voter turnout has traditionally been very high, 85% to 90%, but was only just above 80% in the last two elections, which has led to an intensive debate as to whether democracy is in crisis (Müller, 2002).

Some Historical Notes

It is rather difficult to select a few historical fragments to say anything significant about the Sweden of today that we are about to explore in this chapter. It can be argued that "history" is in itself always a gross oversimplification of immensely complex and irreducible processes, constantly being rewritten and edited for contemporary interests and purposes. Then, in a chapter like this one, we have the added challenge of reducing and simplifying further what is already oversimplified, while also trying to say something meaningful. What selection criteria should be used? We decided to take the historical themes and events that the Swedish Institute[3] uses in presenting Sweden to other countries, and that most Swedes would refer to

[1]A minority of private alternatives coexists with the public services.
[2]Municipalities and county councils.
[3]The Swedish Institute (SI) is a public agency "entrusted with disseminating knowledge abroad about Sweden and organizing exchanges with other countries in the spheres of culture, education, research, and public life in general." Sources for the historical notes can be found on their Web site at http://www.si.se.

in everyday talk (self-representation). In other words, the selection itself may say as much about contemporary Sweden as its actual content does.

The Viking Age, 800–1050 AD, was a period of expansion directed primarily eastward. Many Viking expeditions set off from Sweden for the combined purposes of plunder and trade along the coasts of the Baltic Sea and up the rivers extending deep into present-day Russia. The Vikings active in the east traveled as far as the Black Sea and the Caspian Sea, where they developed trading links with the Byzantine Empire and the Arab dominions. The Vikings were thus the pioneers in establishing Sweden's foreign trade and international relations.

In the Middle Ages, the loose federation of provinces constituting Sweden became part of the cultural sphere of Catholic Europe. In 1397, Scandinavia was united under Queen Margaret in a union that lasted until the early years of the 16th century, when the Danes besieged Kalmar and Stockholm. Gustav Vasa (1523–1560), one of the most prominent political leaders in Swedish history, regained control over the country and was proclaimed King.

The foundations of the Swedish national state were laid during the reign of Gustav Vasa, who gave Sweden a strong central government in an administration reorganized along German lines, and established Protestantism as the state religion.

In 1818, Jean Baptiste Bernadotte, a French Marshal and opponent of Napoleon, was crowned King of Sweden. The present Swedish Royal Family, which is greatly respected by Swedes but that has no formal political influence, are his direct descendants.

During the later part of the 19th century Sweden was one of the poorest countries in Europe. The majority of the population, 90%s earned its livelihood from agriculture. One consequence of this situation was emigration, mainly to North America, which in relative terms was very substantial: Out of a population of a mere 3.5 million in 1850, and approximately 6 million in 1930, about 1.5 million Swedes emigrated between 1850 and 1930.

Late but Rapid Industrialization

The technical advances achieved during the 16th and 17th centuries were mainly attributable to the immigration of skilled craftsmen, merchants, and professionals—among them many Germans, Scots, Dutch, and Walloons.

In the late 19th century, the Swedish engineering industry entered into a period of rapid industrialization and expansion, unparalleled before or since. Sweden had rich domestic supplies of iron ore, timber, and waterpower. The next few decades witnessed the creation of a number of companies that were to attain a dominant role in Swedish industry through a successful combination of inventors, entrepreneurs, and financiers (Jönsson, 1995a). Industry did not begin to grow until the 1890s, but then developed very rapidly between 1900 and 1930. After the World War II, Sweden became one of Europe's leading industrial nations.

With pride, Swedes recall the achievements of engineers and entrepreneurs like Lars Magnus Ericsson (1846–1926), who together with a partner started a company manufacturing telephones and telephone equipment in 1878. As early as the 1890s, the company established subsidiaries abroad, and the products attracted international attention. Ericsson developed into one of the leading telecom companies in the world today. Other inventors and/or entrepreneurs who started important enterprises at about the same time included Alfred Nobel[4] (1833–1896), the inventor of dynamite (Nobel Industries); Nils Gustav Dalén[5] (1869–1937), who invented the automatic maritime beacon (AGA); Gustaf de Laval

---

[4]Alfred Nobel's will created the Nobel Prizes in physics, chemistry, medicine/physiology, literature, and peace, to be given to those who had "conferred the greatest benefit on mankind" the preceding year. The Nobel Prizes were awarded for the first time in 1901.

[5]Dalén was awarded the Nobel Prize for physics in 1912.

(1845–1913), who invented the cream separator (Alfa Laval); and Sven Wingquist (1876–1953), who is the father of the modern ball-bearing and founder of AB Svenska Kullagerfabriken (SKF), which remains the world's leading producer of industrial bearings.[6]

Because Swedish companies commanded a small domestic market, they were forced into international expansion at an early stage. Today, Swedish-owned multinational firms account for about half of total Swedish exports and manufacturing output. Many of these firms are extensively global, with almost 90% of sales in foreign markets and with more than 60% of their staff employed outside Sweden.

Access to raw materials, skilled workers, and innovative talent helped Sweden achieve the same level of per capita income as Great Britain by the outbreak of the Second World War. Sweden was fortunate enough not to be drawn into the war. Its industry and infrastructure thus remained intact and were well equipped to take advantage of the upswing in world trade during the postwar period.

Nineteenth-century Sweden was also characterized by the emergence of strong popular movements such as the free (i.e., nonstate) churches, the temperance and women's movements and, above all, the labor movement. The latter, which grew concurrently with the industrialization of the later 19th century, became reformist in its outlook after the turn of the century and by 1917 the first representatives of the Social Democratic movement joined the government. Universal suffrage was introduced for men in 1909 and for women in 1921, and this later date also marked the breakthrough for the principle of parliamentary government.

Building the Welfare State: *Folkhemmet* and the Swedish Model

An important concept in describing the evolution of Sweden as a modern welfare state is the political Utopia of a "People's home"—or *Folkhemmet*—as envisioned around 1930 by the Social Democratic Party, which was the ruling political party for more than four decades after 1932.[7] *Folkhemmet* is a metaphor of society as the good home, a nationwide community in which "equality, concern for others, co-operation and helpfulness"[8] (as in any good home) should prevail. It was a vision of a decent and socialist society, entailing economic and social justice, and equality. It proved possible to realize these plans in all their essentials after the World War II.

Important figureheads during the postwar *Folkhemmet* period were the Social Democratic leaders Per Albin Hansson, Tage Erlander, and Olof Palme, all of them prime minister in turn.[9] Hansson and Erlander in particular became national father figures, with powerful leader profiles. Palme enjoyed similar status but was much more controversial, partly because his political focus stretched well beyond the domestic arena. Palme became famous internationally for his strong commitment to the Third World and the struggle for the right of the emerging nations to self-determination.[10]

These developments in Sweden in general, and the evolution in the country of the modern universal welfare state in particular, are often described in terms of "the Swedish model." As

---

[6]For more comprehensive descriptions of the evolution of seven dominant Swedish companies, see Jönsson (1995a).

[7]The Social Democratic Party held power alone or in coalition during 1932–1976 and 1982–1991, whereas the nonsocialist parties formed coalition governments during 1976–1982 and 1991–1994. After the 1994, 1998, and 2002 elections, the Social Democratic Party has ruled the country with a minority government.

[8]The future prime minister Per-Albin Hansson in a speech in the Swedish Parliament in 1928, appealing to the home-sweet-home sentiments of the general public (Hirdman, 1989, p. 89).

[9]Hansson was prime minister 1932–1946, Erlander 1946–1969, and Palme 1969–1976 and 1982–1986 (opposition leader 1976–1982).

[10]In foreign affairs Olof Palme embarked on new directions, such as disarmament, building global security in a Cold War world full of confrontations, and narrowing the gap between the rich and poor nations. For good or worse, Sweden developed the role of a kind of "world conscience" in international relations. The assassination of Prime Minister Palme in February 1986 has been dubbed by many as Sweden's loss of virginity.

the name suggests, the model embraces certain factors that, taken together, are typical of Swedish society and unique to it. Although the Swedish model has been more or less abandoned today, it is important to offer a brief description of some of its main characteristics in any account of the development of Swedish society and culture since the Second World War, and of the institutional context that this has provided for managerial leadership in Sweden over more than half a century. If typical management styles are seen as sediments of experience over time, then the collective experience of the Swedish model can certainly be said to have permeated the minds of Swedish managers (Jönsson, 1995b).

The Swedish model should not be interpreted as a precise or unambiguous concept. Nevertheless, a 5-year interdisciplinary research program, "The Study of Power and Democracy in Sweden,"[11] did identify a number of distinctive and partially interlocking features that had developed between the end of 1930 and the beginning of 1970, a period coinciding with the years of Social Democratic rule in Sweden. These features can be summarized as follows:

- A non-interventionist stance on the part of the state in the industrial relations system. The labor market actors avoided the threat of state intervention in conflicts, and it is probable that this threat helped to promote cooperation among the actors.[12] In the Swedish model, this cooperation soon became the norm.
- Centralized collective negotiations between the actors on the labor market. This centralization facilitated the pursuit of a wage policy that exhibited solidarity with low-paid workers, in the sense that the general wage level was adjusted and increased to that of the most internationally competitive industries, thus forcing unproductive enterprises either to improve or to close down.
- The potential problem of lay-offs resulting from this wage policy was dealt with by an active governmental labor market policy, aimed essentially at promoting the movement of the labor force from low-productive to high-productive sectors.

To this can be added a unique political climate between the different actors in the labor market, a culture of consensus that prevailed for several decades following World War II. The 1938 "Saltsjöbaden-agreement" was a historical compromise between the two main actors, the Swedish Trade Union Confederation (*Landsorganisationen*, LO) and the Swedish Employers' Confederation (*Svenska Arbetsgivareföreningen*, SAF).[13] This agreement marked the starting point for a period of relatively peaceful industrial relations, cooperation, and mutual trust. The spirit of Saltsjöbaden became the cultural frame within which the Swedish model developed and "signaled the end of worker-employer hostilities and paved the way for the economic basis of the welfare state" (Trädgård, 1990, p. 48; cited in Berglund & Löwstedt, 1996). Economic growth was thus rapid during the postwar period and up to the mid-1970s, during which time Swedish export industry was highly competitive and the Swedish economy was enjoying an exceptional rate of growth.

Sweden's development as a welfare state was thus due, to a large extent, to the Swedish model and its middle-of-the-road strategy between capitalism and socialism, a strategy accomplished in a joint effort by a triad consisting of the state, the labor unions, and the employers. Berglund and Löwstedt (1996) suggest that the Swedish model can be seen as an attempt at realizing a *Gesellschaft* within a *Gemeinschaft* (cf. Tönnies, 1963).

---

[11]*Maktutredningen. Huvudrapport: "Demokrati och makt i Sverige"* (SOU, 1990, p. 44).

[12]Cf. Jönsson (1995a, p. 125).

[13]Besides LO (which represents blue-collar and some clerical occupations) and SAF (representing private-sector employers), there are also several national confederations of white-collar employees and employers covering workplaces in both the private and public sectors.

Although the Swedish model is a crucial feature of any attempt to describe the institutional context in which industry (and managerial leadership) developed in Sweden during this period, it is naturally not the only one. In his comprehensive work on the historical development of a number of large Swedish companies, Jönsson (1995a) indicates several other contributory institutional conditions. Early internationalization was one factor that has already been mentioned. Swedish companies were quick to adapt to foreign markets and different cultures. A second factor was the strong influence of three dominating banking interests,[14] which, as well as supplying risk capital, also provided active long-term ownership, industrial competence, and a network of industrial leaders and directors from companies within their own spheres and representing a major part of Swedish industry. A third factor consisted of the collaboration between the parties on the labor market aimed at combining modernization (new technology) and rationalization with various enriching and participative models of work organization.

In recent decades, like many other Western countries, Sweden has been evolving as a service-oriented and knowledge-intensive society. In the Swedish case, a service-oriented society meant an expanding public sector, because such key services as medical care, child care, and education were provided predominantly by public organizations. As the country moved into the 1990s the economic trends took a downturn, and as the recession deepened unemployment rose from a very low rate in the 1970s and 1980s toward a more average European level[15] (Swedish Institute, 2004b). The public sector, previously a bastion of employment for women, suffered major cutbacks and family policies became less generous.

In the second half of the 1990s, the economy recovered. Unemployment was reduced to the government's target level of 4% by late 2000. Part of the explanation lay in increasing support to local governments (schools, health care, and social services) and national programs such as the Adult Education Initiative (*kompetenslyftet*) to promote higher adult education (Swedish Institute, 2004b). Primarily, however, the reduction was due to the creation of new jobs, mainly within the pharmaceutical and telecommunications industries.

A number of indicators bear witness to the transformation of Swedish businesses into knowledge-intensive operations. These are the only kind of operations to show a growth in jobs during the last two decades (mainly in services and knowledge-intensive manufacturing), and Sweden is established among the top countries on research and development (R&D) spending[16] (Swedish Institute, 2003a). The transformation is also evident in that Sweden was among the leading information technology (IT) nations in the world by the beginning of the 21st century. The exceptionally high rate of IT usage has made a powerful contribution to economic growth overall, to the rapid expansion of IT and the Internet companies, and to the fact that Sweden has become an important test market for international IT companies (Ilshammar, 2000). This expansion has made waves internationally. In 1999, for instance, *Newsweek magazine* devoted a special edition to Stockholm as the proclaimed Internet capital of Europe with regard to its IT industry.

A New Landscape for Swedish Leadership

The institutional context for business management in Sweden has thus changed significantly compared to the situation only a few decades ago. For instance, the increasing dominance of financial investors in the capital market has removed the crucial function of industrial ownership

---

[14]Most notably the Wallenberg sphere of interest.

[15]In 1996, unemployment averaged 8.0%. In addition, 4.5% of the labor force was engaged in employment training, public relief work, and other activities supported by the government.

[16]R&D investments in 2001 equaled close to 4.0% of GDP, with industrial R&D accounting for the lion's share of 3.3% (Swedish Institute, 2003a).

(Jönsson, 1995a, 1995b). This has placed a new emphasis on short-term economic performance and on shareholder values, diverging from the traditional long-term stakeholder perspective that has hitherto prevailed for decades in Swedish businesses. Furthermore, the economic base is now concentrated on large enterprises whose foreign operations represent a considerable share of their activities. Naturally, the interests of a global enterprise are not always compatible with those of the Swedish state, a situation that has generated certain tensions and has reduced the mutual trust that had prevailed for so long. This new landscape obviously shapes the way leadership is enacted, determines what leader qualities are most valued in recruitment situations, affects the expectations and ideals associated with leaders in the public discourse, and so on (House, Wright, & Aditya, 1997). New leadership models and ideals are constantly evolving as an adaptive response to a changing environment, while at the same time they are also actively shaping this environment themselves (Gergen, 1999).

But the landscape is not constituted only by institutional arrangements. Swedish culture in the sense of norms, values, and shared understandings is an equally important component in the landscape that shapes (and is shaped by) the images of leadership as well as the execution of leadership in practice. Before embarking on an exploration of leadership in Sweden (the Images of Leadership section in this chapter), we look first at Swedish culture in this sense, as we analyze the results of the GLOBE study conducted in Sweden.

1. SWEDEN IN THE GLOBE STUDY

The GLOBE project has collected data using multiple methods (cf. House et al., 2004; chap. 1, this volume). This section reports the results that emerged from quantitative data collection, more specifically from a survey of observations and values regarding Sweden as expressed by middle managers in terms of the nine GLOBE culture dimensions. This presentation of results is followed by an elaboration of each dimension drawn from qualitative data such as interview material, public information, and nonobtrusive observations relevant to the different dimensions.

The Swedish questionnaire was distributed among middle managers in 14 business organizations active in three different industries:[17] finance, food processing, and telecommunications. Altogether 896 middle managers answered the questionnaire. Male respondents constituted 82.3%, whereas 17.7% represented female participation. Ages ranged between 25 and 64 years, with a median of 46. As regards cultural conditioning, 97.1% were born in Sweden. Methodological details relevant to this section and an elaboration of the basic demographics of the sample group can be found in the Appendix.

Results for the Swedish Sample

Table 3.1 presents the societal culture dimensions for Sweden. Starting at the higher end, the results show very high aggregated scale scores and rankings (indicated here in parentheses) on the three following dimensions in perceptions of societal cultural ("As Is" scale scores): Institutional Collectivism (Mean [M] = 5.22, Rank 1), Uncertainty Avoidance (M = 5.32, Rank 2), and Gender Egalitarianism (M = 3.84, Rank 8). In an international comparison, we can therefore clearly identify Sweden as a very collectivist society, where equality between men and women is relatively high. The country is further characterized by a large number of institutional arrangements and structures, such as rules and procedures that serve to reduce uncertainty.

---

[17]The data set in the three industries is distributed as follows: finance (4 organizations, N = 373), food processing (6 organizations, N = 301), and telecommunication (4 organizations, N = 222).

TABLE 3.1
Results for Sweden for the Nine GLOBE Cultural Dimensions at the Society Level

Cultural Dimension	Society Culture "As Is"		Society Culture "Should Be"		Diff. "Should Be" – "As Is"
	Score	Band[a] (Rank)[b]	Score	Band[a] (Rank)[b]	
Institutional Collectivism	5.22	A[d] (1)	3.94	C[d] (58)	−1.28
Uncertainty Avoidance	5.32	A[d] (2)	3.60	D[e] (58)	−1.72
Gender Egalitarianism	3.84	A[c] (8)	5.15	A[d] (2)	1.31
Future Orientation	4.39	B[d] (9)	4.89	C[d] (56)	0.50
Humane Orientation	4.10	C[d] (28)	5.65	A[e] (9)	1.55
Performance Orientation	3.72	B[c] (48)	5.80	C[e] (42)	2.08
Power Distance	4.85	B[d] (51)	2.70	C[e] (31)	−2.15
In-Group Collectivism	3.66	C[c] (60)	6.04	A[c] (11)	2.38
Assertiveness	3.38	C[c] (61)	3.61	B[c] (38)	0.23

[a]Bands A > B > C > D > E are determined by calculating the grand mean and standard deviations across all scales. These means and standard deviations are used to calculate high, medium, and low bands of countries (Test Banding, cf. Hanges, Dickson, & Sipe, 2004). [b]Numbers in parentheses (Rank) indicate rank order for Sweden among the 61 GLOBE countries. [c]Three group bands identified ranging from A to C (high–low). [d]Four group bands identified ranging from A to D (high–low). [e]Five group bands identified ranging from A to E (high–low).

In terms of values, or "Should Be" scale scores for the same high-end dimensions, the results show that the middle managers would like to see less emphasis on solutions and practices expressing Institutional Collectivism (M = 3.94, Rank 58) and Uncertainty Avoidance (M = 3.60, Rank 58). In the case of Gender Egalitarianism, there is clear evidence of support for promoting this societal issue even more. Although it is high, it should be even higher (M = 5.15, Rank 2).

At the lower end of Table 3.1, we find very low "As Is" scale scores and rankings on the three following dimensions: Performance Orientation (M = 3.72, Rank 48), In-group Collectivism (M = 3.66, Rank 60), and Assertiveness (M = 3.38, Rank 61). In an international comparison, Swedish society is not apparently organized for emphasizing or rewarding performance. A striking and particularly interesting result is that whereas Sweden is ranked as the most collectivist society in the GLOBE study (Institutional Collectivism), it is also ranked as extremely individualist in terms of the In-Group Collectivism dimension. Finally, Swedes emerge as a very timid and nonassertive society by international comparison.

"Should Be" scale scores for the same low-end dimensions reveal a wish for this to be higher on all three dimensions in absolute terms, but the difference is small for Assertiveness (0.23 score points). The rather big shift in ranking for Assertiveness from 61/61 ("As Is") to 38/61 ("Should Be"), is thus largely a relative one. The opposite effect is evident for the Performance Orientation score. There is a big difference of more than two points between the "As Is" and "Should Be" scores for this dimension, but the shift in international, relative ranking is a modest one only: from 48/61 (As Is) to 42/61 (Should Be). In other words, although there is a clear desire for an increase in emphasis on performance, this follows a universal pattern. Finally, the equivalent results for In-Group Collectivism demonstrate a major shift both in absolute and relative terms, moving from an "As Is" ranking of 60/61, to a "Should Be" ranking of 11/61.

Future Orientation (*M* = 4.39, Rank 9), Humane Orientation (*M* = 4.10, Rank 28), and Power Distance (*M* = 4.85, Rank 51) are the three remaining dimensions where the Swedish scores and rankings do not diverge markedly in any direction, especially with regard to the absolute "As Is" scores. Although the rankings show that Future Orientation is rather high and Power Distance low, with Humane Orientation in the middle, Sweden is still positioned in the middle country clusters on all three dimensions (see Table 3.1, rank columns).

The "Should Be" score for Future Orientation points in two directions, depending on the perspective. The absolute direction is positive: The middle managers think that more attention should be paid to future-oriented activities such as planning and preparing for future events. In relative terms, however, the direction is negative. Ranking for Future Orientation drops from a positioning of 9/61 (As Is) down to 56/61 (Should Be). In other words, Swedish middle managers think there should be more focus on Future Orientation than there is in what they conceive as the present state. This is in line with their colleagues in most other countries, but to a much lesser degree.

Swedish middle managers think there should be less Power Distance and the difference in absolute numbers between "how it should be" and "how it is" is among the greatest within the sample. Yet the shift is only modest in an international comparison. The ranking is thus actually higher for the "Should Be" score (*M* = 2.70, Rank 31), than for the "As Is" score (*M* = 4.85, Rank 51). In other words, values regarding Power Distance seem to follow an international pattern in such a way that a (much) lower Power Distance is universally desired, but to a lesser extent in Sweden relative to most other countries.

Finally, the "Should Be" scores and rankings for Humane Orientation show Swedish middle managers to have a relatively strong preference for increasing arrangements and activities that promote an even more humane society. The "Should Be" ranking is 9/61, which qualifies Sweden for membership in the top country cluster.

Illustrations and Elaboration of the Study Dimensions

In this section, we illustrate and elaborate the results presented previously, using additional data from two sources. One of these entails non-obtrusive measurements using public sources and expert knowledge collected by the Swedish GLOBE team. A second involves direct observations of local expressions relevant to the GLOBE culture dimensions at the society level. These data were collected primarily by the Swedish research team during the spring of 1995, and subsequently supplemented by interviews and observations during 1996–1997.

Institutional Collectivism.   In the preceding section, we found that Sweden was the most collectivist society of all the participating countries. Institutional Collectivism refers here to social arrangements at the societal level that promote conformity and interdependence among (groups of) individuals, and a concern for collective rather than individual interests.

One good indicator of this dimension and the promotion of collective interests is represented by the labor unions, for example, their political influence and their level of membership. Sweden is in fact the leading example in a group of countries including members such as Denmark and Finland, which all have a very high unionization rate. Almost 9 out of 10 (87%) of the wage earners in Sweden are members of a union. Some comparable figures are one out of three (34%) in the UK, and one out of four (24%) in Japan. In France, only 9% of the wage earners are members of a union.[18]

---

[18]Sources are: Sweden: Statistics Sweden (SCB); UK and France: Visser (1996), *Trends in Union Membership and Union Density in OECD Countries 1970–1994*, Centre for Research on European Societies and Industrial Relations, February 1996; and Japan: Japan Institute of Labor. Reported in Kjellberg (1997).

Another expression of Institutional Collectivism is the relatively high-tax situation in Sweden. The public sector, that is, the national government (the state) and the local government (the municipalities and county councils), have assumed extensive responsibility for many services such as education, labor market, and industrial policies, the care of the sick and elderly, pensions and other types of social insurance, environmental protection, and so on. The tax system is thus a key institution for the realization of political goals regarding collective interests. Although this is true for any country, the high level of taxation in Sweden is in line with the high score for Institutional Collectivism.

A third example of Institutional Collectivism is expressed by the Right of Public Access (*Allemansrätten,* which literally means "Every Man's Right"). The law grants each and every individual the right, under responsibility, to enjoy the countryside for recreation and tourism, for example, the right to visit other people's property (and to pick wildflowers, mushrooms, berries, etc.), and to bathe in and travel by boat on other people's water. The individual landowner's interests are thus subordinated to collective interests. The Right of Public Access is unique to Sweden and is a very important base for recreation. It also has an important cultural/historical value as a right going back to medieval traditions.[19] The Right of Public Access with its delicate balance of freedom and responsibility captures something essential in the relationship between the individual and the collective.

One last example illustrating the concern for collective rather than individual interests is the "Principle of public access to official records" (*Offentlighetsprincipen*) that is inscribed in the Swedish Constitution. According to this principle, all official records are to be accessible to the citizens, unless specifically stated otherwise. Openness should be the rule and secrecy the exception. For instance, civil servants and others working for the public authorities are obliged to disclose what they know and to give information to the media, unless the information in question is officially confidential. Court proceedings, parliamentary, and local or regional authority sessions are open to the public and the media. Even the computer logs that track the prime minister's surfing on the Internet, and all of his e-mail correspondence, are publicly accessible.

Uncertainty Avoidance.   Uncertainty Avoidance is defined as the extent to which a collective strives to avoid uncertainty by relying on social norms, structural arrangements, rituals, and bureaucratic practices to alleviate the unpredictability of future events. The mean value scored by Sweden was 5.32, which positions it second out of the 61 countries in this dimension. This result indicates very high Uncertainty Avoidance. Protecting the rights of individuals in their contacts with the authorities is fundamental to the process of law in Sweden, and it is one of many expressions of uncertainty reduction. In this context, the Swedish *ombudsman* system is a guarantee against oppressive measures and misgovernment in the judiciary or the public administration. The parliamentary ombudsmen investigate suspected abuses of authority on the part of civil servants. Other ombudsmen protect the public by keeping a watchful eye on consumer rights, ethnic and sex discrimination, press ethics, and the rights of children, young people, and those with disabilities.

Another example under this heading is that all residents in Sweden are covered by the national health insurance. If someone is ill or has to stay home from work to care for sick children, they receive a taxable daily allowance: 75% to 85% of lost income, depending on the length of the absence. Finally, the social norm that calls for people to be "on time" is related to

---

[19]The right was originally designed to protect people traveling through the vast forests by granting them the right to gather what they needed for survival during their journey (e.g., nuts, berries, wood, or grass for their horses). This was regulated in the provincial laws.

Uncertainty Avoidance, and sticking to an agreed-on time is important to the maintenance of good social relations in both working life and private life. Only deviations by a few minutes are accepted as being "on time": 10 minutes after the agreed-on time counts as being "late."

Gender Egalitarianism.   In the dimension of Gender Egalitarianism—the extent to which a society minimizes gender role differences—Sweden ranks eighth, scoring 3.84. The score indicates that men and women are attributed almost equal status, although there is a slight bias toward the male side.

The 1994 elections in Sweden resulted in a substantial increase in the proportion of women in Parliament. Of the 349 members, over 40% were women.[20] This world record in women's participation was maintained at the subsequent election 1998. The latest election, in 2002, gave women 45.3% of the places in Parliament. Another breakthrough for equality occurred in the cabinet created by former Social Democratic Prime Minister Ingvar Carlsson in 1994, in which half the members were women. The present cabinet headed by Prime Minister Göran Persson also breaks even, with 11 female and 11 male ministers (January 2004). These figures are obviously highly symbolic of the gender-equality ambitions in the Social Democratic movement.

However, the situation in working life in general is still far from equal—at least by Swedish standards. Though labor force participation is more or less equal between men and women,[21] the labor market is segregated, despite a general political consensus on the principle of gender equality.[22] Of all the women in the labor market, 51% are active in the public sector and 49 percent in the private. The equivalent figures for men are 19% and 81% respectively. Although women have gained power over the last decade and hold influential positions more than ever, men still dominate in certain domains. For instance, 56% of the people holding a management position in public organizations are women, but only 19% in the private sector (Statistics Sweden, 2004).

The main statute governing the practical realization of equality between women and men is aimed at working life. The Act on Equality between Men and Women at Work, generally known as the Equal Opportunities Act,[23] came into force in 1980. A new and stricter Equal Opportunities Act replaced the existing one on January 1, 1992.

A separate Equality Affairs Division (*Jämställdhetsenheten*) was established at the central governmental level in the early 1980s. The Office of the Equal Opportunities Ombudsman (*Jämställdhetsombudsmannen, JämO*) is an independent government authority under the Ministry of Labor. It was set up when the first Equal Opportunities Act came into force in 1980. The main purpose of the Act is to promote equal rights for men and women with respect to employment, working conditions, and opportunities for personal development at work. The rules are of two types: those prohibiting an employer from discriminating against a person on account of gender, and second, those requiring an employer to take active steps to promote equality at the workplace.

---

[20]Comparable figures for some other countries are Denmark 37%, Switzerland 25%, United States 15%, and Japan 7% (Inter-Parliamentary Union, IPU, 2005).

[21]In 1999, 78% of all women aged between 16 and 64 were in the labor force, although many worked part-time. In the same year, 84% of men in the same age group belonged to the labor force. Women accounted for approximately half of Sweden's total labor force (Swedish Institute, 2004a).

[22]These principles are also incorporated in to the Swedish Constitution.

[23]It is interesting to note that gender equality policy is fundamentally concerned with creating equal conditions for every individual, to achieve economic independence through gainful employment regardless of gender. The actual redistribution of power, for instance, does not seem to be an end in itself.

One last example concerns an institution that promotes equality in the private domain. When a child is born, its parents are legally entitled to a total of 15 months paid parental leave from work. This leave can be shared between them and can be taken any time before the child's eighth birthday. One of the months is reserved specifically for the father, and is forfeited if he does not use it. Surveys show that more than 50% of fathers utilize their right to paid parental leave during the child's first year. In addition to these benefits, all fathers are entitled to a 10-day leave of absence with parental benefit in connection with the child's birth. About 80% of fathers take advantage of this opportunity (Swedish Institute, 2004a).

Future Orientation.   Future Orientation is the degree to which an organization or society encourages and rewards future-oriented behaviors such as planning, investing in the future, and delaying gratification. Sweden's Future Orientation ranks fairly high (9/61), with a scale score of 4.39. This result suggests a leaning toward a long-term rather than a short-term focus.

One obvious expression of Future Orientation is represented by the investments into various kinds of education and personnel development (competence development, postgraduate education, conferencing, etc). Sweden has been among the leading countries in the world for many years in terms of investment in education (Organization for Economic Cooperation and Development, 2005), and the educational attainment of the population is high. In 1996, only 30% of the population had left school after the primary/lower secondary level. Furthermore, Swedish employees spend more time at internal conferences than their counterparts in any other country in Europe,[24] and the market for executive education such as MBA programs and similar postgraduate courses is growing.

Another expression of a strong Future Orientation is that Sweden is among the top countries in terms of spending on industrial R&D as a percentage of GDP. In 2001, industrial R&D expenditures alone corresponded to 3.3% of GDP (Swedish Institute, 2003a).

Humane Orientation.   Humane Orientation is the degree to which an organization or society encourages and rewards individuals for being fair, altruistic, friendly, generous, caring, and kind to others.

The social concern that is characteristic of Swedish culture is captured in part by this dimension, where Sweden scores 4.10 and ranks 28/61. This result is rather surprising at a first glance, because Sweden is internationally famed for being a very humane society. However, the dimension as defined here focuses on individual humane characteristics rather than on the institutional arrangements that are the primary source of Sweden's reputation. These can be exemplified by the arrangements instituted in Sweden for two groups, namely criminals and disabled people.

The Swedish Prison and Probation Service is the public institution responsible for people sentenced to imprisonment or probation.[25] The basic ideas underlying their operations are summarized in their own words as follows (our translation):

- As little intervention as possible, probation and parole being the best way of rehabilitating offenders.
- Care in prison should be designed to promote the rehabilitation of inmates, to prepare them for their return to society and to mitigate the harmful effects of incarceration.

---

[24]According to Björn Strömberg, manager at a publishing house that publishes the periodical The Conference World (Konferensvärlden).

[25]In 2004, about 10,700 people passed through the institutions of the Prison and Probation Service, with and average of 4,500 people incarcerated on any given day (Kriminalvårdsstyrelsen, 2005).

- During the period in care, time is spent on persuading the inmate to live a life free of crime and drugs on release.
- The regular resources of the community, for example, medical care and the social services, are to be utilized as far as possible. (*Kriminalvårdsstyrelsen, 2005*)

These ideas or principles for the Prison and Probation Service are clearly rooted in an explicit Humane Orientation. With regard to the conditions of prison life, prisoners work while serving their sentences and are paid for it; they have their own TVs in their personal cells; and they have easy access to a physician when necessary.

Another example of the Humane Orientation in Sweden can be seen in the policies regarding disabled people. The very interpretation of the "handicap" concept, which naturally plays a central role in any disability policy, is fundamentally humane. In Sweden a handicap is viewed not as a characteristic of a person, but as something that *arises* when an inaccessible environment confronts a person with a functional impairment. Thus, a common theme in the various policies is to place the responsibility on all organizations to create and sustain environmental conditions as such that an individual disability is not transformed into a handicap. Apart from various rights to financial support and personal assistance, disabled people have their own ombudsman, the Office of the Disability Ombudsman (*Handikappombudsmannen*), an authority that monitors their rights and interests.

Performance Orientation.   Performance Orientation refers to the extent to which an organization or society encourages and rewards group members for performance improvement and excellence. Sweden was ranked rather low in the international comparison: 48/61, with a score of 3.72.

The relatively low score reflects the Swedish approach in relation to this dimension, which is to focus on the performance of organizational units rather than specific members of those units. For instance, a common procedure at universities is to provide regular feedback to faculty departments about their scholarly performance in terms of research projects and publications. On the other hand, the teaching performance of faculty members is generally not evaluated, nor are individual students with the best grades generally honored.

This general observation does not exclude a number of practices for encouraging and rewarding individual performance excellence, for instance, in major companies where promotion is given to individuals on the basis of such excellence. Furthermore, if politicians at the top three levels of the national government happen to have kinship ties with other politicians at the same level, this depends solely on coincidence: What counts is competence in the performance of the duties concerned, and not social connections or any other such criteria. Nonetheless, most organizations avoid applying formal, explicit performance appraisal systems to individuals. Again, the organizational department or equivalent group is the normal unit for performance evaluation.

Power Distance.   Power Distance is defined as the degree to which members of an organization or society expect and agree that power is unequally shared. Sweden scored a mean of 4.85 in the Power Distance dimension and was ranked 51/61, thus being perceived as a low–Power Distance society.

Non-obtrusive measures provided eloquent examples of various characteristics relevant to Power Distance. For instance, most business organizations lack any dress codes based on employee status, and titles are seldom listed on door signs (the door sign for Sweden's prime minister simply gives his name, Göran Persson, on a plain label). Nor are titles generally used

when addressing people. Eating places at work are not generally segregated on a basis of position, although certain privileges such as special parking places or bigger offices are allocated
to senior managerial levels.

Outside the sphere of work, low Power Distance can be revealed in various ways. Burial
grounds, for instance, are generally similar for everyone regardless of family wealth or status.
Nor is ability to get on a bus or any other public transportation helped by personal status, as
everybody is obliged to queue.

Also significant in this context is the absence of pictures of living political leaders in any
public place or on symbolic artifacts such as stamps (apart from members of the royal
family—but then again they have no formal political influence). Only in very special circumstances is there any symbolic recognition of political, business, or religious leaders in
public places. One such case occurred after the murder of the former Prime Minister Olof
Palme in 1986, when the name of the street at the end of which the lethal shot was fired, was
changed to Olof Palme Street. In general, if a street name acknowledges an individual at all,
it is most likely to be of historical origin.

Two phenomena that demonstrate reductions in Power Distance in Sweden are the
country's system of progressive income tax, and the contents of the 1976 Codetermination
Act (*Medbestämmandelagen*), which guarantees the unions the formal right to membership
of company boards.

In-Group Collectivism.   According to Table 3.1, Sweden ranks as one of the most individualistic nations investigated in GLOBE (60/61), in terms of the In-Group Collectivism
scale. This result is very noticeable together with the high Institutional Collectivism score
reported earlier.

Modal values in Sweden stress individual independence and strength. The strong need for
independence can be expressed not only as a wish to be left alone, to "be spared other people,"
but also as a desire "not to be beholden to anyone." The word *ensamhet* (solitude) has a
positive connotation. It suggests inner peace, independence, and personal strength.

Hendin (1964) explains the relation to solitude by reference to the Swedish way of bringing up children. Swedish children are encouraged to become independent at an early stage:
the earlier in life, the greater the sign of what the Swede regards as maturity. It is certainly no
coincidence that the world-famous character Pippi Longstocking (*Pippi Långstrump*) was
created by a Swedish author, Astrid Lindgren. Being able to take care of oneself independent
of a family, as Pippi always does, is regarded as something positive. Consequently, the family
does not occupy a significant role in Swedish society in an international comparison.

It is not therefore surprising that the proportion of single households is the highest in the
world. One reason is that the different generations do not as a rule live together. Widowed parents or older family members do not live with their relatives. Instead, residences for old
people are common in Sweden. It is certainly rare to find unmarried adults living with their
parents, but even the youngest offspring are encouraged to leave the family home early, supported by state loans. In Sweden a 22-year-old person still living with his or her parents is
regarded as being slightly odd.

In 2003 approximately 74% of all Swedish children aged 1 to 3 years, and 96% of all
children aged 4 to 6 years, were spending (at least part of) their day at a child-care institution
of some kind (*Skolverket,* 2004). In the typical Swedish family, both parents are thus working and their children are either at a child-care institution or at school. The grandparents live
on their own. This means that in Sweden family life, as usually understood, is enacted almost
exclusively at the weekends.

Assertiveness.   Assertiveness refers to the degree to which individuals in a society are assertive, confrontational, and aggressive in their relationships with others. Sweden has the lowest international ranking in this dimension (61/61), with a scale score of 3.38. This result suggests that Swedes are typically nonassertive, that is, timid, nondominant, and nonaggressive in social relationships.

This result confirms the findings of previous studies and informed accounts on Swedish culture. Foreigners often regard Swedes as shy, reserved, and "cold-hearted." This does not necessarily mean that Swedes are actually feeling less emotion than other nationalities. It is the way of expressing feelings that is culture-specific, and the subtle signals can be very difficult for foreigners to interpret. Swedes do not reveal their emotions as often or as overtly as people from most other countries, and the importance of keeping control over one's feelings is introduced early, as part of a child's upbringing. In this respect, Swedes are strikingly similar to the Japanese (Daun, 1986). For instance, it is rare to use car horns in traffic unless it is to ward off danger. To blow your horn is generally considered to be an unnecessary, aggressive act. Swedes are internationally famed for their desire to avoid conflict.

Furthermore, there are relatively few hugs and kisses, or verbal expressions of emotion among Swedes. Because strong emotions are rarely expressed openly in Sweden, indirect forms are used instead—something that finds expression in the special love of rituals. For instance, the well-prepared speech made by the managing director to the accountant on retirement, complete with its almost obligatory little joke, may well be the only way of expressing affection and gratitude to a loyal employee, but one that is recognized and appreciated by the recipient as being just that.

Cultural Themes for Sweden

In the following analysis, we synthesize the quantitative and qualitative results presented previously into a number of empirically grounded cultural themes applicable to Sweden: metaphors that together seem to us to capture some particularly important aspects of Swedish culture. We also present some additional information about Swedish society and Swedish culture drawn from a number of ethnographic and sociological accounts.

Two Life Worlds: Socially Concerned Individualism.   The extreme positions of Sweden relative to other countries in the two dimensions Institutional Collectivism (Rank 1) and In-Group Collectivism (Rank 60) are certainly striking and puzzling results. Sweden is at one and the same time an extremely collective and individualistic society. How can we make sense of this paradoxical finding? It can be compared with the result reported by Hofstede (1980), whereby Sweden was labeled an individualistic culture[26] according to the author's IDV (individualism) index. One explanation of this difference is that Hofstede did not distinguish between the small in-groups and the much wider anonymous, institutionalized collective that constitutes society as a whole. This distinction is obviously important in the Swedish case, and Hofstede's measure and definition (which most closely correspond to In-Group Collectivism) reveal only half of the picture.

In ethnographic descriptions of Sweden, it is often asserted that Swedes draw a strict line between public and private life, whereas in many other parts of the world the two are inseparable (Daun, 1989). In many respects the two spheres are very different, and blending them could be problematic. As we have noted, independence and solitude are two concepts with a strong and positive charge among Swedes in general, but they are associated mainly with the

---

[26]Sweden ranked 10th among the 53 countries on the IDV scale in Hofstede's study (1980).

private sphere. One function of the strict borderline between public and private could be to defend the individual's integrity, and guarantee that much-valued feeling of independence vis-à-vis the outside world. The two life worlds are preferably kept apart, in both time and space. It is rare, for instance, for Swedes to socialize with their work colleagues in their spare time—workmates belong to the public sphere.

In a seven-country[27] comparison, Hampden-Turner and Trompenaars (1993) assert that *"more than any other culture examined in this book [Swedes] begin with the individual, his or her integrity, uniqueness, freedom, needs, and values, yet insist that the fulfillment and destiny of the individual lies in developing and sustaining others by the gift of his or her own work and energy"* (p. 239). This energy is translated almost exclusively into engagement in organized activities. We have also found that Sweden is a humane society, first and foremost in terms of institutional arrangements rather than interpersonal (in-group) relationships. We therefore believe that Swedes are fundamentally individualists, with a great concern for fairness and the well-being of others that is expressed in organized activities and institutional arrangements. This delicate balance between, and optimization of, individual and collective interests is captured in the common little word *lagom*[28] or "just right." We have encapsulated it in the notion of the socially concerned individualist.

It is also necessary to note the striking difference between the "As Is" and "Should Be" scores for the middle managers when it comes to the two Collectivism dimensions. Judging from the results, our respondents have a strong preference for replacing socially concerned individualism by stronger social ties within the family or organization, and are much less inclined toward collectivistic solutions on the society level. Should this pattern apply to the population at large, it would mean that Sweden was undergoing a major transformation of the basic foundations of the *Folkhemmet*, affecting all areas of social life and particularly that of working life.

Coping with an Uncertain Future—Rationality and Pragmatism. A second result that stands out distinctly from the quantitative data is the extreme position on the Uncertainty Avoidance dimension[29] (Rank 2) and the high position on Future Orientation (Rank 9). Because uncertainty is by definition connected with the genuinely uncertain future, avoiding uncertainty seems to suggest avoiding the future. In this sense, the results appear contradictory. How are we to understand a culture with a strong Future Orientation that at the same time ranks high on Uncertainty Avoidance? More interestingly, how does such a culture resolve this apparent paradox?

In the ethnographic literature on Sweden a recurrent theme is the pronounced emphasis on reason, objectivity, matter-of-factness, and order. Everything lying beyond reason is awkward, and possibly even immoral (Daun, 1989). Only rational-pragmatic arguments that are straight to the point are legitimate in discussion: "Irrelevant" emotive associations are out-of-bounds. Not surprisingly, the pragmatic Swedes are often regarded as earnest and boring in the eyes of foreigners (Philips-Martinsson, 1991). We thus conclude that the typical Swede is very rational, even though "rationality" can be defined to mean different things. According to Daun (1989) Swedish rationality means putting the emphasis on practical solutions, on action appropriate to the goal pursued, on aiming at one objective at a time. Swedes adopt a practical

---

[27]United States, Japan, Germany, France, Britain, Sweden, and the Netherlands.

[28]The origins of *lagom* are to be found in *Viking* times, when a bowl of a beerlike drink was shared among these seated around the table. Doubts arose about how much to sip: not too much (which would upset the others by not leaving enough drink for them), not too little (as one also wanted to enjoy the drink). A *lagom* sip is "just right" for fulfilling the two conflicting interests.

[29]A comparison of our results with those by Hofstede (1980, 1991) shows the two sets to be contradictory. Sweden was ranked 46/50 in Hofstede's Uncertainty Avoidance index (UAI), indicating low Uncertainty Avoidance.

orientation that some other authors encapsulate in the term *pragmatism* (Czarniawska-Joerges, 1993). We believe that these rational and pragmatic attitudes are an expression of the culture of high Uncertainty Avoidance observed in our study. Rationalism and pragmatism are "solutions" to the problem of coping with uncertainty. Moreover, they offer a perspective that resolves the apparent paradox. Viewed through a rational and pragmatic lens, the focus on the future is narrowed down to the manageable aspects and paying less attention to the unknown. Thus, the future does not *appear* uncertain; rather, it seems predictable and manageable, and something toward which one can quite easily orient oneself.

On the other hand, rationalism and pragmatism are perhaps going to be less important, judging from the big difference between the middle managers' Uncertainty Avoidance "As Is" score (very high) and their "Should Be" score (very low), at least in terms of the "social engineering" culture that prevailed for many decades while the Swedish welfare state was being created.

Consensus—Egalitarianism, Equality, and Timidity.   The Swedish population is unusually homogenous, compared to other countries. Sweden is a low-context culture, a culture in which the situation (context) is not acknowledged as having any significance with regard to the way people act and react. Swedes share the same history, the same language, and the same religion, and the differences between various groups in the country are comparatively small (Daun, 1989). This facilitates communication between different societal groups and opens up the possibility of wide agreement and collective action (Berglund & Löwstedt, 1996).

A third distinct theme to emerge from our findings concerns attitudes to power and influence. Sweden was found to be a relatively equal and egalitarian society (low on Power Distance and high on Gender Egalitarianism). This result is in line with the findings in Hofstede (1980), where Sweden was classified as a low–Power Distance culture (Ranking 43/50) according to the author's Power Distance Index, PDI. One feature of those countries where Power Distance is modest is that everyone is regarded as being "just like everyone else" and status differences are not desired.

From this powerful equality norm, there has emerged a special set of Swedish cultural practices (and rituals) that are often referred to in the relevant literature (Daun, 1989; Jönsson, 1995a; Phillips-Martinsson, 1991). One manifestation is that everyone's opinions, ideas and experiences are respected and listened to, because people are all potential contributors to the accomplishment of the task at hand or to finding a solution to the current problem. Mutual understanding, collective consideration, and compromise solutions are favored. Consensus, albeit regarded primarily as a *condition* for dialogue (Czarniawska-Joerges, 1993), is also seen as one of its desirable *outcomes*. Such an attitude enables a search for creative solutions before the decisions are made, and wide support once they have been taken.

There is a link here with the earlier discussion about assertiveness and conflict avoidance. Rather than seeing conflict avoidance as an end in itself, we believe it is intimately connected with the idea of consensus. Conflict is obviously a threat to the strong norms regarding good conditions for dialogue, so people are consequently expected to be kind to each other and not to quarrel. A kind, polite and neutral attitude is preferred, whereas strong and spontaneous expressions of emotion are regarded as ridiculous and childish (Daun, 1989). As we have noted previously, Assertiveness rates extremely low in Sweden in an international comparison. It seems to us that the egalitarian, equality-oriented, and timid qualities all converge in the consensus concept.

2. IMAGES OF LEADERSHIP IN SWEDEN

In this section, we will explore images of leadership in Sweden using multiple sources of data. A central theoretical construct in the GLOBE project consists of implicit leadership theories. A basic premise from a social-constructivist perspective (Berger & Luckmann, 1966, 1991; Burr, 1995; Gergen, 1999) is that the understandings of leadership, as reflected in implicit theories, are the result not only of individual experiences, but also, and more important, of the interaction between individuals and social networks in the joint construction of the leadership phenomenon. In line with this approach, we see it as important in this chapter to use different sets of data together with a number of comparative results from multiple sources and various types of actors, and to adopt a number of methodological approaches in order to obtain triangulation of data (Alvesson & Sköldberg, 1994).

We start by presenting the data collected from the GLOBE survey of middle managers at the national level. To check for consistency, we also conduct an industry-level analysis. The Swedish data are then analyzed and compared with the global data in a between-country analysis. Together these three analyses enable us to offer a preliminary image of outstanding leadership, to point out variations between different industries, and finally to distinguish such traits as are typical of Sweden from those that are universally endorsed and therefore express globally preferred leadership ideals. The quantitative analyses are then contrasted with an analysis of focus groups and ethnographic interviews with organizational leaders active in widely varying contexts. Finally, we present an analysis of leadership images as constructed by the media, which play an important role in shaping people's views of leadership.

The Implicit Leadership Model Prevailing Among Middle Managers in Sweden

One objective of the GLOBE study was to collect data on attitudes and values relevant to "outstanding leadership," and the country profiles of the leadership scale scores represent the respondents' aggregated implicit leadership model (*cf.* Lord & Maher, 1991). The Swedish results thus provide a preliminary answer to the question: What is the dominating ideal image of leadership in Sweden?

Swedish Conceptions of Leadership From Within.   In the leadership section of the questionnaire, 112 leadership traits and behavior attributes were presented to the respondents. Using several multinational samples from these items, 21 first-order leadership dimensions were extracted that represent the different aspects of leadership (cf. Dorfman, Hanges, & Brodbeck, 2004; House et al., 2004).

The leader dimensions that were rated very high or high[30] by the Swedish middle managers (i.e., factors contributing to outstanding leadership), starting with the highest were: (1) Inspirational, (2) Integrity, (3) Visionary, (4) Team Integrator, (5) Performance Orientation, (6) Decisive, and (7) Collaborative Team Orientation (see Table 3.2).

At the other end of the spectrum we find the dimensions that are rated low or very low[31] (i.e., factors inhibiting outstanding leadership): (18) Autocratic, (19) Face-Saver, (20) Self-Centered, and (21) Malevolent (see Table 3.2).

The survey result suggests that, according to the middle managers, an outstanding leader should inspire and engage the organization members to do their best to achieve a visionary future, and she or he should be honest and trustworthy. Such a leader should work, not for his or her own self-interest, but for the common good, and should also be highly capable at creating a team spirit within the organization. Although these notions clearly portray an influential

---

[30]The operationalization of very high ratings is a total mean > 6.0, and of high ratings is 6.0–5.5, on a 7-point Likert-type scale.

[31]The operationalization of very low ratings is a total mean < 2.0, and of low ratings 2.0–2.5, on a 7-point Likert-type scale.

TABLE 3.2
Swedish Results on Attitudes to Leadership Traits and Behavior

Dimension	Example Item Key Words	Score
Inspirational	Enthusiastic, Positive, Encouraging, Motivational, and Morale booster	6.31
Integrity	Honest, Sincere, Just, and Trustworthy	6.29
Visionary	Future-oriented, Anticipatory, Inspirational, Visionary, and Intellectually stimulating	6.05
Collaborative Team Orientation	Group-oriented, Collaborative, Loyal, Consultative, Mediator, and Fraternal	5.98
Performance Orientation	Improvement-, Excellence-, and Performance-oriented	5.96
Decisive	Willful, Decisive, and Intuitive	5.59
Team Integrator	Communicative, Team builder, Integrator, and Coordinator	5.50
Administratively Competent	Orderly, Administratively skilled, Organized, and Good administrator	5.44
Diplomatic	Diplomatic, Win/win problem solver, and Effective bargainer	5.27
Humane	Generous, and Compassionate	4.96
Self-Sacrificial	Risk taker, Self-sacrificial, and Convincing	4.81
Modesty	Modest, Self-effacing, Calm, and Patient	4.59
Autonomous	Individualistic, Independent, Autonomous, and Unique	3.97
Conflict Inducer	Normative, Secretive, and an Intragroup competitor	3.33
Status-Consciousness	Status-conscious, and Class-conscious	3.30
Procedural	Ritualistic, Formal, Habitual, Cautious, and Procedural	3.19
Nonparticipative	Nondelegater, Micromanager, Nonegalitarian, and Individually oriented	2.51
Autocratic	Autocratic, Dictatorial, Elitist, Ruler, and Domineering	2.41
Face Saver	Indirect, Avoiding negatives, and Evasive	2.39
Self-Centered	Self-interested, Nonparticipative, Loner, and Asocial	1.79
Malevolent	Hostile, Vindictive, Cynical, Noncooperative, and Egotistical	1.52

and willful person, the preferred working mode is team working with collaboration and consultation. This implicit model of leadership is the interpretation that emerges directly from the definitions of the dimensions, the total sample means, and the relative rankings. Thus, according to a large majority of the Swedish middle managers, an outstanding leader possesses qualities that are associated with a charismatic and team-oriented leadership style.

Industry Differences in the Swedish Sample.   By sampling three qualitatively different industries and collecting a larger data sample from each one, more than that which was required for the purposes of the GLOBE between-country analyses, we were able to analyze the homogeneity of the results presented previously in greater detail in the Swedish sample. Data were collected from all three industries studied in the GLOBE project: finance, telecommunications, and food processing. In other words, we were able to investigate whether the image of (outstanding) leadership in Sweden as it emerged from the sample on a national level was consistent with that at the industry level.

Spender (1989) proposes the existence of industry recipes for leadership. He argues that in any given industry there is a recipe, or a prevailing professional "common sense," that guides leaders in their assessments, choices, and so on. Spender shows that leaders in a particular industry share similar cognitive images of that industry and of its particular dynamics and logic, and that this affects leader behavior (cf. Hellgren & Melin, 1992: "industrial wisdom"; Porac, Thomas, & Baden-Fuller, 1989: "cognitive communities"). Thus, industry variations within the Swedish sample would be a plausible finding.

In order to perform the industry level of analysis, we had to obtain scales with sufficient reliability for our purposes. The original GLOBE scales were constructed for maximizing reliable and valid scales for *between-country* analyses. We therefore had to redesign the collection of scales somewhat to serve our particular ends (*within-country* analyses). The final result includes 12 of the original 21 GLOBE leader scales, and 3 additional scales that are modifications of original GLOBE scales: *friendly* (modification of *humane*), *independent* (modification of *autonomous*), and *close supervisor* (modification of *nonparticipative*). The redesign of the scales, based on reliability analyses, is described in further detail in the Appendix.

Table 3.3 further explores the implicit leadership model obtained among Swedish middle managers. An evaluation of the total means naturally re-creates the original model: A leader who is being inspirational, visionary, and performance oriented contributes to outstanding leadership. Strong personal integrity is another important contributing feature, as is the ability to integrate teams. Characteristics inhibiting outstanding leadership are an autocratic attitude, malevolence, and self-centeredness. Furthermore, the exercise of close supervision is a factor that is strongly rejected. However, by analyzing the industry results and by making statistical comparisons, we are able to identify an *industry-specific emphasis* on various factors that extends and modifies the original model.

The *telecommunications industry* is conspicuous for rating *collaborative team orientation* significantly higher, and *administratively competent, procedural, autocratic,* and *self-centered* significantly lower, in relation to the other two industries. The *finance industry,* on the other hand, is conspicuous for rating *performance oriented, independent,* and *visionary* significantly higher than the two other industries. Finally, the *food-processing* industry has a significantly lower rating for the *inspirational* dimension than the other two, and a higher rating for *close supervisor.* In brief, the clearest differences between the industries are associated with (a) the degree of formalization, order and systemization, (b) the relation to performance, and (c) with motivation and encouragement.

The profiles, based on the results by industry, produce rather interesting variations of the original implicit leadership model. For instance, middle managers in the telecommunications industry emphasize such things as teamwork, cooperation, personal freedom (no close supervision), and flexibility (nonprocedural, less administration). A metaphor for outstanding leadership in this industry could be the team leader or team coach. This certainly makes sense in an industry that is characterized by the rapid rate of change in its business environment,[32] such as the deregulation of the telecom markets and the opening up of new business opportunities,

---

[32]In brief, this market was characterized by a complete restructuring in combination with rapid technological development, especially for the mobile phone business area. The state-owned operator *Televerket* enjoyed monopoly status until mid-1980, when deregulation came up on the political agenda. In 1993, Televerket was corporatized and the first Telecommunications Act established, as a stable regulatory framework for greater competition (Kaplan, 1997). As a consequence of the Act, the market became open to any applicant "obviously capable of pursuing operations on a permanent basis" and a stream of new operators entered the market (Kaplan, 1997). In 1998, there were 17 operators covering telephone services, as well as mobile and fixed telephone.

TABLE 3.3

Modified Leadership Scale Means per Industry (Finance, Food, Telecom) Compared

	Total N = 896	Finance N = 374	Food N = 301	Telecom N = 221	z Value (1)	z Value (2)	z Value (3)
Inspirational	6.31	6.36	6.20	6.37	−4.36**	−0.33	−4.19**
Integrity	6.29	6.28	6.30	6.29	−0.07	−0.13	−0.06
Visionary	6.05	6.11	6.00	6.02	−2.46*	−2.14*	−0.05
Team Integrator	5.98	6.00	5.93	6.00	−1.63	−0.27	−1.67
Performance Oriented	5.96	6.08	5.89	5.85	−3.61**	−4.35**	−0.98
Collaborative Team Oriented	5.50	5.46	5.47	5.61	−0.03	−3.24**	−3.15**
Administratively Competent	5.44	5.50	5.55	5.19	−0.76	−5.27**	−5.65**
Friendly	4.68	4.67	4.62	4.77	−0.90	−1.38	−2.18*
Independent	4.33	4.55	4.17	4.19	−3.13**	−2.87**	−0.05
Status-Conscious	3.30	3.34	3.31	3.23	−0.43	−1.31	−0.92
Procedural	3.19	3.24	3.28	2.95	−0.52	−5.08**	−5.10**
Autocratic	2.41	2.52	2.42	2.22	−1.24	−4.09**	−2.90**
Malevolent	1.97	2.00	1.96	1.91	−1.31	−2.96**	−1.72
Close Supervisor	1.89	1.88	2.01	1.75	−1.28	−2.42*	−3.33**
Self-Centered	1.79	1.84	1.84	1.65	−0.57	−4.22**	−3.32**

Note. z value (1) Mann–Whitney U test between Finance and Food sectors; z value (2) between Finance and Telecommunication sectors; z value (3) between Food and Telecommunication sectors.
*$p < .05.$ **$p < .01.$

and the increasing rate of its technological development. A common way of coping with the turbulent environment in this industry is through the adoption of project organization, and certainly our results suggest that team leadership is of key importance.

In contrast to the telecommunications industry, there is an emphasis on performance and independence in the finance industry, combined with high preference for a visionary and inspirational leadership style. In the middle of the 1990s, when this survey was carried out, the industry had recently undergone a crisis and was just starting to recover.[33] The preferred traits and behavior attributes go hand in hand with this situation, with a focus on performance to achieve recovery in the present, and on the visionary in order to determine the future direction. A metaphor for outstanding leadership in this industry is the leader as a high-scoring professional.

---

[33]To add to this market situation, a new wave of mergers was also seen during this period. In 1997 alone, the Swedish bank *Nordbanken* merged with the Finnish *Meritabank,* whereas *Sparbanken* merged with *Föreningsbanken,* and *S-E Banken* with the insurance company *Trygg Hansa.* Furthermore, a number of small banks also started up. They are known as "niche banks," because they concentrate on selected types of services. Internet banking, insurance companies, and start-up banks with a very lean structure are a few of several examples. Within their selected segments, these banks offered serious competition to the major banks (Swedish Bankers' Association, 1995).

Finally, the image of outstanding leadership in the food-processing industry emphasizes direct control more than vision. Given the nature of the industry,[34] with its heavy production-process investment and economies of scale, a focus on efficiency and attending primarily to existing operations certainly makes sense. Perhaps the metaphor of a careful gardener best captures the essence of leadership in the food-processing business: creating the space for some variation at the team level, while always bearing in mind the viability of the whole.

From the industry-level analysis, we can thus conclude that the basic components of the Swedish middle managers' implicit leadership model holds across industries, although we also find support for some variants in the model depending on the industry-specific characteristics.

Swedish Conceptions of Leadership in a Global Perspective.   We now turn to a comparison between the Swedish and the total GLOBE data. Such a comparison enables us to understand the Swedish data from a global perspective, and to identify dimensions that are typical and culture-specific for Sweden. From Table 3.4 we note that all high-end dimensions in the Swedish middle managers' implicit model of leadership (within country) as found in the preceding section, are included in the high-end clusters in the between country analysis: *inspirational, integrity, visionary, performance-oriented, decisive,* and *collaborative team oriented.* However, all these dimensions belong to the universally endorsed dimensions contributing to outstanding leadership (House et al., 1999). Though clearly being important traits and attributes also in the Swedish context, those dimensions do not distinguish any characteristics typical for the implicit leadership model in Sweden.

What instead typifies Swedish outstanding leadership in an international comparison is found in the extreme high-end clusters: *autonomous, humane,* and *team integrator*[35]—a humane orientation and the capability for creating and sustaining teams, and also a relatively high degree of autonomy in the sense of being individualistic and independent. Taken together, this result appears contradictory at first sight but as we show later, they give an important cue to the particular meaning of teamwork in the Swedish context—and more specifically to the relationship between the individual and the collective (team).

Table 3.4 shows further that Sweden is relatively low or very low in the eight following dimensions: *autocratic, face saver, administratively competent, procedural, conflict inducer, self-centered, status conscious,* and *malevolent.* Four of these dimensions are universally viewed as inhibiting outstanding leadership: *autocratic, face saver, self-centered,* and *malevolent* (House et al., 1999). This result suggests that the negative perceptions of these four dimensions are indisputable among Swedish middle managers and among their counterparts in most other countries. The four remaining dimensions (*administratively competent, procedural, conflict inducer,* and *status-conscious*) are culturally contingent dimensions and are

---

[34]The Swedish food industry was subject to far-reaching regulation from the 1930s until the beginning of 1990, when a system of deregulation was proposed by the government and accepted by Parliament. The reform entailed the slow successive phasing out of the rules, with a view to adapting the farmers' production to the internal demand for their products. The new policy implied that the state would abandon its traditional price-setting role. Of the four areas included in the Swedish GLOBE project—slaughterhouses, dairy products, bakeries, and breweries—the first two were still protected, whereas the second two were included in EFTA (European Free Trade Agreement) and EU free-trade agreements (Industriförbundet, 1992). Another characteristic of food industry is its high degree of concentration at the owner, the regional, and the distribution levels. Political restrictions on trade and agriculture have limited the opportunities for growth in this already mature market. Production companies consequently have become fewer but bigger and have been concentrated to the most densely populated regions (Industriförbundet, 1992).

[35]The Diplomatic dimension is a fourth variable that belongs to a high-end cluster (A). The variable simple splits the international sample in two halves, however. It has been removed from this analysis because its cluster membership does not tell us anything typical or modal for Sweden. Rather, being diplomatic is reckoned to be a universally endorsed leader trait (House et al., 1999; 2004).

TABLE 3.4
Swedish Results on Attitudes to Leadership Traits and Behavior Compared
With All GLOBE Data

Leadership Scale (GLOBE)	Band Membership[a] (between countries)	Ranking (between countries)	Ranking[b] (within country)
Autonomous	A[c], Very high	24	Medium high
Humane	A[d], Very high	26	Medium high
Team II: Team Integrator	A[d], Very high	32	High
Diplomatic	A[b], Very high	47	Medium high
Integrity	B[e], High	17	Very high
Charismatic II: Inspirational	B[e], High	18	Very high
Team I: Coll. Team Oriented	B[d], High	32	High
Charismatic I: Visionary	B[e], High	38	Very high
Nonparticipative	B[c], High	37	Low
Performance Oriented	B[d], High	41	High
Charismatic III: Self-Sacrificial	B[d], High	45	Medium high
Decisive	B[d], High	50	Medium high
Modesty	B[c], Medium	50	Medium high
Autocratic	C[d], Low	43	Low
Face Saver	C[d], Very low	52	Low
Administratively Competent	C[c], Very low	51	Medium high
Procedural	C[d], Very low	55	Medium high
Conflict Inducer	C[c], Very low	56	Medium high
Self-Centered	C[d], Very low	58	Very low
Status-Conscious	C[d], Very low	59	Medium high
Malevolent	D[e], Very low	56	Very low

[a]Bands A > B > C > D > E are determined by calculating the grand mean and standard deviations across all scales. These means and standard deviations are used to calculate high, medium, and low bands of countries (Test Banding, cf. Hanges, Dickson, & Sipe, 2004). [b]Rank order of the GLOBE variables in the Swedish sample (cf. Table 3.2). [c]Three group bands identified ranging from A to C (high–low) [d]Four group bands identified ranging from A to D (high–low). [e]Five group bands identified ranging from A to E (high–low).

therefore more pertinent when it comes to distinguishing the typical character of outstanding leadership in Sweden. The results show that these dimensions are rated higher in most other countries. Hence, in a comparative perspective, outstanding leaders in Sweden are not associated with different expressions of formality and order such as administration, organization, routines, and procedures.[36] Nor should they provoke conflict by being secretive or bringing about competition within the team. In addition, the results show that outstanding leaders should not be status- or class-conscious, but should rather play down or even transcend existing differences within the group, the organization, or the community.

---

[36]Administratively competent is a special case, because it is classified as a contributing factor. Though not rejecting administrative competence in absolute terms (M = 5.44), the results show that this variable is rated lower in Sweden than in most other countries, and this result therefore does indicate something typical about outstanding leadership in Sweden.

Leadership Images in Focus Groups and Ethnographic Interviews

As part of the GLOBE study in Sweden, we also worked with focus groups and interviews collecting data on the conceptions and various expressions of leadership (see Interviews and Focus Groups within the Appendix for further details of these studies). One way to capture the essence of an interviewee's conception of leadership is to let them describe what they mean by it in relation to other concepts. The two concepts of management (*chefskap*) and leadership (*ledarskap*) are often used interchangeably in the literature, but for practitioners there seems to be distinct differences. Consider the following selected quotations from the ethnographic interviews, describing the perceived differences between managers and leaders:

*For me, leadership is about having this rather **more overall view** ... and to lead the company or in this case the theater in a certain direction with a **well worked-out idea or philosophy** about how it may be developed as a unit. ... I am of course a manager in the sense that people come to me and say "Paul, what do we do in this situation" ... But, what really interests me is the leadership thing, that is, **to lead one great company as a whole**—and much more in fact than these managerial functions—and that is why to a large extent I go for what's called delegated responsibility ... I fiddle about with details very little. ... (theater director)*

*I think that leadership for me is something more than management. Management, that means making certain decisions. It's about being superior to others, [dealing with] systems of rules. Leadership is something more. It contains many, many elements. It's a question of a kind of **holistic picture**. It is to have an **experience to offer**. It is a question of having an interest in looking a bit further ahead. (bishop)*

*It's **having a vision** about how to develop your company, your workplace or your organization, to lift your eyes, kind of seeing what it takes for us to get there. To look at **the paths of change you have to follow**. ... (secretary of political youth organization)*

*Someone who is formally a manager does not necessarily become a leader. As a manager you may not have that natural authority for leadership or you are not able to build your role as a leader. ... to be a **leader is a way of being** as a person, while a manager is something you are formally. (general manager)*

*This is really compressed as you can see [referring to a policy document]. Leadership is the will and ability to **build enthusiasm and to cooperate**. To share your knowledge. To be **focused on goals** and results. **Develop and change**. (regional director)*

The quotations show that the Swedish conception of management is described almost exclusively in fairly technical terms: It is little more than functional responsibilities, an administrative task. A manager is a person who is formally responsible for a work group or a unit. The conception of the *competent manager* is of someone who has good professional skills and administrative competence. Being a competent manager also includes social competence. When describing desirable interpersonal traits, the interviewees used words like *professionally competent, empathetic, fair, informative, trustworthy, friendly, enthusiastic, good at listening, showing respect for others*—traits that, taken together, describe a supportive management style. Competent managers are expected to give feedback—both positive and negative—to their employees, and to support them socially and technically in their work. When people need advice, a competent manager should always be available.

When it comes to describing *outstanding leadership,* it is clear that this is something that goes well beyond the call of duty and the formal organization (role, goals, methods, etc.). The interviewees mentioned several of the traits and behaviors of competent managers, such as trustworthiness, enthusiasm, respect, and professional competence, but outstanding leaders are also expected to be holistic, visionary, good communicators, team builders, and change agents. This image is clearly consistent with the basic components of the implicit leadership model outlined earlier.

Different Beings: Managers are the Present, Leaders the Future.   An important clue to an enhanced understanding of the different construction of the two related concepts, managers and leaders, was the subtle difference in meaning regarding the notion of the "role model." In the interviews, a competent manager was referred to as a *föredöme,* that is, someone who affects their coworkers' attitudes and behaviors within the present paradigm by their own way of acting.[37] An outstanding leader, on the other hand, was referred to as a *förebild,* that is, someone who demonstrates an attractive, alternative future by their personal way of being and who can thus perhaps shape other people's identity, values, and sense of direction. Outstanding leaders are visionaries in that they challenge the existing paradigm in terms of beliefs, common goals, structures, institutions, and so on. In creating something new, it is necessary to cross borders and break the rules. "Well ... I think that an important part of leadership is also to be adequately go-ahead or unafraid when it comes to rule systems and money" (director-general).

In short, narratives about management are situated to a large extent in the present, whereas leadership is situated in a desired future. In this sense, leaders "come from" the future and give attractive direction in the present. Even if the descriptions of the two related concepts partly overlap, they are apparently expressing two fundamentally different ideas. In the construction of outstanding leaders, for instance, building a team means building a strong commitment to a specific future rather than building a strong and loyal group (management). Likewise, high integrity for leaders means being loyal to the vision rather than, for managers, being loyal to the team (or organization).

However, it is important to note that according to the interviewees the notion of visionary leadership has a variety of possible expressions in practice. We were presented with several different ideas about the exercise of visionary leadership, and about the *origin* of the vision: It could be a case of visions created by the leader, visions created by the leader in dialogue with a vital few, visions expressed as a mission or an assignment (indicating a strong influence of external stakeholders), and visions created collectively.

To summarize, the analyses of the focus groups and the ethnographic data revealed a similar pattern with regard to the basic components of the implicit leadership model in Sweden, and thus gives support to the quantitative findings. In addition to this validation, the data enrich the previous analyses by suggesting that the construction of outstanding leadership is situated in the future, as well as indicating nontrivial variations in the actual enactment of the implicit leadership model.

Leadership Images in the Swedish Media

In the introduction to this section, we stated that images of leadership are the result of an interaction between individuals and social networks in the joint construction of the leadership phenomenon. As many social scientists have pointed out, the media is clearly an important

---

[37]The subtle difference between the two Swedish concepts förebild and föredöme is difficult to translate into English. Literally, a förebild means "preimage," which is not really communicated by the English translation "role model." The concept föredöme is much closer to this translation, namely, someone who acts as a model for someone else in terms of a specific role (e.g., formal position). Föredöme is expressed as a more rationalistic view of role modeling, for instance:

We [i.e., managers/leaders] never do understand clearly enough that we become föredömen (role models) in our organizations, whether we like it or not, or whether we are aware of it or not. "The boss does it, therefore it's all right for me to do it." It really is important to be aware of this, I believe. The way I am dressed ... the time I come to work in the morning. If I come in at nine, it somehow becomes legitimate to come in at nine. (general manager; cf. Kallifatides, 1998)

actor[38] in the shaping of people's views on various social phenomena[39] such as leadership (e.g., McLuhan & Fiore, 1967). This does not necessarily mean, however, that everyone's contributions to such construction processes carry equal weight. Rather, an adaptation of the Orwellian approach to equality gives us a better representation of the implications of a constructivist approach: "All accounts are equal, but some are more equal than others" (Grint, 1997). Perceptions of social phenomena like leadership and organizing as reflected in the implicit theories are thus likely to be determined by interactions with the social agents who affect the availability, salience, and value of the information received (Chen & Meindl, 1991; Salancik & Pfeffer, 1978). The various media are consequently important actors in molding our views of ourselves and of the world we live in. According to Chen and Meindl, the implicit leadership theories produced by the media are an expression of the national culture as a whole. It was thus strongly motivated to undertake a media study as a complement to the studies already pursued as part of the GLOBE project.

In a third study, the images of outstanding leadership as expressed in the Swedish print media were therefore analyzed, using an ethnographic-semantic approach.[40] More than 8,000 articles relevant to the understanding or perception of leadership were collected from five different newspapers and business magazines over two separate periods (for methodological details, see Analysis of Swedish Media within the Appendix). In brief, images of outstanding leadership were distilled from a process of categorization of the data via the selection of key phrases and key words (examples of collected key phrases and key words are exhibited in Table A.2 in the Appendix). Two analyses were performed, the *explicit* model of outstanding leadership in the Swedish media, and the *implicit* model of outstanding leadership.

The first analysis generated 853 key words relevant to leadership extracted from key phrases in the many articles in Swedish newspapers and magazines. The key words were classified into 60 "typification categories" (see summary in Table A.4 in the Appendix). The 10 typification categories with the highest rating among the 60 represent 301 of the 853 key words (35%). These categories obviously describe important aspects of leadership as expressed in the Swedish media, in terms of the way "outstanding" leaders should be, or the way they should act. The top 10 typification categories are "action-oriented," "cooperative," "works for equality," "communicates and has verbal ability," "enthusiastic and inspiring," "accountable," "delegates," "trustworthy," "control," and "humane." These 10 typification categories constitute what could be regarded as the dominant *explicit* model of outstanding leadership in the Swedish media.

In order to explore the data further and to distinguish the possible *implicit* model(s) of leadership in the media, we decided to search for underlying themes in the material or for any patterns in the data related to different contexts. We conducted an iterative process of framing, testing, and reframing the semantic links between the 60 typification categories (cf. the explicit model) produced at the level of the articles and the key phrases, and finally arrived at several clusters, each of which were bound together by an underlying theme relevant to the understanding of leadership (Table 3.5).

According to these themes, an outstanding leader should be *performance and action oriented, charismatic and visible inside and outside the organization, honest, modest, pragmatic, procedural, a good team builder, and entrepreneurial, and should work for egalitarianism and consensus.* These

---

[38]Other important producers of explicit and implicit leadership models are business schools or leader-training institutions (Engwall, 1992; Trollestad, 1994), management gurus (Huczynski, 1993; Furusten, 1995), and management consultants and firms (Brulin, 1997; Czarniawska-Joerges and Joerges 1988; 1990).

[39]For a comprehensive review, see Roberts and Maccoby (1985).

[40]For a full report on this study, see Holmberg and Åkerblom (2001).

TABLE 3.5
Underlying Themes Relevant to the Understanding of Leadership

Leadership Theme	Brief Explanation
Performance Orientation	Found in articles describing leaders as goal oriented, hard-working, ambitious, and acting with self-confidence
Action Orientation	Found in articles describing leaders as decisive, demanding, and action oriented
Charisma	Found in articles describing leaders as visionary, inspiring, charismatic, enthusiastic, and having unusual verbal ability
Visibility	Found in articles describing leaders as accessible, visible, figureheads, and role models
Team Building	Found in articles describing leaders as cooperative, relational, loyalty inducing, personnel oriented, and network builders
Egalitarianism	Found in articles describing leaders who give fair and equal treatment to others, work for equality, delegate, and are nonauthoritarian
Consensus	Found in articles describing leaders as willing to compromise and seek consensus, and as being empathetic, humane, and good listeners
Pragmatism	Found in articles describing leaders as rational, reasonable, pragmatic, patient, and tolerant
Honesty	Found in articles describing leaders as honest, trustworthy, ethical, and moral

qualities could be regarded as a preliminary dominant model of leadership (re)produced in the Swedish media—a culturally grounded image of leadership that defines leadership in the Swedish context, and that constrains, moderates, or facilitates the exercise and evaluation of leadership.

Comparing the Media Image With the Implicit Leadership Model. How does this image of outstanding leadership as expressed in the Swedish media compare with the previously presented quantitative results, that is, the Swedish middle managers' implicit leadership theories? To enable such a comparison we first needed to calibrate the concepts from the two studies for equivalence in meaning. Because the studies used different methodological approaches—a deductive approach (the questionnaire) and an inductive approach (the media analysis)—this calibration could only be done *post hoc* by comparing the underlying basic units (items and key words, respectively) that constituted the concepts used in the two studies. Table 3.6 summarizes our analysis of equivalence between the themes generated by the media analysis and the leadership dimensions used in the questionnaire. Of the 12 leadership themes generated by the media analysis and listed in Table 3.5, 6 were immediately found to have equivalent leadership dimensions. Three themes were found to have equivalent meaning to *pairs* of leadership dimensions (charisma, team building, and consensus). Finally, three themes had no equivalent leadership dimension, and thus qualify as concepts that say something important about leadership—at least in a Swedish context—and that were not covered in the leadership questionnaire (egalitarianism, pragmatism, and visibility).

TABLE 3.6
Comparing Meanings Between Leadership Themes (Media Analysis) and
Leadership Dimensions (Questionnaire)

Leadership Themes From Media Analysis	Leadership Dimensions From GLOBE Questionnaire Data
Charisma	Visionary + Inspirational
Honesty	Integrity
Team Building	Collaborative Team Oriented + Team Integrator
Performance Orientation	Performance Oriented
Action Orientation	Decisive
Procedural	Administratively Competent
Consensus	Humane + Diplomatic
Modesty	Modesty
Entrepreneurial	Self-Sacrificial
Egalitarianism	*No equivalent dimension*
Pragmatism	*No equivalent dimension*
Visibility	*No equivalent dimension*

In conclusion, we find that the results from the two separate studies are mutually supportive, insofar as they are comparable. The media analysis also enabled us to identify three additional themes that are essential to an understanding of leadership in Sweden.

Context-Bound Variations.   The greater majority of the selected articles contained information on leadership in two specific and different settings, namely the political and the business domains. By employing this context-based distinction in the analysis, the common assumption of one dominant model of leadership was called into question (see Holmberg & Åkerblom, 2001). The analysis clearly showed the existence of multiple coexisting models. For instance, in the political context the emphasis on action and the maintenance of a common purpose rather than results (performance) and team building is very striking. The expression "a man of action" frequently occurs in articles that discuss outstanding political leadership, and lack of action is equally often proposed as an explanation for an observed failure in political leadership (see Table A.3 in the Appendix).

In summary, the images of political and business leadership clearly differ in a number of nontrivial aspects. And yet they evidently share a core of leadership attributes that are revealed repeatedly across our studies.

Conclusions

We have reported on results and analyses from three studies, all concerned with images of leadership in Sweden. Overall, we found mutual support for the results across the studies, but some interesting variations were also noted. We now summarize the findings so far.

From the within-country analysis, we concluded that the contributory traits and behavior attributes to outstanding leadership in Sweden are the following dimensions: *inspirational, integrity, visionary, team integrator, performance orientation, decisive,* and *collaborative team orientation.* At the other end of the spectrum, the dimensions inhibiting outstanding leadership were found to be *autocratic, face saver, self-centered,* and *malevolent.*

It is important to keep in mind, however, that this image of outstanding leadership is not restricted to Swedish managers only. All these dimensions belong to the (almost) universally endorsed implicit model of outstanding leadership reported by GLOBE (Dorfman et al., 2004; House et al., 1998). Nevertheless, it gives essential input to the conception of outstanding leadership in Sweden. Indeed, the importance of our findings was verified in our subsequent study of leadership images in the Swedish media.

Subsequent analyses, putting the Swedish data in contrast with the international comparative data, shed light on dimensions that capture something typical or culture-specific about leadership in Sweden, because "typicality" can best be distinguished in relation to other instances. *Team integrator, autonomous,* and *humane* were concluded to be contributing factors and *administratively competent, procedural, conflict inducer,* and *status-conscious* were the inhibiting factors. In addition, the media study supplemented this result by introducing *egalitarian, pragmatic,* and *visible* as important concepts to be included in the culturally specific version of outstanding leadership.

Drawing from several data analyses and results from different methodologies, we have captured both the important and, in an international perspective, distinguishing characteristics of the implicit model of outstanding leadership in Sweden. The findings are summarized in Table 3.7.

Our findings can be compared with those reported in Tollgerdt-Andersson (1989), which among previous studies is the one most closely related to ours. The author investigated naive (or spontaneous) leadership theories, a concept very close to the notion of implicit theories used in GLOBE. She surveyed the spontaneous leadership theories of approximately 100 top managers, in terms of "important" leader characteristics and behaviors. Generally speaking, the qualities that these managers considered important for a good leader were an ability to be enthusiastic, decisive, cooperative, honest, and able to delegate. This result is very much in line with the general implicit leadership model proposed here (cf. Table 3.2), suggesting that Swedish top and middle managers are in agreement on the most important characteristics that make an outstanding leader.

Further comparisons with previous studies are quite encouraging. Distinguishing characteristics of Swedish leadership as reported in previous results, include an ability to create commitment to a communicated vision (Jönsson, 1995a; Källström, 1995), a strong focus on performance and a preference for teamwork and cooperation (Zander, 1997), the acceptance of challenges and risk taking (Edström, Norbäck, & Rendahl, 1989), and consensus as a condition for and a preferred outcome of direct dialogue with organization members (Czarniawska-Joerges, 1993; Edström & Jönsson, 1998).

Altogether, we find that the implicit model of outstanding leadership is an informative and useful analytical construct for which there is wide support not only across methodologies and managerial groups, but also across research projects and studies. Nontrivial variations depending on contexts such as industries or the political and business domains respectively have also been shown previously. We would argue that the images (notions) of outstanding leadership are always defined from and within the specific context.

3.   "PRIMUS INTER PARES": THE IMPLICIT LEADERSHIP MODEL IN RELATION TO SWEDISH CULTURAL CHARACTERISTICS

The next issue addressed is the relation between the cultural characteristics (see the section Sweden in the GLOBE study) and the dominant implicit model of leadership in Sweden (see the section Images of Leadership in Sweden). Before embarking on a more detailed discussion of this relationship, we need to clarify the view of culture that we have adopted in our study. It is not possible to separate the implicit leadership theories from societal culture. Rather, we have

TABLE 3.7
Summary of the Implicit Model of Outstanding Leadership in Sweden From Both a
Within- Country and Between-Country Perspective

Important Dimensions		*Distinguishing Dimensions*	
Contributing Attributes	*Someone Who Is …*	*Contributing Attributes*	*Someone Who Is …*
Inspirational	Enthusiastic, Positive, Encouraging, Motivational, and Morale booster	*Autonomous*	Individualistic, Independent, Autonomous, and Unique
Integrity	Honest, Sincere, Just, and Trustworthy	*Humane*	Generous, and Compassionate
Visionary	Future oriented, Anticipatory, Inspirational, Visionary, and Intellectually stimulating	*Team Integrator*[a]	Communicative, Team builder, Integrator, and Coordinator
Team Integrator	Communicative, Team builder, Integrator, and Coordinator	*Egalitarianism*	Treating others fairly and equally, Works for equality, Delegates and is Nonauthoritarian
Performance Orientation	Improvement, Excellence, and Performance oriented	*Visibility*	Accessible, Visible, a Figurehead, and Role model
Decisive	Willful, Decisive, and Intuitive	*Pragmatism*	Rational, Reasonable, Pragmatic, Patient, and Tolerant
Inhibiting Attributes	*Someone Who Is …*	*Inhibiting Attributes*	*Someone Who Is …*
Autocratic	Autocratic, Dictatorial, Elitist, Ruler, and Domineering	*Administrative Competency*[b]	Orderly, Administratively skilled, Organized, and Good administrator
Face Saver	Indirect, Avoiding negatives, and Evasive	*Status Consciousness*	Status- conscious, and Class-conscious
Self-Centered	Self-interested, Nonparticipative, Loner, and Asocial	*Procedural*	Ritualistic, Formal, Habitual, Cautious, and Procedural
Malevolent	Hostile, Vindictive, Cynical, Noncooperative, and Egotistical	*Conflict Inducer*	Normative, Secretive, and an Intragroup competitor

[a]Team Integrator is found to be both important and typical and is therefore included on both lists. [b]Though Administrative Competence is not rejected as inhibiting in absolute terms, our findings show that this variable is rated lower in Sweden than in most other countries and should therefore typically be less pronounced.

regarded these theories as *cultural expressions*. Our analysis thus has to focus on the linkages between typical expressions of the cultural characteristics and the implicit leadership model found in this study, that is, the enactment of leadership in organizational settings.

We distinguished three important cultural themes in the second section: *socially concerned individualism* as a summary notion for the relationship between the individual and social groups (collectivities), *rationality and pragmatism* as means for managing the future and coping with uncertainty, and *consensus* as an expression of egalitarianism, equality, and timidity. The first two cultural themes in particular were found to be in the process of revision, reformulation, and possible transformation, which we elaborate on in the concluding section.

In order to discuss how the implicit leadership model is enacted in organizational settings, we use the arena of project teams as an illustration. A reason for this choice is that throughout our studies and analyses the concept of "team" has shown importance for Swedish managers and also a remarked typicalness in an international comparison.

In a project team, and in the preferred leadership that goes with it, several aspects of the cultural theme of socially concerned individualism are expressed. There is a strong statement of belief in the power of teams and the indispensability of team leadership. Leaders should be able to build, integrate, and coordinate teams, and to create an empowering team spirit (cf. *team integrator* and *collaborative team orientation*). At the same time there is a relatively high preference for autonomy that complements—and seemingly complicates—this picture. Leaders must allow for individuality and independence even in a team setting (cf. *autonomous*). However, this seemingly paradoxical picture with a combination of autonomy and team integration can be understood as a mirror of the Swedish combination of individualism and independence on the one hand, and collectivism and cooperation on the other.

A distinctive feature of teams in Sweden, allowing for the paradox to dissolve, is that the social ties within a work team stem from a common commitment to some particular cause or goal, rather than from strong interpersonal ties between the team members. The unifying component in the team is a common desired future. We have found that leadership necessitates an exceptional ability to communicate the vision (cf. *visionary* and *inspirational*), or alternatively to manage its collective creation. This is a way for a leader to promote the sense of unity, and yet not to stand out as a commanding person (i.e., being *assertive*).

A challenge for any leader in Sweden is to balance the desire for bold vision, direction, and inspiration with the deeply rooted end values of egalitarianism and equality. These last are intertwined with the established tradition of consensus, our second cultural theme, and with the norm of low power distance. The notion of consensus as a condition for dialogue as well as its desired outcome is directly relevant to the understanding of team leadership in Sweden. The commitment and consent of all the members of a Swedish organization are valued equally. Thus, according to Swedish managers and to others commenting on their leadership style, decision making in Sweden is naturally participative (cf. *egalitarian* and *status-conscious; neg.*). The ideal of participative leadership is expressed as a readiness to listen to others, and willingness to compromise when necessary. It is rare that decisions are enforced on a basis of formal authority. Instead, there is a marked preference for informal, consensual decision making without "unnecessary" tensions or conflicts (cf. *conflict inducer; neg.*).

One way for leaders to handle potential conflicts is to separate the factual from the personal, thus paying heed to both pragmatism and timidity. Leaders are expected to be able to translate emotional issues or arguments into matters of fact. The depersonalization of an issue makes it much easier to handle, and the sense of consensus is preserved. Reasoning based on facts and logic, and the ability to enact practical solutions are celebrated leader qualities (cf. *pragmatic*). This obviously links up with the third cultural theme, rationality and pragmatism, but there is also an interesting departure from the cultural framework when it comes to the procedural aspects.

We have learned that Swedish society ranks high on Uncertainty Avoidance, with an inclination to create rules and routines for almost any issue of social importance. One might therefore assume that the leader role would automatically include accommodating and managing uncertainty by administrative means. But not at all: According to our findings outstanding leaders are regarded particularly informal (cf. *procedural; neg.*), and order and structure being typically less pronounced in the Swedish context (cf. *administrative competence*). One possible interpretation, supported by the ethnographic interviews, is that Swedes perceive their lives to be somewhat restricted by laws, regulations, rules, and procedures. However justified these may be as symbolizing and re-creating important achievements from the past, the possibility in the present of building for the future is nonetheless limited. Hence, the implicit notion of the leader, who personifies the better future, is of someone with the willingness, the courage, and the ability to break with the existing rules and procedures, rather than reinforcing them. Leaders are expected to show determination and support the team to deliver results (cf. *performance orientation* and *decisive*), and should not let established procedures get in the way.

By preference, new ideas are first approached in quite general and vague terms, in order to invite others to join the process. In other words, Swedes are generally very suspicious of ready-made ideas or solutions. It is also a question of the "ownership" of the idea. If Swedes have not been involved in the generation process, then no one should take it for granted that they will involve themselves in the implementation process either. It would be a sign of a lack of confidence to tell another person how they should perform a certain task, and leaders are certainly aware of this norm. When situations occur that require some sort of specific instruction, good leaders are expected to show great skill in providing the necessary information, but subtly and without being too specific. In light of these qualities—rationality and pragmatism, and consensus—vagueness (in the sense of a lack of ready-made ideas or solutions) is enacted as a way not only of inviting others to participate actively but also of rendering status differences invisible. Vagueness thus has a positive connotation in the Swedish language, because it creates a freedom to act and to take initiative by oneself (*autonomous*).

In Essence: First Among equals

The strong egalitarian values, preferences for pragmatic solutions, and socially concerned individualism thus suggest that the Swedish version of a team is a group of equal individuals, in which everyone expects to be consulted. The role of a leader is to skillfully balance between acting as a team member *and* simultaneously taking the lead by communicating visions, guiding sense-making processes, representing collective ambitions and interests, and framing the challenges ahead. This implies an idea of the leader as the *primus inter pares*, or first among equals.

Discussion—Swedish Leadership in Transition?

What are the likely future directions for leadership in Sweden, and what contemporary issues can provide us with further insights into this matter? We have already noted that the institutional context for leadership in Sweden is undergoing some rather dramatically changes (see the section Sweden in the GLOBE study). The social welfare system is still considered to be of great importance but it is apparently challenged by a more individualistic ideology, captured by the extreme positions and shifts for the cultural dimensions Institutional Collectivism and In-Group Collectivism. Another noticeable value change deals with the mind-set regarding the future, portrayed in the less pronunciation of arrangements to reduce uncertainty. The rational and pragmatic approach to uncertainty is still viable, but inspirational leader qualities are apparently offering a refreshing alternative. We conclude this chapter on culture and leadership with a more speculative discussion on changes in the Swedish value and belief systems, and possible implications for leadership.

In the late 1990s, people preaching the message of a new economic order invaded the public space. Much of the talk about "the new economy" was concerned with the new business logic due to rapid IT development and the breakthrough for Internet. By the end of the millennium, a new generation of business leaders emerged as figureheads. Despite their industry's relatively small share of the total economy, this new breed of leaders had a tremendous impact on the public discourse, as well as on the political agenda (Holmberg, Salzer- Mörling, & Strannegård, 2002).

The kind of leadership that these figureheads expressed and promoted was extraordinary in the Swedish context. They were young, energetic, and bold individualists with an entrepreneurial spirit recalling the heroes who transformed Sweden into an industrial nation over a century ago (an image that was actually used in their rhetoric in order to attract political interest and investor capital). Entrepreneurship became almost synonymous with outstanding leadership (Holmberg & Strannegård, 2002). One of the figureheads published a book[41] in 1999, proclaiming this attitude in its very title: *Nothing Can Stop Us Now! A New Generation Takes Command.* The ideological tension between this new generation of entrepreneurs stressing individual talent and success, and the established business leaders representing corporate collective action, was obvious.

How can we understand the enormous attention that these leaders received in the media, and the admiration they generally received from the public? We believe that one explanation lies in the vision of a future for Sweden as an advanced and affluent information society. This was very attractive, given the harsh economic situation of the 1990s. As already mentioned, the young business leaders paid tribute to the historical heritage by rhetorically linking their visions to the entrepreneurial and innovative spirit of the early 20th century. Though admittedly individualistic and egocentric when speaking of a visionary and compelling future for the IT industry in general and for their own companies in particular, they also included society as a whole in their vision. This new bread of leaders expressed an alternative way of running business, reformulating individualistic interests and yet preserving collectivistic ideals on the society level. Thus they timely articulated and embodied the values shifting toward a more individualistic ideology in organizational life.

By 2001, the IT hype was over, and many renowned dot-com companies suddenly went bankrupt. As we write these words Sweden, with its heavy dependence on the world economic situation, is under pressure from a new recession. The figureheads of the large corporations have regained the available space in the media, as the experimental and expansionary period is over. But leadership as a cultural expression was certainly not unaffected by this short yet intensive period. Although the momentum may have been interrupted, we believe that Swedish leadership is undergoing a process of transition in the directions outlined here.

The IT hype surfaced not only a transition in the leadership ideals, but also a new set of organizational ideals. A perspective emphasizing shareholder value challenged the stakeholder model that had prevailed for many decades. Remuneration policies were called into question and modified to meet the criteria of a new economic order, resulting in individual bonus systems with practically no limits. The rationales were often adjustments to international remuneration standards and acknowledgment of individual talent. In several infamous cases, these new ideals reached a limit in relationship to the Swedish norms of reasonableness

---

[41]von Holstein, J. S. (1999), *Inget kan stoppa oss nu! En ny generation tar plats.* Stockholm: Ekerlid.

and fairness however. Although there is a growing acceptance for individualistic values, perceptions of sheer greed are not well received in the public space. This example shows that working life ideals are still very much rooted in the Swedish social welfare system, and the process of cultural change in the balance between individual and collective interest that we have identified is slow and leads to obvious tensions.

REFERENCES

Agar, M. H. (1986). *Speaking of ethnography* (Sage Qualitative Research Methods Series, Vol. 2). Newbury Park, CA: Sage.

Agar, M. H. (1995). *The GLOBE project: Ethnography manual for leadership studies.* College Park: Ethnoworks, University of Maryland.

Agar, M. H. (1996a). *The GLOBE project: Qualitative research manual II.* College Park: Ethnoworks, University of Maryland.

Agar, M. H. (1996b). *The professional stranger: an informal introduction to ethnography* (2nd ed.). San Diego, CA: Academic Press.

Alvesson, M., & Sköldberg, K. (1994). *Tolkning och reflektion: Vetenskapsfilosofi och kvalitativ metod* [Interpretation and reflection: Philosophy and qualitative methodology]. Lund, Sweden: Studentlitteratur.

Berger, P. L., & Luckmann, T. (1991). *The social construction of reality: A treatise in the sociology of knowledge* (Reprint). London: Penguin. (Original work published 1966)

Berglund, J., & Löwstedt, J. (1996). Sweden: The fate of human resource management in a "folkish" society. In T. Clark (Ed.), *European human resource management* (pp. 215–243). Oxford, England: Blackwell.

Brulin, G. (1997). *Företagsledningskonsulternas kunskapsbas* [The knowledge base of management consultants]. In Å. Sandberg (Ed.), *Ledning för alla? Om perspektivbrytningar i företagsledningar* (3rd ed., pp. 291–314). Stockholm: SNS Förlag.

Burr, V. (1995). *An introduction to social constructionism.* London: Routledge.

Chen, C. C., & Meindl, J. R. (1991). The construction of leadership images in the popular press: The case of Donald Burr and People Express. *Administrative Science Quarterly, 36,* 521–551.

Czarniawska-Joerges, B. and Joerges, B. (1988). How to control things with words. On organizational talk and organizational control. *Management Communication Quarterly,* 2(2): 170–193.

Czarniawska-Joerges, B. and Joerges, B. (1990). Linguistic artifacts at service of organizational control. In: Gagliardi, P. (ed.) *The symbolics of corporate artifacts.* Berlin: de Gruyter, pp. 509–548.

Czarniawska-Joerges, B. (1993). *Sweden: A modern project, a postmodern implementation.* In D. J. Hickson (Ed.), *Management in Western Europe: Society, culture and organization in twelve nations* (pp. 229–247). Berlin: Walter de Gruyter.

Daun, Å. (1986). *The Japanese of the north—The Swedes of Asia? Ethnologia Scandinavica, 16,* 5–15.

Daun, Å. (1989). *Svensk mentalitet* [Swedish mentality]. Stockholm: Rabén & Sjögren. (English edition: *Swedish mentality* (1996) J. Teeland, trans. University Park: Pennsylvania State University Press).

Dorfman, P., Hanges, P. J., & Brodbeck, F. C. (2004). Leadership and cultural variation: The identification of culturally endorsed leadership profiles. In R. J. House, P. J. Hanges, M. Javidan, P. Dorfman, & V. Gupta (Eds.), *Leadership, culture, and organizations: The GLOBE study of 62 societies* (pp. 669–719). Thousand Oaks, CA: Sage.

Edström, A., and Jönsson, S. (1998). *Svenskt ledarskap* [Swedish leadership]. In B. Czarniawska (Ed.), *Organisationsteori på svenska.* Malmö, Sweden: Liber.

Edström, A., Norbäck, L.-E., & Rendahl, J.-E. (1989). *Förnyelsens ledarskap: SAS utveckling från flygbolag till reseföretag* [The leadership of renewal: The development of SAS from airline to travel company]. Stockholm: Norstedt.

Engwall, L. (1992). *Mercury meets Minerva: Business studies and higher education—the Swedish case.* Oxford, England: Pergamon.

Furusten, S. (1995). *The managerial discourse: a study of the creation and diffusion of popular management knowledge.* Unpublished doctoral thesis, Uppsala University, Uppsala, Sweden.

Gergen, K. J. (1999). *An Invitation to social construction.* London: Sage.

Grint, K. (Ed.). (1997). *Leadership: Classical, contemporary, and critical approaches.* Oxford, England: Oxford University Press.

Hampden-Turner, C., & Trompenaars, F. (1993). *Sweden's social individualism: Between raging horses.* In *The seven cultures of capitalism: Value systems for creating wealth in the United States, Japan, Germany, France, Britain, Sweden, and the Netherlands* (pp. 233–260). New York: Doubleday.

Hanges, P. J., Dickson, M. W., & Sipe, M. T. (2004). In R. J. House, P. J. Hanges, M. Javidan, P. Dorfman, & V. Gupta (Eds.), *Leadership, culture, and organizations: The GLOBE study of 62 societies* (pp. 219–234). Thousand Oaks, CA: Sage.

Hellgren, B., & Melin, L. (1992). *Business systems, industrial wisdom and corporate strategies.* In R. Whitley (Ed.), *European business Systems: Firms and markets in their national context* (pp. 180–197). London: Sage.

Hendin, H. (1964). *Suicide and Scandinavia. A psycho-analytic study of culture and character.* New York: Grune & Stratton.

Hirdman, Y. (1989). *Att lägga livet till rätta: Studier i svensk folkhemspolitik* [Putting life into order: Studies in Swedish people's home policies]. Stockholm: Carlsson.

Hofstede, G. (1980). *Culture's consequences: International differences in work-related values.* Beverly Hills, CA: Sage

Hofstede, G. (1991). *Organisationer och kulturer—om interkulturell förståelse* [Cultures and organizations: Software of the mind]. Lund, Sweden: Studentlitteratur.

Holmberg, I., & Åkerblom, S. (2001). The production of outstanding leadership—An analysis of leadership images expressed in Swedish media. *Scandinavian Journal of Management, 1*(17), 67–85.

Holmberg, I., Salzer-Mörling, M., & Strannegård, L. (Eds.). (2002). *Stuck in the future: Tracing "the new economy."* Stockholm: Book House.

Holmberg, I., & Strannegård, L. (2002). The ideology of the new economy. In I. Holmberg, M. Salzer-Mörling, & L. Strannegård (Eds.), *Stuck in the future: Tracing "the new economy"* (pp. 23–53). Stockholm: Book House.

House, R. J. (1994). *Global Leadership and Organizational Behavior Effectiveness Program prospectus.* Philadelphia: University of Pennsylvania, Wharton School of Management.

House, R. J., Hanges, P. J., Javidan, M., Dorfman, P. W., Gupta, V., & Globe Associates (2004). *Culture, leadership, and organizations: The GLOBE study of 62 societies.* Thousand Oaks, CA: Sage.

House, R. J., Hanges, P. J., Ruiz-Quintanilla, S. A., Dorfman, P. W., Javidan, M., Dickson, M., et al. (1999). Cultural influences on leadership and organizations: Project GLOBE. In W. Mobley, M. J. Gessner & V. Arnold (Eds.), *Advances in global leadership* (Vol. 1, pp. 171–234). Stamford, CT: JAI.

House, R. J., Wright, N. S., & Aditya, R. N. (1997). Cross-cultural research on organizational leadership: A critical analysis and a proposed theory. In P. C. Earley & M. Erez (Eds.), *New perspectives in international industrial organizational psychology* (pp. 535–625). San Francisco: New Lexington.

Huczynski, A. A. (1993). *Management gurus: What makes them and how to become one.* London: Routledge.

Ilshammar, L. (2000). *Sweden as an IT nation* (Current Sweden Series No. 430). Stockholm: Swedish Institute.

Industriförbundet (1992). *Sveriges industri* [Sweden's industry]. Stockholm: Förlags AB Industrilitteratur.

Jönsson, S. (1995a). *Goda utsikter: Svenskt management i perspektiv* [Good outlooks: Swedish management in perspective]. Stockholm: Nerenius & Santérus Förlag.

Jönsson, S. (1995b). *Management style seen as sedimentation caused by change and stability: the case of Sweden* (GRI Reports 1995:3). Göteborg, Sweden: Gothenburg Research Institute.

Kallifatides, M. (1998). *Leadership and the ethics of late modernity* (Research Paper Series, 1998/2). Stockholm: Centre for Advanced Studies in Leadership.

Källström, A. (1995). *I Spetsen för sin flock: Normer för svenskt management* [At the forefront: Norms for Swedish management]. Göteborg, Sweden: Gothenburg Research Institute, Förlags AB Industrilitteratur.

Kaplan, M. (1997). *Liberalisation and privatisation in telecoms: Does sequencing matter?* Stockholm: Stockholm School of Economics, Department of Marketing, Distribution and Industry Dynamics and EFI.

Kjellberg, A. (1997). *Fackliga organisationer och medlemmar i dagens Sverige* [Union organizations and membership in contemporary Sweden]. Arkiv Förlag.

Kriminalvårdsstyrelsen. (2005). Information published on Internet. Retrieved October 10, 2005, from http://www.kvv.se

Lord, R., & Maher, K. J. (1991). *Leadership and information processing: Linking perceptions and performance.* Boston: Unwin-Everyman.

McLuhan, M., & Fiore, Q. (1967). *The medium is the message: An inventory of effects.* New York: Bantam.

Möller, T (2002). *Election year 2002: Sweden's Social Democrats consolidate their dominance.* Stockholm: Swedish Institute.

Organization for Economic Cooperation and Development. (2005). *Education at a glance 2005.* Report from OECD Directorate for Education. Retrieved October 5, 2005, from http://www.oecd.org

Phillips-Martinsson, J. (1991). *Swedes as others see them—facts, myths or a communication complex?* Lund, Sweden: Studentlitteratur.

Porac, J. F., Thomas, H., & Baden-Fuller, C. (1989). Competitive groups as cognitive communities: the case of Scottish knitwear manufacturers. *Journal of Management Studies, 26,* 397–416.

Roberts, D. F., & Maccoby, N. (1985). *Effects of mass communication.* In G. Lindzey & E. Aronson (Eds.), *Handbook of social psychology* (pp. 539–598). New York: Random House.

Salancik, G. R., & Pfeffer, J. (1978). A social information approach to attitudes and task design. *Administrative Science Quarterly, 23,* 224–253.

Skolverket. (2004). *Report No. 248.* Stockholm: Swedish National Agency for Education.

SOU, Statens offentliga utredningar. (1990). *Maktutredningen. Demokrati och makt i Sverige: Maktutredningens huvudrapport* [Democracy and power in Sweden: Final report from the study of power and democracy in Sweden]. (1990:44). Stockholm: Allmänna Förlaget.

Spender, J.-C. (1989). *Industry recipes: An enquiry into the nature and sources of managerial judgement.* Oxford, England: Basil Blackwell.

Statistics Sweden. (2004). *På tal om kvinnor och män* [Talking about women and men]. Stockholm: Statistiska Centralbyrån.

Statistics Sweden. (2005). *Population figures for July 31, 2005.* Retrieved October 7, 2005, from http://www.scb.se/eng/index.asp

Swedish Bankers' Association. (1995). *The Swedish credit market.* Stockholm: Svenska Bankföreningen.

Swedish Institute. (2003a). *Swedish industry.* Stockholm: Svenska institutet.

Swedish Institute. (2003b). *Swedish trade policy.* Stockholm: Svenska institutet.

Swedish Institute. (2004a). *Equality between women and men.* Stockholm: Svenska institutet.

Swedish Institute. (2004b). *The Swedish economy.* Stockholm: Svenska institutet.

Thomas, J. (1996). *A GLOBE pilot study of the media analysis method in USA* (Internal project report). College Park: University of Maryland.

Tollgerdt-Andersson, I. (1989). *Ledarskapsteorier, företagsklimat och bedömningsmetoder* [Leadership theories, corporate climates, and assessment methods]. Unpublished doctoral dissertation, EFI, Stockholm School of Economics.

Tönnies, F. (1963). *Community and society: Gemeinschaft und Gesellschaft.* New York: Harper Torchbook.

Trollestad, C. (1994). *Människosyn i ledarskapsutbildning—en empirisk studie* [Conception of human nature in leadership training programmes—an empirical study]. Nora, Sweden: Nya Doxa.

Zander, L. (1997). *The licence to lead: An 18 country study of the relationship between employees' preferences regarding interpersonal leadership and national culture.* Stockholm: Institute of International Business, Stockholm School of Economics.

Appendix A

Notes on Methodology

THE GLOBE QUESTIONNAIRE

As part of the preparation for collecting our data, we translated the preliminary version of the English questionnaire into Swedish. We then translated our Swedish version back into English, a process that meant that problematic items could be identified and either modified or removed completely in the final version. Two independent professional translators did most of this work under our supervision. The translators and the Swedish GLOBE team also had the expert support of a social scientist with extensive experience of business surveys. English was his mother tongue, but he was also fluent in Swedish.[42]

The data were collected during the first 5 months of 1996. A contact person at each participating organization handled the distribution of the questionnaires, in order to reduce distribution costs while also increasing the legitimacy of the questionnaire. The responses were returned directly to the research team by mail. Because we wanted to enable within-country analyses as well as international comparisons (between-country), the Swedish sample was considerably larger than that required for the GLOBE purposes (House, 1994).

The final version of the Swedish questionnaire was distributed to middle managers in 14 business organizations active in three different industries: finance (4 organizations, $N = 373$), food processing (6 organizations, $N = 301$) and telecommunications (4 organizations, $N = 222$). Altogether, almost 900 middle managers responded to the questionnaire. The overall response rate was 75% which was very satisfactory for a study of this type. All questionnaire responses were coded into a computer with the help of six research assistants during May and June 1996.

BASIC DEMOGRAPHICS OF THE SWEDISH SAMPLE

The most important demographic characteristics of the sample of middle managers can be summarized as follows:

- Gender: 82.3% of the respondents were male; 17.7% were female.
- Age: The respondents were aged between 25 and 64 years, with a median of 46.
- Cultural conditioning: 97.1% were born in Sweden and 85% had never lived abroad for more than a year.
- Working experience: The full-time working experience of the middle managers ranged from 4 to 49 years with a median of 25; 12 years was the median for holding a management position. Managers who had worked for a Swedish or foreign multinational corporation at some point accounted for 26.4%.

---

[42]Associate Professor Peter Docherty at the Stockholm School of Economics. We are very grateful for his generous contribution to the development of the Swedish GLOBE questionnaire.

- Education: Around 23% had received the basic compulsory education only (9 years) and 37% had the equivalent of a college diploma (12–13 years of formal education), or less. The remaining 40% had gone on to earn a university degree. Around half the middle managers reported that, regardless of the educational level concerned, they had specialized in business and administration, and an additional 25% had studied engineering.
- Training: 90% of the managers reported that they had participated in formal management training of some kind.
- Staff: The median number of people directly reporting to the manager was six, and the average number of subordinates was 55.

REDESIGNING THE SCALES FOR INDUSTRY COMPARISON PURPOSES

In order to make the industry comparison (within-country) we had to obtain scales with sufficient reliability for our purposes. The original GLOBE scales were constructed for maximizing reliable and valid scales for between-country analyses. We therefore had to redesign the collection of scales somewhat to serve our own ends.

The following original scales were retained in the industry comparison: *administratively competent, autocratic, charismatic I: visionary, charismatic II: inspirational, integrity, malevolent, performance oriented, procedural, self-centered, status conscious, team I: collaborative team oriented, and team II: team integrator.* Reliability (Chrombach's alpha measure) for these scales varied between 0.56 and 0.80, with an average of 0.66.

Three additional scales (included items in parentheses) were constructed, using reliability analyses as a basis for detecting items that had great influence on low alpha values, and factor analysis to investigate the within-country factor structure: *friendly* (generous, compassionate, sensitive, caring: 0.56), *independent* (independent, autonomous: 0.72), *close supervisor* (micromanager, nondelegater: 0.71).

INTERVIEWS AND FOCUS GROUPS

During the first phase of the project we operated with two focus groups, one made up of managers and one of students (February and March 1994). The manager group consisted of four men and two women. The group members represented different industries (mainly telecommunications, food, banking, and insurance) and held various managerial positions (one managing director, two general managers, one project manager, and two functional managers). The second focus group comprised of seven final-year students of business administration. All reported that they had at least 2 years of work-life experience.

The participants of both groups were asked to carry out a preparatory assignment, reflecting on their personal experiences of outstanding leaders and competent managers respectively.

The focus group interviews lasted about 2 hours each and concentrated on three themes defined in the GLOBE study: the definitions of (outstanding) leadership and (competent) management, the difference (if any) between the two concepts, and examples of outstanding leadership.

Four semistructured interviews were also conducted at the start of the project with individuals in managerial positions in different industries. They were asked about their perception and experience of outstanding leadership, and if there was any difference between outstanding leaders and competent managers. The average duration of the interviews was 1.5 hours. The guiding questions covered the same three themes as in the focus groups.

At a later stage in the project, we also conducted ethnographic interviews, in line with the GLOBE qualitative research manual (Agar, 1995). Six high-ranking officials from very different formal organizations were asked to develop their views on leadership and on what constitutes successful leadership, and to give their views on how their organizations work. The interviewees were chosen to represent a wide range of societal sectors, all of them outside or on the margins of the sphere of privately or publicly owned corporations. The interviewees were: a bishop in the Swedish Church, a director-general in a national authority, a secretary of a political party's youth organization together with one of her colleagues, a general manager of a nationwide lobbying organization, a regional director of another national authority, and a theater director. The duration of the interviews varied from 1.5 to 2.0 hours. Every interview consisted of the interviewee's own account of leadership and leadership behavior, combined with stories from their own experience of successful and unsuccessful leadership. The six interviews were tape-recorded and the interviewer subsequently typed full transcripts (Kallifatides, 1998).

The four semistructured interviews and the six ethnographic interviews were transcribed and structured into text segments covering different ideas/topics. All the interviews were first analyzed individually, before frame building was conducted at the group level. The data were analyzed in to different sets of categories: the person-specific characteristics (traits and behavior), leader–follower relations (values and norms regarding leader–follower interactions), and organizational issues (the leader's role within the organization, and organizational practices).

The interviews were checked for intrapersonal consistency between what the interviewee said about leadership in general and what they described in the stories about good and bad leadership.

ANALYSIS OF SWEDISH MEDIA

The research strategy and methodology for the analysis of the media were described in three internal GLOBE project documents, namely two research manuals (Agar, 1995, 1996a) and one document describing a pilot study which applied the methodology to the media in the United States (Thomas, 1996). The approach is referred to as "ethnographic semantics" (Agar, 1986, 1996b). Ethnographic semantics belongs to semantics because it deals with word meanings, and to ethnography because the aim is to create and resolve "rich points," empirical observations that do not make sense from the researcher's point of view and that therefore suggest a surfaced gap between two worlds of knowledge. A rich point represents an opportunity to learn something about the view of the world that is held by the studied group of people (Agar, 1996). Central to this approach is the idea that an understanding of a particular culture emerges from an exploration of the system of concepts within that culture, and of the links that tie the concepts together. In language, concepts are expressed in linguistic labels, mainly words. Thus, words label concepts, and the system of concepts (relevant to leadership) is the primary focus for this type of study. In short, the aim of the procedure described is to help the researcher to extract the most important strings of words from a large volume of text. Concepts and relationships between them can then be further explored from this extracted data.

The Swedish newspapers and magazines that best fitted the criteria given in the research manual (Agar, 1996) were (a) *Dagens Nyheter* (Daily News), the largest and most respected national daily newspaper with an average daily circulation of 357,000, (b) *Dagens Industri* (Business Today), the only general business newspaper distributed nationally (100,000), (c) *Expressen* (The Express), at the time of data collection the largest daily national newspaper aimed at the general public (339,000) and with a reputation as one of the main newspapers prone to sensational journalism, (d) *Veckans Affärer* (Business Weekly), the largest weekly magazine aimed at the general business community (33,000), and (e) *Månadens Affärer* (Business Monthly), a glossy business magazine often containing specials on management issues, as well as leader profiles. Circulation is based primarily on the magazine's position as a monthly supplement to subscribers of *Veckans Affärer*.

Data for this study were collected over two periods (weeks): March 15–23, 1996, and July 12–18, 1996. The periods were determined in advance, and to our knowledge at the time of the selection these could be expected to be two very "normal" weeks with no major national events such as political elections, nor any important anniversaries that would take up a large proportion of the news space or the journalistic focus.

During the month of July *Dagens Industri* was published only on Fridays, due to the summer season (vacations). Thus only one issue of *Dagens Industri* was collected during the second collection period. *Veckans Affärer* was not published at all during July, so the latest issue from June was collected instead as a replacement. Table A.1 displays a frequency summary of the empirical material resulting from the chosen collection periods.

TABLE A.1

Summary of the Empirical Material That Was Analyzed for Images of Leadership

	Dagens Nyheter	Dagens Industri	Expressen	Veckans Affärer	Månadens Affärer	Total
Newspapers/journals	14	8	14	2	2	40
Articles	4,732	744	1,575	363	650	8,064

TABLE A.2

Examples of Key Phrases Collected and Key Words Subsequently Highlighted
From the Five Swedish Newspapers and Journals

DI 960315, p.5	He was **seen as a visionary** and someone who **initiated** a number of projects. He **aroused enthusiasm in his coworkers** but, according to DI sources, was **dependent** on having competent people around him.
DI 960316, p. 40	**Women are less prestige-minded than men.** It is easier for them to **delegate** than it is for men, and they are often **good organizers.**
DI 960318, p. 3	[The Prime Minister] Göran Persson is a **brilliant pedagogue.** He has realized that he needs **co-operation** to succeed.
DN 960317, p. B4	There is a big editorial staff working at **high tempo,** and **decisions are being taken by the minute.** Not everyone can handle it. The **personal confidence** of the journalist **in you as the manager** is also needed, if things are to work.
DN 960317, p. B5	I want to **give this plan for gender equality,** with all its elegant words, **a real meaning.** The mission is to **make sure the measures** described in the plan **are accomplished.**
EXP 960317, p. 2	The problem troubling the new chairman is that he has been so **convincing in his previous roles.**
MA March, 1996, p. 78	[As a leader] you also have to **know the business** you are leading, and to **care about the people** at the workplace, and to have the **ability to recruit good people who work well together.** A good leader must be **interested in people** and must not be **self-centered.**
VA week 12, p. 6	Many people have great hopes, but if [Prime Minister] Persson is going to succeed it will chiefly be a matter of **changing old attitudes.**

Note. Text is originally in Swedish and was translated by the authors.

TABLE A.3

Two Emergent Implicit Models of Leadership, Depending on
Context

Political Leadership	*Business Leadership*
Charisma	Charisma
Pragmatism	Pragmatism
Procedural	Procedural
Action orientation	Performance oriented
Egalitarianism	Team building
Consensus	Entrepreneurial
Modesty	Visibility
Honesty	

TABLE A.4

Summary of the 60 Typification Categories Generated From the Media Analysis,
Together Representing 853 Key Words

Typification Category	Freq.	Typification Category	Freq.	Typification Category	Freq.
Action oriented	43	Good listener/Sensitive	16	*Providing guidelines*	9
Cooperative	38	PR/image figurehead	16	Strategic & tactical	9
Works for equality	32	Visionary	16	Humorous	8
Communicates & verbal ability	31	Performance oriented	15	Popular/common touch	8
Enthusiastic & inspiring	31	Relational	15	Patient & tolerant	8
Accountable	26	Network builder	14	Prone to risks/Bold	8
Delegates	26	Flexible & change oriented	13	Coordinator and organizer	7
Trustworthy	26	Informing	13	Cultured	7
Control	25	Charismatic	12	Induces loyalty	7
Humane	23	Autonomous	11	Competent	6
Compromise & consensus	22	Determined	11	Creative	6
Risk avoiding/careful	22	Accessible & visible	10	Effective bargainer	6
Ethical/moral	21	Careful & orderly	10	Self-confident	6
Humble, low-key, modest	20	Encouraging/motivational	10	Empathic	5
Elucidate & simplify	20	Respectable & respectful	10	Family oriented	5
Fair/equal treatment	18	Balanced/harmonic	9	Planning	5
Honest	18	Entrepreneurial	9	Informal	4
Nonauthoritarian/hierarchic	18	Generalist	9	Evaluate	3
Reasonable & pragmatic	18	Long-term oriented	9	Personnel oriented	3
Ambitious	16	Open	9	Role model	2

Culture and Leadership in Finland

Martin Lindell
Swedish School of Economics and Business Administration

Camilla Sigfrids
Center for Leading Competence Oy, Helsinki, Finland

A salient feature of Finnish society is its position between West and East. One of the prerequisites for understanding leadership and culture in Finland is to understand the historical development of Finnish society with its influences from both directions. The country's geographic vicinity to both Sweden and Russia has also had an impact on Finnish politics and the economy. A nation derives its culture from four principal sources: history, language, religion, and climate (Lewis, 1997). In the following section, a brief description of the Finnish historical background is given.

1. THE BACKGROUND AND DEVELOPMENT OF FINNISH CULTURE

Early History

The first inhabitants of Finland lived along the coast in the south and west of the country. From the Middle Ages Sweden exerted the strongest and most immediate influence. The Åland Islands (between Sweden and Finland) were inhabited around 500 A.D. by settlers from Sweden and ever since have had a Swedish-speaking population. Swedes ruled Finland for about 500 years. Finland was incorporated into Sweden in 1155 under the leadership of the Catholic St. Hendrick, Finland's first Bishop of Turku. During that period Nordic institutions and traditions, religious practices, education and public administration were introduced in Finland (Häikiö, 1992). Also, the Swedish civil and criminal codes, approved at a meeting of the Swedish-Finnish Estates in 1734, remained in force during the period of Russian rule (Häikiö, 1992).

But at the beginning of the 19th century Russia and France wanted to form an alliance against Britain, wanting Sweden to be included in that alliance. Sweden, however, refused and Russia declared war on Sweden. Finland was occupied in 1809 and became a Grand Duchy of Russia. Alexander I, the Russian Emperor, was the first Grand Duke.

In order to increase Russian influence, the capital of Finland was moved from Turku to Helsinki in 1812, and the university followed in 1828. Generally, however, Finland maintained a high degree of autonomy. Russia's leaders relied on the Finnish language and way of thinking to act as a barrier against the West (TAT Group, 2001). The Finns' feeling of national pride grew ever stronger. The Finnish national epic, the *Kalevala,* written by Elias Lönnrot, was published in 1835. J. L. Runeberg became Finland's national poet and the author of the national anthem. At that time J. V. Snellman was one of the most visible statesmen and he advocated that the Finnish language should gradually become an official language alongside Swedish.

But the situation in Europe changed in the 1860s and 1870s. Russia's leaders felt the need to impose more direct control over the countries on their borders. In Poland and the Baltic countries Russian became the official language and the countries Russian provinces. In Finland the strongest Russification period occurred in 1899–1917. A long range of measures was implemented. Finns had to serve in the Russian army, and Russian became an official language in Finland. It was also planned to bring Finland's laws into line with those of Russia and that any new laws would have to be approved by the Russian Emperor. Russian opinions were published in new Russian newspapers in Finland. Many Finnish newspapers were withdrawn from circulation. Russian stamps had to be used on mail sent abroad. There were also plans to eliminate the customs border between the two countries and Finnish money (Nyberg, 1995). Under the plans Finland was to become an integrated part of Russian society. When Russification was stepped up, resistance also increased. The most serious event was the assassination of the Russian Governor General Bobrikov in 1904. Finland never became an integrated part of Russia, but 100 years did not pass without leaving a mark.

Independence

The military setbacks of the First World War led to several changes in Russian top leadership. The Russification drive in Finland ceased at the beginning of 1917 and finally Lenin and the Bolsheviks seized power. The Finns then saw their chance to gain independence and on December 6, 1917, Finland was declared independent. The Parliament approved a declaration earlier made by the Senate. Although a high point in Finnish history, the situation was unstable. There was a civil war lasting three months between a right-wing loyal to the government and a communist left-wing. The war ended in May 1918 with victory for the government troops led by General Gustaf Mannerheim. About 30,000 people died in the war and also in the executions following it (Häikiö, 1992). In 1919, Finland became a republic and K. J. Ståhlberg was elected as the first President.

Economically, Finland developed rapidly between the two World Wars. However, the positive trend was broken by the world depression at the beginning of the 1930s, but became a boom by the end of the decade. The most rapid growth took place in the paper and metal industries.

In 1939 a non-aggression pact was signed between the Soviet Union and Germany, and in November 1939 the Soviet Union invaded Finland in the so-called Winter War. After the Second World War the basis of the new foreign policy was the Treaty of Friendship, Co-operation and Mutual Assistance signed in 1948. Finland was once more integrated more closely into the Soviet Union's security sphere. However, any assistance from the Soviet Union was to be agreed upon separately and Finland could in fact be considered a neutral country. The military agreement remained in force for more than 40 years. In September 1990 the Government declared the Treaty of Paris (1947) obsolete. The Treaty imposed restrictions on the size of the armed forces and military hardware. In 1992, following the changes in the former Soviet Union, a new Treaty on cooperation between Finland and Russia was signed.

This new Treaty did not contain any military provisions and the previous Treaty on Friendship, Co-operation and Mutual Assistance was rescinded.

Finland Integrates Closer Into Europe and Attains Greater Sovereignty

After the Second World War a period of stronger internationalization and orientation towards Europe started. The first steps were slow and minor. It was not until the end of the century before a real breakthrough took place. Below some of the important international organizations that Finland has joined during the last six decades are mentioned.

Finland joined the International Monetary Fund in 1948 and became a member of GATT (General Agreement on Tariff and Trade) two years later. The trend of internationalization and alignment with other countries continued and Finland became a member of the United Nations and the Nordic Council in 1956, followed by the joining of the OECD (the Organization for Economic Cooperation and Development) in 1969. Finland was recognized as a neutral country both by East and West and therefore acted as host to many large international conferences. In 1975 the Conference on Security and Co-Operation in Europe (CSCE), with 35 heads of state from Europe and North America, was held in Helsinki where the Helsinki Final Act was signed.

Rapid and perhaps most significant international integration, however, took place at the end of the 1980s and in the 1990s. In 1986 Finland became a full member of EFTA (European Free Trade Agreement, consisting of Finland, Sweden, Norway, Iceland, Switzerland, and Austria) and in 1989 the country also became a member of the Council of Europe. In 1992 Finland applied for full membership of the EU (European Union). The European Parliament voted in favor of Finnish membership two years later. The European integration continued with the European Monetary Union (EMU) at the beginning of 1999, with Euro notes and coins being introduced in 2002. From the start, eleven EU member countries (including Finland) joined EMU. As a result several positive effects of EU membership have been evident: food prices, inflation and interest rates have decreased (Torvi, 1999). Finland has also been active in European cooperation. From July to December 1999 Finland held the presidency of the Council of the EU for the first time.

To conclude, the influence of Sweden has been significant over the last eight centuries. The Russian influence was notable and had both a direct and indirect effect on the period beginning from the 19th century until around 1990. After that Western influences have held sway of Finland, mostly from Central Europe.

Finland Today

The foundations of a Scandinavian welfare state system in Finland were lain in since the beginning of the 1960s, with services being provided by public funds. Welfare and social security are guaranteed for all citizens. But welfare has also brought with it a high level of taxation. The gross tax ratio is higher than in most other OECD countries. In Sweden it was 53% in 1998, in Denmark 49.3%, in Finland 46.9% and in Norway 43.6% (Statistical Yearbook of Finland, 2000). Taxes are channeled to provide health care, social services and free education. More and more Finns become dependent on social income transfers in order to maintain their standard of living. In 1998, 28% of household incomes consisted of social benefits (Salonen et al., 2001). One of the most important parts of the social service system is the pension system. The basic national pension system guarantees everyone an equal minimum income.

Generally, the prosperity of the Finnish population has improved significantly. If 100 are used as the real purchasing power of wages in 1964, the index was 1838 in 1999 (*Statistical Yearbook of Finland*, 2000). The life expectancy of women is 81 years and for men 73.7 years (Salonen, Kääriäinen, & Niemelä, 2001, p.16). But in society as a whole the development has not always been as positive as outlined above. In the 1980s the unemployment rate in Finland was rather low at about 5%. However from 1991 unemployment went up very rapidly, reaching a peak of 16.6% in 1994. Since then unemployment has decreased slowly and was around 8% in August 2001.

Finland has gained a reputation in a number of areas. The country is perhaps best known today for its rally, Formula 1 drivers and the sauna (there are 1.5 million saunas in Finland, one for every four inhabitants). But Finland is also known for Lapland (as being the homeland of Santa Claus), for its architects (e.g., Eliel Saarinen), composers (e.g., Jean Sibelius), and designers of elegant fabrics, furniture, silver, ceramics, and glassware. The environment is clean. In a 122-nation study by the Earth Institute's Center for International Earth Science Information Network (CIESIN), Finland, Norway and Canada were ranked highest in environmental sustainability (CIESIN, 2001).

Industry is putting in a strong performance at the end of 1990s. Finland today is seen as a high-tech country. A scoreboard found that Finland and Sweden outstrip the U.S. and the rest of the EU in applying for patents for high-tech applications (Hargreaves, 2000). Those two countries also score highest on business expenditure on research and development as a percentage of gross domestic product (GDP)—3% percent in Sweden and just below 3% in Finland. Over the last decade the Finns have been best known for their advances in electronics and mobile communications. Nokia is recognized all over the world as the largest and most profitable manufacturer of mobile phones and Linus Torvald as the inventor of the Linux operating system. Nokia accounts for almost a fourth of Finland's exports (Annual report of Nokia, 2000, *Statistical yearbook of Finland*, 2000).

At the end of 1999, there were 121 personal computers (PCS) with an Internet connection per thousand citizens. Around half of all households have a PC and 78% a mobile phone (Salonen et al., 2001). In the UN Human Development Report (UNDP) for 2001, Finland is ranked as the most highly developed country technologically. As early as in 1896–1897 the Spanish Consul in Finland, Axel Ganivet, devoted an entire chapter of his book on Finland to the "excessive" interest Finns had with technology. Phones were almost as common as kitchenware. In the 1920s and 1930s there were more than 800 separate telephone companies in the country (Leonard, 2000).

Educational System

The majority of the population was already literate during the nineteenth century, and comprehensive schooling became compulsory more than 150 years ago. The first university was founded in 1640 (Häikiö, 1992). In the early 1970s a uniform system of basic education was implemented. There is a 9-year comprehensive schooling system. Children begin their formal education at the age of 7. After completing comprehensive school, there are two alternatives. Either pupils continue in a vocational school for 2 to 6 years or they attend a 3-year upper secondary school. About half of the school-leavers select vocational school and the other half, upper secondary school. A large number of those selecting upper secondary school continue at universities and polytechnics. Of the total population, 57.7% have some form of qualification other than a comprehensive school leaving certificate. In 2000, the universities had 157,000

TABLE 4.1
Members of Different Religious Communities in Finland at the End of 1999

Religion	Absolute Numbers	Percentage of Total Population
Lutheran	4.40 million	85.3
Orthodox	0.05 million	1.1
Other communities	0.05 million	1.0
No religious community	0.63 million	12.6

Note. From Statistical Yearbook of Finland (2001).

students at different levels. In addition, there were 88,000 Open University students and 105,000 executive education students. That means that more than 10% of the active population is participating in university level education each year (Ministry of Education, 2001). In comparison with the Nordic and other European countries Finland had the most students at higher level per 100,000 inhabitants in 1994 and 1995 (*Statistical Yearbook of Finland*, 2000).

The education policy of the state is that education should be equal for all citizens, and that means that education is largely free of charge. Finland invested 5.7% of its GDP in education in 1998. In this respect Finland's position is towards the average of the OECD countries (OECD, statistics).

As already mentioned, national cultures are defined besides history, by language, climate, and religion (Lewis, 1997). These three factors are briefly discussed next.

Religion

Finland was largely Roman Catholic until the Protestant Reformation. Lutheranism became the state religion in 1593. In 1923, freedom of religion was guaranteed. Citizens were then free to found religious denominations (H. Heino, 1998). They also had the right not to subscribe to any denomination at all. The state took a neutral attitude to religion. Schools give religious education according to the confession of the majority of the pupils.

The Finns have a positive attitude towards the church; 64% of the Finns are of the opinion that the church is necessary. But the Finnish population does not take a very active part in the activities of the church. Only half of the population attends the church at least once a year (Salonen et al., 2001). Active members of the Lutheran church attend services at least once a month and vote in parish elections. The majority of Finns prefer to marry in church, have their children baptized, and have them confirmed. They also want a Christian burial for themselves and their relatives (H. Heino, 1998). For frequency distributions of the various Religions in Finland, see Table 4.1.

Although most of the population is Lutheran the Finnish society is mostly secular. Over the last 30 years the numbers of those belonging to no religious denomination have increased by almost 10% (Salonen et al., 2001).

The Finnish Orthodox church is strongest in the east of Finland, with the monastery at Valamo as its center. When Finland became independent the administrative links to the church were broken, but reestablished in 1923. In Helsinki, the Uspenski Cathedral is a monument from the Russian era. It was consecrated in 1868 and is well known and visited by Finns and foreigners even today.

Language and Climate

Unlike most European languages, Finnish is neither a member of the Indo-European language family nor is it related to the other Nordic languages (Swedish, Norwegian, and Danish). Finnish belongs to the language family known as Uralian, whose two branches include Finnish and Estonian in the Finno group and Hungarian in the Ugric (TAT Group, 2001). Finnish is also related to several minority languages in Russia, such as Karelian, spoken along the Finland - Russian border (Gordon, 1991). About 94% of the population of Finland speaks Finnish as their main language and 6% Swedish. During the Swedish era, soldiers, officials, and priests stationed in Finland settled in the country. Swedish businessmen and artisans migrated to Finnish towns. Swedish continued to be the official language and kept its position as the language of cultural life. Swedish was used in official bodies during the 19th century. In 1902, Finnish also became an official language.

In the 1880s, more than 14% of the population had Swedish as their mother tongue (Nyberg, 1995). But emigration to Sweden in the 1950s and 1960s significantly reduced the rank of the Swedish speaking population. Traditionally there has been tension between the two language groups and there is still a Swedish party defending the rights of the Swedish-speaking Finns.

The climate in Finland is characterized by great variety. The summers are warm and beautiful, the winters often very cold. Of the world's populations, only the Finns have settled an entire population of more than five million above 60 degree N (Lewis, 1997). The mean temperature in Finland is several degrees (as much as 10°C in winter) above that in other areas at the same latitude, e.g., Siberia and south Greenland (R. Heino, 2001). The main reason for this is the airflows from the Atlantic are warmed up by the Gulf Stream.

According to Lewis (1997), the effects of the climate are that these latitudes engender sturdy, resilient people with an inordinate capacity for self-reliance and an instinct for survival. Arctic survivors need stamina, tenacity, self-dependence, and resourcefulness that the Finns are well known for (see, e.g., Laine-Sveiby, 1987; Simon, Bauer, & Kaivola, 1996). The temperature can vary between more than plus 30°C in July to minus 30°C in January. The country is large, with a surface area of 338,000 km².

2.   THE COMPETITIVE POSITION OF FINNISH INDUSTRY

The historical background and the present situation of Finland today were outlined above. In the following, attention is focused on the development of industry and economic life within the country. Systematic industrial policy dates back to 1616, when Finland was still under Swedish rule. In that year an iron foundry was built in the western part of Uusimaa (Laakso, 2000). However, the first modern factory was a cotton-spinning mill in Tampere. In the 1850s it was the biggest industrial company in Scandinavia. There was an industrial breakthrough in the 1860s and 1870s. Growth was spearheaded by the sawmill industry, and was initially slow in gaining momentum. The pulp and paper industry took off at a later stage. The wealth generated by the forest industry was reflected in society at large and propelled the development of other industries, notably textiles, metals and engineering. Finland was being changed more and more from an agricultural country to an industrial one. Järvinen, Korkala, and Åman (1978) identify the existence of three cultures in the 1800s; (a) a farming culture, (b) a trade culture and (c) an artisan culture.

At the turn of the 20th century, and in spite of her geographical and Russian connection, Finland was surprisingly international in outlook. From 1890 to Finnish independence in 1917, the eastern Baltic was one of the most international areas in the world. Helsinki, Viipuri (Vyborg) and St. Petersburg were lively centers of artistic excellence and multilingualism. In Viipuri many people spoke four languages (Lewis, 1997). In those days foreigners contributed significantly to the development of Finnish industry, including names such as Fazer (German), Hackman (German), Finlayson (Scot), Gutzeit (Norwegian), Sinebrychoff (German from St. Petersburg) (Alho, 1961).

The years since the Second World War to the beginning of the 1990s were years of continuous growth. War reparations to the Soviet Union in the form of industrial products contributed to a transformation in Finnish industry (Laakso, 2000). A strong metal and engineering industry grew up alongside the traditionally powerful forest industry. Shipyards and especially icebreakers were success stories of this period. Finland's trade with its eastern neighbor smoothed out the effects of worldwide fluctuations within the forest industry (Laakso, 2000). Metal products, textiles and clothing were exchanged for raw materials from the east. In particular, declining oil prices in the 1980s were the first danger signals of the vulnerability of Finland's trade with the Soviet Union.

A new and modern era started at the end of the 1980s with closer integration into Western Europe. The emerging positive trend was broken by the deep recession at the beginning of the 1990s. Waves of bankruptcy swept through industry; many small and medium-sized enterprises went under. The banking system was saved only by substantial government support. The national debt grew rapidly during the recession. It has since decreased somewhat, but was still 47.1% of the GDP at the end of 1999.

However, in spite of the difficulties, the process of deregulation and privatization continued both in Europe and North America. There were major regulatory changes affecting airlines, financial services, public transport, and telecommunications, to mention just a few (Lindell, 1998). One of the key events for the Finnish economy was the early deregulation of telecommunications. Competition in the mobile network started in 1990 when the Finnish firms Radiolinja and Sonera obtained licenses to build their own GSM (Global system for mobile communications) networks alongside the existing networks. Competition on long-distance calls began in 1994. Nowadays there are 13 different operators (Ahonen, 2001). According to Ahonen, all the European Union countries have followed Finland's example in the development of data communications infrastructure and deregulation of the telecommunications sector. He also argues that in these areas Finland has been, and will be, at the leading edge of developments. The globalization of markets and the drive for European unification have enlarged the market of Finnish companies and created new possibilities, but it has also increased competition and risks and stressed the need to develop new ways to respond to free competition.

The successes in the telecommunications sector are best illustrated by the success of the Finnish flagship Nokia. The group has gone through a transformation from an unfocused conglomerate to a global leader. A couple of decades ago, its product range included rubber boots, cables, lavatory paper and televisions. CEO Ollila explained Nokia's success to the *Financial Times* in the following way: "We were earlier than most in understanding the benefits of focusing the business portfolio in a global world, that in order to be really successful you have to globalize your organization and focus your business portfolio. We have also been able to grow and be global and maintain our agility and be fast at the same time" (Brown-Humes, 2001, p. 4). Nokia has adapted to the market more effectively than its competitors.

Productivity in industry has improved substantially. A productivity index that stood at 48 in 1975 had increased to 159 in 1998 (*Statistical Yearbook of Finland,* 2000). This is a better performance than that for the USA, Japan, Germany, France, the UK, and Sweden. Exports have become more diversified. Earlier exports consisted mainly of forest products, but in the 1970s the share of metal products increased significantly to around one-third of total exports and now telecommunications is one of the fastest growing export sectors. According to the World Economic Forum, Finland was the most competitive country in the world in 2000 (Takala, 2001).

In this section, we have described the history of Finland and some data on economic performance. This description will serve as a setting for understanding and interpreting the quantitative and qualitative GLOBE results which, are based on systematic evaluations of Finnish societal culture, organizational cultures and leadership ideals (cf. House et al., 2004).

3.   THE GLOBE STUDY IN FINLAND

Sample and Procedure

A questionnaire was distributed to middle managers in the financial services, food production and telecommunications companies in Finland. In all, 438 managers in seven companies completed the questionnaire (telecommunications, 2 companies, $n = 108$; food production, 2 companies, $n = 187$; financial sector, 3 companies, $n = 143$). The companies chosen were all large and important in their respective industries. Although the industries chosen are central in most countries, they employed no more than about 7% to 8% of the labor force in Finland in 1999 (Statistics Finland, Labor Force Survey, 2000).

The GLOBE questionnaire measured social and organizational cultural norms and leadership concepts. The cultural norms were built around Hofstede's (1980) four cultural dimensions: Power Distance, Uncertainty Avoidance, Gender Differentiation and Collectivism. In the GLOBE study, Gender Differentiation was subdivided into Gender Egalitarianism and Assertiveness and Collectivism was subdivided into Institutional Collectivism and In-Group Collectivism (see House et al., 2004). Further dimensions were developed, namely Future Orientation, Performance Orientation and Humane Orientation. In the leadership part of the questionnaire managers responded to 112 items by rating the degree to which each listed leadership attribute facilitates or impedes "outstanding leadership." All items were rated on a 7-point Likert-type scale that ranged from low to high. A contact person was nominated by a top manager in each participating company in order to increase legitimacy and motivation for the GLOBE research project. She or he handled the distribution and collection of the questionnaires and sent them to the researcher. Further mostly qualitative methods were used for data collection.

The following sections detail the findings of the survey of middle managers' opinions about outstanding leader behavior and attributes and existing and ideal values in Finland. The presentation of the quantitative data is elaborated by adding qualitative data and observations relevant to the different GLOBE dimensions.

Demographics

Following, some demographic characteristics of the sample of middle managers used in this study are given:

- Gender: 74.5% of the respondents were male.
- Age: The age of the respondents varied from 25 years to 68 years, with a mean age of 42.3 years and a median of 42 years.
- Cultural background: 99.9% were born in Finland and 85.3% had not lived abroad for more than a year.
- Religious affiliation: As much as 24.2% said that they did not belong to any religious affiliation, 75% were Lutherans, 0.4% Orthodox, 0.2% Catholics and 0.2% Baptists.
- Working experience: The full-time working experience of the middle managers ranged from 0 to 43 years, with a mean of 18.8 years and a median of 18 years. The median for occupying a managerial position was 11 years. The managers had been in their current company for a long time. The median period with their current employer was 10.5 years. Around one-fourth (25.8%) had experience with a multinational corporation.
- Education: The median length of formal education was six years. Around 40% of the respondents mentioned their educational specialization. Education in business and administration accounted for 50% of respondents, 40% were educated as engineers and the remaining 10% had education in many different areas.
- Training: Middle managers that reported they had participated in formal management training of some kind consisted of 60%.
- Hierarchy: The median number of people reporting to the managers was six and the average number of subordinates was 56. There were two organizational levels between middle managers and chief executives and one level to non-supervisor personnel.

4.   GLOBE RESULTS ABOUT SOCIETAL CULTURE

Table 4.2 presents the Finnish country score (mean of individual ratings) for societal culture "As Is" and societal culture "Should Be" and its rank on each dimension compared to the other 61 participating countries.

Finnish society scores highly on societal culture "As Is" in comparison with the other GLOBE countries on Uncertainty Avoidance (Rank 8, Band A)and Institutional Collectivism (Rank 10, Band A). Finnish society relies on social norms and procedures to alleviate the unpredictability of future events. Finland is a collectivist society where equality between men and women is relatively high.

Finnish society scores low on In-group Collectivism (Rank 54, Band C) and Humane Orientation (Rank 35, Band C) and medium to low on Assertiveness (Rank 47, Band B), Power Distance (Rank 47, Band B) and Performance Orientation (Rank 46, Band B). The family unit (In-Group Collectivism) ranks low by international comparison, which is contrary to the general requirement of high Institutional Collectivism. Although group behavior is generally stressed, in the family context (In-Group Collectivism) strong individualistic behavior is highly valued. Humane Orientation describes the degree to which a society encourages and rewards individuals for being fair, altruistic, generous, caring, and kind to others. Despite the comparatively low rank in Humane Orientation, Finns perceive themselves as low on Assertiveness. Also Power Distance is relatively low, which means that according to the middle managers, society mostly maintains equality among its members with respect to power, authority, prestige, status, wealth, and material possessions. Finally, low Performance Orientation means that society does not encourage or reward groups for performance improvement and excellence.

TABLE 4.2
Societal Culture "As Is" and "Should Be"

Dimensions	Perception ("As Is")			Values ("Should Be")		
	Score[a]	Band[b]	Rank[c]	Score	Band	Rank
Uncertainty Avoidance	5.02	A	8	3.85	C	53
Institutional Collectivism	4.63	A	10	4.11	C	55
Future Orientation	4.24	B	14	5.07	C	51
Gender Egalitarianism	3.35	B	31	4.24	B	45
Performance Orientation	3.81	B	46	6.11	B	20
Assertiveness	3.81	B	47	3.68	B	35
Power Distance	4.89	B	47	2.19	D	60
Humane Orientation	3.96	C	35	5.81	A	2
In-Group Collectivism	4.07	C	54	5.42	B	47

[a]Country score for Finland based on mean of individual ratings.
[b]Letters A to D indicate the "Band" of countries Finland belongs to (A > B > C > D). Countries from different bands are considered to differ significantly from each other (GLOBE test banding procedure, cf. Hanges, Dickson, & Sipe, 2004).
[c]Finland's position relative to the 61 countries in the GLOBE study; Rank 1 = highest; Rank 61 = lowest.

On further two dimensions, Finland scores in the higher middle out of the GLOBE countries that participated. These are Future Orientation (Rank 14, Band B) and Gender Egalitarianism (Rank 31, Band B). Future Orientation refers to the extent to which a society rewards future-oriented behavior such as planning, investing in the future and delaying gratification. Gender Egalitarianism measures the extent to which a society minimizes gender role differences.

In terms of values (societal culture "Should Be") the most sought-after positive changes in culture compared to the existing situation, both absolutely and relatively, were in Performance Orientation (change in ranking from 46 to 20) and Humane Orientation (change in ranking from 35 to 2). The most sought-after negative changes in ranking were found in Future Orientation (from 14 to 51), Institutional Collectivism (from 10 to 55), and in Uncertainty Avoidance (from 8 to 53). The ranking moved in a negative direction, but somewhat less, for Power Distance (from 47 to 60). A minor difference between the "As Is" and "Should Be" was observed for the three dimensions Assertiveness, Gender Egalitarianism and In-group Collectivism. We discuss the changes below in connection with the various dimensions.

Performance Orientation

The current level of Performance Orientation in the study [Mean (m) = 3.81, Rank 46] is relatively low, but Finnish managers would like to see this reversed in the future (m) = 6.11, Rank 20. The explanation for the current low level is that, although results are stressed, there are many counteracting factors, especially at the society level. There is a desire to even out differences in earnings through a re-distributive taxation system and high rates of taxes. The social security system is good and guarantees a minimum standard of living.

There is now a general desire to reduce government expenditure and that will probably mean the result for orientation will be higher in the future. Because Finland is a member of EMU, it will not be possible to use monetary policy tools such as devaluation to correct future setbacks in the economy. Therefore the pressure to achieve will be much greater in the future (cf. "Should Be" in Table 4.2). Another feature of the 1990s already mentioned is deregulation, with many state-owned companies being privatized (Kivikko, Lindell, & Naukkarinen, 1997; Lindell, 1998).

Some changes producing greater efficiency can already be observed. In an investigation of 84 large Finnish companies during the 1990s, only 5 companies produced economic value-added to their owners in 1992, when including industry risks and a 4.5% risk premium in the calculations. By 1996, the number had increased to 25 companies (Veranen & Junnila, 1997). Since 1994, unemployment has improved gradually but is still quite high. It was 8.7% in September 2001, whereas on average 7.6% in all of the other 15 EU countries.

The wide use of telecommunication aids has helped to facilitate and speed up government services. According to Kahila (2001), Finns spend less and less time trudging to government offices and dealing with bureaucrats. About a decade ago Finns made 7 million trips a year to central registry offices for things like registering address changes, filling out pension forms, and replacing lost ID cards. That figure is now down to about half a million visits. Advances in telecommunications have allowed Finland to cut its national civil service headcount while increasing the service's productivity by 3.5% per year.

Future Orientation

The absolute direction for Future Orientation is positive, with a change in the mean from 4.24 to 5.07. Managers at the middle level are of the opinion that more forward planning is required. Future Orientation is at a high level in Finnish society compared to many other countries, but planning for the future still needs to be improved. Central government ran a deficit during much of the 1990s. Government subsidies to municipalities have been cut, and this has also stressed the need for more achievement orientation but above all more future planning.

The political stability of Finland means that societal forecasts can be made. Therefore there has been a need for long-range 3-year wage agreements between employers' associations and employees' representatives in order to increase the ability to make reliable forecasts. On the other hand, one can argue that the increased turbulence in society in general, and the faster and more radical changes taking place, will make it perhaps less possible to plan for many years ahead. That might be one reason why the sought-after increased mean on Future Orientation is not more than 0.77.

However, it is interesting to note that on an international comparison the direction has been negative for Finland. Although in absolute terms the mean has increased from 4.24 to 5.07, Finland's ranking has dropped from 14 to 51. While Finnish managers believe that more emphasis should be placed on Future Orientation, when compared to the present, they act like middle managers in the other countries that took part in the study, but to a much lesser degree. The most obvious explanation for this is deregulation, the decrease in tax rates, and the objective of keeping the national budget at a relatively low level. This means that there is not much scope for large future investments at the society level.

Assertiveness

Finland scored 3.81 on Assertiveness and ranks 47th among the 61 GLOBE countries, indicating that the Finns are rather nondominant and non-aggressive in their social relationships. Lewis (1993), who has studied cultures in many different countries, has characterized Finland as a "cultural lone wolf." According to Lewis, Finns are a warm-hearted people who long for loneliness. He stresses too that Finnish men do not speak very much and they are slow in their communication. Perhaps this is because Finland is a large, sparsely inhabited country. They admire a peaceful mentality, are introverted and tolerant. They are also truly democratic. Against the above background, we can understand the score indicating nonaggressiveness.

The "Should Be" score is 3.68 and ranks 35. This means that Finnish middle managers want to see a change toward less dominance and aggressiveness in social relationships. However, this wanted change is quite minor in comparison with many other Globe countries.

Institutional Collectivism

Finnish managers score highly on Institutional Collectivism (m = 4.63, Rank 10), which is explained by a number of factors. Firstly, Finland's centralized economy was not immediately aligned with the decentralized market economies in the immediate post-war years due to its geopolitical context (Steinbock, 1998). Instead an economy was developed largely behind protective and regulatory barriers, dominated by a few big companies. It also had influences from the east European command economies. There was strong pressure for consensus, which gave rise to conformism and intolerance toward differences of opinion. The gross taxation rate is among the highest in the Western countries, at 46.9% in 1998 (OECD, revenue statistics).

Secondly, Finland still has quite strong labor unions. The current system was established after World War II. Significant importance was placed on a stabilization agreement made in March 1968, and was largely adhered to throughout the 1970s. The period starting in 1968 is known as the "period of incomes policy" in the Finnish industrial relations system (Lilja, 1983). The labor market organizations and political forces have essentially remained unchanged to the present day. A system of exchanges between the government and interest organizations has contributed to the stability of the macromanagement of Finnish society.

Thirdly, teamwork has been highly valued throughout the 1990s, both in firms and in government bodies. Cooperation, teamwork and shared decision-making are seen as desirable (Simon et al., 1996). In fact a law exists on cooperation within companies too. Employees have the right to influence decisions affecting them, their work, and working conditions. A strong top manager is looked for only in a crisis situation (cf. the strong Finnish heads of state in history). Mutual respect, direct communication, discussions, and flat organizational structures are features of Finnish industry today.

Fourthly, Finland is a small country, which facilitates consensus. It is possible for all the influential people in different spheres of society to know each other and meet personally both in an official and unofficial capacity. The discipline of political groups is strong. Sometimes members are excluded from a political party if they vote against the party line on an important issue.

But although Institutional Collectivism is strong in Finnish society, bringing prosperity and an acceptable standard of living to most Finns, there are also signs of individuality. In particular, Finns value heroes in different areas. Finland has produced leading personalities in sport, architecture, art, and music. A long line of Finnish athletes has become world-famous figures, from Paavo Nurmi in the 1920s, to Lasse Viren in the 1970s. Among musicians, painters and architects, Sibelius, Kajanus, Saarinen, Järnefelt, Gallen-Kallela, and Alvar Aalto have assured the country's position at the highest artistic levels. The prospect of reduced Institutional Collectivism in the future supports this view; cf. the "Should Be" mean of 4.11 and rank of 55. An investigation by Salonen et al., (2001) suggests that a change took place in the middle of the 1990s in the Finns' feeling of community and that the attitudes changed in favor of more individuality. Hofstede´s study (1980) indicated rather high individuality among Finnish managers.

Institutional Collectivism seems, at least to some extent, to go in waves. When times are good in society individuality will be stronger, and in bad times collectivism is stronger.

Gender Egalitarianism

On Gender Egalitarianism, Finland's position is situated in the middle of the GLOBE countries ("As Is" m = 3.35, Rank 31). Its score is also in the middle of the scale, but somewhat more on the masculine side. That is interesting because in Hofstede's study (1980), Finland was in the most feminine cluster. The most likely reason for this deviation would appear to be that in the GLOBE study, egalitarian aspects are stressed more, whereas in Hofstede's study the whole scale of masculinity and femininity was used. Finnish society has for a long time striven for equality between the genders and that trend has also continued since Hofstede´s study.

Universal suffrage was introduced for men in 1902 and for women in 1906. Finland was the first country in Europe to grant women the right to vote in parliamentary elections. Social justice, solidarity, and egalitarianism are valued as part of the Scandinavian way of thinking (Nurmi, 1989). Finland now has its first female President. Equality is based on history but is also enshrined in law (The Equality Act).

The emancipation of women has been moving in a more equal direction between the sexes for many decades. The share of women elected at the last General Election was 36.5%. The share of female professors increased from 14.6% in 1992 to 20.1% in 2000 (Ministry of Education, 2001). The gap in earnings between men and women has also decreased somewhat. In 1980, the monthly earnings of salaried industry employees were FIM 5,276 for men and FIM 3,210 for women. The corresponding figures in 1999 were FIM 16,633 for men and FIM 12,108 for women (Confederation of Finnish Industry and Employers, 2000).

However, it is a fact that there are still relatively few women in top positions in either society or business. Our interpretation is that the demands of domestic tasks, education of children etc., have an effect here. Although Finnish women work much more outside the home, they still perform most of the domestic tasks, which seems at least to some extent to prevent them from pursuing a career in society and business. In 1998, women made up 48% of the total work force out of 2.5 million (*Statistical Yearbook of Finland*, 2000). The trend is clearly in a more equal direction. But there is still some way to go. The legislation in place is appropriate, but efforts have to be made on the practical side and in terms of changing attitudes. The ideal society would require a higher feminine input (m = 4.24, Rank 45). So, Finnish society has still to be improved in terms of gender egalitarianism.

Humane Orientation

When it comes to Humane Orientation, Finland has an average ranking among the GLOBE countries (m = 3.96, Rank 35). In an investigation by the Finnish Tourist Board (1988), tourists found Finnish people friendly and ready to help.

Interestingly, Finnish managers would like to see a very significant increase in Humane Orientation: Finland scored second highest on the "Should Be" ranking (m = 5.81, Rank 2). Why this desire for more Humane Orientation? There have been cuts in social welfare, and society is not felt to be as generous as it once was. The gap between the rich and the poor has widened.

Earlier high unemployment has contributed to this perception of a less Humane Orientation. Temporary employment too is a phenomenon that increased dramatically in the early 1990s. According to an investigation of the work environment, almost one in five employees was still on temporary contracts in 1997 (Salonen et al., 2001). Since then the situation has improved but many people are still stigmatized by the past. Within 10 years, however, it has been forecast that there will be a labor shortage in Finland.

Migration from rural areas into the cities has also increased insecurity and people's ability to plan for the future. Secularization and increased stress may have added a perception that people do not matter. Idyllic rural life and large family units are mainly things of the past. The number of households on a very small annual income has increased. In 1995, 121,000 persons lived in households with a very low income. By 1998 the number of such persons had increased to 196,000 (Salonen et al., 2001). The majority of this group consisted of students and unemployed persons. Many young people who tend to move away from their parents more or less immediately after matriculation at the age of 18 or 19 naturally are on a low income when studying. These may be some of the reasons behind the desire for a radical improvement in Humane Orientation in the ideal society.

Power Distance

Power Distance in Finland is in the middle (but at the lower end of that category) compared to the other GLOBE countries (m = 4.89, Rank 47). Power Distance was found to be short in Hofstede's (1980) investigation, somewhat shorter than the GLOBE study indicates. However, the results of these studies support each other. The general trend in very many countries seems to be towards less and less distance between levels in organizations and society. In a recent study, Lindell and Arvonen (1996) found that a dominant feature of the Scandinavian management style is delegation of responsibility. The interesting point here is that in spite of the rather low ranking (Rank 47), Finnish managers would like to see a significant decrease in Power Distance (from 4.89 to 2.19, and in ranking from 47 to 60).

There was a trend toward more decentralization in society before Finland joined the EU, and before the recession at the beginning of the 1990s. There was more teamwork in society. Managers were no longer venerated as before. All members of firms and other organizations were important for the achievement of results, and managers were not necessarily the ultimate authority on every matter. Networks, project groups etc., were appreciated more and more. People were well educated, and the authority inherent in a position meant less and less. The distance between managers and their subordinates was short and communication was direct. That trend was interrupted when many decisions had to be made quickly at the center. For instance, when the entire banking system was at risk at the beginning of the 1990s and the national debt was rising steeply. A fairly large gap appeared between expectations and reality, which explains the desire for a significant improvement in Power Distance.

Recently, it has furthermore become established that Finnish governments are broad-based and that they govern for the whole term. Nowadays it is rare for there to be a mid-term change of government. It is difficult for the opposition to have any real impact on the work and decisions made by the government. The relatively strong labor unions and collective bargaining agreements lasting several years compound this trend. Membership of the European Union and the transfer of decision-making in some issues to Brussels might be perceived by the Finns as meaning more centralization. All of this might have influenced perceptions of a relatively high Power Distance.

In-Group Collectivism

Middle managers rate Finnish society as low on In-group Collectivism (m = 4.07, Rank 54). The migration from rural areas to the cities has had the effect that different generations no longer live together. Dwellings are now much smaller than they had been previously in rural areas, which places a lot more pressure on families. Both parents have to work in order to maintain the family's finances and standard of living, and most children of pre-school age spend a half or full day in some kind of child care institution. Family unity has decreased.

Cohabiting partners has also become more commonplace. In 1999 there were 68.2% of couples married, 18.2% were cohabiting partners and 13.2% of families were single-parent units (*Statistical Yearbook of Finland,* 2000). Many marriages end in divorce. Therefore it is not at all strange that the Finns would like to see an improvement in family loyalty ("Should Be" m = 5.42, Rank 47). Family loyalty is a quality that will be more appreciated in future.

Uncertainty Avoidance

Finland scores high on Uncertainty Avoidance (m = 5.02, Rank 8). In many sectors such as banking, insurance, and food manufacturing competition has been limited. A deregulation process has started and many state-owned companies have been privatized or are in the process of privatization. But the Finns are also time-conscious and therefore punctuality and keeping appointments is important. Prior appointments are necessary for business visits. Finnish managers also like to have their responsibilities and authority well defined.

There is a substantial difference in the ideal society or "Should Be" position (m = 3.85, Rank 53). Finnish managers at the middle level are of the opinion that risks should be increased dramatically. The welfare system has been generous and living standards are at an acceptable level even for those without a job. The Government has taken steps to reward work. Income tax has been reduced by a few percentages. There has also been some reduction in social welfare. The first steps toward higher risk-taking have been taken. These actions are in accordance with Hofstede's (1980) investigation, which ranked Finland toward the middle on Uncertainty Avoidance.

Conclusions

The general observation that can be made is that a change in a more individualistic and risk-taking direction is desired and that a more rewarding society is required. Culture at the society level should be changed to make it more demanding. Deregulation seems to have had some impact here. To counterbalance this, a significant increase in Humane Orientation is desired. Finnish people should be more caring and kind to one another.

In comparison with the other GLOBE countries, Finnish society scores highly on Uncertainty Avoidance, Future Orientation, and Institutional Collectivism. That indicates that forward planning is an important feature, but working in teams is important too. The showing of a higher need for Institutional Collectivism in this investigation is interesting. In Hofstede's study (1980), Finland scored quite high on individuality, which is contrary to the findings of the GLOBE study. What is the reason for this difference? Either there has been a radical change in values since Hofstede's investigation or there are differences in the studies' operationalization of individuality and collectivism. The more likely explanation is the latter, because the Finns rate relatively low on In-Group Collectivism "As Is" and much higher on

Institutional Collectivism "As Is." Evidence for this comes from the GLOBE validation studies, showing that GLOBE's Institutional Collectivism "As Is" scale does not correlate with Hofstede's Individualism scale ($R = .15$) whereas GLOBE's In-Group Collectivism scale "As Is" correlates highly ($R = -.82$, cf. House, et al., 2004, p. 475).

The greatest improvement sought after in the ideal society, relative to the current situation, is in Performance Orientation and Power Distance. Finnish managers feel that in the future competition will be tougher and that more efficiency and innovation will be required to meet future challenges. Finns want to see a flat societal structure and want to be involved in decisions with hardly any Power Distance. Important problems and issues should be discussed, planned, decided on, and implemented together.

5.   FINNISH LEADERSHIP CHARACTERISTICS AND LEADERS

The study of societal cultural practices and values has outlined the environment in which companies operate. Below, a more detailed study is described concerning leadership characteristics central for leader acceptance and leader effectiveness in Finland. We search for answers to the question how an outstanding leader might behave in Finland and his attributes and characteristics.

Previous Research on Finnish Leadership

Finnish leadership attributes were not studied very systematically before the 1980s and 1990s. Below some of the main findings from some studies over the two latest decades are reported.

Airola, Kulla, Lumia, Nyström, and Snow (1991) concluded a study among the 250 largest industrial and trading companies in Finland. They interviewed 128 leaders. In answer to the question asking what are the three most important tasks managers had to learn in order to fulfil their role as a leader, the ranking of the five most often mentioned ones was as follows: (a) leading people, (b) capacity to cooperate, (c) the creation of a holistic vision, (d) goal-oriented business, and (e) delegation. According to the study the most important factor that a leader has to learn is how to motivate and manage people. Lewis (1993) also found that the Finns do not lead by giving orders, but by motivating and setting an example to subordinates. In order to commit Finnish managers, the following factors were important:

- Tasks which correspond to the managers' own abilities.
- Participation in decision making.
- Loyalty between foremen and top management.

In the Airola et al., (1991) study leaders were also asked to describe "effective leaders" they know in two or three words. The ranking of the most important features was (a) goal-orientation, (b) mastering of a complex entity, (c) motivating, (d) visionary, (e) charismatic, (f) diligent, (g) experienced, (h) able to make decisions, (I) capacity to cooperate, (j) capacity to communicate, (k) controlling, and (l) delegating.

Kivistö (1989) studied the behavior of around 1,000 Finnish foremen. Four factors emerged from the data: (a) taking care of human relations, (b) performing the tasks of a foreman, (c) flexibility, and (d) manager's ethics. The two most important factors explaining 44% and 13% of the variance were the two well-know behavior dimensions relations-orientation and task-orientation (cf. for instance Yukl, 2002). Lindell and Rosenqvist (1992) question the exclusive use of task- and relations-orientation that has dominated leadership research. In a study of 439 Finnish managers, they identify a third dimension, development orientation, using confirmatory factor analysis and structural equation modeling (LISREL 7).

In a small study, Simon et al., (1996) interviewed 20 Finnish managers with international experience. They found three characteristics for Finnish companies:

- Clear and simple ways of doing business.
- Fast decision-making process.
- Fairness and responsibility in business.

Their research findings also show that Finnish leaders are characterized by traits such as integrity, energy, reliability, and straightforwardness, and foster a corporate culture of openness and respect for individuals. Apart from honesty, characteristics such as stamina, professionalism, reliability, a high level of education, and perfectionism also describe the Finns. Finnish leaders value cooperation, teamwork, and participatory decision-making. They emphasize the development of skills, creativity, and networks of collaborative relations between different organizational levels (Simon et. al., 1996).

Zandler (1997) surveyed the leadership preferences of 17,000 employees from a Swedish multinational, with a substantial sample from Finland. Zandler's results show that the Finnish results differed from the Scandinavian nations in respect of a desire for a lower frequency of interaction with superiors. This preferred interpersonal leadership is characterized by low intensity. Employees prefer their managers to focus on coaching. To make individuals and the department perform to their outmost, managers should encourage cooperation and teamwork. However, managers need not communicate frequently, unless it is about personal matters. In addition, employees have only limited interest in being empowered and supervised. Zander named the preferred profile "silent coaching."

Aaltonen (1998) has analyzed descriptions of leaders in the national epos Kalevala and other historical books illustrating Finnish leadership. The most important features in this study were acceptance of subordinates, friendship, setting an example, and avoidance of giving more orders than necessary. A universal feature was the importance of paying attention to subordinates as human beings and individuals, and valuing their feelings and opinions.

Lewis (1996) associates Finns with many positive attributes. He states that Finns have high standards of cleanness, honesty, stamina, workmanship, reliability, hygiene, safety, and education.

Outstanding Finnish Leaders

Three people were seen as outstanding leaders in the political life of independent Finland: The Presidents Carl Gustaf Mannerheim (1867–1951), Juho Kusti Paasikivi (1879–1956), and Urho Kaleva Kekkonen (1900–1986). Can we learn something about outstanding leadership from them?

Carl Gustaf Mannerheim.   Mannerheim came from a Dutch merchant family. He was ambitious and purposeful, graduating as an officer in the cavalry from a riding academy in St Petersburg. He continued to serve there for 14 years. In order to gain experience of war he volunteered for the Japanese War of 1904–1905. He attained the rank of General in 1911 and returned to Finland in 1917 (TAT Group, 2001). In 1918, Mannerheim was selected as commander-in-chief of the government troops and also stood as a presidential candidate in the election of 1919. He was unsuccessful and thereafter concentrated on civilian tasks. He was elected as President of the Finnish Red Cross and the Central Union of Child Welfare, founded in 1920. He was given the title Marshal of Finland on his 75th birthday in 1942. During World War II he was elected President and retained that position until March 1946, when he resigned owing to poor health. Mannerheim was a highly respected man in Finland (TAT Group, 2001). He had a vast all-round education and was well versed in languages. He was flexible, adaptable, diplomatic, and a political realist. He had the ability to rise above the everyday political arguments and distance himself from his original reference group. Even after Word War II he was able to refocus himself and see new opportunities, and had the capacity and flexibility to make others see things his way. He became an institution; a great man in the history of Finland.

Juho Kusti Paasikivi. Juho Kusti Paasikivi was quite the opposite of Mannerheim. He was the son of a farmer and his mother died when he was only 4 years of age. After his mother's death his father moved to Lahti where he founded a draper's shop. The father wanted his son to continue with the shop and sent his son to school. Juho was a brilliant pupil and moved on to high school. But his father had financial problems and quite soon after he too died. In spite of that, Juho Kusti succeeded in graduating with the highest grades and went on to university, where he studied languages, literature, philosophy, and law. Even at school he was interested in Russian history and its impact on the historical development of Finland. He made several trips to Russia early on and got a thorough picture of the country from a grass-root perspective complemented later on with the perspective of diplomats and politicians. During World War II Paasikivi was involved in the political negotiations between the Soviet Union and Finland. In 1944, Paasikivi was elected Prime Minister of Finland, although he was already 74 years old, and 2 years later President. Paasikivi was a pragmatist. He understood that politics are the art of the possible and that recognition of the facts is the beginning of all wisdom (Vihavainen, 2000). He realized that Finland was powerless to confront the military superiority of the Soviet Union. For a very long time the Treaty of Friendship, Cooperation and Mutual Assistance signed in 1948 was one of the cornerstones of Finnish foreign policy. Paasikivi was one of the chief architects of that agreement.

Urho Kaleva Kekkonen. In his early days, Kekkonen showed gifts both as a writer and a sportsman. He realized that sports could be a strength, which could be used to unite and strengthen the country, a political potential to be used. He felt strongly for the Finnish language, and that colored his actions both in sports and politics. He obtained his PhD in Finnish Law in 1936. Kekkonen was elected President on March 1, 1956, and continued as President for 25 years. Kekkonen was very popular among the country's citizens. The presidential term is normally 6 years. However, in 1973 Kekkonen was "selected" for a further 6 years by special legislation, which required a two-thirds majority in Parliament.

Finnish foreign policy became more active. One of the fundamental insights of Kekkonen's policy was the "Finnish paradox": the closer Finland's relationship with the Soviet Union, the freer it was to develop relations with the West (Vihavainen, 2000). Kekkonen and others took the initiative of declaring the Nordic countries a nuclear weapon-free zone. In 1975 Finland hosted the Conference on Security and Cooperation in Europe. Soviet archives have shown that the initiatives were developed in cooperation with representatives of the Soviet Union (Vihavainen, 2000).

Kekkonen used his power and possibilities to influence very actively. He controlled the composition of governments and the appointments of high officials. He also intervened in labor disputes. He sent letters to other politicians and important people in order to influence their decisions and opinions.

In summary, all of the above-mentioned leaders were strong, but in different ways. They were appropriate for the situation in Finland at the time. When Finland was struggling for its independence and was involved in several wars, a President with a military background was needed. Mannerheim was head of the Finnish armed forces in the World Wars I and II. He had a military eye. After the wars it was important for Finland to build up and regain the confidence of the Soviet Union. Both Paasikivi and Kekkonen were both appreciated for their foreign policy and good relationships with Soviet politicians although they were different as leaders. Their foreign policy approach is called the Paasikivi-Kekkonen line and centered on: (a) good relationships with the Soviet Union, (b) cooperation with the Nordic countries, (c) economic connections with the Western market economies, (d) work within the United Nations.

Without any doubt Mannerheim had a military strategy competence, Paasikivi a more social competence, whereas Kekkonen was an individualist who could handle the political game. To summarize this review of outstanding Finnish leaders, we could say that the political leaders acted differently, but were outstanding in particular situations and were able to understand the demands of the surrounding environment. Linna (a very well known author in Finland) wrote literary classics in which Finnish leaders are portrayed. He strongly suggests that leaders are respected solely on the basis of their own achievements rather than because of their title or position. Thus independence may be valued over deference. This short review also indicates that little systematic evidence is yet available regarding distinctive Finnish attributes.

6. GLOBE STUDY ABOUT LEADERSHIP IN FINLAND

A comprehensive questionnaire was used to collect data for this study on Finnish leaders' behavior and attributes (cf. House, et al., 2004). In total, 438 completed questionnaires were received from three industries: food production ($n = 187$), telecommunications ($n = 108$) and the financial sector ($n = 143$). The respondents were asked to evaluate people (outstanding leaders) who are exceptionally skilled at motivating, influencing, or enabling themselves and others. A 7- point scale was used, 1 indicating behavior or characteristics that greatly inhibit a person from being an outstanding leader, and 7 behavior or characteristics contributing greatly to a person being an outstanding leader. Results for Finland are summarized in Table 4.3, which lists the country's scores for each dimension from the highest to the lowest.

GLOBE Leadership Dimensions

On four leadership dimensions Finns scored very highly, both in absolute and relative terms (in comparison with the other GLOBE countries): Integrity, Inspirational, Collaborative Team Oriented and Visionary. Most of these features are elements of transformational leadership, especially the "charismatic" factor, but also to some extent the "individualized consideration" factor (cf. Bass, 1985; Burns, 1978).

Integrity. The Finns value integrity; an outstanding leader should be honest, sincere, just, and trustworthy. A good leader means what he or she says. The proverb "honesty is the best policy" is valid for outstanding leaders. Honesty seems to be a feature of a good leader in many cultures. Tollgerdt-Andersson (1996) conducted a European-wide investigation and found that honesty is also a very important attribute for leaders in Germany and the UK.

TABLE 4.3
Leadership Scales

21 First-Order GLOBE Leadership Dimensions	Score	Rank
Integrity	6.52	4
Inspirational	6.42	6
Collaborative Team Oriented	6.35	3
Visionary	6.29	9
Performance Orientation	6.04	35
Decisive	5.97	23
Team Integrator	5.54	27
Diplomatic	5.4	40
Administrative Competency	5.32	55
Modesty	4.52	53
Self-Sacrificial	4.22	59
Autonomous	4.08	18
Humane	4.06	54
Status-Conscious	3.15	60
Conflict Inducer	3.10	60
Procedural	2.87	60
Autocratic	2.11	52
Nonparticipative	2.08	57
Face Saver	2.05	61
Self-Centered	1.55	61
Malevolent	1.47	59

Note. Country scores are listed from highest (*contributes outstanding leadership greatly* = 7, *somewhat* = 6, *slightly* = 5, *via no impact* = 4) to lowest (*inhibits outstanding leadership slightly* = 3, *somewhat* = 2, *greatly* = 1).

Inspirational. An outstanding Finnish leader should also inspire his or her subordinates, i.e., be enthusiastic, positive, encouraging, and build confidence. In addition he or she should encourage and give advice and support, provide feed-back on successful work and show confidence in subordinates. An outstanding Finnish leader generates energy in the organization and cooperates with subordinates in order to attain goals at an even higher level.

Collaborative Team Oriented. Outstanding Finnish leaders have to be good team integrators, i.e., be able to build teams, integrate and coordinate teams, and communicate within them. Teams are considered to be responsible for their own tasks and therefore a leader is expected to be able to integrate and cooperate. As Lewis (1997) stresses, the Finns like the idea of profit centers and accountability. However, creating a good team demands a lot of the leader because there may be tension between teamwork and individuality. Laine-Sveiby (1987) found that the Finns are keen on spontaneity and value consensus at the society level, but individuality at the personal level. Therefore there should also be scope for individuality in teams. Lewis (1997) says that when working with Finns one should set clear goals, define objectives, and appeal to the inner resources of individuals to achieve the task within their own team and to be fully accountable for it.

Visionary.   Besides being inspirational, a good Finnish leader is also required to be visionary, i.e., to have foresight, be intellectually stimulating, and plan ahead. Visionary leadership does not resort to orders or coercion. The more subordinates are aware of the vision, the less external supervision is needed. Visions generate creativity, motivation, and thus efficiency.

In summary, it is worth noting that integrity, inspiration, collaborative team orientation, and vision are all features that apply to good leaders universally (House et al., 1999), not only to Finnish leaders. In addition to these four attributes, two other attributes received high scores internationally: "performance orientation" and "decisive." The scores by Finnish middle managers were average by international comparison: "performance orientation" (m = 6.04, Rank 35) and "decisive" (m = 5.97, Rank 23).

There were also several leadership features on which the Finns score very low, both in absolute and relative terms, compared to the other GLOBE countries. They are Malevolent (i.e., hostile, dishonest, vindictive, irritable, cynical etc), Self-Centered, Face Saver, Nonparticipative, and Autocratic. Aaltonen (1998) characterizes poor leaders as being unable to put themselves at the level of the subordinates, get close to them, or understand them. Good leaders, on the other hand, interact with their subordinates and employees, tell them where the organization is going, encourage subordinates in their tasks, and build up a working team and organization structure. Good leaders also seem to create both a positive climate and positive values in the organization. As argued above, the Finns have a high level of education and are good on innovation and technology. That means that subordinates are knowledgeable people and hence the leader cannot be the one with the best knowledge in all issues. It is up to him or her to support subordinates and inspire them in order to bring out their best. For Finnish firms this is extraordinarily important because Finland is very dependent on exports and international trade. The competence of the employees of companies must be utilized in order to be internationally competitive. The previously mentioned factors are attributes, which are not connected with outstanding leadership internationally.

Leadership Perceptions in Different Industries

In Table 4.4, the similarities and differences in leadership dimensions between the three industry sectors, Finance, Food, and Telecommunications, are described. Generally, the results for all three sectors mirror quite closely the results for all sectors together. The most important attributes for an outstanding leader are still integrity, inspirational, collaborative team oriented, and visionary. Behavior styles to be avoided in all sectors are malevolent, self-centered, face saver, autocratic, and nonparticipative. However, some significant differences do exist between the three sectors. These differences seem to be caused by industry-specific factors more than by culture factors. In the finance sector customer-orientation and external effectiveness are stressed, while in food production and telecommunications internal efficiency is of greater importance. Against that background it is not at all strange that integrity and a leader's capacity to inspire and function as a collaborator and team-builder are emphasized more in finance than in the other two sectors. Similarly, bad attributes such as malevolent, self-centered, autocratic, and procedural are rated even lower than in the other two sectors. Therefore, the industry context as well as the country culture seems to have quite a strong impact on leader behavior too.

TABLE 4.4
Leadership Scores in Different Industry Sectors (Test of Differences, One-Way ANOVA)

Attribute	Total (n = 438)	Finance (n = 143)	Food (n = 187)	Telecom. (n = 108)	F-value	Sig.
Integrity	6.52	6.52	6.47	6.50	(2.34)	
Inspirational	6.42	6.50	6.33	6.41	(11.13)	$p < .001$
Collaborative, Team Oriented	6.35	6.43	6.27	6.36	(5.03)	$p < .01$
Visionary	6.29	6.33	6.27	6.27	(0.61)	
Performance Orientation	6.04	6.07	6.03	6.01	(2.32)	
Decisive	5.97	6.09	5.90	6.03	(4.71)	$p < .01$
Team Integrator	5.54	5.57	5.49	5.57	(1.16)	
Diplomatic	5.41	5.38	5.36	5.47	(0.61)	
Administrative Competent	5.32	5.25	5.36	5.37	(2.88)	
Modesty	4.52	4.46	4.47	4.58	(2.04)	
Self-Sacrificial	4.22	4.11	4.20	4.37	(3.76)	$p < .05$
Autonomous	4.08	4.12	4.14	4.20	(1.06)	
Humane	4.06	4.29	3.98	4.10	(1.34)	
Status-Conscious	3.15	2.97	3.31	3.17	(1.16)	
Conflict Inducer	3.10	2.88	3.17	3.07	(1.31)	
Procedural	2.89	2.77	2.94	2.85	(3.03)	$p < .05$
Autocratic	2.11	1.90	2.26	2.29	(9.51)	$p < .001$
Nonparticipative	2.08	2.00	2.15	2.07	(1.81)	
Face Saver	2.05	1.90	2.03	2.14	(1.21)	
Self-Centered	1.55	1.54	1.61	1.63	(3.19)	$p < .05$
Malevolent	1.47	1.42	1.53	1.47	(3.23)	$p < .05$

7.   QUALITATIVE RESULTS ABOUT LEADERSHIP

To deepen our understanding of the characteristics of Finnish leaders, two additional studies were performed media analysis, several interviews, and focus group discussions.

Finnish Leadership Behavior Based on Media Analysis

In the media analysis a sample of data was taken from the leading Finnish daily financial newspaper *Kauppalehti* and the leading Finnish weekly financial magazine, *Talouselämä*. The first period was in May 1996 and the second in May and June 1997. The magazines and newspapers were read in full. Extracts were selected which illustrated what leaders do, but also how they are evaluated. Our aim was to locate verbs and adjectives describing leaders who influence others in an organizational and societal context. A total of 163 text extracts were selected. The important verbs, adjectives, and phrases relevant to leadership were highlighted. The highlighted phrases were typified with one word which best described their content. The following characteristics were derived from the texts and the frequency at which they were used is expressed a percentage (see Table 4.5).

TABLE 4.5
Leadership Attributes: A Brief Description

Theme	Description	Relative Frequency
Visionary	Describes a leader as far-sighted, or as being able to project the future position of the company several years ahead, or a picture of the company or unit several years ahead	17.7
Performance Oriented	Ideas about how to improve performance, results, and efficiency	12.9
Action Oriented	A leader who undertakes actions, e.g., making decisions, giving speeches, communicating, making changes	12.9
Organized	A leader who demonstrates good administrative skills and order	9.5
Clear	A leader who is explicit and clear about rules, values, and policies in the company	9.5
Cooperative	Networking, cooperation between companies and leaders	8.2
Decisive	Strong statement by the leader what is to be done, and how to behave in the firm	7.5
Team Oriented	Team builder, team creator, organizes projects	4.8
Self-Developer	Activities through which he or she develops him or herself mentally or physically	3.4
Inspirational	Leader encourages, rewards his or her subordinates, is enthusiastic	2.7
Sensitive	Leader shows his or her feelings	2.0
Risk-Avoiding	Leader avoids risky steps or positions for his or her company	2.0
Communicator	Leader communicates his or her ideas and/ or creates good conditions for meeting with subordinates and customers	1.4
Autocrat	A leader dictatorial and not open to criticism	1.4
Others		4.1

The most frequent leadership issue mentioned in Finnish business publications analyzed was "visionary." The notion that managers are forward-looking is not at all strange. The very deep recession at the beginning of the 1990s followed by continuous growth for many years meant that speculating about the future and one's company's position in the market had a high priority.

A second frequent theme was performance and action oriented. A recurrent issue was how to improve the efficiency of companies by means of investments, for example. The link between results and methods of rewarding people was also often discussed and stressed. More generally, the importance of a healthy financial structure and cash flow was underlined. The speed of change seemed to be increasing continuously. Therefore leaders had to be very active and appear to be undertaking some form of initiative at all times.

Leaders were organized; they had ideas about what a good organization should be. Organizing comprised decentralization, participation, teamwork, and flexibility, and creating networks and an open organizational climate. Finns want to work in small groups or individually; compare the quantitative study. Nurmi (1989) states that Finns are satisfied with their work when their entitlements and responsibilities are defined and they can work undisturbed. Their self-discipline is high, and they dislike being closely monitored or ordered about. Thus they are happy to enjoy their independence in a structure that gears their work to the objectives of the organization or society at large. This characteristic of the Finns may explain the many references to organizing.

Another strong feature in the media analysis was clear. Leaders knew how to be successful in their sector and what values to project to their subordinates. They seemed to govern more through values than through orders. Therefore they were also decisive. They followed principles that were critical for development of their company.

Finally cooperation and networking were words that characterized Finnish managers in many articles. For Finnish firms, which are small internationally, cooperation and sometimes also acquisitions and mergers were a necessity. Cooperation was mentioned much more often than competition, competitiveness, and competitive advantage. All in all these features seem to indicate a low organizational structure that is held together with values and visions.

Of the leader attributes identified in the media analysis, several are also included in the GLOBE questionnaire, such as visionary, performance oriented, administratively competent (organized), decisive, team oriented, inspirational, and autocrat. However, there are also several attributes with no equivalent dimension. These are action oriented, clear, cooperative, self-developer, sensitive, communicator, and avoids risks. There are several reasons for the differences identified. One is that the leader attributes identified in the media analysis were characteristic of leaders in general, and not only outstanding leaders. Another reason might be that not all important leader attributes are included in the GLOBE questionnaire. Finally, a third reason could be that some of these attributes might be emic Finnish attributes.

Interviews and Focus Group Discussions

The second part of the qualitative research was to conduct six interviews and two discussions with focus groups on what is understood by the terms *leader, manager, competent manager,* and *outstanding leader,* with particular emphasis placed on the characteristics of outstanding leaders and their behavior. All the interviews were tape-recorded and the transcripts analyzed in full. The interviewees comprised three men and three women aged between 30 and 60. All had at least profit center responsibility and therefore management experience. The interviews lasted an average of 1½ hours and were conducted in an office environment.

The focus groups were of two different types. The first consisted of middle managers at a large insurance company, six women and two men aged between 40 and 50. The second was a group of managers participating in an 8-week management education course. There were 15 managers in that group with varying positions and functions, several presidents of their companies. All the managers were from different companies and aged between 40 and 60, most of them men. Both focus group discussions lasted 2 hours.

In the interviews Finnish managers were characterized as people who do not easily give in. They are hard-working. Work has been, and still is, a central value for the Finns. This obviously stemming from Finnish roots in the agrarian society, when hard work was a necessity to survive, earning a living from the land. Finnish Manager's ideas may be questioned and decisions are increasingly being taken at lower levels in organizations. Finns are also quite good at improvising.

It also emerged that Finns experience difficulty in showing their feelings. Their ego tends to be vulnerable and they are below average when it comes to small talk. They are serious, somewhat "gray," and reserved. They are not good at establishing close personal relationships with customers in other countries, which in some parts of the world is considered very important. They are more authoritarian than Swedish managers. Swedish mangers are better able to discuss, and want to establish contact by talking first about other things than business. The Finns tend to go straight to the matter at hand during meetings.

As regards to competent managers, in particular it was stressed that they have a thorough knowledge of their own areas and build on that. They communicate their ideas to subordinates, that is, they mediate, inform, and translate the ideas of top management in an understandable form to employees. Competent managers are above all task managers. They implement the strategies of the firm, supervise, and ensure that things get done. They work in teams and therefore also have to be people oriented. They select subordinates and have to rely on them. They give feedback and can, if necessary, also change their own views.

Compared to the Swedes, the interviewees thought the Finns to be more flexible and able to improvise. In Sweden it is important to have clear rules, norms and systems. Hierarchies are lower in Finland and it is hoped that they will be even lower in the future. In comparison with Central European managers the interviewees thought the Finns to be more specialized. Central European managers were thought to have a broader humanistic education.

The features that characterized outstanding Finnish leaders in the interviews and focus discussions are shown in Table 4.6. The marks indicate in which interviews and focus discussions, and how often the different behavior traits and features were stressed. In some interviews and focus discussions the same feature was encountered several times, but the number of times within an interview or a focus discussion is not specified.

The three most important personal characteristics raised in the interviews were to get subordinates involved and develop their "self-esteem," "integrity and honesty," and "ability to make fast decisions." An outstanding Finnish leader should be honest, just, reliable, trustworthy, and enthusiastic, but also be able to make decisions fast. The first group of characteristics has to do with commitment and development of subordinates, together with personal features and behavior traits of the leader. The second important group of qualities concerns especially relations with subordinates: "good listener," "gets people to do more than expected," "inspires the subordinates," "has communication skills," and "gets people to follow him or her." An outstanding Finnish leader should above all have excellent skills in handling relationships with his or her subordinates.

The ability to make fast decision is an interesting feature. Especially in comparison with the Swedes, Finnish leaders are known for making decisions faster and more individually (cf. Laine- Sveiby, 1987). Finnish society has previously been quite authoritarian. Finland has been involved in two world wars and one civil war. Many of the military leaders in the wars subsequently became managers of companies. Källström (1995) argues that Finnish business leadership is characterized by a military culture that was formed during the two world wars. In many sectors of industry officers and noncommissioned officers were supervisors, which had an effect on the style of management and organization. The former CEO of the Swiss-Swedish industrial group ABB, Percy Barnevik, also gives quite an authoritarian picture of Finnish management. He said in an interview (Källstrand): "When you arrive in Finland, you are expected to say how things should be, the employees like to know where they are going and what the top manager

TABLE 4.6

Features of the Outstanding Finnish Leader

Themes	Interviews						Focus Groups		Total
	1	2	3	4	5	6	7	8	Total
Gets subordinates involved and develops self-esteem	x			x		x		x	4
Honesty and integrity		x					x	x	3
Ability to make fast decisions	x			x				x	3
Charisma			x				x		2
Reliable			x				x		2
Good listener, knows and notices his or her subordinates		x						x	2
Communication ability	x						x		2
Gets subordinates to follow him or her	x						x		2
Capacity to take calculated risks			x		x				2
Inspires subordinates	x				x				2
Gets people to do more than expected								x	1

wants, because the manager makes the final decision." (p. 141) But this authoritarian picture has gradually changed over the last two decades. As one interviewee said: "We try to get people to understand that everyone is a specialist in his own area, and that he has to present his own ideas and thoughts about the work that is very important for the firm. Subordinates may question the way things are done; indeed it is their duty to do that".

For older generations that are more used to the authoritarian era it has not always been easy to adapt their behavior and way of thinking. Nowadays delegation is strongly encouraged.

In conclusion it can be said that the quantitative and qualitative studies produced fairly similar results. *Integrity* and *charisma* were emphasized in both types of studies. An outstanding Finnish leader is inspirational and instills a positive and creative climate in which to work. She or he sets an example and selects the right people. Nurmi (1989) stresses that failure in this figurehead role makes leaders also appear untrustworthy in their other roles. The "visionary" factor was supported strongly both in the media analysis, focus group discussions and the quantitative studies. The term *team integrator* was mentioned in the qualitative study, but not emphasized as strongly as in the quantitative part. One reason for this could be that the interviewees were mostly managers at the middle level who do not work with the "charismatic," "visionary" top leader on a daily basis. Also the "team integrator" factor is quite a complicated concept with many different dimensions of team working. The qualitative studies indicate that an outstanding Finnish leader works in a group, selects the right employees, utilizes the ideas of the team, and blends them with his or her own ideas to produce good proposals and plans.

8. EFFECTIVE FINNISH LEADERSHIP, IMPLICATIONS
   FOR CROSS-CULTURAL PRACTICE AND RESEARCH

In summary, the personal features of outstanding leaders are *integrity, inspiration, team integrator,* and *visionary.* An outstanding leader stays at a high ethical level, encourages his or her subordinates, is good at coordinating the efforts of different teams and is future-oriented. Authority can be delegated, creating the conditions for positive and creative work. Ken Olsen, the founder and CEO of Digital Equipment Corporation, illustrates some of the behavioral qualities of successful leaders (Savage, 1990): "From our point of view, the companies that will survive are going to move from an environment of management control to one that allows a large number of people, all using their creative ability, their education, and their motivation, to take part" (p. 72).

According to House, Wright, and Aditya (1997), Americans appreciate two kinds of leaders. They seek empowerment from leaders who grant autonomy and delegate authority to subordinates. But they also respect bold, forceful, confident, and risk-taking leaders as personified by John Wayne. That seems to be very much the case for Finnish employees also. They want both autonomy and authority at the same time. Leaders have to be some sort of figurehead and be in the forefront. Such as in wars, the top leader has to make the risky and final decisions. But outstanding Finnish leaders bring forth energy in to the organization and cooperate with subordinates.

The implementation of ideas and plans is decentralized to the middle and lower levels. The actions and behavior of an outstanding leader at those levels will be to select good employees, inspire subordinates, set an example to them, get them involved and get them to follow the leader, pay attention to the subordinates and be a good listener, develop subordinates' self-esteem, get them to go beyond the call of duty, and finally, to implement ideas by being receptive to others' ideas and motivating subordinates. At the lower levels of organizations, outstanding Finnish leaders are good at managing people and have superior social skills. Issuing orders and direct supervision are to be avoided since Finns expect to have freedom in their tasks.

The quantitative questionnaires did not catch all the central emic Finnish characteristics. In the qualitative studies the poor communication capability was emphasized several times. However, in the questionnaire there was only one item about communication ability.

Finnish Leadership Between West and East

The history of Finland has very clearly placed the country borderline between the west and east. Finnish societal culture has been influenced, and to some extent created, by the culture of Sweden. The Swedish and Nordic influence has been very strong lasting over more than 800 years. Finns have moved especially to Sweden, but also moved back again. There has been an intensive interaction between Finland and Sweden. But the influence of the east should not be neglected. This influence was direct over more than 100 years before World War I. After World War II, the influence was more indirect up until the 1990s. The Finns had to take into consideration the opinion of Soviet leaders. After the disintegration of the Soviet Union relations have been normalized. Nowadays Russian tourists are one of the largest visitor groups to Finland. But what has be the effect been of Finland's position between Sweden and Russia, between West and East?

The figures from the quantitative study in the GLOBE project indicate larger differences between Finland and Russia than what exists between Sweden and Finland. For instance, checking the figures for society "As Is," Future Orientation is very low, Uncertainty Avoidance is also very low, Power Distance is higher, and Collectivism higher in Russia than that for both Finland and Sweden. The very significant differences might have to do with the large changes going on in Russian society.

The dilemma for Finns is that they have Western values but an Asian communication style (see next paragraph). Lewis (1997) stresses that the Finns' strengths lie in their values and code of behavior, not in their expressiveness. The two are in a sense incompatible. European values are determinate, logical and often Hegelian (idealistic). In Northern Europe in particular, the values tend to be "black and white." Asian values are less cut-and-dried, and are more ambiguous. The communication style is more Asian in character. Nurmi (1989) describes it as follows:

> "Finns do not think aloud as much as in Anglo-Saxon cultures, they are less open and slower to communicate, and they are relatively more synthetic than analytic in their thinking. What is communicated is meant to be more certain, serious and reliable than in more fluent cultures." (p. 12 ff)

Why are the social skills of Finns perhaps weaker than those of Nordic and European leaders? Nurmi (1989) emphasizes that a decade ago Finland was a relatively closed country on the European scene. One other factor is the Finnish language. It is very different from almost all other languages except Estonian, which can be understood at least partly by Finnish speakers. Language has been one reason for the historical isolation of the Finnish-speaking Finns. Another explanation is that Finland is a relatively large country with a small population (the surface area of Finland is 338,000 km2, and the population density is 15 persons/km2). The large area and small population contributed to a situation where remote settlements lived in isolation with little contact with people from other countries.

In Table 4.7 a summary from Lewis (1997) work about the values and communication styles used in the West, the East and in Finland is given.

Practical Implications

What should a foreign leader expect and how should s/he behave when dealing with Finnish leaders? Foreign leaders should find employees hard-working if they are correctly motivated. They are honest, reliable, punctual, quite modest, and have the ability to take initiatives. But their social competence is at a lower level.

The Finns are quite individualistic. In most Finnish companies the culture is open and individuals are respected. The distance between leaders, managers and subordinates is short. Many firms have open-plan offices, which facilitate direct communication. Finns are well educated and do not like close supervision. Finnish managers and subordinates want to have their responsibility and authority well defined. Simon et al. (1996) point out that Finnish managers will be committed if they receive work tasks according to their own capabilities, they are involved in the decision-making, and if there is a loyalty between the top management and management at lower levels in the organization. However, Finns are also able to work in a team, but the teams are to combine teamwork and individuality. Lewis (1997) stresses that you should try to appeal to the inner resources of individuals to achieve the task under their own stream and to be fully accountable for it.

Leaders should state clear goals and generate visions, but let the subordinate find the means of how to reach those goals. The leader should discuss the decisions with the subordinate, but the leader makes the decisions and is also responsible for them. The decision making should be fast. Status and hierarchy mean less than in many other Central and Latin European counties.

TABLE 4.7

Finnish Values and Communication Style

U.S.A./Western EU Values	Finnish Values	Asian Values
Democracy	Democracy	Hierarchies
Self-determinism	Self-determinism	Fatalism
Equality for women	Equality for women	Males dominate
Work ethic	Work ethic	Work ethic
Human rights	Human rights	Inequality
Ecology	Ecology	Exploits environment
Western *Communication Style*	*Finnish* *Communication Style*	*Asian* *Communication Style*
Extrovert	Introvert	Introvert
Forceful	Modest	Modest
Lively	Quiet	Quiet
Thinks aloud	Thinks in silence	Thinks in silence
Interrupts	Doesn't interrupt	Doesn't interrupt
Talkative	Distrusts big talkers	Distrusts big talkers
Dislikes silence	Uses silence	Uses silence
Truth before diplomacy	Truth before diplomacy	Diplomacy before truth
Overt body language	Little body language	Little body language

Note. From Lewis (1997, p. 4). Copyright 1997 by Lewis and The Institute of Cross-Cultural Communication. Adapted and modified by permission.

The managers have usually taken great responsibility for their employees. However, during the most recent years the globalization of many branches and introductions to the international stock exchange market have forced the Finnish companies to stress more the financial results than has been known earlier. Internationalization has increased significantly during the 1980s and 1990s. The Finnish managers are positive towards the European Union markets. The strategic goals are customer oriented and are based on good technology and a high quality level (Simon et al., 1996). Generally Finns are quite technology and innovation oriented but perhaps are somewhat weaker on the marketing.

Källström finds the national culture stronger in Finland than in Sweden. Therefore it is harder for Swedish leaders, for example, to be leaders of Finns.

Limitations and Suggestions for Future Research

This is a research project investigating the perceptions and views of middle managers in Finnish firms. The results might be somewhat different when investigating CEOs in Finnish organizations, because the tasks are different and the view of a CEO is more holistic and usually also more global. Also their experiences as managers are different. One could expect that culture differences might be somewhat less pronounced at the highest level. Managers at the highest level travel widely and have been influenced by many cultures. Their understanding of other cultures might be greater.

Our study did not cover all of the significant industries in Finland. The paper and metal industries are two of the largest employers in the country. There is a need for further research in order to gain a complete picture of Finnish management behavior and Finnish culture and outstanding leadership in Finland.

REFERENCES

Aaltonen, M. (1998). Suomalaisen johtamisen kuvia Kalevassa, Vänrikki Stoolin tarinoissa, Seitsemässä veljessä ja Tuntemattomassa sotilassa [Descriptions of Finnish Leadership in Kalevala, in the stories of second lieutenant Stool, in Seven brothers and in Unknown soldier]. *The Finnish Journal of Business Economics, 47*(2), 236–246.

Ahonen, P. (1999). *Finland: A communications superpower.* Retrieved July 27, 2001, from http// virtual.finland.fi/finfo/english/ahoneng.html.

Airola, V., Kulla, J., Lumia, M., Nyström, L., & Snow, J. (1991). *Suomalainen johtaja 1991* [Finnish leader 1991]. Helsinki: PA Consulting Group Oy.

Alho, K. (1961). *Suomen teollisuuden suurmiehiä* [The heroes of Finnish industry]. Helsinki: Werner Söderström Osakeyhtiö.

Arbetsgruppen för konferensen för utvecklandet av församlingen (1995). *Till tusen sjöars land och folk. En undersökning om finländarnas adliga tillstånd och utvecklingsmöjligheter för församligarna* [The report of the working group for a conference about development of a congregation. An investigation of the Finn's religious state and development possibilities of congregations]. Helsingfors, Finland: Seurakunnan kasvu ry.

Bass, B. M. (1985). *Leadership and performance beyond expectations.* New York: The Free Press.

Brown-Humes, C. (2001, Feb 2). The challenges of globalization, part 3. Nokia sets the standards. *Financial Times,* p. 4.

Burns, J. M. (1978). *Leadership.* New York: Harper & Row.

Center for International Earth Science International Network. (2001). *Study shows Finland, Norway and Canada rank as top countries in environmental sustainability.* New York: Earth Institute, Colombia University.

Confederation of Finnish Industry and Employers. (2000). *Facts about the Finnish economy 2000.* Helsinki, Finland: Esa Print Oy.

Gordon, P. (1991). *Report from Finland* (UFSI Field Report No. 11). Indianapolis: Universities Field Staff International.

Häikiö, M. (1992). *A brief history of modern Finland.* Lahti, Finland: University of Helsinki, Lahti Research and Training Centre.

Hanges, P.

Hargreaves, D. (2000, November 9). Scandinavia "best for business." *Financial Times.*

Heino, H. (1998). *Religion and churches in Finland. Virtual Finland.* Retrieved May 21, 2001, from http://www.finland.fi/finfo/english/uskoeng.html

Heino, R. (2001). *Finland's climate.* Retrieved July 27, 2001, from http://virtual.finland.fi/finfo/ english/ilmaeng.html

Hofstede, G. (1980). *Culture's consequences: International differences in work-related values.* Beverley Hills, CA: Sage.

House, R. J., Hanges, P. J., Javidan, M., Dorfman, P. W., Gupta, V., & Globe Associates. (2004). *Culture, leadership, and organizations: The GLOBE study of 62 societies.* Thousand Oaks, CA: Sage.

House, R. J., Hanges, P. J., Ruiz-Quintanilla, S. A., Dorfman, P. W., Javidan, M., Dickson, M., et al. (1999). Cultural influences on leadership and organizations: Project GLOBE. In W. Mobley, M. J. Gessner, & V. Arnold (Eds.), *Advances in global leadership* (Vol. 1, pp. 171–234). Stamford, CT: JAI.

House, R. J., Wright, N. S., & Aditya, R. N. (1997). Cross-cultural research on organizational leadership. A critical analysis and a proposed theory. In P. C. Earley & M. Erez (Eds.), *New perspectives in international industrial organizational psychology* (pp. 535–625). San Francisco: New Lexington.

Järvinen, J., Korkala, P., & Åman, R. (1978). *Suomalainen työnjohtaja* [Finish manager]. Espoo, Finland: Johtamistaidon Opistory.

Kahila, P. (2001, March). Meanwhile, in Finland: The $45,000 traffic ticket and other tales from Finland, home to the most wired government on earth. *eCompany Now.*

Källström, A. (1995). *I spetsen för sin flock: Normer för svenskt management* [In front of his crowd: Norms for Swedish management]. Göteborg, Sweden: Gothenburg Research Institute. Handelshögskolan vid Göteborgs universitet.

Kivikko, L., Lindell, M., & Naukkarinen, A. (1997). *Kilpailu strategisena valmentajana—kokemuksia markkinoiden murroksesta* [Competition as a strategic coach—experiences from reconstructed markets]. Helsinki, Finland: WSOY.

Kivistö, M. (1989). *Esimiehen johamiskäyttäytyminen* [Superior's management behavior]. Helsinki, Finland: JOT tutkimuksia, Series 3.

Laakso, A.-U. (2000). *Finnish industry—a modern day cinderella story.* Retrieved July 27, 2001, from http://virtual.finland.fi/finfo/english/teollisuus.html

Laine-Sveiby, K. (1987). *Nationell kultur som strategi—en fallstudie Sverige-Finland* [National culture as strategy—a case study Sweden-Finland]. Helsingfors, Finland: Näringslivets Delegation (EVA).

Leonard, A. (2000). *Finland the open-source society.* Retrieved March 2, 2001, from www.salon.com

Lewis, R. D. (1993). *Mekö erilaisia? Suomalainen kansainvälisissä liikeneuvotteluissa* [Are we different? The Finn in international business negotiations]. Helsinki, Finland: Kustannusosakeyhtiö Otava.

Lewis, R. D. (1996). *When cultures collide: Managing successfully across cultures.* London: Nicholas Brealey.

Lewis, R. D. (1997). *Cross cultural letter to international managers: Finland, Europe's hero nation.* Hampshire, England: Institute of Cross Cultural Communication.

Lilja, K. (1983). *Workers' workplace organizations: Their conceptual identification, historically specific conditions and manifestations.* Unpublished doctoral dissertation, Helsinki School of Economics, Series A: 39, Finland.

Lindell, M. (1998). The reorientation process following deregulation in some Finnish companies. *The Finnish Journal of Business Economics, 47*(2), 229–235.

Lindell, M., & Arvonen, J. (1996). The Nordic management style of investigation. In S. Jönsson (Ed.), *Perspectives of Scandinavian Management* (pp. 11–36). Gothenburg, Sweden: Gothenburg Research Institute, Gothenburg School of Economics and Commercial Law.

Lindell, M., & Rosenqvist, G. (1992). Management behavior dimensions and the development orientation. *Leadership Quarterly, 3*(4), 355–377.

Matkailun Edistämiskeskus (1988). *Suomi ulkomaalaisen silmin* [Finland in the eyes of foreigners]. Helsinki, Finland: MEK Sarja A:62.

Ministry of Education. (2001). *Yliopistot 2000* (Annual report). Helsinki, Finland: F. G. Lönnberg.

Nokia. (2000). *Annual reports.* Available at http://www.Nokia.com

Nurmi, R. (1989). *Management in Finland* (Report 29/1989). Turku, Finland: Turku School of Economics and Business Administration, Institute of Administration and Marketing.

Nyberg, F. (1995). *Autonomi och självständighet: Det moderna Finlands tillkomst* [Autonomy and independence: The birth of the modern Finland]. Borgå, Finland: Söderström & CO Förlags AB.

Salonen, K., Kääriäinen, K., & Niemelä, K. (2001). *Kyrkan inför ett nytt årtusende: Evangelisk-lutherska kyrkan I Finland åren 1996–1999* [The church on the eve of a new millennium: Evangelilcal-Lutheran church in Finland the years 1996–1999]. Jyväskylä, Finland: Gummerus Kirjapaino Oy.

Savage, C. M. (1990). *Fifth generation management: Integrating enterprises through human networking.* Boston: Digital Press.

Simon, H., Bauer, B., & Kaivola, K. (1996). *Europpalainen johtaja johtamiskulttuurit ja menestymistekijät* [European manager management cultures and success factors]. Porvoo, Finland: WSOY.

Statistical Yearbook of Finland. (2000). Keuruu, Finland: Otavan Kirjapaino.

Steinbock, D. (1998). *The competitive advantage of Finland: From cartels to competition.* Helsinki, Finland: Taloustieto Oy.

Takala, P. (2001, October 18). Suomi maaliman kilpailukykyisin [Finland the most competitive country in the world]. *Kauppalehti.*

TAT Group. (2001). *The story of Finland.* Helsinki, Finland: Vartia, P., Ylä-Anttila, P., & Hämäläinen, U.

Tollgerdt-Andersson, L. (1996). *Svenskt ledarskap I Europa* [Swedish leadership in Europe]. Malmö, Sweden: Liber-Hermods.

Torvi, K. (1999). *EU membership has benefited Finnish economy: Virtual Finland.* Retrieved May 21, 2001, from http://virtual.finland.fi/finfo/english/eu_econ.htlm

Veranen, J., & Junnila, P. (1997). Lisäarvoa tuo vain joka neljäs yritys [Only every fourth company generate value]. *Talouselämä, 20,* 28–31.

Vihavainen, T. (2002). *Finland's relations with the Soviet Union 1944–1991.* Retrieved November 7, 2000, from http://ww.finland.org/after.html

Yukl, G. (2002). *Leadership in organizations.* Upper Saddle River, NJ: Prentice-Hall.

Zandler, L. (1997). *The licence to lead—an 18 country study of the relationship between employees' preferences regarding interpesonal leadership and national country.* Stockholm, Sweden: Stockholm School of Economics, Institute of International Business.

II

GERMANIC EUROPE CLUSTER

Austria, Germany (former East and former West), the Netherlands, and Switzerland (German-speaking) formed the Germanic Europe cluster in the GLOBE Research Program. All four of these countries are included in this volume. The use of the German language is an obvious commonality that runs through these countries, with the exception of the Netherlands, which has a distinct language of its own though a basic grasp of German is usually found in the Netherlands also.

The Germanic Europe cluster scores high on Assertiveness, Future Orientation, Performance Orientation, and Uncertainty Avoidance. It is in the mid-score range for Gender Egalitarianism, and Power Distance. It scores low on Human Orientation, Institutional Collectivism, and In-Group Collectivism.

This cluster endorsed Participative leadership very positively, the highest among all 10 clusters. Participative leadership is seen to be as important as Charismatic/Value based leadership and more important than Team Oriented leadership. Countries in this cluster view Self-Protective leadership more negatively than in all other cultural clusters. Autonomous leadership is viewed positively except in the Netherlands (House et al., 2004). Participation seems to be a key value in the countries of this cluster. The middle managers' view of their society and ideal leadership seems to be considerably influenced by the current models of cooperation between "labor" and "capital" of these countries (Szabo et al., 2002). These countries also show the strong impact of societal culture in preference to political or economic philosophy.

REFERENCES

House, R. J., Hanges, P. J., Javidan, M., Dorfman, P. W., Gupta, V., & GLOBE Associates. (2004). *Culture, leadership, and organizations: The GLOBE study of 62 societies.* Thousand Oaks, CA: Sage.

Szabo, E., Brodbeck, F. C., Den Hartog, D. N., Reber, G., Weibler, J., & Wunderer, R. (2002). The Germanic Europe cluster: Where employees have a voice. *Journal of World Business, 37,* 55–68.

5

▼▼▼▼▼▼▼

Culture and Leadership in Austria

Erna Szabo
Gerhard Reber
Department of International Management,
Johannes Kepler University,
Altenberger Strasse 69, A-4040 Linz, Austria

1. SOCIETY AND CULTURE IN AUSTRIA

Introduction

Based on several extensive image studies in 30 countries, Schweiger (1992) presented Austria's image in the world: Austria is considered *the* country of classical music and world famous for the Viennese Waltz. In response to the question "Which famous Austrians do you know?" most respondents (above 20% in all countries, 75% in the United States) named the composer Wolfgang Amadeus Mozart (1756–1791), followed by Johann Strauß, Senior (1804–1849) and Johann Strauß, Junior (1825–1899). Historical and contemporary political leaders, business leaders, and famous Austrian scientists fell far short.[1]

Indeed, Austria is famous as the land of music and a tourist attraction with its Vienna Boys' Choir (founded in 1498 by Emperor Maximilian I), the Vienna Philharmonic Orchestra, and the Vienna State Opera. Yet is Austria just a pure country of culture, in the sense of art and literature? What about the second aspect of culture originating from anthropology, that is, the shared way people in a society feel, think, and behave? Who knows which forces have shaped Austrian societal culture, which practices and principles make Austrian organizations work, and which leadership styles are accepted and preferred among Austrians? The following

---

[1]Historical leaders most frequently mentioned were the Emperor of the Austrian Hungarian Empire, Kaiser Franz Joseph I (1830–1916) and Adolf Hitler (1889–1945). According to the study, contemporary well-know Austrian leaders and Bruno Kreisky (former federal chancellor of Austria; 1911–1990) and Kurt Waldheim (former secretary general to the United Nations and former federal president of Austria; born 1918). The one Austrian scientist named repeatedly was Sigmund Freud (1856–1939), founding father of psychoanalysis.

chapter sheds light on these issues. We start with a brief summary of Austria's history and its contemporary economic and social structure (Appendix A gives basic information on Austria) and then report findings of the GLOBE project related to societal culture and business leadership in Austria.

Historical and Political Developments

Settlements in the Alpine region and the fertile plains of the Danube date back to prehistoric times: The Celts prospered from the rich mineral resources (most notably salt and iron); the Romans conquered the region around the birth of Christ; up to the late 8th century waves of migrating peoples, among them Germanic tribes, Huns, and Slavs, repeatedly crossed the land; toward the end of the 10th century Charlemagne established the Carolingian Mark in the area of present-day Austria.

From the 10th century onward, Austria's history was dominated by two dynasties: the Babenbergs, who died out in the middle of the 13th century, and the Habsburgs, who originated from Switzerland. The Habsburgs were very successful in enlarging their territories, for example, by strategic marriages. At the beginning of the 16th century, the dynasty split into a Spanish and an Austrian line and the Austrian Habsburgs added Bohemia and Hungary to their empire. Throughout the 16th and 17th centuries, the dominant theme of Austrian history was confrontation with the Ottoman Empire, whose vast armies twice laid siege to Vienna.[2] After these threats were over, Austria acquired new territories and emerged as a major European power. Its lands, which were inhabited by a rich body of different peoples, extended from the Netherlands to the West to Sicily in the South and to Poland in the East. Austria in this period covered a region that largely overlapped with today's European Union (EU), but without the British and Irish Isles and Scandinavia. Conquests in Central America under Karl V led to the notation of the empire in which "the sun never sets." In the second half of the 18th century, Empress Maria Theresia and her son Joseph II implemented massive programs of reform, laying the foundations for a modern state administration. The General School Regulations decreed by the Empress in 1774 laid the cornerstone for Austria's education system; mandatory school attendance for children starting from the age of 6 years was introduced.

In the 19th century, Austria suffered a succession of defeats against other European powers; at the same time the Habsburg administration was forced to make concessions to both the rapidly growing nationalist and democratic movements. In 1867, Emperor Franz Joseph I acceded to demands for the creation of the Double Monarchy of Austria-Hungary. Meanwhile, Germany was founded after Prussia won a military victory over France. Austria, that is, the House of Habsburg, was excluded from this new construction of a "Little German Solution" and remained a nation of many peoples (*Vielvölkerstaat*) with increasing nationalist conflicts, which finally led to the beginning of World War I (1914–1918). The war had started as an internal Austrian issue, triggered by the assassination of the successor to the throne by a Serbian nationalist.[3] The main rivals in the war were Austria and Germany on one side and the "Triple Entente" (Great Britain, France, and Russia) on the other side. After the victory of the Entente and the end of the war, the Habsburg empire was dissolved under the Versailles Treaty and Austria was proclaimed a republic in 1918.

---

[2] What remained of this time is the traditional Viennese coffee house.

[3] In 1919, the Austrian writer Karl Kraus (1874–1936) finished the drama "*Die letzten Tage der Menschheit*" ("The last days of mankind"), which gives a critical record of the events leading to and during the war.

The so-called First Republic provided the foundation for today's democracy. However, in 1933 unstable economic and political conditions led to the imposition of a dictatorship under Engelbert Dollfuss, whereas civil war in 1934 resulted in suppression of the Social Democratic Party and Dollfuss's assassination by National Socialists.[4] Hitler "invaded" Austria in March 1938 and formally incorporated its territory into the German Reich. Hitler was welcomed by a large part of the Austrian population. However, historians have been debating since whether the invasion was a hostile annexation by Nazi Germany or a voluntary joining (*Anschluß*) by the Austrians.

What followed was World War II and Austria's probably darkest period in history, including the *Holocaust* with the murder of 66,000 Austrian Jews. Even today, this period of Austrian history has not been completely overcome and "healed up." In particular, Austrian citizens' active role in the holocaust still leads to defensive reactions among parts of the population. Decades after the fact, some Austrians still view Austria as the first victim of Adolf Hitler and have therefore, compared to Germany, never really accepted the culpability or responsibility of their country.

In 1945, after the victory of the Allied Powers (Britain, France, the Soviet Union, and the United States) over Nazi Germany, Austria was revived as a republic (the so-called Second Republic) but remained occupied by the Allied armies for another 10 years. The economy was stimulated with international help; in particular the Marshall Plan[5] enabled a successful recovery.

In 1955, the Austrian State Treaty was signed, reestablishing Austria as a *sovereign* nation. In accordance with the treaty, Austria became a permanently *neutral* state after adopting a law in parliament that ruled out military bases on Austrian soil and the accession to any military alliance. Austria followed a policy of active neutrality and joined the United Nations (Sully, 1995b, p. 67). The Austrian capital, Vienna, became one of the permanent seats of the UN (United Nations), hosting the IAEA (International Atomic Energy Agency), the UNIDO (United Nations Industrial Development Organization), and several UN departments. Vienna was also selected to host the OSCE (Organization for Security and Cooperation in Europe) and OPEC (Organization of Petroleum Exporting Countries). Vienna has frequently been chosen as the venue of key superpower summit meetings and of other important international negotiations. For many years now Austria has made an active contribution to the United Nations' peace- keeping missions.

Coalition governments between the Social Democrats and the People's Party endured under a succession of chancellors until 1966, when the People's Party won a legislative majority and organized a single-party government. In 1970, the Social Democrats came to power as a minority government under Bruno Kreisky. Subsequent elections in 1971, 1975, and 1979 yielded majority mandates for Chancellor Kreisky. International negotiations, for example, between Israel and the Palestine Liberation Organization (PLO), took place in Austria and social reforms were undertaken. Their focus was on full employment rather than budgetary consolidation: *"If you were to ask me how I feel about public debt, I would say over and over that a couple billion Schillings of public debt causes me fewer sleepless nights than to think of the hundred thousands of unemployed"* (Bruno Kreisky, quoted on Austrian television, 1990).

---

[4]Former chancellor Bruno Kreisky is quoted saying, "If we had known of the dangers threatened by Germany in 1930, history would have taken a different turn" (Österreichischer Rundfunk [ORF], 1990).

[5]The plan was initiated by U.S. Secretary of State George Catlett Marshall.

The 1980s were again characterized by coalition governments between the Social Democrats and the People's Party. The election of October 1994, however, radically altered the parameters of the postwar system. For the first time since 1945, the two main parties failed to secure a two-thirds majority of the seats in Parliament; the old two-party system gave way to a pentagonal model: Overall five parties secured parliamentary seats (Sully, 1995a, p. 219), among them the Green Party and the Freedom Party (FPÖ), whose chairman at that time Jörg Haider is by some considered a mere populist, by others a far-right nationalist (Banks, Day, & Muller, 1997).

After the 1999 election, the Freedom Party became even stronger and was able to form a coalition government with the People's Party. This constellation led to criticism and protests nationally and internationally and the EU imposed sanctions on Austria. In an EU report covering the new Austrian government's commitment to the common European values and the evolution of the political nature of the FPÖ, Ahtisaari, Frowein, and Oreja (2000, p. 27) state:

> *The FPÖ has been described as a "right wing populist party with extremist expressions." This description is, according to our judgement still applicable after the party joined the Federal Government. This must give rise to concern, since Governments are the organs of the European states which have the direct responsibility to implement their positive obligations concerning the protection and promotion of human rights, democracy, and the suppression of any kind of ethnic or racial discrimination.*

It is ironic that at the formal level Austria had become a less "corporate state" (see the section on social partnership later), and thus had moved closer to other European democracies' political realities. The irony is that the move obviously needed a party that leaves doubts as to their own democratic principles.

After 1999, local and provincial elections saw continuous losses for the Freedom Party. It became obvious that a large number of Austrians had been in favor of strengthening the Freedom Party as a form of protest against the old party system, yet they did not approve the new political course in similarly large numbers as the federal election would have suggested. What followed were better fights and intrigues within the Freedom Party, which finally led to the breakup of the coalition government. The following elections saw the Freedom Party reduced to one third and fewer of the votes the party had managed to secure in 1999.

In summary, Austria has, over time, moved from a world power to a small country, from a monarchy to a democratic republic. In this sense, Austria might be considered a social construction rather than an entity and has a background that concerns issues and territories that are no longer part of the modern state: *"Austria as an entity that spans centuries, religions, classes, dynasties, regions, and ethnic groups is an invention naturally: a 'Kopfgeburt' (a figment of your imagination), projected from the present to the past, with sites set on the future. Of course, in this respect Austria is no different from France or Portugal or the Netherlands or Switzerland. All 'nations' are political inventions"* (Pelinka, 1995, p. 8).

On a humorous note, Austrian-born Paul Watzlawick concluded that Austria's history has brought about very special people:

> *In the heart of Europe there was once a great empire. It was composed of so many and so widely different cultures that no common sense solution to any problem could ever be reached, and absurdity became the only possible way of life. Its inhabitants—the Austro-Hungarians, as the reader may already have suspected—thus were proverbial not only for their inability to cope reasonably with the simplest of problems, but also for their ability to achieve the impossible*

somehow almost by default. Britain, as one bon mot claimed, loses every battle except the decisive ones; Austria loses every battle except the hopeless ones. (Small wonder, since the highest military decoration was reserved for officers who snatched victory from the jaws of defeat by taking some action that was in flat contradiction to the general battle plan.) The great empire is now a tiny country, but absurdity has remained its inhabitants' outlook on life. For all of them, life is hopeless, but not serious. (Watzlawick, 1983, p. 9)

We conclude this excursion into history with a recapitulation of the leaders who have most significantly *shaped* the history and development of Austria:

- Various emperors of the Habsburg dynasty: The most popular ones were Maria Theresia, the first woman to the throne, her son and successor Joseph II, and Franz Joseph I, a well-liked father figure.[6]
- Adolf Hitler: Born and raised in Austria,[7] Hitler began in Germany to transform his ideas for the *Third Reich* into deeds. Later, his charisma had a similar effect on Austrians as it had on the Germans; disillusioned by the political and economic situation, the Austrian population was more than ready to accept his promises for a reconstruction of the Austrian economy. Hitler also successfully constructed images of national pride and power that were based on the institutionalization of schemes of racism and anti-Semitism in public culture and political action.
- The first generation of politicians in the Second Republic: Among them were survivors of the concentration camps as well as returning emigrants, described as possessing honesty and integrity rather than political expertise. Across political party lines they were united in the conviction that social unrest based on economic inequality (which had enabled Hitler's success in Austria) had to be avoided in the future, and that cooperation in economic matters was an effective means to grant stability.
- Bruno Kreisky: Of Jewish descent, Kreisky was a young member of the Socialist Party when the Second Republic was established. He is described as a strong-willed person acting on socialist ideology. He was federal chancellor from 1970 to 1983, built the Austrian welfare state, shaped the European Social Democratic landscape together with Willy Brandt in Germany and Olaf Palme in Sweden,[8] and was internationally highly respected for his mediation in peace negotiations, in particular in the Middle East.

The Current Economic and Societal Situation

The Economy

The *primary* sector (agriculture) accounts for 1.8% of Austria's gross domestic product, whereas the *secondary* sector (industry) makes up 30.4%, and the *tertiary* sector (services) accounts for 67.8% (2004 estimate; *World Factbook*, 2006). Austria has a per capita GDP of about U.S.$32,500 (2005 estimate; *World Factbook*, 2006) and ranks 14th place on the human development index[9] (Human Development Report, 2006).

---

[6]After a journey to Europe in 1910, the American President Theodore Roosevelt is quoted saying that apart from the Austrian Emperor no other European leader of state had impressed him (Kleindel, 1978).

[7]Hitler wanted to become an artist but was not accepted as a student by the Art Academy of Vienna.

[8]Both Kreisky and Brandt lived in exile in Sweden during World War II.

[9]This index is measured by life expectancy, educational attainment, and adjusted income per capita in purchasing power parity U.S. dollars.

Austria draws on the following resources: timber, few metals and minerals, salt, a dense river network serving as the base for hydroelectric power[10] and mass transportation, and the beauty of the different Austrian regions. Altogether this is a rather poor basis, making Austria heavily dependent on foreign trade. Education and the quality of the workforce are Austria's most valuable assets. For instance the LD process,[11] invented in Austria, has dominated steel production around the world. Two thirds of the steel production worldwide (about 800 million tons per year) are based on the LD process.

During World War II, the Nazis had taken over all industry of significant size. In 1946, this former Third Reich industry became state owned to avoid a transfer of assets to the Soviet Union (Dana, 1992, p. 127). Most of these firms remained in the ownership of the state until the beginning of the 1990s, when privatization programs were started. Recent trends have included deregulation and privatization of many sectors, such as that of major industries, including steel, oil, chemicals, as well as the railroads and major banks.

One of the areas in the tertiary sector that reports especially high rates of foreign-currency earnings is tourism. In contrast to countries where hotels tend to be large and parts of chains (e.g., Holiday Inn, Hilton), most of Austria's thousands of hotels are family owned and operated, in some cases for decades or even centuries; for instance, the *Ortner family* has owned the Hotel *Weisses Kreuz* in Innsbruck since 1465 (Dana, 1992, p. 129).

As in tourism, the predominant feature of Austria's overall economy is its high proportion of small and medium-size enterprises. Most firms are traditional small businesses that employ a substantial portion of the population: 97% of Austrian businesses have fewer than 50 employees; 46% of the labor force works for such firms. Most small firms are unincorporated sole proprietorships (Dana, 1992, p. 126). Other countries' governments have encouraged mergers of existing firms into larger units; in contrast, Austrian business did not go through a "big is better" stage. Only in the wake of EU membership have mergers taken place in some sectors, for example, the financial sector.

Austria and Neighboring Germany.   The two countries are characterized by populations of predominantly Germanic origin, sharing a common language. Thus, it is not surprising that the Austrian economy is closely tied to its German neighbor. This link goes back to the time between the two world wars, when Germany's economic influence on impoverished Austria grew substantially; by the 1930s, commercial law in Austria and Germany had become almost identical. The close ties to the German market economy remain today and facilitate business transactions between the two countries. To eliminate foreign exchange risk, to facilitate trade and to support the small-business sector, the Austrian government ensured that the Austrian schilling had a stable exchange rate with the German mark (Dana, 1992, pp. 127–128) long before the euro was introduced as the common currency. Germany's leading export to Austria is the automobile, essential parts of which are manufactured in Austria, for example, the Diesel engines for the BMW models. Germany's main contribution to Austria's economy is in tourism.[12]

---

[10]In a referendum in 1978, a close majority of the Austrian population voted against the use of nuclear power.

[11]LD stands for Linz and Donawitz, the two Austrian cities hosting steel plants.

[12]The year 2004 saw 117.3 million overnight stays of foreigners in Austria, among them 51.0 million stays by guests from Germany (Statistisches Jahrbuch Österreichs, 2006).

The Fall of the Iron Curtain. With the collapse of Eastern European communism in 1989, Austria was favorably positioned to regain its role as an economic power in the region. During 1990 alone, exports to Czechoslovakia increased by 72%. In addition, Austrian exports to Hungary, Poland, and Czechoslovakia more than doubled during the first 3 years after the fall of the Iron Curtain (Smith, 1992, p. 108). In the years immediately following the opening of the borders, some 40% of all direct foreign investments in the former communist countries came from Austria (Bundeskanzleramt, 1996). Austrian businesses began taking advantage of *cheaper labor* (e.g., in Austria the average monthly salary was about seven times higher than the equivalent in Hungary); many manufacturers shifted their production sites across the borders. Vienna's proximity to the Central and Eastern European markets also meant that many international firms began to use the city as a *base* from which to coordinate Central and Eastern European operations (C. Smith, 1992, p. 108).

Austria in the European Union. Austria joined the EU in 1995 after a national referendum had produced a solid positive result of 66.6% "Yes" votes. From the start the "Yes" campaign had significant advantages: It was better organized and financed, the two coalition parties were at leadership level for membership, and the social partners (see next subsection) were also in favor (Fitzmaurice, 1995). Although Austria trades with some 150 countries, the countries of the EU account for about two thirds of foreign trade, which made the step to join the union even more reasonable. The transition has not been a completely smooth one, however: Hundreds of laws have had to be changed, protection of industries had to be given up, concessions to lower environmental standards had to be made, and dealing with the EU bureaucracy had to be learned.

Social Partnership and Codetermination

Consensus politics has been one of the hallmarks of postwar Austrian life, its predominant manifestation being the *social partnership model.* This model was created after World War II, mainly as a result of a lack of confidence in the political extremes on the capitalism/socialism continuum (Child, 1981). The model substantially contributed to the social peace that was essential for the reconstruction of Austria after the destruction of the war and Austria's subsequent development into a modern industrialized country (Bundeskammer für Arbeiter und Angestellte, 1996, p. 5). Specific contingencies supported the success of the model: the distribution of economic and political power among the two camps of the Social Democrats and the Conservatives, the smallness of the economy, and the high percentage of state ownership (Nowotny, 1991).

The social partnership model is a system of economic and social cooperation at the national level between the representatives of employers (Chamber of Commerce), employees (Chamber of Labor), farmers (Chamber of Agriculture), unions, and government. This cooperation is at the top level ("Parity Commission") based on the principle of voluntarism and carried out in an informal way. The general idea of the system is that the basic aims of economic and social policy are recognized by all partners and can be better realized through cooperation and coordinated action rather than through confrontational means such as strikes or lockouts. Social partnership is not a means of denying conflicts of interests; it is a model that aims at mutual problem solving and balancing interests through achieving mutual strategies and through its readiness to compromise and find consensus (Bundeskammer für Arbeiter und Angestellte, 1996, p. 7).

This form of partnership could not function unless the sections of the working population concerned belong virtually en bloc to their representative organizations (Bundeskanzleramt, 1996). Membership to the Chambers of Commerce, Labor, and Agriculture is obligatory (in 1996 the members of the different chambers voted in large numbers for a retention of obligatory membership), whereas trade union membership is voluntary (about 43% of the workforce were union members in 1999; Österreichischer Gewerkschaftsbund, 2001). Austrian unions are closely linked to political parties and are influenced by social ideologies, including Catholic and socialist ones (Tannenbaum, Kavcic, Rosner, Vianello, & Wieser, 1974). The centralization of the Austrian political system together with the cooperation with the (also) centralized social partners fits Crispo's (1978) term of a "corporate state."

Ever since Austria became a member of the EU, the role of the social partnership has been continually changing because some responsibilities/decisions that were at the discretion of Austria and its social partners before are now handled at EU level. Also, since the federal election in 1999 (see the earlier discussion on political development) the role of the social partners is being further debated, in particular originating from the Freedom Party. However, despite these attempts to keep the social partners at distance, or even eliminate them from decision-making processes, we can state that the ideas of the social partnership model are still very much anchored in the Austrian system. In addition, nothing has changed in terms of arrangements concerning codetermination and works councils (see the following).

As in Germany, Luxembourg, Denmark, Norway, and Sweden, legally mandated *codetermination* is in place within Austrian organizations. The Austrian form of codetermination in large enterprises takes the form of two-tiered management structures: Workers' representatives sit on the *supervisory board,* which sets corporate politics, approves major investments, mergers, expansion and plant closures, and also appoints members to a *management board,* which actually manages the enterprise (Hammer, 1996, p. 1923).

Works councils in Austria are given three kinds of rights: the right to information, the right of consultation in economic and financial matters, and the right of consent in social and personnel affairs. Works council members are elected by the workers; in practice, they often have close union ties (Hammer, 1996, p. 1923).

Codetermination and works councils are the logical consequences of the social partnership idea at the national level as it filters down into the individual organization. However, recent developments (e.g., the transfer of operations across the border to decrease labor costs) also show that the stable foundation on which employer–employee relations were built so far might have already developed its first cracks. In the wake of increasing competition, purely economic interests are sometimes given higher priority than long-term social partnership ideas. However, such changes are not restricted to Austria. The following quote regarding management in Europe confirms this opinion:

> *Despite the Europolitical tradition of social protection of "the weak" at the government level, in the 1990s there is not as much protection of weak workers within organizations as was common in Europe's recent past (in contrast with North American labor practices). In response to intensified competition, major reorganizations are continuously carried out, and a fairly consistent rate of 10 percent unemployment can be observed for the European work force in the 1990s.* (Wilderom, Glunk, & Inzerilli, 1997, pp. 5–6)

2. METHODOLOGY OF GLOBE RESEARCH IN AUSTRIA

The GLOBE research in Austria consisted of questionnaire-based data collection, focus groups, semistructured as well as ethnographic interviews, and a qualitative media analysis.

TABLE 5.1
Demographic Characteristics of the Manager Sample

Attribute	Mean	Range
Age	40.03	25–59
Years of formal education	13.44	9–22
Years in managerial position	9.62	0–31
Number of subordinates	9.56	0–99
Native speakers of German	100%	
Female managers	11.8%	

Only a triangulation of different data (Webb, Campbell, Schwartz, & Sechrest, 1966), quantitative as well as qualitative, allows for the interpretation of *holistic* concepts such as culture and leadership. This strategy has been at the core of the GLOBE project from the beginning (House et al., 1999). In this sense, the Austrian research team applied specific *ethnographic principles,* in particular bringing in various types of data, collecting and analyzing these data in several rounds, and gradually narrowing the focus (Agar, 1996). This strategy assured that patterns in the data could be found, frames could be built, and an Austria-specific model of leadership could be generated.

Questionnaires

The questionnaire-based data included the three standard GLOBE Phase II questionnaires for the three levels under study: societal culture ("As Is" and "Should Be" items), organizational practices ("As Is" and "Should Be" items), and leadership attributes. We report the findings of the societal culture and leadership attributes questionnaires in this chapter.

A total of 169 Austrian middle managers completed the questionnaires in 1995. Table 5.1 shows their demographic characteristics. All participants completed the leadership attributes questionnaire, whereas about half of the managers ($N = 91$) filled out Version A of the questionnaire including the organizational practices items, and the other half ($N = 78$) completed Version B containing the societal culture items. The managers were members of 18 organizations within the two industries *financial services* and *food processing.*

Focus Groups

In early 1994, we conducted two focus groups, one with managers and professionals, the other with part-time students. The managerial group consisted of six alumni (two women, four men) from Johannes Kepler University, three of whom also held an MBA degree from a North American university. They represented various industries and functional areas. The second focus group comprised of eight part-time students (one woman, seven men) studying business administration. These students worked in different fields; none of them reported any managerial experience. Participants of both groups were asked to complete preparatory assignments concerning their personal definition of leadership. The actual focus group discussions lasted about 2 hours each and focused on three themes as defined by the GLOBE team: the definition of management and leadership, the difference (if any) between these two concepts, and finally, examples of outstanding leadership.

TABLE 5.2
Demographic Characteristics of the Interviewees

Interviewees Attributes	1	2	3	4	5	6	7	8	9	10
Industry:										
Banks					x	x	x			
Food								x	x	
Other	x	x	x	x						x
Hierarchical level:										
Top management						x				x
Middle management		x		x			x	x	x	
Employee	x		x		x					
Sex:										
Female		x		x						x
Male	x	x		x		x	x	x	x	
Age:										
Younger than 35					x					x
35–50	x		x	x			x		x	
Older than 50		x				x		x		
Type of interview:										
Ethnographic						x	x	x	x	x
Semistructured	x	x	x	x	x					
Number of interviews:										
One interview	x	x	x	x	x					x
Interview and follow-up						x	x	x	x	

Interviews

Semistructured interviews took place right at the start of the project in early 1994. Five interviewees (two women, three men), in managerial as well as nonmanagerial positions in different industries, were asked about their perception of management and leadership. The average duration of the interviews was about 40 minutes. The guiding questions covered the same three themes that were used in the focus groups.

Ethnographic interviews were conducted during a later phase of the project, namely in 1995. They were based on the *Qualitative Research Manual* prepared for the GLOBE researchers by the anthropologist Michael Agar. Based on the strategy of *maximizing differences*,[13] five managers were asked to participate in the interviews. Table 5.2 shows their demographic characteristics. The duration of the interviews ranged from 45 minutes to 1.5 hours. Interview themes focused on the interviewees' concepts of leadership in general as well as on stories of successful and unsuccessful leadership from their own experience. Four interview partners also described their industry. Furthermore, four of the participants agreed to participate in follow-up interviews (see the following discussion on validation process).

---

[13]According to this strategy, the benefit of selecting interviewees who are different from each other in some important ways is "to force differences to show up; if they don't, then you know that the patterns that are common across all interviewees are more likely to be common to managers, however else they might differ from each other" (Agar, n.d., *Qualitative Research Manual I*, p. 27).

TABLE 5.3
Austrian Media Analysis Data

Name of Print Media	Frequency	Readership	Circulation (in 1,000s)
Die Presse	Daily	General	88–143
Der Standard	Daily	General	87–191
Profil	Weekly	General	105
Trend	Monthly	Business	90
Wirtschaftswoche (initial sample)	Monthly	Business	48
Gewinn (validation sample)	Monthly	Business	95

Note. Gewinn was sampled in addition to *Wirtschaftswoche,* as *Wirtschaftswoche* was no longer in print in September 1997 when the validation data were collected. The two journals are comparable in terms of topics and readership.

The five semi-structured interviews and the nine ethnographic interviews (five initial, four follow-up) were transcribed and the resulting texts were restructured into text segments covering one idea each. All interviews were first analyzed *individually,* before frame building was applied during the subsequent *group* analysis. The interview data were analyzed separately for *person-specific characteristics* (character traits and behavior), *leader–follower relations* (values and norms concerning the followers as well as leader–follower interactions), and *organizational issues* (the leader's role inside and outside the organization as well as organizational practices).

The interview data were *validated* in four ways:

1. About a month after the initial transcribing process the tapes were listened to again and necessary modifications made.
2. The interviews were checked for intrapersonal consistency between what the interviewee said about leadership in general and what she or he described in the stories as good or bad leadership. Consistency was found in all 10 cases.
3. During the follow-up interviews, the managers were confronted with the researchers' analysis of the initial interviews and were asked to make corrections and improvements. Some minor adjustments were necessary, but overall the interview partners were satisfied with the way their statements had been interpreted.
4. The interview data were assigned to theme-specific categories. These categories were not predefined by the researchers but emerged from the data. The transcripts were recoded a couple of weeks after the original coding and the results were compared with the initial categories.

Media Analysis

The media analysis covered material from the Austrian print media and consisted of three types of data: (a) articles related to the nine GLOBE societal culture dimensions, (b) articles concerning the two industries under study (financial services and food processing), and (c) articles referring to leaders and/or leadership.

Articles for inclusion in the media analysis were collected from six print media during one week in December 1996 (December 9–15) and one week in September 1997 (September 8–14). The data of the second week comprised the validation sample. Table 5.3 describes the selected media in more detail. The sampling strategy followed Michael Agar's guidelines for qualitative data analysis. Overall, 443 articles were selected (229 in the initial sample, 214 in the validation sample) and organized into 2,960 distinctive text segments. The analysis was conducted separately for the three types of data.

The media data were *validated* in the following ways:

1. Data collection consisted of two samples. The second sample was used to verify patterns that had emerged from the original sample.
2. About two months after the initial data collection, the chosen issues were scanned a second time to check whether the selection of relevant articles had been complete. Some additional articles were added to the sample.
3. Within the three large categories (societal culture, industry characteristics, and leadership) the text segments were assigned theme-specific codes, which were not predefined but emerged from the data. The coding of the initial sample was reexamined and adjusted after the collection of the validation sample.

3. FINDINGS

We first present the findings concerning societal culture and then continue with the description of the leadership results. In each of these two subsections, the results of the questionnaire-based data collection are introduced followed by the findings of the qualitative part of the study (focus groups, interviews, and media analysis) whenever applicable. Results and conclusions from other research are brought in as well.

Societal Culture

The questionnaire-based results for the nine societal scales for Austria are displayed in Fig. 5.1 and Table 5.4. The "As Is" scales represent the *perception* of how the respondents view societal culture, whereas the "Should Be" scales indicate their *values,* that is, how the managers think their society ought to be. These two types of scales are not unrelated. For instance, the higher a person values gender equality, the more critical she or he will perceive actual gender equality practices, which might lead to lower scores on the "As Is" scale. Likewise, if a person perceives a dimension, for example, Power Distance, to be unsatisfactorily high, she or he will rate the "Should Be" dimension even lower. In other words, the person will value power egalitarianism even higher.

Where applicable, we compare our findings to Hofstede's (1980) results, although his data concerning Power Distance, Uncertainty Avoidance, Individualism, and Masculinity tap at a mixture of perceptions and values. In other words, Hofstede does not explicitly distinguish between "As Is" and "Should Be" scales. For instance, two of the three items used to calculate the Power Distance score are parallel items concerning the real-life ("As Is") versus the ideal ("Should Be") boss.

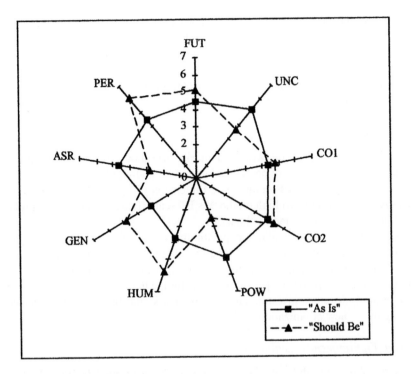

Figure 5.1   Societal Culture GLOBE Dimensions

TABLE 5.4
Societal Culture Dimensions

Dimensions	Perceptions ("As Is")			Values ("Should Be")		
	Score	Band	Rank	Score	Band	Rank
Future Orientation	4.46	A	6	5.11	C	50
Uncertainty Avoidance	5.16	A	6	3.66	D	57
Assertiveness	4.62	A	6	2.81	C	60
Performance Orientation	4.44	A	14	6.10	B	21
Institutional Collectivism	4.30	B	27	4.73	B	31
In-Group Collectivism	4.85	B	42	5.27	C	51
Power Distance	4.95	B	44	2.44	D	48
Gender Egalitarianism	3.09	B	45	4.83	A	18
Humane Orientation	3.72	C	46	5.76	A	4

Note.   Score: Country mean for Austria on the basis of aggregated scale scores. *Band*: Letters A to D indicate the country band Austria belongs to (A > B > C > D). Countries from different bands are considered to differ significantly from each other (GLOBE test banding procedure, cf. Hanges, Dickson, & Sipe, 2004). *Rank*: Austria's position relative to the 61 countries in the GLOBE study; Rank 1 = highest; Rank 61 = lowest score.

For the description of the results, we grouped the nine GLOBE scales (cf. House et al., 2004) in accordance with Kluckhohn and Strodtbeck's (1961) classification of value orientations: time orientation (Future Orientation), human–environment orientation (Uncertainty Avoidance), relational orientation (Power Distance, Gender Egalitarianism, Humane Orientation, Institutional Collectivism, In-Group Collectivism), and activity orientation (Performance Orientation, Assertiveness).

Time Orientation

The scale *Future Orientation* (axis FUT in Fig. 5.1) shows that the Austrian middle managers reported a medium level of perceived Future Orientation (4.46), whereas they expressed a preference for higher scores on the value dimension (5.11). However, compared to other countries Austria is positioned high on the "As Is" scale (Band A, Rank 6), yet relatively low on the "Should Be" scale (Band C, Rank 50).

The Austrian media data parallel the quantitative findings: 9 out of 13 text segments relating to this dimension give accounts of initiatives that target an actual or planned increase of Future Orientation. An example is the foundation of an agency for innovation that specializes in helping start-up companies by providing funds for the market entry of innovative new products, by bringing together investors and entrepreneurs, and by offering assistance with the structuring of the new organization.

Human–Environment Orientation

Figure 5.1 shows a high level of *Uncertainty Avoidance* (axis UNC) for the "As Is" scale (5.16) and a considerable gap to the "Should Be" scale (3.66). In addition, Austria's position relative to the other GLOBE countries is in the top group for the "As Is" results (Band A, Rank 6). This finding corresponds with Hofstede's (1980, 1993) research that placed Austria in the upper third country cluster (Uncertainty Avoidance score of 70) among 53 countries and regions. Concerning the "Should Be" scale, Austria ranks very low (Band D, Rank 57), meaning that the middle managers in the Austrian sample indicate a preference for an increase in flexibility and risk taking.

A high level of Uncertainty Avoidance is usually reflected in the desire to control one's environment, in high levels of standardization, in regulations and laws even for specific details, and in bureaucracy. Drastic examples that exist in Austria are the bureaucratic hurdles entrepreneurs usually face during the start-up of a company, or the necessity of people visiting Austria, including tourists, to register with the police within 48 hours after entering the country. It is interesting that the findings for *Uncertainty Avoidance* seem to somehow contradict those for *Future Orientation*. Whereas on the one hand initiatives such as starting one's own business are encouraged (high Future Orientation), the actual process is then very formalized (high Uncertainty Avoidance). The Austrian media data reflect these general observations: 12 out of 26 text segments concerning Uncertainty Avoidance present a picture of a somewhat slow and complicated bureaucratic process, illustrated by the first and second of the following quotes. However, the media data also provide some examples of active appeals to change the current situation, as the third quote shows:

Bureaucracy and mentality barriers are the largest handicaps for the economic site of Austria, revealed an opinion poll by the economic forum of executives. (Die Presse, December 12, 1996, p. 19)

Well, there is a problem I am struggling with: the omnipresent bureaucracy. It is really not easy for an entrepreneur in Austria. There are the authorities, red tape, licensing proceedings, requirements and so on. This paralysis, costs a lot of time and money. If the time, energy and money required by bureaucracy is too high, an enterprise is no longer competitive. That's the point. (Frank Stronach about his plans to establish Magna's European headquarters in Austria, his birth country; *Wirtschaftswoche,* December 5, 1996, p. 54)

Let us find the courage to not regulate everything, but rather let us find the courage for planned omission. (Statement by the President of the Austrian Lawyers Association; *Die Presse,* September 10, 1997, p. 6)

In addition to bureaucracy, manifestations of high Uncertainty Avoidance in Austria include for example:

- A comparison among the OECD (Organization for Economic Development and Cooperation) countries shows that the savings rate[14] for Austria is 26.0, as compared to the United States at 14.4 or Japan at 34.6. Within Europe only the Swiss show a higher rate (33.0). A low-interest, low-risk savings account (*Sparbuch*) is the traditional and common way for many Austrians to invest their money. Only recently have other and more risky forms of investment, such as stocks, become more popular.
- There are explicit laws regulating the workplace. Examples include the *Arbeitnehmerschutzgesetz* (law regulating working conditions), the *Arbeitszeitgesetz* (law setting working hours), the *Mutterschutzgesetz* (law protecting mothers-to-be and nursing mothers), and *Kollektivverträge* (collective agreements) negotiated between employers and unions at industry level. In addition, the *Unternehmensverfassung* (governance structure) defines, based on the type of organization (private vs. public), whose interests have to be represented in the decision-making bodies (management and supervisory boards) and what the procedures have to look like. Also, the rights given to the works councils are stated explicitly, as mentioned earlier.

Relational Orientation

The dimensions *Power Distance* (axis POW), *Gender Egalitarianism* (axis GEN), *Humane Orientation* (axis HUM), *Institutional Collectivism* (axis CO1), and *In-Group Collectivism* (axis CO2), all concern social relations: among people at different levels in the social hierarchy; among women and men, the poor/disadvantaged, and groups. In general, the data suggest a strong preference for *more democracy* in society: Whereas the perception represented in the "As Is" scales is one of inequality, the "Should Be" scales show that power should be distributed more equally ("As Is" 4.95, "Should Be" 2.44), women given more opportunity ("As Is" 3.09, "Should Be" 4.83), and the poor/disadvantaged provided with better support ("As Is" 3.72, "Should Be" 5.76). Only the two collectivism scales show small gaps between "As Is" (Institutional Collectivism: 4.30, In-Group Collectivism: 4.85) and "Should Be" (Institutional Collectivism: 4.73, In-Group Collectivism: 5.27), both reflecting a slightly collectivistic rather than individualistic orientation.

---

[14]Gross national income minus public and private consumption, in percentage of the gross domestic product. Statistics by the OECD, published in *Der Standard,* October 4, 1994.

A possible explanation for the wide gaps could be that political correctness and social desirability accounted for the results. Maybe the managers in our sample reported espoused rather than enacted values (cf. Argyris & Schön, 1978). In order to answer this question, we need to look at the dimensions in more detail and bring in additional findings from the qualitative part of the study.

Power Distance.   Hofstede (1980) reported a Power Distance score of 11 for Austria (ranking Austria as the country with the lowest score overall). The GLOBE data give Austria a medium score on the "As Is" scale (Score 4.95, Band B, Rank 44), and place Austria in a low group for the "Should Be" scale (Score 2.44, Band D, Rank 48). When the "As Is" and "Should Be" scales are taken together, our findings do not contradict Hofstede's earlier results. Low Power Distance also goes along with Trompenaars's (1993) findings concerning the reason for having an organizational structure. Respondents in this multicountry study were offered two alternative explanations:

> Option A: *"The main reason for having an organizational structure is so that everyone knows who has authority over whom."*
>
> Option B: *"The main reason for having an organizational structure is so that everyone knows how functions are allocated and coordinated."*

Austrian respondents opted for Option B by 94%, thus following a rational and coordinative logic of subordination, in contrast to looking at the organization as a legitimization for power differences.

However, the low level of *Power Distance* found in research is still puzzling Austrian scholars as well as Austrian students of cross-cultural management. Examples for and against the low level of Power Distance are usually produced without hesitation: On the one hand, *participation in decision making* is accepted and expected among Austrians; it is represented at the societal level in the social partnership model as well as at the organizational level through codetermination. On the other hand, Austrians are familiar with the importance of status symbols, in particular *titles*. Both participation in decision making and status symbols are believed to be indicators of a society's level of Power Distance, the former for a low level, the latter for a high level. How can such inconsistencies be explained? A possible explanation could be that societal changes take place over time and what we observe today might be artifacts of the past. During the monarchy ranks and titles were *awarded* by the Emperor. Those awarded a title most likely felt very proud and displayed the new title as an extended and audible symbol of the recognition given to them. Examples can still be found in the older parts of Austrian cemeteries, where titles such as "k.u.k. Hofbäckermeister"[15] are listed on gravestones. Also, traditional store owners still display these titles in their logos. More than 80 years after the end of the monarchy, titles in recognition of seniority and status (*Amtstitel*, e.g., *Hofrat*) are still awarded in public institutions, to the amusement of other parts of the population (Corti, 1994, p. 135). However, times are changing. The younger generation, in particular, do not honor titles as much nowadays. Also, the majority of today's titles are no longer *awarded,* but *achieved,* especially in the form of academic degrees. Whereas with the older generation achieved titles are treated similarly to awarded ones, titles do not have the traditional connotations for the younger generation as they had earlier. In more general terms, a

---

[15]The term stands for *kaiserlich and königlicher Hofbäckermeister,* which in translation means "the exclusive baker to the Austro-Hungarian Emperor's Court."

change might have taken place from *status by ascription* to *status by achievement* (Trompenaars, 1993); that is, it is today a person's own achievement that accounts for a high status rather than one's affiliation with a particular group.

Gender Egalitarianism. Austrian women account for 64.1% of the official labor force, mainly in sales, agriculture, and unskilled manufacturing. Whereas only 4.2% of all employed men work part-time, women constitute 28.8% (Bundespressedienst, 2000). Women have held about 10% of Federal Assembly seats in recent years, with more than twice as many serving in provincial government (Banks et al., 1997, p. 52). These numbers support the low level of Gender Egalitarianism found in the quantitative "As Is" data (Score 3.09, Band B, Rank 45). Similar to Power Distance, a wide gap exists between the "As Is" and the "Should Be" data (Score 4.83, Band A, Rank 18). The GLOBE "As Is" data show the same tendency as Hofstede's (1980, 1993) Masculinity scale, although less pronounced. This earlier research had placed Austria in the upper third country cluster (score of 79) among 53 countries and regions.

In recent years, gender-related topics have been hot issues on the public agenda. In 1997, a referendum[16] was held for more rights for women (*"Frauenvolksbegehren"*). It was initiated by a committee of women, including politicians, artists, and journalists, who claimed the right for women to 50% of the public influence, power, and money. The referendum was successful: It received 645,000 votes. However, from today's (2006) perspective, it has to be said that despite the referendum's success, hardly any of its claims have been put into practice by supporting legislation.

Participant observation confirms that there is much *talk* about equal chances for women. However, practices often show a different picture. The following example illustrates this point. One of the few female Austrian university professors is quoted as saying at a conference on gender equality at Johannes Kepler University in 1997: "We've done a wonderful job in training our male colleagues. They have become experts on gender-neutral language. Unfortunately, their behavior has not changed a single centimeter."

All data considered, one might assume that what our (predominantly male) respondents ($N = 68$) articulated in the questionnaires is likely to be *espoused* rather than *enacted* values. The female sample is too small to conduct a comparative empirical analysis, but a comparison of the mean scores gives a rough impression. The mean score of the 10 female respondents is 3.52 for the "As Is" scale (male sample: 3.02), and 5.40 for the "Should Be" scale (male sample: 4.74). Thus, although we might find some lip service on behalf of the male respondents, the female managers opt for even higher levels of gender equality.

Humane Orientation. This dimension shows similar patterns to Gender Egalitarianism, namely a medium level for the "As Is" scale (Score 3.72, Band C, Rank 46), and a very high one for the "Should Be" scale (5.76, Band: A, Rank: 4). Similar to Gender Egalitarianism, there is a lot of public and private discourse considering humane issues. A good example is the treatment of refugees. In the past, the official Austria as well as individual citizens often helped beyond the call of duty, for example, during the Hungarian crisis in 1956 (when 152,000 refugees came to Austria). The opening of the borders to the former communist neighboring countries and the civil war in the former Yugoslavia has recently brought refugees to Austria once again. This time, however, there is increasing resentment against the

---

[16]A referendum is a form of direct democracy anchored in the Austrian Constitution. If a referendum exceeds more than 100,000 votes, it has to be dealt with in the Federal Parliament.

(temporary) newcomers, which goes along with changes in legislation that make it more difficult for refugees to attain political asylum.[17]

Espoused values concerning Humane Orientation are usually numerous in preelection times. The following quotes are taken from media reports on campaigns for provincial elections: "Fighting unemployment, homelessness, and poverty is our primary goal" (People's Party); "In addition to ecology, women and humanitarian issues are the main topics on our agenda" (Green Party); "No one should be discriminated against because of a disability" (Social Democratic Party). Thus, there are proclamations for Humane Orientation, yet enacted values often show the contrary. The media even provide a pattern of *decreasing* solidarity:

- "It is increasingly difficult to get active support for foreigners in need" *(Die Presse, December 10, 1996, p. 2)*.
- Another headline says: "We are unable to cope. The state tends to look away and leave charity assistance to private organizations such as Caritas [Caritas is a private charity with close links to the Catholic Church]" *(Die Presse, September 11, 1997, p. 11)*. In the article itself, the director of Caritas warns readers about the "privatization" of distress and about the increasing economization of all areas, which leads to a "loss of humanity."

Collectivism. The two dimensions *Institutional Collectivism and In-Group Collectivism* show corresponding results. In both cases the "Should Be" scales (Institutional Collectivism 4.73, In-Group Collectivism 5.27) are slightly higher than the "As Is" scales (Institutional Collectivism 4.30, In-Group Collectivism 4.85). Hofstede (1980, 1993) also positioned Austria on the more collectivistic side of the individualism–collectivism continuum (score of 55).

Collectivistic societies are characterized by an economic system that is designed to maximize collective interests. The Austrian model of social partnership fits with this concept. Citizens of collectivistic societies also take pride in being members of their society and it matters to them that their country is viewed positively by people of other societies. Wodak et al. (1998) conducted an extensive discourse analysis concerning national identity. They located distinct national pride and patriotism in Austria: *"Preferred objects of national pride are the Austrian landscape, political, social and ecological achievements, political security, cultural and scientific achievements, victories in sport, and national symbols like the anthem and the Austrian flag"* (p. 345).

Traditionally, there have been long-lasting employer–employee relationships in Austria. It is not uncommon for someone to begin work for a company as an apprentice and then retire from the very same company. A curriculum vitae indicating a number of different employers is still looked on with suspicion. Unlike countries such as the United States where a change of workplace indicates flexibility, Austrians accentuate loyalty, although the situation is slowly beginning to change.

---

[17]The number of refugees seeking asylum in Austria went down from 27,306 in 1991 to a mere 6,719 in 1997. It increased again in the following years, mainly because of large numbers of refugees from former Yugoslavia (Statistisches Jahrbuch Österreichs, 2006). However, Amnesty International Österreich (2001) criticizes the restricted asylum policy of Austria, with only one third of all applications being accepted, often only after a very lengthy process.

Moving from the workplace to the families, pride exists at this level, too. In a representative survey among the Austrian population,[18] 60% of respondents stated that family and children are very important for them. A typical Austrian manifestation of family ties is the *Sonntagsausflug:* Parents and their children, frequently accompanied by grandparents or other family members, use Sundays to make an outing to the countryside, hike or go for a walk, and have lunch or dinner together. Adolescents often dislike this tradition, but it is a "must" in many Austrian families.

The fact that the "Should Be" scales are higher than the "As Is" scales, meaning more collectivism is preferred, is interesting: According to Triandis (1994), modern and complex societies become increasingly individualistic; Hofstede and Bond (1988) note that individualism follows economic success. Both factors apply for Austria, yet the trend at the individualism–collectivism dimension points to the opposite direction. What shows in our data might be the fear of loss of even more of the collectivistic values and therefore the respondents expressed heightened awareness to keep what is left.

Activity Orientation

The Austrian results show a high level of *Performance Orientation* (axis PER) at the "As Is" scale (Score 4.44, Band A, Rank 14) and an even higher level at the "Should Be" scale (Score 6.10, Band B, Rank 21). This comes as a surprise, because other studies (e.g., Trompenaars, 1993; Zander, 1997) do not report on similarly high levels of Performance Orientation for Austria. An indicator of a society's orientation to performance and achievement is *entrepreneurship*. We described earlier that some initiatives exist to support company start-ups, whereas bureaucracy clearly provides major barriers. Dana (1992, p. 126) concluded that although innovative entrepreneurship has occurred in Austria, for example, the invention of modern skis, one cannot describe the Austrian society as extremely entrepreneurial. Moreover, entrepreneurship is not as highly *valued* in Austria as in many other countries. One might add that conditions in Austria have indeed never been very favorable for entrepreneurs and inventors. What is commonly known as the *österreichisches Erfinderschicksal* (Austrian inventors' fate) stands for the fact that in the past inventors were usually not given credit for their work while still alive; many of Austria's most remarkable inventors died in poverty.

However, recent developments in business organizations indicate a trend toward more Performance Orientation, in particular in the form of new incentive systems and performance-based pay structures. They are already common for Austrians working for multinational companies and are becoming increasingly popular in Austrian businesses as well.

Finally, the dimension *Assertiveness* (axis ASR) shows for Austria a relatively high score on the "As Is" scale (Score 4.62, Band A, Rank 6), yet a very low score on the "Should Be" scale (Score 2.81, Band C, Rank 60). Assertiveness was a part of Hofstede's (1980) Masculinity index, where Austria also ranked very high (score of 79). It is treated as a separate dimension by the GLOBE study. The low level of "Should Be" Assertiveness might hint at a possible trend toward a more egalitarian society, as was discussed in the section concerning relational orientation.

---

[18]The survey was conducted in 1994 and published in *Der Standard*, December 19, 1994, p. 5.

TABLE 5.5
Translating the Terms Leader and Follower into German

German Term	Closest English Translation	Frequency	Percent
Manager	Manager	114	84
Führungskraft	Person in a leading position	19	14
Führer	Leader	3	2
Mitarbeiter	Coworkers	99	86
Arbeitnehmer	Employees	14	12
Bedienstete	Employed persons	2	2
Untergebene	Subordinates	0	0

Leadership

A chapter on *leadership* and *leaders* in a German-speaking country would not be complete without a discussion on the translation of these two terms into German. The direct translation of the English word *leader* into German is *Führer*. It carries a heavy weight because it refers to Hitler and Nazi Germany. The word root *"führ"* is present in Austrian German but the noun *Führer* is cut out of the language, in particular when referring to an individual. Words including *Führung* (leadership), however, are frequently used, for example, *Führungsstil* (leadership style), *Führungskultur* (leadership culture), *Führungsteam* (managerial team); and so are words including *Führer* when referring to *organizations,* for example, *Marktführer* (market leader) or *Branchenführer* (industry leader).

The stigmatization of the term *Führer* opens a gap for alternative terms. The questions then are: (a) Which terms do people use when they talk about leaders, (b) do these terms bear the same or similar connotations as in English, and (c) is there a difference between the English *manager* and *leader*? An analysis of our two *media* samples provided the terms listed in the upper part of Table 5.5.

The media data might present a slightly distorted distribution of language use, because they mostly talk about top managers. Our interviewees, for instance, used the term *Führungskraft* much more frequently than the media analysis suggests. However, both data types suggest that the gap left by the stigmatization of the term *Führer* is filled with the two terms *Manager* and *Führungskraft*. Is there a difference in concept between a *Manager* and a *Führungskraft*? This question was asked to the focus group participants and the five managers with whom we conducted semistructured interviews. Their answers do not provide a clear picture: Some of the interviewees matched "task orientation" with the *Manager* and "leading people" with the *Führungskraft;* others considered the two terms to be synonymous. Among those to whom the terms differed there was no consensus as to whether an outstanding *Führungskraft* had to be a good *Manager* at the same time. Some considered *Führungskraft* the overarching concept, whereas others assumed that an outstanding *Führungskraft* did not necessarily have to be professionally competent at the same time. Some concluded that an outstanding *Führungskraft* is needed in exceptional situations only and a competent *Manager* is required to run daily operations (cf. Appendix B for the different definitions of outstanding leadership).

Similar translation difficulties as those found with leader occurred for the English term *follower.* The direct translation into German is *Geführte,* again, a word hardly ever used by the media or our interview partners. The term *Mitarbeiter* is the one word most frequently

TABLE 5.6
Leadership Factors and Subscales

Second-Order Leadership Scales First-Order Subscales	Score	Band	Rank Between Countries	Rank Within Country[a]
Participative leadership	**6.00**	A	**3**	**2**
Nonparticipative (reverse scored)	*2.11*		*55*	*(3)*
Autocratic (reverse scored)	*1.90*		*60*	*(1)*
Autonomous leadership	**4.47**	A	**6**	**5**
Autonomous	*4.47*		*7*	*13*
Charismatic leadership	**6.02**	B	**12**	**1**
Integrity	*6.46*		*9*	*1*
Inspirational	*6.34*		*13*	*2*
Performance Orientation	*6.23*		*15*	*4*
Visionary	*6.13*		*29*	*6*
Decisive	*5.96*		*24*	*7*
Self-sacrificial	*5.03*		*29*	*10*
Team Oriented leadership	**5.74**	B	**38**	**3**
Diplomatic	*5.43*		*36*	*3*
Team Integrator	*5.34*		*42*	*5*
Administratively Competent	*5.80*		*32*	*8*
Collaborative Team Oriented	*5.67*		*46*	*9*
Malevolent (reverse scored)	*1.54*		*55*	*(4)*
Humane leadership	**4.93**	B	**28**	**4**
Humane	*4.80*		*30*	*11*
Modesty	*5.05*		*30*	*12*
Self-protective leadership	**3.07**	F	**49**	**6**
Status-Conscious	*3.86*		*43*	*14*
Conflict Inducer	*3.57*		*49*	*15*
Procedural	*3.36*		*51*	*16*
Face Saver	*2.56*		*40*	*18*
Self-centered	*1.99*		*40*	*20*

Note.   Score: Country mean for Austria on the basis of aggregated scale scores. *Band*: Letters A to D indicate the country band Austria belongs to (A > B > C > D). Countries from different bands are considered to differ significantly from each other (GLOBE test banding procedure, cf. Hanges, Dickson, & Sipe, 2004). *Rank*: Austria's position relative to the 61 countries in the GLOBE study; Rank 1 = highest; Rank 61 = lowest score.
[a]A scale's score position compared to the other scales on the same level.

used; the media as well as the interview data suggest that this is the correct word to address followers in a business context. In the past, employees were frequently called *Untergebene* (subordinates), a term that is not common any more. The lower part of Table 5.5 shows the frequency of language use in the two media samples.

Questionnaire-Based Data Collection

Table 5.6 gives an overview of the six second-order leadership factors and their corresponding 21 first-order subscales. They are based on an overall 112 leadership items that were ranked by the middle managers in our sample ($N = 169$) on a scale between 1 (attribute greatly inhibits a person from being an outstanding leader) and 7 (attribute contributes greatly to a person being an outstanding leader). Data were collected in two industries, namely food processing and financial services. However, comparative analyses did not reveal any major differences in the managers' responses (for a discussion of the industry-level results, see Brodbeck, Hanges, Dickson, Gupta, & Dorfman, 2004).

Among the contributing second-order leadership factors (Mean > 4.5) are *Charismatic* (6.02), *Participative* (6.00), *Team Oriented* (5.74) and *Humane Leadership* (4.93). These four factors include four facets of leadership, namely personality (e.g., integrity), cognitive skills (e.g., administratively competent), leadership style (e.g., participative), and concern for the team (e.g., team integrator). This suggests that the managers in the Austrian sample view leadership as a holistic concept, and do not, for instance, focus exclusively on personality or leadership behavior. Compared to many other countries in the GLOBE study, it is in particular the scale *Participative leadership* that stands out (Band A, Country Rank 3). These findings are in line with the relatively low power distance scores we found earlier in the discussion of societal culture, and also with the results of research based on the Vroom–Yetton (1973) model for managerial decision making.[19] The model has recently been employed to compare leadership styles between seven European countries (Reber, Jago, Auer-Rizzi, & Szabo, 2000), between Polish, Austrian, and U.S. managers specifically (Maczynski, Jago, Reber, & Böhnisch, 1994), and of country samples over time (Reber & Jago, 1997). The studies consistently show Austria as very participative, similar to its neighbor countries Germany and Switzerland (Brodbeck et al., 2000; Szabo, Reber, Weibler, Brodbeck, & Wunderer, 2001), and significantly different from Finland, France, the Czech Republic, Poland, Turkey, and the United States.

Autonomous leadership is neither clearly contributing to nor clearly hindering from outstanding leadership (4.47). However, Austria ranks higher on this dimension than most other countries (Band A, Country Rank 6).

Self-protective leadership is the one clearly inhibiting second-order leadership factor (3.07). This holds true in absolute as well as relative terms (Band F, Country Rank 49). The five scales comprising self-protective leadership suggest consistency with the contributing factors mentioned previously: A *self-centered* person would not be *open for participation* but would rather act *autocratically,* and *face saving* would inhibit the open discussion of problems and conflicts that participative interactions require.

Media Analysis

Table 5.7 gives an overview of the most frequency occurring leadership categories in the two Austrian media samples. Most of the categories concern person-specific characteristics, whereas two categories relate to leader–follower relations, in most cases in the specific form of negotiations between employers and works councils. The categories give a hint as to the areas of media focus. Much is said about the leaders themselves and the role they play in the organization and the outer environment. However, little is said about how leaders actually relate to and interact with their followers on a daily basis.

---

[19]The Vroom–Yetton (1973) model is based on a problem set containing 30 decision-making situations, which are administered to managers who are unfamiliar with the model at the time of data collection. Respondents are asked to choose their behavioral responses to each of the 30 situations; their answers are from a set of five alternative strategies (ranging from highly autocratic to highly participative). The model also consists of seven diagnostic questions that help the manager to understand the situational characteristics of a decision-making situation. Finally, the model comprises behavioral rules. The application of these rules calls for the exclusion of certain strategies and thereby assures decision quality and decision acceptance.

TABLE 5.7
Leader Descriptions in the Media

Leadership Categories	Person-Specific Characteristics	Leader-Follower Relation	Frequency: Articles/Segments[a]	Ranked by No. of Articles	Austria's Score on Leadership Scales	Ranked by Scale Score[b]
Decisive	x		37/70	1	5.95	7
Integrity	x		28/47	2	6.46	1
Negotiations and conflict solving at the org. level		x	24/45	3	no equivalent	
Visionary	x		21/37	4	6.13	6
Technical/factual competence	x		20/43	5	no equivalent	
Working as a team/ team integrator		x	15/24	6	6.14	5
Performance oriented	x		12/18	7	6.23	4
Social competence	x		12/18	7	no equivalent	

Note. The table includes only the leadership categories most frequently mentioned in the media.
[a]Frequency refers to the number of articles (initial sample and validation sample taken together) and text segments in which a particular category occurred. [b]Scale Rank is taken from Table 5.6.

Table 5.7 allows for a comparison between the media data and the questionnaire-based data. It ranks the frequency of categories retrieved from the media and the means of the corresponding leadership scales. The rankings show that the most frequently mentioned media categories are at the same time among the top seven leadership scales. It follows that what is considered highly contributing to outstanding leadership in the questionnaires also finds a high representation in the media.

Because the media texts concerned all types of leaders, we checked for possible differences between *business* and other types of leaders: Most findings were in accordance. The only major difference was that *integrity* was significantly more often mentioned in a *political* than a *business* context. Recent scandals in different political parties may explain the wish/request for more integrity as part of political leadership.

Interview Analysis

In contrast to the media data, the interview data provide more insights into the daily interactions between managers and their employees. Table 5.8 gives an overview of how the interviewees described the leader as a person: Descriptions of *specific* personality traits are rare. Rather, more general descriptions are the norm, ranging from the possession of *integrity* and *personality* (without going into more detail) to the necessity of the leader to serve as a *role model* and possess *social competence*. Another theme related to the individual concerns the *managerial* side of behavior, namely *technical/factual competence* as a prerequisite for success. However, there was no consensus among the interviewees whether this type of competence really contributed to a good leader. This finding parallels the initial description of the diffuse difference between *Führungskraft* and *Manager.*

TABLE 5.8
Person-Specific Characteristics in the Interviews

Categories[a]	N of Interviewees[b]	Consent[c]	Content of Shared Versus Differing Opinion(s)
Technical and factual competence	7	No	Competence required vs. not necessarily; broad knowledge vs. expert knowledge.
Integrity	6	Yes	Essential set of values, includes honesty, trustworthiness, ethical behavior.
Personality (unspecified)	6	Yes	Considered essential.
Role model	5	Yes	Values and behavior of leader influence followers, in the positive as well as negative sense.
Social competence	5	Yes	An absolute must for successful leadership; includes the ability to solve conflicts and the knowledge of employees' problems.

[a]Topics mentioned by five or more interviewees. [b]Refers to the number of interviewees who mentioned a particular category. [c]Consent: Yes = the interviewees had similar opinions concerning a category; No = the interviewees were of differing opinions.

The leader–follower relationship was what the interviewees talked about in great detail (compare Table 5.9). This may have to do with the format of the interviews, because we had asked for events of successful versus unsuccessful leadership.

The different categories tie into one another and include *orientation to people* as well as *task orientation,* with *communication* being the "vehicle" and *trust* and *respect* being the underlying prerequisites. Whereas *decisions* are preferably made as a team, the leader is expected to *coordinate* and *supervise* the work. It is interesting how well these results (derived from interviews with managers) fit with Zander's (1997)[20] profile of Austrian employees' preferences regarding interpersonal leadership (derived from questionnaires):

> The employees in Austria prefer their managers to communicate with them more frequently and they are not as uninterested in personal communication as the employees in the Germanic-Latin-Japanese cluster. In addition, the employees in Austria also prefer that their managers supervise, review and make them proud of their work more frequently than the employees in the countries in the [Germanic-Latin-Japanese cluster]. This preferred profile of [interpersonal leadership] is nicknamed "communicative directing." (Zander, 1997, p. 289)

4.   PATTERNS IN AUSTRIAN BUSINESS LEADERSHIP

In this section, we are going to integrate the findings from the different sources concerning leaders and leadership obtained so far: questionnaire-based data, media analysis, and

---

[20]This study explores how employees in 18 countries prefer to be managed (named *license to lead*), and whether culture affects their preferences.

TABLE 5.9
Leader–Follower Relations in the Interviews

Categories[a]	N of Interviewees[b]	Consent[c]	Content of Shared Versus Differing Opinion(s)
Communication	10	Yes	Frequent communication is necessary and helpful, requires a small group size.
Handling problems	10	Yes	The leader should initiate the solving of task specific problems (supervision, followed by coordination) as well as personal problems (by using social competence).
Decision making	9	No	The more participation, the better vs. autocratic behavior would sometimes be more efficient, but will most likely not be accepted by employees.
Motivation	9	Yes	Leader should motivate employees, give support.
Goal setting, planning, supervision at work	8	Yes	This function is with the leader, not the team.
Respect	6	Yes	Leader should respect followers.
Trust	6	Yes	Trust in followers is essential (is a requirement for the "long leash" concept, innovations); has to be enacted and not just talked about (role model).
Coordination of a team	5	Yes	The leader is the process agent of the team.
Room for action (long leash)	5	Yes	Supervision is important, but within the given boundaries employees should be allowed to do their work quite independently.

[a]Topics mentioned by five or more interviewees. [b]Refers to the number of interviewees who mentioned a particular category. [c]Consent: Yes = the interviewees had similar opinions concerning a category; No = the interviewees were of differing opinions.

interview data. To start with, if there were a prototypical type of Austrian business leader, what would such a person look like?

Characteristics of a Leader

Demographics. In terms of demographic characteristics, the person would most likely be male (as suggested by the findings concerning Gender Egalitarianism at the societal practices level) and of middle age (as suggested by the media and also reflected in our sample of middle managers itself), although both gender and age are contingent on the industry (the primary and secondary sectors are traditionally male dominated, whereas the services sector allows for better chances of women) and the level within the organizational hierarchy (the higher up in the ranks, the fewer women).

Education.   As for education, this person's curriculum vitae would likely provide for a sound education and possibly a university degree. However, there is a shift in focus. According to media and interviews, continuing training is becoming increasingly important. But whereas until about 20 years ago the *area of concentration* was not extremely important (there are, e.g., many lawyers among Austrian business leaders) and Tannenbaum et al. (1974) concluded that "Austria lacks training facilities for managers," the focus today is on business studies. A large number of public and private training programs supplement university education. Most management training occurs in the area of technical/factual competence, whereas less consideration is given to personality development and social competence. An analysis of course offerings for "more success in business" (based on our media samples) confirms this pattern: About 70% of all offered courses focus on the person (about 50% of the courses aim at an increase in the manager's competence through technical/factual knowledge; 20% concern personality factors and behavior), whereas only 30% aim at an improvement of the manager–employees interaction. Is the basic assumption then that a leader is "born" as compared to "trained/educated?" According to the data, a leader is required *personality* (as was stressed in the interviews), in particular *integrity* and *trustworthiness* (as questionnaire-based data and media data indicate). *Vision, decisiveness,* and *social competence* also seem to be important. Let us look at these attributes in a little more detail before we come back to the question concerning "born versus "trained/educated" leaders.

Integrity.   Integrity is the characteristic scoring the highest in the questionnaire-based data. It was also mentioned as a preferred leader attribute in 30% of all media articles describing leader characteristics, as well as by 6 of our 10 interviewees. The relevance of integrity shows in particular in leader–follower relations and in references to negotiations. The term *"eine Person mit Handschlagqualitäten"* ("a person with handshake qualities") refers to the symbolic act of finalizing a deal by shaking hands and then sticking to the agreement. The following quote from the media provides a good example: *"They both have an extremely polite and extremely pleasant way of dealing with people, they are exceedingly correct and reliable. They are just the way business partners should be"* (quote from a portrait of the two "managers of the year"; *Wirtschaftswoche,* December 1996, p. 40).

Having said that, the interview and focus group data also suggest that there are not too many leaders in Austrian business, let alone in politics, who indeed possess personality and integrity. Focus group discussants had problems naming suitable contemporary leaders; concerning politics, the men founding the Second Republic after World War II were attributed integrity, whereas today's politicians are not as well respected.

Vision.   Vision, according to the questionnaire-based data, is another highly favorable leader attribute. Along the same lines, discussants of both our focus groups and part of our interviewees (implicitly) included vision into their definitions of outstanding leadership (cf. Appendix B). Also, most of the success stories in the media contain one or the other aspect of visionary thinking. Vision is described as a characteristic that someone possesses or does not; there are no references that visionary thinking could be trained in any way. Interestingly enough, however, none of the real-life examples described by our interviewees was labeled as visionary, not by the interviewees themselves or by us, the researchers, when we sorted the text segments into categories. The media data indicate that there are three kinds of barriers that hinder Austrian leaders from being visionary or prevent the translation of a leader's vision into deeds:

- The high level of *Uncertainty Avoidance* found at the societal level: A substantial majority of Austrian business leaders seem to be plagued by a fear of new situations: *"'A strong fear of anything new'—for more than one third of 1000 managers questioned by Fessel+Gfk on behalf of the economic forum of executives (WdF) this is the main reason why there are so few Austrian enterprises with international business relations"* (*Die Presse,* December 12, 1996, p. 19).
- The general assumption that leaders must be *realistic:* The data suggest that being visionary and being realistic are two extremes of the same dimension. If someone is realistic, the thinking is, she or he is probably lacking vision. This pattern was first detected in the initial media sample and later confirmed in the validation sample. It is illustrated in the following two quotes: *"It is my task to find practicable solutions. This has nothing to do with a lack of creativity"* (statement by a political leader; *Profil,* December 9, 1996, p. 28); and *"[He lacks] visionary imagination. He is a mere administrator of the city budget, unable to set clear, forward-looking major points of emphasis"* (Criticism aimed at the political leader quoted previously; *Profil,* December 9, 1996, p. 29).
- *Organizational structures,* which might not be adequate for and supportive of the leader's vision, and/or *followers* who might not go along: "The regulations set by Minister E. are boycotted by a xenophobic bureaucracy" (*Der Standard,* December 12, 1996, p. 5).

To summarize, visionary thinking seems to be an ideal in Austria, according to the questionnaire-based data more so than other attributes, yet there is a wide gap between the "Should Be" and the "As Is." In other words, visionary thinking is considered an important ingredient of outstanding leaders, yet only few of them fit the ideal, for either personal reasons or constraints posed by the environment.

Decisiveness.   This is yet another characteristic for which consistency between the media and the quantitative results was found. In the media sample, leaders were often characterized as being dynamic, determined, and making decisions and defending them. The media sample also included a couple of course offerings to gain more decisiveness, among them a workshop specifically for women. Our interviewees, on the other hand, did not *explicitly* define decisiveness as prerequisite for good leadership. Their *examples,* however, indicate that the attribute is desired and that real-life cases also exist:

> *I think it's crucial that the leader of such a project is very, very convinced of the project from the very beginning. Maybe even more than the team members who work on the project with great enthusiasm. If this is the case the leader also endures criticisms and opposition from the outside.*

> *We [solved the problem of the unbalanced cash account] within two days, together with the teller, the area coordinator, and the branch manager. You don't "fiddle around" at different hierarchical levels, you do it directly. You have to solve it and that's what we did.*

Social Competence.   With Austrian society placing heavy weight on the family and the economy, characterized by small to medium-size companies often owned and run by families, it is no surprise that the data frequently refers to existing or hypothetical family ties; one of the media articles, for instance, described the relationship of fellow business leaders "as if they were brothers." Along the same lines, our interviewees also stressed trust, reliability, and support, that is, attributes very similar to the ones described for actual family relations, and used these concepts in their stories of good leadership, as the following quote by one interviewed manager shows:

> *There was our senior boss, the late Engineer S. He possessed personality and technical skills, but you also could come to see him when you had private problems, and he sat down with you and said, "Listen, it's gonna be all right." He supported us in whatever way he could. S. really motivated us.*

Let us now return to the initial question concerning "born" versus "trained/educated" leaders. It seems from the data that the basic assumption is that leaders are "born." Decisiveness and social competence are the attributes one can learn to a certain extent; the other factors (integrity and vision), however, are considered to be within the person and therefore have no connection to education and training.

Preferred Leadership Behavior

After this exploration of what a prototypical business leader in Austria could look like, the follow-on questions would of course concern likely leader–followers relations: How could the leadership style be described? How are decisions made?

Decision Making.   The questionnaire-based results suggest which style Austrians are definitely not in favor of, namely an autocratic style. Likewise, the autocratic style was the one style repeatedly described in the media as being rated negatively by followers and having negative consequences for the climate of the group, as the following quote shows: *"Since Mr. H. put this man in charge in 1991, the internal climate has steadily worsened. He won't have any argument; everything is dictated from the top"* (statement by a member of the Freedom Party; *Profil,* December 9, 1996, p. 40).

The interviewees talked about different styles they preferred and also exercised. Among them were the democratic, the participative, and the collegial style. The latter style was described with possible downsides, as the following quote by a middle manager shows: *"When the collegial leadership style is concerned, it's sometimes a bit difficult, so to say, to come up with a peremptory order and to say, 'Friends, OK, from now on we'll do things differently.' But I'm still convinced that this style is the better one."*

The interviewees used different terms, but what these terms have in common is a focus on democratic relations. From the interviews and other research we know that traditionally leadership in Austria was often paternalistic, sometimes autocratic. Today, however, more cooperative ways to lead are in favor, at least at the level of espoused values. The German term *Mitarbeiter* (coworker) is another indicator, as was already suggested earlier. The trend goes along with the societal shift toward more democracy as described in the section about societal culture.

Our findings fit well with the findings for Austria in the Vroom–Yetton (1973) studies, as mentioned before. Interpreting detailed findings, Maczynski et al. (1994) suggest the following reasons why Austrian managers prefer participative strategies:

1. Austrian managers seem to use participation to bring *greater information* and *different perspectives* to bear on the substantive problems they face; they are tapping subordinate "resources" for what they believe will be a benefit to the organization.

2. Austrian managers typically respond to *conflict* among subordinates by becoming more participative; thus, they seem to assume that participation provides the opportunity for a conflict to be expressed and resolved.[21]

That the *group* is seen as a forum that allows for conflict resolution shows in the GLOBE data as well. The item "intragroup conflict avoider" in the leader attributes questionnaire was rated as hindering a person from being an outstanding leader (Mean = 2.05). Why is conflict not considered negative in Austria? The German word *Streitkultur* (culture/norms stating how to handle disagreement/conflict to reach a positive result) comes to mind. Conflict is not a threat to the leader or the group and there is confidence that it will not escalate, but be solved in a cultivated manner. The leader plays a significant role here, because, as the interview data shows, it is the leader who is responsible for initiating and coordinating problem solving.

Is there more to be learned about participation? Participation seems to be contingent on the type of decision and this pattern of "contingent" participation shows in the interviews as well as in the media:

1. Whenever followers are *directly* affected by a decision they want to be involved in all relevant aspects of the decision-making process; if this does not happen, conflict/frustration is the consequence.
2. If *group internal* matters are concerned but the leader interferes, problems may arise as well.
3. Certain topics, in most cases strategic decisions, seem to be considered in the *sole discretion* of management. The characteristic decisive was often mentioned in this context.

Supervision. This type of behavior was part of neither the questionnaire-based data collection nor the media data. However, it came up repeatedly in the interview data. For the majority of the interviewees, it seemed to be an integral part of their managerial role. The degree of supervisory behavior differed from story to story and from interviewee to interviewee, but it was there in any case. One interviewee called it "leading on the long leash." This metaphor refers to a person walking a dog on the leash. A long leash gives the dog some freedom and space to explore its environment, but obviously only within a certain radius. Applied to the work life, a "long leash" means giving the employees space to come up with their own ideas and solutions. It does not mean, however, to let them work without any control, as the following quote by an interviewee shows: *"The long leash to me does not mean that I lean back as a leader and just watch what's gonna happen"*.

The overall process, from planning to results, is steered and coordinated by the leader, although allowing some input from the employees. In other words, although employees are supposed to work relatively independently, coordination and control seem still necessary, but with a benevolent touch: Mistakes on behalf of the employees can occur and then it is the leader's role to steer toward the right direction again.

Likewise, the degree to which employees participate in the process also varies and ranges from hierarchical control behavior on the one hand, to a common effort of manager *and* team

---

[21]The Austrian managers' behavior is in contrast to French, Finnish, U.S., Polish, and Czech managers, who become more autocratic when conflict is likely to arise among subordinates (Maczynski et al., 1994; Reber et al., 2000).

on the other. Responsibility for the outcome was in all cases described as the individual responsibility of the leader, never as the group's responsibility. Because the leaders are personally held responsible for the projects/tasks that are undertaken by their group, the basic assumption probably is that they better control the process, in their own and the group's interest. Supervision in this form then is no contradiction to participation and to low Power Distance as found at the societal level, because it is part of the managerial role and not a means to exercise power.

Communication Style.   As the interview data show, communication is one of the functions considered highly important by the interviewees, most of them in leading positions themselves: "[An open conversation] allows you to bring an argument to the open, so to say, I can fight the argument or come up with better ones myself." Or, *"We have these weekly talks, where we say, OK, what have we accomplished, where do we stand, what are we going to do next week?"* And, *"If people never come and say, I would like to know about this or that, or, could we talk about this, it's an extremely bad sign."*

In addition to that described previously, Zander (1997) found that Austrian employees prefer their managers to communicate with them *frequently* and show interest in *personal* communication. Thus, the focus on communication exists on both sides: It is stressed by superiors as well as expected by subordinates. The Vroom–Yetton (1973) studies confirm this pattern. The data show that Austrian managers, along with Germans and Swiss, have a stronger preference for CII (consulting with the group) and GII (group decision) strategies compared to the other countries in the study. And even when the normative model does not recommend the GII group strategy, as is the case when organizational goals are not shared by the group (goal congruence rule), Austrian managers still have a high tendency to go for GII (Reber et al., 2000). Staying within the framework of the Vroom–Yetton model, one may argue that Austrian managers seem to assume that by bringing the group together they might be able to convince them of the goals to share. Coming together as a group and talking things over might also be such a habit for the participants that it overwrites the question whether in a particular case a group discussion makes sense at all.

Consensus Orientation.   Communication patterns as described previously serve as a basis for this final pattern that emerged from the data. A saying in Austria is *"Durch's Reden kommen d'Leut zsamm"* (talking brings people together; meaning communication solves problems). In this sense, the pattern described in the following has to do with negotiating and problem solving. The questionnaires included a couple of items that tackle these matters. The Austrian respondents rated these items as contributing greatly to a person being an outstanding leader: diplomatic (6.43), worldly (6.11), win/win problem solver (6.22), and effective bargainer (6.34).

But what do consensus-oriented negotiations "made in Austria" actually look like? The following two summaries are examples as found repeatedly in the media:

- The *Vienna Philharmonic Orchestra* was described as having a dispute with the director of the prestigious *Salzburg Music Festival*. The musicians threatened not to participate in the festival. The dispute was covered extensively by the media. The musicians were described as clever negotiators, the festival director as having brought himself into a weak bargaining position. Politicians stepped in and took part in the negotiations. Finally, the festival director gave in and the orchestra was ready to play. The papers cited both sides as being satisfied: the musicians because all their conditions were met, the festival director and the politicians because the result was "in the best interest of Austria" (*Die Presse,* December 10, 1996, p. 21).

- The members of the supervisory board of Bank Austria met to give their approval to place a take over offer for the CA, another large Austrian bank, which was to be privatized. The general director brought the topic to the agenda; the board followed his advice by a majority vote. One board member abstained from voting. The majority of the board members was described as being affiliated with the Social Democratic Party; the president of the Vienna Chamber of Commerce, who was against the deal and abstained from voting, was the only representative of the Conservative Party (*Der Standard,* December 12, 1996, p. 19; *Die Presse,* December 12, 1996, p. 15).

Both stories hint at consensus orientation and long-term orientation. In the first case, a compromise was found that satisfied both sides. In the second story, a bank's board member disagreed with a decision, yet did not vote against it. In both examples, the parties likely wanted to "keep their doors open" for the future.

Consensus orientation is not an isolated pattern found in the leadership data. As described earlier, we also found evidence for consensus orientation at the societal and organizational level, that is, in the form of the social partnership model and codetermination.

5.   CONCLUSION

Limitations of the Study and Suggestions for Future Research

Data were collected in 1995. Since then the political landscape in Austria has changed considerably. The consistency that shows in our data, that is, consensus and partnership orientation, seems to have been replaced by contradictions. If these values are indeed so deeply ingrained in Austrian society, then why did so many Austrians in the federal election of 1999 vote for the Freedom Party with an autocratic leader like Haider? Why are there today so many voices criticizing the social partnership model? Would the results of the survey look differently today? We think they would not, for the following reasons:

1. The election likely reflects protest against the status quo rather than the desire for fundamental political change, as was argued in the section on historical and political development. Maybe the pendulum will swing back, as the elections at the local and provincial levels indicate.
2. Cultural data do not change easily and quickly, as Reber and Jago's (1997) longitudinal study of leader behavior in several countries indicates. Very likely it is way too early to tell whether the recent political developments will have an impact on Austrian societal culture at all. It would be highly interesting to conduct a follow-up study in a couple of years from now.

Managers are specific populations of any society. The question is whether the results they produce also hold true for other cohorts of a society. An initial comparison of managers and students in Austria and Ireland (Keating, Martin, & Szabo, 2002) suggests that similarities as well as differences exist between cohorts. The study indicates that the country effect is more dominant than the cohort effect in respect of both practices and values. However, there are also significant differences between the two cohorts, in particular concerning the dimensions Future Orientation, Gender Egalitarianism, and Collectivism. These differences may be attributed to cultural change, generational differences, and/or an idealized worldview of the younger population. Further studies are needed to explore these within-country variations and their underlying causes.

At the current stage, the GLOBE research concentrates on leadership ideals. These concepts are distant from actual leadership behavior and do not seem to be the best predictors for action. Future studies need to examine the link between values and practices in more detail (Szabo et al., 2001). What is also missing is contextuality, that is, the definition of the context under which leaders display particular behaviors (P. B. Smith et al., 2002[22]).

Practical Implications

As described in the section on patterns in Austrian business leadership, leaders are expected to be consensus oriented, place a focus on communication, and practice a participative leadership style. It follows that employees are frequently involved in the leadership process, not just because it is the personal decision of the leader, but also because the structure of the Austrian system (social partnership model, codetermination, works councils) calls for it. The system gives Austrian employees "a voice" (Hirschman, 1970), similar to how the systems in Germany, Switzerland, and the Netherlands, that is, the other countries of the Germanic Europe cluster (Szabo et al., 2002), operate.

At a more general level, one can argue that there will most likely be a good understanding between Austrian managers and business partners from abroad at the *managerial skills* level, because technical/factual knowledge is in Austria, as in many other countries, influenced by Western management competence, often popularized by the United States. When person-specific or interpersonal issues *(social skills)* are concerned, however, differences should be expected, because it is in this area that culture comes into play. In a world of continuous globalization and convergence toward professionalism of managers, one should not underestimate cultural diversity. The goal should not be to try to harmonize the differences in the values area, or in an extreme case to allow that one type of value orientation dominates divergent views (Reber, 2001). It is not acceptable (and likely to be impossible anyway) to train managers to completely change their values and behavioral leadership pattern. Rather, managers with different cultural backgrounds should be allowed to stay like they are, but should ideally be equipped with an increased awareness of their differences. Training is useful and possible in the area of cultural awareness: Cultural patterns reside in the unconscious, but making them explicit is a step toward improved interactions of people of different origin, in business as well as in political and social interactions.

REFERENCES

Agar, M. H. (1996). *The professional stranger: An informal introduction to ethnography.* San Diego, CA: Academic Press.

Agar, M. H. (n.d.). *Qualitative research manual, I and II.* GLOBE Research Project. Unpublished manuscript.

---

[22]This study presents data showing how middle managers in 47 countries report handling eight specific work events. The data are used to test the ability of cultural value dimensions to predict the specific sources of guidance on which managers rely.

Ahtisaari, M., Frowein, J., & Oreja, M. (2000). *Report: The Austrian government's commitment to the common European values and the evolution of the political nature of the FPÖ.* Paris: European Union.

Amnesty International Österreich. (2001). http://www.amnesty.at/

Argyris, C., & Schön, D. A. (1978). *Organizational learning: A theory of action perspective.* Reading, MA: Addison-Wesley.

Banks, A. S., Day, A. J., & Muller, T. C. (1997). *Political handbook of the world: 1997.* Birmingham, NY: CSA.

Brodbeck, F. C., Frese, M., Akerblom, S., Audia, G., Bakacsi, G., Bendova, H., et al. (2000). Cultural variation of leadership prototypes across 22 European countries. *Journal of Occupational and Organizational Psychology, 73,* 1–29.

Brodbeck, F. C., Hanges, P. J., Dickson., M. W., Gupta, V., & Dorfman, P. W. (2004). Comparative influence of industry and societal culture on organizational cultural practices. In R. J. House, P. J. Hanges, M. Javidan, P. Dorfman, & V. Gupta (Eds.), *Leadership, culture, and organizations: The GLOBE study of 62 societies* (pp. 654–668). Thousand Oaks, CA: Sage.

Bundeskammer für Arbeiter und Angestellte. (1996). *The chamber of labour—an Austrian solution.* Vienna: Author.

Bundeskanzleramt (Österreich). (1996). *Austria: Facts and figures.* Vienna: Bundespressedienst.

Bundespressedienst. (2000). *Tatsachen und Zahlen* [Facts and figures]. Vienna: Author.

Child, J. (1981). Culture, contingency and capitalism in the cross-national study of organizations. In L. L. Cummings & B. M. Staw (Eds.), *Research in organizational behavior* (Vol. 3, pp. 303--356). Greenwich, CT: JAI.

Corti, A. (1994). *Der Schalldämpfer: Texte aus den Jahren 1970–1993* [The sound absorber: Texts from 1970 to 1993]. Vienna: Kremayr & Scheriau.

Crispo, J. (1978*). Industrial democracy in Western Europe: A North American perspective.* Toronto: McGraw-Hill Ryerson.

Dana, L. P. (1992). A look at small business in Austria. *Journal of Small Business Management, 30,* 126–130.

Fitzmaurice, J. (1995). The 1994 referenda on EU membership in Austria and Scandinavia: A comparative analysis. *Electoral Studies, 14*(2), 226–232.

Hammer, T. H. (1996). Industrial democracy. In M. Warner (Ed.), *International encyclopedia of business and management* (pp. 1921–1930). London: Routledge.

Hanges, P. J., Dickson, M. W., & Sipe, M. T. (2004). Rationale for GLOBE statistical analyses: Societal rankings and test of hypotheses. In R. J. House, P. J. Hanges, M. Javidan, P. Dorfman, & V. Gupta (Eds.), *Leadership, culture, and organizations: The GLOBE study of 62 societies* (pp. 219–234). Thousand Oaks, CA: Sage.

Hirschman, A. O. (1970). *Exit, voice and loyalty.* Cambridge, MA: Harvard University Press.

Hofstede, G. (1980). *Culture's consequences: International differences in work related values.* Beverly Hills, CA: Sage.

Hofstede, G. (1993). Intercultural conflict and synergy in Europe. In D. Hickson (Ed.), *Management in Western Europe: Society, culture and organizations in twelve nations* (pp. 1–8). New York: de Gruyter.

Hofstede, G., & Bond, M. H. (1988). The confucius connection: From cultural roots to economic growth. *Organizational Dynamics, 16*(4), 4–21.

House, R. J., Hanges, P. J., Javidan, M., Dorfman, P. W., Gupta, V., & Globe Associates. (2004). *Culture, leadership, and organizations: The GLOBE study of 62 societies.* Thousand Oaks, CA: Sage.

House, R. J., Hanges, P. J., Ruiz-Quintanilla, S. A., Dorfman, P. W., Javidan, M., Dickson, M., et al. (1999). Cultural influences on leadership and organizations: Project GLOBE. In W. H. Mobley, M. J. Gessner, & V. Arnold (Eds.), *Advances in global leadership* (Vol. 1, pp. 171–233). Stamford, CT: JAI.

Human Development Report (2006). http://hdr.undp.org/hdr2006/

Keating, M. A., Martin, G. S., & Szabo, E. (2002). Do managers and students share the same perceptions of societal culture? *International Journal of Intercultural Relations, 26*(6), 633–652.

Kleindel, W. (1978). *Österreich Chronik: Daten zur Geschichte und Kultur* [Austria chronicle: History and culture]. Vienna: Ueberreuter.

Kluckhohn, F. R., & Strodtbeck, F. L. (1961). *Variations in value orientations.* New York: Harper & Row.

Maczynski, J., Jago, A. G., Reber, G., & Böhnisch, W. (1994). Culture and leadership styles: A comparison of Polish, Austrian, and U.S. managers. *Polish Psychological Bulletin, 25*(4), 303–315.

Merz, C., & Qualtinger, H. (1988). *Der Herr Karl* [Video]. Vienna: BMG Ariola Musik. (Original work published 1961)

Nowotny, E. (1991). Wirtschafts- und Sozialpartnerschaft in Österreich—Gesamtwirtschaftliche und einzelbetriebliche Formen und Effekte [Economic and social partnership in Austria – Economic and Organizational forms and effects]. *Die Betriebswirtschaft, 51*(3), 286–308.

Österreichischer Rundfunk. (1990). *Der Weg nach oben. Dr. Bruno Kreisky 1911–1990* (Video) [The way to the top. Dr. Bruno Kreisky 1911–1990]. Vienna: Author.

Österreichischer Gewerkschaftsbund. (2001). ÖGB-*Mitgliederstatistik 1999* [Austrian union membership statistics 1999]. Retrieved from http://www.oegb.at

Pelinka, A. (1995). Nationale Identität [National identity]. In Projekt-Team "Identitätswandel Österreichs im veränderten Europa" (Ed.), *Nationale und kulturelle Identitäten Österreichs. Theorien, Methoden und Probleme der Forschung zu kollektiver Identität* (pp. 28–33). Vienna: Internationales Forschungszentrum Kulturwissenschaften.

Reber, G. (2001). Divergenzen im Führungsverhalten [Diversity in leadership behavior]. In S. Klein & C. Loebbecke (Eds.), *Interdisziplinäre Managementforschung und -lehre: Herausforderungen und Chancen. Norbert Szyperski zum 70. Geburtstag* (pp. 49–77). Wiesbaden, Germany: Gabler.

Reber, G., & Jago, A. G. (1997). Festgemauert in der Erde … Eine Studie zur Veränderung oder Stabilität des Führungsverhaltens von Managern in Deutschland, Frankreich, Österreich, Polen, Tschechien und der Schweiz zwischen 1989 und 1996 [Walled up in the earth so steady … A study on change and stability in leadership behavior of managers in Germany, France, Austria, Poland, the Czech Republic, and Switzerland between 1989 and 1996]. In R. Klimecki & A. Remer (Eds.), *Personal als Strategie: Mit flexiblen und lernbereiten Human-Ressourcen Kernkompetenzen aufbauen* (pp. 158–184). Bern: Haupt.

Reber, G., Jago, A. G., Auer-Rizzi, W., & Szabo, E. (2000). Führungsstile in sieben Ländern Europas—Ein interkultureller Vergleich [Leadership styles in seven European countries—Across-culture comparison]. In E. Regnet & L. M. Hofmann (Eds.), *Personal management in Europa* (pp. 154–173). Göttingen: Verlag für Angewandte Psychologie.

Schweiger, G. (1992). *Österreichs Image in der Welt: Ein Vergleich mit Deutschland und der Schweiz* [Austria's image in the world: A comparison with Germany and Switzerland]. Vienna: Service Fachverlag.

Smith, C. (1992, September). When the curtain went up. *Management Today,* p. 108.

Smith, P. B., Peterson, M. F., Schwartz, S. H., with E. Szabo and 42 other coauthors. (2002). Cultural values, sources of guidance and their relevance to managerial behavior: A 47 nation study. *Journal of Cross-Cultural Psychology, 33*(2), 188–208.

Statistisches Jahrbuch Österreichs. (2006). http://www.statistik.at/jahrbuch_2006/englisch/start.shtml

Sully, M. (1995a). The Austrian election of 1994. *Electoral Studies, 14*(2), 218–222.

Sully, M. (1995b). The Austrian referendum 1994. *Electoral Studies, 14*(1), 67–69.

Szabo, E., Brodbeck, F. C., den Hartog, D., Reber, G., Weibler, J., & Wunderer, R. (2002). The Germanic Europe cluster: Where employees have a voice. *Journal of World Business, 37*(1), 55–68.

Szabo, E., Reber, G., Weibler, J., Brodbeck, F., & Wunderer, R. (2001). Values and behavior orientation in leadership studies: Reflections based on findings in three German-speaking countries. *Leadership Quarterly, 12*(2), 219–244.

Tannenbaum, A. S., Kavcic, B., Rosner, M., Vianello, M., & Wieser, G. (1974). *Hierarchy in organizations.* San Francisco: Jossey-Bass.

Triandis, H. C. (1994). *Culture and social behavior.* New York: McGraw-Hill.

Trompenaars, F. (1993). *Riding the waves of culture: Understanding cultural diversity in business.* London: The Economist Books.

Vroom, V. H., & Yetton, P. W. (1973). *Leadership and decision-making*. Pittsburgh, PA: University of Pittsburgh Press.

Watzlawick, P. (1983). *The situation is hopeless, but not serious: The pursuit of unhappiness*. New York: Norton.

Webb, E. J., Campbell, D. T., Schwartz, R. D., & Sechrest, L. (1966). *Unobtrusive measures: Nonreactive research in the social sciences*. Chicago: Rand McNally.

Wilderom, C., Glunk, U., & Inzerilli, G. (1997). "European management" as a construct. *International Studies of Management & Organization, 26*(3), 3–12.

Wodak, R., de Cillia, R., Reisigl, M., Liebhart, K., Hofstätter, K., & Kargl, M. (1998). *Zur diskursiven Konstruktion von nationaler Identität* [About the construction of national identity via discourse]. Frankfurt, Germany: Suhrkamp.

World Desk Reference. (3rd ed.). (2000). New York: Dorling Kindersley.

World Factbook. (2006). https://www.cia.gov/cia/publications/factbook/

Zander, L. (1997). *The licence to lead: An 18 country study of the relationship between employees' preferences regarding interpersonal leadership and national culture*. Stockholm: Stockholm School of Economics.

Appendix A

Basic Information on Austria[23]

LOCATION

Austria is located in Central Europe and has a land surface of 82,730 square kilometers (31,942 square miles). Austria is topographically dominated by the Alps in the south and west, whereas its eastern provinces lie within the Danube basin. Although small in size, Austria shares borders with eight countries, namely Germany, the Czech Republic, Slovakia, Hungary, Slovenia, Italy, Switzerland, and Liechtenstein.

POPULATION

The Austrian population totals 8.19 million (July 2006 estimate; *World Factbook,* 2006), some 98% of whom are German-speaking, the official language of the Republic of Austria. There are six ethnic and linguistic minority groups officially recognized in Austria. These groups are concentrated in the eastern and southern parts of the country and have been accorded specific rights by federal law. In terms of religious allegiances, 74% of Austrians are Roman Catholic, a further 5% Protestant. About 9% of the population belongs to a different faith, 12% to no religious group at all (2001 census; *World Factbook,* 2006). Life expectancy is 76 years for men and 82 years for women; the fertility rate amounts to 1.36 (2006 estimates; *World Factbook,* 2006).

Austrians are stereotypically described as *gemütlich* (sociable), having a communication style that includes *Schmäh* (a concept in between humor and biting irony; in particular the Schmäh of the Viennese population is legendary) and *sudern* (similar to complaining, finding a negative aspect in even the brightest situations), and sometimes showing behavior that is called *durchwursteln* (muddling through).[24] We would like to stress that these factors, like all stereotypes, might not apply to the individual Austrian, however, a little truth might still be found in these stereotypical attributes.

CONSTITUTION AND GOVERNMENT

Austria's constitution provides for a federal democratic republic embracing nine provinces including the capital Vienna; that is, Vienna is a city *and* a province. The national government consists of a president whose functions are largely ceremonial, a cabinet headed by a chancellor,

---

[23]Unless otherwise state, the information in Appendix A is taken from the statistical profile of the GLOBE society sample (House et al., 2004) and *World Desk Reference* (2000).

[24]A wonderful example of this type of Austrian is *"Der Herr Karl,"* a satiric figure portrayed by the late Austrian actor Helmut Qualtinger (Merz & Qualtinger, 1961/1988).

and a bicameral legislature. The chancellor and the cabinet members are appointed by the president usually from the party with the strongest representation in the lower house, the National Council (*Nationalrat*). The upper house, the Federal Council (*Bundesrat*), represents the provinces and is restricted to a review of legislation passed by the National Council. Its decisions have only delaying powers. The two houses together constitute the Federal Assembly (*Bundesversammlung*), whose approval in full sitting is required in certain contingencies, for example, the recall of the federal president prior to the end of the term of office. Although most effective power is at the federal level, the provinces have some latitude in local administration. Each province has an elected legislature (*Landtag*) and an administration headed by a governor (*Landeshauptmann*) designated by the legislature. The judicial system is headed by the Supreme Judicial Court (*Oberster Gerichtshof*) and includes two other high courts, the Constitutional Court (*Verfassungsgerichtshof*) and the Administrative Court (*Verwaltungsgerichtshof*). There are four higher provincial courts (*Oberlandesgerichte*), seventeen provincial and district courts (*Landes-und Kreisgerichte*), and numerous local courts (*Bezirksgerichte*).

EDUCATION

Total government expenditure spent on education is close to 8%. Compulsory schooling lasts nine years. Austria's school system is governed by uniform regulations nationwide. No fees are charged for attendance at state-run schools. Austria has nineteen universities, including the University of Vienna, which was founded in 1365. The successful completion of the final, rather comprehensive and demanding high school examination ("Matura") gives the student the right to study at any national university she or he selects. As of the 2001/2002 academic year, students are required to pay a modest tuition fee for each term they attend university.

Appendix B

Definitions of Outstanding Leadership

Focus Group 1	An outstanding leader is a charismatic person who possesses high social competence and is able to lead her/his people with less direct motivation and control than a competent manager needs. An outstanding leader has to be a competent manager at the same time. Every organization needs an outstanding leader intermittently to survive in the long run.
Focus Group 2	An outstanding leader is a visionary, a charismatic person who acts according to her/his principles. Her/his time horizon is wider. Whereas a competent manager integrates the tomorrow, an outstanding leader shapes the day after tomorrow as well.
Interviewee 1	An outstanding leader has to possess technical/factual knowledge and also the capability to lead people.
Interviewee 2	An outstanding leader is competent in his subject. He lets subordinates participate in his decisions and do their own work rather independently, but intervenes whenever necessary. He has to possess absolute integrity.
Interviewee 3	An outstanding leader possesses high inter-personal competence, whereas technical/factual competence is not so important.
Interviewee 4	An outstanding leader is an outstanding personality and more than just an expert is his field.
Interviewee 5	Outstanding leadership and competent management are ideally combined in one person, including personality and technical/factual competence. An outstanding leader is a role model for his subordinates and interacts with them in a climate of trust and openness.

6

Societal Culture and Leadership in Germany

Felix C. Brodbeck
Aston Business School, Aston University, Birmingham, UK

Michael Frese
University of Giessen, Germany, and London Business School

"The Germans make everything difficult, both for themselves and for everyone else."

—J. W. Goethe

"The German Riddle: Is it Solvable?" is the title of the epilogue in the German 1991 translation of Hofstede's (1980) *Culture's Consequences.* In their epilogue, the translators point toward the potential usefulness of cross-cultural studies to overcome the typical difficulty of Germans in not being able to describe who they are: a difficulty, the French, the Italians or the Britons never had with their identity. Historians and authors, from Tacitus to Thomas Mann, have meticulously pondered the difficulties they had when attempting to describe Germany and the Germans—so had we! However, instead of pondering about the difficulties, we set out the present chapter to help solving the German riddle by using empirical cross-cultural studies.

We provide an analysis of culture and leadership in Germany based on the GLOBE study and relevant data from other sources. The first part describes the German societal culture by considering the German population, economy, political system, history, the reunification in 1990, and the GLOBE questionnaire survey (conducted in the second half of the 1990s) about societal cultural practices and values based on a total of $N = 471$ German middle managers in three different industries (food, finance, and telecommunications). The second section concentrates on leadership perceptions in Germany. It begins with a description of leadership practice and research in Germany. Then, leadership prototypes (i.e., culturally endorsed perceptions of outstanding leadership) are described, again on the basis of the German GLOBE questionnaire survey. In addition, results from content analyses of print media, semistructured interviews, focus group discussions, job-postings analyses, and biographical analysis of popular leaders in Germany are used to complete the picture. In the final section, commonalties and differences among East and West German societal culture and perceptions of excellent leadership are summarized and discussed. The chapter ends with an integrative account of culture and leadership in Germany, limitations of our studies, practical implications and suggestions for future research.

1.   CONTEMPORARY GERMANY

Contemporary Germany lies at the heart of Europe. With a population of 82 million citizens (80% West, 20% East Germany), it is the most populated country in Europe. Ninety percent of the population is German. About 28 million people belong to the Roman Catholic Church (predominantly inhabiting the southwest of Germany) and another 28 million follow the Protestant doctrine (predominantly inhabiting the northeast). The rest are Moslems and others, or with no confession.

Germany is heavily dependent on foreign trade due to a lack of natural resources. The strongest industrial sectors are automobiles, engineering, electronics, and chemicals. In the year 2000, Germany was the world's second largest exporter after the United States (World Economic Forum, 2000). That year the country's gross domestic product (GDP) amounts to over U.S.$2 trillion and its GDP per capita of U.S.$ 23,742 is one of the highest in the world.

Germany's Current Dilemma

Germany is the biggest economy in the European Union (EU). However, its economy, educational system, and social fabric are slipping. In 1990, the American economy was 3.7 times bigger than the German one, but in 2002 the American economy has become five times bigger than the German one ("An Uncertain Giant," 2002). Following the postunification boom in 1994, growth has slowed averaging only 1.6% a year—the lowest rate in the EU ("An Uncertain Giant," 2002). Hourly labor costs are higher than in the United States (13%) or Britain (43%) and productivity is reducing. "Germany has far too many rules and regulations" ("An Uncertain Giant," 2002, p. 10). Germany spends more on pension than most other developed countries; its regulations of the labor market are stronger and more ossified than those of other countries.

Still, poverty is low and people live comfortably in modern Germany. In addition, companies are able to compete on the market. Much of Germany's strength is due to small and medium-size firms (Simon, 1996). Though managers of medium-sized firms are often complaining that government is not helping them, they still prove to be quite resilient even in bad times. "With so much to complain about, how do so many German firms still manage to do so well? The answer lies in good old-fashioned hard work, efficiency, attention to detail and precision, and high standards, particularly in engineering" ("An Uncertain Giant," 2002, p. 10).

Germany's Social Market Economy

In Germany, as in the other Germanic countries of Austria and Switzerland (Szabo et al., 2002), the relationship between "labor" and "capital" is shaped by the fundamental assumption, enshrined in law, that economic prosperity and growth can be best attained through cooperation between labor and capital. The labor–management system is designed to give employees a "voice." The doctrine of social market economy ("*soziale Marktwirtschaft*") defines obligations of government, trade unions, and companies to maintain public welfare, social justice, and cooperative industrial relations. The free-market capitalist system is constrained by the principle of social responsibility, which is anchored in the German Constitution. An important element of the labor–management relations is codetermination. Regulated by law, it takes the form of a democratic management structure with presence of both the employer and the labor side on supervisory boards of large enterprises, which set corporate policies and approve major investments, mergers, expansion, and plant closures. The employer side can only overrule the resistance of the labor side in deadlock situations. Another important feature of the German system is the workers' councils. These councils are elected by the employees and often have close union ties. They enjoy three types of rights: the right of information, the right of consultation, and the right of consent, depending on whether or not economic, social or personnel affairs are concerned. (For more information on these issues see Appendix A.)

In recent years, the social nature of the market economy has been subject to criticisms from within and outside Germany as being too cost intensive, idiosyncratic, and too constraining for management, thereby impeding Germany's economic development. Is the German culture prepared to cope with the necessary changes in the social welfare principle considering its current profile in societal values? Moreover, are German managers prepared for taking up leadership roles that support such a change from a state-granted social market to a private- initiative-based system? These are questions we address in the present chapter as well. For a deeper understanding of the answers suggested later in the chapter, a brief overview of the geo-cultural history of Germany is given.

2. GEO-CULTURAL HISTORY OF GERMANY

Where Germans Live

Writers from the Roman Empire acknowledged *Germania* about 2,000 years ago; for example, Gaius Julius Caesar mentions the Germans in his book *De bello gallico* (51 BC) and Tacitus, the Roman historian, writes about the origin and habitat of the Germans in his book *De origine et situ Germanorum* (AD 98). The German words nowadays used to decipher German (*Deutsch*) and Germany or German Nation (*Deutschland*) underwent considerable semantic changes in history. Their changing meanings document the various roots of the idea of a German Nation (Berschin, 1993). In 786, *theodiscus* (German) is first documented to mean the language spoken by ordinary people in contrast to the Latin language spoken by the scholars at the court of Karl the Great. In 1090, *diutischin liute* (German People) is first documented to mean the German people that live in the East Franconian Empire. The idea of a singular German State appears quite late in history. In the 15th century, Germany and Austria became the *Heiliges Roemisches Reich Deutscher Nation* (Holy Roman Empire of German Nation). But this Empire is a lose federation of states that falls apart rapidly. Usually the plural form, "Deutsche Lande" (German Countries), is used. It means people of German language and the regions where they live. Until the nineteenth century, *Deutschland* (Germany) and *Deutsche Nation* (German Nation) meant the geographical area inhabited by German-speaking people. In combination with *German* the word *Nation* did not refer to the idea of a political unit or a singular state. It rather meant the *cultural unity* of German-speaking people in various central European states.

During the 19th century the cultural concept of German changed into a political one, partly because German territory was defended in the Napoleonic Wars and partly due to the German National Movement against feudalism that resulted in the Constitutional Convention in Frankfurt in 1848. The practical impossibility of a German Nation as a cultural *and* political unit became apparent when the German Empire was founded in 1871. Many people of German culture and language were not part of it (e.g., Germans in Switzerland or in Austria)

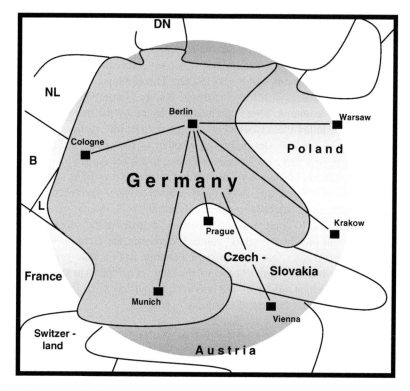

Figure 6.1   Germany with Central Europe, before 1945 (adapted from Schäfer, 1989)

and some people other than those of German culture and language formed ethnic minorities within the geographical boarders of the German Empire (e.g., French, Danish, and Polish minorities).

During the first three decades of the 20th century, the concept of a German Nation was highly ambiguous and allowed for interpretations in various directions. First, it could mean the narrow German state that was enforced after World War I (Weimarer Republic, 1919–1932). Second, it could mean the territory of German culture, including the geographical areas that belonged to the German Empire before World War I. Third, it could mean the even greater territory inhabited by people of German language and cultural background, and fourth, it could mean the extended territory inhabited by people of German descent, a principle that became popular in the Wilhelmenian period of the German Empire (1890–1918). The ideal of an extended German nation became more and more popular when the ethnic and territorial interpretations of German were combined—*"Ein Volk, ein Reich"* ("One Nation, one Empire"). This became particularly virulent in the megalomaniac political program of the *Third Reich* promoted by the Austrian-born Adolf Hitler—*Der Führer* (The Leader)—which resulted in the Holocaust.

The strong geopolitical position of Germany in central Europe before 1945 is illustrated in Fig. 6.1. The state territory showed a regional unity in the west and a large extension toward the east, where German and Slavic populations mixed. The capital city, Berlin, was mainly oriented toward the east and southeast (Schäfer, 1989).

The 2,000 years of geo-cultural proximity of the "German people and culture" should have left its traces in the countries of today's Central Europe and indeed cross-cultural research from the 1960s to the late 1990s suggests the existence of a Germanic cultural cluster in Central Europe (Brodbeck, Frese et al., 2000; Hofstede, 1980; Jago et al., 1993; Ronen & Shenkar, 1985; Szabo et al., 2002), comprising Austria, former East and West Germany, Switzerland, and in some studies also the Netherlands. Even though cultural differences between these countries are identifiable, their citizens seem to share cultural characteristics, work attitudes, and leadership perceptions to a considerable extent, especially when compared to other cultural entities, so that they are distinguishable as a cultural cluster within Europe (Brodbeck, Frese et al., 2000) and worldwide (Gupta & Hanges, 2004; Gupta, Hanges, & Dorfman, 2002).

Chronically Torn and Divided

We want to argue that Germany is a country that has been torn apart in history several times and, therefore, has a history of division. We think that one effect is that Germans tend to be anxious about the future, uncertainty avoidant, and uncomfortable with their identity. Some of the more powerful divisions were between uneducated barbarism and civilization, between Catholicism and Protestantism, between the eastern states and the western states, and between Romanticism and Rationality. Furthermore, Germany has been torn between an overenthusiastic Germanic identification to feelings of inferiority to the other large European countries—France and England.

Uneducated barbarism has existed beyond the Limes—a wall that the Romans built to keep the barbarian Germans out and to demarcate their empire (roughly the regions of Bavaria, Baden-Württemberg, Palatinate, and a large part of Hessia—farther north the border followed the Rhine—were part of the civilization of the Roman empire). The Limes went through the middle of what is Germany today. Some of the same divisions appear again and again between the eastern German states, which were less influenced by Western countries, particularly France and Britain. Therefore, it was mostly the western states that followed French revolutionary and democratic ideals and that led the revolt for democratic Germany in 1848 (and chose the western city of Frankfurt as their capital). The eastern states of Germany were less influenced by democratic and revolutionary ideas and idealized the state and its influence (particularly in Prussia).

Although there was an east–west divide in this sense, there was a north–south divide along the lines of Catholicism and Protestantism. After Luther started his revolt against the Pope, Protestantism became a powerful force. (Incidentally Luther also developed High- German as the language that he created to produce a German Bible; High-German would eventually be understood by all Germans.) Many states became Protestant (it was usually the decision by the ruler of the state who decided whether a state would be Protestant or Catholic). In 1618, the 30-year war started between the Catholics and Protestants; it was mainly fought on German soil with an influx of powerful forces from Spain, France and Scandinavia; the soldiers lived off the land through which they passed. Famines, killings, foraging, destruction, and the plague decimated and destroyed much of Germany during these 30 years—historians estimate that a third of the population was killed during this time. Those states most affected suffered tremendous causalities. Württemberg's population was reduced from 400,000 to 48,000; Palatinate lost four fifths, and Bohemia's 3 million were reduced to 780,000 people (Craig, 1991). German angst (*anxiety*) may well be related to this period of time, which left traces in many sayings, for example, "Schwedentrunk" (peasants were given boiling hot manure to drink until they divulged where they had hidden their money). This might also have contributed to a certain degree of xenophobia, which resulted in anxiety of other surrounding countries.

After the 30-year war, 300 sovereign states were to exist. The nobility reigned and the power of the commercial cities was reduced. Any threat to upset the order produced high anxiety in the populace because of the experience of the 30-year war. Obedience was, therefore, important to uphold social order. These 300 German states were powerless vis-à-vis their neighbors but a high degree of differentiated cultural development resulted from the competition between these states (e.g., many dukes employed their own orchestra or a composer). On the other hand, most of Germany was provincial with little knowledge about the world. It was against this background of backwardness that anti-Semitism flourished, supported by Luther's diatribes against the Jews.

Quite some time later and after many wars (particularly between Prussia in the northeast and Austria in the south) Germany started to become a nation. In 1866, Prussia defeated Austria, leading to the North German Confederation under Prussian control. In 1870, Prussia went to war with France, defeating her, leading to the declaration of the first German nation in 1871 (after the southern German states Barvaria, Würtemberg, Baden, and the Palatinate were cajoled and bribed into the new German Empire). Thus, national unity was achieved by the state with military might, not by popular will and revolt. Similarly, industrialization was set off, supported, and channeled by active interventions from the state. Though Germany had a free-market economy, the state's power was strong and influential in every area of industrial activities at a time, when industry was much freer in Britain and the United States. The state also subsidized newspapers, which made them dependent on state support. Similarly, the state organized schools and universities. Thus, there were few private initiatives that were not at least condoned by the state. Therefore, the general concept of the all-powerful state was developed and underpinned philosophically (e.g., by Hegel). We assume that the post-30-year-war importance of the local princes, the romantic notion of community, and the de facto importance of the modern (Prussian) state all reinforced a traditional power distance and institutionalized uncertainty avoidance.

Although Germany managed to develop its industry after the forced unification by Prussia, it was unsure of itself and its position in Europe. Up to Wilhelm II—the emperor who started World War I in 1918—Germany had the impression that it had come too late to get its rightful place as a part of Europe's imperialism (e.g., by accumulating colonies in other continents).

Another conflict issue was the tradition of Romanticism versus Rationalism. German literature, arts, and music were heavily romantic (e.g. in literature, early Goethe, Schlegel, Tieck, Brentano, the Grimm brothers, E. T. A Hoffmann, von Eichendorff). Romanticism emphasized the irrational, mystical, and emotional, the imaginative and the visionary. And it was directed against enlightenment and materialism. It was past oriented and against modernity (cf. the importance of fairy tales and German sagas). Romanticism was also related to nationalism in Germany. There were romantic notions of leadership and state (Hegel), which may have contributed to the acceptance of high power distance (and which were important for the development and rise of National Socialism in Germany). Romantic authors also used the German language systematically (instead of Latin or French) and started a literature for the normal population. Romanticism was in stark contrast to a rational approach, which was the basis of science and technology that bloomed during the same period of the 19th century. National Socialism has been described to make use of "high technology romanticism" (Thomas Mann).

The German readiness to romanticize the state and to be obedient to the state may look like collectivism but this is not correct. We follow Dumont (1994), who argues that Germany did not develop a modern concept of organized society because Germans were individualistic. However, their concept of the collective togetherness was one of *Gemeinschaft* (community). Thus, there was a romantic notion of togetherness that went alongside a keen interest in individual development and individual self-improvement. Luther's reformation strengthened individualism. A community was one that did not allow conflicts and that served as an immediate reference point to which one had to be subservient. The Nazis used this when they talked about the *Volksgemeinschaft* (people community). German culture was already integrated into this idea of community. The community developed spontaneously; it was not developed as a social contract. Thus, Germans are easily organizable: Dumont (1994, p. 41) quotes Troeltsch, "the liberty of the German is willed discipline, advancement and development of one's own self in a whole and for a whole" (the whole being the people community).

From this short historical introduction, we assume that German culture is state oriented and the default expectation of Germans is a high degree of activity by the state instead of individual activities (e.g., in the area of general welfare or entrepreneurial activities). This may translate into moderate to high power distance. The uncertainties and divisions may have increased and supported high uncertainty avoidance (to avoid anxiety) and high future orientation; that is, people save to be able to deal with future problems.

A discussion of Germany cannot be complete without pointing to the significance of Adolf Hitler, anti-Semitism, and World War II. Although the Second World War was of obvious significance for every German, Hitler and National Socialism was not really worked through until the 1960s in which the German youth revolt included a revolt against the elders' obedience and "organizability" during the Third Reich. From foes and defenders alike, the 68-generation revolt is seen as a cultural watershed. In our view, it means that a Westernization has taken place, increasing individualism, reducing the romantic notions of community (however, keeping romantic notions of the changeability of humans), and increasing values of risk taking, innovation, cultural heterogeneity, and disobedience. Cultural changes are slow and, therefore, we expect to see smaller changes in the culture as it is perceived (societal culture "As Is") but steeper changes in what people aspire to (societal culture "Should Be").

The cultural revolution of the 1960s did not take place in East Germany, which in spite of the communist regime displayed a higher cultural continuity from Hitler's time to the late 1980s. All the more, was there a cultural break and shock when the Eastern part of Germany was integrated into the West in 1990. The shock waves of this reunification are still with Germany today.

Separated in 1949 and Reunited in 1990

The separation and the ready acceptance of separation into East and West was only the latest of the divisions of Germany. As a result of the Second World War and the beginning of the Cold War between the communist and the Western world, two German states emerged with different economic and political systems: the Federal Republic of Germany (FRG, Bundesrepublick Deutschland, also called West Germany), embedded in the Western economic system and the NATO military alliance, and the German Democratic Republic (GDR, Deutsche Demokratische Republick, also called East Germany), embedded in the communist economic system (COMCON) and the Warsaw pact.

In 1949, both the Federal Republic of Germany (May 24, 1949) and the German Democratic Republic (October 7, 1949) were founded. Figure 6.2 illustrates to what extent the powerful geopolitical positioning of Germany within central Europe before 1945 (see

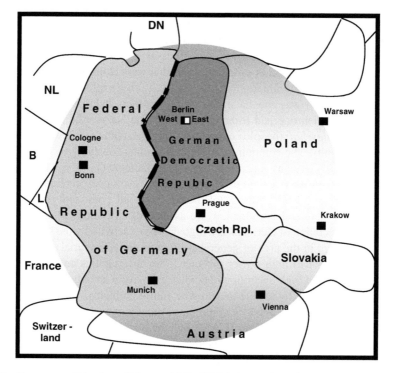

Figure 6.2   Germany within Central Europe 1949–1990 (adapted from Schäfer, 1989)

Figure 6.1) had dramatically changed by 1949. A major geopolitical border, the "iron curtain" between East and West, separated Germany into two different states, which were part of very different geopolitical and economic systems.

In 1949, the goal to unite Germany again was made part of the West German Constitution. This constitutional law formed the legal basis of reunification (October 3, 1990), which was initiated by popular uprising and the highly symbolic act of the fall of the wall in Berlin (November 9, 1989). Since East Germany joined the West German Federal Republic, there has been little apparent change for West Germans, but dramatic changes for East Germans in their political, economical, and social environment. For a more detailed description of former West and East Germany and the German reunification process, see Appendixes A, B, and C, respectively.

We argue that East Germany did not have the same cultural developments and breaks in the 1960s as West Germany. The present chapter therefore also explores the extent to which differences in societal culture and leadership perceptions between former East and West German managers exist.

Still Carrying the Costs of Reunification

The process of rebuilding the economy in the eastern part, which has yet to be completed, has been very expensive and laborious (see Appendix C). Between 1990 and 2001, more than 800 billion euro (a trillion dollars; "An Uncertain Giant," 2002) were transferred from the West to the new eastern states. The infrastructure was modernized, private-sector economy was established, and the West German health care and social welfare systems were installed in the East. It is now clear that the time frame and the costs of updating the collapsed former East German economy and social systems were initially drastically underestimated. Moreover, the West is still developing faster than the East. East German unemployment was between 18% and 22% with some areas higher than 30% at the end of 2002. Moreover, productivity was 70% of the West in 2002 ("Abbruch Ost," 2003); GDP per person is 27,000 euros per person in the West and 16,500 euros in the East ("Europe Has a Problem," 2002). Thus, improving the economy and reducing high unemployment rates in the East are set to be major challenges in the years to come.

It can be assumed that the unsettling times following German reunification based on Germany's comparatively high level of uncertainty avoidance (Hofstede, 1980) contributed to cultural practices of consolidation, risk avoidance, and overregulation.

In the present chapter, characteristics of the societal culture, work attitudes, and leadership perceptions in contemporary Germany (East and West) are investigated on the basis of the GLOBE data and further sources.

3.   METHODS, SAMPLES, AND PROCEDURES

The empirical approach taken here is both quantitative and qualitative in nature. Quantitative data based on the GLOBE questionnaire survey (see chaps. 1 and 2, this volume; House, et al. 2004) are supplemented with qualitative data from content analyses of print media, job-postings analyses, semistructured interviews, focus group discussions, biographical analysis of popular leaders in Germany, as well as from unobtrusive measures, participant observation, and reviewing the literature about German culture and leadership.

GLOBE Questionnaire Study in Germany

Samples from former East and West German territory were drawn during the years 1995 and 1996. Using the German companies by industries listing, a random sample of 500 organizations (including the 50 top organizations) was contacted by mail, fax, and telephone (in this sequence). Thirty organizations agreed to participate in the study. Eighteen of these delivered sufficient data for further analyses (see Table 6.1). Twelve companies continued to collaborate after results were available. They received written evaluation feedback about perceptions of culture and leadership concepts within their organization in relation to the aggregated results for Germany.

The sample of respondents comprises altogether 471 middle managers (East German: $N = 54$; West Germany $N = 417$, see Table 6.1). With 11.5% of the total sample, East German managers are somewhat underrepresented because the former East German population constitutes about 20% of the total population in contemporary Germany. All respondents are middle managers with substantial work experience (on the average about 22 years) and leadership experience (average about 11 years). The sample in former East Germany shows a higher average age (46 years) and a higher percentage of female managers (30% women) than the sample in former West Germany (43 years, 12% women). Although the East German managers sampled have more work experience (26 years) and more leadership experience (15 years) than their West German counterparts (21 years and 10 years respectively), the level of hierarchy and responsibility they had approached by the time of the study is somewhat lower (average levels to top = 1.3, average levels to bottom = .07, average number of reporting staff = 8.2, average size of unit = 106. 5) than for West German managers (see Table 6.1).

TABLE 6.1
Sample Characteristics of the GLOBE Questionnaire Study in Germany

Organizations in the Sample[a]	West Germany	East Germany	Total Germany
N in food industry	5	3	7
N in finance industry	6	1	6
N in telecom industry	5	1	5
Total N of organizations sampled	16	5	18
Individual respondents[bc]	$N = 417$	$N = 54$	$N = 471$
Percent female[**]	12	30	14
Age (in years)[*]	42.6	45.6	42.9
Years education[**]	14.1	16.1	14.3
Years work experience[**]	21.0	25.6	21.6
Years as manager[**]	10.5	14.6	10.9
N of hierarchy levels to top	1.1	1.3	1.1
N of hierarchy levels to bottom[*]	1.2	0.7	1.1
N of direct reports	11.1	8.2	10.9
Average size of organizational units	131.1	106.5	128.3
Respondents stating that their organization is multinational	67 %	67%	67%

Note. Significant differences between East and West Germany: [*]$p < .05$, [**]$p < .01$
[a]In each industry, one organization had subsidiaries in East and West Germany. Two organizations (both from the food industry) originated in East Germany. [b]All West and East German respondents were born, socialized, and educated in West or East Germany respectively. A total of 75% of East German and 74% of West German respondents held leadership positions before the reunification in 1990. [c]West German sample: highest $N = 417$, lowest $N = 408$; East German sample: highest $N = 54$, lowest $N = 50$, depending on variables analyzed.

There are several possible reasons for disparities in sample size and sample characteristics. Many East German companies were still in the process of being closed down after the German reunification in 1990. We encountered several instances in which the willingness to cooperate with the GLOBE program was signaled, however, top management felt that enduring collaboration may not be maintainable because negotiations with potential new owners were in progress and considerable redundancies had to be made—especially among the senior workforce. Further disparities in sample characteristics are partially due to differences in the formal education and career systems. Note that in the average, East German managers have 2 more years of formal education than West German managers. However, this does not fully account for the difference in work and leadership experience of about 5 and 4 years respectively. The remaining disparities are likely to be due to the higher promotion rates for West German as compared to East German managers. After the reunification mainly West German companies "took over" (see Appendix C), and the predominant assumption was that East German managers were not experienced enough with Western market economy principles. Hence their prospect for promotion was reduced. The gender difference described in Table 6.1 finds an explanation in the traditionally larger representation of the female workforce in East Germany as compared to West Germany.

   In order to protect the GLOBE results from potential sampling bias, the previously described differences in demographic variables were taken into account in our statistical analyses. First, the respective variables were used as covariates when comparing questionnaire data from East and West. Second, a West German twin sample was drawn by matching West German with East German managers one by one on the basis of the aforementioned variables. As is shown in the results section, all comparative results remain stable after the demographic differences were taken into account.

Industry (finance, telecommunication, food) had no significant effects on the GLOBE results neither for societal culture, nor for organizational culture and leadership in Germany. On the one side, this increases our confidence in the sample to represent the perceptions and values of German middle managers fairly well, and on the other side, it makes it obsolete to engage in detailed subgroup analysis with respect to industry and organizational culture. The reader who is interested in overall relationships between industry, societal culture, and organizational cultures (organizational culture mainly is predicted by societal culture) may find the respective GLOBE results informative that are reported by Brodbeck, Hanges, Dickson, Gupta, and Dorfman (2004). The case of how societal and organizational culture are linked in contemporary Germany has recently been addressed empirically by Armbrüster (2005).

The GLOBE standard questionnaire was used (cf. House et. al., 2004; see also chap. 1, this volume). Note that for evaluating perceptions of societal culture, respondents were asked to rate the GLOBE questionnaire items about societal culture by considering the reunited contemporary Germany and not with reference to either of the two former German states alone. In our interpretations of the results this peculiarity is taken into account.

Content Analysis of Print Media

East and West German print media were analyzed during the 25th and 29th week of 1996. The following print media were chosen: *Frankfurter Allgemeine Zeitung* (daily newspaper, mainly West German staff), *Bild Zeitung* (daily popular press, mainly West German staff), *Die Zeit* (weekly newspaper, mainly West German staff), *Wirtschaftswoche* (weekly business magazine, mainly West German staff), *Handelsblatt* (weekly business paper, mainly West German staff), *Wochenpost* (weekly newspaper, mainly East German staff), and *Freie Presse Chemnitzer Zeitung* (daily newspaper, mainly East German staff). The sections of news, politics, economy, society, comments, and so on, were used for content analysis. Sports, travel, theater, cinema, and foreign issues were disregarded. Job advertisements for executives were analyzed separately (see next subsection). Every article's headline was read and classified whether leadership issues were mentioned. Texts concerning either business leadership or political leadership were selected. The selected articles were read and central phrases that contained information about what leaders "should do" or "should be like" or about leader attributes and actions that were identifiably as an "accepted standard" were typed into a data file. A list of all phrases was created, and to each phrase the central verb or adjective, representing the predominant leadership attribute, was added. Beginning with the list of phrases from East German print media ($N = 189$) categories were inductively generated. The same was done for the West German sample ($N = 360$ phrases). Most of the categories were found in both samples, so that a common category system could be employed comprising altogether 13 categories (see Appendix D). Two trained individuals (the first author and a postgraduate student) independently rated all 549 phrases according to the 13 categories resulting in high reliability coefficients (Cohen's κappa: East Germany = .96; West Germany = .98).[1]

---

[1]The contributions from Markus Schmidt are thankfully acknowledged.

Job Advertisement Analysis

Leadership requirements for German managers in 1981 and 1996 were compared by using content analysis data from executive-level job postings published in three major German print media (*Frankfurter Allgemeine Zeitung, Die Zeit,* and *Handelsblatt*). For the year 1996, we used the print media that were text analyzed (see previous subsection). For the year 1981, issues from the same weeks (25th and 29th) as in 1996 were chosen. Comparison with East German print media in 1981 and 1996 were not possible. In 1981, job offerings for executives were not announced in public print media, and in 1996 the number of identifiably East German job advertisements was too small. The comparison of 1981 and 1996 allows establishing the degree of stability and change in job requirements over a period of 15 years in West Germany. Only advertisements from domestic companies offering an executive position in Germany were selected. Up to 20 advertisements per print media were randomly chosen so that an approximately equal sample size could be drawn for the years 1981 and 1996. Analyses were conducted by a group of postgraduate students in the social science department (Institute of Psychology) at the University of Munich. They attended a course in cross-cultural research methods conducted by the first author. The students were unaware of the GLOBE dimensions and hypotheses at the time of conducting the study. On their own, they developed a categorization system to classify the total of $N = 402$ executive job requirements obtained. Sixteen categories emerged (see Appendix E).[2]

Interviews and Focus Groups

Six semistructured interviews with West German managers (two female, four male) from various branches and two focus group discussions involving nine experienced managers and consultants from different West German companies and branches were conducted. It was intended to use the contacts to East German managers that develop during the course of the acquisition of organizations in former East Germany to set up interviews and focus groups with East German managers as well. However, it was not possible to obtain a satisfactory number of cooperating managers within the set time window for the GLOBE study.

The interviews and focus groups were conducted to evaluate expectations about unusually effective leaders versus average managers. Heterogeneity among respondents, for example, in organizational background, gender, and age, was purposefully maximized. This decreased the likelihood that prototypical attributes for excellent leadership overlap among respondents due to similar background. Written protocols from the tape-recorded interviews were analyzed and interpreted by an ethnologist who was unaware of the GLOBE dimensions and hypotheses.[3] Her task was to identify and categorize characteristic attributes for an unusually effective leader versus an average manager. Group discussions were tape-recorded and all attributes and examples given were listed and subsequently classified according to the categorical system developed on the basis of the interviews.

Bibliographical Data About Popular Leaders

Twelve persons (West Germans) of various ages, gender, and social and educational background were interviewed in 1998 to create a list of unusually effective and commonly known

[2]The contributions from Silvia Specht de Huber, Gabriele Kessler, Oswald Moosmann, Alexandra Muz, and Nadja Töpper are thankfully acknowledged.

[3]The contributions from Natalie Goeltenboth are thankfully acknowledged.

leaders in politics and business from the end of World War II until today. For three approximate time periods (from 1945 to mid-1960s, from mid-1960s to early 1980s, and from the mid-1980s to the 1990s) the most often mentioned leaders were selected for biographical analysis. Biographical books and articles were used to derive predominant leadership attributes commonly attributed to these persons.[4] Note that the process of generating the list of popular leaders is based on West Germans' perspectives. Therefore, the results are not meant to represent East German views in any way.

4.   SOCIETAL CULTURAL PRACTICES AND VALUES IN GERMANY

Box-plot statistics are used to show the distributions of societal cultural practices scores ("As Is," Fig. 6.3) and societal cultural values scores ("Should Be," Fig. 6.4) for all GLOBE countries (see Appendix F and chap. 1 and 2 of this volume for more detailed descriptions of the GLOBE dimensions; cf. House et al., 2004). Differences between societal cultural practices scores (Fig. 6.3, "As Is") and values scores (Fig. 6.4, "Should Be") reflect the discrepancy between the perceived ("real") societal culture and the desired ("ideal") societal culture.

Each figure allows for a direct comparison of East and West Germany's societal culture scores with the distribution of scores within the GLOBE sample of countries. In the cylinder-shaped box-plots, four quartiles are distinguished (lowest 25%, low 25%, high 25%, highest 25%) and the median is given (vertical black bar indicating the midpoint of the distribution with 50% above and 50% below). The range of country scores is represented by the total length of the cylinders. In cases where societal cultural practices are similarly perceived by East and West German managers, an oval-shaped blimp is shown for Germany, as in the case of *Uncertainty Avoidance* cultural practices (see Fig. 6.3). Here East and West Germany rank among the top 25% of all countries. In cases of differences between East and West (e.g., *Future Orientation,* Fig. 6.3), the blimp's thick end represents the perceptions of West German managers (80% of the total population) and the blimp's thin end represents the perceptions of East German managers. Country scores, test banding positions, and ranks for Germany East and West are given in Table 6.2.

Power Distance in Decline

The GLOBE results on *Power Distance* point to an interesting overall finding: The "As Is" cylinder (Range 3.9–5.8, Fig. 6.3) and the "Should Be" cylinder (Range 2.0–3.7, Fig. 6.4) don't overlap at all. Quite understandably middle managers in all GLOBE countries seem to prefer lower levels of power distance than they actually experience. Germany's moderate to high ranking on *Power Distance* "As Is" (above the median of box-plot in Fig. 6.3) is in line with our historical analysis in which it was assumed that the post-30-year-war importance of the local princes, the romantic notion of community, and the de facto importance of the modern (Prussian) state all reinforced a strong state orientation with traditional power distance. However, the noticeably low positioning on *Power Distance* "Should Be" (below the median of box-plot in Fig. 6.4) seems to indicate that there is a preference for a more egalitarian approach to status in the modern German society, which is more pronounced than the global trend. The desire for less privilege for people in position of power is reflected in a report in the February 22, 2001, issue of *Business Week* that discusses the sudden departure of BMW's CEO and the no. 2 executive:

---

[4]The contributions from Claudia Sold are thankfully acknowledged.

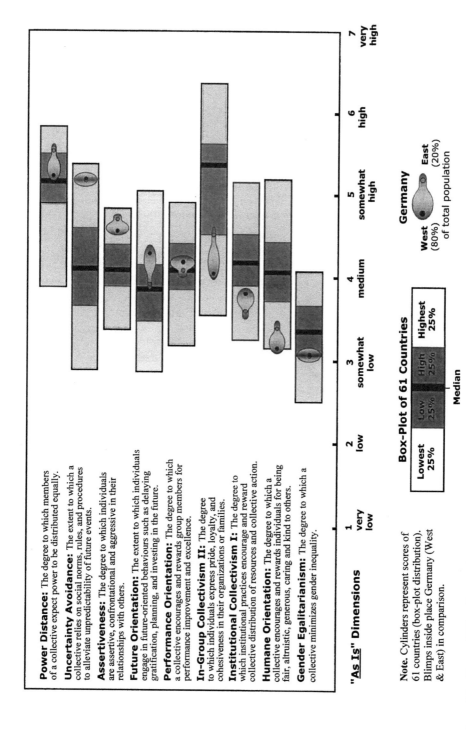

"As Is" Dimensions

Power Distance: The degree to which members of a collective expect power to be distributed equally.

Uncertainty Avoidance: The extent to which a collective relies on social norms, rules, and procedures to alleviate unpredictability of future events.

Assertiveness: The degree to which individuals are assertive, confrontational and aggressive in their relationships with others.

Future Orientation: The extent to which individuals engage in future-oriented behaviours such as delaying gratification, planning, and investing in the future.

Performance Orientation: The degree to which a collective encourages and rewards group members for performance improvement and excellence.

In-Group Collectivism II: The degree to which individuals express pride, loyalty, and cohesiveness in their organizations or families.

Institutional Collectivism I: The degree to which institutional practices encourage and reward collective distribution of resources and collective action.

Humane Orientation: The degree to which a collective encourages and rewards individuals for being fair, altruistic, generous, caring and kind to others.

Gender Egalitarianism: The degree to which a collective minimizes gender inequality.

| 1
very
low | 2
low | 3
somewhat
low | 4
medium | 5
somewhat
high | 6
high | 7
very
high |

Box-Plot of 61 Countries

| Lowest
25% | Low
25% | High
25% | Highest
25% |

Median

Germany

West (80%)   East (20%)

of total population

Note. Cylinders represent scores of 61 countries (box-plot distribution). Blimps inside place Germany (West & East) in comparison.

Figure 6.3 East and West Germany's societal culture, "As Is" dimensions, within box-plot distributions of 61 GLOBE countries (Brodbeck, Frese & Javidan, 2002, p. 18. Reprinted with permission from Academy of Management).

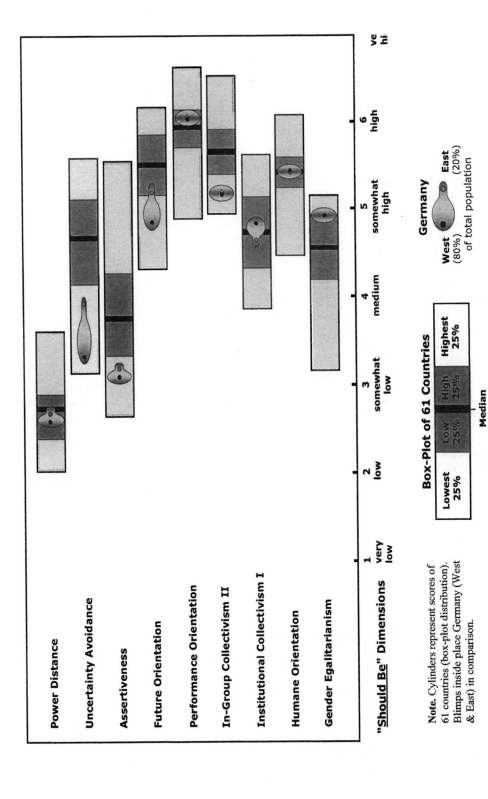

Figure 6.4 East and West Germany's societal culture, "Should Be" dimensions, within box-plot distributions of 61 GLOBE countries (Brodbeck, Frese & Javidan, 2002, p. 19. Reprinted with permission from Academy of Management)

TABLE 6.2
Country Means for Societal Culture Dimensions "As Is" And "Should Be"

Dimensions Society "As Is"	West Germany (W)			East Germany (E)			Sig. Diff.[b]
	Score	Band[a]	Rank	Score	Band[a]	Rank	
Power Distance	5.25	B	29	5.54	A	13	W<<E
Uncertainty Avoidance	5.22	A	5	5.16	A	7	
Assertiveness	4.55	A	10	4.73	A	4	
Future Orientation	4.27	B	13	3.95	B	25	W > E
Performance Orientation	4.25	B	22	4.09	B	33	
Institutional Collectivism I	3.79	C	54	3.56	C	59	
In-Group Collectivism II	4.02	C	54	4.52	B	46	W<<E
Humane Orientation	3.18	D	61	3.40	D	56	
Gender Egalitarianism	3.10	B	44	3.06	B	47	
Society "Should Be"							
Power Distance	2.54	C	44	2.69	C	34	
Uncertainty Avoidance	3.32	D	59	3.94	C	52	W<<E
Assertiveness	3.09	C	55	3.23	B	53	
Future Orientation	4.85	C	57	5.23	B	42	W<<E
Performance Orientation	6.01	B	29	6.09	B	22	
Institutional Collectivism I	4.82	B	28	4.68	B	34	
In-Group Collectivism II	5.18	C	55	5.22	C	53	
Humane Orientation	5.46	B	30	5.44	B	33	
Gender Egalitarianism	4.89	A	15	4.90	A	14	

[a]Bands A > B > C > D are determined by calculating the grand mean and standard deviations across all society "As Is" and "Should Be" scales respectively for the GLOBE sample of countries. These means and standard deviations are than used to calculate low, medium, and high bands of countries (GLOBE standard procedure, cf. Hanges, Dickson, & Sipe, 2004).
[b]Symbols ">" or "<" indicate the direction of significant differences between Germany East and West (one-sided test, $p < .05$) obtained by MANOVA and MANCOVA (i.e., differences in demographics are statistically controlled for) and for sibling samples (samples with equal distributions in demographics are used). Symbols ">>" or "<<" indicate a match in significant differences between East versus West *and* differences in bands.

Unceremoniously axing a top exec just wasn't done—till now. In the old days, a CEO practically had to steal money from the company to lose his job, says Frank F. Beelitz, head of Lehman Brothers Inc.'s German unit. "Now, the life expectancy of an underperformer is getting shorter."

High Uncertainty Avoidance in Decline

Germany's scores for societal culture practices ("As Is") are particularly high on the dimensions *Uncertainty Avoidance* (Fig. 6.3). West Germany ranks fifth highest and East Germany seventh highest in *Uncertainty Avoidance* among the 61 GLOBE countries (see Table 6.2). These findings are higher than what Hofstede (1980) reports. In his study, West Germany ranks only 29th among 53 nations. The GLOBE findings for *Uncertainty Avoidance* "As Is" are in line with our assumption that Germany's long history of many divisions may have increased and supported high *Uncertainty Avoidance* (to avoid anxiety), which contributed to cultural practices of consolidation, risk avoidance, and overregulation. Furthermore, the traditionally Prussian state orientation, resulting in formalization and institutionalization, constitutes a means of reducing uncertainty through structures. Similarly, Warner and Campbell (1993) conclude that Germany's "desire to be grounded in clear and unambiguous principles may be seen as a cultural response to the uncertainties which have characterized German history" (p. 91). Contemporary Germany is again facing uncertainties due to the unsettling times following German reunification and increasing globalization.

High *Uncertainty Avoidance* means that Germans prefer their lives to be structured, well orga-nized, and secure. They rely on rules and institutionalized procedures to reduce stress and anxi-ety when facing ambiguity and uncertainty. These findings are quite consistent with other studies. In its comparative study of 59 countries, the World Economic Forum (2000) ranked Germany 43rd (the higher the number the more pronounced the issue) in terms of burdensome regulations, 49th in terms of the negative impact of the tax system on business investment, 48th in terms of inflexibility of employment rules, and second to last in terms of employer discretion in hiring and firing decisions. The country is ranked 42nd for its low flexibility and adaptability.

Interestingly, in the GLOBE sample, although Germany ranks among the highest 25% on *Uncertainty Avoidance* "As Is" (Fig. 6.3), it ranks among the lowest 25% on *Uncertainty Avoidance* "Should Be" (Fig. 6.4). In other words, compared to the GLOBE sample as a whole, German managers would like to get rid of the many rules, regulations, and constraints. The stark differences between "As Is" and "Should Be" are an example of the divergence between the traditional culture and recent changes in cultural aspirations. The meaning of a disparity between "As Is" and "Should be" country scores is further discussed in chapter*** (i.e. the final Chapter Brodbeck, Chhokar, House, in this Volume).

High Assertiveness in Decline

Germany shows a high degree of *Assertiveness,* which is similar to Hofstede's (1980) finding of high masculinity in Germany. East Germany is the 4th highest and West Germany the 10th highest amongst the 61 GLOBE countries (see Table 6.2). Note that the GLOBE empirical data suggests partitioning Hofstede's masculinity dimension into *Assertiveness* and *Gender Egalitarianism* (House et al., 2004). Apparently, there is a high degree of stability of assertiveness from Hofstede's study time to GLOBE. High *Assertiveness* means that Germans are more confrontational in their relationships with others than members of most other soci-eties. Interpersonal interactions at work tend to be aggressive and assertive. The language tends to be straightforward and stern. This also means that conflict and confrontational debate are acceptable approaches at work. There is a story of Siemens CEO, Dr. Henrich von Pierer, who yelled at his teammate in a tennis match: "You have to hate your opponent!" (*The Wall Street Journal,* February 2, 2001). It seems that open verbal aggression and confrontational behavior is tolerated in German society more than in many others.

On the "Should Be" *Assertiveness* dimension, Germany ranks very low (Fig. 6.4), which is considerably lower than the respective "As Is" score for cultural practices (Fig. 6.3). The downward trend from "As Is" (top quartile) to "Should Be" *Assertiveness* (bottom quartile) is considerably stronger than the global trend. This may reflect a strong desire for a less con-frontational approach to interpersonal relations in Germany. It seems that German managers wish to abandon the traditional "tough on the person" approach.

Zeitgeist of Consolidation

Traditionally, high *Performance Orientation* has been seen as an "ideal" in Germany society. This view is still reflected by the highest score for *Performance Orientation* "Should Be" compared to the scores of all other cultural dimensions in Germany (see Fig. 6.4). However, Germany ranks around the median in *Performance Orientation* "As Is" (see Fig. 6.3). It seems to be no longer or (not yet again) a leading country in that respect. Middle managers in Germany perceive the current "real" society to be lower in *Performance Orientation* than it "Should Be."

West Germany's *Future Orientation* "As Is" ranks among the highest 25%, whereas the "Should Be" score ranks within the lowest 25% of all GLOBE countries. This trend is actually opposite to the global trend of a higher "ideal" than "real" future orientation (the range of the future orientation "Should Be" cylinder shown in Fig. 6.4 is placed considerably higher on the scale than the range of the "As Is" cylinder in Fig. 6.3). It seems that middle managers in West Germany believe that a nonrisky attitude of delayed gratification, planning, and investment into the future should be reduced. Interestingly, East German managers perceive less *Future Orientation* "As Is" and more *Future Orientation* "Should Be" than West German managers. In German history, many uncertainties and divisions have supported an ideal of high future orientation, which was most prominent during the post–World War II period. The current discrepancy between high "As Is" and low "Should Be" scores on *Future Orientation,* which is against the trend among all GLOBE countries, suggests a culture of hesitation and consolidation that is rather recent in nature, possibly a consequence of the post-reunification period (see Appendix C).

Individualism With Collectivistic Elements

Germany's comparatively low ranking on *In-Group Collectivism* and low to moderate ranking on *Institutionalized Collectivism* speak to a mainly individualistic society. Differences between cultural practices (Fig. 6.3) and values (Fig. 6.4) on these dimensions are not particularly pronounced. The *Institutionalized Collectivism* "Should Be" score for West Germany, which is slightly above the median, relates well to the ideal of a "Gemeinschaft" and the social welfare state in Germany (see earlier discussion and Appendix A, respectively). Low scores on collectivism scales are typical for highly developed Western societies, such as the United States or the UK. Individualism means that resources and rewards tend to be distributed on the basis of individual rather than collective achievements, that individuals express pride in their individual achievements rather than in group achievements, and that they value individual self-esteem higher than group loyalty, cohesiveness, or group viability.

Advancement of the Female Workforce

A comparison between this dimension's cylinders in Figs. 6.3 and 6.4 reveals an interesting global trend. *Gender Egalitarianism* is more highly valued than actually practiced in almost all societies studied. The "As Is" cylinder in Fig. 6.3 is positioned at the lower end of the scale whereas the "Should Be" cylinder in Fig. 6.4 is positioned considerably higher. Germany's "Should Be" *Gender Egalitarianism* ranks in the highest 25% of all countries whereas the "As Is" score ranks in the low 25%. The difference between "ideal" and "real" for *Gender Egalitarianism* in Germany exceeds the magnitude of the global trend. German middle managers seem to be particularly strongly in favor of a society that is more equal in opportunities for men and women than it currently is, perhaps favoring a degree of reverse discrimination. Thus, in the decades to come women will probably experience a steeper social advance in Germany than in most of the other GLOBE countries. This seems timely because although the first female leader in a German parliament appeared in 1919 (seventh rank among the GLOBE countries), there are only 5% female representatives in German government today (50th rank among GLOBE countries). Perhaps it is a case in point, that about 8 years after the

GLOBE data was sampled, the Germans voted a political constellation into parliament in September 2005, which resulted in a female Bundeskanzlerin (chancellor or premier) for the first time in Germany's history.

Lowest on Compassion

Germany ranks surprisingly low on *Humane Orientation* "As Is" (see Fig. 6.3, West Germany being the lowest among the 61 countries) and not higher than moderate on *Humane Orientation* "Should Be." A more detailed inspection of what "Humane Orientation" actually means seems appropriate. The GLOBE concept of *Humane Orientation* measures the degree to which a society is perceived ("As Is") and expected ("Should Be") to encourage individuals to be fair, altruistic, generous, caring, and kind to others. The items in the GLOBE scale address mainly prosocial behavior in interpersonal situations (e.g., concern about others, tolerance of errors, being generous, being friendly, and being sensitive toward others). Social interaction in German companies tends to be more task oriented, straightforward, and less "kind" than in many other countries. Germans tend to be perceived by other countries as being driven by abstract principles. The principles are used as (often absolute) guidelines that need to be executed even if individual cases merit another treatment. This decreases a flexible approach toward personnel issues. The low level of humane orientation is in line with the high *Assertiveness* cultural practices reported for Germany earlier. Getting the task done, minimizing errors, and achieving high-quality standards seem to be more important at work than compassion and interpersonal consideration.

The Paradox of Low Compassion and Social Welfare

The findings here seem to present a paradox. On the one hand, Germany scores low on interpersonal humane orientation and compassion at work. On the other hand, Germany enjoys institutions and legal practices, tracing back to the pioneering social welfare laws introduced in the late 19th century, that take care of people's social welfare to a much larger extent than in many other countries (see previous discussion and Appendix A). The German approach to humane orientation seems to be manifested in institutionalized societal caring for people (*Solidargemeinschaft*, or solidarity community), especially the working class and the disadvantaged, rather than in the nature of interpersonal relations at work. The strong tendency to avoid uncertainty in people's lives may have prompted the development of very elaborate institutionalized social systems to take care of people and to reduce risks to individuals and institutions (e.g., the country ranked second in the world in terms of total expenditures on health as a percentage of GDP in 2000). Apparently, there is an institutionalization of altruism, generosity, and caring in Germany that in other countries tend to be taken care of on an interpersonal level. In Germany, humane orientation is seen to be taken care of by state institutions (as part of the *Solidargemeinschaft*) and it seems that therefore, humane orientation on an interpersonal level is perceived (and "Should Be") of lesser importance.

East Meets West

Overall, the societal cultural similarities found in this study of East and West German managers outweigh the differences. Only a few significant differences were found (see Table 6.2). As compared to West German managers, East German managers perceive the reunited German culture to be significantly higher in Power Distance "As Is," In-group Collectivism "As Is," Uncertainty Avoidance "Should Be," Future Orientation "Should Be," and significantly lower in Future Orientation "As Is."

When interpreting these differences, we should keep in mind that both East and West German managers were asked to evaluate the culture in contemporary Germany as a whole and *not* the respective subcultures (East or West German, respectively) they were part of at the time of the study. This leaves us with some ambiguity for interpretation.

The differences in perceptions of *Power Distance* may be related to historical East–West differences; for example, the (Prussian) East has traditionally shown a higher degree of Power Distance than the West. Moreover the differences may be due to the fact that a cultural change toward Western ideals of liberty and self-actualization took place only in West Germany in the 1960s which, for example, reduced Power Distance. A third reason for differences may be related to current perceptions of discrimination on the part of the East Germans as a consequence of the inequalities of the reunification. East Germans receive lower wages, and many of the East German leaders were not promoted or were even downgraded and many were facing unemployment at the time of the GLOBE study. Obviously, we cannot test these different hypotheses with our data set. However, we think that the first two reasons are more likely to explain sustained cultural differences between East and West Germany than the third.

The same three reasons may have contributed to differences of In-Group Collectivism leading to higher "As Is" scores in the East. Note that no differences were found for In- Group Collectivism "Should Be."

We assume that differences in the "As Is" dimensions are probably based on long-term differences in culture (either because of culture change of the 1960s or because of historical East–West differences) whereas differences in the "Should Be" category are more likely to be related to current issues of East–West relations after the reunification. Thus, the higher "Should Be" Uncertainty Avoidance in the East may be the result of the higher objective economic uncertainty that affects East Germans and has contributed to higher levels of anxiety. Higher "Should Be" Future Orientation in the East may similarly be related to higher anxiety levels, as planning for the future (e.g., differed gratification) is one way to reduce anxiety and uncertainty.

Finally, a specific methodological dilemma of a comparison of East and West German managers (still in office) has to be pointed out. Managers from former East Germany, who where still active after the reunification (and thus responded to the GLOBE questionnaire), may not be representative for the typical East German manager before reunification (because many Communist Party members among the managers were fired or demoted—and many of them were party members), whereas the post-reunification West German managers are most likely to be representative of the West German management before reunification.

Overall, the substantial societal cultural overlap found for the East and West German samples investigated by our study is in line with the Germanic cultural cluster that has been consistently reported in cross-cultural studies from the early 1960s to the late 1990s (e.g., Gupta et al., 2002; Ronen & Shenkar, 1985; Szabo et al., 2002). Therefore we feel confident in saying that the contemporary East and West German societal cultures are strikingly similar despite 40 years of separation into rather different economical and political spheres.

The Paradox of Germany's Twin Accomplishments in the Past

The paradox of West Germany's twin accomplishment in the second half of the past century, high economic success and high standards in social welfare, may be related to the paradox of low interpersonal compassion at work and high institutionalized social welfare described earlier. It is quite possible that West Germany's past economic success resulted from high performance orientation and assertiveness paired with low interpersonal compassion at work. This combination allows for higher levels of conflict and controversy at work and such task-focused conflict is likely to contribute to high performance and quality. It is known that, if constructively used, task conflict is productive and does not turn into dysfunctional relationship conflict (Simons & Peterson, 2000), especially when mutual trust is maintained, in Germany, for example, via the institutionalized cooperative capital–labor relationships. Anxiety and stress, usually resulting from interpersonal conflict and controversy, should not have surfaced in Germany to the expected extent because it is counteracted by the institutionalized social welfare systems and labor protection laws, which satisfy personal needs for security and job safety in Germany's high *Uncertainty Avoidance* culture.

An interesting question is whether Germany can reproduce its historic twin accomplishment in the future. Since the late 1990s, Germany has received much criticism from many corners. Otmar Issing, the European central bank's chief economist, has criticized German policymakers for their failure to tackle the overly generous welfare system. The magazine the *Economist* identified the causes of Germany's recent economic malaise as "a Byzantine and inefficient tax system, a bloated welfare system, and excessive labor costs" ("The Sick Man of the Euro," 1999, p. 21). The report also complained about the country's excessive regulations: "Germany is still smothered in regulations that crimp markets. Many prices are regulated and consumers remain 'protected' in bizarre ways" (p. 21). Similarly, the World Economic Forum reported the German tax system and regulations as a major source of competitive disadvantage for German firms. The *Economist*'s recipe: "In the longer term, … it is still more vital that Germany, along with most of Europe, attack the high taxes, over-generous welfare benefits, onerous labor market restrictions and red tape that are choking growth in output and jobs" (p. 21).

Is the German culture prepared to cope with the necessary changes in the social welfare principle considering its current profile in societal values? The GLOBE societal culture findings presented here support the conclusion that the *Economist*'s recipe may not be easy to implement in Germany. Underpinning the high taxes, the excessive regulations, the high labor costs, and the expensive social safety net is a set of cultural values and practices (e.g., high uncertainty avoidance, high assertiveness, low interpersonal humane orientation, high institutionalized social welfare, and strong labor representation). These cultural practices and values have not changed very much over the last four decades. Even more important, these characteristics of the German culture may have actually contributed to Germany's economic and social success in the past, in close interaction with factors such as high performance orientation and high tolerance for conflict and controversy among the workforce.

The apparent trends in Germany's societal culture "Should Be," the declining Power Distance, Uncertainty Avoidance, and Assertiveness, and the advancement of the female workforce and interpersonal Humane Orientation justify some optimism. However, Germany's traditional high Performance and Future Orientation have declined in the 1990s and the previously described cultural practices and values, still endorsed in contemporary Germany, show a better fit in stable times dominated by large industrial companies and labor unions and a stable environment. How will German firms compete in a faster changing global environment? Even more important, is the German leadership culture prepared to promote the necessary changes?

5. LEADERSHIP IN GERMANY

A direct translation of the English term *leader* into the German word *Führer* is inadequate (see also the respective discussion in chap. 5, this volume). The word *Führer* is very negatively connoted in German-speaking countries, and worldwide, because it is associated with Hitler and the Nazi regime in World War II. Interestingly, today there are many German words used in business that contain *Führung* ("leadership," the depersonalized version of *Führer*) and are positively connoted, for example, *Führungskraft* (someone who leads), *Führungseigenschaften* (leadership characteristics), *Führungsanspruch* (attempting to lead), or *Führungsposition* (leadership position). Moreover, German citizens who receive a good *Führungszeugnis* (official document stating that a person had not been in conflict with the law) can hope to be hired as a state employee, and German prisoners who have shown *gute Führung* (good conduct) can hope for an early release to liberty. As Brodbeck (2004) has pointed out, leadership terminology that uses the depersonalized and deindividualized term *Führung* is favored in Germany over the simple word *Führer,* which is semantically the most precise word for a person who leads. Does this mean that "Leadership Made in Germany" is seen as less personal and less interpersonal and more institutionalized and more depersonalized then leadership elsewhere in the world? The GLOBE results can give an answer to this question.

Before we address the respective GLOBE results, we reflect on what the literature has to say about German leadership practice and research, which can be classified according to three phases of economic and cultural development in Germany: (a) the classic period of economical growth and strength in the 1950s, for West Germany as one of the leading economies in the world and for East Germany as a leading economy in the COMCON, (b) the rise of postmaterialistic values and the intake of Anglo-American management philosophies in West Germany with the early 1970s, as compared to no detectable developments with respect to leadership in East Germany, (c) the period of a perceived mismatch between East and West German approaches to work and leadership after the reunification in 1990.

The Post War Period

Research about the relationship between leader attributes and leadership effectiveness was not as strongly endorsed within Germany (Müller, 1995) as, for example, in the United States (e.g., Yukl, 2005). Wunderer explains this with reference to the existence of a *Führerallergie,* which means that German management plays down the positive impact of the leader (cited in Martin et al., 2004, p. 47). This is in contrast, for example, to British and Americans who praise leaders for "single-handedly turning around a company's fortunes" (Stewart, Barsoux, Kieser, Ganter, & Walgenbach, 1994, p. 187). Such a perspective must be seen within its historical context. Since the Holocaust, the term *Führer* (leader) has a negative connotation— worldwide and especially in Germany.

The stereotypical German business leader of postwar Germany is described as a person with a formal interpersonal style and straightforward behavior, technically skilled, a specialist rather than a generalist, neither bureaucratic nor authoritarian, and one who emphasizes *Technik* (i.e., technical excellence) as both means and ends. He or she is a believer in the motto that "well-made products will be eagerly bought" (Lawrence, 1994).

Westernization of Management Principles in the 1970s and 1980s

Since the mid-1970s, concepts like interpersonal skills, delegation, participation, inspiration, and empowerment have become popular among German managers (Wiendick, 1990), which reflects the broader changes in West German attitudes from materialistic to postmaterialistic values and their consequences for leadership practice. The more traditional work values, for example, the fulfillment of materialistic needs, discipline, and orderliness declined and values such as self-fulfillment, life satisfaction, and personal growth became more popular (Maier, 1990; von Rosenstiel, 1995; Zander, 1995). Also apparent is the acceptance of more generalist "Anglo-American" competencies in management, such as social competency, delegation, and participation, together with a focus on motivating and inspiring followers (Lawrence, 1994; Regnet, 1995; Wiendick, 1990).

Post-Reunification Leadership Research

Despite these developments, post-reunification German management style has lately been characterized by the "competence first" principle again (Glunk, Wilderom, & Ogilvie, 1997). Similarly, Hammer (1999) reports on the basis of case studies of German and Swiss managers in which emphasis is still put on the technical expertise of leaders and the bureaucratic rule-setting role of management, than on the communicative and interactive processes of people-oriented leadership.

The importance of participation through systems such as codetermination is emphasized in the German leadership literature. For the whole Germanic cluster (Austria, Switzerland, the Netherlands, East and West Germany), Szabo et al. (2001) report acceptance of the fact that participation "serves as a good means to achieve individual and organizational goals" (p. 239). In Reber, Jago, Auer-Rizzi, and Szabo's (2000) multicountry comparison, participation is identified as a central attribute of German leadership style. Bass (1990) suggests that West German participative leadership is based on the subordinates' expectation to be consulted about decisions. Once the leader makes the decision, subordinates prefer to carry it out autonomously to the best of their ability. This is consistent with the negatively perceived *Führerprinzip* (Bass, 1990, p. 786), and also with the subordinates' preference for high autonomy. German employees are relatively autonomous in carrying out work and have comparatively high job discretion (Glunk et al., 1997; Warner & Campbell, 1993), which is matched with their usually high levels of education, knowledge, and skill.

The centrality of technical competence seems to go hand in hand with a wide span of control in German management, which provides both leaders and subordinates with the level of autonomy necessary to bring technical competency to bear on the task. The principle of participation seems to play a central role in that it delivers the means by which autonomous and technically competent leaders and followers negotiate their contributions to performing the tasks at hand to the highest standards possible.

Empirical research of East German leadership prior to German reunification is difficult to retrieve (cf. Andersch-Niestedt & Lilge, 1981) and to West Germans even more difficult to interpret. Independent leadership research was suspended by the East German SED (*Sozialistische Einheitspartei Deutschland,* or the Socialist Unitary Party of Germany) in 1971, because leadership was perceived to be an intimate and exclusive task of the SED (Zwarg, 1995). The difficulty in appropriately contextualizing the meaning of "business leadership" in former East Germany becomes apparent when considering its political role. The major requirement for East German "leaders" was educating the work force in the political-ideological (SED) doctrines of a socialistic society (Andersch-Niested & Lilge, 1981; Hiebsch & Vorwerg, 1978; Zwarg, 1995). Hiebsch and Vorwerg report empirical data that are in line with this view. Based on factor analyses of leadership functions, they identify three major leadership tasks: "interpersonal cooperative tasks," "technical cooperative tasks," and "political-ideological maturity." The first two factors match with the classic dimensions of "consideration" (people orientation) and "initiating structure" (task orientation) that were popular within the behavior-oriented tradition of Anglo-American leadership research (for a review, see Yukl, 2005). The third factor implies the willingness to indoctrinate others into *socialist* principles. It may be an intriguing research program to explore the Western capitalistic counterpart to socialist "political-ideological maturity." It probably would focus on Western leaders' willingness to indoctrinate others into *capitalist* principles.

In general, research about leadership values and practices in former East Germany is difficult to interpret from a West German perspective. We therefore point out a few highlights about pre- and post-reunification research comparing East and West German leadership that seem valid because they are derived from multiple sources, part of which are from East German and non- German scholars.

Overall, it seems that within the East German system, leadership tasks were more concerned with maintenance and implementation as opposed to initiation and goal setting, which is more predominant within market-economy-driven organizations. Lawrence (1994) describes the former East German ethos as one of "bureaucratic inefficiency," and Warner and Campbell (1993) write of a culture that was "bureaucratic, disciplined and oriented toward control" (p. 90).

In the post-reunification years, some research has focused on comparisons between East and West German work attitudes and leadership styles. The literature seems to converge on only a few characteristics that distinguish East and West German leadership. The majority of findings are in line with the previously described influx of Anglo-American management principles into West Germany during the 1970s and 1980s. Generalist competencies such as motivating followers were considered more important leadership attributes by West German as compared to East German respondents (e.g., Wuppertaler Kreis, 1992). Schulz-Gambard and Altschuh (1993) report higher authority orientation and lower levels of competition among East German managers. Frese, Kring, Soose, and Zempel (1996) show in a longitudinal study that personal initiative and organizational spontaneity are lower among the former East German workforce, providing evidence that bureaucratic socialism can produce work conditions that constrain the development of personal initiative.

More interestingly, a number of studies (Boehnke, Dettenhorn, Horstmann, & Schwartz, 1994; Heyse, 1994; Macharzina, 1993) have demonstrated that East and West German work attitudes and value systems are surprisingly similar in spite of the strong polarization between the East and West evident during the 1990s. Very shortly after the reunification in 1990, the Wuppertaler Kreis (1992) conducted an interview study with $N = 95$ managers from 10 East German organizations near Magdeburg (mean age 47, in occupation 27 years, leadership functions 16 years) and $N = 104$ managers from 35 organizations in North-Rhine-Westphalia (mean age 45, in occupation 23 years, leadership functions 14 years). They reported technical competency and task orientation to be leadership values dominating both East and West German companies. This is in line with recent characterizations of German leadership as being guided by the "competence first" principle (cf. Glunk et al., 1997).

In summary, contemporary leadership research in Germany indicates the enduring importance of technical competence and a strong task/product commitment. Although there seem to be some differences between East and West German leadership values, the principle of participative leadership seems to unite the Germanic cultural cluster in Central Europe, which includes former East and West Germany. What we see within Germany is an institutionalization of leadership, with the existence of systems and structures for participation to depersonalize leadership (Martin, Keating, & Brodbeck, 2004).

In the following, we present the findings from the GLOBE quantitative and qualitative studies about leadership perceptions and prototypes in East and West Germany that were conducted in the second half of the 1990s.

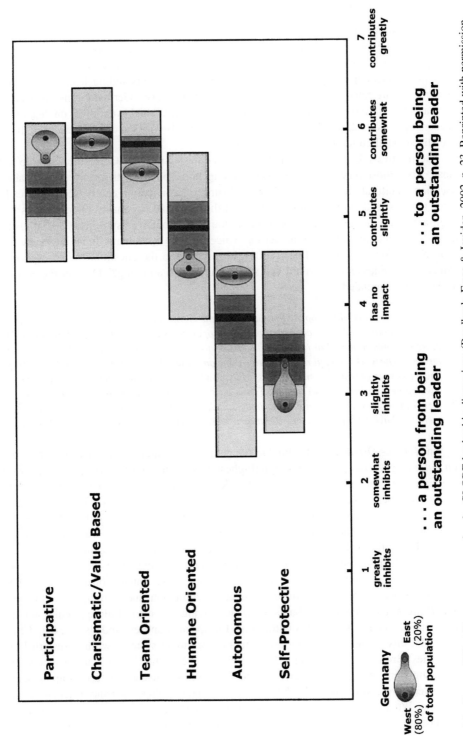

Figure 6.5 East and West Germany on second-order GLOBE leadership dimensions (Brodbeck, Frese & Javidan, 2002, p. 23. Reprinted with permission from Academy of Management)

The Six Second-Order Leadership Dimensions From GLOBE

Figure 6.5 shows the box-plot cylinders representing the scores of all GLOBE countries for the six-second order leadership dimensions. Germany's scores are again represented as blimps (see note to Fig. 6.3). In all GLOBE countries, *Charismatic/Value Based* and *Team Oriented* leadership are perceived as clearly facilitating outstanding leadership. And these dimensions are rated highest in Germany as well. However, Germany ranks just below the median in *Charismatic/Value Based* leadership (low 25%) and even lower on *Team Oriented* leadership (lowest 25%). The latter finding corresponds with the comparatively high individualistic societal cultural values in Germany.

The relatively high ranking on *Participative* leadership sets German leadership cultures apart from most other countries. This finding corresponds with prior research about the Germanic cultural cluster as was described earlier. Participation can be seen as a leadership style that responds to high individualism on the one hand (by making negotiations between high-autonomy parties manageable), and to the institutionalized systems of social justice and labor representation giving employees a "voice," on the other hand. In an interview with the *Wall Street Journal* ("Boss Talk," 2001), in response to the question, "What aspects of the American business model would you say are not worth adopting?" Dr. Von Pierer, the CEO of Siemens responded:

> *The way one deals with people. One example is the German co-determination. Today I met with 30 representatives of works councils from all the operations in Berlin. In Anglo-Saxon world that always sounds so nice. But today the discussion focused on large drives, which we are restructuring…. The works council representative came and said, "We've taken a look at the master plan and we have suggestions from our plant, which is where our know how lies, about where we could develop new business." That's great. That's part of codetermination that the people come with their own suggestions…. You have to understand, you come into a German board meeting and there you have 10 capitalists and 10 labor representatives. That demands different behavior.*

On *Humane Oriented* leadership Germany ranks comparatively low (lowest 25%) whereas on *Autonomy* it ranks particularly high (highest 25%). This pattern corresponds very well with the high levels on assertiveness and the low levels on humane orientation reported earlier for Germany's societal cultures. *Self-Protective* leadership is perceived to clearly inhibit effective leadership in Germany. High self-protective behavior of a leader would inhibit open conflict and controversy (to the benefit of saving face), and thus would also undermine true participation. Interestingly, East German managers (they rank around the median) seem to be somewhat more lenient toward *Self-Protective* leadership attributes than West German managers are (they rank in the lowest 25%). This is probably a consequence of the East Germans not having been exposed to institutionalized codetermination and participation. Interestingly, *Self-Protective* leadership attributes (e.g., face saving) are overall more popular among (former) planned economy systems within East European countries (and also in, e.g., China, see chap. 24, this volume) than they are in market economy systems within Western European countries (Brodbeck, Frese et al., 2000) and others (e.g., the United States, Canada, etc.).

In summary, in line with the global trend, effective and outstanding leadership in Germany is perceived to be charismatic/value based, which includes high performance orientation and decisiveness. What sets the German business leadership culture apart from the leadership cultures in most of the other GLOBE countries is the combination of high participation, high autonomy, and low self-protection along with relatively low interpersonal humane orientation. Altogether, the German profile of attributes and behaviors associated with ideal leadership matches substantially with the profiles of societal culture in Germany. Hallmarks of German cultural practices are high levels of performance orientation, uncertainty avoidance, and assertiveness, along with low levels of interpersonal humane orientation, all soothed by institutionalized participation and social welfare. Compassion is low and interpersonal relations are straightforward and stern—not only at work. It seems that conflict and controversy moderated by institutionalized participation and social welfare are part and parcel of the German societal and leadership cultures.

The 21 First-Order Leadership Dimensions From GLOBE

Differences between East and West German leadership concepts emerge only when a detailed analysis based on the 21 first-order GLOBE leadership dimensions is undertaken (see Table 6.3). Note that the 21 leadership scales formed the basis for the six second-order leadership dimensions (cf. House et al., 2004).

In a two-step process, we established the basis for comparing the samples of East and West German managers on these 21 scales by using individual-level variance.[5] First, we conducted a confirmatory factor analysis (individual level of analysis) in order to establish scale reliability and construct validity for the leadership scales across the East and West German subsamples. Sixteen out of the 21 GLOBE leadership scales were retained (indicated by superscript *a* in Table 6.3) because their reliabilities and factor loadings were satisfactory (see Appendix F). Second, we compared East and West German scores on these 16 scales by using an analysis of variance (ANOVA) for comparing the original East and West German samples, a multiple analysis of covariance (MANCOVA) (statistically accounting for the demographic differences between the two samples reported in Table 6.1), and an ANOVA based on the original East German sample plus the West German twin sample of similar size, in which West German respondents were matched with East German respondents on the basis of the previously identified demographic variables that differed between the two samples (see Appendix G).

Note that the GLOBE scales were designed to measure organizational or societal level variability (Hanges & Dickson, 2004). The scales were not intended to meaningfully differentiate among individuals within a particular society. However, even though the scales were not constructed to provide such information, in some cases it is interesting to assess whether similar factors differentiate individuals within a society especially when subcultures are assumed to exist. However, it should be noted, that because of the within-society restriction of the GLOBE scales true-score variability (which was based on between-society differences) the loadings of the GLOBE scale's items on within society factors should be lower than between societies (cf. Hanges & Dickson, 2004). Furthermore, one should not interpret the within-society factor analyses as replications of the GLOBE factor structure. And the absence of a GLOBE factor within a society should not be automatically interpreted as the factor being irrelevant to the people in that country. Rather, a factor may fail to emerge within a society even when that theme is extremely critical, because there was no variability in how the individuals from a single society rated the items (e.g., they all rated the items a 7). Factor analysis requires variability and so a factor could fail to emerge because it is extremely critical or completely irrelevant to the people within a society.

---

[5]The contributions from Oswald Moosmann in calculating and drafting the tables in Appendixes F and G as part of his diploma thesis supervised by the first author are thankfully acknowledged.

TABLE 6.3

Country Means and Ranks for First- and Second-Order GLOBE Leadership Dimensions

Dimensions Subdimensions	Mean: Germany		Rank: Germany	
	West	*East*	*West*	*East*
Charismatic/Value Based	**5.84**	**5.87**	**42**	**39**
Performance Orientation[a]	6.11	6.33	26	12
Visionary[a]	5.99	5.86	43	47
Inspirational[a]	6.15	6.10	31	34
Integrity[a]	6.12	6.11	30	32
Self-Sacrificial	4.87	5.08	41	26
Decisive	5.78	5.81	37	34
Team Oriented	**5.49**	**5.51**	**56**	**55**
Team Integrator[a]	5.05	5.08	57	56
Collaborative Team Oriented[a]	5.48	5.37	53	56
Administratively Competent[a]	5.51 W < E	5.74	48	34
Diplomatic	5.08	5.10	57	56
Malevolent[a]	1.68	1.71	38	34
Self-Protective	**2.96**	**3.32**	**53**	**38**
Self-Centered[a]	2.10 W < E	2.20	31	24
Status-Conscious[a]	3.72 W << E	4.45	49	27
Conflict Inducer	3.59	4.14	48	26
Face-Saver	2.36	2.46	53	48
Procedural[a]	3.00 W << E	3.40	58	50
Participative	**5.88**	**5.70**	**9**	**14**
Autocratic[a]	1.95	2.06	57	55
Nonparticipative[a]	2.28	2.53	51	35
Humane	**4.44**	**4.60**	**53**	**49**
Humane[a]	4.27	4.36	49	48
Modesty[a]	4.61	4.81	49	41
Autonomous	**4.30**	**4.35**	**10**	**8**
Autonomous[a]	4.30	4.35	10	8

[a]Indicates the first-order scales that were found to be reliable and valid on the individual level of analysis of the German sample (see Appendix F). > / < indicate the direction of significant differences between Germany East and West obtained by MANOVA, MANCOVA, twin sample (see Appendix G). >> / << indicate a match in significant differences between East and West and respective differences in ranks and test bands.

The most significant difference (effect size $\eta^2 > .03$) is that East German managers perceive outstanding leadership to be more positively associated with *Status Consciousness* than do West German managers. Three further significant differences of weaker effect sizes (η^2 range between .01 and .02) were identified: East German managers perceive outstanding leadership to be more positively associated with attributes of *Administrative Competency, Self-Centeredness,* and *Procedural* leadership (see Appendix G). All four significant differences relate to an officious leadership concept in the sense of Max Weber's bureaucratic organization, which matches other reports about leadership in East Germany (e.g., control orientation, Warner & Campbell, 1993; authority orientation, Schulz-Gambardt & Altschuh, 1993).

The here established differences between East and West German leadership perceptions are also in line with GLOBE findings across 22 European countries. There, bureaucratic-type leadership attributes (administrative skill, face saving, procedural, status consciousness) are more positively perceived in Eastern European (formerly planned economy) countries, than in Western European market economy countries (Brodbeck et al., 2000). This is indicative of a specific divide in leadership perceptions at the interface between East and West Europe where Germany is located.

Overall, however, the GLOBE results for Germany demonstrate that the leadership prototypes of contemporary East and West German managers are highly similar to each other. This is in line with several other post-reunification studies of leadership and work values in Germany (Boehnke et al., 1994; Heyse, 1994; Macharzina, 1993; Wuppertaler Kreis, 1992). According to the GLOBE results, in both parts of Germany middle managers perceive outstanding leadership as high in *Performance Orientation,* high in *Autonomy,* and high in *Participation,* as well as medium in *Team Orientation,* and low in *Self-Protection* and *Compassion.*

Profiles of Leadership Types in East and West Germany

In order to better understand particular types of leadership within Germany, we undertook further analyses. On the basis of the 16 leadership scales that were identified to be reliable and valid within the total German sample, profiles of leadership types were empirically formed by using a combination of multidimensional scaling (MDS) and cluster analysis (e.g., Brodbeck et al., 2000; Smith, Dugan, & Trompenaars, 1996). First, MDS was conducted with the 16 scales for each of the two German samples. A two-dimensional structure with an almost perfect fit was obtained for East Germany ($R^2 = .998$) and for West Germany ($R^2 = .996$). The MDS results for East and West Germany are nearly identical (see Appendix H). Dimension 1, termed "Positive vs. Negative," represents the extent to which leadership attributes are perceived to facilitate or inhibit outstanding leadership. Dimension 2, termed "High Independence vs. Low Independence," represents the extent to which leadership attributes are related to social independence on the one side (autonomy, individualistic, independent, unique), and to sociability on the other side (concern about others, tolerance, generous and sensitive toward others). Second, a cluster analysis (average linkage method) was performed to identify groups of leadership scales that are related to each other and distinct from those in other clusters.

Each circled cluster in Fig. 6. 6 represents a leadership type for West Germany. Altogether five leadership types are distinguishable. We termed them (from right to left in Figure 6 *Charismatic, Humble Collaborator, Individualist, Bureaucrat,* and *Oppressive* leadership.

In Fig. 6.7, the clusters and their interrelationships for East Germany are displayed. These differ from the West German clusters in three particular respects: (a) the link between *Status-Conscious* leadership and the *Humble Collaborator* cluster, (b) the link between *Procedural* leadership and the *Oppressive Leader* cluster, and (c) the *Bureaucratic Leader* is not perceived as a distinct leadership type among East German managers. They connote *Status Consciousness* (note it resembles "class consciousness" in communist societies) more positively than West German managers do.

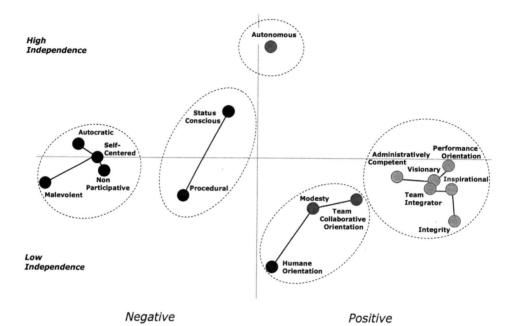

Figure 6.6   West German leadership types (Brodbeck, Frese & Jaqvidan, 2002, p. 25. Reprinted with permission from Academy of Management).

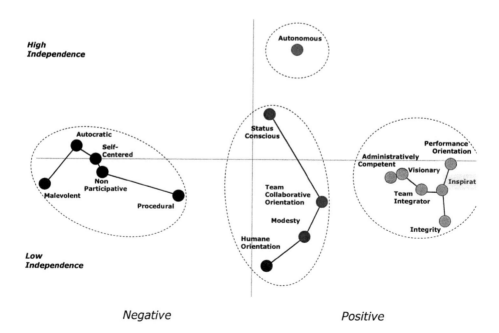

Figure 6.7   East German leadership types (Brodbeck, Frese & Javidan, 2002, p. 25. Reprinted with permission from Academy of Management)

The Charismatic Leader

The most positive leadership type in East and West Germany comprises the attributes of integrity, inspiration, performance orientation, vision, administrative competence, and team integration. We termed this type *charismatic* because three of the attributes listed are described in various theories of transformational and charismatic leadership (inspirational, visionary, performance orientation; e.g., Bass, 1985; an overview is given in Yukl, 2005). The respective clusters shown in Fig. 6.6 (West Germany) and Fig. 6.7 (East Germany) seem to represent a particularly German version of charismatic leadership, which incorporates administrative competence and team-integrative behaviors. As was pointed out by Martin et al. (2004), the importance of these attributes links in with Gurowitz's (1998) assertion of a lingering presence of notions such as authority and position within German society, which are incompatible with newer Anglo-American concepts of leadership that focus on inspiring others via an appealing vision. Another explanation of the administrative and team-oriented blend of charismatic leadership in Germany can be derived from Stewart et al.'s (1994) assertion that—compared with its British and American counterparts—German management downplays the leader's impact. This may be due to the historically negative associations of the concept of *Führer* (a dark charismatic with an evil vision). The consequence is a marked absence of truly charismatic business leaders in contemporary Germany. This was put in clear terms by Swatch founder Nicholas Hayek: "We have too many managers, in other words, people who can conduct a good orchestra and play Mozart or Beethoven clinically and without emotion. However, we no longer have any Mozarts or Beethovens" (Gurowitz, 1998, p. 135, translated by Martin et al., 2004). There seems to be deep fear and constant suspicion in Germany that a visionary leader may turn out to be a dark charismatic.

The Humble Collaborator

The second and also positively perceived leadership type comprises collaborative orientation, modesty, and humane orientation as its central attributes. We termed this type *humble collaborator* because the attributes emphasize leadership on an equal basis with followers, be it in team collaborative work (e.g., group oriented, loyalty, fraternal, consultative, mediator), in personal temperament (modesty, self-effacing, patient), or in interpersonal humane orientation (concern about others, tolerance, generous, sensitive toward others). In contrast to West Germans, East German managers perceive status consciousness to be a positive leadership attribute and they perceive it to be part of the *humble collaborator* cluster (see Fig. 6.7).

Although the *humble collaborator* leader is not as positively perceived as the charismatic leader, this type is clearly desirable in Germany. The perceived importance of humility and collaboration reflects the German value of participation. A *humble collaborator* leader encourages participation and collaboration in organizations. It is noteworthy that attributes of Humane Orientation are the least positive in this leadership type (they are positioned nearest to the midpoint of the positive–negative scale in Figs. 6.6 and 6.7). This can be seen as reflecting the low scores on *Humane Orientation* in Germany's societal culture (see Table 6.2) and second-order leadership dimensions (cf. Fig. 6.5 and Table 6.3).

The low endorsement of humane orientation as compared to high performance orientation indicates that among German managers, task orientation is still perceived to be more important than people orientation. This does not mean that inhumane leadership behavior is tolerated. It rather means that Germans treat interpersonal relationships at work in a distanced and institutionalized way. A strong task orientation does not necessarily denote an eschewal of human relations. As Stewart et al. (1994) have pointed out, in Germany a different approach to motivating workers is taken. If employees hold the same assumptions about interpersonal conduct then "no one feels hard done by when feelings take second place to task" (p. 185). We have already pointed out the positive aspects of low levels of interpersonal compassion at work. For example, task conflict is less likely to turn into dysfunctional relationship conflict. If constructively handled, task conflict is likely to result in high quality and efficiency at work. The humble collaborator seems to be the perfect leadership type for managing such a process in German culture.

The Individualist

Not surprisingly, *individualistic* leadership (autonomous, individualistic, independent, unique) ranks highest on the independence scale. Despite the fact that the *individualist* prototype is opposite the previous type of the *humble collaborator,* it is still viewed somewhat positively by West German managers and even more so by East German managers. It represents the unique, independent, and individualistic manager who stays apart from the crowd. A typical representative of an individualist leader can be seen in Alfred Herrhausen, former president of the Deutsche Bank, who was murdered in 1989 by German terrorists (he was also named as one of the most prototypical German business leaders; see Table 6.8). His impressive career began in 1970 when he became a member of the board of directors. In biographies and the public press reports of his time, he is described as a courageous risk taker, rational in thinking and straightforward, energetic, enforcing, and purposive in temperament, with high performance and power orientation. Most prominently, he was described as an individualist, an outsider, often reserved and distanced with a high need for recognition. Interestingly, he claimed to waive the debt for the poorest developing countries, which was, in his time, for a banker, a quite exceptional position that stood against popular views.

The positive endorsement of autonomous leadership in both parts of Germany is in line with individualism (opposite of collectivism) as a marker of German societal culture (see Table 6.2). On the surface, it seems to conflict with the strong endorsement of participation in the German (work) culture. However, as was noted earlier, institutionalized participation offers a mechanism to attain individual and group goals while monitoring leaders' actions closely (thus allowing for more autonomy) and giving employees a voice in the process (the principle of codetermination). The emphasis on technical competence leads to a wider control span and greater autonomy on part of the employees. However, as Warner and Campbell (1993) note, professionalization on all levels within German organizations reflects (and requires) a considerable degree of self-discipline and self-programming. Independence within agreed-on parameters characterizes the preferred mode of working or managing in Germany (cf. Warner & Campbell, 1993, pp. 99–100). Thus, autonomy granted for leaders in Germany finds its counterpart in the expectation that autonomy is also granted for employees. Institutionalized participation, technically competent personnel, and low self-protection on part of the leaders (and followers) seem to be necessary ingredients to make autonomous leadership (and followership) work effectively in Germany.

The Bureaucrat

The *bureaucratic* leader, comprising the attributes of status consciousness and procedural (ritualistic, formal, habitual, and cautious), seems to exist as a leadership type only among West

German managers. East Germans perceive, on the one side, procedural leadership nearer to the *oppressive leader* and on the other side, status consciousness as part of the *humble collaborator*. The *bureaucratic* leader is perceived by West German managers to slightly inhibit outstanding leadership. This leadership type scores in the middle of the independence scale. Leaders who are visibly attracted to status and privilege, and are focused on rules and procedures, are seen neither as outstanding, nor as particularly ineffective in West Germany. In contrast, status and privilege seems to be part of a more positive leadership image among East German managers. The dislike for procedural leaders in both East and West Germany seems to be rooted in the strong desire for performance orientation and the desire for reduced prevalence and intrusion of rules and procedures that is apparent in the low *Uncertainty Avoidance* societal cultural values ("Should Be," see Table 6.2).

The Oppressive Leader

The *oppressive* leader unifies the attributes of a German leader who is neither trusted nor loved by the followers. An *oppressive* leader tends to be nonparticipative, a micromanager, autocratic, elitist, vindictive, cynical, and hostile, among other attributes. The *oppressive* leader does not recognize the followers' views or contributions, partly due to his or her complete self-absorption, and partly because of his or her cynical and malevolent views toward others. Oppressive leaders are disliked by followers partly because of a negative impact on their emotional well-being and partly because they are the ultimate representations of high self-protection and low participation.

Mixed Leadership Types

The GLOBE data about leadership cannot give direct evidence for actual prevalence rates of these leadership types in Germany (or any other country) because the managers' ratings in the GLOBE questionnaire focused on "outstanding leadership"; that is, they described "very effective" leaders, not necessarily "average" leaders. A perceived "outstanding" leadership style fits the implicit leadership concepts held by followers. Leadership is most effective when the fit between attributes of a leader and the followers' leadership concepts is high because followers are more motivated and committed when their leadership expectations are met and misunderstandings and reluctance against influence attempts are less likely (cf. Lord & Maher, 1991).

For Germany, the charismatic leader (also administrative competent and team integrative) and the humble collaborator (also encouraging participation and compassion) seem to fit the leadership concepts held by middle managers best. However, leadership types are seldom found in purity. They overlap with each other and their relationships to societal cultural values are of particular relevance to predicting which leadership style will be successful—even if not all too positively valued.

For example, some of the oppressive leader's attributes resemble attributes of an individualistic leader (e.g., loner, asocial). The latter is perceived to contribute to outstanding leadership; the former is not. However, oppressive leaders can gain some emotional and motivational commitment from followers due to the conceptual overlap with individualistic leadership. This overlap can raise the likelihood that East and West German middle managers are tolerant toward oppressive leaders. In contrast, this conceptual overlap can also lead to unjustified intolerance toward individualistic leadership styles (e.g., misperceived as dark charismatic).

For another example, a person with high *Assertiveness* and low *Humane Orientation* may still be perceived as a *charismatic* leader in East and West Germany (and may get away with poor interpersonal behavior) because interpersonal humane orientation is less highly valued in German society and organizations than, for example, performance orientation and decisiveness. In other countries, where humane orientation is more highly valued than in Germany, a manager displaying a lack of compassion will never be perceived a charismatic leader.

Leadership Perceptions in East and West German Print Media

Altogether 13 categories were used (see Appendix D) to analyze leadership perceptions evident in a sample of German print media in 1996 (for details, see section 3 in this chapter). The relative frequencies and rankings per category for business leaders in West and East German print media are presented in Table 6.4.

In the predominant West German print media, the three attributes described most often for business leaders are "determined" (13.1%), "high integrity" (9.6%), and "future orientation" (8.8%). For East German print media the three highest ranking categories are "evaluating" (14.0%), "rational" (11.6%), and "confronting" (11.6%). Values and behaviors of business leaders that imply personality characteristics of determination, assertiveness, and masculinity (altogether 21.9%) are about four times more often expressed in West German than in East German print media (altogether 4.7%). In contrast, values and behaviors that imply rationality, evaluation, and opinion expression (altogether 34.9%) are about two times more often expressed in East German than in West German print media (altogether 14.4%). It seems that

TABLE 6.4
Relative Frequencies and Rankings of Leadership Attributes (in 13 Categories) From West and East German Print Media (Business Leaders)

Characteristics	West Germany		East Germany	
	%	Rank	%	Rank
Determined	**13.1**	**1**	4.7	9
High Integrity	**9.6**	**2**	9.3	4
Future Oriented	**8.8**	**3**	7.0	7
Firm	6.4	6	0.0	13
Communicating	6.4	6	9.6	4
Confronting	6.4	6	**11.3**	**3**
Rational	6.4	6	**11.6**	**2**
Evaluating	5.6	8	**14.0**	**1**
Visionary	5.6	8	2.3	10
Collaborating	4.0	10	7.0	7
Optimistic	3.2	11	0.0	13
Opinion Expression	2.4	12	9.3	4
Masculine	2.4	12	0.0	13
Total %	80.3		85.5	
N Phrases	(125)		(43)	

prototypes for business leadership in West German print media are expressed in terms of personal characteristics referring to high task commitment (e.g., leaders are determined, assertive, masculine). In East German print media, business leadership seems to be more a matter of interpersonal exchange and rationality (e.g., leaders express their opinions, evaluate the opinions of others, and confront others with their views).

West German print media portrait business leaders as individuals with high task commitment and determination (cf. *charismatic leader*); East German print media portray business leaders as individuals who express opinions within certain contexts of interaction (cf. *humble collaborator*). The latter can also be related to the significantly stronger endorsement of status consciousness in East as compared to West German leadership prototypes. East German print media seem to be more inclined to attribute leadership to an ascribed status, a position within a social system, rather than to a self-determined individual. On the part of the West German press, the results indicate a partial neglect of the dialectical nature of exchanging opinions in search for higher levels of rationality in business. On the part of the East German press, the results indicate a partial neglect of the business leader as a self-determined person.

For political leadership (see Table 6.5) the differences between East and West German print media are less pronounced. Political leaders are most often described to be "Confronting" (West 18.6%; East 13.6%) and "Determined" (West: 13.6%; East: 12.7%), followed by "Communicating" (9.0%) and "Collaborating" (8.1%) in West German print media, and by "Collaborating" (12.7%), and "Evaluating" (12.7%) in East German print media. The

TABLE 6.5
Relative Frequencies and Rankings of Leadership Attributes (in 13 Categories) From West and East German Print Media (Political Leaders)

	Political leaders			
	West German		*East German*	
Category	*%*	*Rank*	*%*	*Rank*
Confronting	**18.6**	1	**13.6**	1
Determined	**13.6**	2	**12.7**	2
Communicating	**9.0**	3	3.4	8
Collaborating	**8.1**	4	**12.7**	2
High Integrity	**8.1**	4	5.1	6
Firm	7.2	6	1.7	10
Evaluating	5.4	7	**12.7**	2
Future Oriented	5.0	8	1.7	10
Rational	4.5	9	**7.6**	5
Masculine	4.1	10	1.7	10
Opinion Expression	3.6	11	4.2	7
Visionary	1.8	12	3.4	8
Optimistic	0.9	13	0.0	13
Total percent	92.4		80.5	
Total N	(221)		(118)	

higher commonality of East and West German print media in describing political leadership as compared to business leadership may be due to the fact that the leaders being described were most often federal politicians of predominantly West German descent, whereas the business leaders were more likely to be of regional origin. It is also possible that in the public arena of politics task commitment (i.e., determination) and the exchange of ideas in search for better solutions (e.g., confronting) are more evidently displayed for both East and West German print media than in the business arena.

Leaders Versus Managers in West Germany: Interviews

On the basis of content analyses of interview transcripts (see Section 3 for details) altogether eight categories were derived that describe outstanding leaders (left-hand column in Table 6.5) and eight categories that describe average managers (right-hand column in Table 6.6). The two halves of the table read like the "do" and "don't do" of leadership because respondents were asked to contrast attributes of leaders to attributes of managers. The latter turned out to be uniformly seen as "average" and the former as outstanding in at least some respect (as is reflected in the column headlines of Table 6.6).

Outstanding leaders are expected to develop and attain higher order goals (visionary). In comparison, average managers are expected to attain proximate or small goals set by others (administrative). Leaders are described to be convinced and convincing (inspirational), managers to hide (or not act in accord with) their personal convictions (procedural). Usually high personal integrity of leaders can be contrasted to self-centered motives and behaviors ascribed to managers (self-protective). The remaining contrasting categories are: collaborative team orientation versus autocratic and power orientation, self-critical versus face saving, and consideration versus task orientation. So far, all the categories associated with leadership match well with the leadership dimensions GLOBE has identified throughout the world (Dorfman, Hanges, & Brodbeck, 2004). Note that, in the interviews, no category was evident for interpersonal *Humane Orientation,* comprising attributes like generous, compassionate, or being fair, altruistic, caring, or kind to others. This is in line with the GLOBE questionnaire results according to which interpersonal humane orientation is not particularly strongly associated with outstanding leadership in Germany.

Two categories were identified that have not been used in the overall GLOBE study: high transparency (which includes straightforwardness, open communication, and explaining decisions) and a broad knowledge base, for example, knowing the essentials or a wide mental and educational horizon. Both can be related to the central role of autonomy, technical competency (also not part of the GLOBE leadership dimensions), and participation in German organizations, which requires low self-protection (i.e., straightforwardness, transparency, and open communication) and high professionalism (knowing the essentials of the job and a broad knowledge and education).

When asked for publicly known persons who exemplify excellent leadership in their domain, some personal characteristics (e.g., future oriented, visionary, disciplined) and many interpersonal behaviors (e.g., inspirational, motivating, transparency, straightforward, social welfare orientated) were mentioned. When asked for critical incidents from the respondents' personal experience, leadership attributes that are relevant to interpersonal relationships were most often given, for example, open-mindedness, combines job and private life well, motivating, sensitive, convinces others, overcoming hierarchy, trusting, and showing weakness and errors.

TABLE 6.6
Attributes of Outstanding Versus Average Leaders—Interviews

Outstanding Leader	*Average Manager*
Visionary • attains higher order goals • has personal convictions & charisma • knows a lot about recent trends • sensitive for new developments • can abandon old structures and secure paths	*Administrative* • attains proximate goals • has small goals and plans in mind • sticks to rules and traditions • passes the pressure from above to his or her employees
Inspirational & motivating • convincing, shows and gives security • supports employee identification • raises intrinsic motivation • presents him or herself positively to others	*Procedural* • not really convinced about goals • doesn't display personal convictions • problems in own decision making
High integrity • stable self-concept, calm, self-possessed • sure of him or herself, not fearful • modesty, high integrity, trustworthy • a strong soul and mind • disciplined in work and private	*Self-centered* • emotionally unstable • insensitive, superficial, inflexible • switches "chief"/"companion" role • tries to attribute responsibility for errors to others
Collaborative and team oriented • delegates responsibility • participative • able to compromise • empowering • social responsibility • solves conflicts win/win	*Personal power oriented* • no critique of higher management • leads by command, status oriented • doesn't or can't delegate • non-participate, feels as a "king" • wants to do by him or herself • no trust in others doing job right
Critical about him or herself • can take criticism, shows weakness • admits errors or deficiencies • knows his or her limits	*Face saving* • hides errors • changes direction without explicitly telling, is indirect
Considerate of people • committed to his or her employees • doesn't give employees a feeling of being used for something • defines attainable goals • backs one up, caring, sensible, open • personal interest, sympathy, respect	*Task oriented on cost of people* • seldom time to talk to employees • instrumentalizes employees • puts pressure on employees
Transparency • clear communicator, explains decisions • straight forward, relentless when necessary • openly communicates task criteria and controlling mechanisms • displays the paths to the goal clearly	*Unclear* • doesn't explain decisions/motives • unclear, distanced • keeps information secret • low on feedback • actions not clear to understand
Broad knowledge • high competence in field of expertise • knows the essentials right away • wide mental and educational horizon • talented, genius	*Specialized knowledge* • knows much about company • knows much about market

Leaders Versus Managers in West Germany: Focus Groups

The attributes of leaders versus managers from two focus group discussions are described in Table 6.7 (details about the procedures are described in Section 3). They were categorized using the schema that was developed on the basis of the semi-structured interviews described previously. The average manager is perceived as a somewhat autocratic, task-oriented specialist who controls a complex system by attaining the goals specified ("does things right"). A leader is mainly perceived to be "more" than a competent manager, by being wise and visionary ("doing the right thing"), by dealing especially well with people (considerate, empowering), and by being an outstanding person in character (integrity, authentic), in dedication and vision (enthusiastic, innovative), and in education (broad knowledge). These results are very much in line with the results found in the semistructured interviews.

Overall, the focus group discussions resulted in a somewhat narrower range of attributes than in the semistructured interviews. Also, fewer negatively valued attributes of an average manager were given. In particular, negative attributes of interpersonal relations, for example, self-centeredness, being unclear, face saving, and personal power orientation, were more often reported in the "private" context of the semistructured interviews than in the somewhat more "public" context of the focus group discussions. In the focus group setting, the average manager was described to be basically a good person who is trying to do things right, who is personally responsible for the correct procedure, but who does not feel personally responsible to develop a vision of what the right things are (and forms no aspirations that contradict higher management). In the interview setting, the average manager was mainly described as a person who is "doing things right," however, also as a person of questionable personal characteristics (e.g., self-centered, emotionally unstable) and of questionable interpersonal qualities (e.g., nonparticipative, using others for own purpose), that is, not treating people particularly well.

Particular care should be taken when interpreting findings elicited by just one qualitative evaluation method. For example, we contrast findings from the interviews and the focus groups. One can distinguish all attributes found into two broad categories: *intra*personal or personality characteristics like traits or abilities, and *inter*personal characteristics, like social competency, motivating others or being considerate of others. By counting the number of attributes per category, a ratio of about 60% interpersonal attributes to 40% intrapersonal attributes resulted from the interview setting. In the focus groups, the ratio was the reverse: 40% interpersonal and 60% personality attributes. It seems that personal and interpersonal attributes of leaders are differentially salient depending on the social setting imposed by the evaluation method. To go one step further, we also computed the relative frequencies of interpersonal (e.g., communicating, collaborating) and intrapersonal categories (e.g., rational, optimistic) from the results of the print media analysis. A ratio of about 35% to 65% respectively was found. Thus, interpersonal aspects of leadership seem to be least salient in print media (35%) and less salient in focus group discussions (40%) than in semistructured interviews (60%). The more intimate (or the less public) the social setting the more likely it is that interpersonal attributes of leaders are reflected and discussed.

In summary, the interview and focus group data, which was categorized by individuals naive to the GLOBE hypotheses, replicate nearly all GLOBE dimensions for Germany. Interestingly, Humane Orientation did not emerge as a category in the qualitative analyses, which is probably due to the comparatively low salience of interpersonal conduct at work in Germany. Some further categories for outstanding leadership, namely high transparency and broad knowledge base, were found. High transparency fits well with the ideal of participation

TABLE 6.7
Attributes of Outstanding Versus Average Leaders—Focus Groups

Outstanding Leader	*Average Manager*
Visionary • clear vision • knows about new trends	*Administrative* • organizes and commands • encourages new ideas but not against the higher management
Inspirational & motivating • enthusiastic • charismatic	*Procedural* • keeps things going • controls a complex system
High integrity • trustworthy, authentic, modest • high discipline • can deal with chaos while not being chaotic • brave • non-materialistic orientation	
Collaborative and team oriented • delegates by task and not by formal procedures • doesn't rely on formal power • cnflict resolving • a servant of the company • teamwork competency • empowers others • committed to others	*Personal power oriented* • dominating • a person who wants power
Considerate of people • sensitive • supports ideas of employees • trusting employees • loyal toward employees • open, tolerant, and fair • communicative	*Task oriented on cost of people* • some social competency • delegates • not very good in criticizing • flexible
Transparency • shares vision with others	
Broad knowledge • broad education • creative • multiculturally oriented but not other cultures • wise • spirited when it becomes difficult	*Specialized knowledge* • specific knowledge • specialist • knows his or her own culture quite well
Does the right thing	*Does things right*

and constructive conflict and broad knowledge base fits well with the ideal of autonomy requiring professionalism and high task competency. When asked to describe public leaders or leaders the respondents have firsthand experience with, interpersonal attributes dominate over personal attributes. They comprise aspects of charismatic leadership, high transparency in communication, and humane orientation (e.g., inspirational, motivating, open communicator, straight forwardness, social welfare orientated). Differences in relative proportions of intrapersonal versus interpersonal attributes seem to be a result of the evaluation method used. The more direct and face-to-face the evaluation method is (print media–focus group–personal interview), the more interpersonal attributes for describing leaders are elicited.

Job Requirements for Executive Positions in West Germany

Table 6.8 lists the relative frequencies of job requirements published in job advertisements in West German print media for the 16 categories identified (see Appendix E, for details about the procedures used, see Section 3). From 1981 to 1996, the average number of attributes listed per advertisement increased from 2.57 to 3.84. Despite this quantitative increase, the relative frequencies and rankings are remarkably stable. In 1981 and 1996, West German leaders are mainly expected to take initiative (13.5%, 11.8%), to be purposive (12.8%, 12.2%), and to communicate effectively (11.5%, 10.2%). The demand for collaborative qualities has increased significantly, from the fifth position in 1981 (7.7%) to the first position (14.2%) in 1996. In contrast, "responsibility" is less often listed in 1996 (2.0%) than in 1981 (6.4%). A similar negative trend exists for administrative skills (1981: 9.6%; 1996: 7.7%).

It seems that the old-fashioned leadership ideal of individual responsibility within a clear hierarchy (bureaucratic, administrative orientation) is changing toward a leadership ideal of interpersonal competencies and team orientation. Furthermore, "firmness" and "future orientation" are listed nearly twice as often today (6.5% and 6.9%) than 15 years ago (3.8% and 3.8%). Finally, "willingness to learn" (2%) has emerged as a new characteristic that was not listed in 1981.

Commonly Known Leaders in West Germany

Sixteen outstanding business leaders were suggested by a convenient sample of 14 West German respondents (basically random people on the street). Table 6.9 (right-hand side) describes the three most frequently suggested persons, Axel Springer (for the postwar period and somewhat later), Alfred Herrhausen (for the 1970s to late 1980s), and Leo Kirch (for the mid-1980s to the late 1990s—his company went bankrupt in 2002 several years after the GLOBE evaluation took place). Twelve outstanding political leaders were mentioned. Table 6.9 (left-hand side) describes the predominant attributes for the three most frequently mentioned political leaders: Ludwig Erhard (for the postwar period), Willi Brandt (for the 1970s to early 1980s) and Helmut Kohl (for the mid-1980s to the mid-1990s; at the time of evaluation he served as Bundeskanzler, i.e., chancellor or premier).

The leadership attributes described in Table 8 cannot be viewed as representative; however, each person seems to exemplify a "Gestalt" of an outstanding leader in a certain historical and contemporary period of Germany.

With the exception of Alfred Herrhausen (see the subsection Individualist Leader), all leaders in politics and business were reported to have a vision. The vision was either very appealing to all ("combining economic growth and social justice" by Ludwig Erhard, or the "ideal of peace and reconciliation" by Willy Brandt, or "supporting social economy" by Axel Springer), or it was appealing to a very large proportion of the public (e.g., "reunification of Germany and its integration in Europe," by Helmut Kohl), or it was a vision of some

TABLE 6.8
Percent of Attributes per Category in West German Executive Job Advertisements

Characteristics	1981		1996	
	%	Rank	%	Rank
Initiative	**13.5**	1	**11.8**	3
Purposive	**12.8**	2	**12.2**	2
Communicating	**11.5**	3	10.2	4
Administrative Skill	**9.6**	4	7.7	5
Inspirational	7.7	5	6.9	7
Collaborative	7.7	5	**14.2**	1
Leader Experience	7.1	7	6.9	5
Responsible	6.4	8	2.0	12
Motivating	5.8	9	3.3	11
Firm	3.8	11	6.5	9
Flexible	3.8	11	4.9	10
Future Oriented	3.8	11	6.9	7
Rational	3.2	13	2.0	12
Enthusiastic	1.9	14	1.2	15
Directive	1.3	15	0.8	16
Willingness to Learn	0.0	–	2.0	12
N of categorized attributes	156		246	
Total N of attributes	177		261	
Total N of advertisements	69		68	
Attributes per advertisement	2.57		3.84	

self-grandiosity ("creating a media monopoly in Germany," by Leo Kirch) that provoked distrust and harsh criticism from various groups in society. All leaders were admired or at least respected for mainly three different classes of personal leadership characteristics:

- Purposive goal attainment, high performance orientation.
- High expertise, realism, rationality, and reliability.
- Courage and straightforwardness.

Positively valued *inter*personal attributes were mainly associated with Willy Brandt, who was said to have displayed the "most human form of power" (Eppler, 1992), including trustworthiness, collaborative, and humane orientation, and somewhat associated with Ludwig Erhard (the "father" of Germany's social market economy) for his social justice and social welfare orientation. Most of the interpersonal leadership behaviors ascribed to the remaining political and some of the business leaders were pointed out in the biographical publications to be questionable to at least some extent, for example, they were said to instrumentalize personal

TABLE 6.9
Leader Attributes of Publicly Known Leaders in West Germany

Political Leaders	Business Leaders
1945 to 1960s: Post World War II, a Period of Privation and Beginning Economic Growth	
Ludwig Erhard (1897–1977): German Minister of Economy (1945–1963) as a member of the conservative party (CDU). Known as the father of the "soziale Marktwirtschaft" his (social economy) and the German "Wirtschaftswunder" (engl., economic mystery).	**Axel Springer (1912–1985):** Most successful publisher (popular press, e.g. Bild-Zeitung) during the German postwar area and the 1960s and 1970s. Known for his conservative attitudes, fight for German Reunification, reconciliation with Israel, and supporting the social economy.
Leader attributes: • Visionary, "highly prognostic in economics" • Realistic and constructive optimist • Performance orientation • Social justice orientation, "Gemeinwohl" • Firm, imperturbable • High expertise in economics	**Leader attributes:** • Visionary, missionary • Moralist, religious • Patriarchal, micromanager • Seeking for harmony • "Publishers task ... of 'grounding' ideals • often excludes materialistic thought and action."
1960s to 1970s: A Period of Social Change (e.g., Student Revolt) and Steady Economic Growth	
Willy Brandt (1913–1992): German Chancellor (1969–1974) as a member of the social democratic party (SPD). Known for his "Versöhnungspolitik" (politics of reconciliation) with East Germany. Received the Nobel Peace Prize in 1971.	**Alfred Herrhausen (1930–1989):** Known as president of the Deutsche Bank who was murdered in 1989. He became member of the board of directors, Deutsche Bank, in 1970. His high rise ("high profile," "sharply rising") career extended until the late 1980's when he became president of the Deutsche Bank.
Leader attributes: • Visionary, "ideal of peace," inspirational • High integrity, trustworthy, loyalty • Collaborative, cooperative, mediator • Social and humane orientation • Convincing speaker, excellent listener • Ambitious, highly self-critical	**Leader attributes:** • Risk taker, courageous, straightforward • Energetic, enforcing, purposive • Peformance oriented, individualist, outsider • High need for recognition and confirmation • Micromanager, power oriented, autocratic • Rational, reserved, distanced.
1980s and 1990s: A Period of Geopolitical Change (Reunification) and Reduced Economic Growth	
Helmut Kohl (1928): German Chancellor (1982–1998) as a member of the conservative party (CDU). Known to be the driving force of the Reunification of Germany in 1989 and its integration in the European Union. Despite intense investigations, he was never sentenced for obvious deception.	**Leo Kirch (1927):** Known as "media tycoon" who created an empire consisting of several private TV stations and several TV-production and trading companies. His activities were subject to public suspicion in the early 1990s. He lost his whole empire right after the turn of the century.

(Continued)

TABLE 6.9 (*Continued*)

Political Leaders	*Business Leaders*
Leader attributes:	**Leader attributes:**
• Politically instinctive and far-sighted • Purposive, enforcing, "a doer" • Firm, consistent, reliable, autocratic • Ambitious, micropolitician • Realistic with common sense	• Vision of himself as a media monopolist • Instrumentalizing personal relationships • Firm, hard, smart, cunning • Personal power and status oriented • Patriarchal, autocratic, micromanager

relationships, play micropolitics, be autocratic, display patriarchal behaviors and high power orientation at the expense of people orientation. However, the popularity of these leaders and the fact that they were commonly chosen as examples for outstanding leadership underlines the quantitative GLOBE results for Germany, which indicate a leniency toward leadership that displays deficiencies in interpersonal conduct and humane orientation. This view is also in line with the argument described earlier, that leadership in Germany seems to be depersonalized and institutionalized (Martin et al., 2004).

6. SUMMARY

The GLOBE program has demonstrated that characteristics attributed to outstanding leaders match closely with cultural values and practices (cf. House et al., 2004). Our analysis shows that this holds true for Germany as well. Hallmarks of German cultural practices are high levels of *Uncertainty Avoidance, Assertiveness,* and *Performance Orientation,* along with low levels of *interpersonal Humane Orientation*, all moderated by institutionalized social welfare and code-termination of capital and labor. Effective German leaders are characterized by high *Performance Orientation,* high *Autonomy,* high *Participation,* low *Self-Protection,* and low *Compassion.* Conflict and controversy seem to be built into the German work culture, soothed by institutionalized participation and social welfare. In short, the phrase, "tough on the issue, tough on the person, participative in nature," appears to best characterize the GLOBE findings for leadership "Made in Germany" at the turn of the 20th century (Brodbeck, Frese, & Javidan, 2002).

Is the German culture prepared to cope with the necessary changes when considering its current economical profile? The GLOBE societal culture findings presented here can lead to the conclusion that the *Economist*'s recipe, "attack the high taxes, over-generous welfare benefits, onerous labor market restrictions and red tape that are choking growth in output and jobs" ("The Sick man of the Euro," p. 21) is not easy to implement because a set of historically rooted cultural practices and values (uncertainty avoidance, assertiveness, performance orientation, institutionalized welfare, and strong labor representation) underpins the status quo that the *Economist* suggests to "attack." The decline of Germany's traditionally high performance and future orientation in the 1990s—Zeitgeist of consolidation—worsens the case. We assume that it is much more difficult to change national culture than organizational cultre. Since the issues of high uncertainty avoidance, high assertiveness and low humane orientation may be more important in the companies because it makes it difficult to manage change, we suggest that organizations should work hard on changing their organizational culture. Managers in Germany should not wait (or hope) for societal changes to happen any time soon.

What is on the positive side then? Apparent positive trends in Germany's societal culture ("Should Be") indicate, on the one hand, declining levels of power distance, assertiveness, and uncertainty avoidance and, on the other hand, an increased popularity of gender egalitarianism and interpersonal compassion at work. These trends justify some optimism. Altogether we think that our analysis can serve as a first step toward a societal cultural SWOT (strengths, weaknesses, opportunities, threats) analysis for another twin accomplishment for Germany (world-class economy *and* social welfare) in the new millennium.

Are German managers prepared for taking up leadership roles that support the necessary changes? The current "tough on the issue, tough on the person" leadership approach in combination with institutionalized participation appears to explain Germany's twin accomplishments of economical and social welfare in the second half of the 20th century. However, whereas this period was dominated by large industrial companies and labor unions and a stable environment, the present and the future look different. The old-fashioned "tough on the issue, tough on the person" leadership approach is unlikely to be effective in a future that requires to respond to the challenges of globalization and to change the "Germany AG" from a state-granted social market to a private-initiative-based modern social economy.

What can be done? A "tough on the issue, *soft* on the person" leadership approach seems to be a better recipe for future generations of German managers. It requires a careful development of Germany's business leaders that enables them to promote and effectively manage declining levels of power distance and uncertainty avoidance, on the one hand, and to capitalize on the increased popularity of gender egalitarianism and the apparent request for more compassion, interpersonal competence, and team orientation at work, on the other hand. It also requires the preservation of the traditional benefits of constructive conflict at work by keeping the balance of high autonomy (for leaders and employees), high participation (codetermination), and low self-protection on part of the leaders, as well as working toward even improving levels of professionalism, technical competency, and broad knowledge on the part of both leaders and followers.

A lot can be learned, not only from the West, where business leaders are portrayed in the public press as determined, future oriented, and assertive, but also from the East, where business leadership is portrayed as dialectical in nature, a constant exchange of opinions in search for higher levels of rationality and effectiveness. Overall it seems that the valuable principles of codetermination and humane orientation, which traditionally have been institutionalized in Germany, need to find their way onto the interpersonal levels of face-to-face social behavior in small groups, company networks, and international partnerships, guided by principles of direct participation and compassion.

7.   PRACTICAL IMPLICATIONS

The strong relationship between societal culture and leadership perceptions, which are evident across all GLOBE countries and in Germany as well, finds an explanation in the following processes: Culture defines a set of acceptable and unacceptable behaviors. Individuals learn to conform to these norms through acculturation and socialization. Over time, individuals become particularly skilled at acceptable behaviors. Successful managers are well socialized and acculturated. They tend to be good at acceptable behaviors.

Cultural adaptation can also be dysfunctional, for example, when managers are placed in a different cultural environment or when change is forced on organizations or whole societies. Successes (and failures) in the past generate experiences and formerly successful behaviors will be repeated elsewhere—even when change is required.

Considering Cultural Differences

GLOBE has produced a database that can help us identify the similarities and differences among countries and organizations. When two cultures are relatively similar in content, that is, their dimensional profiles have considerable similarities (rather than markedly different), transacting business is easier with not much change in behaviors (for a detailed discussion of GLOBE results in relation to knowledge transfer across cultures, see Stahl, Javidan, Brodbeck, & Wilderom, 2004).

However, even when it comes to apparently very similar cultures, we have learned that it is useful to take a more detailed look. For an example, the GLOBE data show the cultural profiles of Austria, German-speaking Switzerland, and Germany to be highly similar to each other and dissimilar to 19 other Pan-European countries (Brodbeck et al., 2000). To a manager from Japan or any other culture distant to the Germanic cultures, representatives from these three Germanic countries appear very much the same. However, there can be subtle but disturbing differences when representatives from highly similar cultures are working together. Closer inspection of the GLOBE database revealed that leadership concepts of German-speaking Swiss managers differ in some subtle ways from their German counterparts. They rank slightly lower on autonomy and somewhat higher on modesty, diplomacy, and team orientation than their German counterparts. Although the differences on each dimension are small, their combined effects may have severe consequences in particular situations (Weibler et al., 2000). According to the author's observations, German-speaking Swiss managers find it disturbing when German managers tend to present their views in a confrontational manner (low compassion, low modesty, low team orientation, high straightforwardness), thereby stressing the differences between others and their own position (high autonomy) by making statements like, *"Yes! But I think X and Y."* In German-speaking Switzerland, different views are usually presented in a compromising way (higher compassion, modesty, and team orientation) stressing the common basis (lower autonomy) by a statement like, *"Yes! And we should also consider X and Y."* The same factual issue, introduced with a *"Yes, but I ..."* approach, is less likely to be impartially considered by Swiss managers than when it is introduced with a *"Yes, and we ..."* approach.

When cultures are different in content, that is, their dimensional profiles are significantly different, adjustment is generally necessary in proportion to the cultural distance. It will be more difficult to adjust to another culture if the cultural differences are large and manifold because it implies that people need a higher amount of cognitive and behavioral restructuring, especially when larger cultural regions are trespassed (the 10 cultural regions identified by GLOBE; cf. House et al., 2004). This can be attained via training, coaching, and experience within the country. Knowledge about specific cultural characteristics (e.g., the type of constructive conflict and controversy at work endorsed in Germany) can help expatriate managers to better anticipate potential benefits (constructive controversy leads to high quality) and potential problems (interpersonal conflict leads to stress and emotional strain) in cross-cultural interactions. The knowledge derived from GLOBE about the particular leadership profiles that most strongly differentiate two or more target countries can be used for the development of cross-cultural management training and coaching.

For example, the empirical evidence for German managers being perceived as lower in humane orientation and as higher in autonomy than UK managers can be used to tailor-make trainings for the managers from these two countries by identifying and developing critical role-play situations that embody the particular differences GLOBE has identified.

Another implication is that a manager successful in one culture may not be able to adjust well to another culture. Or the other way around, a technically well-qualified manager who is socially maladjusted at home might actually be a good fit in another culture.

For example, assertiveness in Germany is associated with straightforwardness, tolerance for conflict, and controversy. Paired with low interpersonal humane orientation, this might lead to a manager humiliating an employee from a higher humane orientation culture like the UK. In contrast, the same set of factors paired with high performance orientation can be highly efficient with employees from a high performance orientation culture like Germany. A UK manager with high tolerance for conflict and controversy and high performance orientation, who is not the perfect fit within his or her mother culture, can actually be a successful manager in Germany, particularly if he or she is not easily disturbed when facing conflict and low compassion in interpersonal behavior.

Considering Change

Germany may have to change its culture to be able to compete successfully in the global markets of the 21st century. However, societal culture is difficult to change. Some cultural dimensions are so deeply rooted in history and society that any change will take a long time and require widely distributed efforts. Germany's high uncertainty avoidance, high individualism, high assertiveness, and reliance on state intervention seem to be deeply rooted in its history. Both parts of Germany rank similarly on these dimensions in various studies from the early 1960s to the late 1990s. However, prompted by the demands of the free-market economy and globalization in the 1990s, Germany has witnessed a questioning of the ideals of a welfare state in favor of neo-liberal concepts of self-reliance and of individual commitment to smaller, organically grown units such as family, work groups and networks. The country has entered a postmodern type of democracy, in retreat from state intervention and disenchanted with the welfare state (Hahn, 1995). First steps to such a change are visible; Germany is currently reducing resources to its social programs by using additional private pension schemes (*Private Zusatzrente*) and increasing private contributions to the health care system. Note that the 2005 elections in Germany resulted in a pat situation for the two major political parties (the socialist SPD and the conservative CDU), which the media currently interpret to promote stagnation rather than reforms. If major reforms can be brought on their way at all, it seems it will take a broad consent within society and across political camps.

Our own data support the view that some cultural aspects are already valued differently than some decades ago. German society and organizations want to advance more female participation in work and management. This could even change the comparably low levels of perceived humane orientation because a more feminine ideal of leadership could bring more interpersonal compassion to work. The German Zeitgeist of consolidation, in part a consequence of the tremendous monetary and psychological costs of the reunification process, seems to be a major obstacle. A critical challenge is how to restructure the traditionally institutionalized mechanisms for maintaining social welfare, cooperative capital–labor relationships, and personal safety while at the same time cutting down on high taxes, high labor costs, and a cumbersome bureaucracy.

Last but not least, there are consequences to tolerating managers who are insensitive to the feelings of employees and are so task focused that learning and development are not on their agenda. Especially in these times of globalization and multicultural work forces, the so-called soft skills (e.g., consideration of people, compassion in interpersonal conduct, team orientation, and cross-cultural flexibility) become critical attributes for success. Though conflict and controversy have their merits in a highly task-focused and performance-oriented society, German managers need to be aware of the pitfalls of their current "tough on the issue, tough on the person" approach. This is particularly true when institutionalized systems to deal with social welfare and the peoples' *angst* are in decline.

Developing the perceived strength of outstanding leadership *Made in Germany* (i.e., high performance orientation, low self-protection, high participation, high autonomy, open communication, technical competency, and a broad knowledge base) and changing the weaknesses (medium team orientation, low interpersonal humane orientation) seems to be the route to go. The benefits of developing leaders to be "tough on the issue, *soft* on the person, and participative in conduct" need to be intensively explored in future practice and research. Further practical implications for doing business with Germans, which relate to GLOBE findings, are described by Schroll-Machl (2005). The author looks at two sides of business partnerships—on the one hand, when people are working from their home country or as expatriates with Germans; and on the other hand, when Germans have business relationships with people from all over the world, wether face to face or at a distance.

8.   LIMITATIONS AND FUTURE RESEARCH

Though ambitious in scope and design, the GLOBE project has set clear limitations on the samples and methods used within each country. The strengths of the quantitative and comparative design of GLOBE sets clear limits to the study of a particular country's societal and leadership cultures because data from only three industries and only middle managers were obtained. Clearly this does not constitute a representative sample. However, note that, in the overall GLOBE study, in fact all the societal cultural and leadership dimensions have been triangulated on the country level of analysis with a whole variety of additional data about the countries studied (cf. House et al., 2004). With the additional qualitative analyses, using a whole range of respondents (e.g., managers, journalists, and ordinary people from different strata in society) and several different methods for data gathering, at least some triangulation was possible for Germany. The quantitative and qualitative findings about Germany described in the present chapter converge in nearly all respects. This increases our confidence in the validity of the findings and the conclusions.

Even more ambitious is the attempt to describe a nation's history, economy, societal culture, and leadership concepts in just a couple of pages while not being an expert in the relevant disciplines of political science, history, economy, management, anthropology, and sociology. The reader who is an expert in one of these disciplines may accept our apologies for not being aware of further relevant resources. We can only hope that the results described and the interpretations given stimulate further and improved quantitative and qualitative research into the issue of how leadership concepts held in Germany relate to its societal culture, the effectiveness of its organizations, and the economic situation as a whole.

The following suggestions for future research are based on our psychological background in the subdisciplines of basic and applied social, cross-cultural, work, and organizational psychology.

First, obviously the GLOBE data generated to date does not allow stringent predictions about actual leadership behavior in organizations and cross-cultural situations. This requires further in situ investigation of how a particular cultural background influences leadership behavior and effectiveness within and across certain cultures' boundaries.

Second, an intriguing consideration about leadership made in Germany becomes evident when considering that the interpersonal dimension of leadership is becoming more critical around the world. Traditional power distance, competition, and conflict-based models of how human beings relate with each other are no longer functional in a highly interconnected world (Clark & Matze, 1999). Thus, members of certain cultures may be better suited to the new challenges of global leadership than others are. For example, Martin et al. (2004) argue that German managers (as compared to Irish) may be less geared to operating as multinational executives because of the very specific cultural context of their country's success (cf. Warner & Campbell, 1993). Also, too few of them have worked or studied abroad. Assuming that a global company's success is clearly linked to the emotional intelligence of its leaders (cf. Adler, 2002), comprising empathy and social skills for successfully managing relationships, the German leadership concept with its dominant task focus and low interpersonal humane orientation does indeed not seem to match particularly well to the future global challenges.

However, our outlook to the potential of international success of leadership made in Germany is actually less grim than that reported in Martin et al.(2004). There are clear strengths in German leadership concepts, as there are particular leadership strengths to discover within any societal culture. Within Germany, outstanding leadership is associated with high performance orientation, technical competency, autonomy, straightforwardness, constructive controversy, and participation. When adequately managed (e.g., *soft* on the person), these attributes can provide for work outcomes of the highest ambition and quality—anywhere in the world. These and similar hypotheses, which emphasize the notion that there is a grain of "truth" (about what makes people live well) in every viable societal culture and leadership approach around the world, seem worthwhile to be further investigated by sound empirical testing and practice.

REFERENCES

Adler, N. J. (2002). *International dimensions of organizational behavior* (4th ed.). Cincinnati, OH: South-Western.

Abbruch Ost. (2003, February 6). *Der Spiegel.*

Andersch-Niestedt, H., & Lilge, H.-G. (1981). *Betriebliche Führung im Vergleich: Bundesrepublik Deutschland—Deutsche Demokratische Republik* [Comparing business leadership: Federal Republik of Germany—German Democratic Republik]. Berlin: Verlag Volker Spiess.

Armbrüster, T. (2005). *Management and organization in Germany.* Bodmin, Cornwall, England: MPG Books.

Bass, B. M. (1985). *Leadership and performance beyond expectations.* New York: The Free Press.

Bass, B. M. (1990). *Bass and Stogdill's handbook of leadership: Theory, research, and practical applications* (3rd ed.). New York: The Free Press.

Berschin, H. (1993). Deutschlandbegriff im sprachlichen Wandel [Semantic changes of the concept of Germany]. In W. Weidenfeld & K.-R. Korte (Eds.), *Handbuch zur deutschen Einheit* (pp. 139–147). Frankfurt, Germany: Campus.

Boehnke, K., Dettenborn, H., Horstmann, K., & Schwartz, S. (1994). Value priorities in the United Germany: Teachers and students from East and West compared. *European Journal of Psychology of Education, 9,* 191–202.

Boss talk: Goal is game, set, and match—Siemens' CEO allies tactics of tennis to management: Rules of winning, losing. *The Wall Street Journal.* (2001, February 2).

Brockhaus Encyclopedia. (1997). *Deutsche Einheit* [German reunification], *5,* 289—290.

Brodbeck, F. C. (2004). Führung—made in Germany. *Die Mitbestimmung, 4 (April),* 10–18.

Brodbeck, F. C., Frese, M., Akerblom, S., Audia, G., Bakacsi, G., Bendova, H., et al. (2000). Cultural variation of leadership prototypes across 22 European countries. *Journal of Occupational and Organizational Psychology, 73,* 1–29.

Brodbeck, F. C., Frese, M., & Javidan, M. (2002). Leadership made in Germany: Low on compassion, high on performance. *Academy of Management Executive, 16*(1), 16–29.

Brodbeck, F. C., Hanges, P. J., Dickson., M. W., Gupta, V., & Dorfman, P. W. (2004). Comparative influence of industry and societal culture on organizational cultural practices. In R. J. House, P. J. Hanges,

M. Javidan, P. Dorfman, & V. Gupta (Eds.), *Leadership, culture, and organizations: The GLOBE study of 62 societies* (pp. 654–668). Thousand Oaks, CA: Sage.

Clark, B., & Matze, M. (1999). A core of global leadership: Relational competence. In W. H. Mobley, M. J. Gessner, & V. Arnold (Eds.), *Advances in global leadership* (Vol. 1, pp. 127–161). Stamford, CT: JAI.

Craig, G. A. (1991). *The Germans.* New York: Putnam's Median Book.

Dorfman, P., Hanges, P. J., & Brodbeck, F. C. (2004). Leadership and cultural variation: The identification of culturally endorsed leadership profiles. In R. J. House, P. J. Hanges, M. Javidan, P. Dorfman, & V. Gupta (Eds.), *Leadership, culture, and organizations: The GLOBE study of 62 societies* (pp. 669–719). Thousand Oaks, CA: Sage.

Dumont, L. (1994). *German ideology.* Chicago: University of Chicago Press.

Eppler, E. (1992). Die humanste Form der Macht [The most human form of power]. *Der Spiegel, 42,* 26–28.

Europe has a problem—and its name is Germany. (2002, January 19). *The Economist,* p. 9.

Frese, M., Kring, W., Soose, A., & Zempel, J. (1996). Personal initiative at work: Differences between East and West Germany. *Academy of Management Journal, 39,* 37–63.

Glunk, U., Wilderom, C., & Ogilvie, R. (1997). Finding the key to German-style management. *International Studies of Management & Organizations, 26,* 93–108.

Gupta, V., & Hanges, P. J. (2004). Regional and climate clustering of societal cultures. In R. J. House, P. J. Hanges, M. Javidan, P. Dorfman, & V. Gupta (Eds.), *Leadership, culture, and organizations: The GLOBE study of 62 societies* (pp. 178–218). Thousand Oaks, CA: Sage.

Gupta, V., Hanges, P. J., & Dorfman, P. (2002). Cultural clusters methodology and findings. *Journal of World Business* [Special Issue on GLOBE], *37,* 11–15.

Gurowitz, E. M. (1998, October). Ohne Worte [No words]. *Manager Magazin,* pp. 133–134.

Hahn, H. J. (1995). *German thought and culture. From the Holy Roman Empire to the present day.* Manchester, England: Manchester University Press.

Hammer, T, (1999). Developing global leaders: A European perspective. In W. H. Mobley, M. J. Gessner & V. Arnold (Eds.), *Advances in Global Leadership* (Vol. 1, pp. 99–113). Stamford, CT: JAI.

Hanges, P. J., & Dickson, M. W. (2004). The development and validation of the GLOBE culture and leadership scales. In R. J. House, P. J. Hanges, M. Javidan, P. Dorfman, & V. Gupta (Eds.), *Leadership, culture, and organizations: The GLOBE study of 62 societies* (pp. 122–151). Thousand Oaks, CA: Sage.

Heyse, V. (1994). Führungskraefte-Orientierungen und Weiterbildung in ostdeutschen Unternehmen [Leaders' orientations and training in East German companies]. In L. v. Rosenstiel, T. Lang, & E. Sigl (Eds.), *Auswahl des Fach—und Führungskräftenachwuchses in den alten und neuen Bundesläendern* (pp. 323–331). Landshut, Germany: Schriften der Sommerakademie.

Hiebsch, H., & Vorwerg, M. (1978). *Sozialpsychologie* [Social psychology]. Berlin: VEB Deutscher Verlag der Wissenschaften.

Hofstede, G. (1980). *Cultures' consequences: International differences in work-related values.* London: Sage.

House, R. J., Hanges, P. J., Javidan, M., Dorfman, P. W., Gupta, V., & Globe Associates (2004). *Culture, leadership, and organizations: The GLOBE study of 62 societies.* Thousand Oaks, CA: Sage.

Jago, A. G., Reber, G., Böhnisch, W., Maczynski, J., Zavrel, J., & Dudorkin, J. (1993). Cultures' conseqeunces? A seven nations study of participation. In D. F. Rogus & A. S. Ratmi (Eds.), *Proceedings of the 24th Annual Meeting of the Decision Sciences Institute* (pp. 451–454). Washington DC: Decision Sciences Institute.

Lawrence, P. (1994). German management: At the interface between Eastern and Western Europe. In R. Calori & P. de Wood (Eds.), *A European management model: Beyond diversity* (pp. 133–165). New York: Prentice-Hall.

Lord, R. G., & Maher, K. J. (1991). *Leadership and information processing.* London: Routledge.

Macharzina, K. (1993). *Werthaltungen in den neuen Bundesläendern: Strategien fuer das Personalmanagement* [Values in the new German states: Strategies for personnel management]. Wiesbaden, Germany: Gabler.

Maier, G. (1990). Füehrungsgrundsäetze: Ein Ausdruck der Unternehmenskultur [Principles of leadership: An expression of organizational culture]. In S. Hoefling & W. Butollo (Eds.), *Proceedings of the 15th Congress for Applied Psychology of the German Psychological Association* (BDP) (pp. 135–144). Bonn, Germany: Deutscher Psychologen Verlag.

Martin, G. S., Keating, M., & Brodbeck, F. C. (2004). Organisational leadership in Germany and Ireland. In M. Keating & G. S. Martin (Eds.), *Managing cross-cultural business relations: The Irish-German case* (pp. 41–69). Blackhall, Ireland: Dublin.

Müller, W. A. (1995). Führungsforschung/Führung in der Bundesrepublik Deutschland, in Österreich und in der Schweiz [Leadership research/leadership in Germany, Austria and Switzerland]. In A. Kieser, G. Reber, & R. Wunderer (Eds.), *Handwörterbuch der Führung* (pp. 573–586). Stuttgart, Germany: Schäffer-Poeschel.

Reber, G., Jago, A. G., Auer-Rizzi, W., & Szabo, E. (2000). Führungsstile in sieben Ländern Europas—Ein interkultureller Vergleich [Leadership styles in seven European countries—A inter cultural comparison]. In E. Regnet & L. M. Hofmann (Eds.), *Personalmanagement in Europa* (pp. 154–173). Göttingen: Verlag für Angewandte Psychologie.

Regnet, E. (1995). Der Weg in die Zukunft: Neue Anforderungen and Führungskräfte [Pathways to the future: New requirements for managers]. In L. von Rosenstiel, E. Regnet, & M. Domsch (Eds.), *Führung von Mitarbeitern: Handbuch für erfolgreiches Personalmanagement* (pp. 43–54). Stuttgart, Germany: Schäffer-Poeschel.

Ronen, S., & Shenkar, O. (1985). Clustering countries on attitudinal dimensions: A review and synthesis. *Academy of Management Review, 10,* 435–454.

Schäfer, P. (1989). Der Raum—seine territorial-politische und seine wirtschafts—und kulturgeographischen Veränderungen [Space—its territorial political and its economical and geo-cultural change]. In M. Overesch (Ed.), *Die Gründung der Bundesrepublick Deutschland: Jahre der Entscheidung 1945–1949, Texte und Documente* (pp. 19–44). Hannover: Landeszentrale für politische Bildung, Niedersachsen.

Schroll-Machl, S. (2005). *Doing business with Germans: Their perception, our perception* (2nd ed.). Göttingen: Vandenhoeck and Ruprecht.

Schultz-Gambard, J., & Altschuh, E. (1993). Unterschiedliche Füehrungsstile im geeinten Deutschland [Different leadership styles in the united Germany]. *Zeitschrift für Sozialpsychologie, 24,* 167–175.

The sick man of the euro. (1999, June 5). *The Economist,* p. 5.

Simon, H. (1996). *Hidden champions.* Boston.: Harvard Business School Press.

Simons, T. L., & Peterson, R. S. (2000). Task conflict and relationship conflict in top management teams. The pivotal role of intra group trust. *Journal of Applied Psychology, 85,* 102–111.

Stahl, G., Javidan, M., Brodbeck, F. C., & Wilderom, C. (2005). Transferring knowledge across cultures: Lessons learned from project GLOBE. *Academy of Management Executive, 19*(2), 59–76.

Stewart, R., Barsoux, J. L., Kieser, A., Ganter, H. D., & Walgenbach, P. (1994). *Managing in Britain and Germany.* London: Macmillan.

Szabo, E., Brodbeck, F. C., den Hartog, D. E., Reber, G., Weibler, J., & Wunderer, R. (2002). The Germanic Europe cluster: Where employees have a voice. *Journal of World Business, 37,* 55–68.

An uncertain giant: A survey of Germany. (2002, January 19). *The Economist,* pp. 1–20.

von Rosenstiel, L. (1995). Führung durch Motivation in Zeiten sich wandelnder Wertorientierungen [Management via motivation in times of changing value orientations]. In H. Kasper (Ed.), *Post-Graduate-Management-Wissen* (pp. 75–146).Wien, Germany: Wirtschaftsverlag Ueberreuter.

Warner, M., & Campbell, A. (1993). German management. In D. J. Hickson (Ed.), *Management in Western Europe: Society, culture and organization in twelve nations* (pp. 89–108). Berlin: de Gruyter.

Weibler, J., Brodbeck, F. C., Szabo, E., Reber, G., Wunderer, R., & Moosmann, O. (2000). Führung in kulturverwandten Regionen: Gemeinsamkeiten und Unterschiede bei Führungsidealen zwischen Deutschland, Österreich und der Schweiz [Leadership in culturally similar regions: Similarities and differences of leadership prototypes in Germany, Austria and Switzerland]. *Die Betriebswirtschaft, 5,* 588–604.

Wiendick, G. (1990). *Führung im Wandel. Neue Perspektiven für Führungsforschung und Führungspraxis* [Leadership under changing conditions. New perspectives of leadership research and leadership practice]. Stuttgart, Germany: Enke.

World Economic Forum. (2000). *The global competitiveness report.* New York: Oxford University Press.

Wuppertaler Kreis. (1992). *Führungsverständnis in Ost und West* [Concepts of leadership in East and West]. Köln, Germany: Deutscher Wirtschaftsdienst.

Yukl, G. (2005). Leadership in organizations (6th ed.). Upper Saddle River, NJ: Pearson Prentice Hall.

Zander, E. (1995). Führungsstil und Personalpolitik im Wandel [Changes in leadership style and personell policy]. *Personal, 47,* 238–241.

Zwarg, I. (1995). Führung in den neuen Bundesländern [Leadership in the new states of Germany]. In L. von Rosenstiel, E. Regnet, & M. Domsch (Eds.), *Führung von Mitarbeitern: Handbuch für erfolgreiches Personalmanagement* (pp. 739–750). Stuttgart, Germany: Schäffer- Poeschel.

Appendix A

West Germany

The political system of the Federal Republic of Germany was—and still is today—a constitutional, representative, and pluralistic democracy, similar to other Western democracies. In the early days after World War II, the Western allies, especially the United States of America, took a major part in helping the West Germans to build a modern democracy. The GARIOA scheme (Government and Relief in Occupied Areas) and, most well known, the Marshall Aid (ERP, i.e., the European Recovery Program) granted financial aid, stability, and favorable conditions for building a constitutional democracy granting the basic rights of freedom of opinion, freedom of the press, liberty, and protection of the private sphere and their recoverability by law. The German constitution, though not specifying any particular economic system, constrains a free-market economy with the doctrine of the *social* market economy (*Soziale Marktwirtschaft*). It defines legal obligations for the government, the trade unions, and the companies for maintaining public welfare (e.g., education, health, retirement), social justice (e.g., social security, equal opportunities, protection of minorities), and cooperative industrial relations (e.g., codetermination, industrial democracy). A key feature of industrial relations is exemplified in the wage-bargaining process. It is simple in structure, only two partners, one trade union and one employer. It is predictable—a timetable of industries and states is sequentially followed—and it is stable—wage bargaining has the force of law and strikes inevitably occur in particular seasons of the year (cf. Lawrence, 1994). Another key feature of industrial relations is the system of codetermination that is regulated by law. It grants mutual control and participation for employees by defining rights and duties for worker representatives in the companies' supervisory boards and for elected employee representatives on the work council. The social market economy is one important factor for the stable and solid economical and social development in post–World War II Germany. To some foreigners this system appears to be overburdened with formal procedures. However, the strengths are its high reliability, straightforwardness, and legally enforced procedural justice, criteria that meet the formal and task-oriented interaction style maintained in West German companies (cf. Lawrence, 1994).

Appendix B

Former East Germany

The constitution of the German Democratic Republic (according to its revision from October 7, 1974) described a socialistic state of workers and farmers under leadership of the Marxistic- Leninistic unitary party, SED (*Sozialistische Einheitspartei Deutschland*). Legally, this party was constructed according to the principle of "democratic centralism"; practically, centralism dominated, although officials from other parties (CDU, Christian Democrats, LDPD, Liberal Democrats) were also involved. The political bureau of the SED-party (*Politbüro*) and its first secretary, decided about the political, economical, educational, and cultural life in former East Germany. It controlled the trade unions, the so-called "transmission belt" of the party, in which 95% of German workforce were members, the German youth organization (FDJ) in which about 70% of German 14- to 17-year-olds were organized, the people's own companies (VEBs and combines), the educational system (university entry was based on a subject quota basis, graduates were located to jobs by the state), and the media (e.g., no foreign print media and no foreign TV or radio was officially allowed to be consumed). The basic rights, freedom of opinion, freedom of the press, liberty, and protection of the private sphere were constitutional, however, practically they were not fully recoverable by law (e.g., no free traveling abroad). In contrast, however, the basic social rights (e.g., the right to work, the right to health protection, the right to education) were highly effective in principle and in practice.

The planned economy system determined the level of productivity to be fulfilled by the VEBs and the aggregates of VEBs (combines) in all industries. Research and development activities were also performed in VEBs and combines. The structure was centralistic, meaning groups of combines reported to industry ministers and the ministers in turn reported to the Plan Commission, which was an organ of the SED political bureau. The planned market was controlled the reverse way; the Plan Commission defined the expected productivity output per industry and the combines and VEBs had to fulfill the plan. About 98% of the industries were "publicly owned" in this manner and only some private economy was allowed for a very small proportion of entrepreneurs (e.g., craftsmen) and private gardeners.

East German authors tend to describe the economic system as "double headed" (R. Lang, personal communication as part of a written review of an earlier draft of this chapter, 2000), that is, bureaucratic and tayloristic at its surface, but informal, bargaining oriented, with strong emphasis on informal contracts and pacts in its real functioning.

Appendix C

The German Reunification

As a result of the German reunification in 1990, East Germany stopped existing. The two "Germanies" did not merge; rather, East Germany joined West Germany and, therefore, adopted the legal system, fiscal policy, employment policy, external trade policy, and so on from West Germany (*Brockhaus Encyclopaedia*, 1997, pp. 289–290). Aside from the geopolitical situation and the Russian *Perestroika*, one reason for the reunification is seen in the near collapse of the East German economy in the late 1980s. After the reunification the productivity levels of East German companies dropped again and unemployment—unknown in the former East Germany—rose sharply. A significant problem was the privatization of the state-owned companies; this led to the closing of many companies. By the end of 1994 more than 20,000 organizations were privatized.

From 1991 to 1995, West Germany transferred about a trillion German marks (about 500 billion euro/dollar to East Germany), from which 25% went into the economy and 11% were spent for developing infrastructure (e.g. transport, telecommunications, etc.). The largest proportion, however, went into unemployment, health care, and social welfare funds. On the one hand, German reunification triggered a consumer boom (which actually masked the beginning structural crisis of the West German economy). On the other hand, it exhausted West Germany's economy to considerable extent.

The cultural change and social psychological consequences of the reunification concerned mainly East Germans, who carried the primary share of change ("modernization shock"). They gained the basic constitutional rights of a Western democratic society and they gained in living standards. However, the reunification also resulted in disillusionment and the experience of high uncertainty. Furthermore, the markedly lower income level of East Germans as compared to West Germans (47% in 1991; 67% in 1994; 77% in 2002) led to feelings of injustice and unfairness among East Germans (however, household income is higher in East Germany because of higher female participation in the labor market).

Additional hard feelings were produced by criminal activities in the changeover process from state ownership into private hands and the mass restitution of those possessions that had been expropriated by the communist regime (2.7 million titles had to be processed). For example, renters of flats suddenly had to deal with different owners or owners of houses were expropriated in favor of the original owners. Women, who were highly integrated in the former East German workforce, saw an end to their favored status (e.g., the well-developed East German kindergarten system was completely destroyed). One of the darkest chapters in East German history was that millions of secret personal files collected and used by the former East German state security system (*Stasi = Staatssicherheit*) were released to the people who had been subject to prosecution. Thus, in addition to the modernization shock, many East Germans learned that their best friends, neighbors, coworkers, and so forth reported private and personal details to the Stasi. In short, the whole past and future life of many East Germans was called into question—for some of them totally—virtually overnight.

The dramatic changes in East Germany have not led to instant adaptation of the Western culture. Expressions of an East German cultural identity can be seen in their voting behavior. The PDS, a successor party of the former Communist Party, used to be rather strong in the East and practically nonexistent in the West. Furthermore, as part of the GLOBE survey in 1995–1996, East German managers tend to disagree with questionnaire statements like, "Citizens of the former East Germany should learn as quickly as possible from West Germans," whereas West German managers tend to agree. On the other side, East German managers tend to agree to statements like "Citizens of the former East Germany should consider the strengths of the former East German culture"; West German managers tend to disagree.

An East versus West polarization became apparent that is still existent today. Stereotyped attributions of responsibility for the social and economical problems were often expressed in public media. West Germans stereotyped East Germans as showing little initiative, being unproductive, and exhibiting a welfare mentality of "taking from but not actively giving to society." On the other hand, East Germans stereotyped West Germans as pretending to know everything better (*Besserwessis*) and as highly individualistic and self-centered.

Appendix D

Categories for Content Analysis of Print Media

Category Name	Text Phrases Containing the Following Characteristics
Determined	behaviors and expressed attitudes that imply determined decisions and actions.
Firm	behaviors and expressed attitudes that imply firm defense or resolute execution of goals, plans, ideas and beliefs.
Masculine	attributes like strength, courage, fighting, fatherly or paternal.
High integrity	attributes like modesty, socially responsible, humane, loyalty, trustworthiness or sense of responsibility.
Future oriented	behaviors and expressed attitudes that aim towards the future, planning for the future, anticipation of future events, or preparing for the future.
Visionary	behaviors and expressed attitudes that inspire or stimulate others, e.g. to surpass their limits, to change their attitudes and behavior.
Optimistic	behaviors and expressed attitudes that imply confidence in, or generally positive views of facts, events and future developments.
Confronting	attitude expressions in a highly confronting or agitating manner.
Rational	behaviors and expressed attitudes that imply objectivity, pertinence, rationality, realism, analytical competency and being well informed.
Evaluating	attitude expressions in an assessing or evaluative manner.
Opinion expression	attitude expression in a neutral manner.
Communicating	behaviors and attitudes that imply communication with others, informing oneself and others, and maintaining good relationships.
Collaborating	behaviors and attitudes that imply cooperation, or stress common goals, win/win situations and compromise.

Appendix E

Categories for Content Analysis of Executive Job Posting

Category Name	Text Phrases Containing the Following Characteristics
Initiative	engagement, entrepreneurship, intrinsic and performance motivation.
Purposive	high energetic impetus and strength in goal attainment.
Communicating	effective interaction and bargaining, affiliation motives, intercultural interests.
Administrative skill	structuring and controlling complex systems, implementing goals and plans.
Inspirational	convincing, being a positive model and thus influential, "a real personality."
Collaborative	cooperative, participative, social competency and team orientation.
Leader experience	experience in leadership.
Responsible	willingness and awareness of taking responsibility seriously, committed, liable.
Motivating	motivating, supporting and developing employees.
Firm	persistence and stress resistance.
Flexible	adaptability, creativity, being nimble and movable.
Future oriented	planning ahead, prepared, modern, being a "signpost."
Rational	thinking analytically, critical and realistic, broad knowledge.
Enthusiastic	enjoying to work.
Directive	straight, strict, and controlling leadership style.
Willingness to learn	motivation to learn, to acquaint with new tasks.

Appendix F

Factor Analysis Results of the 21 GLOBE Leadership Scales for Germany, East and West, and a West German Twin-Sample

No.	GLOBE-Scale	Item # Item Attributes—Descriptions (in German)[c]	Germany (total) (n = 471)		East Germany (n = 53)		West Germany (n = 417)		West (twin sample) (n = 53)	
			Cronbach α/r[b]	Eigen-value > 1	Cronbach α/r	Eigen value > 1	Cronbach α/r	Eigen-value > 1	Cronbach α/r	Eigen-value > 1
1	Administrative Competency [*]	2-19 —Administrationstalent—Kann die Arbeit einer großen Anzahl von Personen (mehr als 75) planen, organisieren, koordinieren und kontrollieren 2-34—Systematisch—Ist organisiert und methodisch bei der Arbeit 4-2 —Organisiert—Gut organisiert, methodisch, systematisch 4-52 Guter Administrator—Hat die Fähigkeit, komplexe Büroarbeit und Verwaltungseinrichtungen zu handhaben	.607	1,873	.632	2,038	.599	1,842	.562	1,837
2	Autocratic [*]	2-4 —Herrisch—Sagt MitarbeiterInnen auf gebieterische Weise, was zu tun ist 2-36— Selbstherrlich—Trifft Entscheidungen diktatorisch 4-33— Herrschsüchtig—Bestrebt, andere zu beherrschen 4-37— Elitär—Glaubt, daß eine kleine Zahl von Leuten mit ähnlichem Hintergrund höherwertig ist und Privilegien genießen sollte 4-48— Herrscher—Hat das Sagen und toleriert Widerspruch oder Nachfragen nicht, erteilt Befehle 4-54 —Diktatorisch—Zwingt seine/ihre Werte und Ansichten anderen auf	.778	2,904 (1,118)	.757	2,860	.780	2,907	.871	3,669
3	Autonomous [*]	2-7 —Autonom—Handelt selbständig, verläßt sich nicht auf andere	.555	1,823 (1,118)	.356	1,885	.577	1,837 (1,130)	742	2,268

APPENDIX F (CONTINUED)

No.	GLOBE-Scale	Item # Item Attributes—Descriptions (in German)[c]	Germany (total) (n = 471) Cronbach α/r^b	Germany (total) Eigen-value > 1	East Germany (n = 53) Cronbach α/r	East Germany Eigen value > 1	West Germany (n = 417) Cronbach α/r	West Germany Eigen value > 1	West (twin sample) (n = 53) Cronbach α/r	West (twin sample) Eigen value > 1
		2-8 —Selbständig—Verläßt sich nicht auf andere, ist autonom								
		2-29—Einzigartig—Eine ungewöhnliche Person, hat Verhaltensmerkmale, die sich von den meisten anderen unterscheiden								
		4-55—Individualistisch—Verhält sich anders als vergleichbare Personen (ITEM DELETED)[a]	.644	1,816	.643	1,807	.739	1,816	.614	1,975
4	Charismatic I-Visionary[*]	2-12—Anregend—Inspiriert Gefühle, Meinungen, Werthaltungen und Verhalten anderer; inspiriert andere, zu harter Arbeit motiviert zu sein	.751	3,213 (1,088)	.653	2,874 (1,434) (1,081)	.763	3,318 (1,097)	.848	4,280 (1,116)
		2-13—Vorausschauend—Versucht Ereignisse vorherzusagen, bedenkt, was in der Zukunft passieren könnte								
		2-35—Vorbereitet—Ist bereit für bevorstehende Ereignisse								
		2-56—Intellektuell stimulierend—Ermutigt andere zum Denken und zum Gebrauch ihres eigenen Verstandes; fordert Meinungen, Klischees und Einstellungen anderer heraus								
		4-10—Voraussichtig—Antizipiert zukünftige Ereignisse								
		4-11—Plant im voraus—Antizipiert und trifft Vorkehrungen im voraus								
		4-19—Fähigkeit zu antizipieren—Fähigkeit, zukünftige Anforderungen erfolgreich vorauszusehen								
		4-46—Visionär—Hat eine Vision und eine Vorstellung von der Zukunft								
		4-51—Zukunftsorientiert—Macht Pläne und ergreift Maßnahmen auf Basis zukunftsorientierter Ziele								

APPENDIX F (CONTINUED)

	No.	GLOBE-Scale	Item # Item Attributes—Descriptions (in German)[c]	Germany (total) (n = 471)		East Germany (n = 53)		West Germany (n = 417)		West (twin sample) (n = 53)	
				Cronbach α/r[b]	Eigen-value > 1	Cronbach α/r	Eigen value > 1	Cronbach α/r	Eigen-value > 1	Cronbach α/r	Eigen-value > 1
	5	Charismatic II –Inspirational *	2-5 — Positiv—Im allgemeinen optimistisch und zuversichtlich	.735	2,856 (1,128)	.663	2,602 (1,302) (1,212)	.744	2,927 (1,150)	.788	3,417 (1,171)
			2-31—Ermutigend—Macht Mut, gibt Zuversicht und Hoffnung durch Bestätigung und Ratschläge								
			2-32—Stärkt die Moral—Erhöht die Moral der Mitarbeiter durch Unterstützungsangebote, Lob und/oder durch seine/ihre Zuversichtlichkeit								
			2-48—Begeistert—Zeigt und vermittelt starke positive Gefühle für die Arbeit								
			4-20—Spornt an—Mobilisiert und aktiviert eine Gefolgschaft								
			4-26—Schafft Vertrauen—Erweckt Vertrauen bei anderen durch starkes Vertrauen in andere								
			4-35—Dynamisch—Stark engagiert, tatkräftig, voller Begeisterung, motiviert								
			4-42—Motivierend—Spornt andere dazu an, sich über ihre normale Pflicht hinaus anzustrengen und persönliche Opfer zu bringen								
	6	Charismatic III Self-Sacrificial	2-14—Risikobereit—Ist gewillt, größere Ressourcen in Bemühungen zu investieren, die keine große Erfolgswahrscheinlichkeit haben	.088	1,080	–.168	1,118 (1,017)	.117	1,105	.354	1,379
			4-22—Überzeugend—Ungewöhnlich begabt im Überzeugen anderer von seinen/ihren Standpunkten								
			4-30—Selbstaufopfernd—Übergeht Eigeninteressen und bringt persönliche Opfer im Interesse eines Zieles oder einer Vision								

APPENDIX F (CONTINUED)

No.	GLOBE-Scale	Item # Item Attributes—Descriptions (in German)[c]	Germany (total) (n = 471)		East Germany (n = 53)		West Germany (n = 417)		West (twin sample) (n = 53)	
			Cronbach α/r[b]	Eigenvalue > 1	Cronbach α/r	Eigen value > 1	Cronbach α/r	Eigen-value > 1	Cronbach α/r	Eigen-value > 1
7	Conflict Inducer	2-6 —Wettbewerbsorientiert—Versucht die Leistung anderer in seiner oder ihrer Arbeitsgruppe zu übertreffen 2-37—Geheimniskrämerisch—Neigt dazu, anderen Informationen zu verheimlichen 4-12—Normenkonform—Verhält sich gemäß den Normen seiner oder ihrer Gruppe	.243	1,222	.471	1,479	.194	1,181	.356	1,374 (1,062)
8	Decisive	2-44—Entscheidungsfreudig—Trifft Entscheidungen entschlossen und schnell 4-8—Logisch—Denkt folgerichtig 4-15—Intuitiv—Hat Fingerspitzengefühl 4-47—Eigenwillig—Willensstark, entschlossen, resolut, hartnäckig	.372	1,439	.483	1,687	.357	1,413	.455	1,587 (1,095)
9	Diplomatic	2-1 —Diplomatisch—Ist geschickt in zwischenmenschlichen Beziehungen, taktvoll 2-17—Weltoffen—Interessiert sich für aktuelle Ereignisse, hat einen sehr umfassenden Horizont 2-18—Konfliktmeider—Weicht Auseinandersetzungen mit anderen Mitgliedern seiner oder ihrer Gruppe aus (ITEM DELETED) 2-21—Gewinn/Gewinn-Problemlöser—Kann Lösungen ausfindig machen, die Individuen mit verschiedenen und widersprechenden Interessen befriedigen 4-5 —Effektiver Verhandlungsführer—Kann wirksam verhandeln, kann Geschäfte mit anderen zu günstigen Bedingungen abschließen	.058 .349	1,555 (1,032) 1,372	.033 .470	1,847 (1,252) 1,584	.054 324	1,515 (1,046) 1,350	.187 .394	1,502 (1,153) 1,429

No.	GLOBE-Scale	Item # Item Attributes—Descriptions (in German)[c]	Germany (total) (n = 471)		East Germany (n = 53)		West Germany (n = 417)		West (twin sample) (n = 53)	
			Cronbach α/r[b]	Eigen-value > 1	Cronbach α/r	Eigen value > 1	Cronbach α/r	Eigen-value > 1	Cronbach α/r	Eigen-value > 1
10	Face Saver	2-2 —Ausweichend—Sieht davon ab, negative Kommentare zu machen, um gute Beziehungen zu erhalten und das Gesicht zu wahren	.404	1,375	.319	1,294	.419	1,393	.253	1,251 (1,073)
		4-16—Indirekt—Kommt nicht direkt zum Punkt, benutzt Metaphern und Beispiele beim Kommunizieren								
		4-45—VermeidetNegatives—Tendiert dazu, etwas nicht abzulehnen, auch wenn er/sie es nicht erfüllen kann								
11	Humane Orientation[*]	2-40—Selbstlos—Ist gewillt, anderen Zeit, Geld, Ressourcen und Hilfe zu geben	r = .423	1,422	r = .563	1,563	r = .407	1,407	r = .648	1,648
		2-51—Mitfühlend—Hat Einfühlungsvermögen, ist bereit zu helfen, zeigt Barmherzigkeit								
12	Integrity[*]	2-15—Aufrichtig—Meint auch was er/sie sagt, ehrlich	.806	2,562	.827	2,696	.805	2,553	.823	2,644
		2-16—Vertrauenswürdig—Hat Vertrauen verdient, man kann ihm/ihr glauben und seinem/ihrem Wort trauen								
		2-20—Gerecht—Handelt danach, was richtig und fair ist								
		4-32—Ehrlich—Spricht und handelt aufrichtig								
13	Malevolent[*]	2-43—Intelligent—Klug, lernt und versteht schnell	.747	3,181 (1,197)	.699	3,011 (1,682)	.754	3,250 (1,182)	.748	3,802 (1,292)
		2-46—Reizbar—Launisch; leicht aufgebracht								
		2-50—Rachsüchtig—Nachtragend; trachtet nach Vergeltung, wenn ihm/ihr Unrecht getan wurde								
		4-6 —Selbstgefällig—Eingebildet, von den eigenen Fähigkeiten überzeugt								

APPENDIX F (CONTINUED)

No.	GLOBE-Scale	Item # Item Attributes— Descriptions (in German)[c]	Germany (total) (n = 471) Cronbach α/r[b]	Germany (total) Eigen- value > 1	East Germany (n = 53) Cronbach α/r	East Germany Eigen value > 1	West Germany (n = 417) Cronbach α/r	West Germany Eigen- value > 1	West (twin sample) (n = 53) Cronbach α/r	West (twin sample) Eigen- value > 1
		4-7 —Nicht kooperativ—Nicht bereit, gemeinschaftlich mit anderen zu arbeiten								
		4-39—Zynisch—Neigt dazu, das Schlechteste über Leute und Ereignisse anzunehmen								
		4-49—Unredlich—Betrügerisch, unaufrichtig								
		4-50—Feindselig—Bewußt unfreundlich, handelt anderen zuwider								
		4-53—Verläßlich—Zuverlässig								
14	Modesty*	2-26—Ruhig—Gerät nicht so leicht in Besorgnis bzw. in Verzweiflung	.561	1,744	.744	2,284	.524	1,669	.495	1,749
		2-42—Bescheiden—Prahlt nicht, präsentiert sich selbst in zurückhaltender Art und Weise								
		4-18—Zurückhaltend—Präsentiert sich auf zurückhaltende Art und Weise								
		4-31—Geduldig—Hat und zeigt Geduld								
15	Nonparticipative*	4-13—Individuell ausgerichtet—Interessiert sich mehr für die Erfüllung seiner/ihrer eigenen Bedürfnisse als für die der Gruppe	.518	1,709 (1,135)	.338	1,554 (1,047)	.539	1,742 (1,156)	.609	1,853 (1,134)
		4-14—Nicht egalitär—Glaubt, daß nicht alle Menschen gleich sind und nur einigen dieselben Rechte und Privilegien haben sollten	.523	1,600	.487	1,547	.523	1,600	.455	1,492
		4-43—Mikro-Manager—Extrem detaillierte Supervision; jemand, der/die darauf besteht, alle Entscheidungen zu treffen (ITEM DELETED)								
		4-44—Nicht delegativ—Nicht bereit oder nicht fähig, die Kontrolle über Projekte oder Aufgaben abzugeben								

209

APPENDIX F (CONTINUED)

No.	GLOBE-Scale	Item # Item Attributes—Descriptions (in German)c	Germany (total) (n = 471)		East Germany (n = 53)		West Germany (n = 417)		West (twin sample) (n = 53)	
			Cronbach α/rb	Eigen-value > 1	Cronbach α/r	Eigen value > 1	Cronbach α/r	Eigen-value > 1	Cronbach α/r	Eigen-value > 1
16	Performance Orientation*	2-11—Verbesserungsorientiert—Strebt nach kontinuierlicher Leistungsverbesserung 4-24—An excellenter Leistung orientiert—Bemüht sich um hervorragende Leistungen bei sich selbst und bei Anderen 4-40—Leistungsorientier—Setzt hohe Leistungsstandards	.571	1,622	.634	1,749	.562	1,610	.589	1,689
17	Procedural*	2-41—Förmlich—Handelt gemäß Regeln, Konventionen und Zeremonien 4-1—Vorsichtig—Geht mit großer Sorgfalt vor, geht keine Risiken ein 4-17—Gewohnheitsorientiert—Neigt zu gleichbleibender, fahrplanmäßiger Routine 4-25—Regelfixiert—Folgt etablierten Regeln und Richtlinien 4-56—Rituell—Geht nach festgelegten Ordnungen vor	.663	2,190	.642	2,168	.667	2,210	.720	2,474
18	Self-Centered*	2-23—Eigennützig—Verfolgt eigene Interessen am stärksten 2-38—Ungesellig—Meidet Menschen und Gruppen, bevorzugt das Alleinsein 2-47—Einzelgänger—Arbeitet und agiert getrennt von anderen 4-29—Nicht partizipativ—Beteiligt andere nicht	.594	1,867	.588	1,821 (1,184)	.596	1,877	.591	1,884 (1,023)
19	Status-Conscious*	4-9—Statusbewußt—Ist sich des gesellschaftlichen Status anderer bewußt 4-28—Klassenbewußt—Ist sich Klassenunterschieden und Statusgrenzen bewußt und handelt entsprechend	r = .443	1,441	r = .303	1,299	r = .445	1,443	r = .578	1,575

APPENDIX F (CONTINUED)

No.	GLOBE-Scale	Item # Item Attributes—Descriptions (in German)[c]	Germany (total) (n = 471)		East Germany (n = 53)		West Germany (n = 417)		West (twin sample) (n = 53)	
			Cronbach α/r[b]	Eigen-value > 1	Cronbach α/r	Eigen value > 1	Cronbach α/r	Eigen-value > 1	Cronbach α/r	Eigen-value > 1
20	Team I: Team Collaborative Orientation*	2-3 —Vermittler—Interveniert, um Probleme zwischen Individuen zu lösen	.626	2,192	.674	2,394	.623	2,182	.390	1,629
		2-28—Loyal—Hält zu Freunden und unterstützt sie, wenn sie große Probleme oder Schwierigkeiten haben				(1,073)				(1,330)
		2-30—Kooperationsbereit—Arbeitet bereitwillig gemeinsam mit anderen								
		2-39—Brüderlich—Ist bestrebt, ein guter Freund seiner/ihrer MitarbeiterInnen zu sein								
		2-45—Ratsuchend—Berät sich mit anderen, bevor er/sie Pläne macht oder in Aktion tritt								
		4-27—Gruppenorientiert—Kümmert sich um das Wohlergehen der Gruppe								
21	Team II: Team Integrator*	2-22—Klar—Gut und leicht zu verstehen	.456	2,313	.442	2,528	.536	2,322	.444	2,457
		2-25—Intergrativ—Fügt Menschen oder Dinge zu einem eng verbundenen, funktionierenden Ganzen zusammen								
		2-52—Ist kontrolliert/beherrscht—Hält an sich, ruhig (ITEM DELETED)	.631	2,155	.629	2,330	.651	2,156	.648	2,283

APPENDIX F (CONTINUED)

No.	GLOBE-Scale	Item # Item Attributes—Descriptions (in German)[c]	Germany (total) (n = 471)		East Germany (n = 53)		West Germany (n = 417)		West (twin sample) (n = 53)	
			Cronbach α/r[b]	Eigen-value > 1	Cronbach α/r	Eigen value > 1	Cronbach α/r	Eigen-value > 1	Cronbach α/r	Eigen-value > 1
		4-4 —Informiert—Gebildet, gut unterrichtet bzw weiß Bescheid								
		4-23—Kommunikativ—Kommuniziert gern häufig mit anderen								
		4-36—Koordinator—Integriert und organisiert die Arbeit der Mitarbeiterinnen								
		4-38—Teambildner—Kann Gruppenmitglieder zur Zusammenarbeit bewegen								

*Scales marked with * are kept for further analyses (Cronbach a > .50 or Pearson r > .40).

[a](ITEM DELETED) means that the scale statistics were calculated without the respective item.

[b]Pearson r is calculated when N of Items per scale equals 2.

[c]Items are listed in full German wording in order to stimulate future research. The numbers indicate item location in the GLOBE Questionnaire (parts 2 & 4). Items were developed in collaboration with Erna Szabo (chap. 5, this volume) and Jürgen Weibler (chap. 8, this volume).

[d]Eigenvalue of first emerging factor is listed. Eigenvalues of further factors that emerged are given in brackets.

Appendix G

Comparison of East vs. West German Leadership Scores (16 Scales from Factor Analysis, see Appendix F)

Reliable leadership scales for Germany	Germany (n = 471)		East (n = 53)		West (n = 417)		West-twin (n = 53)		East/West (ANOVA) $F = 2.81^{**}$ (1,450)	$Eta^2 = 0.09$	East/West-twin (ANOVA) $F = 1.18$ (1,98)	$Eta^2 = 0.19$	East/West (MANCOVA) $F = 2.32^{**}$ (1,428)	$Eta^2 = 0.08$
	M	SD	M	SD	M	SD	M	SD	F	Eta^2	F	Eta^2	F	Eta^2
Administratively Competent	5.53	.71	5.74	.74	5.51	.71	5.60	.69	7.84^{**}	.017	2.15	.021	4.26^{*}	.010
Autocratic	1.95	.77	2.07	.79	1.94	.77	2.03	.99	1.05	.002	.02	.000	2.34	.005
Visionary	5.98	.50	5.91	.49	5.99	.50	6.05	.56	.69	.002	1.38	.014	2.46	.006
Inspirational	6.15	.48	6.11	.49	6.15	.48	6.15	.51	.12	.000	.01	.000	2.65	.006
Humane Orientation	4.26	1.09	4.27	1.14	4.25	1.09	4.39	1.14	.00	.000	.15	.002	.73	.002
Integrity	6.11	.81	6.03	.87	6.12	.81	6.13	.79	.32	.001	.16	.002	2.48	.006
Malevolent	1.68	.48	1.70	.47	1.68	.48	1.68	.48	.00	.000	.00	.000	.79	.002
Modest	4.62	.75	4.69	.91	4.61	.73	4.67	.72	.69	.002	.06	.001	.20	.000
Self-centered	2.15	.70	2.33	.78	2.13	.69	2.10	.67	4.09^{*}	.009	2.93	.029	6.46^{*}	.015
Performance Oriented	6.13	.60	6.29	.58	6.11	.60	6.21	.62	6.36^{*}	.014	1.27	.013	2.39	.006
Procedural	3.03	.74	3.28	.81	3.00	.73	2.97	.76	5.22^{*}	.011	3.22	.032	5.32^{**}	.012
Nonparticipative	2.12	.72	2.21	.78	2.11	.71	2.17	.76	.85	.002	.06	.001	1.82	.004
Status-Conscious	3.79	1.09	4.37	.95	3.72	1.09	3.91	1.22	16.43^{**}	.035	4.48^{*}	.044	15.95^{**}	.036
Team Collaboration Oriented	5.04	.65	4.98	.70	5.05	.65	5.09	.56	.88	.002	.77	.008	2.72	.006
Team Integrator[1]	5.95	.52	5.91	.61	5.96	.51	5.93	.53	.01	.000	.08	.001	.78	.002
Autonomous[1]	4.39	1.39	4.71	1.35	4.35	1.39	4.43	1.47	3.51	.008	1.28	.013	.15	.001

[1]Scales were shortened by one item to improve reliability (see Appendix F).
Country means may differ from the country scores obtained by GLOBE (House et al., 2004) because sample sizes differ for methodological reasons.
* $p < .05$. ** $p < .01$ (two-sided tests).

Appendix H

Regression Analysis for Two Dimensional MDS Solutions in East and West Germany, and West German twin sample

16 Leadership Scales (Germany)	East Germany (n = 53)			West Germany (n = 417)			West Germany (twin sample) (n = 53)		
	DIM 1 (β)[1]	DIM 2 (β)	Adjusted R²	DIM 1 (β)	DIM 2 (β)	Adjusted R²	DIM 1 (β)	DIM 2 (β)	Adjusted R²
Malevolent	–.85	.07	.76**	–.84	–.05	.67**	–.87	–.11	.65**
Self-Centered	–.74	–.13	.49**	–.63	.04	.41*	–.63	.18	.54**
Autocratic	–.72	.20	.63**	–.65	.22	.58**	–.63	.25	.63**
Nonparticipative	–.71	.11	.54**	–.75	.11	.64**	–.78	.06	.65**
Inspirational	.69	–.01	.46**	.76	.15	.50**	.80	.20	.46**
Team Integrator	.69	.07	.42**	.79	.22	.52**	.84	.25	.50**
Visionary	.63	.24	.34**	.72	.28	.43**	.85	.59	.46**
Performance Orientation	.62	.40	.37**	.59	.33	.29**	.63	.29	.24**
Administratively Competent	.55	.16	.24**	.47	.23	.18**	.62	.42	.22**
Integrity	.54	–.44	.62**	.66	–.17	.55**	.55	–.22	.48**
Procedural	–.40	–.30	.14**	–.48	–.17	.18**	–.47	–.03	.17**
Autonomous	.13	.86	.67**	.25	.91	.69**	.29	.92	.60**
Humane Orientation	–.10	–.63	.34**	.23	–.48	.38**	.30	–.37	.33**
Modest	.39	–.50	.50**	.33	–.37	.35**	.32	–.32	.30**
Team Collaborative Orientation	.24	–.46	.30**	.51	–.20	.38**	.30	–.36	.32**
Status Conscious	–.07	.36	.11**	–.25	.30	.22**	–.31	.40	.37**

Note: The β-weights for each leadership scale are highly similar between the East and West German samples indicating a high model fit across Germany
[1] β-weights of multiple regression with the two MDS-dimensions used as predictor variables for each leadership scales (cf. Smith *et al.*, 1996).

7

▼▼▼▼▼▼▼

Culture and Leadership in a Flat Country: The Case of the Netherlands

Henk Thierry
Tilburg University, the Netherlands

Deanne N. den Hartog
University of Amsterdam

Paul L. Koopman
Vrije Universiteit Amsterdam

Celeste P. M. Wilderom
University of Twente, the Netherlands

Summary

Dutch GLOBE data are presented in this chapter with an overview of the history of Holland and later the Netherlands. From the Middle Ages onward, Dutch cities had substantial local autonomy, which led their educated citizens and merchants to rule themselves to a large extent. This relative autonomy stimulated independent thought and judgment, a climate that helped Protestantism to gain much ground. Foreign trade facilitated the rise of a liberal culture. Later on, religious denomination became an important societal organization principle. After the Second World War industrial relations were characterized by an economic order that emphasized mixed capitalism (in which the government has a strong role), consultation among major parties, and a welfare state.

GLOBE data on societal and organizational culture show that collective economic interests, low power distance, gender egalitarianism, and group loyalty are still endorsed in the Netherlands, although values like performance and assertiveness are gaining ground. This reflects a process of cultural transition in which individualization and flexibility become increasingly dominant values. Dutch middle managers' perceptions of outstanding leaders stress the importance of consensus building, support, and power sharing, but also of visionary, motivating, and decisive qualities.

This chapter ends with 10 "commandments" on what leaders from abroad should and shouldn't do in the Netherlands.

1.   OVERVIEW

When descending by aircraft toward Amsterdam airport (Schiphol), the traveler gets a characteristic view of The Netherlands, regardless of the direction of the approach. Green meadows are orderly intersected by rivers, canals, and lakes; growing cities and towns surround agricultural areas; roads and highways expose heavy traffic; and the country is clean and flat. In fact, a large part of the country is below sea level: The Dutch are well known for their technical expertise in building dikes and dams to protect vulnerable areas and in gaining land from the sea. Additionally, some parts of the country are slightly hilly, but that feature is not visible to the air passenger: It reveals itself only to the traveler with a slower pace of transport. All in all, the country looks very organized.

Having read KLM's in-flight magazine, the air passenger is informed that the Netherlands covers 13,433 square miles. It houses slightly more than 16 million inhabitants and it is consequently the country with approximately the highest population per square mile in the world. The Dutch language is spoken throughout the country, but there are remarkable differences between regions with regard to pronunciation. Even bordering villages or towns may sizably differ from one another in their vocabulary. Often, historical and cultural factors explain most of these differences, for example, the extent to which a community was exposed to French influences during the French Revolution, or the religion (Protestantism or Roman Catholicism) most inhabitants (used to) adhere to. Dutch is also spoken by the Flemish people in Belgium. Not only their pronunciation, but also their construction of sentences is different; some "Dutch" words originate in Belgium, and are only used in Flemish. When somebody from South Africa (speaking "Afrikaans" rooted in 17th-century Dutch) is interviewed on Dutch TV, subtitles are shown. In one of the 12 counties, Friesland, the "Fries" language is spoken besides Dutch, and the names of towns in that county are spelled in both Dutch and Fries. Major current minority languages are Turkish, Moroccan, Surinam, and Papiaments (originally from the Dutch Antilles). Larger cities, like Amsterdam and Rotterdam, are home to former inhabitants of more than 130 countries, resulting in many other languages being heard as well, making Dutch culture in these areas increasingly multicolored and pluriform in nature.

The Netherlands is also the home base for several large multinational enterprises in different sectors, including Philips, Shell, Unilever, AKZO/Nobel, DSM, CORUS (former Hoogovens), KLM, ING Bank, ABN/AMRO Bank, and Ahold. Yet, company (and political) leadership is not often a hot item in the country. Many people even find it difficult to mention an outstanding Dutch leader, not because good leaders are lacking, but much more because a leader tends not to be recognized as such. As a well-known saying goes "a leader should remain to be an ordinary person." Dutch organizations emphasize training and educating the workforce, and keeping people "employable." Many commercial and noncommercial training institutions are active on the Dutch market. Many companies make extensive use of the help of organizational consultancy agencies. The average productivity level (combining both labor and capital productivity) was comparatively high in the past two decades, but the level of growth is gradually decreasing. Also, a sizable part of the employable population is partly or fully disabled and cannot work. Only around 40% of the people aged between 55 and 65 years are still employed. The country was successful in reducing its unemployment rate to less than

5% (effective 1998 onward), primarily through increasing the amount of part-time jobs. However, the slowing down of the economy has recently caused many organizations to reduce their labor force.

Characteristic to the country is having an organized, businesslike climate rather than a powerful leader-oriented atmosphere. To a certain extent there is even an antihero attitude. Dutch prime ministers usually do not present themselves as stars, but tend to emphasize trustworthiness, thoroughness, and commonness (such as "shopping like the next-door neighbor") in their behavior. Often, they stress the general interest (in terms of "being the prime minister of all inhabitants of the country") rather than favoring the interests of the political party they adhere to. The relative inexperience with stardom in politics surfaced in 2002 as a charismatic opposition leader "Pim Fortuyn" challenged the dominant "purple" coalition (constituted by the Conservative and the Social Democratic parties). He was killed briefly before the parliamentary elections in that year (which evoked distress on a national level), and even after his death his party still got the largest turnout of votes that any new party ever gained in Dutch parliamentary history.

The air passenger, with whom this introductory overview started, made the ground successfully. Inside and outside the airport the country looks orderly and clean; the Dutch language provides the passenger with mysterious feelings as it sounds so unfamiliar, but luckily most people master the English language. The country looks flat, and the passenger wonders whether this impression holds beyond its literal, geographical meaning.

Let's expose our guest first to an essay about some historical features of Dutch societal culture, (Section 2). Next, the industrial relations system is described (Section 3), focusing especially on how it developed itself after the Second World War. Section 4 highlights current characteristics of societal culture, including the data assembled in the GLOBE study, whereas Section 5 describes results relevant to the culture of the organizations participating in the Dutch GLOBE study. Section 6 returns to the theme of leadership, and presents the Dutch GLOBE data on this theme. Section 7 deals with several specific manifestations of Dutch societal culture, some limitations of the current study, as well as some suggestions for future research. Section 8 addresses some current challenges for Dutch organizational leadership. Finally, in the concluding Section 9 the guest should have at least learned which behaviors leaders from abroad should engage in, and abstain from, when exposed to Dutch employees.

2. DUTCH SOCIETAL CULTURE AND POLITICS: A BRIEF HISTORICAL PERSPECTIVE

The Dutch are not known as people who regularly commemorate figures of historical importance. Suppose you as a reader were to ask a Dutch citizen living in one of the cities, which of his or her past or current countrymen is considered to be a person of historical importance? Probably, the first reply would be in terms of another question: "What is meant by 'historical' importance?" Assuming that this problem would be solved satisfactorily, the second reply would probably also embody a question: "Why commemorate him or her?"

One of the "solid" ways to commemorate historical figures and to support the societal values they modeled would be to erect a statue for them. Such statues in the Netherlands are scarce, but there are several, such as the one for William, Prince of Orange, murdered in 1584 in Delft; Van Oldenbarnevelt, an influential legal consultant to the Counties of Holland, also murdered (1619); Michiel de Ruyter, a famous Navy Commander in the 17th century; William III, King of the Netherlands, 19th century; and Van Heutsz, Army General and colonial ruler in the Indies,

19th and 20th century. Perhaps because of her role during the Second World War, Queen Wilhelmina, grandmother of the current Queen Beatrix, received more than one statue. Interestingly, some influential philosophers are also "petrified," including Erasmus (Rotterdam), Spinoza, and Comenius (the latter from Czech decent). Quite a few statues are found along the Dutch coast, such as the one showing a small boy keeping his thumb in the hole of a dike, thus preventing the inundation of a larger part of the country. Some other statues show an old woman, sadly stretching her arm to the vast waters. Such statues express the constant concern of the "low countries" with the North Sea: a fishing area for some, a graveyard for too many, and an unpredictable nibbler of the coastline, causing a continuous fight for land.

Yet, the "harvest" of statues commemorating historical figures is modest. This is not because there weren't Dutch persons of historical national or international importance: Time and again Dutch inhabitants gained prominence in whatever domain, and painted portraits of some of these people are found in museums and castles. Rather, in Dutch culture outstanding individuals are usually not *identified* as a hero: It runs counter to important values and habits that attribute unusual performance mainly, let alone exclusively, to individual characteristics. The root of this conception probably dates back many centuries. To gain more insight into such roots we briefly need to review the political and economic culture of "Holland," from the early 14th century onward (cf.; Blonk, Romein, & Oerlemans, 1967, 1978; Braudel, 1979; Koeningsberger, 2001; D. Langedijk, 1948a, 1948b; Rijpma, 1952; Schama, 1987).

Citizens and Merchants

Although the terms "Holland" and "the Netherlands" are nowadays used interchangeably to identify the same nation-state, there is a vast historical difference. Holland refers to the western part of the country, roughly encompassing the current counties North-Holland (capital: Haarlem) and South-Holland (capital: The Hague). During previous centuries Holland sometimes went to war against neighboring counties, but more often cooperated with them (such as Friesland, Zeeland, and Utrecht), and established a small nation - state for quite a long period of time. Some counties that currently belong to the state of Belgium joined the cooperation with Holland for a while, but other counties opted for temporary liaisons with "enemy states" such as France or Spain. Holland got its fair share of wars, against or in cooperation with England, Prussia, France, and, for quite a period, Spain. During Napoleon's regime Holland and other counties were made part of France for several years. Shortly afterward, as King William I was inaugurated (1814), the Netherlands was established as a country, also encompassing current parts of Belgium (the so-called South - Netherlands) as a consequence of the ruling by the Viennese Congress (1815). Later Belgium received its independence in 1831.

Around AD 1300 the cities of Holland got *municipal rights*. These rights allowed a city to govern itself and to determine its own jurisdiction. If a plan for action was very expensive, good custom held that citizens were consulted. Generally, merchants favored the high extent of the cities' "local autonomy." As merchants became more prosperous through effective trading, they asked the count for protection against gangs of robbers or foreign invasion. Perhaps because of this, but also because an increasing number of counties became involved (Holland and other counties including French Burgundy), a strong centralized government was installed at the time Jacoba van Beieren was countess (early 15th century). Each region got a *stadtholder* (the word probably being a combination of the Dutch *stad* [city] and the English *holder*), representing the authority of the count. The nobility, the clergy and the cities were consulted in the Regional Estates (*Gewestelijke Staten*). All counties together convened every now and then in the Estate General (*Staten Generaal*).[1] The Dutch Estate General is among the oldest democratic institutions in Europe, established in 1464 by representatives of the Regional Estates (Koeningsberger, 2001).

These developments strengthened the position of the citizens (and the farmers) at the expense of the power of the nobility and the clergy. Trade and commerce flourished. The position of merchants was an issue of debate, however, because some people held that the price of a product would be lower if it were to be established without the interference of a "third (merchant) party." So the government took care that products were bought and sold for a *fair price*. This early form of capitalism was also practiced in the early 16th century in Northern Italy. Dutch trade focused on fishing (in particular herring), whereas freight was taken when the fishing season was over. Gradually, Dutch merchants started to trade independently (e.g., in grain). Also, wage laborers were attracted to the clothing industry (cloth was purchased in Calais from English merchants). As the art of printing was developed (Gutenberg, in Germany, 1450), citizens in the wealthy cities founded their own schools, and reduced the power the clergy traditionally enjoyed in this domain. Pupils were educated in bookkeeping and other applied subjects, which prepared them for a merchant career. Wealthier cities also raised their own mercenary armies, thus controlling the power the nobility usually possessed there. It is small wonder that the onset of the Renaissance met fertile soil in the cities in Holland with their relatively wealthy, educated, and independent citizens. These citizens were used to carry personal responsibility and to making their own judgment, as they were rather independent from the clergy and the nobility.

Yet, it is not so much the Renaissance but more so the onset of Protestantism that is most important to the further development of Holland. Early in the 16th century Luther attached his 95 "statements" to the Chapel of Wittenberg, Germany (1517). In Holland and adjacent counties, the assumptions and ideas of Calvin ("Calvinism") became more influential, as these diffused from Switzerland to France and other European countries from 1550 onward. During that period, Roman Catholic Spanish kings ruled Holland: Karel V reigned for a rather long time, and was succeeded by his son Philips II. A nobleman, William, Prince of Orange, became the leader of the opposition in Holland. Lower nobility joined with this opposition, because they **too** had adopted the Calvinistic faith. Moreover, the Bartholomew night (1572) that had taken place in France in which many Protestants were killed, had brought quite a number of those Protestant survivors to Holland. Major issues for the opposition to contest were:

- The introduction of new (Roman Catholic) dioceses.
- A change in civil administration.
- The presence of the Spanish army.

A long period of strenuous fights followed, partly underground. Groups of *Geuzen*[2] battled repeatedly with the Spanish army. When a city joined the Orange opposition, it meant that its citizens would adopt Protestantism. Usually this implied that a new government was

---

[1] Up to the present day, the Dutch Parliament (which is composed of two chambers) is called the "Estate General." Each of the current 12 countries is ruled by the "County Estate" (whereas each city or town is headed by the City Council).

[2] The word *geus* probably stems from the French term *des gueux,* which means "beggar" or "vagrant," a term perhaps used by an underling in the Spanish court to identify the "Protestants" from Holland. Interestingly, the English word for *geus* is *Protestant.* In Dutch, *geus* has the connotation of a courageous person.

appointed from the lower classes, which did not tend to obey the nobility and the Catholic Church. William, Prince of Orange was excommunicated by the pope in 1580, and was murdered in 1584. His son Maurits became the new stadtholder. Battles with Spain continued every now and then until the peace treaty of Münster in 1648.

Let's briefly recap the key ideas from the preceding sections. The cities in Holland already enjoyed a large amount of autonomy by the end of the Middle Ages. They took care of their administration as well as of their jurisdiction. Trade prospered, accompanied by a concern to achieve fair prices. Wealthier cities founded their own schools and raised mercenary armies. The role of the Catholic Church and of noblemen was much weaker than in many other countries: the educated citizen was capable of *judging for him or herself* how to behave and what to think, and was not inclined to accept somebody else's authority. Protestantism, in particular the Calvinistic faith, was very much in line with most of these values: Each citizen should read the Bible him or herself, should make his or her own judgment, and can practice faith in the local parish where "Presbyters,"[3] and not priests, should have influence.

It is this background against which the 17th century—the Dutch Golden Age—took off. The Republic of Holland had by and large prospered during the war against Spain. Merchants established trading societies with shares for each participant, thus sharing profits and losses with one another. In 1602, the East Indies Company was founded, followed by the West Indies Company in 1621. Their shares were traded at the stock exchange. New Amsterdam (the later New York) was established in 1625. Holland was the sole country with a permanent foothold in Japan (Decima). The Northern Company ruled the whale fishery around Scandinavia. Sea traders sailed the world seas.[4] Sciences, arts, and literature were cultivated at a high level (e.g., Huijgens, Spinoza, Vondel, and Rembrandt van Rijn). The Republic ruled itself through the Estate bodies mentioned earlier: The county of Holland had the most power (interestingly, the clergy was not represented in the States of Holland; the nobility had one vote). It is a matter of debate whether the Estate General of the Republic or the stadtholder wielded most power; anyway, they repeatedly struggled about the delineation of the other party's and their own rights and responsibilities (cf. Koeningsberger, 2001; van Deursen, 2004). In the domain of religion, a strongly debated and divisive subject related to the extent to which the Bible should be understood "literally," for example, as to whether personal salvation is predetermined by God.[5] Yet, many pleas were made to be tolerant and "liberal" to people with other beliefs or opinions (among those the people without a particular faith or religion), and "equal rights" were advocated for the "common people," the handicapped, and the poor. Such pleas were even more important as the seizure of the Edict of Nantes in France (1685) expelled many French Protestants. As many of these "Huegenots" were skilled craftsmen, the economies in the countries to which they fled profited sizably (e.g., parts of Germany and Holland).

In the 18th century, the Republic showed a tremendous amount of decay in many domains that had flourished during the Golden Age. Wealthy merchants showed off their possessions and lived off the interests and rents. Regents divided the best jobs and positions among themselves and their offspring. The army was corrupt, and a debate continued about the required size of army needed. Moreover, many foreign countries became strong economic competitors, outperforming the Republic in many ways. Yet, trade remained a strong sector. Humanism strengthened the dislike of authority. Rousseau's ideas about the people's sovereignty and

---

[3]Senior, recognized church members, appointed or elected by the parish community.
[4]Even nowadays a strong characteristic of the Dutch economy is the transport sector for international trade.
[5]The so-called "predestination."

Montesquieu's conception about the "trias politica"[6] were attractive to many regents. Then France occupied the Republic in 1794–1795, shortly before Napoleon started to battle with many other European countries.

Holland lost its independence for quite a while. The country—called the Batavian Republic until 1806—had to pay heavy duties to France. Trade collapsed, civil administration changed drastically, and the country became engaged in a war against England. Yet, various innovative laws were enacted, such as those on taxes and basic education. Between 1806 and 1810, Napoleon's brother—Lodewijk Napoleon—was King of Holland. From 1810 onward, Holland became a part of France. But in 1814, King William I of Orange was inaugurated and a new Constitution was introduced: The country of the Netherlands was born, which also incorporated major parts of Belgium until 1831. Trade started to flourish again. This new-found unity did not, however, lead to a centralized power structure. Most important for the administrative structure of the country was the new Constitution of 1848, primarily designed by the Liberal politician Thorbecke, who was appointed prime minister shortly afterward. It marked the onset of the *parliamentary aristocracy* (cf. Blonk et al., 1978). The Constitution addressed, for instance, direct election of the Second Chamber (Parliament), the rights and responsibilities of both Chambers, the public (open) character of all governmental institutions, and the inviolability of the king. Counties and cities again acquired substantial autonomy in the administration of their own affairs. Besides the Liberal Party, there was a Conservative, a Protestant, and a Roman Catholic Party. In the second part of the 19th century, social and socioeconomic issues became main points of concern, for example, child labor, industrial nuisance, and the self-organization of workers in labor unions. Manufacturing industries were innovated, and transport by train and by boat was provided with a better infrastructure. Farm produce was not protected against cheaper foreign imports, because the government favored free world trade.

In the next two sections, some main trends and characteristics of the 20th century are highlighted. First, the foreign policy of the Netherlands continued with its neutrality in international conflicts. This kept the country largely outside World War I, but it didn't offer protection against German occupation in World War II, which left the country devastated in 1945. Second, the life and work of many were organized along *denominational segregation lines*. This applied primarily to the Protestant and to the Roman Catholic denominations: Many societal organizations and institutions belonged to a particular denomination, implying, for instance, that citizens selected retail shops, leisure-time pursuits, health care, their political party, cultural events, their union, and even their employer more or less according to their "religious" color. Such segregation was previously thought to have hindered societal development, as the principles of "sovereignty in one's own circle" (Protestant) and "subsidiarity" (Roman Catholic: What is better done down the hierarchical chain should not be handled at a higher level) would make citizens less open to developments in other societal domains. Nowadays, the perspective is taken that denominational segregation may not only have facilitated the "emancipation" of minority movements, but may also have contributed to balancing parties in conflict and integrating citizens into society. Denominational segregation has probably played a key role in the development of a large *middle class,* which helped to stabilize the country and led to continued modernization. After a period of desegregation in recent decades, some new denominational categories have surfaced in Dutch society, like the Islamic, Liberal, Christian (Roman Catholics and Protestants combined), and Socio-Democrat movements.

---

[6]The "trias politica" holds that the legislative power, the judicial power, and the executive power should be independent from one another.

No Heros?

Why is it that the Dutch usually do not tend to recognize countrymen of particular "historical" importance as heroes, or even manifest an antihero attitude? Why is it that they frequently detest observing outspoken symbols of officialdom, resent prerogatives of leaders, and sometimes even question the acceptability of persons in more powerful positions? Furthermore, why did they tend to disregard high performers or discourage outstanding achievers (as is highlighted in the typically Dutch saying: "Being ordinary is sufficiently awkward.")? There is, of course, not one, single, fully adequate answer to these questions. However, the historical perspective taken in the preceding section identified some core themes, which may jointly apply:

1. From at least the Middle Ages onward, cities possessed or gained much power to settle their own affairs in various respects. They were most often not subject to a strong, single-person type of leadership structure: the count or the king usually resided abroad and left affairs to be handled by a *remplacant,* for example, a stadtholder. The more educated citizens were thus accustomed to a relatively large amount of autonomy and shared their power, to a certain extent, with others. Thus, these citizens were never very dependent on emperors, the clergy, and/or the nobility. In addition, Holland never had very distinct class differences although in later centuries, a large middle class developed.

2. Merchants created a lot of wealth for the cities. This strengthened the opportunities for cities and their citizens to regulate their own affairs, for example, through founding their own schools or setting up an army of mercenaries. As merchants very often went abroad and foreign traders frequently visited the Republic of Holland, a liberal, tolerant climate developed, open to different views (and, sometimes, some variety in religion).

• This culture of self-determination, of decentralized administration and of relative wealth for the "cultured," educated citizens was open to the Protestant faith, in particular as represented by Calvin. It is probably a bit too simple, as Weber (1947) tended to say, that Calvinism provided fertile ground for capitalism (also as many other, non-Protestant countries adopted capitalism). Rather, a certain embarrassment with the visible prosperity of many may have been more characteristic (Schama, 1987). Schama coined the term "moral ambiguity of prosperity" to refer to the problem of how to reconcile a luxurious lifestyle with the endorsement of the values of soberness and charity.

• Children were usually raised at home and not in a boarding school. Generally, women aspired to be housewives, including taking on the full-time care of their children. As for a boarding school, this would be typical of a more masculine environment (stressing values like disciplined behavior, obedience, courage, achievement, etc.), but such values were not dominant. Moreover, the people of Holland were not used to royal courts with pomp and circumstance.

3. Taken together, these core themes may have cradled the "germs" of the shared perception, in Dutch society, that a "person of historical importance" should be looked upon in terms of the social network—the *context*—she or he is embedded in. Favorable *situational conditions* rather than outstanding individual qualities should be considered crucial to their accomplishments.

4. The emphasis on decentralization and local autonomy got reestablished in the Constitution inspired by Thorbecke in the midst of the 19th century. This "tradition" was markedly changed immediately after World War II. The national government gained a very important role in rebuilding Dutch society and contributed to a "mixed economy" in which capitalism met government interference. The next section, on industrial relations, highlights some of these features. However, the last decade of the 20th century witnessed a gradual changeover. A retreating government, favoring a stronger role of market forces was seen, along with an emphasis on "intermediary societal institutions" (like the family and the local community) that should provide for the integration of citizens in a "multicultural" society. These ideas are to a large extent in line with the principles that governed Dutch society in previous centuries.

Translated to the dimensions of GLOBE research (cf. House et al., 2004), the preceding description suggests the following dimensions to be characteristic of the developments in Dutch society during the second part of the 20th century:

- (Societal and organizational) culture: relatively higher scores on individualism, femininity, tolerance of uncertainty, power egalitarianism, and humane orientation, and a relatively lower score on the performance orientation can be expected. There is no particular expectation regarding future–present orientation.
- Leadership: higher scores on attributes such as being humane, diplomatic, having integrity, and a collective orientation are expected along with lower scores on autocratic and status conscious behavior.

3. DUTCH INDUSTRIAL RELATIONS AFTER WORLD WAR II

The First Part of the 20th Century: Some Features

The kingdom of the Netherlands—with Queen Wilhelmina and the two chambers of Parliament—was not strongly affected by the First World War, because the nation had maintained its neutral foreign policy. During the 1929 Great Depression, many people suffered from unemployment, sudden loss of wealth and property, and a gloomy outlook for the future. For sure, the government provided some relief work projects. Vocational guidance was started (also initiated by some nongovernmental institutions and groups) to facilitate job openings for unemployed people through additional education, and to match abilities and skills of those who entered the labor market with the requirements of available jobs (e.g., Van Strien, 1988). However, the country did not have much industry. Of course, there were exceptions, like the ship-building sector, agriculture, textiles, and the Philips company. But many employers were traders rather than industrial entrepreneurs.

The country suffered severely from the German occupation during World War II (1940–1945). The Royal Family and the Dutch cabinet went abroad. During the last years of the war, representatives of different political parties secretly met to consider opportunities for joint political action when the war would end.

A new era began in May 1945 after the country was liberated: The government got a strong "centralized" position in rebuilding the country, in reshaping civilization, and in raising a strong industrial infrastructure, the latter with the help of the U.S. Marshall Funds. *Mixed capitalism* (in which governmental control and market forces are the main factors), a *consultation economy*[7] (which means that major interest groups are frequently consulted about their views), and a substantial *welfare state* were to be the main characteristics of Dutch (socio-)economic policy for many years to come.

Industrial Relations

Dutch industrial relations after World War II were strongly influenced by the need to rebuild society. The government, the major political parties, the employers' federations, and the unions worked together (initially harmoniously) to achieve rapid industrialization (cf. Industrial Democracy in Europe International Research Group, 1981). The government played a dominant role, first through its authority to control wages and prices: For more than 15 years wage and price increases were set (and usually controlled and maintained) at a national level. Second, the government enacted legislation in various domains, such as that concerning industrial democracy at the level of the enterprise. Yet, most decisions that were eventually taken at the national, sector, or individual organization level went through a dis- cussion and preparation phase in *councils* and *committees,* which were composed of employer federations and union representatives. During the 1950s some of the major characteristics of Dutch Industrial Relations were (Industrial Democracy in Europe International Research Group, 1981):

1. *Differentiation:* Both employer federations and workers' unions were patterned according to their industrial sector, and, in addition, also split into three segregated "denominations": Roman Catholic; Protestant; nondenominational (employers), respectively Social Democrats (union).
2. *Integration and consensus:* Despite the segregation, the unions and the employer fed- erations cooperated closely, and rather harmoniously, with one another. They held similar, or at least compatible, views on the goals of socioeconomic policy as well as on the objectives and the ways to implement industrial relations.
3. *Centralization:* A rather unique feature was the emphasis on (collective labor) agree- ments at the national level, in which the government was a powerful party (mostly mediating between employer federations and unions).

Objectives in the Post–Second World War Period

These included rebuilding the national economy, achieving full employment, and strongly expanding social legislation to further the development of a welfare state. The latter led to a comparatively high level of social security coverage, for example, a base pension for all citi- zens of 65 years or over and allowances in the case of sickness, unemployment, disability, and so forth. The consensus on objectives caused discussions and bargaining to focus primarily on ways and means. The three parties maintained frequent and intensive communication, in particular in the Social and Economic Council (SER) and the Foundation of Labor. This foun- dation was established in 1945 by employer federations and unions, and was accepted by the government as an important advisory body on socioeconomic subjects. The SER took shape in 1950 and became the main institution for advising the government on social and economic

---

[7]Some favor the term *consensus economy.*

problems.[8] It is composed of 45 members: Employer federations and unions account for 15 members each respectively, and 15 independent experts are appointed by the government.

Major conflicts were rare during the 1950s and early 1960s; if one occurred, a solution was reached by consultation. In order to establish the level of wages for the next year, a government planning bureau performed econometric calculations and estimated the wage increase the national economy could afford (e.g.,Windmuller, 1968). Institutions and industrial firms were stimulated to adopt a system of job evaluation (cf. Thierry & De Jong, 1998) that would facilitate company-internal equity as well as conformity to market rates (external equity). Instead of free bargaining, government control (and consultation with parties concerned) prevailed.

At the level of the enterprise, two formats for workers' participation prevailed. In 1950, the first Works Council Act was enacted. This Act describes the Works Council as a consultation body, primarily concerned with the general, common interests of the enterprise, having the managing director as its chairperson. The second format referred to the introduction of job consultation (*werkoverleg;* cf. Koopman & Wierdsma, 1998) at the shop-floor level in an increasing number of work organizations.

The early 1960s saw the onset of a drastic change in the industrial relations climate. The national economy did rather well. The standard of living had risen sizably. The labor market was very tight, in particular in areas of the country bordering (former West-)Germany: The economic boom in the rebuilt German industry allowed companies in that country to pay rather high wages, which attracted many Dutch workers. The former forces pressing for integration, like rebuilding the economy and providing for full employment, were burning out. Industrial relations became slightly more decentralized. Unions adopted a more independent attitude, were less concerned about economic growth, and focused more on workers' interests. This was apparent not only in the field of wages and employment conditions, but also in the domain of participation and power relations within the company. Moreover, around 1966, employer federations and unions agreed to eliminate the traditional distinction between white- and blue-collar workers and, consequently, to "harmonize" the differences in employment conditions. The growing diversification in jobs (and job requirements) had blurred this distinction, though it was widely held that most employment differences[9] did not keep up with the shared conceptions of social justice.

In France, a "cultural revolution" surfaced around 1968, primarily among students at universities (e.g., Paris and Nanterre). It reverberated rather strongly at Dutch universities: The student movement protested against what they perceived to be authoritarian attitudes and rigid, bureaucratic structures (Albeda, 1984). The new ideology called for "democratization" and a less unequal power distribution. The Dutch government reacted rather quickly and enacted a new law on the administration of the university—which ruled that students would be

---

[8]The Social and Economic Council is an example of the so-called *cooperate industrial organization* (CIO; *Publiekrechtelijke Bedrijfsorganisatie*), which was implemented at the level of an (industrial) sector. Its aim is to let the relevant employer federations and unions concerned arrange the "infrastructure" of that sector. Like the SER, some of the CIOs are still in existence. Some people expect that the increasing socioeconomic interdependence among countries within the European Union (EU) will make the CIO obsolete.

[9]White-collar employees got a monthly salary, whereas blue-collar workers were paid a weekly wage. White collars usually got a flat salary, whereas blue-collar pay was often partly based on performance. Regulations on absenteeism, pension schemes, and so forth also differed sizably. This harmonization movement took off much later in other European countries (Thierry, 1998).

represented in committees and boards—an effect of which was that the aftermath of the "revolution" took much longer (until the mid-1990s) than in any other European country. But the new ideology also affected industrial relations. Unions placed more emphasis on activities at the shop-floor level, consequently at the expense of the role they played at the industry and national level. The notions about a more equal distribution of power geared to the widely shared idea that income differences should be less steep. Remarkably, unions bargained with many industries in order to expel pay for performance, and achieved success (cf. Koopman-Iwema & Thierry, 1981). *Job evaluation* was considered to be a more fair strategy. In the 1970s, the government enacted a law to further the use of job evaluation, extending its application not only to higher management and senior executives in work organizations, but also to the free professions (like lawyers, accountants, medical doctors, etc.) and self-employed people. It sought to achieve both nationwide control of incomes and a fairer income distribution.

These developments can be characterized as a change in industrial relations from a "harmony model" to a "coalition model" (Peper, 1973). A harmony model is known for its consensus on goals, a large degree of cooperation, a low level of conflict, and the use of consultation as the main mechanism for the resolution of a conflict. A coalition model features partial consensus, some cooperation in a few restricted domains, a moderate level of conflict, and the use of bargaining as the main vehicle to solve conflicts. Some evidence in support of this change during those years is (Industrial Democracy in Europe International Research Group, 1981):

- A larger number of employees and firms were involved in the strikes.
- The content of collective labor agreements was shifting, as noneconomic issues got more emphasis (e.g., the *"quality of work"*).
- The process of bargaining was becoming tougher.
- The demand was made that the managing director should no longer be a member, let alone the chairperson, of the works council.

The new Act on the Works Council (1971) stated in particular that the task of the council was consultation, and representation of *employees'* interests. Research in the 1970s showed that a considerable number of works councils had potential influence on the company's decision-making process. However, this influence proved to be rather limited in practice (cf. Hövels & Nas, 1976; Industrial Democracy in Europe International Research Group, 1981). Decisions about appointments of senior executives, investments, and reorganization were hardly influenced by these councils (Andriessen & Coetsier, 1984; Koopman, 1992; Andriessen, 1998). Yet, most key informants at all levels of organizations believed that the works council had made a contribution to informing people better about what was going on in their organization. Also, they held that decisions were more easily accepted after having been discussed by the council (Industrial Democracy in Europe International Research Group, 1993).

The Works Council Act was amended in 1979, and again in 1982. The 1979 amendment made works councils more independent of the employer in organizations that totaled 100 or more employees: The managing director was no longer the chairperson, and the works council got more discretionary power on some subject matters. In 1982, the works council was made obligatory for organizations that employed 35 or more employees. Job evaluation schemes were still very much in use, if not at an increasing rate. Yet, the objective changed: Rather than effecting distributive justice, the *acceptance* of its results by employees (and their representatives in the works council) was emphasized. Consequently, the order of job values (and of corresponding basic salaries) that was considered to be acceptable in one organization could be seen as unfair in a neighboring company. This was one of the early signs of the need for decentralization, deregulation, and "company-tailored" conditions, which would manifest itself more strongly in the years to come.

Also in 1982, the coalition of political parties represented in the Dutch cabinet of ministers changed: The Christian Democratic Party constituted a new government jointly with the Liberal Party, whereas the Social Democrats went into the opposition. The new government was less interested than its predecessors in regulating industrial relations and furthering industrial democracy. As in several other countries, the era of "no-nonsense policymaking" took off. The economy—which faced a severe recession in that period—was stimulated by cutting back government spending and decreasing state intervention in trade and industry (Industrial Democracy in Europe International Research Group, 1993). In practice, it proved to be hard to reduce the role of the government in the industrial relations domain. Cabinets in later years did not drastically alter the main line of policy set during the 1970s. Remarkably, the coalition of Liberal and Social Democratic parties that ruled the country at the end of the 20th century and the onset of the 21st century strongly favored a *market* economy, in which the role of the state is modest (more facilitating in nature), service organizations and state firms were privatized as much as possible, flexibility in employment conditions (and various other areas) was pursued (e.g., "employability"), and decentralization and deregulation were enacted. As stated earlier, these values seem to be reminiscent of some of the major themes in Dutch history until the early 20th century, implying that the post–World War II period with a strong centralized position of the government may have been an exception to the rule.

Interpreting Evidence

How should Dutch industrial relations in the last 15 years of the 20th century be characterized? Hofstede's data (1984) on national culture show that the Dutch, in the early 1980s, scored high on individualism, and low on power distance and masculinity. Average scores were reached on tolerance of uncertainty, and long-term orientation. The "leader" was seen as somebody who is modest, favoring consultation of employees, work autonomy, training, the use of skills, the support of his or her group, and the contribution of all toward the success of the organization. Interestingly, these observations are in support of the GLOBE dimensions suggested to be characteristic for the Dutch in the historical overview (Section 2, No Heros?).

As previously outlined, centralized control prevailed until the early 1980s: The government was active in enacting new legislation on employees' participation in decision making. Pleas and initiatives to increase the opportunities for participation also came from companies, unions, and academics. However, one of the consequences of the economic recession in those times was a severe weakening of the position of the main unions in the Netherlands as an effect of both the loss of many members and diminishing bargaining power. Also, "competing" unions (e.g., for executives and managers) were gradually gaining power, sometimes at a sector level, but mostly at the organizational level. Democratization and participation lost their position on the public agenda. Nationwide agreements and initiatives regarding industrial relations subjects became scarce: Formerly held societal values were wearing out and getting fragmented or were replaced by norms and values of interest groups operating at all levels of the society. Yet, research evidence showed that the extent of participation in practice, both direct and representative, was not smaller in the 1980s than in the 1970s (cf. Pool, Drenth, Koopman, & Lammers, 1988).

In the 1990s, the industrial relations climate was becoming more of an intense issue at the sector and organization level. The use of job evaluation (advocated in an earlier decade with an eye on nationwide objectives and values) was recommended, because it allowed ordering jobs (and thus base salaries) in accordance with the particular, if not *unique,* "strategic" conditions of each company. Employer's federations merged, and attuned their activities much more to local companies, regional markets, and international conditions. Also, major trade unions were in a merging process. Collective labor agreements were more often set at the company level, containing "boundary conditions" the framework of which was to be elaborated within a firm or business unit: It is here that the role of the (local) works council was emphasized. Some firms, for example, in the commercial services branch, tended to do without the involvement of unions, favoring individual labor contracts. Indeed, an important question is whether the Dutch industrial relations system can be characterized as a consultation economy since the 1990s.

In terms of GLOBE research, this overview suggests that the following dimensions characterize the postwar period until the early 1990s:

- Cultural practice: relatively high scores on collectivism, gender egalitarianism, uncertainty avoidance, and humane values; and a very high score on power egalitarianism; and a moderate score on performance orientation as well as on future–present orientation.
- Leadership preferences: a relatively high score on attributes like team orientation, diplomatic, and humane, and a rather low score on autocratic, self-centered, and status-conscious.

The next three sections deal in particular with data from different sources—most of which were gathered in the context of the GLOBE study—on how societal culture, organizational culture, and outstanding leadership were perceived to be in the Netherlands during the second part of the 1990s.

4. CONTEMPORARY SOCIETAL CULTURE

During the pilot phase the provisional GLOBE questionnaires were carefully translated into Dutch and back-translated into English. The final questionnaires were administered to 287 middle managers, randomly selected from three companies in the food sector, and three companies in the banking/insurance sector. All items appeared to be clear and provided no observable problems of interpretation. The six companies had cooperated on an earlier occasion in a project with a member of the CCI team. Within each sector the three companies differed greatly from one another in size, location, products and services, and the like. A total of 146 managers filled out the national culture questionnaire and 141 completed the questionnaire on organizational culture.

In the first column of Table 7.1, the mean scores of Dutch managers on current societal culture *practices* are shown. The second column lists the group category: The scores of all 61 countries sparticipating in GLOBE were assigned to so-called Bands (cf. Hanges, Dickson, & Sipe, 2004). Band A is the highest, Band C (or D) the lowest. The third and fourth columns contain the maximum, and respectively, minimum scores given to any country. Thus, the first row indicates that Dutch managers rate Performance Orientation in their societal culture as slightly above the midscale point (running from 1 "very low" to 7 "very high") positioned in Band B.

Table 7.1 reveals that Dutch managers consider societal cultural practices as higher on Uncertainty Avoidance, Future Orientation, and Institutional Collectivism, and lower on

TABLE 7.1
Societal Culture Scales ("As Is")

	Mean	Band[a]	Maximum	Minimum
Performance Orientation	4.32	B	4.94	3.20
Future Orientation	4.61	A	5.07	2.80
Assertiveness	4.32	A	4.97	2.79
Institutional Collectivism	4.46	B	5.22	3.25
Gender Egalitarianism	3.50	B	4.33	2.50
Humane Orientation	3.86	C	5.23	3.18
Power Distance	4.11	C	5.80	3.59
In-Group Collectivism	3.70	C	6.36	3.18
Uncertainty Avoidance	4.70	B	5.37	2.85

[a]Bands A > B > C > D are determined by calculating the grand mean and standard deviations across all society "As Is" and "Should Be" scales respectively for the GLOBE sample of countries. These means and standard deviations are than used to calculate low, medium, and high bands of countries (GLOBE standard procedure, cf. Hanges, Dickson, & Sipe, 2004).

Humane Orientation, In-Group Collectivism, and Gender Egalitarianism. They understand Dutch society as being characterized by rules and orderliness, planning ahead, collective economic interests, and group loyalty, but not so concerned with sensitivity toward people—a society, moreover, in which individual accomplishments of children are favored, and moderately equal opportunities exists for female citizens. The comparative scores add to this picture that Dutch people are seen as relatively dominant and tough (Assertiveness), and not so strongly inclined to accept hierarchy (Power Distance). The emphasis on self-reliance and individual autonomy (Participant Observation Questionnaire [POQ], Items 9 and 10), collective economic interests, and consensual decision making is in accordance with a part of Dutch history (Section 2) and the industrial relations system described earlier. The data on *Gender Egalitarianism* are to some extent in contrast with Hofstede's study (1984), in which Dutch society was found to be feminine. Also, the results from the POQ (items 40, 60, and 88) indicate that occupations of women are predominantly of a lower status, like homemaking, child care, and serving others. National heroes, on the other hand, are predominantly male. Yet, the percentage of women among politicians at the highest two levels of government is increasing (currently around 25% to 30%).

It is interesting to compare these results with the middle managers scores on societal cultural *values*, which reflect what they feel the dimensions should look like. Table 7.2 contains these data.

According to Table 7.2 Dutch managers have higher scores on Performance Orientation, Humane Orientation, In-Group Collectivism, and Future Orientation, and lower scores on Uncertainty Avoidance and in particular Power Distance. Thus, they value in their society an emphasis on innovativeness and effective performance, a sensitive and tolerant concern for people, loyalty to family and organization, an eye on future events and longer term planning, a climate of experimentation and freedom, and a concern for sharing power. The comparative scores show in addition that Dutch managers stress the importance of feminine opportunities, but less so of dominance and toughness.

TABLE 7.2
Societal Culture Scales ("Should Be")

	Mean	Band[a]	Maximum	Minimum
Performance Orientation	5.49	B	6.58	2.35
Future Orientation	5.07	B	6.20	2.95
Assertiveness	3.02	C	4.94	2.40
Institutional Collectivism	4.55	B	5.65	3.80
Gender Egalitarianism	4.99	A	5.17	3.18
Humane Orientation	5.20	B	6.09	3.39
Power Distance	2.45	D	4.35	2.04
In-Group Collectivism	5.17	B	6.52	4.06
Uncertainty Avoidance	3.24	D	5.61	3.16

[a]Bands A > B > C > D are determined by calculating the grand mean and standard deviations across all society "As Is" and "Should Be" scales respectively for the GLOBE sample of countries. These means and standard deviations are than used to calculate low, medium, and high bands of countries (GLOBE standard procedure, cf. Hanges, Dickson, & Sipe, 2004).

When cultural practices (Table 7.1) are confronted with cultural values (Table 7.2) it appears that values like sharing power, feminine values, family and organizational loyalty, experimentation and freedom, sensitivity to people, and achievement should be emphasized more than they are now.[10] These results suggest that Dutch society is involved in a process of *cultural transition,* in which more classical values, such as collective economic interests, loyalty, being humane, sharing of power, and gender egalitarianism, are still endorsed, whereas values of individual achievement and autonomy are gaining prominence. Let's see whether the perspectives on organizational culture reflect a comparable dual emphasis.

5.   ORGANIZATION CULTURE

As previously mentioned, 141 managers completed the questionnaire on organizational culture. Table 7.3 contains the scores given based on *practices* in both the financial and food sectors.

Table 7.3 shows that the scores of managers in the financial sector are not very different from those of managers in the food sector. The largest difference occurs with regard to Gender Egalitarianism. Thus, organizational culture practices are characterized by higher scores on Future Orientation, In-group Collectivism, Assertiveness, Humane Orientation, and Performance Orientation, and a lower score on Power Distance. In other words, to some extent middle managers describe cultural practices within their organization to be in accordance with societal culture practices, as a comparison with Table 7.1 reveals. Yet, more emphasis is put on future events, longer term planning, and humane values, and less on power distance and uncertainty avoidance. Table 7.4 lists the middle managers' scores on organization culture *values.*

Again, the scores of managers in both sectors hardly differ from one another, as Table 7.4 shows.

---

[10]All *t* values concerned are significant.

TABLE 7.3

Organization Culture Practices ("As Is") in the Financial and Food Sector

	Financial Sector	*Food Sector*
Performance Orientation	4.56	4.29
Assertiveness	4.63	4.38
Future Orientation	5.20	5.29
Gender Egalitarianism	3.71	3.01
Humane Orientation	4.77	4.57
Institutional Collectivism	4.33	4.63
Power Distance	3.14	3.07
In-Group Collectivism	4.90	4.92
Uncertainty Avoidance	3.85	3.91

TABLE 7.4

Organization Culture Values ("Should Be") in the Food and Banking/Insurance Sector

	Financial Sector	*Food Sector*
Performance Orientation	5.99	5.76
Assertiveness	4.15	4.51
Future Orientation	5.65	5.70
Gender Egalitarianism	5.22	5.12
Humane Values	4.50	4.82
Institutional Collectivism	4.54	4.57
Power Distance	3.07	3.12
In-Group Collectivism	5.72	5.60
Uncertainty Avoidance	2.98	3.30

The results indicate that Performance Orientation, Future Orientation, and In-Group Collectivism get higher scores, whereas Power Distance and Uncertainty Avoidance get lower scores. In comparison with Table 7.3 on organization culture practices, it appears that values such as Performance Orientation, family and organization Collectivism, and Gender Egalitarianism receive higher scores, whereas Uncertainty Avoidance gets a lower score. Thus, middle managers prefer their organization's culture to be more focused upon innovation and effective performance, on planning for the future, on equal opportunities for women, and on loyalty to the family and their own organization. With a view on the relatively high scores on a humane as well as a collective orientation, the suggestion put forward at the end of the preceding section is supported: Dutch societal and organizational culture seems to be in a transitional phase. Classical values concerning loyalty, collective economic interests, being humane, sharing of power, and gender egalitarianism are still endorsed, whereas individual achievement and innovation are becoming more important. This transition occurs against the background of the changeover from the post–Second World War political and industrial relations climate—which was rather "collective" in nature—toward the contemporaneous more "individualized and flexible" climate (as described in Sections 2 and 3). An interesting question is which leadership attributes are considered to qualify outstanding leaders in this transitional phase. This is the subject of the next section.

6.   ON LEADERSHIP

In this section the results from some qualitative and quantitative data on leadership are discussed. First, the outcomes of Dutch media analysis are presented. Then the main themes from a series of interviews in a major Dutch daily newspaper with Dutch CEOs on decision making and leadership are summarized. Next, the responses given in individual as well as focus group interviews on characteristics of outstanding leadership are highlighted. Subsequent to this, data on GLOBE questionnaires relating to preferred attributes of outstanding leaders are analyzed. In conclusion, some data from another Dutch study on leadership characteristics are discussed.

Media Analysis

One of the qualitative sources for learning more about contemporary leadership values and required leader characteristics is provided by the *analysis of media*. Data for this analysis were collected in Week 32 (August 4–11) of 1996. It started with *NRC/Handelsblad* (a prominent national newspaper, with a liberal character). Then *Het Financiële Dagblad* (the Dutch equivalent of the *Wall Street Journal*) was added, as well as *Intermediair* (including its postings of management vacancies), *Elsevier, HP/De Tijd,* and *Vrij Nederland* (four weekly magazines with a wide distribution throughout the Netherlands). Finally, a monthly glossy management magazine was included called *Quote.* All these weekly and monthly magazines are especially popular among people in middle-managerial positions.

In these media we hardly found any articles on *good* leaders; moreover, in Dutch media very few leaders are associated with events in society or in organizations. Probably, this observation relates both to Dutch culture in general and to the prevailing Dutch media culture. Most journalists tend to be factual and fairly neutral in their reporting style with little speculation about possible managerial or leadership influences. Also, details about a leader's private life are not made public or at least only to a moderate extent (a similar reserve is taken by most media regarding the private life of the Queen and the Royal Family).

The media portray good Dutch leaders/managers as fulfilling a modest role; they tend to be trustworthy, down-to-earth, well-organized, hard-working, competent, and inconspicuous. At the same time, they are strong-willed, ambitious, inspirational, pragmatic, and demanding on their personnel and on suppliers. They feel they should take time to consult major parties before implementing plans; they tend to mediate well between various stakeholders and they attribute success to teamwork. Some consider many Dutch leaders to be intellectually mediocre and some such critics think they should say that in public. Often, leaders get more public criticism than praise in the Netherlands. Perhaps that explains, in part, why most leadership figures are slightly inconspicuous or nonflamboyant.

Table 7.5 lists leadership attributes that are specified in managerial job postings. Three frequency categories are distinguished: (a) all postings, (b) often listed, and (c) mentioned several times.

TABLE 7.5
Leadership Attributes Listed in Intermediair's Managerial Job Postings

Listed in All Postings	Often Listed
Leadership experience	Good communicator
Expertise (that fits the particular job)	Flexible

Mentioned Several Times	
Consideration	Achievement orientation
Motivator	Self-confidence
Empathy	Independent, yet team player
Convincing	Commercial skills
Tactful/diplomatic	Hard-working
Coach	Entrepreneur
Trustworthy	Strong personality
Change/Innovation	Decision maker
Creative negotiator	Planning & Control
Innovator	Risk controller
International experience/interest	Planner
Experienced change manager	Organizing talent
Vision implementer	Eye for detail
Initiating capacity	
Inspiring	

Table 7.5 shows that "expertise" is emphasized as a major leadership attribute required. Managers need to have a particularly strong background in the contents of the jobs they will be managing. In addition, they should have gained some managerial experience, to show they are capable of leading others. Moreover, they need to be socially astute. Less frequently mentioned attributes relate to consideration, achievement orientation, change and innovation, and planning and control.

It should be kept in mind that the postings refer to a rather large variety of leadership positions and managerial jobs. Many of the requirements just mentioned change from time to time and are prone to (especially Anglo-Saxon managerial) fads and fashions. After all, Dutch people have a great interest in (popular English) managerial literature, which has, of course, an impact. Yet, this impact does not seem to pervade the media culture very strongly, as these requirements are rather general in nature. Let's see how Dutch CEOs are characterized by several journalists.

Interviews With Dutch CEOs

In the spring of 1994, *NRC/Handelsblad,* the daily newspaper, ran a series of feature articles titled "The Decision Makers." This 15-part series consisted of 14 interviews with Dutch CEOs of diverse and rather large companies. The smallest organization, DTZ Zadelhoff, is a brokerage agency, at that time still led by the entrepreneur who had started the business in 1961. When the interview was held it consisted of 1,700 employees in nine different countries. With 96,000 employees at the time of the interview KPN, the Dutch telecommunications and postal giant (later privatized), is the largest independent employer on the Amsterdam Stock Exchange. Other well-known companies whose CEOs participated in the series include Heineken (beer), KLM (Royal Dutch Airline), ING (banking), and Akzo-Nobel (chemicals).

The interviews highlight the opinion of Dutch business leaders on topics such as unemployment, government regulations, and competition from low-wage countries. It was also intended to give an impression of how these CEOs lead their own organization. The series concluded with one final article by journalists and business consultants that comprised of more general comments based on Dutch business leaders and outlined the demands faced by Dutch business leadership in the past and future decade.

In general, several points are noteworthy. First, it is remarkable that the articles do *not* give much personal information about CEOs. Some prior work experience is mentioned for all CEOs, their educational background and age for most, but further personal details, income, or family are hardly discussed. This seems consistent with Dutch tradition (as we also noted in the media analysis in the previous section), where even royalty and public figures are "entitled" to some privacy and in which leaders are not considered or treated as heroes (Section 2).

All CEOs interviewed are *men*. This still reflects the current situation in which only a very few women are found in the higher echelons of large corporations. Recent figures also show, for instance, that Dutch universities are among the lowest ranking in the world with regard to women holding a full professorship. Most of the interviewed CEOs commented on political issues in the interviews and several were actively involved in national politics and political decision making, mainly through their role in political parties or employers federations. All 14 have a *university* degree. However, they were educated in diverse fields such as economics and business, engineering, or law. Most started their career in another organization, earning their merits before taking over as CEO in their current organization. Two of the CEOs are entrepreneurs who started their own business and are still in charge.

Another striking aspect in the articles is the strong *international* focus of all CEOs and of the company strategies they represent. Asia and especially China are seen as offering many new and important business opportunities; the same goes (to a lesser extent) for Central or Eastern Europe. It is not surprising that Dutch business often has an international orientation; the Netherlands is a small country with a limited domestic market. The tradition of intensive trade with many other nations started many centuries ago (Section 2). Also, an international orientation seems to be a typical feature of the Netherlands, which is reflected, for instance, in the fact that most Dutch speak two or often even three languages to a certain degree (Dutch, and usually English and/or some German). The educational system emphasizes the importance of learning these different languages. Also indicative of this international focus is that newspapers and broadcasts present a lot of international news, especially regarding other countries in Europe, the United States, Asia, and the Middle East.

The interview with each CEO includes many company-specific situational elements. For instance, in companies that had recently experienced a crisis, restructuring, or turnaround in which many employees had to be made unemployed, this provided the background for the interview. In companies that recently merged or were taken over by others, this constituted the main setting.

CEOs often referred to the company in terms of a collectivity: *"we at ..."* Other elements that were often mentioned regarding leadership and decision making were the necessity of *support, consensus, and acceptance* by lower level managers and employees. Remarks such as "consensus is an important prerequisite to realize goals" and "ideas need acceptance, otherwise they will not be realized" reflect this concern. This emphasis on a combination of *autonomy and consensus* is a feature strongly associated with the way in which the Dutch have been governed for many years. Hofstede (1984) has also described this Dutch emphasis on consensus (see Section 3 as well).

If an organization faces a crisis, leaders need to show optimism, vision, decisiveness, and *credibility*, need to care about the people they work with, and should emphasize team building. Examples of remarks made are:

> In crisis a leader must be energetic and decisive and be the one to see the light at the end of the tunnel. Such a period of restructuring is always unpleasant. The credibility of leadership is increased immensely by pulling an organization through a crisis. One must display a certain optimism; for if the organizations feels their leaders don't believe in the future, you cannot expect them to believe in it.

> In such a period you have to brace yourself. Eat in the works canteen with everyone. Show interest in the people they work with. One should not lock oneself in an ivory tower to be pampered, but show you are one with the organization. Demonstrate trust. We do it together.

Other remarks on the demands that a crisis places on management were: "A clear agreement on goals of the reorganization is very important, and so is making people *responsible* for goal attainment." This was followed by the remark: "A second element is working as a *team*, gaining consensus." Another translated quote: "In the team we listen well and keep talking until everyone agrees. That goes for the board of directors but also for the levels below that. Of course knots must be cut [hard decisions made]. That is my role. Everyone understands that at a certain point talk is over."

According to the CEOs, *visioning* is part of the job. Many talk about their ideas for the future, new markets, a new strategy, as well as what they learned from the past. A more general remark reflecting the importance the CEOs put on vision is:

> Having a certain vision is an important asset for leaders and entrepreneurs: where is my organization positioned on the market, what is my dream. You also need tenacity, like a terrier and love people a little. Do not only sit in your room, but get out there, motivating they call that. You can't motivate people if you do not care about them.

People skills, motivating, and social responsibility are also mentioned several times as important leadership skills.

In the concluding article, the journalists show that until recently the top echelon of Dutch business was recruited from a small "reservoir," a sort of old boys network. Many companies were also still run by the family that had once started the corporation. However, in the 1980s the situation changed. The barriers of the "silent ruling class" in business were broken and the influence of families in their businesses diminished to make way for what one of the CEOs describes as *"professional management."* The appealing entrepreneurs, the immensely committed heads of the family business, and the social reformers in top administrative positions were replaced with hard-working, analytical, and careful problem solvers. These new top managers had an almost mathematical method of leading, in which communicating with the outside world is hardly done except where company figures and acquisitions are concerned. However, according to the journalists the coming years will place new demands on leaders. These ever faster changing times call for more inspirational "stimulators" who are willing to take risks and have a vision that integrates the activities of the many business units the modern corporation is composed of. The writers summarize their impression with remarks such as "after the shepherds, technocrats and caretakers we now need *pioneers* to run large businesses in The Netherlands."

We assume that the final conclusions of the journalists concerned are in accordance with the ideas expressed by the CEOs. Remarkable, then, is the agreement with the results of the media analysis (Section 6) regarding managerial job postings. It seems that *in addition* to traditional practices and values concerning consensus, acceptance, support, and work autonomy, an outstanding CEO is expected to be a decisive team player, tenacious and dreaming, motivate people, and pioneer the organization. In Section 3, several leadership dimensions were suggested as characteristic for the Dutch postwar period until the early 1990s. The preceding qualitative findings are only partly in agreement with these. Against the background of the transition in Dutch societal and organizational culture (Sections 4 and 5) these findings may suggest the beginning *demise* of a leadership pattern that seems to have been developed during the postwar period. This pattern combined two distinct, though interrelated, features:

1. Leadership behavior is not very "personalized": The leader's behavior is not particularly outspoken, and not primarily attuned to a group member's particular behaviors or attitudes. Rather, the leader's actions are usually oriented toward creating *conditions* for influencing the group members. The behaviors of many leaders are focused on fairness for the group members and equality in treatment; as a consequence, leadership behavior is often a bit bureaucratic in nature. Power is obviously enacted, but subdued, not blatant; rule making and rule enactment prevail rather than personal views and preferences. The new emphasis on the tenacious, motivating, and pioneering leader signals perhaps that "personal" qualities are perceived to be more needed nowadays and are thus becoming more valued or "acceptable."

2. Leadership behavior (and policymaking in institutional settings) is oriented at combining different viewpoints. Balancing between opposite stands, compromising between different plans, making a coalition with an opponent party, socializing with "the enemy"—these themes seem to qualify many acts of leaders. Such behaviors serve, to some extent, to make leadership less based on "personal" choices and decisions. These behaviors are legitimized by the "constituents" to the extent that they recognize some of their own interests and goals. Yet, a balancing leadership style that encompasses the making of compromises also "softens" the *countervoice*. Perhaps the new emphasis on risk taking, decisiveness, creative negotiation, and vision indicate a trend toward less compromising and more assertive leadership behaviors.

Focus Interviews and Questionnaire Data

Individual interviews were held with five middle managers. Focus group interviews involved an additional 15 managers. Table 7.6 indicates which aspects are mentioned more and less frequently as characteristic of outstanding leadership by all 20 respondents.

Almost all respondents say that an outstanding leader should have a clear vision of the direction in which the organization ought to go, including the way to achieve the objectives and goals set. The leader should moreover continuously adapt to the organization's internal and external changes, solving occurring problems creatively. In doing so the leader must be

TABLE 7.6

Characteristics of Outstanding Leadership Assembled by Interviews and Focus Groups

Mentioned Attributes of Outstanding Leadership	Frequency
Visionary	19
Creativity/innovative behavior	17
Inspiring	12
Risk taking/courage/nerve	11
Self-insight/knowing one's limitations	11
Open communication	10
Calm	9
Open to situation/environment	8
Creating group feeling	8
Attention to private life of follower	7
Long-term oriented	7
Trustworthy	7
Expressiveness/radiating	7

able to inspire followers, motivating them to work hard and to give 100% in their job. That also requires the courage to stick out one's neck, accompanied by a good self-insight and a sense of one's own limitations. Half the respondents refer to open communication, which includes the discussion of policy matters with followers, the clarification of difficult issues, the ability to listen, and honesty toward followers. In summary, the outstanding leader should be a *visionary* and a *decent* person who involves his or her followers incisively. Remarkably, an attribute like integrity was not mentioned at all: When asked, respondents indicated that all human beings should show integrity (and not only outstanding leaders). Also, achievement was hardly stressed. Slightly different from the results of the media analysis (Section 6), it appears that change/innovation is strongly emphasized, whereas achievement is not.

The same respondents also rated 10 leadership characteristics (derived from performance appraisal instruments) regarding their importance to outstanding leadership. Table 7.7 lists these characteristics and the mean scores.

Creativity and innovation are considered to be most vital to outstanding leadership, according to the results of Table 7.7. Interpersonal relationships is rated second (as is quality of output), getting a slightly more prominent place than open communications in Table 7.6. Reliability is among the less outspoken dimensions (as is trustworthy in Table 7.6). All in all, these outcomes support the main conclusions derived from the interviews with middle managers.

GLOBE Questionnaire Results

As indicated earlier, 287 middle managers from the food and the banking/insurance sector took the questionnaire on leadership attributes. Table 7.8 shows the results, also in comparison to the scores of all other countries. This table shows that Dutch managers consider

TABLE 7.7
Importance Ratings of Leadership Characteristics

Dimensions	Mean
Creativity and innovative behavior	3.0
Quality of output	3.3
Interpersonal relationships	3.3
Planning	5.1
Cooperative attitude	5.9
Cost control	6.0
Expertise	6.1
Reliability	6.3
Quantity of output	7.3
Work habits	8.7

Note. $N = 20$ managerial raters. 1 = most important.

characteristics such as integrity, inspirational, and visionary as crucial for success as a leader. On the contrary, attributes such as malevolent, self-centered, and autocratic get very low scores. In comparison with all other countries, the attributes team integrator, decisive, diplomatic, and humane orientation also characterize Dutch perceptions of outstanding leaders. Malevolent, Autocratic, and Face saving get comparatively low scores.

Table 7.9 shows the results of an exploratory factor analysis[11] on the Dutch data. Jointly, these four factors explain 55% of the variance. The higher loadings on Factor I reveal that a generous, *group-oriented,* modest, and sincere style characterizes one pattern of leadership. A second pattern combines foresight, *mission orientation,* willfulness, enthusiasm, and a concern for excellence. Interestingly, the attribute face saving (which represents evasive, indirect behaviors) has a negative loading on this second factor. The third pattern is characterized by a nonparticipative, *individualistic,* domineering style. The fourth pattern reflects a formal, cautious, and *orderly* style of leadership. Some attributes have rather high loadings on more than one factor (like self-sacrifice and face saving); other attributes (e.g., status-conscious) have rather low loadings on all factors.

---

[11]Principal components analysis with Varimax rotation was used. Note that the GLOBE scales were designed to measure organizational or societal level variability (Hanges, Dickson, & Sipe, 2004). The scales were *not* intended to meaningfully differentiate among individuals within a particular society. However, even though the scales were not constructed to provide such information, in some cases it is interesting to assess whether similar factors differentiate individuals within a society. Country-specific factor analysis is intended as an exploration of the themes captured by GLOBE in a new domain, that is, individual differences within a society. It should be noted, that because of the within-society restriction of the GLOBE scales true-score variability (which was based on between-society differences) the loadings of the GLOBE scale's items on within-society factors should be lower than between societies (cf. Hanges, Dickson, & Sipe, 2004). Furthermore, one should not interpret the within-society factor analyses as replications of the GLOBE factor structure. And the absence of a GLOBE factor within a society should not be automatically interpreted as the factor being irrelevant to the people in that country. Rather, a factor may fail to emerge within a society even when that theme is extremely critical because there was no variability in how the individuals from a single society rated the items (e.g., they all rated the items a 7). Factor analysis requires variability and so a factor could fail to emerge because it is extremely critical or completely irrelevant to the people within a society.

TABLE 7.8
Outstanding Leadership Attributes

Dimension	Mean	Band	Maximum
Integrity	6.52	A	6.79
Inspirational	6.38	A	6.63
Visionary	6.30	A	6.50
Team Integrator	6.01	A	6.43
Performance Orientation	5.95	B	6.64
Decisive	5.87	A	6.37
Diplomatic	5.43	A	6.05
Admin. Competent	5.43	C	6.42
Team Orientation	5.42	B	6.09
Humane Orient.	4.98	A	5.68
Self-Sacrifice	4.79	B	5.99
Modesty	4.71	B	5.79
Status-Conscious	3.93	C	5.93
Autonomous	3.53	B	4.65
Conflict Inducer	3.26	C	5.01
Procedural	3.22	C	4.89
Nonparticipative	2.41	B	3.68
Face Saving	2.23	D	4.53
Autocratic	2.08	D	4.16
Self-Centered	1.75	C	3.41
Malevolent	1.62	D	2.67

Note.   N = 287.

TABLE 7.9
Four Leadership Factors: Attributes and Factor Loadings

I		II		III		IV	
Humane Orientation	.75	Visionary	.76	Self-Centered	.72	Procedural	.79
Team Orientation	.73	Decisive	.72	Autonomous	.71	Administratively Competent	.73
Modesty	.71	Inspirational	.69	Autocratic	.71		
Integrity	.53	Performance Orientation	.67				
Diplomatic	.50						

In the typical Dutch *polder model*,[12] a group-oriented leadership style is important, in which consultation with other parties and integration of different opinions stands out. Therefore, a relatively low score on the orderly leadership style (which represents a focus on attributes as autocratic, self-centered, and nonparticipative) could be expected. Also, status consciousness is not very helpful to become an excellent manager in the Netherlands. Sharing visions and being a team player are more required. Observations in line with these results can also be found in the Unobtrusive Measurement Questionnaire (UMQ) and the Participant Observation Questionnaire (POQ); for example: Burial places are not separated according to the status of the deceased (Item 3). Pictures of living political leaders are not normally displayed in bars during nonelection times (Item 4), nor displayed on postage stamps (Item 16). Eating places in large companies are mostly *not* separated according to the status of the employees (Item 22). Also, individuals are generally expected to voice their personal opinions, even when in disagreement with the majority of the people with whom they interact.

A separate study done in the Netherlands (den Hartog, 1997; den Hartog, Koopman, & Van Muijen, 1998) asked a nationwide sample ($N=2,161$, at least 19 years of age, with work experience) on characteristics seen as important for Dutch top and middle managers. Results show that the most important characteristics for *top managers* in the Netherlands are: eye for innovation, long-term orientation, vision, convincing, trustworthy, communicative, confidence builder, and courage. Dominant, formal, but also modest behaviors are not considered as characteristics of successful top leaders. For good Dutch *middle managers,* important characteristics are: trustworthy, communicative, concern for subordinates' interests, team builder, participative, and confidence builder. Again, dominant and formal behaviors have very low scores.

In other words, this confirms again that the Dutch culture appears to be a bit aversive against a large power distance and strong leaders. Formal leadership does not guarantee commitment. Leaders have to consult, and to convince in order to be trusted and followed. As was shown in Table 7.6, characteristics mentioned most in the interviews and the focus group interviews were: visionary, creativity/innovative behavior, and inspirational leadership. Dominant, formal, and authoritarian leadership is less accepted in the Netherlands, perhaps unless special situations, such as a crisis or a decline of operations, are faced. Yet, it is important to keep in mind that a trend in Dutch societal and organizational culture seems to be emerging in which increasing emphasis is placed on values like individualism and flexibility (Sections 4 and 5). Apparently, outstanding leaders with a strong group orientation and an emphasis on intellectual stimulation, orderly in nature but low on individualism, are considered to be able to cope with these upcoming changes.

7. SPECIFIC MANIFESTATIONS OF DUTCH SOCIETAL CULTURE

One way to characterize the dominant current culture in Dutch society is its *egalitarian* nature. Leaders of companies and institutions ought to satisfy pretty high requirements in order to be qualified for their job, but should still behave as their next-door neighbor, without pretense, pomp, particular prerogatives, or a high income. Good leaders are expected not to behave distinctively, and their style of living should be kept a rather private issue, according to

---

[12]The term poldermodel refers literally to pieces of land gained from the sea. Symbolically, it reflects a concern for consultation and joint decision making in the industrial relations area.

many citizens. Dutch people tend not to monitor individuals in high-power positions, excellent performers, or talented youngsters. Rather, their heart goes out to human beings in deprived conditions (abroad or at home), to mediocre or poor performers, to students at school staying behind: These people should get supportive aid within a climate of "equal opportunities for all." Many citizens hold the strong belief that the creation of *facilitating conditions* results in better, more mature personal development of individuals. The enactment of rules and regulations at different societal levels helps to further these conditions as well as a climate that favors humane, social values.

One of the manifestations of egalitarianism is the dislike for authority within Dutch society. Obviously, a few officials with some authority are needed to get society moving, but the authority sources should not be too personalized. Dutch citizens favor a high degree of individual *autonomy:* They tend to follow only those rules (e.g., in traffic) that they consider to be worthwhile and "relevant" to their personal situation. The need for autonomy is apparent in the tendency not to accept "directives from above," but to engage in discussion and deliberation in order to better negotiate personal and group interests. On a societal level this tendency is exemplified during the past two decades by the *poldermodel,* the Dutch term for "consensual" decision making between (socio) political parties with diverging interests. The *poldermodel* is built on the assumption that parties concerned are willing to form coalitions with one another, to make compromises, to give and to take, thus achieving their objectives and interests eventually better than through pushing these separate from each other. As a consequence, the *poldermodel* absorbs countervoices to some extent: It smoothes extreme points of view. But it has also enabled Dutch industry from the early 1980s onward to create an unprecedented increase in employment—for instance, through introducing flexible working conditions on a large scale, part-time jobs, and the like—jointly with very moderate annual wage and salary increases.

A particular characteristic of Dutch societal culture is the belief that Dutch culture is *not so important.* Many citizens in the Netherlands are not very well informed about the history of their country or major achievements (and failures) in earlier ages, let alone heroes of the past. They doubt moreover whether it is necessary to teach Dutch history extensively at school. Various new developments and trends have often been rapidly accepted and introduced, as the high average rate of Internet facilities at home and cellular phones shows. Some feel this reflects the traditional liberal climate in the country: open to innovations and imports from abroad, tolerant of different beliefs and habits of immigrants, and thus exemplifying the features of a modern, multicultured society. Others tend to interpret this development as "nihilistic," betraying a loss of shared values and norms without the occurrence of a coherent set of new and different beliefs and ideals. Dutch people's self-image stresses their being *open, friendly, and hardly discriminatory.*

In earlier sections, the suggestion was made that Dutch culture is in a process of transition from a focus on classical values (like collective interests) toward more emphasis on modern values such as individualism, flexibility, and autonomy. Because many people do not esteem their culture in high terms, this process is probably creating quite some ambivalence.

8. LIMITATIONS OF THE CURRENT STUDY AND SUGGESTIONS FOR FUTURE RESEARCH

The GLOBE project is unique in its scope and the number of countries and researchers involved. Aiming to compare countries almost inevitably means that some of the uniqueness of different cultures is lost. Some features—sometimes those that are very central to specific cultures—are moreover hard to translate (a Dutch example is the word *gezelligheid,* a very common term describing a cozy, pleasant, rather "intimate" social climate within a group). To ensure that GLOBE also captures some of the culture-specific elements, qualitative research was done alongside the quantitative study. This combination of methods offers a rich data set that is explored in this volume. However, the emphasis in most publications from the GLOBE study is on the quantitative data gathered with questionnaires, with all the associated methodological advantages and drawbacks. We do not go into general methodological issues, but describe a few limitations of the GLOBE study (as a whole and the Dutch part) and provide some suggestions for future research.

GLOBE focuses on universals and culture-based differences in preferred leadership attributes by asking middle managers to rate whether showing certain leader characteristics and behaviors would help or hinder a person in being an outstanding leader. A possible bias in this study stems from the fact that when *middle managers* rate characteristics for effective leadership, they are likely to think of top management, as those are the leaders from the middle-management vantage point: "The perceptual processes that operate with respect to leaders are very likely to involve quite different considerations at upper versus lower hierarchical levels" (Lord & Maher, 1991, p. 97). As demands, tasks, and responsibilities at different hierarchical levels are quite diverse, it seems likely that preferred leader attributes also differ for the different levels. Thus, more research on perceptions of different types of leadership (including, e.g., political and military leadership) may also be of interest. Also, all respondents in the GLOBE study are currently employed within middle management in organizations from two industries. This leads to a restriction regarding variables such as age, gender, and education. A specific problem with the Dutch sample is that the managers were virtually all men. Although women are underrepresented in the samples from many countries, this is obviously extremely so for our sample. There may well be differences in the perceptions and preferences of women and men where culture and leadership are concerned.

To illustrate the possible biases resulting from the chosen sample, another study was done. The aforementioned study on perceptions of top and middle managers used a representative sample of the Dutch population older than 19 years of age. The study shows there are clear differences in preferred leadership attributes for leaders at top-management level and managers at lower levels in the hierarchy. It also explores whether there are greater gender differences. Some gender differences were indeed found; for example, women rated the importance of characteristics such as concern for subordinates' interests, compassionate, and participative higher than men, and characteristics such as dominant and rational were scored higher by men than by women (den Hartog, 1997). Besides the gender diversity, the ethnic diversity of the workforce is also rapidly changing in the Netherlands. Future research, using different and diverse samples, can help create more insight into the expectations that different groups within our society have of their leaders. A related question is the extent to which perceptions of people from different ethnic backgrounds are influenced by both the norms and values of their former "home" country and the country they currently live in. Are their views typically "Dutch" or have such groups perhaps developed a unique hybrid culture, combining Dutch norms and values with those from their home country?

As stated, GLOBE focuses on leadership perceptions: What are characteristics that people associate with highly effective leaders? Future research should also take actual leader behavior into account. An interesting question is whether leaders need to match their behavior to cultural expectations to be effective. House, Wright, and Aditya (1997) advanced three propositions in this area. First, they propose that leader behaviors that are accepted, enacted, and effective within a collective are the behaviors that most clearly fit within the parameters of the cultural forces surrounding the leader. They also suggest that leader behavior that deviates slightly from dominant cultural values will encourage innovation and performance improvement, as such behaviors are nontraditional and unexpected. Finally, they hold that some leader behaviors may be universally accepted and considered effective, regardless of the specific cultural values of the collective. More research in this area is needed in order to shed more light.

The Dutch GLOBE data were gathered at one specific point in time. They present a snapshot of perceptions of leadership and culture in the Netherlands, seen through the eyes of a very specific group in organizations (middle managers). In addition to studying the perceptions of other groups, as suggested earlier, repeating data collection every few years might yield interesting information on how the perceptions of leadership and culture changes over time. Given the changing organizational landscape in the Netherlands (due to, e.g., technological developments, more flexibility and less hierarchy, and increased globalization), the demands placed on leaders of and within organizations may well change too.

9. CURRENT CHALLENGES

The trend toward more individualism and flexibility confronts Dutch society with values and practices that are slightly at odds with the dominant societal and organizational culture outlined in previous sections. This trend is briefly discussed next under two headings: Flexibility and Action Organizations. Some potential implications for outstanding leadership values and practices are touched on.

Flexibility

This term has gained momentum in the past 20 years. The original meaning of *flexibility* is that the core of something remains unchanged, whereas the particular form or application of that something is tailored to specific, local conditions or requirements. Current usage is quite different: Flexibility has become some "container" concept, referring to many domains of what is commonly understood to be "organizational change." At least seven areas of flexibility in organizations may be distinguished and are described in the following subsections.

Work Content.   This area is often referred to as work structuring, job redesign, quality of work, and the like. It covers changes in the content of somebody's work as a result of job rotation, job enlargement, and job enrichment, but also as a consequence of moving toward a second or third career. It highlights the management of competences and of multiskills, intending to increase and support employability.

Workplace.   This area literally bears upon the geographical location of somebody's place(s) of work. In addition to the fixed or stable location, we distinguish the mobile workplace (such as when technical maintenance is carried out at a client's home), the "flying brigade" (whose members are assigned to units with a temporary shortage of manpower), tele-work (where the employee or manager is working at home or at a particular shop, communicating electronically with his or her company), and the "flexible bureau" (in which employees plug in their PC at a spot that happens to be available in their organization).

Labor Relations.   Both internal and external relations constitute this domain. Internally, it covers themes like the less hierarchical organization chart (with fewer layers than previously) and self-steering units (semiautonomous work teams). These examples reflect that the locus of power, in particular concerning knowledge, is moving downward in many organizations. Externally, we refer to what was said earlier regarding collective labor agreements: They tend to become decentralized (toward the firm level), deregulated (defining merely boundary conditions), or even "traded" for individual agreements. Increasingly, company-internal and -external groups tend to negotiate about working conditions that are tailored to their own interests.

Work Time.   Many changes are occurring in this area, for instance, an increase in the application rate (and the diversity) of shift work and irregular working schedules (Thierry & Jansen, 1998), of part-time arrangements, and of compressed schedules (working more hours per day and fewer days per week). There is also a slight increase in flexitime schedules (core and optional work hours), in permanent night and weekend shifts, in work hour budgets that specify the annual amount of hours (allowing much variation per day or week), and the like.

Labor Contract.   This area borders the preceding one. For decades, contracts mirrored the tradition of having permanent employment (in most cases after a probation period). Increasingly, contracts are made that limit employment to a fixed period, for example, the min–max contract (in which merely the minimum and the maximum amount of hours per week or other time period are specified), and the zero hours contract (a worker may work no hours at all in one week, and work full-time with overtime the following week), and so forth. Organization of Economic Co-operation and Development (OECD) figures show that "flexible" contracts apply to around 12% of the employed people in the Netherlands.

Work Conditions.   Flexible pay usually concerns employee benefits, allowing employees and managers some choice on how to spend part of their income, such as in the cafeteria plan (M. C. Langedijk, 1998; Thierry, 2002). Yet, a more recent usage also includes gain sharing (making a relatively large proportion of base salary dependent on the organization's financial results), performance - related pay, and reducing social security provisions to a slightly smaller core package.

Personal Career.   As an outcome of changes in the preceding areas, the working life of the individual executive, manager, and employee is increasingly showing a diversified pattern. Continued education and training are necessary to make up for the increasingly rapid obsolescence of acquired skills and abilities. Periods of work and care taking (e.g., parental leave) will alternate. Two or more careers per individual are going to be the rule rather than the exception.

This "flexibilization of work and private life" occurs in some sectors (as well as in some countries) much faster than in others. Yet, it will probably pervade industrialized countries to a greater extent in the years to come. Flexibility seems to be the visible, manifest outcropping of incisive, partly latent societal changes. These changes necessitate at least a partly different *legitimation* process of leadership decisions on both company strategy and policy implementation. Related to this is another factor: Markets are becoming more global, competition is increasingly on an international basis, and technological innovations occur more frequently, one of the consequences of which is the need for flexible organizational adaptation, involving one reorganization after another.

It is far from evident which *outstanding leadership* practices and attitudes are required to manage this flexible life. Probably, they differ according to different segments of an organization's workforce. Thus, it might be argued that a visionary, change-oriented, and consulting style would apply to the core, highly educated employees in organizations facing high levels of uncertainty. Transactional leader behavior would best suit the temporary managers and employees, who are hired from employment agencies. A more formal, orderly oriented style would qualify the approach to workers on a hire-and-fire basis. Career planning would be facilitated by a humane, collaborative style. This theme—the mix of outstanding leadership practices—is hopefully a major subject for comparative future research, in which one important question would be whether outstanding leadership should be conceived in terms of simultaneously needed, *contradictory* practices (e.g., visionary *and* transactional, change oriented *and* an emphasis on more formal control).

Action Organizations

In the mid-1990s, the Dutch—British multinational Shell Petroleum Company intended to dump the worn-out oil platform Brent Spar at the bottom of one of the deep seas. Greenpeace, very well known because of its stands and actions to protect the ecological environment, objected heavily. Greenpeace held, for instance, that the platform would severely pollute seawater, and that Shell greatly underrated the amount of oil and other substances left in Brent Spar. Shell management disputed Greenpeace's point of view, with among other things expert data, but Greenpeace maintained its stand, supported by much publicity in various countries. Gradually, members of Parliament started to pose critical questions; regular customers of Shell (i.e., at gas stations) changed to competing oil companies, and so forth. Eventually, Shell gave in and agreed to search for another solution for Brent Spar, while a joint Shell–Greenpeace committee of experts would reanalyze the debris within the former platform. This was widely acclaimed as a Greenpeace victory; incidentally, the joint committee reported later that data initially published by Shell were in fact correct.

Of course, this account does not "accuse" or "applaud" any of the parties mentioned. It serves as an illustration of what seems to become a major change in the (Dutch) industrial relations system and climate since the early 1990s: the onset of *action organizations* confronting larger enterprises with their points of view (cf. Tieleman, Van Luijk, Van Noort, & Van Riemsdijk, 1996). Current action organizations cover a great variety of themes, such as, human rights, the policy toward a particular developing country, social policy, child labor, anti-racism, baby nutrition, DNA manipulation, peace keeping, the aged, and so forth. Of course, action or interest groups are nothing new: Olson (1982) made the intriguing argument that the decline of large nations—such as the Roman or the British Empire—might have been brought about by the falling apart of the society in a multiplicity of action groups. What appears to be new is that more and more action organizations[13] voice very particular concerns against larger companies— such as *protesting* against specific policy measures or putting *pressure* in favor of a stand or action—as a consequence of which they become involved in bargaining processes with companies. An action organization expresses a particular concern (e.g., genetically manipulated soy beans) as a theme of *general* interest (i.e., health risks for the population at large). It has a smaller or larger constituency whose members are usually well educated. The action organization embodies and expresses to some extent the countervoice (cf. Section 6).

---

[13]The term *action organization* stems from Cor. J. Lammers (*Organiseren van bovenaf en van onderop* [Organization downwards and upwards], 1993, Utrecht: Het Spectrum.

Although action organizations deal primarily, until now, with larger companies, medium-size organizations may be affected as well in the near future. Traditionally, a large (multi-)national enterprise enters into agreements with the government and the unions of one or more countries (and, obviously, with banking corporations and perhaps transnational political authorities). This continues to be the case. But it doesn't suffice anymore: Agreed-upon plans for action (e.g., investments or a new plant) do not reach the operational phase; more bargaining is needed. Why? The national government occupies a more peripheral position than in the 1970s and 1980s, and has lost quite a bit of power and legitimizing authority. The same argument applies to many unions: They have moved from a natural countervailing power position toward the role of discussion partner (cf. Tieleman et al., 1996). Action organizations—sometimes called single-issue nongovernmental organizations—question indeed the *credibility* of the company in some particular subject matter, and require at least public recognition of their particular concerns. As a consequence, the company enters new territory: facing particular actions, being engaged in tense debates, negotiating for an agreement with one or more counterparties who are able to commit many resources. In other words, the company has to search for *legitimation* of its policy and activities from other, and more, sources than they were used to.

How should the company go about achieving this? Should they act quickly, and engage immediately into negotiations with action organizations' representatives? Or is it better to avoid rapid action? Is one governance structure (e.g., the divisional form; cf. Mintzberg, 1983) more suited than another? Tieleman et al. (1996) suggest that a company should not focus its business plan exclusively on financial results: This implies, of course, a serious discussion with the shareholders about their concerns. Rather, major subject matters of action organizations could be made part of the company's business policy (cf. Ackerman, 1975). Shell's former CEO seems to have followed Ackerman's advice: He testified in 1996 that his company had been rather arrogant in reaction to environmental, and other, concerns of action organizations. Thus, Shell enacted early 1997 an *ethical statute,* outlining norms and lines of conduct applying to top managers in any country where Shell has economic interests. Many other organizations followed Shell's example.

Why has the government lost much of its power and legitimizing authority? Various perspectives may be taken here: One line of explanation holds that the increased role of the market economy, combined with the globalization and internationalization of doing business, has more or less *caused* the decrease in governmental authority. Self-steering work teams are the contemporaneous expression of the historical trend of Dutch educated citizens to rule themselves as much as possible. As a consequence, the government's primary role is being reduced to facilitate this. Another explanation stresses changes that reverberate at both the societal and the individual citizen level: The increasing individualization (and flexibilization) reflects that almost no values and norms are shared by the whole society, but rather by members of interest groups, clubs, committees, action organizations, and the like. Moral behavior, according to Tieleman et al., is democratized. Thus, there is hardly any moral authority left for the government. At the individual level, people are usually engaged in many different activities; yet, these activities are kept separate. The loyalty felt for one activity (e.g., being an employee of a construction firm) does not relate to the loyalty felt for another activity (e.g., being a member of an action organization fighting the construction firm's activities in a particular neighborhood). Moral behavior is thus *individualized.*[14] Within this perspective, action organizations are filling a 'moral gap'.

---

[14]It is an interesting question whether individualized behavior can acquire a moral quality by definition.

10. IN CONCLUSION: 10 COMMANDMENTS

This chapter started with presenting the views of an air passenger descending into Amsterdam airport. One concern of the passenger proved to be whether the initial impression of a flat country would also apply to its culture, politics, leadership, and achievements. The journey through the preceding sections has shown how misleading first impressions might be. As a summary of the discoveries made during that journey, the passenger has some clear notions on what she or he, as a foreigner, should *(not)* do, were she or he planning as a next step in his or her career to manage and to provide leadership to Dutch employees and supervisors. Having learned quite a bit about Dutch history, she or he voices these notions in the form of 10 commandments.

As a leader from abroad; thou should:

- Consistently try to reach consensus with all stakeholders.
- Act as a team player with an open style of supervision, willing to share power with colleagues and employees.
- Recognize the strong need of Dutch employees and workers to experience autonomy.
- Balance the development of employees' personal growth plans with the design of situational conditions facilitating a permanent learning process.
- Reward your employees primarily according to the value of their job without applying steep pay differentials.
- Recognize that agreements and decisions made on courses of actions will probably be interpreted merely as one of the contributions to a still ongoing discussion.

As a leader from abroad; thou should not:

- Take pride in status symbols, extravagant spending, and manifest use of power.
- Control closely the behavior of coworkers.
- Publicly announce and list the top achievers.
- Engage in joking on gender discrimination.

REFERENCES

Ackerman, R. W. (1975). *The social challenge to business.* Cambridge, MA: Harvard University Press.

Albeda, W. (1984). European industrial relations in a time of crisis. In P. J. D. Drenth, H. Thierry, P. J. Willems, & C. J. de Wolff (Eds.), *Handbook of work and organizational psychology* (pp. 401–428). Chichester, England: John Wiley.

Andriessen, J. H. E. (1998). Industrial Democratization and Industrial Relations. In P. J. D. Drenth, H. Thierry, & C. J. de Wolff (Eds.) *Handbook of work and organizational psychology* (2nd ed., Vol. 4, pp. 955–977). Hove, England: Psychology Press.

Andriessen, J. H. E., & Coetsier, P. L. (1984). Industrial democratization. In P. J. D. Drenth, H. Thierry, P. J. Willems, & C. J. de Wolff (Eds.), *Handbook of work and organizational psychology* (pp. 955–977). Chichester, England: John Wiley.

Blonk, A., Romein, J., & Oerlemans, J. W. (1967). *Hoofdwegen der Geschiedenis* [History's major avenues] (Vol. 1). Groningen, Netherlands: Wolters.

Blonk, A., Romein, J., & Oerlemans, J. W. (1978). *Hoofdwegen der Geschiedenis* [History's major avenues] (Vol. 2). Groningen, Netherlands: Wolters.

Braudel, F. (1979). *Civilisation matérielle, Economie et Capitalisme Xve-XVIIIe siècle. Tome 3: Le temps du Monde* [Material civilization, economy and capitalism in the 15–18 century. Part 3:A world developing]. Paris: Colin.

den Hartog, D. N. (1997) *Inspirational leadership.* Amsterdam: Vrije Universiteit. Doctoral dissertation.

den Hartog, D. N., Koopman, P. L., & Muijen, J. J. (1998, August) *Implicit theories of leadership at different hierarchical levels.* Paper presented at the 24th International Congress of Applied Psychology, San Francisco.

Hanges, P. J., Dickson, M. W., & Sipe, M. T. (2004). Rationale for GLOBE statistical analyses: Societal rankings and test of hypotheses. In R. J. House, P. J. Hanges, M. Javidan, P. Dorfman, & V. Gupta (Eds.), *Leadership, culture, and organizations: The GLOBE study of 62 societies* (pp. 219–234). Thousand Oaks, CA: Sage.

Hofstede, G. (1984). *Culture's consequences: International differences in work-related values.* London: Sage.

House, R. J., Hanges, P. J., Javidan, M., Dorfman, P. W., Gupta, V., & GLOBE Associates. (2004). *Cultures, leadership, and organizations: The GLOBE study of 62 societies.* Thousand Oaks, CA: Sage.

House, R. J., Wright, N. S., & Aditya, R. N. (1997). Cross-cultural research on organizational leadership: A critical analysis and a proposed theory. In P. C. Early & M. Erez (Eds.), *New perspectives on international industrial/organizational psychology.* San Francisco: The New Lexington Press.

Hövels, B., & Nas, P. (1976). *Ondernemingsraden en medezeggenschap* [Work councils and codetermination]. Nijmegen, Netherlands: Busser.

Industrial Democracy in Europe International Research Group. (1981). *European Industrial Relations.* Oxford, England: Clarendon.

Industrial Democracy in Europe International Research Group. (1993). *Industrial democracy in Europe revisited.* Oxford, England: Oxford University Press.

Koeningsberger, H. G. (2001). *Monarchies, states general, and parliaments.* Cambridge, England: Cambridge University Press.

Koopman, P. L. (1992). Between economic-technical and socio-political rationality: Multilevel decision making in a multinational organization. *The Irish Journal of Psychology, 13*(1), 32–50.

Koopman, P. L., & Wierdsma, A. F. M. (1998). Participative management. In P. J. D. Drenth, H. Thierry, & C. J. de Wolff (Eds.) *Handbook of work and organizational psychology* (2nd ed., Vol. 3, pp. 297–324). Hove, England: Psychology Press.

Koopman-Iwema, A. M., & Thierry, H. (1981). *Pay for performance in the Netherlands: An analysis.* Dublin, Ireland: European Foundation for the Improvement of Living and Working Conditions.

Langedijk, D. (1948a). *Geschiedenis der Volkeren* [History of the People]. (Vol. 2). Groningen, Netherlands: Wolters.

Langedijk, D. (1948b). *Geschiedenis der Volkeren* [History of the People]. (Vol. 3). Groningen, Netherlands: Wolters.

Langedijk, M. C. (1998). *Flexibele beloning: De keuze voor arbeidsvoorwaarden op maat* [Flexible compensation: The choice of tailored working conditions]. (2nd ed.). Assen, Netherlands: Van Gorcum.

Lord, R. G., & Maher, K. J. (1991). *Leadership and information processing.* London: Routledge.

Mintzberg, H. (1983). *Structures in fives: Designing effective organizations.* London: Prentice- Hall.

Olson, M. (1982). *The rise and decline of nations: Economic growth, stagflation, and social rigidities.* New Haven, CT: Yale University Press.

Peper, B. (1973). *De Nederlandse arbeidsverhoudingen, continuïteit en verandering* [Dutch labor relations: Continuity and change]. Rotterdam, Netherlands: Universitaire Pers.

Pool, J., Drenth, P. J. D., Koopman, P. L., & Lammers, C. J. (1988). De volwassenwording van medezeggenschap [Coming of age of codetermination]. *Gedrag en Organisatie, 1,* 37–58.

Rijpma, E. (1952). *De Ontwikkelingsgang der Historie* [As History Develops Itself]. (Vol. 3). Groningen, Netherlands: Wolters.

Schama, S. (1987). *The embarrassment of riches.* New York: Knopf.

Thierry, H. (1998). Compensating work. In P. J. D. Drenth, H. Thierry, & C. J. de Wolff (Eds.), *Handbook of work and organizational psychology* (2nd ed., Vol. 4, pp. 291–319). Hove, England: Psychology Press.

Thierry, H. (2002). Enhancing performance through pay and reward systems. In S. Sonnentag (Ed.), *Psychological management of individual performance* (pp. 325–347). Chichester, England: John Wiley.

Thierry, H., & Jansen, B. (1998). Work and working time. In P. J. D. Drenth, H. Thierry, & C. J. de Wolff (Eds.), *Handbook of work and organizational psychology* (2nd ed., Vol. 2, pp. 89–119). Hove, England: Psychology Press.

Thierry, H., & de Jong, J. R. (1998). Job evaluation. In P. J. D. Drenth, H. Thierry, & C. J. de Wolff (Eds.), *Handbook of work and organizational psychology* (2nd ed., Vol. 3, pp. 165–183). Hove, England: Psychology Press.

Tieleman, H. J., van Luijk, H. J., van Noort, W. J., & van Riemsdijk, M. J. (1996). *Conflicten tussen actiegroepen en ondernemingen* [Conflicts between action organizations and companies]. Scheveningen, Netherlands: Stichting Maatschappy en Onderneming.

van Deursen, A. T. (2004). *De last van veel geluk* [The load of much happiness]. Amsterdam: Bert Bakker.

van Strien, P. J. (1988). De ontwikkeling van de A & O Psychologie in Nederland [The development of I & O psychology in the Netherlands]. In P. J. D. Drenth, H. Thierry, & C. J. de Wolff (Eds.), *Nieuw Handboek Arbeids-en Organisatiepsychologie* (pp. 1.4-1–1.4-49). Houten, Netherlands: Bohn, Stafleu, Van Loghum.

Weber, M. (1947). *The theory of social and economic organization.* New York: The Free Press.

Windmuller, J. P. (1968). *Labour relations in the Netherlands.* Ithaca, NY: Cornell University Press.

Leadership and Culture in Switzerland—Theoretical and Empirical Findings[1]

Jürgen Weibler
University of Hagen (FernUniversität in Hagen),
Chair of Business Administration,
Leadership and Organization, Germany

Rolf Wunderer
University of St. Gallen,
Institute for Leadership and Human Resource Management,
Switzerland

> *Nothing is more fragile and questionable than judging and assessing a culture or a mentality.*
>
> —Rüdiger Görner

In the following chapter, we seek a closer look at the understanding of leadership and how this understanding relates back to the specific culture in Switzerland. Because being Swiss does not mean to belong to a special ethnic group that has a distinct religion or language and because Switzerland is—under a historical perspective—a multicultural gathering of people from its neighboring countries with the will to form an own nation ("a nation of will") as the only common grounds,[2] we concentrate our analysis especially for the empirical findings on the German-speaking area of Switzerland, which accounts for nearly two thirds of the population.[3] This allows us to focus our statements on a comparatively cohesive part of the Swiss population. Although we are aware that every country conceives leadership in many different

---

[1] We concentrate our analysis on the German-speaking area of Switzerland.

[2] This later discussed fact had already been meritoriously emphasized by a reviewer.

[3] 1990: 63.6% (Bundesamt fü Statistik, 1998) and 1997: 71.7% of the resident population (oral information obtained from the Bundesamt für Statistik in 1998). Also 73.26% of the national income for 1995 can be ascribed to the German-speaking area (authors' own calculation after consultation with the Bundesamt für Statistik). Cantons were classed according to the linguistic majority. Thus any statements and comments are valid only for this part of the country and do not apply to the three other language areas (French, Italian, and Rhaeto-Romanic).

ways, we are trying to illustrate the core elements. The objective of our reflections is to discover what characterizes an outstanding leader in Switzerland and what, in particular, might be the cultural reason for this. The answer to this question is based on two assumptions: (a) Leadership is an attribution process that itself depends on implicit theories about leadership in the mind of the observer, and (b) These so-called "leadership prototypes" and manifestations do not occur in a vacuum but are developed and shown in a broader cultural context.

These assumptions, which are dominating features of the GLOBE study (for details, House, Hanges, & Ruiz-Quintanilla, 1997; House et al., 1999; Lord & Emrich, 2001), are based on research findings by Shaw (1990) and Lord and Maher (1991). Their theoretical work suggests that individuals have implicit theories of leadership in their minds. Experimental evidence in various settings has shown that these implicit leadership theories (which culminate in the picture of an outstanding leader) guide the construction and evaluation (attributes and behavior) that define an outstanding leader. They define the path on which varying forms of leadership can be accepted and tolerated, and moderate relationships between leadership attributes, behaviors, and effectiveness. The more a leader appears and acts in congruence with the expectations of the attributing observer, the more the observer is willing to recognize his or her leadership. Although it cannot be assumed that national culture alone has an influence on leadership (e.g., Bass, 1990; Dorfman & Howell, 1988; Haire, Ghiselli & Porter, 1966; House, Wright, & Aditya, 1997; Reber & Jago, 1997; Smith & Peterson, 1988), various authors demonstrate impressively that implicit theories of leadership are culturally endorsed (House et al., 1999) and we know "that even very subtle differences can complicate a cross-cultural encounter" (Szabo, Reber, Weibler, Brodbeck, & Wunderer, 2001, p. 241). Therefore, as leadership researchers we need to set out for a better understanding of culturally specific implicit leadership theories, in our case, Switzerland.

The cultural context in which leaders operate can be described both by shared values (Kluckhohn & Strodtbeck, 1961), measured by indicators assessing what "Should Be," and by observed perceptions of modal practices, measured by indicators assessing "what is" or "what are" ("As Is") common behaviors, prescriptions, and institutional practices inside a nation. In sum, we call this "national culture." So, "Should Be" and "As Is" data on culture both may be helpful in interpreting this ideal leadership construction.

Despite the demonstrated effect of national culture on the perception of outstanding leadership, it is unclear to what extent culture affects the impact of certain leadership behaviors/attributes on performance and to what extent it is the outcome of other factors such as organizational culture, task environment, and market situation.[4] However, we mainly focus our study on the level of national culture because research has been widely neglected in this field. Where it seems necessary, we add other factors.

The chapter is divided into four principal sections. After the presentation of some interesting and useful facts about Switzerland, we start on our tour to explore the concept of leadership in Switzerland with a brief introduction to the long history of this country, then add some general economic and political information, thereby providing a context in which to present the GLOBE study. The second section informs about the methodology of GLOBE research in Switzerland. Section 3 investigates its societal culture on the basis of GLOBE's findings. We then concentrate on specifically the Swiss attributes and behaviors of outstanding leaders with

---

[4]For example, compare House, Hanges et al. (1997), Weibler (1996, 2001), Wunderer and Grunwald (1980), and Wunderer (2001, 2006).

reference to the empirical research conducted within the framework of GLOBE. Conclusions are presented in the final section.

2. EVOLUTION AND SALIENT CHARACTERISTICS OF THE SWISS NATION

Geography/Demography

Switzerland is a country of about 41,300 square kilometers in the center of Europe, surrounded by Germany, Austria, Italy, France, and Liechtenstein. The country consists of three geographical areas: the Alps (60%), the Midlands (30%) and the Western Jura region (10%); the two big chains of mountains account for more than half of the country's surface. There are four different linguistic areas in Switzerland (German, French, Italian, and Rhaeto-Romanic): In 1990, 63.6% of the population had German as their main language, 19.2% French, 7.6% Italian, and 0.6% Rhaeto-Romanic (other languages: 8.9%). Switzerland is divided into 26 autonomous states—so-called cantons. Its capital is Bern. At the end of 2000,[5] Switzerland had 7,204,100 inhabitants (women: 51%, men: 49%), among them 1,424,370 foreigners (19.8%), which in comparison with the international average is quite a high proportion, but is in part due to very strict laws for gaining citizenship. Being born in Switzerland does not lead to Swiss citizenship, a fact that led to a growing second and third generation of foreign residents. The average age in 1996 was 39 years. The average household consisted of just under 2.5 persons. As far as the religious denominations are concerned, 46.1% of the 1990 population belonged to the Roman Catholic Church and 40.0% were Protestants (non-denominational part of the population: 7.4%; other religions: 5.0%; no response: 1.5%; (Bundesamt für Statistik, 1998).

History

The earliest signs of human activities in Switzerland can be traced back to the Old Stone Age (cf. Fahrni, 1988; Im Hof 1991a, 1991b). Until the Romans expanded their empire to the north, the areas of present-day Switzerland were inhabited by different Celtic tribes. The most important among them were the Helvetians, who lived in the Midlands, and the Rhaetians, who lived in the Grisons. After their defeat by Julius Caesar in the battle of Bibracte (58 BC), the Celtic areas came under Roman rule. About 400–600 AD, Germanic tribes conquered the western part of the Roman Empire. The southern part of Switzerland was inhabited by Lombardian tribes, the Langobards. In contrast to the Burgundians and the Langobards, who adopted Christianity and the Roman language, Latin, the Alemanns, who made up the largest part of the immigrants, retained their culture and language. However, they did not succeed in conquering Rhaetia; the Roman Rhaetians who were resident there successfully resisted them. Over time, they withdrew into the high alpine valleys of the Grisons, where they could live without any great outside interference. Thus the foundations of Switzerland's multilingualism were laid.

In the Middle Ages, Switzerland became part of the Holy Roman Empire. Assisted by the decline of the Emperor's power, some Swiss dynasties succeeded in taking larger areas and acting as sovereigns up to the 13th century. The founding of cities was an important

---

[5]If possible up-to-date data are used. Deviations are due to delay of publication.

instrument of aristocratic territorial policy. Though trade and craft in the cities provided the cities' rulers with new sources of revenue, the cities also served as garrisons and places of jurisdiction. Acquiring more economic power, the cities succeeded in becoming more and more independent, and finally, they attained the position of free imperial cities.

The small and remote valleys in the Alps had always been autonomous and free. This situation seemed to be endangered when the Austrian Hapsburgs started appointing governors in order to collect their revenues and secure their rights. So, as the story goes, three representatives of the so- called Waldstätte, the original "forest cantons" around Lake Lucerne (Uri, Schwyz, and Unterwalden), gathered on August 1st, 1291, in a field called Rütli to enter into a mutual assistance pact against imposed administration. This pact is regarded as the birth of the Eidgenossenschaft or Confederation. August 1st later became a Swiss national holiday and the Rütli has often served as a place for important national ceremonies.

In the course of the 14th century, some city-states (Lucerne, Glarus, Zug, and Bern) joined the Waldstätte pact in order to free themselves of the cities' sovereigns. Niklaus von Flüe (1417–1487), one of the most prominent figures of the epoch, unified litigant cantons and is therefore associated with the further enlargement of the Confæderatio Helvetica (see Box 8.1). As a consequence, a state with a certain degree of independence emerged within the Holy Roman Empire. Having driven out the Hapsburgs and weakened the local nobility, a civilian society arose. The power and the land were passed over to cities, guilds, and rural villages.

After its military successes, the Confederation sought to expand its territories. Initially successful, the Confederates were defeated in 1515 by French and Venetian troops in the battle of Marignano. As a result of this, they retreated from the international scene, withdrawing their expansionist policies and declaring their neutrality, something that has been practiced up to the present day (as it was during the two world wars).

At about the same time one of the most famous Swiss precursors of the Reformation in Europe lived in Switzerland: Huldrych Zwingli (1484–1531). In 1525, the Grand Council of Zurich adopted Zwingli's demands for a reform of the church, as well as his demands for political and economic change, particularly the secularization of monasteries, and the reform of the interest system and land utilization rights. Another remarkable fighter for religious reformation was Jean (John) Calvin (1509–1564). His ideas influenced the economic development of the Confederation in the centuries that were to follow insofar as he explicitly related personal success in life to a positive selection by God. Among other things, this belief led to a very ascetic lifestyle in a large part of the country where investment was valued more highly than consumption. Despite the fact that the Reformation split Switzerland into two camps, it had an important positive outcome for the identity of Switzerland as a nation as it also promoted a gradual separation of the Confederation from the German Empire. After the Thirty Years' War, which was caused by religious conflicts, the Treaty of Westphalia (1648) made Switzerland "de jure" independent.

In the 17th and 18th centuries, the political activities in the cantons of the "Old Confederation" became more and more ossified. The government was led by a few clans. The referenda (electoral devices that enables voters to express their opinion directly on an issue), which were often conducted at the time of the Reformation, totally disappeared. In the social and economic sectors, however, far-reaching changes occurred. The population quadrupled (from 400,000 to 1.6 million between 1700 and 1800) and the first industries developed (textiles, and watch and clock making). Switzerland was the most industrialized country in Europe (second only to England). Above and beyond this, scientists generated an intellectual upswing in Switzerland, among them Johann Bernoulli, Leonhard Euler, Albrecht von Haller, and Johann Heinrich Pestalozzi.

After the country was occupied by Napoleon in 1798, Switzerland entered a state of crisis that was to last 50 years. This was the starting point of a long and arduous development toward the foundation of a federal state in 1848. The Constitution, which came along with the changes in the political system during that time, introduced a number of new rights: the right to choose one's domicile freely, the freedom of association, the principle of equality in law, and the rights of minorities. The rights of the people were increasingly strengthened, albeit with differences from canton to canton. In 1874, the Constitution of 1848 was amended. Since then it remained largely unchanged until recently. A review process was started to modernize the Swiss Constitution. There was one peculiarity in this process of democratization, which was also accompanied by many improvements in the sociopolitical sector: Only in 1973, 123 years after the introduction of universal and equal suffrage for men, was female suffrage introduced at national level. In 1981, equal rights for both men and women were guaranteed by the Constitution. As far as its commitment to international relations was concerned, Switzerland remained largely inactive. Switzerland did not join the United Nations for a long time (2002), yet it has played an active role in UN organizations (e.g., the *World Bank, the International Monetary Fund, World Trade Organization* (WTO), *Organization for Economic Cooperation and Development* (OECD), *Organizzazione per la Cooperazione Economicae Per lo Sviluppo* (OSCE), and the *Partnership for Peace*) and currently holds 14th place as a financial contributor to the United Nations (Edgenössisches Department für Auswärtige Angelegenheiten [ETA], 2005).

Efforts toward Switzerland's European integration were not approved by the people, consequently it did not participate in the founding of the European Council in 1949. It also rejected membership in the European Economic Community (EEC) in 1957. However, in 1959, Switzerland, together with other non-EEC states, set up the European Free Trade Association (EFTA), whose purely economic objectives did not clash with Switzerland's policy of neutrality. Switzerland has also actively cooperated in different development aid programs since the early 1950s. In 1986, the bid to join the UN was narrowly defeated in a referendum. In 1992, the referendum on the membership of the European Economic Area was also narrowly rejected. But in 2002, the bid to join the UN was accepted by the Swiss people and Switzerland finally became a member. Despite its partial reluctance to formally join international associations, Switzerland is actually among those 10 countries in the world that most extended their memberships of international organizations between 1980 and 1990 (Schneider, 1998, p. 14). In 1995, Switzerland was a member of 64 intergovernmental organizations, which gives the country a leading position in the list of OECD states. Switzerland has sometimes mediated in international conflicts. In addition, it is a member of more than 2,600 international nongovernmental organizations (Schneider, 1998). It also claims the seat of the International Committee of the Red Cross, founded by the Swiss Henri Dunant in 1863, which is independent of the government. Its executive members are exclusively recruited from Swiss citizens, which illustrates its typical conflict between detachment and cooperation. According to Schneider, this was a natural consequence of its geography. South and North European traders often had to cross the Alps and were dependent on the help of the people living there. A flourishing barter system developed. This cooperation and the extensive interaction with many cultures resulted in the desire among the natives to retain their own identity, which simultaneously promoted a degree of detachment. Also, observers should not forget that Switzerland found—while practicing such an ambiguous behavior—a way to get the needed protection from the German Empire without being a part of it. Not without reason did the development of alpine passes give rise to the first myths about the origins of Switzerland (Schneider, 1998, p. 20).

The Current Situation

A detailed characterization of present-day Switzerland is beyond the scope of this chapter, but we try to go beyond the picture-postcard view, which is influenced by tourists and largely constitutes Switzerland's international image.[6] More specifically, we concentrate on the political and the economic systems.

The Political System

The Swiss Confederation—Switzerland's official name—has been a federal republic since 1848 (cf. earlier discussion). The basic political values of present-day Switzerland, which according to Riklin and Möckli (1983, pp. 18, 116) can be characterized in more detail by the key words *security, democracy, rule of law,* and *welfare state,* are already discernible in their historical genesis. According to those authors, security—a very old Swiss basic value—is explained as follows: "The alliances of the old federation were mainly held together by the idea of internal and external security." The "ancient Swiss freedom" meant the independence of the collective from the "outside" (Riklin & Möckli, 1983, p. 116). Neutrality was one of the key instruments supporting the maintenance of independence from the outside (Riklin & Möckli, 1983, p. 22). On the inside, this meant, at the same time, avoiding extreme positions, in particular, and an awareness of the fragility of this polyglot country: "The practice of moderation between the extremes, which came to be vital under the Swiss conditions of natural and historical diversity and difference, can be seen as the central and most general Swiss trait" (Weiss, 1946, p. 364; cited in Riklin & Möckli, 1983, p. 96, footnote 434, translated). From this, it is also possible to deduce the necessity of a development that has, at least, not maximized an orientation toward the individual; rather, "moderation" and "avoidance of extreme positions" seem more compatible with a collective orientation. Thus "moderation" suddenly becomes a noble virtue (Bader, 1998, p. 3), nowadays unfortunately an often forgotten insight (remember the Assertiveness scale), which was already in high esteem in the ancient world. Switzerland is one of the last countries in the world that has substantial elements of direct democracy. According to the political scientists Riklin and Möckli "Switzerland is considered worldwide to be the country with the most extended, differentiated and traditional institutional structure of direct democracy" (p. 39). Combined with the federal principle, this underlines the Swiss aversion to central authorities and indirectly accentuates the autonomy of its citizens. Together with the personal, not only institutional, disapproval of power relations that are not voluntarily accepted, a strong aversion to power that is not legitimized by qualifications (power by privileges, e.g.) or reason can be noted. The principle of subsidiary is well established: "Only what the individual family cannot do, the community should do; only what the community cannot do, the canton should do; only what the canton cannot do, the Federal State should do" (Hilb & Wittmann, 1992, p. 526). Apart from elections, there are two possibilities for the Swiss population to exert influence on political decision making: the "initiative" and the "referendum." The initiative denotes the right of the people—providing that the necessary number of signatures has been collected to put forward proposals on governmental enactments and to cause the relevant institutions to vote on these proposals.[7] The referendum

---

[6]In a representative survey, 80% of interviewees declared that Switzerland is first of all a long of mountains, watches, and chocolate; cf. Stamm, Arend, and Lamprecht (1997, p. 17).

[7]Having collected 100,000 signatures, Swiss citizens are able to demand a total or partial revision of the constitution at *national level* withing 18 months. In order to carry out such a revision, there has to be an approving majority in both chambers of Parliament. At the *cantonal and local levels,* there are possibilities for further initiative rights, particularly the possibility to initiate laws (cf. Huber, 1988, p. 131).

is a direct vote by all eligible citizens (plebiscite) on governmental enactments such as amendments to the Constitution, and laws or issues relating to financial policy.[8] Both lead to continual votes by Swiss citizens on many political issues. These mechanisms provide a relatively high degree of self-determination in political and societal issues (for further details; see Neidhart, 1970).

A brief characterization of the political institutions suffices for our purposes. The Bundesversammlung or Federal Assembly consists of two chambers: the Nationalrat or National Council, whose members represent the population, and the Ständerat or Council of States, whose members represent the cantons. Decisions by the Bundesversammlung become law only if both chambers have passed them. The Bundesrat or Federal Council constitutes the government. Its seven members are representatives of the four biggest political parties. The Bundesrat is elected every 4 years by the Bundesversammlung immediately after the elections for the Nationalrat. An unwritten law demands that the linguistic minorities of Western Switzerland and of the Ticino are always represented. The Bundesrat is a so-called collegial authority, which means that all important decisions are made by the Bundesrat as a whole, and that there is no actual head of government in Switzerland. Rather, the president of the Confederation or Bundespräsident, who is elected from among the members of the government for a term of just 1 year (after which another member will accede to this office), is not a head of state but a primus inter pares. Switzerland is the only country in the world where a collegial authority serves as the head of state, as head of the government, and as the government itself. This approach toward an uncharismatic leadership in governance is very characteristic of Switzerland's leadership culture. The seat of the Bundesrat is Bern.

The Economic System: General Information

Switzerland had 312,449 privately owned companies in 1998; 99.7% were so-called small and medium-size enterprises with fewer than 250 full-time employees. Nearly 69% of all employees worked there. However, some of the biggest companies worldwide are Swiss.

In terms of per capita gross national product (GNP), Switzerland is among the world's wealthiest nations. In 1998 (2003), the per capita GNP amounted to $39,980 (39.880) which is much higher than the average of the rest of the world. According to a 1997 World Bank report (Finfacts, 2005; "Schweiz," 1998, p.19), Switzerland had even the absolutely highest per capita gross income in the world ($44,320 as compared with $28,747 in the United States). In terms of the indicator of "quality of life," which transcends the one- sided economic orientation of international comparisons, Switzerland regularly leads the world ratings, too.

Apart from water, Switzerland does not possess any considerable raw materials. For economic reasons alone, Switzerland maintains numerous foreign trade relations. Its import and export quota are among the highest in the world. The lion's share of cross-border trade is accounted for by the OECD countries. In 1996, 90% of all imports originated from OECD countries, and 79% of all exports were sent there. The most important export goods are machines, electronics, chemicals, precision instruments, watches and clocks, and jewelry. Tourism is another very important industry in terms of foreign trade. It produces about 8% of export revenues, thus occupying third place behind mechanical engineering and chemicals. A look at the financial volume for 1993 illustrates the importance of trade (import and

---

[8]There are two types of referenda at the national level: (a) an obligatory referendum (compulsory in certain situations) and (b) and optional referendum (takes place if more than 50,000 citizens' signatures are collected of if eight cantons demand this within the so-called "referendum term," i.e., within 90 days after a law has been published in the Federal Official Journal).

export): Amounting to CHF 14,000 (= $9,500) per capita, it was by far higher than in countries like the United States or Japan (both less than CHF 5,000 = $3,400). The strong international commitment of Swiss industry can also be observed in foreign direct investments. Switzerland is one of the key actors (Schneider, 1998). For instance, it maintains above-average commitments in the new German Länder (former East Germany).

Yet another typical feature is the fact that many industries successfully managed to cut themselves off from competition for a long time (cartels, subsidies, etc.). This has led to the problem that a lot of firms in these sections got into serious difficulties when they were forced by legislation directly (law) or indirectly (globalization) to open the market. These processes of adaptation are still going on.

In 2000, an average of 3,879,000 people were employed in Switzerland: 1,707,000 women (44%) and 2,172,000 men (56%); 908,000 (23.4%) of them had only part-time jobs. This corresponds to an employment rate of 53%. Foreigners employed were 25.1% and employment in the so-called third sector, that is, trade and services, was 69.1%. Industry accounted for 26.4%, and only 4.5% worked in agriculture. Average working hours per week were 41.8 hours in 2000. This is above average compared to most other European states. In 2000, 106,000 people were registered as unemployed. This corresponds to an unemployment rate of 2.7%. After this brief overview of the economic situation in Switzerland, we now pay more detailed attention to the three industries surveyed in the GLOBE study: financial services, telecommunications, and food processing.

The Economic System: Specific Information (GLOBE Industries)

Financial Services.   The financial services is one of the most important industries in the Swiss economy. In 2000, there were 375 banks in Switzerland: 24 Cantonal Banks, 3 "big" banks, 103 regional and savings banks, 17 privately owned banks, 23 affiliates of foreign financial institutions and, finally, 205 other banks (Schweizerische Nationalbank, 1997, p. 22). The major banking centers are Zurich, Basel, and Geneva. All in all, Switzerland is considered to be "overbanked" (one important reason is the bank secret, i.e., no information about accounts are released; another reason until recently is the cartelization of this industry), which will lead to a massive increase in competition and concentration in the years to come, particularly with foreign banks. Since then mergers have happened and in combination with a more restricted law the process of consolidation has started.

The employment rate has risen above the average in the last few decades. Between 1960 and 1994, there was an increase of 398% in the number of people employed in banks, compared to an increase of 39% in the entire Swiss working population. An unfavorable economic situation, increased competition, and various mergers of enterprises, however, has caused the employment rate to fall in the last few years. Thus in 1996, the number of employees fell to 119,771 people (cf. Schweizerische Nationalbank, 1997, p. 49). The biggest employers in the financial services are UBS and Credit Suisse, which both have their head office in Zurich.

The banking sector's share of Switzerland's GNP is relatively high. Between 1988 and 1993, it amounted to an average of 8.6%, whereas in other European countries it amounted to only 3% to 4%. Only in Luxembourg does the financial sector have an even larger share of the GNP, namely 33% (Gratzl & Kaufmann, 1996; quoted in Schweizerische Bankiervereinigung, 1996, p. 12). Of the Swiss working population 3.8% were employed in the banking sector in 1995 and thus twice as many as that, for example, in Italy, France, and Great Britain, or around one third higher than in Germany and in Austria (Schweizerische Bankiervereinigung, 1996, p. 12). The importance of the banking system for foreign trade cannot be estimated directly because the relevant values are not listed separately in the figures of the national accounting. But according to reliable estimates, the banks may well contribute half of the amount of Switzerland's foreign trade (Schweizerische ankiervereinigung, 1996, p. 12).

Telecommunications.   Switzerland has one of the world's most efficient infrastructures in telecommunications. Private users and enterprises have access to the most modern communication systems. Like many other European countries, Switzerland's telecommunications sector is at the moment characterized by deregulation. The years 1992 and 1993 marked the definite end of the Swiss Radio and Television Company's (Schweizerische Radio- und Fernsehgesellschaft [SRG] monopoly; SRG, 1994, p. 8). On July 1, 1995, another step toward liberalization was taken; since then private suppliers and foreign companies have been allowed to offer telephone services by renting public wires. Finally, on January 1, 1998, the telecommunications market was liberalized at a European level.

Swisscom is the market leader in the telecommunications industry. The company has an annual turnover of around 11 billion Swiss Francs and employs 21,000 people (2002). The formerly public-sector company was transformed into a joint-stock company under special law on January 1, 1998—just in time with regard to the total liberalization of the telecommunications industry. The company went public in 1998. Swisscom is the only full-service supplier present in all parts of Switzerland. It is at the same time one of the country's biggest employers. In 1998, however, two large private competitors (orange, diAX) entered the market (see, for further details, Swiss Federal Office of Communication, 2002).

Food Processing.   The Swiss food-processing industry developed out of small trade at the end of the 19th century. Some enterprises—with Nestlé at the top—have grown considerably since. Numerous small enterprises survived by pursuing a specific policy of "market gaps." In the last few decades, the food-processing industry has developed continuously within a framework of stable and predictable conditions in Switzerland. The high quality of the products offered by the Swiss food-processing industry was a very central strategic success factor for international growth (Hodler, 1994, p. 8).

The food-processing industry is primarily oriented toward the home market. In the last few years, however, there has been a clearly recognizable trend toward growing exports. Nevertheless, its export share exceeds 50% only in some areas such as soups and sauces, cheese spreads, and candies (cf. Hodler, 1994, p. 5). The food retail market, to give an enriched description, constitutes a typically Swiss and unique duopolistic situation that reduces the possibilities in an already small home market.

With about 70,000 employees, the food-processing industry comes fourth among the secondary-sector industries (after mechanical engineering, electronics, and the chemical industry). Some 100,000 jobs in agriculture, packaging, and transportation are indirectly dependent on the food-processing industry. The biggest food producers are: Migros (head office: Zurich), the Coop Group (head office: Basel), the Nestlé combine (head office: Vevey), and Toni Lait (head office: Winterthur) (HandelsZeitung, 1995, p. 3).

3.   THE METHODOLOGY OF GLOBE RESEARCH IN SWITZERLAND

The GLOBE research for the understanding of leadership and culture in Switzerland was based on, and inspired by, the conceptual and methodological framework of the GLOBE study as a whole (for details, se' House, Hanges et al., 1997; House, Wright et al., 1997; House et al., 1999, 2004; Javidan & House, 2001; Szabo et al., 2002; see also chap. 1, this volume).

In the GLOBE study, several methods were combined to describe and analyze societal (and organizational) culture and leadership prototypes. In this respect, we followed Hofstede (1980), who stressed that every method has its own advantages and disadvantages, and therefore a multimethod approach was employed in order to gain valid insights into culture and leadership. Specifically, it consisted of a literature analysis, a questionnaire-based data collection, focus groups, semistructured interviews, ethnographic interviews, and unobtrusive participant observations. For all the methods and instruments, we relied on the previous work done by the project as a whole (e.g., an international validation of the questionnaire, ideas and rules for conducting interviews, etc.; House, Hanges et al., 1997; House, Wright et al., 1997; House et al., 1999).

The questionnaire-based data included the three standardized GLOBE questionnaires for the three levels under study: societal culture ("Should Be" and "As Is"), organizational culture ("Should Be" and "As Is"), and leadership attributes/behaviors ("Should Be").[9] For the societal and organizational level, GLOBE refers to value-belief theories of culture (Hofstede, 1980; Triandis, 1995), which suggest that the commonly shared values and beliefs held by members of a collective (e.g., a nation) influence the behavior of individuals and other entities (groups and institutions). They also influence the degree to which an observed behavior is viewed as legitimate. To describe the culture of a nation, GLOBE investigates the cultural dimensions in accordance with Hofstede's work: Uncertainty Avoidance, Power Stratification, Collectivism; two scales are used, the Collectivism scale from Triandis (1995), and Gender Egalitarianism and Assertiveness (both replaced the former Hofstede scale of Masculinity). In addition to these six scales, two dimensions derive from McClelland's (1961, 1985) theories of implicit human motivation and economic development: Humane Orientation and Performance Orientation. Finally, the dimension of Future Orientation was included, originating from the work of F. R. Kluckhohn and Strodtbeck (1961). The 21 leadership scales, which were made up of 112 leadership items, ultimately derive from an intercultural factor analysis.[10]

Three hundred and twenty-one Swiss middle managers[11] completed the questionnaire (societal culture items: 159; organizational culture items: 162; leadership items: 112). The middle managers worked in 19 organizations in three different industries (financial services: 26.5%; food processing: 32.4%; telecommunications: 41.1%). The respondents' sex was predominantly masculine (91.3% men, 8.7% women), and their age was between 27 and 65 years (average age: 44.48 years). On average, they had held managerial positions for 12.89 years (range between 1–35), and had an average of 6.23 subordinates reporting to them.

Three focus groups[12] and several interviews were mainly created to evaluate expectations about unusually effective leaders versus normally effective managers. Heterogeneity among respondents, for example, in organizational background (rank, experiences in different industries) and age (mid-20s to 60s), was maximized deliberately (Agar, 1980). These data-collecting processes on the occasion of post-graduate seminars (focus groups) and specially made contacts (interviews) were carried out at the beginning of our project and followed GLOBE guidelines.

---

[9]No "As Is" evaluations were collected in our context.

[10]The 21 leadership scales are presented later.

[11]Middle managers in this study are defined as being at least one hierarchical level below the top hierarchical level and at least on hierarchical level above the first hierarchical level.

[12]Focus groups are moderated discussion groups where the participants (experts, representatives of the object in focus, here managers) talked about and reflected on — in this case — various management and leadership phenomena.

The three 1-hour focus group discussions were taped, and all the relevant statements and examples were subsequently listed. During the group session, the 12 female and male participants, who were doing this postgraduate course in general management at the University of St. Gallen, were asked to rank their own answers on special topics on a group consensus basis: definition of leadership and management, the possible difference between these two constructs, and examples of outstanding leadership.

Nine semistructured interviews were conducted with middle managers in different industries (e.g., insurance companies, financial services, and publishers). The interviews were taped, and the interviewees were asked about their understanding of management and leadership in a way similar to that used in the focus groups. The average duration of these interviews was 45 minutes.

Three ethnographic interviews were conducted at a later stage of the project in the three GLOBE branches. They were based on a qualitative research manual prepared for GLOBE by Michael Agar. Written protocols from the taped 60-minute interviews were analyzed and interpreted by two people, both experienced in interview analysis. The aim was to identify and categorize attributes and behaviors that were characteristic of leadership and management, to learn about the interviewees' experiences of successful and unsuccessful leadership, and to gain insights into their hidden basic assumptions about leadership. Stories and illustrative examples were very helpful in this respect. The categories that were found were not predefined but emerged from the analyzing process. Thus we wanted to check if any aspect of the leadership phenomenon was mentioned that we were not aware of, while gaining a deeper insight into the possible variance of leadership prototypes. In a follow-up interview, all interviewees were asked if they were able to "recognize" themselves in our analysis. With the exception of very minor changes, the interview partners were satisfied with our interpretation.

The GLOBE researchers' very soundly reasoned assumption has been to combine quantitative and qualitative data. Only this offers the possibility for a holistic interpretation of culture and leadership. To intensify the culture research and to obtain a more in-depth picture of the leadership ideal in Switzerland, we also collected information by means of unobtrusive measurement techniques (e.g., House, Hanges et al., 1997; Webb, Campbell, Schwartz, & Sechresl, 1999). These measures do not rely on people to report data (as do interviews, e.g.) and are nonreactive to this extent. We decided to concentrate our analysis here mainly on two unobtrusive measures: street names and statues and legends/myths. However, other forms of research are shortly mentioned to illustrate the full range of our data collection.

Typically, in street names or in statues, persons are honored who were considered to be exceptional or outstanding for a society. Thus it might be interesting to see what kind of persons were honored in Switzerland. If one knows more about such people' thoughts and actions, then one can get—or so we assumed—more information on the valued aspects with regard to outstanding leaders in this culture. In addition, this method assumes that the central aspects of a current culture have developed over centuries or decades. This leads to the final underlying assumption that knowing more about the past will enable us to gain more insights into the present. The five biggest (German-speaking) Swiss cities were included in this analysis. The research was done on the basis of street-name registers and travel guides (statues[13]).

---

[13]This was done in a research seminar at the Institute for Leadership and Human Resource Management at the University of St. Gallen, Switzerland. Following the GLOBE framework, we conceptualized the procedure in more detail. The work was done by a student (Roth, 1996). Statues were found in the city guides. Street names were gleaned from either special registers or telephone directories (for this, cf. Cavalli 1995, p. 20). More detailed analyses were conducted for the cities of Bern, St. Gallen, and Zurich.

Another research method was used to assess the impact of culture on leadership: myths and legends.[14] Those standards still hold their own in today's value structure. "Legends" means oral tales that sometimes refer to historical events, which were passed on orally in former days, and are meant to explain, remind, and advise. This points to the significance of the values and standards presented in those legends, which are preferably packaged in impressive images. Legends are only worth telling if taboos are broken. Such an instance of taboo breaking can easily accommodate a moral lesson, and comprehensive ethical values can be identified. This makes legends suitable for the identification of culturally rooted leadership ideals.

Also a media study was conducted. The objective of the media study was to find information that would help us to continue to build our leadership frame.[15] Thus we were interested in repeated patterns of leadership. The underlying assumption here is that the media very prominently represent the values of a kind of leadership that is honored in a society, at least from the viewpoint of people who work in this media industry; however, it may be assumed that these persons also try to articulate the opinion of other people in society, possibly even the majority. The analysis focused on three print media (*Neue Zürcher Zeitung, Weltwoche,* and *Blick*). They were selected because of their range with respect to readers and their particular variety of clients.

Additionally, participant observation—following GLOBE guidelines—was carried out on the basis of a fully structured questionnaire. First, three persons completed the instrument by themselves, asking experts for further information, if and when necessary. Afterward, a consensual agreement was made between these persons in respect of the items contained in the questionnaire so that at the end one version existed. Literature analysis in different fields completed our efforts to describe and interpret Swiss culture and outstanding leadership during the whole project.[16]

4.   FINDINGS

After providing a first impression of the Swiss peculiarities and a comprehensive survey of the methodological basis of our study, we now turn to the findings of our analysis. This section is structured according to the two main levels under scrutiny: societal (national) culture and leadership. In each subsection, the results of the questionnaire-based data collection are presented first. In the Leadership subsection, we integrate qualitative results additionally.

Societal Culture

Table 8.1 presents the findings in respect of Swiss societal culture in terms of (a) absolute mean scores on a 7-point Likert-type scale, (b) an indication of country membership clusters for each country dimension, (means: relative position out of a maximum five distinct country clusters A > B > C > D > E), and (c) the rank order on each dimension compared to the other 60 participating countries. An absolute score indicating the difference between the two

---

[14]This was done in a research seminar at the Institute for Leadership and Human Resource Management at the University of St. Gallen, Switzerland. Following the GLOBE framework, we conceptualized the procedure in more detail. The work was done by a student (Jäger, 1996) A very good overview of Swiss legends is given in Keckeis (1995).

[15]This was done in a research seminar at the Institute for Leadership and Human Resource Management at the University of St. Gallen, Switzerland. Following the GLOBE framework, we conceptualized the procedure in more detail. The work was done by a student (Jüstrich, 1996). No separate analysis is given here.

[16]No separate analysis is given here. Selected points are integrated into the text as and when useful.

TABLE 8.1

Societal Culture of Switzerland: "Should Be" and "As Is" Scores

Societal Dimensions	"Should Be"			"As Is"			Difference		
	Score	Band	Rank	Score	Band	Rank	Delta	t Value	Sign.
Future Orientation	4.79	B	59	4.73	A	2	.06	.47	ns.
Uncertainty Avoidance	3.16	E	61	5.37	A	1	−2.21	−24.06	***
Institutional Collectivism	4.69	B	33	4.06	B	38	.63	7.32	***
In-Group Collectivism	4.94	C	61	3.97	C	56	.97	11.50	***
Power Distance	2.44	D	48	4.90	B	46	−2.44	−27.85	***
Humane Orientation	5.54	B	22	3.60	D	53	1.94	22.94	***
Gender Egalitarianism	4.92	A	13	2.97	B	54	1.95	25.95	***
Assertiveness	3.21	B	54	4.51	A	14	−1.30	−13.51	***
Performance Orientation	5.82	C	39	4.94	A	1	.88	11.88	***

Note.   *Score*: Country mean for Switzerland on the basis of aggregated scale scores. *Band*: Letters A to D indicate the country band Switzerland belongs to (A > B > C > D). Countries from different Bands are considered to differ significantly from each other (GLOBE test banding procedure; cf. Hanges, Dickson, & Sipe, 2004). *Rank*: Switzerland's position relative to the 61 countries in the GLOBE study; Rank 1 = highest; Rank 61 = lowest score. *Difference*: The difference was computed by subtracting "As Is" scores from the respective "Should Be" scores. A positive difference indicates that the society wishes to have more of a particular attribute or dimension whereas a negative score indicates the opposite.

* $p < .05$, ** $p < .01$, *** $p < .001$, ns. = nonsignificant.

societal culture measures is provided: "Should Be," the espoused value placed on how the participants would like it to be, and "As Is," observations of practices on how it is at present. The analysis of the statistical significance of the difference is also shown in Table 8.1.

According to F. R. Kluckhohn and Strodtbeck's (1961) value classification system, we grouped the nine societal culture scales loosely under four prominent headlines for easier access (Szabo & Reber, chap. 5, this volume): time, human–environment, relational, and activity orientation (see also Szabo et al., 2002). Using this classification, we followed a suggestion made by our Austrian GLOBE colleagues. Time Orientation describes the way in which a society uses time, and whether a society is oriented toward the past, present, or future. Human–Environment Orientation describes people's relationship with the world. Relational Orientation describes the way in which people in a society define themselves and others. Activity Orientation describes, among other things, the way people try to force things or influence life (e.g., doing vs. being).

Time Orientation

Future Orientation (similar to the Confucian Dynamism dimension by Hofstede & Bond, 1988) measures the degree to which a society encourages and rewards future-oriented behaviors (for all the scale definitions, House et al., 1999). The "As Is" score for Future Orientation stands at a very remarkable 4.73, ranking the Swiss in second position among all of the countries participating (2/61). The "Should Be" value for Future Orientation does not differ significantly (Mean [*M*] = 4.79,) but the comparative rank drops to 59/61, suggesting that many other countries are also, and much more concerned about, becoming stronger in future oriented. With respect to the high level of economic development (which also means planning, investing, and saving), the predominant educational standards (which also means delayed material gratification) and the religious roots of a partly Calvinist society (which also means hard work and less fun in the present), it was to be expected that Switzerland should have fairly high results here. The "Should Be" data, which could be interpreted as medium to high, meets this expectation to a considerable extent. However, at first sight, we would have assumed a higher score. This is reinforced by the fact that the worldwide ranking is extremely low (see previous discussion). But in contrast to many other countries, the perceived ("As Is") orientation to the future is on the same level as the expectation expressed. This result reflects our theoretical considerations (Wunderer & Weibler, 2002). The expression of the Swiss's orientation toward the future includes their outstanding thrift. Their saving rate is among the worlds highest. Money is invested in long-term objects rather than spent on short-term amusement: "rather on house and a car than for dinner, rather on streets and buildings than on personal staff" (Bergmann, 1990, p. 364, translated). The Future Orientation manifests also in investments for education, which have increased to $16.1 billion (Swiss Federal Statistical Office, 2003).

The reason for the discrepancy of 57 positions between the "Should Be" versus "As Is" global ranking can mainly be seen in a nonexisting need for a more extreme position on this dimension. Because every dimension also symbolizes a function for the survival and progress of society, one has to realize that this problem-solving attitude works pretty well. So why change it?

Human–Environment Orientation

Uncertainty Avoidance measures the degree to which a society strives to avoid uncertainty by norms, rules, rituals, plans, bureaucratic practices, and so on. Uncertainty Avoidance in Switzerland reaches a level of 5.37, the highest of all the "As Is" values worldwide. The "Should Be" value is much smaller, with a mean of 3.16; no other country has a lower value. A paradox? Not at all.

On the one hand, the explanation for this finding is that the contemporary willingness to take risks is rather low (see also Wunderer & Weibler, 2002). One's own actions are guided by rules, given structures, and so forth. Hofstede's work (1980) revealed a comparable result, although not as pronounced. The reason might be that Hofstede uses a slightly different operationalization of this dimension. The Swiss work ethic and Swiss values even reinforce this tendency. For instance, insurance policies for every possible event in life are widely offered and taken out; a great many laws regulate nearly every sphere of life. If something is not regulated, regulations will almost certainly be called for as soon as they are required. This instance, too, is due to historical circumstances: "Switzerland was a poor country for a long time; today, it is a small country surrounded by big neighbors. Accordingly, one is used to preventing, neutralizing and avoiding risks" (Bergmann, 1990, p. 364, translated). Owing to political and economic reasons, Switzerland faced the necessity of making the environment more predictable and more controllable for centuries. This led to numerous precautions, norms, and rules, which has obviously had a bearing on the fact that present-day societal culture is perceived as extremely uncertainty avoiding. This underlying basic position is reflected in business politics. Swiss companies are commonly less eager to conquer new markets than they are to enforce quality standards by continuous improvement and thereby maintaining their hold on the market by means of the "Swiss Quality" label (cf. Bergmann, 1990).

On the other hand, it can be observed that people want to change this risk-averse orientation. This can be explained by the fact that for a long period of time, unpleasant "side effects" (such as inflexibility, the obstruction and delay of innovation) of these Uncertainty Avoidance strategies occurred to an increasing extent. Switzerland is seen to be inadequately experimental and innovative, although it holds the highest rate of patents (Bundesamt für Statistik [BFS], 2005), as well as the highest number of Nobel Prize winners per capita (Kanton Zurich, 2005) which contrasts sharply with the preceding sentence at a first glance. The point is obviously that the connection of thinking (inventing) and the acting (implementing) is insufficient. For instance, too few people try to set up their own businesses. The mental constitution for risk taking is lacking and the excessively regulated environment is a significant barrier. The impressive wish for a reduction of these constraints is a clear indication of a perceived need for fundamental change. This change can mainly be achieved through improved background conditions at the societal and economic-political levels. A possible starting point might be a reduction in unnecessary regulations, the enforcement of self-responsibility, ideological support for encouraging the willingness to run risks, a reduction in nonfunctional power in favor of fluctuating hierarchies, and favorable attitude toward training the critical faculty in good time (Weibler, 1999).

Relational Orientation

The dimensions of Power Distance, Gender Egalitarianism, Humane Orientation, and Collectivism (subscales: Institutional Collectivism = Collectivism I/In-Group Collectivism = Collectivism II) belong to this category. They all describe different qualities of social relations, whether with respect to the relations between those who have or do not have power, between the sexes, between people in general, or between a single person and a group. To summarize, the Swiss people prefer a more democratic, humane, and group-oriented society where men and women play an equal part than that which is perceived right now. In detail:

Power Distance.   Power Distance measures the degree to which a society expects and agrees that power Should Be unequally shared (or distributed.) The Swiss respondents express the view that their society has quite a high level of Power Distance (4.90) "As Is" and that it needs much less, 2.44 "Should Be." This leads to a difference of nearly 2.5 points. However, this discrepancy is on average virtually identical in all the other countries so we must not detect any special cultural reasons that are responsible for it. To us, this represents a reference to worldwide power stratification where individual wants and societal practices are at odds. But we are able to add some insights that will nevertheless reveal some cultural aspects. Because democracy, freedom, and self-determination are known to have been basic and stable cornerstones of the Swiss national consciousness for centuries, it is explicable that Power Distance—just like in Hofstede's research (1980)—achieved a low grade on the "Should Be" scales. This fits clearly with the historical development of Switzerland. Typically, the best-known Swiss stories—the legends of William Tell and the Foundation of Switzerland—have as protagonists individuals (like William Tell) or groups (the representatives of the cantons Uri, Schwyz, and Unterwalden) who successfully revolted against authority and the abuse of power. In 1998, the political commentator Höpli stated, *"If we are proud of anything at all, then it still tends to be the descent from an alpine herdsman and farmer culture whose leaders knew how to defend themselves successfully in their valleys against the yoke of foreign lords and judges" (p. 2, translated)*—as opposed to the constitution or a republican myth[17] (Weibler & Wunderer, 1997). Even today, an emphasis on power differentials—for example, status symbols—is felt to be annoying in many places (Müller, 1990, p. 374). Accordingly, a leader's authority is accepted as long as he or she displays competence and honorable behavior. This presupposes that leaders *"have to work as long and as hard as their employees; they are not supposed to see themselves as more valuable than others because of their position … they Should Be there for their employees at all times, they should not ask for any privileges and deference … and they have to be willing and able to help out if necessary"* (Bergmann, 1990, p. 368, translated).

Gender Egalitarianism.   Gender Egalitarianism measures the degree to which a society minimizes gender role differences (a medium score means that masculine and feminine roles are recognized to the same extent; i.e., differences are minimized). The respondents recognize a high level of emphasis on the male role "As Is" ($M = 2.97$), ranked 54/61, but would like to see significantly more emphasis on gender equality ($M = 4.92$), ranked 13/61. This reveals that in fact men still dominate and gain more attention. This was already noted by Hofstede (1980). This current desire for greater egalitarianism, even slightly preferring feminity, reflects a shift that can be observed in many GLOBE countries. It fits with basic Swiss values like autonomy, equality, and loyalty. Yet it must be noted that in the past few decades, a convergence toward equal rights has been taking place in almost all of Western society. Thanks to this development, more importance has been accorded to women's concerns. So far, it is virtually impossible to point out which results can be traced back to cultural influences or cross-national trends in the evolution of values.

However, until now basic Swiss values such as self-determination and loyalty have little influence on an equal gender distribution of important positions in society. Indicators for this include the extremely late introduction of women's rights to vote (cf. The discussion in Section 2) and women's underrepresentation in public offices. At the Parliamentary elections in 1995, the proportion of women among the Nationalräte rose to 21.5% (Bundesamt für Statistik, 1998). However, participant observation confirms that currently, a great number of discussions and attempts to secure equal opportunities for women are going on; in 1995, an Equality Act was passed. This Equality Act supports the implementation of constitutional equal rights designed to protect women against discrimination, mainly in economic life (Segesser, Sonderegger, & Stampfli, 1996). However, an enormous number of discussions and publications on the subject of equal rights are concurrent with a recognizably smaller number of specific actions (Wunderer & Dick, 1997). The central obstacle in the way of equal rights is an inadequate infrastructure, which if removed would enable the unity of family and work. The supply of places in kindergarten and day nurseries in Switzerland is clearly below that of many other European countries. In addition, there is nothing like a legally guaranteed maternity leave (i.e., vacations for looking after a child during the first months), and working mothers thus still have to face prejudices (such as being called a "bad mother") although this issue has been of public concern for at least two decades. Switzerland's position with respect to Gender Egalitarianism is still on a low level. In this regard, Switzerland, which is otherwise highly developed, has remained an underdeveloped country (cf. Hollstein, 1989).

---

[17]The nonemotional relationship with the Constitution fits in quite well with the emotional distance many German-speaking Swiss seem to have toward their national anthem (Sauser, 1998, p. 5).

Humane Orientation. Humane Orientation measures the degree to which a society encourages and rewards individuals for being fair, friendly, caring, and compassionate. The "As Is" score for Humane Orientation stands at a moderate low 3.60, ranking Switzerland at the absolute lowest quartile of GLOBE countries. The "Should Be" value for Humane Orientation records a significantly higher 5.54 and the comparative rank rises to 22/61, suggesting that "softer" and "fuller" thinking and behavior might be an asset for this country. The expressed values in this dimension are closely related to an element of its national identity: Solidarity, whose importance can be deduced directly from Swiss history.[18] This was for example, demonstrated in Swiss people's great helpfulness during and especially after the two world wars (Im Hof, 1991a, p. 268), although as we know today, the solidarity of some parts of the population during the two world wars was only one side of the medal (the other side stands for economic interest). Today, tolerance and responsibility are the central educational goals in Switzerland (Pagnossin Aligisakis, 1991, p. 108)—two virtues that refer to the constructs of Humane Orientation and solidarity in functional relationships.

However, it is completely unclear if the values for politeness, generosity, and tolerance will have a chance to develop at a more intensive quality. We can speculate wildly about the discrepancy between the "As Is" and "Should Be" scores. Presumably, one major instance is the high score of Performance Orientation for Switzerland, which would be partly opposed to Humane Orientation although many substantial reforms originated in Switzerland, for example, the maintenance of industrial health and safety.[19] To make matters worse, the common concentration on individual achievement supports competition rather than cooperation and solidarity. The tense economic situation and increasingly fierce competition (the increase in job performance assessment in companies being a case in point) intensify this fundamental problem even more. In addition, the high degree of institutional Humane Orientation (public welfare) intensifies an individual's feeling that the responsibility for any social problem can be passed on to one of the many public institutions. The attributes of willingness to help, empathy, friendliness, tolerance, and generosity are obviously more easily propagated than practiced—worldwide. This doubt is supported by the results from a study by Berthouzoz (1991, p. 162), who showed that 52% noticed a decrease in people's willingness to help in Switzerland. Increasing individualism, materialism, loss of guiding ethical values—which are shared unquestioned by the vast majority—a domination of economic thinking, also in matters that are not economic in origin, indubitably erodes the foundations of solidarity. The fact that, as repeatedly reported in the media, it is becoming increasingly difficult to fill honorary offices, points in the same direction. From a foreign affairs point of view, it is remarkable that as in other Western European countries, some people display resentment toward persons entering the country without official documents. Changes in legislation have made it more difficult for refugees to be granted asylum in the last few years. However, one should not forget that Switzerland has the highest rate of foreigners in the whole of Europe (which is partly forced by the restricted law to get the Swiss nationality) and is currently very helpful in giving refugees a temporary safe haven.

---

[18]Through mutual solidarity and reciprocal support, the old Confederates often achieved major victories against supremacy and repression (cf. the subsection History).

[19]One of Switzerland's pioneering works wast eh Federal Law on Factories passed on March 23, 1877, which contained regulations on working hours. In the area of international industrial health and safety standards, Switzerland was also the first to take different initiatives, such as the initiative for the first International Labor Convention (1891) and the proposal for the creation of an international authority for industrial security and health standards (1896); Switzerland was also a cofounder of the International Association of Industrial Security and Health Standards (1900). Another pioneering work was collective labor agreements protected by law (cf. Riklin & Möckli, 1983, p. 84).

In-Group Collectivism and Institutional Collectivism.   In-Group Collectivism denotes the degree to which individuals express pride, loyalty, and cohesiveness in their organizations, work groups, or families. Institutional Collectivism refers to the extent to which social institutions or institutional practices encourage and reward collective distribution of resources and collective action. A mean "As Is" score of 4.06 (Institutional Collectivism) and 3.97 (In-Group Collectivism) suggests that Switzerland is neither on the collectivistic nor on the individualistic side. In contrast, the In-Group-Collectivism score for Switzerland ranks low (56). This expresses a comparably stable focus on individuality, which German-speaking Switzerland has in common with its direct neighbors Germany and Austria as well as with some Northern European and Anglo-American nations. Therefore, we interpret Switzerland's score to be rooted in religious, political, and industrial characteristics that are shared with several nations from these country clusters. The respective states are all well known for more or less appreciating rights of the single person with respect to intended influences from the state. Nonetheless—and despite some method differences in the scale compositions (House et al., 2004, p. 461ff), the "As Is" and "Should Be" scores for Collectivism indicate that the participants of the GLOBE survey wish to enhance the collectivistic values from a nearly balanced score to higher levels (Institutional Collectivism: 4.69, Rank 33; In-Group Collectivism: 4.94, Rank 61), though this raise is undoubtedly not very strong based on the international average. It appears that Swiss people feel quite comfortable being integrated within groups of manageable size, yet they also seem unwilling to give up their identity in this "collectivistic" constellation. This fits in quite well with tendencies that we identified in our historical analysis: the principle of emotionally favoring affairs that are close at hand, not excessive in size, and understandable (first the community, then the canton, then the Confederation). In summary, Swiss people seem to have a clear imagination about being embodied in social entities and society as a whole while maintaining their own individuality and respecting autonomy and freedom. The societal cultural practices do not differ from the respective societal cultural values as much as they do in other nations.

Activity Orientation

Performance Orientation.   Performance Orientation measures the degree to which a society encourages and rewards group members for performance improvement and excellence. The "As Is" score for Performance Orientation stands at a high 4.94, ranking Switzerland at the absolute top position of GLOBE countries (1/61). The "Should Be" value for Performance Orientation records a significantly higher 5.82, but the comparative rank drops to 39/61, suggesting that many other countries are also concerned about becoming more performance-oriented. After all that we have learned about Switzerland's historical and religious roots, this high Performance Orientation cannot be surprising.

An important explanation for the high degree of Performance Orientation can be seen in the traditionally strong work motivation, which is presumably mainly rooted in Protestant Calvinism:

> *Endeavoring to show signs to be the chosen one, the Calvinist developed a joy in work, persistence and energy, unknown to the people in the Middle Ages. This inevitably led to success in matters economic. Because of the strict morality that he was forced to abide by, the Calvinist was unable to spend his wealth on any sort of enjoyment of life ... there was not anything left to do besides investing the money in his own or in a related company. This was the cause for quick corporate expansion and the foundation of capital investment.* (Widmer, 1977, p. 216, translated)

To this extent, Calvinism was one of the major driving forces behind the distinct Swiss work ethic (see also Weber, 1972a, 1922/1972b) and we cannot conceive the modern Switzerland without the immigration of the "huguenotian" watch makers in the 17th century.[20]

Like scientific research, daily observation also reveals even today that work is valued highly within Swiss society. "The Swiss are plain, thrifty and have an obsession with work" (Riklin & Möckli, 1983, p. 95, footnote 432, translated). In a representative survey, 87% out of 1,400 people stated that work was a very important or quite important part of their lives (Melich, 1991, p. 6). An initiative to reduce working hours failed in a plebiscite in December 1988 (Pagnossin Aligisakis, 1991, p. 116). These findings alone suggest that Performance Orientation ranks highly in Swiss society. The distribution of answers to the question "Should better performance at work command higher pay?" in the aforementioned survey shows this even more clearly: 72% of the men and 65% of the women interviewed answered in the affirmative. Agreement is particularly high among the German- Swiss (men: 77%; women: 71%) (Pagnossin Aligisakis, 1991, p. 110). Outside the working sphere, Performance Orientation manifests itself in the great importance ascribed to primary and secondary education. In 1984, a total of 84% of the interviewed parents regarded performance motivation as an important or very important educational goal (Sieber, 1984). The level of education in Switzerland is correspondingly high: four out of five 25- to 64-year-olds continued their education beyond the compulsory number of years; however, only 10% have a university degree (Bundesamt für Statistik, 1998, p. 417). The importance of education in Switzerland however might not be reflected in the percentage of university degrees obtained (which actually is quite low as compared to other developed countries). Far more typical is a broadly supported apprenticeship where Swiss teenagers learn to value professional achievements.[21]

The high priority given to work by the Swiss can also be traced back to Switzerland's particular history. As a poor, barren, and mountainous country, the Swiss had to show a great deal of effort and skill in their struggle with nature. Like many other countries, Switzerland had its own special problems with the economic situation and with poverty at the beginning of the century. In the reconstruction period after the First World War, hard work and an understructured industry seemed to be the main driving force behind economic upswing. The Swiss Farmers' Newspaper announced in January 1924: *"Abroad, daily working hours grew longer to overcome the post-war crisis. Switzerland, with a lack of coal and other raw materials, had to follow this example to survive the pressure exerted by competition on foreign and Swiss markets. Prosperity of the people through work!"* (quoted after Lalive d'Epinay, 1991, p. 18, translated).

During the Second World War, an additional predicament occurred: Surrounded by the Axis powers, the Swiss workforce became a major source of independence to the Swiss people. In 1940, the head of the federal office in charge of food logistics in times of war, Friedrich Wahlen, worked out a survival plan with the goal of *"achieve the greatest possible autonomy in the supply of the country through a gigantic national effort in rational use and ... widely improved management of all reserves and deposits of raw materials and a strict employment organization, and he went so far as to convert public parks and gardens into arable land"* (cf. Lalive d'Epinay, 1991, p. 40).

Swiss efficiency, always in close connection with security, order, and seriousness in life's affairs, comes through in our research. But what might be the reason for the fact that Performance Orientation tends to be high, but lags behind its own claims ("As Is" vs. "Should Be")? If we want

---

[20]This was stressed by a reviewer.
[21]This was especially mentioned by a reviewer.

to explain the results, we have to examine the operationalization of this dimension. The actual result of Performance Orientation is measured (a) by the extent to which rewards are based on performance and other factors, and (b) by the extent to which innovative actions that aim to improve performance are rewarded. Several things have to be mentioned: Performance is becoming decidedly an important basis for rewards in Switzerland, but it is not the only one. Informal relationships, for instance, play a major role, as does—or rather did—military rank. Innovative behavior that aims at performance improvement, and is always also linked with a certain risk, is definitely not invariably rewarded by the Swiss, who tend to be rather careful (cf. Uncertainty Avoidance). In addition, existing structures in many places obstruct innovative behavior rather than supporting it (Wunderer & Weibler, 2002).

A glance at the international "Should Be" ranking with regard to Performance Orientation reveals that the highest ranks/top positions are occupied by many countries, such as El Salvador, Zimbabwe, Slovenia, and Venezuela, which rank far behind Switzerland in terms of economic development and in which a great deal of development work remains to be done. This is exactly a matter that is bound to require a high level of Performance Orientation. The need for Performance Orientation is much higher in those countries than in more highly developed countries with comparatively stable economies like Switzerland. Almost half of the Swiss interviewees stated that they wished work would become a less important part of their lives. In particular, the younger generation—the economic beneficiaries of their parents' hard work—are less ready to make sacrifices for the benefit of work (Ulrich, Probst, & Studer, 1985; Widmaier, 1991).

However, observers might ask how a balanced, egalitarian ideal can cohabit with the high rewards for performance that leads to social and economic differences inevitably? One explanation could be that Swiss people perceive higher monetary rewards not as an implement to buy more hierarchical power but as a substitute for it. For instance, Frey and Kucher (2001) demonstrated that Swiss state employees are better paid in cantons with more direct democracy and therefore less individual discretionary power. We need more kinds of such approaches to understand paradoxes in societal culture dimensions. We are just at the beginning.

Assertiveness.   Assertiveness measures the degree to which individuals in society are allowed to be dominant, aggressive, and confrontational in social relationships. The Swiss respondents express the view that their society has just a slightly high level of Assertiveness (4.51 "As Is") and that it needs much less, 3.21 "Should Be." This shift mirrors a tendency in the international comparison, although the comparative rank of the "Should Be" score at 54/61 suggests that other countries are more focused on the reduction of Assertiveness at this point in time. We think that the wish to reduce assertive behavior is more related to face-to-face relationships (e.g., leadership relations) than to structural forces that coregulate a working community. For this face-to-face relationship a lower score, as it is intended for Switzerland, seems to be the most advantageous in this respect: In a strongly federalist country with largely autonomous cantons, diverse ethical groups, and different languages and religions, it is always necessary to weigh up the various interests, to find compromises, to keep the balance between adaptation and steamrolling. This is the only way a pluralist society made up of several autonomous entities is able to continue existence peacefully. On the other side, it is evident that on a more abstract level this kind of cooperation might be forced by structures to protect it from the unpredictable movements of fate. Swiss people call this "forced consensus."[22] The need to build bridges and to smooth the edges is omnipresent in Swiss society. Only a few, but remarkable examples of this Swiss way

---

[22]This very helpful example was formulated by a reviewer and partly elaborated independently in a separate publication by the authors.

are selected: a multilinguistic school system where every Swiss learns at least one of the other national languages; a military service where every young Swiss man learns to overcome ethnic, religious, and especially social barriers and to tie an informal network; an institutionalized social dialogue between managers, politicians, and workforce unions that Swiss call "work peace" (for the last point, see Hilb & Wittmann, 1992); a collective "bottom-up" decision making in political institutions (which Swiss call "principle of collegiality"). Here, the Swiss quest for a balance culminates into a regulative called "magic formula," which enables most ethnic, religious, geographical, and political fractions to be represented (Wunderer & Weibler, 2002). This in turn is a very Swiss paradox: Though all major fractions take part in the decision, each one is a minority by itself.

However, this cooperative behavior is easier to realize in the political section than in the economical one where competition in and between organizations is still the leading principle. So you cannot be astonished that the respondents experience Assertiveness in their daily occupational life, primarily on the personal face-to-face basis, as we assume. A shift according to the value numbers of the "Should Be" dimension seems to be more realistic when more cooperative behaviors are practiced on the economic structural level, for example, between firms and when success of this behavior is seen. The current discussion in management about "co-opetition" (Brandenburger & Nalebuff, 1996) or "interorganizational cooperation" (Buckley, 2000) or "networks" (Provan & Milward, 1995) leads to this direction.

So far, we have had an intensive look at societal culture in Switzerland as presented by the findings of our survey, and discovered a clear relationship between these findings and the historical cultural development in Switzerland. After this inevitably extensive description and analysis of the basis of Swiss societal culture, we would like to turn the focus on to the kind of Swiss leadership that is regarded as outstanding.

Leadership

The challenge of this chapter is to outline a picture of an insight into outstanding leadership in Switzerland in terms of the interpretations of societal culture laid down previously. As we said in the introduction, we rely on the implicit leadership approach (Lord & Emrich, 2001; Lord & Maher, 1991; Shaw, 1990). This theoretical work suggests that individuals have implicit theories of leadership in their minds that distinguish leaders from nonleaders, effective leaders from noneffective ones, and so on.

Results of the Quantitative Study

As mentioned earlier, the middle managers who formed part of the Swiss sample were asked to rate various leadership items on a scale between 1 (greatly inhibits a person from being an outstanding leader) and 7 (greatly contributes to a person being an outstanding leader). The items were internationally grouped into 21 leadership scales (cf. House et al., 2004).

Figure 8.1 gives an overview of the 21 leadership scales used in our study, which enables us to have a deeper look at expected leadership attributes and behavior. To begin with, we would like to note that the vast majority of these leadership scales are not statistically influenced by industry, age, or sex ($N = 321$).[23]

---

[23]In terms of the comparison of industries, it is worth mentioning that in telecommunications, an outstanding leader scored lower on the leadership scales of conflict inducer, procedural, and status consciousness. The financial service industry's "performance orientation" achieved the highest score in both absolute and relative terms. Women are seen to be significantly more administratively competent, more inspirational, diplomatic, and modest, and less autocratic.

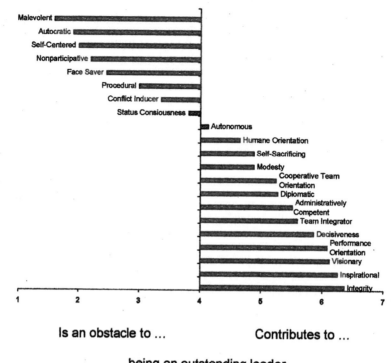

Figure 8.1   Values and positions of leadership scales in Switzerland (prototypes)

Contributing factors: The characteristics of leaders that are deemed by the respondents to contribute to outstanding leadership are seen as a mixture of personality traits (e.g., performance orientation, decisive, administratively competent, modesty, autonomous, and integrity) and attributes and behaviors that are only or mainly relevant in interpersonal relationships (inspirational, visionary, diplomatic, self-sacrificial, humane, team integrator, and collaborative team orientation). In this regard, Switzerland does not hold any clearly special position worldwide, particularly if we take a look at the absolute distinction. One might even say that the attributes regarded as a characteristic of outstanding leadership in Switzerland are (on average) compatible with most other countries, especially as there are no extremes to identify (see Table 8.2). As Weibler et al., (2000) have shown, this does not mean automatically that the meaning of scales is identical for each culture. However, further research is needed to clarify this point.

Inhibiting factors: At the end of the rating scale, we find self-protective, autocratic, inconsiderate, lone wolf/unsociable, and anti-innovation attributes and behaviors. They are partly also judged negatively in an international comparison. Autocratic and nonparticipative behavior in particular prevents leaders from being acknowledged in Switzerland to an extreme extent. This is in line with our description of Swiss culture, which was generally characterized by the negative classification of this element.

TABLE 8.2
Values of Leadership Scales in Switzerland

Leadership Dimensions	Score	Rank	Band
Integrity	6.36	13	B
Inspirational	6.25	26	B
Visionary	6.12	30	B
Performance Orientation	6.08	31	B
Decisive	5.86	30	A
Team Integrator	5.59	50	B
Administratively Competent	5.51	49	C
Diplomatic	5.27	46	A
Collaborative Team Oriented	5.25	49	B
Modesty	4.88	38	B
Self-Sacrificial	4.88	39	B
Humane	4.65	38	B
Autonomous	4.13	16	A
Status-Conscious	3.81	46	C
Conflict Inducer	3.36	54	C
Procedural	3.00	57	D
Face Saver	2.46	49	C
Nonparticipative	2.20	54	C
Self-Centered	2.00	39	C
Autocratic	1.91	59	D
Malevolent	1.60	46	D

Note. Score: Country mean for Switzerland on the basis of aggregated scale scores. *Band*: Letters A to D indicate the country band Switzerland belongs to (A > B > C > D). Countries from different Bands are considered to differ significantly from each other (GLOBE test banding procedure; cf. Hanges, Dickson, & Sipe, 2004). *Rank*: Switzerland's position relative to the 61 countries in the GLOBE study; Rank 1 = highest; Rank 61 = lowest score. *Difference*: The difference was computed by subtracting "As Is" scores from the respective "Should Be" scores. A positive difference indicates that the society wishes to have more of a particular attribute or dimension whereas a negative score indicates the opposite.
Scale ranging from 1 = greatly inhibits a person from being an outstanding leader, to 4 = has no impact on whether a person is an outstanding leader, to 7 = contributes greatly to a person being an outstanding leader (for a detailed description of the scales, cf. House, Hanges et al., 1997; House *et al.*, 1999, 2004).

As in the GLOBE analysis of all the countries (House et al., 1999), our analysis also revealed some statistically meaningful interrelationships among the 21 leadership scales, hence the need to create a second-order factor structure. The second-order solution by House et al., revealed four factors for the present (1999, p. 210):

(1) charismatic/value-based leadership that is team-oriented, (2) autonomous leadership, (3) humane leadership, and (4) non-participative self-protective leadership. Guided by prevailing theory, we divided Factor 1 into charismatic/value-based leadership and team-oriented leadership to create two dimensions. We also divided Factor 4 into two dimensions: self-protective leadership

and participative leadership (the scores of the non-participative subscales were reversed to reflect participative leadership). (GLOBE now uses the six-second order factor structure.)

The aim was to find out if the worldwide second-order factor solution was also valid for Switzerland or if we could discover some Swiss specialties. So the question was if there are significant differences, and how could it be interpreted in this case?

We therefore conducted a maximum likelihood exploratory factor analysis with a varimax rotation (cf. Appendix A).[24] The second-order factor analysis produced four factors that were completely identical with the worldwide factor solution before House et al. (1999) decided to split two factors to preserve conceptual clarity. However, we did not see this necessity for our data set, but we preferred to use a different labeling [25] from that employed by House et al., (1999, 2004). We focused more strongly on the leader type (cf. later discussion). The single scales differed slightly in going into one factor or another. The four second-order factors that were identified explained a total of 56.9% of the variance of the former leadership scales.[26] However, we were not satisfied with the semantic consistency of the fourth factor. First, the autonomous subscale had almost the same high loading—or rather, an equally low loading— on Factor 1, and the other subscale, self-sacrificial, also had a loading below <.50. Thus we came to the conclusion that we should enforce a factor solution with only three factors. This led to a more stable result with respect to our second-order solution (cf. Appendix C). In total, 51.07% of the variance was explained after this revision.[27]

We labeled the three second-order factors as follows:

- Great Leader [28] (visionary, inspirational, self-sacrificial, performance orientation, decisive, diplomatic, administratively competent, and team integrator).

---

[24]For the complete 21-scale solution, cf. Appendix A. The main point of this analysis is that the fourth second-order factor found in the worldwide rating was partly corroborated. The other very remarkable point is that the solution is very much in line with worldwide findings in general. Note that the GLOBE scales were designed to measure organizational or societal level variability (Hanges & Dickson, 2004). The scales were *not* intended to meaningfully differentiate among individuals within a particular society. However, even though the scales were not constructed to provide such information, in some cases it is interesting to assess whether similar factors differentiate individuals within a society. Country-specific factor analysis is intended as an exploration of the themes captured by GLOBE in a new domain, that is, individual differences within a society. It should be noted that, because of the within-society restriction of the GLOBE scales true-score variability (which was based on between-society differences), the loadings of the GLOBE scale's items on within-society factors should be lower than between societies (cf. Hanges & Dickson, 2004). Furthermore, one should not interpret the within-society factor analyses as replications of the GLOBE factor structure. And the absence of a GLOBE factor within a society should not be automatically interpreted as the factor being irrelevant to the people in that country. Rather, a factor may fail to emerge within a society even when that theme is extremely critical because there was no variability in how the individuals from a single society rated the items (e.g., they all rated the items a 7). Factor analysis requires variability and so a factor could fail the emerge because it is extremely critical or completely irrelevant to the people within a society.

[25]At least for the time being.

[26]The commonalities are unsatisfactorily weak in part (cf. Appendix A).

[27]It is important to stress that these three factors have quite satisfactory reliabilities. To calculate these reliabilities for the second-order factors (the partly insufficient ones for the original scales are shown in Appendix B; here we have to remember that their well-documented strength is tested on an aggregated international level), we used the following formula (thanks to Paul Hanges for his support!): reliability = $1 - (a-b)/sigma^2$, where a = sum of the first-order scales variances multiplied by their weight squared (here: 1.0), and where b = sum of the first-order scales variances multiplied by their weight squared (here: 1.0) and by their reliability, and where $sigma^2$ = variance of the second-order factor. Thus the reliabilities are: Factor 1= .72, Factor 2 = .74, and Factor 3 = .83.

[28]This labeling is somewhat different in substance from the "Great Leader" by Bales and Slater (1955).

- Human Leader (integrity, humane, collaborative team oriented, modesty).
- Ego Boss (autonomous, autocratic, malevolent, nonparticipative, procedural, self-centered, status conscious, face saver, conflict inducer).[29]

The first two factors contribute towards being an outstanding leader in Switzerland; the third is a rather powerful inhibiting factor in this respect. With regard to one theoretical assumption of GLOBE (culture fit and success), one might call him or her a "Failure Generating Leader." To us, this factor solution appropriately reflects two main streams in leadership research. First, we can see support for the often replicated OHIO dimensions (e.g., Hemphill & Coons, 1957) when we consider the Performance Orientation subscale in the first second-order factor and the Humane Orientation second-order factor (of course, in a somewhat more modern version). Second, the whole charismatic leadership discussion, restarted after Weber (1922/1972b) by House (1977) up to Bass (1985), fits in with the results quite well. Value, performance, and people orientation (fair, competent, and team oriented) may be the shortest description for an outstanding leader on the basis of these results. At the same time, outstanding leaders have to avoid everything which puts them in the center of attention or leads to solitary decision making, possibly justified only by formal power sources.[30]

After analyzing the quantitative part of our study, we now want to look into our qualitative findings. This is done as briefly as possible. In particular, we are interested in seeing the extent to which we are able to corroborate our findings and, possibly, add new knowledge.

Results of the Qualitative Study

Focus Groups, Semistructured and Ethnographic Interviews.   On the basis of the focus group research and the content analysis of the semistructured and ethnographic interviews, several findings are presented in respect of leadership characteristics in Switzerland. To get a more comprehensive picture of the results we decided to present the findings not separated by method; also because no significant differences in the perception of leadership could be revealed between methods. At best supplements could be found. The views expressed in focus groups and interviews correlated broadly.

The opening question for us to answer was if a difference between leaders and managers is perceived, like it is often mentioned in leadership literature. For example, Zalesnik (1990, pp. 14, 22) wrote on this topic:

> *Whereas managers focus on process, leaders focus on imaginative ideas. Leaders not only dream up ideas, but stimulate and drive other people to work hard and create reality out of ideas ... They [the managers] brought what they learned from the business schools, namely, principles of bargaining, emotional control, human relation skills, and the technology of quantitative control. They left behind commitment, creativity, concern for others, and experimentation. They had learned to be managers instead of leaders.*

---

[29]The suggestion by House et al. (1999) to divide the "nonleadership" second- order factor into narcissistic and participative leadership (the scores for the latter had been reversed before) and to split the team-oriented parts from the charismatic-value-based leadership in order to obtain a separate scale to preserve conceptual clarity and fit in better with existing leadership theories, is not discussed here.

[30]However, we have to refer to two remarkable differences with regard to the worldwide solution in this second-order factor composition. First, "integrity" is classed with the second-order factor, Humane Leader, instead of with the Value-Based leadership factor. Second, "collaborative team oriented" (group oriented, loyal, consultative) and "team integrator" (clear, informed, coordinator, etc.) is statistically distinguishable. Thus at least for Switzerland, this constellation requires further investigation.

Indeed, our empirical findings caused us to conclude that the vast majority of people almost unanimously consider leadership and management to be different, too. When people think about outstanding leadership, they usually associate leadership with the top of a corporation or of a political or military organization.[31] If you compare an outstanding leader with a manager, the first is spontaneously given a higher rating. Nevertheless, finding examples and situations of outstanding leadership was generally difficult. The interviewees were of the opinion that leadership is something more complex and more difficult. Leadership deals with formulating and achieving goals with people—particularly through the creation of meaning (sense), whereas management has something to do with shaping frames, resources, and processes for efficient goal achievement—particularly in the long run. Leaders, in this view, have a direct impact on followers, whereas managers need not necessarily. A manager's position is more closely associated with goal achievement, technical competence (e.g., problem-solving skills), and the ability to make decisions and enforce problem solutions. Thus the main difference between leadership and management is the orientation of leadership toward people and ideas, whereas the orientation of management is toward objects, processes, and systems. The essence is that both aspects are included in every organizational position, but the importance of the aspects changes: With every step up the hierarchical ladder, leadership becomes more important. However, it seems that this distinction is not always manifest in the participants' consciousness. Once people reflect on this issue, however, they often arrive at a specific distinction between the two terms.

Other questions and emerging topics dealt with attributes and behaviors of outstanding or worse leaders. It was mentioned consensually that leaders Should Be able to inspire people (Bass, 1985), act as role models, and possess credibility. Also, they should have a fair amount of social competence, particularly the ability to communicate, combined with the readiness to listen to followers. Communication is seen as a duty to inform followers but also as a duty for followers to inform the leader; it is thus never a one-way system. Another important dimension of social competence is the ability to work in a team. This means two things: First, leaders must themselves be able to work in a team; keywords in this respect are *cooperation, delegation, and coordination* (Humane Orientation and Collectivism; see also Wunderer, 1995; Wunderer & Kuhn, 1992). Second, they Should Be sensitive to team creation, team development, and team maintenance (Margerison & McCann, 1985).[32] This point is quite interesting because it highlights other descriptions whereby outstanding leadership is not a "one-man show" (Collectivism). Moreover, leaders are straight (constant over time, direct in the things they want to communicate) and fair. Important tasks are the motivation of people, human resource development, and the establishment and maintenance of a culture. Leaders who do not mainly act in this way will face different problems such as frustration, resignation, demotivation, and rejection of suggestions, and they will have to cope with declining acceptance. Such leaders are unable to persuade followers and to produce the feeling that leader and followers can reach a goal together. They are unable to convey the ideal fact that everyone is crucial to success and to imbue the follower's position with meaning.

---

[31] It is interesting that as regards the Armed Forces, interviewees adduced examples that referred to their immediate superiors, whereas in the working context, they usually mentioned higher positions such as their or another company's CEOs.

[32] See the significance of Team Orientation on the political level by Bütler (1997), who vehemently supports the "collegial principle" and explains its function, for example, within Switzerland's direct democratic tradition.

The same phenomenon—fascination and mistrust—applies to what is often called a "charismatic leader." When we asked people about the attributes of an outstanding leader, very often "charisma" was a typical answer. Presenting a vision, optimism, and perspectives evokes admiration but must always be combined with specific goals and steps (Future Orientation). Then again, people are afraid that charismatic leaders will be too dominating and lose contact with their followers after some time, or—even worse—try to manipulate them (Power Distance). This consideration is also reflected, among other things, in the fact that the head of Switzerland's federal government changes every year, by the job rotation of the seven members of the government (this position packs much less power than a "presidency," it is more that of a spokesperson and representative of the government).

When we asked for prominent outstanding leaders, they were often labeled as people "who master the art of playing to the gallery," get something moving, and demonstrate independence. Conversely, the followers are afraid that these people may forget their roots and concern for others (Humane Orientation). For this reason, charisma is also viewed in negative terms in Switzerland, presumably much more so than in other countries.[33]

The interview results confirm the recent findings whereby integrity (the leader as a symbol; Weibler, 1995), credibility (being a good role model), or general social competencies rank high. Ideally, leaders Should Be able to demonstrate occasionally what they require from others in person; this will earn them a great deal of recognition. Three impressive examples are given next:

During a military ops exercise, the weather changed, and the question arose whether to leave or to stay. The leader decided to leave and drove the truck through a very muddy and dangerous terrain himself. In another case, a company's purchasing department was not very effective. The CEO then assumed the controlling functions in person and bought goods himself. In a very short time, he was able to sharpen employee consciousness in the direction of effectiveness and demonstrate the importance of their department to the whole company. In a final example, a leader in a company also worked at weekends because he had also expected the same of his or her followers for a certain period of time.

Additionally, it is very important that leaders speak the language of their followers and act in accordance with the situation. Followers in Switzerland are often quite skeptical when a leader is very eloquent, which may be fascinating but also produces mistrust. The reason seems to be that a leader who speaks very eloquently tends to be removed from his or her followers (Power Distance).

As we have seen, there is a close link between the leader and the led. Outstanding leaders function as role models. Leaders do not ideally make a distinction between their own person and their followers. No demonstrative privileges are accepted (Müller, 1990, and his empirical findings for leadership in Switzerland). A demonstration of power, such as a new leader moving his or her deputy into a smaller office, would be received very negatively. This result may be valid independently of rank, function, age, or sex, as Reber and his colleagues found, relying on a revised Vroom–Yetton model in a different leadership study that also included Swiss managers. Their empirical findings provide an impressive corroboration of the nonauthoritarian and participative style of Swiss leadership (see also Reber, Jago, Auer-Rizzi & Szabo, 2000; Szabo, Reber, Weibler, & Wunderer, 2001). They found that more than 70% of the variance could be explained by societal culture factors. However, in contrast to GLOBE, they did not differentiate between these societal culture factors but treated them as

---

[33]The area of conflict concerning charismatic leadership has been discussed intensively in the literature; compare, for instance, Weibler (1997a) and Steyrer (1999).

an amorphous category (Reber, Jago, 1998; Reber, Jago, & Bönisch, 1993).[34] Bad leaders lead based on their position or formal power, and this form deserves the label of "headship" (Gibb, 1965) at best.[35]

Leadership as a social function is generally accepted. It seemed to be clear to our interviewees that someone has to coordinate things and to bear the responsibility for them. Yet they expected leaders to inform their followers in good time, to ensure that communication is open, and to take the group's or the followers' opinions into consideration and—if there is time— to discuss them. The aim of the discussion process is to find a consensus. However, it is evident in all the interviews that ultimately there must be economic success ("when all is said and done, we want to earn money."). Anything else is a means of reaching this end. Ethic considerations (Kuhn & Weibler, 2003; Weibler, 2001, pp. 395–460) were not mentioned. The best strategy for leaders and followers is therefore the rational discussion on the basis of facts and figures, as Wunderer and Weibler (1992) found out in another leadership study with Swiss managers. This will also enable followers to execute certain leadership functions ("managing the boss"; Kipnis, Schmidt & Wilkinson, 1980; Yukl & Falbe, 1990; Wunderer, 1992). If this is possible, a leader may expect acceptance and support.

Leaders can gain additional credit by following the opinion of the group, participants said. This applies when the group is greatly interested in an objective and has very good arguments for pursuing a different course (e.g., problem solving). In such a situation, where they follow the opinion of the group, leaders can gain a great deal of respect for the future. The same holds true for leaders who are able to change their minds after obtaining better information than they had previously; an illustrative example (military) was provided by an interviewee:

One squad had bad shooting results. The battalion commander was quite angry and said to people standing next to him: "I'll go and let them know what I think about that kind of performance." He then ran over to that particular squad, who were far away from his current position. When he returned, he said: "I gave them a rest because they were totally exhausted."

Consensus is a highly valued maxim and was mentioned fairly frequently. Only when a leader is unable to accept such a compromise, that is, a different opinion regarding the right way to proceed, or when a decision has to be made under pressure of time, will assertive behavior be accepted. But this leader will be expected to explain the reasons afterward. This is another good example where the history of a country can influence present conceptions: Consensus was always a necessity for good and sustained cooperation between the relatively high-autonomous but small states (cantons) of the Swiss Confederation (Collectivism). One is able to underpin this assessment with a slightly different remarkable point. To criticize someone in public—especially in a destructive manner—is not liked (face saving). This also seems to be true at times after someone has left a position. For instance, a former member of the government was criticized from different quarters because he officially expressed an opinion that ran counter to that of the current holder of his office.[36] Open communication is often required between the leader and the led, but Should Be restricted to the people who are actually involved. Once a decision has been made, the result should no longer be commented on in public.

---

[34]Please note that this result is also valid in a longitudinal view.

[35]This is the reason why in Switzerland's most famous legend, the hero, William Tell, fought against what the authorities had imposed on him and his compatriots, which involved having to do something that made no sense but required formal obedience only.

[36]Compare, for instance, the leader in the newspaper, *Tagblatt* (1998), regarding a financial problem.

Generally speaking, outstanding leaders are expected to think along entrepreneurial lines and in terms of alternative worlds and scenarios. They Should Be ready to put up with inconveniences and be capable of overcoming obstacles on the way toward realizing their ideas. We were told repeatedly that outstanding leaders should have unambiguous opinions. Outstanding leaders should also react fast and flexibly. They are task oriented (Performance Orientation), open-minded (Uncertainty Avoidance), and promote innovation (Performance Orientation). They are expected to bear responsibility, have a clear point of view, be able to make decisions, and have a modicum of technical competence (more so in lower management positions). It is regarded as particularly important that leaders should have a clear point of view. Leaders who are swayed by every idea, act without thinking, change their minds too often, are judged to be bad leaders. In situations where making a decisions is difficult, leaders are expected to run only moderate risks. We have heard many times that Swiss people—as mentioned before—are very cautious and have a high need for security (Uncertainty Avoidance).

Unobtrusive Measures.   As mentioned in our methodological discussion earlier, we decided to concentrate our activities here mainly on two aspects: street names and statues, and legends/myths.[37] Both possess symbolic significance and bear witness to the importance and appreciation of lead figures and their behavior in and for Switzerland.

1. *Street Names:* With respect to the street names, it was observed that between 13% and 23% of the streets in selected Swiss cities were named after persons. Of these streets, between 44% and 64% were identified as being named after leaders. The distribution for the kinds of leaders (political, religious, military, or intellectual/educational) varies. It can be assumed that historical reasons are responsible for this (St. Gallen, as a traditional monastery city, has nearly one third religious leaders; Bern, Switzerland's capital since 1848, has one third political leaders; in Zurich, a traditional university city, we found more educational leaders than in St. Gallen).

The five most prominent leaders (all men) who are immortalized in street names in at least four of the five cities are the following:

- Henri Dufour (1787–1875, general, politician, engineer, geographer).
- William Tell (legendary figure who refused to salute the hat put up for this purpose by one Gessler, a Hapsburg governor. A salute would have been a symbol of personal humiliation or acceptance of this authority by arms. He fought this foreign authority without fear).
- Arnold Winkelried (died ca. 1386, legendary figure who died for his country by sacrificing himself in a dramatic act, thus enabling the troops of the original Swiss Waldstätte to defeat a Hapsburg army).
- Heinrich Pestalozzi (1746–1827, educationalist, humanist).
- Werner Stauffacher (ca. 1291, legendary figure, one of the three persons who swore the original oath binding the first three cantons in faith, truth, and life to driving out foreign authorities; this oath is regarded as the very beginning of the Swiss state).

---

[37]This was done in a research seminar at the Institute for Leadership and Human Resource Management at the University of St. Gallen, Switzerland. Following the GLOBE framework, we conceptualized the procedure in more detail. The work was done by students (Jäger, 1996; Roth, 1996).

If we take a closer look at their biographies, we can conclude that these men stand for the following attributes: They are willing to make personal sacrifices for others; they are oriented toward other people; they fight against the abuse of power; they serve the community; they show integrity and are willing to improve the prevailing situation. This also applies to those who were next on the list: First, General Henri Guisan, who was the great national integration figure and symbol of resistance in the Second World War and who formulated the strategy of defending Switzerland, should the need arise, against its enemies from Switzerland's historical core territory, which he termed the réduit; Second, Henri Dunant, who fought for humanity and institutionalized the world's best-known charitable organization, the International Red Cross. Our first two second-order leadership factors can easily be recognized (great leader and human leader). This also means that some of the societal culture dimensions discussed earlier (e.g., Humane Orientation, Power Distance) can be observed in the way we analyzed before.

2. *Statues:* The analysis of statues was complicated insofar as none of the cities keep a register of statues of persons. This fact is meaningful in itself because it demonstrates the relative unimportance of admiring former leaders. On the basis of city guides, 37 leaders were identified. Most of them were politicians and people who had worked in education.

    In sum, it must be noted that, in comparison with France or the former Soviet Union, Swiss leaders are rarely immortalized in this manner. This is in line with our findings in the corresponding dimension of societal culture, where a very low degree of Power Distance was observed. Also, it was stressed several times in our interviews that outstanding leaders act together with their working groups and Should Be more "one of them" instead of being remote. The merit they earn invariably depends on the efforts of all. So why give prominence to one person alone? If this is done, then it is likely to happen in the case of people who served the community/society in a very important way.

3. *Legends/Myths:* Before reporting on our findings as regards legends/myths, we would like to present a very prominent, classical example of a Swiss legend. Its only purpose is to demonstrate what kind of material was used for this part of the study:

BOX 8.1

Example of a Famous Swiss Legend (Friar Klaus)

After the Burgundy Wars, the Swiss were respected as a nation abroad, but at home, quarrels and discord were predominant. This was on account of the spoils of war, which proved impossible to divide peacefully. At the same time, Freiburg and Solothurn desired to be members of the Swiss Confederation because they had fought on the side of the Swiss. Whereas the city cantons favored integration, the rural cantons did not because they were afraid of the predominance of the cities. A peaceful settlement of this dispute should have been brought about by the Tagsatzung or Diet, a cross between a senate and a confederate government, at Stans in 1481. Instead of an agreement, however, there were heated arguments between the city and rural cantons. Discord was mounting, and they wanted to break up.

This is why a priest, Imgrund von Stans, hurried to see Friar (i.e., brother) Klaus, a man from Unterwalden with the real name of Niklaus Leuenbrugger. He had served the country as a soldier

(Continued)

and a government official. It happened very often at that time that men led a very secluded life to serve God undisturbed. At the age of 50, Niklaus von Flüe (brother Klaus) became a hermit and went to live in Ranft, a canyon in Melchtal, where his compatriots built him a cell and a chapel.

Father Imgrund lamented the trouble of their native country to this pious man. In great haste, Niklaus went to Stans. As the old man in his simple clothes approached the Tagherren (envoys to the Diet), they rose in awe. In a serious speech, he admonished them to make peace and choose unity instantly. His words had such an effect that the litigious matters were settled peacefully, and Freiburg and Solothurn were included in theSwiss Confederation.

A detailed analysis of legends leads to the following results: First, if a leader uses power at the expense of the led, this is judged negatively.[38] We can see a clear reference here to Humane Orientation. Any selfish exploitation of positional power to increase one's own advantage, which implies isolationist behavior, is definitely rejected. Second, the person who is led is at the same time not presented as completely dependent, but as a subject that has a separate personality and individuality. The legends positively emphasize native shrewdness and disrespect as a sign of independent individualism. Third, the mutual dependency between the leader and the led is emphasized, too. Fourth, the leader's behavior must generally be linked to the values and standards of the culture. This is an obvious reference to the necessity of leaders to behave in accordance with legitimate values and standards. Previous research did not reveal this integration of behavior in moral/ethical standards in such an obvious manner.

In conclusion, the profile of societal leadership that emerges from the quantitative study (questionnaire) strongly echoes many of the results identified within the qualitative study. We found a lot of indicators that forced our consideration that societal culture has an influence both on single leadership scales and on all of the three leadership second-order factors that were distilled by factor analysis, namely the Great Leader, the Human Leader, and the Ego Boss.

Fortunately, other researchers commendably examined parts of the Swiss leadership culture in the recent past (Bergmann, 1986, 1990; Dachler & Dyllik, 1988; Krulis-Randa, 1984; Müller, 1988, 1990; Wunderer, 1990; Wunderer, 2006; Wunderer & Dick, 2006; Wunderer & Kuhn, 1992). Their findings are usually a perfect fit for our empirical results. We frequently integrated their ideas in our reflections. This is not retraced or described in detail here. Besides, we already expressed our appreciation of their contributions before (Weibler & Wunderer, 1997).

5. CONCLUDING COMMENTS

We have tried to draw a picture of the specific Swiss understanding of outstanding and successful leadership, and have made use of several sources and perspectives. Some findings result in quite distinct silhouettes, which have been yielded independently by other researchers in the same way. There is clear evidence for an influence of culture, particularly concerning how leadership and its context are understood.

---

[38]Compare also our findings from the interviews and the questionnaire data mentioned earlier.

Switzerland's strategic situation in the heart of Europe has always catapulted this country into a socioeconomical role that usually only big countries can play. Therefore, Switzerland has always needed to find ways to deal with powerful nations without having the means to defend itself.

The ideal Swiss culture is characterized by a strong orientation toward performance and people. Behavior Should Be clearly orientated toward the needs of the group without, however, surrendering individuality in favor of the collective. It is a culture in which, ideally, living and thinking are orientated toward a planned future. This includes the willingness to abstain from short-term hedonistic desires. In this ideal culture, stereotype male and female patterns of thought and behavior both tend to play an important part. The Swiss desire a culture that does not overweight the importance of assertiveness. They like a culture that is not drowned by excessive formalism, rules, and regulations and in which ostentation and the exertion of illegitimate power is not highly appreciated. By an international comparison, in particular, perceived reality in Switzerland reveals serious differences in interpersonal relations that are experienced as an excessive power distance, an overly masculine orientation of society as a whole and, above all, a perception of society as being dramatically overregulated. The latter one is concomitant with distinctive safeguarding behavior (Uncertainty Avoidance). This gap between aspired and actual culture shows a potential conflict that will enhance the probability for changes in Swiss society in the future.

Practical Implications

Whether modifications in the leadership behavior are likewise probable cannot be illuminated by our study. We were interested in the expectations middle managers have about outstanding leaders and how these relate to the cultural peculiarities in Switzerland. Knowledge about similarities and differences to other cultures "can help the parties at ease" (Javidan, Stahl, Brodbeck, & Wilderom, 2005, p. 72). Swiss leaders as well as expatriates can play a proactive and constructive role in shaping a leadership relation.

Outstanding leadership can be characterized by three second-order factors, which are labeled as leader types: the Great Leader (particularly charismatic/value-based leadership, including Performance Orientation), the Human Leader (particularly integrity, team orientation), and the Ego Boss (nonparticipative/narcissistic leadership, as an inhibiting factor). From this, behaviors can be derived, that Should Be considered by managers in Swiss enterprises:

Hierarchy as a concept of control is recognized and obeyed, if it is connected to a humane role taking, minor claim for authority, and very low formal distance. An Ego-Boss is not favored. In contrast, transformational leadership in terms of Bass and Steidlmeier (1999) is highly favored, whereby the component of charisma is to be classified ambiguously. Instead, the new discussion about authentic leadership (Avolio & Gardner, 2005) leads to a more appropriate description. Outstanding leadership is accepted only if it is connected with high ability for consent and modest manners. Furthermore, an efficiency-oriented pragmatism is expected. Leaders as positive "learning models" are appreciated.

A close link between the leader and the led is preferred, where leaders do not forget their roots and where leaders are striking for goals and decisions, which are accepted by the followers. Therefore, harmonizing, ideally consensus, is valued often.

An "alpha leadership" (i.e., dominant "headman") comprehension, as can be observed in some cultures, contradicts the general understanding and nature of the Swiss Constitution (here particularly: direct democracy). Therefore "leadership by delegation" is strongly preferred but seldom practiced (cf. Weibler & Wunderer, 1997). Ideas of democratic leadership (Weibler, 2004a), for example, avoiding a know-it-all attitude, information sharing, or discussions without coercion (Weibler, 2004b; Wunderer 2006) are a good path to take in Switzerland.

It is not a contradiction, rather, one of the existing paradoxes in Swiss leadership (at first glance), that hierarchy as an accepted control concept is vivid, too and supported by a social network formation. The small territory of Switzerland, the multiple commitments of the citizens in clubs, training seminars, and so on, as well as the regional roots of citizens, promotes remarkable social networking. In such networks, one learns quickly of the possibilities of multiple encounters in life. Those who are not merged into networks are often isolated. Also in companies, this leads to the creation of visible and reliable connections. Here expectation exists that clear and long-term regulations guarantee equal treatment, justice, and fairness. For this reason, conflicts are carried out rarely in the open. Leaders are well advised to act considerately, not too formally and respectfully.

Limitations

There are certain limitations to generalize our findings. First of all, we cannot speak of Switzerland as a whole, but only for its German-speaking part (which makes up, however, 63.6% of the population, and 71.7% of the resident population). Also, we must concede that the quantitative data comes from the (dominantly male) middle management (maximal 3% to 5% of the workforce) of medium-size and big enterprises in three industries, whereas typical for Switzerland are small-scale companies with a share of over 99%. Except for the banking sector, the investigated industries are not as typical as, for example, insurances, chemistry, and mechanical engineering.

So, our discussion mainly dealt with economic leadership. Even so, we do not think that our interpretation has been merely selective. On the one hand, our reflecting remarks on history, which were used to corroborate the findings, are universally applicable. This is also true for the evaluation of the two realized unobtrusive measurements. Findings by other researchers who conducted surveys involving different types of subjects in the economy are not at variance with our arguments. Even Hofstede's (1980) study, which was carried out more than 30 years ago and was based on data mostly, acquired from employees of one company (IBM) and not from executives, is supported partially by our research (Hofstede, 2001). On the other hand, there are propositions about the values and views of the Swiss population that have been put forward by researchers in other disciplines and go beyond the economic sector, thus providing our results with a wider basis than a mere first impression would suggest. In our opinion, we have therefore offered a well-founded interpretation, which can be examined and put in a more concrete form by other researchers.

Future Research

The objective of the analysis of outstanding leadership was twofold: to acquire scientific knowledge and to determine the importance of leadership prototypes in order to enable people to lead effectively in a country. With this the question arises another: whether leaders who conform to cultural values and standards are able to change factors of successful leadership, such as performance, satisfaction, loyalty, and motivation; and if they are, to what extent (Wunderer, 2006). This also concerns the evaluation of the relative importance of societal culture compared to other variables. The GLOBE study will hopefully present further insights on this in the near future.

We further recognize that there are conceptual schemas of leadership (House et al., 1999, 2004), which do not differ very much anywhere in the world. This means that the idea of a Global Leader acquires a "gestalt." This is a very interesting result regarding the globalization of the economy. And Switzerland has much to say on this point. Following a recent survey on this field it ranks worldwide 2 (after Singapore) in globalization, measured by four hard facts (e.g. economic integration via trading or direct investments; Schwarz 2007). Thus, it is evident that special traits and behaviors will produce acceptance and possibly success in many other countries. However, as "prototypes are seldom found in purity" (Brodbeck, Frese, & Javidan, 2002, p. 26) leader behaviors and followers reaction will differ from the ideal in reality. So, leaders will always face uncertainty.

GLOBE was able to answer the "what" questions (integrity, inspirational, performance orientation, etc.). The question as to "how" remains open. Here, we can assume that there are significant differences between countries (how to build trust—e.g., Weibler, 1997b); how to inspire people, how to show Performance Orientation, etc.). However, because we know now what matters most, we are able to evaluate and integrate the rich literature on intercultural communication in a much more focused manner. Likewise, it is now possible to select international leaders based on relevant traits and behaviors, for example, in the course of an assessment center (with respect to more general training efforts; e.g., Kammel & Teichelmann, 1994; Sciuchetti, 1994; Stahl, 1998; Dorfman, Hanges, & Brodbeck, 2004). The following consideration would appear to be very important in this context: Global leadership skills may hardly be acquired by means of training, or only in parts (the global "what" aspect). However, for persons who possess these skills, leadership-training courses make sense because intercultural transfer is then—besides, for instance, empathy and willingness—mainly a cognitive problem that can be solved comparatively easily (the local "how" aspect). Thus, if both these requirements are met successfully and transferred into practice, we can speak of a Global [*sic!*] Leader.

Certainly, after answering the "what" and the "how" questions, one is inclined to inquire about the "why" in even more detail. What are the reasons for the emergence of a specific culture? Here, joint efforts with exponents of other disciplines, such as ethnologists, philosophers, or historians, are necessary to support the answers found so far, to make them more precise, or to revise them.

The philosopher Kohler (University of Zurich, 1996), for instance, regards the Swiss national identity as based on neither ethnic nor linguistic features, but on the will to political unity. The jurist Schindler (University of Zurich, 1995) underlines this by resorting to the shared fundamental political beliefs, which led to the Confederation and are responsible for its durability. According to Kohler, this gave rise to a fundamental susceptibility to interference, which calls for caution and consideration. According to Schindler, the Confederates therefore developed early mechanisms for settling disputes between the cantons. Is this the root of the request for consensus (for ironing things out, finding a compromise) in leadership, too? And is people's traditional participation in the decision making of political leaders in Switzerland's direct democracy, which is unique in Europe (Neidhart, 1995), also the cause for their request for participation in leadership decision making that directly affects the individual? Are the mental reservations about strong leadership, about leadership concentrated in one single person, rooted in history, as we tried to show? Schindler reminds us that the cantons became Confederates to maintain their independence and not to subjugate themselves to a larger unit. Is this an explanation for the reservations about strong leaders, which can also be seen in the rotating position of the president of the Confederation, who has no institutional influence above and beyond that of his or her colleagues and whose period of office is very short? The "cantonal clause"[39] is another example from a different context, namely the idea of federalism, of the limitation of power, which once again symbolizes the virtue of considerateness.

---

[39]The "cantonal clause" of the Federal Constitution provides that only one member of the *Bundesrat,* the federal government, may be elected from any one canton.

Concentration of power in the field of leadership evokes similar reservations, although reality is somewhat different, but the cultural conceptions of what Should Be point in a clear direction.

We are aware that such a macroscopic view cannot embrace all of the details. In case the view becomes more microscopic, increased inconsistencies and paradoxes occur. These inconsistencies and paradoxes led Switzerland during the world exhibition in Sevilla 1992 to present itself under the slogan "La Suisse n'existe pas" (Switzerland doesn't exist) (Altwegg, 2002, p. 41). If this may be a manifestation of an identity crisis on the level of national culture, for the "leadership landscape" of Switzerland this means that general estimations can have their perfidies.

However, the actual function of contributions such as this one is to trigger fundamental reflections, which necessarily cannot measure up to the complexity involved. When all is said and done, we are forced to think our own thoughts and find our own way.

ACKNOWLEDGMENTS

We would like to thank Dr. Petra Dick for her contributions to this study, particularly for her comments on the historical part and her support for the statistical analysis. We also acknowledge our appreciation to Dr. Wendelin Küpers for his comments on an earlier version of this work. Two anonymous reviewers are thanked for their helpful comments.

REFERENCES

Agar, M. H. (1980). *The professional stranger: An informal introduction to ethnography.* San Diego, CA: Academic Press.

Altwegg, J. (2002). Ringsum Feinde [Round about enemies]. *Frankfurter Allgemeine Zeitung, 52,* 41.

Avolio, B. J., & Gardner, W. L. (2005). Authentic leadership development: Getting to the root of positive forms of leadership. *Leadership Quarterly, 16,* 315–338.

Bader, U. (1998, April 15). Zur Legende geworden (Nebelspalter) [Becoming legend] (Bodensee). *Tagblatt,* p. 3.

Bales, R. F., & Slater, P. E. (1955). Role differentiation in small decision-making groups. In T. Parsons & R. F. Bales (Eds.), *Family, socialization, and interaction process* (pp. 259–306). New York: The Free Press.

Bass, B. M. (1985). Leadership: Good, better, best. *Organizational Development, 13,* 26–40.

Bass, B. M. (1990). *Bass & Stogdill's handbook of leadership—Theory, research & managerial applications* (3rd ed.). New York: The Free Press.

Bass, B. M., & Steidlmeier, P. (1999). Ethics, character, and authentic transformational leadership behavior. *Leadership Quarterly, 10,* 181–217.

Bergmann, A. (1986). Management Schweizer Art [Swiss way of management]. *Die Unternehmung, 40,* 289–294.

Bergmann, A. (1990). Nationale Kultur—Unternehmenskultur [National culture—corporate culture]. *Die Unternehmung, 44,* 360–370.

Berthouzoz, R. (1991). Die moralischen Werte [The moral values]. In A. Melich (Ed.), *Die Werte der Schweizer* (pp. 125–165). Bern, Switzerland: Lang.

Brandenburger, A. M., & Nalebuff, B. J. (1996). *Co-opetition.* New York: Doubleday.

Brodbeck, F., Frese, M., & Javidan, M. (2002). Leadership made in Germany: Low on compassion, high on performance. *Academy of Management Executive, 16,* 16–29.

Buckley, P. J. (Ed.). (2000). *Multinational firms, cooperation and competition in the world economy.* Basingstoke, England: Macmillan.

Bundesamt für Statistik. (1998). *Statistisches Jahrbuch der Schweiz.* Zürich, Switzerland: Neue Zürcher Zeitung.

Bundesamt für Statistik. (2005). Retrieved August 25, 2005, from http://www.bfs.admin.ch/bfs/portal/de/index/themen/systemes_d_indicateurs/indicateurs_science/indikatoren.indicator. 20401.html?open=2#2

Bütler, H. (1997, June 4/15). Verunsicherung und politische Führungsschwäche [Uncertainty and political leadership weakness]. *Neue Zürcher Zeitung,* p. 17.

Cavalli, R. (1995, October 4). Wie Prominente zu Strassen kommen. *Schweizer Woche,* 18–22.

Dachler, H. P., & Dyllick, T. (1988). "Machen" und "Kultivieren" [To make and to cultivate]. *Die Unternehmung, 42,* 283–295.

Dorfman, P. W., & Howell, J. P. (1988). Dimensions of national culture and effective leadership patterns: Hofstede revisited. *Advances in International Comparative Management, 3,* 127–150.

Eidgenössisches Departement für Auswärtige Angelegenheiten. (2005). Retrieved August 25, 2005, from http://www.eda.admin.ch/washington_emb/e/home/politic/basics.html

Fahrni, D. (1988). *Schweizer Geschichte. Ein historischer Abriss von den Anfängen bis zur Gegenwart* [Swiss history. A historical survey from the beginnings to present] (4th ed.). Zürich, Switzerland: Edition Pro Helvetia.

Finfacts. (2005). Retrieved August 25, 2005 from http://www.finfacts.com/biz10/globalworldincomepercapita.htm

Frey, B. S., & Kucher, M. (2001). *People pay for power.* Unpublished manuscript, Institute for Empirical Research, University of Zurich, Switzerland.

Gibb, J. R. (1965). Fear and facade: Defensive management. In R. E. Farson (Ed.), *Science and human affairs* (p. 40). Palo Alto: Science & Behavior.

Haire, M., Ghiselli, E. E., & Porter, L. W. (1966). *Managerial thinking: An international study.* New York: Wiley.

HandelsZeitung. (1995). *Top 500, 26,* p. 3ff.

Hanges, P. J., Dickson, M. W., & Sipe, M. T. (2004). In R. J. House, P. J. Hanges, M. Javidan, P. Dorfman, & V. Gupta (Eds.), *Leadership, culture, and organizations: The GLOBE study of 62 societies* (pp. 219–234). Thousand Oaks, CA: Sage.

Hemphill, J. K., & Coons, A. E. (1957). Development of the leader behavior description questionnaire. In R. M. Stogdill, & A. E. Coons (Eds.), *Leader behavior: Its description and measurement* (pp. 6–38). Columbus: Bureau of Business Research. Ohio State University.

Hilb, M., & Wittmann, S. (1992). Switzerland. In C. Brewster, A. Hegewisch, L. Holden, & T. Lockhart (Eds.), *The European human resource management guide* (pp. 524–555). London: Academic Press.

Hodler, B. (1994). Die schweizerische Nahrungsmittelindustrie: Herausforderungen und Chancen. *SWISS FOOD, 16*(12), 5–8.

Höpli, G. F. (1998, July 31). Warum nicht der 12. September? [Why not 12 September?]. *Tagblatt* (Bodensee), p. 2.

Hofstede, G. (1980). *Culture's consequences: International differences in work related values.* Beverly Hills, CA: Sage.

Hofstede, G. (2001). *Culture's consequences: Comparing values, behaviors, and organizations across nations* (2nd ed.). Thousand Oaks, CA: Sage.

Hofstede, G., & Bond, M. H. (1988). The Confucius connection. From cultural roots to economic growths. *Organizational Dynamics, 16,* 4–21.

Hollstein, W. (1989). *Der Schweizer Mann* [The Swiss man]. Zürich, Switzerland: Werd.

House, R. J. (1977). A 1976 theory of charismatic leadership. In J. G. Hunt & L. L. Larson (Eds.), *Leadership. The cutting edge* (pp. 189–207). Carbondale: Southern Illinois University Press.

House, R. J., Hanges, P. J., Javidan, M., Dorfman, P. W., Gupta, V., & Globe Associates. (2004). *Culture, leadership, and organizations: The GLOBE study of 62 societies.* Thousand Oaks, CA: Sage.

House, R. J., Hanges, P. J., & Ruiz-Quintanilla, S. A. (1997). GLOBE. The global leadership and organizational behavior effectiveness research program. *Polish Psychological Bulletin, 28,* 215–254.

House, R. J., Hanges, P. J., Ruiz-Quintanilla, S. A., Dorfmann, P. W., Javidan, M., Dickson, M., et al. (1999). Cultural influences on leadership and organizations: Project GLOBE. In W. Mobley, M. J. Gessner, & V. Arnold (Eds.). *Advances in global leadership 1* (pp. 171–233). Greenwich, CT: JAI.

House, R. J., Wright, N. S., & Aditya, R. N. (1997). Cross-cultural research on organizational leadership. In P. C. Earley & M. Erez (Eds.), *New perspectives on international industrial/organizational psychology* (pp. 535–625). San Francisco: New Lexington Press.

Huber, A. (1988). *Staatskundelexikon* [Encyclopedia of statesmanship] (3rd ed.). Luzern, Switzerland: Keller.

Im Hof, U. (1991a). *Geschichte der Schweiz* (5th ed.). Stuttgart, Germany: Kohlhammer.

Im Hof, U. (1991b). *Mythos Schweiz. Identität—Nation—Geschichte 1291–1991* [Myth Switzerland. Indentity—Nation—History 1291–1991]. Zürich, Switzerland: NZZ.

Jäger, U. (1996). *Sagen und Legenden* [Sagas and legends]. St. Gallen, Switzerland: Seminararbeit Universität St. Gallen.

Javidan, M., & House, R. (2001). Cultural acumen for the global manager: Lessons from project GLOBE. *Organizational Dynamics, 29,* 289–305.

Javidan, M. Stahl, G. K., Brodbeck, F. & Wilderom, C. (2005). Cross-border transfer of knowledge: Cultural lessons from Project GLOBE. *Academy of Management Executive, 19,* 59–76.

Jüstrich, J. (1996). *Das Führerbild in den Schweizer Medien* [The image of leaders in Swiss media]. St. Gallen, Switzerland: Seminararbeit Universität St. Gallen.

Kammel, A., & Teichelmann, D. (1994). *Internationaler Personaleinsatz.* München, Germany: Oldenbourg.

Kanton Zurich. (2005). Retrieved August 25, 2005 from http://www.standort.zh.ch/internet /vd/awa/standort/de/dienste/neuzuzueger.html

Keckeis, P. (Ed.). (1995). *Sagen der Schweiz* [Sagas of Switzerland]. Zürich, Switzerland: Limmat Verlag.

Kipnis, D., Schmidt, S. M., & Wilkinson, I. (1980). Intraorganizational influence tactics: Explorations in getting one's way. *Journal of Applied Psychology, 65,* 440–452.

Kluckhohn, F. R., & Strodtbeck, F. L. (1961). *Variations in value orientations.* New York: HarperCollins.

Kohler, G. (1996, June 8/9). Über Bürgertugend und Patriotismus [Virtues of citizen and patriotism]. *Neue Zürcher Zeitung, 131,* 17.

Krulis-Randa, J. S. (1984). Reflexionen über die Unternehmenskultur [Relections on corporate culture]. *Die Unternehmung, 38,* 358–372.

Kuhn, T., & Weibler, J. (2003). Führungsethik: Notwendigkeit, Ansätze und Vorbedingungen ethikbewusster Mitarbeiterführung [Ethics of leadership: Necessity, approaches, and presuppositions of ethic conscious leadership]. *Die Unternehmung, 57,* 375–392.

Lalive d'Epinay, C. (1991). *Die Schweizer und ihre Arbeit. Von Gewissheiten der Vergangenheit zu Fragen der Zukunft* [Thw Swiss and their work. From the certainties of the past to the questions of the future]. Zürich, Switzerland: Verlag der Fachvereine.

Lord, R. G., & Emrich, C. G. (2001). Thinking outside the box by looking inside the box: Extending the cognitive revolution in leadership research. *Leadership Quarterly, 11,* 551–579.

Lord, R. G., & Maher, K. J. (1991). *Leadership and information processing: Linking perceptions to performance.* Boston: Unwin Hyman.

Margerison, C., & McCann, D. (1985). *How to lead a winning team.* Bradford, England: MCB University Press.

McClelland, D. C. (1961). *The achieving society.* Princeton, NJ: Van Nostrand.

McClelland, D. C. (1985). *Human motivation.* Glenview, IL: Scott-Foresman.

Melich, A. (1991). Nationale Identität [National identity]. In A. Melich (Ed.), *Die Werte der Schweizer* (pp. 1–43). Bern, Switzerland: Lang.

Müller, W. R. (1988). Führungslandschaft Schweiz [The Swiss landscape of leadership]. *Die Unternehmung, 42,* 246–262.

Müller, W. R. (1990). Das Schweizerische Führungsselbstverständnis und seine Wirkungen auf die Wettbewerbsfähigkeit [The Swiss self-conception of leadership and its effects on competitiveness]. *Die Unternehmung, 44,* 371–381.

Neidhart, L. (1970). *Plebiszit und pluralitäre Demokratie* [Plebiscite and pluralistic democracy]. Bern, Switzerland: Francke.

Neidhart, L. (1995, October 7/8). Stimmbeteiligung—Legenden und Realitäten [Polling—Legends and realities]. *Neue Zürcher Zeitung, 233,* 89.

Pfister, T. (1995). Poker mit Einsatz aller Mittel. *HandelsZeitung, 31,* 3.

Pinchot, G. (1985). *Intrapreneuring: Why you don't have to leave the corporation to become an entrepreneur.* New York: Harper&Row.

Provan, K. G., & Milward, H. B. (1995). A preliminary theory of interorganizational network effectiveness: A comparative study of four community mental health systems (pp. 158–184). *Administrative Science Quarterly, 40,* 1–33.

Reber, G., & Jago, A. G. (1997). Festgemauert in der Erde ... Eine Studie zur Veränderung oder Stabilität des Führungsverhaltens von Managern in Deutschland, Frankreich, Österreich, Polen, Tschechien und der Schweiz zwischen 1989 und 1996 ["Firmly bricked in the earth" ... A study about change or stability of leadership behavior of managers in Germany, France, Austria, Poland, Czech Republic, and Switzerland between 1989–1996]. In R. Klimecki, & A. Remer (Eds.), *Personal als Strategie.* Neuwied, Switzerland: Luchterhand.

Reber, G., Jago, A. G., Auer-Rizzi, W., & Szabo, E. (2000). Führungsstile in sieben Ländern Europas— Ein interkultureller Vergleich [Leadership styles in seven European countries—An intercultural comparison]. In E. Regnet & L. M. Hofmann (Eds.), *Personal management in Europa* (pp. 154–173). Göttingen, Germany: Hogrefe.

Reber, G., Jago, A. G., & Bönisch, W. (1993). Interkulturelle Unterschiede im Führungsverhalten [Intercultural differences in leadership behavior]. In M. Haller (Ed.), *Globalisierung der Wirtschaft* (pp. 217–241). Bern, Switzerland: Haupt.

Riklin, A., & Möckli, S. (1983). Werden und Wandel der schweizerischen Staatsidee [Becoming and change of Swiss idea of the state]. In A. Riklin (Ed.), Handbuch Politisches System der Schweiz: Vol. 1. Grundlagen (pp. 9–118). Bern, Switzerland: Haupt.

Roth, C. (1996). *Führerpersönlichkeiten in den Strassen und Denkmälern deutschschweizer Städte* [Leader personalities in the Street names and monuments in Swiss-German cities]. St. Gallen, Switzerland: Seminararbeit Universität St. Gallen.

Salzkorn. (1998, June 2). *Tagblatt* (Bodensee), 1, 7.

Sauser, M. (1998, July 31). Unser Problem mit der Hymne [Our problem with the national anthem]. *Tagblatt* (Bodensee), 5.

Schindler, D. (1995, December 30/31). Die Schweiz unter Veränderungsdruck [Switzerland uder the pressure to change]. *Neue Zürcher Zeitung, 303,* 17.

Schneider, G. (1998). *Vom Sonderfall zum Normalfall: Eine Einführung in die Außenpolitik der Schweiz* [From special to normal case. An introduction to Swiss foreign policy]. Zürich, Switzerland: Pro Helvetia.

Schwarz, G. (2007) Hoher Globalisierungsgrad der Schweiz (High degree of globalization in Switzerland]. Neue Zürcher Zeitung, No. 265, p. 19.

Schweiz bleibt reichstes Land. (1998, October 5). *Tagblatt* (Bodensee), 19.

Schweizerische Bankiervereinigung. (1996). *Der schweizerische Bankensektor: Entwicklung, Struktur und internationale Position* [Swiss banking sector. Development, structure, and international position]. Basel, Switzerland: Author.

Schweizerische Raio- und Fernesehgesellschaft. (1994). *Geschäftsbericht 1994* [Business report 1994]. Bern, Switzerland: Author.

Schweizerische Nationalbank. (Ed.). (1997). *Die Banken in der Schweiz 1996* [The banks in Switzerland 1996]. Zürich, Switzerland: Schweizerische Nationalbank/Zürichsee Zeitschriftenverlag.

Sciuchetti, G.-C. (1994). *Multikulturelle Führungskräfteentwicklung on the job* [Multicultural management development on the job]. Unpublished doctoral dissertation, Universität St. Gallen, Switzerland.

Segesser, J., Sonderegger, C., & Stampfli, M. (Eds.). (1996). *Neues Staatskundelexikon für Politik, Recht, Wirtschaft, Gesellschaft* [Encyclopedia of statesmanship for policy, law, economy, society] (p. 107). Aarau/Zürich, Switzerland: Sauerländer/Sabe.

Shaw, J. B. (1990). A cognitive categorization model for the study of intercultural management. *Academy of Management Review, 15,* 626–645.

Sieber, M. (1984). *Einstellungen und Werthaltungen in der schweizerischen Bevölkerung* [Attitudes and value orientations of the Swiss population]. Sekundäranalysen von Umfragedaten. Bern/Zürich, Switzerland: Schweizerischer Nationalfonds.

Smith, P. B., & Peterson, M. F. (1988). *Leadership, organizations and culture.* London: Sage.

Stamm, H., Arend, M., & Lamprecht, M. (1997, October 18/19). Postkartenimage oder hässliche Schweizer? *Neue Zürcher Zeitung, 242,* 17.

Steyrer, J. (1999). Charisma in Organisationen—Zum Stand der Theorienbildung und empirischen Forschung [Charisma in organizations. State of the art of theory development and empirical research]. In G. Schreyögg & J. Sydow (Eds.), *Führung—neu gesehen, Managementforschung 9.* Berlin: de Gruyter.

Swiss Federal Office of Communication (2002). *Analyse der Preisentwicklung im schweizerischen Telekommunikationsmarkt seit 1998* [Analysis of trend of prices in Swiss telecommunication market since 1998]. Bern, Switzerland: Author.

Swiss Federal Statistical Office. (2003). *Public financing of education* [Press release]. Neuchâtel, Switzerland: Author.

Szabo, E., & Reber, G. (1998). *Culture, organizational practices, and leadership in Austria.* Unpublished manuscript, Linz, Switzerland.

Szabo, E., Reber, G., Weibler, J., Brodbeck, F., & Wunderer, R. (2001). Values and behavior orientation in leadership studies: Reflections based on findings in three German-speaking countries. *The Leadership Quarterly, 12,* 219–244.

Szabo, E., Brodbeck, F., den Hartog, D. N., Reber, G., Weibler, J., & Wunderer, R. (2002). The Germanic Europe cluster: Where employees have a voice. *Journal of World Business, 37,* 55–68.

Triandis, H. C. (1995). *Individualism and collectivism.* Boulder, CO: Westview Press.

Ulrich, H., Probst, G., & Studer, H.-P. (1985). *Werthaltungen von Studenten in der Schweiz* [Value-orientations of Swiss students]. Bern, Switzerland: Haupt.

Webb, E. J., Campbell, D. T., Schwartz, R. D., & Sechrest, L. B. (1999). *Unobtrusive measures.* Thousand Oaks, CA: Sage.

Weber, M. (1972a). Die drei reinen Typen der legitimen Herrschaft. In M. Kunczik (Ed.), *Führung: Theorien und Ergebnisse* [Leadership: Theories and results] (pp. 40–51). Düsseldorf, Germany: Econ.

Weber, M. (1972b). *Wirtschaft und Gesellschaft* (5th ed.). Tübingen, Switzerland: Mohr. (Original work published 1922)

Weibler, J. (1995). Symbolische Führung [Symbolic leadership]. In A. Kieser, G. Reber, & R. Wunderer (Eds.), *Handwörterbuch der Führung* [Handbook of leadership] (2nd ed., pp. 2015–2026). Stuttgart, Germany: Schäffer-Poeschel.

Weibler, J. (1996). Führungslehre—Ursachensuche für die Heterogenität einer Disziplin [Leadership theory—Searching for causes of heterogeneity of a discipline]. In W. Weber (Ed.), *Theoretische Grundlagen der Personalwirtschaftslehre* (pp. 85–219). Wiesbaden, Germany: Gabler.

Weibler, J. (1997a). Unternehmenssteuerung durch charismatische Führungspersönlichkeiten—Anmerkungen zur gegenwärtigen Transformationsdebatte [Management by charismatic leaders]. *Zeitschrift für Führung und Organisation, 66,* 27–32.

Weibler, J. (1997b). Vertrauen und Führung. In R. Klimecki & A. Remer (Eds.), *Personal als Strategie* [Personell as strategy] (pp. 185–214). Neuwied, Switzerland: Luchterhand.

Weibler, J. (1999). Bedeutung der Landeskultur für die Förderung des Mitunternehmertums—Theoretische und empirische Befunde [Significance of national culture for promoting co-intrapreneurship—Theoretical and empirical findings]. In R. Wunderer (Ed.), *Mitarbeiter als Mitunternehmer* (pp. 107–121). Neuwied, Switzerland: Luchterhand.

Weibler, J. (2001). *Personalführung* [Leadership]. München, Germany: Vahlen.

Weibler, J. (2004a). Democratic leadership. In G. R. Goethals, G. Sorenson, & J. R. Burns (Eds.), *The encyclopedia of leadership* (pp. 331–338). Thousand Oaks, CA: Sage.

Weibler, J. (2004b). Discourse ethics. In G. R. Goethals, G. Sorenson, & J. R. Burns (Eds.), *The encyclopedia of leadership* (pp. 340–345). Thousand Oaks, CA: Sage.

Weibler, J., Brodbeck, F., Szabo, E., Reber, G., Wunderer, R., & Moosmann, O. (2000). Führung in kulturverwandten Regionen: Gemeinsamkeiten und Unterschiede bei Führungsidealen in Deutschland, Österreich und der Schweiz [Leadership in culturally akin regions: Commonalities and differences in leadership ideals in Germany, Austria, and Switzerland]. *Die Betriebswirtschaft, 60,* 588–605.

Weibler, J., & Wunderer, R. (1997). Zur Führungskultur der Schweiz [Culture of leadership in Switzerland]. *Die Unternehmung, 51,* 243–272.

Weiss, S. (1946). *Volkskunde der Schweiz* [Folklore of Switzerland]. Zürich, Switzerland: Erlenbach.

Widmaier, S. (1991). *Wertewandel bei Führungskräften und Führungsnachwuchs. Zur Entwicklung einer wertorientierten Unternehmensgestaltung* [Value shift among managers and trainees. Development of a value orientated business management]. Konstanz, Switzerland: Hartung-Gorre.

Widmer, S. (1977). *Illustrierte Geschichte der Schweiz* [Illustrated history of Switzerland] (4th ed.). München, Germany: Beck.

Wunderer, R. (1975). Personalwesen als Wissenschaft [Human resource management as science]. *Personal, 27,* 33–36.

Wunderer, R. (1990). Mitarbeiterführung und Wertewandel [Leadership and shift of values]. In K. Bleicher & P. Gomez (Eds.), *Zukunftsperspektiven der Organisation* (pp. 271–292). Bern, Switzerland: Stämpfli.

Wunderer, R. (1992). Managing the boss—"Führung von unten." *Zeitschrift für Personalforschung, 4,* 287–311.

Wunderer, R. (1995). Kooperative Führung [Cooperative leadership]. In A. Kieser, G. Reber, & R. Wunderer (Eds.), *Handwörterbuch der Führung* (2nd ed., pp. 1369–1386). Stuttgart, Germany: Schäffer-Poeschel.

Wunderer, R. (2001). Employees as "co-intrapreneurs"—a transformation concept. *Leadership and Organization Development Journal, 22,* 193–211.

Wunderer, R. (2006). *Führung und Zusammenarbeit* [Leadership and co-operation]. (6th ed.). Müchen, Germany: Luchterhand.

Wunderer, R., & Dick, P. (1997). *Frauen im Management* [Women in management]. Neuwied, Switzerland: Luchterhand.

Wunderer, R., & Dick, P. (2006). Personal management—Quo vadis? Analysen und Prognosen bis 2010, 4th. ed., Münch 2006 (HRM—Quo vadis? Analyses and prognoses)

Wunderer, R., & Grunwald, W. (1980). *Führungslehre: I. Grundlagen der Führung* [Leadership: I. Basics of leadership]. Berlin: de Gruyter.

Wunderer, R., & Kuhn, T. (1992). *Zukunftstrends in der Personalarbeit. Schweizerisches Personalmanagement 2000* [Future trends in HRM. Swiss HRM 2000]. Bern, Switzerland: Haupt.

Wunderer, R., & Weibler, J. (1992). Vertikale und laterale Einflußstrategien [Vertical and lateral influencing strategies]. *Zeitschrift für Personalforschung, 4,* 515–536.

Wunderer, R., & Weibler, J. (2002). Risikovermeidung und Vorsorge als Schlüssel der schweizerischen Nationalkultur? Eine Bestandsaufnahme und ausgewählte Folgen [Risk aversion and precaution as key of Swiss national culture? State-of-the-art and selected consequences]. In W. Auer-Rizzi, E. Szabo, & C. Innreiter-Moser (Eds.), *Management in einer Welt der Globalisierung und Diversität: Europäische und nordamerikanische Sichtweisen* (pp. 159–178). Stuttgart, Germany: Schäffer-Poeschel.

Yukl, G. A., & Falbe, C. M. (1990). Influence tactics and objectives in upward, downward, and lateral influence attempts. *Journal of Applied Psychology, 75,* 132–140.

Zalesnik, A. (1990). The leadership gap. *Academy of Management Executive, 4,* 7–22.

Appendix A

Factor Analysis Based on 21 Leadership Scales

Initial Eigenvalue	Factor 1	Factor 2	Factor 3	Factor 4
Total	5.657	3.332	1.736	1.235
% of Variance	26.94	15.87	8.27	5.88

Rotated Component Matrix

	Factor 1	Factor 2	Factor 3	Factor 4
Administratively Competent	.297	.217	.417	−.132
Autocratic	−.349	.747	.040	.208
Autonomous	−.011	.222	.165	.296
Charismatic II: Inspirational	.274	−.240	.644	.048
Charismatic III: Self-sacrificial	.114	.040	.169	.373
Charismatic I: Visionary	.163	−.265	.717	.101
Conflict Inducer	.027	.580	.07	.065
Decisive	.126	−.005	.698	.179
Diplomatic	.156	.173	.505	.067
Face Saver	.007	.508	−.153	.054
Humane	.754	−.078	.060	.316
Integrity	.541	−.455	.222	−.057
Malevolent	−.401	.647	−.291	.161
Modesty	.561	−.117	.166	−.030
Nonparticipative	−.283	.665	−.104	.108
Performance Orientation	−.065	−.040	.642	.103
Procedural	.245	.707	−.046	−.185
Self-centered	−.112	.716	−.129	.163
Status-conscious	−.104	.477	.115	−.225
Team I: Collaborative Team-oriented	.661	−.082	.310	.085
Team II: Team Integrator	.191	−.172	.636	.053

Commonalities

Administratively Competent	.33
Autocratic	.73
Autonomous	.16
Charismatic II: Inspirational	.55
Charismatic III: Self-sacrificial	.18
Charismatic I: Visionary	.62
Conflict Inducer	.35
Decisive	.54
Diplomatic	.31
Face Saver	.28
Humane	.68
Integrity	.55
Malevolent	.69
Modesty	.36
Nonparticipative	.55
Performance Orientation	.43
Procedural	.60
Self-centered	.57
Status-conscious	.30
Team I: Collaborative Team-oriented	.55
Team II: Team Integrator	.47

Note. Maximum likelihood, Kaiser rotation.

Appendix B

Reliabilities of the Leadership Scales (Switzerland)

Scale	Alpha
Administratively Competent	.66
Autocratic	.79
Autonomous	.53
Charismatic I: Visionary	.76
Charismatic II: Inspirational	.70
Charismatic III: Self-sacrificial	−.11
Conflict Inducer	.30
Decisive	.42
Diplomatic	.16
Face Saver	.34
Humane	.48
Integrity	.77
Malevolent	.73
Modesty	.51
Nonparticipative	.59
Performance Orientation	.57
Procedural	.71
Self-centered	.57
Status-conscious	.63
Team I: Collaborative Team-oriented	.53
Team II: Team Integrator	.35

Appendix C

Forced Three-Factor Solution Based on 21 Leadership Scales

Initial Eigenvalues	Factor 1	Factor 2	Factor 3
Total	5.657	3.332	1.736
% of Variance	28.94	15.87	8.27

Rotated Component Matrix

Leadership Scales	Factor 1	Factor 2	Factor 3
Administratively Competent	.295	.161	.381
Autocratic	−.325	.780	.081
Autonomous	.008	.263	.210
Charismatic II: Inspirational	.276	−.257	.639
Charismatic III: Self-sacrificial	.130	.093	.225
Charismatic I: Visionary	.152	−.277	.727
Conflict Inducer	−.006	.583	.083
Decisive	.130	−.003	.717
Diplomatic	.170	.164	.506
Face Saver	.025	.516	−.138
Humane	.700	−.063	.124
Integrity	.541	−.479	.199
Malevolent	−.374	.688	−.253
Modesty	.565	−.140	.152
Nonparticipative	−.256	.688	−.080
Performance Orientation	−.076	−.047	.657
Procedural	.228	.633	−.067
Self-centered	.082	.743	−.096
Status-conscious	−.088	.427	.070
Team I: Collaborative Team-oriented	.677	−.092	.313
Team II: Team Integrator	.197	−.186	.631

Note: Maximum likelihood, Kaiser rotation.

Commonalities

Administratively competent	.33
Autocratic	.65
Autonomous	.19
Charismatic II: Inspirational	.52
Charismatic III: Self-sacrificial	.15
Charismatic I: Visionary	.55
Conflict Inducer	.33
Decisive	.47
Diplomatic	.36
Face Saver	.36
Humane	.45
Integrity	.55
Malevolent	.66
Modesty	.34
Nonparticipative	.53
Performance Orientation	.38
Procedural	.46
Self-centered	.55
Status-conscious	.29
Team I: Collaborative Team-oriented	.50
Team II: Team Integrator	.44

III

ANGLO CLUSTER

The Anglo cluster in the GLOBE Research Program consisted of Australia, Canada (English speaking), England, Ireland, New Zealand, South Africa (White sample), and the United States. All of these countries except Canada are represented in this volume with the chapter on South Africa also representing the Sub-Saharan cluster.

The Anglo cluster scored high on Performance Orientation. It was in the midscore range for Assertiveness, Future Orientation, Gender Egalitarianism, Humane Orientation, Institutional Collectivism, Power Distance, and Uncertainty Avoidance. The only cultural dimension it scored low was on In-Group Collectivism. (House et al., 2004).

The Anglo cluster endorsed Charismatic/Value-based leadership very strongly, the highest of all clusters. It also endorsed Team Oriented leadership and elements of Participative leadership enacted in Humane Oriented manner quite strongly. Self-Protective behaviors were viewed rather negatively. A "person oriented" leadership is endorsed in all Anglo countries where a leader is expected to deliver results by operating as a part of a team or a clan. However, there are significant differences among countries in how the leaders are expected to achieve this. In England, for example, a consultative and informed approach is preferred whereas in Ireland a leader is expected to uphold values with integrity, loyalty, and conceptual decision making without flaunting his or her authority. In both Australia and New Zealand, "tall poppies" usually get cut down. A leader in Australia needs to be seen as "one of the boys" and be highly egalitarian. A strong autocratic leader seems preferable in New Zealand to a sensitive facilitator. The United States seems to prefer the "heroic" leader, promoting team spirit and also caring about people. The White population of South Africa seems to prefer strong, direct, fair, and firm leaders.

This cluster is a very interesting example of culture overcoming geographical distances as it is based on ethnic and linguistic similarities and old migration patterns, among other factors. It is often said that the cultural distance between England and France or Germany is much higher than that between England and Australia. This also reflects after-effects of colonization.

REFERENCES

House, R. J., Hanges, P. J., Javidan, M., Dorfman, P. W., Gupta, V., & GLOBE Associates. (2004). *Culture, leadership, and organizations: The GLOBE study of 62 societies.* Thousand Oaks, CA: Sage.

9

The Australian Enigma

Neal M. Ashkanasy
The University of Queensland, Australia

1. ABSTRACT

This chapter provides an analysis of Australian culture and leadership at societal and industry levels. The chapter is based on the results of the author's participation in the GLOBE project (cf. House et al., 2004), but interpretations are supplemented by reference to the extant historical and anthropological literature and interviews with key experts in these fields. The analysis of leadership was supplemented with analysis of text-based media. Results present Australian culture and leadership as an enigma, full of contradiction and change. For instance, Australians have traditionally valued egalitarianism, "mateship," and "a fair go," but have a history of discrimination that belies this image; and Australians see themselves as egalitarian, but seem also to value individual rewards. The GLOBE results support this view, but also indicate that Australian national culture is strongly performance oriented. Australian leaders reflect the enigma, supporting the GLOBE hypothesis that leadership is derived from implicit theories derived from societal culture. Thus, effective Australian leaders must be inspirational, but at the same time must not be seen to be too charismatic. They must be performance oriented, but still must be "one of the boys."

2. THE AUSTRALIAN ENIGMA

Australian culture and leadership provides a fascinating study, full of contradictions and change. In this chapter, I provide an overview of culture and leadership in Australian society, together with a closer look at culture and leadership in two Australian industries: telecommunications and finance. Using anthropological, historical, and industrial literature, I discuss prominent themes in Australian societal and industry cultural development in the context of the Australian results from the GLOBE study, supplemented with other relevant data.

This chapter deals first with societal-level analysis, and then with the industry-level data. In addition, the two foci of the GLOBE study, culture and leadership, are discussed separately, although I recognize that the two processes are inextricably linked. Leadership is born out of and plays a part in maintaining culture (Schein, 1992). The links between culture and leadership are therefore highlighted where possible. The first section describes the Australian society, beginning with an outline of Australian history, economy, and society. The nine cultural dimensions of the GLOBE project are then discussed, together with interview data from experts in the field of anthropology and economic history. The next section, dealing with societal leadership, begins with a review of recent Australian research on leadership, followed by an analysis of two notable Australian prime ministers: Sir Robert Menzies and Robert Hawke. This section ends with a discussion of the results of the GLOBE survey in the context of data obtained from a national media analysis. Discussion of industry-level results for the Australian telecommunications and finance industries completes the chapter.

3. SOCIETAL CULTURE

When presenting an overview of Australian society, one cannot help but be struck by the apparent contradictions that riddle Australian culture: the most sparsely populated inhabited continent on Earth, yet one of the most urbanized societies; a pluralist nation, but with a history of restrictive immigration; a humane, democratic developed country, but with a history of persecution of its Aboriginal people; an island physically distanced from its British and Irish heritage, but historically distinct from its Pacific neighbors. The short but filled history of Australia since European settlement in 1788 appears as complex and conflicting as the current diversity of its society. The Australian national identity is a complex entity, and different aspects of it have been expressed throughout its modern life (see Melleuish, 1996).

One of the most recurring themes of Australian culture, and of the present chapter, is the concept of *egalitarianism,* which has been proposed by Thompson (1994) as fundamental to the self-concept of Australians. According to Thompson, Australian egalitarianism has at least two components: sameness and equality. The notion of sameness rests on the belief that Australians are racially and culturally homogeneous. This has had the dual effect of engendering simultaneously a suspicion of differences and promotion of an illusion of tolerance and acceptance. Once people have been deemed "Australian," they are "one of us" (see national media analysis). Equality refers to a belief in equality of access for all Australians. For example, the belief that anyone can have their own home is very important to Australians, although Thompson, in her book on the phenomena of egalitarianism and all its contradictions in Australian society, proposes that this belief is changing from an expectation to an aspiration in contemporary Australia. Reflecting the "enigma," however, Thompson notes that Australian egalitarian values are balanced by the widespread use of individual rewards across most sectors of the Australian economy.

Australian Pre- and Early-Settlement History[1]

The indigenous population of Australia, arguably the oldest continent in the world geologically, is the Aborigines. It is estimated that human habitation in Australia commenced some 40,000 to 60,000 years before British settlement, although the current Aboriginal race appears

---

[1]This section was largely based on interview with key figures in the anthropology and history disciplines. Where appropriate, data have been source from he Microsoft *Encarta Encyclopaedia,* 1996, World English Edition.

to have migrated to Australia between 20,000 and 60,000 years ago. They eventually came to inhabit every part of the (mostly arid) continent, and lived a technologically and economically simple, but socially complex, life. At the time of European settlement, there were somewhere between 300,000 and 1 million Aborigines living in Australia.

On January 26, 1788, the First Fleet landed at Port Jackson, bringing the first transportation of British and Irish convicts. This event marked the beginning of European settlement of Australia and the start of its modern history. January 26 is celebrated as Australia's National Day.[2] It is also marked as the beginning of a disastrous period for the Aborigines, culminating in their virtual extermination from the island state of Tasmania and the southeast of the mainland. The introduction of diseases and policies further reduced the Aboriginal population (see Stone, 1974). Since the 1950s, the Aboriginal population has recovered to near the number at settlement, although most Aborigines today are of mixed race.

Transportation of convicts continued until the mid-19th century. During this time, the free settlers and emancipated convicts did not settle easily together. This was exacerbated when the colonial governor of the time, Lachlan Macquarie, began to appoint exconvicts to positions of authority. The disquiet surrounding these appointments had a profound effect on the society, but is cited as a source of the nondeferential egalitarianism, which characterizes modern Australia. These appointments meant an individual's past and familial heritage were effectively to be forgotten (Thompson, 1994). Other emancipists were given land grants that had the effect of gradually expanding the colonies. During this period, there were also rapid changes that set the foundations for Australia's development: The colonies, later to become states, achieved distinct identities; large-scale grazing was expanded into the interior; and gold and other minerals were discovered.

In summary, the scene was set for the *Australian enigma* in the earliest days of European settlement. On one hand, Australia's indigenous inhabitants were subject to discrimination and near-extinction; on the other, convicts and free settlers from Britain and Ireland forged a spirit of egalitarianism out of the necessity to survive in a harsh and remote environment.

Government and Politics

The federation of Australia, marking the uniting of the six original colonies under a national flag, was achieved in 1901. The culmination of several decades of change and political maturity, the process was nevertheless peaceful and gradual. The 1901 Constitution, which underpins modern Australia, is based on British parliamentary traditions, but also contains elements of the U.S. system.[3] In particular, a Senate ensures state representation. Australia is now a federal parliamentary democracy with six independent self-governing states and two territories. It is currently a member of the British Commonwealth of Nations, and has British sovereign as head of state. Despite strong moves to achieve republican status, it appears unlikely that Australia will become a republic in the near future.[4]

The political parties in contemporary Australia are the descendants of those that were formed soon after federation (Graetz & McAllister, 1994). The Australian Labour Party

---

[2]This is despite the fact that Australian federation actually took place on January 1, 1901.

[3]The Australian Constitution has proved remarkably difficult to amend, requiring both a majority of the voting population and a majority of the six states. One of the more notable changes to the Constitution was in 1967, when it was amended to give recognition to the Aboriginal population (Clarke, 1992).

[4]Following a constitutional convention in February 1998, a referendum on a republican model was conducted, and was defeated.

(ALP) has dominated the political left, whereas the conservative side of politics has been represented by a variety of parties, consisting, since the 1940s, of a coalition of the city-based Liberal Party[5] and the rural-based National Party. The social-class basis underlying the distinction between the two arms of the political system in Australia is similar to that of Britain: Labour's base of support issuing from the working class; and the Coalition's from a coalition of city-based middle class and country-based graziers and farmers. In particular, support from Australia's strong trade union movement has contributed to the ALP being the dominant party for much of the century. Since the Second World War, however, the two main parties have been steadily becoming less distinct, which, combined with a national trait of distrust of politics and politicians, has rendered contemporary Australia an essentially cohesive, but conservative, society in which control of wealth is the driving force of politics (Graetz & McAllister, 1994). The media analysis conducted as a part of the present study (see later discussion), however, indicates that there are feelings that a more fundamental political philosophy may be needed in Australia to guide it through into the 21st century.

Economy[6]

Although an industrialized nation with a high standard of living, Australia's trade profile—Australia predominantly exports primary products and imports manufactured goods—in many respects resembles that of a developing nation. The economy is therefore particularly vulnerable to inflation and commodity price fluctuations (see M. T. Jones, 1990). Nevertheless, the makeup of the Australian domestic economy has changed substantially since World War II. Agriculture and mining now play a less central role, and have been largely displaced by manufacturing and, more recently, service industries. Financial services rival the extractive industries as the most important economic sector, whereas tourism and education have flourished since the 1980s. Strangely, though Australia is an archetypal industrial/urbanized nation, the image of Australians as tough and silent farmers is still widely maintained and promulgated (Warwick & Scales, 1996).

Australia as a Pluralist Society

Australia is now widely regarded as a multicultural, tolerant, and pluralist society (Jupp, 1996), despite the fact that, for most of the time since federation, the history of Australian immigration has been actively biased against non-Europeans. A discriminatory "White Australia" policy was effective until 1966, and the multicultural aspect of modern Australia has not been easily achieved (Jupp, 1996).

The drive for immigration in Australia has consistently followed the need to expand Australia's relatively small population, with the admonition "populate or perish." Transportation of convicts from Britain and Ireland remained the main source of immigration for the first 50 years of European settlement until free settlers gradually achieved majority status. The gold rush of the 1850s saw the arrival of the first significant wave of non-British/Irish immigrants. In general, however, these newly arrived cultural groups were similar in background to the original settlers, so that ethnic conflicts, although present, were not significant. A notable exception, however, was resentment toward the Chinese, which

---

[5]Despite its name, the Australian Liberal Party, founded by conservative leader Robert Menzies after the Second World War, is inherently in the mold of the British Tories.

[6]Source: *Microsoft Encarta Encyclopaedia,* 1996. World English Edition.

would at times erupt into violence on the gold fields in the late 1800s, and with whom distinctions were almost certainly made based on race (Thompson, 1994). Seemingly in contradiction to these first incidents of racism, nonetheless, the gold rush had the impact of ensuring wide accessibility to wealth across the small population, and thereby acted simultaneously to reinforce the egalitarian side of Australian society (Serle, 1963; Thompson, 1994).

Despite these periods of population growth, Australia continued to experience labor shortages. Consequently, from the mid- to late 19th century, assisted immigration schemes were put in place, which were still bringing British immigrants a hundred years later. Concern about non-European immigration directed most of Australia's immigration policies: most notoriously with the introduction of the White Australia Policy through the Immigration Restriction Act at federation. This policy explicitly aimed to assist and to encourage British settlement; to discourage other Europeans; and to exclude all non-Whites (Jupp, 1996). A shift in policy after World War II, fueled by the need to expand the population and a view that insufficient numbers of immigrants were arriving from the preferred British Isles, retained the exclusion on non-Whites but did mark the first significant number of non-English-speaking immigrants. This process accelerated with the repatriation of large numbers of European refugees from World War II (Jupp, 1996).

The White Australia Policy was finally lifted in 1966, and non-White immigration began in earnest in the 1970s. The makeup of contemporary Australia was then established. In particular, Asian immigration increased rapidly, and Asians now represent a significant portion of the Australian population. Statistics from the 1991 census show that Australia's population of 18 million represents people from over 160 countries (Costa, 1996), 21% born overseas, and over 50% of non-British backgrounds.[7] The ramifications of these shifts in immigration reflected a generation that was coming to terms with its racial past. Notably, there has been a recent awareness of the validity of Aboriginal culture and concerns and, like other countries with a history of colonization, for the government to address past treatment (NAC/UNESCO, 1973). In particular, critical High Court judgments in 1992 and 1996 have finally recognized Aboriginal land rights.[8] There has been a recent backlash against Asian immigration and Aboriginal welfare by vocal sectors of the society.[9]

Relationships with Other Countries

Despite the early evolution of a distinct national culture, and governmental moves to foster national development, Australians have traditionally tended to relate closely to their colonial identity and to focus on their geographically distant British and Irish heritage. This has left Australia culturally detached, even estranged, from its Asian neighbors.

---

[7]Source: Australian Bureau of Immigration, Multicultural and Population Research. (1996). *Overseas born.* Canberra: Australian Government Publishing Service.

[8]The High Court is Australia's Constitutional Court. In 1992, the "Mabo" decision established for the first time the legitimacy of Aboriginal land rights.

[9]Although there have been other advocates for reduced immigration, on of the most talked about politicians at the time of writing was Pauline Hanson, the leader of the One Nation Party, which launched the nation into a divided debate on immigration and Aboriginal welfare. Originally, a member of the Liberal Party, Pauline Hanson was expelled from the party in 1996 and won her seat as an independent candidate. She then formed the One Nation Party, which was briefly the third most popular party in the country and the leading minor party (Bulletin, July 29, 1997). The party's policies on reducing immigration and welfare benefits distributed on race have provoked criticism internationally (Reuters, July 21, 1997) and bitter disputes and rallies nationally.

The British connection prompted Australia's early entry into two world wars. In World War I, Australia suffered per capita casualty rates higher than that of most other countries, but gained an enduring image of national identity with the heroism of the "ANZACs."[10] At this time, the British heritage was still the driving force of Australia's international relations and the attachment between the countries was strong. World War II had different ramifications however. The absence of British aid during the Pacific War and the threat of Japanese invasion saw Australia establish an important alliance with America. The postwar era saw maintenance of a sentimental attachment to Britain, although international relations began to be more oriented toward the Pacific and America, culminating in participation in the Vietnam War as an American ally, and Prime Minister Holt's proclamation in 1969 of "All the way with LBJ!"

Today, there is more awareness of Australia as a nation. It is seen to be emerging from the time when the political, social, and economic development of the country was closely tied to that of Britain and America, to one where national events and achievements are given more prominence (Mackay, 1993). In its newfound independence, Australia is finally turning toward neighboring Asia for its economic development (Mackay, 1993). In this respect, Australia has been significantly affected by the Asian economic downturn of 1997.

Nonetheless, Australians continue to value their colonial identity and to see their political origins in geographically distant Britain and Ireland. This trend continues, despite the ongoing evolution of a distinct national culture, and governmental moves to foster a unique national perspective. For instance, Australians in 1999 rejected a referendum on a republican model that would have cut their last constitutional links with Britain. This has had the effect of further isolating Australia culturally from its Asian neighbors.

In summary, Australia is a nation with a relatively short history as a modern civilization, and continues to be in a state of flux. An egalitarian spirit characterizes the country, although this is contrasted against a history of active discrimination. Australia, by the beginning of the Second Millennium however, has become a pluralist society, and this trend can be expected to continue once Australia finally cuts its constitutional ties with Britain.

Australian Culture: Quantitative Results From the GLOBE Study

The societal-level results for Australia from the GLOBE study are presented in Table 9.1. These results include Australia's ranking on each of the three assessments and the difference between these measures. Following presentation of these results is a discussion and interpretation of findings, based on interviews with three experts in Australian society, from the areas of economic history, commerce, and culture.[11] These interviews involved presenting the quantitative results from the project to each interviewee, and asking for their views and theories to provide a context for interpretation of the GLOBE data. There was considerable overlap in

---

[10]The *Australian and New Zealand Army Corp.* During World War I, these soldiers suffered immense casualties at Gallipoli, Turkey, and their heroism is marked by a national memorial day. Accompanying the image of bravery is that of soldiers who refused to give deference to (often British) officers unless they had earned it, a symbol of the egalitarian nation (Thompson, 1994). Today, people of all ages join the parades and attend dawn services across the country on the public holiday devoted to the remembrance of the ANZAC's landing at Gallipoli, Turkey, on April 25, 1915. Contemporary celebrations of ANZAC Day, however, which saw resurgence in the early 1990s, have more to do with a desire to recognize Australia's heritage and identity than to remember Gallipoli (Mackay, 1993).

[11]Two of the three experts are Australian by birth, with Anglo-Saxon backgrounds. The third arrived in Australia 3 years ago from Germany and has specialized in German–Australian cross-cultural business.

TABLE 9.1
Australian Societal Culture Scores and Rankings for the Nine Cultural Dimensions

Dimension	"As Is" Score[a]	Rank[b]	"Should Be" Score[a]	Rank[b]	Difference Score[c]
Performance Orientation	4.36	16	5.89	38	1.53
Uncertainty Avoidance	4.39	19	3.98	51	−0.41
Future Orientation	4.09	19	5.15	49	1.06
Humane Orientation	4.28	21	5.58	19	1.30
Institutional Collectivism	4.29	28	4.40	42	0.11
In-Group Collectivism	4.17	52	5.75	26	1.58
Gender Egalitarianism	3.40	30	5.02	8	1.62
Assertiveness	4.28	22	3.81	25	−0.47
Power Distance	4.74	53	2.78	25	−1.96

Note. $N = 144$. [a]Items were rated on a Likert-type scale from 1 (very low) to 7 (very high). [b]Ranks are out of the 61 countries that participated in the GLOBE study and have results available for these dimensions. [c]Difference is "Should Be" score minus "As Is" score.

the information obtained, so that the views presented here represent an integration of the interviews.

Performance Orientation. The quantitative results indicate that compared to other countries, Australia rates high in the GLOBE study on this dimension. Furthermore, Australians aspire to even higher levels of performance, although not so much as many of the other countries in the GLOBE study.

The Performance Orientation of Australians can be understood from a historical perspective. Despite the image of Australia as an egalitarian nation, there is nonetheless considerable evidence that a coexisting class system, based on wealth and reward, has existed in Australian society throughout its history (Thompson, 1994). Performance Orientation, as expressed by wealth and material gain, is therefore well established.

Most recently, there has been another development of the Performance Orientation of Australia. Emerging Australian nationalism has led to an increased awareness of a need to achieve, and to contribute to, the success of Australia as a nation (Mackay, 1993). Economic structures have been put in place to reward individuals more for high achievement. For example, Australia has become a strong advocate for removing international trade barriers, and has significantly reduced its own tariffs, many of them in place since federation. This is illustrative of confidence in the ability of Australians to compete successfully in the world market.

Although high on present Performance Orientation, Australians do not seem to want this level to increase as much as many other countries. This may be viewed as an interaction of the idealism of the country and its belief in fair play (see later discussion), with a history which has kept away some of the harsher realities of economy. Australians live on an isolated island continent, and are used to wealth and a high standard of living, largely generated from the land. This is quite different from the reality that 97% of Australians live in large cities. The majority of the population, therefore, may not feel the more dire warnings about the vulnerability of the Australian economy, especially to international commodity price fluctuations. It seems that the mentality of the "lucky country" (Horne, 1965) persists (see Mackay, 1993).

Uncertainty Avoidance.   The results of the GLOBE study indicate that Australians feel that their society ought to take more risks. This result may reflect the present recognition that Australia needs to change to achieve more as a nation although, historically, Australia has preferred a risk-aversive strategy (White, 1992). Notable agendas for Australia have been to imbue the society with security both from other countries (e.g., restriction of immigration from specific cultures and protection against imports through tariffs) and within the nation itself (e.g., minimum wages, welfare, and other mechanisms designed to control volatility and reduce dissatisfaction). Similarly, as Mackay (1993; see also Karpin, 1995) notes, business sectors of Australian society have a history of not being prepared to invest in risky or innovative ventures. Consequently, innovative ideas generated in Australia often need to be exported for the realization of their potential. With the move toward service sectors and the need to compete internationally, however, it may well be that the previous complacency of Australia needs to change.

Future Orientation.   Australia's Future Orientation results show a similar pattern to its Performance Orientation. Australians would like to see more Future Orientation than is currently happening, but this discrepancy does not indicate too much dissatisfaction with the present state. The level of Future Orientation is lower than that of Performance Orientation, despite the similar rankings of these results compared to other countries.

These results indicate that the traditional emphasis placed by Australians on future planning is not as strong as it has been historically. In the past, Australia has had a political agenda based on preparing for the future, with policies focusing on protection against perceived threats of invasion, protection against internal disturbances through minimum wages, and a goal of increasing growth through tariffs. Such "nation building" has been an identifiable policy since the turn of the century, especially since World War II (Clarke, 1992).

With the changing nature of Australian society and its place in the international arena, however, these policies have largely been overturned. The current move has seen a push to remove the infrastructure previously so enthusiastically embraced. Instead, the traditional "planning" mechanisms are now seen as obstacles to a nation that is open to global market forces. On an individual level, Mackay (1993) has argued that Australians have lost their strong Future Orientation in their preoccupation with coping with all the myriad changes in the present society. These changes include a redefinition of gender roles, a high divorce rate, high unemployment, high retail credit, a shrinking middle class, and multiculturalism. They are so endemic, claims Mackay, that there is hardly an institution or a convention of Australian life that has not been subject to revolutionary change in the past two decades.

Humane Orientation.   Australia's moderate results on Humane Orientation may represent another manifestation of the Australian enigma: interplay between historical and recent trends of two extremes of Humane Orientation. One aspect of the Australian heritage is the egalitarian fair nation; the other is the history of exclusion and inhumane treatment of certain sections of society. Similar contradictions have emerged in contemporary history. Thus, whereas general affluence may promote a Humane Orientation, the recent backlash against welfare and immigration suggests another orientation. According to Mackay (1993; see also Horne, 1965), Australians have traditionally been self-congratulatory over their Humane Orientation. The societal safety nets protecting the underprivileged, such as the welfare role of the government, have been enforced by policies and have largely been successful. For instance, it is rare to encounter a beggar in Australia, even in the large cities. Australian vernacular contains prevalent references to this cultural dimension; to be "un-Australian" has connotations of not giving others "a fair go" (Mackay, 1993).

There is another side to the story, however. First, as noted earlier, a perennial blight on the history and development of Australia has been its treatment of Aborigines (see Healey, 1998). There is popular condemnation of the current prime minister's refusal to issue a national apology to the Aboriginal people for their turbulent past and, in particular, for the "stolen generation" of the 1920s to 1950s (the practice of removing children from their natural parents for a "better life" with nonindigenous foster parents). At the same time, many people support the view that reparation is not necessary. Anti-immigration/anti-Aboriginal Welfare movements, and moves to be less liberal with welfare, reflect the feeling that Australia may be too humane as a society, to the detriment of the greater good of the majority. More recently, this view has been reinforced in Australia's treatment of Middle East asylum seekers. Refused entry to the country, they are shipped for status assessment to the tiny Pacific nation of Naru.

Nevertheless, many Australians, particularly professionals and managers (representative of GLOBE respondents), do appear to want their society to be more humane than it is at present.[12] Mackay (1993) has noted that the 1990s have presented a time of unprecedented change in Australian history, and that there is a need now for integrity and caring from our political leaders.

Institutional Collectivism.   Australia's score on this dimension indicates that the country places a moderate level of emphasis on Collectivism, and that, in practice, is fairly close to national values on this dimension. This is in contrast to scores on the In-Group Collectivism dimension (see next subsection), where Australians score relatively low in relation to other countries. These scores would appear to reflect the relatively high levels of social welfare in Australia (see Mackay, 1993).

In-Group Collectivism.   The GLOBE data indicates a low score on the In-Group Collectivism dimension. Like other secular Western nations, Australia has seen a recent trend toward individuals making decisions that focus less on the family unit. For example, decisions not to have children, to marry later, to work from an office rather than home, all have the effect of decreasing the importance of the family in Australian society. Australia has a well-developed welfare system and therefore may be seen to disdain the need to be a collectivist society in order for individuals to survive and thrive (see M. A. Jones, 1996).

The data also indicate that Australia has a relatively wide discrepancy between "As Is" and "Should Be" scores on this dimension. This may reflect popular disquiet about the effect of an individualistic society and an acknowledgment that it carries disadvantages. The divorce rate is higher today than at any other point in Australian history, and unstable marriages mean unstable families (Mackay, 1993). In his analysis of Australian society, Mackay reports that even people in favor of easier divorces find it hard to approve of the instability of family life,

---

[12]Like many developed countries around the world, Australia has become a destination for asylum seekers. The Australian government in 2001, however, instituted a policy of not admitting asylum seekers until after they had obtained refugee status. Letters to the editor in Australia's newspapers in 2001 were heavily in favor of admitting the asylum seekers, in contrast to talk-back radio callers, who supported the government's stand in an election year (see *The Weekend Australian,* September 29–30, 2001, for an analysis of election issues).

and there is widespread community concern about the long-term effect of divorces on children. It appears then that the image of Australia as an ideal country in which to raise a family is now at risk. Moreover, of course, at the other end of the generations, the Australian family unit has never specifically included the extended family members, a situation that is compounded by the increasing mobility of the population and segregation of families through divorce. These factors all contribute to less contact between family members who do not cohabit (Mackay, 1993).

The high difference score for Australia on this dimension may be attributed to a wish to revert to the collectivist underpinnings of egalitarianism that is being lost in the drive toward the individual success of a developed country. Australian's egalitarianism rests on a collectivist approach. Government institutions have traditionally been used to achieve equality for Australians, as manifested by the welfare system, in contrast to the individualistic commitment to equality of opportunity that characterizes America (Thompson, 1994). With recent Australian governmental moves to reduce welfare and encourage small businesses, the still pervasive collectivist notion of egalitarianism may have contributed to the discrepancy between the actual and ideal scores on this dimension.

Gender Egalitarianism.   Despite the popular conception of Australia as a male-orientated culture, the results obtained in the GLOBE study indicate that Australia does not particularly emphasize male roles in society, although, as with almost all other nations, there would ideally be an equal stress placed on male and female roles. On the surface, these results are surprising. Australian language highlights the stereotypes of male "ockers" who once talked about women as "Shielas" and still like to be "one of the boys." Certainly, the tough, male image of rugged farmers is a familiar Australian stereotype (Warwick & Scales, 1996). This image, however, may not be truly representative of contemporary Australian society, or even historically true. Australia, for example, was the second country (after New Zealand) to introduce universal suffrage for women.

This apparent contradiction may be associated with the stereotypical image of Australia as an essentially rural society. In fact, though Australia still relies on primary industry for much of its wealth, it is also one of the most urbanized societies in the world;[13] 90% of the population lives in only 3% of the land area, especially in the major cities along the eastern seaboard. The rural- based masculine stereotypes therefore bear little resemblance to the everyday life of the large majority of Australians.

The trend for an ideally less sexist society is noticeable in Australia, but maybe no more so than in other Western societies. The ideology of successful Western democracies places equal stress on male and female roles, and the results indicate that Australians are following the general trend in this area. For example, since 1990, two women have already achieved the office of state premier.

Assertiveness.   Results in respect of Assertiveness show one of the rare instances of a negative difference between "As Is" and "Should Be" scores. Australians rank relatively highly in terms of "As Is" scores on this dimension, but they do not aspire to more Assertiveness, as represented by the "Should Be" scores. This finding is consistent with the Australian cultural mores discussed earlier, where Assertiveness is seen to be "showing off" or putting oneself ahead of others.

---

[13]Source: *Microsoft Encarta Encyclopaedia,* 1996. World English Edition.

Power Distance.   Relative to other countries, Australia is low on Power Distance. The relatively large negative difference score shows, however, that more stratification exists in society than Australians may consider ideal. Again, there are contradictions evident in the Australian attitudes toward Power Distance. On the one hand, there is the perception of Australia as an egalitarian society, evident in colloquial language, such as the use of the term *mate* as a form of address; and themes and folk heroes in the national literature. Historians believe that "mateship" may be related to the harsh conditions of life for early male settlers, which are assumed to have reinforced a complex mixture of collectivist and egalitarian values, manifest in actions such as loyalty to one's mates, support during crises, sharing, and companionship (Feather, 1986). More recently, Ashkanasy and O'Connor (1997) identified "mateship" as a uniquely Australian dimension of organizational culture.

On the other hand, there is evidence that, in practice, Australian organizations tend to be stratified and hierarchical in structure (Dunphy & Stace, 1990). Given the evidence that Australian society is characterized by a class system based on wealth and materialism (Galvin & West, 1988; Mackay, 1993), this may not be very surprising.

Conclusion.   Results from the GLOBE study in respect of societal culture indicate that Australians see themselves as performance and future orientated, humane, and risk adverse; and also somewhat collectivist and gender egalitarian. The results also reveal that Australians do not see themselves as living in either a highly stratified or a collectivist society in the sense of In-Group Collectivism. Nevertheless, Australians would ideally like to see a trend toward less stratification, more Gender Egalitarianism, more Performance Orientation, and more In-Group Collectivism. Several themes emerge when discussing these results. Notably, the pervasive impact of the egalitarian myth in Australia seems to be often at odds with the reality as revealed in the GLOBE results. Overall, Australians are aware of the need for Australia to adapt to changing economic, cultural, and social environments. Australia appears to be at the brink of change in many of these dimensions, and will need leaders and leadership to make this transition. In the following section, I discuss Australian leadership in the context of the GLOBE results.

4.   LEADERSHIP

Current Australian research in leadership has been motivated by the realization that the country is poised to make some important choices about the future, both politically and economically. In 1995, the Australian government sponsored a major report on leadership and management skills in Australian industry, led by industrialist David Karpin. The resulting report, officially titled "The Report of the Industry Task Force on Leadership and Management Skills," is known colloquially as the "Karpin Report." Although subsequently shelved by the government, the report has nevertheless been described by Clegg and Gray (1996) as probably the world's most comprehensive and recent analysis of leadership and management needs. Central to the report, and the research on which it is based, is the message that Australia needs leaders with a vision for the future to give it an edge in the competition for the world's market share (Sarros, Butchatsky, & Santora, 1996).

Contemporary Australian studies in leadership have identified both transformational and transactional leadership (Bass, 1985; Burns, 1978) as necessary elements in successful organizational development (see Irurita, 1996; Parry, 1996; Parry & Sarros, 1996). Nevertheless, the need for transformational leaders has received particular weight (Dunphy & Stace, 1990;

Lewis, 1996), reflecting Karpin's (1995) call for vision and future orientation. A few studies have indicated distinctive features of transformational leadership in Australia. For example, Sarros et al. (1996) described a related concept, which they termed "breakthrough leadership." This concept stresses innovation and vision, and was developed based on extensive interviews with Australia's top business leaders. The authors noted similarities between Australian executives and their peers in America, Britain, Asia, and Europe, but stressed key differences from the Asian approach to leadership.

Other research has specifically addressed the issue of intercultural differences in transformational leadership between Australian and other cultures. These include studies by Ashkanasy (1997), Parry and Sarros (1996), and Sarros (1992). This work has suggested that transformational leadership in Australia may be distinct from its American counterpart, based on the ubiquitous value placed on equality by Australians (Feather, 1994a, 1994b). Ashkanasy, for example, concluded that, compared to Canadians, Australian leaders are achievement oriented and individualistic, but also value equality.

Studies discussing the distinctive elements of Australian transformational leadership are in the minority. The trend of most Australian studies is to retain variables that are prominent in international research, such as credibility, vision, charisma, communication, decisiveness, role modeling, team building, and collaboration (Parry, 1996). Much of the focus of this research has been on application in the Australian context of internationally grounded research, such as feminization (Clegg & Gray, 1996) and relational models of leadership (e.g., Ashkanasy & Weierter, 1996; Carless, Mann, & Wearing, 1996; Gardiner, Callan, & Terry, 1996).

Outside the area of transformational leadership, Australian research has more strongly emphasized the unique aspects of Australian society relevant to perceptions and development of Australian leaders. Particularly important is the contribution of social psychologist Norman Feather's (1986, 1993, 1994a, 1994b) work on Australian social phenomena, including the notion of the "tall poppy syndrome," defined as a propensity to denigrate high achievers in society. Feather's results suggest that the tall poppy syndrome is prevalent in Australian society, but is dependent on a number of contingency variables. These include the leader's status (Feather, 1994a), perceived deservingness of the leader's achievements (Feather, 1993, 1994b; Feather, Volkmer, & McKee, 1991), responsibility for the leader's fall (Feather, 1993, 1994a, 1994b), and the personal characteristics of those making judgments (Feather, 1994a, 1994b; Feather et al., 1991).

Reflecting the pluralistic aspect of Australia, which features so prominently in current discussions on Australian society, Clegg and Gray (1996) challenge the translation of a strong organizational culture to a unified culture. They suggest instead that Australian leaders need to be able to capitalize on the diversity they have at hand, and that this will lead to innovation. In this case, Australia may have a unique opportunity to utilize its diversity to achieve the type of innovative leadership identified by Karpin (1995) as necessary for the success of Australian industry in the next century.

Another theme in Australian leadership literature has been the perceived need for development of leadership skills. Karpin's report (1995) detailed education and training issues for managers and leaders. Other studies have looked at the role of self-learning and continuous learning in the development and maintenance of leadership skills (e.g., Dickinson, 1996). It has been noted that the degree of reform and change in public administration in Australia renders it essential that leaders continue to learn and update their skills and knowledge. The results of the national media analysis (see later discussion) indicate that the need for reform is pervasive across Australian society.

In conclusion, though Australian leaders have been shown to exhibit some unique characteristics, especially a belief in equality, it is recognized that there is a need for visionary leadership if the nation is to make its way in the global arena (Karpin, 1995). One result of this has been the Australian interest in research based on American models of transformational leadership. A second stream of research has attempted to identify the uniquely Australian aspects of leadership. In particular, the opportunity available to Australian leaders to capitalize on the diversity of the society and to incorporate distinctive aspects of Australian culture, such as the need for equality, presents the key challenge for the future.

Two Eminent Leaders in Australian Society

To illustrate some of the characteristics of leadership in the Australian context, I discuss next two post–World War II political leaders. These brief vignettes illustrate both the nature of Australian attitudes to leadership and, especially, present another example of the Australian enigma.

Australia's history has several heroic figures, but not in the sense that other countries have heroes (Galvin & West, 1988). This is a part of the Australian enigma. The strong leveling tendency among Australians based on their egalitarian and meritocratic heritage has promoted a cynicism about promoting personalities to the status of heroes. Those who have become representative of this national identity, such as Ned Kelly and Peter Lalor,[14] tended to be reviled during their lifetime and seen as antiheroes. The exception lies in sporting heroes, such as Donald Bradman,[15] for whom nationalism is allowed to surface.

Nonetheless, Australia's general reluctance to elevate individuals to heroic status is particularly manifested in the political arena. The cynicism surrounding Australian politics has meant there are no recognizable presidential-style heroes and the most well-known politicians invariably invoke different feelings from different individuals. Politicians are nevertheless among the most influential leaders in Australian society and politics is the area of Australian life most replete with figures of national standing. Throughout Australian history, politics has been the arena for the conversion of statesmen to leaders (Galvin & West, 1988), and the party leader is now an integral part of the political system (Graetz & McAllister, 1994).

Two politicians who achieved close to heroic status in Australian history are Sir Robert Menzies and Robert (Bob) Hawke. Together, these leaders capture some of the anomalies that I argue underlie Australian society and they therefore make interesting study.

Sir Robert Menzies, (prime minister 1939–1941, 1949–1966) was Australia's longest serving leader. A self-made lawyer and political leader, he promoted nationalism and the collective use of the state for economic purposes (Thompson, 1994), and delivered prosperity and stability to Australia (Clarke, 1992). He was also an anglophile who loved luxury and leisure and was dedicated to the British Royal Family. His nationalism revolved around Australia as a colony and he was a fierce defender of its place in the British Commonwealth, rather than a man with great vision for its national future. He was a great orator, and sometimes managed to overturn the traditional two-party rivalry of the Australian system and persuade his opponents that his policies had merit (Galvin & West, 1988).

---

[14]Kelly was a bandit ("bushranger") who achieved national hero status before his hanging in 1880. Lalor, the leader of the "Eureka Stockade" of 1854, Australia's only armed insurgency, later became a respected legislator.

[15]Donald Bradman (1908–2001) was Australia's greatest cricketer during a playing career that stretched from 1929 to 1953. His batting average of 99.94 is considered so famous that "PO Box 9994" is the official post office box number of the Australian Broadcasting Corporation!

Whereas Menzies preferred the "old school tie network" to being "one of the boys" (Thompson, 1994), Bob Hawke was the archetypal Australian male. Australia's second-longest-serving prime minister (1983–1988), he promoted his drinking prowess,[16] male chauvinism, sporting preferences, and union allegiances in a personification of Australian-ness. A populist throughout his term, he gained widespread personal support even while his policies and party were unpopular, and his contemporary popularity eclipses those of most leading figures in Australian history (Galvin & West, 1988). In contrast to Menzies, he had authoritarian tendencies and would often ignore the sensitivities of his party and embark on actions without consultation.

How can one country have had two leaders so disparate and both have captured the public's imagination and support (Thompson, 1994)? I see this as yet another indicator of the Australian enigma; a manifestation of the fundamental contradictions in the "egalitarian" nation that values wealth, but has a disdain for deference and recognizes the need for every individual to find his or her own place in the world.

Australian Leadership: National Media Analysis

As a part of the process of understanding Australian leadership, an analysis was carried out of media reports on leadership during 1996 and 1997. The results of the media analysis are used to aid interpretation of the quantitative results from the GLOBE study as well as revealing other issues discussed here.

The content analyses are proposed to represent espoused values, an assumption supported by recent study of text analysis research (Kabanoff & Holt, 1996; Kabanoff, Waldersee, & Cohen, 1995). An advantage of content analyses is it allows qualitative, indirect observations of organizational values to be combined with the quantification of the data (Kabanoff, 1993), maintaining the multimethod approach of the GLOBE project.

Methodology.   Three collection periods were selected for the national media analysis—May 1996, October 1996, and May 1997. During each period, four print media sources were analyzed for articles pertaining to leadership. These were the national Australian newspaper (*The Australian*), the national financial newspaper (*The Australian Financial Review*), the most popular daily newspaper in the state of Queensland (*The Courier Mail*),[17] and a major business magazine (*Business Review Weekly*). Leaders or leadership did not have to be explicitly labeled in the article, but direct reference of the article to either a person or general characteristic of Australian leadership was necessary. To ensure Australian leadership only was the subject of discussion in the articles, world news, other articles focusing on international events or character, and articles from foreign correspondents were excluded from the analysis. In total, 273 text extracts were selected. During the third collection period, two international raters also scanned the media for leadership references to obtain a measure of validity for the selection of articles. Presented with the same newspapers, their interrater reliability was 84%.

The words or phrases in the selected text extracts that pertained to leaders or leadership were Q-sorted by the two Australian researchers involved in the GLOBE project. A reference could be coded under more than one category if this was appropriate. Codings were then cross-checked by the two researchers to optimize validity. These codings were sorted initially

---

[16]Hawke was listed for many years in the Guinness Book Of Records as the world-record holder for downing a "Yard" (2.5 pints) of beer.
[17]The author is based in Queensland.

into 17 GLOBE leadership dimensions. The remaining extracts were separately categorized into dimensions of uniquely Australian leadership. In effect, these Australian dimensions emerged after controlling for the GLOBE categories.

The GLOBE leadership and Australian leadership models and coding for the text references were then entered into the *Nudist®* program for analysis. This allows for the iterative building and expanding of models during the three separate collection periods. The program also has the capacity to include text selections, referenced at numerous nodes at once, which allows detailed analyses of content in subsequent research.

Results of the Media Analysis.   The results of the media analysis are presented in Tables 9.2 and 9.3. Table 2 shows the frequency of references in respect of the 17 GLOBE dimensions current at the time of the study.[18] Table 9.3 lists the frequency of reference according to the uniquely Australian dimensions (after removing the references based on the GLOBE dimensions). Discussion of these results is incorporated into the dimension-by-dimension results based on the qualitative GLOBE results.

Australian Leadership: GLOBE Dimensions.

The national-level results for perceptions of leadership in Australia from the GLOBE study are presented in Table 9.2, with the results of the media analysis in column 2. The dimensions are presented in descending order of frequency of coding in the media analysis. The GLOBE survey mean scores are given in the third column, with the order of each variable within the GLOBE dimensions listed in column 4. This permits a direct comparison of the two sets of results. The final column in Table 9.2 shows Australia's ranking on each dimension relative to other countries involved in the GLOBE study. The results of the media analysis were used to aid interpretation of the quantitative results from the GLOBE study as well as to reveal other issues warranting discussion.

The national-level GLOBE results for leadership dimensions indicate that effective Australian leaders are seen to be inspirational, of high integrity and vision, as well as being decisive and performance oriented. They are not, however, seen to be self-centered, autocratic, procedural, or face saving. Compared to the scores across the other countries in the GLOBE study, Australian leaders rank high on inspiration, performance orientation, integrity, vision, and humanity. They rank low on being autocratic, procedural, self-centered, administratively competent, and status-conscious. On the surface, this profile appears to be entirely consistent with the portraits of Australian leaders presented earlier, especially with the notion of Australia as a society that values egalitarianism. These characteristics were largely supported in the media analysis, which characterized Australian leaders as decisive, performance

---

[18]Results are presented here in terms of the 17 leadership factors (or dimensions) that were current at the time of the media analysis. The final GLOBE publications refer, however, to 21 leadership factors. As the media analysis reported in this chapter was structured around the original 17-dimension model, I have retained this structure in this chapter. The differences between the 17- and 21-dimension models make no difference to the conclusions that I reach. For reference, the final 21-dimension model differs from the 17-dimension model in a number of ways. First, the Malevolent, Conflict Inducer, and Nonparticipative dimensions have been added. Second, Procedural has been replaced by Administratively Competent, Individualism has been replaced by Autonomous, Equanimity has been replace by Modesty, Face Saving has been replace by Face Saver, Humane Orientation has been replaced by Humane, Bureaucratic has been replaced by Procedural, and Charismatic has been replace by Self-Sacrificial. Last, Collective has been split into two dimensions, Collaborative Team Oriented and Team Integrator.

TABLE 9.2
Leadership Results Comparing Rankings from GLOBE Survey and
National Media Analysis[a]

Leadership Dimension	Frequency of Coding[b]	GLOBE Score	Within country Ranking[c]	GLOBE Ranking[d]
Decisive	73	6.02	5	18
Performance Orientation	58	6.35	3	10
Diplomatic	57	5.56	6	30
Collaborative Team Oriented	56	5.52	7	30
Inspirational	51	6.40	1	7
Integrity	46	6.36	2	12
Visionary	41	6.24	4	14
Autocratic	28	2.28	16	49
Modesty	25	5.09	11	29
Humane	25	5.12	10	15
Face Saver	24	2.67	15	36
Autonomous	23	3.95	12	25
Procedural	20	3.56	14	44
Self-Centered	15	1.91	17	49
Self-Sacrificial	14	5.14	9	20
Administratively Competent	12	5.41	8	53
Status-conscious	8	3.82	13	44

[a]Based on 17-factor model (see Footnote 18). [b]Frequency of coding in media analysis indicates that this dimension either exists or should exist. [c]Rank order of GLOBE variables within the Australian sample. [d]Rank position within the sample of 61 GLOBE countries.

orientated, diplomatic, collaborative team oriented, and inspirational. The media analysis also showed that Australian leaders are rarely described as procedural, self-centered, self-sacrificing, administratively competent, or status-conscious.

There were some contradictory results evident in the media analyses that provide further insights into the Australian enigma. These are in respect to the dimensions of face saving, autocratic leadership, and self-sacrificial. Face saving and autocratic leadership scored low in the GLOBE survey results, but appeared as influential dimensions in the media analysis. By contrast, self-sacrifice scored high in the GLOBE results, but ranked low in the media analysis. An explanation for these contrary findings may once again be found in the enigmatic nature of Australian leaders. It is clear from the earlier discussion that Australians, consistent with their egalitarian image of "mateship," try to avoid criticism and confrontation, and seek to downplay personal qualities. The stories presented in the media typically involve reports of these sorts of antagonistic situations. In this case, it is likely that Australian leaders represented in the media are displaying characteristics that they usually try to avoid. This was also clear from the anecdotal evidence provided in the interviews, where it was suggested that Australian leaders could become tough and aggressive if confrontation does occur. The high scores on decisiveness in both the GLOBE results and the media analysis also bear relevance here, as does the media analysis identification of a tendency toward male characteristics in leaders.

TABLE 9.3
Uniquely Australian Leadership Dimensions from the
National Media Analysis

Dimension	Frequency of Coding
Game Metaphor	12
Mateship	10
Work Ethic	7
Caution	5
Adversarial	5
One of Us	5
Tall Poppy	4
Underdog	4
Pragmatic	2

Another characteristic of Australian leaders was also apparent from a qualitative analysis of the media experts. This was a perception that, whereas many Australian leaders are visionary and inspirational, others seem to have reached their positions of eminence despite a lack of vision and inspirational qualities. One explanation for this result is that the vision of many Australian leaders may be focused on specific problems, rather than on long-term strategic issues. This was especially apparent in the interviews conducted for the present project, where there was agreement that Australian leaders often display vision and inspiration, but usually do so only in respect to short- to medium-term issues. This observation is given credence by Australia's impressive track record in research and development innovations, coupled with a failure in many instances to convert the new technologies into manufacturing success (Mackay, 1993). Similarly, the anecdotal evidence relates examples of leadership distinguished by innovative and often successful solutions to crises, rather than strategic thinking and prediction of future situations that would avoid the crises. Indeed, successful short-term remedies serve to reinforce the idea that leadership involves a focus on short- to medium-term solutions. This idea also links with the historically maintained characterization of Australia as a "lucky country" (Horne, 1965), where the notion of "she'll be right" replaces long-term strategic vision.

In summary, the results of the GLOBE analysis, supported by the national-level media analysis, present effective Australian leaders as people of integrity and vision who are decisive with a strong performance orientation. They tend not to be status-conscious, procedural, or self-centered. Some anomalies between the GLOBE results and the media analysis, however, suggest that Australian leaders can become more aggressive and face saving in confrontational and crisis situations. Overall, Australian leadership appears to be consistent with the picture presented earlier of a society that values egalitarianism and "a fair go" for all, but that lacks a truly long-term future orientation. These themes are taken further in the following analysis of the uniquely Australian dimensions that emerged from the media analysis.

Uniquely Australian Dimensions of Leadership From the Media Analysis

The media analysis revealed nine dimensions of Australian leadership that could not be categorized using the GLOBE dimensions (Table 9.3). Although the frequencies of the Australian dimensions are not as high as the GLOBE dimensions, they indicate distinctly Australian aspects of leadership that are pervasive and referred to in the national media. For example, the four distinctive references to "tall poppies" are over and above those that relate to the syndrome, but can be categorized under the GLOBE dimension of modesty, such as equanimity and lack of pomposity.

The uniquely Australian dimensions break down into three categories: (a) dimensions linked with the traditional Australian concepts of "mateship" and egalitarianism; (b) dimensions linked with leadership and the new work ethic; and (c) dimensions that have surfaced in response to contemporary issues in Australian political leadership.

Traditional Australian Themes.   Four of the unique characteristics can be linked back to the underlying theme of egalitarianism in Australian society: "mateship," "one of us," "tall poppies," and leaders as "underdogs."

This dimension can be conceived as the quintessential expression of egalitarianism (Ashkanasy & O'Connor, 1997; Thompson, 1994), and has already been discussed as an underlying characteristic of Australian societal culture.

This dimension is a more general phrase for the more traditional symbol of Australian culture "just one of the boys," first used in Capper (1853) (cited in Thompson, 1994). Its importance to modern leaders is highlighted by Thompson: "It has such potency that some of those in positions of enormous economic or political power still affect its trappings, drawing on a wellspring of legitimacy not usually available to them" (p. 2). Bob

Hawke's leadership was an outstanding example of this trait. Some examples of the phrases in the media analysis database are as follows:

- *"People are soothed by her [a noted female public figure] limitations, reassured by her inability to articulate. Not for her, the language used by a Prime Minister at the dispatch box. She speaks, instead, from the laundry, the kitchen, the barbecue."*
- *The boy [another well known public figure] … is the man credited with what one colleague describes as "an uncanny sense of what the punters think."*

The extracts coded as indicative of the tall poppy syndrome reflect the deeply rooted nature of this phenomenon, identified by Feather (1994a) and other researchers. The syndrome is often moderated by other Australian characteristics, and reinforces the enigma of Australian leadership. Mackay (1993), for example, has noted that Australians do not necessarily dislike success, and only demonstrate the tall poppy syndrome when success is accompanied by arrogance and any inherent implication of superiority.

Finally, Australians have had a traditional tendency to support the weaker party, especially when that party represents their own position and aspirations (Thompson, 1994). Leaders of the "underdogs" are traditionally seen to display the characteristics of integrity and forbearance that Australians admire and respect (Mackay, 1993).

Work Ethic.   Since the 1970s, unemployment has been a perennial problem in the Australian economy. The unemployed are reviled in the press as "dole bludgers."[19] This negative attitude has become further reinforced with the ongoing breakdown of family life and

---

[19]The term *dole bludger* is derived from *dole,* a reference to the doling out of welfare payments, and *bludger,* a Cockney term for "pimp."

redefinition of gender roles, so that work has become more important to most people (Mackay, 1993). Nevertheless, the harsh reality of structural unemployment has also meant that the traditional source of identity, dignity, structure, and purpose for many people's lives has been taken away. Against this background, leaders are seen to have a special responsibility to address the issue of work (or the lack of it). The specific references in the media excerpts make it clear that this is now an important role of Australian leaders.

Contemporary Australian Leadership.   Finally, and tied together as a group, are themes in Australian leadership that are related to contemporary political life. These include the concepts of pragmatic, cautious, and adversarial leadership, and political "game playing." These aspects of Australian leadership have received media attention under the general rubric of public disenchantment with the lack of distinguishable political philosophies in recent years (Mackay, 1993). In particular, the pragmatic nature of Australian politics appears to have overtaken an ideological basis to such an extent that Mackay, in his analysis of Australian society, coined this "the era of pragmatics politics." It is an era where leadership has more to do with management and reaction to events than with vision, conviction, or deeply rooted philosophies. In addition, pragmatic politics appears often to be an end attained through political game playing by Australia's leaders. In the media analysis, these features of Australian leadership appeared over and above the GLOBE dimensions. Examples of text excerpts from the media analysis are:

- *"The pendulum has swung late and decisively from radical reform to [a] blend of clever caution, but the pragmatic politics of the Prime Minister's tariff plan are nonetheless positive."*
- *"Closely connected to pragmatic politics is gamesmanship and game playing, expressed as game metaphors in the national and regional press."*

A further dimension emergent from the media analysis was the adversarial nature of Australian leadership, expressed in public verbal abuse, and the aggressive nature of interpersonal relationships. This behavior is distinct from the GLOBE dimension of decisiveness, which was identifiable in references to terms such as "tough stand" and "fortitude." The adversarial nature of Australian leadership was evident in terms like *attack, fight,* and *vicious tirade.*

A caveat to this interpretation is that these comments resulted from a general awakening that politics ought to be more than game playing and pragmatism. Australians are instead expressing the need for debate about ideals, convictions, and policies, hoping that this will reflect real emotional and intellectual resources in the leaders who are going to lead Australia at this time of rapid and widespread change (Mackay, 1993). Although there is an admission that the adversarial nature of politics is born of the two-party system, the blurring of the parties' political philosophies has removed this legitimacy, so that Australians appear now to attribute aggressive leadership to the personality of the individual leaders, rather than to the system itself.

This need for more vision and integrity from Australia's leaders is not a mass movement (Mackay, 1993), and the quantitative results from the GLOBE study on dimensions such as Future Orientation indicate that many respondents are equivocal. Nevertheless, the national media analysis, through the definition of the Australian leadership dimensions of caution, pragmatism, game metaphor, and adversarial, attests to the earlier discussion of a lack of long-term vision and conviction within Australian society. Fortunately, the results also reflect the Australian enigma. They attest to a general recognition that Australian leaders are still capable of vision and integrity. The issue is whether they will use these qualities in guiding the nation in this age of change.

5.   INDUSTRY LEVEL ANALYSIS

The two Australian industries involved in the project were telecommunications and finance. Both these industries are integral to the Australian economy: Finance is the single largest sector in the Australian economy and telecommunications is one of the fastest growing sectors.[20] Moreover, both industries provide services on which so much of business in general depends, and they are interdependent. For example, the financial sector is heavily reliant on an efficient, sophisticated telecommunications network. The importance of these industry sectors to Australian business is one reason why they are particularly worthy of study. In addition, they were ideal for inclusion in the GLOBE project because both have undergone substantial and fundamental changes in the last decade, and their response to these changes provide insights into contemporary Australian culture. Both industries have also been through substantial restructuring in the latter part of the 20th century, sometimes led by powerful expatriate chief executive officers (CEOs; see Blount, Joss, & Mair, 1999).

Discussion of the backgrounds of the industries, and the results obtained through both the GLOBE study and subsequent explanatory research appears in the following sections. As with the societal analysis, the two foci of the GLOBE study, culture and leadership, are discussed separately, supplemented by the data from interviews with industry experts and an analysis of industry text media.

Telecommunications Industry

For decades, telecommunications services in Australia have been provided by a government monopoly. Although telecommunications had seen significant changes, such as the separation of telecommunications and postal activities in 1975, it is only in the 1990s that the industry has seen truly fundamental changes. Firstly, in 1989, the regulatory power was taken away from the telecommunications carrier (then Telecom, now named Telstra) and given to an independent body, the Australian Telecommunications Authority. In 1991, Telecom and the Australian international carrier, OTC, merged. Then, in 1992, the monopoly held by Telstra in its various forms since the beginning of the century was broken, and Optus, an Australian–American–British consortium became a new competitor in the field. Deregulation was fully realized in 1998 with the entry of more competitors. There is, however, general optimism regarding the future of Telstra and its new competitors, especially regarding the role of Australia as the leading telecommunications center in the Asia-Pacific region.[21]

Although no longer the sole national provider, Telstra is still currently Australia's only full-service telecommunications provider. Traditionally tied to the government, and operating in many ways like a public service, Telstra has undergone a series of transitions to render it more similar to a private-enterprise organization (see Blount et al., 1999). Large-scale restructuring to centralize the organization and to downsize has, however, led to much unease within the organization. The downsizing is expected to pare down the corporation to half its 1996

---

[20]Source: *Microsoft Encarta Encyclopaedia,* 1996. World English Edition.

[21]It should be noted, however, that the present analysis was carried out in 1996–1997.

administrative staff complement of 26,000 (Bromby, 1996). In its present state, Telstra is a corporation with an independent board and has recently been privatized and listed as a public company with a highly successful 30% sell-off.[22] Since then, Telstra shares have sagged after two public share floats, but Telstra management remains optimistic about its long-term future (Telstra Corporation, 2000).

As part of the deregulation of the industry, Telstra is operating under competition policies put in place and monitored through a regulatory body, the Australian Communications Authority. The justification for these regulations has centered on the need to identify the level of competition needed for the industry and how this can be achieved or maintained (Fels, 1997). Fels has noted that, in many ways, Telstra is much further ahead than other industries in Australia, offering full access, whereas others do not even have laws pertaining to such access.

Despite the new competitors, Telstra is generally expected to remain the major telecommunications carrier in Australia (Bromby, 1995; Chow, 1997). Currently, Telstra is the largest integrated telecommunications carrier in the Asia Pacific, and is already Australia's largest listed company. Telstra has expressed the goal of being a major driving force in regional and global telecommunications and is eager to leverage the multicultural makeup of modern Australia to help achieve that goal.

The second telecommunications carrier in Australia, founded in 1992, is Optus. Optus has introduced several major technological innovations and has had considerable impact in the areas of pay TV and the international-call market (Bromby, 1995). Optus, and other operators such as AAPT, have only recently entered the local-call market.

There are good indications that Australia's telecommunications industry will continue to expand its influence as a dynamic sector of the economy. First, Australia's expertise in designing, implementing, and managing telecommunications networks in the Asia Pacific region have made it a significant telecommunications center. Second, Australia offers leading-edge technology coupled with a sophisticated domestic market and a broad range of engineering skills. It has a very strong base in communications and information technology (IT) support firms, with the second largest IT market in the region, seven times larger than either Singapore's or Hong Kong's (Chow, 1997). It can be expected, therefore, that there be will considerable interest from potential international competitors who wish to enter a strong market. Such transformations, however, are bound to affect the state and culture of the telecommunications industry.

Results

The preceding discussion provides a context within which the quantitative results from the GLOBE project can be viewed for the Australian telecommunications industry. The telecommunications industry culture results appear in Table 9.4. These results were interpreted with the aid of key individuals from the telecommunications industry. Two experts from the industry were presented with the results and asked to discuss each of the dimensions separately. The focus of this section is on Telstra because this was the primary area of expertise for the interviewers and, given the size and dominance of Telstra, the Australian industry is still critically tied to the fortunes of the national carrier (Eason, 1995).

The industry-level culture results for the Australian telecommunications industry from the GLOBE study appear in Table 9.4. These results include Australia's ranking on each of the

---

[22]The present study was conducted 1 year before the share market listing and sell-off.

TABLE 9.4

Telecommunications Industry Results for the Nine Cultural Dimensions With Rankings for Australia Compared to the Scores of 29 Countries

	"As Is"		"Should Be"		Difference
Dimension	Score[a]	Rank[b]	Score[a]	Rank[b]	Score[c]
Performance Orientation	4.04	22	6.42	5	2.38
Uncertainty Avoidance	3.76	23	3.64	23	–0.12
Future Orientation	4.18	22	5.52	17	1.34
Humane Orientation	4.08	24	5.17	12	1.09
Institutional Collectivism	3.97	24	4.53	26	0.56
In-Group Collectivism	4.10	26	5.81	16	1.71
Gender Egalitarianism	2.77	21	5.34	4	2.57
Assertiveness	3.86	18	3.80	21	–0.06
Power Distance	4.52	7	3.25	23	1.27

Note.   N = 4 organizations.
[a]Items were rated on a Likert-type scale from 1 (*very low*) to 7 (*very high*). [b]Ranks are out of the 30 countries that provided data for the telecommunications industry in the GLOBE study. [c]Difference is "Should be" score minus "As is" score.

three assessments: "As Is," "Should Be," and the difference between these measures. Table 9.5 describes the telecommunications industry leadership results in conjunction with results from a media analysis of the 1996 annual reports from the four telecommunications organizations included in the study. Kabanoff (1993) has shown that annual reports provide an appropriate source for measuring the espoused organizational values, although only some sections of the reports were relevant for the present study of leadership. These results have therefore been presented together with the measures of perceived leadership in the telecommunications industry obtained by GLOBE. Researchers coded 102 relevant text extractions.

Telecommunications Industry Culture.   The GLOBE results show that the Australian telecommunications industry respondents value a performance orientation, but see it as not being achieved at the current time. These results need to be taken in the context of the massive restructuring of the primary telecommunications corporation, Telstra, and the consequent job insecurity of many employees. Furthermore, most workers in the telecommunications industry have continually changing portfolios, and are working long hours. As a result, they feel unable to place a high priority on Performance Orientation.

The industry experts commented that this effect might also be a result of complacency. In particular, Telstra is expected to profit from deregulation in the long term (Bromby, 1996). Thus, a short-term effect of deregulation has been to enable Telstra to exploit the new flexibility in the industry, and to dominate at all quarters. Such dominance does little to promote a need to perform beyond current levels.

The rating of both the existing and the desired measures of Uncertainty Avoidance is low in the Australian telecommunications industry. Indeed, there seems general satisfaction with the levels of uncertainty avoidance. This may in part reflect the limitations under which the

TABLE 9.5
GLOBE Study Leadership and Media Analysis Results for Telecommunications Industry[a]

Leadership Dimension	Percentage of Coding[b]	GLOBE Score	Variable Ranking[c]	GLOBE Ranking[d]
Performance Orientation	28	6.31	3	=6
Visionary	15	6.29	4	6
Collaborative Team Oriented	10	5.64	6	=10
Decisive	10	5.96	5	=11
Administratively Competent	7	5.42	8	24
Integrity	7	6.54	1	3
Humane	5	5.22	10	7
Autocratic	5	2.11	16	24
Diplomatic	4	5.57	7	=14
Inspirational	4	6.43	2	2
Procedural	1	3.39	14	22
Autonomous	1	3.99	12	=14
Modesty	1	5.27	9	11
Face Saver	1	2.43	15	24
Self-Centered	1	1.75	17	=27
Status-Conscious	0	3.46	13	25
Self-Sacrificial	0	4.86	11	=23

[a]Based on 17-factor model (see Footnote 18). [b]Frequency of coding in media analysis indicates that this dimension either exists or should exist. [c]Rank order of GLOBE variables within the Australian sample. [d]Rank position within the sample of 30 GLOBE countries that provided data for the telecommunications industry.

primary telecommunications carrier is operating. Regulatory bodies also restrict the room for risk taking in the current telecommunications industry in Australia, and any business dealings are constrained by the rules of fair competition (see Standing Committee on Industry, Science, and Technology, 1997). The distinction between regulated and nonregulated aspects requires that these components remain segregated and further reduce potential for change.

The restraint may be in some respect alleviated with the deregulation of the industry and privatization of Telstra. So long as Telstra's shares remained 100% government owned, the leeway for the organization to take risks with uncertain outcomes remained limited.

The telecommunications industry in Australia is largely event driven, with little implementation of planning in areas other than finance or marketing. This lack of planning is evident in GLOBE results for current Future Orientation and the desire expressed for more Future Orientation. The recent introduction of competition to the market has encouraged more "product planning" and business plans stretch into the next year. Despite this, size, politics, and novelty of the present industry environment all contribute to render planning less effective than might otherwise be expected. The high perceived levels for Future Orientation might be recognition of the very real prospects for capitalizing on an ever-changing market and technology. In particular, the convergence of technologies (combination of computers, telecommunications, and broadcasting) and broadband services indicates that Australia could be following the example of America and European countries and developing strategic approaches to capture the potential of this market (Wilson, 1995). In addition, the likelihood is that deregulation of the industry will see considerable international competition from international alliances and mergers that will need to be met with anticipation by Australian carriers (Eason, 1995). Indeed, part of the rationale for deregulation itself lies in the need for future orientation; that is, that telecommunications reform was necessary to prepare the national industry for participation in increasingly competitive global markets.

Although the pattern of Humane Orientation is behind what is felt to be ideal, it is still relatively high. This result contradicts the generally expressed belief in the industry that competition has had the effect of substituting a community focus with economic considerations. Telstra started to centralize its operations before deregulation (Blount et al., 1999), and the result has been increasing distance between head office and the places where the work is carried out. Cost cutting was the stated rationale for centralization, but it may well have resulted in the marginalization of consumer interests (Goggin, 1995). Wilson (1995) has suggested that the competitive nature of the current regulations is reducing the community basis of the industry. He cites the need for better service to country areas, and for affordability measures to assist people on low incomes.

Given the strong union culture of the telecommunications industry (see Blount et al., 1999), it is somewhat surprising that Australia does not rank higher on this dimension. A possible explanation may be that, through the process of constant structural change that has taken place in the telecommunications industry over the past 20 years, members no longer see societal collective values as important (see also Wilson, 1995). Remembering that the GLOBE respondents were middle managers, these values are likely to be reinforced.

Telecommunications employees believe that their organizations ought to be more loyal than they are currently. As with many industries, telecommunications firms appear to espouse team values (see media analysis), but direct the majority of their performance reward mechanisms to performance at the individual level. The atmosphere of change and large-scale restructuring may also have fostered an "individual-over-team" focus. This may therefore have undermined group loyalty because of the number of individual jobs under threat.

With regard to the industry and the community, there are two opposing views. One is that the corporatization of the industry has removed the community focus of Telstra. A second, however, is that competition will, or at least should, serve to increase efficiency and the sharing of these savings between the producers of the service and the Australian consumers (Lee, 1995; Wilkinson, 1995). The Australian telecommunications industry has traditionally been a male-dominated culture, with a strong engineering, technical background. The results from the quantitative GLOBE study indicate that respondents see the need for more gender equality. Although women's career progression is recognized in the industry, the culture remains based on assertive, tough behavior. Indeed, the anecdotal evidence from the industry experts interviewed suggests that female leaders in the industry need to be tougher, and even more aggressive, than their male counterparts to succeed. This reliance on tough and assertive behavior therefore appears to be continually reinforced, with the current leader role models fitting the industry's traditional roles.

Consistent with the society-level results, Australians view their Assertiveness levels to be close to their ideal. The telecommunications industry is broadly representative of this. Interestingly, Australians in this industry score relatively highly in comparison to other countries on "As Is," but much lower than the others in terms of "Should Be." This result, however, may be what one could expect, given the highly unionized nature of the industry (especially at the time this analysis was done), where Australian values of "mateship" and "one of the boys" is especially evident (see Blount et al., 1999).

The perceived stratification in the telecommunications industry is high, and is seen to be higher than desirable. It seems that restructuring may not only be affecting collectivism but also power distance. This is particularly so in view of the difference between those with knowledge of impending changes and those without. In addition, the threat to the jobs of executive employees may render the imbalance even more accented; fear may induce managers to demand more of those who work underneath them.

Leadership in the Telecommunications Industry.   It is clear from the GLOBE survey results that leadership in the telecommunications industry is a derivative of societal-level attitudes. Effective leaders are seen to be inspirational, of high integrity and vision, decisive, and performance oriented. Effective leaders in the telecommunications industry, on the other hand, are not seen to be self-centered, autocratic, procedural, or face saving. These findings are reflected in the media analysis, although the inspirational dimension is notable for its low ranking. Overall, the leadership results for the telecommunications industry reflect the cultural emphasis on achievement discussed earlier.

As noted previously, Inspirational leadership ranks incongruously low in the media analysis. Furthermore, the dimension of Self-Sacrifice ranked low in the GLOBE survey results and did not rate a mention in the media analysis. This is consistent with the national media analysis, and reinforces the view of the traditional Australian value of egalitarianism. Thus, although approval of self-sacrifice is evident at the societal level (Self-Sacrifice scored relatively high in the societal-level GLOBE results), it appears this leadership trait is not valued at the organizational level.

Conclusion

The picture emergent from the analysis of the Australian telecommunications industry is consistent with the analysis of societal culture values reported earlier in this chapter, and reflects the underlying themes of Australian culture. In particular, the results reinforce the inherent contradictions within the culture. The telecommunications industry is undergoing an intense and seemingly unending process of change, which is reflected in a short-term future orientation and an emphasis on achievement. As a result, effective leaders in the telecommunications industry are seen to be performance oriented and decisive (e.g., see Blount et al., 1999). At the same time, however, they need to be diplomatic rather than self-sacrificing. In effect, they need to be inspirational, without being seen to put themselves ahead of their fellow employees.

Finance Industry

The finance system in Australia is largely accounted for by the banking system, incorporating government-owned and private commercial banks, savings banks, and special-purpose banking institutions. Building societies, trustee companies, credit unions, insurance companies, and merchant banks represent other sections of the finance system.

Before 1980, the finance industry had been relatively stable, with the notable exception of the successful fight against nationalization of the banking system after World War II (Singh, 1991). In the last 15 years, however, there have been considerable changes implemented that have altered forever the face of the Australian finance industry. First, in 1983, amid an environment inclined toward deregulation, the AUD was floated. In 1985, there were four main banks, operating under the supervision and regulation of the Reserve Bank of Australia. Then, corresponding with deregulation in the total finance industry, the federal government issued 16 banking licenses, instead of the expected 6. Consequently, the late 1980s saw a huge growth in employment and competition, riding the wave of an economic boom accompanied by rising inflation.

In the retail market, the effect of the competition rendered banks more competitive. Recently, the trend has been for building societies to convert to banks and the market share of nonbank institutions is becoming smaller. The four main banks (the "four pillars"; see Willetts, 1999) continue to dominate the market and have actually prospered from deregulation (Singh, 1991). The international banks that have attempted to establish retail arms in Australia have generally had limited success. In wholesale banking, new entrants had a notable and lasting impact, especially in corporate lending, in money markets, and in foreign-exchange operations.[23] Today, the wholesale banking industry in Australia is sophisticated and competitive despite the relatively small size of the Australian market.

The late 1980s and early 1990s, however, was a generally difficult period for the finance industry. All banks suffered especially because of large loans issued to entrepreneurs and their ventures, which frequently failed during the recession. In response, the finance industry has downsized strenuously (Singh, 1991). In recent years, the Australian economy has recovered and stabilized, yet the finance industry remains very competitive. Margins have continued to fall, new entrants have kept competition fierce, and the trend has been for greater investment in technology rather than people.

Results

The industry-level culture results for the Australian finance industry, as measured by the GLOBE survey, appear in Table 9.6. Following is an interpretation of these results based on interviews with two experts from the Australian finance industry. These experts from financial institutions were presented with the results by dimensions and asked to discuss their interpretations of the figures, given their knowledge of the industry, for each dimension in turn. In addition, the researchers used information from the interviews conducted by Singh (1991) in his book: The finance industry leadership results (Table 9.7) appear together with information gathered through a media analysis of the annual reports from key finance industries.

The media analysis was conducted by analyzing the 1996 annual reports of 10 finance companies for references to leadership. Represented in the analyses are the four main national banks, smaller banks, insurance bodies, and building societies. As was the case for the telecommunications industry analysis, the reports largely focused on descriptions of contributions made by various employees or board members to the companies, the codes of conduct expected of the board and leaders, and details of leadership schemes being undertaken. There were only limited sections of the annual reports that were relevant for study. Again, however, I argue that annual reports provide a useful index of espoused values, and has been shown to be applicable in the specific instance of the banking industry (see Kabanoff, 1993). These results have been presented together with the measures of perceived leadership in the finance industry obtained by GLOBE. Table 9.7 shows the results from this analysis. The researchers made 129 codings.

---

[23]Source: 1996 annual report of the National Australia Bank.

TABLE 9.6
Finance Industry Results for the Nine Cultural Dimensions With Rankings for Australia
Compared to the Scores of 52 Countries

	"As Is"		"Should Be"		Difference
Dimension	Score[a]	Rank[b]	Score[a]	Rank[b]	Score[c]
Performance Orientation	4.59	26	6.23	16	1.64
Uncertainty Avoidance	4.03	39	4.49	29	0.46
Future Orientation	4.54	33	5.76	21	1.22
Humane Orientation	4.71	14	4.91	27	0.20
Institutional Collectivism	4.41	12	4.57	41	0.16
In-Group Collectivism	4.36	44	5.75	30	1.39
Gender Egalitarianism	3.28	26	5.03	10	1.75
Assertiveness	3.92	29	3.84	28	−0.08
Power Distance	4.20	19	3.45	34	−0.75

Note. N = 14 organizations.
[a]Items were rated on a Likert-type scale from 1 (very low) to 7 (very high). [b]Ranks are out of the 53 countries that provided data for the finance industry in the GLOBE study. [c]Difference is "Should be" score minus "As is" score.

TABLE 9.7
GLOBE Study Leadership and Media Analysis Results for the Australian Finance Industry[a]

Leadership Dimension	Percentage of Coding[b]	GLOBE Score	Variable Ranking[c]	GLOBE Ranking[d]
Collaborative Team Oriented	26	5.49	7	=25
Performance Orientation	16	6.28	3	=13
Diplomatic	13	5.48	8	27
Administratively Competent	10	5.54	6	39
Integrity	9	6.30	2	=18
Humane	8	5.17	9	11
Visionary	6	6.13	4	=26
Inspirational	5	6.35	1	18
Procedural	4	3.83	13	43
Status-Conscious	1	4.07	12	32
Autonomous	1	3.71	14	36
Autocratic	1	2.19	16	=41
Decisive	0	5.91	5	=28
Modesty	0	5.09	10	27
Self-Sacrificial	0	4.88	11	33
Face Saver	0	2.59	15	33
Self-Centered	0	2.02	17	=28

[a]Based on 17-factor model (see Footnote 18). [b]Frequency of coding in media analysis indicates that this dimension either exists or should exist. [c]Rank order of GLOBE variables within the Australian sample. [d]Rank position within the sample of 53 GLOBE countries that provided data for the telecommunications industry.

Finance Industry Culture. The GLOBE survey results indicate that the Australian finance industry is achievement oriented, but would like to be considerably more so. Part of the explanation for such an emphasis on performance may lie in the nature of the finance discipline: Profit oriented and capitalistic in ideology, the structure of the finance industry clearly necessitates a performance orientation.

The competitive nature of the finance industry may also contribute to its perceived Performance Orientation. With so many of the features of financial institutions, such as interest rates, being tightly controlled and regulated, the scope for attracting customers is necessarily limited and must rest on individuals performing optimally in their work capacity. Performance of individuals may thus be the only way to differentiate between financial institutions that cannot offer substantially different corporate performance.

Finally, the extent of finance industry regulation may also serve to explain why an even higher level of performance is desired. Controls would tend to limit the scope for high performance of individuals within institutions, and employees may feel dissatisfaction with this restriction on their aspirations.

The results on Uncertainty Avoidance for the Australian finance industry are particularly interesting. The pattern here contrasts with that of telecommunications industry and society; finance industry respondents expressed a desire for a more conservative environment. This may reflect the national perception that banking should be a safe industry. This perception in turn is reinforced by the general practice of Australian banks, differing from international trends, to profit from the interest and fees transactions generate rather than to speculate on the market. When the State Bank of Victoria collapsed in 1990, indicating that banks are not guaranteed to be safe, the effect was felt throughout the smaller banks, with customers migrating to the "four pillars." Risk taking is therefore not a part of the banking culture in Australia, nor is risk taking perceived to be desired (see also Singh, 1991).

The finance industry results indicate that the future orientation of this industry is perceived to be higher than either that of the Australian telecommunications industry or of society in general. The ideal ratings for Future Orientation maintain this pattern.

One distinctive feature of the finance industry is that, at an industry level, it is constrained by the economic cycle; there is always the fear that the next financial downturn will lead to organizational failure. Future orientation therefore is an inevitable and necessary component of the industry.

Another factor affecting future orientation in the finance industry is the increasing emphasis placed on technology, rather than personnel. The experts interviewed expressed the commonly held industry belief that the future of finance lies in optimizing technology.

The Humane Orientation results from GLOBE indicate that the present level is perceived to be similar to the desired level of humane orientation. Historically, the finance sector in Australia has had a very public, caring face (Mackay, 1993). The network has an unusual rural penetration, born from its growth during the goldfields in the 1850s and the opening of wheat lands in the 1860s (Singh, 1991). The rural focus gave banks a service orientation toward the Australian community similar to that recounted by Telstra employees. One effect of the competitive environment of deregulation, however, has been to make personal relationships between institutions and customers less important in the name of survival. With deregulation, the caring face of banks is less evident than is the drive for service and more market share. Customers of Australian banks envision a future with fewer big banks, becoming increasingly centralized and less personal, with a developing market for the small and medium-size banks to establish personal relationships and service (Mackay, 1993).

Rather surprisingly, Australians in the finance sector score relatively highly on this dimension. This is compensated for, however, by the finding that the "As Is" score is almost the same as the "Should Be" score. As I have argued previously, this variable is consistent with the union-based nature of Australian industry and the strong element of welfarism in the Australian economy (see Mackay, 1993). In the banking sector, the union element remains relatively strong, despite restructuring (see Blount et al., 1999; Singh, 1991).

The finance industry appears to be replicating the pattern of the telecommunications and societal results for In-Group Collectivism. More collectivist than individualistic at present, the ideal appears nonetheless to be that the industry becomes more collectivist in orientation.

The qualitative results indicate that the finance industry operates predominantly on a team basis, both within and between institutions. The latter is particularly distinctive for the finance industry, because banks can own other banks, and the larger banks often support building societies. Furthermore, the introduction of technology has tended to increase collaboration between banks irrespective of competition, because of the need to use the same technological infrastructure (Singh, 1991). The needs of the industry therefore can override achievements of individual enterprises.

Contrary to this impetus for a group orientation, however, are two matters already discussed. The first of these is the reward for individual performance within the institutions. The second is the effect of deregulation and competition, which is acting to de-emphasize relationships in the banking world. As Singh (1991) relates, banks are "competing for business rather than following old loyalties; once the corporates [sic] learnt to play the game equally well, they would go for where they got the best price and the best service" (p. 76). This conflict may in part explain the perceived wish for more collectivism than is presently practiced. A 1992 report on the Australian banking market concluded that, as a direct result of deregulation, Australians view their banking system as aggressive and commercial, in marked contrast to the community view that survived through the mid-1980s (Mackay, 1993).

The Gender Egalitarianism results from GLOBE suggest that the finance industry is characterized by a medium level of emphasis on stereotypically male characteristics, but would like to see much more gender equality. Although the industry is largely male dominated in the upper echelons of management, it is probable that the pervasive impact of technology would have contributed to mute a strong male emphasis. Technology has brought an increased emphasis on collaboration and communication, especially within the IT area itself (Clegg & Gray, 1996).

As was the case for the telecommunications industry, the Assertiveness result mirrors the societal culture results, in that the finance respondents are generally happy with their level of assertiveness, although it appears that assertiveness is valued slightly more in this industry sector. Consistent with Singh's (1991) observations, finance industry respondents in Australia take a generally aggressive approach, more so than in other industries.

The finance industry is traditionally replete with hierarchical institutions, so it is not surprising that the GLOBE results show a perception that Power Distance is higher than it should be. This ties in with the predominance of references to the board and executives in the annual reports used in the media analysis. It is also notable that the level of reported ideal power distance is higher than in the telecommunications industry, and the societal results. Possibly, the high level of regulation necessitates, to some degree, a hierarchical management structure, and this is therefore seen as more appropriate than in other sections of Australian society. As automation becomes increasingly a part of banking, it appears that banks will centralize and the authority and power of local branches decrease (Mackay, 1993).

Leadership in the Finance Industry.   The results in respect of leadership in the finance sector, as for the telecommunications industry, reflect the societal results. Effective leaders are seen to be inspirational, of high integrity and vision, decisive, and performance oriented (see Blount et al., 1999). Effective leaders, on the other hand, are not seen to be self-centered, autocratic, autonomous, or face-saving. These findings are reflected in the media analysis, with the exception that the annual reports place the most emphasis on collaborative team orientation, reflecting the values discussed earlier. In this respect, the finance industry in Australia appears to be following the trends, discussed earlier, toward a participatory team approach to management.

An interesting aspect of the finance industry leadership results is the relatively low ranking of the Australian scores compared to other countries participating in the GLOBE study, with the possible exception of Performance Orientation, Humane, Integrity, and Inspiration. This is consistent with the results from the telecommunications industry, where the Australian scores on dimensions such as Integrity and Inspirational were among the highest. This consistency with the telecommunications industry is further supported in respect of the Self-Sacrificial dimension, which ranked low in the GLOBE survey results and did not rate a mention in the finance media analysis. This provides additional evidence that overtly expressed self-sacrifice is not a desirable trait in Australian leaders.

Conclusion

It is clear from the analysis that the finance industry is somewhat different from the telecommunications industry, and provides an interesting contrast. The organizational cultures expressed in the two industries reflect this difference. Employees in both industry sectors are experiencing a continuing high rate of change, but there appears to be a much higher level of acceptance of the status quo in the finance industry. The evidence from observers such as Singh (1991) suggests that this may arise from the high level of regulation in the industry, which lowers aspirations. Another factor is that the finance industry is subject to the vagaries of the economic cycle, which promotes a lower level of risk taking.

Finally, the leadership results reflect once more the underlying cultural characteristics of Australians, but at the same time suggest that the current trend toward higher levels of collectivism are having an effect. This was particularly evident in the finance industry media analysis, where, in contrast to the telecommunications industry results, collaborative team-oriented views appeared in more than a quarter of the text excerpts.

Summary of Industry Results

One of the primary hypotheses of the GLOBE project is that leadership is reflected in implicit theories, which are embedded in national culture. My analysis of the Australian telecommunications and finance industries provides support for this proposition. The patters of cultural practices and beliefs that were evident from the analysis of societal culture and leadership were evident in the industry studies. This is despite the differences between the two industry sectors, which are subject to markedly different environmental pressures (see Blount et al., 1999).

The results also reinforce the underlying themes of Australian culture, discussed earlier in this chapter. In particular, Australian leaders need to be performance oriented in a society that values achievement, but at the same time need to do so in a manner that does not set them too far apart from their fellow organizational members. Being seen to stand out from peers, for example, was consistently ranked one of the least desirable characteristics of Australian industry leaders. It seems that the need for leaders to "perform" is at odds with the need for them to appear to be "one of the boys."[24] In particular, leaders who are seen to over perform are likely to find themselves in the position of the "tall poppy," ready to be cut down.

Finally, the industry-level results reinforce the idea of an Australian enigma. Australian leaders must aim high, but not be "seen" to do so. They must be inspirational, but not too self-sacrificial. They must be humane, but still prepared to make the hard decisions if required. They must be recognized as leaders, but still be seen to be "one of us." Overall, it seems that successful leadership in Australia is far from easy to achieve.

6. CONCLUSIONS

The title of this chapter is *"The Australian Enigma."* This was deemed appropriate because Australia turns out to be a land of contradiction and paradox. It is a vast and mostly empty land, where most of the population lives in a small number of large urban centers. It is a country with a catch cry of "a fair go," but with a record of discrimination and exclusion that is anything but fair. Australians see themselves as the embodiment of the egalitarian society, but at the same time, according to social commentators such as Mackay (1993), they crave wealth and success. Australians are proud of their egalitarian culture, but at the same time also value rewards for high achievers. Its leaders are expected to inspire high levels of performance, but must do so without giving the impression of self-sacrifice or of not being anything more than "one of the boys." Australians are inventive and expect their leaders to show visionary qualities, but seem to have little conception of anything more than a short- to medium-term future.

In this chapter, I have presented evidence for these seemingly contradictory qualities, and attempted to provide some understanding of their origins. Australia is a young country, but with an eventful history. Many of the reasons for the enigmatic qualities can be traced in Australian history, starting with the original convict settlements. In particular, Australia has been influenced by successive waves of immigrants who have shaped a diverse society, which is only now beginning to deal with many of its more fundamental issues, including relationships with its Aboriginal population, its British/Irish heritage, its role as a political refuge, and its place in the Asia Pacific region. Nevertheless, Australia is an advanced industrialized nation, with a well-entrenched work ethic.

Results from the GLOBE survey have shown that Australians value performance orientation, future orientation, a humane orientation, and uncertainty avoidance, but would like their society to be less stratified and collective. Australians also see their leaders as being achievement orientated, visionary, and inspirational.

Some of the more interesting results of the present study were produced in the national media analysis. Though most characteristics of Australian leaders matched the GLOBE dimensions, some anomalies provided additional insights into Australian leadership. In particular, a number of uniquely Australian leadership qualities appeared. Some of these are related to contemporary events and the new work ethic, but others appeared to relate to the underling Australian value of egalitarianism. I called these traits "mateship," "one of us," "tall poppy," and "underdog." These traits also appeared to underpin many of the findings of the

---

[24] I have deliberately used *boys* here. The evidence from interview with industry experts was consistent in making the point that, to be successful, female leaders needed also to be seen as "one of the boys."

industry-based part of the present study. These findings offer interesting potential for future research. Indeed, Meng, Ashkanasy, and Härtel (2003) found, in a follow-up study, that "tall poppy" attitudes directly affect the application of American value-based leadership theory in Australia. Additional research along these lines holds potential to understand further the role of unique cultural values and attitudes on leadership and management in Australia.

Finally, I note that this research has some important limitations. The sample of respondents was limited, only two industries were surveyed, and the research was done as a cross-sectional study. Indeed, the world, and Australia in particular, is experiencing a state of rapid change, so that the conclusions presented in this chapter must be taken in the context of the world as it was in the late 1990s—prior to the Asian financial crisis, the "Tech Wreck" of the later 1990s, the events that followed September 11, 2001, and the subsequent political and economic upheavals. Nonetheless, the consistencies of the industry representative interviews and the media analysis with the results of the survey data, give confidence that the results are broadly representative of Australian cultural values and leadership.

To conclude, it appears that effective leadership within the context of the Australian culture may be especially difficult. The principal implication for managerial practice emerging from the study is that Australian leaders must balance the competing demands of egalitarianism and achievement, and at the same time appear to be "one of the boys." In addition, and as Parry (2001) has also noted, Australian leaders emphasize integrity and consideration for followers while at the same time rejecting American-style grand charisma. The further primary concern for Australian managers is a need to develop a truly long-term future orientation; in a changing world where Australia is yet to find its place, this may yet prove to be the most difficult challenge.

ACKNOWLEDGMENTS

The author acknowledges contributions by Sara Falkus, who assisted with data collection. Also acknowledged with thanks are the members of the GLOBE team and anonymous reviewers who provided valuable suggestions and ideas for improving the chapter. This research was conducted with funding from a University of Queensland "Quality" Grant.

REFERENCES

Ashkanasy, N. M. (1997). A cross-national comparison of Australian and Canadian supervisor's attributional and evaluative responses to subordinate performance. *Australian Psychologist, 32,* 29–36.
Ashkanasy, N. M., & O'Connor, C. (1997). Value congruence in leader–member exchange. *The Journal of Social Psychology, 137,* 647–662.
Ashkanasy, N. M., & Weierter, S. J. (1996). Modelling the leader–member relationship: The role of value congruence and charisma. In K. Parry (Ed.), *Leadership research and practice* (pp. 105–112). Melbourne, Australia: Pitman Press.
Bass, B. M. (1985). Leadership: Good, better, best. *Organizational Dynamics, Winter,* 26–40.
Blount, F., Joss, B., & Mair, D. (1999). *Managing in Australia.* Sydney, Australia: Lansdowne Press.
Bromby, R. (1995). Australia: Deregulation: A distant dream. *Telecommunications International Edition, 29*(10), 157–158.
Bromby, R. (1996). Antipodean competition for Telstra. *Telecommunications International Edition, 30*(6), 24.

Burns, J. M. (1978). *Leadership*. New York: Harper & Row.

Carless, S., Mann, L., & Wearing, A. (1996). Transformational leadership and teams: An examination of the Bass and Kousez–Posner models. In K. Parry (Ed.), *Leadership research and practice* (pp. 77–90). Melbourne, Australia: Pitman Press.

Chow, L. (1997). Take no chances. *Far Eastern Economic Review, 160*(6), 49.

Clarke, F. G. (1992). *Australia: A concise political and social history.* Sydney, Australia: Harcourt Brace.

Clegg, S., & Gray, J. (1996). Leadership research and embryonic industry: Harvesting competitive advantage. In K. Parry (Ed.), *Leadership research and practice* (pp. 29–40). Melbourne, Australia: Pitman Press.

Costa, W. G. (1996). An Australian call center answers the need for Novell support. *Telemarketing and Call Center Solutions, 14*(7), 88–91.

Dickinson, C. (1996). Maintaining leadership effectiveness in the senior executive service. In K. Parry (Ed.), *Leadership Research and Practice* (pp. 139–152). Melbourne, Australia: Pitman Press.

Dunphy, D., & Stace, D. (1990). *Under new management: Australian Organisations in transition.* Sydney, Australia: McGraw-Hill.

Eason, R. (1995). A union view on regulating multi-carrier environment. In I. Wilson (Ed.), *Converging on telecommunications: Conference proceedings of the consumers' telecommunications network* (pp. 75–82). Surry Hills, Australia: Consumers' Telecommunications Network.

Feather, N. T. (1986). Value systems across cultures: Australia and China. *International Journal of Psychology, 21,* 697–715.

Feather, N. T. (1993). The rise and fall of political leaders: Attributions, deservingness, personality and affect. *Australian Journal of Psychology, 45,* 61–68.

Feather, N. T. (1994a). Attitudes toward high achievers and reactions to their fall: Theory and research concerning tall poppies. In M. P. Zanna (Ed.), *Advances in experimental social psychology* (Vol. 26, pp. 1–73). New York: Academic Press.

Feather, N. T. (1994b). Values and national identification: Australian evidence. *Australian Journal of Psychology, 46,* 35–40.

Fels, A. (1997, June 3). Interview. Journalist: Mark, Hollands. *The Australian,* 56–57.

Galvin, M. & West, P. (1988). *A changing Australia: Themes and case studies.* Sydney, Australia: Harcourt Brace.

Gardiner, J., Callan, V., & Terry, D. (1996). Communication, leadership and organizational change. Some conceptual links and practical implications. In K. Parry (Ed.), *Leadership research and practice.* (pp. 153–162). Melbourne, Australia: Pitman Press.

Goggin, G. (1995). Faith no more: Comprehensive universal service and consumer interests under competition. In I. Wilson (ed.) *Converging on telecommunications: Conference proceedings of the consumers' telecommunications network* (pp. 131–137). Surry Hills, Australia: Consumers' Telecommunications Network.

Graetz, B. & McAllister, I. (1994). *Dimensions of Australian society.* South Melbourne, Australia: Macmillan.

Healey, K. (Ed.). (1998). *The stolen generation.* Balmain, Australia: Spinney Press.

Horne, D. (1965). *The lucky country: Australia in the sixties.* Sydney, Australia: Angus & Robertson.

House, R. J., Hanges, P. J., Javidan, M., Dorfman, P. W., Gupta, V., & Globe Associates. (2004). *Culture, leadership, and organizations: The GLOBE study of 62 societies.* Thousand Oaks, CA: Sage.

Irurita, V. (1996). Optimizing: A leadership process for transforming mediocrity to excellence. A study of nursing leadership. In K. Parry (Ed.), *Leadership research and practice* (pp. 125–138). Melbourne, Australia: Pitman Press.

Jones, M. A. (1996). *The Australian welfare state: Evaluating social policy* (4th ed.). St. Leonards, Australia: Allen & Unwin.

Jones, M. T. (1990). *Real exchange rates and Australian export competitiveness.* Sydney: Reserve Bank of Australia.

Jupp, J. (1996). *Understanding Australian multiculturalism.* Canberra: Australian Government Publishing Service.

Kabanoff, B. (1993). An exploration of espoused culture in Australian organizations (with a closer look at the banking sector). *Asia Pacific Journal of Human Resources, 31*(3), 1–29.

Kabanoff, B., & Holt, J. (1996). Changes in the espoused values of Australian organizations 1986–1990. *Journal of Organizational Behavior, 17,* 201–219.

Kabanoff B., Waldersee, R., & Cohen, M. (1995). Espoused values and organizational change themes. *Academy of Management Journal, 38,* 1075–1104.

Karpin, D. (1995). *Enterprising nation: Renewing Australia's managers to meet the challenges of the Asia-Pacific century* (Report on the Industry Task Force on Leadership and Management Skills). Canberra: Australian Government Publishing Service.

Lee, M. (1995). Opening address: The impact of rapidly changing communications technology on consumers. In I. Wilson (Ed.), *Converging on telecommunications: Conference proceedings of the consumers' telecommunications network* (pp. 19–28). Surry Hills, Australia: Consumers' Telecommunications Network.

Lewis, D. (1996). New perspectives on transformational leadership. In K. Parry (Ed.), *Leadership research and practice* (pp. 17–28). Melbourne, Australia: Pitman Press.

Mackay, H. (1993). *Reinventing Australia: The mind and mood of Australia in the 1990s.* Sydney, Australia: Angus & Robertson.

Melleuish, G. (1996). Who owns the national identity? *IPA—Review, 49*(2), 17–18.

Meng, Y. K., Ashkanasy, N. M., & Härtel, C. E. J. (2003). The effects of Australian tall poppy attitudes on American value-based leadership theory. *International Journal of Value- Based Management, 16,* 53–65.

NAC/UNESCO. (1973). *Australian Aboriginal culture* (2nd ed.). Canberra: Australian Government Printing Service.

Parry, K. W. (1996). Leadership research: Themes, implications, and a new leadership challenge. In K. Parry (Ed.), *Leadership Research and Practice* (pp. 163–170). Melbourne, Australia: Pitman Press.

Parry, K. W. (2001). Conclusions, implications, and a leadership profile. In K. W. Parry (Ed.), *Leadership in the Antipodes: Findings, implications, and a leader profile* (pp. 225–241). Wellington, New Zealand: Institute of Policy Studies and the Centre for the Study of Leadership.

Parry, K. W., & Sarros, J. (1996). An Australasian perspective on transformational leadership. In K. Parry (Ed.), *Leadership research and practice* (pp. 105–112). Melbourne, Australia: Pitman Press.

Sarros, J. C. (1992). What leaders say they do: An Australian example. *Leadership and Organization Development Journal, 13*(5), 21–27.

Sarros, J., Butchatsky, O., & Santora, J. (1996). Breakthrough leadership: Leadership skills for the twenty-first century. In K. Parry (Ed.), *Leadership research and practice* (pp. 41–52). Melbourne, Australia: Pitman Press.

Schein, E. H. (1992). *Organizational culture and leadership* (2nd ed.). San Francisco: Jossey- Bass.

Serle, G. (1963). *The golden age : A history of the colony of Victoria, 1851–1861.* Parkville, Australia: Melbourne University Press.

Singh, S. (1991). *The Bankers: Australia's leading bankers talk about banking today.* Sydney, Australia: Allen & Unwin.

Standing Committee on Industry, Science, and Technology. (1997). *Finding a balance: Towards fair trading in Australia.* Canberra: Australian Government Printing Service.

Stone, S. N. (Ed.). (1974). *Aborigines in White Australia: A documentary history of the attitudes affecting official policy and the Australian Aborigine, 1697–1973.* South Yarra, Australia: Heinemann Educational.

Telstra Corporation. (2000). *Annual report.* Melbourne, Australia: Author.

Thompson, E. (1994). *Fair enough: Egalitarianism in Australia.* Sydney, Australia: University of New South Wales Press.

Warwick, M., & Scales, I. (1996). Ups and downs down under. *Communications International. 23*(2), 4–7.

White, C. (1992). *Mastering risk, environment, markets and politics in Australian economic history.* Melbourne, Australia: Oxford University Press.

Wilkinson, R. (1995). Consumers and the 1997 review: Telecommunications after 1997. In I. Wilson (Ed.), *Converging on telecommunications: Conference proceedings of the consumers' telecommunications network* (pp. 47–52). Surry Hills, Australia: Consumers' Telecommunications Network.

Willetts, B. (1999). *The "four pillars policy" and major Australian bank mergers.* Unpublished honors thesis, University of Queensland, Australia.

Wilson, I. (1995). Introduction. In I. Wilson (Ed.), *Converging on telecommunications: Conference proceedings of the consumers' telecommunications network* (pp. 7–18). Surry Hills, Australia: Consumers' Telecommunications Network.

10

▼▼▼▼▼▼▼

Inspirational Variations? Culture and Leadership in England

Simon Booth
University of Reading, United Kingdom

Over the last three generations there has been significant cultural change in England as a result of both external and internal factors. An observer looking at the dominant cultural characteristics of England in the early 1900s would find it very difficult to recognize such characteristics in the early years of this century. To understand the changing culture of England and its influence on organizations and individuals it is important to look at the historical context. This will help us distinguish what is unique to the English way of doing things today. It may help us prescriptively suggest how its leaders need to work in order to be successful.

In the broadest sense, the success of plays such as *Henry V* may be partly due to how well Shakespeare understood and described characteristics of outstanding leadership, which chimed with popular opinion. That this play is equally popular today, despite a very different cultural context, suggests that there may be some characteristics that have remained constant over time and during periods of cultural change. We are interested in asking questions about what people today understand by the term outstanding leadership. Are there still a number of constant, dominant characteristics, or is this too simplistic in view of the highly cosmopolitan culture we live in?

1. ENGLAND IN CONTEXT

Cultural change in England in the 20th century has been rapid during periods of war and slow during periods of peace. Change has been influenced, however, not just by war and conflict, but also by a number of other elements.

First, the arrival of migrants from the Commonwealth and many different parts of the world led to England becoming a far more multicultural and cosmopolitan society than it had been before the Second World War. Second, the rise to power of the "baby boomers" (the generation of children born in the period 1945–1960) provided the conditions in which social and economic reform was high on the political agenda. This generation was committed to a welfare state, but not to the dependency relationships that had characterized the first phase of the welfare state. This generation was more willing than the previous generation to accept a greater tolerance of difference; they were less xenophobic and more committed to equality of opportunity.

Third is, the rise of regional and ethnic influences. Regional differences began to grow in significance (Curtice, 1996). The agreement to establish a new Scottish Parliament in Edinburgh and an Assembly in Wales spoke of the recognition of the political, social, and cultural importance of these parts of the UK. Similarly, the differences between England and Northern Ireland have been identified as significant in political and cultural terms (Gallagher, 1992).

There are also differences between many ethnic communities, which make up substantial populations in some parts of England. There is a need to be cautious, therefore, in making generalized claims about a uniform English "culture." Indeed by the start of the 21st century, any observer of the culture of England would have to take into account the importance of its multicultural aspects.

Finally, a continuing debate has raged about the importance of science and technology in the cultural fabric of the nation. The dimensions of this argument go back to C. P. Snow (1963), who suggested that two mutually exclusive cultures were developing in society. One culture was made up of an essentially progressive scientific elite. The other culture was based on the traditional intellectual elite that had no understanding of science or technology and no interest in promoting the values associated with the scientific endeavor. Writers such as F. R. Leavis (1972; Leavis & Thompson, 1960) represented the traditional literary elite and the culture on which it was based. Snow and Leavis represented two poles of this division in English culture (Johnson, 1979). Mant (1977) developed this argument by suggesting that a similar division was to be found in business culture.

The influence of these four sets of forces on English culture can be seen in a number of ways. Some writers have suggested that society is now divided into a number of different groupings (Johnson, 1979; Storey, 1994), in which there is no clear cultural predominance. In contrast, the argument explored here is that these forces have had a strong influence that can be summed up as a battle between progressives and traditionalists. Looking back over the last 50 years we can see that two cultural archetypes have been striving for supremacy.

Traditionalist Culture

Traditional culture was based on social and economic inequality in society that supported and maintained the idea of class as a differentiating factor (E. P. Thompson, 1978). The traditionalist culture had a number of classes within it, including the social elite of the aristocracy and landed gentry, a significant middle class, and a large working class. This culture was held together by a general acceptance of inequality, the support of the Church, as well as by law and custom.

The traditionalist culture showed a tendency toward, or acceptance of, authoritarianism, high power distance and in-egalitarianism. There was a predominantly masculine, individualistic, achieving ,and class-based orientation. Members of this culture preferred the known, learned, or experienced truths with which they were raised. The precise nature of the social rules, which governed behavior, depended on the class to which an individual belonged. Managers and leaders subscribed to middle- and upper-class norms. Some of these included putting an emphasis on values such as personal discipline and morality, politeness, keeping to the rules even when no one else is checking, telling the truth, and acting as a "gentleman" or "lady." These attributes were at the heart of an "establishment" view of the world, reproduced by the "public school education" system, which was intended to breed the leaders of society (Leavis, 1972).

Boys were often sent away to boarding school from the age of 7 until 18. Boys had to learn both formal and informal rules, behaviors, and conventions in order to survive. The result of this form of education was a class of people who showed a certain reserve, a "stiff upper lip," and an adherence to a code of honor, behavior, and manners, which has been seen as stereotypical of the ruling class (Marnham, 1982). These characteristics were seen as important because of the need to be seen to abide by the rules of society and to accept without question the place one had in the class system. Fulfilling the obligations imposed by the class system, even when such rules did not lead to personal advantage, was considered important. This culture was, therefore, based on an internalization of a set of formal and informal rules. Contravention of the rules could lead to loss of face, dishonor, and social ostracism.

Liberal Culture

An alternative culture developed based on a mixture of liberal and collectivist values. An important element in this was the acceptance of community norms and collectivist activity (M. Young & Willmott, 1957). With the development of the welfare state and new laws banning discrimination on the basis of race or sex in the 1970s, the liberal culture was beginning to pose a threat to the hegemony of the traditionalist culture.

There were a number of different threads that differentiated groups within the liberal culture. Most people who subscribed to the main tenets of the liberal culture rejected inequality replacing it with an emphasis on humane and egalitarian attitudes and a belief in cooperation, consensus, and individual freedom. Those who adopted this outlook had a general belief in progression through merit and were happy to work in a performance-oriented environment. They rejected high power distance. Collectivist variants of this subculture were led by writers such as Raymond Williams (Johnson, 1979). He was a variant who rejected the class-based views, arguing that new opportunities permitted the rise of a meritocracy (M. Young, 1958).

Recent Cultural Change in England

Against this general background it can be seen that between 1945 and 2000 major cultural changes took place in England. Hall, Held, and McGrew (1992) and Halsey (1995) suggest that these changes are leading to the construction of new meanings and identities that are likely to influence the actions of both organizations and individuals in ways that cannot easily be identified.

The old ruling class has lost much of its once dominant position. Even the traditional characteristic of reserve or reluctance to show feelings in public has changed. For example, the importance of the idea of the "stiff upper lip" was challenged by the remarkable public grief shown at the death of Princess Diana in 1997. This reflected a growing recognition in society that it was acceptable to show emotions in public.

An example of the rise of the challenge to the dominance of the male role model can be seen in the social and economic emancipation of women. By the 1990s, women had the opportunity to play a much greater role in society and contribute to a reorientation of culture. With at least a minimum welfare state, the dominant fear of poverty and illness found in the 1930s had been significantly reduced for women, who had found new ways of raising children without the need for a man to provide for the family.

With such massive changes by the end of the 20th century, the relevance of traditionalist culture was being seriously questioned (Hobsbawm & Ranger, 1983).

The rise and widespread use of satirical humor in a variety of media has acted as a mirror for those questioning the relevance of dominant cultural norms. Humor has been an acceptable tool to prick the pomposity and overweening pride of leaders in society. Not even the Queen, as head of state, has been immune to this. Humor and self-mockery has also been used by leaders in business as an effective way of cutting through hierarchies in order to establish relationships. Humor provided the safety valve through which social, economic, and political inequalities could be addressed. It is a route by which the traditional deference and reserve, which still pervades parts of society, can be challenged. British culture has never been immune to change. Migration, regional consciousness, the rise of science, the increasing role of women, and the openness of the mass media have all played a part in change over the period between 1950 until 2000. As a result, some have questioned how culturally united England really is (Corner & Harvey, 1991; Hewison, 1995). These recent cultural changes have made England into a far more varied and cosmopolitan society than was the case in the 1950s. This does not mean, however, that there are not identifiable bastions of the traditionalist culture. There are also other parts of society that emphasize a liberal culture.

It is fairly easy for people to recognize the images and actions that represent these different cultural archetypes (Halsey, 1995). We briefly outline some unobtrusive measures that give a qualitative insight into British culture. These measures are concerned with the GLOBE concepts of Power Distance, Collectivism (Individualism), Gender Egalitarianism, Humane Orientation, Future Orientation, and Performance Orientation.

Power Distance.   In the past there has been a high degree of Power Distance among those who felt they belonged to the class-based culture of British society. In the period since the Second World War, there has been a decline in the rigidity of this system. The royal family and landed aristocracy lost a great deal of their power and influence. The royal family, based on the hereditary principle, appears to many as something of a contradiction in modern Britain. It maintains a system of hierarchy and honors that seems rather out of place in a democratic state. However, there is very widespread public support for the monarchy, without which its existence would be called into question.

Since World War II, politics in Britain has often revolved around the power distance debate. The advent of the Thatcher government led to radical change and the promotion of individual power rather than state power. The period from 1979 to 1997 was characterized by the privatization of state enterprises, the development of an "enterprise culture," deregulation, tax reduction, the abolition of foreign exchange controls, and a cutback on the welfare state. The aim was to change the culture from dependency to individual freedom, enterprise, and responsibility (Randlesome, 1995). The emphasis on deregulation extended to trade unions. The right not to join a union and legal control of the right to strike transformed the industrial relations environment. There was a fall in the membership of trade unions from 10.9 million in 1984 to 8.27 million in 1994. More significant, the power of the unions was significantly reduced. The number of working days lost through strikes went down from 4.12 million in 1989 to 278,000 in 1994. The number of workers involved in strikes went down from 887,000 in 1987 to 107,000 in 1994, and the number of disputes went down from 1,074 in 1986 to 205 in 1994 (Office for National Statistics, 1997).

The deregulation emphasis on enterprise and individualism characteristic of the Thatcher governments of the 1980s was seen as a watershed to some and an aberration to others. Thatcher was a good example of a prime minister who made radical changes and provided innovative leadership. But such an approach was exceptional. The main political parties have, in the 1990s, changed tack, and proclaimed their wish to transform Britain into a "classless" society. This approach retained some elements of Thatcherism, such as recognition of the importance of private enterprise, but it also included funding to provide a better system of education, creating more equal opportunities and a measure of redistribution. In the 1990s, social scientists such as Anthony Giddens had a significant influence on the thinking of leading Labor politicians. He sketched out what became known as "the third way" (Giddens, 1994, 1998, 2000). This suggested that a new and different approach to politics could be developed that would leave behind the traditional fight between right and left. Indeed, research by Peter Saunders (1996) suggests that England is already largely a meritocratic society. He found that the most important factors accounting for social-class division was individual ability and motivation rather than family background or social situation.

Collectivism (Individualism).   There is a streak of individualism to be found in England. To some this can be explained by simple characteristics such as the fact that being an island there has been an emphasis on self-reliance. Others would suggest that an explanation can best be found in the legal system and the long tradition of liberalism going back to the Bill of Rights in 1688, which has provided a degree of personal liberty not found elsewhere. At the same time, it would be equally true to say that there is also acceptance of community values that governments have attempted to support in a variety of ways. An example of the individualism of the British is in their attitude toward obeying the law when it comes to matters of conscience. In a recent survey (Brook & Cape, 1995) only 36% would obey the law if it clearly went against their conscience, whereas 57% would follow their conscience rather than the law.

There is generally a belief that individuals should be allowed to do what they want, so long as it does not adversely affect others. For example, the issue of the illegality of some "soft" drugs has been a matter of debate, with public opinion showing signs of change. Recent evidence (Gould, Shaw, & Ahrendt, 1996) suggests that attitudes have changed over the period from 1983 to 1995. Those wishing to keep cannabis illegal have declined from 78% to 58%. Those wishing for a change in the law have risen from 12% to 31%. Such results indicate growing support for the right of the individual to make choices in this area.

Finally, the opposite of an individualist approach is perceived as an authoritarian orientation, for this denies the right of individuals to make choices. Ahrendt and Young (1994) found that people in England over the age of 60 years were more than twice as likely to hold authoritarian views than those under 34. Their evidence indicates that whereas authoritarian attitudes are fairly strong amongst older and less well-educated people, among the younger and better-educated, authoritarian attitudes are held only by a minority (19%). Despite this general picture, people in England still take an authoritarian approach to punishment and law breaking, especially over serious crimes. There is a strong public view that the law should be obeyed, and that crime should be punished.

Gender Egalitarianism.   Traditionally there has been a strong emphasis on masculinity in English culture with women playing a subordinate role. Until the end of the 1950s, it was still considered that "the woman's place is in the home." Even in the 1990s, women still did not have equal representation in leadership positions in many areas of economic and political life. The advent of equal opportunities and the economic emancipation of women has, however, led to significant change. Now most women work and only 27% of people think that the wife should stay at home and look after the children. It has been suggested that this increased participation in the labor force has shaken the foundations of traditional family life (Scott, Braun, & Alwin, 1993). One of the consequences of the emancipation of women has been a change in the nature of relationships and a decline in the need for the traditional family bound by marriage. For example, the number of births outside marriage increased steadily from 218,000 in 1990 to 240,000 in 1995. By the mid-1990s almost one in two children were born outside marriage. There is a trend, at least among younger people, toward a greater tolerance of different ways of bringing up children. Living together outside marriage does not bring the stigma and social isolation that it did in the 1960s.

Humane Orientation.   It would appear that there has been a general move toward a more humane or liberal approach in many social aspects of English culture. For example, the death penalty was abolished in the 1960s, abortion was legalized, and the laws have been used to try to stamp out discrimination.

There is generally a good health service, which is free at the point of need, funded through taxation. Increasing numbers of people, however, recognizing its shortcomings, are also using private health insurance. There is a fairly poor state-funded pension scheme, but strong encouragement exists for those in work to take part in private pension schemes. Overall it can be said that the welfare state does still provide some assistance for the basic needs of most of the vulnerable and deprived sections of the population, on at least a minimal level. In addition there is a significant and relatively thriving voluntary sector, which provides assistance for many special needs.

Future Orientation and Performance Orientation.   There has been a relatively low level of consideration for the longer-term future, partly because of the welfare state safety net. It was thought by many that the funding provided through taxation would cover for most future needs (including education, unemployment benefit, and pensions). The attack on the welfare state in the 1980s and 1990s has led to an increased concern for the future. Among the middle classes delayed gratification is still important. For many millions of people who have average or lower than average incomes, the most important concern is deciding which bills to pay at the end of the week. For the majority, therefore, dealing with the present provides enough problems without having to think about the long-term future.

Linked to a willingness to plan for the future is often a concern to achieve. Many companies say they recognize and reward performance among employees. For some this amounts to little more than tokenism, but for others, this can make a significant difference to their take-home pay. A recent survey indicated that on average nonmanagers in the private sector gained an 8.9% increase on their base pay and senior managers gained an increase of 13.6% (Chartered Institute of Personnel and Development [CIPD], 1999). Almost all firms now have some sort of performance measurement, monitoring, and appraisal system.

2.   THE CONTEXT OF MANAGEMENT AND LEADERSHIP IN ENGLAND

Many authors have tried to identify the main characteristics of English business culture and its influence on management in business (Adler, 1991; Child, 1981; Cooper & Hingley, 1985; Lazonick, 1986; Mant, 1977; Trompenaars, 1993). One of the most interesting and influential contributions, was by Geert Hofstede (1980, 1991), who provided a useful comparative analysis of managers and their cultural attitudes. His research on managers at IBM in Britain showed a comparatively high score for Individualism and Masculinity, but a comparatively low score on Uncertainty Avoidance and Power Distance.

In the 19th and early 20th, centuries there was an aristocratic aversion to industry (Lazonick, 1986). The predominant form of enterprise was the family-run business, which lacked any professional training. The professionalization of management can be traced back to the growth of "red-brick" universities such as Leeds (textiles), Birmingham (engineering), and Reading (agriculture and land management), which provided a new group of professionally qualified managerial staff. It was not until 1947 that the British Institute of Management was formed to try to promote management education, and it was over 10 years later that the first state-supported business schools, London Business School and Manchester Business School, were established. Even in the late 1960s and early 1970s, managers were not seen as professionals (Lazonick, 1986).

Between 1970 and 2000, British managers became professionalized. This period saw a huge increase in management education, training, and development. For example, the number of business graduates in British universities rose from virtually none in 1960 to 124,000 in 1994–1995. During this period, however, most top British managers had at best, technical rather than business qualifications. As a group, it was said that they showed some typical characteristics such as politeness, tenaciousness, resourcefulness, and self-discipline (Terry, 1979). Terry also suggested that they had a generally ethnocentric attitude toward their foreign counterparts, and most could hardly speak a foreign language. Although not common in most large firms, even in the 1980s, Newitt (1989) suggested that some managers still had an ignorant, arrogant, narrow minded colonial and nationalistic attitude. Most large and multinational firms had moved on from such stereotypes many years before. They had been exposed to international competition, learned from best practice from around the world, and some were leading the way in innovative management training, in diversity management, and in promoting equal opportunities. These open-minded, professional managers reflected some of the more positive aspects of the British character of honesty, frankness, trust, self-control, self-discipline, and politeness (Tayeb, 1993). In the late 1980s and early 1990s, managers who worked in such organizations were studied by Trompenaars (1993), who commented that the characteristic corporate culture in Britain could be called a "guided missile" model. This is essentially egalitarian, impersonal, and task oriented. However, the professionalization of business management was still seen by many as having little to do with leadership. Management was a matter of administration, procedures, and abiding by rules and regulations. British authors such as John Adair were influential in challenging this view, arguing that every manager needed leadership skills. Indeed he suggested, "leadership is an essential ingredient in effective and successful management." (Adair, 1984, p. ix). His ideas about developing leadership skills were widely adopted in business and the public sector in the 1980s and 1990s.

The work of Cooper and Hingley (1985) showed that many of the most successful leaders in business adopted an open, honest, charismatic leadership style. Successful corporate leaders were often highly motivated individuals who were driven by anger and frustration with the status quo. Essentially these people were active leaders who did not simply respond to circumstances, but who were determined to change circumstances and to triumph over adversity. This type of approach echoed the inspirational and aggressive approach taken by leaders such as Churchill, Montgomery, and Nelson. In difficult circumstances, they were single-minded and determined to do what they thought right and carried their followers with them. These attitudes led to some terms in popular speech, such as "the bulldog spirit" to express admiration for an individual's determination to fight against a much more powerful opponent. Another was "the Nelson touch" in which Nelson ignored orders to stop an attack and carried on a battle to victory. This sort of individualism was not new. In earlier times, leaders such as

Sir Francis Drake, and later Cecil Rhodes were seen as outstanding, not so much for their inspirational qualities, but for the ruthless single-mindedness with which they achieved their aims. Such approaches are still adopted by some business leaders in England.

Many others seem to prefer a more anonymous approach, which may hide the significant changes they make. In the public sector, for example, Clement Atlee was seen as quiet, diplomatic, and procedural. He was noted for not using one word where none would do. Yet he presided over some of the most significant political, social, and economic changes of the century.

In looking at leaders in British history, we cannot see any one dominant approach, but there are a variety of approaches. In schools and popular culture, there is much more discussion of the different ways people can lead organizations than 50 years ago. People aged over 50 learned in school about the great military and royal leaders of conquest and empire. Today leadership qualities from other walks of life are recognized. People such as Florence Nightingale and Isambard Kingdom Brunel are considered as worthy of attention as military leaders like Haig or Wellington.

3.   THE GLOBE STUDY

Media Analysis Findings

The aim of this analysis was to identify key features of leadership as reported in the British media. A systematic analysis of press stories about the actions or intentions of business leaders was made. These were distilled into a number of simple categories. Details of the method used can be found in Appendix A. Table 10.1 outlines the main results.

The most frequently cited characteristic was energy, followed by change, action, facilitation, and direction. The results reveal that the lowest ranking scores were for vision, innovation, authority, communication, results orientation, and setting a challenge.

Over 70% of the stories selected were from either the *Financial Times* or *Management Today*. This reflects a greater concern for leadership issues in these two publications. They were also the only two media that reported on innovation within the context of leadership. This may in part be due to their more in-depth concentration on UK business issues than other national news media. *Management Today* also shows higher figures for *facilitate, direction,* and *culture,* highlighting its focus on modern organizational leadership issues.

The findings of this media analysis show that the most prominent characteristic of British leadership is the energy (or dynamism) that leaders showed together with their focus on a positive action orientation. From this study, it can also be concluded that leaders appear to be strong promoters of change, providing clear direction and inspiration for their followers. Perhaps it is not surprising, therefore, that leaders also attract a significant degree of criticism. They are generally realistic in identifying failure. British leaders are goal oriented and usually set realistic targets. The articles indicate that these leaders prefer not to exercise authority or power in public, but to get things done or fixed in private. They have collective skills (e.g., group decision making) that complement this sort of style. They tend to use flat rather than tall hierarchies, and methods that empower employees seem to be preferred. Masculine and feminine characteristics are evident but with few extremes. Leaders are seen to be dynamic, energetic, action orientated, flexible go-getters. They have an ability to induce change and are promoters of future strategies but the stories show they tend to want to go ahead and get things done as soon as possible.

TABLE 10.1
Media Analysis by Source

| Categories | Media Source | | | | | Total | % |
	Fin Times	Independent	Daily Mail	Economist	Mgt. Today		
Energy	8	9	3	2	13	35	23.7
Change	8	5	0	0	8	21	14.2
Action	8	4	0	2	6	20	13.5
Facilitate	5	1	1	0	9	16	10.8
Direction	6	2	1	0	7	16	10.8
Objectives	5	3	3	0	0	11	7.4
Culture	0	1	0	0	5	6	4.1
Vision	3	0	0	0	2	5	3.4
Authority	1	0	2	1	0	4	2.7
Communication	1	0	0	0	3	4	2.7
Challenge	1	0	0	0	2	3	2
Innovate	3	0	0	0	0	3	2
Results	0	0	0	0	3	3	2
Control	0	0	0	0	1	1	0.7
Total	49	25	10	5	59	148	100

They did not show a high level of vision, innovation, and long-term planning. They did not rely on authority structures, and there was little evidence of their ability to communicate within their corporations.

Overall, this media analysis shows that British business leaders do not reflect traditional culture; if anything, they seem to fit more within what was earlier termed a liberal culture. They do not talk about high power distance or tall hierarchies, but they do seem concerned to show energy and an action orientation that empowers and motivates employees.

The Empirical Survey

English Culture.   This section outlines the findings of the survey carried out among middle-level managers in England in 1996. This was a relatively small sample ($N = 81$) and no generalizations can be drawn from it. Nevertheless, the responses do provide interesting findings of the views of a sample of middle managers in some leading British companies, at what appears to be a time of cultural transition. We have used the Mean (M) scores of the responses in this section. Respondents were asked to give their responses using a 7-point Likert-type scale with 1 as the minimum score and 7 as the maximum.

The results of the survey concerning societal culture show that the respondents felt that England was a stratified, individualistic, masculine society. There were significant differences of power. There was little humanity, sharing, or kindness (see Table 10.2).

TABLE 10.2

Results for Britain on the Nine GLOBE Cultural Dimensions at the Societal Level

Culture Dimensions	Society "As Is"			Society "Should Be"			Difference[d]
	Mean[a]	Band[b]	Rank[c]	Mean[a]	Band[b]	Rank[c]	Should Be–Is
Power Distance	5.15	B	36	2.80	C	24	–2.35
Uncertainty Avoidance	4.65	B	14	4.11	C	47	–0.54
Assertiveness	4.15	A	29	3.70	B	33	–0.45
Collectivism 1	4.27	B	30	4.31	C	47	0.04
Future Orientation	4.28	B	11	5.06	C	53	0.78
Collectivism 2	4.08	C	53	5.55	B	37	1.47
Gender Egalitarianism	3.67	A	12	5.17	A	1	1.50
Humane Orientation	3.72	C	48	5.43	B	34	1.71
Performance Orientation	4.08	B	34	5.9	B	37	1.82

Notes: N = 81.
[a]Mean score on a 7-point Likert scale. [b]Letters A to E indicate distinguishable bands of country clusters (cf. Hanges, Dickson, & Sipe, 2004), with A (highest) > B > C > D > E (lowest). [c]Rank position for England relative to the 61 GLOBE countries. [d]Absolute difference between the "Should Be" and "As Is" scores.

The middle managers in the survey felt that society was only moderately encouraging (M = 4.08) people toward Performance Orientation. They saw in society moderate Future Orientation (M = 4.28). They considered there was a significant degree of Assertiveness in society (M = 4.15) and a fairly low score for Gender Egalitarianism (M = 3.67), indicating a significant masculine orientation in society. They also felt that society was not particularly of a Humane Orientation (M = 3.72). These responses complement their view that there was a substantial Power Distance in British society (M = 5.15). However, at the same time they recognized that there was a significant degree of Collectivism at the societal level (M = 4.27), perhaps reflecting the influence of the welfare state. They also saw that family Collectivism was of at least some significance (M = 4.08). Both these responses may explain to some degree the mean of 4.65 given for Uncertainty Avoidance, indicating that there was some basic provision to help people deal with most of the commonly accepted uncertainties in daily life.

The interesting part of this survey was concerned with how middle managers felt society "Should Be." They were asked to express their views about what society should be like. We can see in their responses something of a reflection of the changes from a traditional to a liberal culture. Perhaps the most striking example of this was that there should be less Power Distance in society ("As Is" M = 5.15, "Should Be" M = 2.80). Supporting this they said that there should be much more Gender Egalitarianism (M = 5.17), and a much more Humane Orientation in British society (M = 5.43). These results indicate that the middle managers were in favor of cultural change. At the same time, however, they also felt that there should be greater reliance on Performance Orientation (M = 5.90), family Collectivism (M = 5.55), and a Future Orientation (M = 5.06). These results seem to indicate a strong wish for greater equality of opportunity for all, reward for performance, and a rejection of the inequalities based on power distance and gender.

Organizational Culture "As Is" and "Should Be"

In this section, we consider the survey responses by middle managers in the financial services sector and the food-processing sector in England. Eighty-one middle-level managers from leading financial institutions and food companies took part in this. Although the numbers are small and generalizations cannot be made, the results do provide an insight into the views of middle managers in the organizations taking part.

As in the previous section the same 7-point scale was used.

Financial Services.   In the 1980s and 1990s, there has been a significant reduction in the number of middle-level managers in British industry and an increase in their responsibilities for the achievement of goals. In the financial services industry, in particular, there has been very significant organizational change in which middle managers have been squeezed to improve performance with fewer resources (see Appendix B for details). Performance is important ($M = 4.36$, cf. Table 10.3, "As Is"), but there should be an even stronger emphasis on performance in the industry ($M = 6.31$, "Should Be"). Managers wish to plan for the future and believe in delayed gratification ($M = 4.75$), but they suggest that there is significantly more that should be done ($M = 5.68$) to support this aspiration to invest in the future.

Traditionally there was a strong masculine culture in the management of the banking and finance industry. This has declined to a significant degree, and some firms have made great efforts to recruit and promote female managers. It is clear from the survey, however, that there is still a feeling that at present there is only limited Gender Egalitarianism ($M = 3.44$). The managers in the survey felt that there should be a significant change to ensure gender equality ($M = 5.11$). It was also clear that although there was recognition of the need for fairness and a caring or humane approach in their organizations ($M = 4.38$), they felt that more needed to be done ($M = 5.04$). Linked to this the managers said there was some Power Distance in their organizations ($M = 4.61$), which in their view should be reduced ($M = 3.39$). Almost as a corollary of this, the emphasis on the individual was considered to be less important than the need for group pride and loyalty ($M = 6.18$). Respondents felt their organizational culture aimed at avoiding Uncertainty ($M = 4.37$), but the managers perceive there should be less Uncertainty Avoidance ($M = 3.73$).

TABLE 10.3
Organizational Culture in Financial Sector Companies

Culture Dimension	"As Is"	"Should Be"	Difference
Power Distance	4.61	3.41	−1.20
Uncertainty Avoidance	4.77	3.73	−1.04
Assertiveness	3.82	3.98	0.16
Humane Orientation	4.38	5.04	0.66
Institutional Collectivism	4.08	4.82	0.74
Future Orientation	4.75	5.68	0.93
Gender Egalitarianism	3.44	5.11	1.67
In-Group Collectivism	4.37	6.18	1.81
Performance Orientation	4.36	6.31	1.95

Note. $N = 81$.

TABLE 10.4

Organizational Culture in Food Companies

Culture Dimension	"As Is"	"Should Be"	Difference
Power Distance	3.80	3.58	−0.22
Uncertainty Avoidance	4.08	4.27	0.19
Assertiveness	4.63	4.86	0.23
Humane Orientation	3.43	3.91	0.48
Institutional Collectivism	3.47	4.11	0.64
Future Orientation	5.06	5.76	0.70
Gender Egalitarianism	4.00	4.89	0.89
In-Group Collectivism	4.64	5.79	1.15
Performance Orientation	4.43	6.31	1.88

Note.   N = 81.

The Food-Processing Sector.   The managers in the food-processing industry responded in a similar way to the managers in the finance industry (see Appendix C for details of the food industry). Like their colleagues in the financial services industry, they felt that Performance Orientation was of some importance ($M = 4.43$, cf. Table 10.4, "As Is"), but there should be a significant increase in the recognition and rewards for improvements in Performance ($M = 6.31$, "Should Be"). The frustration at a lack of a strong Performance Orientation was important, showing the greatest difference between "As Is" and "Should Be" scores. They said the culture of their organizations was Future Oriented ($M = 5.06$), but this should have a still greater emphasis ($M = 5.76$). Traditionally in the food services sector, men have been dominant in the managerial levels. The respondents thought there should be much more equality between the sexes ($M = 5.11$). Managers felt that the organizational culture supported fairness and a humane approach to dealing with problems ($M = 4.63$) and little more should be done ($M = 4.86$). The score on Power Distance showed that the firms in this sector do not have highly stratified power levels ($M = 3.80$) and there was little need for change ($M = 3.58$). The respondents felt that there was a reasonable degree of group pride and loyalty ($M = 4.64$), but there should be changes to put greater emphasis on this ($M = 5.79$). The respondents were reasonably tolerant of Uncertainty Avoidance ($M = 4.08$) but, if anything, they thought there should be less uncertainty and risk in their organizations ($M = 4.27$).

Organizational Characteristics "As Is" Across Both Sectors.   In looking at the means of organizational characteristics "As Is," it is clear that there are no very strongly suggested characteristics. The lowest means are for Variables 1-22 and 1-34. These ask respondents to give their perceptions on factual matters. Variable 1-22 asks whether most tasks are done by men or women, with men as 1 and women as 7 ($M = 2.80$). Variable 1-34 asks how many positions are filled by women (with possible responses ranging from less than 10% as 1 and with more than 90% as 7. The mean on this variable of 2.37 indicates respondents thought that women filled about 10% to 25% of positions. This shows under-representation of women in the workforce of these firms. All the other means fall within a range of 3.42 to 5.50. The highest means show that organizations are generally seen as slightly unfriendly places (Variable 1-24 stated "in this organization staff are generally very friendly" [1], to very unfriendly [7], and the mean response was 5.50). Management does not encourage continuous improvement (Variable 1-15 asked if staff in this organization are encouraged to strive for continuous improvement with 1 as strongly agree and 7 as strongly disagree, and a respondent mean of 5.45). There is a tendency toward taking events as they occur rather than planning ahead (variable 1-3 asked if the way to be successful in this organization was to plan ahead [1], or to take events as they occur [7]). The respondent mean was 5.05. This suggests that respondents feel that to be successful organizations need to be flexible, pragmatic, and concerned with the short term rather than making plans for the future.

Organizational Characteristics "Should Be."   The means of responses provided evidence of some strong views. For example, Variable 3-5 stated, "in this organization a person's influence should be based primarily on: one's ability and contribution to the organization (1), or the authority of one's position (7)." The mean response was 1.81, indicating a strong unwillingness to be influenced by position rather than ability. However, on the other hand, there was some reluctance by managers to be involved in constant performance improvement. Variable 3-15 said, "in this organization people should be encouraged to strive for continuously improved performance," with 1 as strongly agree and 7 as strongly disagree. The mean response was 6.7. These responses seem to show that respondents wanted to be free to perform and contribute, but still wanted some stability and security in their work without the pressure of the need to constantly improve. The responses suggested that people should be assertive, self-centered, and not concerned for (nor sensitive about) others in the workplace. They felt they should obey the boss without question, but they did not feel any great loyalty to the organization.

Overall, the results of the analysis at the organizational level indicate a wish for smaller power distance, less risk taking, less gender differentiation, and less individualism. They also suggest the need for a more future and performance orientation, more collectivism, and more of a humane approach. These results support and perhaps mirror the cultural changes that are taking place in society, with managers appearing to support elements of a liberal culture with lower power distance, greater gender equality, and a more humane and collectivist approach.

Empirical Survey of Leadership

Characteristics of Leaders in Society.   This section discusses the results of the empirical survey, which asked managers to outline what they considered to be the attributes expected in leaders in their organization and in society as a whole. The means outlined in Table 10.5 have been calculated from the validated combination of individual attributes. The attributes most expected in outstanding leaders complement the views outlined earlier. In commenting on leadership, respondents valued highly the ability to provide inspiration, vision, encouragement of a performance orientation, and team integration. Personal integrity, decisiveness, diplomacy, and administrative competence were also valued. The results show that individualists who were autocratic, status-conscious, and who used bureaucratic methods were not favored.

If these results are compared with the results of the media analysis, there are similarities. The media analysis evaluated what leaders said they had done, were doing, or would do. The most commonly used characteristic was energy. The expression of energy, linked with direction, action, and change, provides a complementary support for the survey results concerning the importance of inspiration and performance orientation. An action and change orientation can be seen as related to performance and decisiveness. The leading attributes found in the

TABLE 10.5
Means and Ranking of First-Order Leadership Scales in the Finance and Food Companies

Characteristics	Finance		Food	
	Mean	Rank	Mean	Rank
Inspirational	6.44	1	6.27	1
Performance Orientation	6.41	2	6.27	2
Visionary	6.23	3	6.17	3
Integrity	6.20	4	6.08	5
Team Integrator	6.16	5	6.16	4
Decisive	5.96	6	6.03	6
Diplomatic	5.40	7	5.36	9
Team Collaboration	5.33	8	5.45	8
Administrative Competent	5.15	9	5.75	7
Self-Sacrificial	5.02	10	4.72	12
Humane orientation	4.95	11	4.91	11
Modesty	4.80	12	5.15	10
Autonomous	3.85	13	3.88	13
Status-Conscious	3.61	14	3.85	15
Conflict Inducer	3.47	15	3.31	16
Procedural	3.38	16	3.88	14
Face Saver	2.48	17	2.62	18
Autocratic	2.42	18	2.98	17
Nonparticipative	2.27	19	2.24	19
Self-Centered	1.88	20	2.02	20
Malevolent	1.71	21	1.77	21

media analysis do appear to generally support the attributes expressed by managers in the survey.

In the empirical survey, it is clear that vision is seen as a critical attribute, providing a link between some of the personal qualities of individuals such as intelligence, competence, and performance orientation and the need to look outward to how best the firm could deal with the business environment. As a trading nation, England is subject to often rapid and turbulent change so the link between inspiring employees, emphasizing competitive performance, and using vision to anticipate future changes fits in well with the needs of the business environment.

Individualism is not rated highly by the respondents as an attribute of leaders (Autonomy ranks only 13th out of 21 in both Finance and Food, cf. Table 10.5). Similarly, the survey shows that Status Consciousness (Rank 14/15) and authoritarian approaches are not rated highly (Autocratic: Rank 18/17). This provides more evidence of the challenge of the liberal culture to the traditional culture, which relied on status and class.

Factor Analysis of Leadership Variables.[1].   The purpose of factor analysis is to summarize the interrelationships among a set of variables as an aid in conceptualization. Factor analysis provides an understanding of the interdependence among a large set of variables and their dependence on a number of unobservable common factors. It is not within the scope of this chapter to go into a detailed discussion of factor analysis, but there is some debate about the extent to which conclusions can be based on the relationship between variables and the underlying themes (Kinnear & Gray, 1997). An exploratory factor analysis was carried out on the 112 leadership variables based on the total sample size of $N = 168$ respondents. Using principal component analysis, we extracted four main components. There were many other components but they accounted for a very small amount of variance. We briefly outline the four main underlying dimensions, which are derived from the factor analysis of the empirical survey responses (see Appendix D for the component matrix).

1. *The Inspirational Coach:* The key elements of this approach to leadership include a strong encouraging and morale boosting emphasis, combined with honesty and trust. This dimension is also characterized by dependability, and a consultative and informed approach that is excellence oriented and inspirational. These characteristics suggest support for low power distance and an approach that delegates and builds confidence in employees. An example of a business leader who used this sort of approach in the 1990s was Richard Branson, who became well known in England for his inspirational qualities, low power distance, and a coaching attitude. Such an approach may be most suited to situations where there is scope for the individual to make an impact, or where external or internal regulations are limited or permit significant discretion. Nevertheless, inspirational individuals may be outstandingly successful despite being hemmed in by restrictions or regulations.
2. *The Orderly Organizer:* The underlying characteristics of this dimension included orderliness, patience, use of procedures, and cautiousness. These leaders are essentially rule based, making decisions based clearly on established procedures, and they operate "by the book." They try to work with others in a collaborative fashion and are aware of the need for sensitivity. These leaders are risk averse and modest as individuals. They are not provocative or egotistical but prefer order, formality, and organization. Some of the elements of this approach are found in business leaders such as Arnold Weinstock, who successfully led General Electric in the 1980s and 1990s.
3. *The Merchant Adventurer:* The characteristics of this underlying dimension are high power distance and self-centered individualism. The main elements include ruthlessness,

---

[1]As discussed in Hanges and Dickson (2004), the GLOBE scales were designed to measure organizational or societal level variability. The scales were *not* intended to meaningfully differentiate among individuals within a particular society. However, even though the scales were not constructed to provide such information, in some cases it is interesting to assess whether similar factors differentiate individuals within a society. Country-specific factor analysis is intended as an exploration of the themes captured by GLOBE in a new domain, that is, individual differences within a society. It should be noted that, because of the within-society restriction of the GLOBE scales true-score variability (which was based on between-society factors should be lower than between societies (cf. Hanges & Dickson, 2004). Furthermore, one should not interpret the within society factor analyses as replications of the GLOBE factor structure. And the absence of a GLOBE factor within a society should not be automatically interpreted as the factor being irrelevant to the people in that country. Rather, a factor may fail to emerge within a society even when that theme is extremely critical because there was no variability and so a factor could fail to emerge because it is extremely critical or completely irrelevant to the people within a society.

egotism, and nonegalitarianism. A domineering elitism is found in this category. These elements have a great deal in common with the self-made millionaires who grew rich during the 1980s. Individuals such as "Tiny" Rowlands, Robert Maxwell, and James Hanson showed how the individualistic merchant adventurer spirit could be successful in modern England. They were successful through a combination of intelligence, ruthlessness, and cunning.

4. *The Compassionate Visionary:* The underlying dimension can be seen as a humane orientation that is inspirational and self-sacrificial. There is also a future and improvement orientation found in this dimension. These leaders show compassion and to a lesser degree dynamism and enthusiasm. They may not be very good administrators but they have vision. It could be suggested that this category is reflected in the leadership style of Anita Roddick, who won widespread praise in the 1990s for building a highly successful business while at the same time emphasizing the importance of social and ethical values. She seemed to represent some of the emerging liberal culture. She was egalitarian and passionate about business ethics. She stood in clear contrast to the merchant adventurer approach. That Anita Roddick succeeded in England indicates that women could win through and capitalize on the opportunities they had created. It provides a clear indication of change in British culture.

4.   MANAGING IN MODERN ENGLAND: LESSONS LEARNED

In the light of the analysis outlined herein, the question that might well be asked is "what should a foreign manager coming to England expect?" How should a manager coming into England from some other country deal with employees?

The first point to make is that from the evidence it is clear that there would be acceptance of such a manager whatever their gender. The cultural bias, which in the past made it hard for a female manager to succeed, has been significantly reduced. There are laws to prevent gender and racial discrimination acting as a barrier to successful performance. Today business organizations are open to all.

The second point is that such a manager would be more likely to gain respect if they had some of the attributes considered characteristic of outstanding leaders. The survey suggests that what matters is personal ability, effort, and the capacity to motivate and lead others. The ability to inspire and arouse motivated activity in others is paramount, but in addition the respondents suggested that outstanding leaders needed to have some other personal qualities such as trustworthiness, diplomacy, modesty, and integrity. Such leaders are likely to be positive, intelligent, and clear communicators who are performance and excellence oriented. If managers coming to England had some of these characteristics, they would have a good chance of being accepted.

What might managers from another country expect to find when they come to England? First, there are a wide variety of organizational cultures in England, which reflects the cosmopolitan nature of English society. At one extreme, some organizations may still show a very traditional class culture, such as Morgan Cars. At the other extreme, some firms may exhibit some special characteristics. For example, as England has been successful in attracting foreign investors, so there are many firms that have strong cultural attributes linked to a foreign national culture. Some of the Japanese firms in England, such as Toyota, use Japanese management styles, and the English workforce has successfully adopted the cultural norms required. In between these two extremes there is a huge variety of cultural practices, so the first important lesson for a foreign manager should be not to prejudge the organization, but to be sensitive to its specific cultural attributes.

The second most important lesson, which this research suggests, is that a manager coming from abroad will find that organizations in England are generally only slightly performance oriented. Middle managers would wish to see their organizations as being much more performance oriented. This could be very significant in combination with the view that firms should also be more future oriented. For a manager coming from abroad this evidence clearly provides scope for action.

The third lesson that a manager coming into England can learn from this research concerns how to deal with employees. There is a need for more collectivism rather than individualism in the organizations surveyed. This translates into a wish for more group-based working, and more team-based approach in the workplace.

The fourth lesson also relates to people management. Managers in this research feel that there should be less differentiation based on gender, and a more humane orientation with less power distance. Learning these lessons would give managers an excellent start in understanding how they could be successful in dealing with employees at present and in working out strategies for future direction.

The final lesson is that respondents feel there is not one best way to lead. Instead they have identified four main approaches, each of which has specific characteristics. Each approach may be best suited to different industry or organizational characteristics, but an understanding of these approaches should help in assessing what may be possible and what may be most appropriate in a given situation. The inspirational coach and the compassionate visionary types may be seen as representatives of the new world of work, which is based on a liberal culture where individual employees are seen as critical to the success of the company. It could be suggested that the orderly organizer type reflects the professionalization of management and the influence of business education in England. The merchant adventurer type might be seen as more representative of older cultural stereotypes but may still be successful in certain circumstances.

5.   LIMITATIONS

There are limitations to this research that should be mentioned. The first main limitation is that we have talked about England rather than Britain or the UK as the main focus of this study. Britain is, of course, a mixture of different cultures. Scotland has a vibrant national culture. There are also regional and ethnic cultures that overlay the English, Scottish, or Welsh cultures. For example, Jewish, Quaker, Islamic (religious-based cultures), and Chinese, African, Indian and Pakistani (ethnic-based cultures) have been influential in some areas of business life in different parts of Britain. The influx of populations from many parts of the world has created a diversity of cultures. Tayeb (1993) suggested that the values of these communities fuse with those of the English to create nuances in business style and practice which can be significant. The research presented here is concerned, however, with the findings that derive from a study of firms in England. Questions about the relative importance and influence of different national, regional, religious, or ethnic cultures are, however, important.

A second limitation is that we have taken a once-in-time snapshot of English culture. One of the main points that we make is that cultural change is taking place. It would be sensible to follow up this snapshot with further research to measure the changes over time.

A third limitation is that we have been concerned to gain a general view, from the perspective of middle managers and from the media. The survey of middle managers was limited and it would be incautious to make any generalizations from such a small survey. To get a balanced view of firms it would be necessary to have good survey data from other groups such as lower-level employees and top management. In order to get a balanced view of societal culture, it would be useful to have a representative sample of the population. Although this would be likely to provide more accurate data, undertaking such a large data-gathering exercise was well beyond the resources available. It is to be hoped, however, that this research will provide a stimulus to others to carry out such work in the future.

Nevertheless, within these limitations, we have attempted to define and characterize some of the common aspects of English culture. Measuring the nature of the relationship between culture, organization, and leadership is a huge task. In this research, we have made one small contribution to what should be a growing wealth of research findings.

6. CONCLUSIONS

The results of this study provide new evidence of a transformation that is taking place in the attitudes, norms, and expectations of English managers, as expressed in the empirical survey. In some ways, this reflects cultural changes that are taking place in society. The English managers surveyed show a movement toward what we have called a liberal culture from the dominant traditionalist one. They expect leaders in their organizations to reflect the main attributes expected in leaders in the rest of society. The main attributes that leaders need to demonstrate, in order to have a chance of success, are a decisive, inspirational, and visionary performance orientation, in which integrity and diplomacy are also found. This view is largely confirmed from the media analysis, where leaders exhibit great energy. They have an action orientation and are change makers, setting and directing the organization to achieve objectives.

The results found confirm the work of Cooper and Hingley (1985), Trompenaars (1993), Terry (1979) and, to some extent, Hofstede's results concerning Uncertainty Avoidance, but goes further in suggesting that managers would like to see less Uncertainty Avoidance in their working lives. The research also suggests that whereas managers find England to be a high Power Distance society they expect outstanding leaders to have a low Power Distance orientation. The managers in the survey wish to see less masculinity and a more equally balanced gender orientation. In addition, they would expect a more Humane Orientation in organizations.

The research shows that England has undergone significant cultural change since the 1970s. The once dominant traditionalist culture has been challenged by the liberal culture. In the ranks of middle management, the end of class as a means of differentiating people has meant that individuals are expected to be able to succeed on the basis of merit rather than social origin. Old styles of leadership will be less likely to be accepted. There will be a need for more education and training on how best to motivate and encourage excellence in the workforce. It is clear that managers are searching for more motivation in the workplace. The attributes expected in organization leaders mirror these changes. The managers in the survey wanted leaders to reflect the need for equality of opportunity, reward for performance, and to reduce the power distance found within some organizations.

What is clear from this research is that the business leaders of the future will need a rather different set of attributes, compared to those of the past. They can no longer rely on loyalty; instead they have to earn it. They are not so likely to succeed by using an authoritarian or individualistic approach but must understand how to provide vision, energy, inspiration, and encouragement. This provides a tremendous challenge to educators to try to help develop the skills that can unlock the potential of business leaders to be able to flourish in the changing environment of the 21st century.

REFERENCES

Adair, J. (1984). *The skills of leadership.* Aldershot, England: Gower.

Adler, N. J. (1991). *International dimensions of organizational behavior.* Boston: PWS-Kent.

Ahrendt, D., & Young, K. (1994). Authoritarianism updated. In R. Jowell, J. Curtice, L. Brook, D. Ahrendt, & A. Park (Eds.), *British social attitudes: The 11th report* (pp. 75–93). Aldershot, England: Social and Community Planning Research, Dartmouth.

Brook, L., & Cape, E. (1995). Libertarianism in Retreat ? In R. Jowell, J. Curtice, L. Brook, D. Ahrendt, & A. Park (Eds.), *British social attitudes: The 12th report* (pp. 191–209). Aldershot, England: Social and Community Planning Research, Dartmouth.

Chartered Institute of Personnel and Development. (1999). *Performance pay trends* (IPD survey report). London: Author.

Child, J. (1981). Culture, contingency and capitalism In the cross national study of organisations. In L. L. Cummings & B. M. Staw (Eds.), *Research In organisational behavior* (Vol. 3, pp. 303–356). New York: JAI.

Cooper, C., & Hingley, P. (1985). *The change makers.* London: Harper & Row.

Corner, J., & Harvey, S. (Eds.). (1991). *Enterprise and heritage.* London: Routledge.

Curtice, J. (1996). One nation again ? In R. Jowell, J. Curtice, A. Park, L. Brook, & K. Thomson (Eds.), *British social attitudes: The 13th report* (pp. 1–16). Aldershot, England: Dartmouth.

Gallagher, T. (1992). Community relations In Northern Ireland. In R. Jowell, J. Curtice, A. Park, L. Brook, & K. Thomson (Eds.), *British social attitudes: The 9th report* (pp. 155–173). Aldershot, England: Dartmouth.

Giddens, A. (1994). *Beyond left and right: The future of radical politics.* Cambridge, England: Polity Press.

Giddens, A. (1998). *The third way: The renewal of social democracy.* Cambridge, England: Polity Press.

Giddens, A.(2000). *The third way and its critics.* Cambridge, England: Polity Press.

Gorsuch, R. L. (1983). *Factor analysis* (2nd ed.). Hillsdale, NJ: Lawrence Erlbaum Associates.

Gould, A., Shaw, A., & Ahrendt, D. (1996). Illegal drugs: Liberal and restrictive attitudes. In R. Jowell, J. Curtice, A. Park, L. Brook, & K. Thomson (Eds.), *British social attitudes: The 13th report* (pp. 93–114). Aldershot, England: Dartmouth.

Hall, S., Held, D., & McGrew, T. (1992). *Modernity and its futures.* Cambridge, England: Polity Press.

Halsey, A. H. (1995). *Change In British society.* Oxford, England: Oxford University Press.

Hanges, P. J., Dickson, M. W., & Sipe, M. T. (2004). Rationale for GLOBE statistical analyses: Societal rankings and test of hypotheses. In R. J. House, P. J. Hanges, M. Javidan, P. Dorfman, & V. Gupta (Eds.), *Leadership, culture, and organizations: The GLOBE study of 62 societies* (pp. 219–234). Thousand Oaks, CA: Sage.

Hanges, P. J., & Dickson, M. W. (2004). The development and validation of the GLOBE culture and leadership scales. In R. J. House, P. J. Hanges, M. Javidan, P. Dorfman, & V. Gupta (Eds.), *Leadership, culture and organizations: The GLOBE study of 62 societies* (pp. 122–151). Thousand Oaks, CA: Sage.

Hewison, R. (1995). *Culture and consensus.* London: Methuen.

Hobsbawm, E., & Ranger, T. (1983). *The invention of tradition.* Cambridge, England: Oxford University Press.

Hofstede, G. (1980). *Culture's consequences: International differences In work-related values.* Beverly Hills, CA: Sage.

Hofstede, G. (1991). *Cultures and organisations: Software of the mind.* London: McGraw-Hill.

Johnson, L. (1979). *The cultural critics.* London: Routledge.

Kinnear, P. R., & Gray, C. D. (1997). *SPSS for Windows* (2nd ed.). Hove, England: Psychology Press.

Lazonick, W. (1986). Strategy, structure and management development In the United States and Britain. In *Development of managerial enterprise* (pp. 101–146). Tokyo: University of Tokyo Press.

Leavis, F. R. (1972). *Nor shall my sword.* London: Chatto & Windus.

Leavis, F. R., & Thompson, D. (1960). *Culture and environment.* London: Chatto & Windus.

Mant, A. (1977). *The rise and fall of the British manager.* London: Macmillan.

Marnham, P. (1982). *The private eye story.* London: Andre Deutsch.

Newitt, S. (1989, September 27). *Executive post, No. 460,* p. 3.

Office for National Statistics. (1997). *Annual Abstract of Statistics* (No. 133). London: The Stationery Office.

Randlesome, C. (1995). *Business cultures In Europe.* London: Butterworth.

Saunders, P. (1996). *Unequal but fair.* London: Institute of Economic Affairs.

Snow, C, P. (1963). *The two cultures.* New York: Mentor.

Storey, J. (1994). *Cultural theory and popular culture.* New York: Harvester Wheatsheaf.

Tayeb, M. (1993). England. In D. Hickson (Ed.), *Management In Western Europe* (pp. 47–64). Berlin : de Gruyter.

Terry, P. (1979). *An investigation of some cultural determinants of English organisation behavior.* Unpublished doctoral dissertation, University of Bath, England.

Thompson, E. P. (1978). *The making of the English working class.* Harmondsworth, England: Penguin.

Trompenaars, F. (1993). *Riding the waves of culture.* London: Nicholas Brierley.

Young, M. (1958). *The rise of the meritocracy.* Harmondsworth, England: Penguin.

Young, M., & Willmott, P. (1957). *Family and kinship In east London.* Harmondsworth, England: Penguin.

Appendix A

Methodology for Media Analysis

For this study, five forms of news media with a national circulation were used: *The Financial Times, The Independent, The Daily Mail, The Economist,* and *Management Today.* These provided a variety of viewpoints.

The periods chosen for data collection were a 2-week period from May 20–31, 1996 and a 1-week period from June 24–29, 1996. All articles concerned with UK news were scanned using the following criteria:

- What a leader In an organization does, has done, will do, could do, or should do.
- How a leader was viewed as a result of the aforementioned acts.
- Articles about leaders In Britain only.

Articles about leadership In the public sector as well as the private sector were used and about leadership In business, politics, and society. The periods that were selected did not cover any major event. The period was average, except for one issue, which has come to be known as the "BSE crisis." This was not important enough during the survey period to necessitate excluding all articles referring to it from the study. The same criteria were used In selecting articles on the BSE crisis as with any other. If the piece described what a leader In the UK was doing, had done, and how their actions were viewed, then it was included In the study.

Once all the data had been collected and referenced, the most characteristic attributes were used to categorize the phrases. Where possible these were chosen from the verbs and adjectives within each phrase where this accurately summarized the meaning of the phrase. This reduced the mass of data to a number of words that clearly illustrated the phrases chosen.

Testing of the categories was a difficult task. To test whether the categories were seen as reasonable (i.e., an accurate reflection of the phrases) it was agreed that a test should be set up using students. They were asked to comment on a series of phrases and say how they would categorize them. The results from this were very favorable. A majority of students used the same or a related word to describe a phrase as had been used by the researcher. None of the category names used had to be changed.

Initially, while going through the phrases and categorizing them, it was decided that a second label should be added In some cases. This was used mainly when a phrase represented a negative attitude toward the first category label. The following are some examples: "He is not performing" (energy/negative); "we tried a bit of everything and most of the time we did not do particularly well" (direction/negative); "Leave that to the other lot" (action/negative).

On reviewing these, however, it was realized that each of these "negative" secondary labels could also be seen as indicating a need for a more positive approach. So "he is not performing" indicated a need for more positive performance. "We did not do particularly well" indicates the need to have better direction; and "leave that to the other lot" indicates that the individual had his or her own positive direction.

One major problem with this method of analysis was consistency In applying the secondary labels. The test of a sample helped to confirm that there was consistency. It was possible to build a set of loose guidelines when applying the secondary labels. For example, if the phrases actually contained a key word such as *culture, challenge, vision,* or *change* this usually meant that it would be categorized by the same word. Many phrases had a clear category label such as "action," "objective," or "result" where these were clearly illustrated In the phrase and the context of the articles.

Once all the articles had been typified and added to the listings it was possible to calculate the number of times each category appeared. The protocol suggested that the quantity of each category label gives an indication of how leaders are represented In the media. Clearly this view could be challenged. For example, it may well be that one category label is given only occasionally, but, perhaps because it is a word reserved for important occasions, it should have a weighting attached to it. For example, some important statements may only be made at an annual general meeting, and unless the sample covered the period of reporting to shareholders, some significant activities of leaders may not appear In the press. This issue does deserve serious attention.

The issue of bias was a concern—not just the bias resulting from making interpretations of categories without having a weighting, but that of the media sources used. Most articles from the media were written or edited by journalists. They are normally concerned with "newsworthy events" which could skew the findings toward an extreme issue or event, simply because such things make headlines.

Another problem with using popular media is that the journalists writing many of the articles are not usually qualified experts In that particular field. The article might not reflect what a leader intended it to, or what actually happened.

There are, therefore, some potentially significant methodological issues that researchers need to be aware of In conducting media analysis. The analysis did provide, however, a secondary form of independent evidence that was useful to compare with the results obtained from the empirical survey.

I would like to acknowledge Rachel Arnold for her research assistance In carrying out this element of the study.

Appendix B

The Financial Services Industry

There have been three major changes In the finance sector In the UK In the period from 1970 to 1997. These can be summarized as environmental change, technological change, and personnel change.

The first main change has been In the environment of the financial services sector. Perhaps the most important element of this has been the change In the law that allowed foreign banks to establish a presence In Britain and to compete for certain types of customer. Linked to this was the abolition of foreign-exchange controls, which allowed citizens to take money abroad and to bring money In. The effect of these changes was to break the cozy almost noncompetitive relationships between clearing bans In the UK. This led to much greater competition and a need to change the product mix and to market aggressively to customers. The main result of these environmental changes was a wave of takeovers and mergers In the 1980s and 1990s, and the increased integration of the industry. This mostly affected building societies and mortgage companies, but some of the main clearing banks (such as the TSB, the Royal Bank of Scotland, and the Midland Bank [HSBC] were also affected. The number of building societies declined from 167 In 1985 to 94 In 1995.

The second major change was the advent of technology, which led to a huge reduction In the need for retail outlets and backroom staff. As a result, there were very large staff reductions In almost all financial institutions In the 1980s and large investment In computerized systems. The whole retail banking system was threatened by the advent of banks with no retail outlets, where all business could be conducted over the phone. By the mid-1990s, banks were also beginning to establish "virtual banking" In which business could be conducted over the Internet.

The third major change has concerned those who work In the financial services sector. There has been a change In the culture of banks and financial institutions that has gone together with the need to compete for business. Staff were properly trained and organizations were structured to be able to compete. There has been a very large decline In the number of staff, and those that remained have had to be retrained to meet the needs of customers. Far fewer men were employed, but there was a significant increase In part-time female labor.

The three areas of change outlined briefly herein have left banks and other financial institutions appearing quite differently In 1997, compared to 1970. The revolution began by deregulation, and it is still In progress and will change not only the industry itself, but also the habits of consumers and the face of the high streets of towns throughout Britain as retail outlets close down.

Appendix C

The Food Industry

The dominant force In the period 1970–1997 was the European Union and the Common Agricultural Policy (CAP). The consistency of the CAP allowed many larger farmers In Britain generally to prosper In the 1980s. The food-processing companies had a steady supply of raw materials. Over the period, there was a significant integration of retailing with the dominance of major supermarkets such as Tesco, Sainsbury's, Safeway, and Somerfield.

There was also significant integration among food processors In Britain. By 1997, the six top processors were dominant In the market. There were also a large number of small enterprises, but relatively few medium-size firms. In 1992, about 564,000 people worked In the food, drink, and tobacco industry. Within the food sector, the three most important areas of manufacturing and sales were meat production and preserving, bread and cakes, and chocolate and confectionery. Most produce was sold In the UK or European market.

With the advent of the Single European Market, there have been threats from competition and increased opportunities for sales within Europe, In addition to traditional markets. The most significant issue, which has affected the food industry as a whole, has been the increased demand for high-quality produce and food safety. As the supermarket's power has increased, so farmers and processors have had to respond with cost-effective, high-quality products. A series of problems concerning food safety has led to political action to increase protection and regulation to ensure a higher degree of control In some areas. The main issue that has dominated the industry over the period 1989–1997 has been the contamination of the human food chain with a disease of cattle, BSE (Bovine Spongiform Encephalopathy and variants). This has had a devastating effect on those most closely affected and has led to changes In the way In which risk is assessed by companies and by the state.

Appendix D

Factor Analysis of Leadership Items

Inspirational Coach		Orderly Organizer	
Morale booster	.767	Procedural	.677
Confidence builder	.719	Formal	.646
Encouraging	.711	Patient	.606
Trustworthy	.686	Orderly	.550
Honest	.678	Cautious	.546
Plans ahead	.647	Organized	.537
Intelligent	.587	Collaborative	.521
Informed	.583	Risk averse	.505
Foresight	.566	Habitual	.487
Intellectually Stimulating	.563	Modest	.476

Merchant Adventurer		Compassionate Visionary	
Ruthless	.515	Team building	.438
Ruler	.463	Inspirational	.423
Able to anticipate	.448	Compassionate	.416
Organized	.431	Self-sacrificial	.409
Egotistical	.421	Motivational	.387
Dictatorial	.421		
Wilful	.420		
Nonegalitarian	.417		
Domineering	.404		
Self interested	.403		

The percentage of total variance explained by each factor was: Inspirational coach, 17.5%; Orderly organizer, 7.1%; Merchant adventurer, 6.2%; Compassionate visionary, 4.1%.
Note $N = 168$. Key extracted items are listed. Kaiser–Meyer–Olkin measure of sampling adequacy = .642. Approximate chi-square = 12,756.67 (df 6,216, p <.0001).

11

▼▼▼▼▼▼▼

Leadership and Culture in the Republic of Ireland

Mary A. Keating
Gillian S. Martin
*School of Business Studies and Department of Germanic Studies,
University of Dublin, Trinity College, Ireland*

The contemporary Irish writer, Seamus Deane, has interpreted W. B. Yeats's observation that "Ireland belonged to Asia before the Battle of the Boyne" (cited in Deane, 1984, p. 90) as underlining Ireland's membership of an old and worldwide culture.[1] The island of Ireland is situated to the extreme northwest of Europe and is separated from Britain, its closest neighbor, by the Irish Sea. Celts, Vikings, Normans, and the English have inhabited Ireland since the Stone Age. At the 2002 census, the population of the Republic of Ireland stood at 3.92 million and is predicted to increase to 5.1 million by 2021 (Central Statistics Office, 2004). In 1841, shortly before the Great Famine, the area now comprising the present Irish State had a population of over 6.5 million. The 1851 census revealed a massive decline to 5.1 million due to death from starvation, disease, and emigration. This outflow established a pattern, which has only recently begun to change. Former President Mary Robinson, in a speech to a joint sitting of the two houses of parliament on February 2, 1995, noted that there are some 70 million people of Irish descent living outside Ireland, who assert a strong cultural allegiance to their land of origin, yet have adapted and contributed richly to the countries in which they now reside. Indeed, while geography has destined Ireland to remain peripheral, this diaspora has also enriched the country's heritage in ensuring that "Irishness is not simply territorial" (Robinson, 1995).

Culture is defined by the GLOBE (Global Leadership and Organizational Behavior Effectiveness) study as "the common experiences of individuals which result in shared motives, values, beliefs, identities, and interpretations (meanings) of significant events" (House et al., 1999, p. 5). The following chapter sets out to explore leadership in the Republic of Ireland within its cultural and organizational context and to consider the interrelationship between societal and organizational culture as they have impacted on the implicit leadership perceptions held by Irish middle managers. It also investigates the extent to which these perceptions have been

---

[1]The Battle of the Boyne was fought in 1690.

shaped by recent and past history. The study is informed by the insights that have emerged from analysis of both quantitative and qualitative data generated within the framework of the GLOBE project. The corpus includes questionnaires, focus groups, and qualitative interviews alongside a review of unobtrusive indicators of culture. The organizational focus of the Irish study is located in the financial services and the food-processing sectors.

The chapter is divided into six principal sections. The first seeks to introduce Irish cultural identity from a social, historical, political, and economic perspective and thereby to provide a context in which to locate the field study. The second section introduces the GLOBE research in the Republic of Ireland. The third presents the findings of the empirical study of Irish societal culture. In the fourth, the focus is on leadership. The section begins with a review of leadership research in Ireland, before reporting on the leadership perceptions of Irish middle managers and investigating one of the core research questions set by the GLOBE project, specifically, how societal culture influences such perceptions. The fifth section addresses this question at an industry level with a view to exploring the interrelationship between societal and organizational culture and leadership perceptions in the food processing and financial services sectors. Conclusions are presented in the final section.

1. IRELAND: SOCIETY, HISTORY, POLITICS, AND ECONOMY

Perspectives on Ireland

Ireland has undergone vast changes since independence in 1921 and, perhaps most particularly, since the 1960s (Breen, Hannan, Rottman, & Whelan, 1990). The past 40 years have seen much turbulence as Irish society has moved away from being a traditional, socially conservative society and sought to redefine what it means to be Irish in a new millennium. Membership in the European Union (EU), global influences, the impact of new communication and information technologies, shifting demographic patterns, and higher levels of education have all contributed to this change.

Historians and psychologists use terms such as national psyche and collective psyche. Concepts such as the "Irish personality" or "Irish psyche" can generate stereotypes and appear static, suggesting that variations across social groups, historical time, and life span do not exist (Moane, 1994). At the same time, such concepts bear the "imprint of bygone circumstances" (Lee, 1994, p. 248). Lee exhorts that all generalizations about national psyche should be based on comparison; for Ireland, the English connection has been central to our historical experience. The fundamental difference between the historical experience of the Irish and English is that the English have been a conquering people and the Irish a conquered (cf. Lee, 1994).

Ireland has been studied from a variety of viewpoints including the postcolonial, the nationalist, and the religious, that is, Roman Catholic perspective. Lee (1989) mentions the following postcolonial characteristics of late twentieth century Irish society: "extreme centralization; resistance to change and to new ideas, a lack of self-reflection, internal fragmentation; lack of self confidence" (cited in Moane 1994, p. 254), all of which add up to a national inferiority complex. Kane (1986) observes that a group's ethnic identity is more likely to hold positive and negative assumptions about itself when it is part of a "conquest culture" and when these assumptions are instilled in part by the conquering culture (pp. 540–541). In this vein, Ruth (1988) has suggested that many of the changes that have taken place in Ireland are typical of a postcolonial society. He identifies in this respect psychological patterns such as the acceptance of anti-Irish stereotypes (dim-witted, drunken, aggressive) and, ensuing lack of pride, mistrust with this, and divisiveness between Irish people, a narrow identity definition of being Irish, a lack of assertiveness, and a tendency to oppress. Liberation from such patterns may, according to Ruth, involve anger and grief followed by pride, assertiveness, and acceptance of all members of society.

Within the stages of evolution prescribed by postcolonialism, it would appear that the process of liberation is under way. There has been a remarkable growth in self-confidence since the early 1990s, prompted to some degree by success in the artistic, literary, and sporting spheres, but most notably by economic growth. Furthermore, a sense of anger among the Irish people toward many of the institutions that have influenced their lives, most notably the Roman Catholic Church, has given way to a questioning of their moral authority.

The Roman Catholic Church continues to exert influence on the Irish psyche. To some, being Roman Catholic is synonymous with being Irish. The rate of religious practice among Irish Catholics is one of the highest in the world, although it is much lower than the statistics suggest. According to one commentator, the social project of the Roman Catholic Church in Ireland has been the maintenance of social stability (Nic Ghiolla Phádraig, 1995). To this end it provided the state with independent legitimization; the state, in turn, instituted laws and policies in keeping with Catholic teaching. Moreover, it has been closely involved in the provision of education, health, and welfare services. Much of this involvement is being renegotiated as the Church redefines its mission in the light of dwindling vocations, its implosion in the wake of internal scandals, and the emerging voice of a more pluralist society.

History: Ireland in the 20th Century

Following 800 years of domination, the Easter Rising of 1916 saw the final rebellion against British rule in Ireland. It unleashed a bitter War of Independence (1919–1921) after which the Anglo-Irish Treaty was signed and 26 counties gained independence from the British Crown as the Irish Free State. Six counties were granted their own parliament in Belfast and remained within the United Kingdom. The "troubles" in Northern Ireland have been the legacy of this division.

On independence, the Irish Free State inherited a number of important assets including "an extensive system of communications, a developed banking system, a vigorous wholesale and retail network, an efficient and honest administration, universal literacy, a large stock of schools, houses and hospitals and enormous external assets" (Haughton, 1995, p. 26). Yet, the new state faced a number of serious problems, most notably, the need to establish a new government in the wake of a destructive and divisive Civil War (1921–1922).

Eamon de Valera, who played a major role in the development of modern Ireland, entered office in 1932 as head of government. He embraced the role of protector of Irish nationalism and creator of the Irish nation and, to this end, instituted a policy requiring the use of the Irish language wherever possible. In 1937, he introduced a new constitution, declaring Ireland to be a sovereign, independent, and democratic state. In keeping with its independence from Britain, Ireland remained neutral during the Second World War and thus escaped the worst effects of the conflict. In 1948, the Republic of Ireland Act was passed, severing Ireland's last constitutional links with Britain.

From the late 1950s onward, the country underwent rapid economic expansion under de Valera's successor, Séan Lemass. Post-1965, following a free-trade agreement between Ireland and Britain, there were significant developments in Irish trading patterns, which were positively influenced by accession to the European Community in 1973. Such developments marked the beginning of an opening up of the Irish economy, which helped to pave the way for the emergence of the "Celtic Tiger" in the 1990s and a period of sustained economic growth.

Legal and Political Framework

The basic law of the Irish State is the Constitution of Ireland, adopted by referendum in 1937, which asserts that all legislative, executive, and judicial powers of government derive under God from the people. Freedom of conscience and the free profession and practice of religion are, subject to public order, constitutionally guaranteed and the state guarantees not to endow any religion. In a referendum held in 1972, the Irish people voted overwhelmingly to delete those clauses in the Constitution that recognized the "special position" of the Roman Catholic Church as guardian of the faith of the majority of citizens.

Duncan (1994) observes that "it is a feature of certain areas of Irish law that there exists, or has existed, a considerable divide between legal aspiration or principle and social fact, but that this divide has been mitigated by a remarkable flexibility in the operation of those principles" (p. 450). His commentary poses interesting questions about Irish attitudes to law and how Irish society resolves certain deep conflicts, most notably, divorce, abortion, and homosexuality. He suggests that our Catholic heritage of condemning the sin but not the sinner may go some way toward explaining this flexibility, but concludes that a more acceptable explanation, also influenced by our Catholic heritage, may lie in the Church's view of the civil law as an important mainstay of moral living. That laws should be used to shape moral behavior has subsequently given way to the more subtle idea that change in the law may create an environment that makes the individual's path to virtue a more difficult one (Daly, 1993; cited in Duncan, 1994).

Many areas of Irish law have been honored in the breach rather than in observance. Evidence presented at ongoing tribunals investigating political and financial scandals in Ireland supports the view that a culture of noncompliance existed in respect of commercial and company law. In spite of rules and regulations to manage all aspects of public life, a culture of bending these rules prevailed: Who you were and who you knew mattered in terms of how you were treated if you were caught. Some have attempted to explain this practice with reference to the aforementioned Catholic heritage of forgiving the sinner or by evoking our colonial past where, much in line with the literary parallel of servant–master relations it was deemed a feather in your cap if you could dupe the master! However, the past 10 years have seen an attempt to modify Irish attitudes and behavior in terms of compliance with rules and regulations.

Irish political decision making is shaped by a highly centralized bureaucracy, an executive monopoly of legislation, and a tightly controlled political party system within the context of a personalist political structure (Coakley & Gallagher, 1993). Though local government plays a minor role in Irish political life, some would argue that the Irish electoral system, which is based on proportional representation coupled with multiseat constituencies, "gives too much weight to the constituencies rather than the country" (Guiomard, 1995, p. 163). The personalist political environment has nurtured a culture of direct-contact clientelism between government ministers, senior administrators, and organized representative groups.

British rule in Ireland left a significant legacy in terms of public policies. Similarly, the agricultural heritage of the country, together with its strong Catholic tradition, has ensured the maintenance of an essentially conservative base within politics. The current government consists of a coalition between two center right parties. Many scholars contend that Ireland displays a distinctly corporatist pattern of group–state relationships, particularly in the economic sphere; indeed, some go so far as to suggest that it displays a closed corporatist pattern of interest representation (Galligan, 1998). However, it is becoming apparent that Europe will increasingly determine Ireland's public policies.

The Irish Economy

Ireland is now classed as a high-income economy by the World Bank on the basis of gross national income (GNI)/capita of $27,010 (World Bank, 2005). As an island, the Irish economy is very open and heavily dependent on trade: exports of goods and services amount to 94% of gross domestic product (GDP; World Bank, 2005). It is widely accepted that the slow growth of the Irish economy in the 1950s was largely because of the inefficiency of the industrial sector developed in the 1930s. The main elements of Ireland's current industrial policy were introduced in 1958 in the country's first comprehensive plan for economic development. These were: the introduction of substantial capital grants and tax concessions to encourage export-oriented manufacturing, the inducement of direct investment by foreign export-oriented manufacturing enterprises in Ireland, and a transition to free trade. On joining the European Economic Community (EEC) in 1973 (now the EU), Ireland was classified as a peripheral nation and benefited greatly from European structural and cohesion funds as well as becoming part of a large economic area with free movement of goods, services, people, and capital.

Since the 1980s, policies have been implemented to curb imbalances in the public finances. O'Higgins (2002) summarizes the situation in the mid-1980s as a time when Ireland "was beset by prolonged recession, low living standards, a negative trade balance, high inflation, unemployment of over 17 percent, a hostile industrial relations climate, and weak revenues" (pp. 104–105). Since then, living standards have been converging with European levels and by 2000 GDP per capita had risen to 115%.

The "vicious circle of Irish industrialisation" (Mjoset, 1992, p. 13), based on a weak national system of innovation and continual population decline, appears to have been finally overtaken by a "virtuous circle," at the center of which lies a corporatist, consensual approach. This strategy has resulted in rapid development and economic stability. The growth of the Irish economy since 1994, dubbed "the Celtic Tiger," has been three to four times the average of the EU countries and higher than the OECD (Organization for Economic Cooperation and Development) average. Indeed, economic growth continues at a rate of over 5%, whereas other Western European countries struggle to attain less than half this figure (Federation of European Employers, 2005). Such high levels of growth over the past 10 years have, in turn, led to skilled inward migration. This inward migration will become even more critical in the future if current levels of growth are to be supported (Federation of European Employers, 2005).

Gray (1997) has proposed a number of reasons for Ireland's economic turnaround. These are labor force skill and education, an English-speaking workforce, the importance of foreign investment coupled with a shift in the balance of international trade, the provision of European subsidies, the role of convergence, and the prospect of peace in Northern Ireland. A favorable corporate tax regime and the emergence of the Single European Market have also contributed to this turnaround, as has the social partnership. The *Programme for National Recovery* (1988–1990) secured trade union support for cuts in public spending and was followed by a series of partnership programs involving all stakeholders in Irish economic well-being.

Two major tasks face Ireland in the new millennium: The first is to address the problems of social inequality; the second is to stimulate an Irish system of innovation that encourages the development of indigenous firms while reducing the country's dependency on mobile foreign direct investment.

Education

One of the main catalysts of social change in Ireland has been education. Education and learning have always been valued and, for many, a good education represented the passport to a better life. This view has become more pronounced with the "shift from family property to education as the principal means of reproducing social status" (Fahey, 1995, p. 218). According to Nic Ghiolla Phádraig (1995), schools are "important tools of religious socialisation" (p. 603) and, traditionally, the Catholic Church has been the dominant player in educational provision at primary and second level. This influence has diminished with increasing secularization of schools. Free secondary education was introduced in 1966, with Irish children remaining in obligatory full-time education until the age of 15. O'Higgins (2002) notes that, "[b]y the late 1990s, over 80 per cent of workforce entrants had completed secondary education and 40-plus per cent experienced some third-level education"; this latter figure compares favorably with the EU average of 20% (p. 106).

The aim of the Operational Programme for Human Resources Development 1994–1999 (Government of Ireland, 1995) has been to maximize the potential of Ireland's people and to facilitate the shift to a knowledge-based service society. Much of the funding to achieve these objectives has come from the European Social Fund. The recognition that Ireland's human resources will constitute the key to the country's economic competitiveness in the next millennium has prompted a shift within educational thinking toward the notion of continuous learning and, with this, awareness of the imperative of ongoing training within industry. In 2000, Professor Michael Porter stressed the need for more executive training and better managerial skills if Ireland is to remain competitive (*The Irish Times,* October 27, 2000, p. 4).

Summary

The preceding section has provided an overview of Ireland's social, economic, and political development over the last century. In particular, it is important to emphasize the ongoing significant changes within Irish society, most notably the move toward a more secular, pluralist, and transparent society, the unprecedented levels of economic growth, and the sense of confidence that this has instilled in the Irish people. The path of change and growing self-confidence, attested by many Irish "success stories" on the world stage in the economic, diplomatic, literary, and artistic spheres, is expressed forcefully by one commentator:

> *The final quarter of the twentieth century saw extraordinary changes in the Irish psyche and in Irish society. The transformations touched virtually every aspect of life in Ireland—personal, educational, economic and political. Changes that were working their way through the body politic and the body social in the seventies and eighties came to the surface in the nineties, catching many people unawares.* (Walshe, 1999, p. 1)

It is against this backdrop of change that we now turn to the GLOBE study in Ireland. This is preceded by a brief summary of Ireland's profile within existing cross-cultural comparative management literature, including Hofstede's (1980) research. The latter has retained its benchmark status as the most extensive quantitative empirical study of the dimensions of Irish societal culture until the GLOBE project.

2. GLOBE IN THE REPUBLIC OF IRELAND

Ireland in Cross-Cultural Management Research

Recent cross-cultural empirical research has paid scant attention to Ireland, lumped it together with Britain, or hinted at a more schizophrenic profile (Martin, 2001). Ronen and Shenkar's (1985) review of eight cross-cultural studies, including that conducted by Hofstede (1980), generated five main clusters within Europe. Ireland is assigned to the Anglo cluster, alongside the United Kingdom. The authors propose that geographical proximity, shared language or language groups, and religion are determinants of cultural clustering; they also explore the influence of modernity in the areas of economic, social, political, and educational development as it has an impact on individualism, uncertainty avoidance, and gender equality (cf. Brodbeck et al., 2000). More recently, in a survey of top managers' views on the diversity of management systems in Europe, Calori (1994) notes that Ireland "probably belongs to a broader Anglo-Saxon block, but … may also share some Latin characteristics" (p. 21), a view also suggested in the Cranfield study of management styles in eight European countries (Myers, Kakabadse, McMahon, & Spony, 1995, pp. 22–23; cf. also Hickson & Pugh, 1995). Other commentators to have hinted at "Latin rim" characteristics include Mahon (1994), who refers to indicators such as late industrialization and postcolonialism.

Hofstede's (1980) research classifies Ireland as low on Power Distance, high on Individualism, weak on Uncertainty Avoidance, and high on the Masculine Index, a profile similar to that of Great Britain. Whereas Hofstede's findings suggest similarity, the inhabitants of these countries would recognize that there are fundamental differences in their outlook on life and in the conduct of business. Such differences may emerge more clearly through the inclusion of qualitative research tools, which were absent from Hofstede's study.

When contemplating the findings of the GLOBE study of societal culture, it is useful to consider these varied observations on Ireland's cultural profile, together with the social, economic, and political changes, which we have documented in the first section of the chapter. GLOBE provides a lens through which to view the Ireland of the mid-1990s. Critically, unlike previous cross-cultural comparative research, GLOBE can establish the direction of desired change in a culture by focusing on "As Is" scales (i.e., societal practice or perceptions of one's society) and "Should Be" scales (i.e., espoused values concerning one's ideal society).

The GLOBE Dimensions and the Irish Sample

At the center of the GLOBE study has been the development of scales for the evaluation of societal cultural norms. The scales build on Hofstede's (1980) four cultural dimensions and include Power Distance, Uncertainty Avoidance, Gender Egalitarianism, which replaces Masculinity/Femininity, and Institutional Collectivism in place of Individualism/Collectivism. It introduces Assertiveness, which was previously part of Hofstede's Masculinity/Femininity dimension, but treats it as a separate index. Four further dimensions are included: Future Orientation (Kluckhohn & Strodtbeck, 1961), Performance Orientation (McClelland, 1961), Humane Orientation (Kluckhohn & Strodtbeck, 1961; Putnam, 1993), and In-Group Collectivism, that is, Collectivism as an orientation discrete from Individualism. Definitions of

TABLE 11.1
Definition of the GLOBE Dimensions of Societal Culture

Dimension	Definition
Power Distance	The degree to which members of a society expect power to be distributed equally
Uncertainty Avoidance	The extent to which a society relies on social norms, rules, and procedures to alleviate the unpredictability of future events
Humane Orientation	The degree to which a society encourages and rewards individuals for being fair, altruistic, generous, caring, and kind to others
Institutional Collectivism	The degree to which societal institutional practices encourage and reward collective distribution of resources and collective action
In-Group Collectivism	The degree to which individuals express pride, loyalty, and cohesiveness in their families
Assertiveness	The degree to which individuals are assertive, dominant, and demanding in their relationships with others
Gender Egalitarianism	The degree to which a society minimizes gender inequality
Future Orientation	The extent to which a society encourages future-orientated behaviors such as delaying gratification, planning, and investing in the future
Performance Orientation	The degree to which a society encourages and rewards group members for performance improvement and excellence

the dimensions are summarized in Table 11.1. The methodological parameters of the GLOBE study are set out in House et al. (2004).

The GLOBE study in the Republic of Ireland is based on analysis of 156 questionnaires collected during 1995 and 1996 in two wholly indigenous sectors, namely the food-processing and financial services sectors. The Irish sample is drawn from 8 indigenous financial services companies and 10 food-processing companies. The sample reflects an urban and provincial spread. Respondents were middle managers aged between 23 and 56; the age range was virtually identical in both sectors. The average age of the respondents was 37 years; 84% were male. In addition, two focus groups and two semistructured qualitative interviews were conducted with middle managers in these sectors. A review of unobtrusive indicators of culture and leadership, including stamps, banknotes, and statues, was also undertaken in an attempt to explicate features of Irish identity that impact on attitudes toward leadership within social and organizational settings.

There are two GLOBE questionnaires. Questionnaire Alpha concentrates on the measurement of leadership and organizational culture. Questionnaire Beta measures leadership and societal culture. An equal number of respondents to Alpha and Beta questionnaires was sought in each organization taking part in the study. Using a 7-point scale, informants were asked to state their perceptions of items relating to the nine cultural dimensions, concerning how things "are" (observed practices) in their society or organization and how things "should be" (values). In this way, the questionnaire distinguishes between practices ("As Is") and espoused values ("Should Be"), allowing us to comment on trends in societal and organizational practices and values.

On the leadership scales, the middle managers were asked to rate 112 leadership items on a scale between 1 (greatly inhibits a person from being an outstanding leader) and 7 (greatly contributes to a person being an outstanding leader). Based on exploratory factor analysis and prior theorizing, the items were distilled into 21 leadership scales, which constitute culturally endorsed perceptions of leadership.

The following section reports on the findings of the questionnaire-based study of societal culture. On the basis of the profile of Irish society emerging from the questionnaires, we briefly consider some of the possible implications for preferred leadership styles.

3. IRISH SOCIETAL CULTURE

Findings of the GLOBE Study

Table 11.2 presents the findings in respect of Irish societal culture in terms of absolute mean scores for practices ("As Is") and espoused values ("Should Be") scores on a 7-point scale. The results represent aggregated scale scores on each of the dimensions. Ireland's ranking on each dimension relative to the other participating cultures is also indicated, together with the band to which Ireland belongs. Countries in Bands A or B are very high or high on the particular dimension, whereas those in Bands C and D are low or very low respectively, compared to all other countries. An absolute score indicating the difference between the two culture measures, "As Is" and "Should Be," is also provided.

If we examine each of these dimensions within the context of the issues discussed in the first part of the chapter, we can posit a number of explanations as to the emergent trends within the data set and assess their possible implications for preferred leadership styles.

TABLE 11.2
Country Means for Societal Culture Dimensions

Culture Dimensions	Society "As Is"			Society "Should Be"			Difference[d]
	Mean[a]	Band[b]	Rank[c]	Mean[a]	Band[b]	Rank[c]	Should Be /As Is
Power Distance	5.15	B	36	2.71	C	30	−2.44
In-Group Collectivism	5.14	B	39	5.74	B	28	0.60
Humane Orientation	4.96	A	3	5.47	B	29	0.51
Institutional Collectivism	4.63	A	9	4.59	B	35	−0.04
Performance Orientation	4.36	A	17	5.98	B	30	1.62
Uncertainty Avoidance	4.30	B	22	4.02	C	49	0.28
Future Orientation	3.98	B	21	5.22	B	43	1.24
Assertiveness	3.92	B	41	3.99	B	19	−0.07
Gender Egalitarianism	3.21	B	39	5.14	A	3	1.93

[a]Country mean score on a 7-point Likert-type scale. [b]Band letter A–D indicating meaningful country bands for the scales A > B > C (>D); see Hanges, Dickson, and Sipe (2004). [c]The rank order for Ireland relative to 61 countries. [d]Absolute difference between the "Should Be" and "As Is" score.

Power Distance.   Power Distance specifies the extent to which the members of a society expect power to be shared equally in that society. Hofstede's (1980) study classified Ireland as a low Power Distance society, whereas the GLOBE data reveal that perceived levels of Power Distance within our society are high (Mean [M] = 5.15, Rank 36, Band B) and that middle managers would like to see much lower levels (M = 2.71, Rank 30, Band C). In fact, the highest absolute difference between "As Is" and "Should Be" is recorded for this dimension (–2.44). The espousal of lower levels of Power Distance mirrors the worldwide trend. Interestingly, however, when juxtaposed with the other sampled countries, Ireland's relative score on "As Is" suggests that levels of Power Distance in Irish society are moderate.

One factor, which might explain the respondents' perceptions of Power Distance within Irish society, is centralization. Faced in the 1980s with a galloping national debt and rising unemployment, central government and its various departments assumed greater powers as a means of tackling these problems (cf. the subsection *Legal and Political Framework*). Other organs of centralized power include the EU and the Roman Catholic Church. Where the locus of power is perceived to be defined centrally, those who are affected by its mandate may discern its influence to be greater.

On the surface, Ireland does not appear to be a very formal society. People do not use titles, prefer first-name terms, and tend to relate to each other as equals in a familiar way, regardless of position or status. Yet, underlying this behavior is an awareness of the power relationship and a sense that everybody knows their place. Irish society cannot be described as elitist and, generally, status is achieved nowadays rather than ascribed (cf. the subsection *Legal and Political Framework*) and class determined to a large extent by occupation. However, in the past it has been argued that people were rewarded for their possessions, notably land, jobs, education, and wealth, rather than for their performance or enterprise (Lee, 1989). Warnes (1979) observed the prevalence in the late 1970s of "class distinctions, class-prejudices, nepotism, obsequiousness, back-biting, rigid stratifications, procrastination, social rituals, authoritarianism, inquisitiveness into who your father was, [and] what kind of school you attended" (p. 330). Indeed, the much more recent scandals within Irish public life have revealed the abuse of power by named politicians, members of the judiciary, the banking and accounting professions, and well-known chief executives in the agricultural and financial services sectors and government departments, and have demonstrated that status can confer certain privileges. Furthermore, they underpin the fact that clientelism and networking have always been an accepted part of life in Ireland (cf. the subsection *Legal and Political Framework*). This may help to explain perceptions of higher Power Distance.

Attitudes to Power Distance may also be linked to the latent disrespect for authority held by Irish people. Attempts to impose new regulations on different aspects of daily life have traditionally been ignored on a widespread basis and form part of the culture of noncompliance. This situation has changed as structures are being imposed to modify behavior across a variety of fronts. The growing confidence of a younger, more highly educated generation, coupled with the many scandals within the Church, has fundamentally altered this sense of acquiescence.

Gender Egalitarianism.   Gender Egalitarianism is defined as the extent to which gender differences in a particular society are minimized. Ireland's score for practices on this dimension (M = 3.21, Rank 39, Band B) would imply that, in absolute terms, Irish middle managers perceive Irish society to have a low level of gender equality. For values, Irish middle managers espouse high levels of Gender Egalitarianism (M = 5.14, Rank 3, Band A), in both absolute and relative terms. Indeed, the second highest absolute difference between practices and espoused values is on the dimension Gender Egalitarianism (1.93).

Hofstede's (1980) study classified Ireland as high on masculinity. Until recently, Ireland could be regarded as a predominantly patriarchal society. It had earned this reputation because of its traditional stance on reproductive rights and the low participation of women in the labor force. Scannell's (1988) study of the position of women subsequent to the enactment of the 1937 Constitution found that "for almost thirty years after the Constitution was adopted, the position of women in Irish society hardly changed at all" (p. 127). Education has facilitated greater gender equality, although some academics would argue that sex role models are reinforced by schools and may have implications for the career choices made by women.

In the 1970s, a liberal agenda of policy reform dominated public discourse and was strongly influenced by European Community directives. Since then, the dismantling of discriminatory legislation and expanding participation of women within the workforce have altered the profile and role of Irish women in society. Between 1991 and 2002, female participation in the Irish labor force increased from 35.9% to 47% (Browne, 2005), while the rate of employment among women (54%) represents a 15% increase since 1994 and is now higher than most OECD countries (European Employment Observatory, 2003). Nonetheless, they remain underrepresented at the senior management level across a number of sectors. By contrast, women are extremely active in a voluntary capacity at local level in their communities (Coulter, 1993) and, at the time of the GLOBE survey, some 53% of adult women in Ireland were home workers (K. Lynch & McLaughlin, 1995, p. 266).

The findings attest that the country has made some progress in achieving greater gender egalitarianism, although the "Should Be" scores echo the widespread and explicit view that we still have considerable distance to travel. Such a view may also be reinforced by the constitution of the GLOBE sample: The workforce within the food industry remains predominantly male and respondents to the questionnaires in this particular sector were 100% male.

Performance Orientation.   Performance Orientation describes the degree to which people are encouraged and rewarded for performance improvement and achievement of excellence. On the "As Is" scale, the respondents record moderate scores in absolute terms, but, viewed relatively, the country belongs in the highest band ($M = 4.36$, Rank 17, Band A). In absolute terms, the "Should Be" score for Performance Orientation is substantially higher ($M = 5.98$, Rank 30, Band B)—it is, in fact, the highest absolute score on any of the value dimensions— but in relative terms the data suggest that many other countries are more performance oriented.

Lee's (1989) reference to an inadequate "performance ethic" in Irish life (cf. the subsection *Power Distance*) may have characterized past attitudes, when "it was accepted that profits could be made, not by means of enterprise, but rather by financial engineering and tax avoidance" (O'Higgins, 2002, p. 105). The GLOBE findings suggest that Ireland has become very performance oriented. Factors contributing to this include the country's continued economic development, the shift from an inward- to an outward-focused economic policy, membership in the EU, the number of foreign direct investment firms located in Ireland and the global economic environment (cf. the subsection *The Irish Economy*), all of which stress the importance of remaining competitive on a global level. There has been a growth in performance-management-oriented systems in work organizations and this trend is expected to continue in order to facilitate labor market flexibility. In the *Financial Times* (May 26, 1995) Ireland was recorded as having a productivity record that "would be the envy of the Germans, and a balance of payments surplus in line with Switzerland and Japan," a trend reiterated by an ILO (International Labour Organization) study of global labor trends (Doohan, 1999). Notwithstanding the recognition that transfer pricing can distort national figures in a small economy (Stewart, 1997), Ireland has grown fast and the Irish respondents appear to recognize that maintaining such levels of performance and growth will be the challenge of the future.

Future Orientation.   Future Orientation measures the extent to which future-oriented behaviors (e.g. planning, investing, delay of gratification) are encouraged and rewarded. On practice scores ($M = 3.98$, Rank 21, Band B), the absolute and relative positioning implies that Irish society is moderately future oriented. For values ($M = 5.22$, Rank 43, Band B), they espouse significantly higher levels of Future Orientation, although in relative terms, other countries are more focused on the future at this point in time.

With increased economic prosperity, the stability offered by continuity of employment provides a more solid foundation on which to plan for the future. The efforts and success of the Irish Investment and Development Agency in pursuing a policy of attracting targeted multinational corporations (MNCs), specifically in the technology sectors, cannot be under-estimated. Central planning to sustain economic performance and growth is also evident, together with higher levels of investment in training and executive education and in research and development (R&D) within industry, a figure that has more than quadrupled since 1982. However, the percentage remains modest when juxtaposed with other European countries and is lower in indigenous Irish firms than in foreign companies (J. J. Lynch & Roche, 1995, pp. 48–52). As O'Higgins (2002) has pointed out: "Mindful that Ireland lags behind the EU average on R&D government spending as a percentage of GDP, the state invested ∈ 1 billion-plus in Ireland's R&D future in 2001, to fund basic research in information and communications technology, biotechnology, and center of excellence standard R&D in universities and colleges" (p. 107). Within organizations, strategic planning has assumed new dimensions, even if the Anglo-Saxon model of shareholder as opposed to stakeholder value remains pre-dominant amongst the larger publicly quoted companies. Individuals within Irish society have also become more proactive in making independent provision for their future and taking con-trol of their own destiny (Jupp & O'Neill, 1994) as evidenced by the increase in numbers pur-chasing health insurance and making pension arrangements.

Such shifts are reflected in the Irish GLOBE data, together with possible recognition of the lag between policymaking for the future and present reality, which is most clearly evinced in the area of infrastructural development. There is a realization that infrastructural weaknesses could ultimately compromise Ireland's attractiveness as a location for inward investment.

In-Group Collectivism.   In-Group Collectivism describes relationships among members of families or organizations. On practices ($M = 5.14$, Rank 39, Band B), Irish middle man-agers report in absolute terms high levels of In-Group Collectivism. Viewed relatively, Ireland has moderate levels of In-Group Collectivism. The "Should Be" ($M = 5.74$, Rank 28, Band B) indicates a moderate desire for greater In-Group Collectivism.

This profile may be traceable to the increasing fragmentation of Irish society in the wake of shifting values, coupled with economic development, attendant urbanization, and the sense of displacement and anonymity that this can produce. Family patterns in Ireland have undergone considerable change since the 1960s, marking a growing distance between public religious observance and personal decisions. In line with European trends, the number of children born outside marriage had risen to 31% by 2002 (National Center for Policy Analysis, 2002).

The changing role of women and their increased presence in the workforce, together with the growing phenomenon of spousal separation prior to the introduction of divorce in 1996 have had repercussions for the stability of family life and the traditional patterns of family organization. Yet, although the traditional family group may be under stress, the role of family remains very important in Ireland as a form of social support. Society continues to place a high value on mothers, who exercise great influence both within and beyond the family circle (cf. the subsection *Gender Egalitarianism*). Equally, kinship ties remain strong in both rural and urban families and many people obtain important levels of support from their family and neighbors; for example, care of the elderly continues to be assumed largely by the family. K. Lynch and McLaughlin (1995) note that although the Republic of Ireland is unusual insofar as it does make some provision for carers in its social security system, the actual sharing of costs between carer and the state remains minimal (p. 283).

Humane Orientation.   Humane Orientation describes how much a society rewards or encourages its members for being fair, altruistic, and caring toward others. Looking at the score for practices ($M = 4.96$, Rank 3, Band A), Ireland is considered by the respondents to place a very high value on these qualities, in both absolute and relative terms. For values ($M = 5.47$, Rank 29, Band B), we see a desire for higher levels on this dimension, although in relative terms the ranking drops.

The high "As Is" score ($M = 4.96$) is probably attributable to our strong Christian and Catholic heritage and the size of the country. For decades, Irish missionaries have ministered to the needs of those in developing countries and nowadays are assisted by many young volunteer workers. There is a long tradition of charitable institutions being funded by the government and run by religious orders, also representing a pragmatic solution to the problems of cash shortages.

The higher values score ($M = 5.47$) may be explained by the perception that the "softer," gentler characteristics of life in this country are being sacrificed to the "Celtic Tiger" through economic success and emphasis on performance and individual achievement. According to Collins and Kavanagh (1998), "There has been a marked increase in the level of inequality (in Ireland) over the past twenty years" (p. 172). Whereas the wealthiest 20% of the population has increased its share of national income from 46.7% in 1972 to 52.5% in 1994, income distribution for the lowest 50% fell from 18% to 11.5% (Collins & Kavanagh, 1998, p. 172). A comprehensive welfare system does exist, but, as in many other developed nations, it fails to catch all in its net. Many of those who remain outside the system are reliant on services provided by voluntary organizations.

Through economic prosperity, there are signs that Irish people are beginning to forget their own diaspora. Already, the impact of an increasing number of refugees seeking either political or economic asylum in the wake of the country's prosperity is being felt. Until recently, Ireland was shielded by its relative economic weakness and its island geography from immigration and, thus, Irish society has remained remarkably homogeneous. Whereas there is a tolerance of difference within the "in-group," this not necessarily replicated with respect to "outsiders" from other cultures who seek refuge in Ireland (cf. Jupp & O'Neill, 1994). Jupp and O'Neill suggest that in the future, Irish people expect fear and greed to be more apparent and politeness, generosity, and tolerance to wane. They record: "Our socio-cultural values will be severely tested as twice as many people expect us to be less caring by the next millennium" (p. 12).

Uncertainty Avoidance.   Uncertainty Avoidance captures the degree to which reliance is placed on social norms and procedures to reduce the unpredictability of future events. For practices ($M = 4.30$, Rank 22, Band B), the respondents record moderate scores both in absolute and relative terms. For values ($M = 4.02$, Rank 49, Band C), lower levels of Uncertainty Avoidance are espoused. Whereas Hofstede (1980) categorized Ireland as low on Uncertainty Avoidance, the GLOBE findings indicate that we have become less tolerant of uncertainty, but wish to become more tolerant.

As societies mature, they become better at managing uncertainty (Hofstede, 1980). Examples of Ireland's attempts to manage uncertainty can be seen in the area of macroeconomic planning, the emergence of the social partnership in the 1980s and early 1990s (cf. the subsection *The Irish Economy*), improved educational policies linked to future prosperity, and efforts to build a culture of compliance with rules and regulations for the good of the country and its citizens. Additionally, people now insure their lives and possessions more comprehensively against risk, which also ties in with the desire for greater Future Orientation. Though Ireland has been described as having a "lightly regulated environment" with respect to employment regulation and benefits (Sedgwick Noble Lownes, 1998), the desire for a lower level of Uncertainty Avoidance may reflect a sense of constraint, which is imposed by increased regulation and structure in the era of freedom of information and accountability.

Communication has a strong basis in the oral tradition with evidence of recourse to metaphor, euphemism, and legend and is "particularly suited to the expression of ambivalence and ambiguity" (Bourke, 1999, p. 206). Much value is still attached to the notion of a word-of-mouth culture, although the indispensability of written documentation both in the workplace and in dealing with public institutions has gained in importance as the country has evolved socially and economically. Nonetheless, off-the-record conversations remain intrinsic to how we communicate with each other, together with subtle signaling known as "nodding and winking," which has close ties to the clientelist approach. Keeping situations open-ended, providing loopholes, bending rules, and avoiding closure are mechanisms that are often used to manage uncertainty at the individual level.

Assertiveness.   Assertiveness refers to the degree to which individuals in a society are allowed to be aggressive or dominant. Nonassertiveness refers to nonconfrontational, nondominant social relationships. For both practices ($M = 3.92$, Rank 41, Band B) and values ($M = 3.99$, Rank 19, Band B), the scores suggest in absolute and relative terms moderate to low Assertiveness and the desire not to alter this.

V. Kenny (1985) elaborates on social relations in Ireland. He talks of social withdrawal, in other words, superficial compliance, indirect communication, the lack of self-revelation, and the elaboration of secret worlds. These can result in such behaviors as understatement, evasiveness, the avoidance of conflict and self-exhibition, passive aggression (cited in Moane, 1994, p. 259), and nonassertiveness, which are symptomatic of a postcolonial mind-set (cf. Ruth, 1988, in the subsection *Perspectives on Ireland*). This can be disconcerting for people who speak the same language, but do not use language in the same way, including our closest neighbors within the British Isles. In face-to-face negotiation, issues are generally not dealt with head-on and confrontation is avoided (Martin, 2001). Indeed, the nature of communication points to the fact that Ireland may have more in common with high-context cultures (Hall, 1976). Often what is *not* said is more important than what *is* said and an ability to read between the lines is essential. This would also appear to tie in with our collectivist orientation.

Institutional Collectivism. Institutional Collectivism refers to the degree to which societies reward collective endeavor. Hofstede's (1980) classification of Ireland as individualistic does not match the view held by respondents in the Irish GLOBE study. In both absolute and relative terms, the score for practices indicates high levels of institutional collectivism ($M = 4.63$, Rank 9, Band A) and the minor shift on values ($M = 4.59$, Rank 35, Band B) suggests that the respondents are happy with these existing levels. The drop in ranking from 10 on "As Is" to 35 on "Should Be" reflects the international shift toward espousal of higher levels of Institutional Collectivism. Similar trends are evident for Humane Orientation and Future Orientation.

The high level of Institutional Collectivism is compatible with our size and colonial history. There is a strong sense of belonging to a parish, of community-level interdependence especially in a rural context. Most indigenous Irish sports are team based and membership in collectives, such as trade unions, is high. Roche and Ashmore (1997) estimated trade union density at 53%. Additionally, positioning on this dimension may be influenced by the collective sense of national pride and self-esteem evident in the Ireland of the mid-1990s as a consequence of the success of the "corporatist partnership" (Sweeney, 1998). O'Higgins (2002) observes: "Smallness is an advantage in maintaining partnership because of familiarity, informality, and close personal relationships among the stakeholders, all helpful preconditions for successful bargaining and compromise" (p. 105). However, she draws attention to the growing inequalities within Irish society between rich and poor as a result of espousal of the capitalist model (cf. the subsection *Humane Orientation*), which might "weaken the social solidarity that has been such a cornerstone of Irish development" (p. 117).

There has also been a move toward encouraging greater collective responsibility in dealing with a variety of societal administrative and behavioral matters such as drinking and driving and tax evasion. It is suggested that this trend is symptomatic of a desire to foster an independence rather than a dependence culture and also mirrors the trend toward Irish individuals accepting collective responsibility for what is acceptable in our society.

One economist presents an alternative view on collectivism in Irish society: "Our rhetoric stresses the community over the individual, upbraiding the upstart and the self-starter, implicitly requiring that everybody stay in his or her appointed place" (Guiomard, 1995, p. 186). Such a commentary also raises a number of interesting issues in respect of Irish attitudes to failure and to Power Distance (cf. the subsection *Power Distance*). Peter Sutherland, ex-head of GATT (General Agreement on Tariffs and Trade) and Ireland's previous EU commissioner, observed in 1990: "We have a capacity for excessively admiring noble failure. We seem sometimes to be inured to coming off worst and almost to wallow wilfully in this" (cited in Guiomard, 1995, p. 188). The notion that we like to see others fail is a theme to which we return in our discussion of the literature on leadership in Ireland and in the qualitative study of leadership.

Summary. The Irish GLOBE data confirm the fact that Ireland is a country that has undergone radical and rapid change since the 1960s and is reflecting on how to proceed beyond the crossroads at which it currently finds itself. This involves some degree of reconciliation and recalibration of old and new practices and values. There is evidence of divergence from Hofstede's (1980) conclusions, in particular, regarding assumptions about individualism and collectivism.

The information presented in the preceding sections provides the context for one of the central objectives of the GLOBE study, namely the investigation of the impact of societal culture on implicitly held perceptions of leadership. In summary, Irish society is characterized *inter alia* by moderate Power Distance, high Collectivism, high Humane Orientation, high Performance Orientation, moderate levels of Assertiveness, Future Orientation, Uncertainty Avoidance, and Gender Egalitarianism. In absolute terms, Irish middle managers want more Gender Egalitarianism, a more humane society, more In-Group Collectivism, stronger Future Orientation, and higher Performance Orientation. They espouse similar levels of Assertiveness and Institutional Collectivism and lower levels of Power Distance and Uncertainty Avoidance.

What are the implications of this profile for leadership in Ireland? Certain initial assumptions as to the style of leadership, which is compatible with Ireland's positioning on the GLOBE societal dimensions, can be distilled from the findings. They suggest the importance of a participative, nonassertive, consensus-based style, which manifests a strong humane underpinning, together with a focus on performance. In the following sections, we explore such assumptions empirically, with reference to unobtrusive indicators of culture, as defined by Webb et al. (1973), the focus groups, the qualitative interviews, and the quantitative study of leadership. The presentation of the empirical study is preceded by a review of leadership research conducted in an Irish context.

4. LEADERSHIP IN IRELAND

Research on Leadership in Ireland

Whereas many of the other country chapters within this collection can draw on studies of leaders and leadership in their particular societies, there is a lack of any large empirical study or incisive theoretical analysis of leadership in Ireland. This is, in part, due to the preponderance of the self-analytic, autobiographical, and biographical approach to the study of leaders.

An early study in the 1960s, conducted by researchers at the Irish Management Institute and the Institute of Personality Assessment and Research (Berkeley, California), involved self-and other assessment of the personal attributes of 37 Irish business leaders using a battery of psychological tests (Barron & Egan, 1966, p. 13). All the leaders were male. The emergent attributes are "the achievement motive, personal dominance and leadership, and freedom from self-doubt" (Barron & Egan, 1996, p. 20); moreover, "independence is balanced by conformity" and there is an element of "feminine nurturance" (Barron & Egan, 1966, p. 22), which Barron and Egan see as challenging their assumptions about Irish leadership. In their conclusion, they observe: "There is an odd combination of masculinity and sense of the poetic in them. Their vision is of conquest, mastery, personal dominance, [and] command" (p. 29).

As already mentioned, much of the literature on leaders within Irish society and business is biographical in focus. Examples include Farrell's *Chairman or Chief* (1971), and I. Kenny's *In Good Company: Conversations With Irish Leaders* (1987), *Out on Their Own: Conversations With Irish Entrepreneurs* (1991), and *Leaders: Conversations With Irish Chief Executives* (2001). Farrell focuses on the constitutional, legal, and administrative position of *Taoiseach* (i.e., head of government). He categorizes five Irish heads of government as either "Chief" or "Chairman." Chiefs are exceedingly dominant, even authoritarian, figures. They believe in the concentration of power and centrally controlled decision making. The Chief is "dynamic, an activist and a promoter of action" (p. xi). Conversely, the Chairman adopts a consensual, procedural style of leadership. He believes in the sharing of responsibility and collective decision making: "He is a routine leader, more conscious of methods than goals" (p. xi). Eamon de Valera, perhaps the most famous of Ireland's political leaders, is classified as a Chairman. His governments "moved slowly, at the pace of the last man to be convinced" (p. 30). By contrast, Séan Lemass was the perfect Chief. His leadership was undisputed and his dominance uncontested. He favored the quick decision and believed "that the task was to hold the team together and to press forward with an active, even controversial, programme" (p. 58). Farrell's study emphasizes the importance of context and time in understanding leadership and submits that the position of *Taoiseach* was designed for a Chairman and not a Chief.

I. Kenny (1987) records a number of leadership attributes and behaviors characterizing the 15 male leaders from business, religious, and media spheres appearing in his book *In Good Company: Conversations With Irish Leaders.* It is worth noting that the individual whose name is mentioned most as having been a successful leader in Irish society is Séan Lemass, classified by Farrell (1971) as a Chief:

> They have the ability to listen and they have the ability to be tough. A high value is put on trust and loyalty. They are not, or at least do not like to be, remote figures: several are happiest among the troops. They think of themselves as pragmatic and practical but with a high level of conviction. They see this conviction as an essential element in influencing others. While they are far-sighted and can see the big picture, they believe ideas come from all over the place. They are themselves decisive—they abhor indecisiveness in others. They have definite views about the qualities needed in a chief executive: he must be the all-round man, both managerial and entrepreneurial; have a good track record; have integrity and be a good communicator; and be totally and exclusively dedicated to the job. (I. Kenny, 1987, pp. 6–7)

Other attributes and behaviors include the importance of being able to delegate and to use the talents and skills of others, to build a strong team, to set goals and see clearly where they are going, to seek consensus, to possess determination and patience, and to take risks. In a recent survey of nine Irish business leaders (*Excellence Ireland,* 2001) and in I. Kenny's *Leaders: Conversations With Irish Chief Executives* these attributes and behaviors are reemphasized. Kenny defines a leader as "someone who has willing followers" (p. 2); leadership is "a combination of character (who you are) and competence (what you can do)" (p. 2). Interestingly, Kenny's interviewees also refer to the begrudgery of success in Irish society, a point noted in our discussion of the societal cultural dimensions (cf. the subsection *Institutional Collectivism*).

In the past few years, a number of autobiographies and biographies of Irish business leaders have been published, including those of Tony O'Reilly,[1] and Bill Cullen.[2] Yet, alongside this, a recent publication, which presented perspectives on Irish identity from 100 very diverse people (Logue, 2000), did not feature a business leader. The omission is striking, considering the economic changes that the country has undergone and the contribution of the business community to this development. It is worth reflecting in this context on I. Kenny's

---

[1]Former CEO of Heinz.
[2]CEO of Renault Distributors, Ireland. This book topped the Irish bestseller list for a number of weeks.

(1991) observation that "it is the peasant culture which attributes lesser value to business, than, for example, the professions" (p. 4).

A further omission is striking, namely the absence of female leaders from available literature on leadership and Irish leaders. I. Kenny (2001) notes: "While there may be anecdotal evidence that women are beginning to break through, few indeed have reached the top floor—women constitute two percent of the chief executives in the leading 100 Irish companies" (p. 5).

The contextual nature of leadership underscored by Farrell (1971) and I. Kenny (1987) is further elaborated by Leavy and Wilson (1994), who use a multilevel approach to explore how "leadership, context and history interact in the formation of an organization's strategy and how this changes over time" (p. 2). Their analysis of leaders is focused less on attributes and more on the challenges, which they face within their organizational and historical context. Leaders, they posit, are "tenants of context and time" (p. 3). They classify the leaders who form part of the study into four generic groupings, *viz.* builders, revitalizers, turnarounders, and inheritors (p. 113) and identify the contextual factors that seem to have exerted the greatest influence on strategy within the organizations under scrutiny. The authors draw attention to the shift in the 1960s away from the leader as "nation-builder" who was "driven by values forged during the revolutionary times" and in times of peace had harnessed this "nationalistic passion and leadership talents to the practical patriotism of laying down the economic infrastructure of the new state" (p. 165). The new direction of leadership was towards "careerism, managerialism and professionalism" (p. 163), epitomized by Tony O'Reilly: *"Under his [Lemass's] leadership a new kind of hero or economic patriot, the professional manager, began to rise in stature. The men who rose to govern the country in the post-Lemass era had come to power because they were men of ambition rather than of destiny who had chosen politics as a career"* (p. 164). Such a shift is arguably a worldwide rather than a specifically Irish phenomenon.

The findings of a survey on best practice in Irish top management, jointly conducted by the Cranfield School of Management and the Irish Management Institute in 1991, concluded that the key competencies of top managers/CEOs were generating a vision for the future, molding a top team, communicating effectively, generating a positive success-oriented culture within the organization, and practicing the personal qualities and skills required for effective performance (Kakabadse, Alderson, & Gorman, 1995). The authors of the survey submit that, in comparison with other European samples, Ireland has produced talented business leaders, Irish management is one of the better educated professional cohorts in Europe, and Ireland does not have a leadership capability problem; the challenge is the development of top teams (p. 23). This view is supported by another recent study based on interviews with CEOs and a survey of the top-management team, of core knowledge employees, and of human resource managers in multinationals and indigenous software and telecommunications companies. The authors of this study conclude that the interviewed leaders recognize the need to move from the solitary leader model to a more collective and mutually accountable leadership style (Flood, MacCurtain, & West, 2001).

There are a number of themes emerging from the literature on leadership in Ireland, which resonate with points raised in our exposition of society, the economy, and politics, and with the findings of the quantitative study of Irish societal culture. These include the growing importance of performance; the espousal of lower Power Distance; the existence of consensus-based models of decision making, which correlate with a strongly collectivistic society; the importance of lower Uncertainty Avoidance; and recognition of the traditionally patriarchal nature of society and its implicit assumptions about gender roles.

The existence of begrudgery is a further theme, which surfaces in the literature and may be embedded in higher levels of collectivism and attitudes to Power Distance. We can also observe that the study of leadership in Ireland mirrors trends in research worldwide with its shift from a focus on the characteristics of leaders to a concentration on leading the top team.

In the following sections, we turn attention to the qualitative components of the GLOBE study in Ireland, which include a review of unobtrusive indicators of leadership, focus groups, and qualitative interviews. The findings are contemplated alongside the trends emerging from the literature on leadership and the quantitative study of societal culture.

The Qualitative Study of Leadership in Ireland

Unobtrusive Indicators of Culture and Leadership. Stamps, statues, and banknotes possess symbolic significance. They "recall, evoke the sentiments of, or otherwise render recognizable the cultural mappings of basic social and ecological relationships in human society" (Garrison & Arensberg, 1976; cited in Kane, 1986, p. 549); they bear witness to the historical and social evolution of Ireland and to its continuing transition and shaping of a new identity.

The emergence of the Irish State and its path from a small, inward-looking economy to a fully integrated member of the EU is charted by its stamp design (cf. Miller, 1986). In particular, stamp design has chronicled in recent decades the changing face of nationalism and the burgeoning self-confidence of the Irish nation. The semiotic value of stamps as an assertion of nationhood cannot be disputed. The first stamps to emerge post-1922 thus reinforced, through their use of motifs and symbols traditionally associated with Irish heritage, the religious and scholarly self-image possessed by Ireland (Scott, 1995, pp. 87–88). Up until the Republic of Ireland Act in 1948, which Scott sees as a watershed in Irish stamp design, stamps continued to mirror those themes that were ideologically close to the young state, most notably religion and nationalism. The Irish language also featured prominently, although after 1949 there is a move toward bilingual stamps, connoting the growing self-confidence and international outlook of the Irish nation. This also found expression in a broadening of the motifs depicted by Irish stamps: Literary and artistic motifs together with a greater emphasis on themes that attest to Ireland's technological and scientific accomplishments are in evidence.

Banknotes, like stamps, have tended overwhelmingly to depict male figures. Although Ireland has produced a significant number of prominent women in both the literary and political spheres, the representation of women as contributors to the country's development is limited to their participation within the caring professions, in religious life, and as homemakers, reasserting the centrality of the family together with its Catholic ethos within Irish society (cf. the subsections *Gender Egalitarianism, In-Group Collectivism*). In spite of the erosion of the position of the Roman Catholic Church, the achievements of founders of religious orders continued to be commemorated on banknotes right up to the introduction of the euro in 2002.

Ireland's history is also reflected by its public art. Many of the classical monuments, erected by dukes and viceroys to the honor of kings or military prominents of the British Empire, were removed after independence or blown up. At the time of their erection, the arbiters of "the politics of public space" were the landowning and politically influential Protestant class, although it is important not to confound "Protestant" with "British." By the mid-19th century, there was general support among Catholics and Protestants for the need to forge an Irish identity through monuments, even if the conception of this identity was not always shared. The monuments erected during this period thus paid tribute to those who had furthered either constitutionally or at arms the cause of Irish sovereignty. In the 20th century, the heroes of 1916 provided the symbolism with which to shape the identity of the newly independent state. Independence monuments frequently adopted religious imagery, which also underpinned the ideal of the nationalist Catholic state. Nowadays, artists and literary figures are immortalized in stone, but they exist alongside sculptures, which address issues that have had an impact on everyday people in both the present and past, such as the Great Famine.

Smyth (1985) charts an important evolution within Irish commemorative art in the 20th century away from a narrow ethnic view of public memory to searches for Irish identity across different traditions in politics, institutions, art, and thought (cited in Hill, 1998, p. 201). Other forces have been at work in determining the changing orientation of public sculpture. The process of its selection has become more democratic. There are new patrons amongst the business community who wish to emphasize their links with art and thereby to provide the "philistine" pursuits of commerce with a more acceptable face and to reinforce their own status within the community. Yet, there is a continued lack of public recognition of achievements and achievers in the business world, recalling our comments with respect to Logue's (2000) omission of a business leader in his recent publication on Irish identity (cf. the subsection *Research on Leadership in Ireland*). We have indicated that this might be attributable to the country's relatively recent commercial success or to our "peasant culture" (I. Kenny, 1991, p. 4).

In summary, stamps, banknotes, and public monuments point to an ideal of leadership that is clearly centered on the notion of the romantic or patriot hero and liberator, possessing vision and willingness to risk his or her life for the freedom of the country. The evolution of public commemoration again encapsulates the crossroads at which the country now finds itself: Growing self-confidence coexists with a sense of nostalgia and looking to the past rather than the present for inspirational leader figures. The absence of prominent business leaders from public memory is noteworthy. In the next subsection, we consider the view of leadership emerging from the focus groups and qualitative interviews.

The Focus Groups and Qualitative Interviews.   Two focus groups were conducted during 1995. The participants were drawn from a cross-section of industrial sectors and did not know each other. In total, 13 middle managers, both male and female, participated. They were asked to define management and leadership, to identify the behavioral characteristics of an average manager, an above-average manager, and an outstanding leader, and to indicate whether successful Irish managers would have to alter their behavior to be successful abroad. Participants were also asked to reflect on incidents involving a strong leader and a strong manager who was not a strong leader. The focus groups were both audio- and videotaped for the purposes of transcription. The researchers also conducted two semistructured qualitative interviews with middle managers, which sought to elicit views of outstanding leaders. These interviews were also audiotaped and transcribed and are used to supplement observations recorded from the focus groups.

Leadership was perceived to be a top-level or very senior management characteristic. A characteristic of the outstanding leader is an ability to see the big picture—the so-called "helicopter view"—and to take a global approach, recalling the profile described by I. Kenny (1987; cf. the subsection *Research on Leadership in Ireland*). Thus, when the participants were asked whether they could identify leaders at different societal or organizational levels, identification was almost solely confined to the highest echelons of society and organizations. The outstanding leader fulfills a strategic function as opposed to the competent manager, who is effective on the operational level and doesn't take too many risks. Outstanding leaders are seen to be visionary, charismatic, inspirational, and tenacious, and to exhibit a willingness to take risks. They possess intelligence and drive, and are outstanding motivators. Leaders adapt to situations and choose to get around the red tape that may stand in the way of achieving a goal. Such characteristics are compatible with lower levels of Uncertainty Avoidance (cf. the subsection *Uncertainty Avoidance*). By contrast, an inability to delegate, being overly task centered, getting bogged down by issues of procedure and administration, aggressive, dominant, and face-saving behavior together with steam-rolling ideas and opinions are the hallmarks of ineffective leadership, but are attributes sometimes used to describe a normally effective manager. Verbs used to describe leaders include *to inspire, to guide, to stimulate, to direct,* and *to communicate.* There was general agreement that leadership involved influencing people to do something.

Leaders have an ability to command respect and to take tough decisions. Though it was recognized that the leader must on occasions be assertive, consensus was seen as the preferred decision-making style for Irish leaders. The opinions expressed in the qualitative interviews correlate with those documented in the focus groups and reflect the preference for a consensus- based leadership style. Moreover, they provide support for trends emerging from the quantitative study of societal culture, for example, low Assertiveness and high levels of Institutional Collectivism. In the rejection of authoritarian leadership, we see the preference for lower Power Distance relationships in Ireland.

Some of the participants noted that good leaders do not have to be liked, but, critically, they must enthuse people to follow. Charisma was seen as a critical trait. Recognition of the importance of followers in the achievement of goals or strategy was a recurrent theme, which resonates with the old adage that Irish people cannot be led, but must be inspired. Indeed, as noted in our discussion of Power Distance, Irish people tend to be low on obedience to authority and, consequently, they do not always make good followers. A view reiterated in the focus groups was that outstanding leaders are often those who remain in the background, rather than flaunting their authority.

In Ireland, powerful people are frequently seen as leaders, yet the feeling in the focus groups was that it is important to distinguish between having power and being a leader; the difference resides in the use to which power is put. Such a view is also expressed by Gardner (1996, p. 16). There is a strong awareness of the negative side of leadership. Indeed, the participants reject the abuse of authority, conferred by what might be designated as position power, although it was also suggested that leaders need to manipulate people and that leadership sometimes consists of negative control with leaders concealing their real objectives. In the words of one participant: "I think being an outstanding leader is not seeming to manipulate, but [he] is manipulating all over the place. And he's not seen to control, [yet] he is controlling. He's using all sorts of techniques [and] methods to get his own way."

The role of the leader in creating versus implementing an existing vision was discussed in the focus groups. A leader can take an idea and create a vision around it, much like Gardner's "innovative leader" (Gardner, 1996, p. 10): Examples given by the participants include the former prime ministers, de Valera and Haughey. Yet, this, in turn, raises the question as to whether implementing the vision is a function of management or leadership. In general, it was felt by participants that leadership is more about getting people to follow or to buy into the vision than actually creating it.

A further theme concerns the notion that leadership is context framed, a view that we have already documented with reference to Farrell (1971), I. Kenny (1987), and Leavy and Wilson (1994) (cf. the subsection *Research on Leadership in Ireland*). The participants in both the focus groups and the qualitative interviews were unable to divorce leadership from its context, irrespective of whether the context is generated by a political party or an organization. Leaders stand out from the crowd in their own microculture and their status is achieved both by an ability to inspire and by knowledge of the industry. The desirability of competence in a particular leadership context ties in with the desire for the leader to deliver and perform.

It was considered difficult to achieve consensus on who is or is not an outstanding leader in Ireland. Similarly, the participants had reservations about conferring prominent Irish business figures with leadership status, with the exception of Tony O'Reilly. There was great dissent as to whether the outstanding business people in both the Irish and international business sphere could be considered as outstanding leaders. The conclusion was that they were outstanding business people but not outstanding leaders. We have noted the absence of business people in public memory in our discussion of unobtrusive indicators and suggested that our relatively late emergence as an industrialized nation implies less experience of prominent business figures. Unwillingness to laud success in business may be embedded in Irish culture in the guise of begrudgery (Guiomard, 1995; I. Kenny, 2001; cf. also the subsections *Institutional Collectivism, Research on Leadership in Ireland*). It resurfaces in both the focus groups and qualitative interviews and is perhaps not unrelated to the lack of confidence in Irish business leaders at home and the general belief that they perform well abroad. Abroad they are perceived to be adaptable, versatile, and unbureaucratic.

Many of the outstanding leaders identified by the focus group participants and the interviewees are not Irish: They include Richard Branson, Margaret Thatcher, Lee Iacocca, and John F. Kennedy, the latter albeit with Irish roots. Irish nationals mentioned include a number of political figures, such as Lemass, de Valera, Haughey, and Mary Robinson—the sole female figure of Irish nationality considered to personify outstanding leadership. Noteworthy is the naming of ex-Prime Minister Haughey in the light of the scandals that have shadowed his career. During his period of office, shadiness in political and personal dealings were never far away, although he continued to enjoy a great deal of support among the grass-roots members of his party and the broader electorate. Haughey is recognized as having possessed vision and charisma. Although recently, the many tribunals of inquiry (cf. the subsection *Legal and Political Framework*) have assumed an almost cathartic, countercultural function; some sneaking regard for the duplicity and rule bending successfully practiced by Haughey would appear to linger.

Summary.   On the basis of the qualitative study of leadership, several preliminary observations can be presented with respect to leadership characteristics together with a number of apparent paradoxes. Interestingly, the participants in the focus groups and qualitative interviews were able to identify the characteristics of leaders, but had difficulty in naming leader figures other than those from the political sphere. The memory of past political figures is very much alive and they are generally credited with the shaping of modern Ireland. Vision and charisma are amongst the central tenets of outstanding leadership and the image of the romantic or patriot hero continues to hold a dominant place in collective memory and in perceptions of leadership qualities.

Consensus-based leadership is seen as the preferred decision-making style, although the frequent naming of Lemass, classified as a Chief by Farrell (1971) by virtue of his more authoritarian leadership style, underpins the importance of context. This style of leadership may be more appropriate in times of economic crisis such as existed during Lemass's period of office.

The view that leaders within the business community are not outstanding leaders within society is widespread and they also remain absent among the unobtrusive indicators of culture and leadership. Such a perception again underpins the contextual focus of leadership, which might also explain why leaders often remain in the background, that is, within their own context, and why business leaders are not widely recognized beyond their context. Ireland's economic turnaround has evidently been steered by leaders in the business community and their absence from the list of named figures would support the notion that they are acting in the background. Alongside this, we have noted higher levels of identification with Irish business leaders who have gone abroad. We might speculate that this is, in part, a consequence of many decades of emigration, which have seen individuals with low Uncertainty Avoidance go abroad, thereby leaving behind those with higher Uncertainty Avoidance. Those who have gone abroad thus fulfill one of the expectations attributed to outstanding leaders, namely risk taking.

There is broad consistency between the findings emerging from the narrow literature base on leadership in Ireland and the issues raised by the participants in the focus groups, qualitative interviews, and the review of unobtrusive indicators. Moreover, the profile of Irish society generated from the quantitative study supports the view of leadership that is articulated in the qualitative research, specifically a preference for consensus-based and participative leadership, a willingness to take risks, together with a nonauthoritarian and nonassertive style. These preferences correspond with strong endorsement of Institutional Collectivism, low Uncertainty Avoidance and Power Distance, and moderate Assertiveness. Such a profile is now juxtaposed with results of the quantitative study of leadership in Ireland.

The Quantitative Study of Leadership in Ireland

Findings. Irish middle managers rated the 112 leadership items on a sclae between 1 (greatly inhibits a person from being an outstanding leader) and 7 (greatly contributes to a person being an outstanding leader). Using exploratory factor analysis (see House *et al.*, 2004) these items were grouped intially into 21 first-order leadership dimensions which, in turn, were consolidated into 6 second-order global leadership dimensions, namely *autonomous, charismatic, humane, self-protective, participative* and *team-oriented* leadership. Table 11.3 shows the 6 global second-order culturally endorsed leadership theory dimensions together with the 21 first-order leadership dimensions. Together they constitute the attributes and behaviors culturally perceived to contribute to or inhibit outstanding leadership.

When we consider the scores for each of the 21 first-order leadership dimensions, the dimensions rated as most important for Irish middle managers and, therefore, deemed by the respondents to contribute significantly to outstanding leadership include performance orientation ($M=6.38$), visionary ($M=6.33$), inspirational ($M=6.33$), integrity ($M=6.19$), collaborative team oriented ($M=6.19$), and decisive ($M=6.14$). Also of importance are: administratively competent ($M=5.60$), team integrator ($M=5.46$), diplomacy ($M=5.44$), modesty ($M=5.11$), self-sacrificial (i.e., foregoing self-interest in the interest of the goal or vision) ($M=5.11$) and humane ($M=5.01$). Based on the global culturally endorsed leadership theory dimensions these findings suggest that Irish middle managers espouse a charismatic/value based leadership style. They also endorse a team-oriented style coupled with a participative and humane approach. By contrast, dimensions which are perceived to act as significant inhibitors of successful leadership include malevolent (egoistic, cynical, dishonest, vindictive), conflict inducer, self-centered, nonparticipative face-saving and autocratic behavior. A self-protective or narcissistic leadership style is not acceptable to Irish middle managers.

TABLE 11.3
Country Mean Scores for Leadership Dimensions

First-order and Second-order Dimensions	Mean
Charismatic	6.08
Performance Orientation	6.38
Visionary	6.33
Inspirational	6.33
Integrity	6.19
Self-Sacrificial	5.11
Decisive	6.14
Team Oriented	5.81
Team Integrator	5.46
Collaborative Team Oriented	6.19
Administratively Competent	5.60
Diplomatic	5.44
Malevolent (reversed)	1.66
Self-Protective	3.00
Self-Centered	1.99
Status-Conscious	3.63
Conflict Inducer	3.36
Face Saver	2.48
Procedural	3.50
Participative	5.64
Autocratic (reversed)	2.48
Nonparticipative	2.24
Humane	5.06
Humane	5.01
Modesty	5.11
Autonomous	3.95
Autonomous	3.95

Note. The six higher order dimensions of Leadership, shown in the body of the table, are the result of second-order factor analysis on the 21 subdimensions. See den Hartog *et al.* (1999) and House *et al.* (2004).

Discussion. The profile to emerge from the Irish qualitative and quantitative data indicates that charismatic value-based leadership is endorsed. Such characteristics—visionary, inspirational, performance orientation—have already been highlighted in the qualitative research and the review of unobtrusive indicators. They also resonate strongly with the profile emerging from the quantitative study of societal culture and with the findings of previous research, including "the achievement motive" (Barron & Egan, 1966, p. 20) and qualities such as integrity, decisiveness, performance, vision, and team integrator (*Excellence Ireland,* 2001; I. Kenny, 1987).

Such preferences must be considered against the backdrop of societal change in Ireland. It is not difficult to understand why performance-oriented leadership is valued if one considers the dynamic imposed by social and economic progress. Emphasis on decisiveness and integrity may reflect expectations of greater clarity of vision coupled with the shift away from the clientelist approach toward transparency within Irish society. Indeed, trust is perceived to be a critical attribute of all leadership relationships: it is asserted by the focus group participants and in the leadership literature (cf. the subsection *Research on Leadership in Ireland*). Furthermore, the belief that decisiveness substantially enhances leadership effectiveness marries well with the view expressed in the qualitative research that a leader is someone who "sees things through." The recognition that administrative competence enhances leadership can be linked with the broader thrust toward performance orientation. The desirability of inspirational leadership underpins the notion that Irish people need to be inspired rather than led by a directive or authoritarian leader, a point raised in the focus groups and in our discussion of power relationships in Irish society. So too, willingness on the part of leaders to sacrifice themselves for the common good may connote some form of residual adherence to the image of the romantic hero, which features so prominently in collective memory.

The importance attributed to the characteristic "collaborative team oriented" attests to the centrality of getting people to buy into the vision and the ability to ensure commitment to the vision. This characteristic was identified by Farrell (1971) and echoed in the research findings of Kakabadse et al. (1995) and Flood et al. (2001), and in the qualitative research regarding the leader–follower relationship.

Unlike Barron and Egan (1966), who found that "feminine nurturance" challenged their expectation of leadership, various explanations can be offered that potentially account for the value attributed to a more humane style of leadership. Within the societal culture data, Ireland enjoys one of the highest rankings on the "As Is" scale for humane orientation and there is belief that Irish society should be even more humane. Contributing to this profile is the fact that modesty and diplomacy are seen as positive dimensions of leadership. It has already been documented in the findings of the quantitative study of societal culture that Ireland is a relatively nonassertive society with a preference for indirectness in interpersonal communication. In the focus groups, the participants observed that leaders do not flaunt their authority. The impression that they should adopt a consultative style, not induce conflict, and involve team members in decision making, is evidenced in both the quantitative and qualitative findings.

Face-saving behavior, with its implications of evasiveness and ambiguity, is negatively evaluated. This possibly signals a desire to move away from a feature of Irish society characterized by Lee (1982) as the "peasant residue in the Irish psyche" which "confuses the distinction between necessary confidentiality and furtive concealment," thereby underpinning "suspicions grounded in the face to face nature" of society in Ireland (cited in Leavy, 1993, p. 145). The tendency to conceal may also be a legacy of Ireland's colonial past. The dissimulation of truth, revealed in the previously mentioned investigative tribunals, has undermined the credibility of some recent Irish political and business leaders.

Narcissistic, self-centered leaders have never been endorsed within Irish society, which may also be a consequence of several centuries of occupation by a colonial power. Despite the fact that autocratic leadership is not deemed desirable, Ireland has had autocratic leaders who were "tenants of history and time" (Leavy & Wilson, 1994). The focus groups concurred that such a style exists, especially in times of crisis, even if it is not desirable. Not surprisingly malevolence is seen as a significant inhibitor of leadership.

Another characteristic that has a slight inhibiting function is the focus on procedure. Again, this perception corresponds with a view expressed in the focus groups and qualitative interviews that outstanding leaders can cut through red tape in order to achieve their goals: Emphasis on procedure was identified as characterizing managers, not leaders. The fact that the questionnaire respondents eschew bureaucratic procedures is not surprising if one considers the tendency, which has been inherent within Irish society, to circumvent rules and regulations (cf. the subsection *Legal and Political Framework*).

In conclusion, the profile of leadership issuing from the quantitative study broadly echoes many of the trends that we have identified within the qualitative components of the research, the quantitative study of Irish societal culture, and the leadership literature.

The preceding sections complete the review of societal culture and of middle managers' implicit perceptions of leadership. The following section presents an industry-level analysis of the data, reporting the findings of the quantitative study of organizational culture and leadership in the food-processing and financial services sectors. To recap, data were collected from middle managers in 10 indigenous food-processing and 8 indigenous financial services companies. Central to our reflections is a consideration of the interrelationship between societal culture and organizational culture and their impact on perceptions of leadership in the two sectors.

5. ORGANIZATIONAL CULTURE IN THE TWO SECTORS

Findings

Organizational culture was measured on the same nine dimensions as those employed in the societal culture survey, with the "As Is" scores reflecting organizational practices and the "Should Be" scores espoused values. The GLOBE study posits that organizational culture and practices will affect how leaders in these organizations are expected to behave. Specifically, it is hypothesized that organizational culture will have a stronger impact on leadership perceptions than societal culture as the organizational culture is more proximate. Table 11.4 presents the findings for the two industries with respect to the nine GLOBE dimensions.

With the exception of Uncertainty Avoidance, the direction of desired change from "As Is" to "Should Be" across the remaining eight dimensions is similar in the two sectors. For Performance Orientation, Future Orientation, Humane Orientation, Gender Egalitarianism, Institutional Collectivism, and In-Group Collectivism, the trend is toward the espousal of higher values. With respect to Assertiveness, respondents in the food sector espouse slightly lower levels ("As Is" $M = 3.47$; "Should Be" $M = 3.27$) and those in the financial services sector seem content with existing levels ("As Is" $M = 3.83$; "Should Be" $M = 3.77$).

Both the food-processing and financial services sectors face challenging futures, requiring greater Performance Orientation (Food Processing "As Is" $M = 4.53$, "Should Be" $M = 6.36$; Financial Services "As Is" $M = 4.32$, "Should Be" $M = 6.14$) and Future Orientation (Food Processing "As Is" $M = 5.07$, "Should Be" $M = 5.75$; Financial Services "As Is" $M = 4.67$, "Should Be" $M = 5.62$). Margins are low in the food commodity sector, giving rise to continuing pressures to be more efficient and cost-effective; hence the trend toward implementing change management strategies such as world-class manufacturing. In the financial services sector, middle managers recognize the need to become more performance oriented in order to deliver anticipated shareholder value, to meet financial targets, and to prevent takeovers by larger predator institutions. The thrust toward greater Future Orientation signals recognition of the necessity to plan ahead. For the food-processing industry, the scores may reflect awareness of the challenge of managing the shift away from primary processing toward producing value-added consumer foods and the need for investment in product development and innovation.

Middle managers in the two sectors also espouse higher organizational loyalty, that is, In-Group Collectivism (Food Processing "As Is" $M = 4.67$, "Should Be" $M = 6.13$; Financial

TABLE 11.4
Country Mean Scores for Organizational Culture Dimensions

Organizational Culture Dimensions	Food			Finance		
	"As Is"[a] (a)	"Should Be"[a] (a)	Absolute Difference[b] (b)	"As Is"	"Should Be"	Absolute Difference
Future Orientation	5.07	5.75	0.68	4.67	5.62	0.95
Performance Orientation	4.53	6.36	1.83	4.32	6.14	1.82
In-Group Collectivism	4.67	6.13	1.46	4.44	5.82	1.38
Institutional Collectivism	4.50	4.73	0.23	4.20	4.89	0.69
Humane Orientation	4.26	4.59	0.33	4.26	4.71	0.45
Gender Egalitarianism	2.72	5.11	2.39	3.11	4.93	1.82
Power Distance	4.00	3.42	−0.58	4.53	3.40	−1.13
Uncertainty Avoidance	4.09	4.33	0.24	4.44	4.17	−0.27
Assertiveness	3.47	3.27	−0.20	3.83	3.77	−0.06

[a]Country Mean score on a 7-point Likert-type scale. [b]Absolute difference between the "Should Be" and "As Is" score.

Services "As Is" $M = 4.44$, "Should Be" $M = 5.82$). This is particularly so in the food-processing sector, mirroring the fact that the food sector organizations are already very collectively focused due to their location in tightly knit rural communities. In both sectors, there is a clear desire for greater cohesiveness and a more collective, shared vision. The espousal of higher levels of Institutional Collectivism (Food Processing "As Is" $M = 4.50$, "Should Be" $M = 4.73$; Financial Services "As Is" $M = 4.20$, "Should Be" $M = 4.89$) support this trend.

Both industries embrace higher Humane Orientation (Food Processing "As Is" $M = 4.26$, "Should Be" $M = 4.59$; Financial Services "As Is" $M = 4.26$, "Should Be" $M = 4.71$). One explanation for such a view within the financial services sector is that many of these organizations are large mature bureaucracies, where regardless of excellent procedures and practices, there can be a lack of human kindness. According to the results of the quantitative studies of societal culture and of leadership in Ireland, humane qualities are valued highly within Irish society.

Respondents in both sectors recognize the importance of improving Gender Egalitarianism (Food Processing "As Is" $M = 2.72$, "Should Be" $M = 5.11$; Financial Services "As Is" $M = 3.11$, "Should Be" $M = 4.93$). However, this is felt more strongly in the food sector companies in which fewer women are employed, and those who are have traditionally operated in sex-segregated roles. Gender imbalance is apparent at senior levels in financial institutions and most of the organizations surveyed are implementing "valuing diversity" and "employment equality" strategies in order to make the espoused value a reality.

Middle managers in both sectors want Power Distance to be reduced (Food Processing "As Is" $M = 4.00$, "Should Be" $M = 3.42$; Financial Services "As Is" $M = 4.53$, "Should Be" $M = 3.40$), with the financial services sector endorsing this reduction more significantly. As machine bureaucracies, financial institutions have a stronger sense of hierarchy and formality than food sector processing plants. Dismantling hierarchies and focusing staff around the concept of customer service will necessitate a more collaborative approach to work in financial services.

On Uncertainty Avoidance, the organizational cultures of the two industries diverge (Food Processing "As Is" $M = 4.09$, "Should Be" $M = 4.33$; Financial Services "As Is" $M = 4.44$, "Should Be" $M = 4.17$). Respondents in the food sector organizations wish to become slightly better at managing uncertainty, which reflects the increasingly regulated environment in which these companies operate. Certification, validation, and evaluation are required to meet the demands of accountability and transparency to multiple stakeholders. Financial services companies, on the other hand, wish to become less uncertainty avoiding. As an industry dominated by rules and procedures, these organizations wish to become more innovative and to encourage staff to become more responsible and self-reliant in order to deliver a speedy and efficient customer service.

In summary, the organizational culture data from both sectors broadly mirror each other. The mean scores on each of the dimensions reflect recognition of the reality of the macroenvironment in which the industries are operating and of future challenges. Significantly, when juxtaposed with the findings for the societal cultural data, we can see clear parallels in the direction of espoused change. In the organizational culture data we find, not surprisingly, a stronger focus on "Should Be" for Future and Performance Orientation, whereas for Power Distance and Humane Orientation, the societal cultural scores are significantly higher on "As Is" and "Should Be," respectively. In conclusion, the findings demonstrate the strong interrelationship between societal and organizational culture. In the next section, we examine perceptions of effective leadership within the two industries.

Leadership in the Two Sectors

The results of the industry-level analysis of perceptions of leadership are presented in Table 11.5.

The charismatic/value-based cluster of attributes, including inspirational, visionary, performance orientation, decisive, self-sacrificial, and integrity, are positively endorsed in both sectors. The leadership dimension receiving the highest mean score in the food sector is performance orientation ($M = 6.63$), reflecting the pressure to perform and deliver shareholder value. Complementing performance, which is a feature of all cost-competitive strategies, are the leadership attributes "inspirational" and "visionary." These attributes are self-explanatory if one takes account of the task facing the leaders of Irish food sector companies to effect radical change in an industry that is critical to the Irish economy and psyche. The profile of charismatic leadership also distinguishes the financial services industry, where "inspirational" ranks highest ($M = 6.32$). Personal integrity ($M = 6.14$) is judged to be very important and represents a value that has always been esteemed in financial service leaders. Indeed, poor performance and lack of personal integrity have resulted in the recent removal of leaders from leadership positions in this sector.

Team orientation is highly valued in both industries and provides evidence of the necessity for leaders in Irish business organizations to have the ability not just to create the vision but to inspire their followers to accept their vision. Given the pluralist allegiances within these industries in terms of stakeholders and the strong support for a collective orientation, the task facing leaders is to ensure that the organization is fully committed to and inspired by their vision. Skills in team leadership will be imperative for food sector leaders, who will have to secure acceptance of their future vision of a drastically changing industry in the face of European expansion and globalization, as well as motivating and empowering highly unionized, middle-aged, and inward-looking staff. Equally important in both industries are skills of diplomacy (Food $M = 5.49$; Financial Services $M = 5.33$) in orchestrating the shift

TABLE 11.5

Comparison of the Organizational Means for Leadership Characteristics in the
Food-Processing and Financial Services Industries

	Food		Finance	
Characteristics	*Mean*	*Rank*	*Mean*	*Rank*
Performance Orientation	6.63	1	6.26	3
Inspirational	6.44	2	6.32	1
Visionary	6.43	3	6.29	2
Team Integrator	6.30	4	6.18	4
Decisive	6.19	5	6.12	6
Integrity	6.15	6	6.15	5
Administratively Competent	5.94	7	5.41	7
Collaborative Team Oriented	5.64	8	5.33	8
Diplomatic	5.49	9	5.33	9
Modesty	5.22	10	5.17	10
Self-Sacrificial	5.10	11	4.96	11
Humane	5.00	12	4.91	12
Autonomous	4.24	13	3.78	13
Status-Conscious	3.68	14	3.43	14
Procedural	3.63	15	3.38	15
Conflict Inducer	3.51	16	3.23	16
Autocratic	2.75	17	2.43	17
Face Saver	2.44	18	2.34	18
Nonparticipative	2.32	19	2.30	19
Self-Centered	1.87	20	1.94	20
Malevolent	1.63	21	1.70	21

from managing internal stakeholders to delivering external shareholder value. Communication
can be very political and clientelist in business circles and this might help to explain the high
value placed on diplomacy as a desirable attribute for leaders in the two sectors. Given the
increasing requirements for transparency, accountability, and compliance with national and
international regulations in the food and financial services sectors, senior managers will need
to adopt a team-oriented, participative approach. Administrative competence is rated particularly highly, especially in the food sector ($M = 5.93$), where there is perhaps a perceived need
for such expertise to guide the industry successfully through a period of turbulent change.

Finally, in both sectors leaders are expected to demonstrate a humane orientation. Given
the small size of Irish food sector companies and their location in small rural communities,
this emphasis is understandable. Modesty was ranked as an important characteristic of Irish
business leaders and may coincide with the fact that food and financial services' chief executives have not been public figures in the past. They have been acknowledged within their

context but not in the wider society, although this situation is changing. It is worth recalling the reservations expressed in the focus groups about accepting prominent business figures as leaders: "They're outstanding in the area which is important for them to operate in—not in the huge arena but in the micro-culture environment of their organization or industry." This statement rings true in the food industry, where leaders are household names, especially in their regions and local community, and it brings us closer to an understanding of the contextual basis of leadership.

A self-protective, narcissistic, nonparticipative style of leadership is not acceptable in either industry. Factors perceived to impede effective leadership in the two sectors include malevolent, self-centered, nonparticipative, autocratic, and face-saving behavior. We might recall the suspicion voiced by the focus group participants regarding the misuse of power to influence followers: This view is wholly endorsed in both industries, with malevolence ranked as the factor most likely to impede leadership.

In summary, middle managers in both food-processing and financial services organizations in Ireland expect their corporate leaders to practice charismatic, value-based leadership. This expectation is underpinned by an assumption that leadership will be focused on team integration using a participative style and humane orientation. Both sectors agree that being malevolent, self-centered, nonparticipative, face saving, and autocratic are not the characteristics of the leaders they wish to follow in their respective industries. The emergent profile of leadership in the two sectors has strong parallels with that documented in previous research and also elaborated in the focus groups and qualitative interviews. The findings point to a high degree of congruence regarding the espoused profile of leadership between the two industries. Taking into consideration the finding that there is a strong interrelationship between societal and organizational culture, we might conclude that societal culture is potentially more influential in shaping perceptions of effective leadership than organizational culture.

6. CONCLUSION

The Irish GLOBE study set out to explore, describe, and explain leadership in the Republic of Ireland within its cultural and organizational context and to consider the interrelationship between societal and organizational culture as they have an impact on leadership. The research embraced both quantitative and qualitative approaches in addressing these questions.

In Ireland, the quantitative and qualitative studies of leadership point unambiguously to the espousal of a charismatic value-based leadership style. This style of leadership is underpinned by a constellation of leadership attributes, which are strongly influenced by the dimensions of Irish societal culture. However, the imprint of history still casts a shadow over perceptions of leadership.

There is a clear view among Irish middle managers about the substance of leadership. This clarity is evidenced in the findings of the quantitative study, the focus groups, and qualitative interviews and, additionally, in the findings of previous research. Irish leaders are performance orientated, have vision, possess a so-called "helicopter view," and are focused on the future. They are expected not just to inspire their followers, but to get them "to buy into their vision." They achieve this by participative, consensual decision making, integrity, trust, and loyalty: in short, by playing the role of *chairman* as described by Farrell (1971). There is a strong expectation that leaders will behave in a humane, modest way, will not flaunt their authority, and will be self-sacrificing in the interest of their organization. By contrast, an authoritarian leadership style, based on narcissism and self-centered, face-saving behavior, is perceived to be an inappropriate style.

This profile resonates strongly with findings of the quantitative study of societal culture. Ireland emerges as a performance- and future-oriented society, which is not surprising for a country that has recently been ranked for 3 years in succession as the world's most globalized economy (A. T. Kearney, 2004). It manifests strong Collectivism, which, together with moderate Power Distance, explains the preference for participative, consensual decision making. The "Should Be" scores on the dimensions Institutional Collectivism, In-Group Collectivism, and Power Distance indicate that this style of leadership will continue to be endorsed. Furthermore, Irish society is deemed to be very humanitarian and wishes to remain so, suggesting that the expectation for Irish leaders to behave in a kind, humane way will also persist. Some tension between this value and the demands for performance, driven by the global imperative, may ensue.

In contrast, there is little or no consensus on who might be designated as having leader status in contemporary Irish society. The people most named were political or historical, demonstrating that the image of the romantic patriot hero continues to infuse perceptions of leadership qualities. Collective memory is also more firmly focused on an ideal of leadership centered on the patriot-hero and liberator, as commemorated *inter alia* by stamps and monuments, who is symbolic of Ireland's struggle for and transition to independence. Such an ideal would appear to remain valid within Irish society in the 1990s. Moreover, it attributes little value to female figures, who notwithstanding their prominent role in the family, in caring, and in the community, seem not to be lauded as leaders, the exception being ex-president Mary Robinson. This scenario may change if we consider the "Should Be" scores for Gender Egalitarianism coupled with the increased participation of women in the labor force.

Business leaders are not accepted as leaders except in their business context and they have not yet earned a place in public memory. Their absence is noteworthy in a society in which business leadership has clearly been evidenced. The most obvious examples include the emergence of the "Celtic Tiger" and the major social and economic changes that Ireland has undergone in the past quarter of a century. Why are business leaders not recognized or, indeed, visible other than in the context of their organizations? One possible explanation is the country's late industrialization, which might explain the preoccupation with historical and political figures and the reluctance to elevate prominent business figures to the status of societal leaders. Alternatively, based on the GLOBE "As Is" findings, Irish society's strong collectivist orientation, moderate Power Distance relationships, and nonassertiveness might militate against leaders standing out from their context. This particular nexus of societal factors might lead us to conclude that in a small collectivist society the leader remains in the background; they are known in context to the selected team/in-group and influence performance and outcomes through networking and clientelist relations, often eschewing bureaucracy and regulation behind closed doors. This latter insight has been glimpsed through the workings of the many tribunals currently investigating business and political life in Ireland.

There is also a strong sense emerging from the quantitative and qualitative data that although leadership is about performance and vision, it will occur in Ireland only if the followers choose to follow the leader, who will be one of the team, who will not be entitled as the leader to flaunt authority, who will encourage and influence the team members, who will not induce conflict, and who will know her or his place. Knowing one's place again raises the issue of context, but also recalls the theme of begrudgery, which features strongly both in the literature on leadership and in the qualitative research. Ruth's (1988) discussion of the post-colonial psyche notes that the process of internalized oppression means that we have "unrealistically high expectations of leaders" (p. 436).

What then might the practical implications of our findings be for foreign nationals who lead organizations in Ireland? There are dangers associated with the interpretation of the findings of large-scale cross-cultural studies. The practitioner may assume that where an attribute is universally endorsed, it is enacted in an identical manner the world over. It is critical for managers who operate across borders to be aware that even where cultures are clustered, for example, in the case of Ireland, the United States, Canada, Great Britain, Australia, New Zealand, and White South Africa (Anglo cluster), the enactment and acceptability of certain behaviors differs among the countries within that cluster. There are, however, a number of features that non-Irish managers operating in Ireland will need to consider if they are to lead organizations and motivate their staff to buy into their vision. In Ireland, the findings of the GLOBE research suggest that success and performance rely on people and that interpersonal relationship building and maintenance are critical components in ensuring that the task is fulfilled. This approach can result in some blurring of the task and relational levels, which means that criticism can be taken personally, that conflict and confrontation are avoided, and therefore that interpersonal exchanges need to be appropriately modified. Moderate levels of assertiveness help to explain this behavior. The importance of relationships and social competence is underpinned by strong collectivism, which creates higher expectations of team integration and participation in decision making among followers. Moderate levels of uncertainty avoidance mean operating with fewer rules and regulations or accepting the tendency to find a way around these rules and regulations and to keep all options open. The expectation that rules will be followed unquestioningly may be a misplaced assumption on the part of the non-national manager.

Though understanding cultural dimensions and their impact on organizational leadership can guide expatriate or international managers toward identifying areas where they must adjust their behavior, ultimately the degree of adjustment will depend on their interpretation of the range of prevailing organizational, situational, and personal contingencies. In other words, any kind of cultural or leadership dimensions that are used in cross-cultural training or orientation should not create the assumption of within-culture homogeneity. Integrating the theory with practitioner experience is a critical consideration (cf. Keating & Martin, 2004). The Irish GLOBE findings also have implications for national managers working in organizations that have become increasingly multicultural over the past 10 years.

The advantages of combining quantitative and qualitative methodologies are clearly demonstrated by the GLOBE study (cf. Martin et al., 1999). Qualitative methods can help to elicit the many permutations of the cultural context in which quantitative findings are embedded; they can enrich, challenge, or confirm quantitative data and in this way they can reveal new relationships. Though they may appear "messy, incomplete, unvalidated, and not readily amenable to the neat control that is taken for granted with abstract concepts and laboratory data" (Gulliver 1979, pp. 63–64), the focus groups, qualitative interviews, and review of unobtrusive indicators of culture in the current research provide a valuable explanatory framework and help us to explicate some of the complexities of the context in which the findings of the quantitative surveys of societal culture and leadership are presented.

One methodological question raised by the GLOBE study concerns the issue of sampling. Is it possible to select a sample from a particular group, such as middle managers, that might be considered to represent the values held more broadly by the members of that society? This question has long preoccupied researchers and there is no clear answer (Schwartz, 1992, 1994). Large-scale cross-cultural studies tend to rely on "convenience sampling" (Kim, Triandis, Kagitcibasi, Choi, & Yoon, 1994, p. 9) for comparative purposes; clearly, in the case of GLOBE it would be both desirable and interesting to replicate parts of the study using other samples. The authors of this chapter and the Austrian chapter have already taken steps in this regard (Keating, Martin, & Szabo, 2001). Nevertheless, at the societal level, unobtrusive indicators confirm the GLOBE middle manager reports with respect to all core GLOBE dimensions.

In the course of this chapter, we have made ongoing reference to the significant reshaping of Irish society over the last quarter century, not least the leap from a pre- to a postindustrial society. Yet, it would appear that we have not made the transition from lauding "men of destiny" toward recognizing "men of achievement." Might it be the case that members of Irish society look to the past for their role models as their expectations are too aspirational to fit the "postrevolutionary" reality? Answers to this and other similar questions may lie in the search for self-identity in the new century; there is a need to reconcile the legacy of a colonial mind-set with the far-reaching social and economic changes within Irish society. Looking toward external role models or the "ideal" figures of the past (Kane, 1986) are manifestations of this search. The GLOBE study in Ireland has captured some of the dilemmas within Irish society and attitudes toward leadership in the closing decade of the millennium. The new millennium will confront business leaders with new strategic challenges. The process of shaping self-identity is continuous and responds to the changing sociocultural context; it remains to be seen for how long our perceptions of leadership bear the "imprint of bygone circumstances" (Lee, 1994, p. 248).

ACKNOWLEDGMENTS

The authors wish to acknowledge support received from the Trinity College Dublin Arts and Social Sciences Benefactions Fund.

REFERENCES

Barron, F., & Egan, D. (1966). *Leaders and innovators in Irish management: A psychological study.* Dublin: Irish Management Institute.

Excellence Ireland. (2001). *Best practice.* Dublin, Ireland.

Bourke, A. (1999). *The burning of Bridget Cleary.* Dublin, Ireland: Pimlico.

Breen, R., Hannan, D. F., Rottman, D. B., & Whelan, C. (1990). *Understanding contemporary Ireland: State, class and development in the Republic of Ireland.* Dublin, Ireland: Gill & Macmillan.

Brodbeck, F. C., Frese, M., Akerblom, S., Bakacsi, G., Bendova, H., et al. (2000). Cultural variation of leadership prototypes across 22 European countries. *Journal of Occupational and Organizational Psychology, 73,* 1–29.

Browne, M. (2005). *Family matters ten years on.* Dublin, Ireland: Comhairle.

Calori, R. (1994). The diversity of management systems. In R. Calori & P. de Woot (Eds.), *A European management model: Beyond diversity* (pp. 11–30). Hemel Hempstead, England: Prentice Hall.

Central Statistics Office. (2004). *Population and labour force projections 2006–2036.* Dublin, Ireland: Stationery Office.

Coakley, J., & Gallagher, M. (1993*). Politics in the Republic of Ireland.* Dublin, Ireland: Folens.

Collins, M., & Kavanagh, K. (1998). For richer, for poorer: The changing distribution of household income in Ireland, 1973–1994. In S. Healy & B. Reynolds (Eds.), *Social policy in Ireland: Principles, practices and problems* (pp. 163–192). Dublin, Ireland: Oak Tree Press.

Coulter, C. (1993). *The hidden tradition: Feminism, women and nationalism in Ireland.* Cork, Ireland: Cork University Press.

Deane, S. (1984). Remembering the Irish future. *The Crane Bag, 8*(1), 81–92.

Den Hartog, D., House, R. J., Hanges, P. J., Ruiz-Quintanilla, S. A., Dorfman, P. W., et al. (1999). Culture specific and cross-culturally generalizable implicit leadership theories: Are attributes of charismatic/transformational leadership universally endorsed? *Leadership Quarterly, 10*(2), 219–256.

Doohan, J. (1999 September/October). Working longer, working better? *World of Work, 31.* Retrieved July 6, 2006, from http://www.ilo.org/public/english/bureau/inf/magazine/31/work.htm

Duncan, W. (1994). Law and the Irish psyche: the conflict between aspiration and experience. *Irish Journal of Psychology, 15*(2–3), 448–455.

European Employment Observatory. (2003). *Increasing the participation of women in the labour market: The situation in the EU15, acceding, candidate countries and Norway.* Retrieved August 30, 2005, from http://www.eu-employment-observatory.net/resources/meetings/MISEP_2003_11.doc

Fahey, T. (1995). Family and household in Ireland. In P. Clancy (Ed.), *Irish society: sociological perspectives* (pp. 205–234). Dublin, Ireland: Institute of Public Administration.

Farrell, B. (1971). *Chairman or chief? The role of Taoiseach in Irish government.* Dublin, Ireland: Gill & Macmillan.

Federation of European Employers. (2005). *Feeding the tiger. How will Ireland's tiger economy keep up its momentum?* Retrieved August 30, 2005, from http://www.feedee.com/celtictiger.shtml

Flood, P., MacCurtain, S., & West M. (2001). *Effective top management teams.* Dublin, Ireland: Blackhall Press.

Galligan, Y. (1998). *Women and politics in contemporary Ireland: From the margins to the mainstream.* London: Pinter.

Gardner, H. (1996). *Leading minds. An anatomy of leadership.* London: HarperCollins.

Government of Ireland. (1995). *Operational programme for human resources. 1994/1999.* Dublin, Ireland: Stationery Office.

Gray, A. W. (Ed.). (1997). *International perspectives on the Irish economy.* Dublin, Ireland: Indecon Economic Consultants.

Guiomard, C. (1995). *The Irish disease and how to cure it: Common-sense economics for a competitive world.* Dublin, Ireland: Oak Tree Press.

Gulliver, P. H. (1979). *Disputes and negotiations: A cross-cultural perspective.* New York: Academic Press.

Hall, E. T. (1976). *Beyond culture.* New York: Doubleday.

Hanges, P. J., Dickson, M. W., & Sipe, M. T. (2004). Rationale for GLOBE statistical analyses: Societal rankings and test of hypotheses. In R. J. House, P. J. Hanges, M. Javidan, P. Dorfman, & V. Gupta (Eds.), *Leadership, culture, and organizations: The GLOBE study of 62 societies* (pp. 219–234). Thousand Oaks, CA: Sage.

Haughton, J. (1995). The historical background. In J. W. O'Hagan (Ed.), *The economy of Ireland: policy and performance of a small European country* (pp. 1–44). Dublin, Ireland: Gill & Macmillan.

Hickson, D. J., & Pugh, D. S. (1995). *Management worldwide: The impact of societal culture on organizations around the globe.* London: Penguin.

Hill, J. (1998). *Irish public sculpture: A history.* Dublin, Ireland: Four Courts Press.

Hofstede, G. (1980). *Culture's consequences: International differences in work related values.* Beverly Hills, CA: Sage.

House, R. J., Hanges, P. J., Ruiz-Quintanilla, S. A., Dorfman, P. W., Javidan, M., Dickson, M., et al. (1999). Cultural influences on leadership and organizations: Project GLOBE. In W. H. Mobley, M. J. Gessner, & V. Arnold (Eds.), *Advances in global leadership*(Vol. 1, pp. 171–233). Stamford, CT: JAI.

House, R. J., Hanges, P. J., Javidan, M., Dorfman, P. W., Gupta, V. & GLOBE Associates. (2004). *Cultures, leadership, and organizations: The GLOBE study of 62 societies.* Thousand Oaks, CA: Sage.

Jupp, R., & O'Neill, G. (1994). *Reflections on Ireland in the year 2000.* Dublin, Ireland: Landsdowne Market Research and Henly Center Ireland.

Kakabadse, A., Alderson, S., & Gorman, L. (1995). Irish top management—competencies and team dynamics. In B. Leavy & J. Walsh (Eds.), *Strategy and general management: A general reader* (pp. 3–24). Dublin, Ireland: Oak Tree Press.

Kane, E. (1986/Winter). Stereotypes and Irish identity: Mental illness as a cultural frame. *Studies,* 539–551.

Keating, M., & Martin, G. (2004). Managing cross-cultural business relations: The Irish-German experience. Dublin, Ireland: Blackhall.

Keating, M., Martin, G., & Szabo, E. (2002). Do managers and students share the same perceptions of societal culture? *International Journal of Intercultural Relations, 26*(6), 633–652.

Kenny, I. (1987). *In good company: Conversations with Irish leaders.* Dublin, Ireland: Gill & Macmillan.

Kenny, I. (1991). *Out on their own: Conversations with Irish entrepreneurs.* Dublin, Ireland: Gill & Macmillan.

Kenny, I. (2001). *Leaders: Conversations with Irish chief executives.* Dublin, Ireland: Oak Tree Press.

Kenny, V. (1985). The post-colonial personality. *The Crane Bag, 9,* 70–78.

Kim, U., Triandis, H. C., Kagitcibasi, C., Choi, S.-C., & Yoon, G. (1994). *Individualism and collectivism: Theory, method, and applications.* Thousand Oaks, CA: Sage.

Kluckhohn, C., & Strodtbeck, F. L. (1961). *Variations in value orientation.* New York: Harper & Row.

Leavy, B. (1993). Ireland: Managing the economy of a newly independent state. In D. J. Hickson (Ed.), *Management in Western Europe: Society, culture and organization in 12 nations* (pp. 125–148). Berlin: De Gruyter.

Leavy, B., & Wilson, D. (1994). *Strategy and leadership.* London: Routledge.

Lee, J. J. (1982). Society and culture. In F. Litton (Ed.), *Unequal achievement: The Irish experience 1957–1982* (pp. 1–18). Dublin, Ireland: Institute of Public Administration.

Lee, J. J. (1989). *Ireland 1912–1985, politics and society.* Cambridge, England: Cambridge University Press.

Lee, J. J. (1994). The Irish psyche: A historical perspective. *The Irish Journal of Psychology, 15*(2–3), 245–249.

Logue, P. (2000). *Being Irish.* Dublin, Ireland: Oak Tree Press.

Lynch, J. J., & Roche, F. W. (1995). *Business management in Ireland: Competitive strategy for the 21st century.* Dublin, Ireland: Oak Tree Press.

Lynch, K., & McLaughlin, E. (1995). Caring labour and love labour. In P. Clancy (Ed.), *Irish society: Sociological perspectives* (pp. 250–292). Dublin, Ireland: Institute of Public Administration.

Mahon, E. (1994). Ireland: A private patriarchy. *Environment and Planning, 26,* 1277–1296.

Martin, G. S. (2001). *German–Irish sales negotiation: Theory, practice and pedagogical implications.* Frankfurt: Peter Lang.

Martin, G., Donnelly-Cox, G., & Keating, M. (1999). Culture, communication and organisation: what can linguists, psychologists and organisation theorists learn from each other? In D. O'Baoill & A. Chambers (Eds), Intercultural communication and Language Learning (pp. 265–278). Dublin: IRAAL/RIA.

McClelland, D. (1961). *The achieving society.* New York: Irvington.

Miller, L. (1996). *The Dolmen book of Irish stamps.* Mountrath, Ireland: Dolmen.

Mjoset, L. (1992). *The Irish economy in a comparative perspective* (National Economic and Social Council, 93). Dublin, Ireland: National Economic and Social Council.

Moane, G. (1994). A psychological analysis of colonialism in an Irish context. *Irish Journal of Psychology, 15*(2–3), 250–265.

Myers, A., Kakabadse, A., McMahon, J. T., & Spony, G. (1995). Top management styles in Europe: Implications for business and cross-national teams. *European Business Journal, 7*(1), 17–27.

National Center for Policy Analysis. (2002). *In Europe, little stigma attached to children born out of wedlock.* Retrieved March 27, 2002, from http://www.ncpa.org/iss/soc/2002pd032702e.html

Nic Ghiolla Phádraig, M. (1995). The power of the Catholic Church in the Republic of Ireland. In P. Clancy (Ed.), *Irish Society: Sociological perspectives* (pp. 593–619). Dublin, Ireland: Institute of Public Administration.

O'Higgins, E. (2002). Government and the creation of the Celtic Tiger: can management maintain the momentum? *Academy of Management Executive, 16*(3), 104–120.

Putnam, D. (1993). Making democracy work. Princeton, NJ: Princeton University Press

Robinson, M. (1995, February 2). Cherishing the Irish diaspora. *Address to the Houses of the Oireachtas.* Retrieved July 6, 2006, from http://www.oireachtas.ie/viewdoc.asp?fn=/documents/addresses/2Feb1995.ht

Roche, W. K., & Ashmore, J. (1997). *The changing shape of trade union membership in the Republic of Ireland 1990–1996* (Working paper). Dublin, Ireland: University College Dublin, Smurfit School of Business.

Ronen, S., & Shenkar, O. (1985). Clustering countries on attitudinal dimensions: A review and synthesis. *Academy of Management Review, 10*(3), 435–454.

Ruth, S. (1988). Understanding oppression and liberation. *Studies, 77*(308), 434–443.

Scannell, Y. (1988). The Constitution and the role of women. In B. Farrell (Ed.), *De Valera's constitution and ours* (pp. 123–136). Dublin, Ireland: Gill & Macmillan.

Schwartz, S. H. (1992). Universals in the content and structure of values: Theoretical advances and empirical tests in 20 countries. In M. Zanna (Ed.), *Advances in experimental social psychology* (Vol. 25, pp. 1–65). Orlando, FL: Academic Press.

Schwartz, S. H. (1994). Beyond individualism/collectivism: New cultural dimensions of values. In U. Kim, H. C. Triandis, C. Kagitcibasi, S. C. Choi, & G. Yoon (Eds.), *Individualism and collectivism: Theory, method and applications* (pp. 85–119). Thousand Oaks, CA: Sage.

Scott, D. (1995). *European stamp design: A semiotic approach to designing messages.* London: Academy Editions.

Sedgwick Noble Lownes. (1998). *The guide to employee benefits and labour law in Europe 1997/8.* Croydon, England: Author.

Smyth, A. (1985). The floozie in the jacuzzi. *Circa* (November/December 1989), 32–38.

Stewart, J. C. (1997). Multi-nationals and transfer pricing. *Journal of Business Finance and Accounting, 4*(3), 353–371.

Sweeney, P. (1998). *The Celtic Tiger: Ireland's economic miracle explained.* Dublin, Ireland: Oak Tree Press.

Walshe, J. (1999). *A new partnership in education: From consultation to legislation in the nineties.* Dublin, Ireland: Institute of Public Administration.

Warnes, H. (1979). Cultural factors in Irish psychiatry. *Psychiatric Journal of the University of Ottawa, 4*(4), 329–335.

Webb, E. J., Campbell, D. T., Schwartz, R. D., & Sechrest, L. (1973). *Unobtrusive measures: Non-reactive research in the social sciences.* Chicago: Rand McNally.

World Bank. (2005). Country data retrieved August 30, 2005, from http://www.worldbank.org/data/countrydata.html

12
▼▼▼▼▼▼▼

Leadership and culture in New Zealand

Jeffrey C. Kennedy
Nanyang Business School, Singapore

> *Everything that was good from that small, remote country had gone into them—*
> *sunshine and strength, good sense, patience, the versatility of practical men.*
> —Mulgan (1984, p. 15)

This chapter begins with an overview of New Zealand's historical development, and the cultural themes that have emerged since European settlement in the 1800s. The GLOBE methodology in New Zealand is then described, and New Zealand's pattern of responses to the GLOBE cultural scales is discussed. The next section provides a summary of research into organizational leadership, followed by presentation of the qualitative and quantitative findings of the GLOBE study. The concluding section summarizes the results, provides suggestions for expatriate managers in New Zealand, and identifies limitations of the study.

1. NEW ZEALAND SOCIETY AND CULTURE

New Zealand is a country consisting of two main islands, two thirds the size of California, in the far corner of the earth's largest ocean, the Pacific. With a population of 4 million, it has fewer people than cities such as Bangkok, London, New York, or Sydney.

New Zealand comprises the last islands of any size to be reached by people. The original inhabitants, the Maori, came from Polynesia around a thousand years ago. About 800 years later, Britain colonized New Zealand, and waves of immigrants from Britain subsequently established settlements. Discovery of gold in 1861 led to an influx of miners from the declining gold fields in Australia and China, followed in 1870 by another wave of assisted immigration from Germany, Scandinavia, and France, as well as the British Isles. The period between the two world wars saw an increase in immigration from Central Europe, whereas the period after the Second World War was characterized by a significant inflow from the Netherlands and Poland. More recently, immigration from Pacific nations (such as Samoa, Tonga, and Fiji) has increased, and the Asian population has been boosted by new arrivals from Indo-China, Hong Kong, Singapore, Taiwan, Korea, and other neighbors to the north. In the 1996 census, almost 20% of the population claimed identification with two or more ethnic groups. Around 80% of the population are of European descent, and almost 15% are Maori. Pacific Islanders and Chinese ethnic groups comprise 6.5% and 2.9% respectively of the overall population (Statistics New Zealand, 2001).

Although these figures suggest that it makes little sense to talk of one culture for New Zealand, New Zealanders (self-styled "Kiwis") will argue strongly for the existence of a unique identity, for the existence of something that sets them apart from others, a "Kiwi culture." Though some of the components of this identity may be found in other cultures and nations, New Zealanders' shared experiences and history create a distinctive pattern. In the following paragraphs, a summary of New Zealand's historical development provides insights into some of the key elements of this pattern.

The earliest inhabitants of New Zealand migrated from Polynesia around 1000 AD. The Maori retained aspects of their Polynesian culture, while adapting to the challenges of a less tropical and more rugged physical environment. Maori social organization is largely communal, with social groupings being based on *whanau* (extended families), *hapu* (subtribes), and *iwi* (tribes), usually based on descent from a common ancestor. Communities were ruled by chiefs (*rangatira*), who generally held their position subject to the community remaining satisfied with their continued good performance. The literal meaning of *rangatira* is "to weave people together"—a definition of leadership that neatly encapsulates the interdependent and communal nature of Maori society.

In 1642, a Dutch East India Company expedition under Abel Tasman became the first recorded European voyagers to discover New Zealand. Detailed European exploration took place during the 1770s, with several expeditions by the British explorer James Cook. In 1788, a British prison colony was established across the Tasman Sea in New South Wales (now a state in present-day Australia), facilitating greater access to New Zealand. American and British whalers and sealers began to establish bases on the New Zealand coast, and several of these expanded into larger settlements involved in farming and trade in timber and flax.

A British governor was appointed in 1840, and in February he began gaining Maori signatories to the "Treaty of Waitangi." This document provided for the indigenous Maori to cede aspects of sovereignty to Queen Victoria, gaining the rights and privileges of British subjects, while retaining ownership of their land, forests, and fisheries. It is considered by many to be the founding document of the nation of New Zealand.

Originally an extension of the British colony in New South Wales, New Zealand became a British colony in its own right in 1841. Increasing numbers of settlers arrived, principally from Britain, and a number of planned settlements began to take shape. In the four decades following 1840, the European settler (Pakeha) population grew from 2,000 to almost 500,000. In contrast, but not coincidentally, the Maori population decreased from around 120,000 in pre-European times to 42,000 in 1896, causing some commentators to view them as a "dying race" (Belich, 2001).

Conflict over land and trade, characterized by breaches of trust and Pakeha disregard of the Treaty of Waitangi, sparked off the New Zealand land wars, a bloody series of military actions that reached their peak in the 1860s. The Maori became increasingly marginalized as the Crown confiscated land, and passed legislation that undermined Maori land ownership, language use, education, and health. Although the Maori had continued to seek redress under the Treaty, an 1877 court decision declared it to be a "simple nullity." It was not until the 1970s and 1980s that increasing Maori activism brought the Treaty back into national consciousness. In 1975, the Waitangi Tribunal was established to deal with claims against the Crown under the Treaty, but it was 1985 before the Tribunal was empowered to hear claims dating back to 1840. By 2001, close to U.S.$380 million had been paid or committed to claimants for historical grievances relating to return of land, fisheries, and cultural resources (Office of Treaty Settlements, 2001).

As an integral part of this settlement process, different ethnic groups in New Zealand have had to reassess their identities and relationships with each other. The concept of partnership inherent in the Treaty has been actualized in legislation and policy. The special standing of Maori and Pakeha (as signatories to the Treaty) has generated pressure for greater sharing of power and resources between the two cultures (O'Reilly & Wood, 1991). This trend is not without its critics. Biculturalism, by definition, relegates cultural groups that have arrived in New Zealand since 1840 to a lower standing. Moves to empower such groups through a greater emphasis on multiculturalism are often viewed as attempts to discredit biculturalism, and the claims of Maori under the Treaty (Jones, Pringle, & Shepherd, 2000). Political and economic pressures have increasingly turned New Zealand toward a greater reliance on Asian neighbors, and recent immigration policies encouraging greater Asian investment have served to further energize the debate over cultural identities.

The rapid growth of New Zealand during its early colonial history affected political and economic structures. In an arrangement akin to the American federal system, six provincial governments were established in 1852, but these were abolished in favor of a central government in 1876. A centralized approach was needed in order to fund and coordinate the expensive business of developing the new nation's transport and communications infrastructure.

During the last decades of the 19th century, the central government began to take a much broader and socially progressive role in running the country. In 1877 it provided for a system of free, compulsory education. In 1879 it introduced universal male suffrage, and in 1893 New Zealand became the first country in the world to extend the vote to women.

The Industrial Conciliation and Arbitration Act was passed in 1894 as a response to public concern about exploitative working conditions. It has been described as "one of the most dramatic contributions New Zealand has made to conceptions of humanitarian democracy" (Hansen, 1968, p. 58). The 1894 Act provided a compulsory system of state arbitration "aimed at preventing class conflict by ensuring the workers an adequate share of the national wealth even as it assured adequate incentive to the employer" (Hansen, 1968, p. 58).

The passing of this Act provides a number of insights into aspects of New Zealand societal values that are still relevant today. The changes it introduced (together with the earlier widening of the electoral franchise) reflect a degree of willingness by the well-off to give up some privilege, wealth, and power. Hansen (1968) argues that this illustrates a gap between the values of the settlers and those dominant in their countries of origin. In particular, the settlers placed greater emphasis on equality, freedom, and individual dignity: "In comparison with England and the United States, and even Australia, New Zealand has most actively and consistently emphasized equalitarianism" (p. 58).

The New Zealand concept of egalitarianism is not restricted to the sense of equal opportunity; it extends to the idea that people should be considered as equal in all aspects of life: "Not only should one person not inherit greater life chances than another; none should be allowed to accumulate a great deal more than another through his own efforts or luck. Exceptional performances or capacities are deprecated by both individuals in a relationship" (Hansen, 1968, p. 60). The phrase "tall poppy syndrome" refers to a tendency in New Zealand to find fault with high achievers, to "cut them down to size" if they act as though their achievements make them better than anyone else. Few academic research studies have been conducted on the phenomenon in New Zealand, but Australian studies of contingencies influencing the tall poppy syndrome are likely to be relevant to New Zealand (see, e.g., Feather, 1993, 1994a, 1994b).

Another aspect of egalitarianism was captured in the feeling held by many working people that they could work their way out of wage dependency and into property ownership on the basis of their individual effort (Fairburn, 1989). Class barriers to upward mobility did not exist to the same extent as in Victorian Britain, and there was little requirement for social or family connections, patronage of the wealthy, intellectual accomplishments, or attendance at the "right" schools. Deeks, Parker, and Ryan (1994) comment on the structures imported into New Zealand from English common law (e.g., the master–servant relationship), but note their comparative weakness. Few households had servants, and there was not the same expectation of deference and servility in such relationships.

Egalitarianism is also apparent in New Zealand labor law, which until 1991 enforced a strict system of awards that acted to ensure uniform minimum pay rates and conditions for the same jobs across all employers. Differentials between skill levels were based on negotiation (by centralized employer and employee organizations) rather than market considerations, and pay for seniority was far more prevalent than pay for performance.

Economically, New Zealand was dependent almost entirely on agricultural exports. Early trade in flax and seafood (primarily with Australia) gave way to exports of meat, wool, and dairy products to Britain. Throughout the period from 1875 until World War II, around 80% of New Zealand exports were sold to the United Kingdom, and over half its imports came from that country (Department of Statistics, 1990). Dependence was not limited to the economic sphere; many political and social institutions and customs had English origins, and settlers continued to refer to Britain as "Home" with a capital *H*.

New Zealand participation in the South African War (1899–1902) and World War I (where 103,000 served abroad, from a total population of around 1 million) led to a greater sense of national identity. New Zealanders compared themselves favorably with their British regular-force counterparts. In particular, heroic actions of the Australian and New Zealand Army Corps (ANZACs) at Gallipoli in 1915 are still recalled in annual ceremonies marked by a glorification of Australasian exploits, and a diminution of British (and other Allied) contributions. The dominant and enduring cultural theme portrays New Zealanders as self-reliant pioneers, brave and heroic, demonstrating initiative under pressure. These characteristics were said to engender leadership based on example rather than insistence on "red tape," by officers who were "'democratic' and modest—one of the boys" (Phillips, 1989, p. 96).

The pioneering-settler history, combined with the dependence on farming, gave rise to a strong self-image of New Zealand as a country of rugged individualists in a dramatic rural landscape. The literary incarnation of this theme has a dark side, with an underlying sense of alienation and of distance. This imagery has been used metaphorically in describing interpersonal relationships, and conveys "uncertainties about the influence of the past as well as a lack of confidence in the future" (Lealand, 1988, pp. 29–30). At a more popular level, the rural theme is the setting for much New Zealand humor, is used in locally made television dramas, and is portrayed in many different ways in commercial advertisements (Carter & Perry, 1987).

Another important element of this cultural archetype is a practical, problem-solving approach to life. This involves the willingness to tackle problems and take on responsibilities outside one's normal role. Innovative solutions using tools or materials at hand are valued. Kiwis take pride in being able to fix anything with "a piece of No. 8 fencing wire." Edmund Hillary was the first person to drive a motorized vehicle overland to the South Pole, and he used converted farm tractors for the expedition (Booth, 1993). Richard Pearse was a farmer who attempted powered flight 9 months before the Wright brothers, in an airplane (featuring a variable pitch propeller, wing flaps, and rear elevator) and petrol engine he constructed with home made tools from scrap metal and other oddments (New Zealand Department of Internal Affairs, 1996; Ogilvie, 1973). More recently, John Britten created the world's fastest four-stroke superbike using innovative design and materials technology (Bridges & Downs, 2000). As Holm has noted (1994), this celebrated trait of "Kiwi ingenuity," of devising innovative, practical, cost-effective solutions, is now no longer confined to the use of such prosaic materials as fencing wire.

The lasting strength of this masculine, rural image, of the practical man in tune with the elements, belies the level of urbanization in New Zealand. A peak of 75% of the population lived in rural areas in 1871, but this figure has steadily declined. At the most recent census, 85% of New Zealanders lived in urban areas (Statistics New Zealand, 2002).

The introduction of television broadcasts and international passenger jet services (both in the early 1960s), coupled with ongoing improvements in communications technology, contributed to the ongoing reduction in New Zealand's isolation and insulation from the rest of the world (Belich, 2001). Following a period of prosperity during the 1950s and 1960s, New Zealand entered a period of uncertainty during the 1970s. External factors, such as oil price shocks, weakened New Zealand's terms of trade, inflation threatened people's standard of living, government debt increased, and unemployment began to rise. Britain, which had hitherto been the main market for New Zealand exports, entered the European Economic Community, and by 1975 was only taking one fifth of the country's total exports.

Governments during the 1970s responded to these economic problems by providing tax incentives and financial subsidies for agricultural production, and by increasing the size of the state sector in the economy. In 1979, Robert Muldoon's National (center-right) government embarked on a multibillion-dollar plan that targeted import substitution through investment in petrochemical plants (synthetic petrol, natural gas, and oil refining), steel refining, and aluminum smelting. Known colloquially as "Think Big," the projects failed to meet their ambitious economic and employment targets.

A snap election was called in 1984. A Labour (center-left) government gained power, and immediately faced a foreign-exchange crisis that precipitated a 20% devaluation of the New Zealand dollar. There was, by this time, widespread agreement that significant economic restructuring had to be undertaken. The new minister of finance, Roger Douglas, capitalized on this feeling by initiating a breathtakingly fast-paced, far-reaching program of reform aimed at reducing the role of the state in favor of a more free-market economy. Although consistent with a global shift toward free-market policies, this "radical experiment in a remote part of the Pacific Rim" (Yergin & Stanislaw, 1998, p. 140) went further and faster than comparable programs in other developed countries.

The reforms encompassed financial deregulation, state sector reorganization, and removal of subsidies for agriculture and industry. Controls were removed from areas such as foreign-exchange transactions, interest rates, banking, overseas investments, and the share market. A goods and services tax was introduced and income tax was reduced and simplified in a manner that (contrary to the principle of egalitarianism) benefited the rich more than the poor. Tax concessions, import controls, tariff protections, subsidies, and other restrictions on free trade were phased out.

Government departments that provided a service were "corporatized"—restructured along private-sector, market-oriented lines. Telecommunications, air traffic control services, government research agencies, the postal service, banks, valuation, rail transport, and numerous other activities were transformed into state-owned enterprises and, in many cases, subsequently privatized. Charges were introduced (or increased) for many government services, in an attempt to limit demand as well as to raise revenue. The National government of 1990 continued the reform process, extending the policy of "user pays" for government services, making cuts to welfare spending, and restructuring public hospitals along private-sector corporation lines.

The National government also deregulated the labor market, passing the Employment Contracts Act in 1991. This Act removed legislative recognition of unions, contributing to a halving in union membership from 45% of the workforce in 1989 to 23% in 1994 (Belich, 2001). By promoting flexibility in employment arrangements and responsiveness to market conditions, and through its use of a new vocabulary replacing traditional terms, the Act highlighted the transactional, impersonal aspects of the employment exchange (Peel & Inkson, 2000).

The significant shift in New Zealand's political, social, and economic landscape since 1984 has often clashed with New Zealanders' underlying cultural values. Though the pioneering sense of self-reliance shows in an intolerance of those considered to "bludge" off the welfare state, the sense of egalitarianism rebels at the thought that some sections of society are unduly benefiting from reforms, whereas others are being unfairly marginalized. Many New Zealanders' sense of "fair play" has been challenged by evidence of poverty and social exclusion among low-income and Maori households (Stephens, Frater, & Waldegrave, 2000), of absolute declines in the real income of low-income households (Dalziel, 2002), and of the widening income gap between rich and poor (Gendall, Robbie, Patchett, & Bright, 2000).

These concerns led to changes in government priorities at the end of the 1990s. The National government promoted a Code of Social and Family Responsibility, and the Treasury (the department responsible for economic advice to government) introduced "social cohesion" as an element that should be "at the heart of government policy" (Ansley, 2000, p. 16). A Labour-led coalition of center-left parties came to power at the end of 1999, and introduced a raft of changes in areas such as taxation, superannuation, and the health sector, aimed at restoring social equity. The Employment Contracts Act was replaced by legislation that promoted the role of unions and collective bargaining, and imposed a duty of "good faith" on parties in their employment negotiations.

Foreign Policy

Following World War II, New Zealand's identification with Britain as the "Mother Country" weakened. The United States protected New Zealand in the Pacific, whereas most New Zealand troops were fighting in the Mediterranean theater. Over 100,000 Americans were stationed in New Zealand during latter stages of the war, and in the following decades New Zealand's foreign policy became more aligned with that of the United States. New Zealand signed the ANZUS security treaty with Australia and the United States in 1952, and fought alongside both countries in Korea and Vietnam. Since 1971, defense ties with Asian countries have been further reinforced by New Zealand's active participation as a member (with Australia, Malaysia, Singapore, and the United Kingdom) of the Five Power Defense Arrangements (FPDA).

New Zealand is still supportive of traditional allies, offering military support in the Falklands campaign (1982), in the Persian Gulf War (1991), and in Afghanistan (2001). Increasingly, however, the military orientation is toward peacekeeping, with New Zealand personnel having been deployed with UN peacekeeping or mine-clearing missions to East

Timor (the largest commitment of troops since the Korean War), the former Yugoslavia, the Middle East, Mozambique, Sierra Leone, Bougainville, Laos, and other regions. In 2000, 31% of the Army was committed to UN operations, and in recent years the Defense Force's strike capacity has been reduced by disbanding the air combat force, whereas emphasis is being given to modernizing transport and maritime surveillance roles (Hughes, 2001; Ministry of Defense, 2001; New Zealand Government, 2001).

New Zealand is now more prepared to take an individual stand on issues rather than uncritically adopt the views of Britain or the United States. A high-profile example was the 1984 Labour government's introduction of a nuclear-prohibition policy in the face of considerable opposition from Western allies. Despite pressure from the United States (including cuts in military cooperation, suspension of the ANZUS treaty, and a downgrading of New Zealand's diplomatic status) the policy passed into law in 1987 (Ware & Dewes, 2000). This policy gained momentum largely because of concern at the effects of ongoing nuclear testing in the Pacific, New Zealand's "back yard." It illustrates how New Zealand increasingly views its sphere of influence as lying in the southwest Pacific. This shift in political orientation has also led to new themes for our cultural identity. The European linkage is weaker, and a renaissance in Maori culture and traditions coupled with acknowledgment of New Zealand's geographic location, is creating a new identity as a "self-confident, multicultural Pacific nation" (Lealand, 1988).

It is clear from this brief overview that dramatic shifts have taken place in New Zealanders' conception of their place in the world. The country has moved from dependence to independence, from a Euro-focused worldview toward one centered more on the Asia-Pacific region. It should also be apparent that the dominant cultural themes are not truly representative of the diverse population. Many of the themes are masculine in origin, with pioneering, rural, and military provenances. The perspectives of women and Maori are underrepresented. Similarly, women and Maori are underrepresented in management within New Zealand organizations. In common with the cultural themes presented in this section, the GLOBE research discussed in the next section reflects a primarily male (and New Zealand European) perspective. This does not make the perspective any less important, but it serves to delimit it.

2. THE GLOBE STUDY—SOCIETAL CULTURE

As described in the first chapter in this volume, the GLOBE project used both quantitative and qualitative methods to gather data on cultural values and perceptions of effective leader behaviors. The following section reports results from the surveyed middle managers' ratings of New Zealand society in terms of the GLOBE dimensions, followed by a discussion incorporating additional material from public information and observations.

In line with the overall GLOBE methodology, the questionnaire was distributed to middle managers in business organizations operating in three different industries: finance ($N = 69$), food processing ($N = 53$) and telecommunications ($N = 62$). A description of each industry is provided in the Appendix. Personal contact was used to ensure close to 100% return rates and, in order to increase representativeness of the sample, only four to six questionnaires were completed within each company or business unit.

Key demographic characteristics of the sample of 184 managers can be summarized as follows:

- Gender: 79% of the respondents were male, and 21% female.
- Age: The age of respondents ranged between 22 and 63, with a median of 38 years.

TABLE 12.1
Results for New Zealand on the Nine GLOBE Cultural Dimensions, Society Level

Cultural Dimension	"As Is" Ratings		"Should Be" Ratings		Difference
	Score[b]	Band[c] (Rank)	Score[b]	Band (Rank)[c]	
Institutional Collectivism	4.81	A[e] (5)	4.20	C[e] (51)	−0.61
Uncertainty Avoidance	4.75	A[e] (12)	4.10	C[f] (48)	−0.65
Performance Orientation	4.72	A[d] (5)	5.90	B[f] (34)	1.18
Power Distance	4.89	B[e] (47)	3.53	A[f] (3)	−1.36
Humane Orientation	4.32	B[e] (19)	4.49	E[f] (61)	0.17
Gender Egalitarianism[a]	3.22	B[d] (38)	4.23	B[e] (47)	1.01
In-Group Collectivism	3.67	C[d] (59)	6.21	A[d] (3)	2.54
Future Orientation	3.47	C[e] (48)	5.54	B[e] (31)	2.07
Assertiveness	3.42	C[d] (60)	3.54	B[d] (41)	0.12

[a]Low = male oriented. [b]Country mean on a 7-point scale (range 1 to 7). [c]Represents band of countries New Zealand falls into (from a high of A to a low of C, D, or E); bands identify meaningful differences between groups of countries (cf. Hanges, Dickson, & Sipe, 2004). The number in parentheses is New Zealand's rank order out of the 61 countries. [d]Group span ranges from A to C. [e]Group span ranges from A to D. [f]Group span ranges from A to E.

- New Zealand residence: 79% had lived in New Zealand all their life, whereas 16% had spent more than 3 years out of the country.
- Working experience: The full-time working experience of the sample ranged between 2 and 45 years with a median of 20 years, and with 8 years being the median for holding a management position. Years spent with the current employer ranged from less than 1 through to a maximum of 41, with a median of 11 years. Thirty-eight percent had worked for a multinational corporation, either in New Zealand or overseas.
- Staff: The median number of people directly reporting to the manager was 5, with only 9% of the sample having more than 10 subordinates. The maximum number of levels from the manager to his or her CEO was four, with a median of two.

The GLOBE study included a quantitative assessment of societal cultural values, seeking information on the extent to which values are reflected in current practices in society ("As Is") and the emphasis that respondents felt should be given to each value ("Should Be"). Details on these measures can be found in the introductory chapter. Table 12.1 presents the results for New Zealand in terms of absolute scores (on a rating scale from 1 to 7) and comparative rankings with other countries on the GLOBE cultural dimensions.

In considering the current situation ("As Is"), New Zealand ranked in the highest 20% of countries on the dimensions of Performance Orientation (Rank 5), Institutional Collectivism (Rank 5) and Uncertainty Avoidance (Rank 12). In an international context, New Zealand therefore stands out as being a society that places importance on high standards of performance, while supporting practices that encourage collective distribution of resources and collective action. It is also characterized by a reliance on social norms, rules, and procedures to reduce unpredictability and uncertainty.

In contrast, it ranked at the low end of the sample in regard to Power Distance (Rank 47), Future Orientation (Rank 48), In-Group Collectivism (Rank 59), and Assertiveness (Rank 61). These rankings indicate that New Zealand society values egalitarianism more highly than most other countries in the sample, and is second only to Sweden in the importance placed on individualism—on independence as opposed to family cohesiveness and loyalty. The emphasis on planning or investing for the future and willingness to delay gratification is lower than in most countries. Finally, New Zealand managers show one of the lowest levels of acceptance of assertiveness, confrontation, and aggression in relationships with others; only Swedish managers rated this dimension lower.

Comparison of New Zealand's "As Is" scores with "Should Be" scores indicates a desire for change in several areas. The managers in the sample expressed a strong desire to place much more emphasis on values consistent with In-Group Collectivism, increasing the rating given to this dimension by 2.54 (on a 7-point scale), producing the third-highest "Should Be" rating of all countries. They also wanted to see a much greater emphasis on Future Orientation, lifting the rating given to this dimension by 2.07, and changing the "As Is" ranking of 48 to a "Should Be" ranking of 31. Although there was a desire for further emphasis on Performance Orientation, other countries sought to increase more, and New Zealand's "Should Be" ranking dropped back to 34.

Though New Zealand managers reported a low level of Power Distance, and wanted to see emphasis on this value further reduced, managers in most other countries wanted an even larger reduction in Power Distance. As a result, New Zealand ranks highly in regard to the "Should Be" value of Power Distance (Rank 3). This suggests that New Zealand managers are, in comparative terms, reasonably satisfied with existing levels of Power Distance.

The discussion of the dominant cultural themes in New Zealand indicates the emphasis placed on male views of society. The majority of survey respondents were male; they acknowledged that New Zealand society is male oriented, and expressed a desire to see a greater shift toward a more gender-balanced orientation.

In regard to Humane Orientation, the managers saw New Zealand as being around the mid-point of the scale, and expressed little desire to shift from this position. Most other countries felt they needed to emphasize this dimension more, and as a result the New Zealand ranking shifted from 19 ("As Is") to 61 ("Should Be").

The following paragraphs explore these findings, using examples from public sources, interviews, and observations.

Institutional Collectivism.   An example of New Zealanders' concern for collective interests comes from a recent survey undertaken as part of a global study of social policy issues (Gendall et al., 2000). Most of the respondents were in favor of a progressive tax system, with 70% believing that taxes on those with low incomes are too high. Large proportions of the sample were in favor of increased government spending on health (90%), education (85%), assistance to the unemployed (60%), and pensions (60%), even if this meant an increase in taxes.

New Zealand's long history of a collective approach toward workplace bargaining is also consistent with this value. For almost a century prior to 1991, employment conditions for different classes of work were determined by comprehensive collective bargaining between employer and union representatives, resulting in a binding agreement known as an "Award." The shift to an individualistic, contractual focus (with the 1991 Employment Contracts Act) has now been reversed with legislation that explicitly encourages collective bargaining (Employment Relations Act, 2000).

Uncertainty Avoidance. Hofstede ranks New Zealand as 39 out of 53 countries on his measure of Uncertainty Avoidance (2001, Exhibit 4.1). As discussed by Hanges and Dickson (2004), the Hofstede scale corresponds to the GLOBE values ("Should Be") scale, where New Zealand is also ranked in the bottom quartile. In terms of practice ("As Is"), however, New Zealand is ranked in the highest quartile of countries. This scale includes items such as the extent to which laws or rules exist to cover most situations, the tendency for people to lead structured lives, and the relative emphasis on orderliness and consistency.

Writers have often attacked the pressure for conformity in New Zealand. Charles Brasch (quoted in Geraets, 1984, p. 81) writes of "the pressure of conformity." Author Dan Davin vividly captures elements of the emphasis on structured lives and consistency (1984, p. 105): *"In New Zealand everyone knows everyone more or less: those you don't know personally you might just as well because they're bound to be very like the people you know already; or think you know, because of course everyone's different deep down but in New Zealand the stereotype that controls what you can say or be seen to do is very strong."* The New Zealand Survey of Values found that of a list of six important life qualities (comfort and prosperity, excitement, security and stability, accomplishing things, being respected, salvation) security was ranked first, accomplishing things second, and comfort/prosperity third. In regard to important job characteristics, job security and good pay were ranked at the top of the list (Gold & Webster, 1990).

In a recent international study of entrepreneurship (Frederick & Carswell, 2001), New Zealand ranked 15th out of 29 countries in tolerance for uncertainty—further evidence that the Hofstede work underestimated the extent of Uncertainty Avoidance in New Zealand society.

A comprehensive state-funded accident insurance and rehabilitation scheme reduces uncertainty for all New Zealanders by removing the right to sue for personal injury, in return for providing universal coverage for injuries. Many commentators have argued that government has been too involved in the detailed regulation of everyday life ("regulomania" in the words of James Belich, 2001) and of business activities (Easton, 2000).

It is possible that uncertainty engendered by the dramatic economic restructuring of the past 20 years has created a desire for greater stability. Weariness with change is setting in, and this may be reflected in a desire for greater certainty and predictability (Ansley, 2000). However, the existence of a "nanny state" creating security for its people "from cradle to grave" appears to be congruent with underlying values in New Zealand, and with the comparatively high ranking on Uncertainty Avoidance.

Performance Orientation. New Zealanders have always taken pride in the world-beating achievements of people from such a small (in population terms) country. New Zealanders have been the first to split the atom (Ernest Rutherford), to climb Mt. Everest (Ed Hillary), to fly direct from England to New Zealand (Jean Batten). Twenty years ago, V. S. Naipaul wrote of the contribution New Zealand has made to the world, proclaiming that "more gifted men and women have come from its population of three million than from the 23 millions of Argentines" (1980, p. 153). A comparative study of national pride in 23 countries revealed that New Zealanders ranked second in the amount of pride they displayed in their country's sporting achievements, and third in pride in science/technology and arts and literature (Smith & Jarkko, 2001).

Expectations and encouragement for high performance are evident particularly in the sporting arena, where New Zealanders have performed creditably on the international stage in athletics, yachting, rugby, softball, rowing, swimming, and other events. Athletes have very high expectations placed on them by the public, and are severely criticized when their performance drops.

In the business arena, rapid deregulation of the economy from the mid-1980s has opened domestic firms to international competition, and removed almost all governmental subsidies and protection. New Zealand was recently ranked first out of 47 countries on the criteria of lack of protectionism, lack of price controls, and accessibility to foreign financial institutions (IMD International, 2000). These factors, together with geographical isolation from most trading partners, have put pressure on companies to lift their performance to (or above) international standards.

This emphasis on performance may seem at odds with the "tall poppy syndrome" discussed in the opening section of this chapter, but an important issue is the attitude displayed by the high achiever. A contributor to an Internet discussion on the topic expressed it this way: *"New Zealanders do not resent success; what we do despise, and will cut down to size, is the braggart and the show-off. You can be as successful as you like and you will be respected for it, but the moment that you let it go to your head and start acting as if you are better or more important than other people ... you will lose our respect"* (Watson, 1994).

There is an interesting tension between Performance Orientation and Egalitarianism. A high performer, by definition, stands out from the crowd. McKinlay (2000) discusses the experience of New Zealand investment bankers, who note a reluctance in New Zealand entrepreneurs to build their personal wealth beyond the U.S.$5million–$10 million mark. Many seem concerned that it is not socially acceptable to build major private wealth (even though it may lead to significant employment and wealth gains for other New Zealanders as well). The market-based reforms of the 1980s and 1990s encouraged a "winner take all" mentality that sits uneasily with many New Zealanders. The chief executive of a government department recently scrapped a performance-pay system on the grounds that it was unfair, proving more generous for those in senior positions than for those at the bottom (Watkins, 2003). Such concerns may underlie the lower ranking of New Zealand managers on the "Should Be" Performance Orientation scale.

Assertiveness. At the other end of the scale, New Zealand scored second-lowest of all countries on the Assertiveness dimension. The Survey of Values, in looking at the values emphasized in child training, found a high level of national consensus regarding the importance of pleasantness, politeness, and good manners (Gold & Webster, 1990).

It is difficult to locate objective international comparisons of business practice that might illustrate this dimension further, but there are many examples of New Zealanders believing they lack the aggression of international trading partners. This is well illustrated by comparisons with our closest neighbor, Australia—a nation that shares many historical experiences and cultural attributes with New Zealand. On the GLOBE cultural scales, the biggest absolute scale difference between the two countries is on Assertiveness, where Australia ranks 22nd with a rating of 4.28, compared to New Zealand's score of 3.42 and rank of 60. Consistent with this difference, Australians are viewed by many New Zealanders as more aggressive in sporting, political, and business domains. High-profile examples include their willingness to exploit a loophole in the rules to ensure they won a cricket match (using an underarm bowl), the Australian government's reneging on an "open skies" deal so as to deny New Zealand's national airline access to the Australian domestic air travel market, the Australian Rugby Union's success in gaining full hosting rights for the 2003 rugby world cup, and the aggressive tactics used by Australian airline Qantas in its efforts to dominate the trans-Tasman travel market.

In contrast with the low Assertiveness ranking, values of aggressiveness, competitiveness, and domination are commonly portrayed and encouraged by "male" sports in New Zealand (Gidlow, Perkins, Cushman, & Simpson, 1994). The dominant sporting code in New Zealand is rugby, a physically aggressive variety of football played by teams of 15, without the benefit of helmets or padding. Perhaps its popularity is partly due to the outlet it provides for socially acceptable aggression, whether by participants or (vicariously) by spectators.

In-Group Collectivism.   The middle manager sample also rated New Zealand very low on In-Group Collectivism. Though the average score of 3.67 is just below the scale midpoint, it is the third-lowest rating of all countries in the sample. It contrasts markedly with the high ranking (fifth) on Institutional Collectivism. This pattern of high Institutional Collectivism and very low In-Group Collectivism is also found in Sweden, Denmark, and Finland.

There is a theme of independence running through the dominant New Zealand European cultural archetypes, and this carries over into attitudes toward the family. Young New Zealanders are keen to leave the family, to make their own way, often starting with a period of "OE" (overseas experience). It is uncommon for adults (whether single or married) to share their home with older generations. State support (in the form of universal superannuation, unemployment benefits, payments to single mothers, study allowances, sickness benefits, etc.) reduces the financial obligation on family members to support relatives. There may also be a historical pattern, with those immigrants willing to come to New Zealand being the ones who were more prepared to sever family ties with relatives left behind.

In a critical commentary on the insular nature of many New Zealand families, popular author Gordon McLauchlan suggested that there are *"few secure traditional extensions to the nuclear group, either sideways to brothers, sisters, cousins or through marriage to in-laws; and there are no extensions vertically to those who have gone before and who will come after; so that we have no identity in place or time"* (McLauchlan & Morgan, 1976, p. 40).

Several statistics reflect the lack of closeness and support prevailing in many New Zealand families—New Zealand has the highest level of youth suicide among comparable OECD countries (Ministry of Youth Affairs, 2002), and one of the highest rates of teenage births of any industrialized country (Ministry of Youth Affairs, 1998). Though most dependent children under 18 years of age live with two parents, the proportion has declined over time, from 84% in 1986, to 76% in 1996. Over the same period, the proportion of dependent children living in mother-only families rose from 14% to 21%, and the proportion living in father-only families increased from 2% to 3% (Child, Youth and Family, 1999).

Hofstede's study (conducted in the 1970s) ranked New Zealand as sixth out of 53 countries on his individualism scale (2001). In a study conducted after the GLOBE data were gathered, New Zealand ranked second out of 23 countries using the Hofstede measure of individualism (Spector et al., 2001). Given the communal nature of traditional Maori society, it is important to note that this stable, distinctive characteristic of individualism is a mark of the dominant New Zealand European culture. Geographic isolation, the separation of pioneer settlers from families in their homeland, and the literary themes of "man alone" all resonate with the importance of "the independent self" and a subordination of relatedness needs to the primacy of individual goals and preferences.

The desire for greater emphasis on In-Group Collectivism indicated by the "Should Be" score reflects a yearning for a sense of family connectedness. This desire may also be underlying the trend toward greater acceptance and introduction of "family friendly" workplace policies (Rotherham, 1998).

Power Distance. New Zealand's low Power Distance rating is consistent with the key theme of egalitarianism emerging from the discussion of New Zealand culture in the introduction to this chapter. It would be wrong to categorize New Zealand as classless, but there is an inherent dislike of elitism. Historian Keith Sinclair talks of the "common colonist's" "distaste for privilege" and how this "distinguished the New Zealanders even among the peoples of America and Australia." Although acknowledging that New Zealand is not a classless society, he claims that it "must be more nearly classless ... than any advanced society in the world. Some people are richer than others, but wealth carries no great prestige and no prerogative of leadership" (Sinclair, 1969, p. 285).

In the years since those words were written, the gap between rich and poor has increased significantly (Ansley, 2000). Power Distance is positively correlated with the size of the salary range between the top and bottom of organizations across different societies (Hofstede, 2001). As would be expected in a country with low Power Distance, 80% of New Zealanders consider the increasing differences in wealth to be "unacceptable" (Gold & Webster, 1990), and a majority would like to see income gaps reduced (Gendall et al., 2000).

Hierarchical differences between levels in New Zealand organizations are not as clearly marked by symbols or language as they are in higher Power Distance cultures. Use of first names is common, even between senior managers and junior employees, and extreme perks of office (such as executive washrooms, elevators, or dining rooms) are almost nonexistent. In universities, students usually address academic staff by first names. In one New Zealand University, staff teaching into a degree program in Malaysia (a higher Power Distance country) were asked not to encourage the students to use first names as it made them uncomfortable.

Future Orientation. New Zealand's rating on this dimension ranks 48th among the surveyed countries. The average of 3.47 suggests that we place a comparatively low emphasis on future-oriented behaviors such as planning, investing in the future, and delaying gratification.

New Zealand household saving is low by OECD standards, and has been falling in recent years (Savage, 1999). Saving requires a person or household to forego the pleasure of current expenditure in order to provide for some possible event in the future, and savings decisions are therefore partly a reflection of Future Orientation. Historically New Zealand has had a comprehensive social welfare scheme financed from general taxation; wage and salary earners are not required to pay regular contributions to a social security fund. This reduces the risks associated with nonsaving, and may encourage a "live for the day" mentality. In September 1997, a referendum on the possible introduction of a compulsory retirement savings scheme was held. Eighty percent of eligible voters participated, with over 90% voting against the scheme.

In an organizational context, recent surveys suggest that New Zealand companies are not paying sufficient attention to long-term planning. A study of manufacturing companies found evidence of a short-term orientation among many of the sampled firms (Knuckey, Leung-Wai, & Meskill, 1999). A more comprehensive survey of all sectors concluded that managers were excessively focused on short-term goals and need to take a longer-term strategic view in order to achieve sustainable adaptation (Wevers International Ltd/Centre for Corporate Strategy, 1996).

These examples are consistent with the relatively low rating given to Future Orientation by the managers in our sample. They also suggest the reasons for such a high emphasis being given to the "Should Be" rating. Over recent years, increasing public attention has been paid to the inadequacy of most households' preparations for the future. Demographic trends and government reductions in social security provision have highlighted the need for individuals to adopt a longer time horizon for their planning, whereas economic deregulation and removal of subsidies have created similar pressures on businesses.

Humane Orientation.   New Zealand's low "Should Be" ranking on the Humane Orientation scale may be a reflection of complacency with its past reputation as a welfare state. The country introduced its first state-funded welfare assistance (an old-age pension) in 1898, extending into additional programs that culminated in the 1938 Social Security Act, "a bold and daring experiment that deeply influenced the course of legislation in other countries" (Briggs, 1965, p. 67). Such initiatives gave New Zealand a deserved reputation as one of the leading welfare states in the immediate postwar period.

Contrasting with this early emphasis on social security is the cultural theme of independence, and the value placed on people achieving success through their own efforts. This perspective has resulted in people on welfare payments being criticized as lazy, and labeled as "dole bludgers." Gold and Webster's survey (1990) asked for perceptions of whom or what is responsible for poverty and deprivation in New Zealand. Although most respondents attributed it to external causes (unfairness, injustice, bad luck), the single most popular explanation was laziness. The authors concluded that "sympathy for the poor and deprived in New Zealand is not as deeply rooted as it might be" (p. 19).

New Zealand's position as a leading welfare state has declined since the 1960s. In the mid-1980s, the government reformed the welfare system, shifting from one of universal assistance to one that provided a "safety net" for those in the greatest of need, and that encouraged self-sufficiency (Statistics New Zealand, 1995). In the period since completion of the GLOBE data gathering, New Zealanders have become more concerned about the evidence of increasing social disadvantage, and there is greater support for more government spending on core welfare state activities. However, this humane attitude is kept in check by concern regarding possible negative effects of welfare on self-reliance, and on the willingness of people to help each other—40% of New Zealand respondents to the International Social Survey Programme study on social equality believed that less generous welfare benefits would encourage people to "stand on their own two feet" (Gendall et al., 2000). The GLOBE respondents gave very similar ratings to both the "As Is" and "Should Be" Humane Orientation scales, suggesting satisfaction with the current balance between support for the needy and encouragement of independence.

Themes

The GLOBE societal culture scales present a pattern that is consistent with the preceding discussion of underlying cultural themes in New Zealand. The importance of Egalitarianism is captured in the low rating given to Power Distance. When coupled with Performance Orientation, it becomes clear that people are more likely to be judged on their accomplishments than by their background. The cultural emphasis on performance also makes it clear that New Zealanders like winners, but the winners need to be humble. Assertiveness, especially if it shades into aggressiveness in pursuit of personal goals, is unwelcome. People take pride in belonging to the wider collective, to social groupings or the country as a whole. However, there is a sense of dislocation, of being unhappy at a perceived lack of family collectiveness, which echoes some of the literary cultural themes of "man alone." Finally, the independence of the pioneer, the expectation of having to make one's own way, lives on in the responses to the Humane Orientation scale.

Several of these themes underpin the culturally implicit theory of leadership held by New Zealanders. The next section begins with an overview of organizational leadership research in New Zealand, and is followed by discussion of the GLOBE leadership study.

3. LEADERSHIP RESEARCH IN NEW ZEALAND

During the 1970s George Hines, a psychologist at Victoria University of Wellington, carried out a program of survey research into the background, business practices, motivation, and psychological characteristics of over 2,400 New Zealand managers (Hines, 1973). He reported that New Zealand managers placed a significantly greater weight on interpersonal relationships than did North American and European managers. He suggested that this finding related to the small size of New Zealand companies, the opportunities for frequent interactions between people at all levels, and the lack of arbitrary class differences. Individuality and independence were valued, together with an emphasis on performance rather than social status. New Zealand (at that time) also lacked large salary differentials within organizations.

In small organizations, employees know managers personally, decisions are generally conveyed face-to-face, and there is nowhere to hide when problems arise. Sir James Wattie, founder of Wattie's Foods, is a good example of these attributes. As chief executive, he used to eat in the staff cafeteria, and placed a high value on the information he gained from informal interaction with staff at all levels in his factory. This approach contrasts markedly with the more formal, individualistic culture imposed on Wattie's by the multinational Heinz company, after it acquired Wattie's in 1992 (Irving & Inkson, 1998).

Hines's survey was consistent with other research that had found New Zealand managers to be conservative in outlook (Wilson & Patterson, 1968). He commented on the association between conservatism and other factors, including adherence to rules and regulations, resistance to change, compliance with existing norms, and a preference for stability, predictability, and security—attributes consistent with a high level of Uncertainty Avoidance.

Prior to 1984, it may have been possible for managers in New Zealand's protected economy to avoid uncertainty; after 1984 it was no longer an option. The qualities reflected by leadership research and practice during the 1970s would not suffice for the 1990s or beyond. The sense of sharp transition, of a watershed in the demands on leaders, is clear:

> *If our past existence had created an environment where the basic parameters for leadership were set, where the solid virtues, sound administration, transactional leadership, and strong control were sufficient for success, then the new environment has changed things irrevocably. Qualities previously unnecessary in New Zealand management suddenly became critical not for spectacular success, but for mere survival: innovation, lateral thinking, vision, entrepreneurship (and its organization corollary, "intrapreneurship"), networking ability, international orientation. (Inkson & Henshall, 1990, p. 164)*

Transformational leaders became more visible at the helm of many New Zealand companies (Inkson, Henshall, Marsh, & Ellis, 1986), the prevalence of "high commitment" management practices increased (Hamilton, Dakin, & Loney, 1992), and research began to indicate the increased value subordinates placed on transformational behaviors (Singer, 1985).

In 1993 and 1996, the New Zealand Institute for Economic Research (NZIER) published studies that examined the ways in which New Zealand private-sector management had adjusted to the structural changes and deregulation of the preceding decade (Campbell-Hunt &

Corbett, 1996; Campbell-Hunt, Harper, & Hamilton, 1993). These reports found evidence of increasing emphasis on teamwork, training, and performance rewards (with a dramatic increase in the use of performance-linked pay systems since the introduction of the Employment Contracts Act in 1991). Consequently, longer-term issues such as career development, labor planning, and the link between training policy and strategic planning received insufficient attention. This pattern is consistent with the high Performance Orientation and low Future Orientation scores of New Zealand managers.

The NZIER studies revealed that managers showed increasing awareness of the need to create more flexible organization structures, to improve the communication of their vision to staff, and to involve people more effectively in the development of strategy. Evidence suggested, however, that many managers did not know how to transform this awareness into action (Frater, Stuart, Rose, & Andrews, 1995; Wevers & Company, 1994). Campbell-Hunt and Corbett concluded, in 1996, that New Zealand managers were "only part-way through a change in style from a hierarchical, 'command and control' mentality to an empowering, 'delegate and coach' style" (p. 98).

Rippin (1995) explored managerial behavior in more depth, seeking to identify the characteristics of effective New Zealand managers. She used the repertory grid technique (Stewart, 1981) to elicit constructs underlying chief executives' perceptions of the effectiveness of senior managers. The broad pattern of competencies emerging from her study was similar to that identified in studies carried out in other countries. One difference she noted was the high contribution of perceived technical skills to judgments of the effectiveness of senior managers—something she suggested might be a function of the New Zealand culture, the "Colonial spirit" (p. 133).

Rippin (1995) developed a questionnaire containing over 300 items to measure the constructs identified in the repertory grid study, and administered it to 185 senior managers. Analysis revealed a six-factor structure, with the first factor (Interpersonal Skills) accounting for 40% of the variance. The 20 highest loading items on this factor reveal a pattern of inclusive, egalitarian, and participative attributes. Key words from these items include: takes a genuine interest in people, makes people feel at ease, is consultative, sensitive, empathetic, accessible, treats all people as their equal, is compassionate, can laugh at themselves, is a team player, has a harmonizing effect, and has a basic respect for all staff in the organization (1995, p. 152).

Cammock, Nilakant, and Dakin (1995) also used repertory grid interviews to develop items for a questionnaire survey exploring perceptions of managerial effectiveness. They located their study in a large New Zealand public-sector organization and interviewed staff from all levels, not just managers. The resulting model placed more emphasis on personal characteristics (as opposed to skilled behavior) than most (non-New Zealand) competency studies. Two broad factors (Conceptual and Interpersonal) emerged. Effective managers were seen as positive, visible, approachable, friendly, supportive, consultative, willing to learn from others, and honest in their dealings with staff. In regard to conceptual abilities, they instilled a clear sense of purpose, constantly looked for new approaches, considered the long term, did not get bogged down in detail, had a good sense of priorities, and displayed high levels of drive and enthusiasm (p. 456).

In both of these studies (Cammock et al., 1995; Rippin, 1995), the researchers created leadership models based on the responses of their subjects. In contrast, Parry and Proctor (2000) surveyed over 1,300 private- and public-sector managers in New Zealand using standard leadership and organizational questionnaires, including the Multifactor Leadership

Questionnaire (MLQ) (Bass & Avolio, 1990) and the Organization Description Questionnaire (ODQ) (Bass & Avolio, 1993). The managers scored at a generally high level in regard to the display of transformational leadership behaviors (in line with norms for other Western countries). They differed, however, in displaying more "contingent reward" behaviors than managers in similar countries. These behaviors are transactional in nature, focusing on an exchange between leader and follower, rather than the development of shared values and vision. Parry and Proctor viewed this comparatively high use of contingent reward by New Zealand managers as a cause for concern. They speculated that the 15 years of economic reform (since 1984) may "have created a generation of very transactionally-minded and contractually-oriented people" (p. 32)—a view that is consistent with Peel and Inkson's (2000) evidence for a shift from relational to transactional employment contracts during this period.

Contemporary leadership research is beginning to reflect the "Maori renaissance," emerging Pacific cultural themes, and the increasing diversity of New Zealand society. With the Treaty of Waitangi settlements leading to greater Maori investment in property, tourism, and fishing industries, there is an increased interest in Maori leadership (Tapsell, 1997). Henry (as cited in Jones et al., 2000) identified a range of leadership styles adopted by Maori women. These include, for example, *kuia* (wise elder-grandmother) authoritarian leadership, and *whaea* (mother) guiding and leading from behind. These styles stem from family position and traditional precolonial leadership roles, and were distinct from the leadership roles identified in a study of Pakeha women-run organizations. Pfeifer and Love (2004) compared Maori and Pakeha leadership styles using the MLQ (Bass & Avolio, 1990) and found evidence of differences in perceptions of leadership styles between these two cultural groups. Ah Chong and Thomas (1997) compared Pacific Island and Pakeha leaders, and identified style variations attributable to cultural differences (especially in regard to task-oriented behaviors).

These emergent themes are likely to influence the mainstream model of business leadership in New Zealand over the coming years. The GLOBE methodology lends itself to explorations of culture- and gender-based variations, and Pfeifer (2005) has used the framework to identify similarities and differences in how Maori and Pakeha followers perceived the outstanding leadership behavior of culturally similar leaders.

The following section assesses the predominant implicit leadership theory currently held by New Zealand middle managers.

4. THE GLOBE STUDY—LEADERSHIP

The leadership component of the GLOBE study in New Zealand consisted of interviews, a focus group, media analysis, and questionnaire-based data collection. The focus group was conducted with 10 participants, including 2 women. Five were chief executives of companies (representing food, manufacturing, finance, and the service sectors), three were company directors with previous management experience, one was a human resource manager, and one was a partner in a financial services firm. Introductory comments by the facilitator set the scene, encouraging the participants to discuss their views of leadership, contrasts between management and leadership, and aspects of leadership unique to New Zealand. Minimal guidance was provided during the discussion, which was tape-recorded and transcribed for subsequent analysis.

Semistructured interviews were conducted with one female and two male senior managers; the interviews included broad, open-ended questions about the characteristics of effective leaders, behaviors associated with ineffective leaders, examples of outstanding leaders, and contrasts between management and leadership. Interviewees were given freedom to discuss widely around these topics. The interviews were taped, transcribed, and analyzed in order to identify key themes.

Additional qualitative insights into New Zealand leaders were gained from analysis of leadership references in print media during a 1-week period at the end of 1997 (Godfrey & Kennedy, 1998). The sample media comprised two business magazines (*Management* and *New Zealand Business*), two business weekly newspapers (*The Independent* and *National Business Review*), and three daily newspapers (Auckland's *New Zealand Herald,* Wellington's *Dominion,* and Christchurch's *The Press*). All references to New Zealand leaders (in political, commercial, and community spheres) were identified and coded, before being analyzed to identify emergent themes.

Finally, the GLOBE quantitative leadership scales were administered to 184 managers. Details of the sample demographics are summarized in the earlier section on the societal culture survey, whereas development of the questionnaire is described in the first chapter in this volume.

Focus Groups and Interviews

Similar themes emerged from the focus group and interviews (Fearing, Heyward, Kennedy, & O'Sullivan, 1995); these are summarized in Table 12.2. Average managers were described as primarily maintaining the status quo through control and enforcement of existing policies and procedures. They were considered better managers of things than of people, and some members of the focus group felt this characteristic was often associated with a weakness in regard to understanding human nature. They did not have an innate understanding of how to motivate people, and tended to be ineffective delegators.

More effective managers shared some of these characteristics, but were regarded as willing to question goals, procedures, and processes in order to explore opportunities, and seek lateral alternatives. They typically had greater people skills, and were able to lead effectively by example. They were more willing to take risks than were average managers, and could marshal resources to achieve results over and above routine expectations.

Average managers were viewed as controllers, whereas leaders were more democratic and team oriented. The focus group was convened shortly after the death of one of New Zealand's celebrated war heroes, double–Victoria Cross winner Charles Upham. One of the group participants noted that Upham always claimed his team was "very hard to control, but a lot easier to lead." This captures the ambivalent feeling many New Zealanders have in regard to formal restraint and control.

In distinguishing leadership from management, participants also emphasized the importance of developing a clear vision, and a set of beliefs that are passed on to peers and subordinates. Leaders were seen as high achievers, with their success leavened by humility. New Zealanders like "humble winners." Several participants expressed reservations about setting any leader up as a role model for others, commenting that this could result in the leader "play acting" or focusing on meeting others' expectations at the expense of integrity and commitment to their job. Rather than a role model to aspire to, New Zealanders prefer a leader they can relate to; modesty and quiet confidence are respected. Furthermore, leaders were not expected to be successful leaders for all time, or in all situations. Charles Upham, for example, returned to a farming life after his successful wartime leadership role.

TABLE 12.2

Manager and Leader Characteristics Identified by Focus Group

Characteristics Reported by Focus Group Participants		
Average Manager	*Above-Average Manager*	*Outstanding Leader*
• Concerned with maintenance	• Has flair for growth and opportunity	• Total commitment ("love") for people
• Better at managing things	• Uses lateral thinking	• Articulate and persuasive
• Policies and procedures	• Good with people and involves them as a team	• Possess high degree of integrity
• Controller, not expander		
• Maintains status quo	• Communicates well	• High achiever, both in and outside of work
• Regular (e.g., works 9a.m. to 5p.m.)	• Growth oriented: sets some goals	• Charismatic—has the "X" factor
• Not completely focused	• Uncertain about projecting visions and beliefs throughout the organization	• Consistent
• Compromises		• Democratic
• Doesn't fully understand human nature	• Not visionary: works on a day-to-day or yearly basis	• Trusting of others
• Problems with delegation	• More focused than average manager	• Team player
• Patterned		• Have strong communication and people skills
• Controlled outcome, standard requirement	• Prepared to take risks to some extent	• Customer oriented
	• Leads by example	• Humble
	• Not afraid of making important decisions	• Imperfect, but knows own weaknesses
	• Has better understanding of people and the business than the average manager	• Have respect for self
		• Experienced and well-rounded
	• Aims to achieve a result beyond given expectations	• Pragmatic
	• Uses resources effectively	

A cluster of traits emerging from the focus group discussion concerned the personal characteristics of modesty, humility, and recognition of one's own weaknesses, balanced with a healthy respect for self and others. Outstanding leaders in New Zealand are not self-absorbed, "cocky," or bent on Machiavellian control of others. They see their leadership role as being based in the team, not outside it. They evidence a strong commitment to the value of teamwork, a willingness to be a "team player" themselves, and to actively contribute their own efforts and ideas, rather than try to lead from a distance. As one participant noted: *"They get around their troops a lot, they make sure they talk to everybody; they make people really feel part of a team, as though they're important. It's their people skills; they understand the strengths and weaknesses of the team."*

Media Analysis

A total of 557 data elements (from 320 separate text extracts) were categorized iteratively, starting with fine-grained categories containing only a few items. These were combined progressively into broader groupings in successive rounds, resulting in a final number of 25 categories. Table 12.3 lists the categories grouped into five main facets of leadership—organization management, people management, personality, ability, and image. The most frequently represented categories are listed first in each column whereas categories containing less than six data elements (equivalent to 1% of the total set) are printed in italics. Categories including elements referring only to political leaders are labeled (P).

The largest category, representing 30% of the data elements, was that of personality traits. Within this cluster, the largest subcategory referred to determination, resolve, "stickability" and perseverance toward accomplishment of goals. Confidence was the second-largest subcategory, encompassing belief in oneself, and an optimistic outlook. Passion, energy, and commitment comprised the next cluster of attributes. Several attributes were presented as being undesirable; these included arrogance, emotionality, panic, and weakness.

The second-largest category (12%) referred to aspects of taking action. Being active, responsive, and proactive were viewed positively, whereas negative connotations applied to behaviors such as delaying, reneging on commitments, and becoming complacent.

The next most common category (8%) was strategic management, which included data elements relating to vision, planning, policy, strategy, and purpose.

The importance of personality traits in describing leaders is consistent with some of Rippin's work, in which she found that "the effectiveness of managers is largely assessed on personality dimensions" (1995, p.190). The nature of the positive and negative evaluations of traits and behaviors is consistent with New Zealand managers' endorsement of transformational leadership characteristics (Parry & Proctor, 2000).

TABLE 12.3
Categories Emerging From Media Analysis

Organization Management	People Management	Personality	Ability	Image
Taking action (12%)	Motivator	Traits (30%)	Abilities	Impression management
	Communicator	Leader style	Knowledge and understanding	Conduct
Strategic management (8%)	Relationship builder	Realism (P)	Worthiness	Public image
Development				
	Team player		Information management	Consistency
Change management	Director			Political expediency (P)
			Cultural awareness	
Setting ethical standards	Information provider (P)		Conceptual thinking	

Note. Categories in italics each contain less than 1% of the total number of text elements. Categories including elements relating only to political leaders are labeled (P).

The Leadership Scales

The GLOBE leadership questionnaire asked respondents to rate various leadership behaviors and traits on a 7-point scale according to the extent they contributed to "outstanding leadership" in New Zealand. Table 12.4 presents the mean score for each of the 21 first-order leadership factors, grouped under their respective second-order factors (in bold). The numbers in parentheses are New Zealand's rankings in comparison with the other 61 countries. As with the cultural scales, countries have been grouped into a number of bands according to their scale score, and the standard error of difference. Countries within the same band on a scale do not differ meaningfully from each other on that scale.

Within-Country Comparison. The six second-order factors in Table 12.4 represent culturally generalizable implicit leadership theories (CLTs) that emerged from analysis of the complete GLOBE data set (Den Hartog et al., 1999; House et al., 1999, 2004). Two of these CLTs (Charismatic/Value Based and Team Oriented) are universally viewed (in all countries) as contributors to effective leadership, whereas the Self-Protective CLT is perceived as an impediment to outstanding leadership. The New Zealand responses are consistent with this macrolevel pattern—average ratings on scales comprising the first two CLTs are all above the scale midpoints, whereas Self-Protective scale ratings are all below the midpoint.

In terms of absolute scale values, New Zealand managers gave three scales average ratings in excess of 6.0 on the 7-point scale: Inspirational, Performance Orientation, and Visionary. A further two scales (Team Integrator and Decisive) were rated 5.5 or higher. At the low end Malevolent, Self-centered, Nonparticipative, and Face Saver all had average ratings lower than 2.4 and were thus seen as seriously inhibiting effective leadership.

At a simple level then, an outstanding leader in New Zealand is seen as a positive, optimistic person who is able to generate confidence, enthusiasm, and excitement among followers, challenging them to exceed expectations in pursuit of future goals. He or she is a good communicator, sharing information to ensure common understanding among followers, and encouraging them to work as an integrated team. The leader must be prepared to make decisions firmly and resolutely, whether based on logic or intuition. This decisiveness needs to be balanced, however, by recognition of the individual abilities of team members (without regard to their status); the leader must not be a micromanager, and must be willing to share the decision making with capable team members. Personal qualities such as irritability, cynicism, conceitedness, or lack of sincerity undermine leadership effectiveness.

Between-Country Comparison. The leadership qualities valued by New Zealanders will now be compared with other countries in the sample. Within the Charismatic/Value Based CLT, New Zealanders placed more emphasis on the Inspirational scale than managers from all but two other countries. This scale picks up items relevant to the leader's optimism, energy, confidence, and motivation, and his or her ability to inspire these characteristics in followers.

New Zealand is also in the highest band for the Visionary, Decisive, Performance Orientation, and Humane scales. The first three of these scales were noted in the discussion of within-country rankings. The importance of Humane is consistent with the finding by Toulson (1990) that New Zealanders in work organizations strongly endorse humanistic work beliefs. Furthermore, the large-scale redundancies occasioned by the economic reforms commenced in 1984 and the share market crash of 1987, may have heightened respondents' sensitivity to the importance of a humane dimension of leadership.

TABLE 12.4
New Zealand Leadership Styles

Dimensions- Subdimensions	Country Score	GLOBE Band	(Rank)[a]	Within – Ranking[j]
Charismatic/Value Based	5.87	C[i]	(34)	–
Visionary	6.23	A[e]	(16)	3
Inspirational	6.50	A[e]	(3)	1
Self-Sacrificial	4.88	B[d]	(39)	10
Integrity	5.49	C[e]	(55)	6
Decisive	5.69	A[d]	(45)	5
Performance Orientation	6.31	A[d]	(13)	2
Team Oriented	5.44	D[g]	(57)	–
Collaborative Team Oriented	5.21	B[d]	(50)	8
Team Integrator	5.71	B[d]	(41)	4
Diplomatic	5.22	B[b]	(52)	7
Malevolent (Recoded)	1.83	C[e]	(21)	21
Administratively Competent	4.79	C[c]	(59)	11
Self-Protective	3.19	F[h]	(45)	–
Self-Centered	2.23	C[d]	(22)	20
Status-Consciousness	3.56	C[d]	(55)	16
Conflict Inducer	3.74	B[e]	(40)	15
Face Saver	2.39	C[d]	(51)	18
Procedural	3.86	B[d]	(34)	13
Participative	5.50	C[f]	(23)	–
Autocratic (Recoded)	2.63	C[d]	(31)	17
Nonparticipative (Recoded)	2.38	B[e]	(47)	19
Humane	4.78	C[e]	(37)	–
Modesty	4.57	B[c]	(51)	12
Humane	5.09	A[d]	(18)	9
Autonomous	3.77	B[d]	(36)	–
Autonomous	3.77	B[c]	(36)	14

Note   Second-order leadership factors are shown in bold, with the corresponding first-order scales grouped below them (in italics).
[a]Countries are grouped into clusters, based on the standard error of difference for each scale. Countries within each cluster do not differ meaningfully from each other on the scale. Cluster A > Cluster B (> C > D > E > F). Each cluster spans 2 standard errors of differences; as the standard error of difference varies across the scales, the number of clusters for each scale also varies (cf. Hanges, Dickson, & Sipe, 2004). [b]Group span ranges from A to B. [c]Group span ranges from A to C. [d]Group span ranges from A to D. [e]Group span ranges from A to E. [f]Group span ranges from A to F. [g]Group span ranges from A to G. [h]Group span ranges from A to H. [i]Group span ranges from A to I. [j]Rank order of GLOBE dimensions within the New Zealand sample.

In contrast, New Zealand managers' ratings on six of the leadership scales were among the lowest 10 countries. The rating of 4.79 given to Administratively Competent ranks 59th among all the countries, falling into the lowest band. The scale reflects an organized, methodical approach to work, underpinned by skills in coordinating and managing complex administrative systems. The mean is just above the midpoint, suggesting that most managers view this scale positively, but it is valued much less as a contributor to effective leadership than in other countries. As noted by the focus group, Administrative Competence is something required by an average manager, and is not a distinguishing characteristic of an outstanding leader.

The New Zealand sample also gave lower ratings to Integrity than most other countries—an average of 5.49 giving a country ranking of 55th. This scale had the highest standard deviation for the New Zealand leadership scales, suggesting a wide spread of opinion about its relevance to leadership. The focus group saw integrity as essential for a leader (Table 12.2), and Parry and Proctor (2000) found very high levels of perceived integrity in their survey of New Zealand leaders. New Zealand is also consistently ranked among the three or four least corrupt societies in the world (Transparency International, 2002). Perhaps New Zealand managers consider honesty and trustworthiness to be the norm in New Zealand, rather than a special quality useful for distinguishing effective leaders.

Status Consciousness, with a rating of 3.56, also ranked 55th out of the 61 GLOBE countries. The rating is below the midpoint of the scale, indicating that most managers take a negative view of leaders who are conscious of class or status boundaries, and who allow these to influence their actions. The items comprising this scale showed very large differences in country means, ranging from 1.92 (impedes leadership effectiveness) to 5.77 (contributes to leadership effectiveness) (den Hartog et al., 1999). New Zealand's low score is therefore an important, distinctive attribute of leadership in this country.

The final three scales on which New Zealand ranks low compared with other countries are Diplomatic (52nd), Face Saver (51st), and Modesty (51st). The Face Saver characteristics (e.g., being indirect in communication to avoid giving offense) are seen as inhibiting effective leadership more by New Zealanders than by respondents in other countries. The other two dimensions are rated as contributing to effective leadership, but are seen as less important contributors than in other countries.

Factor Analysis of Leadership Scales. Although the 21 GLOBE leadership factors provide a fine-grained picture of effective leadership in New Zealand organizations, people typically use fewer dimensions to make judgments about people. Factor analysis is a statistical technique that can help identify the underlying dimensions (or latent constructs) related to assessments of leader behaviors. This section summarizes the results of a principal axis factor analysis of the New Zealand leadership questionnaire responses.[1] On the basis of parallel analysis (Fabrigar, Wegener, MacCallum, & Strahan, 1999; O'Connor, 2000) four factors were extracted, and the scale loadings are summarized in Table 12.5.

All of the scales comprising the GLOBE Team Oriented and Charismatic/Value Based CLTs have their largest loadings on the first factor, with the exception of Inspirational. This factor has been labeled "Team Leader." It reflects a style of leading that encompasses transformational leadership attributes firmly based in a cooperative, high-performing team context.

---

[1]The GLOBE scales were designed to measure organizational- or societal-level variability (Hanges & Dickson, 2004). The scales were *not* intended to meaningfully differentiate among individuals within a particular society. However, even though the scales were not constructed to provide such information, in some cases it is interesting to assess whether similar factors differentiate individuals within a society. Country-specific factor analysis is intended as an exploration of the themes captured by GLOBE in a new domain, that is, individual differences within a society. It should be noted that, because of the within-society restriction of the GLOBE scales true-score variability (which was based on between-society differences), the loadings of the GLOBE scale's items on within-society factors should be lower than between societies (cf. Hanges & Dickson, 2004). Furthermore, one should not interpret the within-society factor analyses as replications of the GLOBE factor structure. And the absence of a GLOBE factor within a society should not be automatically interpreted as the factor being irrelevant to the people in that country. Rather, a factor may fail to emerge within a society even when that theme is extremely critical because there was no variability in how the individuals from a single society rated the items (e.g., they all rated the items a 7). Factor analysis requires variability and so a factor could fail the emerge because it is extremely critical or completely irrelevant to the people within a society.

TABLE 12.5

Exploratory Factor Analysis of New Zealand Leader Attributes

Scale	Team Leader	Straight Talker	Self-Promoter	Bureaucrat
Decisive	.78			
Team Integrator	.72			
Admin Competent	.68			
Integrity	.62			
Collaborative Team Oriented	.54			
Malevolent	−.53	−.41	.45	
Visionary	.49			
Diplomatic	.47			
Performance Oriented	.47			
Inspirational		.76		
Face Saver		−.61		
Status-Conscious		−.42		
Conflict Inducer			.72	
Autocratic		−.43	.65	
Self-Centered		−.43	.59	
Modesty			−.55	
Nonparticipative			.42	
Procedural				.74
Eigenvalue	3.92	2.74	2.71	1.02
Variance explained (%)	18.6	13.0	12.9	4.9

Note. Principal axis factor analysis, extracting four factors with varimax rotation. Only loadings greater than 0.4 are shown. Three scales (Self-Sacrificial, Humane, and Autonomous) failed to reach this level on any factor and do not appear in the table.

The Team Integrator, Collaborative Team Oriented, and Diplomatic scale items emphasize the importance of working together, resolving individual and intragroup conflict, giving time and energy to help others, being skilled and tactful in interpersonal relations, and being loyal to the group even in times of trouble.

The factor also has significant loadings from the Decisive and Performance Oriented scales. These capture elements of effective behaviors—the ability to make decisions firmly and logically, to be determined and persistent, and to strive for increasingly high levels of performance. The team has to be an efficient and effective one, a winning team, not an unstructured or directionless group. The high negative loading of Malevolent indicates the undesirability of attributes such as irritability, dishonesty, egotistical behaviors, cynicism, and uncooperativeness.

The second factor ("Straight Talker") shows that the New Zealand managers' implicit model of leadership includes an underlying construct in which inspirational motivation and concern for followers are coupled with a willingness to communicate honestly, candidly, and without undue deference to status. The highest loading scale on this factor is the Inspirational scale. Scale content includes the extent to which leaders display (or generate in their followers) positivity, encouragement, enthusiasm, high morale, confidence, and energy. The Face-Saving and Status-Conscious scales (both components of the GLOBE Self-Protective CLT) have strong loadings in the opposite direction to the Inspirational and Humane scales. An egalitarian approach coupled with clear and direct communication is an important part of the leadership perspective captured by this factor.

The third factor (labeled "Self-Promoter") includes elements of both the Self- Protective and Participative (negatively loaded) CLT dimensions. It captures a self-centered, directive leadership style. A strong loading from Autocratic captures both leadership style (bossy, domineering, dictatorial, and intolerant of questioning) and belief in elitism. The other four scales loading positively on this factor are Conflict Inducer, Nonparticipative, Self-Centered, and Autonomous. These reflect attributes such as an emphasis on one's own interests rather than the groups, an insistence on making decisions personally, a tendency to conceal information from the group, and a preference for independence. Finally, the high negative loading of Modesty reflects New Zealanders' dislike of boasting, and the value placed on a self-effacing manner.

The fourth factor ("Bureaucrat") differs markedly from the GLOBE second-order factors. It highlights a unique aspect of the way in which New Zealand managers evaluate their leaders. The factor is dominated by the Procedural scale, which includes items relating to formality, caution, maintaining a habitual routine, and a preference for following established rules. Reliance on formal rules goes against the New Zealand preference for managing the team rather than the process, and has been identified as a weakness in many New Zealand managers (see Parry & Proctor, 2000).

The contribution of the four factors to perceptions of effective leadership can be assessed. The leadership scales are based on variables rated from 1 ("greatly inhibits a person from being an outstanding leader") to 7 ("contributes greatly to a person being an outstanding leader"). By taking the average score of each of the leadership scales loading on each factor, we can assess the extent to which a high factor score is positively or negatively associated with leadership.

On this basis, the cluster of leadership scales represented by the Team Leader factor are the ones most highly valued in New Zealand leaders, with an average rating of 5.65. This factor also accounts for the largest amount of variance in the model (18.6%). The "Straight Talker" factor has an average of 5.41, and accounts for 13% of variance. This cluster of attributes is therefore highly valued, and an important component of the New Zealand leadership model. The Self-Promoter factor (accounting for 12.9% of variance) captures behaviors that detract from effective leadership, with an average rating of 3.03; the Autocratic, Self-centered, and Nonparticipative scales in particular are viewed as inimical to good leadership. Finally, behaviors associated with the Bureaucrat factor (3.86) detract from perceptions of effective leadership, but account for only 4.9% of variance.

The New Zealand factor structure replicates the GLOBE Charismatic/Value Based and Team Oriented CLTs, although these factors emerge as one in the New Zealand sample. The remaining New Zealand factors differ from the GLOBE factor structure, and thus provide insights into unique aspects of the New Zealand leadership model. The factor structure highlights the importance of honest, candid communication with people, transcending status or class boundaries (Straight Talker). It also underscores the importance of a leader being seen to actively engage with his or her team, to encourage participation, to place the team and its goals ahead of personal ambition, and to maintain an appropriate level of humility (Self-Promoter). Finally, the negative connotations of the Bureaucrat factor are consistent with the pragmatic, problem-solving attitude discussed in the section on culture.

Many of the people honored by being featured on New Zealand banknotes epitomize these qualities—in particular, the willingness to forego self-interest and to make personal sacrifices in the interest of a goal or vision, often coupled with a challenge to existing privilege or control structures. Kate Sheppard was the most prominent leader of the campaign for universal suffrage in New Zealand at the end of the 19th century; Sir Apirana Ngata led the revival of Maori people and culture in the early 20th century; Ernest Rutherford is internationally recognized as the "father of the atom"; and Sir Edmund Hillary was the first person to climb Mt Everest, and to drive overland to the South Pole.

Discussion

The findings of the qualitative and quantitative analyses provide a consistent picture of the leadership behaviors valued most highly by New Zealand managers. High levels of performance must be balanced by a somewhat modest, self-deprecating attitude. Involvement of team members using an egalitarian, participative style is expected, together with flexibility in the application of rules and processes. The leader must enthuse and inspire followers, but this is best done through personal commitment, perseverance, and example, rather than by exhortation or flummery.

The cultural emphasis on low In-Group Collectivism, high Institutional Collectivism, low Power Distance, and low Assertiveness distinguish New Zealand from most other GLOBE countries. The value placed on collectivism at the work group and societal level contrasts markedly with the individualist values apparent in the in-group and family context. The managers' view of work group pride seems linked more to utilitarian considerations than to an innate need for affiliation. Performance is paramount. In line with the pioneering cultural strand, people are considered to determine their own fortune; they stand or fall on their ability to achieve, whether as individuals or as contributors to a wider group enterprise.

New Zealanders don't look favorably on rules, detailed administrative procedures, or being controlled by micromanaging bureaucrats. On the other hand, the cultural values evidence a high need to reduce uncertainty, to increase the level of stability and predictability. This is achieved more by conformity, by a desire to avoid being different, than by subordination to a set of externally imposed or class-based "rules." Effective leadership in New Zealand is therefore likely to require a "clan control" rather than "bureaucratic control" approach to controlling people and channeling their efforts (Bartol & Martin, 1998).

Though New Zealanders dislike autocratic leaders, they also spurn leaders who pull their punches, who aren't prepared to "call a spade a spade." There is a potential dissonance between this avoidance of the autocrat, and the desire for a leader who can reduce uncertainty, provide a sense of security, and instill confidence. Performance is valued highly, and accolades are given to those who achieve at the highest level (as long as they don't act as though their achievements make them better than others). New Zealanders want to follow a leader who can succeed, who can perform at an exceptional level, and who gives hope that followers can share in this success. They want to be told what to do by a successful (albeit self-effacing) leader, not by a bureaucrat with a policy manual.

A strong leader can reduce uncertainty, and make people feel they are on the winning team. Perhaps this accounts for what Pearson has called New Zealanders' "lurking respect for the dictator" (Pearson, 1974), the willingness to allow a leader to be dictatorial if he or she achieves results, and if those results benefit the dominant group. Dictators usually have a passion, they are driven to control people to an end, and they are enthusiastic about their goals.

At various times in the past New Zealand has willingly endorsed authoritarian Prime Ministers (most recently, Sir Robert Muldoon). The media study identified emotionality, panic, and weakness as negative characteristics—the country's pioneering background seems to make a strong autocrat preferable to a sensitive facilitator.

Traditional attributes are still valued, such as strength of character, resolve, determination, and commitment. Increasing importance is being placed on the ability to inspire and enthuse staff, on Future Orientation, and on development and communication of a compelling vision. The high importance placed on having a leader with vision reflects the overall concern at the low level of Future Orientation in society. Leaders are valued for demonstrating foresight, planning ahead, and taking actions in consideration of future goals, perhaps in compensation for the low emphasis given to these behaviors by society as a whole.

There is an important aspect of our cultural identity that is not adequately captured by the GLOBE questionnaire. The rural archetype encompasses a practical, down-to-earth approach to problem solving, colored by "Kiwi ingenuity." The GLOBE items, by focusing on generic leadership behaviors, do not address technical skills, yet this seems to be an area that may further distinguish New Zealand leaders from their international counterparts. Rippin (1995) found that technical skills were an important contributor to judgments about senior managers' perceived levels of overall effectiveness. Her finding contrasts with similar overseas studies, and she speculates that the value placed on technical skills may be a function of the New Zealand "colonial spirit" (p.133), requiring managers to demonstrate greater versatility than is the case in other countries.

This summary has implications for overseas managers who come to New Zealand to assume leadership roles. The large individual differences that exist within cultures make it hard to be definitive about the likely experiences of expatriate or immigrant managers in New Zealand. Furthermore, such managers will find an increasingly multicultural workforce—a typical New Zealand manufacturer in the Auckland region might comprise 20% New Zealand European, 15% Maori, 15% Samoan, 10% Cook Islanders, 10% Tongans, 10% Chinese, 10% Malaysian, 5% Korean, and 5% Indian (Thomas, Ravlin, & Barry, 2000).

However, managers from cultures that differ markedly from the values espoused by New Zealand managers are likely to experience greater dissonance than those from similar cultures. Comparison of GLOBE values for other countries is a useful starting point, and the cluster analysis by Gupta, Hanges, and Dorfman (2002) gives an overview of broad cultural similarities and differences. Even within the same cluster, however, important differences exist. Australia, the United States, and South Africa (White sample) all belong (with New Zealand) to the Anglo cluster, but managers from all of these countries scored significantly higher on Assertiveness than did New Zealand managers.

Australians, Americans, and South Africans who use levels of assertive behavior consistent with norms in their home countries are likely to be viewed negatively in New Zealand. Their actions may be considered "pushy," arrogant, or domineering, resulting in lowered cooperation and respect from locals.

Managers from cultures that are high on Power Distance or status consciousness must be prepared for greater levels of informality in New Zealand. The apparent lack of deference shown by New Zealanders is driven by egalitarian values, and should not be interpreted as lack of respect. Similarly, the new leader has to be careful in choosing how to establish credibility. Personal statements about his or her experience and expertise may be seen as "skiting," as self-promotion inconsistent with the value placed on humility and modesty. Understated, objective descriptions of experience or achievements, giving acknowledgment to the contributions of others, are less likely to engender skepticism.

Gaining the acceptance of followers is critical for leaders in New Zealand, as the low level of Power Distance makes it difficult for leaders to maintain their position based only on legitimate authority. Acceptance requires openness, integrity, straightforward communication, and willingness to subordinate personal ego for the good of the group.

New Zealanders' high level of Institutional Collectivism is consistent with their strong sense of national pride (Smith & Jarkko, 2001). It is important that expatriate managers recognize this, and minimize actions that belittle or undermine this sense of unique identity. Unthinking application of international HR policies, value statements, diversity programs, and similar initiatives can have unintended effects (cynicism, lowered trust, resentment) unless the local context and values are taken into account (Jones et al., 2000).

Finally, the egalitarianism that pervades New Zealand culture creates challenges for expatriates seeking to recognize and reward individual performance. The sense of "fair play" dictates that individuals are acknowledged and rewarded for their contribution, whereas the emphasis on teamwork and egalitarianism creates strong pressure for team-based rewards. The composition of work teams, levels of interdependence, and opportunity for individual contribution need to be carefully balanced against these values of egalitarianism and team loyalty.

Limitations and Suggestions for Future Research

The use of GLOBE quantitative and qualitative tools to explore cultural values and preferred leadership behaviors provides a strong foundation for international comparisons. However, by collecting quantitative data from only three industries, care must be taken when generalizing results within New Zealand. The sample size (184) prevents more fine-grained analysis. Future research into the differences in values and implicit leadership models of men and women, of different ethnic groups in New Zealand, as a function of age, or of geographic location will contribute to our understanding of effective leadership in organizations.

Data collection took place following one of the most significant periods of economic and social restructuring in New Zealand's history. As noted in several places during this chapter, it is possible that some responses may have been influenced by reaction to these events. Future studies using the GLOBE scales will be needed in order to clarify the stability of the pattern identified.

5. CONCLUSION

This chapter began with a quotation from John Mulgan, a New Zealand writer and diplomat who studied and worked in England during the 1930s. He described the qualities that characterized New Zealand soldiers he met during the desert campaign of World War II. We have seen how some of these attributes closely fit the culturally endorsed model of outstanding leadership in New Zealand. This implicit model combines inspirational enthusiasm ("sunshine"), low assertiveness, pragmatism, and perseverance. Low Power Distance and the strength of egalitarian beliefs mandate a style of leadership that is participative, grounded in the team, and provides the opportunity for shared success.

To the extent that leadership is "the process of being perceived by others as a leader" (Lord & Maher, 1991, p. 11) then New Zealand leaders must conform to the cultural expectations of their followers. New Zealand's cultural identity, however, has been determined in part by the actions of leaders (in military, cultural, sporting, political, and commercial spheres). Culture can therefore be viewed both as a constraint on what is acceptable and as a supporting structure amenable to further development as New Zealanders build and extend their concept of effective leadership. Another New Zealand writer, Katherine Mansfield (1960, p. 127), described New Zealand as *"a little land with no history (Making its own history, slowly and clumsily. Piecing together this and that, finding the pattern, solving the problem, Like a child with a box of bricks)."*

New Zealand leaders have found patterns and solved problems in ways that both reflect and help to define "Kiwi culture." Though many of the building blocks for New Zealand's leadership style can be found in other countries, the overall pattern is unique. The problems to be solved will continue to change, and leaders will need to continue finding new bricks to extend the pattern. The GLOBE study provides a snapshot of existing cultural themes and leadership styles, and a basis from which to explore future evolution of Kiwi leadership as New Zealand continues to develop and refine its sense of identity and place in the world.

ACKNOWLEDGMENTS

This chapter was written while I was in the Commerce Division of Lincoln University, New Zealand. Peter Cosgriff, Mark Fearing, and Dan Sauers contributed to the early planning and data-gathering stages of GLOBE in New Zealand and their contribution is gratefully acknowledged. I also thank Kerr Inkson, Jagdeep Chhokar, Ken Parry, Peter Cammock, and Ramzi Addison for their constructive and thoughtful comments on a draft.

REFERENCES

Ah Chong, L. M., & Thomas, D. C. (1997). Leadership perceptions in cross-cultural context: Pakeha and Pacific Islanders in New Zealand. *The Leadership Quarterly, 8*(3), 275–293.

Ansley, B. (2000, March 25). Human values. *Listener,* 16–19.

Bartol, K. M., & Martin, D. C. (1998). *Management* (3rd ed.). New York: Irwin/McGraw-Hill.

Bass, B. M., & Avolio, B. J. (1990). *Transformational leadership development: Manual for the Multifactor Leadership Questionnaire.* Palo Alto, CA: Consulting Psychologists Press.

Bass, B. M., & Avolio, B. J. (1993). Transformational leadership and organizational culture. *Public Administrative Quarterly, 17*(1), 112–121.

Belich, J. (2001). *Paradise reforged : A history of the New Zealanders from the 1880s to the year 2000.* Auckland, New Zealand: Allen Lane Penguin Press.

Booth, P. (1993). *Edmund Hillary: The life of a legend.* Auckland, New Zealand: Hodder Moa Beckett.

Bridges, J., & Downs, D. (2000). *No. 8 wire: The best of Kiwi ingenuity.* Auckland, New Zealand: Hodder Moa Beckett.

Briggs, A. (1965). The welfare state in historical perspective. In M. Zald (Ed.), *Social welfare institutions* (pp. 25–45). New York: Wiley.

Cammock, P., Nilakant, V., & Dakin, S. R. (1995). Developing a lay model of managerial effectiveness: A social constructionist perspective. *Journal of Management Studies, 32*(4), 443–476.

Campbell-Hunt, C., & Corbett, L. (1996). *A season of excellence? An overview of New Zealand enterprise in the Nineties* (Research Monograph No. 65). Wellington: New Zealand Institute of Economic Research.

Campbell-Hunt, C., Harper, D., & Hamilton, R. (1993). *Islands of excellence? A study of management in New Zealand* (Research Monograph No. 59). Wellington: New Zealand Institute of Economic Research.

Carter, I., & Perry, N. (1987). Rembrandt in gumboots: Rural imagery in New Zealand television advertisements. In J. Phillips (Ed.), *Te Whenua Te Iwi—The land and the people.* Wellington, New Zealand: Allen & Unwin/Port Nicholson Press.

Child, Youth and Family. (1999). *Strengthening families: Report on cross-sectoral outcome measures and targets.* Wellington, New Zealand: Author.

Crocombe, G., Enright, M., & Porter, M. (1991). *Upgrading New Zealand's competitive advantage.* Auckland, New Zealand: Oxford University Press.

Dalziel, P. (2002). New Zealand's economic reforms: An assessment. *Review of Political Economy, 14*(1), 31–46.

Davin, D. (1984, November). Cassino casualty. *Islands, 1 New Series.*

Deeks, J., Parker, J., & Ryan, R. (1994). *Labour and employment relations in New Zealand* (2nd ed.). Auckland, New Zealand: Longman Paul.

den Hartog, D. N., House, R. J., Hanges, P. J., Ruiz-Quintanilla, S. A., Dorfman, P. W., Kennedy, J. C., et al. (1999). Culture-specific and cross-culturally generalizable implicit leadership theories: Are attributes of charismatic/transformational leadership universally endorsed? *The Leadership Quarterly, 10*(2), 219–256.

Department of Statistics. (1990). *New Zealand Official Yearbook* (94th ed.). Wellington, New Zealand: Author.

Easton, B. (2000, March 25). Value added. *Listener,* pp. 20–21.

Fabrigar, L. R., Wegener, D. T., MacCallum, R. C., & Strahan, E. J. (1999). Evaluating the use of exploratory factor analysis in psychological research. *Psychological Methods, 4*(3), 272–299.

Fairburn, M. (1989). *The ideal society and its enemies: The foundations of modern New Zealand society 1850–1900.* Auckland, New Zealand: Auckland University Press.

Fearing, M., Heyward, J., Kennedy, J. C., & O'Sullivan, D. (1995). *The GLOBE study of management and leadership in New Zealand.* Unpublished manuscript, Commerce Division, Lincoln University, Christchurch, New Zealand.

Feather, N. T. (1993). The rise and fall of political leaders: Attributions, deservingness, personality and affect. *Australian Journal of Psychology, 45,* 61–68.

Feather, N. T. (1994a). Attitudes toward high achievers and reactions to their fall: Theory and research concerning tall poppies. In M. P. Zanna (Ed.), *Advances in social psychology* (Vol. 26, pp. 1–73). New York: Academic Press.

Feather, N. T. (1994b). Values and national identification: Australian evidence. *Australian Journal of Psychology, 46,* 35–40.

Frater, P., Stuart, G., Rose, D., & Andrews, G. (1995). *The New Zealand innovation environment.* Wellington, New Zealand: Business and Economic Research Ltd.

Frederick, H. H., & Carswell, P. J. (2001). *Global entrepreneurship monitor New Zealand 2001.* Auckland: New Zealand Centre for Innovation and Entrepreneurship (UNITEC).

Gendall, P., Robbie, P., Patchett, S., & Bright, N. (2000). *Social equality in New Zealand.* Palmerston North, New Zealand: Department of Marketing, Massey University, International Social Survey Programme.

Geraets, J. (1984). An interior landscape: Charles Brasch's "Indirections" and "The Universal Dance." *Islands, 1 New Series*(1), 71–84.

Gidlow, R., Perkins, H., Cushman, G., & Simpson, C. (1994). Leisure and recreation. In P. Spoonley, D. Pearson, & I. Shirley (Eds.), *New Zealand society: A sociological introduction* (2nd ed., pp. 253–267). Palmerston North, New Zealand: Dunmore Press.

Godfrey, K., & Kennedy, J. C. (1998). *Media portrayal of leadership in New Zealand: A GLOBE study.* Unpublished Manuscript, Commerce Division, Lincoln University, Christchurch, New Zealand.

Gold, H., & Webster, A. (1990). *New Zealand values today.* Palmerston North, New Zealand: Alpha.

Gupta, V., Hanges, P. J., & Dorfman, P. W. (2002). Cultural clusters: Methodology and findings. *Journal of World Business, 37*(1), 11–15.

Hamilton, R. T., Dakin, S. R., & Loney, R. P. (1992). Economic deregulation and general managers: New Zealand's experience. *Personnel Review, 21*(7), 14–23.

Hanges, P. J., & Dickson, M. W. (2004). The development and validation of the GLOBE culture and leadership scales. In R. J. House, P. J. Hanges, M. Javidan, P. W. Dorfman, V. Gupta, & GLOBE Associates (Eds.), *Culture, leadership, and organizations: The GLOBE study of 62 societies* (pp. 122–151). Thousand Oaks, CA: Sage.

Hanges, P. J., Dickson, M. W., & Sipe, M. T. (2004). Rationale for GLOBE statistical analyses: Societal rankings and test of hypotheses. In R. J. House, P. J. Hanges, M. Javidan, P. Dorfman, & V. Gupta (Eds.), *Leadership, culture, and organizations: The GLOBE study of 62 societies* (pp. 219–234). Thousand Oaks, CA: Sage.

Hansen, D. (1968). Social institutions. In A. McLeod (Ed.), *The pattern of New Zealand culture* (pp. 49-67). Ithaca, NY: Cornell University Press.

Harris, P. (1996). *The changes banks face.* Wellington, New Zealand: The Finance Sector Union (FinSec).

Hines, G. (1973). *The New Zealand manager.* Wellington, New Zealand: Hicks, Smith & Sons Ltd.

Hofstede, G. H. (2001). *Culture's consequences: Comparing values, behaviors, institutions, and organizations across nations* (2nd ed.). Thousand Oaks, CA: Sage.

Holm, M. (1994, November 5). Secrets for success. *Listener,* pp. 16–24.

House, R. J., Hanges, P. J., Ruiz-Quintanilla, S. A., Dorfman, P. W., Javidan, M., Dickson, M., et al. (1999). Cultural influences on leadership and organizations: Project GLOBE. In W. H. Mobley, M. J. Gessner, & V. Arnold (Eds.), *Advances in global leadership* (Vol. 1, pp. 171–233). Stamford, CT: JAI.

House, R. J., Hanges, P. J., Javidan, M., Dorfman, P. W., Gupta, V., & GLOBE Associates (2004). *Culture, leadership, and organizations: The GLOBE study of 62 societies.* Thousand Oaks, CA: Sage.

Hughes, T. (2001). *Statement by the New Zealand Deputy Permanent Representative, Friday 10 November 2000.* Paper presented at the Special Political and Decolonisation Committee (Fourth Committee), United Nations, New York.

Hyde, T. (1991, September). How they sold Telecom, why they sold Telecom. *Metro,* pp. 54–69.

IMD International. (2000). *The world competitiveness yearbook.* Lausanne, Switzerland: International Institute for Management Development.

Inkson, J. H. K., & Henshall, B. (1990). Transformational leadership and management development. In P. Boxall (Ed.), *Function in search of a future: Perspectives on contemporary human resource management in New Zealand* (pp. 157–171). Auckland, New Zealand: Longman Paul.

Inkson, J. H. K., Henshall, B., Marsh, N., & Ellis, G. (1986). *Theory K: The key to excellence in New Zealand management.* Auckland, New Zealand: David Bateman Ltd.

Irving, D., & Inkson, J. H. K. (1998). *It must be Wattie's: From Kiwi icon to global player.* Auckland, New Zealand: David Bateman.

Jones, D., Pringle, J., & Shepherd, D. (2000). "Managing diversity" meets Aotearoa/New Zealand. *Personnel Review, 29*(3), 364–380.

Knuckey, S., Leung-Wai, J., & Meskill, M. (1999). *Gearing up: A study of best manufacturing practice in New Zealand.* Wellington, New Zealand: Ministry of Commerce.

Lattimore, R. G. (1994). Assessing the international competitiveness of the New Zealand food sector. In M. Bredahl, P. Abbott, & M. Reed (Eds.), *Competitiveness in international food markets.* Boulder, CO: Westview.

Lattimore, R. G. (1997). Deregulation: The New Zealand food industry. In T. Wallace & W. Schroder (Eds.), *Government and the food industry: Economic and political effects of conflict and cooperation.* Boston: Kluwer.

Lealand, G. (1988). *A foreign egg in our nest? American popular culture in New Zealand.* Wellington, New Zealand: Victoria University Press.

Ledingham, P. (1995). The review of bank supervision arrangements in New Zealand: The main elements of the debate. *Reserve Bank Bulletin (RBNZ), 58*(3), 163–171.

Lord, R. G., & Maher, K. J. (1991). *Leadership and information processing: Linking perceptions and performance.* Boston: Unwin Hyman.

Love, P. (1996, September 14). Changing times bring upheaval for financiers. *The Evening Post,* p. 15.

Mansfield, K. (1960). To Stanislaw Wyspianski. In A. Curnow (Ed.), *The Penguin book of New Zealand Verse* (pp. 127–128). Harmondsworth, England: Penguin.

McKinlay, P. (2000, June). *Social responsibility—business challenge.* Paper presented at the Redesigning Resources Conference, Christchurch, New Zealand.

McLauchlan, G., & Morgan, J. (1976). *The passionless people.* Auckland: Cassell New Zealand.

Ministry of Defense. (2001). *Report of the Ministry of Defense for the year ended 30 June 2001.* Wellington, New Zealand: Author.

Ministry of Youth Affairs. (1998). *Options for enhancing the effectiveness of government policy on young people's sexual and reproductive health.* Wellington, New Zealand: Ministry of Youth Affairs Te Tari Taiohi.

Ministry of Youth Affairs. (2002). *Building resilience: Briefing to the incoming minister.* Wellington, New Zealand: Ministry of Youth Affairs Te Tari Taiohi.

Mulgan, J. (1984). *Report on experience.* Auckland, New Zealand: Oxford University Press.

Naipaul, V. (1980). *The return of Eva Peron with the killings in Trinidad.* London: Andre Deutsch.

New Zealand Department of Internal Affairs. (1996). *The dictionary of New Zealand biography 1901–1920* (Vol. 3). Auckland, New Zealand: Auckland University Press.

New Zealand Government. (2001). *Government defense statement: A modern, sustainable defense force matched to New Zealand's needs.* Wellington: Author.

O'Connor, B. P. (2000). SPSS and SAS programs for determining the number of components using parallel analysis and Velicer's MAP test. *Behavior Research Methods, Instruments, & Computers, 32*(3), 396–402.

Office of Treaty Settlements. (2001). *Quarterly report to June 2001.* Wellington, New Zealand: Office of Treaty Settlements Te Tari Whakatau Take e pa ana ki te Tiriti o Waitangi.

Ogilvie, G. (1973). *The riddle of Richard Pearse.* Wellington, New Zealand: AH & AW Reed.

One-third of bank branches closed. (1999, May 5). *The Press,* p. 29.

O'Reilly, T., & Wood, D. (1991). Biculturalism and the public sector. In J. Boston, J. Martin, J. Pallot, & P. Walsh (Eds.), *Reshaping the state: New Zealand's bureaucratic revolution* (pp. 329–342). Auckland, New Zealand: Oxford University Press.

Parry, K. W., & Proctor, S. B. (2000). *The New Zealand Leadership Survey, 1999.* Wellington, New Zealand: Centre for the Study of Leadership, Victoria University.

Pearson, B. (1974). *Fretful sleepers and other essays.* London: Heinemann Educational Books.

Peel, S., & Inkson, J. H. K. (2000). Economic deregulation and psychological contracts: The New Zealand experience. In D. M. Rousseau & R. Schalk (Eds.), *Psychological contracts in employment: Cross-national perspectives* (pp. 195–212). Thousand Oaks, CA: Sage.

Pfeifer, D. (2005). *Leadership in Aotearoa New Zealand: Maori and Pakeha perceptions of outstanding leadership.* Unpublished Master of Management thesis, Massey University, Wellington, New Zealand.

Pfeifer, D., & Love, M. (2004). Leadership in Aotearoa New Zealand: A cross-cultural study. *PRISM, 2.* Retrieved August 30, 2005, from http://praxis.massey.ac.nz/number_2_1.html

Phillips, J. (1989). War and national identity. In D. Novitz & B. Willmott (Eds.), *Culture and identity in New Zealand* (pp. 91–109). Wellington, New Zealand: GP Books.

Rippin, S. (1995). *The competencies used to assess the effectiveness of New Zealand managers.* Unpublished doctoral dissertation, Victoria University of Wellington, Wellington: New Zealand.

Rotherham, F. (1998, September 2). Is the Kiwi corporate culture wrecking our family life? *The Independent.*

Savage, J. (1999). *Savings in New Zealand* (No. 99/1). Wellington, New Zealand: Office of the Retirement Commissioner.

Sinclair, K. (1969). *A History of New Zealand* (2nd ed.). Harmondsworth, England: Penguin.

Singer, M. (1985). Transformational vs transactional leadership: A study of New Zealand company managers. *Psychological Reports, 56,* 816–818.

Smith, T. W., & Jarkko, L. (2001). *National pride in cross-national perspective.* Chicago: National Opinion Research Center, University of Chicago.

Spector, P., Cooper, C. L., Sanchez, J. I., O'Driscoll, M. P., Sparks, K., Bernin, P., et al. (2001). Do national levels of individualism and internal locus of control relate to well-being: An ecological level international study. *Journal of Organizational Behavior, 22,* 815–832.

Statistics New Zealand. (1995). *Facts NZ* (2nd ed.). Wellington, New Zealand: Author.

Statistics New Zealand. (1997). *New Zealand official year book 1997.* Wellington, New Zealand: GP Print.

Statistics New Zealand. (1999). *New Zealand official yearbook on the Web 1999.* Retrieved April 26, 2000, from http://www.stats.govt.nz

Statistics New Zealand. (2001). Retrieved August 29, 2005, from http://www.stats.govt.nz/quick-facts/people/default.htm

Statistics New Zealand. (2002). New Zealand official year book 2002. Wellington, New Zealand: GP Print.

Stephens, R. J., Frater, P. R., & Waldegrave, C. (2000). *Below the line: An analysis of income poverty in New Zealand, 1984–1998.* Wellington, New Zealand: Graduate School of Business and Government Management, Victoria University of Wellington.

Stewart, V. (1981). *Business applications of repertory grid.* London: McGraw-Hill.

Tapsell, S. (1997, October). Is Maori management different? *Management, 44,* 46–50.

Telecom Corporation of New Zealand. (1993). *The Telecom turnaround: The deregulation of the telecommunications industry.* Wellington: Author.

Thomas, D. C., Ravlin, E. C., & Barry, D. (2000). Creating effective multicultural teams. *Auckland University Business Review, 2*(1), 11–24.

Toulson, P. K. (1990). *Perceptions, practices, and productivity: An assessment of personnel management in New Zealand.* Unpublished doctoral dissertation, Massey University, Palmerston North, New Zealand.

Transparency International. (2002). *Corruptions Perceptions Index 2002.* Retrieved January 27, 2003, from http://www.transparency.org/cpi/2002/cpi2002.en.html

Ware, A., & Dewes, K. (2000, September). *Nuclear weapons-free zones: From symbolic gesture to statutory ban: The Aotearoa-New Zealand experience.* Paper presented at the Nuclear Weapons-Free Zones: Crucial Steps Towards a Nuclear-Free World, Uppsala, Sweden.

Watkins, T. (2003, January 9). Big pay rises replace bonus system. *The Dominion Post.*

Watson, L. (1994). *The "tall poppy" myth.* Retrieved January 29, 2003, from soc.culture.new-zealand archives in http://groups.google.co.nz

Wevers & Company. (1994). *The Index of Human Resource Management Performance.* Wellington, New Zealand: Author.

Wevers International Ltd/Centre for Corporate Strategy. (1996). *New Zealand Index of Human Resource Management & Organisational Effectiveness.* Wellington: New Zealand Institute of Management.

Wilson, G. D., & Patterson, J. R. (1968). A new measure of conservatism. *British Journal of Social and Clinical Psychology, 7,* 264–269.

Yergin, D., & Stanislaw, J. (1998). *The commanding heights: The battle between government and the marketplace that is remaking the modern world.* New York: Simon & Schuster.

Appendix A

Background Information on the Food-Processing, Finance, and Telecommunications Industries

In order to improve comparability among the various countries of the GLOBE study, the research was carried out in three selected industries—food processing, financial services, and telecommunications. This section provides brief background material on each sector in New Zealand.

FOOD PROCESSING INDUSTRY

New Zealand, as a temperate country with low population density, has a long history as an agricultural producer and exporter. Its ability to attain high levels of self-sufficiency in food products led to an early emphasis on exporting (Lattimore, 1994). In the late 19th century, export activities were oriented largely toward supplying the British market, and many food-processing companies (especially in the meat sector) were established with British capital (Lattimore, 1997). Today, New Zealand exports of sheep meat account for 54% of the world export trade, and the country is one of the top five dairy exporters in the world (Statistics New Zealand, 1999). New Zealand export industries are dominated by companies in the food and beverage sector (Crocombe, Enright, & Porter, 1991) and, in 1996, food products made up 38.5% of the total value of New Zealand's exports (Statistics New Zealand, 1997).

Acting in the role of "Britain's Farm," New Zealand supplied bulk commodities (such as sheep meat and butter), with little in the way of added-value processing. The guaranteed market (and good returns) meant there was little pressure to develop greater sophistication in food processing, or to enter more competitive markets. At the same time, domestically oriented food-processing industries (such as wheat, bakery, and cereal products) were protected from international competition by a system of state import monopolies, consumer restrictions, and phytosanitary restrictions (Lattimore, 1997).

Britain's entry into the European Common Market during the 1970s meant the loss of New Zealand's largest market for agricultural products and resulted in increased exports to new trading partners, particularly in Asia. Firms have had to develop greater awareness of diverse customer requirements, and make technological innovations to serve them effectively, while adjusting to significantly higher levels of international competition.

Agriculture was one of the first sectors to lose government protection and support during the economic deregulation program that began in 1984. New Zealand is now unique among developed countries in that farmers receive no subsidies from government while having to compete with subsidized production from other producing countries (Statistics New Zealand, 1999).

FINANCIAL SERVICES INDUSTRY

The banking and financial services sector in New Zealand is now highly competitive but it hasn't always been that way. Until the mid-1980s, only four commercial banks operated in the country, and these were subject to governmental controls over their interest rates, investments, and lending portfolios. Other organizations (such as savings banks, building societies, and finance companies) offered a more limited range of banking services, and were also subject to tight government control. Strong restrictions on foreign-exchange transactions effectively protected New Zealand banks from overseas competition, and the lack of any effective competition in the sector meant that little innovation occurred. Ledingham (1995, p. 163) has characterized the sector at this time as being "boringly stable."

The large commercial banks developed multileveled hierarchies and mechanistic cultures appropriate for the stable and predictable environment. They were cautious and conservative, with cultures ill-suited to rapid or radical change (Harris, 1996). During the 1970s and 1980s, competition developed outside the banking sector, with finance companies and other organizations beginning to capture an increasing share of the deposits and lending markets. These institutions lobbied for access to other activities (e.g., foreign-exchange dealing) that government regulations excluded them from. The distinction between banks and nonbanks began to diminish and, in 1984–1985, the government carried out major reforms of the financial sector. Foreign-exchange and interest rate controls were removed, and, in 1986, new banks were allowed to set up in New Zealand. A total of 21 new banks were approved. The government sold the banks that it controlled (1989–1992) and withdrew its explicit guarantee of deposits at trustee savings banks (1988).

During this time banks also had to cope with major changes in technology. The extensive introduction of electronic payments systems, development of new products, and exposure to international innovations placed pressure on managers whose past experience was in a more stable and predictable world.

During the 1990s, the financial sector continued to evolve as a result of pressures to increase cost efficiencies and improve customer service. Large mergers resulted in closure of branches, and staff redundancies, although accelerating uptake of telephone banking, ATMs (automatic teller machines), and other technology, contributed to reduced staffing levels. More than one third of New Zealand's bank branches were closed between 1993 and 1998, with staffing being reduced by 11%. The number of ATMs increased by over 30% in the same period (Harris, 1996; Love, 1996; "One-third of bank branches closed," 1999).

The New Zealand finance sector is now dominated by overseas-owned companies. Three of the five major banks are owned by Australian parent companies, one operates as a branch of an Australian bank, and the other has a British parent.

TELECOMMUNICATIONS INDUSTRY

Prior to April 1, 1987, all telecommunications services, both domestic and international, were provided by the state-controlled New Zealand Post Office. The Post Office's statutory monopoly also extended to the provision of telecommunications equipment, such as domestic telephones and commercial switchboards. In the mid-1980s, New Zealand experienced rapid growth in the demand for telecommunication services, and the national network was severely overloaded. At times it was impossible to get a call through from New Zealand's largest city, Auckland, to the capital, Wellington. Long delays in the provision of telephone services were common, with customers having to wait 6 to 8 weeks for a telephone to be installed (Telecom Corporation of New Zealand, 1993).

In 1986, the Labour government, as part of its economic restructuring programme, split the Post Office into three separate state-owned enterprises. Telecom Corporation assumed responsibility for the telecommunications role, and began operating on April 1, 1987. Telecom's first priority was to restructure the company in preparation for deregulation and eventual competition. The centralized bureaucracy was replaced with a decentralized organization structure and Telecom invested in programs aimed at improving service quality, network reliability, personnel productivity, and profitability. Cost-cutting programs were put into place, a substantial number of jobs were made redundant, and outdated systems were replaced with computerized alternatives (Telecom Corporation of New Zealand, 1993).

In 1990, Telecom Corporation was privatized through sale to a consortium headed by two American telecommunications companies, Ameritech and Bell Atlantic, for over U.S.$2.5 billion. This was the sixth-biggest deal in the world in 1990 and, until recently, the biggest deal in New Zealand history (Hyde, 1991).

Deregulation allowed new competitors into the market, with companies such as Clear Communications, BellSouth, Telstra, and Vodafone seeking to compete in different parts of the domestic, international, and mobile markets. International companies (including Motorola, Nokia, and Ericsson) began selling telecommunications equipment, and New Zealand companies (such as Ben Rumble) entered the retail equipment sales and servicing sector.

In summary, all three of the industries surveyed in this part of the GLOBE project have experienced significant pressures to increase effectiveness and efficiency, as they operate in an environment characterized by increasing competition, greater demands for technology investment, and reduced governmental support and protection.

13

▼▼▼▼▼▼▼

Culture and Leadership in South Africa

Lize A. E. Booysen
University of South Africa

Marius W. van Wyk
University of South Africa

1. HISTORICAL OVERVIEW OF THE CULTURE AND LEADERSHIP IN SOUTH AFRICA

Introduction

South Africa is a land of contrasts (Booysen, 1994; Booysen, 2001, 2005). The country is multicultural and comprises 11 official languages. Though South Africa is a relatively rich land and the economic giant in Africa, it is a developing economy—it has severe shortage of jobs. Almost half of the country's population is without work. With economic, sport, and cultural sanctions lifted, apartheid legislation scrapped, and a new constitution, a truly democratic government was elected in 1994. Despite this, management power resided almost exclusively with White men; in 1994, white men held more than 80% of management positions (Central Statistics Service [CSS], 1995a, 1995b, 1996). A comparison between the 2000 and 2002/2003 Commission for Employment Equity reports shows that whereas there is an increase in the employment of Blacks in management, White men are still overrepresented (Commission for Employment Equity, 2003).

Figure 13.1 depicts the percentage distribution of "legislators" by race and gender. The category "Legislators" refers to decision makers who provide the direction of a critical technical function, such as postmaster, dean, school principal, and so on.

Due to the dominance of White men in management in South Africa, especially in 1995 when this sample was drawn, this chapter is mainly based on a White male sample only. However, some subsequent GLOBE-related research that includes Black as well is discussed in the section Eurocentric Versus Afrocentric Leadership.

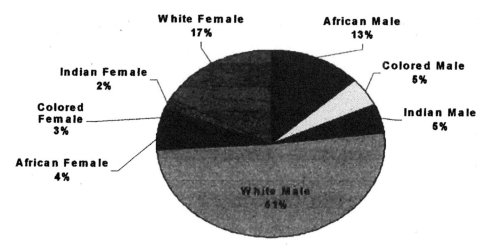

Figure 13.1.   Percentage distribution of legislators by race and gender. From South African Department of Labor. (2003). *Annual Report—Commission for Employment Equity 2002–2003.*

Historical Overview of South Africa[1]

In this section, major historic developments of South Africa and its different groups are highlighted as background.

Prehistory Up to 1652.   Although the debate on the "Out of Africa" hypothesis[2] continues, there is clear evidence that the first group that populated South Africa were the San (colloquially referred to as "Bushmen").[3] These Stone Age people were "hunter-gatherers" and some San communities started keeping cattle and sheep that they acquired from the Bantu-speaking groups. The Khoikhoi (the name used for the pastoralist San) and the San (reserved for that subgroup that remained hunter-gatherers) continued to reside separately, though at the end all merged into one group called Khoikhoi—"Hottentots" according to the Dutch in the 17th century.

Khoikhoi leadership rested with a "khoeque" ("rich man") who was often assisted by a second-in-command. The leadership position passed from father to son. The Khoeque was

---

[1]An overview such as this does not allow the author the luxury of posing opposing views of history, and evaluating these in lengthy scholarly fashion. Given South Africa's history, it is surprisingly difficult to find good reference works that are not biased. This discussion is largely based on a work coauthored by 12 writers with the assistance of a respected historian as historical advisor and a consulting editor, Oakes. The authors are of the opinion that this collaborative effort succeeded in producing a book that is as ideologically neutral as one could hope to find at this juncture in our history.

[2]Major palaeontological discoveries such as the "Tuang child" (in 1924 at Tuang in the northern Cape) and "Mrs. Ples" (in 1947 at Sterkfontein in Gauteng) as well as a wealth of other finds prove that a species of early man inhabited the African continent millions of years ago. Fossilized remains of *Australopithecus Africanus, Homo Habilis, Homo Erectus,* and *Homo Sapiens Sapiens* have been found at a number of sites in South Africa.

[3]The San called themselves "Khoikhoi," which means "men of men" or "real people."

not ostentatious and important decisions and the dispensing of justice was the domain of the chief in conjunction with a council of clan leaders and/or all the male members of the tribe. A Khoeque who abused his authority was quickly sanctioned by the group. A plausible description of the Khoikhoi communities was that of collectivism and egalitarianism. For the San, everything was regarded as communal property until the communities developed into pastoralists, where individual ownership started to emerge (Oakes, 1994, pp. 20–25).

The indigenous Bantu-speaking groups in the northern regions also reared cattle, cultivated crops, mined gold, tin, iron, and copper, and coexisted with the Khoisan tribe peacefully. "Bantu" is the scientific term for the language group to which all indigenous South Africans, except the Khoisan, belong. Two main language subgroups, namely, Nguni and Sotho language groups, can be distinguished, leading to numerous further groupings based on history and tribal loyalties. Members of this language group migrated to the Transvaal and Natal by 300 AD (Oakes, 1994, pp. 26–31).

Historically, White South Africans are descendants from English, Dutch, French, German, and Portuguese settlers. Men of different colors, "Coloreds," who are the descendants of slaves, the indigenous Khoisan people, and White settlers, may be said with some justification to represent the only group that can truly lay claim to being South Africans.

The First Europeans in South Africa. About 500 years ago, the first Europeans visited the eastern and southern African coasts in their quest to find a sea route to the east. Portugal took the lead in these explorations, and in 1488 Bartholomew Dias opened the sea route to the east for Europe by rounding the southernmost tip of Africa. He named the Cape the "Cape of Good Hope." Following Dias, other Portuguese explorers came, such as Vasco Da Gama and De Saldanha. Although the sporadic contact between the European seafarers and the Khoikhoi were mostly of a peaceful commercial nature, clashes continued when the Dutch superseded the Portuguese (cf. Oakes, 1994, pp. 32–35).

The Dutch East India Company established a refreshment station at the Cape of Good Hope in 1652 under the command of Jan van Riebeeck, a merchant. Within 60 years of interaction, the Khoikhoi's social and economic order had been more or less being destroyed. (A major contributing factor was the outbreak of a smallpox epidemic in 1713.)

The Period 1652–1948. Van Riebeeck had strict instructions to preserve peace with the Khoisan. These "Vryburghers" ("free citizens") were not permitted to enslave the local Khoisan. Consequently slaves primarily came from present-day Java, Bali, Timor, Malaysia, Madagascar, China, and parts of India to cultivate the land. In the early years of the colony, many White men married female slaves. Such marriages were later regarded as socially undesirable and the White man was punished. Male chauvinism dictated that White women who indulged in sexual intercourse with male slaves were subjected to criminal sanctions.

From 1660 onward, a new breed of Dutch settlers emerged, namely the "Trekboers," who can be called the first White Africans. They inadvertently caused the official area of the colony to expand, reaching the Great Fish River by 1778. In 1688 French Huguenot, poor, unemployed, and landless refugees arrived in the Cape to further swell the ranks. The defining characteristics of the Trekboers can be encapsulated by the words "fiercely independent," "defiance of authority," "poor," "nomadic," "religious fundamentalism," and "illiterate" (cf. Oakes, 1994, pp. 54–56).

From 1771 onward, the Trekboers came up against the Xhosa. Both groups were mainly cattle farmers and the first of eight "frontier wars" between the colonialists and the Xhosa broke out in 1781.

As a result of political events in Europe, the British colonized the Cape in 1795 until 1802, thereafter a brief return to Dutch rule, and then the British reoccupied the Cape in 1806. Many Dutch colonialists could not accept this and for various other reasons migrated north, which culminated in what became known as the "Groot Trek" (the "Great Trek"). The Great Trek must surely be the single most important origination point of Afrikaner nationalism, "Afrikaner volk" (the other being the Anglo Boer War, battles with indigenous nations, and the emergence of the Afrikaans language). The Trekboers, or "Voortrekkers" (as these migrating Trekboers were called), wanted to establish their own independent state because they saw themselves as the modern version of the biblical people of Israel—the "chosen people." This explains the Voortrekkers' view of the Blacks they encountered on their migration as being heathens.

In successive frontier wars, the British sided with the colonialists against the Xhosa resulting in the latter's final defeat in 1858. In the early 1800s, African societies of Southern Africa were beset by upheavals caused by chieftains fighting each other for political supremacy, cattle, and grazing territory. One such leader was Shaka, generally regarded as the father of the Zulu nation. By the time of Shaka's murder, by his half-brother Dingaan in 1828, the different tribes formed the most powerful and feared military machine in Southern Africa.

In 1854, representative government was granted to the Cape colony. All adult males, irrespective of race, had the franchise provided they occupied property worth at least 25 British pounds. The Black vote (restricted to men) in the Cape Province was later abolished in 1956 by the National Party Government.

In 1854, the Boer Republic of the Orange Free State came into being. In 1860, the Zuid Afrikaansche Republiek (the "South African Republic") was established. By 1870, the Cape colony had 200,000 White inhabitants and the two Boer Republics approximately 45,000. The discovery of diamonds in 1867 near the banks of the Orange River and the Witwatersrand gold strike in 1886 have important consequences, which are listed next.

First, the need for labor and the transformation of the Voortrekker republics' was stimulated. To obtain the necessary labor, Blacks were stripped of their property rights and huts; other taxes were introduced to force them to work on the mines. The embryonic system of migrant labor (which exists to this day) was expanded. Second, the unimaginable mineral wealth of the Boer republics caused the British government to annex the republics. Third, large conglomerates such as De Beers and Anglo American owe their existence to the diamond and gold industry. Fourth, the small White populations of the Boer republics were swelled by the influx of immigrant fortune seekers. Fifth, these immigrants brought with them the notions of trade unionism. The first recorded strike took place in 1871. The trade union movement played a decisive role in the transformation of South Africa in the 20th century.[4]

Two of the people most closely associated with the diamond industry are Barney Barnato and Cecil John Rhodes. Rhodes went on to become the prime minister of the Cape colony. Rhodes, an ardent imperialist, had the vision of constructing a railway from "Cape to Cairo."

---

[4]See the discussion in the subsection A Historical Overview of Industrial Relations in South Africa.

The establishment of new colonies farther to the north (present-day Zambia and Zimbabwe, respectively) can all be traced to Rhodes's imperialist ambitions.

One of the most significant Afrikaner leaders in Afrikaner mythology is Paul Kruger. Kruger was elected as president of the Zuid Afrikaansche Republiek in 1883 and remained head of state until his exile in 1900. Kruger enacted all sorts of preconditions before "Uitlanders" (foreigners) could be granted the franchise. Kruger's effective disenfranchisement caused the British government to invade the Zuid Afrikaansche Republiek. After failed negotiations, war was declared on October 11, 1899—the Anglo-Boer War. After initial victories by the Boer forces, the superior numbers of the British forces began to come. The war then moved into a second phase by the decision of the Boers to avoid pitched battles in favor of guerrilla tactics. These proved highly successful but elicited a vicious response from the British, burning all farms and forcing women and children into concentration camps, where approximately 28,000 Whites died. These inhumane actions provided another impetus for Afrikaner nationalism. African farm workers were also placed in concentration camps, with deaths in these camps totaling at least 14,000. No recognition was given to the Blacks nor was mention ever made of the existence of Black concentration camps. Eventually, on May 31, 1902, a peace treaty was signed at Pretoria, bringing an end to the Anglo-Boer War.

South Africa also has a small but politically influential Indian population. When sugar cane was first produced in Natal in 1851 the farmers lacked a source of cheap labor. Consequently, Indian ("coolie") indentured labor (152,000) was imported between 1860 and 1911 and approximately 52% decided to remain. In addition, some Indians came to Natal at their own expense, mostly as traders. This group formed the elite (commercial) of Indian society. In 1893, a young lawyer came to South Africa. His name was Mohandas Karamchand Gandhi. His ejection from a first-class railway carriage, reserved for Whites, was "the most important factor" for his struggle against racist laws using his philosophy of "passive resistance."

On May 31, 1910, the Cape and Natal colonies united to form the Union of South Africa. The Act of Union excluded Blacks who formed the forerunner of the ANC (African Natinoal Congress), the South African Native National Congress (SANNC), in 1912 . In 1913, the notorious Natives' Land Act was passed by the Union government, which in time meant that Blacks, the majority group, were entitled to a meager 13% of the total land mass of South Africa.

Afrikaners started to rebuild their community around political and financial institutions. Their sense of being unjustly treated only served to fire their nationalism, which culminated in 1948 in victory at the polls.

The Period 1948–1994. "Although total separation on every level between black and white became official policy only after the National Party election victory in 1948, its foundation had been laid nearly half a century previously in a policy then known as segregation—not by Afrikaners but by British Government officials" (Oakes, 1994, p. 312).

It indeed is true that many of the pillars of what later became to be known as "apartheid" (literally meaning "separateness") were laid long before 1948, such as the Mines and Works Act (1913), the Natives' Land Act (1913), the Native Affairs Act (1920), the Natives (Urban Areas) Act (1923), and the Industrial Conciliation Act (1926).

The National Party (NP) won the election in 1948 on promises to preserve White power in general, and Afrikaner power in particular. The NP instituted a battery of legislation, and introduced laws such as the Prohibition of Mixed Marriages Act and the Immorality Act (outlawing sexual and marriage unions between people of different races), the Population Registration Act (allowing for the classification of people according to race), the Group Areas Act and the Reservation of Separate Amenities Act (reserving residential suburbs and public areas for the exclusive use of designated race groups), the Pass laws (requiring Africans to carry "reference books" at all times), and the Bantu Education Act (introducing a system of inferior education for Africans).

The NP government successes at the polling booth can be ascribed to many factors, some of which are: events in the rest of Africa where independence from colonial rule was accompanied by instances of massacres, one-party rule, the ascendancy of dictators, and the adoption of "African socialism"—all of which played in to the hands of a party that built its support on "swart gevaar" ("black danger") propaganda; the economic boom experienced in the country; the cold war between the superpowers; and the increased support of English-speaking White South Africans for the NP.

In the early years, the courts opposed many of the apartheid legislative but the government started to appoint judges sympathetic to its cause. The major surviving achievement of the South African judiciary was the notion that the courts remain a separate branch of the state. A curious characteristic of the NP government was its ostensible respect for the law. It took the government no less than 4 years to achieve its aim of depriving the Coloreds of their vote in the Cape Province.

In 1961 South Africa became a republic, after having left the commonwealth. It was also in this year that the ANC adopted the strategy of the armed struggle. During the 1960s and 1970s the South African economy grew rapidly.

In total an estimated 3.5 million people were uprooted in the name of apartheid. The scheme was that Blacks should realize their political aspirations in Black "homelands" while still being available as inexpensive labor pool. However, apart from being too small to sustain large numbers of inhabitants, the homelands had very little infrastructure and mismanagement. Due to these, an unstoppable stream of Blacks migrated to the cities.

By the late 1980s, South Africa's economy was in tatters and it became clear that although the overthrow of the government was not possible, neither was a decisive victory over the liberation forces. Two events provided a window of opportunity to break this stalemate. First, the events in Eastern Europe removed the perceived threat communism posed; and second, after having suffered a stroke, P. W. Botha, a staunch apartheid regime state president, was replaced by F. W. de Klerk as leader of the government in 1989. On February, 2, 1990, De Klerk announced in parliament that organizations such as the ANC and the SACP would no longer be banned and that Nelson Mandela was to be released from prison, thereby opening the way for negotiating a new democratic constitutional dispensation.

Present-Day South Africa: The Post-Apartheid Era (1994–).   After the first democratic elections in 1994, Nelson Mandela was inaugurated as the first Black state president and leader of South Africa. He served a crucial and vibrant 4 years, then Thabo Mbeki became and still is the president of South Africa.

The ANC is still, however, reaping what it had sowed in the 1980s when it had called for the townships to be made ungovernable. Despite calls from Mandela himself, township residents largely refuse to pay for services such as electricity and municipal services and infrastructural upgrading. Also, in what has become known as the "lost generation" (those school children who abandoned their schooling in the wake of the 1976 riots) poses a major danger to stability with millions of Black adults having very little education.

Unemployment is in excess of 30%; crime and violence remains unresolved impeding economic growth. Violence and killings between ANC and Inkatha supporters continue in the Natal province. Also, whereas the different ethnic groups were united in their struggle against apartheid, indications are that tribalism is now coming to the forefront. Corruption by senior government officials, appointed not on ability but rather as reward for their participation in the struggle, is rife. More worrisome is the ANC's apparent failure to appreciate that for democracy to flourish, a free press and vigorous public debate must be tolerated. The tendency too frequently is for the government to react angrily to well-founded criticism by branding it as "undemocratic," "unpatriotic," or "racist." Under such conditions, elections in South Africa for the foreseeable future will amount to nothing more than a "racial/ethnic census," with the Inkatha Freedom Party drawing its support from Zulus, the White political parties being supported by Whites and Coloreds, and the ANC being supported by Xhosa speakers and some other ethnic groupings.

Despite these negatives, South Africa presently probably has the best government it ever had. Under the constitutional regime adopted as a result of the negotiations between the ANC and the NP that preceded the 1994 elections, South Africa has a model Constitution and a constitutional court with the power to review parliamentary legislation. Also, though much is made of corruption by government officials, this must be placed in context. Under the NP rule corruption was hidden from public scrutiny; under the new Constitution, the corruption is at least exposed.

There is a rapid rise in a new Black elite with considerable pressure being brought to bear on private industry to appoint Blacks and to enter into empowerment deals and joint ventures with Black business. However, due to a rigid labor market and continued trade union militancy, millions of people remain unemployed with little hope that any of the fruits of political liberation will translate into an increased standard of living for them. Further exacerbating the unemployment and crime problems is the fact that large numbers of Africans from the rest of Africa flock to South Africa as illegal immigrants.

In 1996, 57% of the population were living in poverty, two thirds of whom were African black. The general income distribution of South Africa was among the most unequal in the world, and the White per capita income was almost nine times higher than that of Africans. For the first time in history, in August 2001 the total income of the Black majority outstripped the total income of White minority (Census 2003, South African government Web site).

Although whites as a group still hold on a relative basis greater economic power than other groups in South Africa, there are numerous corporate and government initiatives aimed at redressing the economic status of blacks, most notably affirmative action, equal employment opportunities, and Black economic empowerment (BEE) measures.

A *Finance Week* study on the progress of BEE, published April 2005, showed that in regard to the direct and indirect shareholding and control on the Johannesburg Stock Exchange (JSE), South African Whites effectively own and control a little more than 50% of the JSE (Rautenbach, 2005).

As happened elsewhere, one could expect that whereas the disparities in wealth between groups will decrease, the disparities in wealth within the beneficiary groups will increase, because the acts, in all likelihood, will have the affect of benefiting the least disadvantaged among the previously disadvantaged groups, rather than accelerating the absorption of the millions of uneducated poor into the labor market.

South African Demographics.   In this section, some telling demographics of South African society are summarized. The overall picture is one of inequality on a number of

TABLE 13.1
National Demographics by Population Group

Year	Asian	African	Colored	White	Black	Total
1996	1	32.2	3.5	5.2	36.7	41.9
	(3%)	(77%)	(8%)	(12%)	(88%)	(100%)
2001	1.4	35	4.1	4.5	40.5	45
	(2.5%)	(79%)	(8.9%)	(9.6%)	(88%)	(100%)

Note. Numbers are in millions. The term *population groups* is used to designate Asians, Africans, Coloreds, and Whites. The term *Black* is used as a collective noun referring to Asians, Africans, and Coloreds. From A. Roux (1996).

important indicators, which is not surprising given the country's apartheid heritage. However, it is fairly certain that inequalities within the Black group will soon, if this has not already happened, overtake the inequality prevalent in society as a whole. In Table 13.1 the proportional population group composition of the total South African population (1996 and 2001 figures) is depicted.

South African people are still classified by population group. However now, different from in the past, membership of a racial group is based on self-perception and self-classification, not on a legal definition. The total classification of the population in the Census 2001 (Census, 2003) was based on, African Black, 79%, Colored 8.9%, Asian or Indian, 2.5% and White 9.6%. Black Africans constitute more than three-fourths of the total population. There are 53% females and 47% males; we have 31 different cultures, and 45 million people in total.

The educational level of Africans has improved over recent years with proportionally more completing 12 years of schooling (matric) and postmatric qualifications. From the October 1995 Household Survey (CSS, 1995, p. 75) some data regarding levels of education of the population 20 years and older by population group are summarized in Table 13.2.

For the first time, in 1995, the majority of university students were Black, constituting 51% of all university students. This is estimated to increase to 72% by the year 2020. In 1995 Blacks, Coloreds, and Asians made up 63% of university enrollment.

The passing of the Employment Equity Act by Parliament in 1998 should have a major impact on the composition of the labor force in years to come. In terms of the 1998 act, Africans, Indians, Coloreds, women, and people with disabilities must be adequately represented in an employer's labor force so as to reflect the national demographics of the country. Various administrative control measures as well as punitive measures are provided for and employers are required to submit "employment equity plans" and annual reports to account for their efforts in reaching affirmative action goals. Companies that do not comply with the provisions of the act are excluded from public-sector tenders and noncompliance constitutes a material breach of existing contracts. The antidiscrimination provisions of the act are applicable to all employers, whereas the affirmative action provisions are applicable to companies employing 50 or more employees as well as smaller employers whose annual turnover exceeds stipulated maxima, depending on the sectors in which they operate.

A Historical Overview of Industrial Relations in South Africa.   With the discovery of gold and diamonds round about 1867–1870, South Africa entered its own unique industrial

TABLE 13.2
Level of Education by Population Group

Level	African	Colored	Asian	White	Black	Total
Matric (12 years of school)	2,110,000 (51.1%)	268,000 (6.5%)	207,000 (5%)	1,545.000 (37.4%)	2,586.000 (62.6%)	4,131,000 (100%)
Diploma/Certificate with Std. 10	634,000 (48.8%)	78,000 (6.0%)	39,000 (3.0%)	549,000 (42.2%)	751,000 (57.8)	1,300,000 (100%)
Degree	188,000 (28.3%)	24,000 (3.7%)	35,000 (5.4%)	403,000 (62.1%)	246,000 (37.9%)	649,000 (100%)

Note. From 1995 Household Survey data (Central Statistics, 1995).

revolution, due to large numbers of immigrants, industrialization, and the development of unions happened simultaneously. The first union in South Africa, the Society of Carpenters and Joiners, was formed on December 23, 1881. This union had only White members, who were mainly British mine workers. The secondary industries created a large demand for skilled, mainly White, overseas labor. Consequently, White mine workers received high salaries in comparison with the unskilled Black workers and thus color and skill became synonymous. The concept of the "color bar" arose between the mining companies and the White unions. The mining companies tried to lower the requirements into relatively simple tasks so that unskilled (Black) workers could perform them. In this way, the mining companies were able to replace some skilled workers with semiskilled or even unskilled workers. Guild unions protected skills by regulating the admission of apprentices against the huge Black unskilled labor force.

The war with Britain (1899–1902) virtually destroyed the economies of the two Boer Republics by the plundering of farms and the destruction of large numbers of livestock. The White farmers, who were also unskilled or semiskilled, were therefore forced to move to the towns with scarce job opportunities, competing with Black workers who were willing to work for lower wages. This was the beginning of the so-called "poor White" problem. In the 1920s there was a drop in the gold price and a recession in the international and South African economies, which was further worsened by large-scale unemployment among the soldiers who had returned from World War I.

The government introduced relief schemes at the end of 1920 to help the unemployed Whites. In 1920, the Low Grades Mines Commission recommended that the expensive White labor be replaced by Black labor. This caused widespread strikes involving approximately 23,000 White workers. Martial law was declared and bloody fights broke out between strikers and government forces. When the strike ended on March 18, 1922, altogether 247 people had died and the unions were defeated, which resulted in the Smuts government being defeated and replaced by the so-called PACT government with General Hertzog as prime minister. The new government gave preference to the appointment of Whites. The large-scale employment of Whites led to the White labor force being increasingly associated with the political status quo. One of the direct results was the promulgation of the Industrial Conciliation Act, Act 11 of 1924, on March 3, 1924. This act made provision for, among other things: the appointment of industrial councils; the implementation of a system for the registration of unions, employers' organizations, and industrial councils; the exclusion of Black workers (White, Asian, and Colored benefited) from the definition of an "employee" under it. The objectives of the act were to provide for collective bargaining, to prevent or solve industrial disputes, and to create a framework within which unions and employers' organizations could regulate their relations. But exclusion of Black workers polarized the South African labor force into "Black" and "non-Black." The Industrial Conciliation Act was replaced in 1956 by a new act. The following are some of its important provisions: Job reservation gained unequivocal statutory authority; any further registration of racially mixed unions was prohibited; an industrial tribunal was created to hear labor disputes and act as arbitrator; strict restrictions were imposed on the constitutions and finances of unions; and restrictions were imposed on the political activities of unions.

Black workers went on strike countrywide in 1973. For the first time, there was a realization of the actual power of black workers. Because no unions were officially involved in these strikes, it dramatically pointed out the shortcomings in existing Black labor legislation (Finnemore & Van der Merwe, 1986, p.7).

From 1973 to 1977, the real power of unregistered unions grew steadily and employers increasingly recognized and negotiated directly with unregistered unions. Other factors that exerted pressure were the Soweto riots of 1976, overseas disinvestment in South Africa, as well as the growing shortage of skilled workers (Finnemore & Van der Merwe, 1986, p. 8). The strikes of 1973 and the strong growth of unions necessitated the former state president to appointed the Wiehahn Commission of Inquiry into Labor Legislation on June 21, 1977.

One of the most important recommendations made by the commission was that freedom of association had to be granted for all workers: The commission also recommended that all racial prejudice should be removed from the Industrial Conciliation Act, Act 28 of 1956, and more specifically that all workers have absolute freedom, that statutory job reservation be abolished immediately, that certain job reservation measures be removed through consultation between employer and employee parties, that Blacks should be allowed as apprentices, and that an Industrial Court be established with equitable jurisdiction. This last recommendation proved to have far-reaching effects of "unfair labor practice" to confer a myriad of new rights on employees and unions. Furthermore, legal provisions that made it compulsory to have separate amenities for Whites and non-Whites at workplaces were to be repealed. Separate or shared amenities would therefore not be compulsory but be regulated by means of collective bargaining.

The government's reaction to the commission's report was generally positive. The Wiehahn Report empowered the trade union movement (most notably the Congress of South African Trade Unions [COSATU]) to bring pressure to bear on employers and the National Party government to effect political changes.

After the democratic elections in April 1994, a new Labor Relations Act (Act 66 of 1995) came into force. This act extended its ambit to cover almost all workers (the public sector, farm and domestic workers), including job security for employees participating in a legal strike, and awarded further organizational rights to trade unions. It created the Commission for Conciliation, Mediation and Arbitration (CCMA) to speedily resolve labor disputes. The creation of the National Economic, Development and Labour Council (NEDLAC) in which the state, labor, and capital negotiate, formally institutionalized social corporatism in the country.

Today South Africa has one of the most progressive labor law dispensations in the world, although there is concern about unemployment, new jobs, and foreign investment. Other legislative interventions include the Labour Relations Act 1995, which took effect in 1996; the

Constitution of South Africa, 1996; the Basic Conditions of Employment Act in 1997; the Employment Equity (EE) Act and its antidiscrimination provisions, which came into effect on Women's Day, August 9, 1999; the Skills Development Act of 1998; and the Skills Development Levies Act of 1999. The intention of the last two acts is to shift the focus away from only affirmative action appointments to also recruitment, succession planning, and development and training of persons in the designated groups (Blacks and women) and to address the skills gap. These changes were followed by the establishment of the Broad-Based Black Economic Empowerment (BEE) Commission in 1999, and the subsequent strategies and policies set by government and industry alike. The Black Economic Empowerment Act was implemented in 2003 and the Black Economic Empowerment industry charters with proposed quotas for Black ownership and management followed. In 2004, the government sensed disparities and possible clashes between different industry charters and published a draft Code of Practice aimed at providing guidelines to the various branches of industry on how to set up their BEE schemes (Booysen, 2005).

2.   GLOBE STUDIES IN SOUTH AFRICA

Methods and Procedures

The South African data were collected over a 4-year period, from 1994 to 1997. It included the collection of qualitative and quantitative data from junior, middle, and senior White men from one organization in the telecommunications sector (Telkom[5]) and two organizations in the financial services sector (Standard Bank[6] and Sanlam[7]), as well as participant observations, unobtrusive measures, and media analysis on culture and leadership in South Africa. A total of 666 respondents participated in this research, comprising a sample of 232 White male South African managers, 426 management students of mixed race and gender, of which 82% were White men, and 8 South African leadership specialists.

Quantitative Data Collection: September–October 1995.   The collection of the quantitative data with the Societal and Organizational Culture and Leadership Questionnaire was done in September and October 1995. The sample consisted of a total of 183 White men, 130 from the telecommunications sector and 53 from the financial services. The data collection with the Organizational Questionnaires was done in September and October 1996 involving 15 White male senior managers, 5 in each organization sampled. A total of 198 respondents participated in the quantitative research.

Qualitative Data Collection: February 1994– June 1997.   The collection of the qualitative data spanned an entire 4-year period, and included six consecutive measures and four

---

[5]Telkom used to be a public institution accountable to a cabinet minister. In recent years, it was transformed into a company with the government as its only shareholder. It also brought in foreign partners as minority shareholders and in 2003 it became a truly private company when share were sold on the open stock market to individuals. It is a national organization with a monopoly in the telecommunications sector, but the government is presently considering tenders for allowing competitors to enter this sector.

[6]Standard Bank is one of the three largest banks in South Africa and operates nationally.

[7]Sanlam is the second-largest life insurer in South Africa and was started in the first half of the previous century as art of the Afrikaners' effort to uplift Afrikaners. It used to be perceived as an Afrikaans organization serving the interest of members of this group. This has changed in recent years. The company operates nationally.

different data collection techniques. A total of 468 respondents participated in the qualitative research.

Pilot Focus Groups and Interviews: February 1994.   The preliminary qualitative pilot data, in the form of focus groups, was collected in February 1994. A total of 70 focus groups were conducted involving 430 management students, who were representative of all nine provinces in South Africa and included Blacks and women as well. Ten white men were randomly selected from the 70 focus groups for in-depth individual interviews.

In-Depth Focus Groups and Interviews: March 1994.   These pilot data were used as input to focus group and individual interviews with 20 White male middle managers representative of the nine provinces of South Africa.

Two in-depth focus groups, with seven participants per group were held, together with six individual interviews. In preparation for the focus group discussions, the participants had to complete the "Management Effectiveness Exercise," which provided each participant with an opportunity to express his own views on behavior that distinguishes outstanding leaders from competent managers. During the focus group the participants had to: (a) discuss the terms *leadership* and *management,* (b) define these two terms, (c) list the attributes that distinguish outstanding leaders from competent managers, and (if time permitted) (d) describe how managers in their culture differ from managers in another country that is a major trading partner.

Six individual interviews were held. The purpose of the individual interviews was to explore, in some depth, how South African middle managers define leadership implicitly and explicitly. After an explanation of the study, the interviews were conducted by means of an interview schedule, which included the following 10 questions:

1. The first question concerns the difference between competent managers and outstanding leaders. What do you see this difference to be?
2. Now we are interested in your perception of the opposite of outstanding leadership. If the person is in the position of leadership and does not exercise outstanding leadership, what would be the kinds of behaviors in which they engage?
3. Can you think of a critical incident that illustrates outstanding leadership?
4. Can you think of another such incident?
5. Were there any obstacles or constraints faced by the leaders in these incidents? Any opposition, resistance, bureaucratic red tape, or lack of resources, for example.
6. Can you think of two or three well known outstanding leaders? Who are they? (7) Is there anything that these leaders have in common that make them outstanding and that distinguishes them from others who have been in similar positions?
8. How is the behavior of these leaders similar?
9. Can you think of a specific behavior, something each leader did, that illustrates his or her leadership?
10. Can you think of something a leader did that resulted in your strong acceptance or support of the leader, or in significantly increased motivation on your part, or in willingness to go above and beyond the call of duty in the interest of the leader's vision, objective, or mission?

Intensive Individual Interviews: March–November 1995.   Ten White male middle managers were selected from the three organizations; in-depth and follow-up interviews were held. The purpose of the in-depth individual interviews was to further explore, in more depth, how South African middle managers define leadership implicitly and explicitly to ascertain their implicit leadership models. The interviews were taped, transcribed, and content analysis was done.

Unobtrusive Measurement and Participant Observations: November 1996. The unobtrusive measures and participant observations were intended to explore the South African environment and to identify implicit indicators indicative of the prominence of specific leader dimensions comparable to others. These data were collected by means of the Unobtrusive Measurement Questionnaire and Participant Observation Questionnaire. The two questionnaires were conducted on eight leadership specialists; a content analysis followed.

Media Analysis: May–June 1997. The sample for the media analysis comprised the following newspapers, business periodicals, and industry-specific journals over the period May 21 to June 20, 1997: *The Star* (the largest English-language daily newspaper in South Africa with a circulation area covering the economic hub of the country, primarily Gauteng province, but also with a circulation in a number of other provinces); *The Sunday Independent* (an English-language Sunday paper with a national circulation); *The Financial Mail* (an English-language weekly business periodical with a national readership); *Finansies en Tegniek* (an Afrikaans language weekly business periodical with a national readership); *The Sowetan* (the largest English-language newspaper focused on a Black readership with a circulation primarily in the Gauteng province); and an in-house publication of each of the three organizations used as representative of the financial and telecommunications industries respectively.

For this phase of the research project, use was made of two research assistants who, independently of each other, identified and coded relevant quotations from the media sample. Their respective coded texts were then compared and in the case of differences between the two research assistants, a quotation was included in the final database only if the researchers could reach consensus on the relevance of the quotation and the appropriateness of its coding. An initial list of "code filters" (i.e., a list of key terms used to identify and code quotations) was generated by one of the authors for use by the research assistants. This initial list was generated by scanning a presample from the selected newspapers and periodicals. Words and phrases that appeared frequently in the media were noted, as well as using the definitions of the GLOBE Societal Culture Dimensions and Leadership Attributes as guidelines and combining these two for a total of 74 potential code filters. This initial list was refined and consolidated into a final one, but only after a dummy run had been executed by the research assistants in order to determine the completeness and relevance of the initial list.

The media analysis was accomplished by making use of the "Atlas" software program. "Atlas" is a computer-aided text interpretation and theory-building software package. The program serves as a powerful utility for qualitative analysis of large bodies of text. The media sample yielded a total of 1207 usable quotes that were linked to 55 code filters. As the last step in the media analysis, one of the authors performed a content analysis on this coded database to group the coded data into a more manageable number of clusters that cohered on a conceptual level. Groupings of quotations that did not fit these schemas and comprised only a small number of quotations were discarded at this stage. Essentially an inductive methodology was used by referring to the GLOBE Societal Culture Dimensions and the Leader Attributes. This second-order coding yielded a number of clusters that were ranked in terms of the total number of quotations each contained. The data were then ranked and compared with the South African rankings of the GLOBE Societal Culture Dimensions and Attributes.

3.   SOCIETAL CULTURE: SOUTH AFRICA

This section focuses on the results of the Societal Culture of South Africa and then on the results of the Leadership dimension in South Africa. The quantitative results of the GLOBE project are discussed and supplemented with the qualitative data, namely focus group and individual interview data, participant observations, unobtrusive measures, and media analysis of the cultural dimensions and leadership encountered in the South African society.

Cross-cultural leadership studies clearly show that cultural differences influence individual expectations and assumptions about management (Dorfman, 1996; Hofstede, 1980, 1991, 1994; House, Wright, & Aditya, 1997) and that those management philosophies typically evolve in harmony with the cultures within which they function. However, it is evident from the earlier historical overview that even though South Africa is a complex amalgam of several cultures and subcultures, the South African management and leadership philosophies did not evolve in harmony with all the cultures and subcultures in South Africa. In fact, for historical reasons it evolved in line with Western thinking and the dominant management practices today are Anglo-American, as practiced by the dominant White male group in management.

The manifestation of the nine cultural dimensions as reviewed in House et al. (2004) (see also chap. 1, this volume) in South African White male leadership is discussed next. The quantitative GLOBE results are discussed and supplemented with results from participant observations, unobtrusive measures, and media analysis of the respective cultural dimensions.

Results From Quantitative Study

The South African (White sample) scores and ranks for the nine societal cultural dimensions are provided in Table 13.3. GLOBE distinguishes perceptions of societal cultural practices ("As Is") and perceptions of societal cultural values ("Should Be").

Assertiveness.   South Africa shows well above average levels of Assertiveness and is ranked 8th out of 61 countries on this dimension. South Africa falls in the Band A with countries like Germany (East 4, West 10), Hong Kong (5), Austria (6), El Salvador (7), Greece (9), United States (10), and Turkey (12). Albania (1), Nigeria (1), and Hungary (2) measured higher on Assertiveness than South Africa; Japan (58), French Switzerland (59), New Zealand (60), and Sweden (61) measured the lowest on Assertiveness.

South Africa's "Should Be" score of 3.69 on Assertiveness ranks average but is much lower than the "As Is" score. The South African "As Is" score ranked 34, which is also average and which indicates that South Africans are of the opinion that they are probably too assertive.

Institutional Collectivism.   Higher scores on this dimension reflect the degree to which organizational and societal institutional practices encourage and reward collective distribution of resources and collective action. Essentially it reflects a society's level of autonomy versus

TABLE 13.3
South Africa (White Sample): Societal Cultural Dimensions

Dimensions	Society "As Is"			Society "Should Be"			Dev.
	Score	Band	Rank	Score	Band	Rank	
Assertiveness	4.60	A	8	3.69	B	24	0.91
Institutional Collectivism	4.62	A	11	4.38	C	43	0.24
Future Orientation	4.13	B	19	5.66	B	26	1.53
Performance Orientation	4.11	B	30	6.23	B	13	2.12
Uncertainty Avoidance	4.09	B	32	4.67	B	32	0.58
Power Distance	5.16	B	35	2.64	C	38	−2.52
Gender Egalitarianism	3.27	B	35	4.60	B	30	1.33
In-Group Collectivism	4.50	B	48	5.91	B	16	1.41
Humane Orientation	3.49	D	54	5.65	B	8	2.16

Note. Score: Country mean for South Africa on the basis of aggregated scale scores. *Band:* Letters A to D indicate the country band Austria belongs to (A > B > C > D). Countries from different Bands are considered to differ significantly from each other (GLOBE test banding procedure, cf. Hanges, Dickson, & Sipe, 2004). *Rank:* South Africa's position relative to the 61 countries in the GLOBE study; Rank 1 = highest; Rank 61 = score. *Dev.:* The "Deviation Score" was computed by subtracting "As Is" scores from the respective "Should Be" scores. A positive difference indicates that the society wishes to have more of a particular attribute or dimension whereas a negative score indicates the opposite.
[a]A scale's score within-country position compared to the other scales on the same level.

collectivism. With a score of 4.62 and a ranking of 11th, South Africa is well above average on the scale and slightly to the top end of the Band A countries on this dimension. Countries grouped in the same cluster as South Africa include, among others, China (7), Philippines (8), Finland (9), Ireland (9), Zambia, (12), Malaysia (12), and Taiwan (14). It seems as if there is a relatively high degree of integration into groups, within organizations and society, in South Africa. Sweden (1), South Korea (2), Japan (3), and Singapore (4) scored higher than South Africa on the Institutional Collectivism dimension. The countries that scored the lowest on this dimension include Greece (61, Hungary (60), Germany (GRD) (59) and Argentina (58).

Future Orientation.   The essence of this dimension is preoccupation with the future rather than the present and delay of gratification in the interest of future growth, development, or rewards. Higher scores on this dimension indicate a greater degree of Future Orientation. With a score of 4.13 and a ranking of 19, these results indicate a well above average degree of Future Orientation. On this dimension, South Africa is grouped in Band B with such countries such as Finland (14), India (15), Philippines (16), United States (16), Nigeria (19), Australia (19), Hong Kong (21), and Ireland (22). The cluster of countries scoring higher than South Africa on the Future Orientation dimension includes Singapore (1), Switzerland (2), the Netherlands (4), and Malaysia (5). Countries scoring lower than South Africa on this dimension include Poland (59), Argentina (60) and Russia (61). As is generally true for most participating countries, South Africans desire a greater degree of Future Orientation (deviation score = 1.53).

Performance Orientation. Higher scores on this dimension indicate a greater Performance Orientation (i.e., the degree to which a collective encourages and rewards group members for performance improvement and excellence). The ranking of 30th on the "As Is" scale (out of a total of 61 countries) indicate that (White) South Africans are well in the midrange of Performance Orientation grouped together (in Band B) with countries such as Japan (25), Ecuador (27), Zambia (28), Costa Rica (29), France (30), Mexico (32), East Germany (33) and England (34), but South Africans score below such countries like Switzerland (1), Singapore (2), Hong Kong, (3) and Albania (4), and above countries like Hungary (58), Russia (59), Venezuela (60), or Greece (61). Also of interest is the fact that South Africans wish that they were much more achievement oriented (deviation score = 2.12). This desire for a society that is more achievement oriented is in line with the overall GLOBE results and indicates that, generally speaking, most countries want more emphasis placed on achievement in their society.

Uncertainty Avoidance. Uncertainty Avoidance is defined by GLOBE as the extent to which a society relies on social norms and procedures to alleviate the unpredictability of future events. Higher scores on this dimension indicate an aversion to uncertainty (leading to uncertainty-avoiding behavior), whereas lower scores indicate tolerance for uncertainty. With a score of 4.09 and a ranking of 32, South Africa lies on the average of participating countries for this dimension, and at the very bottom of Band B. Sharing Band B on this dimension with South Africa are countries such as Mexico (26), Indonesia (27), Zimbabwe, India, and the United States, all sharing 28, and Zambia (31). The countries that have a higher intolerance for uncertainty, besides South Africa, include Switzerland (1), Sweden (2), Singapore (3), and Denmark (4). The deviation score of 0.58 represents the lowest one for all deviation scores (see Table 13.3). Given the sociopolitical turmoil endemic in South Africa at the time, this is quite remarkable.[8] Intuitively one would have thought that White South Africans at that time would have wanted a greater degree of certainty, rather than being relatively quite relaxed about the future. However, in comparison with the other sample countries, South Africa is ranked in the middle range (32) for this dimension. Maybe this provides a clue as to why the majority of White South Africans were prepared to endorse the revolutionary changes initiated by the De Klerk Government in the early 1990s.

Power Distance. The essence of this dimension is the establishment and maintenance of dominance and control of the less powerful by the more powerful. Higher scores on this dimension indicate a greater degree of Power Distance. Compared to the other participating countries, South Africa scores just below average on this dimension with a score of 5.16. However, this score is still well above the midpoint of 3.5 on the 7-point scale used to measure this dimension. Generally, most participating countries' score on this dimension reflects a perception that Power Distance is high in most countries. Even the country that scores lowest on this dimension, Denmark, weighs in with a score above the midpoint on the 7-point scale, at 3.89. South African society is ranked 35 and is located in the top of the Band B countries,

---

[8]Booysen's subsequent research shows the score on this scale to be significantly higher with a score of 5.11 in 1999. This might indicate that White South Africans were possible, in line with change management theory (Van Tonder, 2004), in denial about the future changes in 1994 when the GLOBE data were collected and more in line with the reality in 1999.

alongside other such countries as Georgia (30), Taiwan (32), Indonesia (33), Malaysia (34), England (36), Ireland (36), Kuwait (38), and Japan (39). Countries with a lower level of Power Distance than South Africa include Denmark (61), the Netherlands (59), Bolivia (58), and Albania (57). The high deviation score of −2.52 indicates a desire for a society that is less stratified and lends further support to the inference that South Africans regard their society as being more stratified than egalitarian, and wishing that we were a more egalitarian society.

Gender Egalitarianism.   Medium scores on this dimension indicate a weak emphasis on gender equality (in the sense of equality for male and female roles). Whereas low scores indicate an emphasis on the male role. High scores indicate a stronger emphasis on egalitarianism. With a score of 3.27 and a ranking of 35, South African society falls slightly below average on this dimension, indicating a slight propensity for the male role. Band B countries grouped together with South Africa on the Gender Egalitarianism dimension include Finland (31), Thailand (31), United States (33), Brazil (34), Indonesia (36), Italy (37), New Zealand (38), and Ireland (39). The cluster of countries that exhibit a greater degree of female orientation compared to South Africa include Hungary (1), Russia (12), Poland (3), and Slovenia (4).

Countries in which greater emphasis is placed on the male role include Zambia (57), Morocco (58), Egypt (59), Kuwait (60), and South Korea (61). The deviance score of 1.33 indicates that South Africans are aware that they should give more encouragement and recognition to female roles.

In-Group Collectivism.   Higher scores on this dimension indicate the degree to which individuals express pride, loyalty, and cohesiveness in their organization or families. With a score of 4.50 and a ranking of 48, South Africa is below the country average on this dimension. Countries grouped in the Band B with South Africa include Israel (44), Japan (45), Germany (GDR) (46), Namibia (46), and France (49). Countries such as the Philippines (1), Georgia (2), Iran (3), and India (4) scored higher than South Africa on the In-Group Collectivism dimension. The cluster of countries that scored the lowest comprises the Netherlands (58), New Zealand (59), Sweden (60), and Denmark (61). The deviation score of 1.41 could be interpreted as a desire for a more In-Group Collectivist orientation and that White South Africans yearn for a society with a greater degree of integration of the individual into small groups and the organization.

Humane Orientation.   Higher scores on this dimension indicate a more Humane Orientation. South Africa is not perceived as a caring or humane society. With a score of 3.49 and a ranking of 54, South Africa is grouped in the Band D together with such countries as Italy (51), Poland (52), Switzerland (53), Singapore (54), Germany (former GDR) (56), France (56), and Hungary (58). The countries that scored lower on the Humane Orientation dimension than South Africa are Germany FRG (61), Spain (60), and Greece (59).

Of all the dimensions, the lack of a more Humane Orientation prevalent in society is most keenly felt by South Africans (deviation score of 2.16). Countries that scored higher than South Africa on this dimension are Zambia (1), Philippines (2), Ireland (3), and Malaysia (4).

Results From Media Analysis

In this section, the South African results of the participants' observations, unobtrusive measures, and media analysis, based on the cultural dimensions, are discussed. The ranked data from the

TABLE 13.4
Comparison of Media Analysis Data With GLOBE Cultural Dimensions (Ranking)

Culture Dimensions	"As Is"	"Should Be"	Media Analysis	Sum of Ranks
Performance Orientation	4	1	2	7
Future Orientation	3	3	1	7
Institutional & In-Group Collectivism	2	2	4	8
Power Distance	1	7	3	11
Uncertainty Avoidance	5	5	6	16
Humane Orientation	6	4	7	17
Gender Egalitarianism/ Assertiveness	7	6	5	18

Note. "As Is" and "Should Be" rankings were obtained by ranking the scores of South Africa on the different cultural dimensions. Rankings from media analysis were obtained on the basis of relative frequencies per category (at the time of media analysis there were only seven GLOBE dimensions, with Gender Egalitarianism and Assertiveness as one dimension and Institutional and In-Group Collectivism as one). Sum of Ranks are used as an indicator of cultural emphasis (the lower the number the higher the relative emphasis).

media analysis are summarized and compared with the South African internal rankings of the GLOBE Societal Culture Dimensions, "As Is" and "Should Be" categories in Table 13.4.

Performance Orientation.   The qualitative data are in accordance with the quantitative data that the South African society places a high premium on the Performance Orientation dimension. From Table 13.4 it can be seen that the media analysis indicates that it is the second highest-ranked cultural dimension. The quantitative data suggest that the Performance Orientation dimension is ranked the fourth highest in South African culture and the desire is that it should be the highest ranking.

Future Orientation.   Future Orientation is ranked as the most prevalent cultural dimension in the media analysis, and it is ranked as third most important in both the "As Is" and "Should Be" categories in the quantitative study. The slightly higher ranking in the media analysis may be ascribed to the emphasis that the South African media placed on the future of South Africa in the years directly after the 1994 elections.

Individualism/Collectivism.   Regarding Individualism/Collectivism, Table 13.4 indicates that it is ranked fourth most important in the media analysis, and even though South Africa scored well below average on this dimension, it is rated as the second most important dimension in the quantitative analysis. It should be taken into account that, when this analysis was done, the scores of Institutional and In-Group Collectivism were still conflated in one dimension, Collectivism.

Power Distance.   Power Distance is ranked 1 in the "As Is" category and 7 in the "Should Be," whereas it is ranked third in the media analysis. Thus, both the quantitative data and the media analysis indicate that South Africans regard our society as highly stratified. The emphasis in our Constitution on the value of equality reinforces the notion that South Africans are very conscious of the need to transform our society into a more egalitarian one.

Uncertainty Avoidance. Uncertainty Avoidance is ranked 6 in the media analysis and 5 in the quantitative data.

Humane Orientation. The quantitative and qualitative data indicate that South Africans perceive their society as less humane. The media analysis ranking for this dimension placed it seventh, and the "As Is" ranking is sixth, whereas the "Should Be" ranking is fourth. The greater emphasis found in the media analysis may be an artifact of the nature of mass-circulation newspapers: Stories of atrocities are more likely to be published to promote circulation figures than Good Samaritan stories. Nevertheless, the quantitative data support the inference that South Africans wish that our society was more humane.

Gender Egalitarianism/Assertiveness. Regarding Gender Egalitarianism, the results show that the cultural emphasis on this dimension is rather low. Both the quantitative data and media analyses indicate that South Africa is a masculine society. The slight difference between the media analysis and "Should Be" rankings is possibly a function of the difference in the sample. Whereas the quantitative data was limited to a sample of White males from management (which is dominated by men), the media analysis represented all population groups in South Africa and didn't focus purely on management. Note that when this analysis was done the Assertiveness and Gender Egalitarian scores were still conflated in the Masculinity/Femininity Dimensions.

SUMMARY

In summary, the White male South Africans ranked 8 out of 61 countries on Assertiveness with well above average levels of assertiveness, however their "As Is" score indicates that they are of the opinion that they are probably too assertive. They ranked 30 and are above average on the Performance Orientation dimension, and they wish that they were much more achievement oriented. A national trait that exemplifies South African's need for achievement is the national obsession with sporting victories and individual achievement in other walks of life.

They ranked 19 on the Future Orientation dimension, scoring well above average; a desire for a greater degree of Future Orientation also emerged. Long-term, short-term, and scenario planning is an everyday event in South African organizations.

South Africa is a masculine society, and indeed management is still dominated by (White) men. In terms of Gender Egalitarianism, South Africans Ranked 35, and fall slightly below average on this dimension; the "Should Be" score indicates that South Africans are mildly aware that they should give more encouragement and recognition to female roles.

South Africa scored relatively low on Humane Orientation, and is not perceived as a caring or humane society (they Ranked 54), however, they are acutely aware of this and wish to move toward a much higher level of Humane Orientation.

Compared to the other participating countries, South Africa scores above average on Power Distance, and is ranked 35. Even though this score is well above the midpoint on the scale, which indicates a high level of Power Distance, the high deviation score indicates a desire for a society that is less stratified and more egalitarian.

South Africa scored above average and ranked 11 on the Institutional Collectivism dimension and ranked 48 with a score of 4.50 on In-Group Collectivism. White male South Africans yearn for a society with a greater degree of integration of the individual into groups and communities.

South Africa ranked 32 and measured average for Uncertainty Avoidance with little difference shown between the "As Is" and "Should Be" scores. The traditional South African organization is noted for its many rules, regulations, and procedures for almost every possible event and contingency.

4.   LEADERSHIP: SOUTH AFRICA

In this section, a brief review of the literature and prior research on leadership in South Africa is given. The quantitative results of the GLOBE project are discussed and supplemented with the focus group and in-depth individual interview data and media analysis.

Prior Research on Leadership in South Africa

Binedell (1992) claims that management philosophies typically evolve in harmony with the cultures within which they function. However, although South Africa is a complex amalgam of several cultures and subcultures, for historical reasons, the dominant management practices are Anglo-American. The South African leadership context is furthermore marred by the socialized assumptions: "White is right," "West is best," and "Think manager, think male" (Lessem, 1994, 1996; Potgieter, 1996; Sonn, 1996; Steyn & Motshabi, 1996). The leadership picture is made even more complex and biased by the skewed representations of managers in terms of the population groups, as already discussed. In the majority of cases, the South African male manager's first experience of leadership and organizational life was during national military service. This situation prompts Christie (1996, p. 35) to say, *"Unfortunately, my view is that the expression 'You're in the army now' applies as strongly in the business sphere as it does in the South African National Defense Forces."* Suffice it to say that, because of the exclusivity of the then national service, similar experiences and value systems are not shared by the majority White women or members of other groups in South Africa.

Leadership research in South Africa is not abundant, which made this review problematic. Prior to De Klerk, South African (political) leaders were seen as strong men who took unilateral decisions with scant regard for consensus seeking (Grobler, 1996; Khoza, 1994; Madi, 1995; Manning, 1997; Sonn, 1996). Grobler points out that the future leaders of companies in South Africa should reflect the population composition of the country, and that the leadership philosophy should be aimed at the future and at achievement based on partnership. He continues by saying that the days of autocratic leadership have gone forever—the concepts of demand and control are simply no longer acceptable. Leadership must include elements such as integrity, fairness, democracy, empowerment, broad consultation, respect for the individual, and sensitivity for cultural diversity. Grobler concludes by saying that *"the future leader must also be caring, show empathy, be willing to serve, and recognise human worth"* (p. 11).

In preliminary research done by Booysen and Van Wyk (Booysen, 1994) on the preferred leadership style of effective leaders in South Africa, they analyzed focus group discussions that involved the participation of 430 first-year Masters in Business Leadership students (all working managers) and 20 middle managers in South Africa. They found that outstanding leaders in

South Africa are perceived to show a strong and direct, but democratic and participative, leadership style. They are perceived to be agents of change, visionaries, and individualists. This indicates a preference for a transformational leadership style. Although they are regarded as moderately charismatic, they are seen as being responsible, rather than as agitators.

These preliminary results indicate that South African leaders are also perceived as being sensitive to their followers' needs and are expected to reflect their followers' ideas, satisfy their needs, and be respectful and understanding. South African leaders are expected to be pragmatic and creative. By utilizing their interpersonal skills and knowledge, they are expected to be reactive as well as proactive, depending on their analysis of any given situation.

Charlton's (1993, pp. 83–93) findings, in his research into 20 of the most senior leaders and 40 of their followers in a large financial organization in South Africa, corresponds with those of Booysen and Van Wyk. He found that excellent South African leaders have superb interpersonal skills, exhibit candor, and delegate authority, which empowers employees. They openly share goals and values that allow collaborative individualism. He also emphasizes the ability of the South African manager to be competent in self-management, self-aware, and committed to self-development, growth, and personal mastery. They also exhibit an internal locus of control.

Charlton (1993, p. 60) maintains that excellent leaders distinguish themselves through five competencies of vision, namely:

- They develop and communicate a clear future vision.
- They expect uncompromising standards of excellence and pursue improvement on previous standards.
- They create focus and transmit clarity concerning expectations.
- They express a sense of mission that catches attention, inspires commitment, and transforms purpose into action.
- They seek to understand current reality.

He adds that there is a link between the aforementioned strategies and the leader's ability to manage him or herself. This involves diagnosing inappropriate or ineffective behavior and assuming personal responsibility for learning, productive growth, and change. He also argues that a business leader needs to create an empowering environment in which followers are willing or motivated, able or trained, and are allowed the responsibility and authority to perform to their potential. Charlton concludes by saying, *"empowerment is both a consequence (indication) and competence of effective leadership"* (p. 5).

Godsell (in Charlton, 1993) expresses the opinion that in South Africa, particularly with its multiculturalism and its multilingual workforce, superb communication is of paramount importance, not only from leaders, but on all levels within and between management and employees.

There is no doubt that affirmative action programs have, and will continue to, lead to more cultural diversity in the South African workforce. On the other hand, researchers have identified that a by-product of diverse workplaces is distrust, negative attitudes toward diversity, and perceived barriers to successful careers for newly disaffected groups. Although the resistance, resentment, and aggression shown toward management by a certain faction of workers must be taken into account, the fears and uncertainties of others must also be considered (Human, 1996; Kemp, 1994; Makwana, 1994; Manning, 1997a; 1997b).

These are among the critical human resources issues that South African leaders must confront in the future. On the one hand, they must meet the needs of a culturally diverse workforce that comprises a massive contingent of illiterate, unskilled, and semiskilled people (mainly Black), whereas on the other hand, accommodate an educated, highly skilled workforce comprising mainly Whites. They will need to get people of different cultures and backgrounds together to negotiate and participate. South Africans have to come to terms with each other's cultural differences, acknowledge them, put them into perspective, and discover the strengths and weaknesses in different ideologies. Only if South African managers succeed in resolving these issues can they improve the aggregate potential of South African organizations—through creating the best prospects of unity through diversity (Avolio, 1995; Booysen & Beaty, 1997; Human, 1996; Khoza, 1994; Madi, 1995; Manning, 1996, 1997a, 1997b; Mbigi, 1997).

Results of THE Quantitative Study

The GLOBE leader attribute questionnaire (House et al., 2004) asked respondents to indicate the attributes (traits or behaviors) that they think distinguish highly effective leaders from others. The leader attribute questionnaire includes a number of attribute items relevant to the seven societal dimensions, plus four additional theoretical leadership attribute dimensions: leader integrity, leader generalized competence, leader value orientation, and leader clarity of direction. This section of the questionnaire measures 21 primary factors and 6 distinct second-order factors (cf. House et al., 2004).

Table 13.5 depicts the first- and second-order leadership dimensions as well as the ranking of South Africans (White sample) on the second-order leadership factors compared to the other countries.

From Table 13.5 it is can be seen that in terms of South Africa's own scores, South Africa's highest score is on Charismatic leadership (5.99), the second highest is on the Team-Oriented leadership (5.80), the third highest score is on Participative leadership (5.62), the fourth highest score is on Humane leadership (5.33), the fifth highest score is on Autonomous leadership (3.74), and the lowest score is on Self-Protective leadership (3.19). White male South African leaders perceive themselves as having very high levels of charisma, team orientation, and participation, a high level of humaneness, and lower levels of self-protection and autonomy in their leadership approach.

When South Africa is compared to the 61 other countries, the rankings look as described in the following subsections.

Charismatic Leadership. Even though South Africa's highest score is on Charismatic leadership, it ranked only 19 on this leadership dimension, and it is the third-highest South African ranking compared to the other countries. Other countries that ranked similar to South Africa are Brazil, Denmark, and Guatemala, all ranking 16 with scores of 6.00. The Netherlands, Italy, and Argentina all ranked 20 with scores of 5.98. The countries that ranked the highest on the Charismatic leadership dimension are Ecuador (1 with a score of 6.46), Philippines, (2 with a score of 6.33), and Israel (3 with a score of 6.23).

Team Oriented Leadership. South Africa's second-highest score is on Team Oriented leadership (5.80). Even though this score is well above average and can be seen as high, South Africa is ranked only 31, quite average in terms if the other countries on this dimension, and the fourth-highest ranking compared to the other countries. Countries that scored higher than South Africa are Ecuador (6.21, Rank 1), Brazil (6.17, Rank 2), Greece (6.12, Rank 3), and

TABLE 13.5
First- and Second-Order Leadership Dimensions (South Africa White Sample)

Second-Order Leadership Scales First-Order Subscales	Score	Band	Rank Between Countries	Rank Within Country[a]
Charismatic leadership	**5.99**	B	19	1
Integrity	*6.35*		*14*	*1*
Inspirational	*6.33*		*16*	*2*
Performance Orientation	*6.01*		*37*	*6*
Visionary	*6.15*		*27*	*3*
Decisive	*6.07*		*15*	*4*
Self-Sacrificial	*5.01*		*31*	*12*
Team Oriented leadership	**5.80**	B	31	2
Diplomatic	*5.43*		*36*	*9*
Team Integrator	*5.61*		*23*	*8*
Administratively Competent	*5.74*		*34*	*7*
Collaborative Team Oriented	*6.02*		*28*	*5*
Malevolent (reverse scored)	*1.81*		*24*	*(21)*
Participative leadership	**5.62**	B	16	3
Nonparticipative (reverse scored)	*2.46*		*43*	*(18)*
Autocratic (reverse scored)	*2.30*		*47*	*(19)*
Humane leadership	**5.33**	A	7	4
Humane	*5.35*		*8*	*10*
Modesty	*5.33*		*14*	*11*
Autonomous leadership	**3.74**	C	40	5
Autonomous	*3.74*		*40*	*14*
Self-Protective leadership	**3.19**	E	45	6
Status Conscious	*3.78*		*46*	*13*
Conflict Inducer	*3.69*		*44*	*15*
Procedural	*3.53*		*46*	*16*
Face Saver	*2.78*		*33*	*17*
Self-Centered	*2.10*		*31*	*20*

Note. *Score:* Country mean for South Africa on the basis of aggregated scale scores. *Band:* Letters A to D indicate the country band Austria belongs to (A > B > C > D >). Countries from different Bands are considered to differ significantly from each other (Globe test banding procedure, cf. Hanges, Dickson, & Sipe, 2004). *Rank:* South Africa's position relative to the 61 countries in the GLOBE study; Rank 1 = highest; Rank 61 = score. *Dev.:* The "Deviation Score" was computed by subtracting "As Is" scores from [a] A scale's score within-country position compared to the other scales on the same level. *Note.* [a]A scale's score within-country position compared to the other scales on the same level.

Bolivia (6.1, Rank 4). Countries that ranked similar to South Africa are Australia, Costa Rica, Ireland, and Namibia (all with a score of 5.81 and Rank 27). Malaysia and the United Sates ranked exactly the same as South Africa, at 31 with a score of 5.8. The countries that scored the lowest on this dimension are France (4.93, Rank 59), Morocco (4.81, Rank 60), and Qatar (4.51, Rank 61).

Participative Leadership. South Africa scored the Participative leadership dimension as the third-highest leadership dimension, and it is South Africa's second-highest ranking leadership dimension compared to the other countries, with a score of 5.62 and a rank of 16. Countries who scored similarly to South Africa are he Netherlands (5.75, Rank 12), Australia (5.71, Rank 13), East Germany (5.7, Rank 14), Ireland (5.64, Rank 15), and United Kingdom alongside Zimbabwe (both Ranked 17, and scored 5.57). Costa Rica and Sweden had scores of 5.54 and ranked 19. The countries that scored the highest on this dimension are Canada (6.09, Rank 1), Brazil (6.06, Rank 2), and Austria (6.00 Rank 3). The countries that scored the lowest on the Participative Leadership Dimension are Albania (4.5, Rank 61), Indonesia (4.6, Rank 60), and Mexico (4.64 Rank 59).

Humane Leadership. Even though the South Africa score on the Humane dimension (5.33) is only the fourth highest of South Africa's own scores, it is ranked as 8 out off all the other countries, and it is the highest ranking compared to the other dimensions. Iran (5.75) ranked the highest on this dimension, with Georgia (5.61) in second, Phillippines (5.53) in third, and Nigeria (5.49) in fourth place. Countries that ranked similarly to South Africa are Indonesia (5.33, Rank 5), Taiwan (5.35, Rank 6), Zambia (5.27, Rank 8), and India (5.26, Rank 7). The countries that scored the lowest on this dimension are Morocco (4.10, Rank 59), Russia (4.08, Rank 60), and France (3.82, Rank 61).

Autonomous Leadership. South Africa scored the Autonomous leadership dimension as the fifth highest (second-lowest) leadership dimension, it is also South Africa's fifth-highest-ranking leadership dimension compared to the other countries. With a rank of 40, South Africa ranked well below average compared to the other countries on this dimension. Countries who scored similarly to South Africa are Namibia and New Zealand, both with scores of 3.77 and ranks of 36, and the Philippines and United States, both with scores of 3.75 and ranks of 38. Japan (3.67, Rank 41), Canada (3.65, Rank 42), Italy and Nigeria, both with scores of 3.62 and ranks of 43 also ranked similarly to South Africa.

The countries that scored the highest on this dimension are Russia (4.63, Rank 1), Kazakhstan (4.58, Rank 2), and Georgia (4.57, Rank 3). The countries that scored the lowest on the Autonomous Leadership dimension are Brazil (2.27, Rank 61), Portugal (3.19, Rank 60), and Hungary (3.23 Rank 59).

Self-Protective Leadership. South Africa's sixth highest score, or lowest score, is on Self-Protective leadership (3.19) and the score is below the scale average. South Africa is ranked 45. The countries that scored the highest on this dimension are Albania (4.62, Rank 1), Iran (4.34, Rank 2), Taiwan (4.28, Rank 3), and Egypt (4.21, Rank 4). Countries that ranked similarly to South Africa are Italy (3.25, Rank 42), Hungary (3.24, Rank 43), Zimbabwe (3.20, Rank 44), New Zealand (3.19, Rank 45), United States (3.15, Rank 47), Portugal (3.10, Rank 48), Austria (3.07, Rank 49), and Australia (3.05, Rank 50). The countries that scored the lowest on this dimension are France and Sweden both with scores of 2.81 and ranks of 58, and Finland (2.55, Rank 61).

Results of Qualitative Study

In this section, the South African results of the focus groups, in-depth interviews, and media analysis, based on the seven cultural dimensions, are discussed.

Focus Groups and Individual Interviews. Prior to conducting the focus group discussions and interviews, the authors did a prestudy in which 430 first-year MBA students had to list the characteristics of competent managers and outstanding leaders. Additionally, they had to indicate how managers from South African differed from those from Russia and Japan. The data obtained in this way were incorporated in the overall qualitative report, because they did not differ significantly from the data derived from the individual interviews and focus group discussions. It was found in the prestudy that the South African graduates, whether Black or White, were unable to differentiate between South African managers and managers in the specified countries, other than in a very vague stereotypical way. There may be various reasons for this: (a) The nature of the question requires stereotyping; (b) South Africans have, in the apartheid years, been so isolated from the international mainstream through sanctions, trade boycotts, travel restrictions, censorship, and demonizing of communist countries, that they cannot be expected to have any authentic or well-informed opinion on this question.

A general observation is that our respondents viewed South African managers as being more similar to Russian managers than to the Japanese. Russian managers are seen to be bureaucratic, conservative, slow-moving, and not particularly innovative. The respondents were also of the opinion that the reality in South African and Russian management/leadership style reflects management, whereas the ideal is that of Japan, which is associated with leadership. Given the results of this large sample, it was decided not to include this international comparison in the focus group discussions. With regard to South Africa's international isolation, a further point needs to be made: All the respondents have some form of tertiary education (management programs, bachelor's degrees, engineering, or postgraduate). Management education in South Africa is largely based on American textbooks and although it was stressed from the outset that this research is not interested in textbook-correct answers, it is suspected that the "American slant" present in our educational system did play a role in the respondents' personal views and opinions.

The following qualitative data were obtained from the interviews and focus group discussions.

Definition of a Leader.

1. A leader is an accepted person who displays a natural ability in a given situation to inspire others to willingly follow an ideal or vision.
2. A leader is a person who leads followers to believe in themselves, their own strengths, abilities and worth, who inspires his or her followers to commitment, motivation, and self-confidence.
3. A leader is a person who is capable of paradigm shifts, takes risks, is a facilitator of people, and empowers people, and who is perceived to be a trustworthy person with high moral values.

The Roles and Behavior Expected of Leaders.

1. A leader has a vision—like a dream, which includes others—a broad vision, not an egocentric vision. Leaders are able to communicate their vision and tangible goals to their followers convincingly—and to inspire them to follow their vision voluntarily. Leaders are excellent team players, effectively utilizing followers through their excellent people skills, like empathy, understanding, effective listening, effective communication on all levels, and delegation. Leaders lead by example, identify with their followers, and instill self-respect and self-confidence into them.
2. Leaders are competent, have good judgment abilities, and understand the process of leading. Leaders are fair and firm, but also flexible and adaptable.

3. Leaders are accepted, popular, respected, and also respectful toward followers and enemies.

4. Leaders are usually bound to a specific situation and emerge naturally in a specific context, where they are accepted as leaders. Leadership is not in a specific position, but lies in the person; a leader earns leadership.

5. Leaders are courageous, willing to take risks and break with conventions and role expectations if necessary (they redefine roles). Leaders tend to be unconventional and individualistic. They are their own persons, but not to the extent that they isolate themselves; they are still accessible and approachable.

6. Some of the outstanding attributes of leaders are: dynamism, confidence, determination, persistence, and energy. They are good strategists, negotiators, and persuaders, without being manipulative or domineering. They show good decision-making skills and are rational and logical. They may be shrewd but not calculating.

7. Their behavior may also be nuanced by their use of a soft approach with people. Leaders know themselves and other people; they know their own weaknesses and strengths. They have integrity, are honest and open, but also direct. They handle situations in a humane, calm, and emotionally appropriate way. Although they are emotionally controlled, they are not cool and aloof.

8. Leaders are accommodating, diplomatic and have integrity. They have credibility, are effective, and follow things through. Leaders give continual feedback to followers, are genuinely interested in their followers, and try to satisfy their followers' needs. They are facilitators—flexible and adaptable. Leaders are responsible persons, not agitators.

Leadership Style in South Africa.

1. Outstanding leaders are perceived to show a strong and direct, but democratic and participative leadership style. They are perceived to be agents of change, visionaries, and individualists. This indicates a preference for a transformational leadership style. Although they are viewed as moderately charismatic, they are also seen as being responsible, not as agitators.

2. South African leaders are also thought of as being sensitive to followers' needs and are expected to reflect followers' ideas, satisfy their needs, and be respectful and understanding. South African leaders are expected to be pragmatic and creative; by utilizing their interpersonal skills and knowledge they must act reactively as well as proactively, depending on their analysis of a situation.

3. Some respondents were of the opinion that South Africa "breeds" managers, not leaders. Some of reasons offered for this are: Formal learning inhibits creativity; external insignia of leadership are regarded as important; ours is a confirmative and rule-bound society; society values technical managerial skills (the "good" employee is promoted to management); development of leadership is limited by finances and economics; bureaucracy; South African society does not value humanities/soft sciences; the South African schooling system is inadequate—it neither stimulates the development of intellect, creativity, and self-confidence, nor identifies children with natural leadership abilities and develop these.

Definition of a Manager.   It was decided to include a paragraph on the manager in this chapter because some of the respondents (apart from making the unremarkable observation that the ideal is that the manager must also be a leader) pointed out that in the end there must be convergence between the leader and the manager. Leaders must be contextualized in that they must have the ability to translate their new idea/vision into an organizationally acceptable format and communicate and sell this to their peers, superiors, and subordinates. Leaders must have the ability to "shift gears": Their vision must be managed in terms of traditional managerial skills such as planning and control.

Managers are trained persons who use their initiative to perform the traditional functions of management—planning, leading, organizing and control to achieve results—within a set time frame and limits. In doing this they must display the ability to listen, communicate, motivate, delegate, and coach. Managers derive their objectives from that of the organization, whereas leaders have more of an "internal locus of control."

Roles and Behavior of the Competent Manager.

1. The manager is: a coordinator; a planner, organizer, and controller; a respected and respectful person.
2. A manager must: be able to lead in a directive way; able to motivate subordinates; knowledgeable in the field of management, not in specialist fields; able to delegate; able to see the bottom line; able to predict; strategic and short-term oriented; an effective listener; a trainer or a coach; honest.
3. A manager must have initiative, empathy, and good communication skills.

Some of the obstacles to leadership mentioned by the respondents related to South Africa's cultural and linguistic diversity, and lack of transcultural empathy, interaction, and accommodation. Whereas it may make sense in a country such as the United States, where the economically dominant group is also the numerically superior group and hence the dominant political group, to take into account only that group's norms, culture, and perceptions, the same cannot be said in a country such as South Africa, where cross-cultural issues may be determinative of leadership effectiveness.

Media Analysis.   In the search for quotations relating to leadership in the media analysis stage of the research, the term *leadership* was interpreted in a wide context to include political, business, and community leaders but excluding references to leaders and leadership in sport.

In the media analysis, visionary leadership (1), performance-orientated leadership (2), decisive leadership (3), collectivist leadership, which include humane leadership (4), inspirational leadership (5), and integrity leadership (6) came out on top in terms of frequency of occurrence in media reports. With one exception, there is a close correspondence with these results and that of the quantitative data. The high ranking of collectivist leadership (4) in the media analysis can be explained by the stress placed on corporatist policies and practices in the business domain. It is neither politically correct, nor commercially prudent, to praise leadership in the corporate world at a time when the unions have gained much ground in their struggle for greater participative management and consultation rights. Another possible explanation for this specific discrepancy is that the quantitative data focused exclusively on Whites, whereas the media analysis also included the other cultures in South Africa. It may well be that the higher collectivistic leadership score is a more accurate reflection of South Africa's larger population's perceptions.

Combined, Overall Profile of Leadership in South Africa

From the preceding qualitative data, focus group, individual interview, and the media analysis discussion, it seems that outstanding leaders in South Africa are perceived to show a strong and direct, but team-oriented and participative style of leadership. In terms of leadership attributes, it seems that the White subgroup shows a strong preference for charismatic and action-orientated leadership and a preference for considerate and humane leadership with a tendency toward a bureaucratic leadership. Although they are seen as being charismatic, they are also seen as being responsible, not as agitators, and to some extent as visionaries. Even though South African leaders place high emphasis on performance, they tend to be perceived as being sensitive to followers' needs and are expected to reflect followers' ideas, satisfy their requirements, and be respectful and understanding. They are seen as quite participative and humane. South African leaders are perceived to be decisive and good negotiators. They are also expected to be pragmatic and creative, by utilizing their interpersonal skills and knowledge. They must act reactively as well as proactively, depending on their analysis of a situation. South African leaders are also perceived to show integrity in their leadership and appear not to be self-protective.

5. EMIC MANIFESTATIONS OF THE CULTURE OF AND LEADERSHIP IN SOUTH AFRICA

Performance Orientation

Achievement on all levels is important to South Africans. Rugby stars and Olympic champions are remembered long after their achievements have been eclipsed by others. Indeed, for a glorious moment in our history, all South Africans were united in triumph when South Africa won the rugby world cup in 1995. In the rural town of Beaufort West, there is even a museum in honor of Chris Barnard, who performed the first heart transplant. Many individuals are remembered and honored for their mythical heroic deeds, among these are Wolrade Woltemade, Racheltjie de Beer, Dick King, and various Voortrekker leaders as well as some of their opponents and Black adversaries. The emphasis seems to fall on individual achievement rather than the heroics of the collective.

Schooling is compulsory up to the age of 15, or the ninth grade, and no pupil may be refused entry to a school simply because of an inability to pay school fees. At the end of each school year, the newspapers carry short résumés with photographs of pupils who achieved the highest grades for their final-year examinations, these achievers are typically awarded with bursaries for university studies. In particular, the press highlights any pupil who overcame personal hardship to attain good marks. However, the dark side of this achieving ethos is that every year yields its tragic crop of suicides among high school students during the examination period. Among all population groups in South Africa an almost exaggerated importance is placed on academic qualifications and achievements.

In South African organizations, Performance Orientation manifests by extensive use of performance appraisals, employee-of-the-month awards, and promotions based on outstanding performance. Performance excellence is emphasized and usually coupled with merit awards. Leadership awards are awarded not only in organizations but also in the greater community, like the Leadership in Practice Award that is awarded to an outstanding business person every year by one of South Africa's prominent business schools. There are an abundance of certificate programs, short courses, and seminars dealing with performance excellence and quality improvement. In the academic world, awards for outstanding research and lecturing are awarded. Merit bursaries are awarded to pupils and students with exceptional grades and talents.

Future Orientation

In looking at South African organizations, the relatively high ranking of South Africa on this dimension is to some extent understandable. South Africa, in the person of Clem Sunter, developed scenario planning, which is a planning model focusing on different scenarios in 10 to 25 years in the future. Strategic planning is very important, if not number one, on most companies' agendas. Companies have annually and some biannually have strategic planning sessions or *bosberade* (the Afrikaans word for strategic planning) or "Indabas" (an African word used for strategic planning), where planning is done for the next year, next 5 years, or even further in the future. These strategic sessions are often planned a year or 6 months in advance.

It is also not uncommon to have a chartered accountant or finance person as executive officer, even in organizations whose core business is not finance. Almost every organization has at least one financial expert on the board of directors. Most companies have strict budgets, are busy with cost-cutting and saving, do long-term planning, and have plans for the next 5 to 10 years.

It is, however, more difficult to explain the relatively high ranking on this dimension, when looking at political leaders and government. Certainly, South Africa's political leaders and their (White) followers have always looked at short-term solutions for the country's internal troubles. Also, the continued export of primary resources rather than enriching it locally for export, so typical of a Third World country, indicates a lack of Future Orientation. On the other hand, the determined search for oil and the development of the oil-from-coal technology and heavy industry in iron and steel may indicate the contrary, although a more plausible explanation for these developments is the international isolation of the country during the apartheid years.

Gender Egalitarianism

In most South African households, the husband is the head of the family who makes almost all the important decisions. The inequality of sharing household chores even where both partners work is a further indication of widespread chauvinism in our society. Until recently, politics, engineering, law, medicine, and other high-profile careers were almost totally dominated by men and these "male occupations" attract good remuneration packages when compared to "female jobs," such as nursing or speech therapists, which are not well-paid occupations. This male dominance is not limited to the Afrikaner group, but a particularly tragic manifestation of the Afrikaner man as the head of, and sole provider for his family, is the fact that among the Afrikaner group, family massacres occur more frequently than anywhere else in the world.

Even though the South African government occupies seventh position out of 179 parliaments surveyed on their involvement of women, with only Sweden, Denmark, Norway, the Netherlands, Finland, and New Zealand ahead of them, men still dominate politics, business, the trade union movement, and the economy in South Africa. The latest statistics (CSS, 1998, p. 41) show that in December 1997, 87% of management in the public service were men, and only 13% women.

From Fig. 13.1 it is evident that in business, very few women are in senior and executive positions. In 1997, women comprised only 1.3% (49) of 3,773 directors of the Johannesburg Stock Exchange's 657 listed companies; only 14 women were listed as either executive directors, chairwomen, or managing directors, and less than 1% as board members. A 2004 Census of South African Women in Corporate Leadership, done by the Business Women's Association of South Africa (BWASA) in association with Catalyst (USA), surveyed the women on boards of directors and in executive management of public companies listed on the JSE as of September 30, 2004 (BWASA, 2005). The results gives a similar picture regarding gender and showed that women constitute only 19.8% of all executive managers and only 10.7% of all directors (Booysen, 2005). In management training, women comprise only 20%, with women lecturing staff on the faculty of business schools only 23%. Because of the historically dominant masculine values in South African organizational cultures, leadership, and leadership training, as well as the minority status of women in management, feminine values in leadership are not yet valued on an equal footing with masculine values.

Humane Orientation

Given South Africa's apartheid history, it is perhaps not surprising that South Africans do not see theirs as a humane society. Paradoxically, the inhumane treatment of other groups ran directly counter to Christian teachings, which meant that the Christian nationalist somehow had to keep a rigid divide between their religious beliefs and their political practices. South Africans regard themselves as conservative Christians and in the latter years of apartheid the churches started (belatedly) to speak up against the apartheid state. Also, because the distribution of crime has become more equally distributed since the abolition of influx control (i.e., it has spread from the Black townships to traditionally White suburbs), the perception is that violent crime has increased.

Power Distance

In most companies, senior staff members enjoy advantages of status such as larger offices, more opulent office furniture, and reserved parking bays. Dress is generally formal and a senior executive is shielded from his or her minions by a formidable private secretary. Organizational structures tend to be more hierarchical, with long power and command lines, and systems and processes in place that support power structures and positional power and authority. Most organizations' cultures value authority, titles, and power displays. However, there are indications that these hierarchical barriers are being relaxed and in some instances completely dismantled. (Mandela's informal and relaxed conduct, casual attire and "African" shirts may act as a role model in this regard.) In the schools, pupils address teachers in a formal and deferential manner and are not likely to challenge authority. Public works and monuments are frequently named for leaders. At a local level, street names would frequently honor local celebrities.

Individualism/Collectivism

The urbanization level of White South Africans has reached a ceiling, and in keeping with relatively affluent Western urbanized societies, the low level of collectivism is unsurprising. This contrasts sharply with the situation two to three generations ago when families were large and extended, and kinship ties were cherished and maintained. In modern urbanized South Africa, the typical core family of four lives in isolation of its neighbors. This causes an interesting dilemma for upwardly mobile Blacks who move to traditionally White neighborhoods. Coming from communities where neighbors were very much a part of one's everyday life, many Blacks find it a lonely and isolated experience to live in a White urban area. However, as discussed in the introduction, it seems that Africans as a group tend to be more collectivistic than the White group, and it is foreseen that the South African Blacks will measure higher on collectivism than the White sample used in the research on which this chapter is based.

Uncertainty Avoidance

South Africa is noted for its many rules and regulations. For many years, there were "control boards" for anything from maize to fruit to regulate market fluctuations. Perhaps this multitude of control boards, with their blatant interference in the free market in a country that professed to foster a capitalist economy, were the clearest indication of our fear of uncertainty and aversion to risk taking. In the labor market, laws were promulgated to provide for minimum standards of employment, unemployment insurance, and compensation for disabilities and diseases arising from employment. Apart from these laws, the system of industrial councils provided for the negotiation, on an industry-wide basis, of a myriad of rules regulating businesses in a particular industry. Most South African organizations also have numerous rules, regulations, and procedures for almost every possible event and contingency that may happen within their organization.

6. LIMITATIONS AND FUTURE RESEARCH

The main limitation of this study is the composition of the sample to which the whole battery of analytic methods could be employed, being exclusively White men. Related to this is the fact that the media analysis included newspapers with a target market other than White men, which makes comparisons between the results of the media analysis and the quantitative data suspect. On reflection, the media analysis should have been done individually, per paper/journal, rather than summing these results combining newspapers and journals. Second, this was done during a time of monumental transition in South Africa, making generalizations across time a risky business. At most, one can say that these results are a snapshot of one sector of our society at a given time and that replication studies will have to be undertaken to determine which conclusions have stood the test of time and which have been overtaken by sociopolitical events.

Possible directions of future research that may be of great significance include the following:

- Interethnic comparisons (the perception that Blacks are a homogenous grouping, though it may have had greater validity in the struggle against apartheid, is an oversimplification and a Eurocentric view; in postapartheid South Africa, ethnic differences and tribal loyalties may reassert themselves). Also an investigation in African management practices, or Afrocentric leadership.
- Investigating the conceptions of leadership between the genders (there are indications that women tend to have a greater affinity for leadership that focuses on relationships and this may correlate with the African concept of "ubuntu," which holds that "I am a person through other persons").

- The conceptions of leadership held in the political sphere (the authors hypothesize that some political decisions of our leaders may be explained by an expanded notion of the obligations of a leader toward his or her subordinates).
- The conceptions of leadership held in traditional communities versus conceptions of leadership held in urbanized communities (South Africa's modern Constitution and its Bill of Rights come into direct conflict with many customs and practices in traditional tribal communities).

7. PRACTICAL IMPLICATIONS

What should a foreign manager expect while dealing with south African managers? Though it is not possible to provide a comprehensive discussion for the visiting manager, because a large part of this research focuses just on White men, and the South African society transformed rapidly since 1999 when the data was collected, some of the most salient and probable features of the South African world of work are listed here. The central theme is diversity management. With the advent of affirmative action and Black economic empowerment initiatives, the South African workforce has become increasingly diverse (with the exception of lower levels of employment, which are dominated by Blacks). Interpersonal communication (including the correct interpretation of body language) is of great importance because it may lead the visitor to draw incorrect inferences if she or he is not careful. A manager from a country where task orientation is focused on should be aware that South Africans will also express concern over the welfare of the person (greetings are mostly phrased in sentences such as "How are you?" to which one must respond appropriately and extend the same courtesy to the speaker). Male South African managers may tend to be authoritarian, in the sense that they make the final decision, but this is typically preceded by a lengthy consultative process. The visitor may also find that strict adherence to starting times of meetings is not the norm and because of the importance placed on giving each person the chance to voice his or her opinion, meetings may also last longer than expected. Also, European visitors may find that the perceived role of a manager as a man is still much more prevalent in South Africa than is the case in Western Europe, although the presence of young well-educated women in managerial positions is sharply on the increase.

8. EUROCENTRIC VERSUS AFROCENTRIC LEADERSHIP

Two different leadership approaches in the country, namely an Afrocentric and a Eurocentric conception of leadership, is one of the dilemmas South African managers face. On the one hand is the Eurocentric/Western approach, which has proven value in improving organizational and work performance worldwide and in South Africa and, on the other is the Afrocentric management approach (Booysen & Beaty, 1997). This dilemma is discussed in more detail by looking at research done in this regard subsequent to the GLOBE data collection mentioned earlier, which focused only on the White male manager in South Africa.

Subsequent to the data collection for the GLOBE study, Booysen (1999; 2001) used an adapted version of the GLOBE questionnaire in combination with interviews and focus groups to measure subcultural differences between race and gender in South African managers. The unit of study was White and African Black management; the levels of management included junior, middle, and senior management, from three of the largest retail banks in South Africa. The target population included a total of 18,449 managers. A disproportional probability sample was used to include comparable numbers in the sample across and within each management level. The respondents were selected on a systematic basis, according to specified quotas and stratified in terms of organization, management level, gender, and race. The quota included 840 managers (4.6% of the total population). A total of 263 managers (1.4% of the total population) across all the banks were sampled. As regards the race distribution across the organizations, 119 (45.2%) respondents were Black managers and 144 (54.8%) White managers. There were 90 (34.2%) White male managers, 54 (20.5%) White female managers, 82 (31.%) Black male managers, and 37 (14.1%) Black female managers in the total sample frame. It should be noted that Booysen's (1999) study does not include the "Should Be" scale and is based only on the "As Is" scale. Furthermore, the GLOBE data discussed earlier were collected from White men in 1995 and 1996, just after the first democratic elections in April 1994, whereas the data for Booysen's (1999) study were collected at the end of 1998 and beginning of 1999, and included African Blacks and women.

In summary, in terms of the cultural dimensions, the findings of Booysen's study showed indeed significant differences between the Black and White racial groups on all the dimensions except Power Distance. The findings are depicted in Table 13.6.

Performance Orientation

Although both groups scored above average on the Performance Orientation cultural dimension, White managers scored well above average and measured significantly higher than Black managers, who scored above average ($p < 0.10$). Some quotations from the qualitative data illustrate this point:

- *"Blacks are not as results driven as whites."*
- *"Whites are performance orientated with the focus on profit margin."*
- *"Whites are bottom line driven—if you do not perform you are out."*
- *"Blacks focus on people instead of skills."*

It is interesting to note that the Performance Orientation in highly individualistic societies, like the Whites in South Africa, lies on the individual level—individuals strive for their own achievement in life. However, in collectivistic societies, like the African Blacks in South Africa, Performance Orientation manifests at the group level. The score of the White group on this scale of 5.28 is higher than the GLOBE "As Is" score of 4.11 and nearer to the GLOBE "Should Be" score of 6.23.

Future Orientation

White managers measured higher than Black managers on Future Orientation ($p < 0.01$). White managers scored well above average, whereas Black managers scored below average and ranked it in seventh place. This finding confirms the arguments of Coldwell and Moerdyk (1981), Meeding (1994), Boon (1996), Prime (1999), and Collier and Bornman (1999), who stress the differences between the linear, sequential, or mono-chronic perception of time by Whites and the cyclical, synchronic, or poly-chronic perception of time by Blacks in South Africa.

TABLE 13.6
T Test Results for Differences Between Blacks and Whites on the Cultural Dimensions
($df = 261$, $N = 119$, White $N = 144$).

Cultural Dimension	Race	Rank	Mean	SD	T Test	Exceedance Probability
1: Uncertainty Avoidance	Black	4	4.75	0.90	3.38	0.00[***]
	White	2	5.11	0.80		
2: Assertiveness	Black	6	4.39	1.10	2.91	0.00[***]
	White	5	4.78	1.11		
3: Gender Egalitarianism	Black	8	3.26	1.14	2.12	0.04[**]
	White	8	3.53	0.83		
4: Future Orientation	Black	7	4.38	1.05	5.50	0.00[***]
	White	3	5.04	0.87		
5: Power Distance	Black	5	4.72	1.18	0.59	0.55
	White	4	4.80	0.87		
6: Collectivism	Black	1	5.40	0.76	11.90	0.00[***]
	White	6	4.36	0.66		
7: Humane Orientation	Black	2	5.36	1.05	9.12	0.00[***]
	White	7	4.24	0.93		
8: Performance Orientation	Black	3	5.04	1.13	1.92	0.06[*]
	White	1	5.28	0.28		

Note.   From Booysen (1999, 2001).
[*]$p < .10$ (90%).
[**]$p < .05$ (95%).
[***]$p < .01$ (99%).
Dimensions are ranked according to group means.
SD = standard deviation.

A linear concept of time that is shared by the Whites is more event related than continuum related. Time is tangible and divisible in this view. Time commitments are taken seriously, and time is seen as a narrow line consisting of discrete, consecutive points. The dominant temporal horizon is the future where consciousness first projects into. Planning and keeping to plans and schedules once made are important. Future planning is important.

Alternatively, if time is viewed as synchronic, poly-chronic, or cyclical, several things can be done at the same time. Time is viewed as a wide ribbon, allowing many things to take place simultaneously; time is flexible and intangible. Time commitments are seen as desirable rather than absolute. Plans can be easily changed and more value is placed on the satisfactory completion of interaction with others than on time commitments. Because of the poly-chronic or cyclical concept of time, Black managers would tend to have a preference for past and immediate or present orientation, and not necessarily focus on planning or making preparations for events to happen in the future (Berger, 1996; Collier & Bornman, 1999; Prime, 1999).

It is also clear that different perceptions of time have implications for organizational practices, for instance, the running of meetings with cultural diverse groups. Sequential cultures, like the White group in South Africa, are likely to upset synchronic cultures, like the African Black group in South Africa, when they insist on running meeting agendas like clockwork. Synchronic people will frustrate sequential people when they seem unable to stay focused on the single specific issue at hand and when relationships are seen as more important than time. The score of the White group on this scale of 5.04 is higher than the GLOBE "As Is" score of 4.13 and more in line with the GLOBE "Should Be" score of 5.66.

Gender Egalitarianism and Assertiveness

White managers measured higher than Black managers on Assertiveness ($p < 0.01$) and Gender Egalitarianism ($p < 0.05$). Whites scored above average on Assertiveness and ranked it in fifth place, whereas Blacks scored below average and ranked Assertiveness in sixth place. Though both groups scored far below average on Gender Egalitarianism and ranked it in last place, there is nevertheless a significant difference between the groups, with Blacks showing more gender differentiation than Whites. The following are illustrations from the qualitative data:

- *"Whites are autocratic and aggressive."*
- *"Blacks are not assertive."*
- *"Blacks do not want female managers."*

As already discussed, Assertiveness and Gender Egalitarianism are the subdivisions of the Masculinity/Femininity cultural dimension. At the organizational level, Masculinity is manifested by aggressive competition, the selection and encouragement of strong-willed and determined management, the pursuit of growth in markets and profits, lean organizational functioning, austere surroundings, and sex role discrimination with respect to higher level positions. Femininity is manifested in participative behavior, power sharing, empowerment, consensus, and collaboration. Networking, teamwork, and cooperation are emphasized, and there is emphasis on feelings, intuition, and relationship building.

The combination of a high level of Assertiveness and a low level of Gender Egalitarianism, as in the case of Whites, indicates a high level of Masculinity. Although Blacks score below average on Assertiveness, they score significantly lower than the already low score of Whites on Gender Egalitarianism, and thus are also high on Masculinity. The score of the White group on assertiveness of 4.78 is higher than the GLOBE "As Is" score of 4.60 and lower than GLOBE "Should Be" score of 3.69. The Booysen score of the White group on Gender Egalitarianism 3.53 is slightly higher than the GLOBE "As Is" score of 4.09 and lower than the GLOBE "Should Be" score of 4.60.

Humane Orientation

Black managers scored well above average, whereas White managers scored below average on Humane Orientation ($p < 0.10$). There is a significant difference on this scale between Blacks and Whites and Blacks tend to be more humane than Whites. The qualitative data support the survey findings as illustrated by the following quotes:

- *"Whites are less accommodating than black managers."*
- *"Whites are more task focused than people oriented."*
- *"Blacks divide/share responsibility in order to protect the non-performer."*

- *"Whites focus on short term financial comfort—whereas blacks focus on the community—more people oriented."*
- *"Blacks affirm more and build employees' self esteem, they focus on people instead of skills."*

The score of the White group on this scale of 4.24 is higher than the GLOBE "As Is" score of 3.49 and more in line with the GLOBE "Should Be" score of 5.65.

Power Distance

Although White managers indeed measured higher than Black managers on the Power Distance cultural dimension, this is the only dimension on which there is no significant difference between the scores of the Black and the White groups. However, both Blacks and Whites scored above the scale average on Power Distance. The score of the White group on this scale of 4.80 is lower than the GLOBE "As Is" score of 5.16 and higher than the GLOBE "Should Be" score of 2.64.

Collectivism/Individualism

Black managers measured higher than White managers on Collectivism ($p < 0.01$). The qualitative data support the survey research and the following themes and patterns emerged from quotes from both groups in regard to this issue:

- *"Blacks are collectivistic—go back to the tribe to obtain input—are experienced as being indecisive."*
- *"Whites are individualistic—obtain input from team players and then take decisions."*
- *"Blacks emphasize the team above the individual."*
- *"The black leader takes responsibility for the whole team."*
- *"Whites are autocratic dictators."*
- *"Blacks are communal, democratic and inclusive."*
- *"Afro-centric—more communal way of doing things, joint problem solving. The contact with the employee is through his/her family. Leader rather than dictator—usually elderly experienced person."*

This research thus confirms the findings of Avolio (1995) and Prime (1999), who claim that in South Africa there appear to be both an individualistic and a communalistic orientation, depending on whether the group is White or Black. It also confirms the research of Koopman (1994), who maintains that Whites give primacy to the individual, whereas Blacks see the need for individuals to find their place in a societal structure. This research furthermore confirms Mbigi's (1995a, 1995b, 1997) argument that Africans (Blacks) share the principles of collective solidarity and not the principles of individual self-sufficiency, like Whites. Note that when this analysis was done the scores of Institutional and In-Group Collectivism were still conflated in the Individualism/Collectivism Dimension.

Uncertainty Avoidance

White managers measured significantly higher than Black managers on Uncertainty Avoidance ($p < 0.01$). This means that White managers show a higher intolerance for uncertainty than Black managers. It is important to note that, although Whites measured higher on Uncertainty Avoidance than Blacks, both groups scored above average on this dimension. Though both groups will display Uncertainty Avoidance behavior, Blacks have a significant higher tolerance for uncertainty than Whites, which is illustrated by quotes from the qualitative data:

- *"Whites are more regimented and non-flexible."*
- *"Whites are more business like, formal and restrictive."*
- *"Blacks are rebellious, want flexibility, want freedom."*

This hypothesis thus confirms the literature (Meeding, 1994; Boon, 1996; Lessem, 1994, 1996) that states that because of several differences between the African and Western worldviews, which can be listed according to causation, time, self, and probability, and the African ontological perspective of not having exclusive control over the future, Blacks tend to have a greater tolerance for uncertainty than Whites.

South Africa is currently going through a transformational period, one that is busy changing the existing intergroup dynamics due to societal power shifts among the different culture groups that took place in South Africa since 1994. Apart from the inherent cultural differences, possible other circumstantial explanations can be given as to why African Blacks show a lower level of Uncertainty Avoidance behavior than Whites. Some of these explanations are as follows:

First, the societal changes that started to take place in South Africa since the first democratic elections and the new Constitution, which guarantees equal rights to all people, gave an enormous amount of power to Blacks that they did not previously have. However, even though the constitutional rights to all people did not formally take away any power from Whites, they now do not have exclusive power anymore and therefore may feel that they have lost some power and opportunities (even to the extent that they feel powerless), which may cause higher levels of uncertainty (Booysen, 2005; Munetsi, 1999; Rowen, 2000; Shapiro, 2001).

Second, in the work situation, changes like the Labour Relations and the Equality Acts and the implementation of affirmative action and employment equity policies can be construed as disempowering to Whites and empowering to Blacks. This may cause lower levels of uncertainty among Blacks, and higher levels of uncertainty among Whites (Helepi, 1999; Pillay, 1999). Third, due to apartheid and the historical dominance of White norms, rules, and regulations, Blacks, being in the subordinate position prior to 1994, learned to cope better with change, uncertainty, and ambiguity. Whites, especially White men, who used to be the dominant group, are still in the process of dealing with their changed status. The score of the White group on this scale of 5.11 is higher than the GLOBE "As Is" score of 4.09 and more in line with the GLOBE "Should Be" score of 4.67.

Cultural Profiles of White and Black South African Managers

The cultural profile of the White South African management group reflects a high level of Performance Orientation, above-average levels of Uncertainty Avoidance, Future Orientation, Power Distance, and Assertiveness, below-average levels of Collectivism and Humane Orientation, and a low level of Gender Egalitarianism. This profile is largely congruent with Western or Eurocentric management systems, which tend to emphasize competition and a work orientation, free enterprise, liberal democracy, materialism, individual self-sufficiency, self-fulfillment and -development, exclusivity, planning, methodology, and structure.

The cultural constellation of the Black South African management group reflects high levels of Collectivism and Humane Orientation, above-average levels of Performance Orientation, Uncertainty Avoidance, and Power Distance, below-average levels of Assertiveness and Future Orientation, and a low level of Gender Egalitarianism. This profile is to a large extent opposed to the Western or European management systems, and comparable to the Afrocentric management system, which emphasizes collective solidarity, inclusivity, collaboration, consensus and group significance, concern for people as well as working for the common good, structure through rituals and ceremonies, patriarchy, respect, and dignity.

A clear parallel can be drawn between the Eurocentric or individualistic models, and transactional leadership. African humanism or Ubuntu is much more closely aligned with transformational leadership. *"Specifically, transformational leaders work to create a climate and culture where each individual and the group can achieve their full potential. In doing so, transformational leaders can facilitate the Africanisation of South African organizations"* (Avolio, 1995, p. 19).

That there are two different leadership approaches in the country is one of the dilemmas South African managers face: on the one hand, Eurocentric/Western approach that has proven value in improving organizational and work performance worldwide including in South Africa and, on the other, the Afrocentric management approach (Booysen & Beaty, 1997). Supporters of the latter approach argue that, for managers to be relevant in South Africa, they must accept concepts embodied in the indigenous African philosophy. The same dilemma applies to foreign companies who want to do business in South Africa.

However, managers do not, and should not, choose between Eurocentric and Afrocentric management approaches in South Africa; rather, these two sets of values must rather hastily embrace each other. However, previous thinking, action and behavior of the South African corporate world and culture were somewhere between Europe and the United States—not at all in Africa. But, as Madi (1995) argues, with the changes taking place in the new South Africa, even corporate culture has started to realize that we are all in Africa, and that the average South African is 15 years old and Black and they, with their sense of values, perceptions, and frames of reference, will be the workforce of tomorrow.

9. CONCLUSION

The results herein focused on the White male subcultural group in South Africa, which historically was, and still is, the dominant group in business. There are, however, several other cultural groupings that need also to be taken into account when analyzing leadership in South Africa, as discussed in Section 5. South Africa is at present in a transitional phase and it is foreseen that because of affirmative action and equal opportunity programs, more people of color and women will enter the leadership echelons, and the leadership culture will change.

The most important findings from the results can be summarized as follows:
In terms of cultural dimensions:

- South Africa has shows an above-average level of Assertiveness and ranked eighth out of all the countries; they are, however, of the opinion that their level of assertiveness is probably too high.

- South African has an above-average score on Performance Orientation, with a ranking of 30, and desires to be even more achievement orientated. The media analysis provides strong support for this conclusion in that Performance Orientation ranked second highest of all the cultural dimensions in the media sample.
- South Africa displays a well above average degree of Future Orientation, with a ranking of 19, and desires an even higher degree of Future Orientation. Strong support for this inference is found in the results of the media analysis in which Future Orientation ranked first.
- South African has a propensity for the male role and masculine values, with a ranking of 35, and South Africans are mildly aware that they should value femininity and recognize female roles more.
- With a ranking of 54, South Africa seems to be a rather inhumane society, and of all the dimensions South Africans felt most strongly the desire to become a more humane society. Humane values were also manifestly absent in the media analysis sample and ranked last of the seven dimensions.
- Although South Africa scores in the midrange of countries sampled, with a ranking of 35 on the Power Distance dimension, its score still reflects high on Power Distance, with a desire to be more Egalitarian. Although Power Distance ranked fifth in the quantitative data analysis, it came out third in the media analysis. A possible explanation of this discrepancy in the results obtained by the different data sets could be that whereas the former comprised only Whites, the media analysis included a Black newspaper as well as reports on Black businesses and the pronouncements of Black business leaders. It may well be that Blacks' sense of Power Distance in society is much higher than that of Whites, thus accounting for the higher ranking obtained in the media analysis.
- South Africa scored well above average and slightly to the top end of the Band A countries on Institutional Collectivism, which shows that there is a relatively high degree of integration into groups and within organizations and society in South Africa. Regarding In-Group Collectivism, South Africa scored below average and is grouped in the Band B countries. The high deviation score could be interpreted as a desire for a higher In-Group Collectivist orientation and that South Africans yearn for a society with a greater degree of integration of the individual into small groups and families. This is also reflected in the media analysis. A possible explanation for this strong collectivistic sentiment from the media analysis could be that, because of our very strong Black trade unions and the nature of our labor laws and industrial relations dispensation, great emphasis is placed on participative management, worker empowerment, and consultative management by spokespersons of corporations. This is good public relations and makes for good copy. Such pronouncements may well have manifested themselves in the media analysis as "collectivist" sentiments.
- South Africa has an average score and ranking of 32 on Uncertainty Avoidance and it seems that there is not really a desire to change this. The results of the media analysis indicate an even lower level of concern with Uncertainty Avoidance. This result is difficult to explain given the transitional phase the society finds itself in; intuitively one would have expected a greater concern with uncertainty but this is not borne out by the empirical data. However, Booysen's (1999) data show a higher level of Uncertainty Avoidance in White men than does the GLOBE study.

In terms of Leadership attributes, it seems that the White subgroup shows a strong preference for charismatic and action-orientated leadership, and a moderate preference for considerate leadership with a tendency to bureaucratic leadership; this fits neatly with the focus group analysis. It thus seems that White male managers in South Africa tend to be charismatic and action orientated in their preferred leader behavior. They are highly future and achievement orientated, showing a high level of Power Distance. Although they also show some tendency toward bureaucratic leadership, they have a moderate tendency to be considerate in their leader behavior. They are showing moderate Uncertainty Avoidance behavior and tend to value Masculinity and the male role slightly more than female roles. White South African managers are not Collectivistic inclined, and perceive the South African society to be rather inhumane.

The discrepancies between the GLOBE data and the media analysis on the cultural and leadership attribute dimensions are probably because the GLOBE data included only the White subgroup, whereas the media analysis included White as well as Black media. It also seems that Blacks have a higher Uncertainty Avoidance propensity and are more Collectivistic than are Whites. The media analysis's findings thus seem more in line with the South Africa's general population, than just that of the White subgroup. The lower ranking on Power Distance is possibly because of the trend toward democratization of the workplace in South Africa.

REFERENCES

Avolio, B. J. (1995). Integrating transformational leadership and Afro-centric management. *Human Resource Management, 11*(6), 17–21.

Beaty, D. T. (1996). Eurocentric or Afrocentric? *Business Day Part 2. Mastering Management.* (March 11, 1996).

Bendix, D. W. F. (1979). *A synopsis of South African legislation. The report of the Commission of Inquiry into Labour Legislation and the Industrial Conciliation Amendment Act* (No. 94 of 1979). Research Series No. 4., Pretoria, Institute of Labour Relations, UNISA.

Berger, M. (1996). *Cross-cultural team building.* London: McGraw-Hill.

Binedell, N. (1992). New approaches. *People Dynamics, 10*(3), 1.

Boon, M. (1996). *The African way. The power of interactive leadership.* Sandton: Zebra Press.

Booysen, A. E. (1994, June 13–14). *An introduction to a multination study on leadership and organisational practices.* Paper delivered at the Congress on Psychometrics for Psychologists and Personnel Practitioners: Evaluation in Diversity—New Challenges. Escom College, Midrand.

Booysen, A. E. (1999). *An examination of race and gender influences on the leadership attributes of South African managers.* Unpublished doctoral dissertation, University of South Africa.

Booysen, L. (2001). The duality in South African leadership: Afrocentric or Eurocentric. *South African Journal of Labour Relations, 25*(3&4), 36–64.

Booysen, L. (2005, June 23). *Social identity changes in South Africa: Challenges facing leadership.* Professorial Inaugural Lecture, Graduate School of Business Leadership. Midrand: Unisa Publishers.

Booysen, A. E., & Beaty, D. T. (1997). Linking transformation and change leadership in South Africa: A review of principles and practices. *SBL Research Review, 1*(1), 9–18.

Business Women's Association South Africa, Catalyst USA. (2005). *South African women in corporate leadership* (Census 2005). Sandton: Nedbank Press.

Charlton, G. D. (1993). *The human race: Leadership* (2nd ed.). Cape Town: Rustica.

Christie, P. (1996). *Stories from an Afman(ager)!* Pretoria: Sigma.

Coldwell, D. A. L., & Moerdyk, A. P. (1981). Paradigms apart: Black managers in a white man's world. *South African Journal of Business Management, 12*(3).

Collier, M. J., & Bornman, E. (1999). Core symbols in South African intercultural friendship. *International Journal of Intercultural Relations, 23*(1), 133–156.

Dorfman, P. W. (1996). Part II: Topical issues in international management research. In J. Punnitt & O. Shanker (Eds.), *International and cross-cultural leadership* (p. 267). Cambridge, MA: Blackwell.

Finnemore, M., & Van der Merwe, R. (1986). *Introduction to industrial relations in South Africa.* Johannesburg: McGraw-Hill Book Co.

Grobler, P. A. (1996). *Leadership challenges facing companies in the New South Africa.* Inaugural lecture, Department of Business Management, University of South Africa, Pretoria.

Hanges, P. J., Dickson, M. W., & Sipe, M. T. (2004). In R. J. House, P. J. Hanges, M. Javidan, P. Dorfman, & V. Gupta (Eds.), *Leadership, culture, and organizations; The GLOBE study of 62 societies* (pp. 219–234). Thousand Oaks, CA: Sage.

Helepi, G. (2000). Moulding strategic affirmative training and development. *People Dynamics, 18*(3), 34–36.

Hofstede, G. (1980). *Culture's consequences: International differences in work-related values.* London: Sage.

Hofstede, G. (1991). *Cultures and organizations: Software of the mind.* London: McGraw-Hill International.

Hofstede, G. (1994). *Uncommon sense about organizations, cases, studies, and field observations.* London: Sage.

House, R. J., Hanges, P. J., Javidan, M., Dorfman, P. W., Gupta, V., & Globe Associates. (2004). *Culture, leadership, and organizations: The GLOBE study of 62 societies.* Thousand Oaks, CA: Sage.

House, R. J., Wright, N. S., & Aditya, R. N. (1997). Cross-cultural research on organisational leadership: A critical analysis and a proposed theory. In P. C. Early & m. Erez (Eds.), *New perspectives on international industry/organisational psychology* (p. 535). San Francisco, CA: New Lexington.

Human, L. (1996). Future competencies of managing diversity: What South African managers need. In M. E. Steyn & K. G. Motshabi (Eds.), *Cultural synergy in South Africa* (p. 171). Pretoria: Sigma.

Kemp, N. (1994). Managing diversity and affirmative action. *Human Resource Management, 10*(4), 26–31.

Khoza, R. (1994). The need for an Afrocentric management approach—A South African-based management approach. In P. Christie, R. Lessem, & L. Mbigi, (Eds.), *African management: Philosophies, concepts and applications* (pp. 117–124). Pretoria: Sigma.

Koopman, A. (1994). Transcultural management—In search of pragmatic humanism. In P. Christie, R. Lessem, & L. Mbigi (Eds.), *African management: Philosophies, concepts and applications* (pp. 41–76). Pretoria: Sigma.

Lessem, R. (1994). Four worlds—The Southern African businesssphere. In P. Christie, R. Lessem, & L. Mbigi (Eds.), *African management: Philosophies, concepts and applications* (pp. 17–40). Randburg: Knowledge Resources.

Lessem, R. (1996). The Southern African businesssphere. In M. E. Steyn & K. B. Motshabi (Eds.), *Cultural synergy in South Africa* (pp. 185–208). Pretoria, Sigma.

Madi, P. (1995, March). Moving the centre. *People Dynamics, 13*(3).

Makwana, M. (1994, July). Growing real talent: Implementing authentic affirmative action. *People Dynamics, 12*(8), 22–25.

Manning, T. (1996, November/December). Part One: Transformation or profit checkmate of SA business? *People Dynamics, 14*(18), 16–20.

Manning, T. (1997a, January). Profit through transformation: Part II. *People Dynamics, 15*(1), 16–19.

Manning, T. (1997b). *Radical strategy: How South African companies can win against global competition.* Sandton: Zebra.

Mbigi, L. (1995a). The roots of Ubuntu in business: A definitive perspective. In L. Mbigi & J. Maree (Eds.), *Ubuntu: The spirit of African transformation management* (pp. 77–92). Johannesburg: Knowledge Resources.

Mbigi, L. (1995b, November). Ubuntu: A new dimension for business. *Enterprise, 93,* 57–58.

Mbigi, L. (1997). *Ubuntu: The African dream in management.* Johannesburg: Knowledge Resources.

Meeding, I. (1994). *Leadership values on middle management level: Similarities and differences between groups.* Unpublished MBL research report, Graduate School of Business Leadership, Pretoria, University of South Africa.

Munetsi, W. (1999, January). Affirmative action—A simplistic view. *People Dynamics,* pp. 26–37.

Oakes, D. (1994). *Illustrated history of South Africa: The real story* (3rd ed.). Cape Town: Reader's Digest.

Pillay, D. (1999, July 20). Equity law is statutory change management. *Business Day.*

Potgieter, C. (1996). Women's lives across culture. In M. E. Steyn & K. B. Motshabi (Eds.), *Cultural synergy in South Africa* (p. 89). Pretoria: Sigma.

Prime, N. (1999). *Cross-cultural management in South Africa: Problems, obstacles and agenda for companies.* Available at http://marketing.byu.edu/htmlpages/ccrs/proceedings99/prime.htm

Rautenbach, F. (2005, April 8). Indirect BEE through the JSE. Is South Africa making progress? *Finance Week Report,* pp. 1–37.

Rous, A. (Ed.). (1996). *Business futures 1996.* Stellenbosch: Institute for Futures Research, University of Stellenbosch Printers.

Rowen, P. (2000, March 18). Black income to outstrip Whites. *Sunday Times.*

Shapiro, T. (2001, August 14). Top executives are still white, male and underpaid. *Business Day.*

Sonn, J. (1996). Rewriting the "White-is-Right" model: Towards an inclusive society. In M. E. Steyn & K. B. Motshabi (Eds.), *Cultural synergy in South Africa* (pp. 1–11). Pretoria: Sigma.

South African Central Statistical Service . (1996). *Living in South Africa: Selected findings of the 1995 October Household Survey.* Pretoria: Government Printer.

South African Statistical Service. (1995a). *October household survey 1994.* Pretoria, CSS.

South African Statistical Service. (1995a). *Statistical Release PO317.* Pretoria: CSS.

South African Statistical Service. (1998). *Women and men in South Africa 21 & 41.* Pretoria: CSS.

South African Department of Labour. (2003). *Annual report—Commission for employment equity 2002–2003.* Pretoria: Government Printer.

South African Government Web site. (2005). http://www.safrica.info/women/womeninparliament

Statistics South Africa. (2003). *Census 2001.* Pretoria: Author.

Steyn, M. E., & Motshabi, K. B. (1996). *Cultural synergy in South Africa.* Pretoria: Sigma.

Van Tonder, C. J. (2004). *Organisational change: Theory and practice.* Pretoria: Van Schaik.

14

▼▼▼▼▼▼▼

Leadership in the United States of America: The Leader as Cultural Hero

Michael H. Hoppe
Center for Creative Leadership, Greensboro, North Carolina

Rabi S. Bhagat
The University of Memphis

The United States is a large country, with more than 3.6 million square miles (fourth after Russia, Canada, and China) and around 300 million inhabitants (third most populous after China and India, but less than 5% of the total world population). Its vastness, natural beauty, and big cities attract visitors from around the world. Its economic strength is still unrivaled and its per capita gross national product (GNP) is higher than that of any other major country in the world. It is celebrated for its technological advances and admired or loathed for its political and military might. Its research and development (R&D) achievements are legend (ca. 4 out of 10 of all the Nobel prizes awarded since its inception were awarded to American researchers) and its legal and political institutions serve as models for old and new societies elsewhere.

Moreover, its cultural, economic, and military imprint is felt throughout the world. Its jazz, ragtime, and popular music, films, TV, videos, books, newspapers, and magazines can be found almost everywhere. Economically, Coca-Cola, IBM, Levi's Jeans, Nike sneakers, and many other products of its consumer culture are omnipresent. Militarily, it recently made its mark in Afghanistan and Iraq. Its influence is mostly welcomed, but often also strongly resisted.

Of course, these are only the immediately noticeable manifestations of U.S. society. With a closer look and over time, it reveals itself as an immensely varied and complex society—historically, politically, and culturally—with many contradictions and partially fulfilled aspirations. Also, nobody can yet tell for sure what the long-term domestic and foreign policy ramifications of the terror attack of September 11, 2001, will be.

A closer look also helps surface the assumptions, values, and beliefs that fuel and reinforce U.S. culture's thoughts and actions and its resulting images of the good society and the good and successful life. Similarly, it enables the cultural assumptions, preferences, and beliefs to emerge that shape its people's perceptions of the ideal organization, career, and leadership.

These latter, implicitly and explicitly culturally endorsed, perceptions of leadership are the focus of this chapter.

In particular, this chapter will highlight the uniquely American images, models, and practices of effective leadership and the underlying cultural orientations that help explain them—based on new quantitative and qualitative GLOBE data and existing findings from multiple sources. For the purpose of this chapter, culture is understood as the "internalized patterns of thinking and behaving that are believed to be 'natural'—simply the way things are" (Stewart & Bennett, 1991, p. x.). The definition of the term *leadership* initially follows the one used by the GLOBE study, that is, "people in your organization or industry who are exceptionally skilled at motivating, influencing, or enabling you, others, or groups to contribute to the success of the organization or task." Later in the chapter, we discuss additional ways of thinking of and enacting leadership.

As the biographical sketches at the beginning of the volume make apparent, the two authors originally are from Germany and continental India, respectively. However, both authors feel that they know the United States and its special brand of leadership rather well, given their nearly 60 years of combined experience in living, working, and traveling across the United States. Equally, the authors feel that they are well aware of the aspirations, hopes, fears, and accomplishments of the American people.

The chapter looks at U.S. leadership through five distinct lenses. First, we provide a brief historical overview and identify recurrent themes and tensions in U.S. society to offer a useful background for the discussion. We then paint a brief cultural portrait of the effective leader, using existing sources, followed by summary descriptions of well-known and admired past and current leaders. Next, we look briefly at leadership research in the United States to distill some pertinent old and new preoccupations and issues that will shape leadership theory and practice for years to come. Finally, through our fifth lens, we present and interpret the quantitative and qualitative U.S. results of the GLOBE study, provide some guidance to men and women from other countries who find themselves working with U.S. managers, briefly address the limitations of the data, and offer some suggestions for future leadership research.

It may be helpful to point out from the outset that our chapter cannot, and is not designed, to do full justice to the immense body of knowledge and practice that is U.S. leadership. We are selective by mainly concentrating on cultural roots and expressions of leadership in U.S. society. Equally important, we try to capture *mainstream,* largely corporate, leadership in America. The rationale for this is quite straightforward. Most of the data, including those of GLOBE, are from that part of society. Furthermore, in today's increasingly "global" business environment, that "face" of U.S. leadership is most visible, as it is exported through research and daily business interactions. However, this limited focus in no way should diminish the tremendous richness of other leadership models and approaches in U.S. culture that deserve to be studied in their own right.

1. THE HISTORICAL AND CULTURAL CONTEXT OF U.S. LEADERSHIP THOUGHT AND PRACTICE

Stages and Themes in U.S. History

No discussion of leadership in the United States can be fully understood without, even if ever so briefly, paying attention to the historical, political, economic, and social context from which it emerged (Hofstede, 1980). As a social construct (Berger & Luckmann, 1967), leadership is deeply embedded in that context. Thus, a very condensed version of major stages in the development of the U.S. society and its recurrent themes and struggles is offered first.

The history of the United States can be described in the following stages (Johnson, 1997; see also *World Book Encyclopedia,* 1981):

- First Stage: Colonial America, 1580–1750.
- Second Stage: Revolutionary America, 1750–1815.
- Third Stage: Democratic America, 1815–1850.
- Fourth Stage: Civil war in America, 1850–1870.
- Fifth Stage: Industrial America, 1870–1912.
- Sixth Stage: America as a melting-pot society, 1912–1929.
- Seventh Stage: Superpower America, 1929–1960.
- Eighth Stage: Economic Superpower in the new millennium, 1960–present.

Colonial America (1580–1750) saw the development of a group of independent settlements and small-scale enterprises, initially made up of those escaping religious intolerance or seeking adventure and/or riches. These settlements and small businesses formed into groups for protection that were primarily concerned with producing goods, which were then sent to the "mother country," England, France, or Spain. The majority of the people would have considered themselves to be members of their home countries, rather than of the new country.

Revolutionary America (1750–1815) not only witnessed the fight for independence from England, but the emergence of a strong sense of a uniquely American culture. Freedom from oppression, relying on and fighting for each other, a deep belief in government by the people, and leading simple but productive lives evolved as some of its cornerstones. Furthermore, there was an abiding conviction of the necessity for a "system of checks and balances" that would ensure that no one group or governmental branch could hold sway for an extended period in violation of the rights of others. The U.S. Constitution (1787) and the Bill of Rights (1791) became the most fundamental expressions of those yearnings. George Washington, James Madison, Alexander Hamilton, Benjamin Franklin, and Thomas Jefferson are examples of individual leaders of lasting recognition for their courage, vision, dedication, sense of justice, and breadth of intellect and experience. Their leadership was rooted in their eastern, well-to-do, privileged heritage and their hands-on experience with managing their own affairs.

Democratic America (1815–1850) is the time of Andrew Jackson and the flood of immigrants that settled and developed the West and the rest of the country. It is the time when frontier spirit, hard work, and a sense of great individual independence shaped the collective consciousness. A belief in a "manifest destiny," that is, the control of all of North America, took hold and the idea of the "common man" emerged, who needed to be protected from the monopoly of government and the rich (Andrew Jackson himself came from a background of very modest means). The women's rights and abolitionist movements, fending for equality of men and women, Black and White, developed strength and the increasing importance of, for instance, railroads, steamboats, and the cotton gin contributed to tremendous economic growth.

Civil War America (1850–1870) was a time when brother fought brother and when North and South inflicted wounds to each other that last until today. Yet, it also saw Abraham Lincoln issue the Emancipation Proclamation (urging that all slaves were to be set free). Lincoln's name continues to be listed among the great leaders of U.S. history for his integrity, persistence, and courage against all odds, humility, and standing up for his beliefs.

Industrial America (1870–1912) saw the development of "Big Business," for example, mass production and tremendous wealth in steel (Andrew Carnegie), railroads (Cornelius Vanderbilt II), cars (Henry Ford), banking (R. R. Morgan), and consumer goods (Richard Sears, R. H. Macy, Montgomery Ward). Leaders in business became major national figures, and management was recognized as a scientific study. It witnessed the country grow from 38 million in 1870 to 100 million in 1916, increasing urbanization, and the emergence of reform movements that sought to ameliorate the widening inequalities between the rich and the poor and the unfettered power of big corporate monopolies that strained the social fabric.

Theodore Roosevelt's (Trust Buster) antitrust laws and the Progressive Era's (1890–1917) efforts to reduce poverty, improve schools, and make government and big business more responsible to people were expressions of that struggle. On the whole, there was a collective feeling of unlimited possibilities in the air and a sense that economic advancement and a better future was available to everyone who worked hard and invested in the future. Yet, two groups that benefited less from these efforts were the Native Americans and the country's Black citizens. The former were increasingly pushed onto less economically viable reservations; the latter, officially freed from slavery, ended up in *de facto* segregation, in particular, in the South.

Melting Pot America (1912–1929) continued the assimilation of immigrants from around the world into a uniquely American culture, reinforced by the ascension of the motion picture industry, professional sports, radio broadcasts, and jazz as its outward expressions. It was also a period of stark contrasts. On the one hand, the United States became an important political, military, and economic player on the world stage, accelerated by its role in World War I, granted women voting rights, and experienced the Roaring Twenties. Overall, life became more fast-paced, urban, and international.

On the other hand, Prohibition (1920) started, W. G. Harding (1921–1923) and his followers pushed for a return to isolationism, traditional American values, and law and order, and the Ku Klux Klan reached a membership of 5 million. Then, of course, the stock market crash (Black Friday) in 1929 had everything come crashing down.

Superpower America (1929–1960) saw even greater changes and tensions across the economic, political, and social spectrum. It witnessed the depth of the Depression and the slow recovery from it through Franklin D. Roosevelt's (1933–1945) New Deal policies. It turned the United States into the economic and military superpower that helped defeat Nazi fascism in Europe and, by dropping the first and only atomic bombs ever on Hiroshima and Nagasaki, made World War II in the Far East come to an end. As the most powerful nation of the so-called free world, it revitalized Western Europe through its extensive Marshall Plan and actively fought against the spread of communism in Korea (and later in Vietnam). Its political and economic leadership came to be felt throughout the world.

On the home front, the country experienced, among many other developments, unprecedented growth in population, accelerated movement from the inner city to the suburbs, the witch hunt of McCarthyism in the early 1950s, the stirring of the civil rights movement in the late 1950s, and the increasing influence of labor unions and the power of television.

Economic Superpower (1960–present) sees the United States, in particular after the implosion of the former Soviet Union in 1989, ascend to the economic, technological, and military leadership role in the new information age. As in earlier historical phases, there is light and shadow: the landing on the moon in 1969 and the externally and internally divisive Vietnam War; the civil rights movement and the assassinations of John F. Kennedy, Robert F. Kennedy, and Martin Luther King Jr.; the stock market boom of the mid-1980s and 1990s and its precipitous decline in 2001 as well as a stubborn poverty rate of 14% or more of the population; a concentration of wealth and power in ever smaller numbers of corporations and individuals and a proliferation of small businesses encouraged by the Internet and venture capital; increasing scientific and academic excellence and crumbling public schools; advances in medical and genetic knowledge and 40 million without health insurance (Prugh & Assadourian, 2003); insistence on equal opportunities for all of its citizens and the incarceration of a disproportionately large number of its so-called minority populations behind bars; the opening of the world through the dynamics of globalization and religious fundamentalism at home; and a call for freedom of the peoples of the world and the tightening of the freedoms of its own people after the shattering of the collective psyche on September 11.

Of course, such a quick run through U.S. history up to the present must remain woefully inadequate in capturing the richness, great achievements, and often wrenching struggles of U.S. society to live up to its ideals. However, it may be sufficient within the purpose of this chapter to highlight political, cultural, and social tensions and/or dilemmas that are inherent in U.S. society and that may help explain not only uniquely U.S. preoccupations and cultural preferences, but also their effects on the theory and practice of leadership. Table 14.1 offers a summary of these recurrent themes and tensions.

The first tension raises the question of whether or not it is possible for the United States to rise above the injustices of its early beginnings and, by the sheer force of its moral and economic performance, atone for them. Unlike other nations whose historical origins are often rooted in obscurity, the United States was formed during the time of recorded history and much of the strains of growth have been open for everyone to see. Throughout its history,

TABLE 14.1
Recurrent Themes and Tensions in U.S. Society

1. Atoning for grievous past injustices	⟷	Creating a just and fair society
2. Pursuing narrow self-interests	⟷	Working for the common good
3. Current realities	⟷	"City set upon a hill"
4. Liberty (free market and free from government)	⟷	Equality (equity and solidarity)
5. Efficiency (big business, government, labor)	⟷	Community ("small is beautiful")
6. Individualism	⟷	Collectivism
7. Existential equality	⟷	Existential inequality
8. Live to work	⟷	Work to live
9. Change	⟷	Stability
10. Data/measurement	⟷	Values/morals
11. Practicality	⟷	Ideas/intellect
12. Action	⟷	Reflection

Note. Items 1–3 are from Johnson (1997). Items 4 and 5 are from O'Toole (1993). Items 6–12 are from Hoppe (2003) and Wilson, Hoppe, and Sayles (1996).

U.S. society has always struggled with balancing grievous wrongs of the past, such as slavery or the decimation of the Native American nations, by erecting a society dedicated to justice and fairness for all. This struggle and the resulting sensitivities on both sides continue to be evident in the divisive debate over affirmative action and diversity and their practice in the workplace. Both issues also continue to occupy leadership theory and action at political and organizational levels.

The second question is, how to balance the desire to build the perfect community with the strong tendency toward individual acquisitiveness and ambition that has been present in all phases of U.S. history. Paul Johnson (1997) asks, "Have the Americans got the mixture right?" (p. 3). Has the United States succeeded in building a nation where the common good triumphs over narrow self-interest? The settlement of what is now the United States was part of a larger enterprise of the best and the brightest of the entire European continent—and later of peoples from around the world. A large majority of them were crossing the oceans in search of purely economic gain and/or freedom from political and religious oppression. However, they were also idealists and, in many ways, for example, in Europe, opportunities were too small for them (in earlier centuries, e.g., the 11th to the 13th, the people of Europe had gone East, seeking to re-Christianize the Holy Land and neighboring countries). This mixture of religious fervor, desire for economic gain, need to escape the narrow confines of their homeland, and the sheer force of adventure that inspired generations of crusaders also characterized the early settlers in the eastern part of the continental United States. This same combination is still recognizable today in Americans' fierce insistence on their right to pursue personal wealth on the one hand and their longing for something greater than their own narrow interests on the other. It can also be detected in models of leadership that stress an entrepreneurial mind-set, passion, ambition, and courage, as well as a sense of communal responsibility as critical characteristics of successful leaders.

The third tension is concerned with the question of whether or not the United States has indeed emerged to be an exemplary country for the rest of humanity. Americans originally visualized an otherworldly "city set upon on a hill," in which "we must delight in each other, make others' conditions our own, rejoice together, mourn together, labor and suffer together, always having before our eyes our community as members of the same body" (John Winthrop, cited in Bellah, Madsen, Sullivan, Swidler, & Tipton, 1985, p. 28). However, U.S. society has found the ideal difficult to achieve. Wide discrepancies in income distribution, poverty, and racial discriminations continue to contrast with crowning achievements in technology, concern for human rights worldwide, and justice and equality before the law for all. Although these incongruencies are not unique to U.S. society, the desire to overcome them and the firm belief that it can be done are mirrored in a can-do attitude, hope-for-success approach, and an emphasis on optimism in U.S. leadership theory and practice.

James O'Toole (1993) describes related tensions in U.S. thought and experience—tensions between liberty and equality and efficiency and community. They represent four different visions of the good or just society, visions that in their entirety are always present, but whose inherent contradictions leadership at any level of society, explicitly or implicitly, struggles to reconcile.

Liberty stresses the absolute political and economic freedom whose only law is that of supply and demand. It invites rugged individualism and freedom from governmental and institutional intervention. It is the world of the entrepreneur who thrives in a free-market environment in which personal freedom, choice, and property are seen as sacrosanct and preconditions for "the pursuit of happiness." It is viewed as the most critical prerequisite for contributing to the higher order good of society.

In contrast, proponents of *equality* tend to loathe the absolute freedom of the market. They focus on the resulting inequities in income and power and strive to minimize them. They see government as having a legitimate and important role in reducing these inequities. They fight for disenfranchised groups and minorities. Theirs is a society of social activists in which solidarity and social justice among its citizens are seen as the higher order good.

Efficiency stresses economy of scale. The good society is seen to be achieved by having business, government, and labor work together to create full employment and growth, with constantly increasing standards of living. Technology, science, capital markets, mergers, conglomerates, and globalization are symbols and mechanisms for achieving maximum efficiency. It is the world of the corporate manager whose purpose is to increase the return on investment for stockholder satisfaction.

On the other hand, proponents of *community* tend to abhor a society of big business, big government, and big unions. "Small is beautiful" is their credo. High quality of life, moral rectitude, service, good stewardship of the planet, collaboration, and face-to-face interaction describe the good society for them. It is the world of the communitarian in which simplicity, preservation, local control, and democracy from the bottom up are cherished.

Taken together, these four themes are deeply embedded in the U.S. Constitution as well as describing some of the inherent tensions in capitalism as an ideological belief system. They are also incisively captured in Bellah et al.'s (1985) discussion of individualism and commitment in American life. Similarly, they can be seen as recurrent tensions in U.S. leadership thought and practice—tensions between competition and collaboration, centralization and decentralization, tasks and relationships. Currently, the ideas of the free (and global) market and efficiency seem to have the upper hand. Simultaneously, the ideal leader tends to be described as an individual go-getter, someone who is clear on his or her direction, gets things done, and strives for efficiency in everything, while struggling to respond to demands by people inside and outside of his or her organization for more input, some balance between work and personal life, and a sense of belonging.

Another, pervasive, theme in U.S. history and today's society is briefly mentioned at this point due to its fundamental impact on many of its institutions and, by extension, its leadership practices: institutional and personal religion. Religion was held to be of supreme importance by virtually all Americans in the first half of the 20th century (Johnson, 1997). Even recent surveys suggest that about 95% of U.S. citizens believe in a God, compared to half of that in many European countries (Halman & de Moor, 1993). Inglehart's (1997) research of cultural, economic, and political changes in societies around the world point to similar findings. Alexis de Tocqueville had already observed during the first half of the 19th century that Americans held religion to be indispensable for evolving free institutions (Pierson, 1938). Today, the political "religious right" or religious groups around the country continue to exert a strong influence on national policies in education, politics, and family planning. Character, integrity, responsibility, and honesty are among the important values in that debate. They also are seen as critical attributes of effective leaders.

A Cultural Sketch of the Characteristics of Effective Leaders in U.S. Society

The remaining themes (6–12) in Table 14.1 are cultural themes to which every society develops its own blend of answers, given their historical, religious, and economic circumstances. Stewart and Bennett (1991) have discussed the unique American cultural patterns in great and most insightful detail. Hofstede (1980, 2001), Hoppe (1990), Schwartz (1994), Merritt (2000), House et al. (2004), and others have largely confirmed them in extensive empirical studies. Overall, mainstream U.S. society consistently falls in the Anglo segment of country clusters (Hofstede, 1980; House et al., 2004; Ronen & Shenkar, 1985), with generally high levels of *individualism, performance orientation, masculinity,* and *assertiveness* and low to moderate levels of *power distance* and *uncertainty avoidance.* In addition, it is described as having distinct preferences for facts/data and a practical and active approach to life's challenges.

Yet, it is apparent even to the relatively untrained eye that the United States is of great cultural heterogeneity, consisting of multiple ethnic and religious groups who have found different answers to the themes and tensions in Table 14.1. For instance, for Native Americans, working for the common good, community, and solidarity play a significantly larger role in their lives than in current mainstream U.S. society. Also, the Society of Friends (Quakers) strives for a more "small is beautiful" approach and actively engages in causes of social justice and the common good. Similarly, the servant leadership model (Greenleaf, 1977) emphasizes values inherent in the right-hand column of Themes 1 to 5 in Table 14.1. Furthermore, there exists also a deeply felt sympathy in U.S. culture for the "underdog" and "antihero," who, against all odds, win the day against seemingly superior challengers. Last but not least, it needs to be kept in mind that no social construct, such as culture, by the very definition as a social construct, is static. Changing circumstances inside and/or outside of a society help new perspectives or even entire new paradigms emerge (Kuhn, 1970). So, it is with the concept of leadership, in general, and perceptions of effective leaders, in particular.

As a highly *individualistic* culture, the United States believes in the right of each individual to pursue his or her own happiness. With this credo comes the obligation and expectation to take care of oneself, and distinguish oneself through one's own personal achievements. Initiative and independence are highly valued. Self-actualization through continuous self-improvement is the goal. Achievement motivation is lauded. In the final analysis, one's identity is due to one's own achievements, or the lack thereof. As we have seen in the brief historical overview earlier, this emphasis on the individual may have well served— and been reinforced by—the early frontier experience and its demands for self-reliance. It conjures images of the "Marlboro Man," John Wayne, or the frequently expressed admonition (or wish?) "lead, follow, or get out of the way."

The slogan *"live to work"* illustrates that U.S. culture has a more *"masculine" or tough* orientation to life (Hofstede, 1980, 2001; Hoppe, 1998; Robinson, 2003). Things that are big, strong, fast, or tangible expressions of success (e.g., money!) are desired and admired. In terms of leadership, a focus on work and career, performance, results, challenge, competition, execution, "going the extra mile," decisiveness, and efficiency are key characteristics that are sought and rewarded in a leader (House et al., 2004). Getting the job done, whatever it takes, is the goal. Good working relationships or conditions, collaboration, or solidarity among coworkers may become mere means toward that end. On the whole, hard work and achievement are considered the basis for a good life. The American author's, Horatio Alger (1832–1899), "rags to riches" books for boys captured this theme at an almost mythical level.

In the area of leadership, the belief in the *existential equality* (small to moderate power distance) of all members of U.S. society visibly dovetails the emphasis on the individual and achievement. You are what you have achieved. Nobody is superior in the eyes of the Creator. Alexis de Tocqueville wrote almost 200 years ago while visiting America: "The greatest equality seems to reign, even among those who occupy very different positions in society" (cited in Pierson, 1938, p. 65). It is assumed that everybody's opinion, input, and personal experience *sui generis* has validity and ought to be considered. Hierarchies are established out of necessity or convenience to get the job done. Informality in dress, speech, and behavior is tolerated or even encouraged. At the same time, there exists a managerial prerogative in the

American workplace. Employees accept, at least more so than in Denmark or Sweden, that the manager, by virtue of having achieved this role and level of responsibility, has the right to exercise his or her power to the exclusion of others (Hoppe, 1993).

In looking at these first three U.S. cultural orientations in their interaction, leadership tends to be viewed as something that an individual in a leadership role does. The task, then, of a leader is to successfully deal with a challenge or opportunity through his or her own initiative, skills, experience, ability to get others involved, and the authority granted to him or her and, in the process, make a mark for him or herself. This mind-set may lead, then, to curricula vitae or stories by managers that claim that they "turned the company around," or "saved the company $50 million," or "made the marketing department number 1 in the industry," even though such successes clearly could not have happened without the significant help from their direct reports and many others. In social attribution theory, it could be called the "me" theory.

Flexibility and openness to change and new experiences are another cultural cornerstone. What is different or new is exciting. Mobility is expected. The newest technology or fashion is welcomed. New leadership models are eagerly explored, for example, leadership as jazz, permanent whitewater, chaos theory, or the learning organization. The admonition "to learn the competency of incompetence" (Vaill, 1996) elevates the need for life-long learning. The advice "if it is not broken, break it" (Peters, 1987) attests to the willingness to experiment and take risks. Creativity, innovation, and out-of-the-box thinking are encouraged. Rules, regulations, and policies are kept only as long as they make sense, given changing circumstances. Overall, men and women with the aforementioned mind-set and characteristics who feel comfortable with change and its resulting uncertainties are thought of as leader caliber.

Not surprisingly, U.S. culture's preference for and practices of individual achievement, hard work, existential equality among its members, and openness to change in its leaders (and, by extension, the entire society) greatly overlap with those described in the brief historical overview. They are deeply rooted, all pervasive, and seen as "natural" requirements of an effective leader. They surface repeatedly in later sections of the chapter.

The strong preference for *data,* that is, empirical, observable, measurable facts, is rooted in an American assumption that "rational thinking is based on an objective reality where measurable results can be attained" (Stewart & Bennett, 1991, p. 30). It is reinforced by a scientific worldview that calls for objective, quantifiable facts. Historically, it might be seen as an expression of the American experience of moving west and experiencing progress in terms of miles traveled, cattle herded, or settlements created. Culturally, it is embedded in the combination of individualism and weak uncertainty avoidance that enables people to "let the facts speak for themselves," because there are fewer social constraints to interpret those in a socially acceptable way and fewer emotional ones, respectively, to shy away from unpredictable outcomes. Thus, effective leaders are expected to use data, provide objective analyses, establish measurable goals, and make fact-based decisions. On the other hand, Behrman (1988) cautions against the overuse of this latter approach. It tends to relegate values, morals, and purpose to secondary roles and perpetuate the fallacy that data are "value-free." In fact, Hofstede in reporting on d'Iribarne's comparative study (1994) of a Dutch, French, and American aluminum production plant observes among U.S. managers the very approach to data that Behrman favors. Whereas the Dutch respect facts the most, "in France, status and power often prevail over facts, and Americans want to make facts yield to moral principles" (Hofstede, 2001, p. 119).

Hofstadter (1969) writes in detail about the anti-intellectualism in American life. Cavanagh (1984) observes that to "to call an American 'impractical' would be a severe criticism" (p. 20). In other words, *practicality* and a corresponding preference for inductive and operational thinking are highly valued. Effective leaders are expected to "get the job done" and be pragmatic, flexible, efficient, good problem solvers, and hands-on. Grand theories or intellectual discourse void of practical application are suspect. The focus is on making quick and effective adjustments to immediate problems. This preference may partly be due to "the American concern with avoiding failure in the future by taking action in the present" (Stewart & Bennett, 1991, p. 36). It is also informed by the dynamics of an individual achievement orientation and the willingness to experiment. Historically, it may be seen in the need for finding workable solutions to conquer and survive in the new land and the belief in the virtue of leading a simple and productive life.

U.S. society's preference for *action* over reflection can be described at two different levels. At one level, it is an expression of the biblical injunction of gaining mastery over the world and the belief that we ought to shape our own destiny. Exerting control over one's life and environment is seen as an individual duty. Making progress is quintessential. On another level, but a closely connected one, the high value for action expresses itself in the ways in which societies like to acquire information and/or knowledge. For example, the United States as a whole tends to favor an active, experimental, and experiential approach to learning (Hoppe, 1990). Solving problems through trial and error, case studies, or experiential exercises, for example, in the development of leaders, are common practice.

Taken together, both aspects can be observed in slogans or proverbs, such as "just do it," "the devil finds idle hands," "life, be in it," "got to stay busy, man," and "fish or cut bait." In terms of effective leadership, leaders are expected to take action, at times, just for the sake of it, because taking no action is seen as worse than taking a less than perfect action. They are also measured on the degree to which they exert control and are forceful, decisive, quick, and assertive.

Not separately listed in Table 14.1, but relevant for this cultural sketch of the ideal U.S. leader, is a society's *orientation to time*. One distinction is between societies that have monochronic or polychronic concepts of time (Hall & Hall, 1990). The monochronic orientation is descriptive of most economically highly developed societies, for example, Germany and the United States. Time is seen as a scarce resource that needs to be used as efficiently as possible, as in the saying "time is money." Effective leaders spend their time purposefully and with intensity. They get to the task quickly, start meetings on time, and meet deadlines. They sequentially work from the present toward the future and generally prefer a shorter time frame. At the same time, U.S. society admires leaders with a vision. However, having a vision is typically understood as having an organizational focus/direction or a personal sense of purpose, not as a long-term approach. Short-term objectives remain important (Nanus, 1992).

In summing up this brief sketch of mainstream U.S. culture, here are some of the key leader characteristics that its people, implicitly and/or explicitly, look for and endorse in their leaders:

- To stand out, leave one's mark, get things done, and succeed.
- To be results-driven, exert control over one's environment, and be decisive, forceful, and competitive.
- To work hard, be action oriented, active, and have a sense of urgency.
- To willingly take risks, and be creative, innovative, and flexible.
- To be objective, practical, factual, and pragmatic.
- To be experienced, seek input from others, and be informal.

Additional Characteristics and Images of Outstanding U.S. Leaders

To be sure, there are many more characteristics of effective leaders in U.S. culture, as the lengthy lists in the U.S. leadership literature attest. However, at this point, this first summary is sufficient for providing the stage for the perceptions and images that surfaced, as we asked U.S. university students and colleagues to describe for us leaders of the past and present from any walks of life whom they admired the most.

The individuals who emerged as the primary examples of outstanding leaders from a group of university students[1] in the domain of **business and commerce** were Bill Gates of Microsoft, Jack Welch Jr. of General Electric, Lee Iacocca of Chrysler, and Thomas Watson Jr. of IBM.

Bill Gates.   Bill Gates, the chairman and until recently the CEO of Microsoft, is currently seen as one of the world's richest and most influential leaders in the field of business and commerce, not only in the United States, but also throughout the world. Under his leadership, Microsoft revolutionized computing and became one of the most important competitors in the Internet and media businesses. During his childhood, Bill Gates was noted for his high intelligence and a special talent for business from an early age. At the age of 21, he dropped out of Harvard and, with Paul Allen, started Microsoft. He is perceived to be a brilliant strategist, but not a particularly empathetic human being. It has been said that he would rather destroy his competitor than attempt to grow the market. At Microsoft, Bill Gates is known as having "incredible processing power," "unlimited bandwidth," and a high skill in "parallel processing" and "multitasking"; that is, he is seen as most adept in accomplishing several tasks at the same time. The students saw Mr. Gates as relentless, extremely intelligent, and someone who reached the pinnacle of success by his sheer force of astute business judgment and personality. He was perceived as the most important business leader in the United States, perceptions shared by many business periodicals, such as *Business Week, Fortune* magazine, and *The Economist.* He was also admired for his huge success and described as highly individualistic and as someone who likes to stand out from the rest of his peers by his sheer will and force of personality.

John F. Welch Jr.   Also known as Jack Welch, the legendary chairman of General Electric (GE) breathed new life into GE in 1981, after being named the company's eighth and youngest chairman at 45. He did so by eliminating over a hundred thousand jobs, breaking up its rigid hierarchy at the time, and shifting assets from mature manufacturing businesses into fast-growing high-technology and service operations. Welch grew up in working-class Salem, Massachusetts, the only son of a railroad conductor. His mother infused him with strong sense of ambition and self-confidence. She told him that his stammering, which persists today, was not a handicap but a sign that his mind worked faster than he could talk. He never dreamed of becoming a big businessman. After earning a doctorate in chemical engineering, Welch

---

[1]The first set of names and characteristics comes from an in-class survey during the 1999 fall semester of 31 students majoring in business administration at the mid-South university where the coauthor teaches. They were asked to think of and then rank outstanding leaders in the following areas: business and commerce; education; politics, public service and government; and sports and entertainment. The students had an average age of about 30 years, 80% were from the United States, and 40% of them were women. Their selection of the following leaders is best understood as examples of outstanding leaders in U.S. society, not as a representative sample.

went to work for GE where he succeeded in transforming a struggling plastics business into a sterling success within GE and in emerging as a brilliant, sometimes abrasive, leader with a great eye for operational details. Had Welch arrived in any GE business other than plastics, the future CEO of GE might have left in a matter of months, because he was the antithesis of everything GE stood for at the time: a young man who had no patience for bureaucracy and wanted things to be done as fast as possible. He is said to rush ahead with a speed marked by impulsive vehemence and is known to flout convention. Welch is also known for putting greater emphasis on substance than on style and to be a man of a remarkably forceful vision. Even though the students and others described him as ruthless at times, Welch was considered one of the great business leaders, because he was successful in bringing about extremely high rates of growth in his company and improving performance in the eyes of Wall Street analysts.

Lee Iacocca.   The students perceived Lee Iacocca, the former chairman of Chrysler Corporation, as the third most important leader. He is considered a legend who saved Chrysler from bankruptcy in the early 1980s, and who became a household word. During his heyday, he was regarded as one of the greatest CEOs in American history, because of his unique ability to rescue the third-largest automobile company in the United States by proposing a unique liaison with the American government. Some historians interpret his approach as a bailout, but there is no doubt that he played a large role in saving Chrysler from bankruptcy. The son of an Italian immigrant, Iacocca worked at various jobs during college before he found an engineering job at Ford Motor Company. When he realized he was better in marketing than manufacturing, he moved to the company's headquarters in Detroit. Widely known as a creator of Ford's successful Mustang, he rose to become president of Ford Motor Company. Not long after he was fired in the late 1970s as president by Ford's chairman, Henry Ford II, he was appointed chairman of the Chrysler Corporation, which he transformed into a profitable corporation in the 1980s. In Iacocca, the students saw a person who is forceful and highly individualistic in orientation, has a knack for marketing, and can turn a company around even under the most difficult circumstances.

Thomas Watson Jr.   Thomas Watson Jr. is known for revolutionizing the computer industry. He transformed IBM from a rather modest manufacturer of typewriters and adding machines into a leading global corporation. He was the first to risk the future of the entire company on the 360 series computers that rendered previous IBM machines obsolete. Thomas Watson Jr. grew up under the tutelage of his father, Watson Sr., the founder of IBM. His early years were plagued by self-doubts as to whether he had the ability to satisfy his overly demanding father. After an unsuccessful stint as a junior salesman in IBM for 3 years, he enlisted to serve in World War II and returned to become the next chairman of IBM. In his mission to excel beyond the accomplishments of his father, he pushed the company to higher levels of profits and productivity. Under Watson, IBM developed a customer-first strategy that enabled the company to anticipate the growing needs of customers as opposed to reacting to them in a knee-jerk fashion. Briefly, the students regarded Thomas Watson Jr. as a highly successful leader who knew how to take risks and who was highly innovative.

In the area of **politics,** the students listed a large number of individuals. We describe three leaders of their choice who are widely recognized by American historians as great public leaders, Abraham Lincoln, Harry S. Truman, and John F. Kennedy.

Abraham Lincoln.   Abraham Lincoln was president of the United States for only 4 years (1861–1865), because he was assassinated 2 months into his second term. He is generally considered the greatest and most influential president that America ever had. Lincoln not only helped abolish slavery, but also kept the United States from splitting into two, and attempted to create a republic that would be forever guided by moral, ethical, and democratic principles. His nickname was Honest Abe, and he was described as a man of great humility and friendliness toward others. At the height of the Civil War, the combination of his deeply felt conviction that slavery was wrong on moral grounds, his iron will, and his ability to express his convictions clearly and with force helped him succeed even in an utmost difficult situation. He complemented his leadership with an ability to completely dedicate himself to his cause and to work extremely hard. Though he was not known for his administrative skills, he was considered an effective delegator and developer of people. Another of his characteristics was that, even though he was a trained lawyer, he tended to rely more on his own intuition in reaching important decisions than on the opinions of experts.

Harry S. Truman.   Harry S. Truman (1945–1953) was thrust into the presidency, when President Franklin D. Roosevelt died in April of 1945. Within his first few months in office, Nazi Germany surrendered and then Japan, after he had ordered to drop atomic bombs on Hiroshima and Nagasaki. He also became known for his improbable reelection victory over Thomas E. Dewey, as well as the Truman Doctrine, the Marshall Plan, the establishment of NATO (North Atlantic Treaty Organization), and the United States's entry into the Korean War. In large part, his policies and actions were intended to combat the spread of communism. Truman was feared for his blunt, outspoken, and combative style, but admired for working hard and for his courage, determination, and self-discipline. His friends and supporters described him as straightforward, honest, loyal, and a devoted family man. Truman deliberately crafted his public image as that of an ordinary man who is "just a country Jake who works the job" or "just an old Missouri farmer." Stephen Goode, a presidential historian, called him an "extraordinary ordinary man."

John F. Kennedy.   John F. Kennedy (1961–1963) is considered a great president and leader because of his profound capacity for articulating a vision that galvanized the citizens of his country, that is, to put a man on the moon. Similarly, his appeal to the American people "ask not what your country can do for you, ask what you can do for your country" offered them a deeper sense of purpose that energized them. Kennedy, the youngest president ever elected (aged 43) and the first of Catholic background, was admired for his wit, charm, and charismatic personality. With his intelligent and attractive wife, Jacqueline, Kennedy's presidency came to be known as Camelot. His depiction as a war hero and being the son of a wealthy and influential family contributed to this image. In addition, his handling of the Cuban Missile Crisis in 1962, his support of the early civil rights movement, and the creation of the Peace Corps helped his political stature, despite the Bay of Pigs blunder during his first year in office. Despite recurring health problems and personal infidelities while in office, his youthful demeanor, informality, optimism, and appeal to the good instincts within each person and the nation as a whole are lasting images of his leadership and presidency. His assassination on November 22, 1963, remains the most vivid and traumatic image of that presidency.

Three leaders emerged in the area of **education.** They were Derek Bok of Harvard University, James Bryant Conant of Harvard University, and Harold Bloom of Yale and New York University.

Derek Bok.   Bok is known for his vision to reform the medical and graduate school programs at Harvard University. During his tenure as president of Harvard in the 1980s, he significantly raised Harvard's endowment and started a university-wide initiative on teaching ethics across all curricula. After his retirement, he wrote *The Cost of Talent,* in which he compares and contrasts the economic-compensation practices in many prominent professions in the United States. He was considered a highly innovative and visionary leader in the field of education in the latter part of the 20th century.

James Bryant Conant.   James Bryant Conant, among many other achievements, a chemistry professor by training and president of Harvard for 20 years, is recognized as an important reformer for popularizing the Scholastic Assessment Test (SAT) and other standardized tests to improve the quality of students admitted to American universities. It was his vision and his actions that also helped improve the economic situation of minorities and other disadvantaged young people, by making it possible for them to get admitted to some of the leading universities in the United States. Because of his vision of administrating standardized aptitude tests, the doors of prestigious American universities opened up to promising, yet poor, students from different segments of U.S. society. He was perceived as one of the most important leaders in the American educational system during the second half of the 20th century.

Harold Bloom.   Bloom, America's preeminent literary critic, is the author of more than 20 books. He is considered to be one of the great thinkers in the field of English literature in contemporary America. His book *The Anxiety of Influence,* is known for popularizing the idea of Freudian philosophy. He is also remembered for making Shakespeare's writings more accessible and understandable to a wider audience. He strongly believed that Shakespeare's work is highly relevant for understanding human behavior in the past and present.

When looking at all three leaders at once, what becomes apparent is that all of them are perceived to be highly innovative and intelligent, visionary, and unconventional in their thinking. By acting on those ideas, they changed what it meant to be educated and, thereby, profoundly influenced the lives of many Americans.

In the domain of **sports and entertainment,** the students listed numerous names, in part due to the immense role that sports and entertainment play in U.S. society and in part because of the passions that they feel for their teams and/or type of sport (of course, the terms *sports* and *entertainment* are largely synonymous within the U.S. cultural context).

Professional and college sports are big business in the United States, on a scale almost unimaginable to the rest of the countries of the world. Professional football, basketball, baseball, and hockey teams dot the U.S. landscape. The Dallas Cowboys, for example, called themselves America's team. The Chicago Bulls, during Michael Jordan's heydays, were known worldwide. At the college level, Duke University in basketball or the University of Oklahoma in football are household names. There are many other well-known teams, such as the New York Yankees, the Green Bay Packers, or the Los Angeles Lakers. All of them continuously look for highly qualified professional coaches and/or general managers, often with high name recognition and an outstanding track record, who can help their organization succeed.

Vince Lombardi, the former coach of the professional football team, the Green Bay Packers, largely epitomizes the successful leader in sports. He won five National Football League (NFL) championships in nine seasons with the Packers. His dictum, "winning is not a sometime thing; it's an all-the-time thing," has become a revered philosophy in American sports, but not just in sports. People's personal and professional lives are full of sports- related values and metaphors, such as "be a good sport," "let's huddle" (i.e., get together and talk about it), "we hit a home run" (i.e., we greatly and quickly succeeded), or "don't throw me a fastball" (i.e., don't surprise/take advantage of me). Also, many successful athletes switch to careers in business and politics and many public leaders, for example, Lincoln and Kennedy, were admired in their youth for their athleticism.

Other leaders who are highly respected by the American public are *Tom Landry,* former football coach of the Dallas Cowboys, and *Phil Jackson,* formerly with the Chicago Bulls, now with the Los Angeles Lakers. They and others are typically described as being highly knowledgeable in their sport (business!), innovators in their field, forceful, passionate about winning, and assertive in exercising their authority.

In entertainment, the students recognized *Ted Turner* of Time Warner, *Steven Spielberg,* the movie director of *Indiana Jones* fame, and *Michael Eisner* of Disney as outstanding leaders. All three were seen as rather unconventional in their approaches, highly creative, and assertive and confident in voicing their visions. They were also singled out for their willingness to take significant risks and succeeding in their fields with flying colors.

The second list of names of outstanding leaders came from staff members of the Center for Creative Leadership in Greensboro, North Carolina.[2] The Reverend Martin Luther King Jr. emerged as the top vote getter. The key reasons why he and the other leaders were chosen follow:

Martin Luther King Jr.: Righted a wrong, rallied a nation, nonviolent, spearheaded a movement, led by example, unfaltering, clear in purpose and values, charismatic, catalyst, visionary, motivator for social change, focused, love for equality, justice, and peace, advocate, courage, inspirational, organized, and had a strategy. Also, "he had some (personal) flaws."

John F. Kennedy: Charismatic, a war hero, asked "what you can do for the country," inspirational, idealism, youthfulness, did not forget the poor, inspired country to greatness, handsome.

Franklin D. Roosevelt: Led the nation out of the Great Depression, led the nation through difficult times, swift, bold action despite criticism, able to get others to work together, his social programs.

Abraham Lincoln: Preserved nation, his Emancipation Proclamation, unreproachable integrity and wisdom, humility, true to himself, courage despite risk to him, strong in difficult times, intelligent, kept eye on the vision, standing up for his beliefs.

Obviously, these two lists of outstanding U.S. leaders are rather selective. Another group of students or staff from another company might have chosen some different names of leaders

---

[2]The second list of names and characteristics is based on a question that was posed in early 1999 to staff members at all levels of the Greensboro campus of the Center for Creative Leadership. They were asked to send to the first author of this chapter "names of three U.S. leaders from past or present, who immediately come to mind (from anywhere—business, academia, politics, entertainment, etc.), and a few words on why you selected each." About one third of them responded and of those 72 respondents about 75% were women. A total of 227 names of leaders were submitted, 116 of which were different. With one exception, men listed names of male leaders only. In contrast, about one third of the names of leaders submitted by women were women. The top vote getters from the 72 respondents were Martin Luther King Jr. (26x), John F. Kennedy (13x), and Franklin D. Roosevelt and Abraham Lincoln (12x each).

and reasons for selecting them. Also, the students and staff members shared their perceptions of these individuals, even though most of them very likely had little direct knowledge of their true-life circumstances and/or actions. However, the leader characteristics that emerged from the analysis of the leaders' backgrounds and achievements are very much in line with those found in U.S. literature, in general, and commonly used U.S. leader questionnaires, in particular. Furthermore, they are reflected in recent cover stories by mainstream news magazines such as *U.S. News & World Report* (Gilgoff et al., 2005) on America's currently best leaders. Together, they add to those from the earlier cultural sketch the following characteristics: It is considered important for an outstanding leader to:

- Have a vision, articulate it well, stand up for and stick with it, and keep his or her eye on it.
- Be charismatic, inspirational, and optimistic, hope for success, appeal to the good in people, care about them, and serve the greater good.
- Be a catalyst, turn things around, and create something new.
- Implement, be efficient, overcome all odds, and persevere.
- Be true to self and own conviction, have integrity and honesty, be straightforward, lead by example.
- Be exceptional, unconventional, have a good track record, and be a winner.

A few additional insights could be gained from the respondents' descriptions of their most admired leaders. For example, *age*, that is, advanced age, did not seem to matter. In fact, the examples of Bill Gates, Jack Welch and, in particular, John F. Kennedy pointed to the attractiveness or, at least, acceptance of youthful leaders. In today's fast-paced Internet and information age, this is clearly visible in places such as Silicon Valley. Furthermore, the United States has always been described as a youth-oriented culture.

Some of the leaders were seen to be ruthless and abrasive (Jack Welch) or blunt, outspoken, and combative (Harry Truman). Although they weren't particularly lauded for these characteristics, members of U.S. society overall tend to think that these types of shortcomings are a small price to pay for a leader's ability to have great impact and/or win. At the same time, studies at the Center for Creative Leadership have repeatedly shown that problems with *interpersonal relationships* are one of the chief reasons why people in leadership roles don't reach their potential in their careers (Leslie & Van Velsor, 1996).

Similarly, *formal education* seemed to be of little concern; for example, Bill Gates dropped out of Harvard at 21. In fact, throughout U.S. history a person's formal education or training has been treated as secondary to getting the job done and being successful.

Personal failings or infidelities in past and current U.S. leaders have received, at times, widespread attention in the U.S. media and worldwide. For example, John F. Kennedy's persistent infidelities were well known. Former President Clinton was impeached because of his sexual involvement with a White House intern and his lying about it. Also, Jesse Jackson, leader of the Rainbow Coalition, admitted to having fathered a child outside of his marriage and briefly withdrew from public life. Although their failings were heavily criticized and their personal lives thoroughly scrutinized by the media, they did not, in the final analysis, greatly erode their approval ratings as public figures performing their jobs. Aside from political motifs, it seems as though Americans prefer their leader to be a person of good intentions and/or high moral convictions, but that they can overlook personal imperfections and failings, as long as the person is highly successful in performing the public office. This applies even more to the corporate world where the media spotlight is less invasive and returns on stockholders' investments are the measure of success.

Even when leaders "fall," past personal failings may become assets, as long as the person has shown remorse and/or genuinely asked for forgiveness from the people around him or her—and has worked hard to succeed in any new endeavor! U.S. society is a "second-chance culture." It cheers the "come-back kid." It admires the person who has picked him- or herself up from failure(s) and has become a success again ("it's not a sin to get knocked down; it's a sin to stay down"). It embraces a person's heroic struggle that ends in victory (Hubbell, 1990).

In short, U.S. society tends to pay limited attention to individual leaders' age, formal education, personal shortcomings or failings, and failures—as long as they succeed and win in the long run.

2. PREOCCUPATIONS AND NEW DEVELOPMENTS IN U.S. LEADERSHIP RESEARCH AND PRACTICE

As we have seen, leadership as a social construct, and as reflected in the perceptions of its people, is deeply embedded in the historical, political, economic, social, and cultural fabric of U.S. society. By extension, the same is to be expected in the field of leadership research. The men and women who conduct and fund the research activities bring their individual and professional propensities with them, but equally important, their cultural lenses. There is no "culture-free" research (Hofstede, 1993). Moreover, a society's cultural makeup influences which academic discipline(s) is drawn to studying the phenomenon. In the United States, the vast majority of leadership scholars are psychologists by training (Hofstede & Kassem, 1976). So, with this in mind, we highlight some of the preoccupations in U.S. leadership research (for more extensive overviews, see Bass, 1990; House & Aditya, 1997; Kellerman, 1984).

Leadership Research in the United States: Cultural Preoccupations

As a social construct that enjoys widespread daily use in U.S. society, definitions of leadership abound. However, most definitions of leadership by U.S. researchers, including the one used by GLOBE, have tended to mirror the one by Ralph Stogdill of Ohio State University who stated that "leadership may be considered as the process (act) of influencing the activities of an organized group in its efforts toward goal setting and goal achievement" (Stogdill, 1950, p. 3). For the purpose of this chapter, one element of this definition is highlighted: Leadership tends to be seen as a process of influence in which the individual leader exercises considerable impact on others by inducing them to think and behave in certain ways. As a result, the study of effective leadership in the American tradition has largely been reduced to what the individual leader does and his or her ability to accomplish in a superior fashion the declared and not so clearly articulated goals of the group or organization or the body politics.

This ability to influence the actions of others could be studied as a function of the leader's positional authority and/or his or her personal qualities and characteristics as individuals (Drath, 2001). Regarding the latter, researchers examined a large number of traits, such as height, intelligence, self-confidence, and introversion/extraversion, as possible predictors of effective leaders. Yet, what Stogdill (1948) had concluded earlier remained largely true.

Though most of the traits were related to the exercise of leadership in a variety of settings and tasks, it was difficult to predict who might become a leader based on the knowledge of individual traits alone. Furthermore, leaders did not necessarily become leaders by possessing some important traits, but by adjusting their pattern of personal characteristics to the tasks and the characteristics, goals, and activities of the people with whom they worked. Thus, effective leaders became to be conceived in terms of the interaction between leader and follower(s) characteristics and the task at hand.

This insight led to a host of *contingency studies* (see Bass, 1990). All of them, despite conceptual, psychometric, and methodological issues and limitations, received varying degrees of support in laboratory studies, that is, under controlled conditions. However, their support in field studies, trying to predict a leader's effectiveness, generated conflicting and ambiguous results. Staw (1975) and Calder (1977) offered a possible explanation. They suggested that attributions of effective or ineffective leadership are largely a function of the feedback that group members receive pertaining to their performance in a given situation. For example, if group members are told that their group had performed well, they tend to attribute this to the group leader's effective leadership and ineffective leadership, when told that they had performed poorly. Staw and Calder concluded that one of the fundamental problems in leadership research is one of making correct attributions in a given situation where social actors are likely to be interested in inferring the causes and consequences of their actions.

A second explanation came from Kerr and Jermier (1978), who showed that even the most effective leaders are not necessarily going to be either successful or even needed in some situations; that there exist many neutralizers in the work situation (intrinsic interest in the task, level of technological control permitted in task accomplishment, high degrees of professionalism on the part of group members, etc.) that can negate or reduce the leadership attempts made by even the most competent individuals. Similarly, Pfeffer (1977) and Schein (1985) noted that situational forces in an *organization's environment* or the *organization culture,* respectively, may be more critical in describing the effectiveness of a leader than what the individual actually does.

This observation was in line with Leiberson and O'Conner's (1972) and also Hunt and Osborn's (1982) earlier contentions that the effect size of a leader's impact on organizational performance is far smaller than most people expect; that performance variation in a firm is more a function of macrovariables in the *external environment,* such as variations in a given industry and in overall economic conditions affecting the firm. Later work on the "power of organizational architecture" (Nadler & Tushman, 1997) integrated much of the work on the importance of the internal *and* external environment for a leader's effectiveness.

Yet, in spite of the ambiguous and conflicting research findings in the leadership research literature and the emergence of the importance of the environment in the leadership effectiveness equation, leadership, in particular, the individual leader, remained a topic of great fascination in U.S. popular and academic culture. Enhanced in the early 1980s by the intuitive appeal of the contingency models to the practitioner and the success of books, such as the *One Minute Manager* (Blanchard & Johnson, 1981) and *In Search of Excellence* (Peters & Waterman, 1982), an endless supply of popular writings on leadership and training products began, with books on charismatic leadership (e.g., by Kousnes & Posner, 1987, and Bennis & Nanus, 1985), the transformational leader (Tichy & Devanna, 1986), the authentic leader (Terry, 1993), and many others. For example, online retailer Amazon.com alone lists currently about 9,000 books under the rubric of leadership.

Though an increasing number of academic models also began to look at leadership from the perspective of systems (Senge, 1990), chaos theory (Wheatley, 1992), learning (Vaill,

1996), teams (Hackman, 1990), or followership (Kelley, 1988), the vast majority of the leadership publications remained deeply steeped in the culturally endorsed image of the individual leader, as discussed earlier. Moreover, it appears that U.S. society, notwithstanding the weaknesses of the leadership construct in academic research, has collectively developed a *causal link* between what leaders do and the impact their actions have on a situation or in galvanizing a group of people toward a collective goal. Meindl, Ehrlich, and Dukerich (1985) call this the "romance of leadership" in U.S. culture (see also Meindl, 1993).

New Dynamics Impacting U.S. Leadership Theory and Practice

U.S. society, like the world at large, has been experiencing many important changes that have begun to shape the ways in which its members are thinking about and enacting leadership. Dramatic changes in demographics within the U.S. in general and the workplace, in particular, helped spawn extensive new directions in research on diversity and women in leadership. The dynamics of globalization encouraged the study of cross-cultural differences and similarities in institutions, cultures, and national governments as contextual factors and their impact on leader styles and effectiveness. The rapid growth in the use of computers and the Internet in people's personal and professional lives is also prompting new leadership paradigms and practices. In this section of the chapter, we take a brief look, therefore, at some emerging insights from three selective areas—women and leadership, leadership in a global world, and leadership beyond the individual leader. Admittedly, the empirical evidence is either still sparse or, due to the inherently ambiguous nature of the leadership concept, ambiguous as well.

The interest in *women as leaders* is part of the larger dynamic of a dramatically changing U.S. workforce over the past 30 years during which the percentage of women in the workforce reached 46% and their proportion in executive, managerial, and administrative roles climbed to more than 44% (U.S. Census Bureau, 1999). The full ramifications of these realities may not become apparent for years to come. However, there is some evidence of how women leaders may shift the images and perceptions of the effective leader in U.S. society.

One of the potential ramifications has to do with women's ways of thinking, relating, and leading. The U.S. literature tends to describe women in leadership roles on the whole as being more relational, cooperative, participative, egalitarian, communal, empathetic, responsive, and open—to name a few (Adler, 1999; Gilligan, 1982; Helgesen, 1995; Powell, 1999; Tannen, 1990). Recent special reports in *Newsweek* (Kantrowitz et al., 2005) on how women lead and the aforementioned *U.S. News & World Report* on America's best leaders, respectively, reinforce these research findings. Women leaders consider close working relationships with others, collaboration, and more balance between their professional and personal life as important ingredients of their effectiveness. These preferences tend to be contrasted with those of men, who are described as being more individualistic, directive, assertive, action oriented, decisive, forceful, and competitive. Not surprisingly, this characterization of male leaders has great similarity with the earlier cultural sketch of U.S. leaders. A straightforward explanation for this observation may be that the vast majority of leaders studied and described in the U.S. academic and popular literature are men, because they were the ones in the past who were elected to public office or reached managerial positions in corporate America. Also, as Maier suggests, there tends to exist a pervasive "corporate masculinity" (Maier, 1999, p. 71) in U.S. organizations that perpetuates a "masculine" image of the successful leader.

The question of which leadership approach makes for the more effective and/or preferred leader is inconclusive in the existing U.S. literature (Butterfield & Grinnell, 1999), mainly due to the limited and limiting nature of the question. As pointed out earlier, a leader's effectiveness is largely a function of the situation (including the people with whom the leader works) and the external environment. In other words, if the situation and the environment call for "feminine" leadership characteristics, women may be preferred and seen as being more effective. The same would apply to men in leadership roles. There is evidence for this expectation (Butterfield & Grinnell, 1999). In terms of being viewed as an effective leader, of course, it would be desirable if women *and* men would acquire the mentality, competence, and style that go beyond any gender stereotype or division. Viewing the male–female debate from an international perspective, Adler (1999) adds that the debate may be a uniquely American preoccupation, because men in other cultures around the world value and practice many of the very characteristics that the U.S. literature describes as typical traits of women leaders in the United States.

A second ramification has to do with the observation that being an effective leader in today's world may increasingly demand more of the characteristics that tend to be attributed to women. The evolving information age and its underlying paradigms (e.g., of quantum physics, relativity theory, and chaos theory) seem to call for more cooperation, alliances, networking, interdependence, nonhierarchical approaches, process orientation, participation, and intentional decision-making among individuals and organizations (Maynard & Mehrtens, 1993). In fact, in his discussion of today's global dynamics that allow people to work together across continents through electronic means, Friedman (2005) concludes that "in the flat world, more and more business will be done through collaboration within and between companies" (p. 352ff). Within the U.S. context, Faludi (1999) notes that the economic transition from manufacturing industry to service industry and information-based industry, or from production to consumption, is highly conducive to creating and sustaining a culture that values characteristics that are currently associated with women. Adler (1999) expands on this theme by looking at women leaders in the global arena. She concludes "the feminization of global leadership—beyond referring strictly to the increasing numbers of women who are global leaders—[will result in] the spread of traits and qualities generally associated with women" (p. 249). In other words, U.S. culture's emphasis on the individual go-getter, toughness, action, measurable outcomes, winning, and career may take on diminishing importance in the years to come—inside and outside of U.S. culture.

The impact of *globalization* on leadership theory and practice received a boost when the iron curtain came down in the late 1980s and people, information, money, and businesses began to travel more and more freely across national boundaries (Friedman, 2000, 2005). Ever since, long lists of traits of the effective global leader have been developed, including cognitive complexity, emotional intelligence, and psychological maturity (Rhinesmith, 1993; Wills & Barham, 1994). In addition, Rhinesmith writes

> The movement from domestic to global leadership involves a transition not only in geographic focus, but also in attention to process over structure, seeking out change rather than defending against it, creating chaos rather than avoiding it, and moving to a more free-flowing, open, integrated systems mindset that stresses adaptability of both people and global corporate culture. ... This involves a fundamental change in style, as well as substance. In fact style—global style— *becomes* substance in producing a competitive edge for the company (p. 165).

Traditionally, this more process-oriented, systemic, and global (and implicitly more cosmopolitan) style has not been considered a particular strength of the American leader.

In a recent empirical study, Dalton, Ernst, Deal, and Leslie (2002) identified cultural adaptability, perspective taking, innovation, and international business knowledge as four critical competencies for a global leader. Whereas the latter two are to be expected, cultural adaptability and perspective taking point to the need of future leaders to be aware of their and others' deeply held assumptions, values, and beliefs, and to be able to, almost kaleidoscopically, see people and events from different perspectives so that they may quickly adjust their actions as needed (see also Rosen, 2000). This is difficult enough to do in one's own culture, but even harder across multiple cultures. Moreover, these characteristics clearly go beyond the descriptions found so far in the earlier historical sketch and images of the effective leader in U.S. society. In the relatively more homogeneous societal and organizational culture of the United States even just 30 years ago, leaders were seldom challenged to come to grips with deeply held differences between themselves and others.

On the other hand, the demands of the tremendous speed with which information can move across the globe and the information technology that makes it possible appear to match the American cultural propensity for action, data, practicality, and openness to change. The fascination with technology, deeply rooted in the American psyche (Behrman, 1988), complements it. As a result, U.S. leaders have more quickly embraced the new information technology than leaders elsewhere, for example, in Germany (Jung, 1997), to gather, store, and disseminate information throughout their organizations, create networks for geographically dispersed teams to efficiently work together, and turn the world, technologically speaking, into their own backyard. The question will be to what an extent future leaders not only can access the world, but equally connect to its peoples through increased cultural sensitivity, adaptability, and cultural self-awareness.

Finally, the most challenging dynamic impacting U.S. leadership thought and practice in the years to come may emerge from U.S. culture's (and the Western world, in general) *view of the individual.* As the anthropologist C. Geertz observes, "The Western conception of the person as a bounded, unique, more or less integrated motivational and cognitive universe … organized into a distinctive whole and set contrastively both against other such wholes and against a social and natural background is, however incorrigible it may seem to us, a rather peculiar idea within the context of the world's cultures" (Geertz, 1979, p. 229; see also Gergen, 1996; Sampson, 1993, 2000). What is worth noting is that this highly individualistic conception of the person, even in the West, did not evolve until about 400 years ago—a rather recent development in terms of human history. It is also useful to realize that the so-called Western world constitutes only about one seventh of the world population (*Oxford Atlas of the World,* 1994). Stated differently, the majority of the world population even today adheres to a more collective view that stresses the *socially* constituted and deeply embedded nature of a person in which, for instance, leadership may be seen not as the sole property of one person, but as that of the collectivity.

Of course, there is nothing inherently "wrong" with this Western perspective. As a view of the individual that grew out of economic, political, and philosophical developments, for example, Descartes's *cogito, ergo sum,* it is culturally as legitimate as any other perspective. Moreover, it has powerfully contributed to the insistence on "the sanctity of the individual [as] fundamental to our values about freedom, responsibility, and accountability" (Drath, 1996, p. 2). However, as with any other cultural "given," it remains mostly unexamined and is in conflict with the emerging emphasis on interdependence, mutuality, systems, process, interconnectedness, or networks of today's global information age, as discussed previously.

Within this latter context, leadership is described and studied not so much through a leader's individual characteristics and actions, but through connections, interfaces, systems, coordination mechanisms, that is, the "in-between" dynamics among and across people and organizations. Borrowing an analogy from the Internet, Levine, Locke, Searls, and

Weinberger (2000) note, "The web is not predicated on individuals. It is a web. It is about connections" (p. 121; see also Sayles, 1993). Similarly, Drath (2003) and McCauley and Van Velsor (2004) suggest that leadership studies and development programs temper their overemphasis on the single leader and pay equal attention to the capacity of the entire organization, that is, its infrastructure and the web of relationships among its people, to engage in such basic leadership tasks as setting direction, creating alignment, gaining and maintaining commitment, and initiating and managing change. In their view, leadership needs to be developed and studied as the property of a social system, not only as that of an individual. Collins and Porras (1997) and Collins (2001) provide an example of this latter approach in their seminal studies of organizations that were "built to last" and that succeeded from being "good to [being] great," respectively. In those companies, leaders had become "architects" and "builders" of their organization for sustained success in the market.

The cultural preoccupation in the United States with the individual leader and leadership in general leads to another blind spot—the neglect of the potential, responsibility, and desire in shared leadership by those who are typically not seen as leaders. Drath (2001) speaks of leadership as a shared process and responsibility in which the challenge for everyone is to help create a "leaderful" environment and partake in it. Heifetz (1994) introduces the notion of "adaptive challenges" in which people are challenged to actively engage in narrowing the gap that they experience between their shared values, needs, or desires and the realities that they face in their organizations or communities, thereby exercising leadership from the "bottom up." Berry (1993) addresses the issue directly by observing that

> [T]he American tendency to see leadership as the remarkable individuals we call leaders creates a profound cognitive barrier inhibiting social progress. Because American eyes see leadership as the expression of individuality, we fail to perceive leadership as an expression of community. Because we see leadership as something *they* do, we fail to see leadership as something *we* do. Because we see leadership as the exercise of power, we fail to see leadership as the exercise of democratic values. (p. 2)

Bellah et al. (1985) add, "When economics is the main model for our common life, we are more and more tempted to put ourselves in the hands of the manager and the expert" (p. 271).

Taken together, this brief look at the U.S. research literature on leadership and the emerging demands of today's world on the current and future theory and practice of leadership in the United States allows for the following additional observations. There is an *emphasis on:*

- The individual, psychology, a "peculiar" view of self.
- Leadership as an individual influence process.
- *Out*standing, charismatic, transformational, authentic leaders.
- A (perceived) *causal* link between what leaders do and outcome(s).
- A "romance" of leadership.

There is an awareness of the:

- Need to consider competence, motivation, preferences of those to be influenced.
- Leader's effectiveness as being partly a function of intrinsic motivation, goal clarity, skills, and so on, of those to be influenced.
- Leader's effectiveness as being partly a function of "followers" attributions.
- Leader's effectiveness as being greatly influenced by internal and external environments.

And there is a need for more:

- Process-oriented, collaborative, systemic, participative, and "global" leadership.
- Technological, electronic savvy in the process of leadership.
- Self-awareness, cultural sensitivity and adaptability, and perspective taking.
- Leadership as something that "we" value and do (shared sense of purpose and action).
- Leadership as an expression and practice of the democratic will.

Additional Insight: The Leader as Heroic Warrior

Overall, the major image that emerges from these various looks at the perceptions of effective leaders in theory and practice of U.S. society is that of the hero, more specifically, the hero as masculine "warrior" (Campbell, 1973; Pearson, 1986). The parallels between the warrior hero and the most admired leaders in U.S. culture are striking. They are summarized in Table 14.2.

TABLE 14.2
The Leader as Hero ("Warrior") in U.S. Culture

Characteristics of a Hero ("Warrior")		*Characteristics of the Admired U.S. Leader*
called to adventure, to distinguish himself, to do what is right, to redeem himself	←→	has a vision, attempts something new, pursues a "dream," has sense of purpose
transcends community, resists pull of conformity, is different	←→	is unconventional, unique, true to himself and his convictions
leaves community, enters "wilderness" by himself	←→	is individualistic, is determined, sticks to his vision, leads by example
acts in and on the world, is active and action oriented, seeks control over environment	←→	is active and action oriented, has sense of urgency, exerts control, is a doer
takes great risks, encounters novel and difficult situations, faces significant enemy, shows courage	←→	takes risks, is a catalyst, breaks through conventions, faces great odds, shows courage, takes on big challenge
possesses extraordinary gifts, talents, strengths, has experience	←→	has a good track record, is outstanding, executes well, has some special talents
gets help from "protective" figure, wizard, special magic	←→	takes advantage of opportunities, has a "mentor," is optimistic
stands tall, faces death, overcomes defeat, is victorious, rescues those in distress	←→	overcomes all odds, learns from mistakes, turns things around, works hard, is forceful, asserts himself, perseveres
can move and/or save lesser people, carries their hopes	←→	is inspirational, galvanizes people, is transformational
faces own demon, comes into his own, reintegrates into community	←→	is positive, shows honesty and integrity, makes changes for the good

Note. From Campbell (1973), Hubbell (1990), and Leeming (1981).

In this image of the leader as warrior hero, leaders are driven by an inner calling and/or that of their organization or community. They have a vision of the journey to be taken or the fight to be fought. They are catalysts of change. They are driven to action, have a sense of urgency, and assert themselves. They are willing or forced to take great risks, encounter numerous trials and tribulations, fail, pick themselves up again, overcome all odds, and through great strength, skill, and experience succeed. Their fight is a lonely one, perhaps even against the wishes of their own people, but their deep convictions pull them through and, eventually, they will succeed, and be recognized and admired. They may become mentors of others in their organization or active contributors to the community. Their names may adorn a building, a highway, or a scholarship fund after the successful completion of their "heroic journey." "In many respects, [Abraham] Lincoln conforms perfectly to [this] archetype of the lonely, individualistic hero" (Bellah et al., 1985, p. 146). Similarly, Collins and Porras's (1997) "built to last" leaders and Collins's (2001) "level 5 leaders," who combine great personal humility with a strong professional will, illustrate the power of this image of the individual leader as hero.

It is implicitly also the image of the leader as savior that in part is "our wish to rediscover hope and, interestingly enough, to have someone else provide it for us" (Block, 1993, p. 14). This tendency carries the risk of people getting disillusioned when the leader fails their hopes and expectations. Paradoxically, it may also make them feel insignificant and, as a result, have them hope for their leaders to fail. Whatever the explanation, mainstream U.S. society believes that

> Deeply rooted cultural and social problems can be solved if only we pick the right [leader] ... [In addition], we like our heroes and villains strong, simple, and clearly differentiated. We distrust ambiguity, equivocation, systems, and complexity. We want a *person* to praise or blame. Problems can be "fixed," and that's why we have leaders. They represent us, and if they can't do the job, we will get someone else. ... Top leaders are granted either god-like or goat-like status as they are paraded across our pages and screens. (Noer, 1994, p. 9)

However, there is a second, complementary, image of the leader emerging in the historical and cultural sketches of U.S. leadership. It is an image that has always been part of the themes and tensions in U.S. society but that in today's changing information and global environment is receiving increasing attention—because it either has been ignored for too long or is needed more than ever (or both). It partly reflects aspects of additional expressions of the mythical hero, that is, the teacher, healer, and visionary (Arrien, 1992). It describes leaders as humble, empathetic, cooperative, communal, participative, and process oriented. Furthermore, it expects leaders to be more culturally sensitive and adaptive and more global in their outlook. Some of these additional expectations surface again in the remaining part of this chapter, in the quantitative and qualitative GLOBE data.

Perhaps more important, U.S. leadership theory and practice are beginning to move away from their overemphasis on the individual leader and to broaden their understanding of lead-er*ship* as a process and organizational capacity that allow people to engage together to create and realize their shared sense of purpose as well as to express their democratic responsibility and will. Given the dynamic nature of U.S. society, and especially the dramatic shifts that are taking place around the world, additional models and practices will evolve. It is hoped that those will be enriched by cultures everywhere.

3. QUANTITATIVE AND QUALITATIVE GLOBE RESULTS

This section of the chapter reports on the quantitative and qualitative GLOBE data in the following sequence. First, we summarize the findings along the nine cultural orientations to provide the backdrop against which the next part of the discussion on GLOBE's leadership scales can take place. We then describe the methodology and findings of the structured interviews, focus groups, and the media analysis. Throughout, we frequently link back to the insights from Sections 1 and 2 and provide selected appendices to supplement the findings.

U.S. Cultural Orientations: Etic Comparisons

The data for this Section were collected in late 1997 from 382 U.S. managers from three U.S. financial services, three food, and two telecommunications services industry companies, all of them under U.S. ownership and located in the United States. The managers were on average 44 years old, had an average of 14 years of managerial experience, and belonged in their vast majority to the middle to upper middle management of their company. About one third of them were women. (See Appendix A for more details.) The following discussion of the U.S. results on GLOBE's *cultural* scales is based on about one half of these managers ($N = 188$), who completed the Beta version of GLOBE's research questionnaire that asked respondents how "things are in your society" ("As Is") and how "things generally should be in your society" ("Should Be").

The discussion uses the definition and operationalization of the cultural scales, as described in the introductory chapter of this anthology and as applied in the other chapters of this book. They are society-level constructs that allow U.S. culture to be described in "cultural space," that is, in comparison to other societies that are part of the GLOBE study. This is an important point to keep in mind, because the different or similar cultural preferences of the United States can best be highlighted by contrasting them with the rest of the countries in the study—or any given society at a time. This clearly constitutes an etic approach to understanding U.S. culture (Hofstede, 2001). Furthermore, it may also be helpful to remember, as we continuously link the findings back to the earlier discussion, that the results in this section are largely based on White male managers from corporate America.

Table 14.3 provides a numerical overview of U.S. society for the "Should Be" and "As Is" cultural scales. In addition to its scale means and standard deviations, it ranks the United States on each cultural scale among the 61 GLOBE countries.

Regarding its desirable or espoused societal norms (Should Be), the United States ranks highest on Gender Egalitarianism, Assertiveness, and Performance Orientation and lowest on Institutional Collectivism, Uncertainty Avoidance, and Future Orientation. A closer look helps deepen this observation. The T-scores, which represent standardized U.S. rankings against an overall "global norm" for each scale (Mean [M] = 50; Standard Deviation [SD] = 10), based on the grand mean of the GLOBE countries for each scale, show a significantly (difference of 1 SD or more) higher desire for more equality of opportunity between men and women in U.S. society ($T = 61$) and significantly greater preference for flexibility and openness to change (i.e., weak Uncertainty Avoidance; $T = 41$) and individual rewards or initiative (i.e., low Institutional Collectivism; $T = 40$) than in the other countries on the whole. There is also a comparably higher degree of preference for Assertiveness ($T = 58$).

At the same time, these preferences ("Should Be") across the nine cultural scales do not completely match the U.S. managers' perceptions of how things are ("As Is"). Compared to the rest of the countries studied, they observed, in particular, high degrees of competitive and aggressive behavior (high Assertiveness Orientation; $T = 61$) and marked emphasis on performance ($T = 60$), but low degrees of concern for or cohesiveness in their society's organizations and families (low In-Group Collectivism; $T = 38$) and relatively small power differentials among members of their society (small Power Distance; $T = 43$).

Table 14.4 provides further insights. It offers a comparison between the realities that the managers experience ("As Is") and how they would like things to be ("Should Be") and, once

TABLE 14.3

U.S. Means, Grand Means, Standard Deviations, T-Scores, and Ranges for
"Should Be" and "As Is" Cultural Scales

"Should Be"	U.S. Mean[a]	Standard Deviation	Rank[b]	Grand Mean[b]	Standard Deviation	T-Scores U.S.[c]	Range min.	Range max.
Assertiveness	4.32	.76	15 B	3.82	.65	58	2.66	5.56
Future Orientation	5.31	.68	39 B	5.48	.41	46	4.33	6.20
Gender Egalitarianism	5.06	.69	7 A	4.51	.48	61[d]	3.18	5.17
Humane Orientation	5.53	.64	23 B	5.42	.25	54	4.49	6.09
In-Group Collectivism	5.77	.72	22 B	5.66	.35	53	4.94	6.52
Institutional Collectivism	4.17	.68	53 C	4.73	.49	40[d]	3.83	5.65
Performance Orientation	6.14	.57	16 B	5.94	.34	56	4.92	6.58
Power Distance	2.85	.73	19 C	2.75	.35	53	2.04	3.65
Uncertainty Avoidance	4.00	.90	50 C	4.62	.61	41	3.16	5.61

"As is"	U.S. Mean[a]	Standard Deviation	Rank[b]	Grand Mean[b]	Standard Deviation	T-Scores U.S.[c]	Range min.	Range max.
Assertiveness	4.55	.82	10 A	4.14	.37	61[d]	3.38	4.80
Future Orientation	4.15	.74	16 B	3.85	.46	57	2.88	5.07
Gender Egalitarianism	3.34	.75	33 B	3.37	.37	49	2.50	4.08
Humane Orientation	4.17	.81	26 C	4.09	.47	52	3.18	5.23
In-Group Collectivism	4.25	.73	51 C	5.13	.73	38[d]	3.53	6.36
Institutional Collectivism	4.20	.84	32 B	4.25	.42	49	3.25	5.22
Performance Orientation	4.49	.89	11 A	4.10	.41	60[d]	3.20	4.94
Power Distance	4.88	.80	49 B	5.17	.41	43	3.89	5.80
Uncertainty Avoidance	4.15	.83	28 B	4.16	.60	50	2.88	5.37

[a]$N = 188$ (respondents with missing data included). [b]$N = 61$ countries. In addition, rank group letters A–C (some scales have a group letter of D) indicate meaningful country clusters. A > B > C > D for each scale. [c]T-scores represent standardized U.S. rankings against overall global norms ($M = 50$, $SD = 10$), based on 61 countries (excluding Czech Republic). [d]1 SD or more below or above global norm.

again, expresses those as standardized U.S. rankings against overall global norms for each scale. In addition, it lists the difference between U.S. "As Is" and "Should Be" mean scores for each scale and ranks those across the other countries.

Whereas the U.S. managers would prefer somewhat diminished stress on assertiveness and performance (even though still more than on average in the other countries), they definitely would like to see more attention paid to the needs of organizations and families (In-Group Collectivism), at least to catch up to the world (from $T = 38$ to $T = 53$). They also look for significantly more gender egalitarianism (in spite of the fact that their "As Is" score is close to the standardized mean for all countries in the study, $T = 49$) and for noticeably more power differentiation among the people of their society (from $T = 43$ to $T = 53$). In contrast, they would like U.S. society to become noticeably less rule driven (weak Uncertainty Avoidance; $T = 41$), less future oriented ($T = 46$), and more individualistic (low Institutional Collectivism; $T = 40$) than, on the whole, the managers in the other countries do.

Some caution is in order at this point not to overinterpret these desired changes in U.S. society. First of all, they may reflect some specific organizational dynamics in the eight

TABLE 14.4

Cultural Orientations—Differences Between "As Is" and "Should Be"

US Means[a]	"As Is"	"Should Be"	Difference	Rank[b]	T-Scores[c] "As Is"	"Should Be"
Assertiveness	4.55	4.32	−0.23	26	61[d]	58
Future Orientation	4.15	5.31	+1.16	46	57	← 46
Gender Egalitarianism	3.34	5.06	+1.72	8	49	→ 61[d]
Humane Orientation	4.17	5.53	+1.36	33	52	54
In-Group Collectivism	4.25	5.77	+1.52	7	38[d]	→ 53
Institutional Collectivism	4.20	4.17	−0.03	44	49	← 40[d]
Performance Orientation	4.49	6.14	+1.65	42	60[d]	56
Power Distance	4.88	2.85	−2.03	17	43	→ 53
Uncertainty Avoidance	4.15	4.00	−0.15	45	50	← 41

[a]N = 188. [b]Rank of U.S. difference scores across 61 countries. [c]T-scores represent standardized U.S. rankings against overall global norms (M = 50, SD = 10), based on 61 countries. Compared to other GLOBE countries, ← = noticeably less desirable than is; → = noticeably more desirable than is. [d]1 SD or more below or above the global norm.

corporations of this study. Second, they may mirror the specific needs of managers in middle to upper middle management positions. Perhaps, most important, they need to be understood against changes that managers worldwide desire, as those look at what is and what they would like to happen in their societies. Table 14.3 already hinted at this reality. For example, the U.S. mean scores for Performance Orientation suggest a marked increase between "what is" and "what should be" (x = 4.49 to x = 6.14). Yet, the size of this desired change ranks only 42 among the 61 countries and, in fact, results in the aforementioned wish for a slightly diminished emphasis on performance, when compared to the global norm (from a T-score of 60 to one of 56).

Figure 14.1, based on the grand means and U.S. means from Table 14.3, helps visualize these dynamics. Four is the midpoint ("neither agree nor disagree") of the 7-point Likert scale used in the GLOBE questionnaire. *The managers from all 61 countries on the whole* (in descending order of the magnitude of the shift from "As Is" to "Should Be") would like their societies to place more emphasis on performance, the future, a kinder society (Humane Orientation), gender equalitarianism, their organizations and families' needs (In-Group Collectivism), collective rewards and action (Institutional Collectivism), and provide more certainty, but would like them to greatly decrease inequality in power among their citizens and be somewhat less aggressive and competitive with one another. The U.S. managers agree with all but two of these desired shifts. As described earlier, they want fewer (not more) rules, regulations, and restrictions and greater stress on individual (not collective) rewards and action. In addition, even though they agree with the general direction of seven of the nine shifts that managers around the world would like to see, U.S. managers, *relatively speaking,* end up wanting their society to emphasize performance somewhat and the future markedly less and power distance a bit more (see Table 14.4).

Summing up, the U.S. respondents in this study, *comparatively speaking,* experience their society (As Is) as highly competitive, demanding, and performance-driven—and somewhat

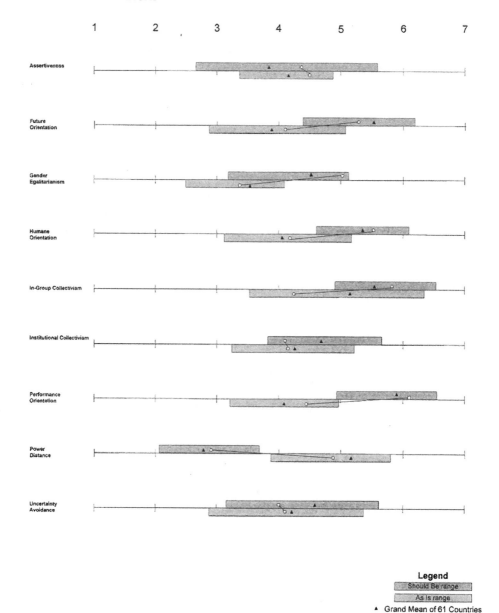

Figure 14.1.   U.S. cultural profile ("Should Be" and "As Is" scales).

future oriented—but little concerned with the well-being of organizations and families and a little bit too much egalitarian (small Power Distance). In terms of the "ideal society" (Should Be), they desire a society that works toward much greater gender equalitarianism as well as the well-being of its organizations and families and creates some more deference and respect for its authorities and leadership (larger Power Distance). Similarly, they would like to see a greater emphasis placed on the present (less Future Orientation) and see innovation, flexibility, and individual initiative and achievement encouraged even more.

Although there are a few minor differences in preferences across the three industries (see Appendix B) and, for instance, findings that women tend to strive for greater gender egalitarianism and somewhat more tolerance for uncertainty and a greater emphasis on the present than men (see discussion in Section 4), this description is very similar to the one that emerged in the earlier parts of this chapter in the image of the U.S. leader as cultural hero. Aspects of it also surface in the structured interview, focus groups, and media analysis results to be discussed later. At this point, selected data, quotes, and references (i.e., emic expressions) deepen the understanding of this cultural profile of U.S. society.

U.S. Cultural Orientations: Emic Manifestations in American Society

Assertiveness Orientation. At the interpersonal level, being assertive in the United States tends to mean standing up for oneself, wanting to be counted, and exercising the right and the obligation to express one's opinions and needs—and to do so in a constructive and kind way that respects the other person's right to do the same. This encourages straightforward, direct, frank or, if unchecked, blunt exchanges among people. At the societal level, it reflects the highly (vertical) individualistic nature of U.S. society (Triandis, 1998) and a high concern for "mastery" (Schwartz, 1999), but when overdone, is seen as aggression, bullying, or an excessive concern with being "number one." The GLOBE results suggest that, indeed, U.S. society is considered significantly more assertive than many other countries—and that it may overdo it. GLOBE's "As Is" scores also correlate significantly at the 0.5 level (Spearman rank) with results from Hofstede's IBM and Hoppe's study of European elites across 16 countries that the three studies have in common. The two latter studies used Hofstede's Masculinity dimension and showed the United States to be the seventh and third, respectively, most masculine country among the 17 countries that those two studies had in common (see Hoppe, 1998, p. 33).

In his book *Understanding Global Cultures,* Gannon captures the essence of U.S. culture in the metaphor of the American football game. He states that "competition seems to be more than a means to an end in the United States and apparently has become a major goal in itself" (Gannon, 1994, p. 308). The exhortation by the legendary football coach, Vince Lombardi (1995), that there is no room for second place makes the same point. George Steinbrenner, owner of the New York Yankees baseball team and former member of the U.S. Olympic Committee, puts it this way: "I want this team to win, I am obsessed with winning, with discipline, with achieving. That's what this country is all about" (cited in Boone, 1992, p. 113). During the Olympic Games in Atlanta in 1996 a Nike billboard announced, "You don't win the silver, you lose the gold." It is no coincidence that all of these quotes come from the field of sports. As described earlier, sports play a dominant role in U.S. culture and sports language and concepts pervade its daily and business interactions.

Moreover, whoever has watched an American football game can attest to its fiercely aggressive nature. It is known as a "collision" sport as opposed to a "contact" sport, such as basketball. Another expression of this aggressive, tough, and domineering orientation in U.S. culture may be seen in its crime and imprisonment rates. Whatever the complex societal and cultural dynamics may be, the United States has a disproportionately much higher number of its citizens commit violent crimes and spend time in prison than any other comparable society in the world (*Oxford Atlas of the World,* 1994, p. 45).

In business, the strong propensity for assertiveness may express itself in working hard to be "number one," a marked competitive drive to get ahead in one's career, a distinct imbalance between professional and personal life, a preference for decisive and forceful leaders, and a short-and-to-the-point communication style. The qualitative data from the structured interviews, focus groups, and the media analysis largely bear this out.

Future Orientation.   As described earlier, the managers in this study, compared to those in the other 60 countries, describe U.S. society as placing relatively great emphasis on the future ($T = 57$ in Table 14.3), that is, planning ahead, investing in the future, and delaying gratification. On the other hand, though wanting society to be even more future-oriented in absolute terms, comparatively speaking, they would like it to be noticeably less so ($T = 46$). This expressed desire by the U.S. managers is more in line with the typical description of U.S. culture as rather short-term oriented—and as surfaced during the brief cultural sketch of U.S. society earlier. At the same time, it may be the constant changes in their work environment that may make them wish for an organizational and societal life that does not always require them to plan for and/or implement the *next* change (e.g., mergers, acquisitions, or organizational consolidation).

Seen through a cultural lens, Stewart and Bennett (1991) discuss Americans' concept of time as "lineal," that is, flowing from past to present to future, with a distinct preference for the present and the future (see also Trompenaars, 1994). They conclude that

> Americans find it important to cope with this flow ("keeping up with the times") and to look ahead ("keeping an eye on the future"), but the temporal orientation downstream should be qualified as "near future." (For businesspeople, six months, or perhaps one year, down river is a reasonable projection. More distant futures are usually considered impractical.) (p. 123)

Similarly, in Hofstede and Bond's (1988) study of 23 countries, the United States showed a relatively short-term orientation, emphasizing consumption and "keeping up with the Joneses" over thrift and long-term investments. This cultural propensity is most visible in a U.S. personal savings rate (as percentage of after-tax income) of *minus* 0.2% in July of 2000 ("Consumer Spending Tops," 2000, p. B8) and the notorious *quarterly* reports that companies are asked to submit to their banks, stockholders, or the government.

The combination of U.S. culture seeing time as a resource that should not be wasted, the availability of increasingly sophisticated information technologies, and the accelerating speed of the global marketplace in which speed has become *the* competitive advantage will most likely reinforce a short-time mentality. Indeed, changes may occur so fast or be so complex that people begin to refuse to engage in activities that extend more than a few months or 2 to 3 years into the future. For example, historian D. Walter found that "students were reluctant to think about the future, a tendency he [also] sees in others" (Blangger, 1999, p. 1). Seen in this light, the U.S. managers in this study may have wished for a comparatively greater focus on the present as a reflection of the complex, sped-up environment in which they do their daily work.

Gender Egalitarianism.   In ancient Greece, women were described as "incomplete men." Only 80 years ago, women in the United States secured the right to vote. About 30 years ago, educational institutions in the United States were federally mandated to provide athletic programs for boys *and* girls (Title IX). In short, present U.S. society has come a long way in creating equal opportunities for boys and girls, men and women, to succeed. For instance, as mentioned earlier, almost half of today's U.S workforce are women and close to 45% hold executive, administrative, and managerial positions. Though still few of today's women occupy top positions in Fortune 500 companies, women currently own and run one third of all American businesses and "employ more people than the entire Fortune 500 list of America's largest companies combined" (Adler, 1999, p. 249). Also, about 4 out of 10 doctorate degrees are awarded to women, of those about 3 out of 10 in the field of business management and administrative services (U.S. Census Bureau, 1999); the U.S. women's soccer team was named team of the year in 1999; and programs of women's studies have become a regular part of academia.

Many more statistics paint a similar picture of great strides toward greater numbers of opportunities and successes for women. Others offer a different story. For example, on average women across occupational and educational groups earn only about 72% of what men of similar background and experience take home ("Household Income," 2000; see also Roos & Gatta, 1999) and Fortune 1000 companies still have only about 10% women on their boards (*American Demographics,* 2000, p. 25). In the political arena, about the same percentage are women senators or Representatives in Congress (Sarin, 2003), even though their proportion is greater at the state level. Furthermore, the "great books" of the past tend to perpetuate masculine images of men *and* women (Rabinowitz & Richlin, 1993).

Overall, the movement toward more egalitarian treatment of men and women will continue. However, it may not automatically make U.S. culture less masculine; in fact, it may reinforce its high degree of cultural masculinity (Hofstede, 1991; Hoppe, 1998). In his reflections on the nature of feminism movements around the world, Hofstede observes that "the masculine form claims that more women should have the same possibilities as men have ... [yet] simply having women work in the same numbers and jobs as men does not necessarily represent their liberation. It could be a double slavery, at work *and* in the home" (p. 102ff).

Humane Orientation.   First-time visitors to the United States often comment on how friendly, open, and generous Americans are. Although there may be noticeable differences between urban and rural areas and north and south and east and west, it tends to be easy to quickly establish, at least superficially, a friendly exchange of information and/or personal history. It is a cultural characteristic that was partly formed early on in American history, when people moved westward and depended on each other for support and survival. It reflects a cultural value that encourages people to transcend their narrow interests "in favor of voluntary commitment to promoting the welfare of others" (Schwartz, 1999, p. 28).

Moreover, this cultural trait expresses itself on a deeper level, when disaster strikes an individual, neighborhood, or community, at home or abroad. This tends to generate a tremendous outpouring of genuine concern and compassion, supported by personal sacrifice and material assistance. Furthermore, it can bee seen in the results of a recent survey in which almost 60% of Americans said that it was *very* important for community life "for people to volunteer money and time to charitable organizations" (The National Commission on Philanthropy and Civic Renewal, 2000, p. 1). In fact, for the year 2000 the total amount of charitable giving reached more than $190 billion (American Association of Fund-Raising Counsel, 2000), encouraged by federal tax laws that allow individuals and organizations to lower their taxes through charitable contributions. About 80% of the contributions come from *individuals.*

Volunteering is an equally deeply ingrained part of the American social fabric. In 1995, more than 90 million Americans were involved in some kind of volunteer work, ranging from help in soup kitchens (to feed those in need), to Habitat for Humanity (to build homes for low-income families), to environmental preservation. Also, corporations routinely sponsor and help staff annual drives for the United Way campaign that raises money for a wide range of community-based, national, and international charitable institutions. They tend to consider it a civic duty—and encourage their employees as well—to contribute to the community in which they are located. Internationally, the U.S. Peace Corps for more than 40 years has been a visible symbol of the genuine American urge to help and to contribute to the greater good of the world community.

In-Group Collectivism.   It may not be much of an exaggeration to assert that many Americans today experience their families and organizations to be under siege. As summarized in Table 14.4, the managers in this study seem to strongly agree with this observation ($T = 38$ for "As Is") and would like their society to be closer to the global mean ($T = 53$ for "Should Be"). One possible explanation for this result may be that they feel caught in the middle of two strong dynamics that describe U.S. society today—the tremendous pressures on the family and the accelerated demands on and by the organizations in which they work.

To understand the family dynamic, it is important to move away from the traditional image of the family as consisting of a married couple with two or three children in which the father was employed outside of the home and the mother stayed at home to take care of the children. In 1998, only 53% of all households with children were headed by a married couple and about 16% by either a single man or woman. The remaining 31% of households were single-male or -female households (U.S. Census Bureau, 1999, p. 873). Furthermore, about 10% of marriages each year end in divorce.

Moreover, in 53% of all married-couple families both spouses work (*Consumer Reports,* 2001, p. 8). In addition, about 6 out of 10 of all married women with children under the age of 6 are employed outside of the home. For single mothers or those from African American communities, the number increases to 7 or almost 8 out of 10, respectively (U.S. Census Bureau, 1999, p. 417). Also, about 8 million men and women hold more than one job, half of them to meet regular household expenses, pay off debts, or save for the future (U.S. Census Bureau, 1999, p. 421). In short, whether married or single, mothers and fathers in large numbers are trying to balance the multiple demands of holding down a job, providing financially for the needs of the family, taking care of their children, and having time for themselves and/or each other. This struggle applies equally to highly successful women in leadership roles (see Kantrowitz et al., 2005; Ruderman & Ohlott, 2002).

This juggling act is exacerbated by the fact that Americans, on average, spend annually between 1 and 3 months more time at work than any other highly economically developed country in the world (International Labor Organization, 1999; Robinson, 2003). Although this trend may be largely due to complex interactions among a number of variables, for example, the dynamics of the free-market system, a volatile labor market, the particular American work ethic, and the cultural propensities related to the strong assertiveness and performance orientation in U.S. society, it has been accelerated by the marked increase in corporate downsizing (i.e., massive job cuts) as an everyday management tool during the past 20 years. In the process, not only have entire layers of middle managers been losing their jobs, but also they have felt deeply betrayed by their companies. The "psychological contract" that they thought they had with their employers—good work and loyalty in return for long-term employment—has been replaced by a new understanding: "We keep you employed as long as your skills and expertise are needed in the changing fortunes of our company."

This new psychological contract has left many of those who lost their job feeling bitter and disillusioned and those who survived the layoffs vulnerable, abused, and overworked. Noer (1993) speaks of the need for "healing the wounds" of the survivors to overcome the traumas of layoffs and to revitalize downsized organizations. In addition, former U.S. Secretary of Labor, Robert Reich observes that "survivors are working harder—that's feeding the whole work frenzy" (cited in McGinn & Naughton, 2001, p. 41). Most likely, globalization and fast-changing technologies, fueled by an economic, free-market mentality, will continue these pressures on companies and its employees to stay nimble and work long hours, respectively. Similarly, the resulting personal economic necessities and the changed nature of the American family will continue to exact its toll on people's time and sense of belonging. In short, pride, loyalty, and cohesiveness in one's family and organization will be hard to come by.

Institutional Collectivism. The U.S. managers in this study confirm what many observers, scholars, and researchers of U.S. culture have maintained for more than the past 200 years. Americans believe that society should primarily encourage and reward *individual* achievements and actions as a means and an end toward the individual and the collective good alike. In the aforementioned studies by Hofstede and Hoppe (see Hoppe, 1998, p. 33), the United States was the most individualistic among 17 countries (Spearman rank correlation with "Should Be" scores across the 16 countries that all three studies had in common was .05 and .01, respectively). In the current one, it is the 9th most individualistic out of 61 countries (i.e., ranked 53 on Institutional Collectivism). The "As Is" scores for the United States are near the global norm ($T = 49$), but as discussed earlier the U.S. managers go against the global trend by desiring a slightly more individualistic orientation of U.S. society. In fact, *comparatively speaking,* they clearly want society to stress individual interests and freedom over those of the collectivity ($Ts = 40$).

In addition to the earlier discussion of individualistic expressions in U.S. life and leadership theory and practice, two observations may help deepen the understanding of this desire for individualism in the United States. The first relates to O'Toole's (1993) distinction between liberty (free market and free from government) and equality (equity and solidarity) in Table 14.1. Both values tend to be cherished in many countries around the world, but typically one is preferred over the other. For example, in a study of nine Western European countries, the respondents in most of them valued on average freedom ("everyone can live in freedom and develop without hindrance") above equality ("nobody is underprivileged and social-class differences are not so strong"). However, when each country's preference for freedom was divided by its preference for equality, the resulting country scores significantly correlated with the individualism scores in Hofstede's IBM study. In other words, "the more individualist a country, the stronger its citizens' preference for liberty over equality" (Hofstede, 1991, p. 72). It is a result that most likely also holds for the United States due to the latter's strong emphasis on individual freedom and initiative.

The second observation stresses the deeply ingrained and interconnected nature of individualism with the political, economic, and philosophical system of mainstream U.S. society (Behrman, 1988). Politically, current U.S. democracy is founded on the premise that only independent, well-informed (and existentially equal, i.e., small Power Distance) citizens, who feel that they have a stake in their community and society at large, can prevent the tyranny of a few. Economically, its embrace of the free-market system is predicated on the enlightened and vigorously pursued self-interest of individuals whose (ideally) free choices determine the flow of supply and demand. Philosophically (and theologically), it assumes free individuals who feel called upon and obliged, to the best of their abilities, to reach for "perfection" in the image of their God. To be sure, there are many shades and permutations of these basic beliefs throughout U.S. history (see Bellah et al., 1985). Furthermore, everyday realities often fail to reflect them. However, as widely espoused beliefs they exert a powerful influence on Americans' images of the ideal person, leader, organization, and society at large, images that may be at odds with those in many other countries, as witnessed by the fact that 70% of the 61 GLOBE countries (economically poor and rich!) want their societies to be *less* individualistic.

Performance Orientation.   Implicitly, this cultural scale is about outcomes and the action, effort, and execution to achieve them—terms that are highly valued in U.S. culture. *E*xplicitly, it is about continuous improvement in individuals and organizations, challenging goals, and effective and innovative behaviors. Related values are facts, data, and measurement as the means of determining the desired and/or promised results. Within a historical and cultural context, this emphasis on performance may be seen as an equitable way of determining a person's standing and identity in a society that has moved away from using tribe, class, or family name to define its members. From an economic perspective, it points to a person's definition as an asset or resource whose value needs to be determined—the citizen as "economic man" (Bellah et al., 1985, p. 271). As a result, there is a heavy emphasis in U.S. culture on measurements of great variety, including national test scores for children in grade school, grade point averages in high school and college, SAT scores to get into college and, in the world of business, assessment centers for selection, performance appraisals and, of course, organizational data of all kinds.

In addition, bonus pay systems and awards to reward the top performers are common. For example, a company in New England gives each December the Extra Mile Award to several of its employees "who have gone above and beyond the call of duty" (Nelson, 2000, p. 43). In sports, there is the player of the week or, of longer-lasting recognition, the induction into the Hall of Fame. Another measure of success for Americans is to be included in the *Who's Who in America.* This attention to the "ceremonial celebration of perfection" is due to "the common belief in the United Sates … that the individual is capable of anything he or she wants to accomplish. Individual achievements, whether earning a degree or scoring the highest number of field goals for one game, are considered precious human deeds and are entitled to commemoration in one type of ceremony or another" (Gannon, 1994, p. 317).

Similarly, the common belief and exhortation that the "sky is the limit" has helped spawn a huge industry of self-improvement books. Books on any topic are available. In the area of leadership, for example, Covey's (1989) book *The Seven Habits of Highly Effective Leaders* has become a runaway bestseller. Other publications, such as the earlier mentioned *In Search of Excellence,* its sequel, *A Passion for Excellence* (Peters & Austin, 1985), or *Good to Great* (Collins, 2001), tell of excellent companies and how to emulate their exemplary practices. Lou Gerstner (2001), CEO of IBM, proclaims, "We have a right to expect excellence" (p. 6). In more recent years, information technologies and globalization have greatly accelerated this trend.

Power Distance.   U.S. culture is typically described as a very egalitarian society whose Constitution not only guarantees the existential equality of every man and woman, of whatever ethnic or national background, but in which people have come to expect that differences in status and power be minimized and hierarchical structures primarily express inequalities in roles established for convenience or efficiency's sake. Therefore, it seems to be somewhat surprising that in other large-scale empirical studies the United States, when compared to Western European countries, consistently shows larger hierarchical differences (i.e., Power Distance) than Denmark, Finland, Norway and Sweden, as well as the Netherlands, the United Kingdom, and Switzerland (Hofstede, 1980; Hoppe, 1998; Schwartz, 1999). The same holds for the "Should Be" scores in the current study. Also, once again, there exists a significant Spearman rank correlation (at the .01 level) between the "As Is" scores and the Hoppe and Hofstede studies (earlier discussion).

One of the explanations for this "surprise" may lie in the observation that Americans' primary mode of distinguishing themselves is their own individual achievement, which makes them stand out and for which they expect tangible, visible rewards. In an organizational environment, the reward may be advancement into a managerial role that signifies the special talent and effort that one has shown and that creates a "legitimate" inequality between manager and employee that is expected to be honored and respected (power values in Schwartz, 1999). The result is the belief (see Section 1) in a "managerial prerogative" that (in combination with the romance of leadership in U.S. culture) is less open to participative management from the *bottom up*—an approach that is more often witnessed in the Northern European countries (Hofstede, 1991). It can be seen in the results that show U.S. respondents consider it less important to be consulted by their manager than those from the aforementioned countries (Hoppe, 1990, p. 225). It can also be observed in the willing acquisition and display of status symbols that come with higher organizational ranks, such as larger offices, cars, or membership privileges and other perquisites (see also Pfeffer, 1981).

A second explanation can be found in the particular version of U.S. capitalism, which has sided over time more than any other country with the demands and promises of the free market *and* the belief in the efficiency of big corporations (O'Toole, 1993; see also Table 14.1). As a result, the prerogative of capital, ownership, and property is largely taken for granted, as directly visible in U.S. society's support and protection of entrepreneurial activities (expression of the liberty theme) and indirectly in its admiration for the corporate manager who can be said to act as the guardian or representative of corporate ownership—be that ownership by individuals, groups, or stockholders (expression of the efficiency theme). In the latter case, managers are expected to run the organization as efficiently as possible and, in the process, protect and enhance the owners' property and/or investments. Inherent in this approach is the notion of hierarchy, because "efficiency requires a division of labor; an orderly division requires a hierarchy based on ability; and people in a hierarchical system will be, by definition, stratified in classes" (O'Toole, 1993, p. 65). In sum, the combination of U.S. culture's emphasis on meritocracy, the sanctity of ownership, and its belief in the importance of efficiency, tends to translate into a managerial prerogative not practiced to the same degree in many Western European countries.

Uncertainty Avoidance. Experiencing and responding to uncertainty, ambiguity, and change with unknown outcomes are part of the human condition. The question is how emotionally comfortable people are in those circumstances and what they do to cope with the inherent unpredictability of their lives. At the societal level of analysis, U.S. society as a whole, more than most societies, accepts uncertainty and its resulting ambiguities and unpredictable changes as a natural part of life. Eric Sevareid, a former American news reporter and commentator, put it this way: "The most distinguished hallmark of the American society is and always has been change" (cited in Boone, 1992, p. 301).

As discussed before, American culture tends to be described as innovative, mobile, flexible, dynamic, and open to change and new experiences even when the outcomes are not predictable. The entrepreneur is idolized, because he or she does not give up despite setbacks and/or outright failure. The leader as heroic warrior is admired for their taking off for unchartered territory and willingly facing great risks without guarantee of a successful ending. Conflict, dissent, and competition are seen as potentially beneficial in spite of their inherently unpredictable outcomes. Overall, it is a description whose roots can be found in U.S. society's historical experience of people taking great risks to reach its shores and conquer its frontiers and a political and economic system that tends to encourage and reward those who dare.

Although this description is not mirrored in this study's "As Is" scores for the United States ($T = 50$), it is clearly the preferred state of affairs ($T = 41$), when compared to the global norm. That is, the U.S. managers of this study want society to become less rule-bound, whereas the other countries as a whole desire significantly more certainty in their lives. This finding is in line with results from the aforementioned studies by Hofstede and Hoppe. They significantly correlate with the "Should Be" scores (Spearman rank at the .05 and .01 level, respectively) and show U.S. society to be highly tolerant of uncertainty—yet, once again, not as much as, for example, Denmark and Sweden or Ireland and the United Kingdom.

An interesting expression of the United States's openness to change and acceptance of uncertainty as a normal part of life can be gleaned from reactions to major layoffs in the U.S. economy. A "striking feature is just how matter-of-factly—even happily—many elite workers are taking their 'reduction in force' notices … many workers have come to accept the risk of layoff as the price of admission to the New Economy" (McGinn & Naughton, 2001, p. 38). Adds a vice president of an outplacement firm: "It's almost a rite of passage … if you haven't lost at least one job in your career today, you haven't taken enough risk" (McGinn & Naughton, 2001, p. 38).

Although these reactions are in marked contrast to those just 10 years ago (see discussion of In-Group Collectivism) and possibly reflective of highly trained professionals in a thriving economy, they are indicative of an American mind-set that can look at a misfortune (e.g., being fired) as an opportunity for something better (e.g., a better job or more time for one's hobby or family). It is also symptomatic of a strong belief in progress and its accompanying general optimism toward the future. Similarly, it helps explain the widely accepted need for life-long learning and its requirements of "a high capacity for change and a high level of [emotional] comfort with that change" (Noer, 1997, p. 89).

In summary, when considered in their entirety, the U.S. results across all nine cultural orientations not surprisingly reinforce earlier descriptions of U.S. culture in Sections 1 and 2. More important, they largely paint a mirror image of the fundamental values and expressions of American democratic capitalism, thereby creating a most helpful backdrop against which mainstream U.S. leadership theory and practice may be understood.

In addition to the insights gained from the discussion of individualism, U.S.-style capitalism requires for its proper functioning not only largely unencumbered freedom for individuals and organizations to compete (weak Uncertainty Avoidance), but also the promise of tangible rewards, such as wealth or recognition, to encourage competition (strong Assertiveness Orientation). Similarly, it depends on measurable criteria and results to declare the winner of the competition, so that everybody understands and accepts the legitimacy of the victorious party ("legitimate inequality"/meritocracy; medium Power Distance). Implicit in all three requirements is an emphasis on performance, continuous improvement, and innovation (strong Performance Orientation) and a deliberate and focused approach to the task or challenge at hand to generate useful results in the foreseeable future (medium Future Orientation). Moreover, American democratic capitalism's long-term viability is fundamentally tied to the individual's moral obligation to seek wealth not only for personal use, but equally for the well-being of the community at large (medium-high Humane Orientation).

At the same time, due to its strong economically oriented philosophy, it subordinates its members' lives to the demands of the market. As a result, individuals' identities become defined in economic terms (e.g., as resources, assets, liabilities) and their families and organizations experience market-induced turbulence and fragmentation (weak In-group Collectivism "As Is"; medium "Should Be"). Similarly, gender equality tends to be narrowly measured either in terms of the degree to which girls and women have access to activities and jobs that were formerly "reserved" for boys and men or in terms of financial compensation (medium Gender Egalitarianism "As Is"; very high Gender Egalitarianism "Should Be"). Thus, by using the particular lens of U.S. society's form of democratic capitalism, it is possible to deepen the understanding of not only its cultural pattern, but simultaneously its inherent tensions and contradictions. Returning to Table 14.1, it also helps make apparent the strong pull that the values and themes in the left-hand column will continue to exert on U.S. culture's approach to leadership. The discussion returns to this overall portrait of American culture during the presentation of the leadership scales and the qualitative results of the study.

U.S. Results on Leadership Scales

The results in this section of the chapter are based on the *total* sample of 382 U.S. managers who responded to the 112 leadership items of the GLOBE instrument (Beta or Alpha version). The managers rated the instrument's 112 leader characteristics on a scale from 1 ("this behavior or characteristic *greatly inhibits* a person from being an outstanding leader") to 7 ("this behavior or characteristic *contributes greatly* to a person being an outstanding leader"). As with the cultural orientations, Table 14.5 provides a numerical summary of the results. Figure 14.2 is the visual representation of Table 14.5.

At first glance, managers around the world agree that for leaders to be seen as outstanding they need to have integrity, stress performance, and be inspirational and visionary (grand mean ratings above six). In contrast, they should not be malevolent, self-centered, autocratic, nonparticipative, and face savers (ratings below three). In addition, they like them to be team integrators, decisive, administratively competent, diplomatic, collaborative, and self-sacrificial (ratings between five and six) and not too autonomous, procedural, and conflict inducers (ratings below four).

Against this cross-cultural ground, the American managers consider it particularly important (top five) for outstanding leaders to have a performance orientation ($T = 62$), integrity ($T = 61$), humane orientation ($T = 59$), vision ($T = 58$), and inspiration ($T = 58$)—and also to a lesser degree to be modest ($T = 56$), decisive ($T = 54$), self-sacrificial ($T = 54$), and a team integrator ($T = 54$)—but to show very low (bottom five) autocratic ($T = 37$), nonparticipative ($T = 37$), status-conscious ($T = 38$), malevolent ($T = 40$), and conflict-inducing ($T = 40$) behaviors. That is, comparatively speaking and applying the specific behaviors that define each leadership scale, the U.S. managers of this study describe leaders as exceptionally good when they

- Demand and extol excellence in performance.
- Are honest, sincere, just, and trustworthy.
- Show compassion for the people who work for them.
- Treat others as equals and are highly informal and participative.
- Are open, pragmatic, friendly, and supportive.
- Have a vision and plan ahead.
- Engage the passions of their followers.

TABLE 14.5
U.S. Means, Grand Means, Ranks, Standard Deviations, *T*-Scores, and
Ranges for Leadership Scales

Leadership Scale	U.S. Mean[a]	Standard Deviation	Rank[b]	Grand Mean[b]	Standard Deviation	T-Scores U.S.[c]	Range min.	max.
Performance Orientation	6.46	.55	3 A	6.02	.37	62[d]	4.51	6.64
Visionary	6.28	.50	10 A	6.02	.36	58	4.62	6.50
Inspirational	6.35	.47	12 A	6.07	.36	58	5.04	6.63
Integrity	6.51	.55	6 A	6.07	.39	61[d]	4.83	6.79
Self-Sacrifical	5.16	.85	19 B	5.00	.41	54	3.98	5.99
Decisive	5.96	.59	25 A	5.80	.44	54	3.62	6.37
Team Integrator	6.03	.45	26 A	5.88	.40	54	4.10	6.43
Collaborative Team Oriented	5.38	.60	40 B	5.46	.32	48	4.42	6.09
Administratively Competent	5.63	.79	44 B	5.76	.39	46	4.53	6.35
Diplomatic	5.46	.48	33 A	5.49	.30	50	4.49	6.05
Malevolent	1.55	.45	52 D	1.80	.28	40[d]	1.33	2.67
Self-Centered	1.97	.71	42 C	2.17	.35	45	1.55	3.41
Status-Conscious	3.60	1.29	54 C	4.34	.64	38[d]	3.15	5.93
Conflict Inducer	3.53	.92	51 C	3.97	.48	40[d]	3.09	5.01
Face Saver	2.66	.97	37 C	2.92	.56	45	2.05	4.63
Procedural	3.90	.76	30 B	3.87	.51	50	2.82	4.89
Autocratic	2.03	.83	56 D	2.65	.46	37[d]	1.89	3.86
Nonparticipative	2.10	.69	56 C	2.66	.44	37[d]	1.86	3.61
Humane	5.19	.94	11 A	4.78	.49	59	3.29	5.68
Modesty	5.24	.76	22 A	4.98	.39	56	4.14	5.58
Autonomous	3.75	1.01	39 B	3.85	.44	47	2.27	4.63

[a]N = 382 (respondents with missing data excluded). [b]N = 60 (N = 61 including Iran, for Humane, Performance Orientation, and Visionary scales). In addition, rank group letters A–D indicate meaningful country clusters. A > B > C > D for each scale. [c]T-scores represent standardized U.S. rankings against overall global norms (M = 50, SD = 10), based on 61 countries. [d]1 SD or more below or above global norm.

- Take a decisive, courageous, and team-oriented approach to the challenges and opportunities at hand.
- Stay calm under pressure and don't take themselves overly seriously.

Table 14.6 reinforces this profile. It offers summary results based on GLOBE's six second-order leadership scales. Here, the outstanding leader combines, in particular, a highly participative with a charismatic and humane set of personal characteristics.

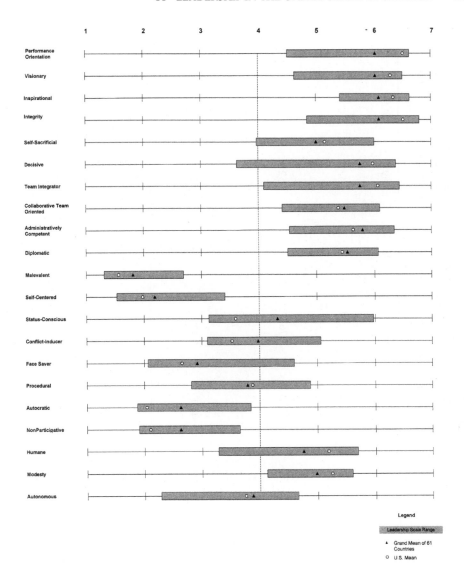

Figure 14.2.   U.S. cultural profile for leadership scales. $N = 382$ (respondents with missing data excluded).

The image of the outstanding leader that emerges from the leader scales is similar to earlier descriptions in this chapter, yet also different. As before, outstanding leaders are seen to have a vision, stress performance excellence, have integrity and convictions, and be decisive, egalitarian, flexible, and pragmatic in their approach to others and their work. However, U.S. managers also describe outstanding leaders as needing to be highly participative, tap into the inner passions of the people who work with them, truly care about them, and be less taken by and be preoccupied with themselves. That is, they do not solely create an image of the individual heroic warrior who

TABLE 14.6
U.S. Means, Grand Means, Standard Deviations, T-Scores, and Ranges for Second-Order Leadership Scales

Second-Order Leadership Scales and Subscales	U.S. Mean[a]	Standard Deviation	Rank[b]	Grand Mean	Standard Deviation	T-Scores U.S.[c]	Range min.	max.
Charismatic	6.12	.39	6 B	5.83	.33	59	4.51	6.46
Performance Orientation								
Visionary								
Inspirational								
Integrity								
Self-Sacrificial								
Decisive								
Team Oriented	5.80	.37	31 B	5.76	.26	52	4.74	6.21
Team Integrator								
Collaborative Team Oriented								
Administratively Competent								
Diplomatic								
Malevolent (reversed scored)								
Self-Protective	3.15	.59	47 F	3.47	.42	42	2.55	4.62
Self-Centered								
Status-Conscious								
Conflict Inducer								
Face Saver								
Procedural								
Participative	5.93	.64	5 A	5.33	.41	64[d]	4.50	6.09
Autocratic (reversed scored)								
Nonparticipative (reversed sc.)								
Humane Orientation	5.21	.71	13 A	4.89	.40	58	3.82	5.75
Humane								
Modesty								
Autonomous	3.75	1.01	39 B	3.85	.44	47	2.27	4.63
Autonomous								

[a]$N = 382$ (respondents with missing data excluded). [b]$N = 61$. In addition, rank group letters A–F indicate meaningful country clusters. $A > B > C > E > F$ for each scale. [c]T-scores represent standardized U.S. rankings against overall global norms ($M = 50$, $SD = 10$), based on 61 countries. [d]1 SD or more above global norm.

is driven to succeed and stand out, but an image that stresses markedly more the organizational realities that work gets done *together* and that people need to feel important and taken seriously in their desire to grow and contribute (see also Manz & Sims, 2001).

What may partly explain these added features of the outstanding leader are the earlier-discussed shifts toward a more process-oriented, cooperative, and participative leadership that today's world seems to be calling for. Also, anecdotally, the first author of the chapter observed a marked change over the past 14 years in the way managers, taking part in leader development activities, approach a competitive group exercise. In the past, the vast majority of the managers tried to have their individual contribution to be judged the best. For the past 10 or so years, participating managers attempt from the outset to develop mutually beneficial outcomes—although the exercise continues to call for individual contributions and remains competitive in nature.

Another plausible explanation has to do with the fact that the U.S. respondents in this study are middle to upper middle managers whose particular role as managers "in the middle" of their organizational environment necessitates that they be participative and sensitive to others' needs. They may also have felt ignored too often in their own needs to have their passions engaged (see discussion of results of In-Group Collectivism). Furthermore, much of the earlier discussion referred to leaders anywhere in U.S. society, whereas the instructions for the leadership items specifically asked the respondents to think of "people in your organization or industry." Thus, the additional characteristics of the outstanding leader that surfaced from the leadership scales may reflect this more organizational focus.

Appendix C provides additional insights, as it summarizes significant correlations between cultural orientations ("Should Be") and the leadership scales. The four cultural scales that correlate most significantly with the leadership scales are Gender Egalitarianism, Uncertainty Avoidance, Power Distance, and Future Orientation. For instance, importance for charismatic leadership and its subscales tend to highly correlate with a preference for gender egalitarianism, but negatively with power distance. The same applies to participative leadership. The latter also correlates strongly with a preference for tolerance for uncertainty and somewhat less with assertiveness and the present. In contrast, self-protective leadership seems to occur more in cultural environments with a preference for strong uncertainty avoidance, an emphasis on the long-term future, and inequality between men and women. Autonomous leadership, not surprisingly, strongly correlates with individualism and to a lesser degree with power distance. In short, U.S. culture with its comparatively strong preference for gender egalitarianism, assertiveness, performance, and tolerance for uncertainty and its medium emphasis on the future and power differential seems to encourage, in particular, a highly participative, charismatic, open, direct, and pragmatic leader style. On the other hand, a clear cultural preference for individualism in U.S. society ($T = 40$ for Institutional Collectivism) does not automatically translate into a clear preference for an autonomous, independent leader style ($T = 47$ and Rank 39 B for autonomous). This latter finding should caution against making direct connections between a country's cultural makeup and its desirable and/or practiced leadership style. There are many other variables—historical, religious, political, economic, or organizational—that play into this dynamic.

Qualitative Data: Structured Interviews, Focus Groups, and Media Analysis

These last sets of data were collected between late 1997 and early 1999. Specifically, the *structured interviews* were conducted with 16 (White) middle to upper middle managers

TABLE 14.7

Structured Interviews[a] Summary of Outstanding Leader Characteristics

GLOBE Leadership Scales and Their Items	U.S. Ranks[b]	Frequency of Outstanding Leader (OL) Descriptions[e]	Representative Quotes
Inspirational (enthusiastic,* positive,* encouraging,* morale booster, motive arouser,* confidence builder;* dynamic,* motivational*)	12 A	84×	…everybody began to feel like a hero working with her … genuinely cares about you and your personal goal … led tremendous amounts of people to do things that they were never really capable of doing by themselves
Visionary (foresight,* intellectually stimulating, future oriented, prepared, anticipatory, plans ahead,* inspirational, visionary, able to anticipate)	10 A	50×	… outstanding leaders [have] the vision and the ability to convey that to others … people who are trying to look forward to the future end up being the leader, because they had foresight … she absolutely saw a big picture … and she drew a picture of where we needed to be
Team Integrator (communicative,* team builder;* informed,* clear, integrator, coordinator,* not subdued)	26 A	43×	… he could take a very, very complex issue and truly communicate it to everybody around him … it is practicing what you preach … it was just mayhem … but … he was able to focus everyone
Integrity (honest,* sincere, just,* trustworthy*)	6 A	35×	… had the gumption to stand up to the powers in a very large corporation … the obligation of leadership is when you see something good you support it no matter where it is … to treat others as you want to be treated, tell the truth, and do your best

(Continued)

TABLE 14.7 (Continued)

GLOBE Leadership Scales and Their Items	U.S. Ranks[b]	Frequency of Outstanding Leader (OL) Descriptions[c]	Representative Quotes
Performance Orientation (improvement oriented, excellence oriented,* performance oriented)	3 A	26×	… he expects nothing but excellence, nothing less … there has got to be a passion to get a little better every day … he demanded very high standards
Self-Sacrificial (risk taker, self-sacrificial, convincing)	19 B	25×	… they are committed to making what I consider sacrificial acts on behalf of others … outstanding are those that … continue to make the tough decisions now that there is a lot of risk involved … the ability to stand in the face of the crowd, if you will, under ridicule, under pressure
Decisive (willful, decisive,* logical, intuitive)	25 A	23×	… leader … is decisive, … firm, has compassion for people, … and is willing to make decisions … you have got to break some eggs and a great leader is one to make that decision … when he came to a decision, that was it, he would fight for it
Collaborative Team Oriented (group oriented, collaborative, loyal, consultative, mediator, fraternal)	40 B	22×	… we are going to win together, it's not just I … was willing to go in and fight for us … a leader is not afraid that some of their staff is better than they are
Humane (generous, compassionate)	11 A	16×	… they also convey to you that they care about you … if you don't have the human aspect, you can't sustain leadership … he never wanted to break you down in front of anyone else

(Continued)

TABLE 14.7 (Continued)

GLOBE Leadership Scales and Their Items	U.S. Ranks[b]	Frequency of Outstanding Leader (OL) Descriptions[c]	Representative Quotes
Diplomatic (diplomatic, worldly, win/win problem solver,[*] intragroup conflict avoider, effective bargainer[*])	33 A	11×	… to see the other point of view and pull two opposing views together … a general recognition and respect for each other's perspective … someone who is always sensitive to group dynamics
Modesty (modest, self-effacing, calm, patient)	22 A	7×	… they are humble. They know that they are not perfect … they remain very calm. They are steady … he is real down to earth
Administratively Competent (orderly, administratively skilled,[*] organized, good administrator)	44 B	7×	… outstanding leaders, I think, are very organized … if you don't carry a day timer you are not going to be here very long … he had … a track record … to believe … that he would get there

[a]Based on 11 interviews with a total of 16 participants and 391 scorable observations. [b]Based on 61 countries. [c]Autocratic (12×) and Malevolent (10×) attracted the most descriptions for *non*outstanding leaders. Remaining leadership scales not separately listed due to low frequencies. [*] = Universally desirable leader characteristics.

518

(12 men and 4 women) between mid-November 1997 and early January 1998. The managers were taking part at the time in a leader development program at the Center for Creative Leadership and volunteered to be interviewed for an hour each on the first evening of the program. They were in their early 40s, worked in the private sector, and all but one were born in the United States (he was from the UK, but had lived in the United States and worked for an American company for the past 20 years). The first author and colleagues of his conducted the interviews by using the interview guide in Appendix D. The interviews were then coded with the help of a graduate student, using the 21 leader scales and their items as a guide. The results are listed in Table 14.7. They are based on 391 scorable observations and 102 different examples of leaders, three fourths of which were presidents or other high public figures (42%), direct superiors, other managers, or coworkers (17%), and corporate leaders (16%).

Inspirational, visionary, team integrator, and integrity are clearly the most frequently mentioned outstanding leader characteristics, followed by being performance oriented, self-sacrificial, decisive, and collaborative. A closer look at the managers' stories revealed a distinct longing for outstanding leaders to appreciate, respect, and deeply care for the dignity and humanity in the people with whom they work. Similarly, leaders were described as outstanding when they helped others grow or mentor them. Moreover, there was an admiration for those who genuinely tried to connect with people who are different from themselves and who encouraged people to freely express their different views, needs, or hopes and fears.

Two additional themes surfaced: the need for outstanding leaders to have great self-awareness, accompanied by a degree of vulnerability, and the importance of timing, luck, and circumstance for outstanding leaders to emerge. As one manager put it regarding the second theme, "I believe that what makes outstanding leaders is often the circumstances, fate, or whatever … there are a lot of competent managers that might have the potential to be outstanding leaders that don't ever get the opportunity."

The total of 14 *focus groups* consisted of 94 middle to upper middle managers (76%), executives (18%), and professionals (6%) who participated in four leader development programs at the Center for Creative Leadership between early August and early October of 1998. Their average age was early 40s, 26% were women, about 10% were members of U.S. minorities, 6% were of different (non-U.S.) nationality, and 94% came from the corporate world.

As part of an exercise during the first morning of the program, they were asked to

Think of the best leadership that you've ever experienced, inside or outside of the workplace, and remember, by yourself and without talking to anyone, all the characteristics, behaviors, etc. that describe this leadership and that makes it still stand out in your mind and heart. As you begin to recall this best-ever leadership, write down each characteristic, behavior, etc., on a separate Post-it note and after 10 minutes post all of them onto the flipchart that has been prepared for your group.

After all characteristics, behaviors, and so on, were posted, small groups of six to eight participants were asked to discuss their results and agree after about 30 minutes on the six to eight descriptors that best captured outstanding leadership for them. The 14 groups generated a total of 387 characteristics, behaviors, and so forth, of which 137 (35.4%) were singled out as particularly descriptive of outstanding leadership. The results were coded in the same way as the structured interviews and are summarized in Table 14.8.

The findings are very similar to those from the structured interviews (Spearman rank at .01 level of significance). They also correlate significantly with the GLOBE rankings for the U.S.

TABLE 14.8
Focus Groups—Summary of Outstanding Leader Characteristics[a]

GLOBE Leadership Scales and Their Items	U.S. Ranks[b]	Frequency of Outstanding Leader (OL) Designations	Examples of OL Characteristics by Members of Focus Groups
Inspirational[c] (enthusiastic,* positive,* encouraging,* morale booster, motive arouser,* confidence builder,* dynamic,* motivational*)	12 A	30 × [61][d]	passionate, seeks buy-in, infectious, enthusiasm, motivator, committed, supportive, praise, nurturing, builds confidence
Integrity (honest,* sincere, just,* trustworthy*)	6 A	22 × [24]	trustworthy, genuine, principled, fair, ethical, moral, respected, credibility
Visionary (foresight,* intellectually stimulating, future oriented, prepared, anticipatory, plans ahead,* inspirational, visionary, able to anticipate)	10 A	18 × [16]	visionary, clear direction, sense of purpose, strategic, facilitates ideas, planning
Team Integrator (communicative,* team builder,* informed,* clear, integrator, coordinator,* not subdued)	26 A	17 × [33]	creates teamwork, goes to bat for team members, communicates frequently, two-way communication, motivates team, listens, ability to build groups, cohesiveness
Self-Sacrificial (risk taker, self-sacrificial, convincing)	19 B	15 × [37]	opportunity seeker, initiative, risk taker, agent of change, courageous, leads by example
Performance Orientation (improvement oriented, excellence oriented, performance oriented)	3 A	13 × [20]	commitment to excellence, sets high standards, focus on end results, accountable, emphasis on success

TABLE 14.8 *(Continued)*

GLOBE Leadership Scales and Their Items	U.S. Ranks[b]	Frequency of Outstanding Leader (OL) Designations	Examples of OL Characteristics by Members of Focus Groups
Decisive (willful, decisive,* logical, intuitive)	25 A	6 × [6]	decisive, decision maker, focused, strong personality
Modesty (modest, self-effacing, calm, patient)	22 A	5 × [12]	patience, emotional consistency, relaxed
Humane (generous, compassionate)	11 A	5 × [12]	compassionate, caring, empathy, humane
Diplomatic (diplomatic, worldly, win/win problem solver,* intragroup conflict avoider, effective bargainer)	33 A	1 × [3]	judgement, consensus builder, recognizes and resolves conflict
Misc. Characteristics		[16]	knowledgeable, experience, personality suited to task, values balance of work and personal life, creating safe environment, early wins

[a]387 scorable observations. 137 (35.4%) designated as OL (i.e., Outstanding Leader). [b]Based on 61 countries. [c]Attracted 5 additional designations of "empowerment" (plus 10 non-OL). [d]In bracket, listed as characteristics of outstanding leaders, but not specifically designated as "OL" * = Universally desirable leader characteristics.

521

managers (.05). Collaborative team orientation is the sole leader scale that did not make the list of the most frequently mentioned leadership characteristics. Overall, inspirational and visionary leaders who show integrity and are team oriented receive the clear majority of the outstanding leadership designations (64%). Compared to the quantitative leadership results, the emphasis on performance excellence is, as in the structured interviews, less pronounced, yet remains among the more frequently cited outstanding leader characteristics.

The data for the *media analysis* were collected between early and mid-December 1998 (Week 1 set of articles) and mid- to late February 1999 (Week 2 set of articles). They came from *The New York Times* (30), *USA Today* (30), *The Wall Street Journal* (26), *Time* magazine (10), and *Business Week* (10) for a total of 106 articles. The articles were selected from a broad spectrum of topics, such as politics, business, sports, and entertainment, that covered individual leaders, but also organizational change, developments in technology, globalization, political events, and so forth. An attempt was made to not a priori limit the portrayal of leadership to the individual leader, but include the broader context in which leadership is embedded. A total of 2,546 (leadership-related) observations were distilled from the 106 articles, coded by a graduate student and, separately, by the first author, and then grouped according to the GLOBE leadership scales and other categories that are presented later. The results for the leadership scales are summarized in Table 14.9. They are based on a total of 505 statements of *individual* leadership characteristics.

The results largely mirror the findings from the structured interviews and focus groups. Performance orientation, sacrificial, inspirational and visionary leadership, decisiveness, and integrity are the characteristics that are most frequently used to describe outstanding leaders in U.S. society, with performance orientation and self-sacrificial attributes, such as taking risks, taking bold steps, or succeeding through repeated trial and error, being emphasized more and integrity somewhat less than in the other two analyses. Diplomatic is also consistently mentioned across the three data sources. In contrast, leadership expressed as being a team integrator did not make the top-10 list at all. Overall, however, the similarities across the qualitative data are more striking than the differences. Appendix E supports this conclusion across all four qualitative and quantitative analyses of the individual leader characteristics.

Table 14.10 below summarizes the frequencies with which the media articles reflect U.S. society's preferences across GLOBE's nine *cultural* orientations. The image that emerges is a society that stresses performance, change, and competition. In combination with information from Appendixes F and G, which rank order major themes and most frequently used terms in the articles, it reinforces the earlier observation that the needs and preoccupations of American-style capitalism (and language!) greatly impact U.S. leadership thought and practice. In this fast-changing environment, all individuals are expected to take risks, compete hard and smart, and excel to achieve tangible results, such as profits, market growth/share, and/or customer loyalty, in the short- to medium-range future.

This type of environment may help explain why self-sacrificial leadership was ranked higher in the media analysis than in the other two qualitative analyses, and significantly higher than in the questionnaire-based findings (see Appendix E). The media analysis illuminates the vagaries of today's environment in which leadership expresses itself, the other three analyses more likely the organizational context in which the respondents worked. The former may be reflected in the markedly greater wish for *tolerance* of uncertainty ("Should Be" score $T = 41$); the latter in the almost 1 *SD* higher "As Is" score ($T = 50$) for Uncertainty Avoidance in Table 14.3.

Summing up the results of the qualitative analyses, it is conceivable that other major U.S. newspapers and magazines might have surfaced somewhat different images of American

TABLE 14.9
Media Analysis: Top 10 Frequencies of Individual Leader Characteristics[a]

---

1. Performance Orientation   (15.2%)
(e.g., improvement oriented, excellence oriented, performance
oriented, plus: persistence, drive, cutting edge, high standards,
staying competitive)

2. Self-Sacrificial   (13.9%)
(e.g., risk taker, self-sacrificial, convincing, plus: courage,
standing up for his or her beliefs, learning from mistakes,
bold steps, taking advantage of opportunities)

3. Inspirational   (12.1%)
(e.g., enthusiastic, positive, encouraging, dynamic, motivational,
plus: giving hope, encouraging others, exciting, imitated
by others, catalyst)

4. Visionary   (9.7%)
(e.g., foresight, intellectually stimulating, future oriented, plans
ahead, visionary, plus: having a business plan, long-term goal,
strategic plan, making priorities, having a master plan)

5. Decisive   (8.1%)
(e.g., willful, decisive, logical, intuitive, plus: assertive,
making quick decisions, firm, exerts his or her authority,
swift action, determined)

6. Integrity   (5.7%)
(e.g., honest, sincere, just, trustworthy, plus: respected, reliable,
fair, trust, consistent, telling the truth, role model)

7. Procedural (reversed)   (4.2%)
(e.g., flexible, informal, situational, plus: pragmatic,
responsive, being nimble, quick, adjusts)

8. Collaborative Team Oriented   (4.0%)
(e.g., collaborative, loyal, consultative, group oriented, plus:
shared purpose, getting input, teamwork, open door,
learning from others)

9. Diplomatic   (3.8%)
(e.g., diplomatic, worldly, win-win problem solver, effective
bargainer, plus: smart negotiation, building alliance, peace maker)

10. Autonomous   (3.8%)
(e.g., individualistic, independent, unique, plus: brilliant, guru,
own style, has his or her own way, making his or her own
decisions, self-styled)

Note.   Additional ranks 11. Self-Centered (reversed); 12. Administratively Competent; 13. Malevolent (reversed); 14. Face Saver (reversed); 15. Modesty.

[a]Based on 505 individual leader characteristics statements (out of 1,648) in *Business Week,* 12/1999; *The New York Times,* 12/9–11/1998 and 2/15–19/1999; and *The Wall Street Journal,* 12/9–11/1998 and 2/16–19/1999. Statements from *USA Today* and *Time* magazine were inadvertently excluded.

society and characteristics of the outstanding leader. However, those included in this analysis are clearly from mainstream publications that mirror mainstream U.S. culture. Similarly, it is

TABLE 14.10
Media Analysis Most Frequently (Explicit and Implicit)
Referenced Cultural Orientations[a]

1. Performance Orientation (e.g., improve performance, setting high goals, striving for excellence, cost reduction, persistence)	**(14%)**
2. Uncertainty Avoidance, *reversed* (e.g., change, innovation, risk-taking, breaking the rules, restructuring, flexibility)	**(13%)**
3. Assertiveness (e.g., domineering, aggressive, being number one, being competitive)	**(11%)**
4. Future Orientation (e.g., long-term, prepared, forecasting, vision, establishing a plan)	**(4%)**
5. Institutional Collectivism, *reversed* (e.g., brilliant, magna cum laude, standing up/out, vocal, causing a stir)	**(2%)**
6. Power Distance, *reversed* (e.g., informality, unconventional, accessible, getting input, encourages others to speak their mind)	**(1%)**

Note. Gender Egalitarianism, Humane Orientation, and In-Group Collectivism did not generate sufficient frequencies to be listed separately.
[a]Based on total of 2,546 statements from 106 articles (see sources of media analysis).

possible that different respondents than those who took part in leader development programs at the Center for Creative Leadership might have generated somewhat different perceptions of the outstanding leader in the structured interviews and focus groups, respectively. However, the results across the three qualitative analyses are strikingly similar. Moreover, they are largely consistent with the previous discussion of U.S. leadership thought and practice. At the same time, they expand and deepen it. Thus, outstanding leaders are additionally seen as able to

- Deeply appreciate and respect the inherent humanity and dignity of each person.
- Help others grow and mentor them.
- Understand their own personal strengths, liabilities, and vulnerabilities.
- Communicate with a wide range of different people and actively encourage them to express their different points of view, beliefs, and values.
- Rise to and above the challenge and/or opportunity at hand.

As pointed out after the presentation of the quantitative leadership results, this creates once again an image of the outstanding leader that includes but also goes beyond that of the individual heroic warrior who is primarily motivated by his or her own needs and values and is driven to succeed and leave behind a legacy. It is an image that highlights the needs and aspirations of those affected by the leader's actions as well and that may be closer to the realities of organizational life than the public's image of the individual heroic warrior may suggest.

4. INTEGRATION OF FINDINGS AND CONCLUSIONS

The major task of this chapter has been to surface major explicit and implicit images and perceptions of leadership in U.S. culture. This was done in Section 1 through brief discussions of the historical context from which they emerged, well-known American cultural patterns that continue to shape them, and outstanding characteristics of prominent past and present leaders. In addition, a selective overview of the leadership literature in Section 2 provided insights into the particular definitions and preoccupations of U.S. leadership thought and practice. This led to the identification of approaches to leadership yet at the fringes of mainstream thinking. Section 2 concluded with a description of the leader as heroic warrior as the preeminent image of the outstanding leader in U.S. society. A similar, yet also different, image of leadership surfaced in Section 3 when U.S. society was placed in "cultural space" along GLOBE's nine cultural dimensions and its 21 (and six second-order) leadership scales, using quantitative as well as qualitative data.

In the remaining part of the chapter, we first provide a snapshot of 10 key U.S. leader characteristics, culled from the previous discussions, to use them as springboard from which to offer selected advice to those from foreign soil who find themselves working with Americans at home or abroad. We then take a brief look at the assets and potential liabilities of mainstream U.S. leadership thought and practice in a changing world and highlight limitations of the study and possible directions for future leadership research.

Summary Profile of the "Ideal Leader" in U.S. Society: Considerations for Leaders Everywhere

When condensed to 10 major characteristics and highlighted against images of outstanding leaders in the other 60 GLOBE countries, exceptional leaders in mainstream U.S. society

1. *Stand out* through their individual achievements. They love to compete, win, and leave a personal legacy. They assert themselves through the force of their personality and/or convictions and lead by example.
2. *Inspire* through their optimism, can-do mentality, and energy. They appeal to the good in people and bring out the best in them. They are comfortable exerting their influence on others.
3. *Stand up for their beliefs.* They stay true to themselves and are authentic and straightforward. They can be trusted. They remain calm under pressure, can laugh at themselves, and may show great humility.
4. *Focus their efforts.* They have an achievable vision, which they pursue against all odds and distractions. They communicate their vision frequently and are able to articulate it to a wide range of different audiences.
5. *Strive for excellence* in their and others' performance. They love challenges and "go the extra mile." They set measurable outcomes, improve on them, and execute efficiently.
6. *Seek change.* They are comfortable with taking risks and making mistakes. They learn from failures and are innovative and flexible. They define challenges as opportunities.
7. *Act quickly.* They exude a sense of urgency and are driven to act. They are decisive and forceful. They prefer swift and approximate over slow and deliberate decisions.
8. *Promote team spirit.* They stress the need to work and succeed together. They communicate team goals and clarify everyone's roles and contributions. They instill pride in the team.

9. *Encourage participation.* They seek input from others and are open to suggestions. They stress informality and create a supportive work environment. They build on people's intrinsic motivations and delegate.
10. *Care about people.* They respect the inherent humanity and dignity of each person. They feel compassion for others and assist them when needed. They encourage and support others to realize their unique potential and strive to serve the greater good.

It is apparent from the other chapters in this volume and GLOBE's overall findings (House et al., 2004) that societies around the world look for these same leader characteristics to varying degrees. Some of them, such as those belonging to the Anglo or the Nordic and Germanic Europe cluster, desire them more; others, for instance, from the Middle East or Confucian Asia cluster, seek them less. That is, an important first step for anyone who finds him- or herself working with someone from another culture it is to gain a deeper understanding of the other person's "culturally acquired implicit and explicit leadership theory and practice" *and* of his or her own. Only by reflecting on both of them and actively trying to understand each other's will the similarities and differences come into focus. Only by striving for greater insights into the other's workplace and the broader societal context in which it is embedded will the similarities and differences begin to make sense. Only by improving one's cultural adaptability and perspective-taking skills will cross-cultural effectiveness ensue.

A fruitful second step is to realize that the aforementioned profile of the leader in U.S. society is a cultural stereotype that needs to be treated as a *provisional* stereotype—not only because cultures change some of their expectations and practices over time, but also because the United States is culturally rather heterogeneous. At the Center of Creative Leadership, the first author uses the term of the "roving anthropologist" to convey the notion that it is essential to continuously check one's own cultural assumptions and keenly and repeatedly assess, hypothesize, and act (AHA principle) when entering and working in a new cultural environment. As Germanic cultures tend to say, "The devil is in the detail" (in the United States, it is said at times that "God is in the detail"). Whatever the case may be, things are not always what they appear to be and often seemingly clear similarities in expected leader behaviors may lead to the greatest misunderstandings and/or conflicts. For example, leaders worldwide are expected to be decisive. However, "decisive" may mean in the United States being "quick and approximate," while in France being "deliberate and precise" and in Japan "consensual and long-term" (see Hoppe, 2004). Similarly, "just" is also seen as a universally desirable leader characteristic. Yet, just may mean in the United States "in accordance with the law or fair" whereas in Mexico "in accordance with my family's or friends' needs."

Beyond these more generic first two suggestions, the third one has to do with the aforementioned observations that American men and women in leadership roles tend to show a strong desire toward action, execution, and getting results. It's a propensity that Yeung and Ready (1995) empirically corroborated in their eight-nations study in which U.S. managers considered "get results-manage strategy to action" the most important leader capability, much more so than managers from France, Germany, Japan, and South Korea. Although this tendency nurtures a "can-do, problem-solving, and just-do-it" approach, it also invites an emphasis on work and career over personal and family life, task over relationship, competition over collaboration. It furthermore tends to encourage a short planning (and quick-to-market approach) and a resulting longer implementation phase during which deficiencies of the new product or service need to be addressed. Men and women from countries such as Denmark, Germany, Norway, the Netherlands, or Sweden need to come to terms with this underlying dynamic in U.S. life, as they work with American men and women at home or abroad.

The final suggestion is based on experiences by the first author over the past 30 years working with participants in leadership roles from all over the world. It is informed by statements that more frequently could be heard from U.S. participants than from any other cultural group, such as "if it is to be, it's up to me"; "make the best of it"; "luck's got nothing to do with it"; "nobody owes me anything"; "I am responsible for my own happiness"; "it's gonna work"; or "if I won't succeed the first time, I'll try again." These expressions of self-agency, positive thinking, and optimism often served up additional energy among the people working together and resulted in a positively charged self-fulfilling prophecy of their activities. Others not infrequently labeled this American spirit as naive, innocent, or ignorant. However, could it not be offered as an antidote to men and women from cultures in which much is invested and expected from the "system," whether the system is the government, the organization, or the family? Stated differently, couldn't a combination of self-agency, positive thinking, and optimism *and* systems thinking, realism, and a concern for the greater good be the more powerful elixir for effective leadership everywhere?

Assets and Potential Liabilities of U.S. Leadership Thought and Practice in a Changing World

It is clear that the aforementioned profile of 10 key U.S. leader characteristics may contain additional lessons for people in leadership roles from around the world who want to be successful in today's fast-changing and increasingly global environment. For example, U.S. leadership's openness to change, its willingness to take risks and try new things, its pragmatic mentality, and its desire to excel in order to achieve tangible results may serve others well, too. Its sense of urgency, its competitive spirit and determination, and its ability to engage the talents and energies of its people may provide them with critical ingredients for success. Its democratic ideals, support of others, and sense of fair play may help them garner greater trust.

Of course, this profile of U.S. leader characteristics constitutes an ideal that may be more in people's head than "real," as the differences between the "Should Be" and "As Is" results of the cultural orientations attest. Also, its characteristics may turn into stumbling blocks when not adjusted to the ever-changing and diverse world or turn into liabilities when overdone. For example, when not properly calibrated, the drive for change may rob people of their need for some stability and undermine their sense of belonging and loyalty in their organizations and communities. Or, when overdone, a healthy competitive spirit may turn into winning by all means at the expense of solidarity and empathy with others (Kohn, 1993). In particular, the emphasis on the *individual* leader who is expected to make the difference in people's and organizations' lives is beginning to show its limitations, as markets have become more global, and assuring the sustainability of planet Earth, in its complexity and long-term implications, requires noticeably more organizational and institutional collaboration (Friedman, 2005; Lodge, 1995).

This over emphasis on the individual leader (and other potential liabilities of leadership thought and practice in U.S. society) has come into sharper focus, as U.S. leadership thought and practice over the past few decades increasingly came into contact with markedly different cultures and the field of intercultural management established itself. For example, looking at the world at large, Hofstede observes, "Collectivism is the rule in our world and individualism the exception" (Hofstede, 1991, p. 54). Similarly, anthropological studies and developments in physics, biology, and computer technologies have led to the realization that the Western world's view of the "self-contained individual" (here, the individual leader) is rather peculiar and predisposes it to commit the "subjectivist fallacy" (Bond, 2000; Sampson,

2000). Or, as Candide in Leonard Bernstein's musical of the same name laments, "It must be me; it must be me."

These are not abstract ruminations. For example, whenever U.S. participants during an exercise in the lead author's leader development work are asked to first describe critical leader characteristics and then their work environment with its typical challenges and opportunities, they tend to end up in a telling dilemma. Inevitably, as a group, they describe a leader who has the aforementioned 10 (or more) characteristics. Inevitably, they also admit that they haven't met anyone yet who had all of those characteristics. Then, when asked to describe the daily realities of their workplace, they speak of great volatility, uncertainty, complexity, ambiguity, and rapid change. Yet, inevitably, the vast majority of them continues to insist that "if there were just that great (heroic) leader, things would be better"—forgetting that today's complex and ever-changing challenges and opportunities are beyond any single person's grasp and abilities and that much of their daily work is already characterized by significant collaboration among them—and their organizations and governments.

Moreover, as discussed in Section 2, the *a priori* definition of leadership as *individual* leadership tends to call forth an image of the leader as a hero and savior, someone who is ascribed superhuman attributes and who carries the hopes and fears of others. Whereas the adulation of the leader as hero may play a useful role in any society by inspiring people to make sacrifices for themselves and others, it tends to undermine the basic requirements of a democratic society whose well-being depends on the active involvement of *the majority* of its members. Is it not much more tempting to leave things up to those who, by default or design, occupy leadership roles? Similarly damaging, it may diminish the sense of worth, personal power, and human dignity that people feel about themselves, when the leaders as heroes occupy the few pedestals that society makes available. Is it not all too human to feel inferior when looking up to these "superhuman" leaders? At its worst, the strong belief in the heroic individual leader, when left unexamined, may lead others astray. Building on a quote by a participant from the structured interviews, "He [the manager] was able to get the staff … to walk on water for him; they would do anything for him." What if what that "charismatic" manager wanted them to do was unethical or immoral? History is full of examples of this kind.

This brief discussion about potential pitfalls of U.S. society's preoccupation with the (heroic) individual leader is embedded in a larger issue. The American romance of leadership on the whole tends to favor social science over politics, psychology over sociology, behavior over structure, data over values (Behrman, 1988; Hofstede, 1993; Lessem & Neubauer, 1994). Comparatively speaking, this is not a minor matter, because many countries around the world express a greater need and/or preference for positional, structural, or systemic leadership. Also, the term *leadership* may not even exist or have very different meanings around the world (Dorfman, 1996), as witnessed by the French's struggle trying to differentiate between leadership and governance. Perhaps even more important, this tendency is of no little consequence within U.S. society either, as the country's problems come to be seen to "stem not from evaded issues of injustice or inequality but from technically faulty administration [i.e., leadership]" (DeMott, 1993, p. 72).

Limitations of the Study and Suggestions for Future Research

The GLOBE study as a whole deserves great credit for attempting to develop an empirically based theory of leadership to help predict the effectiveness of leader and organizational practices in different cultures and, from the outset, embedding its theorizing in data from a wide range of cultures and a set of empirically derived cultural dimensions. By asserting the importance of the cultural context in the understanding of leadership, it is also praiseworthy for implicitly reaffirming the critical role of so-called followership, that is, that "leadership is in the eye of the beholders" (Mintzberg, 2003, p. 10). In addition, and aside from the gargantuan efforts of its key contributors, sustaining the study for more than a decade (and counting) and building up a network of 170 plus scholars from around the world are achievements by themselves. Alas, as with every study large or small, there are research aspects that one would have wished to have done, forget to do, and/or deliberately decided not to do. Here are some that the authors wished to have seen or to see in the future.

The first concerns the overall research methodology of the GLOBE leadership questionnaire that *a priori* invited a definition of leadership as something that an individual does. As this chapter has shown, this introduced a Western and trait-based bias as well as an influence model of leadership that prevented other notions of leadership to come to the fore. If effective leadership is the capacity for carrying out the leadership tasks of setting direction, creating alignment, gaining and maintaining commitment, and facing and resolving adaptive challenges (McCauley & Van Velsor, 2003), then leadership can also be seen as residing in an organization or community as a whole, manifested in its set of competencies, its shared vision and/or passion(s), its structure, and/or culture. This would require studying entire systems, from groups to societies, for expressions of leadership. Similarly, it would call for paying attention to the interconnections between and among people, groups, institutions, and/or functions.

The choice of respondents could be considered a second limitation. The vast majority (90%) were middle managers who had an average of 14 years of managerial experience (for more information, see Appendix A). In some sense, it was a good choice because, as employees in the middle of the organization, they experience themselves as leaders and followers. They were also reasonably well matched across the societies of the entire GLOBE study, coming from the same three for-profit industries. Yet, a managerial bias in their perspective is not unlikely. If one agrees that leadership is in the eye of the beholder, then it would be helpful to learn more about the values, beliefs, and expectations of those not in leadership roles—in particular, as the U.S. workforce has become increasingly diverse (U.S. Census Bureau, 1999). In the same vein, more than two thirds of the U.S. respondents were men. As Appendix H shows, there are some significant differences in cultural norms and leader characteristics that men and women desire. Could this suggest that by relying too much on data from men, who also hold managerial roles and come from the corporate world, the study of leadership across cultures perpetuates a male-dominated image of the leader and the process of leadership? It is a question that needs to be addressed more diligently in future leadership studies.

A definite strength of this study is its combination of different methods, quantitative and qualitative data, and lenses on the past and present that create a mutually reinforcing image of leadership in the United States. Yet, most of the data are still based on surveys, interviews, national statistics, or secondary analyses. What remains missing are complementary data that are collected on site, in real life and leadership situations, and based on actual behaviors— data along Mintzberg's (1973) question of what managers really do, Collins's (2001) work on what makes organizations great, or d'Iribarne's (1994) comparative study of three manufacturing plants of a French aluminum company. These types of data may not only help narrow the often-observed gap between actual and espoused values and beliefs, but also provide nonlaboratory data that more fully capture the complexities and realities of today's leadership challenges and effective approaches.

Last but not least, great benefits may be derived from "de-psychologizing" the study of leadership by more vigorously studying the broader contexts in which individuals, groups, and institutions try to succeed in their leadership tasks, be that their economic, political, cultural, environmental, or historical circumstances. It may turn out that leadership, as largely understood and studied in the United States, is but *one* variable in the total equation of determining people's quality of life and the well-being of the planet earth, perhaps not even the most critical one.

ACKNOWLEDGMENTS

The first author would like to thank for their invaluable assistance Denise Craig, Thomas Engel, Stefan Fazekas, Robert Kaiser, Steffen Obst, Philip Ruerup, Andreas Voigt, Katja Weissbach, and many other colleagues at the Center for Creative Leadership.

The second author acknowledges the summer support provided by the Folgeman College of Business that enabled him to complete work on this chapter. Appreciation is also expressed to Zhenyu Huang, Pamela Dembla, and Karen Moustafa for their assistance.

Apologies to all other Americans, north and south and east and west of the United States of America. The term *American* is used, at times, to help with the flow of the writing, not to expropriate it from other Americans.

REFERENCES

Adler, N. J. (1999). Global leaders: Women of influence. In G. N. Powell (Ed.), *Handbook of gender and work* (pp. 239–261). Thousand Oaks, CA: Sage.

American Association of Fund-Raising Counsel. (2000, May 24). *Total giving reaches $190.16 billion as charitable contributions increase $15.80 billion in 1999.* Retrieved September 27, 2000, from http://www.aafrc.org/News.HTM

American Demographics. (2000, February). *Up the corporate ladder* (p. 25) Available at http://www.demographics.com

Arrien, A. (1993). *The four-fold way: Walking the paths of the warrior, teacher, healer and visionary.* San Francisco: Harper.

Bass, B. M. (1990). *Bass and Stogdill's handbook of leadership.* New York: The Free Press.

Behrman, J. N. (1988). *Essays on ethics in business and the professions.* Englewood Cliffs, NJ: Prentice-Hall.

Bennis, W., & Nanus, B. (1985). *Leaders: The strategies for taking charge.* New York: Harper & Row.

Bellah, R., Madsen, R., Sullivan, W. N., Swidler, A., & Tipton, S. M. (1985). *Habits of the heart: Individualism and commitment in American life.* New York: Perennial Library.

Berger, P. L., & Luckmann, T. (1967). *The social structure of reality: A treatise in the sociology of knowledge.* Garden City, NY: Doubleday (Anchor Books).

Berry, N. (1993). What is our common sense of leadership? *Firethorn Quarterly, 1,* 1–2.

Blanchard, K., & Johnson, S. (1981). *The one-minute manager.* New York: Morrow.

Blangger, T. (1999, December 12). Student hesitancy about the future in stark contrast to that of our fearless forebears. *The Morning Call Newspaper Company.* Retrieved September 28, 2000, from http://www.mcall.com/cgi-bin/slwebsto.cgi

Block, P. (1993). *Stewardship.* San Francisco: Berret-Koehler.

Bond, M. H. (2000, November). *A declaration of independence for editing an international Journal of Cross-Cultural Management.* Unpublished manuscript, Hong Kong: Chinese University of Hong Kong.

Boone, L. E. (1992). *Succeeding in a competitive world.* New York: Random House.

Butterfield, D. A., & Grinnell, J. P. (1999). "Re-Viewing" gender, leadership, and managerial behavior. In G. N. Powell (Ed.), *Handbook of gender and work* (pp. 233–237). Thousand Oaks, CA: Sage.

Calder, B. J. (1977). An attribution theory of leadership. In B. M. Staw & G. R. Salancik (Eds.), *New directions in organizational behavior* (pp. 179–204). Chicago: St. Clair Press.

Campbell, J. (1973). *The hero with a thousand faces.* Princeton, NJ: Princeton University Press.

Cavanagh, G. F. (1984). *American business values.* Englewood Cliffs, NJ: Prentice-Hall.

Collins, J. (2001). *Good to great: Why some companies make the leap and others don't.* New York: HarperCollins.

Collins, J., & Porras, J. I. (1997). *Built to last.* New York: HarperCollins.

Consumer Reports. (2001, January). Des Moines, IA.

Covey, S. R. (1989). *The seven habits of highly effective people.* New York: Simon & Schuster.

Dalton, M., Ernst, C., Deal, J. & Leslie, J. (2002). *Success for the new global manager: How to work across distances, countries, and cultures.* San Francisco: Jossey-Bass.

DeMott, B. (1993). Choice academic pork: Inside the leadership-studies racket. *Harper's Magazine* (pp. 61–77). New York: The Harper's Magazine Foundation.

d'Iribarne, P. (1994).The honor principle in the bureaucratic phenomenon. *Organization Studies, 15,* 81–97.

Dorfman, P. (1996). International and cross-cultural leadership. In B. J. Punnett & O. Shenkar (Eds.), *Handbook for international management research* (pp. 267–349). Cambridge, MA: Blackwell Business.

Drath, W. H. (2001). *The deep blue sea: Rethinking the source of leadership.* San Francisco: Jossey-Bass.

Drath, W. H. (1996). Changing our minds about leadership. *Issues & Observations, 16*(1), 1–4. Greensboro, N.C.: Center for Creative Leadership.

Drath, W. H. (2003). Leading together: Complex challenges require a new approach. *Leadership in Action, 23*(1), 3–7.

Faludi, S. (1999). *Stiffed: The betrayal of the American man.* New York: Morrow.

Friedman, T. L. (2000). *The Lexus and the olive tree.* New York: Anchor Books.

Friedman, T. L. (2005). *The world is flat: A brief history of the twenty-first century.* New York: Farrar, Straus & Giroux.

Gannon, M. J. (1994). *Understanding global cultures.* Thousand Oaks, CA: Sage.

Geertz, C. (1979). From the native's point of view: On the nature of anthropological understanding. In P. Rabinow & W. M. Sullivan (Eds.), *Interpretive social science* (pp. 225–241). Berkeley: University of California Press.

Gergen, K. J. (1996). Psychological science in cultural context. *American Psychologist, 51*(5), 496–503.

Gerstner, L. (2001). Expectation of excellence: We have a right to expect excellence. *Executive Excellence, 18*(2), 6.

Gilgoff, D. (2005, October 31). America's best leaders. *U.S. News & World Report, 139*(16), 18–91.

Gilligan, C. (1982). *In a different voice: Psychological theory and women's development.* Cambridge, MA: Harvard University Press.

Greenleaf, R. K. (1977). *Servant leadership: A journey into the nature of legitimate power and greatness.* New York: Paulist Press.

Hackman, J. R. (1990). *Groups that work (and those that don't).* San Francisco: Jossey- Bass.

Hall, E. T., & Hall, M. R. (1990). *Understanding cultural differences: Germans, French and Americans.* Yarmouth, ME: Intercultural Press.

Halman, L., & de Moor, R. (1993). Religion, churches and moral values. In P. Ester, L. Halman, & R. de Moor (Eds.), *The individualizing society: Value change in Europe and North America* (pp. 37–65). Tilburg, Netherlands: Tilburg University Press.

Heifetz, R. A. (1994). *Leadership without easy answers.* Cambridge, MA: Harvard University Press.

Helgesen, S. (1995). *The web of inclusion.* New York: Doubleday.

Hofstadter, R. (1969). *Anti-intellectualism in American life.* New York: Knopf.

Hofstede, G. (1980). *Culture's consequences: International differences in work-related values.* Beverly Hills, CA: Sage.

Hofstede, G. (1991). *Cultures and organizations: Software of the mind.* London: McGraw Hill.

Hofstede, G. (1993). Cultural constraints in management theories. *The Executive, 8*(1), 81–94.

Hofstede, G. (2001). *Culture's consequences: Comparing values, behaviors, institutions, and organizations across nations* (2nd ed.). Thousand Oaks, CA: Sage.

Hofstede, G., & Bond, M. H. (1988). The Confucius connection: From cultural roots to economic growth. *Organizational Dynamics, 16*(4), 4–21.

Hofstede, G., & Kassem, M. (1976). *European contributions to organization theory.* Assen, Netherlands: Van Gorcum.

Hoppe, M. H. (1990). *A comparative study of country elites: International differences in work-related values and learning and their implications for management training and development.* Unpublished doctoral dissertation, University of North Carolina, Chapel Hill.

Hoppe, M. H. (1993). The effects of national culture on the theory and practice of managing R&D professionals abroad. *R & D Management, 23*(4), 313–325.

Hoppe, M. H. (1998). Validating the masculinity/femininity dimension on elites from 19 countries. In G. Hofstede (Eds.), *Masculinity and Femininity: The taboo dimension of national cultures* (pp. 29–43). Thousand Oaks, CA: Sage.

Hoppe, M. H. (2004). Cross-cultural issues in leader development. In C. D. McCauley & E. van Velsor (Eds.), *Handbook of leadership development* (2nd ed., pp. 331–360). San Francisco: Jossey-Bass.

House, R. J., & Aditya, R. N. (1997). The social scientific study of leadership: Quo vadis? *Journal of Management, 23*(3), 409–473.

House, R. J., Hanges, P. J., Javidan, M., Dorfman, P. W., & Gupta, V. (Eds.). (2004). *Cultures, leadership and organizations: The GLOBE study of 62 societies.* Thousand Oaks, CA: Sage.

Household income hits all-time high. (2000, September 27). *USA Today.*

Hubbell, L. (1990). The relevance of the heroic myths to leadership development. *American Review of Public Administration, 20,* 139–154.

Hunt, J. G., & Osborn, R. N. (1982). Toward a macro-oriented model of leadership: An odyssey. In J. G. Hunt, U. Sekaran, & C. A. Schriesheim (Eds.), *Leadership: Beyond establishment views* (pp. 196–221). Carbondale: Southern Illinois University Press.

Inglehart, R. (1997). *Modernization and post-modernization: Cultural, economic, and political change in 43 societies.* Princeton, NJ: Princeton University Press.

International Labor Organization. (1999, September). Geneva, Switzerland: United Nations.

Johnson, P. (1997). *A history of the American people.* New York: Simon & Schuster.

Jung, B. (1997). *Meeting the new world—influence of globalization and information technology on leadership.* Unpublished manuscript, Center for Creative Leadership, Greensboro, NC.

Kantrowitz, B. (2005, October 24). How women lead: 20 of America's most powerful women on their lives - and the lessons they've learned. *Newsweek, 146*(17), 46–76.

Kellerman, B. (1984). *Leadership: Multidisciplinary perspectives.* Englewood Cliffs, NJ: Prentice-Hall.

Kelley, R. E. (1988). In praise of followers. *Harvard Business Review, 66*(6), 142–148.

Kerr, S., & Jermier, J. M. (1978). Substitutes for leadership: Their meaning and measurement. *Organizational Behavior and Human Performance, 22,* 375–403.

Kohn, A. (1993). *Punished by rewards: The trouble with gold stars, incentive plans, A's, praise, and other bribes.* New York: Houghton-Mifflin.

Kousnes, J. M., & Posner, B. Z. (1987). *The leadership challenge: How to get extraordinary things done in organizations.* San Francisco: Jossey-Bass.

Kuhn, T. (1970). *The structure of scientific revolutions.* Chicago: University of Chicago Press.

Leeming, D. A.(1981). *Mythology: The voyage of the hero* (2nd ed.). New York: Harper & Row.

Leiberson, S., & O'Conner, J. F. (1972). Leadership and organizational performance: A study of large corporations. *American Sociological Review, 37,* 117–130.

Leslie, J. B., & van Velsor, E. (1996). *A look at derailment today: Europe and the United States.* Greensboro, NC: Center for Creative Leadership.

Lessem, R., & Neubauer, F. (1994). *European management systems: Towards unity out of cultural diversity.* London: McGraw-Hill.

Levine, R., Locke, C., Searls, D., & Weinberger, D. (2000). *The cluetrain manifesto: The end of business as usual.* Cambridge, MA: Perseus Books.

Lodge, G. (1995). *Managing globalization in the age of interdependence.* San Diego, CA: Pfeiffer.

Lombardi, V. (1995). In *Estate of Vince Lombardi.* Indianapolis, IN: CMG World Wide.

Maier, M. (1999). On the gendered substructure of organization: Dimensions and dilemmas of corporate masculinity. In G. N. Powell (Ed.), *Handbook of gender and work* (pp. 69–93). Thousand Oaks, CA: Sage.

Manz, C. C., & Sims, H. P. (2001). *The new SuperLeadership: Leading others to lead themselves.* San Francisco: Berret-Koehler.

Maynard, H. B., & Mehrtens, S. E. (1993). *The Fourth Wave: Business in the 21st century.* San Francisco: Berrett-Koehler.

McCauley, C. D., & van Velsor, E. (Eds.). (2004). *Handbook of leadership development* (2nd ed.). San Francisco: Jossey-Bass.

McGinn, D., & Naughton, K. (2001, February 5). How safe is your job? *Newsweek, 137*(6), 36–43.

Meindl, J. R. (1993). Reinventing leadership: A radical, social psychological approach. In J. K. Murnighan (Ed.), *Social psychology in organizations: Advances in theory and research* (pp. 89–118). Englewood Cliffs, NJ: Prentice-Hall.

Meindl, J. R., Ehrlich, S. B., & Dukerich, J. M. (1985). The romance of leadership. *Administrative Science Quarterly, 30,* 78–102.

Merritt, A. (2000). Culture in the cockpit: Do Hofstede's dimensions replicate? *Journal of Cross-Cultural Psychology, 31,*(3), 283–301.

Mintzberg, H. (1973). *The nature of managerial work.* New York: Harper Collins.

Mintzberg, H. (2003). Unconventional wisdom: A conversation with Henry Mintzberg. *Leadership in Action, 23*(4), 8–10.

Nadler, D., & Tushman, M. (1997). *Competing by design: The power of organizational architecture.* Oxford, England: Oxford University Press.

Nanus, B. (1992). *Visionary leadership: Creating a compelling sense of direction for your organization.* San Francisco: Jossey-Bass.

The National Commission on Philanthropy and Civic Renewal. (2000). *Giving better, giving smarter.* Retrieved August 29, 2000, from http://www.centerforrenewal.org/from_the_front__/Rep.../the_need_for_wiser_giving.htm

Nelson, B. (2000). Great leaders inspire action from workers. *Philadelphia Business Journal, 19*(14), 43.

News & Record, Consumer spending tops income growth. (2000, August 29). Greensboro, NC.

Noer, D. M. (1993). *Healing the wounds: Overcoming the trauma of layoffs and revitalizing downsized organizations.* San Francisco: Jossey-Bass.

Noer, D. M. (1994). Of cowboys and leaders. *Issues & Observations, 14*(1), 9–11.

Noer, D. M. (1997). *Breaking free: A prescription for personal and organizational change.* San Francisco: Jossey-Bass.

O'Toole, J. (1993). *The executive's compass: Business and the good society.* New York: Oxford University Press.

Oxford Atlas of the World. (1994). New York: Oxford University Press.

Pearson, C. (1986). *The hero within: Six archetypes we live by.* San Francisco: Harper & Row.

Peters, T. (1987). *Thriving on chaos: Handbook for a management revolution.* New York: Knopf.

Peters, T., & Austin, N. K. (1985). *A passion for excellence: The leadership difference.* New York: Random House.

Peters, T., & Waterman, R. (1982). *In search of excellence: Lessons from America's best-run companies.* New York: Harper & Row.

Pfeffer, J. (1977). The ambiguity of leadership. *Academy of Management Review, 2,* 104–112.

Pfeffer, J. (1981). *Power in organizations.* Boston: Pitman.

Pierson, G. W. (1938). *Tocqueville and Beaumont in America.* Oxford, England: Oxford University Press.

Powell, G. N. (1999). *Handbook of gender & work.* Thousand Oaks, CA: Sage.

Prugh, T., & Assadourian, E. (2003). What is sustainability anyway? *Worldwatch, 16*(5), 10–21.

Rabinowitz, N. S., & Richlin, A. (1993). *Feminist theory and the classics.* New York: Routledge.

Rhinesmith, S. H. (1993). *A manager's guide to globalization: Six keys to success in a changing world.* Alexandria, VA: Business One Irwin.

Robinson, J. (2003). *Work to live: The guide to getting a life.* New York: Perigee.

Ronen, S., & Shenkar, O. (1985). Clustering countries on attitudinal dimensions: A review and synthesis. *Academy of Management Review, 10,* 435–454.

Roos, P. A., & Gatta, M. L. (1999).The gender gap in earnings: Trends, explanations, and prospects. In G. N. Powell (Ed.), *Handbook of gender and work* (pp. 92–123). Thousand Oaks, CA: Sage.

Rosen, R. (2000). *Global literacies.* New York: Simon & Schuster.

Ruderman, M. N., & Ohlott, P. J. (2002). *Standing at the crossroads: Next steps for high-achieving women.* San Francisco: Jossey-Bass.

Sampson, E. E. (1993). *Celebrating the other.* Boulder, CO: Westview Press.

Sampson, E. E. (2000). Reinterpreting individualism and collectivism: Their religious roots and monologic versus dialogic person-other relationship. *American Psychologist, 55*(12), 1425–1432.

Sarin, R. (2003). Women gain political seats, but gap in education and employment persists. *Worldwatch, 16*(2), 8.

Sayles, L. R. (1993). *The working leader.* New York: The Free Press.

Schein, E. H. (1985). *Organizational culture and leadership: A dynamic view.* San Francisco: Jossey-Bass.

Schwartz, S. H. (1994). Beyond individualism/collectivism: New cultural dimensions on values. In U. Kim, H. Triandis, C. Kâgitcibasi, S.-C. Choi, & G. Yoon (Eds.), *Individualism and collectivism: Theory, methods and applications* (pp. 85–119). Thousand Oaks, California: Sage.

Schwartz, S. (1999). The theory of cultural values and some implications for work. *Applied Psychology: An International Review, 48*(1), 23–47.

Senge, P. (1990). *The fifth discipline.* New York: Doubleday.

Staw, B. M. (1975). Attribution of the "causes" of performance: A general alternative interpretation of cross-sectional research on organizations. *Organizational Behavior and Human Performance, 13,* 414–432.

Stewart, E. C., & Bennett, M. J. (1991). *American cultural patterns: A cross-cultural perspective.* Yarmouth, ME: Intercultural Press.

Stogdill, R. M. (1948). Personal factors associated with leadership: A survey of the literature. *Journal of Psychology, 25,* 35–71.

Stogdill, R. M. (1950). Leadership, membership and organization. *Psychological Bulletin, 47,* 1–14.

Tannen, D. (1990). *You just don't understand.* New York: Ballantine.

Terry, R. W. (1993). *Authentic leadership.* San Francisco: Jossey-Bass.

Tichy, N. M., & Devanna, M. A. (1986). *The transformational leader.* New York: Wiley.

Triandis, H. C. (1998). Vertical and horizontal individualism and collectivism: Theory and research implications for international comparative management. *Advances in International Comparative Management, 12,* 7–35.

Trompenaars, F. (1994). *Riding the waves of culture: Understanding diversity in global business.* New York: Irwin.

U.S. Census Bureau. (1999). *Statistical Abstract of the United States.* Washington, DC: U.S. Government Printing Office.

Vaill, P. (1996). *Learning as a way of being: Strategies for survival in a world of permanent white water.* San Francisco: Jossey-Bass.

Wheatley, M. J. (1992). *Leadership and the new science.* San Francisco: Berret-Koehler.

Wills, S., & Barham, K. (1994). Being an international manager. *European Management Journal, 12*(1), 49–58.

Wilson, M. S., Hoppe, M. H., & Sayles, L. R. (1996). *Managing across cultures: A learning framework.* Greensboro, NC: Center for Creative Leadership.

The World Book Encyclopedia. (1981, Vol. 20). Chicago: World Book-Childcraft International.

Yeung, A. K. & Ready, D. A. (1995). Developing leadership capabilities of global corporations: A comparative study of eight nations. *Human Resource Management, 34*(4), 529–547.

Appendix A

U.S. Demographic Data

- Sample Size : N = 382 (respondents with missing data excluded)
- Financial Services Industry : N = 146 (three organizations)
- Telecommunication Services Industry : N = 65 (two organizations)
- Food Industry : N = 171 (three organizations)

- Gender[a] : Male = 68%
  Female = 32%
- Age : $\bar{x} = 44$
- Years of Formal Education : $\bar{x} = 17$
- Years of Managerial Experience : $\bar{x} = 14$
- Years with Current Employer : $\bar{x} = 12$
- Number of Direct Reports : $\bar{x} = 8$

- Respondents in middle and upper middle management (organizational level): 90%
- Respondents who've worked for a multinational corporation in their career: 58%
- Respondents who've received training in Western management practices: 63%
- Respondents in:[b]

HR/Personnel Management	: 12.4%
Manufacturing/Production	: 9.7%
Marketing	: 8.9%
Finance/Accounting	: 8.0%
Administration	: 5.8%
Sales	: 5.8%
R&D	: 4.0%
Support Services	: 3.5%
Planning	: 2.7%
Other	: 39.0%

Notes: [a]Only 285 (or fewer) respondents provided demographic data (gender, age, etc.). [b]226 respondents, only, indicated *one* "kind of work primarily done by your unit."

Appendix B

Cultural Scales, U.S. Industry and Global Norms

Cultural scale	Financial Services Industry[a] T-Score[b]		Telecommunication Services Industry T-Score[c]		Food Industry[d] T-Score	
	"As Is"	"Should Be"	"As Is"	"Should Be"	"As Is"	"Should Be"
Assertiveness	66[e]	60[e]	58	57	56	57
Future Orientation	58	48	50	41	55	46
Gender Egalitarianism	48	61[e]	45	64[e]	53	62[e]
Humane Orientation	55	53	46	53	54	55
In-Group Collectivism	49	53	42	57	40[e]	52
Institutional Collectivism	46	37[e]	45	38[e]	52	41
Performance Orientation	64[e]	56	46	53	60[e]	54
Power Distance	44	51	49	54	46	48
Uncertainty Avoidance	50	40[e]	48	45	46	40[e]

[a]$N = 54$ countries; $N = 3$ U.S. Organizations; $N = 70$ respondents. [b]T-scores represent standardized U.S. industry rankings against global industry norms ($M = 50$, $SD = 10$). [c]$N = 31$ countries; $N = 2$ U.S. Organizations; $N = 30$ respondents. [d]$N = 44$ countries; $N = 3$ *U.S.* Organizations; $N = 88$ respondents. [e]1 *SD* or more above or below global industry norm.

Appendix C

Significant Correlations Between Cultural Orientations ("Should Be") and Leadership Scales[a]

	Positive		Negative	
Gender Egalitarianism	Participative (Second Order)	+.58	Conflict Inducer	−.58
	Inspirational	+.56	Face Saver	−.57
	Performance Orientation	+.51	Self-Protective (Second Order)	−.57
	Visionary	+.51	Nonparticipative	−.56
	Charismatic (Second Order)	+.49	Self-Centered	−.52
	Integrity	+.46	Autocratic	−.51
	Decisive	+.40	Malevolent	−.50
			Procedural	−.43
Assertiveness	Participative (Second Order)	+.34	Face Saver	−.32
			Modesty	−.31
			Humane O. (Second Order)	−.31
			Nonparticipative	−.31
Performance Orientation	Status-Conscious	+.33	Autonomous (Second Order)	−.35
Humane Orientation			Self-Sacrificial	−.27
In-Group Collectivism	Team Integrator	+.40	Autonomous (Second Order)	−.29
	Inspirational	+.30		
Future Orientation	Procedural	+.53	Autonomous (Second Order)	−.37
	Status-Conscious	+.51	Autonomous	−.36
	Self-Protective (Second Order)	+.41	Participative (Second Order)	−.34
	Modesty	+.35		
	Autocratic	+.35		
Power Distance	Self-Centered	+.50	Team Integrator	−.47
	Malevolent	+.35	Inspirational	−.40
	Autonomous (Second Order)	+.33	Integrity	−.40
	Face Saver	+.32	Visionary	−.37
			Charismatic (Second Order)	−.37
			Collaborative Team Oriented	−.32
			Participative (Second Order)	−.32
			Decisive	−.32
Uncertainty Avoidance	Procedural	+.76	Participative (Second Order)	−.62
	Self-Protective (Second Order)	+.76	Inspirational	−.35
	Face Saver	+.64		
	Status-Conscious	+.61		
	Nonparticipative	+.59		
	Conflict Inducer	+.58		
	Autocratic	+.56		
	Administratively Competent	+.48		
	Self-Centered	+.44		
	Malevolent	+.41		
	Team Oriented (Second Order)	+.39		
	Modesty	+.37		
	Humane Orientation (Second Order)	+.34		
Institutional Collectivism	Status-Conscious	+.50	Autonomous	−.51
	Procedural	+.37	Autonomous (Second Order)	−.49
	Collaborative Team Oriented	+.35		

[a]Significant at .01 or higher levels of significance.

Appendix D

Cross-Cultural Interview Guide

Purpose

The purpose of the interview is to explore, in some depth, how managers in your culture explicitly and implicitly define leadership.

QUESTIONS

1. We are interested in determining your personal definition of outstanding leadership. To arrive at this definition we have a number of questions and subquestions. The first question concerns the difference between competent managers and outstanding leaders. What do you see this difference to be?
2. Now we are interested in your perception of the opposite of outstanding leadership. If the person is in the position of leadership and does not exercise outstanding leadership, what would be the kinds of behaviors in which they engage?
3. Can you think of a critical incident that illustrates outstanding leadership?
4. Can you think of another such incident?
5. Were there any obstacles or constraints faced by the leaders in these incidents? Any opposition, resistance, bureaucratic red tape, or lack of resources, for example?
6. Can you think of two or three well-known outstanding leaders? Who are they?
7. Is there anything that these leaders have in common that makes them outstanding and differentiate them from others who have been in similar positions?
8. How is the behavior of these leaders similar?
9. Can you think of a specific behavior, something each leader did, that illustrates his or her leadership?
10. Can you think of something a leader did that resulted in your strong acceptance of support of the leader or resulted in significantly increased motivation on your part, or willingness to go above and beyond the call of duty in the interest of the leader's vision, objective, or mission?

Appendix E

Summary Comparisons Between GLOBE and Qualitative Results

(Rank)	GLOBE[a]		Focus Groups[b]		Structured Interviews[c]		Media Analysis[d]	
(1)	Integrity	(6.51)	**Inspirational**	(7.8)	Inspirational	(21.5)	**Performance Orientation**	(15.2)
(2)	**Performance Orientation**	(6.46)	Integrity	(5.7)	Visionary	(12.8)	*Self-Sacrificial*	(13.9)
(3)	Inspirational	(6.35)	**Visionary**	(4.7)	*Team Integrator*	(11.0)	**Inspirational**	(12.1)
(4)	Visionary	(6.28)	*Team Integrator*	(4.4)	Integrity	(9.0)	Visionary	(9.7)
(5)	*Team Integrator*[e]	(6.03)	*Self-Sacrificial*	(3.9)	**Performance Orientation**	(6.6)	**Decisive**	(8.1)
(6)	**Decisive**	(5.96)	**Performance Orientation**	(3.4)	*Self-Sacrificial*	(6.4)	Integrity	(5.7)
(7)	*Administratively Competent*	(5.63)	**Decisive**	(1.6)	**Decisive**	(5.9)	*Procedural (reversed)*	(4.2)
(8)	**Diplomatic**[f]	(5.46)	*Modesty*	(1.3)	*Collaborative Team Oriented*	(5.6)	*Collaborative Team Oriented*	(4.0)
(9)	*Collaborative Team Oriented*	(5.38)	*Humane*	(1.3)	*Humane*	(4.1)	**Diplomatic**	(3.8)
(10)	*Modesty*	(5.24)	**Diplomatic**	(0.3)	**Diplomatic**	(2.8)	*Autonomous*	(3.8)

[a]Numbers in parentheses = U.S. country mean for that scale. [b]Numbers in parentheses = percent of specifically designated leader characteristic based on 387 observations of which 35.4 percent attracted outstanding leader designation in the 10 leader scales listed. [c]Numbers in parentheses = percent of leader characteristics based on scorable 391 observations. [d]Numbers in parentheses = percent of leader characteristics based on 505 observations from *Business Week*, *The New York Times*, and *The Wall Street Journal*. [e]Leadership scales in bold are part of top 10 of all analyses. [f]Leadership scales in italics not part of top 10 across all four analyses.

Appendix F

Media Analysis Major Themes[a]

Individual Leader Characteristics   **30.6%**
(e.g., hard driving, persistent, competitive, inclusive,
inspirational, risk taker, energetic, firm, decisive, honest)

Growth and Profit   **14.4%**
(e.g., market share, revenue, fast growth, profit, making
money, return on investments, success, bottom line)

Strategy and Doing Business   **14.4%**
(e.g., focusing on core business, restructuring, marketing,
cost cutting, expanding, strategy, differentiate, consolidation)

Free-Market Environment   **12.7%**
(e.g., free-market dynamics, fair competition, changing
times, customer demands, government regulations,
global competition, technological change)

Miscellaneous   **22.8%**
(e.g., back to basics, conspicuous, fast track, capability, pressure,
great complexity, new system, breaking with past, talented)

---

[a]Based on 1,648 key terms in *Business Week,* 12/1998 and 2/1999; *The New York Times*, 12/9–11/1998 and 2/15–19/1999; and *The Wall Street Journal,* 12/9–11/1998 and 2/16–19/1999. Statements from *USA Today* and *Time* magazine were inadvertently excluded.

Appendix G

Media Analysis Most Frequently Used Terms[a]

1. **Market or markets**
    (e.g., market appeal, market share, changing market)

2. **Customers or consumers**
    (e.g., customer demands, customer orientation, consumer tastes)

3. **Profit or profitability**
    (e.g., making profits, profit oriented, profitable management)

4. **Vision or goal**
    (e.g., vision, visionary, setting high goals)

5. **Change or changing**
    (e.g., technological change, ability to change, changing environment)

6. **Efficiency or cutting**
    (e.g., efficiency gains, cost cutting, cutting back)

7. **Growth or expanding**
    (e.g., growth opportunity, expanding market, revenue growth)

8. **Strategy**
    (e.g., long-term strategy, articulating a strategy, growth strategy)

9. **Marketing or advertising**
    (e.g., direct marketing, niche marketing, product advertising)

10. **Long-term**
    (e.g., long-term orientation, thinking long-term, long-term improvement)

[a]Based on 2,546 statements from 106 articles (see sources of media analysis).

Appendix H

Significant Statistical Relationships Between U.S. Demographic Variables, Cultural Orientations (" Should Be"), and Leader Scales

◊ Age × Future Orientation: +.16[*]
◊ Organizational Level × Assertiveness Orientation: +.17[*]
◊ Women lower in Uncertainty Avoidance[*]
◊ Women lower in Future Orientation[**]
◊ Women higher in Gender Egalitarianism[**]

◊ Years of Education × Administratively Competent: −.23[***]
× Modesty: −.18[**]
× Procedural: −.17[**]
× Collaborative Team Oriented: −.16[**]
× Conflict Inducer: −.16[**]
× Diplomatic: −.15[*]
× Malevolent: +.16[**]

◊ Years of Management Experience × Administratively Competent: −.12[*]
× Status-Conscious: −.12[*]

◊ Women less   autocratic[**]
                         face saver[*]
                         procedural[*]
◊ Women more   inspirational[**]
                         visionary[*]
                         diplomatic[*]
                         participative[*]

Note.   There are no significant associations between leader scales and functional belonging of respondents (e.g., sales, R&D, etc.).
[*] < .05, [**] < .01, [***] < .001.

LATIN EUROPE CLUSTER

The Latin European cluster in the GLOBE Research Program consisted of France, Israel, Italy, Portugal, Spain, and Switzerland (French-speaking). In this volume, this cluster is represented by France, Portugal, and Spain.

This cluster scored low on Humane Orientation and Institutional Collectivism dimensions of societal culture and was in the middle range for all the other dimensions: Assertiveness, Future Orientation, Gender Egalitarianism, In-Group Collectivism, Performance Orientation, Power Distance, and Uncertainty Avoidance (House et al., 2004).

Although the overall assessment is that an outstanding leader in this cluster is expected to show Team Oriented leadership supported by Charismatic/Value Based leadership, there is also considerable between-country variation in this cluster. France values Participative leadership the most. Most countries in this cluster were either neutral toward or rejected Autonomous leadership. Humane Oriented leadership is not considered significant in most of these countries. As a matter of fact, it seems to even inhibit outstanding leadership in France. There is significant between-country variation for Self-Protective leadership, although it is generally not endorsed.

The between-country variance on almost all dimensions in this cluster is possibly a reflection of the fact that the culture in each country in the cluster is strong and distinctive. Latin Europe being in some ways the "cradle of Europe," this cluster possibly shows an amalgamation of all the variation that exists in Europe overlaid by the "Mediterranean miracle" (Jesuino, 2002).

REFERENCES

House, R. J., Hanges, P. J., Javidan, M., Dorfman, P. W., Gupta, V., & GLOBE Associates. (2004). *Culture, leadership, and organizations: The GLOBE study of 62 societies.* Thousand Oaks, CA: Sage.

Jesuino, J. C. (2002). Latin Europe cluster: From South to North. *Journal of World Business, 37,* 81–89.

15

Universalism and Exceptionalism: French Business Leadership

Philippe Castel
University of Burgundy–SPMS, Dijon, France

Marc Deneire
University Nancy 2, Nancy, France

Alexandre Kurc
University Nancy 2, Nancy, France

Marie-Françoise Lacassagne
University of Burgundy–SPMS, Dijon, France

Christopher A. Leeds
University Nancy 2, Nancy, France

Universalism and exceptionalism demonstrate the existence of two different management cultures operating within the sectors of industry chosen for this study. Research, including interviews, reveals that both the banking and food-processing sectors are characterized by some companies reflecting classical, commercial leadership/organizational practices whereas other companies follow alternative mutual (banking) and cooperative (food processing) styles.

A media analysis highlights the fact that leaders are part of a system and operate within a set of constraints that they do not always control. Their role is to operate in the background rather than to get involved in their businesses on a regular basis.

Finally, a study of the social representations of exceptional leadership shows similarities with the definitions given by other countries in the GLOBE study. Traits such as "motivation," "competition," "competence," "trust," and "future orientation" all play a central role in the definition of leadership. However, it is personal relations that distinguish the good leader from the exceptional leader.

1. GENERAL BACKGROUND

> Let's adore working together and reject personal power ("Adore le travail collectif et déteste le pouvoir personnel"). (Philippe Dupon, Chairman of a Bank, Le Point, August 6, 1999)

> To get people to perform to the extremes and have the motivation to do so without me having to tell them. (Pierre Bilger, chief executive, major French-British company, about his greatest challenge; The Sunday Telegraph, June 13, 1999, p. 37)

Culture-Generalizable and Culture-Specific Features

The GLOBE project aims to enhance existing knowledge of culture-generalizable and culture-specific aspects of leadership and follower responses to leaders. Processes by which cultural influences are transmitted at two other levels of analysis, societal and organizational, are also important. For the purposes of the project, GLOBE defines leadership as follows: *"the ability of an individual to influence, motivate and enable others to contribute towards the effectiveness and success of the organizations to which they belong"* (House, Wright, & Aditya, 1997).

This section highlights the historical, social, political, and economic features that are relevant to industry and also the key elements of the context in which French leaders operate.

Ongoing GLOBE research confirms the belief that the notion of leadership, and the social status of leaders varies considerably across countries. For example, in contrast to many parts of Northern Europe, leaders are romanticized, glorified, and allowed considerable influence in Arab countries, the United States, Germany, Russia, and France. A marked number of public symbols such as statues, buildings, and streets named in recognition of leaders can be found in France (House, Hanges, & Ruiz-Quintanilla, 1997).

Culture-specific in this study refers not only to leadership traits or styles, where applicable, but also to practices, customs, and norms that influence the nature and profile of French leadership in France. The state and the family play an important role in the French economy, in business, and in management.

Culture-specific features are both the strength of the intellectual tradition in leadership, and the particular nature of industrial relations for many years between many employers and trade unions, especially the combination of two strongly opposed tendencies, namely modernist and antimodernist forces in political and economic life.

The French appreciate two kinds of leaders, the strong charismatic type and the consensus builder or coalition former, as reflected in De Gaulle and Mitterand respectively (House, Hanges, & Ruiz-Quintonilla, 1997). The quotations by Dupont and Bilger, cited at the start of this chapter, are directly relevant to the French mentality. French managers and employees generally dislike being closely supervised. Ideally the French endorse the kind of leader who combines two qualities, a strong dynamic direction and consensual team building. However considerable regional variations exist in France which consequently requires leaders to have the ability to adapt to local conditions (see the Appendix for more detailed information).

Political and Economic Background

Most countries, in varying degrees, possess contrasting features and values, as is the case with France. These features are displayed in geography, history, and culture. Jack (1999) argues that any generalization about France is doomed to contradiction. In France, paradox remains a key feature, depicted through polarities and the interplay between opposing tendencies. Examples are unity–diversity, centralization–regionalism, authority–freedom, dependence–independence, control– autonomy, and in business especially, structured (formal) versus organic (informal) practices.

A broad contrast exists between the values of authority and freedom, whether understood politically or economically. Since the Middle Ages and the Counter-Reformation, centralized government and industry, submission to hierarchy, lack of autonomy, and a strong civil service have remained French features (Bass, 1990). However, this style clashes with the values of freedom and fraternity, originally expressed in the ideals of the French Revolution. The terms *right* and *left* depict these opposing forces, first used politically in 1789 to describe seating arrangements.

Much of the French history of the 19th century, from 1815 onward, mirrored the tension between reaction and authoritarianism on the one hand, and progress and democracy on the other. France continued to maintain two contrasting traditions: first, the aura of elitist aristocratic values, elegance, and grandeur, associated with pre-1789 France, and second, the continuation of egalitarian and radical values associated with the French Revolution.

From 1789 to 1958, France experienced a series of different political systems and new constitutions. Under the Third Republic, the interwar period, and the Fourth Republic (1946–1958) governments were frequently of short duration as a result of the existence of numerous political parties, with opposition parties being able to combine to outvote governments. The constitution of the Fifth Republic (1958) weakened parliament and increased the power of the government. This led to greater political stability and fewer political parties. From 1815 to the present, despite political upheaval, France experienced remarkable stability and continuity in terms of both state governance and stable, effective administrative, legal, and educational structures.

In the economic field, the Catholic Church was, traditionally, reluctant to support commercialism and entrepreneurialism—achieving and profit making implied greed and selfishness. Consequently, the Huguenots (French Calvinists) formed the key business communities, from the Protestant Reformation until the Revocation of the Edict of Nantes (1685). Most Huguenots then, in an attempt to escape persecution, left France. Both in the past, and still today, an important proportion of the political and economic leaders are Protestant in origin.

Various factors delayed industrial modernization: first, the size and key position of the peasantry, owners of small holdings, and agriculture in the economy; second, the antientrepreneurial spirit; and third, the reluctance of the monied class to finance industrial projects, preferring to invest in land, gold, and state bonds. Firms, starved of capital for expansion, tended to remain small or medium-size operations. Industrial progress and socioeconomic development were particularly noticeable at certain periods, such as 1840–1960 and during the 1960s under President De Gaulle.

French Universalism

Myth makers from the time of Clovis, the first King of the Franks, in the eighth century, romantically conceive France in a spiritual sense as the perfect land favored by God. Its borders formed a hexagon, equated with harmony and balance, with the country situated equidistant between the North Pole and the Equator. After initial conflict, the Franks adopted the language of the local people, and Clovis converted to Christianity. As early as the eighth century, the Franks saw themselves as the heirs and custodians of the Greco-Roman classical world. They adopted the idea of Roman Universalism. Lipiansky (1989) observes that throughout their history the French have tended to link their national idea, not with French civilization alone, but with civilization itself. This implies a collection of rules, customs and usages that define civilized behavior. To some extent, France, throughout the early modern period, epitomized values that were associated with the West, namely rationalism, logic, structure, and order, which was reflected in the French approach to education, administration, science, and the arts.

A perennial idea persists that many endeavors are intended to benefit not just the French but the world, exemplified by the key principles stemming from the French Revolution, notably liberty, equality, and fraternity (brotherhood). The historian Jules Michelet (1798–1874) in *The Universal History* portrays France's destiny as the pilot ship of humanity. In a television broadcast during the presidential elections (1998), President Chirac echoed this sentiment, reminding listeners that France was the lighthouse (*phare*) that led the way for all people.

Industrial Relations

The French generally adopt an ambivalent attitude toward authority and employers (Vachette, 1984). Employees, when in need of help, tend to rely on the state or their employer, and respect authority. However, as employers often make decisions with inadequate dialogue with their employees, the latter may eventually challenge authority. Dates of major important political confrontations between the state and the public after the French Revolution, notably through widespread demonstrations in Paris, include 1830, 1848, 1871, 1934, 1958, 1968, 1985 and 1995–19966.

Trade unions, legalized in 1884, were for many years ignored by both the state and an important number of employers. An important section of the union movement developed revolutionary ideas. Of the main industrial countries, only France had as its major labor organization a procommunist union (the CGT), which rejected the idea of bargaining within the "pro-bourgeois" established political framework (Hewlett, 1998). However, violent confrontation between workers and employers were rare, except at moments of major demonstrations. After the student and trade union demonstrations of 1968, Antoine Ribaud, head of a major food-processing company, earned the derision of many fellow leaders when he called upon them publicly to adopt a more social management style toward unions (Jack, 1999).

The dislike of direct, face-to-face relations is visible in many aspects of French economic life. Shop floor workers, for example, reluctant to form teams spontaneously, preferred to cooperate through formal rules established centrally. In the long term, management–union relations considerably improved from the late 1970s, reflected in a change from autocratic to cooperative relationships in many companies (Goetschy, 1998). Today, although French trade union membership continues to be one of the lowest in Europe, approximately 10% of the workforce in France, trade unions remain a formidable force, in both politics and industry. Food processing and banking have been sectors relatively untouched by industrial unrest. To an extent this is due to the influence of decentralized management and cooperative or mutualist ideas in parts of these sectors.

Intellectual and Elitist Traditions

French intellectuals have always occupied a special position in French society. Alexis de Tocqueville, French aristocrat and author of *Democracy in America,* exercised much influence in French politics. He noted that, in the *Ancien Régime,* French intellectuals displayed a more abstract mind-set than their English counterparts. Whereas the British followed the pragmatic and reformist route in political and social matters, French intellectuals preferred more general and abstract plans for reform. Dynamism in French leadership, especially in business, has been tempered, historically, by the existence of a strong intellectual tradition. Top managers are not required to have tremendous charisma or persuasive skills, even if they possess them, or to be visionary (Barsoux & Lawrence, 1997). The mantle of power and authority, associated with their role or ascribed status, guarantees acquiescence from subordinates.

Prestigious higher education is not associated with universities, with the possible exception of the Sorbonne in Paris. Young people aspiring to reach the top in politics, the civil service, or business aim to enter one of the top state-controlled specialist or professional schools, called *Grandes Ecoles*. Over 170 exist, which cater to the technical, administrative, and business needs of both the State and private industry. Distinguished *Grande Ecoles* include the civil service training school (*l'Education Nationale d'Administration*). Normally, students follow 2 years of preparatory courses after the Baccalaureate (high school diploma) before taking a competitive entrance exam. Emphasis is placed at these institutions on mathematical prowess (the main admissions requirement) and logical, abstract thinking.

Products of the very best *Grandes Ecoles* circulate in their careers between the civil service, government, and business. Consequently a powerful elite and old-boy network developed (Barsoux & Lawrence, 1997). The most notable informal club is that of the *Enarques,* graduates of the *Ecole Nationale d'Administration* (commonly called ENA). Major personalities in business move generally in the same circles as leaders, on both the political and social scene, forming altogether a select elite.

Family and State Tradition in Business

Family capitalism remains important in France. The continued paternalism in part of French business is reflected in the number of words connected to management derived from the Latin word *Pater.* Examples are *le patron* (employer, company chief, or boss), *le patronat* (top management), and *le grand patronat* (top business leaders). According to Marseille (1997), France maintained its economic position worldwide due to the dynamism of families, compensating for the defection of the elites. In 1992, 25 out of the 100 leading companies were family controlled. Other scholars have pointed to the importance of family-owned businesses in France (Allouche & Amann, 1997; Barsoux & Lawrence, 1990). The bourgeoisie saw success as based on increasing their wealth and the reputation of their families. They believed their basic duty was to pass on property to their children and to protect family businesses from outside control (Barsoux & Lawrence, 1990).

Altman (1993) places France in a Southern European group for business purposes, metaphorically described as family. At work actors tend to re-create "familial" relationships, which entail conflict resolution based on loyalty, protection, succession, and the exercise of authority.

In Britain and the United States, government and industry traditionally tend to be viewed as two separate areas. Dyson (1983) argues that in France the influence of Roman law and threats from home and abroad, oriented attention toward the state as key actor, with emphasis on values of unity and solidarity. Policies and reforms instituted by Louis XIII, Louis XIV, and their ministers (Richelieu, Mazarin, and Colbert) and by Napoleon Bonaparte, made France the first fully-operative administrative state. The active involvement of the state in economic life (*dirigisme*) was considered both the cause and the effect of the weakness of the private industrial sector.

The state, since industrialization, played an important role in industrial affairs, both as patron and as a model for the business community (Szarka, 1992). As the state has tended to be the principal shareholder in many major companies, the key corporate relationship remains that with the government. The state occasionally rescues important organizations, including banks, that experience serious financial difficulties. The situation has changed in some respects since the mid-1990s, with the state gradually playing a lower profile in industry.

Leading company chairpersons originate from three chief sources, the most important being former higher civil servants. One study found that 15 of the chairpersons of France's top 25 companies (excluding banks and insurance companies) came from this source and a further eight from the second category, founders or inheritors of family firms (Bauer, 1990). In the third and smallest were the "company men," people who had worked their way up in the firms they now headed. The key feature of each of these three groups has been described respectively as intelligence, inheritance, and competence (Barsoux & Lawrence, 1990).

Top civil servants, who wish to ultimately go into business, are appointed as heads of major private companies or public-sector enterprises by the system known as "parachuting" (*parachutage*). According to one estimate, about a third of the top managers in the 200 leading companies come from the *grands corps* in the civil service (Jack, 1999). Working for the state has historically been regarded as noble.

Many company regulations and procedures stem directly from laws. The French word *cadre* (manager) dates from a 1936 law that accords a legally recognized rank to managers along with appropriate status and privileges (Leeds, 1994). In France, *cadre* is the equivalent of a middle (and sometimes upper) managerial position. These ranks are attained only in sectors such as banking, through succeeding in further examinations and interviews as well as possessing a good record. Demonstrated ability does however, still remain the main criterion for promotion to top management.

2. LEADERSHIP IN FRANCE

A large number of persons in senior and top management belong to the political, economic, and social elite. Top managers or leaders have been described as politicized and intellectualized (Jack, 1998).

Leadership Styles

Lebel (1985) identifies six leadership styles: narcissistic, autocratic, paternalist, technical (machine like), consultative, and participative/democratic. In practice, these styles are not mutually exclusive. Most businesses can be characterized by a number of styles operating simultaneously, depending on individual personalities, circumstances, and the level of the hierarchy. According to Lebel, the narcissistic style remains largely confined to parts of the nationalized and public sectors. Three broad leadership styles are evident within French private organizations. The first approximates the classical, Taylorian model, the second reflects paternalism, and the third the participative, consensual style. Weber (1986) combines the first two styles in one model, described as traditional, authoritarian, protectionist, and paternalist. His second model fits within the participative style.

Features of the first model include hierarchy, centralization, bureaucracy, and autocratic quasi-military leadership. Moyet (1989) describes business leaders as akin to army commanders. Managers tend to work in isolation, punctuated by formal meetings (Barsoux & Lawrence,

1997). In a large company, such a person combines the functions of chairperson and managing director, responsibilities that are often separated in large American and British companies. Although, the head is subject to control by the board and by the shareholders, members of the board rarely challenge her or his proposals at meetings. Precision and exactitude pervades the environment, authority being based on status, law, or regulation, and technical competence. The organizational chart corresponds to how people interact and communicate (Graves, 1973). French chief executives do not have to follow long processes of consultation with colleagues or others at various levels of the hierarchy. In this style, managers tend to communicate downward impersonally by written instructions (formal authority).

The second model combines features of traditional French practices such as personalism and paternalism. A closer, more personal nature of superior–subordinate relationship, it softens the hierarchy. The group is considered more of a family than an instrument. Managers concern themselves with the work and personal problems of their staff. Two overlapping forms of family capitalism can be distinguished in this model. The first concerns family-controlled firms, which include some very large companies, for example, Michelin, de Wendel, Schneider, Peugeot, l'Oréal, Pinault, and Dassault. The second applies to firms that create a familial, paternalist or "social concern" atmosphere, still particularly important in many small, some medium-size, and a few large French firms. Sainsaulieu (1997) observes that French bosses may conceive their business as a large family, feeling a personal responsibility for the welfare of employees, which extends to families and dependents.

The third style of leadership clearly has numerous variants, depending on various mixes of directiveness and participation in decision making. Weber (1986) describes his second leadership model as one where a progressive employer is more open to the international economy, accepts trade unions, and combines authoritarian direction with more democratic, participative practices. Hastings (1993) stresses that opposites may exist simultaneously within organizations; examples of this are hierarchy and non-hierarchy, participative decision making, and strong direction. Employees become effective networkers within a collective individualist system. As Brilman (1998) argues, French companies are gradually moving from a Taylorian conception of work toward a post-Taylorian system, reflected by a more horizontal, participative structure with the clientele.

The head is obliged to be a competent administrator in order to cope effectively with the immense volume of regular mail from the government concerning laws, regulations, and other matters. It is he or she, personally, who must make the decisions as to which legislative measures must be respected, resisted, or circumvented for various practical reasons.

French employees dislike being closely supervised and expect a degree of autonomy, even if the organizational chart does not reflect this in theory (D'Iribarne, 1989). The most effective management in such an environment is likely to be of a subtle nature, the head expected to be discreet and unobtrusive. Barsoux and Lawrence (1990) argue that the findings of one survey reflect the need of leaders and managers to communicate instructions in a manner most likely to elicit the cooperation of subordinates. In other words, the latter must feel that leaders have confidence in their ability to carry out their tasks in the way they think is best without being closely supervised.

Although the head of a large company has a board and even a personal group of advisers, he or she may discuss thorny problems with a colleague, friend, or associate from another company or government. Pressures and constraints can sometimes be handled more effectively when resort is made to external council and support. Close cooperation may occur between a group of companies and also between companies and the state. Leading managers of large companies often work closely together, a feature of the *camaraderie* based on the network maintained between former members of the top *Grandes Ecoles.*

3. FOOD PROCESSING AND BANKING—CONTRASTING FEATURES OF TWO SECTORS

Basically three main categories of banks exist. The first category comprises the private or AFB Banks, so-called as they belong to the French Association of Banks, which can undertake all types of banking or credit operations. Although AFB banks started as independent banks, many were nationalized for a time from 1946 or 1982, each becoming independent at various times afterward. The second category covers a special group of mutual and cooperative banks. Since the end of 1999, an important state-controlled savings bank has been in this category along with *Crédit Foncier.* The third category, the state sector, consists of a few banks, such as the Hervé Bank, which have not been denationalized and the Post Office. The latter acts as a minimum universal bank, serving the needs, notably, of modest households.

French private banks belong to a category of multifunctional banks, universal in form, that operate broadly in a similar manner worldwide as commercial entities. The same point applies to private enterprises in food processing. However, organizations with special structures and practices, governed by particular laws and regulations coexist with traditional, private enterprises in both banking and food processing. Many small and some medium-size businesses in food processing are cooperatives. Cooperative and mutual banks vary in size from small to large. Although cooperatives and mutuals are by no means unique to France, they play an important role in the French economy.

Various influences contributed to the origin of cooperatives and mutual organizations. First, during the 19th century humanitarian and radical thinkers looked to alternatives as a means of modifying negative aspects of capitalism. Pierre-Joseph Proudhon, for example, advocated a federal structure that diversified power, the state providing aid or owning the infrastructure. Second, the state supported the mutualist movement and in the 1890s, the state helped to create mutual banks, partly inspired by developments in German banking (Thiveaud, 1977). Third, a strand in French thinking idealizes smallness. France traditionally served as the refuge for small operations, exemplified by the wide variety of small, regionally or locally based banks. In addition, a large number of small craft or artisanal enterprises and cooperatives (strong in areas such as agriculture, construction, and distribution) exist. Private banks did not want such organizations as clients around the early 1900s. Instead, the early mutual and cooperative banks were able to serve the needs of these special sections of the population.

Cooperatives and mutuals operate primarily for their members. When these organizations operate commercially, profits can be made under certain conditions, which preclude speculative activities. Surpluses should directly benefit members or be applied to financing necessary expenses incurred for the long-term benefit of the organization. Cooperatives and mutuals are both financed by the issue of "social shares" (*parts sociales*). Each social share bought by a member has a fixed value. Remuneration, based on the profit or surplus made, amounts to an annual rate of interest, called a dividend. The amount the member receives depends on the quantity of social shares possessed. Each member has only one vote at the annual general meeting (AGM), irrespective of the number of social shares owned.

In medium- to large-scale organizations, financed by share capital, the number of votes that major shareholders have at the AGM correspond to the number of shares each personally owns. Consequently, the influence of the small shareholder is minimal. Shares are often bought and sold for speculative purposes. This aspect of capitalism is not present in cooperative organizations, which are associated with a more democratic ethos. In both cooperatives (food processing) and cooperative/mutual banks, members vote for volunteers to serve on the administrative committee. The latter elect the head of the organization, who can in fact be removed by democratic means should this be necessary.

Mutual and cooperative banks share one advantage in the market economy. They are not funded by share capital. Consequently they may take over a commercial bank or another organization, financed by shares. However, they are protected from the influence of market and globalist pressures themselves in that they cannot be taken over by another organization, hence losing identity and independence.

Within French commercial banks, directive rather than participative decision making prevails within a high power distance environment, approximating civil service or military practices. However, the number of hierarchical levels within branches, regional and divisional centers, and Paris headquarters, resemble the structure in mutualist and cooperative banks. In general, the latter possess considerable autonomy at regional and branch levels. A federal structure links together all the centers and outlets of such banks.

Despite the existence of hierarchies and titles such as general director for bankers holding responsible positions, their importance tends to be less emphasized in cooperative banks as compared to commercial ones. In a small branch, the director will tend to see employees as collaborators rather than as subordinates. At the next level, the senior manager is likely to interpret his or her role as consensual, acting as a coordinator of the various banking centers under his or her responsibility.

Historically, the food-processing sector and mutual and cooperative banks have remained comparatively independent of state intervention. Important food-processing companies were never nationalized and, as a rule, did not require state subsidies. In food processing, particularly in cooperatives and within mutual and cooperative banks, employees have good opportunities for promotion based on their own merits and experience. In contrast, commercial banks have always retained close relations with the state, owing to their importance to industry, a significant and "politically sensitive" area of the economy. Consequently, state intervention has been more significant, particularly during the periods when the major private banks were nationalized. The fact that the state occasionally provides the head of a major bank through the system of parachuting (explained earlier) reduces the prospects of bank employees reaching top-management positions.

For cooperative and mutual banks, group members, such as associations, mutual organizations, and cooperative enterprises, still remain the most important customers. As the latter are run on democratic principles and by law have aims other than profit making, this influences the ethos of the particular banks that serve them, with such banks aiming not to make excessive profits, also referred to as surplus. The corporate or business customers of the private banks are primarily other commercial organizations where the prime motives remain the same, maximizing profits.

In terms of turnover or added value, food processing came first or second, after textiles, based on French industries in the 19th century. From the 1960s, France generally experienced rapid economic growth. She became the first exporter, ahead of the United States, in food-processed products, especially in cereals and wine. Frozen milk products, biscuits, sugar, and meats were also important. Marseille (1997) describes this sector as the new lifeblood of the French economy. Food processing is often the leading sector of French industry in terms of exports.

Mutual banking plays a key role in financing agricultural modernization. Improved technology, mergers and restructuring contribute to the growth of agriculture. In the 1980s, family capital dominated food processing. Indirectly, the state plays an important role by protecting and encouraging the modernization of agriculture, which contributed to the sustained efficiency and dynamism of the food-processing sector.

Structurally a few large firms, a large number of efficient small and medium-size firms, plus small craft businesses characterize the food-processing sector. Small businesses dominate milk, though a few large companies control most of the production. Cooperatives form an important element, comprising 129 out of 489 businesses in milk (Limouzin, 1992). Some large organizations tend to be decentralized and sometimes partially cooperative in form. In the 1980s, families provided the bulk of the capital in this sector.

Food-processing organizations operate in an environment in which cooperation is, to a large extent, the normal procedure. The suppliers of raw materials to this sector, many farmers, suppliers, or intermediaries, are to an important extent organized in some form of cooperative.

Considerable restructuring has taken place in banking since 1996. Mergers have taken place between banks in different or the same categories, aiming to create larger organizations able to compete effectively at home and abroad. Some banks in the mutual/cooperative category gained substantial control over, or bought a small portion of shares in private banks. The result is that the strength and influence of the mutual banks has increased in the economy, compared to the private banks. The state sector of banking has reduced much in size. Mutual and cooperative banks presently control over 50% of the market in French banking.

Both banking and insurance remain simultaneously distinct and intertwined areas of finance. Mutual and private insurance organizations also operate. However, from the start of the 1980s banks began selling insurance products through the creation or purchase of insurance subsidiaries. The tendency has been for equivalents to match up—increased links between mutual insurance organizations and equivalents in banking—followed by the same trend in relation to private insurance companies and private banks. Additionally, the Post Office now also sells life insurance.

Given the diversity and variety of organizations in banking, and to an extent in food processing, the type of leader needed is one who adapts his or her style pragmatically to the work environment. This implies knowing the art of balancing the need to lead and to make changes, and also of adapting to the values of particular organizational cultures. This point becomes all the more relevant given the fact that the two types of organizations in both sectors, the private and the cooperative, no longer necessarily completely exist in pure form. A few of the large food-processing companies now have some branches or subsidiaries structured cooperatively. Some banks in the second category (cooperative or mutual) now possess small or substantial shareholdings in private banks. In addition, both sectors undergo constant evolution and restructuring, requiring flexible, decisive, and visionary leadership.

The banking sector has been, since late 1998, in the process of continuing evolution and restructuring, likely to extend soon to European and global levels as many of the banks look for partners, alliances, or mergers abroad.

4. SUMMARY OF INTERVIEWS

Ten senior managers from the two sectors took part in the interviews, as well as 35 middle managers who completed questionnaires. The age of interviewees ranges from 35 to 52 years

TABLE 15.1
Features of Leaders and Managers as Seen by Middle Managers

Outstanding Leader	Competent Manager	Opposite of Outstanding Leader
• Visionary, can anticipate the future and take a long-term view	• Motivates a team and develops team spirit	• Too individualistic
• Ability not to make her or himself indispensable and who is valued through the success of colleagues	• Is ready to listen to the views of others	• Incompetent; does not know his or her job, product, or market
• Possesses charisma, rigor, and dynamism	• Has technical skills that are indispensable to a team	• Lacks charisma and consideration for others
• Good at relationships, team building, and achieving success	• Diplomatic and rigorous	• Overambitious, authoritarian, and stubborn
• Has empathy, is a good listener and communicates	• A communicator and organizer; ability to make the right decision	• Makes her or himself indispensable and allows no autonomy to his or her team
• Possesses special financial skills related to markets		• Lacks charisma
• Ability to get the maximum support of colleagues in pursuit of achieving objectives set by the leader		

old, with an average age of 42 years. The majority of respondents were men, but a minority of 20% were women. Interviews were also conducted with managers from other sectors. The purpose of these additional interviews was to gather further information to that relating to outstanding leaders, competent managers, and the profile of the opposite of an outstanding leader (see Table 15.1). Such supplementary information has been included in the appropriate sections of this chapter. Information from two focus groups (one from each sector) has been incorporated into this section.

Banking

The general impression gained from the interviews with senior managers in banking was that teamwork pervaded the work environment. Leader attributes included the ability to train colleagues to work in a group or to provide a guiding vision, outlining the direction in which the organization should go and the special technical banking skills required. Outstanding leaders, whether in business or politics, were shrewd and adapted to their professional milieu.

Senior managers saw the primary role of a competent manager as leading a team, encouraging all members to respect the group dynamic. Incompetent or weak managers preoccupied themselves excessively with administrative and task-focused activities, not vital to the business. They were individualists, egoists, or hypocrites.

For middle managers in banking, the outstanding leader possessed charisma and conviction. He or she allowed time to listen to the views of others and acted as the "motor" or dynamizer, who integrated others into working for targets or aims such as increased market share. Skills included good anticipation of future developments in financial markets and the willingness to take risks.

Middle managers emphasized the need for a competent manager to be fully technically skilled in his or her area. Such managers trained others to work in a team for common aims, and were respected by their personnel as their knowledge was vital to group success.

The opposite of an outstanding leader was a person who possessed neither charisma nor real technical competence, even if professionally qualified. Such a leader evaded his or her responsibilities, could not properly train a team, and tended to be dictatorial. He or she appeared as someone on the sidelines, undynamic and unenthusiastic.

Food Processing

"He is at the same time an actor, communicator, visionary, a patriarch who is charismatic and inventive"; and *"He is a visionary, communicator, a consensus-builder, someone remarkable, but after all a humanist who speaks with conviction and has faith in others."*

Two senior managers in the same company, food processing, had the following to say about what makes an outstanding leader:

In food processing, senior managers associated outstanding leaders with qualities such as charisma, dynamism, innovation, vision, and the ability to communicate. As an effective orator, he or she was expected to speak clearly, simply, and effectively in public.

One respondent equated the outstanding leader with the "captain of a ship" or as the patriarchal or father-like figure, who incarnated all the best qualities of the organization. Another stressed the need for a leader to foster solidarity and commitment at all levels of an organization. His particular consensual style included availability at all times ("open door" policy), which facilitated contact with employees and rapid problem solving.

The competent manager was associated with the role of tactician, who found the means of implementing the general goals or targets to be achieved of the leader and senior management.

The opposite of an outstanding leader was seen as a person preoccupied with administrative and task-based activities and as having a nonhumanist orientation that was counterproductive to the interests of the organization.

Based on a focus group and one interview, the image of the significant leader seen by middle managers from two companies (one of which was a cooperative) emerged as a person who reached the top by his or her own efforts, surmounting all obstacles. Such leaders shared common qualities such as courage, honesty, intelligence, sincerity, loyalty, frankness, and cunning.

The power of the leader lay in her or his ability to adapt to people and situations, combined with the capacity to integrate and coordinate the work of employees in the furtherance of group objectives. In the smaller organizations, notably the collectives, employees readily cooperated. Leaders knew that the organization operated on the basis that the team, rather than the individual leader, held the power.

The opposite of an outstanding manager was associated with various profiles. Examples cited were: (a) the person who gained his or her job through connections ("parachuting") and evaded his or her responsibilities; (b) someone who gained a senior post just after graduating from a business school; (c) someone who inherited his or her father's business; (d) the demagogue.

Middle managers from both banking and food processing cited various examples of outstanding leaders in France and elsewhere, including Mother Theresa. The French leader most highlighted was Bernard Tapie, reputed for incarnating the entrepreneurial spirit.

Semantic Analysis of Interviews

An analysis was carried out, based on the interviews, using a technique developed by Benzecri (1976). This organizes data in contingency tables (or cross-tabulation) called "factorial analysis of multiple correspondences." The objective of this method is to produce a statistical study and representation of word distribution after extracting the roots (or lexemes) of the words in a given corpus.

ALCESTE, the program used for this study, was created by Reinert (1993) and based on Benzecri's technique. The program first breaks down the utterances into predicates of equal length using punctuation. These subject-predicate units are called *Unités de contexte élémentaires (UCE, i.e., elementary units of context)*. The program then creates a contingency table using UCEs as one entry and lexical items (lemmas) as the other. Each lexical entry is coded as (1) or (0) based on its presence or absence within the UCEs. A hierarchical classification in a descending order is produced. As a first step in the procedure, the program divides the whole corpus into two classes by maximizing the chi-square of the margins of the table. The procedure is then repeated in an iterative way until all classes are produced, that is, until the best fit between lexical entries and lexical fields is obtained. Each class constitutes a "discourse world." Our analysis using this technique on 75 pages of single-spaced corpus shows a first major opposition between two discourse worlds, that of the managers from the mutualist and cooperative sectors (see Fig. 15.1, Clusters 1 and 3), and that of the managers from large private groups (see Fig. 15.1, Clusters 2, 4, and 5). Within the latter class, a further opposition emerged between the banking (Clusters 4 and 5) and food-processing sectors (Cluster 3). Finally, two different discourse worlds were produced for large state and private banks (Clusters 4 vs. 5). Further descriptions of each cluster are listed in Table 15.

The World of Managers in Mutualist and Cooperative Organizations.   One of the main aspects of managerial work cited in these two discourse worlds is a humanistic orientation, which interviewees oppose to the mechanistic orientation of large private or state concerns that crush the individual. The style of management most often cited is participation and the central idea that decisions are made on the basis of one person, one vote, and not on the amount of capital one possesses.

The terms most used in *Cluster 1, the world of mutualist banks,* are *manager, service, finance,* and *participation.* Managers highlighted participative management. Senior managers consult the heads of service (middle managers) directly concerned with important decisions, such as the hiring or firing of personnel. The following quotation illustrates this type of management:

> Things only work (are accepted) if management is participative. When a decision is made in our headquarters, the personnel are consulted first …. [The top managers] are elected [and not appointed] by the branches and work for them.

Cluster 3, the world of small and medium-size mutuals and cooperatives, best represents the mid-and small-size food-processing cooperatives. The terms most employed in this category

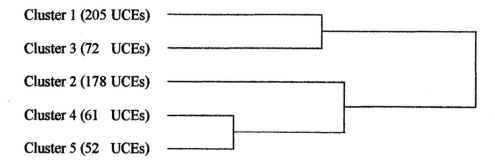

FIG. 15.1.   A dendrogram of five discourse worlds of French middle managers.

TABLE 15.2
Comparative Table of the Five Business Discourse Worlds

Sectors	Description
Cluster 1: Mutual banks	Participative management, top managers are elected, the base is consulted
Cluster 2: Large business private and public (ex-public sector)	Charismatic, competent
Cluster 3: Small food-processing groups	Competence, charisma capacity, values, technical skills
Cluster 4: Public bank / the Post Office	Administrative inertia, lack of understanding of social mechanisms, emotional women's world
Cluster 5: Large private banks	The leader who is able to succeed because of his or her will

are, *commercial, producer, cooperative, assembly,* and *human.* Managers perceive a tension between the human aspects of management and the pressure for immediate results. This humanist orientation leads most managers to emphasize the qualities of the cooperative and mutual sectors. All of the interviewees in this sector insist on the fact that in their company "one person equals one vote" occurs when decisions need to be made, unlike the traditional companies where "voting power" depends on the amount of capital invested:

> But the final decision. How is it made? The final decision depends on the majority of the votes, but the majority one person equals one vote. It is like a referendum. The personnel will vote, and if there are 50 people, it will be 50 votes.

The leader is also a charismatic person who encourages people to work together in a democratic way.

The World of Large Business, Both Private and Public.   The charismatic leader is the one that is most often cited in this category. The competent leader is highly valued as a person who is committed to a team to which he or she brings his or her technical expertise. The large public sector is more marked than others by conflict and conflict resolution (arbitration), by affective relations and sexism.

The terms most often used to describe *Cluster 2, the world of large food-processing companies* are: *qualified leader, significant leader, chief, team, charisma, capacity, values,* and *technical skills.* The interviews also show the importance attached to the charismatic leader for his or her ability to lead, but also to the competent leader who can help and do whatever the workers do:

> The real leader is recognized as somebody who leads his team on a given project. He does not necessarily have the technical ability to substitute for a team member, ... but the team members naturally adhere to his project. A "competent leader" can take the place of any of the team members.... He's the one who helps solve technical problems ... and because he brings a sense of security to his team, he is recognized as a leader, but only for his competence.

Thus, one of the most important traits of the exceptional leader entails keeping a certain distance from the team. The competent leader may be a good leader, but she or he will never become an exceptional leader, lacking the necessary charisma.

Cluster 4, the world of large state banks, best typifies the one large public bank in our sample. People insist on administrative inertia and a lack of understanding of the social mechanisms of management:

"The constraints for the leaders are the structure, whether the social or administrative structure, or just the weight of habits, the weight of the past." Middle managers regularly talk about their relations with upper managers (whether easy or not so easy), which shows a concern for hierarchy. They also express a concern for the evaluation of their work, and the emotional atmosphere of a women's world.

Cluster 5 represents the world of large private banks, one of which is a cooperative bank in the agricultural sector. The words most often used by middle managers are *opinion, succeed, think, idea, question,* and *voluntarism.* The team leader has a stimulating influence, but constantly keeps an eye on objectives that are not the purpose of discussion or argument. He or she insists on hierarchical relations, but is careful to leave enough space for the people working for him or her:

> There are hierarchical relations since we operate in a top-down structure. The general strategy of the company is defined, and once this has been done, the machine comes into play so that all move in the same direction. ... Let us say that we are not in a structure based on self-management. We are in a structure with objectives, with a direction.

5. MEDIA ANALYSIS

This section takes the form of a discourse analysis, focusing on a limited number of extracts. It is not a content analysis of an exhaustive nature, but aims at defining social representations of managers as shown by the way a special section of the media portrays them in its discourse. Special attention is given to the position of the manager as an actor (subject and/or object positions) and the types of verbs associated with this role (factitive, declarative, or stative).

To study the image of a leader in the French press, use has been made of several specialized magazines with of a wide circulation. More specifically, bearing in mind the interpretation of the questionnaires, magazines read by middle managers in the finance and food-processing sectors have been selected. So that the results would not be attributed to specific events, two separate periods of time were chosen—August to October 1998 and June to August 1999.

L'Usine Nouvelle (The New Factory)

L'Usine Nouvelle is the most important magazine aimed at managers in industry and provides up-to-date information on themes such as technical progress, economic developments, financial assessments, and calls for tender. Through a study of this magazine the leader, visualized as a human actor encouraging the progress of his or her organization, is not particularly highlighted. For example, in the 1,300 projects that are analyzed systematically, we note that:

- The projects made no mention of a human actor. Use was made of a nominalized verb, the notion "actor" being understood implicitly. In food processing, for example, 120 out of 171 projects are described without any reference to a human being.
- The agents were described collectively as a group, organization, or enterprise.
- The agent is a specific individual who could be considered a leader (example: "The supplier of Beaujolais wine is required to …").

Le Nouvel Economiste/L'Expansion

The *New Economist* (*Le Nouvel Economiste*) is a magazine, politically center-right, popular with managers specializing in finance. Another magazine, *Expansion* (*L'Expansion*), occupies the same segment of the market and follows the same format as *Le Nouvel Economiste,* but is more right-wing.

To identify the profile of a leader, important portrayals of certain personalities in business have been selected. First, the accounts of the life of similar people were studied in the magazines of 1998. These are Pierre Cardin, "pharaoh-like manager" (*Nouvel Economiste,* October 16, 1998), and Cédric, "manager in fashion" (*L'Expansion,* August 27, 1998). Second, a study was made of the portrayal of the French "among the 200 richest people in the world" (*Le Nouvel Economiste,* July 29, 1999) and of the actors involved in the "explosive revolution of French capitalism" (*L'Expansion,* August 26, 1999, No. 1629).

In *Le Nouvel Economiste,* Pierre Cardin, the fashion designer, is made the subject of a verb in only 11 out of 25 sentences included in the article mentioned previously. In most of these sentences, the agent is portrayed as someone who creates the conditions for production rather than as a producer himself. As the text develops, an image is painted of a manager as someone who exercises a precise activity from the start as the founder of his business. As the creator, he acquired a status that seems to absolve him of all responsibility. For example, in the observation, "In 1949 Cardin created his own business. Fifty years later his organization is present in more than 150 countries," the fashion designer has become a human being who reacts to elements based on this position and who acts through speech.

In the portrayal of Cédric (*L'expansion*), the "fashion manager," the leader is placed only once as the subject of a verb, which is declarative: "He has been able to move towards . ...." Later it is only his professional career that is described. Consequently he is twice the subject, the first of a passive verb—"he is hired …"—and the second of a pronominal verb, "he is content to . ...." In the two cases, he is not the actor in control of events (he is hired only because he has proved himself) and is offered something not very satisfying that he is obliged to accept. Finally, the article concludes with a direct quotation where the manager comments on his situation—"it is most fulfilling"—and describes his work—"my work covers all aspects of the business." In other words, he remains outside and makes no mention of himself as the key actor.

Besides the depiction of leaders as professionals, we also looked at how managers are more broadly portrayed in different articles. Among portrayals of the 200 wealthiest persons in the world (*Le Nouvel Economiste,* 1999), 15 French people are discussed in this study. Leaders' activity is described in one, two, or three sentences (20 propositions in all). Most of the articles provide readers with the latest news on the person described, rather than with his or her specific role in business. Results of this analysis show that the 15 richest French people are quasi-transcendental. Rooted in a family structure, of which they are the heirs or legatees, these out-of-the-ordinary people are content just to possess. Everything happens as if the evolution of their possessions is distinct from them.

Conclusion

The manager is not portrayed in any clearly distinct manner. When he or she is discussed it is rarely as the subject of the sentence, that is, as an initiator. When the manager is the subject, action verbs are rarely used. In fact, these verbs serve as initial acts. A picture is painted of a manager whose importance is (conversely) related to their disengagement from any concrete action. This approach is found not only in an industrial management review, but also in magazines addressed to financial managers of all political orientations. Finally, journalists give their readers (the managers themselves) a view of a leader cut off from events and relieved of work or effort. The manager represents more of an ideal or the vehicle for a dream.

6. QUANTITATIVE ANALYSIS

This section outlines the findings based on a subsection of a survey that was carried out in banking and food industry in 1998/1999 in several areas of France (Paris, the Northeast, and the south). One hundred and eight-five questionnaires were retained for this study. The first part of the analysis deals with Sections 1 and 3 of the questionnaire, which focus on societal and organizational cultural GLOBE dimensions. The second part relates to Sections 2 and 4 of the questionnaire, which focus on the GLOBE leadership dimensions. An item analysis, followed by a factor analysis, allowed us to highlight the features that define good leadership in France.

GLOBE Dimensions in Organizations and Society

The "organizational culture" sample counts 80 subjects and the "societal culture" sample 105 subjects coming from 12 different companies. Age ranges from 35 to 60 with an average of 42. A majority of the respondents were men (149), with a minority of women represented (36). Most of them are French; the nine non-French citizens are Algerian, Belgian, Lebanese, and Polish.

Organizational Culture.   See Tables 15.3 and 15.4 for a statistical breakdown of the organizational results in each of the two industries. Further detail about each of the dimensions follows:

TABLE 15.3
Organizational Culture Results in the Financial Service Industry

| Culture Dimensions | Organization "As Is" | | Organization "Should Be" | | Difference |
	Score[a]	Band[b]	Score[a]	Band[b]	"Should Be" −"As Is"[c]
Uncertainty Avoidance	4.76	A	4.35	B	−0.41
Assertiveness	3.50	B	4.20	A	0.70
Gender Egalitarianism	3.30	B	4.48	B	1.18
Future Orientation	4.96	A	5.40	B	0.44
Power Distance	4.03	C	3.64	B	−0.39
Institutional Collectivism	4.13	B	5.50	A	1.37
In-Group Collectivism	4.22	C	6.20	A	1.98
Humane Orientation	4.05	C	4.60	B/C	0.55
Performance Orientation	4.25	B	5.95	B	1.70

[a]Country mean score on a 7-point Likert-type scale. [b]Band letter A–D indicating meaningful country bands for the scales A > B > C > D; the band width is equal to 2 SD (standard deviation). [c]Absolute difference between the "Should Be" and the "As Is" score.

TABLE 15.4
Organizational Culture Results in the Food Service Industry

| Culture Dimensions | Organization "As Is" | | Organization "Should Be" | | Difference |
	Score[a]	Band[b]	Score[a]	Band[b]	"Should Be" −"As Is"[c]
Uncertainty Avoidance	4.05	C	4.24	B	0.19
Assertiveness	4.01	A/B	4.02	A	0.01
Gender Egalitarianism	3.22	B	4.44	B	1.22
Future Orientation	4.81	A	5.51	A	0.7
Power Distance	3.59	C	3.26	B	−0.33
Institutional Collectivism	4.03	B	4.89	B	0.86
In-Group Collectivism	5.08	B	6.29	A	1.21
Humane Orientation	4.68	B	5.01	B	0.33
Performance Orientation	4.60	A	5.91	B	1.31

[a]Country mean score on a 7-point Likert-type scale. [b]Band letter A–D indicating meaningful country bands for the scales A > B > C > D; the band width is equal to 2 SD (standard deviation). [c]Absolute difference between the "Should Be" and the "As Is" score.

1. *Uncertainty Avoidance:* Uncertainty Avoidance refers to the extent to which the organization relies on rules, norms, and procedures. In the finance sector, middle managers agreed that enough structure and coherence existed in their own workplace. They strongly agreed that precise and detailed instructions needed to be given. However, they also indicated that this should not be done at the expense of innovation and creativity, nor at the expense of emotions; hence the hesitation to argue in favor of more structure overall. Managers in food processing scored slightly lower on this dimension, mainly because they thought that order and coherence were not to be valued to a point where it hindered originality and innovation. The presence of smaller and less formal companies also contributes to this lower score.

2. *Assertiveness:* In the finance sector, respondents indicate perceptions of low aggressiveness. They thought that they ought to be more assertive, and, interestingly, more domineering. However, respondents rejected the idea that they should be more aggressive. Note that the term *aggressive* does not have the positive connotation that it sometimes has in English. Whereas in English, and especially in a business context, the term may have the meaning of "assertive, bold, enterprising" (*American Heritage Dictionary*), in French *aggressif* is always related to aggression, violence, and attacking (*Petit Robert*). In food processing, managers felt self-confident and domineering; they therefore did not perceive any need for more Assertiveness.

3. *Gender Egalitarianism:* Managers in both sectors acknowledged the fact that most physical tasks are performed by men. The survey also shows that only 10% of the managerial positions are occupied by women. Respondents strongly agreed that this situation should change. They even believed that business would be better managed if more women were present. On the other hand, they strongly rejected the idea that special privileges should be granted to women, such as favoring them in terms of training and being more lenient toward them when they failed in their jobs. Respondents also found it normal that some physical tasks should be performed by male employees rather than by their female counterparts.

4. *Future Orientation:* Planning seems to take place in most businesses to the satisfaction of middle managers in general. These managers strongly agree that this should be the case in the future.

5. *Power Distance:* In GLOBE, Power Distance refers to the degree to which members of a collective expect power to be distributed equally. Results for this dimension in finance show that respondents found Power Distance in their own environment to be below average. They also indicate that power relations should be based less on authority and more on competence. Even though respondents believed that they should be allowed to question or challenge their superiors, they also strongly agreed that important decisions ought to be made by senior management and that management generally should "arbitrate" in the case of disagreement between employees or managers of equal rank. In short, what is expected from management is that it provides a broad framework and resolves conflicts to everybody's satisfaction. This is also the case in food processing.

6. *Humane Orientation:* In the finance sector, respondents found their colleagues to be moderately friendly, but also relatively egotistical (self-centered). Understandably, they wish that their colleagues were more altruistic, more sensitive, and more generous toward each other. However, they do not believe that mistakes and errors should be tolerated. The food-processing sector shows a completely different picture on this

dimension. Managers found people in their company to be both altruistic and sensitive toward each other, and friendly and generous day to day.

7. *Performance Orientation:* Performance seems to be highly valued and encouraged by management. However, it does not seem to be rewarded appropriately in the finance sector. Indeed, in food processing, the reward system is reported to be based much more on performance and innovation; this can often be verified on the basis of existing reward systems. In both sectors, respondents agreed that performance should be valued even more highly. They also strongly agree that performance ought to be appropriately rewarded.

8. *Collectivism 1: Societal Emphasis:* Middle managers reported their jobs to be group oriented. Group work is also encouraged by management, notably through the reward system. They thought that this should be even more the case and that management should encourage a positive group atmosphere. In contradiction with what is usually found in the literature on France, managers considered that time spent on reaching consensus was productive rather than unproductive. Food processing displayed a much stronger leaning toward greater Collectivism. Respondents particularly endorsed collaborative projects and attached greater importance to acceptance within the group.

9. *Collectivism 2: In-Group Cohesion and Loyalty:* Respondents were found to have a fairly low degree of identification with their company, especially in banking. However, they believed that managers should identify more with their company. This somewhat contradicts the impression we obtained from the interviews where most respondents seemed to be extremely sensitive to the image of their bank, and strongly believed that its members should defend this image when under attack.

To conclude, considerable agreement was found between the two sectors on the nine dimensions. However, food processing scored lower in Power Distance, and higher on the Humane Orientation and Collectivism. Performance and innovation also seemed to be more valued, or, at the very least, better rewarded. This may be due to the fact that many food-processing organizations in our sample were cooperatives or had decentralized branches.

Societal Culture.   See Table 15.5 for a breakdown of the societal results in each of the two industries. Further detail about each of the dimensions follows:

1. *Uncertainty Avoidance:* France scores fairly high in terms of Uncertainty Avoidance (Band B). The country conforms to the classic pattern of a strong Uncertainty Avoidance, defined by Hofstede (1991), and lives within a highly regulated society of rules and laws. Governments are also known for their output of negative regulations, which highlight what must not be done rather than what should. Many laws or regulations may be ambiguous, out-of-date, or conflict with other stipulations. The French have a name for the general practice of getting around the rules, applied by individuals pragmatically and depending on the situation or context, known as "System D," the "D" standing for *débrouillard* (resourceful, smart).

2. *Assertiveness:* France ranks fairly high in terms of Assertiveness (Bands A and B). This means that relationships are more aggressive than in many other societies. Moreover, the fact that the "Should Be" score is equally high indicates that this style is considered normal, and even desirable in daily interactions. This taste for verbal

TABLE 15.5
Societal Culture Results

Culture Dimensions	Societal Culture "As Is" Score[a]	Band[b]	Societal Culture "Should Be" Score[a]	Band[b]	Difference "Should Be" −"As Is"[c]
Uncertainty Avoidance	4.43	B	4.26	C	−0.17
Assertiveness	4.13	B	3.38	B	−0.75
Gender Egalitarianism	3.64	A	4.40	B	0.76
Future Orientation	3.48	C	4.96	C	1.48
Power Distance	5.28	A	2.76	C	−2.52
Institutional Collectivism	3.93	B	4.86	B	0.93
In-Group Collectivism	4.37	B	5.42	B	2.05
Humane Orientation	3.40	D	5.67	B	2.27
Performance Orientation	4.11	B	5.65	C	1.54

[a]Country mean score on a 7-point Likert-type scale. [b]Band letter A–D indicating meaningful country bands for the scales A > B > C > D; the band width is equal to 2 *SD* (standard deviation). [c]Absolute difference between the "Should Be" and the "As Is" score.

confrontations and sparring corresponds to what has sometimes been presented as "French rationalism." It also results from the educational system where persuasive writing (la "*rhétorique*") and debating are systematically practiced.

In everyday life, to be able to say exactly what one means or feels, in a concise, direct, or forthright manner, tends to be prized. Collectively, the French are reputed for oscillating between two extremes when faced with public authorities: submission and rebellion. When grievances are expressed, the French often do so in no uncertain manner.

3. *Gender Equality:* In state organizations (including the civil service and teaching), in the liberal professions, and in upper management (industry) equality of pay exists for men and women in the same job categories. The law on workplace equality (July 1983) requires every firm above average size to submit an annual report on the relative employment level and pay of men and women employees. However, in spite of this law, only about 30% of managers are women and less than 10% are heads of businesses. Segregation against women is still quite strong. According to the 1999 Eurostat figures, women's salaries are on average 12% below that of men for comparable work (compared to 5% in Portugal and 22% in the UK). Reasons can be sought in the law, which is often vague on this subject, and in the fact that employers often find ways of getting around existing regulations. The French strongly disapprove of this disparity, as the high difference between the "As Is" and the "Should Be" scores indicate.

France is among the countries with the least women in parliament. Only since the last presidential elections (1995) has there been a marked increase in the number of members of parliament (MPs), all left-wing. However in 1998 only 19 of the 321 senators were women and only 59 of the 577 were deputies in the National Assembly. In government, an increasing number of MPs are women, even though the percentage of women in parliament (10.2%) is still one of the lowest in Europe. The fact that women have been admitted to the *Grandes Ecoles* for a number of years (e.g., in 1972 at the *Ecole Polytechnique*) partly explains this evolution.

Women serving in the armed service are able to rise to senior rank. Some are in senior positions in local and regional government. Women first entered the army in 1978; presently, about 20% of the officers up to the level of lieutenant-colonel are women (see <http://defense.gouv.fr/terre/hf/index4.html>).

4. *Future Orientation:* State provisions in areas such as health, pension, retirement, and job security reduce much of the unpredictability or uncertainties of life. The fact that an increasing number of people want to become civil servants (a position that offers absolute job security for life) may explain the relatively low score obtained for Future Orientation. This unique status explains why many people do not need to focus excessively on the long term or to make provisions for the future. For the others, bank advisers are generally allocated to a number of their clients and provide them with information on a range of tax-free, long-term saving schemes and other bank products. Despite the large number of civil servants who do not need to save for the future, the French save, on average, 15% of their income. In consequence, what is sometimes perceived as a lack of clear vision or "strategic planning for the future" needs to be qualified. Indeed, the difference between French Future Orientation and more "Anglo-Saxon" types of Future Orientation is more a qualitative than a quantitative one.

5. *Power Distance:* The French scored moderately high on Power Distance. However, the large difference between "As Is" and "Should Be" scores indicates that they strongly reject the notion of Power Distance altogether.

   To fully understand the notion of "Power Distance" in the French context, the need arises to resolve what may be perceived as an apparent paradox: How can French society resent Power Distance so much while supporting and maintaining such a strong hierarchy in society? This paradox, according to d'Iribarne (1996), is due to the fact that, unlike in the United States and the Netherlands, for example, a distinction needs to be made between *power distance* and *hierarchical distance.* Though Power Distance may be reduced in one part of a business (e.g., within the same office), the distance with those who are higher up in the hierarchy remains high. The very large difference between "As Is" and "Should Be" scores on this dimension shows that most French people resent Power Distance. However, their "logic of honor" and their desire to avoid interference from higher-ups contribute to reproducing and perpetuating hierarchical distance.

6. *Collectivism I—Society:* Results for this dimension indicate that the French value Societal Collectivism moderately ("As Is"). They also seem to be satisfied with the degree of collectivism found in society ("Should Be").

   The term *social economy,* which the French often use to describe their own mode of organization, denotes activities of a charitable or noncommercial nature. This links together associations purely social in nature concerned with aid to the sick, poor, and handicapped, mutualist organizations that supplement the National Health Service, and mutualist and cooperative entities in areas such as transport, building, banking, and food processing. All these entities are particularly oriented toward their customers.

   For the French, the term *collectivism* does not only mean agreeing. It often indicates the right to be heard, for example, through strikes. Not only is the right to strike well protected, but considerable tolerance is shown in conditions when strikers break the law. Basically, the fact that the general public on the whole tacitly supports major strikes reflects a negative form of social cohesion or solidarity.

7. *Collectivism 2—Family:* Large families with three or more children benefit particularly from tax benefits, whereas family businesses may obtain tax concessions to encourage the survival and development of small and medium-size family-run organizations. This applies particularly to businesses where the family members are the direct descendants of the original founders. Despite the fact that divorce rates are high, family values are still at the center of most types of social organization. Not surprisingly, it is in the food sector that respondents believe that family collectivism "Should Be" more developed, in both society and organizations. Indeed, this sector includes a larger amount of smaller paternalistic family businesses.

8. *Humanism:* The score obtained for this dimension is relatively low compared to that of other countries (Bands C and D). However, the high "Should Be" scores show that the French highly value Humanism. Some researchers have argued that the French are primarily moved by self-interest, but that they expect Humanism in the social system and in the business world. This judgment may sound unduly harsh. However, it is true that the French expect fairness and equality to be provided by the political and economic system, and are ready to pay for it, rather than through the generosity of individuals. This results in the relatively higher score for Societal Collectivism (Band B). Today laws and regulations stipulate secure working conditions. For example, employees are protected by minimum-wage legislation (*SMIC*) and an employer cannot fire, at short notice, an employee without providing satisfactory monetary compensation. When French business leaders receive press coverage, emphasis is placed less on personal details reflecting achievement, such as annual salary and size and quality of house, but rather on what they do that is of a positive nature. This concerns the way they have enhanced the efficiency of their organization, how many jobs they have saved, or the number of small companies that they have prevented from going bankrupt.

9. *Performance Orientation:* Understandably, the score obtained for Performance Orientation was lower in society than in organizations. Certainly, it is in the workplace that performance plays a more important role. However, the high "Should Be" score for this dimension indicates respondents' dissatisfaction with this state of affairs. The role of "honor" in all areas of society (in education, among families, etc.) may explain this disparity between "As Is" and "Should Be" scores.

   The French tend to be very competitive while at school, but ascription occurs at an early age based on individual scholastic attainments. Sometimes a person is considered to have already partially succeeded in life when gaining admission to a prestigious institution. Entrance exams are very difficult for the top *Grandes Ecoles* but, having entered, nearly all students pass successfully.

The Social Representation of the Exceptional Leader

The purpose of this section is to determine the representation that French managers have of good leadership in the business world.

The notion of social representation, as defined in France by Moscovici (1961), refers to "common sense knowledge" (Moscovici, 1984), that is, to the whole body of knowledge held by any individual as a member of a social group. Thus, social representation is a form of common ground that is taken for granted, underpinning all forms of behavior and the way these behaviors are rationalized. It is an organized body of denoted and connoted cognitions (Le Bouédec, 1984). According to Flament (1986) and Abric (1984) the semantic content of representations consists of two systems: a central system and a peripheral system. The former revolves around a "hard core" containing the most commonly shared elements, which are therefore the most resistant to change; the latter group contains mainly contextual elements, which are more easily subject to change and transformation. From a functional point of view, the central system ensures the stability and global orientation of the elements of the representation (Abric, 1988), whereas the peripheral system serves to decipher reality. Because the latter constantly adapts to a changing reality, it protects the central system.

Open methods of inquiry are traditionally used to access representation, such as the analysis of nondirective interviews and free verbal association. The first step in the analysis consists of identifying the lexical fields associated with a given term. We then determine how these are structured on the basis of similarities perceived by subjects as a group. Given the way the data were collected in the GLOBE (House et al., 2004) study, certain changes were necessary to examine this particular aspect of social construction. Indeed, we did not try to group items, as was done in other parts of the GLOBE study. Instead, we applied the methodology traditionally used in the study of social representations.

The 112 items in the GLOBE study all refer to the field of leadership. Indeed, they can all be considered as a repertoire of traits that allow us to interpret leaders' behavior (Wetherell & Potter, 1992). However, only the items that received a high score can be considered as belonging to the field of exceptional leadership. On the 7-point Likert scale, 32 items scored 6 or higher and can therefore be taken into account. To be considered as a reflection of a given social reality, these items also need to represent a consensus on the part of the subjects. Items that display too great a variation therefore need to be excluded; standard variations between 0.34 and 1.33 were all considered as weak. For example, even for the item "motivating," which displays the widest variance (1.33), 168 out of 178 subjects attribute scores of 5, 6, or 7. Finally, in order to retain only the items that are part of the core, those items that are too sensitive to context also need to be eliminated. Effects concerning the variable "business sector" comprises eight modalities in the French corpus (four in banking and four in food processing), which were submitted to analysis of variance (ANOVA). The analysis revealed significant effect of a variable on 18 items. These items were therefore ignored. Thirteen items were finally retained as belonging to the core (i.e., non-field-specific) representation of exceptional leadership.

The structure of these elements can be identified through two types of analysis (MacLaury, 1997, 2000; Castel, Lacassagne, & Salès-Wuillemin, 2002), one based on resemblance, and the other on difference. In the former case, an ascending hierarchical analysis is used and represented in a dendrogram displaying similarities. The relation between two elements is considered as similar when it is rated in the same way by a large number of respondents. Relations of difference are obtained through factor analysis.

The dendrogram in Fig. 15.2 shows how groupings are progressively formed, from the bottom to the top. A short distance in the distance of aggregation between two items or blocks of items (y- axis) is shorter when the relation is stronger. The dendrogram displays two unbalanced blocks. The first one (right branch) contains 11 items, whereas the second one contains only 2 items, which are only loosely related.

The first block consists of three subgroups. Subgroup 1 has two poles. In the first one, the item "positive" is close to the item "encouraging"; the item "trustworthy" is also closely

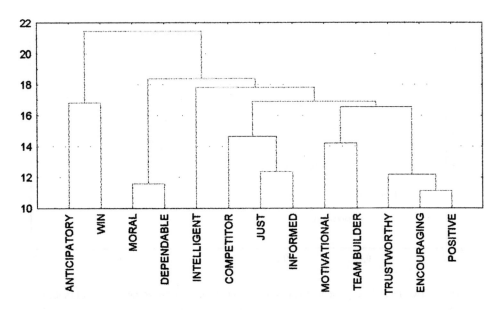

FIG. 15.2.   Dendrogram indicating the relation between items.

related to this pair. In other words, French leaders agree that a positive leader is also an encouraging one; these qualities determine the trust that she or he deserves. These traits are related to the impact that the leader is able to exert on the dynamics of her or his team. Indeed, they are related to the second pole, which includes the items "team builder" and "motivating." Relations in Subgroup 2 highlight the close connection between "informed" and "fair or just"; a third item "intragroup competitor" also closely relates to these traits and makes the connection with Subgroup 1. This means that only people who are likely to use information in a socially acceptable way will be given access to it. The relation between subgroups 1 and 2 shows that a competent and fair leader connects to the relational leader through her or his taste for competition. The third subgroup refers to the traits "morale booster, honest" and "dependable, serious" and loosely connects to the other subgroups through the trait "intelligent." These traits are not sufficient to be an exceptional leader; they need to be rendered more dynamic through intellectual input.

The second block indicates that the items "anticipatory" and "win problem solver" are related, but the relation is fairly loose, which indicates that pragmatic intelligence is not given.

This organization of items, on the basis of consensus, highlights the importance of the relational dimension (the affective component) in the definition of the exceptional leader, but also the subtle relation of this dimension with other attitudinal components (both cognitive and conative). To be informed, that is, to hold knowledge, is not disconnected from human qualities such as fairness. However, this two-dimensional form of "professionalism" is effective only when a competitive dimension is added to the mix. Neither are "dependability, seriousness" and "honesty" by themselves enough to ensure the leader's commitment to tasks on the basis of common interest; they need to be associated with intelligence to contribute to social leadership. The "hard worker" is a good leader only if she or he has the intelligence to adopt the qualities of a "human leader."

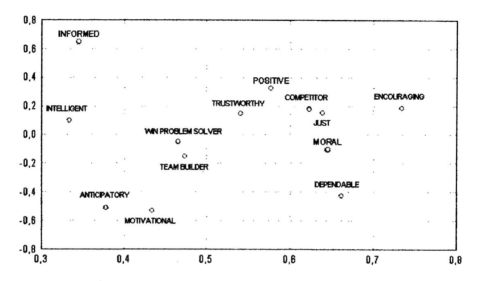

FIG. 15.3.   Two-factorial representation of core attributes of an outstanding leader in France (factor analysis).

Factor Analysis

The factor analysis highlights the opposition between items. Indeed each axis is defined by items whose projections are the most extreme. (See Fig. 15.3.)

In this factor analysis, we identify a first axis (29.36% of the variance), which opposes the items "informed," "intelligence," and "foresight" at one pole, and the item "encouraging" at the other. Between these two poles, we find items such as "motivating," "team builder," and "solution" on the left side, and items such as "competitor," "fair," "honest," and "serious" on the right. By adopting a discriminating vantage (MacLaury, 1997), intellectual qualities can be distinguished from qualities in the management of human relations. As for pragmatic ("win-win problem solver") and collective ("team builder") commitments, they are to be distinguished from more general human qualities such as seriousness ("dependable"), honesty ("moral"), and fairness ("just"). As a consequence, there seems to be an opposition between "cold" and "human" leadership, which affects the way efficiency and team management is perceived. Indeed, problem solving and team building seem to be perceived as less "human" traits than other features that dominate in direct face-to-face relations. The analysis of this first axis confirms the analysis obtained through the dendrogram, and also reveals that the French management of human relations is a relatively complex process, insofar as this dimension tends to infiltrate others. Furthermore, it indicates that more is expected from leaders in terms of individual human relations than in terms of collective relations. This underscores the importance of human sensitivity in leadership.

The second axis (10.81% of the variance) opposes the items "informed," "positive," "trustworthy," and "competitor" to "motivating," "anticipatory," and "moral booster." In other words, it opposes the entrepreneurial but reassuring leader to the serious, future-oriented leader who expects a great deal from his or her subordinates. The fact that respondents make a distinction

TABLE 15.6
Characteristics of Exceptional Leader Among French Managers

Dimensions (First-Order factors) Subdimensions(Second-Order factors)	Mean	Rank
I. Charismatic	**4.93**	**50**
Performance Orientation	5.10	59
Visionary	5.06	59
Inspirational	5.22	59
Integrity	5.14	58
Self-Sacrificial	3.98	61
Decisive	5.06	58
II. Team Oriented	**5.11**	**60**
Team Integrator	4.73	60
Collaborative Team Oriented	5.11	59
Administratively Competent	4.52	61
Diplomatic	5.01	59
Malevolent (reverse for II)	1.95	15
III. Self-Protective	**2.81**	**58**
Self-Centered	1.86	54
Status-Conscious	3.25	58
Conflict Inducer	5.11	59
Face Saver	2.19	60
Procedural	3.17	57
IV. Participative	**5.90**	**7**
Autocratic(reverse for IV)	2.36	44
Nonparticipative (reverse for IV)	1.86	61
V. Humane	**3.82**	**61**
Humane	3.29	60
Modesty	4.27	59
VI. Autonomous	**3.32**	**58**
Autonomous	3.32	58

Note.   Ranks are given in comparison to the 61 GLOBE countries.

between the leader who is simply good, and the one who is good for them, again highlights the importance of interpersonal relations in the representation of the exceptional leader among French managers.

To conclude, the analysis of the organization of the most resistant elements of social representation shows that, for French managers, the exceptional leader is a "people-oriented" person who maintains personable relations in his or her environment. This analysis is confirmed by the following 21 first-order and 6 second-order factors obtained from the GLOBE study.

Table 15.6 shows that some of the major GLOBE leadership dimensions (second-order factors) are valued whereas others are clearly depreciated. Participative leadership stands out as the most appreciated of leadership traits. Indeed, French leaders seem to value everyone participating in decisions as well as task delegation. However, when reading these results, one needs to keep in mind that scores refer to the "nonparticipative" and "autocratic" traits; this means that it is not a direct espousal of "participation" that was expressed, but rather a rejection of nonparticipation (see next section). The next most valued traits in leadership style are "team orientated" (5.11) and "charismatic" (4.93). The former refers to purpose-oriented teamwork based on "diplomacy" and "administrative competence," whereas the latter represents the "visionary," "self-sacrificial," "honest," "decisive," and "performance-oriented" leader. Being "modest" and "humane" appears to be less important and even sometimes slightly negative for good leadership, in that it may affect leaders' credibility. This also applies to "autonomous" leaders, who tend to manage problems on their own. Finally, the least appreciated among leaders is the "self-protected" leader who is "self-centered," "status-conscious," and "procedural," as well as a "conflict inducer" and a "face saver."

7. LEADERSHIP IN FRANCE COMPARED TO OTHER COUNTRIES

When compared with the scores obtained for other countries, French scores lie at both ends of a scale, from the most open or "participative" to the most closed or "self-protective." Indeed, among the six second-order factors, the score obtained for "participation" (Rank 7) places France among the countries that most favor this style of leadership. The other five factors are clearly devalued, ranking between 50th and 61st. Thus, in comparison, only participation seems to be valued whereas other styles are clearly rejected. However, these scores need to be interpreted in light of the general outlook of the results. Indeed, the scores attributed by French middle managers appear to be *systematically* much lower than those obtained for other countries (the higher score for participation results from an inverted low score). Thus, France ranks among the lowest four countries for 18 out of the 21 first-order scales. The other three (where France ranks 54, 44, and 15) refer to items where the other 60 countries also obtain low scores (average <3.5). One possible interpretation is that the middle managers who took part in this study evaluated their own bosses and gave them low scores on most traits. Therefore, it appears that it may not be easy to give a positive opinion about one's superiors in French culture, especially for traits that are most commonly valued.

General Observations

In the interviews, managers endorsed universally approved qualities of leadership, notably vision, dynamism, collaborative, and team orientation, and rejected the negative qualities. In general the findings from the literature research, unobtrusive measures, questionnaire results, and interviews all concur.

Contrary to expectation and what can be found in the literature on France (e.g., Hofstede), France scored relatively low on Power Distance (Bands B and C). This is probably due to recent changes in the business world in France, because many state companies have been recently privatized. However, these results can also be attributed to the fact that most of the literature on leadership in France is based on the study of state industries and large companies, thereby ignoring more than half of the other businesses in the country. The presence of "both worlds" in our sample therefore made it possible to provide another interpretation of French organizations.

Similarly, Uncertainty Avoidance was rated as *moderately* high. However, the study reveals that the French did not want less structure and did not think that more Uncertainty Avoidance would help. Indeed, less structure might, in their view, lead to anarchy rather than favor risk taking.

Humane Orientation was rated relatively low compared to other countries. The following observations might explain this score. First, as explained earlier, managers are only moderately tolerant regarding professional mistakes, which influences the score obtained for Humane Orientation. Second, leaders work within a range of constraints. They are not considered as fully autonomous actors or unique individuals able to achieve, perform, or "move mountains" based on their own volition. They are part of a democratic structure that ensures that the voice of all, including lower level employees, is heard and taken into consideration in decision making.

The results of the media analysis, in which leaders display a low profile, reinforce this viewpoint. In publications, the role of the leader as the main actor is downplayed; the focus is on events that materialize, seemingly independently of the actor's initiative. The key actor in the public domain and business is expected to be rational, intellectual, and objective, conforming to the abstract notions of the system. From that point of view, expectations are similar to those found in other European countries, for example Germany (Brodbeck, Frese, & Javidan, 2002; see also chap. 6, this volume). These "neutral" qualities are important culture-specific traits. The leader is expected to be very well educated, a discreet operator, and a strong silent leader who serves his or her company and country.

Aspects of state industry relations must also be considered. These include the importance of government laws and regulations, many of which form part of the rules of private companies. In many cases, in spite of recent privatizations, the state still maintains a continuing presence as a shareholder, especially in large companies considered of strategic importance. The politicized nature of the state–industry relationship is reflected, for example, in the practice of parachuting.

In spite of this apparently technocratic structure, a series of culture-specific traits reflected a more humanist style of management. Confirmation of the insights of the studies by d'Iribarne (1989) and Amado, Faucheux, and Laurent (1990) were found in that human relations remain important, particularly in the smaller, family-based cooperatives in food processing. A purely commercial and technocratic approach in these companies has often proved to be disruptive, and technocratic leaders have often failed to be reelected because of a lack of knowledge of how human relations function in this sector.

Thus, outstanding French leaders have the ability to adapt to the structure of the workplace, finding their position in the complex network of personal relations of the milieu in which they operate. Many interviewees stressed the need for outstanding leaders to be tuned in on a daily basis to what happens in their organization. This idea of adapting to the milieu becomes all the more relevant because regional differences are still very strong. Indeed, mobility (which is part of the condition of many top leaders) requires modification of leadership styles and techniques for handling management–employee relations.

Thus, for the outstanding French leader, the many rules and regulations that outside observers usually consider as having a paralyzing effect are not perceived as constraints. Rather, these rules constitute a framework that makes creativity and innovation possible. They are the "grammar" of business, or in Pierre Bourdieu's terms, "the rules of the game" (Foster, 1986). The better leaders understand and master these rules, the better players they will be. In short, outstanding leaders do not simply obey rules they use them and build upon them.

Conclusion

Limitations.   On the basis of the overall GLOBE findings, as noted by Hanges (2004), the country scores for France were often identified as outliers. This particular requires further attention. For us, it could be attributed to the way the French relate to power practices. Indeed, the "exercise of power" (*l'exercice du pouvoir*) can be conceptualized in different ways. It can be considered as referring to personal attributes of the source of power. It can be considered through a type of relation linking the source to the target. Finally, it can be considered as result of the interaction between the source and the target. The GLOBE study as a whole focuses on the first conception of power. However, this type of power appears not to be valued by the French. For instance, the individualistic perspective adopted in this study has been contested by many French researchers, a great number of whom in our own research team have refused to collaborate. In the French leadership research tradition, the leader looks like the leader described in the GLOBE study only because his or her subordinates give him or her this role. Thus, a conception of power that focuses on the consciousness of the other's contribution to power would be more acceptable than one that outlines leadership styles. In fact, as we demonstrated in our historical overview, the social conflict between classes is always present in people's minds; as a result, when they answered our questions we do not know what reference group (dominant or dominated) managers had in mind, or more precisely what reference group they chose to adopt, or have adopted, depending on their individual strategy. Despite this fact, which reinforced mental insecurity in responding, managers answered the questionnaire and gave some qualities that they deemed essential in managing French organizations.

These qualities are important in cross-cultural comparisons insofar as they give a unique standard of comparison to determine knowledge. The GLOBE study's reference frame leads the subjects to give an answer. And so they do; they give an image. This image is interesting to explore by comparing one culture to the others. Nevertheless, we should keep in mind that this knowledge does not immediately fit the reality of a particular culture. Consequently, we have to be cautious when we refer to this knowledge in relation to action.

Practical Implications.   Because of the limitations of the research, we believe that the results we obtained differ according to the nationality of managers. For foreign managers, results allow us to provide interpretations for "critical incidents." By critical incidents we refer to conflicts that often emerge between members of different cultures, because they do not have the same reference frame. At work, many problems arise from misunderstanding due to cultural specific perspectives. Considering cultural difference when a problem is emerging allows avoiding interpersonal problems. Thus, foreign managers working in France should appreciate the significance of the following:

- The pervasiveness of intellectualism, planning, and abstraction (see the Appendix).
- The importance of humanism, group orientation, and social forces in the workplace.
- The French ability to reconcile contradictions, such as hierarchy and equality, order, and liberty.
- The extent to which people accept the "system," are bound by it, and find ways to rise above it.

- The fact that horizontal networking and bonding is as important as the more visible hierarchical structure.
- French forms of pragmatism, which include handling uniformity (centralization) and diversity.
- The ability of French managers/supervisors to lead while allowing employees to fulfill tasks on their own (respect of people's sense of honor).
- The French preoccupation with maintaining their own particularism, exceptionalism, and originality.
- The respect for leaders depicting qualities reflecting flair, form, style, charisma, panache, and elegance.

Nevertheless, this knowledge is not really a checklist that can be reduced to one leadership style. The necessity for the leader to be "above the crowd," and therefore, to a certain extent, to be impersonal, invisible, replaceable, and therefore at times bureaucratic and procedural, does not prevent him or her from being human, people centered, and in favor of a team-oriented and humane form of leadership. On the contrary, it is the ability to combine these apparently contrasting qualities that distinguishes the outstanding leader from the "weak leader." In France, leadership style is not entirely the property of the leader because it has to fit with the expectation of the other members of the company. Even if the foreign manager behaves as a manager should behave according to French standards, he or she could be rejected. An outstanding leader is not necessarily associated only with qualities regarded as positive. For example, he or she might possess qualities regarded as marginally negative; certain outstanding leaders have been described as "nice and nasty," "mercenaries," or "pirates."

It is the position of the leader in the entire organization that determines his or her role and consequently the style he or she should adopt. Not conversely, French managers working in the United States can take into account the results of the survey. Thanks to the GLOBE study, they possess, just as managers in other countries do, the expression of (from our viewpoint) the "American framework," and can directly use it. In the same way, but more carefully, French managers can use the results obtained to work with partners all over the world (except perhaps for partners from other "outlier" countries). Explicitly considering the GLOBE questionnaire as referent frame and analyzing the respective distance of its own position, the French position, and the partner country's position, each manager can see what type of effort he or she has to make.

Future Research.   In future research, we would try to be more specific in the identity of our respondents. In sociopsychological terms, we would control the identity concerned by the participation to such a survey. According to self-categorization theory (Turner, Hogg, Oakes, Reicher, & Wetherell, 1987), the consciousness of cultural identity is linked to social identity. When a culture is strongly recognized, social categories emerge. In other words, when people are aware of belonging to the same category at a superordinate level, they strongly show their difference at the ordinate level. As we have seen in our historical overview, French identity is relatively strong. As a result, intragroup conflicts emerge and social categories become salient. Therefore, in their answers, managers tend to activate their social identity by referring to the social group they choose to enhance. To understand what managers are doing when they answer the questionnaire, we would systematically explore the social partitions emerging in the chosen sector (Hight status/Low status; Representative/Nonrepresentative; Minority/Majority) and determine the score for each reference category.

We would also explore leadership in sports contexts. Indeed, it seems that in this field, leaders are viewed differently. They really seem to be responsible for all sport issues, and their individual characteristics are largely developed in the media.

REFERENCES

Abric, C. (1984). L'artisan et l'artisanat: Analyse de contenu et de la structure d'une représentation sociale [The artisan and the craft industry. Analysis of the contents and structure of social representation]. *Bulletin de Psychologie, 37*(3), 861–876.

Allouche, J., & Amann, B. (1977). Le retour triomphant du capitalisme familial [The triomphant return of family capitalism]. *L'Expansion, Management Review, 85,* 92–99.

Altman, Y. (1993). A typology of work relations in the context of contemporary Europe. *Journal of European Industrial Training, 17*(10), 44–50.

Amado, G., Faucheux, C., & Laurent, A. (1990). Changements organisationnels et réalités culturelles [Organizations changes and cultural realities]. In J. F. Chanlot (Ed.), *L'individu dans l'Organisation* (pp. 629–661). Quebec, Canada: Eska University/Laval Press.

Barsoux, J.-L., & Lawrence, P. (1990). *Management in France.* London: Cassell.

Barsoux, J.-L., & Lawrence, P. (1991). Countries, cultures and constraints. In R. Calori & P. Lawrence (Eds.), *The business of Europe—managing change* (pp. 198–217). London: Sage.

Barsoux, J.-L., & Lawrence, P. (1997). *French management: Elitism in action.* London: Cassell.

Bass, B. M. (1990). *Bass and Stogdill's handbook of leadership* (3rd ed.). New York: The Free Press.

Bauer, M. (1990, September 13). Pdg: Les hauts fonctionnaires écrasent les carrières maisons [Chairman and Managing Director: the top civil servants destroy career opportunities in business]. *Les Echos.*

Benzecri, J.-P. (1976). *L'analyse des données* [Data analysis]. Paris: Dunod.

Blondel, J. (1974). *Contemporary France.* London: Methuen.

Brilman, J. (1998). *Les meilleures pratiques de management: Au coeur de la performance* [Best management principles: Based on performance]. Paris: Editions de l'Organisation.

Brodbeck, F. C., Frese, M., & Javidan, M. (2002). Leadership made in Germany: Low on compassion, high on performance. *Academy of Management Executive, 16*(1), 16–29.

Castel, P., Lacassagne, M.-F., & Salès-Wuillemin, E. (2002). Categorial points of view in social representation. *Language Sciences, 24,* 667–678.

d'Iribarne, P. (1989). *La logique de l'honneur* [The logic of principle]. Paris: Seuil.

d'Iribarne, P. (1996). The usefulness of an ethnographic approach to the international comparison of organizations. *International Studies of Management and Organizations, 26*(4), 30–47.

Dyson, K. (1983). The cultural, ideological and structural context. In K. Dyson & S. Wilks (Eds.), *Industrial Crisis: A comparative study of the state and industry* (pp. 26–66). New York: St. Martin's Press.

Flament, C. (1986). L'analyse de similitude: Uune technique pour les recherches sur les représentations sociales [The analysis of similarities: A technique for research in social representations]. In W. Doise et A. Palmonari (Eds.), *L'étude des représentations sociales* (pp. 139–156). Paris: Delachaux et Niestlé.

Foster, S. (1986). Reading Pierre Bourdieu [interview]. *Cultural Anthropology, 1*(1), 103–120.

Girling, J. (1998). *France: Political and social change.* London: Routledge.

Goetschy, J. (1998). France: The limits of reform. In A. Ferner & R. Hyman (Eds.), *Changing industrial relations in Europe* (2nd ed., pp. 357–394). Oxford, England: Blackwell.

Graves, D. (Ed.). (1973). *Management research: A cross-cultural perspective.* Amsterdam: Elsevier Scientific.

Hanges, P. J. (2004). Societal-level, correlations among globe societal culture scales. In R. J. House, P. J. Hanges, M. Javidan, P. W. Dorfman, V. Gupta, & Globe Associates (Eds.), *Culture, leadership, and organizations: The GLOBE study of 62 societies* (pp. 733–736). Thousand Oaks, CA: Sage.

Hastings, C. (1993). *The new organization: Growing the culture of organizational networking.* London: McGraw-Hill.

Hewlett, N. (1998). *Modern French politics.* Cambridge, England: Polity Press.

Hofstede, G. (1991). *Cultures and organizations.* London: McGraw-Hill.

House, R. J., Hanges, P. J., Javidan, M., Dorfman, P. W., Gupta, V., & Globe Associates. (2004). *Culture, leadership, and organizations: The GLOBE study of 62 societies.* Thousand Oaks, CA: Sage.

House, R. J., Hanges P., & Ruiz-Quintanilla, A. (1997). GLOBE: The global leadership and organizational behavior effectiveness research program. *Polish Psychological Bulletin, 28*(3), 215–254.

House, R. J., Wright, N. S., & Aditya, R. N. (1997). Cross-cultural research on organizational leadership: A critical analysis and a proposed theory. In P. C. Earley & M. Erez (Eds.), *New perspectives on international industrial/organizational psychology* (pp. 535–624). San Francisco: New Lexington Press.

Jack, A. (1998). *Sur la France* [About France]. Paris: Odile Jacob.

Jack, A. (1999). *The French exception: France—still so special?* London: Profile Books.

Le Bouédec, G. (1984). Contribution à la méthodologie d'étude de représentations sociales [Contribution to the study of social representations]. *Cahiers de Psychologie Cognitive, 4,* 245–272.

Lebel, P. (1985). *Le triangle du management* [The management triangle]. Paris: Editions d'Organization.

Leeds, C. A. (1994). France. In M. A. Rahim & A. A. Blum (Eds.), *Global perspectives on organizational conflict* (pp. 17–32). Westport, CT: Praeger.

Limouzin, P. (1992). Agricultures et industries agro-alimentaires françaises [French food- processing industries and agriculture]. Paris: Masson.

Lipiansky, E. M. (1989). Discours, représentations de l'identité et relations interculturelles [Discourse, identity representations and intercultural relations]. In *Socialisations et Cultures* (pp. 413–421). Proceedings of the 1st Conference of ARIC (Association for Intercultural Research). Toulouse, France: Mirail University Press.

MacLaury, R. E. (1997). *Color and cognition in Mesoamerica: Constructing Categories as Vantages.* Austin: University of Texas Press.

MacLaury, R. (2000). Linguistic relativity and the plasticity of categorization: Universalism in a new key. In M. Putz & M. Verspoor (Eds.), *Explorations in linguistic relativity* (pp. 249–294). Amsterdam: Bemjamins.

Marseille, J. (1997). *Les industries agro-alimentaire en France* [The food-processing industry in France]. Paris: Le Monde-Editions.

Moscovici, S. (1961). La psychanalyse, son image, son public [(Psychoanalysis, its image, its audience]. Paris: PUF.

Moscovici, S. (1984). Le domaine de la psychologie sociale [The domain of social psychology]. In S. Moscovici (Ed.), *La psychologie sociale* (pp. 3–12). Paris: PUF.

Moyet, S. (1989). *Les commandeurs* [The commanders]. Paris: Stock.

Reinert, M. (1993). Les mondes lexicaux et leur logique à travers l'analyse statistique d'un corpus de récits de cauchemar [Logics of lescical words through statistic analysis of nightmare discourse]. *Langage et Société, 66,* 5–39.

Sainsaulieu, R. (1997). *Sociologie de l'entreprise* [Sociology of business] (2nd ed.). Paris: Presses de Sciences Po and Dalloz.

Szarka, J. (1992). *Business in France: An introduction to the economic and social context.* London: Pitman.

Thiveaud, J. M. (1997). Les évolutions du système bancaire français de l'entre-deux-guerres à nos jours: spécialisation, despécialisation, concentration, concurrence [The development of the French banking system from the interwar period to today: Specialization, de-specialization, concentration, competition]. *Revue d'Economie Financière, 39,* 27–68.

Turner, J. C., Hogg, M., Oakes, P. J., Reicher, S., & Wetherell, M. (1987). *Rediscovering the social group: A self-categorisation theory*. Oxford, England: Basil Blackwell.

Vachette, J.-L. (1984). Le modèle français du changement [The French model of change]. Revue Française de Gestion, 47–48, 119–122.

Weber, H. (1986). *Le parti des patrons—le CNPF* [Organization of the business leaders]. Paris: Seuil.

Appendix B

French Economy and Culture

"France," writes sociologist Stanley Hoffmann, "remains a nation that practices capitalism but harbors a solid anti-capitalist tradition, based on the high value attached to equality, and linked to powerful socialist and Catholic schools of thought" (Hoffman, 2000, p. 78). One should therefore not be surprised to find, behind a rhetoric dominated by anti- Americanism and exceptionalism, a country that, in many ways, resembles most other economic power-houses.

With its 60 million inhabitants, France ranks fourth in the world in terms of gross national product (GNP), after the United States, Japan, and Germany. It is also the fourth largest exporter after the United States, Germany, and Japan with a positive trade balance of 3% in 1999 (Organization for Ecomonic Corporation and Development figures). Most of its activity relates to services (72%), followed by industry (25%) and agriculture (3%). The country is particularly competitive in the areas of new technologies, transportation, equipment, and tourism. It exports goods in agriculture, automotive, civil aviation, transportation, and trains. Its main trading partners are Germany, the United Kingdom, Italy, and Spain. Seventy percent of its commercial exchanges are with these and other European countries.

In June 2002, the international consultants Ernst & Young published a report in which it showed that France, like other European countries, needed to improve its attractiveness if it wanted to counter the ongoing process of delocalization toward central European countries such as the Czech Republic, Poland, Hungary, and Rumania. The 200 international companies consulted for the study resented the labor costs, the poor labor flexibility, and the high taxes that France imposes on foreign investors. Yet France ranked first in terms of quality of life and telecommunication infrastructures, and second, just behind Germany, in terms of quality of labor. Its situation at the center of Europe, and its transport infrastructure were also highly valued. These factors may explain why 266 foreign companies decided to settle in France in 2001 (*Le Monde,* June 25, 2002).

16

Leadership and Culture in Portugal

Jorge Correia Jesuino
Instituto Superior de Ciências do Trabalho e da Empresa,
Lisboa, Portugal

> Portugal, a conflict I have with myself.
> —Alexandre O'Neil

The exergue comes from a poem about Portugal by Alexandre O'Neil (published in 1965). It reflects the *malaise* most of the Portuguese *intelligentsia* feel toward their national culture and identity. José Saramago, Nobel Prize for literature in 2000, has also claimed that he is unlikely to reach a clear understanding of the Portuguese identity in his lifetime. Most of the reflections of Eduardo Lourenço, another famous essayist, have been dedicated to trying to decipher what has already been dubbed as the Portuguese riddle. It is in itself intriguing that so many of the most gifted Portuguese thinkers should espouse such an attitude. There are no apparent reasons for questioning the Portuguese national identity. As Monteiro and & Pinto (1998) remarked:

> Portugal is a political entity that has maintained stable frontiers since the thirteenth century. Its existence as an autonomous kingdom from the twelfth century on was only interrupted for little more than half a century (1580–1640). Portugal, moreover, has never confronted problems of linguistic diversity. All historians, not just those of a nationalist-corporatist bent, have generally taken the nation's existence for granted. (1988, pp. 206–207)

The roots of the intellectual's uneasiness about their own culture has to be sought not in geographical, ethnic, or religious factors but in the "decadence" of the nation that took place after the maritime discoveries of the 15th and 16th centuries, and henceforth never ceased to haunt the Portuguese imaginary. This could also explain the deeply ingrained trend that, at a more popular level, can be observed among the Portuguese for self-derogatory remarks, alongside an acute sensitivity for the ridicule—a culture centered more on shame than on guilt. The example of "Fado, Football, and Fátima" could be given, often invoked as a sarcastic synopsis of the Portuguese cultural profile.

Anyway, the Portuguese now feel very proud of figures like Amália Rodrigues, the famous singer that internationalized Fado, or even football stars like Figo, considered to be the best world player, and Fátima, a holy place where Our Lady was said to have appeared to three shepherds in 1917, recently canonized by the Pope, attracts an ever-growing number of pilgrims.

The "Estado Novo" (New State) that ruled in Portugal under the dictatorship of Salazar (1933–1968) and Caetano (1968–1974) actively promoted the ideal of "national regeneration," which attempted to restore a sense of national pride, mostly grounded on the remains of the Portuguese empire. Another triptych pervading the nationalistic propaganda at the time was: "God, Fatherland, and Family." It is far from sure that the Portuguese societal culture succeeded in internalizing this new ideology, which was in many ways similar to those of European fascist countries such as Italy and Germany. But it certainly succeeded in isolating and alienating the Portuguese from the rest of the world, hence preventing them from developing close links of collective association. In 1974, a revolution led by the military put an end to a regime of 48 years of dictatorship and paved the way for Portugal's integration in the democratic world.

The "Revolution of the Carnations" launched another famous triptych maxim: decolonization, democratization, and development. Essentially this program has now been accomplished, although the enormous handicap at the outset still places Portugal at the tail of the most developed world. Leaders and leadership, both on the political scene and in the multiple organisms of civil society, are central to this process of change and development. Their role and salience depends on the specific features of the situations they face, and their style is to a great extent shaped by the societal and organizational context within which they operate.

In the following chapter, the aim is to examine the interplay of culture and leadership in Portugal within the conceptual framework proposed by the GLOBE project. An attempt is thus made to integrate qualitative, as well as quantitative empirical data gathered from Portuguese middle managers and opinion makers. The chapter is divided into six main sections. The first seeks to present the overall description of the societal culture in terms of the political, social, and economic system. The second section introduces the GLOBE research in Portugal, and the third presents a report of the empirical findings at the level of the societal culture. The fourth section centers on leadership perceptions and in the fifth, two specific sectors are analyzed—food processing and telecommunications. Conclusions are then presented in the final section.

1. PORTUGAL: POLITICAL, ECONOMIC, AND SOCIAL TRENDS

Historical Milestones

The political scene of modern Portugal can be divided in three main periods: the First Republic (1910–1926), the Estado Novo (1933–1974), and the democracy that followed the military coup of April 1974. Portugal was admitted to the European Union (EU; then named European Economic Community EEC) in 1986.

The First Republic. The First Republic is a period characterized politically by the cabinet instability that reflected the efforts to match the political structure to the demands of the emerging capitalism. In 1911, Portugal had a population of about 5.5 million inhabitants. The active population amounted to 2.5 million, 58% of which worked in agriculture, 25% in industry, and 17% in the tertiary sector. The population in 1930 was composed of 80% still living mostly in small towns and villages. The ever-increasing dependence on the African colonies was probably one reason for Portugal's intervention in the First World War,

1914–1918, as England's ally. In spite of the instability, some of the ideals of the republican regime were apparent in a number of political measures, for example, separation of the church from the state, the right to strike, and the approval of civil marriage. The Communist Party was founded in 1921. The economic crisis and the participation in World War I gave rise to social turmoil, paving the way for the implementation of an authoritarian regime.

Estado Novo (New State).   A military coup in 1926 gave rise to the Estado Novo, whose main features were similar to the fascist movements that pervaded a number of European countries. Salazar became the minister of finance in 1928 and president of the Council of Ministers in 1932, a post that he maintained until 1968 when, ill health, following a fall, led to his replacement by his "dauphin" Marcelo Caetano. During the first period between 1932 and the end of World War II in 1945, the project of economic development centered on agriculture and the African colonies were maintained. The structure of the Portuguese economy changed only in the 1940s. Industry came to the forefront. In spite of such structural changes, Portugal was still at the tail end of European countries and was unable to stop emigration. Various attempts to fight the regime were unsuccessful. The Estado Novo was corporatist, and played a central role in institutional structures, ideology, relations with "organized interests," and the state's economic policy. As Costa Pinto (1998) remarked, "The Estado Novo was obsessive about education" (p. 35). This did not mean it wanted to modernize; modernization only became an issue in the 1950s. In 1933, Salazar expressed the opinion that "the constitution of elites is more important than teaching the people to read" (Costa Pinto, 1998, p. 35). The Salazarist ideology was based on the doctrine of God, Fatherland, and Family.

In 1961, the Portuguese settlements in India—Goa, Damão, and Diu—were annexed by the Indian Union. In 1962, the African wars started with terrorist attacks in Luanda. Salazar's order was to embark "rapidly and forcefully" to Angola, an expression that became famous and is still present in the collective memory. The war contributed to disintegrating the regime, and resulted in the "Revolution of Carnations" in April 1974 led by the MFA (Movement of Armed Forces).

Democracy.   The Revolution of 1974 was known as the Revolution of Carnations because no blood was shed. An icon of that period is a famous photo depicting a child putting a carnation in a soldier's rifle. A consequence of the Revolution, if not its very cause, was the independence granted to the African colonies of Guinea-Bissau, Cape-Verde, Angola, and Mozambique in 1975. The transition period was however very complex and conflictive. In April 1976, the Constitution was approved and Mário Soares, secretary-general of the Socialist Party, which won the first free elections, became the prime minister of the First Constitutional Government. After a period of great instability with coalition governments until 1985, there was a period of stability assured by the absolute majority, firstly involving the Social Democratic Party (1985–1995) and then the Socialist Party (1995–2002). On January 1, 1986, Portugal became a member of the EEC (today, EU). Mário Soares was elected president of the republic in February of the same year.

Political Framework

The political structure of Portugal is outlined in Table 16.1.

Political Form and Figures.   In Portugal, representation of political life is still dominated by the continental European concept of left and right wings. The Parliament is a large semicircle

TABLE 16.1
Political Structure of Portugal

	Political Structure
Official Name	Portuguese Republic
Form of State	Parliamentary Republic
Legal System	Based on the Constitution of 1976, amended most recently in 1997.
National Legislature	Unicameral Assembleia da República (Parliament) of 230 members elected for a maximum term of 4 years.
Electoral System	Universal direct suffrage from the age of 18.
National Elections	March 2002; next election due by March 2006.
Head of State	President directly elected for a maximum of two consecutive 5-year terms; currently *Amibal Cavaco Silva* is becoming the First centre-right president since 1974.
National Government	Council of Ministers, led by a prime minister appointed by the president, whose legislative program must be approved by the Assembleia da República. Victory in February 2005 election section went to the Socialist party led by Jose Socrates

where the members sit in accordance to their location in the political spectrum. The two main forces are the Socialists and the Social Democrats, who have been alternating in the government. They differ more in style than in political programs, which, at present, are greatly conditioned by EU directives. Political life in Portugal, like everywhere, is a natural locus for the exercising of leadership. When people are asked to evoke typical examples of Portuguese leaders, political figures come spontaneously to the forefront. Some of them even display charismatic features, making them potential historical figures. This is the case of *Francisco Sá Carneiro,* one of the founders of the Social Democratic Party in 1974, who was killed in an air crash in 1980. The causes of the crash are still controversial, but after more than 20 years of investigation there is no evidence to support sabotage. Sá Carneiro was then prime minister and his tragic death certainly contributed to making him larger than life. His ideas and energetic style are still evoked by the Social Democratic militants. *Cavaco Silva,* who was prime minister for 10 years (1985–1995), and president since 2006 is another respected and authoritative voice. He also displays some charismatic traits of rigor, determination, and austerity.

Another historical and prestigious figure is *Mário Soares,* who founded the Socialist Party in Germany in 1973. It became a party of mass support after the 1974 coup, when it challenged the Portuguese Communist Party (PCP) for the working-class vote. Mário Soares was elected president of the republic for two mandates (1986–1991). Internationally, he is probably the best known Portuguese political actor. Internally, he still exerts an important influence over the public opinion.

Jorge Sampaio, former mayor of Lisbon, is another Socialist leader, who succeeded Mário Soares as president of the republic in 1996, defeating Cavaco Silva, and was then reelected in 2001. *António Guterres,* also from the Socialist area, became prime minister after the Socialist Party's victory in the legislative elections in 1995, repeated again in 2000. Guterres resigned as both party leader and prime minster following a heavy defeat in local elections in December 2001. As a political leader, Guterres fell into discredit due to the profligacy of his economic policy. Guterres introduced a new style of leadership, promoting dialogue with the Parliament, the people, and the media. Apparently, however, communication is not enough.

Another charismatic figure is *Álvaro Cunhal,* the historic leader of the Communist Party. He stood down in 1992, retaining however considerable influence. He is now almost 90 years of age. The PCP was important during the first years of the Revolution. Its support base comes from the industrial suburbs and rural south. But it has steadily eroded since the collapse of the Soviet regime and it is now in a state of crisis. Nevertheless, its influence on the unions, and specifically on those affiliated with CGTP (Confederação Geral dos Trabalhadores Portugueses), is far from being negligible.

Another very active political actor is *Freitas do Amaral,* former founder of the Centre Democratic Party (CDS), now the Popular Party (PP), which lost the presidential elections to Mário Soares in 1986 by a small margin (42.8% vs. 51.2% of the votes). Freitas do Amaral chaired the General Assembly of the United Nations in 2000. The PP, formerly led by *Paulo Portas,* a rather mercurial and controversial figure, formed a coalition with the Social Democratic Party, thus assuring an absolute majority in Parliament until the victory of the Socialist Party in 2005, that became the majority in the Parliament.

Other political actors could be named for the role they played during the period of the Revolution of April 1974—Military figures like *Otelo Saraiva de Carvalho, Vasco Gonçalves, Ramalho Eanes,* who became president of the republic for two mandates (1976–1986), *Vasco Lourenço,* and many others. They became popular heroes for a while, and now are recalled only by the older generation of historians.

Consequently, they contributed to shaping the social representation of the role of leaders and leadership by initiating social change, but they are also a reminder of how elusive and relative an influence is in the final course of history. A final reference concerns *Maria de Lurdes Pintassilgo,* the only Portuguese woman to become head of an independent cabinet that ruled for the short period of just 150 days (July–November 1979).

Many of those figures mentioned were, and most still are, a regular presence in the media, which also contributed to building the leadership culture within the Portuguese "public sphere." Another source is the ever-growing (auto)biographic genre, sometimes in the form of comprehensive interviews, through which the leaders "present themselves" and give a public account of their (sometimes) controversial decisions.

Economic Highlights

Table 16.2 gives an overview of Portugal's economic data, which is discussed in detail in the following.

In the excellent and comprehensive survey of Portugal published in the *Economist* dated November 30, 2000, it is remarked that:

> When Portugal joined the then European Community on New Year's Day 1986, its GDP per head, in terms of purchasing-power-parity (PPP), was a mere 53% of the EU average. Closing the gap has been the stated aim of the Portuguese government ever since, and progress has been swift: GDP is now 75% of the European mean. No other hopeful entrant to the European club—not the big next-door neighbor, Spain; not even Ireland, the Celtic tiger of the 1990s—has made up so much ground in its first few years of membership. Yet the gap has merely narrowed, not disappeared. Between 1987 and 1991, Portugal narrowed the gap with the EU in GDP per head by 10.7%. In the following four years it shaved off only another six percent, and in the four years

TABLE 16.2
Economical Data for Portugal

Economic Indicators 2001	
GDP per head ($ at PPP)	18.580
GDP (% real change)	1.66
Government expenditure (% of GDP)	42.0
Consumer price inflation (%)	4.35
Public debt (% of GDP)	54.90
Labor costs per hour (USD)	5.22
Unemployment (%)	4.05
Current-account balance/GDP	−9.17
Exchange rate (av; US$: Euro)	0.90
Population (m; year-end)	10.36
Main cities & population	
Lisbon (greater urban area)	1.4
Oporto (greater urban area)	1.2
Area (sq km)	92.08
Main trading partners	
Germany (% export)	19.2
(% import)	13.9
Spain (% export)	18.6
(% import)	26.5
France (% export)	12.6
(% import)	10.3
UK (% export)	10.3
(% import)	5.0

Note. From Instituto Nacional de Estatística, OECD Statistics, and Eurostat.

after that, up to 1999, only a further 3.4. With that sort of recent record, and given the European Commission's growth forecasts for 1999–2003 (an average of 3% for the whole EU, a little less for Portugal) "convergence could take 70 years."

Two years later and in part due to the international turbulence, the prospects are even worse with the public finances in crisis, the government has been forced to implement a restrictive and procyclical fiscal policy, which is exacerbating the economic downturn.

Joining the European Community in 1986 did in fact bring major benefits for the Portuguese. It permitted Portugal to rise from about half the European average to three-fourths. The structural funds from Brussels had a significant effect, namely on the country's physical infrastructure. By 1998, Portugal had 840 km of motorway, compared with only 240 km in 1987. Still, according to the *Economist*'s survey, "a second effect of tying itself to Europe was to make Portugal more open to trade and investment. ... Foreign direct investment (FDI) more than doubled between 1985 and 1990, and more than doubled again by 1999." A third outcome of joining Europe "has been to give Portugal macroeconomic credibility."

But structural funds will end in 2006. On the other hand, new candidates, the Eastern European countries, have joined the club. Portugal will have to face a difficult challenge without obvious solutions in sight. Besides, in terms of structural factors such as levels of education, research and development (R&D), investment, productivity, and size of public sector, Portugal has serious handicaps requiring urgent reforms. As reported in an economic survey by the OECD (Organization for Economic Development and Cooperation):

> Portugal's comparative advantage in the production and export of low technology goods made by low-skilled and low-paid labor is not a lasting strength, as competition from developing countries becomes stronger all the time. Policies to encourage the diffusion and implementation of new technologies and production processes are required ... Implementation of competition policy needs to be strengthened, as more competitive markets, especially in network industries, are essential to increase productivity and put downward pressure on prices. (OECD, 2003, p. 108)

A further problem is the relative lack of experience of Portuguese entrepreneurial leaders linked to the tiny size of their companies. Big firms in Portugal have scarcely any weight in the present globalized market. "The Banco Comercial Português (BCP), the biggest private-sector bank in Portugal, ranks only fourth in Iberia and 63rd in Europe. There are only three Portuguese in the Eurotop-300 share index of leading European companies: BCP, Portugal Telecom and Electricidade de Portugal (EDP)" (*The Economist,* November, 2000).

Other important firms belong, as a rule, to well-known families, such as *Belmiro de Azevedo* (SONAE), *José Melo* (CUF), *Espírito Santo* (BES), and *Francisco Balsemão,* a former prime minister turned media tycoon (Impresa), all of them now facing a succession problem. Like the political leaders, the entrepreneurs and CEOs are regularly in the media and they also have fed the biographic genre that contributes to drawing the picture of the Portuguese style of leadership.

Society and Values

Changes in Portuguese society over the last two decades were no less important, giving rise to the emergence of new values and new challenges for management. The first important change concerns the aging of the population with an increase in the number of people aged over 65 years. Simultaneous there has been a fall in birth and fertility rates. A second change is related to the increase of the economically active population due to the entry of women into the labor market. In 1960, 13% of women were economically active. In 1970, that figure had risen to 19% and by 1981 it stood at 29%. In 1991, the figure finally reached 41% (Almeida, 1998). A third factor is the reversal in migration. More than 1 million Portuguese left the country between 1960 and 1980. After 1975 the emigration decreased significantly. From a country of emigrants, Portugal became an importer of labor. In 1974, only 32,000 foreigners resided in Portugal, most of them from other European countries. By 1997, the estimates point to 175,000, half of them from Africa, and the second half from Brazil and from Central and Eastern Europe, these latter often highly skilled (engineers, doctors, nurses, musicians).

Another important change is related to the evolution of the active population characterized by a massive transfer to the tertiary sector. In the period 1960–1990, the tertiary sector rose from 28% to 55%. At the same time, the primary sector fell from 44% to 12%, and the industrial sector also fell but to a lesser extent (from 39% to 33%).

Such a transfer is due largely to the increase in educational standards, leading to the increase of the middle classes. As once again remarked by Ferreira de Almeida:

The development of the "technically" skilled petite bourgeoisie, namely salaried workers engaged in scientific and intellectual work exerted the greatest social impact. In 1960 this group represented 2.6 percent of the total, in 1970 the figure stood at 4.9 percent, in 1981 at 7.9 percent and in 1992 at 16.8 percent. This technically skilled group lives mostly in urban settings and possesses a relatively high cultural capital. (Almeida, 1998, p. 151)

The "feminization" of the economically active population, the growth of the middle classes, along with the entrepreneurial class, high-level managers, and liberal professions, contributed to the appearance of new social values and leadership roles within Portuguese society. Still in accordance with the same author, such new values could be grouped into four clusters: (a) refusal to postpone the fulfilment of personal desires or objectives—"the impatience for happiness"; (b) greater tolerance toward distinct existential models, such as those of a moral, religious, or political nature; (c) a general skepticism toward global, grandiose, and heroic objectives; and (d) a parallel skepticism toward ideologies, such as left and right in the political field.

Portuguese society has become more open, more sophisticated, and more differentiated, but also more skeptical, more demanding, more aloof, and more individualist (see also Ester, Halman, & de Moor, 1993, p. 160).

3. THE GLOBE RESEARCH IN PORTUGAL

Portugal in Cross-Cultural Empirical Research

In this first subsection, we examine some of the most relevant cross-cultural studies on leadership, including Portuguese data.

David McClelland Motivation Profiles. David McClelland is well known as having produced the first map of national cultural indicators using his method of content analysis of stories narrated to children. Four scores were computed from samples collected around 1950 from 42 countries, in which Portugal was included: need for achievement (nAch), need for affiliation (nAff), need for power (nPw), and inhibition (In). This last index indicates the extent to which the need for power is personal (low inhibition) or social (high inhibition). Formerly McClelland (1961) was mostly interested in examining the role of achievement in the economic development of countries, but later he concluded that leadership was more comprehensively related to power than it was to achievement. More precisely, he established a leader motivational profile (LMP) supposed to be related to leader effectiveness. Such a profile is a mix of high concern for (social) power motivation, and power motivation greater than affiliative motivation.

The motivational profile found by McClelland for Portugal is, in standardized figures: nAch = .13; nAff = .72; nPw = −1.17; Inh= −1.38. The findings refer to data collected around the 1950s and were supposed to produce effects one generation later, the time span of youngsters becoming adults and then ready to enact the values internalized along the socialization process. In terms of the LMP, the Portuguese scores could be interpreted as a culture particularly resistant to leadership roles. The high scores on the need for affiliation combined with low need for power and low inhibition suggest that political rulers as well as managers may face problems in structuring the activities of their subordinates who, in turn, are likely to react to strong leadership. At the time of the McClelland study, Portugal was under a dictatorial regime, that was not overthrown until 1974.

Nevertheless, and compared with similar totalitarian regimes, the Portuguese LMP is rather intriguing. Whereas totalitarian regimes either in 1925—Austria, Germany, Japan, Russia, and Spain, as well as in 1950—Argentina, Iraq, Pakistan, Russia, Spain, and South Africa exhibit a pattern of "need for power" higher than the "need for affiliation," in Portugal it was just the reverse that was found.

As remarked by McClelland (1961): "The one exception is Portugal, which at least in some limited sense has been ruled by a dictatorship for a generation [McClelland was writing in the late 1950s] although it may be doubted that it ever has been as ruthless as most of the other totalitarian regimes on the list" (p. 169). The statement—"the traditional softness of the Portuguese morals" ("a tradicional brandura dos costumes portugueses")—has been attributed to Salazar, the dictator who ruled in Portugal from 1932 through to 1968; it is a lasting representation collectively shared, epitomizing the Portuguese national character. These peculiar features seem to fit with the bloodless revolution of 1974 when the dissident soldiers put carnations in the rifles as a symbol of nonviolence (see the introduction).

According to the LMP theory, scoring in the need for affiliation is higher than in the need for power, as found in the Portuguese sample, is negatively related with effective organizational leadership. Affiliative styles give priority to consensus seeking, as well as establishing and reinforcing friendship links, which, more often than not, is incompatible with effective decision making. Leadership is supposedly more related with exerting power rather than governing by consensus.

LMP theory was initially thought to apply mostly to large nontechnological settings as, for example, the government. Some of the validation studies focused on presidential styles as expressed in official speeches (House, Spangler, & Woydee, 1991; Winter, 1973, 1982, 1987). In Portugal, a similar study was conducted by Cruz (1989), who examined the addresses to Parliament of the Portuguese prime ministers from 1976 through to 1987. This study revealed firstly that, as a rule, Prime Ministers expressed the typical LMP profile in their speeches: high nPw, high nAch, low nAff, and high In. Until 1985 the nPw observed was higher than the nAch, but after 1985 the achievement rhetoric became dominant. The highest score on nAff, although lower than the nPw, was observed during the leadership of the only female prime minister—*Maria de Lourdes Pintassilgo*—to perform such a role, even though for a short period of 150 days (July–November 1979, see Section 1).

The study also revealed that scores in nPw were positively related to industrial production as well as a number of approved bills, but also with more conflicts with workers. In terms of unemployment rates, a positive relation was found with nPw and a negative relation with nAff, which led to the assumption that nAff might exert a buffer effect on unpopular measures implemented by political leaders. More recently House, Shame, and Herold (1996) found that LMP was also valid in small entrepreneurial organizations, where leaders with such a profile were perceived by their followers as being charismatic, displaying integrity, and being supportive (House & Aditya, 1997, p. 416).

Considering the persistence and difficulty in changing cultural patterns, it is reasonable to think that weak leadership is expected to be the rule rather than the exception in Portuguese institutions and organizations for years to come. The ambiguity predictable from the LMP theory in the relationship between leaders and followers is coherent, at least in qualitative terms, with other cross-cultural approaches that are examined herein.

Trompenaars's Waves of Culture.   Trompenaars (1993) conducted a cross-cultural study around 1990, collecting data from a sample of about 11,500 managers all over the world in which Portuguese respondents were included. Trompenaars introduces seven fundamental dimensions of culture. Five of those dimensions, pertaining to relationships with people, are: operationalizations of Parsonian dichotomies (Parsons, 1951); universalism versus particularism; individualism versus collectivism; neutral or emotional; specific versus diffuse; achievement versus ascription. The two other dimensions are related to attitudes toward time and attitudes toward environment.

The findings suggest that Portuguese managers are closer to the right pole of the Parsonian dichotomies: They are more particularists, more collective, more emotional, more diffuse, and more ascriptive. In terms of attitudes to time, they tend to be more polychronic than monochronic, and they also tend to be careless toward the environment. In terms of national and corporate culture, Trompenaars introduced two dimensions—equality versus hierarchy and orientation to the person versus orientation to the task—which generate four quadrants: the "family," the "Eiffel Tower," the "guided missile," and the "incubator." These metaphors are useful for summarizing the various patterns of the findings. Within this approach, the Portuguese corporate culture could be described as a "family," clustering with France, Belgium, and Spain—the Latin European cluster (Ronen & Shenkar, 1985)—but also with India and Japan. In "family" cultures, leaders are seen as fathers combining attachment to subordination. It must however be noted that the Portuguese scores are moderate rather than extreme, with 68% of the managers thinking that a good leader "leaves them alone to get the job done" and they also report their organizations as being more horizontal than vertical in terms of hierarchy. These findings are not in contradiction with the McClelland's LMP approach, described earlier. Rather, they seem to confirm each other. Low need for power and high need for affiliation are likely to justify the status ascribed to parent figures who are close and powerful and who "manage by subjectives." On the other hand, the low score in inhibition is likely to considerably reduce the acceptance of leaders, not by direct challenge or confrontation but through devious tactics.

Hofstede's Software of the Mind.   In the Hofstede study (Hofstede, 1984) the Portuguese scores were:

- Power Distance: 63—moderately high.
- Uncertainty Avoidance: 104—very high.
- Individualism: 17—low (more collectivist).
- Masculinity: 31—low (more feministic).

Hofstede did his famous study using data collected around the early 1970s from a sample of more than 116,000 respondents across 53 countries. Although cultural patterns do not change overnight, it could be argued that 30 years later, with so many transformations observed everywhere, the Hofstede indicators would be irremediably dated. More recently an extensive replication was carried out using the responses supplied by 1,544 alumni from 17 Western and Southern European countries plus Turkey and the United States attending a seminar for managers in Salzburg between 1964 and 1983 (Hoppe, 1998). According to the findings, despite some shifts in the relative position of some countries (Austria in Power Distance, France and Italy on Individualism, and France on Masculinity), the rank correlations between the Hofstede and the Salzburg studies are highly significant (above .75). In view of this, and at least for European countries, the overall profile seems to remain basically the same.

As claimed by Hofstede, the most relevant cultural dimensions related to leadership are Individualism and Power Distance. If we combine these two orthogonal dimensions, it is possible to define four cells. Portugal is located in the "large Power Distance" and "Collectivistic" cell. Other countries included in the same cluster are Southeast European countries and also some Asian countries (Hofstede, 1984, p. 159). Scores moderately high on Power Distance and high in Collectivism suggest a preference for benevolent autocratism, as also observed in the Trompenaars study. People in these cultures are expected to bring loyalty to their organizations provided they feel the employer returns the loyalty in the form of protection. In terms of participation, the leader is expected to keep the initiative but, in a collectivistic culture, there will be ways by which the subordinates in a group can still influence the leader.

On the other hand, the most relevant dimensions for organizational configurations are, according to Hofstede (1991), Power Distance and Uncertainty Avoidance. Combining the two dimensions generates four quadrants, metaphorically dubbed as "markets" (low Uncertainty Avoidance, low Power Distance), "families" (high Power Distance, low Uncertainty Avoidance), "well-oiled machines" (high Uncertainty Avoidance , low Power Distance), and "pyramids" (high Power Distance, high Uncertainty Avoidance). The prototypes would be respectively the UK, China, Germany, and France. In accordance with this typology, which is to some extent similar to the one suggested by Trompenaars (1993), Portugal would now be closer to the "pyramid" format than to the "family." It is argued later that this discrepancy might be due to some possible ambiguity in the Uncertainty Avoidance dimension.

The Smith and Peterson Event Management Model.   In accordance with the event management model proposed by Smith and Peterson (1988), leadership behavior depends not only on the structural features of situations but also on the specific events requiring decision making. It can be hypothesized that in national cultures low in Power Distance, there would be greater reliance on participative decision making as well as in national cultures high in Uncertainty Avoidance on rules and procedures. The cross-cultural study conducted by Smith and Peterson initially involved 21 samples of around 100 middle managers from both European and nonEuropean countries. Later it was extended to 35 countries (Smith & Peterson, 1995). The method consisted of presenting eight organizational events, considered as typical to occur often in all countries, and for each of them respondents were asked to indicate the most frequent method on which they relied for making a decision. In total, in 11 out of the 17 European nations examined, respondents reported reliance on their own experience and training. In Portugal as well as in France, the distinctive feature is the higher reliance on unwritten rules (Smith, 1997). Such a finding does not seem to confirm the higher score on Uncertainty Avoidance found by Hofstede for Portugal. The aforementioned study also included questionnaires on role conflict, ambiguity, and overload (Peterson et al., 1995), in which Portugal scored relatively high on role ambiguity. More important, however, was the finding that role ambiguity was not correlated with Uncertainty Avoidance but only with Individualism (.51) and with Power Distance (–.55), which seems to confirm that the Hofstede's scores on Uncertainty Avoidance are to be considered with caution.

Role overload was also found to be negatively related to Individualism (–.60) and positively related with Power Distance (.69). As these are the two dimensions most closely linked to leadership roles, it could be concluded that the combination of high Power Distance with low Individualism (Collectivism) work in conjunction and in a sort of trade-off: Reducing ambiguity through hierarchy and rules can come at the cost of overload.

In short, the various cross-cultural studies reported seem to reasonably cohere, with the exception of Hofstede's Uncertainty Avoidance dimension. Cultural traits suggest that leadership roles in Portuguese organizations are likely to emphasize a paternalistic style more tolerated than actually accepted by subordinates.

The GLOBE Study

The GLOBE study has developed a scale for the evaluation of societal cultural norms. The scale builds on Hofstede's (1984) four cultural dimensions and includes Power Distance, Uncertainty Avoidance, Gender Egalitarianism, which replaces Masculinity/Femininity, and Institutional Collectivism in place of Individualism/Collectivism. It introduces Assertiveness, which was previously part of Hofstede's Masculinity/Femininity dimensions; Future Orientation (Kluckholm & Strodtbeck, 1961); Performance Orientation (McClelland, 1961); Human Orientation (Kluckholm & Strodtbeck, 1961), and Family Collectivism.

The GLOBE study in Portugal is based on the analysis of 79 questionnaires collected from middle managers in two industries in 1996: the food industries which are more traditional and conservative, and telecommunications industries, which are in rapid transformation. Data were gathered from one single organization in each industry.

Qualitative data were also gathered from media and other qualitative studies on culture and leadership with Portuguese managers. The GLOBE questionnaire was split into the Alpha version aimed at measuring leadership and organizational culture. The Beta version measures leadership and societal culture. An equal number of respondents to Alpha and Beta questionnaires were sought in each organization taking part in the study. Using a 7-point Likert scale, respondents were asked to state their preferences of items relating to the eight cultural dimensions, concerning how things "Are" in their society or organization and how things "Should Be." In this way, the questionnaire distinguishes between practices ("As Is") and espoused values ("Should Be").

On the leadership scales, the respondent were asked to rate 112 leadership items on a scale between 1 (greatly inhibits a person from being an outstanding leader) and 7 (greatly contributes to a person being an outstanding leader). Based on an exploratory factor analysis (House et al., 1999) the items were aggregated into 21 leadership scales, which constitute culturally endorsed perceptions of leadership. (For a full display and discussion of GLOBE methods and comparative results, see House et al., 2004.)

Societal Culture

The societal results for Portugal from the GLOBE study are presented in Table 16.3. The results represent the assessments of practices ("As Is") as well as values ("Should Be") and the differences between them. In what follows, comparisons are made both in the overall GLOBE sample and in the European subsample level. The results are assessed in light of the previous cross-cultural studies already examined.

Performance Orientation.   The Performance Orientation describes the degree to which people are encouraged and rewarded for performance improvement and achievement of excellence. Performance Orientation is related both to the issues of external adaptation and internal integration (Javidan, 2002; Schein, 1992). It is an internally consistent set of practices and values that have an impact on the way a society defines success in adapting to external changes, and the way the society manages the interrelationship among its people.

TABLE 16.3
Country Means for GLOBE Societal Culture Dimensions

Culture Dimensions		Society "As Is"			Society "Should Be"			Difference[d]
		Mean[a]	Band[b]	Rank[c]	Mean[a]	Band[b]	Rank[c]	"Should Be" –"As Is"[d]
Uncertainty	P[e]	3.91	C	39	4.43	B	41	0.52
Avoidance	G[f]	4.16	B		4.62	B		0.46
Future	P	3.71	C	38	5.43	B	35	1.72
Orientation	G	3.85	B		5.48	A		1.63
Power Distance	P	5.44	A	17	2.38	D	53	−3.06
	G	5.16	B		2.74	C		−2.42
Institutional	P	3.92	C	47	5.30	A	9	1.38
Collectivism[g]	G	4.25	B		4.73	B		0.48
Humane	P	3.91	C	40	5.31	B	40	2.20
Orientation	G	4.09	C		5.42	B		1.33
Performance	P	3.60	C	54	6.40	A	5	2.80
Orientation	G	4.10	B		5.94	B		1.84
In-Group	P	5.51	A	26	5.94	B	15	0.43
Collectivism	G	5.13	B		5.66	B		0.53
Gender	P	3.66	A	13	5.13	A	4	1.47
Egalitarianism	G	3.37	B		4.51	B		1.14

[a]Country mean score on a 7-point Likert-type scale. [b]Band letter A–D indicating meaningful country bands for the scales A > B > C > D; the band width is equal to 2 *SD*. [c]The rank orders for Portugal relative to the 61 countries. [d]Absolute difference between the "Should Be" and the "As Is" score. [e]Portugal's mean scores. [f]GLOBE's mean scores. [g]High score = more collectivistic; low score = more individualistic.

According to the findings, societies higher in Performance Orientation at the level of practices (As Is) tend to be economically more successful and globally more competitive, additionally with a tendency to enjoy a more positive attitude toward life and live in a more civic society. In contrast, the societies scoring higher on Performance Orientation values ("Should Be") tend to be less competitive, less economically productive, more satisfied with their work lives, and more strongly religion oriented (Javidan, 2002; Schein, 1992).

Portugal's very low score on practices ("As Is") and the higher score on values ("Should Be") seem to reflect the awareness of the respondents about Portugal lagging behind the EU countries. Yet, such a pessimistic view was expressed in a period (1996) when the economy was growing at a relatively fast rate, above the EU average. The value scores also confirm the striving for achievement that were found in the studies of McClelland described earlier. Respondents do not seem to feel happy about the performance of their country and greatly endorse the need for developing more challenging goals. The diagnosis seems realistic in the light of the OECD report (see Section 1).

Future Orientation. This measures the extent to which future-oriented behavior (e.g., planning, investing, delay of gratification) is encouraged and rewarded. The higher the scores, the higher the Future Orientation.

Portuguese scores are lower than the GLOBE average both in practices ("As Is") and in values ("Should Be"). Such findings suggest a relatively moderate striving for the improvement of practices related to organization and planning. Furthermore, observers and analysts tend to denounce the short-term orientation of Portuguese politicians and business people as well. A symptom of this short-term orientation is the rather low investment in R&D. As remarked in the OECD (2003) report:

> Despite the increases recorded in recent years, Portuguese spending on R&D as a percentage of GDP is less than half the OECD average, as in the proportion of researchers in the active population. As in other less advanced OECD countries R&D activities are carried out not so much by the business sector, but rather by the higher education and government sectors, these sectors accounting for almost two-thirds of total R&D expenditure in Portugal, against less than 30% on average in the OECD. (p. 97)

Future Orientation can be related to expenditure practices by either the government, or the public, as well as with savings. Gross domestic savings/gross domestic product (GDP) for 1998 in Portugal was 17%, whereas genuine domestic savings/GDP was 15%. This latter indicator is an overall measure of the degree of sustainable economic growth for society. Although these figures do not significantly differ from other European developed countries, they are far below robust and fast-growing economics such as Singapore (51, 40.7), Taiwan (42, 33.7), or Ireland (37, 32.3).

Gender Egalitarianism.   Within the GLOBE project, the concept is defined as the way in which societies divide rules between women and men. More Gender Egalitarian societies believe that men and women are suited for similar roles, whereas less Gender Egalitarian societies believe that men and women should assume different roles (Emrich, Denmark, & den Hartog, 2004).

Portuguese scores are relatively high—Rank 13 on practices and Rank 4 on values, both higher than the GLOBE average. Among European countries no differences were found between the North-West and the South-East clusters (Koopman et al., 1999). The role of women in Portuguese society has greatly changed over the last four decades. First, there has been a massive entrance of women into the labor market, mainly because the male workforce was depleted due to the colonial war as well as heavy emigration to other European countries. Another reason was the expansion of employment in the process of industrialization. In the 1960s, the rate of feminization of the active labor force increased from 18% to 26% and by 1991 reached 40%.

As remarked by Ferreira (1998):

> Most women are employed in service activities that require no qualification, such as cleaning services (19% of female workers are maids or porters), in subsistence-level agricultural activities (11%), and unskilled industrial workers (25%). On the other hand, technical-scientific professions absorb approximately 11% of economically active women and administrative professions 15.2%. These figures, the lowest in the European Union (the average in Portugal is 19% and in the EU 30%), testify the deficit in intermediary social positions typical of less-developed societies. (p. 169)

This relative subalternation of women within the Portuguese society is also expressed by the indicators relative to the female economic activity—70% in 1998, or 52.3% of the 1998 GDP.

Another relevant indicator is the number of women in Parliament/government. According to the figures in the *Human Development Report* (United Nations Development Programme,

2000), the percentage in 1998 was 11.1 and in 2000 it increased to 18.7. This last figure is slightly above the OECD (15.1%) average but much lower than in countries like Sweden (42.7%), Finland (36.5%), Denmark (37.4%), Belgium (30.2%), or UK (33.0%).

The role and importance of women in Portugal will certainly evolve, sufficing to note their higher rate of school attendance in 1997 that (94% female, 88% male) is even higher in Portugal than in OECD countries (86% for both sexes) or the highly developed world (91% female, 88% male)(United Nationas Developmental Programme, 2000). At the university level, female attendance has risen in 2000 to 63%.

A second qualification concerns the political-juridical framework governing women in Portugal. It is also a fact that the Portuguese legal order on women after the 1974 Revolution can be considered as one of the most advanced in Europe: "Article 13 of the 1976 Constitution universalized the principle of juridical equality. It eliminated the myriad discriminations inherited from the outgoing regime, paving the way for a reform of the legal order, putting paid to discrimination against women" (Ferreira, 1998, p. 174).

But even if such legal changes were introduced without opposition and in spite of the pervading rhetoric of the "equality between the sexes," which, to a certain extent, could explain the results of the GLOBE study, it is worth noting that "in Portugal there is an enormous discrepancy between law on paper and law in action" (Ferreira, 1988, p. 177). In this specific case of the legal equality for women, "the change was imposed from above" (Ferreira, 1988, p. 177). The gap between the law and actual practices is still important. "Many examples can be found of the lack of concrete application of the principle of equality. The sentences passed in crimes against individuals reveal that judges have a different attitude toward women" (Ferreira, 1988, p. 179).

In terms of Gender Egalitarianism in Portugal, much more is still to be achieved. Portugal's integration into the EU might help to close the gap between the practices and the values.

Humane Orientation. Humane Orientation is derived from Kluckholm and Strodtbeck's (1961) work on "human nature is good *versus* human nature is bad" as well as Putnam's (1993) work on the "civic society." It assesses to what extent practices such as being fair, altruistic, generous, caring, and kind to others are promoted in society and organization (House et al., 1999).

The Portuguese results are relatively low for the practices—Rank 40. The difference between "Should Be" and "As Is" is relatively high although not significantly. Both practices and values fall within the GLOBE average. Among European countries no differences were found between the North-West and the South-East clusters (Koopman et al., 1999). Apparently all over the world there is a generalized awareness of the desirability of promoting more human attitudes toward others.

The relatively low score registered at the level of practices may reflect significant changes in conviviality as a consequence of urbanization and modernization. However, it is not clear how to reconcile these findings with the high need for affiliation observed in McClelland's study for Portugal. One possible explanation is that such a high need might reflect a certain affective insecurity instead of expressing the more positive facets of intimacy (McAdams, 1982; McAdams & Powers, 1981a, 1981b).

Power Distance. The Power Distance is derived from Hofstede's Power Distance indicator. It measures the degree to which members of an organization or society expect and agree that power Should Be shared unequally. The Portuguese score on practices ("As Is") is very high (5.44) and significantly higher than the GLOBE average (5.16). Equally for values ("Should Be"), the Portuguese scores are very low (2.38) and lower than the GLOBE average (2.74). The difference between practices and values (–3.06) is the highest registered for Portuguese scores. Apparently the Portuguese respondents consider that at societal level the power stratification is too high and that a significant, if not dramatic, decrease would be highly desirable. In European terms, Portugal is closer to the South cluster together with France, Italy, Spain, and Greece (Koopman et al., 1999).

The aforementioned scores are in accordance with the findings produced by the Hofstede (2000) and Trompenaars (1993) studies. With regards to the low need for power found in McClelland's (1975) study, it can be argued that the correspondence must be applied to the difference observed between practices and values. Power, or at least its representation, is strongly rejected.

Portuguese society is characterized by a large gap between the elites and the masses, by a great distance between the governing and the governed, by pronounced socio-professional segmentation, and by acute inequalities in income and capital, as well as inequalities in formal education (Cabral, 1992, p. 950). A striking indicator is given by the differences of expected incomes between attained education levels. Whereas in Europe the average differential between ISCED 5.7 (higher education) and ISCED-3 (higher secondary) is about 9%, in Portugal the difference jumps to 65% (Lindley, 2000; see also Eurostat).

In terms of the corruption perception index (CPI), found to be highly related to Power Distance (Hofstede, 2000, p. 132–133), in 1998 Portugal scored 6.5 (on a scale of 1 = totally corrupt, 10 = totally clean). Similar scores were found in Spain (6.1) and France (6.7). The relation between Power Distance and corruption perception was found only in wealthy countries but not in the group of the 17 poor countries. Within wealthy countries the higher the CPI values, the cleaner the countries.

In terms of the GINI index—a measure of the inequality in the distribution of consumption (0 = perfect equality, 100 = perfect inequality)—Portugal scores 35.6 slightly above more equalitarian countries such as Austria (23.1), Denmark (24.7), Sweden (25.0), or Japan (24.9) but below the United States (40.8), UK (36.1), or Russia (48.7).

Religion is also related with Power Distance. As suggested by Carl, Gupta, Javidan (2004), Catholic societies, especially the ones that have experienced low growth in private consumption during recent years such as Spain and Portugal, tend to strongly reject the values of power stratification, and favor Power Distance reduction. The authors also suggest that societies with a large, established middle class would have a lower power level of Power Distance than societies with a newly emerging middle class, such as the Iberian countries. It is worth noting, however, that class composition is changing very fast. From 1986 to 1997, according to Eurostat, the numbers of entrepreneurs and professionals increased between 7 and 10 points in the various countries of the EU. In 1997, the percentage of the "middle class" jumped in Portugal by 25%. Such changes will certainly contribute to significant differences in the ways of using power. Participative decision making will likely become more frequent in institutions and organizations.

Collectivism. In the GLOBE study, Collectivism was split into two indicators: *Institutional Collectivism* refers to the degree to which institutional practices at the societal level encourage and reward collective action; *In-Group Collectivism,* on the other hand, is defined as the degree to which individuals express pride, loyalty, and interdependence in their families and close associates. The distinction was found relevant. In Portugal, at the level of practices, In-Group Collectivism was scored much higher than the Institutional Collectivism. At the level of values, respondents would like to reinforce both dimensions of Collectivism.

The Hofstede study also classifies Portugal as a collectivist culture, ranking 39 among 53 countries. The relatively high score on need for affiliation found in the McClelland (1961) study also points in the same direction. But both of these latter studies, according to our interpretation, are more related to Family Collectivism than to Institutional Collectivism.

As remarked in Section 1, Portuguese values seem to be evolving to a more individualistic pattern. Postmodern youngsters are more hedonistic, more disenchanted with traditional ideologies, and more open to diversity. In a word, they are more individualistic, which might raise some intergenerational tensions.

Modernization and economic growth were found to be linked with individualism (Hosftede, 2000, p. 252). Although the Portuguese scores point to classifying this culture as clearly collectivistic, some indicators, as, for example, the high score in lack of inhibition found by McClelland (1975), suggest that socialization practices are not very effective in integrating individuals and society. A frequent impressionistic diagnosis produced by observers and common sense is that Portuguese subjects are better performers as individuals than as a collective body. Such a view is illustrated by the examples of individual subjects excelling when integrated in more developed foreign societies.

Assertiveness. Assertiveness in GLOBE is defined as the degree to which individuals in organizations or societies are assertive, tough, dominant, and aggressive in social relationships (House et al., 1999). The "As Is" score for Portugal is one of the lowest within the GLOBE sample. It ranks 55 among 61 countries in practices. The GLOBE Assertiveness dimension overlaps with Hofstede's Masculinity Index (House et al., 2004). Hofstede's (2000) study also classifies Portugal as low on masculinity. Among 53 countries, Portugal is placed in 44th position, with a score of 31 (mean [*M*] 49, Standard Deviation [*SD*] 18). Nevertheless, the GLOBE respondents would like to even lower the score albeit by a negligible margin. In the "Should Be" dimension, Portugal is close to countries such as Ireland, Netherlands, Sweden, Denmark, and Finland (Koopman et al., 1999). Such findings seem to converge with the high "need for affiliation" and "low inhibition" scores found in the McClelland (1975) study.

The lack of perceived Assertiveness in Portugal could be linked to the relative lagging behind, at least within the EU context, in terms of competitiveness, productivity, and economic prosperity. Along the same vein, the permissiveness and impunity of Portuguese morals, as illustrated by the difficulty in enforcing the law, could also be connected with the weak Assertiveness reflected in the GLOBE scores.

Uncertainty Avoidance. In the GLOBE project, Uncertainty Avoidance was defined in terms of a tendency toward orderliness and consistency, structured lifestyles, clear specification and social expectations, and rules and laws to cover situations. There is no clear correspondence with the similar concept used in the Hofstede study, which is due to different criteria of operationalization. The Portuguese score on Uncertainty Avoidance in the Hofstede study is very high, only second to Greece. In the GLOBE study, the score for Portugal is rather low for practices (3.91), ranking 39, significantly below the GLOBE mean. In terms of values, although remaining low in ranking (41), the Portuguese score is closer to the GLOBE mean. In accordance with the meaning of this concept, the Portuguese respondents believe their society is not sufficiently structured in contrast with Northern countries where more flexibility is desired (Koopman et al., 1999).

The modest difference between "As Is" and "Should Be" suggests that the respondents are not entirely unhappy with the perception they have about the relative lack of structure within the societal environment. This seems to be in line with a widespread commonsense representation shared by the Portuguese of being able to "improvise," a feature very much boasted about. Living comfortably with chaos and ambiguity is considered a competitive advantage. This also suggests that Portugal is a "high context" rather than a "low context" culture (Hall, 1959, 1976; Hall & Hall, 1990), which can be illustrated by anecdotic evidence about the casual and imprecise information within the public space, and the no less casual polychronic way of managing time and opportunity (see also Section 2).

Countries like Portugal that perceive themselves as less structured are, however, less prosperous in terms of consumption and growth. They are also less competitive and less productive. Another relevant indicator is the euromoney credit rating (0 = high risk; 100 = no risk) where Portugal scores 82.8, below the most developed economies.

Summary

The cultural profile that emerges from the GLOBE findings indicates high relative scores for Gender Egalitarianism, In-Group Collectivism, and Power Distance, and low scores in Future Orientation, Humane Orientation, Performance Orientation, Assertiveness, Uncertainty Avoidance, and Institutional Collectivism.

In terms of values, measured by the distance between "As Is" and "Should Be," the Portuguese respondents would like to live in a more Equalitarian as well as more Performing, more Humane, and more Future Oriented society. They do not seem to feel the same need for change in dimensions such as Assertiveness, In-Group Collectivism, and Uncertainty Avoidance.

Such a profile, in rather broad terms, converges with previous cross-cultural findings, and is somewhat intriguing in terms of the requisites for leadership. In fact it aspires for more collective efficiency and effectiveness but within the traditional framework of informality, leniency, and protectionism. The challenge for the exercise of leadership in Portugal seems to give greater priority to the reinforcement of Institutional Collectivism as, to a certain extent, is also salient in the findings.

3. LEADERSHIP IN PORTUGUESE SOCIETY

Research on organizational behavior in which the leadership topic is included is very scarce, indeed almost nonexistent, in Portugal. The only academic study so far published in Portugal is authored by Jesuino (1987). The book presents the results of several empirical studies conducted both in the field and in the laboratory, in an attempt to validate some traditional contingency models on leadership effectiveness. Its added value consists of testing the influence of leadership styles in moderating the polarization effect in group decision making (Jesuino, 1986). A theoretical approach to leadership was also developed by the same author (Jesuino, 1996).

The contribution of these studies to the GLOBE project—relating leadership with societal and organizational cultures—is relatively minor. More relevant is the abundant literature on profiles of political, and to a lesser extent, entrepreneurial leaders, some of them in the genre of comprehensive (auto)biographies. Despite its unconcern with strict scientific criteria, such sources, along with the media, are still the best way of observing the leadership processes that take place in the public sphere. They are addressed in the next subsection.

An intermediate research strategy, inspired by the seminal study of Mintzberg (1973), consists of conducting case studies centered on managerial work through ethnographic individual and group interviews. In the wake of qualitative studies such as the ones carried out by Sayles (1979), Stewart (1979), Kotter (1988), Bennis and Nanus (1985), we also conducted interviews in the late 1980s with 50 Portuguese managers randomly selected from a list of 2,000 national managers—the "Who's Who" in Portuguese business (Jesuino, Pereira, & Reto, 1993).

Ethnographic Evidence

As the only empirical study so far published in Portugal, its main findings are summarized here.

In terms of the characteristics of the sample, 35 of the interviewees were chief executive officers (CEOs) and 15 were general managers. Ages were from 32 to 62 years but the greater majority were aged from 45 to 55 years. The organizations where the interviewees worked were diverse and included banking, insurance, transportation, telecommunications, manufacturing, naval ship building, fisheries, and media. Some of the interviewees worked in branches of multinational corporations.

Private organizations accounted for 28 of the interviewees, 19 were from public enterprises (owned by the state), and 3 belonged to the civil service. Government positions had formerly been held by 10 of the interviewees. Their former and present activities embraced the various domains of managerial activity such as marketing, human resources, production, budgeting, and finance. Only one of the interviewees was female, which reflects the low percentage of Portuguese women in higher managerial positions.

The interviews were tape-recorded and covered a number of topics, such as their views about the concept of leadership, the required leadership attributes for each of the three organizational levels—top, intermediate, and lower (Katz & Kahn, 1978)—strong and weak factors for exerting leadership within the Portuguese organizational context. They ended with a lengthy conversation about their professional careers, agendas, self-assessment, management style, team-building practices, relevant decisions, health/stress, attitudes toward the future, paradigmatic figures (mentors), and self-image.

In terms of the required attributes for the three main organizational levels, the results of the content analysis of the interviews are summarized in Table 16.4

The features identified do not greatly differ from those found in similar studies (Bennis & Nanus, 1985; Katz & Kahn, 1978; Kotter, 1988). Some minor differences are, however, worthy of mention as they might be related to some cultural specificity. Cognitive attributes like intelligence and technical skills across the levels, affective attributes like courage and hardworking at the top level, and honesty at the middle level, are among the most salient differences found.

A likely interpretation could be given in terms of the social and political turmoil that arose in Portugal after the Revolution of 1974. Most of the interviewed managers, in top positions at the time of the interview, had to face difficult situations 15 years earlier, usually in the field of industrial and labor relations. Courage and interpersonal and negotiation skills were a condition for survival, and contributed decisively to the natural selection of managers. Technical skills, whose importance is supposed to decrease from the top downward in the hierarchy, was considered equally important in the present study at all levels. When asked about that, the interviewees appeared to agree with Kotter (1988) in rejecting the principle of the transferability of managers. Most effective managers, they claimed, make their careers in one specific industry or even in one sole company, a necessary condition for dealing with the "competitive edge" and "organizational complexity" that characterizes the present world of business. One last point that

TABLE 16.4
Characteristics of Organizational Leaders According to Portuguese Manager's Views

Responsibilities	Level	Cognitive Attributes	Affective Attributes
Goal setting, strategy, motivating	Top	Vision, intelligence, creativity, diagnostic skills, imagination, technical skills	Charisma, courage, interpersonal skills, self-confidence, hard-working persistence
Coordination, linking	Middle	Intelligence, technical skills, diagnostic skills	Honesty, fairness, equity, loyalty, persuasion skills
Execution	Lower	Technical skills, experience, learning skills	Example, fairness, consideration

the findings suggest is the relative lack of distinction between the middle and bottom levels of the hierarchy. This could also be interpreted as signs of the coming era of flatter organizations.

The next section of the interview asked for a diagnosis of the leadership practices in Portuguese organizations. The aim was to identify the representation developed by managers about the context of their own activity. Table 16.5 summarizes the main characteristics found.

These traits greatly correspond to the stereotypes of the national characteristics and do not necessarily reflect specific constraints at the organizational level. The image herein offered by the Portuguese managers about their subordinates and/or collaborators stands somewhere between Theory X and Theory Y (McGregor, 1960). This image could in itself be a consequence rather than a cause, a sort of self-fulfilling prophecy, legitimizing a paternalistic style of leadership. Subordinates are seen as potentially capable of promptly responding to extreme situations, which is indeed a very positive factor, but on the other hand, and for this same reason, control and supervision are slackened. This sort of vicious circle is perhaps one of the most enduring characteristics of the Portuguese management culture.

Managers were also asked to talk about their careers, their agendas, important decisions they have been involved in, and their espoused philosophies of management.

With regard to the professional career, it was confirmed that most of the managers were "one company men" or, at least, they have always worked in a certain business or industry. As regards routine activities, the findings are quite similar to those reported in the literature by authors like Mintzberg (1973), Sayles (1979), Stewart (1979), and Kotter (1988).

Like their colleagues in other countries, Portuguese managers work very hard, stay at the office 50 to 60 hours weekly, and their work is characterized by "brevity, variety and fragmentation." They also seem to give preference to personal contacts; they travel a lot and have built social networks through which they are able to exert their influence and foster their goals.

With respect to the most important decisions recalled by the interviewees, it was found that the majority of them fall in the area of reorganizing and restructuring—64% of the critical incidents, involving redefinition of functions, downsizing, and collective lay-off. Only 16% of the critical incidents evoked involved strategic decisions such as new investments, diversification of the activity, market expansion, and internationalization. There was occasional mention of technical interventions in the fields of marketing, budgeting, and finances, aimed at improving the effectiveness of the organizations.

TABLE 16.5
Strengthening and Weakening Factors for Leadership Practice in Portuguese Organizations

Strengthening Factors	Weakening Factors
• Adaptability	• Disorganization
• Responsiveness	• Indiscipline
• Improvisation	• Lack of combativeness/discouragement
• "Muddling-through"	• Lack of technical skills/unpreparedness
• Creativity	• Resistance to change/conservatism
• Tolerance	• Dispersion
• Generosity	• Selfishness
• Gentleness	

Although the interviewees considered their actions were important for the outcome of their organizations, it could be argued, in light of their narratives, that the nature of organizational leadership, as claimed by Pfeffer (1977, 1981), is more symbolic than instrumental. Even at the level of the personal perceptions evoked, such as organizational restructuring, executive succession, and organizational development, the examples given were typical of symbolic action. Moreover, the interviewees evaluated themselves in accordance with this criterion, underlying their relationship abilities, their acceptance by the subordinates, and their negotiation skills, all of which are in fact essential for stabilizing a climate dominated by uncertainty. The fundamental task of the manager, and it is here that the leadership factor most clearly emerges, consists of giving meaning to the ambiguous if not threatening environment, as well as acting in a confident manner so as to both inspire and appease those dependent on them. The results of the interviews give substantive qualitative evidence to the major importance of symbolic leadership.

In terms of self-attributions of success in their leadership functions, the results are summarized in Table 16.6.

These reasons for successful leadership were categorized as follows: personal attributes (46%), interpersonal skills (40%), and management of leadership skills (12%).

The list of self-attribution for success fits with the leadership requirements formerly expressed by the interviewees in more abstract terms. Personal and interpersonal attributes by far exceed the management and leadership skills. In accordance with this view, it appears that Portuguese managers consider that their success is due to more personal attributes and interpersonal skills than to strategic vision or management competence.

The answer about decision styles points in the same direction. The great majority (70%) gave preference to the consultative style, which implies obtaining ideas and suggestions from subordinates but making the final decision individually. The most difficult decisions were the ones related to personal matters (60%) followed by economic and financing decisions (18%), jurisdictional ambiguities (16%), and organizational conflicts (6%). Many interviewees explicitly stated that technical decisions are not difficult. Difficult decisions are those associated with the future of people, namely when lay-offs take place or when disciplinary action is required.

With regard to management style, 48% of the interviewees stressed their ability to build effective teams, which they attributed to their motivating skills, their concern for people, and their habit of "managing by wandering around."

Essentially, the management philosophy of the sample interviewed could be described as follows: To manage is to get results through people. This requires the ability to build up effective

TABLE 16.6
Self-Attributed Reasons for Leadership Success Given by Portuguese Managers

Personal Attributes	Interpersonal Skills	Leadership Management Skills
Courage	Tolerance	Vision
Persistence	Easy Contact	Imagination
Strong Will	Democratic	Innovativeness
Rigor	Friendliness	Technical Expertise
Fairness	Communication	Planning Expertise
Patience	Intuition	Decisiveness
Honesty		Hard Working
Ethical Standards		Risk
Tenacity		
Calm		

teams, which implies, in turn, the ability to select people who are loyal, competent, and hard-working. One of the main tasks of leaders is to develop good interpersonal relations and gain the trust of subordinates. In short the "espoused theory" (Argyris & Schön, 1974) of the managers interviewed corresponds, at best, to the human relations philosophy of management.

In terms of biographical data, 50% declared that they had excelled in their youth either in sports, in students associations, or in unions. Also mentioned by 10 interviewees was their experience in the colonial wars in Africa (from 1962 through to 1974) as contributing to the development of their leadership skills.

On health, all the interviewees referred to being in good shape and experiencing moderate levels of stress. As a rule they were optimistic about the future, relying mostly on science and technology for the resolution of the great problems of humankind such as the war, the Third World, or ecological preservation. Asked finally to describe their own personality character-istics, the respondents indicated positive traits like hardworking, persistent, courageous, and honest. Attributes named less often were tolerant, sociable, and open. Such characteristics overlap to some extent with the required features of leadership.

Further Ethnographic Evidence

A more recent empirical study also attempting to examine how entrepreneurs distinguish between management and leadership was conducted by Pereira (2001) using a representative sample of 398 Portuguese entrepreneurs. Covering a vast span of industries, the study adopted the theory of social representations introduced by Serge Moscovici (1961, 1984) as its con-ceptual framework. A widespread technique used within this framework for gathering data consists of asking people to freely evoke associations elicited by a stimulus word/concept. In his study, Pereira (1999) used the words *leader* and *manager* as stimuli. The gathered data were then analyzed using the "similitude analysis," a technique introduced by Flament (1962, 1981) and developed by Degenne and Vergès (1973). The method consists of applying the graph theory, then computing the percentage of joint associations. The technique permits the analysis of the data at various levels (filters) of association. The most comprehensive picture is given by the "maximum tree" showing how the concepts are interlinked without cycling.

According to the representation of managers is centered around the concept of organization. The similitude analysis shows that "organization" is at the center of a "star" to which the quasi-totality of the associations evoked is linked. Through "strategy" the concept of organization is linked to "enterprise," which is at the center of a second and less central "star." But the picture is clear enough. Managerial roles consist mainly of implementing the strategy of the enterprise through organization skills, such as setting objectives, planning, controlling, and coordinating, as well as personal attributes required for the effective management of human resources.

In contrast, leaders are represented through a more complex web of personality traits and interpersonal skills such as influencing, persuading, motivating, and communicating. "Charisma" is strongly associated with "personality," "intelligence," "power," and "influence." Another central concept is "communication," which is linked with "capacity," "understanding," "dynamic," "followers," and "innovator." A third cluster is formed around "group" to which "people," "top," "influence," and "manager" are linked. A fourth central concept comprises "despotic," which is linked to "persuasive," "command," "authority," "confidence," and "intelligent." "Charisma" is linked with "despotic" through "intelligence," and is linked to "group" through "influence." The representations found seem to confirm thepopular dictum that "leaders do the right thing and managers do things right."

These findings, which do not contradict but rather complement the GLOBE cross-cultural universals, could be interpreted in terms of the traditional paradigm of vertical relations between leaders and followers. As the respondents are not reporting about an actual leader common to all of them but to prototypical images, the common ground found could refer to some sort of objective reality reflected by the observers. An alternative view would be that respondents, when asked to express their thoughts about how leaders or managers are expected to behave, do not necessarily evoke some sort of inductive knowledge formed through their own contact with managers, but rather a representation socially constructed through direct horizontal influence processes and exposure to media. The popularity that the concept of charisma has recently been acquired all over the world, as documented by the GLOBE findings, is better understood in terms of social construction than as a significant change in behavior of managers and leaders. In this light, the wide consensus disclosed by the GLOBE results and its convergence with other methodological approaches, as the one presented earlier, could to a large extent be interpreted as the global reach of the American theories of leadership and management.

Media/Discourse Analysis

The media are another important source where the endorsed image of leaders and leadership is reflected. Political leaders use the media to communicate with the general public, mainly through television, but also through radio or even through the press. The press is still the branch of media where the actions of leaders are critically observed with not only perspective but also through conceptual framings. In the GLOBE study, the media analysis is limited to the print press.

In Portugal, during the Salazar regime, the press was not free but submitted to a severe regime of censorship. It was only after the Revolution of 1974 that censorship was suppressed. Many changes have occurred since then in the panorama of the media in Portugal. Liberalization was an important change with the concession of two private TV channels. In Portugal, there are now two public and two private TV channels, two public radio stations, and a number of daily and weekly newspapers, all of them private.

With a literacy rate of 91.4% (HDI), it is not surprising that reading habits are reduced to a small minority. The circulation of the total daily newspapers across the country does not exceed 350,000. The most important papers are the *Diário de Noticias* (DN), *Publico* (P), *Jornal de Noticias* (JN), *Correio da Manhã* (CM), *A Capital* (Cp), *O Comércio do Porto* (CP), and *Diário Económico* (DE). The circulation of weekly newspapers amounts to 450,000, the most important of which is the *Expresso* (EXP). Other weekly newspapers are the *Independente* (IND), the *Visão* (VIS), the *Semanário* (SEM), the *Tal e Qual* (T&Q), and the *Semanário Económico* (SME). These figures do not include the circulation of sports newspapers, which are by far the most sought after by the Portuguese readers.

It was with this corpus of news that a search was conducted in order to trace the image therein projected of leaders' attributes and/or salient leadership initiatives. A comprehensive analysis of the DN, JN, P, DE, and EXP was conducted by a team of four doctoral students for a period of 2 alternate weeks at the end of January and in mid-February 2003. An identical exercise had already been conducted 5 years earlier in June 1998.

In both periods, the search led to very disappointing results. The general impression gathered was that the Portuguese journalists as well as analysts or even opinion makers, although sensitized as they are to observing political action in the making, do not specifically focus on the leadership styles and/or leadership processes.

According to the present widespread structure of the written media, a distinction can be made between the news that, as a rule, is usually transmitted as objective information and the opinion articles, usually undersigned, which address broader issues of political strategy or argue about current controversial issues. Sometimes, and mostly in weekly newspapers, political or business figures are interviewed about several issues, which also contribute to characterizing their styles of leading. Opinion makers as well as public figures very often collect a selection of their interventions or comments together with their speeches, the comprehensive interviews they give, or even retrospective narratives into a book format, where they evoke and very often rationalize their actions. This literature in Portugal has become a genre with apparently certain success.

This sort of media extension offers an alternative for analyzing leadership styles and strategies. A sample of 20 years of editorials from the *Expresso*, spanning from 1982 to 2002, was thus selected as our corpus of analysis. The entries are all related with political figures and events that took place in Portugal over the last two decades. Another selection of interviews, conducted by Luís Osório (1999) with Portuguese political personalities in another elite newspaper, *Diário de Noticias*, and compiled in a book, was also the subject of detailed analysis.

The framing used to analyze leadership is basically dichotomic. Leaders are either charismatic or consensual. Charisma is however understood in rather specific terms, and within the context of the broader distinction between authority and authoritarianism:

> Authority and authoritarianism are to be distinguished. Authority yields respect; authoritarianism yields fear. Why is political authority important? Is it not sufficient for a statesman to be competent, honest, courageous, and to have charisma? It is not enough. And it is not enough, in first place, because that fuzzy quality—and essential—that is called "charisma" is to a great extent constructed by and through authority. In fact, for a politician to have charisma, two things are indispensable: first, that the citizens feel that he is resolute and has decision capacity; ... that he has the necessary personal strength to enforce his decision. (Saraiva, Expresso, October 29, 1988)

Examples of charismatic or preferably authoritative leaders in the Portuguese scene would be Prime Minister Sá Carneiro, who died prematurely in an air crash in December 1980, and

Cavaco Silva, who ruled for two mandates (1985–1995). According to the polls, 62% of the respondents still rate them as being the best Portuguese political leaders since 1974:

> Sá Carneiro was a condottieri, in a certain way "he invented a nation," "an artificial nation"... he aroused dormant energies under the crust of a resigned, accommodating and tamed way of being ... Portuguese are, as a rule, not very courageous. They only act when they feel protected by a strong organization such as the Communist Party or by decisive men ... that is what distinguished Sá Carneiro and other political men, to that breed of men that don't leave a legacy, because their value was due to their personal fascination. (Saraiva, Expresso, December 5, 1981)

Those lines were written when the memory of the condottieri was still alive in the public opinion. But to a great extent it still remains today. Whenever students are asked to name examples of Portuguese (charismatic) leaders, the name of Sá Carneiro is usually invoked. There is an airport in the north of Portugal with his name. Statues, public buildings, and streets also consecrate his memory. The controversy about the cause of his death—accident or bomb attack—also contributes to the maintenance of keeping the myth alive. Apart from his tragic death, Sá Carneiro's distinctive contribution to the making of modern Portugal is that he introduced a new style that became known as bipolarization, a sort of watershed between right and left, opposing the two main political forces that emerged after the 1974 Revolution, instead of attempting to rule through consensus and coalition. This may now appear a little naive but one cannot forget that Portugal was then, and possibly still is, in a process of learning the ropes of democracy.

The strategy together with Sá Carneiro's style was inherited and pursued by Cavaco Silva, a prime minister who ruled in Portugal for a period of 10 years (1985–1995) with the benefit of a parliamentary majority. As a leader and likely future candidate to the presidency of the republic, Cavaco Silva also displays charismatic features, according to the opinion leaders. Not only is he considered without serious contest "the best Prime Minister after the Revolution, but he is continuously described as 'rigorous, highly demanding, competent, and invested by the sense of the national interest and by the dignity of the state'" (Saraiva, *Expresso,* July 6, 1985).

In terms of style, Cavaco Silva, who has a PhD in economics from the University of York (UK), conveyed the image of the "technocrat," more concerned with the economic and financial figures in which he is an expert than with lengthy consultations or explaining his decisions to the general public. Although not very mediatic, he succeeded in turning his aloofness and secrecy into a strength. His inspirational motto was "Portugal cannot stop," paralleling the Sá Carneiro "We have to liberate the civil society." Portuguese leaders, even charismatic, do not appear particularly creative in terms of mobilizing the people through inspirational catchphrases.

This concept of charisma as confounded with authority, if not authoritarianism, is sometimes attributed to the heavy legacy of Salazar's dictatorship. The comparison has sometimes been suggested and also applicable to other figures such as General Eanes, who was elected president of the republic for two mandates (1976–1986). Eanes also projected an image of austerity and rigor although more linked to the military ethic of discipline and loyalty than to concerns of pragmatic efficiency.

Mário Soares, who succeeded Eanes in the presidency and another outstanding political figure of modern Portugal, does not accept the association with Salazar:

> Salazar like Sidónio Paes, were dictators. Ramalho Eanes and Cavaco Silva were and still are democrats. I am not sure that the Portuguese prefer strong rulers. I don't think so. Maybe severe,

aloof, with a sense of mission.... The democratic authority is not incompatible with an affective relationship and closeness with the citizens, as well as with permanent search for dialogue in order to seek possible consensus. (Osório, 1999)

Soares represents an alternative style of political leadership in Portugal. He is considered the "father" of the democratic regime in Portugal. He fought against Salazar and was arrested several times. After the Revolution he fought against the advance of communists. At the international level, he fought for a third way by claiming democratic socialism, which is a combination of socialism and freedom. He has been criticized for being too much of a "politician" in the sense of often giving priority to tactics over strategy while projecting an image lacking in principles, as the famous derogatory expression often used about Soares, "socialism was hidden in a drawer," expresses. In spite of all his qualities and even strategic vision—attested namely by his decisive move on joining the EEC—and notwithstanding his popularity he does not seem to qualify as a charismatic leader, at least in the Portuguese eyes.

The current president, elected after Soares (1996), now in his second mandate, and also from the same socialist family, appears to share similar ideas about charisma. Asked about himself he said, "Some say that I am indecisive. They also say that I don't have charisma.

They don't understand that such would not be compatible, in democracy, to being alive and healthy after 40 years of political life" (Osório, 1999). Implicit in this statement is the idea that charisma is at best brief, instantaneous, and metamorphic, and that sustained charisma in a democratic regime would be a contradiction in terms.

The alternative (socialist) way of leading appears then to enhance communication, dialogue, and participative decision making.

António Guterres, a socialist who in 1995 succeeded Cavaco Silva as prime minister, when asked about the Portuguese preference for "strong fathers" such as Salazar, Eanes, and Cavaco Silva, stated:

There is a collective memory of the Salazarism but I believe that that memory is withering away. But after a period of turmoil (Revolution) that memory emerges again—that was understood by Professor Cavaco Silva.... But I came to Prime Minister when the society was reacting in the opposite sense. They wanted desecrated political power and no more a "muscled democracy"... But there is always a pendulum movement, towards more authority or towards more liberty ... Habermas a German philosopher that I much appreciate, proposed a definition of modern democracy not compatible with the authoritarian appeal, for him the modern democracy is the exercise of power within a logic of permanent intercommunication between the policy makers and the organized civil society. (Osório, 1999)

The words of Guterres became prophetic, in the sense of the unanimous reaction triggered by what was considered *et urbi et orbi* as an excess of dialogue along with erratic, if not lack of decision making. After a few years of governance the media considered Guterres the prototype of the lack of leadership:

The problem of Guterres is not lack of the ability for coordinating. The problem for Guterres is, on the contrary, the tendency to confound coordination with leadership. To coordinate in excess and to not lead at all. The leader by definition goes ahead of the flock, commands respect, chooses the way. But Guterres prefers to walk in the middle of the flock—dialoguing, making contradictory positions compatible, avoiding break ups ... who walks ahead walks alone and can choose the best path. Who walks in the middle is contrived to step the field chosen by others. (Saraiva, May 12, 1997).

The same opinion maker, 2 years earlier, when Guterres won the elections, already anticipated the risks of turning the dialogue into a sort of governance principle *per se:*

> The profession of faith of António Guterres in dialogue is equivocal on three grounds: In the first place it might lead to confuse dialogue with problem solving. But, however comprehensive the dialogue might be, it can never be replaced by decision ... to govern is to decide—and the decisions require courage and imply costs. In the second place, the dialogue can raise false expectations.... In the third place, the idea that the more consensual the idea the better the outcomes will be, is totally false. The consensus leads not to the best solution but, precisely because neutral in order not to make waves, is only likely to be accepted by a large number of people. A governance based on those principles does not attain long term objectives. A government that does not raise discontent will hardly get a place in History. (Saraiva, October 21, 1995)

This idea that leading always implies deciding against some group of interests, that negotiation is only realistic in *win—lose* terms, is now deeply ingrained in the culture, or at least in the mediated culture, of the Portuguese political landscape. It certainly contributes to the image of leadership endorsed by public opinion as well as the frames used for categorizing acts of leadership on a daily basis, be it originated by statesmen or by bosses.

In terms of conclusion after this perusal of the elite press, it appears that the Portuguese attitude toward power is, at best, rather ambiguous. Always oscillating between extremes, they have problems in getting a satisfactory democratic balance between the exertion of power and its sustained legitimacy.

Particularly enlightening for the GLOBE framework is the clarification given for the emic nuances of the concept of charisma. It appears that, at least through the mediated discourse, charisma is a rather fuzzy concept, tending to be reduced, even by responsible policymakers and opinion makers as well, to its literal meaning of "sacred aura" whose effects are limited to commanding a sort of irrational respect. Facets such as "vision" or "inspiration" do not seem to saturate the Portuguese social construct of charismatic leadership. Reexamining the network of concepts in Figure 16.1b, distilling the collective image of entrepreneurs, we also can see that charisma is linked to intelligence, power, personality (the stronger connection), and influence. Vision or inspiration does not seem to spontaneously emerge to the fore of the Portuguese respondents—at least when they are focusing on leaders and leadership.

The Quantitative Study of Societal Leadership

The middle managers who formed part of the Portuguese sample were asked to rate 112 leadership items on a scale of 1 (greatly inhibits a person from being an outstanding leader) to 7 (greatly contributes to a person being an outstanding leader). The items were aggregated into 21 leadership scales (cf. House et al., 2004). The results are summarized in Table 16.7.

The Portuguese scores neither clearly cluster within the Northern European nor the Southern European countries. This can also be observed in a recent study reported by Brodbeck et al. (2000), in which not only Portugal but also the former East Germany appear located on the boundary between Nordic and Latin (Southern) Europe within a semantic space defined by the MDS dimensions of Interpersonal Directness and Proximity, and Autonomy. Portugal is closer to Northern European countries in endorsing attributes such as "inspirational," "integrity," and "performance orientation," and in rejecting less desirable attributes—those that substantially impede outstanding leadership, such as "procedural," "autocratic," "self-centered," and "malevolent." On the other hand, the

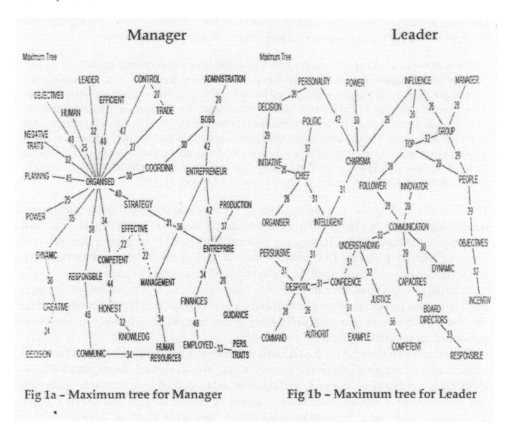

Fig 1a – Maximum tree for Manager   Fig 1b – Maximum tree for Leader

Portuguese scores are closer to the ones from Southern European countries in endorsing the prototype "diplomatic"—an attribute where Portugal ranks very high—and in rejecting attributes such as "self-inducer," "status-consciousness," and "non-participative." For the remaining attributes no differences were found between the two clusters (Koopman et al., 1999).

The correlation of the 21 scales listed in Table 16.7 demonstrated that they were not empirically distinct, which led to a second-order factor analysis. Six second-order factors were obtained. These higher factors are shown in Table 16.8 (den Hartog et al., 1999, p. 236).

In comparative terms, the findings for Portugal confirm the GLOBE hypothesis of universal implicit theories of leadership. Like everywhere, leaders are idealized in terms of the various facets disclosed by the neo-charismatic theories.

In culture-specific terms, the Portuguese scores indicate a particular emphasis on attributes such as "diplomatic," "collective team orientation," "team integration," and "self-sacrificial," as well as on rejecting attributes such as "autonomous," "face- avers," and "procedural," and for the comparatively lower ranking attributed to being "decisive."

In the more synthetic view given by the second-order factors, what appears most distinctive in the Portuguese scores is the relatively higher emphasis on "team oriented" and the relatively lower score on "autonomous" as compared with the scores of the Latin Europe cluster (see also Jesuino, 2002).

TABLE 16.7
GLOBE Results for Leadership Prototypes

	Portugal		GLOBE	North/West	South/East
Attributes	Means	Rank	Range of Means	Rank[a]	Rank[a]
Inspirational	6.27	22	5.0–6.6	19.5*	40.4
Administrative Competence	5.55	47	4.5–6.4	49.0*	24.9
Integrity	6.21	24	4.8–6.8	18.7*	37.0
Performance Orientation	6.18	21	4.5–6.6	25.2	36.4
Modesty	4.78	41	4.1–5.8	43.0	35.1
Procedural	3.19	55	2.8–4.9	54.1*	32.3
Face Saver	2.30	57	2.0–4.5	46.3	33.1
Autocratic	2.30	46	1.9–4.1	50.2*	28.9
Self-Centered	1.97	43	1.5–3.4	44.2*	30.4
Malevolent	1.67	38	1.3–2.7	45.4*	29.8
Visionary	6.12	30	4.6–6.5	25.2	34.4
Diplomatic	5.77	9	4.5–6.0	43.6	20.1*
Team Orientated	5.92	15	4.4–6.0	42.4	29.4
Team Integrator	5.72	11	4.1–6.4	31.3	27.5
Self-Sacrificial	4.33	56	4.0–6.0	35.0	37.8
Decisive	5.31	56	3.6–6.3	25.8	27.2
Humane Orientation	4.45	44	3.3–5.7	38.2	41.1
Conflict Inducer	3.81	36	3.1–5.0	52.2	30.7*
Status-Consciousness	4.33	29	2.4–5.9	47.0	27.0*
Autonomous	3.19	60	2.3–4.6	21.2	30.6
Nonparticipative	2.74	24	1.9–3.7	44.8	28.5*

[a]Mean rank scores for Portugal are calculated in relation to European countries clustered as North/West (Nordic, Anglo, Germanic) and South/East European (Latin, Central, East) by Brodbeck *et al.* (2000).
*significant at 0.05; low rankings indicate higher importance.

Summary

Qualitative and quantitative studies suggest a minimum coherence to the endorsed constructs of leadership. Just looking at the quantitative scores could convey a superficial suggestion that the Portuguese respondents do not dramatically diverge from the more proximal cluster to which they belong. Furthermore, they also respond in accordance with the universal trends revealed by the GLOBE study. The qualitative approach adds however non-negligible intelligence to the slight minimal differences observable in the scores, for example, that "team orientation" and "participation" acquire more relative salience in comparison to "charisma/value based" or "autonomy." In 1996, the political environment in Portugal was striving for a change toward more dialogue, more communication, and more teamwork. The pendulum was swinging then toward a less autocratic orientation. Anyway, a value-based theory of leadership does not seem

TABLE 16.8

Descriptive Statistics for the Second-Order Leadership Factors and the Scales/Items They Are Based On

			All 61 GLOBE Countries		
Scales/Items	Portugal Means	Latin Europe Cluster Means	Min	Max	Mean
Charismatic/Value based *Charismatic 1: Visionary;* *Charismatic 2: Inspirational;* *Charismatic 3: Self-Sacrifice;* *Integrity; Decisive;* *Performance Oriented*	5.75	5.74	4.51	6.46	5.83
Self-Protective *Self-Centered; Status-Conscious;* *Conflict Inducer;* *Face Saver; Procedural*	3.10	3.19	2.54	4.55	3.45
Humane *Modest; Humane Orientation*	4.62	4.24	3.82	5.61	4.87
Team Oriented *Team 1: Collaborative Team;* *Team 2: Team Integrator;* *Diplomatic; Malevolent* *(recoded); Administratively* *Competent*	5.92	5.83	4.74	6.21	5.76
Participative *Autocratic (recoded);* *Nonparticipative (recoded);* *Delegator*	5.48	5.48	4.50	6.09	5.35
Autonomous *Individualistic;* *Independent;* *Autonomous; Unique*	3.19	3.70	2.27	4.65	3.86

to have been actually internalized by the societal political culture. If asked, they obviously concur with its central relevance. But it is more lip service than an actual habitus.

The Portuguese are known as being better followers than leaders. The common sense has it that the Portuguese excel when working as expatriates and when working in multinationals located in Portugal. Portuguese workers apparently have more difficulty in accepting the national than the international managers. In a previous study (Jesuino, 1989), Portuguese as well as foreign managers were asked to brainstorm about what could be considered as "strong factors" and "weak factors" for exerting leadership in Portuguese organizations. Strong factors included adaptability, improvisation, creativity, tolerance and generosity. Among weak factors mentioned were disorganization, indiscipline, easily discouraged, lack of technical skills, resistance to change, and dispersion. Similar to what was found in Eastern countries (Misumi & Peterson, 1985), the old high-high model (high structure/high relationship) could be the most appropriate strategy for foreign managers exerting leadership roles in Portugal.

4. ORGANIZATIONAL CULTURES AND LEADERSHIP

The two Portuguese industries involved in the GLOBE project were food—more traditional and conservative—and telecommunications, which in Portugal, as everywhere, is at present in a boom.

Food Industry

In the 1990s, the production of the Portuguese food industry did not cover the population's food needs. The import of products (both intra- and extra-EU) exceeded the exports by about 90.9%, thus contributing to the deficit of the balance of trade, one of the most important of the country. Industrial food production in Portugal, as in other EU countries, is predominantly oriented to the national market. According to the 1997 data, the total volume of business was 2099×10^9 PTE (1 PTE Portuguese Escudo $\approx$ 5 U.S.$) of which only 12.9% were exports. The market of the Portuguese food industry is thus made up essentially of the 10 million of consumers that live in national territory. In terms of foreign trade in 1997, the exports amounted to 275.4×10^9 PTE (6.6% of the total value produced by the manufacturing industry), and the imports 518.1×10^9 PTE (9.7% of the total value produced by the manufacturing industry). The main countries for export were the former Portuguese colonies in Africa and the countries where Portuguese emigrants live. The imported food products come mainly from the EU countries (71.5%), particularly from Spain and France. The food industry is one of the main employers of the national manufacturing industry, absorbing about 121,000 workers in 1997 (2.5% of the total active population and 11.9% of the total employed in the Portuguese manufacturing industry).

Similarly to the EU, in Portugal the enterprises operating in the food industry are small and medium (SMEs). Out of the total 10,200 enterprises, 9,200 have fewer than 20 workers, whereas only 182 have more than 100 workers. Only 40 enterprises attained a business volume higher than 7.5×10^9 PTEs in 1997. The average in 1997 was 216×10^6 PTEs. The largest employer among those where the GLOBE questionnaires were distributed had 2,075 workers, representing only 1.7% of the total workforce in this industry (see http://193.137.98.84/estudos_agroalimentar/indice.html).

Like the trend observed in the EU, the entrepreneurial fabric of the food industry in Portugal is changing toward a greater concentration of productive forces. An ever-growing number of mergers and acquisitions is observable at both the national and international levels. More than 200 mergers took place in the EU in the period 1993–1995 of which only 8 also included Portuguese firms.

The firm where the GLOBE study was conducted, one of the biggest within the industry, operates in dairy farming. Its workforce amounted to 570 workers and its business budget in 1996 was around 18×109 PTE.

Telecommunications Industry

The telecommunications sector in Portugal was until recently owned and operated by the state. It was characterized by a high dependence on technology, lack of qualified workers at all levels, and weak support of R&D. The new technological paradigm and the rapid and growing domestic demand has led to developing strategies of joint ventures in order to accelerate diversification and modernization (Rodrigues, 1991).

The last decades of the 20th century were a period of dramatic changes in the world. In Europe, the fifteen EU member countries formally entered the European Single Market. Independent domestic monetary policies became something of the past, and macroeconomic convergence led to monetary union with the formal introduction of the euro in January 1999 in 11 countries, of which Portugal is one. The European telecommunications sector became deregulated and liberalized also according to the same strategy.

The resulting growth and variety in telecom services being offered has been so strong that at least up to 2000, and against most forecasts and predictions, no overall job losses in the telecom sector took place; rather, the contrary (Soete, 2002, p. 28).

In Portugal, the telecommunications sector has gone through the same process of change derived from the European strategy. The major Portuguese enterprise operating in the sector is Portugal Telecom (PT), one of three leading Portuguese companies. The other two are Banco Comercial Português (BCP) and Electricidade de Portugal (EDP). Although they've become public, the state keeps "golden shares" of PT, which allows it to veto mergers.

As correctly remarked in the *Economist*'s Survey of 2000, in Portugal, *"There is an obvious appetite for new technology. More than half the population has a mobile phone—a penetration rate lower than in Scandinavia, but higher than in Germany. This is partly because pre-paid mobiles were first developed and introduced in Portugal by TMN, the mobile-phone subsidiary of Portugal Telecom (PT)."*

Portugal has developed an automatic teller machine (ATM) network, the Multibanco system, acknowledged as one of the most sophisticated in the world. Portugal was also a pioneer in prepayment systems for mobile phones, interactive digital television, and call-center software. An electronic motorway toll system has also been developed that directly debits payments from motorists' bank accounts, without requiring them to stop. The system was developed by the Portuguese motorway operator BRISA in a joint venture with the Norwegian company Micro Design, and is considered one of the most advanced in the world ("Portugal, Economy," 2002).

The mobile phone market in Portugal is now shared by three operators: TMN (owned by PT), Telecel (owned by Britain's Vodafone), and Optimus (belonging to the conglomerate SONAE, one of the most important Portuguese economic groups), a newcomer that got 20% of the market. Before launching Optimus, the company asked as many Portuguese households as it could if they wanted to be "pioneers," promising them cheap calls in return for joining Optimus. That gave the company a start-up customer base of 285,000 people.

After the liberalization of the Portuguese telecommunications market on January 1, 2000, the market conditions did not substantially change. Notwithstanding the entry of new operators offering aggressive and competitive conditions and even with innovative products, PT is still the dominant force, similar to what can be observed in other European countries whose telecommunications were liberalized.

For the time being, although the market is liberalized the new operators have only two choices: Either create their own network to directly access their clients, or use indirect access, limited to national and international calls. This latter alternative has been the one preferred so far, but the new operators have plans to develop their own telecommunication infrastructures.

The recommendations of the European Commission for accelerating the liberalization of telecommunications is related with the directives issued from the Lisbon European Summit 2000, setting the priority of a rapid transition to an e-Europe, with an economy based on the information society. But as acknowledged by the European Commission, even in countries where the liberalization started in January 1998, the incumbents have lost some market share in international calls, but maintain 90% to 100% in local calls. According to Andersen Consulting, on average, operators in Europe control 98% of the fixed telecommunications and even in England, the most advanced European country in terms of liberalization, British Telecom still controls 85% of local calls.

According to the Survey of the Telecommunications made by the Instituto Nacional de Estatística in 2001, the income of the services of telecommunication in Portugal amounted to $7,067 \times 106$ _ (Euros) with a homologous variation of 32.2%. The total investment amounted to $1,064 \times 106$ _, 80% of which accounted for equipment and infrastructure (52% for the mobile network and 46% for the fixed network).

The GLOBE study was conducted in two different companies belonging now to the PT universe. One of them, Marconi, operates in the international-call area. The other, PT Innovation, works on R&D and training. The workforce is composed of about 300 people in both of the enterprises. PT Innovation is particularly dynamic. It was here that the prepaid system for mobile phones was developed.

Quantitative Results

Culture. In this last section of the GLOBE study, the organizational cultures were assessed through the second tier of questions also split into practices ("As Is") and values ("Should Be"). The questionnaires were applied to middle managers in two Portuguese industries: food and telecommunications. The results obtained are summarized in Table 16.9.

What immediately strikes one when comparing the results at the organizational level with those at the societal level is that at the organizational level the differences become less extreme. The greatest difference observed in the Portuguese data between practices and values is on Performance, which in both industries is above 2 points. The trend observable in the Portuguese data is parallel to the trend also found in the GLOBE average results. In both cases, the telecommunications industry appear more demanding, at least in terms of desirable performance and desirable future orientation. In the Portuguese results, the contrast between the telecommunications and food industries reveal some specific points. Whereas in telecommunications industries it is considered that the organization should strive for more "future," more "institutional," and fewer norms and procedures (Uncertainty Avoidance), in food organizations more "future" and "institutional" are also desirable, but to a much lesser extent, and there are more, not fewer, norms and procedures. These trends are coherent with the degree of development and corresponding management styles in the two industries. Whereas in telecommunication organizations middle managers seem to prefer a larger amount of decentralization (being left alone to do their job) and at the same time more team building (Institutional Collectivism), in food industries more job ambiguity is perceived, leading to the need for more rules and procedures.

No less striking, both at the GLOBE and at the national level, is the difference in the Power dimension, when we come down from society to organizations. At the organizational level, Power is perceived as much less extreme, and the difference between practices and values, between the actual and the ideal situation, becomes considerably reduced. Instead of a difference of 3 points, observed at the society level, we now have a difference of only half a point as the average for both industries. This finding is somewhat intriguing but also one of the most

TABLE 16.9
Country Mean Scores for Organizational Culture Dimensions

Organizational Culture	Food Industry			Telecommunications Industry		
	"As Is"[a]	"Should Be"[a]	Difference[b]	"As Is"[a]	"Should Be"[a]	Difference[b]
Uncertainty Avoidance	3.30	3.75	+0.45	3.89	3.48	−0.40
Future Orientation	4.81	5.42	+0.61	4.73	5.89	+1.16
Power Distance	3.85	3.58	−0.27	3.97	3.37	−0.60
Institutional Collectivism	4.92	5.33	+0.41	4.58	6.30	+1.72
Humane Orientation	4.11	5.06	+0.95	4.34	5.24	+0.90
Performance Orientation	3.75	6.14	+2.39	4.11	6.59	+2.48
In-Group Collectivism	5.20	5.65	+0.45	5.35	5.82	+0.47
Gender Egalitarianism	3.83	4.53	+0.70	3.66	4.25	+0.59
Assertiveness	3.60	3.54	−0.06	3.70	3.62	+0.08

[a]Country mean score on a 7-point Likert-type scale. [b]Absolute difference between the "Should Be" and "As Is" score.

heuristic contributions of the GLOBE study. It suggests that when asked to describe the amount of power exerted at the societal level, managers do not represent the same entities as the ones they refer to when asked to describe the power at the organizational level.

Power at the societal level is possibly represented as political power. It is more distant and also more abstract. One could speculate that at the societal level respondents activate a social representation that is not directly linked with their direct experience of the organizations where they work. At this latter level, power seems to be much more tolerated or, alternatively, its meaning could change when embedded in a specific working context. Self-protecting rationalizations could also be invoked as an underlying tactic to cope with authority.

Leadership. Table 16.10 summarizes the results of endorsed attributes of leadership, divided between the two industries of food and telecommunications. The findings do not present significant differences between the two industries. The ranking is similar and the differences in the magnitude of the attributes is negligible.

5. LIMITATIONS OF THE CURRENT STUDY

The findings of the present study are obviously subject to qualification. Only two industries were sampled and in both cases the number of respondents was below the amount expected. Media analysis would also benefit from a more extensive and systematic survey in order to detect more detailed descriptions of leadership profiles observable in the public space, as well as in the civil society. Anyway, the substantial convergence found with previous cross-cultural studies suggests that the GLOBE approach could be viewed as a benchmark for the future research of culture and leadership in Portugal.

TABLE 16.10
Leadership Attributes in Portuguese Industries

	Portugal		
Dimensions	Food[a]	Telecommunications[a]	GLOBE Range
Autocratic	2.48 (15)	2.23 (10)	2.89–3.90
Procedural	3.26 (14)	3.17 (13)	2.87–4.89
Self-Sacrificial	4.37 (11)	4.32 (11)	3.98–5.99
Team Orientation	5.69 (7)	5.72 (6)	4.12–6.09
Decisive	5.49 (8)	5.27 (8)	3.62–6.97
Diplomatic	5.79 (5)	5.76 (5)	4.49–6.05
Modesty	4.64 (9)	4.84 (9)	4.23–5.85
Face Saver	2.44 (16)	2.25 (15)	2.05–4.53
Humane Orientation	4.36 (12)	4.48 (10)	3.29–5.68
Autonomous	3.58 (13)	3.04 (14)	2.27–4.73
Inspirational	6.36 (2)	6.24 (1)	5.04–6.63
Integrity	6.44 (1)	6.23 (2)	4.83–6.79
Performance Orientation	6.24 (4)	6.16 (3)	4.51–6.64
Administrative Competence	5.79 (5)	5.47 (7)	4.53–6.42
Self-Centered	2.15 (17)	1.91 (17)	1.55–3.41
Status Consciousness	4.45 (10)	4.28 (12)	2.37–5.93
Visionary	6.32 (3)	6.03 (4)	4.62–6.50

[a]Rank is given in parentheses.

6. CONCLUSION

Comparing the results for both society and industries it can be concluded that there is greater convergence in values than in perceived practices. But even at the level of values, people are more realistic and therefore less demanding when they refer to the job context than when they talk about society in abstract. This distance between the representation of the society and the representation of their own organizations is also an indication of the degree of dissatisfaction or lack of identification with national culture. In Portugal, there is a long tradition of self-derogatory representations about the collective capacity in generating synergy. This could to some extent explain the differences between both practices and values and between the societal and the organizational levels.

Another finding worthy of comment is the ambiguous position of the Portuguese scores within the country clusters. It was seen that in some dimensions Portugal is closer to the North European cluster, whereas in other dimensions the scores tend to be close to the grand mean, which makes the interpretation more difficult. This proximity to the grand mean, also observable in cross-cultural studies on values (Schwartz, 1999), could signify either an eclectic or compromising orientation or, alternatively, some sort of pervasive defensive style.

The Portuguese sociologist Sousa Santos (1994) has suggested a portrait of the Portuguese society as one that is semiperipheral where premodernity, modernity, and postmodernity dynamically coexist. An example could be given by the Portuguese Revolution of 1974. It started with a premodern military putsch, followed by a transitory postmodern period of anarchic social creativity, returning to modernity with the military yielding power to civil society who rapidly enforced the democratic pattern of European societies.

The coexistence of the three orders could also be the determining factor of the Portuguese specificity and even contribute to opening the way to some competitive advantages within the international scene. The GLOBE findings are compatible with, or at least do not contradict, such a hypothesis.

7. FINAL REMARKS

A study about culture and leadership in Portugal would necessarily reflect the huge transformations that took place in this country in the last decades. Portugal is no longer the same. There was a revolution, the transition to democracy, the decolonization of former African territories, and the joining of the EU. In 30 years, the Portuguese people have known periods of political instability but also periods of stability. There has been great economic development but the spectrum of crisis is also always looming.

Portugal is now *a member of the club* of developed countries but it still has the complex of being last in line. Culturally, it is a modern, open society, but with asymmetrical pockets of backwardness.

Such dramatic experiences, however, do not seem to have deeply changed some of the most "basic assumptions" underlying the collective way of life, the Portuguese *Weltanshauung* (i.e. view of the world). Culture never changes overnight. This is also confirmed in the present study through the continuity and convergence of the main findings across the various former cross-cultural studies with their diverse methodologies and conceptual frameworks.

Looking from the perspective of leadership practices and values, it is our understanding that a central feature of the Portuguese collective was captured by the former studies about the LMP where Affiliation scored higher than Power, and Inhibition was found to be low. It could be argued and speculated that this is the central core of the Portuguese *habitus*. Observers of the Portuguese society always confront the excellence of its individual members with the enigmatic negative synergy resulting from their pooled efforts. One possible cause could be the reluctance to both exert and accept leadership.

Leadership density in Portugal, that is, the amount of leadership being exerted within and between social groups, is rather low. It could be argued that suspicion toward power still lingers in the collective memory of the Portuguese people. Almost half a century of dictatorship leaves marks on the collective body. It could also be argued that the process of societal change is slow and that the Portuguese society has not yet had enough time to achieve the reform of its democratic institutions. Such historical handicaps might favor a bent toward a sort of laissez-faire style of leadership whose inertial effects on development are only too well known.

REFERENCES

Almeida, J. F. (1998). Society and values. In A. C. Pinto, *Modern Portugal* (pp. 146–162). Palo Alto, CA: Society for the Promotion of Science and Scholarship.

Argyris, C. & Schön, D. (1974). *Theory in practice: Increasing professional effectiveness.* San Francisco: Jossey-Bass.

Bennis, W., & Nanus, B. (1985). *Leaders.* New York: Harper & Row.

Brodbeck, F. C., Frese, M., Ackerblom, S., Audia, G., Bakacsi, G., Bendova, H., et al. (2000). Cultural variation of leadership prototypes across 22 European countries. *Journal of Occupational and Organisational Psychology, 73,* 1–29.

Cabral, M. V. (1992). Portugal e a Europa: Diferenças e semelhanças [Portugal and Europe: Differences and similarities]. *Análise Social, 27,* 943–954.

Carl, D., Gupta, V., & Javidan, M. (2004). Power distance. In R. J. House, P. J. Hangar, M. Javidan, P. W. Dorfman, V. Gupta, & Globe Associates (Eds.), *Cultures, leadership, and organizations: The GLOBE study of 62 societies* (pp. 513–563). Thousand Oaks, CA: Sage.

Cruz, J. (1989). *Traços motivacionais dos Primeiros Ministros Portugueses (1976–1987) e suas relações com indicadores de natureza económica, social e política* [Motivational traits of Portuguese prime ministers (1976–1987) and its relationships with economic indicators, social and political]. Unpublished manuscript, Instituto Superior de Psicologia Aplicada, Lisbon, Portugal.

Degenne, A., & Vergès, P. (1973). Introduction à l'analyse de similitude [Introduction of similitude analysis]. *Revue Française de Sociologie, 14,* 471–512.

den Hartog, D., House, R., Hanges, P., Ruiz-Quintanilla, S. , Dorfman, P., Javidan, M., et al. (1999). Culture specific and cross-culturally generalizable implicit leadership theories: Are attributes of charismatic/transformational leadership universally endorsed? *Leadership Quarterly, 10,* 219–256.

Emrich, C. G., & Denmark, F. L., Den Hartog, D. N. (2004). Cross-cultural differences in gender egalitarianism: Implications for societies, organizations and leaders. In R. M. House, P. J. Hanges, M. Javidan, P. W. Dorfman, V. Gupta, & GLOBE associates (Eds.), *Cultures, leadership and organizations: A 62-nation study by members of the GLOBE Foundation* (Vol. 1., pp. 343–394). Thousand Oaks, CA: Sage.

Ester, P., Halman, L., & de Moor, R. (1993). *The individualizing society value change in Europe and North America.* Tilburg, Netherlands: Tilburg University Press.

Ferreira, V. (1998). Engendering Portugal: Social change, state politics, and women's social mobilization. In A. C. Pinto (Ed.), *Modern Portugal* (pp.162–188). Palo Alto, CA: Society for the Promotion of Science and Scholarship.

Flament, C. (1962). L'analyse de similitude [Similarity analysis]. *Cahiers du Centre de Recherche Opérationnelle, 4,* 63–97.

Flament, C. (1981). L'analyse de similitude: Une technique pour les recherches sur les représentations sociales [The similarity analysis: A technique for research in social representaitons]. *Cahiers de Psychologie Cognitive, 1*(4), 375–395.

Hall, E. T. (1959). *The silent language.* New York: Doubleday.

Hall, E. T. (1976). *Beyond culture.* New York: Doubleday.

Hall, E. T., & Hall, M. R. (1990). *Understanding culture differences.* New York: Doubleday.

Hofstede, G. (1984). *Culture's consequences: International differences in work-related values* (Abridged ed.). Thousand Oaks, CA: Sage.

Hofstede, G. (1991). *Cultures and organisations: Software of the mind.* London: McGraw-Hill.

Hofstede, G. (2000). *Culture's consequences: Comparing values, behaviors, institutions, and organizations across nations* (2nd ed.). Thousand Oaks, CA: Sage.

House, R. J., Hanges, P. J., Javidan, M., Dorfman, P. W., Gupta, V., & GLOBE Associates (2004). *Cultures, leadership, and organizations: The GLOBE study of 62 societies.* Thousand Oaks, CA: Sage.

House, R. J., & Aditya, R. N. (1997). Social scientific study of leadership: Quo vadis? *Journal of Management, 23*(3), 409–473.

House, R. J., Hanges, P. J., Ruiz-Quintanilla, S. A., Dorfman, P. W., Javidan, M., Dickson, et al. (1999). Cultural influences on leadership and organizations: Project GLOBE. In W. H. Mobley, M. J. Gessner, & V. Arnold (Eds.), *Advances in global leadership* (Vol.1, pp. 171–233). Stamford, CT: JAI.

House, R. J., Shame, S., & Herold, D. (1996). Rumors of the death of dispositional theory and research on organisational behavior are greatly exaggerated. *Academy of Management Review, 21*(1), 203–224.

House, R. J., Spangler, D., & Woydee, J. (1991). Personality and charisma in the U.S. presidency: A psychological theory of leadership effectiveness. *Administrative Science Quarterly, 36,* 364–396.

Javidan, M. (2002). Performance orientation. In R. M. House, P. J. Hanger, M. Javidan, P. W. Dorfman, V. Gupta, & GLOBE associates (Eds.), *Cultures, leadership and organizations: A 62-nation study by members of the GLOBE foundation* (Vol. 1, pp. 239–281). Thousand Oaks, CA: Sage.

Jesuino, J. C. (1986). Influence of leadership processes on group polarization. *European Journal of Social Psychology, 16,* 413–423.

Jesuino, J. C. (1987). *Processos de Liderança* [Leadership processes]. Lisboa, Portugal: Livros Horizonte.

Jesuino, J. C. (1989, April). *Leadership characteristics of top executives.* Paper presented at the 4th European Congress of Psychology of Work and Organizations, Cambridge, England.

Jesuino, J. C. (1996). Leadership: Micro–macro links. In E. H. Witte & J. H. Davis (Eds.), *Understanding group behavior: Small group processes and interpersonal relations* (Vol. 2, pp. 93–125). Mahwah, NJ: Lawrence Erlbaum Associates.

Jesuino, J. C., Pereira, O. G., & Reto, L. A. (1993). Características dos gestores de topo: Uma abordagem qualitativa [Characteristics of top managers: A qualitative approach]. *Análise Psicológica, 2*(11), 179–199.

Jesuino, J. C. (2002). Latin Europe cluster: From south to north. *Journal of World Business, 37,* 81–89.

Katz, D., & Kahn, R. L. (1978). *The social psychology of organizations* (2nd ed.). New York: Wiley. (Original work published 1966)

Kluckholm, F. R., & Strodtbeck, F. L. (1961). *Variations in value orientations.* New York: Harper & Row.

Koopman, P. L., den Hartog, D., Konrad, E., et al. (1999). National cultures and leadership profiles in Europe: Some results from the GLOBE study. *European Journal of Work and Organizational Psychology, 8*(4), 503–520.

Kotter, J. P. (1988). *The leadership factor.* New York: The Free Press.

Lindley, R. M. (2000). Economias baseadas no conhecimento. O debate europeu sobre o emprego num novo contexto [Knowledge based economics: The European debate over employment in a new context]. In M. J. Rodrigues (Coord.), *Para uma Europa da Inovação e do Conhecimento.* Oeiras, Portugal: Celta Editora.

MacCoby, M. (1976). *The gamesman: The new corporate leaders.* New York: Simon & Schuster.

McAdams, D. P. (1982). Experiences of intimacy and power: Relationships between social motives and autobiographical memory. *Journal of Personality and Social Psychology, 42*(2), 292–302.

McAdams, D. P., & Powers, J. (1981a). Intimacy and affiliation motives in daily living: An experience sampling analysis. *Journal of Personality and Social Psychology, 45*(4), 851–861.

McAdams, D. P., & Powers, J. (1981b). Themes of intimacy in behaviour and thought. *Journal of Personality and Social Psychology, 40*(3), 573–587.

McClelland, D. (1961). *The achieving society.* New York: Irvington.

McClelland, D. (1975). *Power: The inner experience.* New York: Irvington.

McGregor, D. (1960). *The human side of enterprise.* New York: McGraw-Hill.

Mintzberg, H. (1973). *The nature of managerial work.* New York: Harper & Row.

Misumi, J., & Peterson, M. F. (1985). The performance-maintenance (PM) theory of leadership: Review of a Japanese research program. *Administrative Science Quarterly, 30,* 198–223.

Moscovici, S. (1961). *La Psychanalyse, son image et son public* [The psychoanalysis, its image and its public]. Paris: PUF.

Moscovici, S. (1984). The phenomenon of social representations. In R. Farr & S. Moscovici (Eds.), *Social representations* (pp. 3–69). London: Academic Press.

Osório, L. (1999). *25 Portugueses.* Lisboa, Portugal: Noticias Editorial.

Parsons, J. (1951). *The social system.* New York: The Free Press.

Pereira, F. C. (2001). *A Representação Social do Empresário* [The social representation of the entrepreneur]. Lisboa, Portugal: Edições Silabo.

Peterson, M., Smith, P. B., Akande, A., Ayestaran, S., Bochner, S., & Callan V. (1995). Role conflict, ambiguity, and overload: A 21-nation study. *Academy of Management Review, 38*(2), 429–452.

Pfeffer, J. (1981). Management as symbolic action: The creation and maintenance of organizational paradigms. In L. L. Cummings & B. M. Staw (Eds.), *Research in organizational behavior* (Vol. 3, pp. 1–52). Greenwich, CT: JAI.

Pinto, A. C. (1998). Introduction. In E. Scheile & A. C. Pinto (Eds.), *Modern Portugal* (pp. 1–40). Palo Alto, CA: Society for the Promotion of Science and Scholarship.

Portugal. Economy, productivity, immigration, absenteeism—and a festa of football. (2000, October 21). *Financial Times.*

Putnam, R. D. (1993). *Making democracy work.* Princeton, NJ: Princeton University Press.

Rodrigues, M. J. (1991). *Competitividade e Recursos Humanos* [Competitiveness and human resources]. Lisboa, Portugal: Publicações D. Quixote.

Ronen, S., & Shenkar, O. (1985). Clustering countries on attitudinal dimensions: A review and synthesis. *Academy of Management Review, 10*(3), 435–454.

Santos, B. S. (1994). *Pela mão de Alice. O social e o político na pós*-modernidade [Led by Alice's hand. The social and political in postmodernity]. Porto, Portugal: Edições Afrontamento.

Sayles, L. R. (1979). *Leadership: What effective managers really do ... and how they do it.* New York: McGraw-Hill.

Schein, E. H. (1992). *Organizational culture and leadership.* San Francisco: Jossey-Bass.

Schwartz, J. H. (1999). A theory of cultural values and some implications for work. *Applied Psychology: An International Review, 48*(1), 23–47.

Smith, P. B. (1997). Leadership in Europe: Euro-management on the footprint of history? *European Journal of Work and Organizational Psychology, 6*(4), 375–386.

Smith, P. B., & Peterson, M. F. (1988). *Leadership, organizations and culture: An event management model.* London: Sage.

Smith, P. B., & Peterson, M. F. (1995, August). *Beyond value comparisons: Sources used to give meaning to management events in 30 countries.* Paper presented at the Academy of Management meeting, Vancouver, British Columbia Canada.

Soete, L. (2002). The challenge and potential of the knowledge-based economy in a globalized world. In M. J. Rodrigues (Ed.), *The new knowledge economy in Europe* (pp. 28–53). Chettenham, England: Edward Elgar.

Stewart, R. (1979). Managerial agendas—reactive or proactive. *Organizational Dynamics, 8*(2), 34–47.

Trompenaars, F. (1993). *Riding the waves of change: Understanding cultural diversity in business.* London: Nicholas Brealey.

United Nations Development Programme. (2000). *Human Development Report.* New York: Author.

Winter, D. G. (1973). *The power motive.* New York: The Free Press.

Winter, D. G. (1982). Motivation and performance in presidential candidates. In A. J. Stewart (Ed.), Motivation and society: *A volume in honour of David McClelland* (pp. 244–273). San Francisco: Jossey-Bass.

Winter, D. G. (1987). Leader appeal, leader performance and the motive profiles of leaders and followers: A study of American presidents and elections, *Journal of Personality and Social Psychology, 52*(1), 196–202.

17

▼▼▼▼▼▼▼

Managerial Culture and Leadership in Spain

Jeremiah J. O'Connell
Bentley College

José M. Prieto
Complutense University, Madrid, Spain

Celia Gutierrez
University of Alcala de Henares, Alcala, Spain

Some Semantic Issues

We begin by firstly clarifying some terms used in this chapter that may produce some confusion as a direct consequence of linguistic drifts between denotations and connotations in cross-cultural settings.

Iberia is the vernacular name for what is now Spain and Portugal. It was a term coined by the nomads traveling from the Sahara to what is known as Basque country. *Sepharad* was the Hebrew name given for this same peninsula that apparently is also mentioned in the Bible (Obad, 20). *Hispania* was the Latin name coined during the Roman Empire and *Al Andalus* the Arab name that was used from the 8th to the 16th century. This multiplicity of names reflects a heterogeneous cultural background.

Also from a historical perspective and in accurate terms, *Hispanic* is an adjective that identifies precisely those persons born in Spain or Portugal. Thus it is highly inaccurate to make use of Hispanic to single out persons from North, Central, or South America because it just so happens that they speak Spanish or Portuguese. In fact, they are not born in Hispania but in America. The confusion continues because, in English, two terms, *Spanish* and *Spaniards,* are used to identify accurately people born in Spain. The confusion with the term Hispanic is obvious in the large majority of research papers published in scientific journals or books whereby many samples have been identified as Hispanic because they speak Spanish or Portuguese, when in fact they are as American as those people who speak English. This distinction is not neutral, but an intentional euphemism leading to an ethnic segregation highlighted, for instance, in 1915 by the philosopher Horace Kallen (1882–1974): "The general notion, 'Americanization,' appears to denote the adoption of English speech, of American clothes and manners, of the American attitude in politics."

In the 21st century the high-minded contrast should be between Hispanic, Anglo-Saxon, or Chinese cultures among American citizens if the idea is of making the point that mother tongues entail different cultures in America among descendants who are second or third generations, almost all of them fluent in American English.

The focus of this chapter is Spain and the Hispanic culture. The purpose of it is to generate a snapshot of Spanish culture in the mid-1990s by looking through the eyes of 173 Spaniards, all middle managers from the financial services and food-processing sectors. They have grown up and belong to the Hispanic culture, chronicled during the last 30 centuries. This emphasis on a strict interpretation of what is meant by Hispanic and Spanish culture makes sense within the GLOBE definition of culture: something deep and enduring and by implication slow to change (House et al., 1999, 2004). A culture cannot be reduced exclusively to the language spoken by a given group of people in a country or a continent. Often, the label *Hispanic Culture* is a typical case of oversimplification because it is attributed to persons who view themselves as Americans and not as Spaniards or Europeans.

In line with the GLOBE policy of focusing on the dominant business culture in a multicultural society, this chapter concentrates on data collected from the Madrid area. In 1561, it became the capital and, for centuries, Madrid has been the melting pot of those better adapted to the highly competitive environment of a metropolis, that is, the royal throne of kings, the seat of government, and the headquarters of important business firms.

We offer one other semantic caveat before we begin. In Spanish, the concepts "leader" and "leadership" appear recently in the business context translated as *lider* and *liderazgo*. As we discuss more fully in the sections dealing with media analysis and the focus group, these labels in Spain have heretofore been reserved for persons and behavior in governmental and other nonbusiness organizations. We caution casual use of these; transliterations could cause unintentional importation of the cultural baggage from their English-language source.

Chapter Outline

In the pages that follow, we offer a sketch of Spanish history and culture as background for our research. Then we turn to Spain today, its geography, demographics, government, and economy. We specifically profile the two industrial sectors, financial services and food processing, in which we did our data gathering. To place our research within the stream of cross-cultural studies, which included data from Spain, we briefly describe the relevant results in their historical context. That done, we report on the quantitative results of our questionnaire inquiry. To round up the results, we present what we have learned from qualitative methods employed: media analysis, focus group, and interviews. We conclude with an appreciation of the significance of what we have learned for other researchers and for managers seeking some guidance in being effective cross-culturally in interactions with Spanish managers and organizations.

1. A SKETCH OF SPANISH HISTORY AND HISPANIC CULTURE

Traditionally, scholars accept the existence of a Proto-Indo-European language, the root of a large majority of languages spoken over the greater part of Europe and Sanskrit. It is the oldest language of religion and scholarship, and is still spoken in India today. Another approach emphasizes the existence of a Proto-African-European language, the root of what is known now as the "Berber-Basque Language Complex," originated in the region of the Sahara, then fertile and rich. Prolonged periods of drought brought about by the winds from the Gulf Stream generated what is now the Sahara Desert and the Sahel, forcing the nomads toward the West (Canary isles), the North (Morocco, Spain, France, Italy), and the East (Egypt, Israel, Crete, Greece). The study of genes' alleles through blood tests and the linguistic study of sentences engraved in funerary stones have confirmed this second lineage (ArnÒiz Villena, 2000; Harrison, 1974). These migratory movements of Iberians in the past persist still via Gibraltar and many companies in Spain and France, for instance, employ them as low-salary labor and via subsidiaries as illegal workers.

Two Semitic groups came to Iberia approximately 25 or more centuries ago: the Phoenicians and the Sephardic Jews. Phoenicians were businessmen who derived their prosperity from trade and manufacturing factories here and there along the Mediterranean border. Their main contribution to the Hispanic culture was the alphabet, very useful for doing the accounts and for writing contracts, and the mercantile mentality that still survives in some regions such as Catalonia and Valencia. The Sephardic Jews observed Babylonian ritual traditions. Their main contribution to Hispanic culture was the collection of legal codes and case law after the tradition started by Hammurabi (about 38 centuries ago) and the formation of professions based on intellectual achievements.

The Hellenic culture arrived at the Mediterranean cities of Spain about 26 centuries ago. Their main contribution was related to navigation techniques as well as the organization of societal life in cities, which implied the active involvement of citizens by mastering the art of logic and rhetoric. Still now a large number of nautical terms in Spanish have a Greek origin. During the Roman Empire the education of children was entrusted to Greek pedagogues and so Hellenic and Hispanic cultures somehow overlapped among educated people. This influence still survives and may be detected when listening to educated Greek people speaking Greek aloud, and educated Spanish people speaking Spanish aloud. The cadence of words, the rhythm of sentences, and the tone are very similar.

Christianity came to Spain by way of two independent channels. Saint Paul the Apostle, in his letter to Romans, announced he planned to visit Spain. He never arrived but his understanding of Christ took root in many Hellenic cities in the Mediterranean coast of Spain by the end of the first century. The second channel was the Visigoths, a branch of the Goths that seized the Roman Empire, and so Hispania. The Visigoths were Christians who followed the doctrine taught by Arius, a Christian priest of Alexandria who died around 336 AD. Arianism featured the finite and created human nature of Christ. The Visigothic understanding of Christianity survived in the regions ruled by the Muslim Moorish Kings in Spain because their understanding of Christ was compatible with the interpretation made in the Koran (which accentuates the absolute oneness of God). The term Mozarab was coined and the Mozarabic rite of the Holy Mass still survives in Spain, especially in Toledo (FernÒndez Arenas, 1978).

In 711 AD, the Muslim kings (Berber descents) came to Spain on a request made by Agila, the son of the Visigothic King Witiza, and became involved in internal quarrels of succession. They decided to stay and controlled the large majority of the country until they reached the zenith by the end of the 10th century, under the Umayyad dynasty (Arab descendents). In the 11th century the decline and political fragmentation began, and the consequence was the consolidation of the Christian kingdoms, which controlled practically all of the country except Granada by the middle of the 13th century. This was the basic social structure: The leading figures and military men were Christians whereas Sephardic Jews devoted themselves to professions requiring prolonged training and formal qualification. The Moorish were employed as farmers, builders, and maintenance workers. This distribution of competences favored the peaceful coexistence of people of different religions in cities and small towns for two centuries. Sometimes it prompted confusion and shock to contemporary outsiders. For instance, people visiting the synagogue of Toledo, built just in that period, cannot understand why there are so many Muslim motifs as ornaments on the walls. The reason is simple: The builders were Muslim and the customers were Sephardic Jews who considered it refinement. So "King of Three Religions" was the honorific title used as a rubric by the Crown of Castile, for instance, stressing a climate of tolerance and heterogeneity, whereas in France or Germany the rubric was "Holy Roman Emperor" of Christianity, stressing homogeneity in that same period. The situation changed drastically in 1492, when the Sephardic Jews were forced to make a choice between the Christian church and the synagogue. About 50,000 Sephardim left for the diaspora in nearby countries. The Kings Ferdinand II of Aragon (1452–1516) and Isabella I of Castile (1451–1504) obtained the honorary title of "Catholic Kings" soon afterward in 1496 from Pope Alexander VI (1431–1503). Moors had to make a similar choice between the church and the mosque during the period elapsed from 1502 to 1614. Letting go of large segments of such professional and occupational groups had very negative consequence in daily affairs during the 16th and 17th centuries.

In 1282, the Hapsburg dynasty established a hereditary monarchy in Austria and in 1452 Frederick III (1415–1493) was the last Holy Roman Emperor crowned by a pope in Rome. The Hapsburg ruled Spain during the 16th and 17th centuries, and so what is called, on the one hand, the Spanish Empire may also be called, on the other hand, the Holy Roman Empire or the Hapsburg Empire in Europe, America, and Asia. For instance, the first emperor, Charles V (1500–1558), was in fact Flemish having been born and raised in Ghent, Belgium. He started to learn Spanish when he became king of Spain in 1517. His first action in Spain was to eliminate those members of local parliaments who refused to subsidize the costs of his crowning ceremonies as emperor. During his term the large majority of resources he had obtained in America were used to pay debts derived from military actions of the Hapsburg dynasty that took place here and there in Europe. His son Philip II also faced several bankruptcies caused by the same transfer of resources that had been obtained in America and used as payment to Northern Europe for services provided by mercenaries to the Hapsburg dynasty. Spendthrift is a term that may be used to categorize the behavioral patterns of the Hapsburgs during their reign in Spain. They spent resources in a rather irresponsible way with scant regard for the safety and the quality of life of the Spaniards.

A large number of Spaniards went to America, but their prevalent profile must be highlighted. The large majority of noblemen who went to America were not the first-born (the formal heir) but the second son, the third, or the Benjamin (i.e. the youngest son). Somehow losers in Spain decided to become winners in America.

By the beginning of the 18th century, the French Bourbon dynasty succeeded the Hapsburg dynasty and the consequence was a centralized concept of government and power. However, as a reaction, the direct consequence has been an increase in the rivalry between Barcelona and Madrid, the first focused on trading and management and the second on lobbying and bureaucracy. The great advantage has been the existence of a bipolar civil society with a mercantile metropolis and an administrative capital separated by 600 km.

At the turn of the 19th century, Spain faced the challenge of the French Revolution. King Carlos IV (1748–1819) was forced to abdicate after a popular rebellion occurred in Aranjuez (1808). Joseph I Bonaparte (1768–1844), brother of Napoleon, was appointed king of Spain immediately afterward with the support of a tiny minority of educated people. This minority favored his fresh ideas about the leading role of monarchy in society, showing preference for top-down policies and actions to reduce inequality and injustice, as well as religious tolerance and freedom of expression. These ideas were based on the Enlightenment movement. However, the large majority rejected his appointment and did not appreciate the consequence of an enlightened monarchy favoring tolerance. British and Spanish troops, led by the Duke of Wellington, defeated the French troops led by Napoleon in 1813. Another king from the Bourbon dynasty was appointed, Ferdinand VII (1784–1833), who led the country under the formula of an "enlightened despotism." It meant that, during the 19th century, it became customary not to comply with regulations or administrative orders enacted by the government or the Crown. Regulations under direct control of military men were the exception. These stipulations were mandatory because the army was in charge of keeping the peace. The direct consequence has been the distinction between regulations and orders enacted by civil or military rulers. There was a double standard: Civil regulations had a descriptive nature whereas military regulations had a prescriptive one.

The 1929 crash of the New York stock market had a direct influence on the Spanish political system a year afterward. King Alphonse XIII (1886–1941) abandoned the country in April 1931, which led to Spain becoming a republic. From 1931 to 1933, the government was entrusted to the leading figures from both the Liberal and the Labor Party. From 1933 to 1935, the government came under the control of the Conservative parties. In July 1936, General Francisco Franco (1892–1975) started the Spanish Civil War (1936–1939). He led a group of military men in an uprising against the republican government and in 1937 he proclaimed himself "Caudillo," that is "Leader," "Fuhrer," "Duce." The main consequence was the exile of about one million left-wing Spaniards and causing the death of about 1 million people from both camps. During his almost four decades in office, backed by the army and the Catholic Church from the beginning, "Leader" was the main title used to identify his top position in the Spanish state and the government. He ruled in an authoritarian form, having outlawed political parties and free trade unions, and having established a Parliament that "had little in common with democratic legislatures" and a Charter of Rights that was "more cosmetic than democratic" (Solsten & Meditz, 1990, p. 42). Franco favored the Catholic Church and restored the central role of Catholic thought in education. There could be no public practice of other religions. He believed in the supremacy of a "unique and great" Spanish nation and so reversed regional autonomy, forbidding the use of the Basque and Catalan languages. The government banned divorce, introduced censorship in all kinds of publications, and required official permission for public meetings. Many military men and members of the only legal organization (Fascism) were employed as top and middle managers in large industries and companies. They insisted on "blind obedience" to immediate supervisors and line managers. By decree, Franco reserved to himself the naming of his successor and did so in 1969 in the person of Prince Juan Carlos de Bourbon. Foreign investment in Spain had increased especially after the UN had lifted its boycott on the regime in 1951, allowing Spain's membership in to that organization in 1955. The direct consequences of economic developments during the 1960s were turbulence and internal tensions. It became evident that new forms of direction and participation in policymaking were necessary. Social movements in universities, illegal trade unions, mass media, and some businessmen and women did call for a convergence with political and administrative standards within the European Union. In this context this comment of Carlos Fuentes, a Mexican observer (who received the Cervantes Award in 1987 and the Prince of Asturias Award in 1994), makes sense: "What is truly important, even singular, about Spain is that Franco never managed to take over the totality of Spanish culture" (Fuentes, 1992, p. 338).

The political transition started in 1977 during the electoral process where all kinds of political parties participated freely, including the Communist Party. This was the initiative of King Juan Carlos I and Adolfo Suarez as prime minister. In December 1978, a new constitution was endorsed by referendum. In 1981, some military men launched a coup d'état that failed. Immediately afterward the Socialist Party obtained an absolute majority and governed from 1982 to 1996 in successive mandates under the leadership of Felipe GonzÒlez as prime minister. In 1996, the Popular Party (Conservative) won the elections and obtained a second term in 2000 by absolute majority under the leadership of Jose Maria Aznar, as prime minister. Felipe GonzÒlez earned a reputation for a charismatic leadership style whereas Jose Maria Aznar is inclined to behave in a rather autocratic style. At first glance this distinctness may be considered idiosyncratic, but an investigation into how discussions and decisions occurred in the respective parties, parliaments, and governments suggests that the distinction is symptomatic of what is considered normal in a left-wing or a right-wing culture in Spain. It is a matter of plurality and tolerance versus conformity and toughness (SÒnchez Soler, 2002; Tussell, 2000, 2001).

It may be stated that from the 15th to the 20th century, Spanish sovereign rulers fostered absolute power and enhanced their leadership by forcing into exile a large number of Spaniards they considered dissidents or nonaligned. For instance, (a) Sephardim in 1492 were compelled to diaspora to avoid the Inquisition, allowing, as an easy way out, for the monarchy and aristocracy to clear debts; (b) troublemakers in the nobility and monasteries were sent to colonize America during the 16th and 17th centuries, (c) Muslims were expelled during these same centuries, (d) free-thinking aristocrats and scholars opposing enlightened despotism were ostracized during the 19th century, and (e) finally by the end of the civil war (1939) citizens considered left-wingers or just liberals had to abandon the country or face several years in prison. Summarizing, it has been a succession of sovereign leaders advocating the eviction or the execution of noncompliant subjects.

In 1981, Spain became a member of NATO and in 1986 joined the European Union (EU). In 1992, Barcelona hosted the Olympic Games and Seville the World's Fair. In 1999, Spain joined the European Monetary Union and in 2002 the euro became the new currency. This has been the only period of tolerance for dissidents and liberals.[1]

2. SKETCH OF SPAIN TODAY

Geography

The geographical center is Madrid, the capital of the Spanish Kingdom, which is located in the extreme southwest of the European continent. It borders France and Andorra in the northeast, Portugal in the west, and Gibraltar in the south. It is bounded by the Mediterranean Sea to the east and southeast and by the Atlantic Ocean to the northwest and southwest. Spanish territory includes the Canary Islands situated in the Atlantic Ocean and the Balearic Islands in the Mediterranean Sea. The total area of the national territory is 194,898 square miles (504,784 square kilometers).

---

[1]The following books are suggested for those interested in a more detailed account of Spanish history and Hispanic culture: Alvarez Junco and Shubert (2000), Brenan (1943), Carr (2000), FernÒndez Arena (1978), Fuentes (1992), Hooper (1995), Solsten and Meditz (1990), Lopez, Talens, and Villaneuva (1994), Ross (1997), and Tussell (2001).

Demographics

The population density in Spain is 79 persons per square kilometer, high compared to 30 in the United States or very low compared to 466 in the Netherlands. The average natural increase rate among the 40 million Spaniards is 0% per year, the same as in other European countries, but very low compared to the average international rate of 1.3%, 0.8% in the United States or 0.3% in affluent societies. About 76% of Spaniards live in an urban milieu, as is the case in the EU and the United States, but this figure is very high compared to the international average rate of 45%. The birthrate is 1.2, very low compared to 2.7, the international average rate, 2.0 in the United States, 1.4 in the EU, and 1.6 in affluent societies. About 2% of the Spanish population account for citizens born in other EU member states and about 0.25% are legal immigrants from Latin American countries. This means that Spaniards are a highly homogeneous population. The Basque people constitute 5% of the Spaniards and, though they have their own unique language, are not so different because they are, in fact, the Iberians who have had descendants here and there in Spain during the last 30 centuries. By 2002, according to the Spanish Sociological Research Center (CIS), about 81% of Spaniards consider themselves Catholics, with a lower percentage in Madrid and Barcelona (69%). Only one out of three taxpayers allocates 0.52% of the taxes they pay in order to help support the Catholic Church; the remaining two out of three prefers to support welfare programs. About 19% of Spaniards go to Sunday mass at least every week and about 12% once a month; close to 50% acknowledge they never attend mass at all, 11% consider themselves agnostic, and 5% state they are atheistic (Bedoya, 2002)

Government

The 1978 Constitution set up a parliamentary monarchy, with a prime minister, a bi-cameral Parliament, a Council of Ministers, and an independent judicial system. A large set of civil and social rights places Spain well within the EU standards. The ultimate responsibility for Spain's defense rests with parliament and the government, and not with the army. Likewise, Spain is a nondenominational kingdom, that is, no state religion at all but guaranteed freedom of religious choice. The Constitution stipulates substantial regional autonomy to the 18 autonomous communities. Spanish is the official language and Basque, Catalan, and Galician languages are also official languages in some of the autonomous communities.

Economy

The gross national product (GNP) in 1999 was $583 billion, which ranked Spain as the 10th largest economy in the world, but it ranked 39th by the measure of GNP per citizen. The gross domestic product (GDP) growth rate in 2001 was 2.9%, higher compared to 2.4% in the EU and 1.5% in the United States. Nine tenths of a percent of the GDP was devoted to research and development (R&D) programs as compared to 1.85% within the EU. This means, among other things, that there are not enough career tracks for researchers at the PhD level. The rate of increase in the retail price index in 2001 was 2.9%, 2.3% in the EU, and 2.6% in the United States. That could imply difficulties ahead in keeping within the track of the euro-zone standards. The unemployment rate was 12.7% in 2001 as compared to 7.8% in the EU and 4.4% in the United States. This suggests the existence of a large network of an invisible workforce in the so-called "black economy" in which many endure a marginal economic existence. About 27% of Spanish homes had a computer in the year 2000 and two out of three had an

Internet connection, using it for information management (82%), e-mail exchange (42%), and chatting (36%). Tourism is the main productivity sector in the Spanish economy and in the year 2000, 48 million people visited the country, producing about $28 billion of income, which ranks Spain third in world after France and the United States as regards to the number of foreign visitors. Spain remains a net beneficiary in the EU, receiving about 1% of the GDP from social funds made available by EU member states (Organization for Economic Cooperation and Development [OECD], 1998, p. 33). Self-employed businessmen own one out of two small or middle-size firms (Prieto, 1990).[2]

Sectors Targeted in this Research

Financial Services Sector.   Within the financial services sector, the Spanish commercial and savings banks have remained largely clear of the international mergers and acquisitions that have so reshaped the banking sector elsewhere. For instance, non-Spanish banks rule only 1 out of 10 banks. After an intense period of concentration within the country, eight Spanish banks are large enough to be included in the *Financial Times* list of the 500 largest enterprises in the world. The size of Spain's core banks and the degree of concentration is in line with European averages (Chislett, 1994, p. 25). The sample of persons who answered the GLOBE survey were employees of Spanish banks, 4 of which are among the 10 largest in the country.

The Spanish financial system is a dynamic arrangement in constant evolution, under the direct supervision of the national government. Interventionism has prevailed during the dictatorship, as well as, more recently, under the leadership of the Socialist and the Conservative Parties (Pérez, 1997). There has been a kind of mutual and latent agreement. If a bank, or an insurance company, is on the brink of insolvency or bankruptcy, the Ministry of Finance formally intervenes to protect the rights of the small savers and investors. In this way, the amount of money in small accounts (about U.S.$10,000) is somehow guaranteed through public subsidies or credits, and a large majority of bank employees keep their jobs, even during the process of a merger. One consequence however is that many top and middle managers in the financial system know that their mistakes do not jeopardize the actual health of the bank. The state plays the role of brakeman and of bodyguard as soon as a critical event emerges (Tamames, 1994).

During the 1980s and 1990s, many mergers between Spanish banks took place. In the 5 years before this research began, four commercial banks and 34 savings banks (accounting for 60% of national deposits) were involved in mergers (Chislett, 1994, p. 107), introducing real turbulence between top and middle managers employed in the merging or the merged bank. About one in three managers were made redundant and negotiated very convenient compensation packages.

In the period 1993–1998, when this research was carried out, several top managers in the bank sector were prosecuted and imprisoned as a consequence of fraud and corruption cases. Top and middle managers in banks not involved directly in such cases experienced a climate of distrust among their customers. The credibility of the bank system was, somehow, under a cloud because many small shareholders lost money they had entrusted to some misled banks.

---

[2]Further details concerning the current political and economic transformations in today's Spain may be found in Lawlor, Rigby, and Yruela (1998) as well in the yearbooks published by newspapers such as El Pais and El Mundo.

Food-Processing Sector. The food-processing sector was characterized by small and medium-size firms (some 70,000), employing about half a million people, less than 4% of the labor force (Solsten & Meditz, 1990, p. 169). The sector is dominated by 150 foreign firms, controlling about half of Spain's total food processing (Chislett, 1994, p. 82). Our sample was drawn from 3 of the top 10 Spanish firms in the sector.

At first glance, mainly family businesses, industrial alliances, as well as small and medium-size firms shape the food sector in Spain. However, these establishments are net-worked through both visible and invisible channels of distribution and accumulation of goods and services. This means that top and middle managers are scarce, because the structure of such networks is rather flat. The exception is multinational firms, mostly foreign owned, which have succeeded breaking into the market by cutting salaries, benefits, and bonuses and serving a stable demand for standard products of average quality. In these settings we do find top and middle managers, many of whom are trained in the doctrine of the multinational firm.

In the food sector, there is also a permanent confrontation between the producers and the processors, between the processors and the distributors, and finally, between the distributors and the retailers. Again, managers are caught in the middle of this strife that occurs in the marketplace. They do not view themselves as the really independent decision makers, but they know that, often, they have no choice but to compromise when they deal with producers or those further down the distribution chain.

In drawing our sample of respondents from the food-processing sector, we focused only on leading Spanish firms in the sector. Following the GLOBE guidelines, we avoided what was thought might "contaminate" the perceived Spanish culture from the influences of the foreign parent. The food-processing sector belongs, somehow, to the merchants tradition where what is important is not what product you have, but from where you buy and to where you sell a product (Prieto & Martinez, 1997).

3. EARLIER RESEARCH RESULTS

O'Connell and Prieto (1998) reviewed the past 50 years of cross-cultural research studies (which included Spain) based on managerial thinking and attitudes, focusing on the issue of leadership in private or public firms. Each of these studies was a snapshot of managerial thinking on leadership styles at a given moment in the Spanish history. The set of studies examined are reclassified here in chronological order to facilitate not only an understanding of statements made by the original authors, but also an understanding of the historical back-ground of the period when the study was carried out.

Research Published in the 1960s

The earliest research was carried out in a political climate that profoundly affected every phase of Spanish life—the 40-year dictatorship of Franco. It only seems reasonable to think that respondent sensitivities may have jeopardized the reliability of some of the findings. In stable societies where the political system has continuity for decades or even centuries, the strategy followed by some international researchers in the area of leadership may be welcome and sound. However, in countries like Spain, where strong political changes and pendulum swings took place during the 20th century, it is important to highlight the background to understand the degree to which the data obtained may be considered more or less meaning-ful (Coverdale, 1979). The historical context facilitates an understanding of the forces at work shaping the actions and comments in a particular time and place. For the research subjects, the political risks and challenges of answering in one or another direction were certainly a front-and-center preoccupation. It is problematic at best to secure reliable results in leadership studies performed in a country where people favoring democracy are persecuted and imprisoned, where military men rule the country, and where citizens cannot freely express their thoughts. In such a setting, the usual promise of anonymity for respondents lacks credibility. Career making was a political experience. During the selection process, candidates for managerial positions had to submit a certificate of "good behavior" issued by the local police. Often the personnel manager was a retired military man. People, including those in managerial positions, were imprisoned or fired if they were incriminated or considered too liberal or too left-minded.

Spanish people in their 40s answering surveys in the 1960s were the same people involved in the civil war (1936–1939) in their 20s. When contacted by a social scientist, how did the large majority of these managers, who were also family men, react and respond? We leave it to the reader to consider which of the findings reported next would be most susceptible to the pressures from the political environment of that period.

The main study written with data from Spain obtained in this period is that of Haire, Ghiselli, and Porter (1966). These are their main findings:

- Spanish managers had very democratic assumptions about information sharing, even though they held much less positive assumptions about people's capacity for leadership and initiative (p. 28).
- Spanish managers gave higher priority to social, esteem, and security needs than to self-actualization and autonomy needs. They expressed the greatest dissatisfaction with social and security needs (p. 94).
- Lower-level managers expressed more dissatisfaction than did higher-level managers. No other researcher reported level-dependent results (p. 160).
- Young managers expressed more dissatisfaction than did older managers (p. 167).
- Company size influenced some results: More democratic assumptions prevailed in small Spanish firms (p.167)

The anthropologists Kluckholm and Strodtbeck (1961) performed another comparative study of management literature where data from Spain were included. They argued that time orientation is a strong differentiating characteristic among cultures, but data from Spanish managers were virtually silent on the matter.

Bass (1968) found that those playing the boss role were strongly dissatisfied with uninvolved subordinates (p. 14).

Research Published in the 1970s

The Spanish political transition had roots back to the late 1960s and early 1970s. In fact, the minority movement included some students, some professors, some priests, some illegal trade unionists, and some journalists from newspapers and broadcasting media. The silent majority was, once again, the passive society, preoccupied and observant but only commenting on some details privately. Franco, old and sick, died in his bed in November 1975. The large majority of Spanish society awaited this very human fate as the only peaceful exit for the regime.

Meanwhile, however, Spain's economic growth favored the presence of foreign firms and foreign investment, in both the service as well as the industrial sector. Tourism became the leading industry and the free expression of ideas started to be an acceptable norm between visitors and guests. Those leading the banking sector started to favor the political transition toward a democratic system because money comes and goes more easily in an open society than in a closed and isolated one. The main barrier to further economic development of the country was at first the dictatorship. After 30 years of military regime (1939–1969), the dictatorship started to decline, pushed, initially, by a tiny but cultivated minority. Still, uncertainty was the prevailing mood.

Cummings, Harnett, and Stevens (1971) are the authors of the first study published in this decade; the highlights of their main findings are as follows:

- Spaniards are more conciliatory than belligerent (p. 292).
- Spaniards are strongest in a belief in fate, very suspicious, and relatively risk adverse (pp. 293–296).
- The Spanish culture may not be homogeneous: Managers from the Barcelona (Catalunia) area were less risk adverse than those from Madrid or the south of Spain (Andalusia) (pp. 298–300).

Bernard M. Bass is the main author of the second study published this decade. He has visited and lectured in Spain several times, and has maintained during the 1980s, and even into the 1990s, regular contacts with schools of management in Spain. His main findings are as follows:

- Bass and Burger (1979) showed service and duty among the strongly preferred life goals whereas wealth, independence, and pleasure among the weak life goals (p. 62).
- Spanish managers express a strong desire to be aware of other people's feelings; and they are more idealistic than pragmatic (p. 62).
- Managers wanted to use less authority to get the work done and wanted to be more participative than political (pp. 184–185).
- Spanish managers are located at a low level in risk tolerance and less concerned for the long term (pp. 184–185).
- Spanish managers favored self-reliance life goals, expressed less desire for group decision making, yet displayed actual group decision-making (pp. 184–185).
- The assertions of the Spanish individualism were tempered with their finding that Spanish managers preferred cooperation to competition with peers (pp. 184–185).
- Spanish managers with the highest rates of advancement displayed unusual self-actualizing, risk taking, and less security-minded tendencies than did other managers (p. 185).

Research Published in the 1980s

In December 1978, the new and democratic Spanish Constitution was voted and welcomed in a national referendum. Still tension and conflicts grew in intensity, fomented by supporters of the old military regime and by a terrorist and nationalist group in the Basque region. In February 1981, military men launched a coup d'etat that failed, among other reasons, as a consequence of the fast reaction against the coup by the young but not so novice king, Juan Carlos I.

It may be stated that a democratic climate started to prevail in the country when the courts imprisoned the military men who supported the coup d'etat. During the 1980s a climate of freedom of speech and expression of thoughts started to germinate throughout the country, except in the Basque region, where, until 1998, a climate of terrorism prevailed.

A clear picture emerges from the first study of Hofstede (1980). It is important to note that the data were obtained some years before (1966–1973). Still, it is probably fair to assert that the Hofstede respondents—all of whom worked for the American multinational IBM in Spain—reflected the earliest evidence of the transition to a post-Franco culture. What was said earlier about the historical context of the 1970s remains relevant here but the fairly predictable shift to the more democratic 1980s was probably already under way among the more cosmopolitan IBM employees. Here are the highlights of Hofstede's findings:

- The Spanish culture showed a relatively large Power Distance as well as strong Uncertainty Avoidance.
- Spain is more individualistic than collective.
- Spanish managers fall on the feminine side.

Hofstede validated the original studies based on single-company (foreign owned) samples, obtaining the samples in public seminars where the company affiliation of participants was not requested (pp. 67–68). In a second book, Hofstede (1991) pursued his findings in greater depth as follows:

- The Spanish sample appeared as exemplars of an individualistic society with a large Power Distance, which produces dependent individualists and subordinates who do not want to participate but expect autocratic style (p. 86).
- High Power Distance and strong Uncertainty Avoidance produce centralized, pyramidal organization structures where a powerful person will be looked for to resolve uncertainties for the others who are risk adverse, and where rules abound that the powerful can ignore (p. 87).
- In more feminine societies, with strong Uncertainty Avoidance, achievement drive will be low and the need for security and love will be strongest (p. 88).

Though Hofstede argues that the "convergence of management will never come" (p. 89), Spain is a good test case because so many of its larger companies are foreign owned. In the Hofstede findings, Spanish managers are the most individualistic of all the managers from the Hispanic (using this term here to group cultures by common language) countries but the least individualistic of the Latin European countries. Organizations and managers in Spain reflect a mix of individualistic and collectivist features, probably reflective of the melange of cultural influences imported to Spain with the vast amounts of direct foreign investment.

Research Published in the 1990s

Politically, the 1990s is a decade of stability and integration of Spain into the European and world communities. In this new era, the large majority of citizens identify themselves as citizens and not as subjects and may express publicly or privately their viewpoints at will. The main evidence of such freedom appears in the large number of interviews and conversations broadcast by mass media where current citizens identify themselves and say whatever is on their mind. Again, the exception has been the Basque region.

Several studies are highlighted next. It is important to note that the respondents in these surveys exclude the large majority of the old regime's managers, who have already retired during this decade. We would therefore expect to observe more reliable results and to garner a more valid picture of societal, organizational, and leadership culture. The review of the studies is as follows:

- McFarlin et al. (1993) found that subordinates wanted to participate even more than those in an Anglo reference group. They also detected that the Spanish managers requested headquarters' policy guidance more than others and that they had the strongest belief in a moral right behind participation practices (p. 373).
- Lewis (1992) reports that Spanish managers, like their U.S. counterparts, underestimated the potential competitive and productivity gains from total quality management (p. 44). U.S. and Spanish managers had very similar perceptions and attitudes about quality (p. 45).
- Boldy, Jain, and Northey (1993) reported that risk taking was not in the top 10 most desirable managerial attributes among Spaniards (p. 163).
- Trompenaars (1993) placed Spanish managers almost as individualist as managers from the United States, on a given scale (p. 48). He described Spaniards as more affective or emotional than neutral (p. 88). He used the high-context/low-context distinction to classify the sample from Spain, which appears among the low-context countries (like the U.S. managers), suggesting that a person needs to know only a little about the situational context before effective communication can occur. No other systematic research elucidates this controversial point. He finds also that Spaniards believed in internal control more than fatalism and believed more in particular than universal rules (pp. 128–135). Spanish Power Distance shows in the classification system of Spanish organizations, which appear in the more hierarchic "family" category, in comparison with many others in a more collectivist society (p. 161). He also indicates that status in Spain is more ascribed to family than to personal achievement.
- Page and Wiseman (1993) add a note of caution with their observation that a Spanish manager's style is less supportive and more punishing than the U.S. managers (p. 167). They argue that Spaniards can be tolerant with autocratic leadership and that style will not affect the positive perception (p. 169). Also, they show that Spaniards have comparatively low levels of participation.
- Pavett and Morris (1995) analyzed data obtained in several plants from a U.S. multinational firm located in five countries, one of them Spain. They reported profiles on participation showing that the plant in Spain was less participative than those in Italy, the UK, and the United States. Their data showed the Spanish plant especially low in the goal-setting and control dimensions of participation.

This review is not to suggest that the studies cited comprise a systematic longitudinal view of the managerial culture on leadership in Spain. Nor do we argue that the studies are strictly comparable. The review is suggestive only, more of tantalizing questions than of secure answers. Just how much did the threatening external environment shape respondent attitudes, perceptions, and values? To what degree was culture itself altered or repressed? To what degree was it merely a case of altered reporting? How reliable is the informal composite profile of Spanish managerial culture that appears to emerge over the past 50 years? Fortunately, we began our research in the mid-1990s in a much more benign environment than did our early predecessors. Our study dealt with a respondent pool where very few of them would have practiced as managers during the Franco period. Almost none had personal scars. They could cite and critique, without political reference, the conventional wisdom or stereotype of

Spanish managerial style: autocratic, male dominated, top down, individualist, risk adverse, assertive but, in the end, conciliatory.

4. GLOBE SURVEY IN SPAIN

Societal Culture

Data Collection

The financial services and food-processing sectors were selected for the GLOBE survey. In total, 96 managers from the financial services sector have been included in the sample for this study and 77 managers from the food-processing sector. As a whole, quantitative data analyses have been carried out with data obtained from 173 respondents.

EUROFORUM (a management training institute) facilitated the data collection process through well-placed contacts who administered the instruments to middle managers separately (Form Alpha and Beta). Further samples were contacted via the department of human resources in several of the firms and middle managers were surveyed on the premises of each company. It was a challenge to raise the percentage of female respondents to 12%. A large number of items in the surveys provoked a negative reaction among the vast majority of potential responders who were contacted. It demanded too much time and concentration, and middle managers insisted they had other priorities. Patience with the niceties of social research is a scarce commodity in Spain. An old saying advances the critical point: "If something is short and brief, then it is twice as good!"

Sample Demographics

Following are the demographic characteristics of the 173 middle managers in the sample:

- The age range was 25 to 35 (60.68%) and 46 to 55 (36.41%) when the samples from the two sectors are combined. Middle managers in the financial services sector were older than in the food-processing sector. In the financial services sector, 27.7% were between 46 and 55 years of age, whereas in the food-processing sector 11.56% were in this age range. This same trend was observed among those above 55 years of age. Middle managers in the food-processing sector were younger than those in the financial services sector. In the food-processing sector, 15.6% were between 25 and 35 years of age whereas in the financial services the percentage was 3.4. No middle manager was younger than 25 years old.
- Middle managers born in Spain constituted 97.68%, 1.15% were born in other EU member states, and the balance were born somewhere else. About 87.2% have resided permanently in Spain and the remainder had spent sometime abroad as immigrants, descendants of immigrants, or students.
- Spanish was the mother tongue for 77.45% of the sample and 15.02% spoke also Basque, Catalan, or Galician language.
- The average seniority was 13 years of full-time work experience. Professional experience in executive posts within national or multinational companies represented 44.5%. Respondents who said they had a formal university degree, and had also received adequate training in the area of business management and administration was 63.5%.

TABLE 17.1

Differences Between Actual Practice and Desired Values at the Societal Level

Culture Dimensions	"As Is"			"Should Be"			Difference
	Score	Band	Rank	Score	Band	Rank	
Performance Orientation	4.01	B	37	5.80	C	41	+1.79
Future Orientation	3.51	C	45	5.63	B	27	+2.12
Assertiveness	4.42	A	17	4.00	B	18	−0.42
Institutional Collectivism	3.85	C	51	5.20	A	12	+1.35
Gender Egalitarian	3.01	B	51	4.82	A	20	+1.81
Humane Orientation	3.32	D	60	5.69	B	5	+2.37
Power Distance	5.52	A	14	2.26	D	59	−3.26
In-Group Collectivism	5.45	A	30	5.79	B	21	+0.34
Uncertainty Avoidance	3.97	C	37	4.76	B	27	+0.79

Note.   Score: Country mean for Spain on the basis of aggregated scale scores. *Band*: Letters A to D indicate the country band Spain belongs to (A > B > C > D). Countries from different bands are considered to differ significantly from each other (GLOBE test banding procedure, cf. Hanges, Dickson, & Sipe, 2004). *Rank*: Spain's position relative to the 61 countries in the GLOBE study; Rank 1 = highest; Rank 61 = score. *Difference*: The difference was computed by subtracting "As Is" scores from the respective "Should Be" scores. A positive difference indicates that the society wishes to have more of a particular attribute or dimension whereas a negative score indicates the opposite.

Results on the Nine Dimensions of Societal Culture

The 173 Spanish middle-manager respondents from the financial services and food-processing sectors made the contrast between actuality (i.e., the existing conditions or facts in the category "As Is" here and now) and desirability (what is valued as intended or expected in the category "Should Be") about the nine dimensions of Spanish culture at the societal level (see Table 17.1).

Country scores (means) for each dimension are reported as well as the position of these responses, vis a vis respondents from 60 other countries by indicating the rank and the band or country cluster (from A to D, cf. Hanges, Dickson, & Sipe, 2004) into which the Spanish means (*M*s) fall. Finally, the difference between average scores of actuality ("As Is") and desirability ("Should Be") is reported. We comment on these results in the following subsections.

Performance Orientation.   This dimension refers to the extent to which a society encourages or rewards group members for performance improvement and excellence. Although the Spanish observations place the culture just below the middle on this dimension ($M = 4.01$), among the 17,000 respondents in 61 countries, the desirability values expressed in the category "Should Be" ($M = 5.80$) suggest significant tension on the subject of Performance Orientation. The Spanish middle-manager sample wants greater encouragement and rewards for improvement and excellence. Still, the large difference of +1.79 leaves our respondents behind the average move in the same direction within the 60 other countries. What is reflected in the Spanish ranking from 37th to 41st is that the Spanish aspiration for change in this dimension is somewhat weaker. These results make sense at this stage of Spanish history because competition in the global economy has been prompting widespread discussion, policy changes, and management education on such issues as continuous improvement, total quality management (TQM), and the "9.9" managerial style that gives appropriate attention to both task and people. Shrewd political maneuvering would no longer carry the day nor would the historical tendency to scramble at the last minute and make do. In-company and public seminars trainees underscored the changes required in Spain to become a globally competitive economy.

Future Orientation.   This dimension describes the degree to which individuals engage in future-oriented behaviors such as planning, investing in the future, and delaying gratification. The Spanish responses again fall somewhat below the middle of the international comparison on this second dimension. This time the difference of +2.12 between the actuality and desirability thrusts Spain further ahead than the average 60 other countries. The Spanish rank changed from a 45th to a 27th pole positioning. Building the future is, to some degree, a matter of will, and so requires voluntary involvement toward intended or planned actions. This distinction makes sense because there is a preference for intended action in the Hispanic culture and for planned actions in the Anglo-Saxon culture. The former focuses on goal attainment with talented and well-trained generalists enjoying freedom in the choice of means. The latter provides trained specialists with a map of prescribed means to attain the goal. Spanish national pride swelled at the successful hosting of the sensitive Arab/Israeli peace conferences in Madrid with scarcely a week's notice. We observed the clash of an old and an emerging culture during the visit of former President Bush to El Escorial. The 22 American security agents responsible for President Bush collaborated with the Spanish security police by exhaustively anticipating every detail covered in their long planning protocol. With glazed eyes, the Spanish police indulged their guests with sorely strained patience. In the Hispanic culture, there must be room for initiative and pride in oneself in the job when we have the right people in the right place and in the right moment performing the tasks and functions they have been trained for. In emergency situations such as September 11, 2001, the accounts of those who survive show that intended actions in some circumstances are more effective than planned actions (Aust & Schnibben, 2002).

Assertiveness.   Assertiveness is the degree to which individuals are assertive, confrontational, and aggressive in social relationships. Again, the Spanish responses position the culture somewhat above the middle ($M = 4.42$) of the international comparison. The expression of desirability shows an aspiration to become slightly less aggressive ($M = 4.00$), an aspiration not unlike the average in the 60 other countries. The Spanish stereotype has some popular appeal despite previous findings by Hofstede (1980, 1983, 1991) where the culture is pictured leaning toward the feminine side and toward a conciliatory style. Often in seminars where these previous findings were discussed, Spanish executives expressed some unease with the more feminine positioning. Daily life seems replete with evidence of strong Assertiveness: me-first driving in roundabouts, flashing lights and blowing horns on the highway, speaking over one another in conversation, baiting and killing the bull in the bull ring, and boisterous labor demonstrations in the street. In the business domain, we observed collective bargaining simulations in management seminars wherein the loud bluster and histrionics almost never ended with a strike. In more than two dozen simulations, conciliation led to settlements in all but four cases.

Institutional Collectivism.   This dimension reflects the degree to which norms and practices encourage and reward collective distribution of resources and collective action.

A higher score favors more collective approaches whereas a lower score promotes a more individualistic approach. The Spanish respondents indicate that actual culture is rather individualistic ($M = 3.85$) whereas it is desirable that it becomes more Institutionally Collective ($M = 5.20$). The shift to the A band from the C band and the rise from 51st rank to 12th rank shows a drastic cultural shift under way. Much historical evidence verifies the individualistic culture. Individual action merited high status, be it in sports, arts, or public life. Hofstede's research in the 1980s evidenced the individualistic strain in the culture. For every example of status earned by collective action, you can find a half-dozen earning status with individual action. For every success in a team sport like the football World Cup, there is the standout performance of the individual athlete in the spotlight. For every famous orchestra, there is the soloist. A matador's success depends on the meticulous choreography of a team of more than a dozen assistants but the spotlight focuses on the strutting matador (Gannon, 1994). In annual studies in OECD countries during the 1980s and 1990s (Prieto, 1993), the following question was asked: "In frail moments and circumstances, do you think the well-being of citizens should depend on individual initiatives or on welfare programs backed by the community?" About two out of three Spaniards favor programs backed by the community (in the United States, two out of three respondents favor individual initiatives, and in France the distribution is 50-50). That reinforces the impression reported later of the Spanish executives' responses in the Lodge questionnaire on ideology where we observed the same situation of current individualism but future collectivism.

Gender Egalitarianism.   This dimension represents the extent to which a society minimizes gender role differences. A midscore on the 7-point scale means gender equilibrium; a low score means leaning toward male standards; a high score means an inclination toward female standards. Ranking 51st ($M = 3.01$), the Spanish middle managers pointed out that the actual culture has a bias toward "masculine oriented standards." However, when they express desirability there is a significant swing to the feminine side ($M = 4.82$), producing a 20th ranking, very close to countries showing higher "feminine oriented standards." Indeed, women are underrepresented in the workforce (about 28% in 2000 and the ratio of unemployment among women doubles compared to that of men) as well as among managers. In the urban milieu and in most regions of the country, men always take care of business affairs and initiatives, in such a way that they take care of all kinds of legal paperwork and register documents by putting their names first. The exception seems to be some regions in the northwest and the northeast where some kind of matriarchy still survives and women are the legal owners of family businesses or farms. Foreigners find it hard to interpret what it means for the status of women in that Spanish women keep their family names when they get married and very rarely use the husband's family name. It can even be confusing during introductions for visitors to identify who is married to whom. By mutual agreement, the mother's family name may appear first in the surname of the children, but this is rarely done. Finally, it is important to recall that less than 12% of our respondents were female managers.

Humane Orientation.   Humane Orientation is the degree to which society encourages and rewards individuals for being fair, altruistic, friendly, generous, caring, and kind to others. It is the idea of a friendly and compassionate society. Our respondents indicated that Spanish culture currently falls far short on this dimension ($M = 3.32$), placing Spain in a very low rank, 60th out of the 61 countries. However, more than in any other dimension, our respondents called for a drastic change in society ($M = 5.69$) where desirability is concerned. Somehow middle managers were repelled by adjectives such as *unfair, selfish, unfriendly, cheap,* and *uncaring.* Evidence of a compassionate society may be found in the fact that

Spaniards rank top in the figures of people donating organs, such that there is an excess of submissions compared to what occurs in other countries.

Power Distance.   Power Distance is defined as the degree to which people expect and agree that power should be shared in a fair manner. Ranked 14th, Spanish culture is pictured as very high ($M = 5.52$) in Power Distance. However, here again our respondents advocate for a radical change, which would rank Spain 59th and shift Spain from the cluster with the highest to the lowest Power Distance. This dimension shows the largest gap (–3.26) between what occurs at present and what should be desirable. In the Spanish language, there is a polite form of addressing those who hold an office and those who are a customer: *usted,* which has some correspondence with *thee* in English, and is different from *you* (*tu*), which is used mainly in inner circles. There is also a long tradition of formal expressions that must be used regularly during interactions held with those in authority, that is, several levels above in the hierarchy. The array of expressions has no direct translation but a certain equivalence may be "Honorable Gentleman," "Honorable Lady," "Your Grace," "Your Lordship," "Excellence," and "Distinguished," which are used very rarely in English but very often in Spanish. These expressions enhance Power Distance. But through history it was also very important to keep a distance from crowned heads and supreme rulers. Very often they needed funding or troops and the first contributors are those standing nearby. The Catholic kings banned the Sephardic Jews in 1492 because, at least in part, their majesties could not afford the huge amounts of money owed to the Jewish creditors. Keeping great distance was the sovereign decision.

In-Group Collectivism.   In-Group Collectivism reflects the degree to which individuals express pride, loyalty, and cohesiveness in their organizations and families. It may also be called tribal culture. Spain was positioned in the middle (30th) of the international comparison. The gap between actuality and desirability in the survey was the narrowest (from $M = 5.45$ to $M = 5.79$), raising Spain's rank to 21st. The identification with the local community in Spain has been legendary (Brenan, 1943). Raiders and invaders became frustrated in centuries past in their efforts to break the nonexistent national spirit, because it was so local that every village and valley had to be subjugated. In the Spanish housing market, the creation of a physical community with its amenities appears to override the concern for suburban sprawl. Even closer to home is the centrality of the family. Family surnames, which combine father's and mother's names, symbolize the close-knit family unit in Spain. Family members know by heart four family names of the father and of the mother in such a way that it is rather easy to trace back lineages when necessary. On the other hand, three out of five daughters tend to stay at home until they get married (often up to 25 years of age and sometimes older). Many "children" and parents still consider this practice wise and acceptable. When we interviewed people belonging to the same age cohort as our survey respondents, they indicated that there is no way to get divorced from older sons and daughters. If children stay at home until a rather late age, parents consider their children's extended dependency as part of responsible fatherhood and motherhood.

Uncertainty Avoidance.   This dimension defines the extent to which people strive to avoid uncertainty by reliance on social norms, rituals, and bureaucratic practices to alleviate the unpredictability of future events. The respondents place Spanish culture almost in the middle of the 61 countries surveyed ($M = 3.97$, Rank 37). Interestingly, our survey sample valued even greater Uncertainty Avoidance in their responses to the "Should Be" questions ($M = 4.76$, Rank 27). If anything typified the self-criticism of Spanish persons in the last quarter-century, it has been the concern for the risk-adverse tendencies, which seemed to stifle Spanish entrepreneurship. As the 1990s dawned, 50% of industrial capacity in Spain was in foreign hands. There were almost no Spanish multinationals. Only 25% of the patents registered in Spain in 1990 were of Spanish origin. The Spanish reluctance to assume risk and invest for the long view may have been cultivated by centuries of top-down governance and dependence on the central authority. To measure Uncertainty Avoidance our survey instruments focused on orderliness and consistency, spelling out requirements and instructions in detail, and rules and laws to cover most situations. It may be understandable, given the pace of change since 1975, that Spaniards pine for some stability even at the risk of dampening that historic Spanish spirit of adventure. This result should be viewed in the light of the rather aggressive shift our respondents expected toward more Future Orientation.

Summary Survey Results

Our middle manager respondents perceived Spanish culture as middle of the road in all dimensions except two. They saw the Spanish culture biased in the male direction in Gender Egalitarianism and selfishness and uncaring in Humane Orientation. The greatest news in the survey is the call for change anticipated in the desirable values expressed by the managers. The major shifts they called for would produce a Spanish culture much less individualistic, much more sensitive to opportunities for women, much more altruistic and caring, and much more committed to equality in power sharing. In many interesting ways Spain, as pictured in the values of the respondents, moves closer to the profile of their central and northern European neighbors. Joining the EU was no empty gesture.

Sector Results on the Nine Dimensions of Societal Culture

The means of the responding managers' societal culture ratings in the financial services sector and the food-processing sector are presented in Table 17.2. There are no significant

TABLE 17.2
"As Is" Culture Dimensions by Sectors

Culture Dimensions Means	"As Is"		"Should Be"	
	Financial Means	Food Means	Financial Food	Means
Performance Orientation	4.06	3.94	5.76	5.83
Future Orientation	3.49	3.53	5.77	5.45
Assertiveness	4.33	4.54	4.04	3.94
Institutional Collectivism	3.87	3.83	5.26	5.13
Gender Egalitarian	2.89	3.15	4.60	4.86
Humane Orientation	4.34	3.53	5.74	5.63
Power Distance	5.71	5.29	2.23	2.29
In-Group Collectivism	5.43	5.48	5.87	5.71
Uncertainty Avoidance	3.95	3.98	4.90	4.60

TABLE 17.3
Scores and Bands of Spanish Data on Leadership Scales

Leadership Dimension	Score	Band
Collaborative Team	6.26	A
Performance Orientation	6.25	A
Decisive	5.95	A
Diplomatic	5.73	A
Team Integrator	5.72	A
Nonparticipative	3.17	A
Inspirational	6.34	B
Integrity	6.11	B
Visionary	5.91	B
Administratively Competent	5.66	B
Self-Sacrificial	4.80	B
Modest	4.76	B
Humane	4.57	B
Conflict Inducer	4.24	B
Status-Conscious	4.23	B
Procedural	4.11	B
Autonomous	3.54	B
Autocratic	2.60	C
Face Saver	2.48	C
Self-Centered	1.84	C
Malevolent	1.77	C

differences on any of the nine cultural dimensions between managers in the two sectors. The largest difference in Humane Orientation (0.81 in Table 17.2) is not significant. Both samples actually perceived society in the same way and held similar desirable outcomes about what the society should be.

Survey Results on Leadership in Spain

When answering the questionnaire the managers were requested to assign a number, between 1 and 7, to 112 distinct attributes and behaviors. The meaning of value 7 was "makes a very important contribution" to making a person an outstanding leader, whereas value 1 meant "this attribute or behavior inhibits the rise of an outstanding leader." Via several samples used by the GLOBE project, these items were grouped into 21 first-order and 6 second-order leadership dimensions (cf. House et al., 2004). Here we report the results for Spain on the 21 first-order leadership dimensions (see Table 17.3).

The implicit theory of leadership among Spanish managers highlights the following attributes (in the parentheses, the average score is given): inspirational (6.34), collective team oriented (6.26), team II (team integrator) (5.72), performance orientation (6.25), integrity (6.11), decisive (5.95), visionary (5.91), diplomat (5.73), team integrator (5.72), administratively competent (5.66), self-sacrificial (4.80), modest (4.76), humane (4.57), conflict inducer (4.24), and status-conscious (4.23).

In the opposite direction, being self-centered (1.84), malevolent (1.77), autocratic (2.60), face saver (2.48) were ranked in the lowest levels, stressing that it contributes very little to what is essential in the process of becoming or being viewed as an outstanding business leader. Being procedural (4.11), autonomous (3.54), nonparticipative (3.17) are nonaligned attributes that neither impede nor facilitate.

Interestingly, the Spanish respondents expressed more negative sentiments toward the four attributes that impede outstanding leadership than did most of the other respondents from the 60 other countries. Note in Table 17.3 that the Spanish means in these four attributes (self-centered, malevolent, autocratic, and face saver) all fell to Group C internationally. By contrast, on the 14 attributes that contribute to outstanding leadership in Spain, the means fell into either Group A or B; that is, Spaniards were in fairly close agreement with those from the 60 other countries. Gutierrez et al. (1999) performed a small replication study with a somewhat expanded proportion of female respondents and essentially confirmed the results presented earlier.

Sectoral Results on Leadership in Spain

As with the results on societal culture, the financial services and food-processing middle managers in Spain showed no significant differences in how they classified attributes as contributing to or impeding outstanding leadership in Spain. The respective mean scores are presented in Table 17.4.

5. QUALITATIVE RESULTS SUPPORTING THE SURVEY RESULTS

We employed three qualitative methodologies—a content analysis of media, a focus group, and several interviews—to better grasp how leadership was understood in Spain. Following, we describe each methodology and explain what each one added to our discernment on the subject.

Media Analysis

By way of context for the media analysis, we must point out that Spanish managers have less dependence (circulation figures support this) on print media than in neighboring countries like France or the United Kingdom. In Spain, oral communication channels predominate over written communication channels. That is, news from the broadcast media reaches larger audiences than printed news by a four to one ratio. Among many top managers this phenomenon may in part be explained by their having grown up in a continuous climate of suspicion against the press and sensitive printed texts. For centuries, Spanish judges have been perceived as being against freedom of expression and even, in the 1990s, they have been perceived as favoring values such as order and authority and depreciating values such as individual freedom and solidarity (Gomez de Liaño, 1999; Navarro, 1994, 1995).

TABLE 17.4
Leadership Dimensions per Sector

Leadership Dimension	Financial Means	Food Means
Collaborative Team	6.27	6.24
Performance Orientation	6.32	6.16
Decisive	5.93	5.90
Diplomatic	5.75	5.69
Team Integrator	5.66	5.56
Nonparticipative	3.30	3.01
Inspirational	6.37	6.31
Integrity	6.01	6.25
Visionary	5.85	5.98
Administratively Competent	5.70	5.62
Self-Sacrificial	4.78	4.83
Modest	4.69	4.85
Humane	4.50	4.66
Conflict Inducer	4..41	4.02
Status-Conscious	4.36	4.06
Procedural	4.16	4.03
Autonomous	3.58	3.49
Autocratic	2.80	2.33
Face Saver	2.49	2.48
Self-Centered	1.92	1.74
Malevolent	1.82	1.71

A second point of context is the perception that the choice of a newspaper by Spanish managers is a political act. In large organizations, the main newspapers are bought by the organization itself and made available to the top managers and civil servants. A second direct way of supporting favorites in the mass media is the pattern of placement of advertising campaigns. Currently there is a correlation above 0.75 between newspapers and magazines bought by the firm, and newspapers and magazines where the firm publishes advertising and circulates marketing strategies.

We used the four newspapers and one magazine in our media analysis. Our sources are the OJD (Oficina Justificación Difusión), AIMC (Asociación para la Investigación Medios de Comunicación), and Diplomaticnet. We studied the following newspapers and periodicals:

- *El Pais,* newspaper; in 2001, per day, the circulation was 433,617; enjoys the leading market share of 14.14%; liberal in the European sense.
- *El Mundo,* newspaper; in 2001, per day, the circulation was 312,366 (second in market share with 8.88%); its evolution parallels the conservative Popular Party's growth, often targeting Socialistic Party leaders.
- *ABC,* newspaper; in 2001, per day, the circulation was 279.050 (7.56% market share); holds conservative, monarchic, and Catholic views.
- *Expansion,* economic newspaper; in 2001, per day, the circulation was 52,645; (1.31% market share); specializes in economy, stock market, and business issues, where it ranks first.

- *Actualidad Economica,* magazine; in 2001, per week, the circulation was 22,739; it ranks 23rd among weekly magazines; devoted to economy and business issues.

We examined the four newspapers for two periods of 2 weeks separated by a 3-week gap. We examined two issues of the weekly magazine, took a 3-week break, and then examined another two issues. All reports that had anything to do with leadership or even referred parenthetically to leadership were marked and selected for an informal analysis.

The content analysis of these newspapers and magazines showed that the term *leader* (*lider*) is not used in Spanish when referring to top managers or CEOs, whereas the more common terms are *executive, general director,* and *big boss.* The term *leader* is used almost exclusively to identify trade union leaders. Also, it is used to identify leaders of a party, but not ministers nor the prime minister. Again, it is used to comment about religious leaders and also "football leader" when talking about the champion team in the Spanish league. During the dictatorship, the title used to refer to General Franco was Caudillo (Leader), and during the monarchy, the term used to identify the Spanish king is *sovereign.* Both expressions are rather unusual in democratic or republican systems. Clearly the term *lider* in Spanish has a restrictive meaning (Prieto, 1989). There is a verb in Spanish, *dirigir,* that just means "to lead" and the derived gerund, *dirigente* (leading person). It has created some problems in the communication process because there are two parallel terms, *lider* and *dirigente,* but they are used separately and in different contexts by managers.

Given the semantic situation in Spanish, managers do not view themselves as "leaders" but as "executives," "supervisors," "superintendents," and "bosses." The term *manager* and the descriptor *charismatic* (which we so often find joined in the Anglo-Saxon press) sound strange to the Spanish ear. Leaders belong to trade unions, the church, the sports, and the army. This is the confusing background in the language when talking about managerial roles and functions in the GLOBE project.

Focus Group

Setting, Data Gathering, and Analysis Method.   During a weeklong organizational behavior module at the training center of Euroforum in the El Escorial, 70 participants (including 8 women) were scheduled to study leadership. All were midmanagers from over 50 Spanish national as well as foreign multinational companies in a wide range of industries including financial services, food processing, and telecommunications. We turned a 90-minute period (which lasted almost 2 hours) into one large focus group and voice-recorded the entire session. The instructor diligently recorded the group comments on flip charts. The instructor's notes and the audiotape served as sources of data for the initial report, which was written within days of the focus group. Later, editing searched for patterns in the focus group report.

Insights From the Focus Group: Management.   Because we started with the task of identifying "management" attributes and defining the concept, that material appears here first as context for the attributes and definition of "leadership." Characteristically, the sample of managers generated a long list of attributes and many partial definitions of management. The group's comments can be grouped into two categories: management attributes, for example, efficient, pragmatic, flexible, and definitional elements, for example, achieving objectives, follow-up/control, selling ideas. As the group members added attributes or definitional elements, each preceding item seemed to be accepted without contest. However, no consensus emerged on another theme discussed at length by the group. Was management earned or given? In other words was it deserved or delegated? The majority of comments favored the classical organizational formalities but a vocal majority insisted on the more modern bottom-up view. At the end, the instructor tried to elicit the consensus definition of management by using what appeared to be the themes with the most group support: "Management means directing persons and groups to achieve results in line with objectives chosen or approved by the owners." The summary statement won modest approval but major definitional difficulties remained unresolved. Many said "management" would mean different things depending on the organizational level where it was practiced—lower, middle, or top. Even at the top, many believed "management" would be defined differently depending on the relationship between the owners and managers in what concerns direction taking, initiative and approval.

Though some participants would imitate the instructor and use *management* in speaking Spanish, the majority used the more pure Spanish words *gestión* for the activity of management and *dirección* for the persons in management. This is very much like French usage.

Insights From the Focus Group: Leadership.   It was more difficult to get down to a tight definition of leadership. Again, guided by the protocol, we began with attributes, for example, charismatic, assumes risk, can gain trust of individuals/group, and then moved to the elements of the leadership definition, for example, catalyst, draws people, saviour.

Speaking about "leadership," by contrast with the discussion on "management," the group totally ignored organizational goal orientation. There was no reference to owners or superordinate bosses. The leader's relationship to the organization was seen in marked contrast to the manager's. The leader is not bound by organizational policies/procedures and he (the masculine was always used!) sells his goals. Furthermore, he emerged by delegation but heightening the personal initiative: "assumes direction … is born of the group … is recognized, acknowledged, and accepted by the group."

For the focus group, the leader's personal attributes differ from the manager's pattern in emotional content and intensity: "passionate … charming … personable … charismatic … enthusiastic … perseverant and stubborn … sees long term … confident … is the soul of the company … the saviour." These last two attributes have a religious connotation—a reference point alluding to the Catholic tradition on the role of leading persons in critical moments for the community. The leadership activities or processes cited included some top-down activities like "vision-taking/presenting … setting the long-term direction/challenge." These expressions also strongly imply more collegial, or at least less hierarchic behaviors toward the followers: "identifies himself with the group … can gain trust of the individuals in the group … involves others … goes in front … draws people … plays a catalyst role … address emotions and not rational thoughts … able to make people follow him … moves others, enhancing a sense of responsibility and duty … has followers who don't rely on rewards or punishments." If anything seemed close to endorsement as a definition of leadership by the majority, it was the act of "drawing people to follow by getting in front with a long-term challenge."

Distinguishing leadership from management would appear to be the leader's act of getting in front and challenging (more emotional than rational) toward the long term. By contrast, management seemed to be less personally risky, relying on relatively short-term means–ends logic, imbedded in a hierarchy of delegated, specific, goal-targeted tasks. Managerial actions seem to be of hierarchic nature, whereas leadership actions seem often to be more collegial.

The focus group members seemed more comfortable with the definitional attempts vis-à-vis the manager, almost as if they were looking in the mirror at themselves or recalling personal development norms associated with their presence in a management development program. Their contributions on leadership seemed remote and neither autobiographical nor drawn from some ideal model for themselves.

Interviews

Data Gathering Method and Analysis. One of the authors trained an assistant by implementing the original interview protocol demonstration, an hour-long, tape-recorded interview with a middle manager known to both parties. The assistant then interviewed and taped six more Spanish middle managers of his acquaintance, using the same protocol. This protocol had a directive tone using several questions comparing management and leadership before moving on to examples of leadership. The assistant then reviewed his tapes and summarized the themes he had heard. Then the audiotapes were transcribed. Two streams of analysis followed with the tapes and the transcriptions. First, the tapes were analyzed by three other assistants both horizontally (by protocol question) and vertically (by respondent for patterns or emerging themes). Second, one of the authors repeated the analysis using the transcriptions.

Insights From the Interviews. Given that the structure of the interview protocol imposed the themes on the respondents, the best patterns emerging from the tapes seemed to be the similarities and differences in the perspectives of the interviewees. Although there was wide consensus, for instance, on the attribute "tough-minded," interviewees were split on the question of whether leaders were a product of nature or nurture.

It was not the intended purpose, but the interviewees did cross the line between borders and identified leaders from business and nonbusiness domains who they understood would be familiar to an international team of researchers. This approach was congruent with the information interviewees had about the GLOBE study on leadership patterns. In this way they singled out well-known leaders among familiar employers, rulers, or authorities. So, during the interview, two managers focused their comments on the CEOs of their firms. Two focused on colleague executives in the same firm, though not direct superiors. The two remaining concentrated on the political domain with Francisco Franco (dictator from 1939 to 1975), Felipe GonzÒlez (prime minister 1982–1996), King Juan Carlos I (1975–), José M. Aznar (prime minister 1996–, then opposition leader), Hitler, and the trio of Clinton, Bush, and Perot (the American election had just been widely reported in the Spanish press).

Despite their different reference points, they seemed to all agree that the leadership style need not be hard or aggressive. It may be soft and nurturing and at the same time be strong and self-confident. Most, though not all, saw the leader as triggered to action by something negative in the environment. Even those who identified leaders who were at the top of organizations denied that position in the hierarchy had anything to do with the emergence of the leader. Despite their different reference points, the interviewees saw some potential downside to leadership if the leader dominated the ideas of the followers or, if the leader caused the followers to attach themselves to the person and not to the cause, thereby condemning the cause to die with him.

The attributes mentioned by the interviewees overlapped substantially with those mentioned in the focus group and did not include any disagreements among the interviewees. One respondent put special stress on a pattern of attributes not so emphasized elsewhere: "The leader is humble and recognizes his mistakes and never does things to benefit himself." Another interviewee added the sensitive note that, "while the manager may be respected by his followers, the leader is loved." In a similar vein, one interviewee said that a manager "gets people to do things because they have to, whereas the leader gets people to do things because they want to."

Another debate divided the interviewees (on an issue raised in the focus group). Was the leader a leader in all aspects of life, personal as well as professional? The minority left room for that possibility but the majority thought that the leader typically sacrificed other aspects of the cause on which he was a leader. It was seen simply as a matter of energy that prevented the leader from having a good equilibrium between personal and professional life, for example. However, following Spanish standards, the private lives of top political leaders very rarely are the subject of a cover page in newspapers and magazines.

6. REFLECTION ON THE BROADER VALUES AND NORMS FROM THE QUALITATIVE STUDIES

In the 1990s, the focus group members and interviewees expected leaders would likely be seen as scarce, counterculture people. Neither the focus group members nor the interviewees seemed to look on themselves as leaders. They tended to look further up the hierarchy for a leadership role, even though some interviewees denied relevance to hierarchy. Most often cited as an outstanding leadership act was King Juan Carlos's brave act in 1981 of standing up to the colonels and thereby saving the nascent democracy. It was the commander in chief reigning over lower-ranking officers. Again, the political perspective corroborates the core idea of leadership. It is important to note that the king's act was position-based from the top of the hierarchy and triggered by a threatening environment launched by some top military men. The king rallied the military men who were not in the plot, the politicians, and the citizens to accept the challenge of making the new democratic system work in the long run despite the short-term difficulties.

Indeed, there are outstanding individuals in Spain (golfers, matadors, mystics, artists, musicians, tennis players, etc.), but these are not seen as leaders because they may have only devotees. The Catholic tradition does not favor the idea of an individual leadership (Prieto, 1989) but of collegiate authorities. It is the Protestant tradition that favors the idea of an individual entrepreneurship. Also, the fate of leaders in Spanish history has been to win and become lords or kings or to lose and get out of the way of the hands of the executioner. This same background is common to British and French monarchies throughout history. The consequence is that Spaniards have some difficulties in identifying actual leaders or entrepreneurs. There is almost surprise when someone pops out of the pack with an entrepreneurial and leadership venture.

In short, leadership as understood by our focus group members and our interviewees would not be a common phenomenon or expectation, given the Spanish values and beliefs. Standout individual acts may be common but not leadership behavior because it has a hierarchic dimension: The person at the top (or "above me") has to be able to lead when the situation (something threatening in the environment, for the most part) calls for that behavior. The 1990s generation of Spanish managers still have memories of the 40 years of dictatorship, which ended only in 1975. The youngest of our respondents were in their midteens when Franco died. In some ways, that period may have dampened what may have been earlier leadership tendencies and expectations. Spain and the Habsburgs dominated much of the world five centuries ago, in part because the second- and third-born were ready to go out of the country and lead specific regions. The privileges of the first-born prevailed in the distribution of properties and the receipt of support. The second- and third-born have authority over specific regions (they were considered "viceroys"). This tradition still survives in the transmission system of the aristocracy (in decline) and in the succession within the monarchy. However, from the 1960s to the 1990s, the dictatorship and the Catholic educational programs in schools have decoupled Spanish executives from the risk-taking mentalities and the initiatives that favor entrepreneurship and leadership.

In many ways, Spain in the 1990s is still in the post-Franco transition. Over the past 15 or 20 years, we have used the George Cabot Lodge ideology questionnaire (*Harvard Business Review,* 1975) as an in-class exercise with Spanish executives. Consistently, they identify the prevailing as well as the preferred ideology as individualistic (though in declining proportions recently). However, they see the ideology emerging in the next 5 years as communitarian. That pattern is consistent with the original Lodge results with American executives. The Spanish executives depart from original American results in response to the question: "Which ideology better fits the problems to be faced in the future?" Whereas the Americans revert to their preferred individualism, the Spaniards in large majorities identified communitarian ideology as the most relevant for the future of Spain. It is, maybe, the consequence of Catholic as well as social-democratic views of what is appropriate for the society. This perspective is also favored by the ideology that prevails within the EU and the financial and institutional support of policies fostering the extension of social rights (much less common in the United States) as a societal commitment once civil rights are guaranteed. The European Social Funds system that exists within the EU highlights the idea that the reduction of social and economic differences between member states and among regions is very important for the feeling of cohesion and belongingness. Core values may indeed be in transition from the traditional individualism, but the passage is far from complete.

Research Limitations and Lessons for Future Research

Though our respondent pool may be accurately labeled *Spanish* and we assume a culturally homogeneous response set, we leave uncovered the potentially interesting regional differences as stressed earlier by the likes of Brenan (1943) in his social commentary and Cummings, Harnett, and Stevens (1971) in their research. Future researchers may wish to explore the more nuanced approach by checking the differences among residents of the four other key autonomous regions aside from Madrid.

Because the female representation in our sample was only 12% (which accurately reflected the gender mix at the mid-manager level in the two business sectors studied at the time of the data gathering), we can say nothing about gender differences. With the feminization of management occurring in Spain at an accelerating pace in the past decade, future researchers may well find different results based on gender. We hypothesize the direction of influence will be to reinforce the major moves from "As Is" to "Should Be" in the descriptors of the societal culture, as well as to reinforce the strong rejection of the four unattractive leadership characteristics.

With the methodologies employed, we leave unexplored the impact of a historical force such as the 40-year Franco dictatorship on the societal culture of Spain. We reasoned how it might have negatively affected the reliability of social science research in that era through intimidation of respondents. The impact on culture is another thing. As in European countries emerging from communist domination or the African nations earlier shedding the colonial yoke, it is not idle curiosity to inquire whether such a generations-long influence changed the culture at its core, changed culture only on the fringes, temporarily repressed cultural expression, or left no traceable impact on the culture. The risk of close proximity to dramatic events is that their influence is overvalued. Future researchers, employing methodologies sensitive to longitudinal changes, may find we have treated culture as too fragile and changeable.

Future researchers in Spain and elsewhere in Europe may wish to monitor the resolution between the historical skepticism over charismatic leaders and the enthusiasm expressed for each dimension of charisma by some academics and indeed by our sample (which parallels the sentiments by other European samples). Some seem to recognize only a positive connotation to the concept. Throughout history, charismatic political leaders in Europe as well as Mediterranean countries have too often been a source of initially stable governments, which later promoted a long series of bloody, criminal, or belligerent actions. It has been the case, in this century, of Bin Laden, Franco, Gadafi, Hassan II, Hitler, Milosevic, Mussolini, Stalin, and Yeltsin. Each of these leaderships combined visionary as well as inspirational perspectives and quietly some citizens became subjects and others become victims. This is the Damoclean sword for dissidents or minority groups under a charismatic leadership in top government or, by inference, in management posts. This reality should at least temper the enthusiasm of some foreign observers who highlight the short-term advantages of charismatic leadership without paying too much attention to the disastrous long-term consequences. From the Spanish optics, when examining charismatic leaders around the world, they too often built their regimes on mass slaughter or reckless destruction of dissidents. Many of the 20th century's immigrants to North America or Western Europe fled from charismatic and sovereign leaders reigning in their home countries.

The focus group and interviews reminded us that in countries with high Individualism and strong Uncertainty Avoidance, researchers might have to distinguish clearly between leadership and entrepreneurship. It seems easy to assert that every act of leadership is not entrepreneurial, but every entrepreneurial act is a source or a symptom of leadership.

In countries such as Spain with large Power Distance, it might be important to be sensitive to the hierarchical character of expectations for leadership behaviors. Great clarity is required in the reference point for our leadership inquiry. If our reference point is in the business firm itself, we will have to specify whether we are focusing on leadership at the top or if we are pointing to the hierarchical techno-structure. Use of such adjectives as *outstanding* will tend to turn attention to the pinnacle of the hierarchy.

The practicalities of doing survey research in Spain (and probably other countries) prompt us to worry out loud that the length of our instruments with their much nuanced shades of meaning in translation may have affected the quality of responses. Many of our respondents certainly voiced their displeasure over the imposition on them. In the search for the greatest validity, we may have inadvertently paid a price in reliability. In any case, future researchers using such methods at least in Spain have been warned.

Implications for Non-Spanish Executives Doing Business in Spain

Without falling into the error of confounding levels of analysis, a visiting executive seeking to be cross-culturally effective in Spain may draw lessons from the descriptions of the societal culture and from the factors identified by our respondents as enhancing the probability of outstanding leadership. It would, of course, be an insult to a Spanish host to stereotype the individual with the expectation of one-to-one correspondence between her or his behavior and the societal culture or our leadership profile research results. Often the experienced international executive can employ the cultural and leadership profiles as working hypotheses guiding her or his observation, inquiry, discussion and even tactical behavior. Such a learning strategy can be a powerful aid in the quest for effectiveness in a new culture. To the degree that one finds our results cogent, one might benefit from experimentation as in the following four examples.

First, in a general sense we assert that mañana has arrived. With all our talk of transition and aspiration for change, one should not assume a time lag before our research results become relevant. Assume rather that the transitions are complete and aspirations fulfilled. See our closing remarks in the next section for some specifics about how this is currently reflected in business practices. Such has been the thrust, zest, and energy behind the transitions and aspirations that to assume anything different would be foolhardy.

If one senses a moral tone in the fact that two of the four top leadership characteristics identified by our Spanish respondents are "inspirational" and "integrity," and that the four attributes that inhibit the rise of an outstanding leader are "self-centered," "malevolent," "autocratic," and "face saver," you would be right. Notice how often conversations take a philosophical turn and move from "what" and "how" to the more challenging "why."

In a fascinating chapter which speaks of bullfighting as a metaphor for Spanish culture, Martin Gannon (1994) points to the liturgy of the bull ring as evocative of the Spanish habit of controlling uncertainty and risk, by the use of ritual. A sensitive guest will be on the watch for the social or business protocol that may be a buffer important to the host's remaining comfort in her or his uncertainty avoidance.

The high value given to In-Group Collectivism among societal cultural characteristics suggests that guest executives not be presumptuous too early about being accepted into the "club." A related faux pas would be for the visitor to "foul his own nest" by casual criticism or expressions of disloyalty to his or her own country, company, and so forth.

7. FINAL REMARKS

Starting in the mid-1970s, Spanish society has approached and overcome important challenges, risks, and changes in a very deep and widely spread democratization process in the country. There has been a transition:

- From a dictatorship toward a monarchic democracy.
- From a centralized to a decentralized political and economic system.
- From ruling roles of military men at the head of the state to rulers in simulations, and in ceremonies, or in NATO or UN peacekeeping forces.
- From a quite isolated and nationalist country toward a rather open and European-minded country after the entrance into the EU in 1986. Nationalist views still survive in very specific regions where close horizons delimit the happy hunting grounds.
- From a strong and conservative influence of the Catholic Church in the private and public life of people and institutions toward a nondenominational state and a rather tolerant society.

The GLOBE study findings—particularly the reported aspirations for change in "As Is" to "Should Be" in Spanish business culture—show what Spanish managers perceive that the Spanish culture sanctions. A foreign businessperson wishing to interact effectively with Spanish colleagues or organizations would be wise to recognize the following deeply held beliefs:

- A bureaucratic approach: by observing as many norms and procedures as might be available because this is a strategic approach to avoid risks and uncertainties.
- A better quality of work and life: Stimulating collaborators and employees to attain higher life standards, superior work habits, and higher performance.
- A climate of industrial democracy: By pushing the participation and loyal involvement of employees in autonomous and semiautonomous groups, identifying themselves with higher quality goods and services produced satisfactorily.
- Altruism and fairness: Through informal channels of communication and collaboration in the workplace, many daily tasks and activities do not fall to the responsibility of the individual but on the work group.
- Egalitarianism in employment: Favoring some policies of affirmative action and support for women rights and (employer) obligations in the interface between work and family life.
- Civil and social rights of employees: Overcoming the past pattern of severe restrictions to civil rights and enhancing welfare measures and public health as well as educational assistance to employed and unemployed citizens.
- Mutual respect and social equality: Reducing the range of salary differences within the same firm or sector, reducing regional differences and eliminating social hierarchies and historical privileges.

Finally, it is important to highlight that the results obtained through this GLOBE study support the hypothesis that leadership styles may be derived from implicit theories of leadership arising from societal priorities and comprehensive conceptions rooted in the culture.

ACKNOWLEDGMENTS

We wish to acknowledge the invaluable assistance of Manuel Rodriguez Cassanueva, founder of Euroforum, and Richard Mukiur, then at Fundesco, Madrid, as well as the research support from Bentley College and Complutense University.

REFERENCES

Alvarez-Junco, J., & Shubert, A. (2000). *Spanish history since 1808.* New York: Edward Arnold.

ArnÒiz Villena, A. (2000). *Prehistoric Iberia: Genetics, anthropology and linguistics.* New York: Kluwer Academic Plenum.

Aust, S., & Schnibben, C. (2002). *11 de Septiembre: Historia de un ataque terrorista* [September 11th, Story of a terrorist attack]. Barcelona, Spain: Círculo de Lectores.

Bass, B. M. (1968). *A preliminary report on manifest preferences in six cultures for participate management* (Tech. Rep. No. 21). Rochester, NY: Office for Naval Research, Management Research Center, College of Business Administration, University of Rochester.

Bass, B. M., & Burger, P. C. (1979). *Assessment of managers: An international comparison.* New York: The Free Press.

Bedoya, J. G. (2002, December 8). Buatizados sí ... pero¿cuÒntos catolicos quedan? [Baptized, yes ... but still how many Catholics?). *El Pais,* p. 6.

Boldy D., Jain, S., & Northey, K. (1993). What makes an effective European manager? A case study of Sweden, Belgium, Germany, and Spain. *Management International Review, 33,* 157–169.

Brenan, G. (1943). *The Spanish labyrinth.* New York: Macmillan.

Carr, R. (2000). *Spain, a history.* Oxford, England: Oxford University Press.

Chislett, W. (1994). *Spain: At a turning point.* Madrid, Spain: Banco Central Hispano.

Coverdale, J. F. (1979). *The political transformation of Spain after Franco.* New York: Praeger.

Cummings, L. L., Harnett, D. L., & Stevens, O. J. (1971). Risk, fate, conciliation, and trust: An international study of attitudinal differences among executives. *Academy of Management Journal, 14,* 285–304.

FernÒndez Arenas, J. (1978). *Imagen del arte mozÒrabe* [Mozarabic art images]. Barcelona, Spain: Poligrafa.

Fuentes, C. (1992). *The buried mirror.* New York: Houghton Mifflin.

Gannon, M. J. (1994). *Understanding global cultures.* Thousand Oaks, CA: Sage.

Gómez-Liaño, J. (1999). *Pasos perdidos: Confesiones en carne viva* [Lost steps: Confessions when my wounds are raw]. Madrid, Spain: Temas de Hoy.

Gutierrez, C., Prieto, J. M., & O'Connell, J. J. (1999). Prototipo de liderazgo en mandos intermedios espanoles [Prototype of leadership in Spanish middle management]. *Revista de Psicología del Trabajo y de las Organizaciones, 15,* 385–406.

Haire, M., Ghiselli, E. E., & Porter, L. W. (1966). *Managerial thinking: An international study.* New York: Wiley.

Hanges, P. J., Dickson, M. W., & Sipe, M. T. (2004). Rationale for GLOBE statistical analyses: Societal rankings and test of hypotheses. In R. J. House, P. J. Hanges, M. Javidan, P. Dorfman, & V. Gupta (Eds.), *Leadership, culture, and organizations: The GLOBE study of 62 societies* (pp. 219–234). Thousand Oaks, CA: Sage.

Harrison, M. (1974). *The roots of witchcraft.* Secaucus, NJ: Citadel Press.

Hofstede, G. (1980). *Culture's consequences: International differences in work-related values.* Beverley Hills, CA: Sage.

Hofstede, G. (1983). National cultures in four dimensions: A research-based theory of culture differences among nations. *International Studies of Management and Organizations, 1–2,* 46–74.

Hofstede, G. (1991). *Cultures and organizations: Software on the mind.* London: McGraw-Hill.

Hooper, J. (1995). *The new Spaniards.* Harmondsworth, England: Penguin.

House, R. J., Hanges, P. J., Javidan, M., Dorfman, P. W., Gupta, V., & Globe Associates. (2004). *Culture, leadership, and organizations: The GLOBE study of 62 societies.* Thousand Oaks, CA: Sage.

House, R. J., Hanges, P. J., Ruiz-Quintanilla, S. A., Dorfman, P. W., Javidan, M., Dickson, M., et al. (1999). Cultural influences on leadership and organizations: Project GLOBE. In W. Mobley, M. J. Gessner & V. Arnold (Eds.), *Advances in global leadership* (Vol. 1, pp. 171–234). Stamford, CT: JAI.

Kluckholm, F. R., & Strodtbeck, F. L. (1961). *Variations in value orientations.* New York: Row Peterson.

Lawlor, T., Rigby, M., & Yruela, M. P. (1998). *Contemporary Spain: Essays and texts on politics, economics, education, employment and society.* Reading, MA: Addison-Wesley.

Lewis, D. A. (1992). A comparison of attitudes of Spanish and American quality assurance managers. *Production and Inventory Management Journal, 1,* 42–45.

Lopez, S. L., Talens, J., &Villanueva, D. (Eds.). (1994). *Critical practices in post-Franco Spain.* Minneapolis: University of Minnesota Press.

McFarlin, D.B., Sweeney, P. D., & Cotton, J. L. (1993). Attitudes toward employee participation in decision making: A comparison of European and American managers in a United States multinational company, *Human Resource Management, 31*(4), 363–383.

Navarro, J. (1994). *La judicatura* [The judiciary]. Madrid, Spain: Acento.

Navarro, J. (1995). *Manos sucias* [Dirty hands]. Madrid, Spain: Temas de Hoy.

O'Connell, J., & Prieto, J. M. (1998). Una lectura vertical de la Investigación Transcultural sobre la dirección de empresa: el caso español [Vertical reading of cross-cultural research on management in Spain] (translated into Spanish by Celia Gutierrez Valero). *Revista de Psicologóa del Trabajo y de las Organizaciones, 14,* 51–63.

Organization for Economic Cooperation and Development. (1998). *OECD economic surveys: Spain.* Paris: Author.

Page, N. R., & Wiseman, R. L. (1993). Supervisory behavior and worker satisfaction in the United States, Mexico, and Spain. *The Journal of Business Communication, 30*(2), 161–180.

Pavett, C., & Morris, T. (1995). Management styles within a multinational corporation: A five country comparative study. *Human Relations, 48*(10), 1171–1191.

Pérez, S. (1997). *Banking on privilege: The politics of Spanish financial reform.* Ithaca, NY: Cornell University Press.

Prieto, J. M. (1989). Liderazgo como enredo en la empresa española [Leadership as a red tape in Spanish firms]. *Boletín de Estudios Económicos, 14*(136), 35–46.

Prieto, J. M. (1990). *Visión de conjunto de los distintos programas de apoyo a la puesta en marcha de pequeñas empresas en España* [Overview of programs supporting start up firms in Spain]. Berlin: CEDEFOP.

Prieto, J. M. (1993). La calidad de Vida, Comentario [Quality of life, a comment]. *Revista de Psicología Social, 8*(1), 119–124.

Prieto, J. M., & Martínez, R. (1997). Those things yonder are not giants, but decision makers in international teams. In P. C. Earley & M. Erez (Eds.), *New perspectives on international industrial/ organizational psychology* (pp. 410–445). San Francisco: New Lexington Press.

Ross, C. J. (1997). *Contemporary Spain: A handbook.* New York: Edward Arnold.

SÒnchez Soler, M. (2002). *Las sotanas del PP: El pacto entre la iglesia y la derecha Española.* [Soutanes in the Popular Party: Agreement between the church and the right wing in Spain]. Madrid, Spain: Temas de Hoy.

Solsten, E., & Meditz, S. W. (1990). *Spain: A country study.* Washington, DC: Library of Congress.

Tamames, R. (1994). *Introducción a la economía española* [Introduction to the Spanish Economy]. Madrid, Spain: Alianza Editorial.

Trompenaars, F. (1993). *Riding the waves of culture: Understanding diversity in business.* London: Economist Books.

Tussell, J. (2000). *El gobierno de Jose Maria Aznar (1996–2000)* [Government of Jose Maria Aznar: 1996–2000]. Barcelona, Spain: Crítica.

Tussell, J. (2001). *Historia de España, la España actual* [Spanish history: Contemporary Spain]. Barcelona, Spain: Labor.

LATIN AMERICA CLUSTER

The Latin America cluster in the GLOBE Research Program consisted of the largest number of countries in any one cluster; namely, Argentina, Bolivia, Brazil, Colombia, Costa Rica, Ecuador, El Salvador, Guatemala, Mexico, and Venezuela. Three of these countries, Argentina, Colombia, and Mexico, are included in this volume.

The Latin America cluster scored high on only the In-Group Collectivism dimension of societal culture. It was in the midrange for Assertiveness, Gender Egalitarianism, Human Orientation, and Power Distance. It scored low on Future Orientation, Institutional Collectivism, Performance Orientation, and Uncertainty Avoidance (House et al., 2004).

Outstanding leaders in Latin America are expected to be Charismatic/Value Based and Team Oriented. Participative leadership and Humane Oriented leadership are also positively endorsed. Between-country variation is high for Participative leadership and low for Humane Oriented leadership. The range of variation of endorsement for Autonomous leadership is fairly wide from negative in Colombia, neutral in Mexico, and positive in Argentina, for example. Self-Protective leadership is generally tolerated but not positively endorsed.

The most common feature running through the countries of this cluster is that of languages: Spanish and Portuguese. The cluster is also generally known for personalism, particularism, and paternalism (Osland, De Franco, & Osland, 1999). Rule of law is often moderated by personal connections. The concepts of in-group and out-group are quite strong.

REFERENCES

House, R. J., Hanges, P. J., Javidan, M., Dorfman, P. W., Gupta, V., & GLOBE Associates. (2004). *Culture, leadership, and organizations: The GLOBE study of 62 societies.* Thousand Oaks, CA: Sage.

Osland, J. S., De Franco, S., & Osland, A. (1999). Organizational implications of Latin American culture: Lessons for the expatriate manager. *Journal of Management Inquiry, 8*(2), 219–234.

18

▼▼▼▼▼▼▼

Argentina: Crisis of Guidance

Carlos Altschul
Marina Altschul
Mercedes López
Maria Marta Preziosa
Flavio Ruffolo
Universidad de Buenos Aires

Argentina, "It is a difficult country" (Schvarzer, in Sábato, 1988, p. 7). Argentina had shown extraordinary growth at the start of the 20th century after stagnation for about 60 years. In the 1990s it underwent major structural changes by developing democratic practices and liberal economic policies. However, the reforms produced neither the economic nor the social results that were expected. The current situation (1995) is characterized by a major debt burden polit- ical and social uncertainty, corporate turbulence, and great personal strain, but growing exports and conservative fiscal policies *that* have helped ease the situation, and the economy is growing steadily, industrial and construction indicators have shown steady growth and unemployment has decreased sensibly. Explanations for the crisis comprise macroeconomic factors, lack of regulatory practices, political mismanagement, and administrative corruption. In May 2003, a new administration was elected which instituted plans and is developing a new balance of political, social, and economic goals and has since taken the country out of economic default, and in search of a new balance. Three major improvements are generally accepted: the renegotiation of the foreign debt, the strengthening of the Supreme Court, and the government's policy on human rights.

This chapter presents a synthesis of Argentine history, culture, and leadership that is meant to help develop an understanding of the idiosyncratic nature of management roles in Argentine business. In particular it deals with the dilemma of leadership that faces the task to develop coherent national and regional strategies in order to meet the global challenges after many decades of economic turbulence.

1. CURRENT DEMOGRAPHY

Located in the southern hemisphere of the American continent (Latin America), Argentina is the eighth-largest country on the planet. It shares borders with Chile, Bolivia, Paraguay, Brazil, and Uruguay and can be portioned into five geographic regions: The pampas and prairies in the north-east which form the economic center of the country, Mesopotamia, the central low lands, the Andean zone in the East, and Patagonia in the south. Most of the country lies in the temperate zone. The total population is 36.1 million and 34% of them inhabit Buenos Aires, the capital city.

Most Argentines come from European ancestry and few aborigines subsist as separate ethnic groups. At the turn of the 19th to 20th century, four million immigrants arrived, 45% from Italy, 32% from Spain, as well as from England, Germany, France, Switzerland, Denmark, Poland, Russia, the Middle East, and Japan; for the past 40 years, immigration from neighboring countries increased, driving a process of Latin-Americanization.

Quality of life may be measured by the facts that Argentina has the highest amount of telephone main lines, and is second highest in personal computers and mobile phones in Latin America. It has the smallest average family size in the region; has 2.7 physicians per 1,000 people, the highest rate for Latin American countries; and life expectancy is 73 years. Still, at the time of the research project, it has the highest rate of unemployment in the GLOBE sample with the exception of Morocco (House et al., 2004).

Argentina is self-sufficient in oil and gas; agriculture is its principal industry and it produces grains and cereals; cattle and sheep are raised on the vast fertile plains of the Central region. Revenues from tourism have grown significantly. Substantial quantities of sugar, fruit, wine, tobacco, cotton, and other internationally marketable products are also produced. Major manufacturing industries include agro industries, food processing, petrochemicals, textiles, chemicals, paper and cellulose, metallurgical (including steel), as well as trucks and automobiles. Between 1995 and 1999, Argentina had a trade surplus against Brazil (mostly manufactured goods), and a significant trade deficit with the United States and the European Economic Union, mostly for food and fuels (CEPAL Foreign Trade data base, 2001).

2. CURRENT POLITICAL SYSTEM

Argentina is a federal republic with 23 provinces and a Federal Capital. The government includes the executive, legislative, and judicial branches. National and provincial governments are democratically chosen and the Constitution of 1853, its latest reform dates back to 1994, is the oldest in Latin America and follows the North American model. Its executive branch includes an all-powerful president; the National Congress consists of two legislative chambers; and the judicial power is exercised by a Supreme Court and courts in the entire territory. Provincial governors are chosen by direct ballot. Women were granted the vote in 1951.

Education plays a high-impact socializing role. The work force has levels of competence comparable to those found in developed countries. Unions were created over sixty years ago and their power has decreased; they have a positive attitude towards foreign investment. Union membership is voluntary and collective bargaining is carried out freely. New ad hoc spontaneous forms of protest and redress have grown, however, since 2003, as has union activity.

3. HISTORICAL DEVELOPMENTS AND THEIR ECONOMICAL IMPACT

Independent Argentina emerged between 1810 and 1816 with a revolutionary war process against Spain. Efforts to institutionally organize the region failed due to an extended confrontation with influential *porteños* (i.e. inhabitants of Buenos Aires), who wanted to hold on to National political power, eliminate federalism and the political autonomy of provinces. Political fragmentation based on irreconcilable positions lasted until 1862, with cruel civil wars interspersed with periods of law and order. In 1853, the provinces agreed to sanction a National Constitution. A federal presidential republic was instituted, but the agreement was fractured and it took many years for the country to reach unification.

Provinces (i.e., the Argentine local political administrative units) were lead by *caudillos,* charismatic leaders who emerged during the wars of independence. Civil war gave them autonomy and made them warrantors of the provincial order. They were locally based, protected the population, owned land and cattle, and were supported by arms. As a product of the militarization of a period when city folk deferred to rural landlords, this process supported a personality cult around caudillo leaders, which influenced the societal culture and leadership practice.

In colonial times the local economy relied on a trade circuit that joined the Peruvian silver mines with Europe. The harbor of Buenos Aires complemented Spanish monopoly with smuggling. The wars of the 19th century destroyed this system, while the plains around the River Plate basin witnessed expansion due to international demands for hides. Cattle ranchers implemented a rational exploitation system called *estancias,* some including rudimentary salting plants. Lacking manpower and capital, landowners increased property size while provincial economies suffered a crisis, showing the unequal economic growth patterns between the prairies and the rest of the country.

After 1863, peace allowed the slow development of a National State and the establishment of a market economy. Political leadership was held by an elite of visionaries, intent on modernizing the country. Through a network of personal loyalties and electoral fraud, protected by power concentration and control of the State, this liberal group became a conservative regime which resisted constitutional norms and warranties until 1916.

Progress required the adaptation of the economy to world market needs. Relying on its natural competitive advantages and following criteria of international division of labor, the Argentine economy specialized in the export of agrarian goods. In the 1850s and 1860s excellent results were obtained by the persistent international demand for wool. In the 1870s decisive organizational changes were brought about, with a successful diversification process which significantly pushed corn, wheat and bovine meat production.

Renewal stimulated the growth of a modern infrastructure. Considerable foreign capital investments contributed to the development of transportation and ports, public, commercial and financial services. Argentina enjoyed exceptional prosperity until 1930. Auspicious circumstances added to sustained growth, trade complementation with England, both a capital and industrial goods supplier and the major market for consumption of Argentine goods. World War I altered this pattern and showed the external vulnerability of an economy based exclusively on food exports.

Major waves of European immigrants settled in the interior, contributed to urbanization and created a prosperous middle class. Producers developed many organizational and technical improvements that favored grain and meat exports. Landowners increased their capacity to accumulate capital, diversified, and introduced flexibility investing in other fields of business. In spite of progress, the conservative order could not resist democratic adherence to a new party, the Unión Cívica Radical, whose leader, Yrigoyen, was elected President in 1916. His party expressed the needs and desires of the rising middle class, formerly excluded from political power. His administration instituted respect for constitutional principles, although it held on to the existing economic and social structure.

Food and textile plants started; trade restrictions from World War I stimulated the emergence of workshops. Vigorous industrial growth and new industries sprouted in the 1920s such as, chemicals, paper, cement, and metallurgy. Manufacturing was oriented toward the local market and relied on imported equipment. Blue collar anarchist and socialist protests activated union growth, and were repressed. Subsidiaries of multinational firms developed as Argentina started oil production.

The world crisis of the 1930s pulverized the economic structures. Collapse contributed to the fall of the government and initiated a series of military coups. Conservative forces held on to power through fraud. Depression interrupted capital entry, international prices plummeted and profits reduced dramatically. The government was slow to apply interventionist measures. Pressures on the currency and fluctuations in exchange rates led to devaluation, and increased unemployment. Balance of payments and foreign trade demanded the establishment of a new relationship between England, the United States, and Argentina, but a weak government privileged English and local landowners' interests.

Thus, Argentina lost the opportunity to open its economy. Although industry grew, protectionism and scarcity of foreign currency stimulated a manufactured imports' substitution program. Industrial plants of medium complexity took advantage of an expanding internal market, which insured investment recovery and high profits. Businessmen disregarded efficiency and quality considerations. A small group of families dominated metallurgy, metal-mechanics, textile equipment, cement, and paper, that is, high profit, dynamic sectors, whereas small and medium-size plants profited through the extensive use of manpower. World War II reinforced this process.

Social unrest and the government's lack of popular support strengthened a group of Army officers who wanted an active and efficient State to promote a program of National industrial development. These ideas gained consensus and lead them to bring down the conservative administration in 1943. General Perón, a charismatic leader, organized blue-collar workers through a vertical union system which was the backbone for the popular movement which lead him to the Presidency twice. In 9 years of government, Perón promoted income redistribution in favor of the workers, strengthened the internal market, and created full employment. The State increased its influence over the productive system and displaced foreign capital. Its progressive welfare programs in education, health, social services, and labor legislation consolidated his power base.

Until the 1950s, global issues stimulated industrial expansion in consumer goods and light manufacturing. In the 1940s, manufactured products were exported, however, this did not last and the imports' substitution approach was reinstated. Factory growth implied an income transfer against land products which continued to be the sector that most contributed to generation of funds needed for technology acquisition. The economy slowed down in the 1950s, with public deficit and inflation increasing. Union pressures deteriorated plant discipline, decreased productivity, and slowed down investments.

Political issues and economic difficulties resulted in Perón's downfall in 1955 and until 1976, the Argentine political process became intricate and unstable. Choices seemed restricted to alternating fragile semidemocratic administrations and military dictatorships, which became more violent as time passed. Argentina was influenced by continental issues. The United States created the Alliance for Progress, which promoted democracy, economic and social progress for Latin America; later the Cuban revolution and Communism affected this strategy, which backed authoritarian regimes through the doctrine of national security. Simultaneously, a new South American institution, the Economic Commission for Latin America, promoted modernizing structural reforms to overcome underdevelopment; at the same time, anti-imperialist feelings came to the fore.

Between 1958 and 1976, administrations adopted a modernizing approach to integrate an industrial economy, termed *desarrollismo* (i.e., developmentalism). It opened the local market to foreign investment, relied on State planning and on scientific and technical renewal. Considerable support was extended to local and foreign investment, which produced major achievements in chemicals, petrochemicals, steel, metal mechanics, automotives, machine tools, paper, cement, and self-supply in oil and energy. Looking backwards, however, one must temper these results. Growth generated industrial development and serviced unsatisfied local demands. Foreign industry introduced state-of-the-art technologies and management, even if imported equipment were expensive. Manufacturing expansion was quick and disorderly. Furthermore, foreign firms had greater productive capacity than required and this affected profitability.

Industrial modernization increased technical and management competence in local firms, many of which acted as suppliers and subcontractors for the foreign corporations. They made up a vibrant entrepreneurial group who built a strong productive network throughout the country. Small firms received active credit policies because they provided employment. Economic indicators show 6% annual growth in 1963/1974. Even in the 1970s, industries exported products and made investments abroad. Low productivity and efficiency were its major weaknesses, however. Businesses were protected, in a vibrant non-competitive market, with captive customers who paid generous prices for low-quality goods. Modernization also extended to the rural context, where after more than 30 years, cultivation and exports grew.

Expansion insured full employment and increased workers' incomes. They benefited even if they did not participate beyond their unions, which retained considerable influence. Every administration acknowledged union power. This explains the relevance of Keynesian policy, although periodic crises emerged with the downfall of currency reserves due to major balance-of-payments deficits, which called for the application of orthodox monetary stabilization measures with authoritarian clout. State participation always was a decisive agent for the promotion of the economy.

In the years following the Great Depression, per capita income rose quicker in Brazil, Mexico, New Zealand, Canada, and Australia than in Argentina, which showed the failure of the imports' substitution strategy to generate sustained growth. In the 1960s, productive forces started to develop, but the economy again stopped after 1975. An analysis of the Argentine case shows three major hurdles: (a) foreign dependency: minimal internal savings capability to finance investments provoked major problems in balance of payments and level of reserves; (b) sector rivalries: permanent conflict over income distribution, between agrarian and industrial sectors, and between corporations and workers; and (c) inflation: where Argentina had one of the highest rates in the 20th century.

The 1970s witnessed a revival of crude violence and authoritarianism. It worsened with the death of Perón during his third term in office. He left a power vacuum which opened the way to the military, which started the most tragic period in the country's history, between 1976 and 1983. An ignominious reign of terror paralyzed Argentina, even as it attempted to transform the bases of the economy. The financial and import sectors were privileged, while a fundamentalist approach opened the market to foreign products and provoked deindustrialization. Simultaneously, the liberalization of the financial market sparked speculative fever, which was exacerbated by inadequate currency exchange policies against the U.S. dollar. This led Argentina to an alarming level of foreign indebtedness. The economic establishment solidified in a group of highly concentrated national and foreign enterprises, diversified in their activities and integrated in their management. Closely linked to the State, these firms obtained lucrative deals. As a powerful business lobby, they became State suppliers and subcontractors. The ravages of inflation hurt employees, workers and small industries.

By 1983, Argentina found itself in a situation fraught with difficulties. Its military government was repudiated for major human rights violations and its wretched economic administration. Its fall was accelerated by the war lost to Great Britain in the Falklands/Malvinas, plus the impact of the crisis of the Latin American foreign debt that interrupted the flow of international loans to the region. A democratic system was instituted and President Alfonsín was chosen. Argentine society recovered its dignity and institutions, overcoming its inheritance of authoritarianism and intolerance.

Reconstructing its economy was one of the major assignments, a task that is currently under way. The new administration wanted to subordinate the economy to the logic of politics, becoming aware too late of the complex and delicate situation of State resources. It did not adequately measure the ability of the financial and monetary systems, nor the degree of power held by the major local and foreign economic groups. Decision making towards sovereign or regionally inspired initiatives was rigorously opposed by the commitments required by foreign debt creditors, in addition to the requirements of the International Monetary Fund.

The first democratic government instituted various economic programs with small successes and major failures. This translated into a learning process for Argentine society, until it finally understood the nature of the crisis and the scope and imminence of the required transformations. The economy became unsettled between 1989 and 1991, with gross price hyperinflation and abrupt devaluation of the currency. These lead to the fall of the government. A new administration took over, lead by President Menem, who expediently ruled during two consecutive periods, 1989/1999.

Increasing economic difficulties caused a loss of autonomy of Argentine rulers. Globalization added to this process, and the weakness of Argentine economy allowed for influence from outside. The economic uncertainty allowed the United States of America, the International Monetary Fund and the World Bank to exercise a monitoring role over the local administration. Control centered on the destiny of international loans, that is, goals and objectives; conditions, results, and periodic inspections to verify compliance. This implied establishing a new relationship with the U.S. government, aligning Argentine policies with its directives and strategies.

President Menem contained the inflationary debacle and solved state bankruptcy. The monetary system was stabilized in 1991, with the satisfactory application of the Currency Board measures. This cleansed the public deficit and gave way to an active program of State offices' re-structuring. An over-arching program of privatization of public companies took place in the first years of his administration.

The scope and intensity of the privatizations were critical, but their results were positive and negative. Considerable investments arrived and technology was modernized, which improved the quality of the services transferred. Still, most privatizations were discretionally assigned and gave way to illegitimate projects resulting in large contingents of workers who lost their jobs and raised unemployment sky high. The rapidity of the process did not allow for rigorous implementation of control mechanisms over quality and tariffs. Besides, privatizations and reforms were carried out through capitalization processes, as well as through recovery of foreign debt titles, which 10 years later duplicated country indebtedness. Foreign commitments became critical with the deregulation and liberalization of the Argentine economy, which although integrated to the global market, is subordinated to the new world order that defines Argentina as a high-risk, emerging country. (1995)

Major macroeconomic achievements must be acknowledged, including real-term 34% gross national product (GNP) growth between 1990 and 1995; and a 22% annual accumulated level of growth since 1991. Market forces did not solve the problems of the Argentine economy. Much to the contrary, evidences show a deepening of the difficulties caused by the effects of adventure capitalism (Weber, 1992).

In 1995 conditions worsened. Unemployment, social marginalization and street violence have increased. A recession is in place since 1997; efforts to combat it only began to emerge in 2003 and are making headway. Depressive trends have not been reversed and major changes are not expected to occur shortly. The democratic election of a new President in 2003 and the need to redefine priorities, however, opened the way to a review of past practices and a search for more balanced forms of economic consolidation.

4. MANAGEMENT IN ARGENTINA

Contemporary Studies

We use two criteria to analyze management studies in Argentina, one chronological, concentrating on those written after the economy opened in 1989, and a second one defined by (a) cultural factors, that is, those centering on the values of the Argentine business leaders and (b) structural considerations, that is, those that govern the link between managerial behavior, and the macroeconomic and social conditions in the country.

Lewis (1993) lists the explanations given for the causes of Argentine decline. The most frequently cited are: (a) the resistance of the traditional oligarchy to accept social and political change; (b) military meddling which exacerbated instability; (c) exploitation by foreign capital; (d) the absence of an industrial class with entrepreneurial skills, (e) the machinations of Perón, and (f) the Argentine national character which impedes cooperation (p. 23ff).

Two interpretations are offered here that relate societal cultural and economic developments to managerial values in Argentina. The first focuses on the absence of an industrial bourgeoisie which is a result of the structural weaknesses of the Latin American economy (e.g., due to their colonial origins or their high vulnerability in the face of world markets given their being primary-goods producers). Within this conception, economic backwardness inhibited capital accumulation in the local markets and required State intervention to mobilize the needed resources to undertake industrialization processes already in place in other countries. The state became a decisive player in economic development and subordinated both the market as a resource allocator as well as the country's industrial strategies to its decisions. Consequently, the emerging and weak industrial bourgeoisies found their growth tied to relationships with the state, which postponed innovation, efficiency, risk taking, and competitive initiatives.

The second interpretation focuses on the basis of factors characteristic of the region and holds that the absence of industrial leadership was due to the fact that in those countries the traditional oligarchic landowning class effectively consolidated its position. Developmental attempts of competing industrial bourgeoisies were rigorously resisted, postponed and inhibited due to the exclusive access to the existing power structures, and the great privileges enjoyed during those decades.

In his analysis of Argentina's economic involution, Sábato (1988) holds that the dominant elite was present in a variety of economic endeavors, had attained unity as a group, and its control of financial and commercial opportunities allowed it to participate in a wide range of productive and speculative activities. In this sense:

> To the degree that if the economy as a whole were subject to pronounced fluctuations or to uneven developments of its component sectors, its extraordinary flexibility to place its excess revenues tended to inhibit the development of specialized fixed investments, investments were only minimally channeled towards productive endeavors, thus postponing the development of the productive capacity of society as a whole and the organization of a capitalist system. (p. 109ff)

Waisman (1987) suggested that the reversal of development was due to the fact that in the 1920s, Argentine institution building was well advanced but the process was maimed by the surge of the Great Depression. The reversal is explained by the combination of structural factors, concentration of agrarian property, lack of manpower reserves, and erroneous political decisions, including indiscriminate industrial protectionism.

In his analysis of Argentine capitalism's future perspectives, Ferrer (1998) identified major trends in the international order, as well as the countries that overcame their relative backwardness and joined the ranks of advanced industrial economies (p. 13ff). He concluded that although the recent Menem administration established a political alliance between local interest groups, popular support, and international power centers, the incapacity to service foreign debt with exports made the country dependent on debtors' decisions (p. 89ff).

Schvarzer (1996) completed a political and social history of Argentine industry and suggested the reasons for it not becoming an effective engine for economic development. More recently, Schvarzer (2001) showed that the poor results obtained in local growth dynamics and distributive equity show that the open economy model firmly implanted since 1975 has not produced desired improvements and new strategies must be evolved (p. 6).

Argentina systematically has a great surplus in food and fuels and a deficit in manufactured goods. Bouzas and Fanelli (2001) believe Argentina must concentrate on multilateral liberalization and regionalism. They see Mercosur, the Southern Cone economic alliance, as a key developmental strategy to face the challenge of globalization and to build the shared economic space that will accelerate productivity growth (p. 250ff).

Developments deriving from the opening of the economy deserve attention: the internationalization of banking and commerce, the corporate purchase of local industries, the onslaught of worldwide competition, the development of communicational and systems technologies, the new legal framework, as well as the de-layering and restructuring of firms, impacted on management practices. However, two tendencies are at loggerheads: the development of organizational learning, as against a winner-take-all mentality.

López (2000) found that an uncertain and ever-changing context produces disciplined subjectivities, the obverse of what the management literature holds: autonomous, creative managers, self-motivated towards permanent growth (Bennis & Nanus, 1985; Schein, 1985; Senge, 1990). Participants defined success as the possibility to strike a balance between professional and personal lives. But instituting a new organization needs new technical contents, as well as the production of disciplined subjectivity. New organizational practices are instituted in a setting of high competitiveness with fierce and open rivalries for jobs; and are based on business criteria, where one may not be able to retain one's job even if one fully satisfies the requirements for the job. Gantman (1994) also points to a management paradigm that increases inequalities and legitimates a two-tier social order, with winners and losers, where total responsibility lies in each individual. A new individualism emerges side by side of a narcissistic paradigm. Etkin (1999) writes about institutionalized corruption: the destructive effects of pragmatism, amorality in management and ethical transgressions.

Corporations are hostile because they create a stage in which pragmatism is the predominant value, people are a resource for goal attainment, demands are exacting, and contracts are precarious. Still, corporate positions are valued because the inverse implies exclusion. Moreover, when interesting work and training is found in companies, growth is enhanced. People must therefore be docile. Future scenarios can only be conjectured. Participants express their hopes and fears; but seem incapable of delving into what is happening because they are overpowered by unpredictability, as well as by the dissolution of former references (López, 2000).

Organizational changes show this dilemma is faced daily by managers, that is, enlightened and narcissistic leadership patterns, at odds with one another. Executives attest to the growing interest in management as an authority system and to the need to institute leadership in complex organizations. Numerous conventions and consulting research projects identify obstacles and show progress made installing rule-oriented behaviors (IDEA, 1992, 1993, 1996, 1999). Still, the pace is slow and the vision emphasizes survival rather than growth. Participants point to contradictions between stated desires to institute empowerment and team work, and the lack of support for such practices. The economy is open, firms incorporate efficient methods, but authoritarian practices remain. Reference should be made to Weber's (1992) reminder to contrast the notions of "modern rational capitalism which has need not only of the technical means of production, but of a calculable legal system and of administration in terms of formal rules" as against "adventurous and speculative trading capitalism" (p. xxxviii) "bound to no ethical norms whatever" (p. 22).

5. RESEARCH RESULTS

Societal Culture: Results Derived From Quantitative Research

GLOBE Questionnaires were distributed during the most conflicting period since the promulgation of the Currency Board system, under which the local peso was tied to the dollar at par. At that time, managers and employees were under great strain. The Mexican financial crisis (December 1994) caused a decrease of economic activity and made access to credit impossible, which accompanied by privatizations, State reform and the incorporation of technologies, increased unemployment from 10.8% in May 1995, to 18.6% twelve months later. Industrial activity stagnated for 9 months.

Besides, it is unusual to carry out industrial research in Argentina, and conditions had to be generated. Preparation required patience and insistence. Purposes and action plans were carefully communicated. Information was circulated to 22 food industry and 20 financial firms; meetings were called to present goals and benefits; and interviews were held with top managers. As a result, 4 food-processing and 5 financial services firms participated: 217 questionnaires were distributed and 153 responses were tabulated, that is, 71% of invitees. The prestige of sponsoring institutions gave GLOBE credibility, but in the light of closings and deactivation of labor laws, it was thought that many would refuse, or would cooperate from fear. Demographic data collection were not collected because it was felt it would diminish participation. Still, an overall sample profile was gathered: All respondents are native Spanish speakers, in second- or third-generation Argentines, and have graduated from High School at least. Sixty-seven percent are under 35 years of age and 85% live in or close to Buenos Aires the capital city.

In the following, information is offered and discussed on each of the nine societal culture GLOBE dimensions (see Table 18.1).

TABLE 18.1
Culture Scales on Society Level

Cultural Dimension	Society Culture "As Is"		Society Culture "Should Be"		Difference "Should Be" – "As Is"
	Mean	Rank	Mean	Rank	
Performance Orientation	3.65	52	6.35	9	2.70
Future Orientation	3.08	60	5.78	19	2.70
Assertiveness	4.22	24	3.25	51	−0.93
Institutional Collectivism	3.66	58	5.32	8	1.66
Gender Egalitarianism	3.49	26	4.98	12	1.49
Humane Orientation	3.99	32	5.58	20	1.59
Power Distance	5.64	5	2.33	56	−3.31
In-Group Collectivism	5.51	28	6.15	7	0.64
Uncertainty Avoidance	3.65	47	4.66	36	1.01

Performance Orientation.   The GLOBE aggregated scale scores indicate that Argentina ranks 52nd out of 61 countries in Performance Orientation: 3.65 for "As Is" and 6.35 for "Should Be." The gap is large and significant. Performance Orientation is a key factor on which change is most desired. Switzerland is the country with the highest "As Is" rating, while El Salvador's "Should Be" values are close to Argentina's.

Argentina flourished taking advantage of its vast natural resources until the 1930s. Since then it tried out many competitive options. All these failed, and Argentines believe that the current downfall (1995) of the major efforts undertaken in the 1990s derive from the lack of a well-conceived and agreed-upon strategic plan. Decision makers, who have direct access to the sources of political and economic power, act barely within the borderlines of legality: "Our genes and our historical education have trained us to despise the law, or at least to handle ourselves subjectively, to speculate, and to try to take advantage of the rules" (Denevi, in Lóizaga, p. 93). Often, executives incorporate the concept of achievement, but it is not prevalent in society. Moreover, whenever mention is made of performance in a public statement, such a reference is suspect, duly interpreted to be inapplicable, and dismissed.

With developing democratic institutions and no inflation, two causes of anxiety have disappeared. Even so, the anomic component is still there in that Argentines are rule breakers (Isuani, 1998). Nino (1992) analyzed the link between inefficiency and underdevelopment and wrote "there is a recurring trend in Argentine society to anomie in general and to illegality in particular," that is, towards the breaking of juridical, moral, and social rules. He considered Argentina "a country outside the law" insofar as "the anomic factor generates reduced levels of efficiency and productivity" (p. 25).

Competition makes it imperative to develop professional ideas in strategy development, goal establishment, resource allocation, time management, weighing of alternatives, results measurement and action plan adjustment. The current explosion in books, specialized magazines, seminars, and postgraduate courses in Business Administration testifies to the need for the assimilation of such criteria. The relevance awarded to the Performance Orientation "Should Be" dimension points to an emerging trend. It places emphasis on achievement and distinguishes power from authority. Argentines value performance and state that it is neglected and not appreciated. Argentines are adept at surviving by their wits. Respondents use them in their individual pursuits, but find they are not applied in Argentine society.

Future Orientation. Argentina ranked 60th out of the 61 GLOBE countries in Future Orientation "As Is" (3.08) and 19th for "Should Be" (5.78). The gap is again large and significant. Future Orientation is a second key factor on which a positive change is desired. Singapore is the state with the highest "As Is" rating, while Russia's "Should Be" rating is as low as Argentina's.

At the start of the century Argentina seemed destined to greatness, but the country slid into a permanent state of vulnerability, economic depression and political instability that gave way to the emigration, in the last 40 years of 2 million university graduates, artists, trades people, scientists, and blue-collar workers who started new lives outside their own country, due to political hardship and to intransigence (Bunge, cited in Barón, del Carril & Gómez, l995, p. 61).

Emigration is still a major concern and many emigrate. Fifty seven percent of the employed fear they may lose their jobs; and respected economists question the common sense behind the measures taken by the government ("They either devaluate or kill the population" Fitoussi, Clarín, June, 2001).

The relevance awarded to Future Orientation dimension merits attention because Argentines live through an apparently unsolvable crisis. The *Economist* (June 23, 2001, p. 11) stated that "Argentina's Currency Board precludes devaluation and puts monetary policy off limits. The country's debt burden leaves no room for looser fiscal policy." This is a major plight as seen by the comment that follows: "Unfortunately, his (the Minister of the Economy) latest decision - to mimic a devaluation by offering exporters a subsidy and importers a tariff, may be a step too far."

Assertiveness. Argentina ranks 24th out of 61 countries in Assertiveness "As Is" (4.22) and 51st for "Should Be" (3.25). Albania is the country with the highest "As Is" rating, while Sweden shows the lowest. The "As Is" score identifies a typical Latin American culture. The position of Argentina lies close to Colombia (25th), Brazil (26th), Venezuela (20th), México (16th), and Ecuador (32nd), and fits also within the Latin European cluster, represented for example, by Spain (17th) and Italy (34th) or France (30th).

"In other modern Western societies, intransigence suggests dogmatism and rigidity. In Argentina it is understood as principled, moral and a defense of the truth. It denotes such orthodox, correct postures that practically all transactions are excluded" (Shumway, 1993, p. 56). This difficulty to reconcile opposing goals is observed in most negotiations, where confrontation is highly valued. As Altschul (1999) observes, "Among us, negotiation defers to harassment and vanquishment, to 'we had to give up,' to 'I couldn't have it my way,' connotes pushy sales techniques, and evokes crooked dealings" (p. 16, 23ff).

Audacity is called for, rather than courage; adventurousness not bravery. Writing about Australia, Ashkanasy (chap. 9, this volume) say about Australia that there is a need to rely on an inspiring leader to carry them to the First World. The past histories of Australia and Argentina, which show parallels in their social development, egalitarianism, discrimination and changes, processes that ride on a history of elimination of aborigines, admiration for individualist leadership, and early women's suffrage, may explain the similar demand for a decidedly assertive style with authoritarian overtones.

Collectivism I: Institutional Collectivism. Argentina ranks 58th out of the 61 GLOBE countries in Collectivism I: Institutional Collectivism "As Is" (3.66) and 8th for "Should Be" (5.32). Sweden is the country with the highest "As Is" rating, while Greece's "Should Be" values are close to Argentina's. The "As Is" position of Argentina lies close other countries of the Latin American cluster, such as Brazil (52nd), Colombia (53rd), Guatemala (56th), El Salvador (55th), and Ecuador (48th), and also lies close to Spain (51st) and Italy (57th).

Hofstede (1984) categorized Argentina as individualistically oriented, and GLOBE scale scores place it at the end of the Collectivism spectrum. This may be attributed to an entrenched feeling of abandonment present in Argentine society. The Menem administration used plenipotentiary powers and promised a future of splendor as a result of the privatization, deregulation, and opening of the economy. The continued demands of new adjustments, a euphemism for junk-job creation, delayering, salary cuts and firings, the Currency Board system had created a sense of despondency; and the repeated schisms in political life contributed to detract from the actual benefits of the program. People feel that society and its structures were destroyed and their values have been laid to waste. People are anxious, feel alienated, feel there is nobody to turn to, or to listen to. They feel menaced by failure. People feel they do not belong, vent their anger after soccer matches. This has improved since the advent of the Kirchner presidency, however. "Cambalache," a popular tango from the 1930s, repeatedly recalls loss of values.

Fundamentalist churches and New Age cults spring up in poorer districts, while 91% say they "believe in God," although only 22.5% are regular church goers. Moreover, 83.7% of Catholic women and 88.1% of Catholic men believe in UFOs and extraterrestrial beings; 60.0% believe in magic-spells, curses, and charms (Baamonde, 2000). Argentine society perceives itself as apolitical: "We have an immature democracy" (74.6%); "We lack years of democracy" (27.3%); "No politician satisfies me" (71.3%).

Gender Egalitarianism. Argentina ranks 26th out of 61 countries in Gender Egalitarianism "As Is" (3.49) and for 12th for "Should Be" (4.98). Hungary is the country with the highest "As Is" ranking, while South Korea ranks lowest. Hofstede (1984) placed Argentina in the middle of the spectrum, though closer to masculinity (20th/21st among 53 countries). Today the gap between the "As Is" and the "Should Be" value stands at 1.49. Altogether, it seems that Argentine managers with mainly urban background feel they are reasonably egalitarian.

Answers correspond to a society with a diminished sexual role division. Today 91.8% of people polled say that a woman may fulfill herself at work and professionally, while 50 years ago only 16.4% thought so; "may go out with her friends or alone" passes from 12.3% 50 years ago to a current 77.9%; and questioned on adultery: "Do you believe men are less loyal than in the past?," 50.8% agree, while the same question on women produces 70.5% agreement, which shows a perceptual change on autonomy.

Significant changes in women's social incorporation include young women leaving parents' homes before young men, contributing significantly to the family budget, and raising families without men's help. Women make up close to 60% of all university students, and they are hired in professional positions previously limited to men. Women occupy more political positions since the Quota Law, in the development and leadership of nongovernmental organizations, and in public welfare institutions. Since October 2001, Argentina has been a country with very high representation of women in legislature (Clarín, July 4, 2001). Furthermore, the paradigmatic role of the Mothers and Grandmothers of Plaza de Mayo in their search for "the disappeared" during the military dictatorship, as well as in social protest manifestations commands respect. In the work environment, women represent 40% of the labor force in Buenos Aires and its outskirts, although this growth is limited to short-term, low-qualification jobs (INDEC, 1999).

Humane Orientation. Argentina ranks 32nd out of the 61 GLOBE countries in Humane Orientation "As Is" (3.99) and 20th for "Should Be" (5.58). Zambia is the country with the highest "As Is" rating, while former West Germany ranks lowest.

Argentina has a long tradition of charitable institutions that maintain continuity by patronage, many of which emerge to complement tasks left unfulfilled by the state. Parents' cooperatives exist in schools and hospitals, neighbors' contributions supplement police stations' and firemen's budgets, and sundry nongovernment institutions subsidize community projects in backward areas whose legitimate revenues do not cover the needs of their inhabitants.

More recently a great diversity of neighborhood, municipal, provincial and national solidarity institutions were created to gather and manage funds for welfare purposes, structured around specific needs of each population: unwed mothers, retirees, AIDS patients, street children, Falklands/Malvinas ex-combatants, and so on. Mostly in silence, they have built a solid reputation, and are now courted by the media, because throughout the years, diverse public institutions had absconded with voluntary contributions.

Argentines value their current level of Humane Orientation, desire to uphold and increase it. Related to the weight assigned to Performance Orientation and Future Orientation greater emphasis is required on developing "crecimiento con equidad," growth-with-fairness mechanisms (Fanelli, 1999).

An interesting opposition emerges from relating the answers to the Humane Orientation and Collectivism I: Societal Emphasis dimensions. Argentina is rated among the most individualist countries in the project but rates high on Collectivism II: Family Collectivism. This is consistent with experience, as for example when the Divorce law was enforced in 1987, the figure for new wedding ceremonies increased in comparison with that of divorces, as a greater quantity of couples legalized their situation, whereas distanced couples had already separated independently of the law (INDEC, 1999). At the same time, executives interviewed define their success primarily in terms of balance between family satisfaction and professional success, and not on the basis of their work performance (López, 2000).

Power Distance.   Argentina ranks 5th out of the 61 GLOBE countries in Power Distance "As Is" (5.64) and 56th for "Should Be" (2.33). This is the dimension with the largest gap between current and desired values. Morrocco and Nigeria are the countries with the highest "As Is" ratings, while Denmark has the lowest ranking. The other Latin American countries, with the exception of Bolivia, which often parallels Argentina's data, cluster around these figures.

Argentina is politically and economically a centralized nation. The essayistic literature holds that the leader manipulates through charisma. Denevi quotes Marañón, a Spanish thinker, as saying that "a good politician should combine lack of scruples, an exaltation of ideas, coolness, obduracy and malice" (Denevi, in Lóizaga, p. 88). The relationship between the leader and the community answers to a direct and informal content. That helps explain why even the most temperate politician adopts a populist style; a feature that extends to the business environment and generates the model of the patrón, very much the lord of the manor. Thus great oversized confrontations, never continuities, persist in Argentina, and divisions circumscribe objectivity, balance, and tolerance.

Within the 53 countries studied, Hofstede (1984) categorized Argentina near Brazil, and far from other Latin American countries. Argentina's GLOBE scale scores display a more central position within Latin American countries. In spite of major macroeconomic achievements, the 1990s show arbitrary use of political and economic power in Argentina: GLOBE responses show this when middle managers interpret that "people in positions of authority wish to exercise power for power itself."

Argentines feel attached to the *barrio* (neighborhood), where a person grew up and where public reputation is anchored. In this context, the *escrache,* which involves soiling a person's house front, searches for reparation by affecting his family reputation. It is a social manifestation that developed as a tool for redress, an ephemeral and preannounced enactment with which a group shames a person held responsible for an injustice or a collective abuse, and constitutes a symbolic action of censure, vilification, and amends. It publicizes indignation in the light of repugnant actions and exhibits moral judgment because existing due process is insufficient to mete out sanctions.

Collectivism II: In-Group Collectivism. Argentina ranks 28th out of the 61 GLOBE countries in Collectivism II: In-Group Collectivism "As Is" (5.51) and 7th for "Should Be" (6.15). The Philippines is the country with the highest "As Is" value, while Denmark's has the lowest. Argentina is positioned within the Latin American culture cluster on the "As Is" Collectivism II, for example, Costa Rica (33rd), El Salvador (32nd), Bolivia (29th), Venezuela (24th), and not too far from Brazil (38th) and Guatemala (17th), and also close to Spain (30th) and Italy (41st).

In Argentina the family constitutes a vital center of social activity; besides being highly media oriented as five of the major pastimes take place in the home, and 50% of people consulted watch between two and three hours of TV per day.

This is extended to the context of friendship, and valued institutions such as the *ronda del mate,* the drinking of *maté* tea, where the tea is sipped through a *bombilla,* a metal tube: the gourd being again replenished after each person drinks, the next person sips through the same *bombilla,* as well as the *asado,* a barbecue where the man of the house prepares food for family and friends. An unobtrusive measure of In-Group Collectivism is seen in airports where it is usual for entire extended families to see a relative off or to wait for them upon their return from a trip: the emotions displayed being independent of the fact that whoever leaves or returns may have been away for a very short period. Recent findings (Markwald, 2005) confirm the strength of this trait. They show that children from Argentina, as compared to those in Brazil, Colombia, Chile, and Mexico, share more activities with friends and that these relationships are critical in the upbringing.

As Cozarinsky (1995) writes: *"Every time I go to Buenos Aires I run into the extraordinary human quality of the Argentines. In Argentine society one immediately and very firmly feels the presence of individuals. One is put in contact with the others. They immediately embrace, kiss, touch. It's not something that I particularly enjoy but it expresses enormous affect related to behaviors of archaic Mediterranean societies. Unfortunately these societies are fully incapable of organizing daily lives"* (Cozarinsky, cited in Barón, del Carril, Gómez, 1995, p. 149).

In the face of globalization, the tendency is to leave the public scene and retreat to the private fold: 78.7% consider that happiness means having a nice family, 50.8% having a nice (marriage) partner; 44.3% having many friends.

Uncertainty Avoidance. Scale scores rank Argentina 47th out of the 61 GLOBE countries on Uncertainty Avoidance "As Is" (3.65) and 36th for "Should Be" (4.66). The gap is large and significant and change is highly desired. Switzerland is the country with the highest Uncertainty Avoidance "As Is" rating, while Russia has the lowest. Again, on "As Is" scores, Argentina is well positioned within the Latin American cluster, for example, Brazil (51st), Colombia (52nd), El Salvador (50th), and not far from Costa Rica (40th), Ecuador (43rd), Bolivia (57th), Venezuela (55th), Guatemala (58th), and lies close to Spain (36th) and Italy (41st). GLOBE figures show a small gap (1.01) between the "As Is" (3.65) and "Should Be" values (4.66).

Improvisation and short-term actions are major part of public and private life, and explain failures in complex endeavors that require a careful evaluation of goals, means, stakeholders, and deriving critical learning from experience. The ability to deal ingeniously and extemporaneously in the face of uncertainty is a prized attribute: from a positive angle it builds flexibility, whereas, from the negative side, it favors makeshift solutions and trickery. These are complementary features that help to construct an identity. This also postpones decision making, which in a changing context implied taking on risks and helps *zafar,* that is, shunning.

In the last decade, and as a result of inflation control, two contradictory processes have arisen in Argentina: a greater degree of planning in the face of uncertainty. However, given the impossibility to conceive the future, skepticism takes over: little credibility is awarded to whatever public figures state and the young identify with pop idols rather than with politicians, business leaders, or intellectuals.

6. REGIONAL AND CULTURAL CONSTELLATION

Argentine scale scores coincide with those of participants of Guatemala, El Salvador and Bolivia, and with those of other Latin American countries, which present a homogeneous cultural cluster in answers to Collectivism I: Institutional Collectivism; Collectivism II: In-Group Collectivism and Uncertainty Avoidance. This attests to the process of Latin Americanization of Argentina (Ogliastri et al., 1999a).

In earlier times, public jobs in health, education, and construction warranted Argentine social mobility. Besides, immigrant communities had founded well-established hospitals, schools, sports, and mutual help associations. Argentina had a large middle class and the quality of its public health and education were superior to those in other countries in the region.

This has changed for the worse. Public opinion speaking of a culture closer to those of neighboring countries is supported by further GLOBE data which shows homogenization of cultural practices and values within Latin American cultures (Ogliastri, et al., 1999a). Middle managers indicate that they live under extremely uncertain conditions with little control over circumstances, and indicate a preference for Uncertainty Avoidance; elitist values predominate, and there is desire to reduce them; Collectivism I and II values are among the highest within GLOBE, and they wish to uphold them; their societies are individualistic, they value social well-being over individual benefits; their societies are reasonably oriented towards performance, but would like to see this enhanced; their societies discriminate against women and egalitarianism should be increased; their societies are present oriented, and would prefer a greater Future Orientation; they prefer a humanist society, whereas the current situation ranks below GLOBE average; they desire to maintain a high degree of interpersonal contact.

In line with societal cultural values ("Should Be"), Latin American middle managers prefer high performance, collaborative, team integrator leaders, and those who are administratively competent and ready to commit themselves to the organization (Ogliastri et al., 1999a, p. 1). In contrast, as will be detailed out in a later section of this chapter, the Argentine concept of leadership runs somewhat "countercultural."

7. SYNTHESIS FOR SOCIETAL CULTURE

A major societal change took place in Argentina: Latin Americanization is driven by immigration from neighboring countries, plus the effects of changes, characteristic of the times, similar to those taking place world-wide are being felt. García Canclini (1995) analyzes the current conflicts in the region as tradition in the face of emergent modernization. Hobsbawm (2000) describes the dilemmas inherent in the "small global world" (p. 82ff). With the onset of new technologies, societies become de-traditionalized. Capital assets fly by night; factories move across continents, foreign financial crises impact globally. Furthermore, social norms are weakened, a sense of the ephemeral prevails, families disintegrate, individualism grows, life is secularized, employment is precarious, and public figures are distrusted. Under these conditions, it is hard to define autonomous national policies, and this influences the behavior of executives and managers who must adapt to perform. This new conjuncture requires attention to be paid both to factors intrinsic and extrinsic to each situation, and makes participants reflective. GLOBE methods capture this richness empirically. This is shown in world wide comparison: Autonomous leadership is highly endorsed in Argentina; within Argentina, it is Participative, Team Oriented and Charismatic Leadership that is most prototypical for outstanding leaders; Self-Protective and Humane leadership are least endorsed.

GLOBE results signal a close relationship between the Argentine profile and those of less developed Latin American nations in Collectivism I: Institutional Collectivism; Collectivism II: In-Group Collectivism, and Uncertainty Avoidance. Facing conditions beyond control, management chooses survival against growth, structural mutilations ensue, and middle managers answer with responses closer to those of traditionally less developed societies.

8. LEADERSHIP IN ARGENTINA: LEADERS AS FIGURAS SEÑERAS

In Spanish, figuras señeras refers to solitary, single, unique, unequaled individuals. Argentina lived through three periods of political pluralism: the constitutional period from 1853; the popular opening of the society from 1916, and the return to democracy from 1983. Intolerance and confrontation predominated at all other times (Massuh, in Lóizaga, 1995, p. 187). This history of discord and rivalries is currently under scrutiny. The present crisis helps the dust settle: it is difficult to further demonize. More reflexive practices are necessary. Leaders need to understand what is happening and why. Still, personalism (Sartori, 1989) persists. Sartori believes that in Latin American democracies people identify with an individual and not with a program. Trust is reposed in a prominent individual who can channel popular will. The emergence of protagonists such as Moreno, San Martín, Rivadavia, Rosas, Urquiza, Alberdi, Sarmiento, Roca, Yrigoyen, Perón, Alfonsín, and Menem, and Kirchner may be explained by the fierce factional confrontations that ended in the death or exile of the contenders throughout the history of the country.

Goldman & Salvatore (1998) indicate that "during Independence, a military career was the shortest road to leadership. Provincial caudillos gained preeminence. They firmly defended the territories they ruled over, did not submit to the rule of law, and ruled each region singularly" (p. 8ff). However, this has changed. Currently, Argentine presidential democracy retains unique characteristics: the concept of control and balance between powers does not exist as rulers see themselves as accountable only to their party, with no institutional accountability towards Congress or the judiciary. With law decrees, the president may disregard the legislature, pay little heed to judicial decisions he deems inconvenient, provoke critical media, and feel free to antagonize others.

The need to synthesize may dramatize the contents. Nonetheless, *cacique* and *caudillo* are Americanisms that distinctly express the overruling leadership mode: the *cacique* leads his people; a *caudillo* takes over in times of war. To govern and to *acaudillar,* to rule as a caudillo (strong man politics)- are never far apart. Thus major contradictions exist, fierce confrontations take place, there are few continuities, and such schisms detract from objectivity, balance, tolerance, and have ominous social consequences. The leader manipulates and his vision fascinates his followers. Graumann (1986) talks of the *meneur,* the *jefe,* the *Fuehrer,* images that connote directive leadership.

In Argentina the resultant relationship between the leader and the community responds to a direct and informal content. That may be why even the most self contained and austere politician adopts populist tactics; and why such a pattern may even extend to the private sphere where the image of the *patrón*, the lord of the manor, persists.

Argentina has produced several dominating figures, yet no books are devoted to Argentine leadership with the exception of Goldman & Salvatore (1998). It may be that "one does not write about the obvious." Lozano (1999) recalls that, whereas Protestant traditions posit a distance between a subjective internal experience and norm ruled external experience, Catholic countries don't separate the personal and social spheres. In the first case, personal self control exemplifies domination over egoistic desires and a balanced external self. However, when Catholicism arrived in Latin America, aborigines were associated with demonic forces, and priests and conquistadors came to redeem them. They were the mythical heroes meant to chastise and conquer barbarism. Contrariwise, Germanic mythology presents the benevolent hero incorporated by Western philosophy, which makes man the subject of history, and interprets confrontation as a transgression against rules drafted by the Creator or the state. This romantic figure reappears in the transformational leader (p. 4).

Popular wisdom may say that mismanagement was explicable in the public sphere where institutions were not expected to deliver, but the current state of competitiveness makes it imperative to identify specific dimensions of Argentine leadership to institute the changes that may help improve motivation and achieve higher performance.

9. RESULTS OF THE QUANTITATIVE STUDY

Mean values of the empirical dimensions of leader behaviors describe respondents' perception of the complexity of the managerial construct in Argentina (see Table 18.2). Distinct sub-constellations are distinguished: responses do not invoke a messianic leader, nor can they be summarized as a management / leadership opposition (Kotter, 1988).

The mean values of the behaviors are patterned, with two extreme clusters and four dimensions that cover a wide mid-range. Malevolent (1.59), self-centered (1.66), nonparticipative (2.02), and autocratic (2.22) all fall below the mean (4.55) and allude to negative behaviors— noncommitted, passive, alienated. They describe sovereign, intemperate, arbitrary, divisive behaviors. This is the image of the abusive leader, who considers himself invested with supreme powers and is narcissistic (Conger, 1989). Within this scheme, malevolent, hostile, dishonest, vindictive, irritable, cynical, undependable, noncooperative, egotistical, unintelligent, self-centered, self-interested, nonparticipative, loner, and asocial are the most critical and can be related to managers who benefit personally from access to positions of authority: "Leaders who serve others, or in the service of their own greed?" illustrates the degree of disbelief. Likewise, autocratic, dictatorial, bossy, elitist, ruler, domineering, nonparticipative, nondelegater, micro manager, nonegalitarian, and individually oriented evoke a "show of epaulettes."

Positive behaviors are above the mean: humane orientation (4.65); modesty (4.68); autonomous (4.68); charismatic III: self-sacrificial (4.85); administratively competent (5.53); collaborative team orientation (5.68); diplomatic (6.07); team integrator (6.08); decisive (6.11); integrity (6.15); charismatic I: visionary (6.17); performance oriented (6.19); charismatic II: inspirational (6.34). They define committed, active, involved behaviors, and as such would comply with organizational and followers' expectations. The fact that most GLOBE countries crowd up to two thirds of all 21 dimensions in this sub-constellation allows us to posit this as

TABLE 18.2
Argentinian GLOBE Leadership Survey

Leadership Dimensions	Mean	Rank	Highest Score	Lowest Score
Autonomous Leadership	**4.55**	**4**	**4.63**	**2.27**
Participative Leadership	**5.89**	**8**	**6.09**	**4.50**
Autocratic	2.23	50	3.86	1.89
(reverse scored) Nonparticipative (reverse scored)	2.00		3.61	1.86
Team-Oriented Leadership	**5.99**	**8**	**6.21**	**4.74**
Team	5.69	16	6.09	4.42
Integrator Collaborative Team Oriented	6.04	38	6.43	4.10
Administrative Competent Diplomatic Malevolent (reverse scored)	6.05		6.05	4.49
Charismatic Leadership	**5.98**	**20**	**6.46**	**4.51**
Performance	6.20	18	6.64	4.51
Visionary	6.20	21	6.50	4.62
Inspirational	6.15	31	6.63	5.04
Integrity	4.72	61	6.79	4.72
Self-sacrifical	4.87	41	5.99	3.98
Decisive	6.13	12	6.37	3.62
Self-Protective Leadership	**3.45**	**32**	**4.62**	**2.55**
Self-centered	6.13	2	6.20	1.55
Status Conscious	3.00	61	5.93	3.00
Conflict Inducer	4.24	18	5.01	3.09
Face-saver	3.00	26	4.63	2.05
Procedural	4.87	3	5.12	2.82
Humane Leadership	**4.70**	**42**	**5.75**	**3.82**
Humane	2.23	61	5.68	2.23
Modesty	4.72	45	5.86	4.14

"a pipe dream," "an expression of fine desires." Besides, subjects recall that "a company pays a salary for your work, it never promises justice."

Thus, internal consistency can be attributed to the ends of the continuum and it becomes easier to assign meaning to the remaining four dimensions in the middle range: face-saver (2.97); procedural (3.75); conflict inducer (4.26); and status oriented (4.49). The sparsely occupied continuum shows a degree of role complexity that rejects self evident conclusions, unless the definition is adapted to our reality, because "to understand us you have to live with us, share our lives, learn how we feel, what we must tolerate." How should one account for these behaviors? Are they the exception that confirms the rule, or do they represent something different? And if they do lead elsewhere, do they indicate a stage on the road to the desirable end, or do they constitute an adaptive response?

Face saver, indirect, avoids negatives, evasive, alludes to the fear of humiliation and to failure due to non-compliance with expectations in the exercise of a position. This translates into maintaining a front and refers to covering up a situation or a feeling so as not to cause a scandal. It alludes to low credibility and inconstancies, and recalls the frequency of unfulfilled

TABLE 18.3
Culture Dimensions on Industry Level

	Finance "As Is"/ "Should Be"	Std. Dev.	Food "As Is"/ "Should Be"	Std. Dev.
Performance Orientation	3.54/ 6.37	0.15/ 0.29	3.88/ 6.40	0.48/ 0.13
Assertiveness	4.44/ 3.67	0.16/ 0.41	4.31/ 3.35	0.36/ 0.37
Future Orientation	3.01/ 5.69	0.20/ 0.15	3.12/ 5.79	0.19/ 0.27
Gender Egalitarianism	3.46/ 4.93	0.12/ 0.23	3.42/ 5.06	0.37/ .09
Humane Orientation	3.82/ 5.43	0.29/ 0.41	4.16/ 5.65	0.29/ 0.28
Institutional Collectivism	3.62/ 5.33	0.09/ 0.34	3.74/ 5.23	0.22/ 0.23
Power Distance	5.69/ 2.34	0.24/ 0.11	5.35/ 2.89	0.48/ 0.17
In-Group Collectivism	5.44/ 6.05	0.27/ 0.24	5.47/ 6.26	0.22/ 0.06
Uncertainty Avoidance	3.61/ 4.69	0.37/ 0.46	3.69/ 4.47	0.31/ 0.55

promises and the repeated use of euphemisms. With procedural, ritualistic, formal, habitual, cautious, conflict inducer, normative, secretive, intragroup competitor, status consciousness, status conscious, and class conscious constitute a subconstellation that identifies entry-level requirements. These are threshold capabilities, socially validated attributes and behaviors, adaptive in that they discriminate merely technical aspects from that which a person must learn what to do upon occupying a position of authority (Heifetz, op cit. 1994). They assume that, to perform within the requirements of the role, a person must exhibit such traits, as they have been found to help based on past experience in similar situations.

Thus, GLOBE respondents construct a complex conception of the leader. The three-pronged constellation signals a change. Whereas the positive end of the spectrum may point to socially well-reputed attributes, and the negative end suggests experienced abusive traits, the middle range identifies adaptive behaviors in the light of major corporate changes that give rise to top management/shareholder discretionary behaviors. The responses differ from Haire, Ghiselli and Porter (1966) and Altschul (1970), and indicate a level of complexity that has not been documented earlier.

10. FINDINGS OF THE ETHNOGRAPHIC RESEARCH

Nine focus groups were held, lasting 45 minutes each with 8 to 10 people, as well as 21 individual interviews of 20 minutes each. Participants were middle managers from leading firms in different industries, each group from one company, with 78% of the participants under 30 years old, representing a broad spectrum of functional areas. "Managerial Effectiveness Exercises" were completed and subjects participated actively in the subsequent ethnographic interviews (Agar, 1994; Agar & McDonald, 1996; Thomas, 1996). All phrases in quotations are comments made in the focus groups.

Focus groups participants were informed of the GLOBE purposes and conversations were held on management, leadership and managerial practices. Participants described the conditions under which Argentines have lived and suggested distinctive attributes and behaviors understood as adaptive responses. They indicated that change is under way: "Now, we live in freedom." They described a history of abundance, of confidence in riches; a young society,

TABLE 18.4

Comparison of Culture Dimensions Between Society and Industries

	Society "As Is"	Industry "As Is"	Society "Should Be"	Industry "Should Be"	Society Difference	Industry Difference
Performance Orientation	3.65	3.61	6.35	6.38	2.70	2.77
Future Orientation	3.08	3.06	5.78	5.74	2.70	2.68
Assertiveness	4.20	4.37	3.25	3.51	0.95	0.86
Gender Egalitarianism	3.49	3.44	4.98	4.99	1.49	1.55
Humane Orientation	3.99	3.99	5.58	5.54	1.59	1.55
Institutional Collectivism	3.66	3.68	5.32	5.28	1.66	1.60
Power Distance	5.64	5.52	2.33	2.61	3.31	2.91
In-Group Collectivism	5.51	5.45	6.15	6.15	0.64	0.70
Uncertainty Avoidance	3.65	3.65	4.66	4.58	1.01	0.93

with an incipient identity: "This was a politically unstable society, with dictatorships, repression, high inflation and constant change. Abuse of power was expected. However, we had work and upward mobility."

Democracy is struggling, because justice is corrupt and inefficient, technical progress dehumanizes, competition provokes social instability, the gap between the poor and the rich increases, and, therefore, a selfish culture flourishes. Advances are being made: one ex-minister in jail for a year, others suffer detention while due process advances, and former President Menem was placed under house arrest and restricted from leaving the country under suspicion of illicit association to conspire.

As a consequence, Argentines develop a strong relationship with family and friends: "We are in solidary with our next of kin," an attribute that generates affect, sociability, passion, expressiveness, and informal behaviors. On the basis of uncertainty, Argentines became competitive, ingenious, flexible, capable in the face of adversity and new situations, but "incapable of establishing long-term goals; they devote little effort to a job. They adapt but don't commit themselves."

A second task required the participants to "think of a person with great motivating power, a capability to influence you and to allow you, or your area, to contribute to the success of your business. How would you call such a person? Think of a specific circumstance and describe the person who you are thinking of."

Stimulated by generic questions, the ethnographic method made it possible to sift singular aspects of the culture. Although no formal typology was developed, discrete and repeated mentions were made of the terms *dueño,* owner; *jefe,* boss; *buen jefe,* good boss; *gerente,* manager; and *líder,* a term used to refer to popular figures, who lead by their example. The term *gerente excepcional* (exceptional manager) came up seldom. These were used as mental composites, were spontaneously repeated in all groups and structured the exchange. We call them icons. Moreover, in the cases in which the use of the term did not correspond to the culturally validated meaning, the speaker would include circumlocutions and clarifications to transmit his ideas.

Prior to describing the icons with illustrative vignettes, the rhetoric used is shown to be consistent with the Collectivism I and II dimensions.

Participants spoke assertively as most information was self referenced. They emphasized their knowledge of the case and its contingencies. They approached phenomena through anecdotes, not data. Rational presentation was accompanied by emotion. Non sequiturs are to be understood as said.

Focus groups devoted 83% of their total time to negative experiences. Only 17% of the protocols refer to *gerentes* or to *buenos jefes,* both required leaders. One participant asked if the research project would take into account "what really happens, as against what management books say." They expressed doubts as to the possibility of change, as well as to the potential impact of the research project.

At first, participants conceptualized in dichotomical terms, not on the basis of dynamic, complex processes; they referred to expressions of whatever is primitive, what emerges naturally, is essentially unchanging and accounts for an observed reality which seems difficult to change. Differences of opinion were dealt with through generating more options and not by overlooking the differences . Once dialogue ensued, participants developed refined categories.

The *dueño/owner* icon: *Dueño* refers to a proprietor, or members of a family structure, and recalls the term *patrón de estancia,* homestead owner. Thus, headship, not professional leadership, is implied. Authority is vested in the individual, and does not imply role performance. Little competence or maturity is attributed to the *dueño,* and it connotes exploitation. Such people "can only tell the difference between making or losing money." A representative vignette is: "The *dueño* here doesn't give a damn. Happy faces, sad faces, they are all the same to him. Wear a happy face, but don't believe his answers. Because when he's happy, he won't tell you anything because he's afraid you might ask for something, and on the day he's made up his mind to fire you, he'll tell you 'we don't need you any more.'"

The characterization emphasizes "here and now," and, in a society that normally prides itself on relationships, for the *dueño,* the other person is unworthy. Thus, the *dueño* icon alludes to absentee leadership and deference implies acritical obedience.

A second example accounts for the complexity of the process. An intermediary figure appears between *patrón* and *peón:* "Out in the country it's different. Out there punishments have no value. When I started fresh out of college, the owner introduced me (to the men) and left me alone. That's where it starts. Because a *gaucho* knows everything! He can drive a herd, build a mill, tighten the wires, shear the sheep, geld, even play the guitar. So you have to hold your own. Because you may have the job, but until you earn it and they acknowledge you as one of them, nothing happens." This vignette introduces the possibilities opened up by the role of an intermediary, the supervisor, who may end up as either *jefe* or *buen jefe,* as will be seen. The speaker acknowledges the difficulty of supervisory work with farm laborers with multiple technical and human talents, and stresses that he will be accepted when and if he contributes with his work. The turning point is established: headship is one matter; but leadership cannot exist without followership.

The *buen jefe/good boss* icon: The *buen jefe* occupies a supervisory position and maintains personal relationships with his wards, that is, he is formally charged with a responsibility but keeps in touch. He "develops chemistry, people follow him," performs within a system of rewards and punishments, is technically competent and sensitive. "The *buen jefe* provides backing, acts as an example, provides work."

Most participants said that they never had a *buen jefe:* "If a fire breaks out the *buen jefe* stays calm, solves problems, shows himself, congratulates. He is interested in people, but his hand doesn't tremble when a person must be fired because he did something that shouldn't have been done." This is critical in times of stress: "If you go right up to him, the *buen jefe* protects you. But in my twenty years I'd have to choose the least bad one. Because *jefes* here have a sense of royalty."

Participants value discerning capabilities: The *buen jefe* knows he is a part of a project in a complex structure. "The *buen jefe* is flexible. He knows how to close his eyes. He has his own merit system, and he evaluates everybody every week end. He uses a points system and he puts them on a tablet so everybody can see."

Interpersonal dynamics make him special: "Above all, the *buen jefe* is tops. And he can tell people apart, knows that a machinist is not a pick and shovel man."

The *jefe/boss* icon: Emphasis on consideration produces two conceptualizations in the supervisor's role. Consequently, two alternative icons are used, *jefe* and *gerente. Jefe* involves the occupant of a position that confers privileges, connotes autocratic style and emphasizes policing behaviors. It is the extension of the shadow of the *dueño,* while *gerente* alludes to a supervisory role in a management system. The *jefe* takes advantage of a slot in a structure where subordination is prevalent; the *gerente* handles himself within the framework of a contract that includes dialogue.

Jefes are overbearing, distance themselves, and keep information to themselves. "Argentines fly as soon as they have a post, or a uniform. They ask for exceptions, they feel free from norms. They make you stay in after hours. And as things stand now, who would dare go home?" And again: "They tell how to behave, but you know what's going on. Still, the *jefes* tries to be at all places, what gets done starts and finishes with him. He often opens without knowing how, not knowing how to follow through. He uses the structure to uphold the fantasy of his leadership."

Impression management places him as a *jefe:* One comment stresses this point: "I suffered under different styles of management. But I make people participate. Other styles never felt good. I replaced a manager who was a *jefe.* He was authoritarian. With him I had to maintain a double standard. I didn't follow his instructions. He said: 'Go kick the shit out of that son of a bitch.' In Argentine firms it is accepted that one has a godfather. You have tactical complicity between the people who have worked together long. It's a mafia."

The *gerente/manager* icon: The *gerente* emerges as a business becomes an organization. Management means "doing things as they should be done," "knowing that a good manager doesn't do everything well." Thus they suggest that a third party establishes goals that the manager must reach. "He is given objectives and can make mistakes." To satisfy this need, the manager "innovates, but not like crazy." Like the *buen jefe* and unlike the *jefe,* the *gerente* includes the notion of an authority system: a *gerente* knows his decisions imply costs and benefits and incorporates feedback.

Professional management is an emerging concept, "He had to renegotiate a contract to establish new prices. He instructed two of us to find fields of mutual benefit, that the others would be interested in. We understood him, saw the mission and the goal, and we did it and it worked." The example shows that even having demonstrated benefits, new practices are not universally adopted.

Gerentes know that norms expect them to include consideration. "This manager had a temp, and it was a bad relationship. But when she got sick, he got her medical coverage, got her a full time position with him, and gave her time to recuperate. He did it because it was expected." He "was a tough cookie" but performed within expected policies and procedures.

Ethnographic data collection reinforced the need for decisiveness, diplomacy, inspiration, vision, integrity, and performance orientation; and the media content analysis added further to this conception. Still it is recalled that in day to day matters decisiveness goes hand in hand with lack of scruples and action orientation can be ruthless. Because "our culture places everything on the man at the top. Everything is asked of him and he is criticized for everything. There is little sense of community and organization, less leaders come up, and *jefes* think that leadership implies opportunism."

In a period of business transformations, strikingly few examples were given of individuals with professional, managerial, and social competences, action oriented persons. An invitation to think of exceptional managers produced few testimonials, and these referred to foreign managers in local endeavors. Exceptions were references to the Minister of Economics of the first years of the Menem administration. "Cavallo is an exceptional manager. He grabbed the country, implemented the Currency Board and is making major changes in the economy. He did what had to be done when the time was right. He has a solid team, he does not improvise. He is capable and committed." But the word *líder* is only used to refer to politicians and soccer coaches, popular leaders with special gifts.

The *líder/maverick* icon: In Argentina *líder* is reserved for public figures endowed with unique gifts, identifies whoever heads a complex process, embodies the masses, needs no intermediaries. "Perón was the only indisputable *líder*. He stayed in people's hearts."

Brief comments refer to the construction of the image of the local leader, as for example: "A leader who 'makes things happen', doesn't seem Argentine." There are some, but very few are commented upon. "We think of people who return us to a time of splendor." In this sense, participants were skeptical as to the existence of this figure, as explained by the only comment on the heroic component in leadership: "The *guapo* (the maverick) goes it alone; he walks forth with his back uncovered. Here, to be a *guapo* you have to be against (them) and you don't last. The *guapos* are in the Chacarita (the popular cemetery)." Boldness and daring are desired but carry huge penalties.

The *líder* is expected to break rules and, alternatively, he will be admired and despised. Participants use *líder* for a person capable of facing a crisis, intimating that crises bring forth the complex relationship between the leaders and the led. Thus a *líder* is relied upon when major changes are needed, "he understands the emotions of the masses, is a trickster, knows how to channel emotions towards a goal," which clashes against the nature of the instrumental relationship required in organizations.

The *líder* recovers territory and imbues it with new meaning. He produces identification because "he does what we like to do ourselves." He becomes an idol, which reinforces the perception of his infallibility. As "he can lead because he is allowed practically everything." Moreover, "he demands exceptional conditions, and as he gains favor through his initiatives, he is awarded more space, but if he fails, he must disappear."

The *líder* is a demagogue and communicates his vision passionately. He develops new tracks, but is trapped by his own rhetoric. "Everybody knows he does not say everything he thinks, nor will do everything he announces." The political *líder* acquires mythical dimensions but "is reviled when he breaks his promises." "*Líder* refers to inborn qualities, to the charisma of the macho. Who does what we would like to do but don't dare."

GLOBE research was conducted during the Menem administration. "I saw President Menem. He talked serenely. He said what people wanted to hear. What had to be done and how. More than a thousand people reacted enthusiastically. They were ready to back him at whatever cost." A complementary vignette: "I don't know Menem personally but he deactivated the power factors that could face him in his desire to accumulate personal power indefinitely. He acts before others, advancing with what the most powerful factions want, and concedes of his own volition, pardoning the military, privatizing and following the dictates of the World Bank to satisfy the owners of the foreign debt, and ceding privatized corporations to local groups. His pragmatism and image as a moral rule breaker fascinate us, and weaken everybody who stands in his way, reinforcing his own power."

The sample included few women. One comment on women as leaders was, "Evita promoted cultural change communicating with the people. She gave a voice to those who didn't have one. She brought a vision, an intuition and feeling to public life in Argentina. People were loyal to her. She was the first woman who put ideas of organization into social work."

Soccer coaches are popular leaders: "Menotti is a coach. His leadership capability is seen in the way the players reacted when he took over. Before he took over, the team played without a plan and lost. Fans and newspapers pressured them. He imposed his method and talked a lot. Generated trust so even in interviews the players talked differently. This self confidence and his technical knowledge helped."

In synthesis, in a context where the State and organizations are illusions, the inclusive leader/follower relationship exists in the *buen jefe, gerente* (including *gerente excepcional*) and soccer coach as *líder* icons, while the *dueño, jefe* and politician as *líder* icons reflect an asymmetrical, excluding relationship. Ten years after the ethnographic data were collected, Menem and Cavallo are reviled.

11. FINDINGS OF THE MEDIA ANALYSIS

Media chosen for content analyses of the written press were: (a) *La Nación,* the traditional daily newspaper; (b) *Clarín,* the largest circulation daily; and (c) *El Cronista Comercial,* a business daily. All enjoy wide circulation and a solid reputation, cover national and international issues, are widely read by middle managers, and include a diversity of opinions, levels of editorial sophistication and control.

Research was carried out in September, 1995. Media data collection was carried out on news printed during the first fortnights of September 1995 and September 2000. In both periods a major crisis was given front page attention. In the first, a dispute between President Menem and his Economics Minister; in the second a scandal in the Senate. They both give evidence of key components of the prevalent leadership model, that of key players in open confrontation.

Leadership issues were chosen, analyses identified the leader mentioned, what he/she did, and enacted behaviors (Ogliastri, chap. 19, this volume). Key paragraphs were chosen and classified by categories. A distinct change is evidenced comparing the 1995 and 2000 data collection periods.

For *Clarín,* leadership implies power brokerage. Relevant behaviors are backing, stalling, closing rank, denying having said what had been recorded, changing sides, maneuvering and persuading. Conflict management is the prevalent mode of exchange. Personality issues are presented in all walks of life. Politicians, ambassadors, policemen and sports figures are key exponents of this dramatic approach. One article in the 2000 period talks of the survival of man who got lost in a snow-storm in Patagonia and survived because "he didn't give up."

Ever more space is devoted to the management of complex governmental or business issues, whereas the intricacies of an instrumental relationship are developed in discussions between football players and their coaches, for example, between the player Maradona, who threatened not to play if his coach was fired, and his coach Bianchi, explaining his leadership model, are extensively given their due. The exception was the case of the crime against María Soledad, where it is reported that after 5 years nobody is held accountable and the article pinpoints the protagonists: the girl's parents and the Catholic nun who headed a new form of protest, the Silent Marches that toppled the governor.

During the first period, from 86 comments on leadership, *Clarín* includes 21 references to the replacement of the minister of the economy and its consequences on the economy (24.5%). In the second, a Senate scandal gets a lot of attention and is discussed in depth. In both cases, emphasis is placed on institution building, and the balance between technical and political considerations in the exercise of authority vested in the functionaries. Negotiation practices are mentioned in two pieces during the September 2000 period, whereas these practices were absent in the September 1995 period. Topics related to Uncertainty Avoidance and Power Distance dimensions are stressed as for example: "I am willing to let you participate in transcendental decision making" (said the Minister of the Economy). "Cavallo left an unusual opening of the Palacio de Hacienda for the business community. His goal was obvious, to consolidate the unprecedented political backing that the establishment gave him through an institutional formula and so remain firmly in his post in spite of the attacks of Ultra-Menemism."

Corruption and misdemeanor issues add to 10 references in the first period, and accounted for over 30% of the headlines during the second, where a major bribery scandal was the focus of public attention. In both *La Nación* and *Clarín,* news included analytical pieces by Argentine intellectuals on the strengthening of institutions if the Senate scandal was investigated and due process followed. Simultaneously, the Army proclaimed contrition "for its responsibilities in the dramatic and cruel events of the past," and the local Catholic Church "confessed its faults and asked for forgiveness."

Performance and Future Orientation topics were practically absent during the 1995 period, but entrepreneurial, scientific and artistic pursuits received more space in the 2000 period with major articles printed on pioneering work in surgery, a major award in literature and the pluck of "Pope John XXIII, a Catholic Church revolutionary."

Humane Orientation and Collectivism I-Institutional Collectivism issues, were expressed by union and church topics (7.0%); and the assassination of a girl in the province of Tucumán occupied 2.4%, the crime of María Soledad. A governor was brought down and 80 Silent Marches were carried out. Five years after the assassination, no one was guilty and there was no one to judge them. On September 10, 1990, the body of a girl of 17 was found in an abandoned lot. She had been beaten and raped. The case moved the country and changed the history of Catamarca.

Beyond soccer results, papers regularly devoted space to players' thoughts and ideas. Transformational leadership concepts appeared in an interview with Bianchi, a coach under the heading; "A winner's prescriptions: Orderliness is the hardest." "We managed by all of us pulling together."

La Nación understands leadership as the exercise of authority. Comments refer to the institutional background within which interactions occur in a complex, changing context. Articles deal with the structure of the economy, concerns about the future, current trends. Two articles in the first period addressed the human aspects of leadership. In the second period, a major article was devoted to an Argentine entrepreneur who successfully developed and sold his company to a German concern.

Out of eight articles on leadership in *La Nación,* seven referred to Power Distance, e.g.,: Diagnosis to foreign investors, the difference between Cavallo's Currency Board and others, is that he relies on his person and is not supported by an institutional framework.

To *El Cronista Comercial,* leadership implies the alignment of third parties to decisions arrived at. It has a financial approach, quotes figures, debates laws and regulations, discusses the actions of shareholders and executives, but devotes little attention to decision making. In both periods, the paper ponders on the costs of depending on the talent of select protagonists for the continuity and well-being of political and economic programs.

12. SYNTHESIS FOR LEADERSHIP

Argentines are habituated to a form of deference based on audacity, lack of scruples and over-simplification. This is accompanied by the self-deprecating "roban pero hacen," "they steal but at least they get things done." Leaders become grandees, heroes, idols, semigods, dicta-tors, and, as such, are inviolate. Action is inhibited by the acritical acceptance of such behav-iors, and the ignorance as to how they are built and reinforced.

Friedrich (1961) suggests that political science "makes sense as long as it differentiates Luther's leadership from Hitler's." Without reaching such extremes, oversimplification clouds the issue of management, which deals with complexity; while leadership deals with change (Kotter, 1988). Current idealizations of leadership lead to value judgments wherein manage-ment deals with the past and is negatively connoted, whereas leadership deals with the future and is positively connoted. Attention should be devoted to the fact that most countries award malevolent the lowest mean values and place visionary and other such behav-iors as high mean values.

Analysis of the Argentine distribution of mean values shows that the middle range mean values express cultural idiosyncrasies and adaptive practices. Moreover, GLOBE quantitative and qualitative data converge to offer an innovative reading into the components of leadership in Argentina and suggest a hypothesis.

To interpret a group's statements, Hofstede (1997) separates desirable from desired: how people believe the world ought to be as against what they wish for themselves. In the case of the desirable, the norm is absolute, while in the case of the desired, the patterns are statisti-cal, because they show majority choice. Similarly Argyris (1992) differentiates between espoused theory, which refers to what a person claims to follow, and theory in use, which may be inferred from action.

Within these frameworks, (a) GLOBE lower mean values refer to abusive leaders, (b) higher mean values refer to a legendary figures, and (c) attributes in the middle range refer to the tolerated leader. Heifetz (1994) reminds us that "scholars might usefully consider that leadership is less an 'As Is' than a 'Should Be'" (p. 286). Our hypothesis holds that the mid-dle mean values are of special interest because they describe a leader who is tolerated within prevalent conditions.

This may be upheld by the fact that all countries place close to two thirds of all leadership dimensions in this high mean category, a matter that merits attention. Within this context, comparing country mean values could suggest expectations placed on vision. For example, the mean value for Albania is 5.02, implying an inordinate degree of hope placed in leader-ship, whereas the mean value for the United States is 4.52. In comparison, the mean value for the Latin American group of countries is 4.61, and for Argentina it is 4.58.

The distribution of mean values for all the Latin America countries identifies differences tol-erated, that is, mid-range behaviors. This pinpoints country peculiarities. The majority coincides in most dimensions, but specific distinctions are to be researched, as for example, autocratic and nonparticipative behaviors seem to be tolerated in Mexico and Venezuela; in Costa Rica decisiveness seems not to be tolerated; in Argentina, Bolivia and Mexico modesty seems not to be tolerated; in Brazil, autonomy and self-centered behaviors seem to be tolerated.

13. SYNTHESIS: THE GLOBE CONTRIBUTION

GLOBE offers empirical dimensions to understand social behavior in Argentine management. Middle managers categorize leadership behaviors through the icons *líder*/politician, *dueño,* and *jefe,* which refer to abusive leaders. *Buen jefe* and *gerente* include significant others but only the first includes attributes that the management literature associates with a leader (Bennis & Nanus, 1985; Schein, 1985; Senge, 1990). The social contract has been broken and skepticism prevails. Respondents think the behaviors of the transformational leader unlikely. Altschul and Carbonell (2003) document how change processes carried out in corporate settings in recent years may balance this view.

14. ADDENDUM

This paper was written in 1995, referee reviewed and corrected in 2003 and in 2005. The downfall of the Argentine economy has been the subject of manifold interpretations. To the authors, the strength of the characteristics of the abusive leader, and the tolerated management behaviors, that is, face saver, procedural, conflict inducer, and status oriented, can best be understood through Weber's notion of the capitalistic adventurer (1992), a figure that can well typify the Argentine context of the 1990s.

15. SUGGESTIONS FOR VISITORS

Argentines say they "descend from the ships." This image illustrates the immigratory composition of the society and may explain why Europeans and North Americans feel at ease. Argentines are educated and identify with Western European values. The high educational level they enjoyed made them cosmopolitan and progressive. Five Nobel Prize winners in the sciences and peace, outstanding opera houses, and active theater and entertainment make Argentines proud of their cultural tradition. People enjoy the amenities of life in a contemporary society: the infrastructure is modern, and computer and communications technologies are extensively applied. Still, Argentines retain their family rooted traditions, where self validating social mores define decision making.

Centuries of Spanish domination left their traces. Spain transferred its institutional system and people considered themselves part of the mother country, not colonizers. In Latin America, status was attained by adapting to such standards. Economy was based on the manorial lifestyle, where status was connected to birth and bloodlines, profit was based on annuities, and loyalty was owed to individuals rather than to laws of the land.

The Latin view of individualism emphasizes each person's uniqueness. The person is valued for who he is, not for what he does. Within this tradition, Argentines are rule breakers, improvise and enjoy the unusual aspects of any event and the free-wheeling discussions that ensue. Debates are charged with affect. Overall, Argentines are ethnocentric, proud of their own country more than of the region.

Leadership is often understood as supremacy. Hegemony is claimed by many that hold public positions and is upheld even through confrontation. This often leads to authoritarian behaviors. Growth crises that in other societies may be understood as stages within a transition cause distress. Argentines find it hard to establish societies and teams. Alternation, or the creation of options are difficult to institute and survive after repeated upheavals.

Power Distance is strong. Upper-status people expect to deal only with individuals of their own standing. Decision making is top down, spontaneous, and impulsive, with an emphasis on concepts. Support from a superior may change if circumstances suggest it, so lower-status persons use caution and do not put forward conflicting ideas. Professionals may not question their superiors although they may know them to be wrong.

Argentines are emotionally sensitive. Words and actions may be interpreted as offenses to a person's inner worth. Argentines use euphemisms and double entendres. They tend to read between the lines, and are good at interpreting messages in their many derivations, and their conclusions are often extreme. They exhibit a refined approach towards reality. They are aware of the "here and now" aspects of an issue, and feel that most matters may change due to actions of third parties beyond their control. This creates a social modality of permanent declamation which translates into poor performance.

Argentines feel that things happen. They conceive of time as abstract, as a resource that helps build relationships, not events in terms of hours and or minutes.

A strong emphasis is placed on personal associations. Networks serve as safety nets and facilitate mobility. When a person needs something done, he will resort preferably to someone he knows. Relationships take precedence over formal contact with institutions, laws and regulations. As such, due process may be regarded with suspicion because it could override informal understandings. The influence of special interests on decision making is expected and condoned.

Participation is vibrant in ongoing discussions on soccer and politics, for example. Expressiveness and emotion in verbal communication are tied to concepts of individualism. The Argentine will impose through eloquence and wit, will rely on charm, and believes that no task is above him. Argentines interrupt as an indication of eagerness to share opinions and enjoy argument. This may dilute efforts to reach concrete simple goals.

Argentines are gregarious. Men, who maintain eye to eye contact, embrace with physical demonstrations of affect. Relationships, based on reciprocity, are informal and stable over time. Visitors are greeted warmly. The expectation of extending a relationship to parties' mutual advantage is present. Personal relationships are established with ease. This does not carry over to the business sphere, however.

Currently, after more than 20 years of democratic regimes committed to low inflation, a free economy, and open trade, Argentina shows change. In the cities, people are always in a hurry and remain active throughout long hours of the day. A feeling of loss of privacy and control of their personal destiny prevails, because, after radical free marketers introduced their normative strictures, the income gap widened, a percentage of Argentines benefited, cities were modernized, and tourism has increased significantly. The middle class is definitely pauperized as expected trickle-down effects of the inclusion of free-market economics had suggested but did not materialize. Civilian governments have not found equitable balances between democracy and efficiency, organizations have become more rigid rather than more flexible, courts are ineffective and corrupt and, with penury, street violence increased. The inability to develop a competitive strategy produced stagnation and frustration. Pessimism ensued and many emigrate: they "return to the ships."

16. A BRIEF COMMENT ON THE LIMITATIONS OF THE CURRENT STUDY

For an analysis of Argentine management practices, purposefully devoid of demographic data collection, we chose the title: "A Crisis of Guidance: Argentine Leadership Icons and Middle Managers Adaptive Responses." Findings need replication but a crisis of leadership can be hypothesized.

Data collection was carried out in 1995, and the downfall of the Argentine economy, after following the prescriptions of international agencies, occurred in 2001. Moreover, the cases of Enron and Worldcom ("Capitalism and its troubles," 2002, "Fallen idols," 2002, Mintzberg, Simons, & Basu, 2002) signaled critical incidents that cause more than attention.

Simultaneously, many transformation projects developed in Argentina (Altschul & Carbonell, 2003) and much has happened since, most especially after 2003: fiscal goals are being met, reserves and industrial productivity have increased year after year since then, and unemployment has decreased significantly.

Further research should relate market conditions and economic guidelines on the emergence of national adaptive behaviors.

ACKNOWLEDGMENTS

Flavio Ruffolo wrote the economic history of Argentina; Mercedes López was instrumental in drafting the final version; Marina Altschul researched and wrote key papers on the development of the banking and food industries; María Marta Preziosa was instrumental in data collection, interviews and revisions.

Special thanks are due to colleagues for the careful review of the first drafts by Héctor Bozunovsky, Claudia d'Annunzio, Victor Lidejover, Juan Magliano, Vicente Miñana, Zita Montes de Oca, Julio Neffa, José Luis Roces, Monique Thiteux; to Adriana Cristensen, Ernesto Gantman, Laura Golpe, Fernando Isuani, Nora Gorrochategui, Marcela Jabbaz, Claudia Lozano, Francisco Suárez and Jorge Walter, researchers at the Instituto de Investigaciones Administrativas, School of Economics, Universidad de Buenos Aires; and to my students in the post graduate programs in Human Resources, School of Economics, Universidad de Buenos Aires, and at the Universidad Siglo XXI, Córdoba for their critical suggestions. Johannes Adams helped make the text readable.

REFERENCES

Agar, M. (1994). Ethnography manual for leadership study. In M. Agar & J. McDonald (Eds.), *Focus groups and ethnography*. Human Organization.

Aguinis, M. (1995). In P. Lóizaga (Ed.), *La contradicción Argentina* (pp. 13, 41). Buenos Aires: Emecé.

Altschul, C. (1970). *Managerial attitudes in Argentina*. Unpublished master's thesis, Iowa State University.

Altschul, C. (1999). *Dinámica de la negociación estratégica*. Buenos Aires: Granica, p. 23ff.

Altschul, C., & Carbonell, R. (Eds.). (2003). *Transformando: Prácticas de cambio en empresas argentinas*. Buenos Aires: Eudeba Universidad de Buenos Aires.

Argyris, A. (1992). *On organizational learning*. Cambridge: Blackwell.

Baamonde, C. (2001). *Proyecto de investigación*. SPES.

Barón, A., del Carril M., & Gómez, A. (1995). *Por qué se fueron.* Buenos Aires: Emecé.

Bass, B. M. (1990). *Bass & Stogdill's handbook of leadership.* New York: The Free Press.

Barzini, L. (1964). *The Italians.* London: Atheneum.

Bennis, W. (1989). *Cómo llegar a ser leader* [On becoming a leader]. Bogotá: Norma.

Bennis, W. (1990). *Why leaders can't lead: The unconscious conspiracy continues.* San Francisco: Jossey-Bass.

Bennis, W., & Nanus, B. (1985). *Leaders: Strategies for taking charge.* New York: Harper & Row.

Bouzas, R., & Fanelli, J. M. (2001). *Mercosur: Integración y Crecimiento.* Buenos Aires: Fundación OSDE.

CEPAL Foreign Trade data base. (2001, June). *In Le monde diplomatique.*

Conger, J. (1989). *The charismatic leader.* New York: Jossey-Bass.

Cozarinsky, E. (1995) . In O. Baron, M. del Carril, & A. Gómez (Eds.), *Por qué se fueron.* Buenos Aires: Emecé.

Denevi, M. (1995). In P Lóizaga (Ed.), *La contradicicción Argentina.* Buenos Aires: Emecé.

Drucker, P. (1954). *The practice of management.* New York: Harper.

Drucker, P. (1964). *Managing for results.* New York: Harper.

Drucker, P. (1993). *Gerencia para el futuro* [Managing for the future]. Bogotá: Norma.

Etkin, J. (1999). *La doble moral de las organizaciones.* Buenos Aires: McGraw-Hill.

Fanelli, J. (1999). *Crecimiento en equidad.* Paper presented at the OSDE conference, Buenos Aires.

Ferrer, A. (1998) *El capitalismo argentino.* Buenos Aires: Fondo de Cultura Económica.

Filmus, D. (1996). *Estado, sociedad y educación en Argentina de fin de siglo: Procesos y desafíos.* Buenos Aires: Troquel.

Friedrich, C. (1961). Political leadership and the problem of charismatic power. *Journal of Politics, 24,* 19.

Gantman, E. (1994). *La evolución de las ideologías gerenciales desde el siglo XIX hasta el presente.* Unpublished doctoral dissertation, Facultad de Ciencias Económicas, Universidad de Buenos Aires.

García Canclini, N. (1995). *Culturas híbridas: Estrategias para entrar y salir de la modernidad.* Buenos Aires: Sudamericana.

Goldman, N., & Salvatore, R. (1998). *Caudillismos rioplatenses: Nuevas miradas a un viejo problema.* Buenos Aires: Eudeba.

Graumann, C. F. (1986). Changing conceptions of leadership: An introduction. In C. F. Graumann & S. Moscovici (Eds.), *Changing conceptions of leadership.* New York: Springer Verlag.

Haire, M., Ghiselli, E. E., & Porter, L. W. (1966). *Managerial thinking: An international study.* New York: Wiley.

Heifetz, R. A. (1994). *Leadership without easy answers.* Cambridge, MA: Belknap Press of Harvard University Press.

Hobsbawm, E. (2000). *Entrevista sobre el sigloXXI.* Barcelona: Crítica.

Hofstede, G. (1997). *Cultures and organizations: Software of the mind.* New York: McGraw-Hill.

Hofstede, G. (1984). *Culture's consequences: International differences in work related values.* Newbury Park: Sage.

House, R. J., Hanges, P. J., Javidan, M., Dorfman, P. W., Gupta, V., & GLOBE Associates (2004). *Cultures, leadership, and organizations: The GLOBE study of 62 societies.* Thousand Oaks, CA: Sage.

House, R. J., Hanges, P. J., Ruiz-Quintanilla, S. A., Dorfman, P. W., Javidan, M., Dickson, M., et al. (1999). Cultural influences on leadership and organizations: Project GLOBE. In W. Mobley, M. J. Gessner, & V. Arnold (Eds.), *Advances in global leadership* (Vol. 1, pp. 171–234). Stanford, CT: JAI.

IDEA. (1992). Coloquio 1992, Cambio organizacional, Informe. Karpf, L. Felcman, I. et al.

IDEA. (1993, May). La empresa en proceso de cambio: ¿Hay experiencias exitosas? Revista IDEA, p. 6f.

IDEA. (1996, November). Renovación del management. Martínez Nogueira, R. Revista IDEA, p. 61f.

IDEA. (1999). Foro sobre Estrategia empresaria. Mimeo.

INDEC (1999). *Anuario Estadístico de la República Argentina.* Ministerio de Economía, de Obras y Servicios Públicos.

Isuani, A. (1998). Anomia social y anemia estatal. Sobre integración social en Argentina. *Sociedad, 10,* 103–128.

Kotter, J. P. (1988). The leadership factor. New York: The Free Press.

Lewis, P. (1990). *The crisis of Argentine capitalism.* Raleigh, NC: The University of North Carolina Press.

Lóizaga, P. (1995). *La contradicicción argentina.* Buenos Aires: Emecé.

López, M. (2000). *Percepciones, valores y significados en el management de empresas de Argentina de fin de siglo.* Unpublished doctoral thesis, Facultad de Psicología, Universidad de Buenos Aires.

Lozano, C. (1999). *Un análisis del colonialismo y del nacionalismo empresarial desde la perspectiva del género.* Mimeo.

Markwald, Lamadrid y Asociados. (2005, August 14). Private research report.

McClelland, D. C. (1961). *The achieving society.* Princeton, NJ: van Norstrand.

Mintzberg, H., Simons, A., & Basu, B. (2002). *"Beyond selfishness."* Available at http://henrymintzberg.com.

Moss Kanter, R. (1983). *The change masters: Innovation and entrepreneurship in the American corporation.* New York: Simon & Shuster.

Nino, C. (1992). *Un país al margen de la ley.* Buenos Aires: Emecé.

Ogliastri, E. (1976). Estudio comparativo sobre movilidad social inter-generacional en las élites regionales de nueve centros urbanos de Colombia [A comparative study of inter-generational social mobility in eight Colombian cities]. *Revista de Planeación y Desarrollo, 7*(2).

Ogliastri, E., & Dávila, C. (1983). Estructura de poder y Desarrollo en once ciudades intermedias de Colombia [Power structure and development in eleven intermediate size Colombian cities]. *Desarrollo y Sociedad, 12.*

Ogliastri, E., McMillen, C., Altschul, C., Arias, M. E., de Bustamante, C., Dávila, C., Dorfman, P., Ferreira de la Coletta, M., Fimmen, C., & Martínez, S. (1998). Cultura y liderazgo organizacional en 10 países de América Latina: El estudio GLOBE. *ACADEMIA. Revista Latinoamericana de Administración, CLADEA, Bogotá, 22,* 29–57.

Ogliastri, E., & Whittingham, M. (2000). El liderazgo colombiano: Un estudio de los medios escritos de comunicación [Colombian leadership: A study of printed media]. In Corporación Calidad, Diálogos sobre Gestión II. Bogotá: Colciencias.

Sábato, J. (1988). *La clase dominante en la Argentina moderna: Formación y características.* CISEA Buenos Aires: Grupo Editor Latinoamericano.

Sartori, G. (1985). *Partidos y participación política.* Madrid: Aguilar.

Schein, E. H. (1985). *Organizational culture and leadership.* San Francisco: Jossey-Bass.

Schumpeter, J. A. (1934). *The theory of economic development.* Cambridge, MA: Harvard University Press.

Shumway, N. (1993). *La invención de la Argentina.* Buenos Aires: Emecé.

Schvarzer, J. (1996). *La industria que supimos conseguir: Una historia político social de la industria argentina.* Buenos Aires: Planeta.

Schvarzer, J. (2001, June 24). Economía Argentina: Situación y perspectivas. *La Gaceta de Económicas.* Buenos Aires.

Senge, P. M. (1990). *The fifth discipline.* New York: Doubleday.

The Economist. (2002, May 4). *"Fallen idols: The overthrow of celebrity CEOs,"* p. 11.

The Economist. (2002, May 18). *"Capitalism and its troubles: A survey of international finance."*

Thomas, J. (1996). *Pilot study: Media analysis and the country study manual.* Mimeo.

Waisman, C. (1987). *Reversal of development in Argentina: Post-war counterrevolutionary policies and their structural consequences.* Princeton, NJ: Princeton University Press.

Weber, M. (1992). *The Protestant ethic and the spirit of capitalism.* London: Routledge.

Wilde, A. (1978). Conversations among gentlemen: Oligarchic democracy in Colombia. In Linz & Stepan (Eds.), *The breakdown of democratic regimes: Latin America.* Baltimore: Johns Hopkins University Press.

19

▼▼▼▼▼▼▼

Colombia: The Human Relations Side of Enterprise*

Enrique Ogliastri
Universidad de los Andes, Bogotá, Colombia,
and INCAE Business School (Costa Rica)
Instituto de Empresa Business School (Spain)

1. COLOMBIA: ECONOMIC, POLITICAL, AND SOCIAL BACKGROUND

Population and Economy

Colombia had a population of 41 million in 1998, and an annual growth rate of 2.2%. The average Colombian household included 5.2 persons, and population density reached 31 inhabitants per square kilometer. The nation's literacy rate was 87%. Per capita income averaged U.S.$1,400 annually, and purchasing power was one fourth that of the United States. Sustained economic growth from 1987 to 1997 surpassed 4% annually. The gross domestic product (GDP) is based on services (51%), industry (28%), and agriculture (20.5%). Foreign trade totals U.S.$23 billion annually and is carried out mainly with the United States (36%), Europe (20%), and the Andean Group (13%). Major exports include petroleum and its derivatives; coffee, coal, and the illegal exportation of cocaine to the major consumption centers. Industrial output is made up of agricultural and food products (30%), textiles and clothing (16%), and transportation and machinery (8%).

The Colombian population is primarily a racial mixture balanced between Native American peoples and descendants of Spanish conquerors, and people of African origin. Although regional social differences still exist, as do traditional aboriginal groups, 75% of the Colombian population now lives in urban areas.

The *GLOBE study,* covering middle managers from three industries (finance, telecommunications, and food processing), was carried out in Bogotá, a city of 7 million inhabitants, half of whom are immigrants from the provinces; the Spanish language and the Christian religion (principally Catholic) predominate. Enormous socioeconomic differences do exist—the poorest 20% of the country's population earned 4% of the national income.

---

*Translated by Steven William Bayless.

History

Although the nation's colonial independence movement began in 1781, full independence from Spain did not come about until 1819. Throughout the 19th century, Colombian leadership alternated between military and civilian types, dedicated to bringing about major changes in society's structures as well as the nature of the state and the government. The first leader in Colombia, after independence was achieved, was of course Simon Bolivar, the hero of the Wars of Liberation in five Andean Republics. Bolivar is remembered as an audacious and visionary leader. His revolutionary counterpart, Francisco de Paula Santander, known as "the Lawmaker," had a reputation for being a cold and efficient leader. Their differences led to Colombia's two-party system. By the mid-19th century, the country was once again in the hands of a military leader—General Tomas Cipriano de Mosquera—whose radical policies and liberal experiments led to civil war. Subsequent political change was personified by President Nuñez, whose visionary statecraft included a national constitution that served the country for more than a hundred years, until 1992. It is worth noting that in Colombia, conservative ideology triumphed at the end of the 19th century, which was not the case in most Latin American countries. The conservative President Reyes headed the movement for national reconstruction at the beginning of the 20th century.

By the 1930s, the Liberal Party had gained control of the government. President Lopez achieved important political reforms that contributed to greater democratic participation and led to more harmonious socioeconomic development. Nevertheless, civil war and widespread violence have continued to plague Colombian society up to the close of the 20th century. By and large, in recent decades the nation followed the economic models recommended by ECLA (Economic Commission for Latin America), which encouraged the protection of domestic industry by means of tariffs. President Lleras—another major liberal reformer—focused on the promotion of exports, and on regional trade blocks, such as the Andean Pact. However, as of 1990 these policies had taken a turn toward the free-market economy and the privatization of state-owned enterprises.

Industries Studied

In the last decades, the *financial sector* in Colombia has been the source of major business opportunities: Starting in 1974, a novel savings program that drew international attention was instituted by the government under which new financial institutions attracted 30% of domestic savings, which in turn were earmarked for new housing construction. This program helped create a network of financial institutions that differed from traditional banks in the sense that they were more dynamic and better organized. In contrast, the banking sector suffered a crisis in 1982, which resulted in the closure of several major banks. This was followed by a period of institutional reforms and control of the financial sector. Beginning in 1990, and as a result of newly formulated free-market guidelines, the financial sector was opened up to foreign investment—mostly from Spain—and due to this increased competition financial institutions have consequently seen their profit margins drop. The financial sector in Colombia has changed from being mostly state owned to being privately operated, and new financial activities have become a major part of this service industry—that is, the management of pension and retirement funds, investment banking, fiduciary services, and cooperative organizations banking. Major financial institutions have been organized under the system of headquarter and specialized subsidiaries, with a tendency to multiple banking services.

Up until the 1990s, the *telecommunications sector* was the almost exclusive domain of the state. Nowadays, cellular telephones, the Internet, satellite communications, new communications services, and data processing have begun to compete with more traditional telecommunications services. TELECOM, the nation's most important communications entity, was state owned up to 1998; however, its privatization process has set off an intense debate among political organizations and labor unions. Furthermore, the telecommunications sector is also being opened up to news media organizations, online suppliers, local telephone companies, and foreign telecommunications companies that possess advanced technology otherwise not available in Colombia, as well as to the largest conglomerates in the nation (three of which are family owned, and a fourth, which is regionally owned).

The *food-processing* industry has traditionally been a mainstay of the Colombian economy. For decades Colombia has been relatively self-sufficient in food production, and national companies have predominated in this sector alongside a small number of multinational corporations (such as Nestlé). Competition has recently increased, and free-market policies have allowed for a greater number of imports and exports that have, in turn, contributed to a more diverse selection of product availability and to a more dynamic business environment in this sector. This growth has gone hand in hand with the sustained development of the national economy as a whole.

Political System

The Colombian political system is an elective democracy in which the executive branch predominates within a centralized state (up to the 1980s). Power is concentrated in the hands of an unchanging, limited elite (Ogliastri, 1976, 1996b; Ogliastri & Guerra, 1980; Ogliastri & Dávila, 1987). It is difficult to clearly define the political system in Colombia because, in spite of having supported democratically elected Governments throughout the entire 20th century (with one exception in 1953), its internal contradictions require paradoxical political terms: "Colombian democracy … in spite of its missing parts … is a surprising reality" (Arrubla, 1978, p. 218). According to Solaún (1980, p. 3), "The country is partially democratic," or barely "a liberal democracy" (Peeler, 1983). Kline (1974) termed it "patrimonial" and "elitist," "a slightly veiled autocracy, managed by an 'oligarchy' or 'elite'" and Bailey (1977) called it a "procedural democracy" (p. 260) and classified Colombia as an example of "elitist pluralism" (p. 275). In addition, Lijphart classified it as "a consociational democracy" (1968, 1977), but later withdrew it from his list and Hartlyn (1988) insists on the same concept. Hoskin and Swanson (1974) agreed that it was "a revolutionary situation in objective terms" (p. 243); but, the term that probably best summarizes the Colombian paradox was coined by Wilde (1978), "Colombia is an oligarchic democracy" (Ogliastri, 1989a, 1989b).

The national Constitution, adopted in 1991, signified an attempt to make the country more democratic and egalitarian within a more just society, but in reality the political situation in the country, in terms of elitist structures, has only slightly been changed and the use of armed force continues to characterize the Colombian government (Peeler, 1994).

A Note on the Narcotics Mafia and the "War on Drugs"

As a result of the demand for narcotics in the United States, minor criminals in Colombia were able to amass sizable fortunes during the 1970s by exporting marijuana; but, when the United States itself became self-sufficient in marijuana production, Colombian marijuana exports dropped dramatically. Colombian narcotics organizations subsequently began to process cocaine (which, until then, had not been cultivated, and which was, as well, little known in Colombia). Illegal cocaine contributed to the growth of wealthy mafias and to the creation of enormous individual fortunes; to increased corruption in the public and private sectors; to the assassination of judges, politicians (including presidential candidates), and journalists; and to a wave of terrorism that forced the government of President Virgilio Barco to declare a War on Drugs in 1989. By 1997, all of the Colombian mafia kingpins were either in prison or dead, while at the same time U.S. drug consumption continued to increase and the illegal narcotics business expanded.

A few individuals involved in drug trafficking possessed a certain charismatic appeal—as was the case of Pablo Escobar in Medellin—but, in general, these criminals have been unsuccessful in finding a place for themselves in the Colombian establishment. This failure can be attributed, in large part, to the oligarchic and closed character of the Colombian ruling class. In particular, the mafia has not been allowed to take control of any banks or financial institutions, nor has the mafia been allowed to acquire interests in the telecommunications or food-processing sectors of the economy. As a result, the narcotics mafia has invested its earnings almost entirely in real estate and livestock, or has left the money overseas (Thoumi, 1994).

The narcotics mafia has also been accused of corrupting government officials and political candidates—particularly in the financing of campaigns—and (many) public officials who have been convicted of making contacts with the mafia have subsequently lost their congressional seats and spent time in prison. This moralization campaign has been directed by the former special prosecutor for the nation in conjunction with the head of the national police, both of whom got nominations as presidential candidates in 1998 (La Figura, 1996).

By 1997, the War on Drugs centered on "illicit enrichment," and on the extradition of Colombian citizens. Financial institutions began to require all clients to declare the origins of their deposits, with no one being exempt from having to prove the source of his or her income under threat of confiscation and imprisonment for failure to comply. The extradition of Colombian nationals has received little support from the general public, which has consistently considered the measure as unfair.[1]

2. THE GLOBE STUDY IN COLOMBIA

Methods and Procedures

In accordance with the parameters outlined by the GLOBE group (see chap. 1 of this volume) research began in Colombia in 1993. It included a combination of qualitative and quantitative methods (Agar, 1994; Glaser & Strauss, 1967; Ogliastri, 1987).

The qualitative side of the research conducted in Colombia consisted of a pilot study, 72 semistructured interviews, three focus groups, 14 case studies, a questionnaire of nonobtrusive indicators, a comparative questionnaire on observations dealing with cultural variables, and content analysis of the printed news media.

The quantitative research consisted of two surveys with 302 middle-level managers from three economic sectors; and an organizational contingency questionnaire with 23 presidents and vice presidents surveyed. Details on each one of these research activities are given later on along with their corresponding results.

---

[1]Most Colombians agree that the country should prosecute its criminals within its own borders instead of extraditing them to the United States; however, the U.S. government has constantly pressured the Colombian government to enforce extradition treaties, a threat that has aided in the dismantling of organized crime in Colombia. The Colombian government has moved to revive extradition through constitutional amendment, a policy that has sparked widespread public debate and that has put the lives and reputations of national leaders at stake—depending on the stance they have taken on the extradition issue.

Once the qualitative pilot study came to an end in 1994, this author, in collaboration with 14 research assistants, interviewed 75 midlevel managers (from the three sectors previously mentioned) during the first semester of 1995. These qualitative interviews used open-ended questions about real-life experiences. All interviews were tape-recorded and transcribed verbatim, which allowed for detailed content analysis of the information. At the same time that these interviews were being conducted, a focus group analyzed case studies of leadership in 14 successful Colombian businesses. The report on this portion of the study was completed before the results of the other GLOBE methodologies were revealed (Ogliastri, 1996a, 1997b; Rodríguez, 1994).

The double-blind "back" translations and the pilot testing of the quantitative questionnaire were completed in 1994 with a group of 56 postgraduate finance students. The final quantitative survey was carried out during the second semester of 1995 with the GLOBE Alpha and Beta questionnaires, to which 302 midlevel managers (from the three economic sectors) responded.[2]

During the first semester of 1996, the Colombian team participated in the development of participant observation and unobtrusive measures questionnaires of the GLOBE study. The final questionnaires were responded to individually by participating researchers who discussed their results and reached a group consensus on the Colombian data.[3]

In the second semester of 1996, data were collected on leadership issues that appeared in the printed news media, specifically, six publications during 1 week in September. The classification, computerization, selection, and handling of these data took place in the months that followed; and the final report, prepared in June 1997, was issued independently from the results of the quantitative survey, which began to appear in May of the same year (Ogliastri, 1997b).

In summary, this study on Colombia's culture and organizational leadership therefore incorporated quantitative (a survey) and qualitative methods (interviews, focus groups, case studies, media analysis) as well as mixed methods (participant observation and unobtrusive indicators questionnaires). Such multiplicity of methods allows for a comparison of results and formulation of general conclusions. In the sections that follow, the results of the Colombian study are presented in the following order: data on Colombian cultural characteristics as expressed in the quantitative questionnaire; unobtrusive observations; results on organizational culture; media analysis of leadership; survey results on leadership; data on case studies, and the results of the focus groups and qualitative interviews.

Colombian Societal Culture: Quantitative GLOBE Survey

The Dutch researcher Geert Hofstede carried out a seminal study on the work-related values of IBM employees in 53 countries, including Colombia. Cultural norms were divided by

---

[2]The author was personally responsible for compiling the data on the financial sector; one half of this was provided by one of the country's largest banks, and the other half was provided by diverse financial institutions. The other two sectors (telecommunications, food processing) were surveyed by research assistants under the direction of the author. These questionnaires, which instead of concentrating on a limited number of business organizations in a given sector, were taken at random, among midlevel managers, from a large number of businesses.

[3]In the first semester of 1996, the back-translation and the development of the organizational contingency questionnaire were carried out in collaboration with the GLOBE study's Spanish team; and data were compiled after interviewing the presidents and vice presidents from the six companies where the greatest number of midlevel managers has been surveyed with the Alpha and Beta questionnaires. The data provided by these corporate presidents and vice presidents will be analyzed for organizational contingency content, as well as for the validation of other results in the GLOBE study that are as yet unavailable.

Hofstede into four areas: equality versus power distance; the need to reduce uncertainty versus tolerance of ambiguity; the individual versus the group; and masculinity versus femininity. Colombia was classified high on the elitist scale, high on group orientation, medium high on being in need of reducing uncertainty, and as a culture oriented toward "masculine" values.

A quantitative section of the GLOBE survey, designated Beta, included the participation of 153 midlevel managers who responded to questionnaire items on the present situation in Colombian society ("As Is," perceived cultural practices), as well as on what they considered Colombian society should become ("Should Be," perceived cultural values). The response items from the questionnaire were grouped into nine dimensions on the basis of literature studies and empirically on the basis of the total sample of 61 GLOBE countries (for details see House et al., 2004): Power Distance, Institutional Collectivism, In-Group Collectivism, Uncertainty Avoidance, Gender Equalititarianism, Assertiveness, Performance Orientation, Future Orientation, and Humane Orientation. Hofstede had originally identified four cultural dimensions (Power Distance, Individualism, Masculinity, and Uncertainty Avoidance), but in the GLOBE study, gender differentiation was broadened beyond just the terms "masculine-feminine" (differentiating equality orientation from assertive "masculine" values), and two different dimensions of collectivism (Institutional vs, In-Group Collectivism) were found. Values were rated from 1 through 7 (the higher the value, the higher the variable content). The data compiled for Colombia appear in Table 19.1.

It is worth mentioning that Colombian culture results were similar to the majority of the 10 Latin American countries of the GLOBE study, except for 3 of the 18 scales.[4] Colombia could be considered in this regard to be the most representative country of Latin America (Ogliastri et al., 1999).

Power Distance. The most remarkable aspects that emerged from the study were the descriptions that Colombian managers gave of their country as being excessively elitist, that is, high in Power Distance "As Is" (Rank 11) and as wanting to see it becoming much less so (Power Distance "Should Be," Rank 61). This desire was so strong that Colombia placed first among all 61 countries ranked, the only one in the extreme E category. Furthermore, they described Colombian society as being highly In-Group Collectivistic ("As Is," Rank 12), in the sense of marked family and group loyalty values—aspects that they wished could be even higher on the values scale ("Should Be," Rank 2). These results coincided with those of Hofstede from two decades earlier, except he did not distinguish between the two different concepts of collectivism considered in the GLOBE scales. The managers are highly unhappy about some individualistic features of their society. Another strongly felt hope among Colombian managers was that Performance Orientation cultural practices ("As Is," Rank 39) should be much higher ("Should Be," Rank 3).

Uncertainty Avoidance. Concerning Uncertainty Avoidance, the data have changed since Hofstede's study in which Colombia earned a medium index rating for Uncertainty

---

[4]In Humane Orientation cultural values ("Should Be"), Colombian managers were among the 3-country minority wishing their country to have above-average (Band B) results, whereas the majority opted for the below-average results (Band C). In Future Orientation, cultural values ("Should Be") Colombia was above world average (top end of Band B) but not as strongly as the majority of Latin American countries classified as Band A countries wishing a higher Future Orientation. (For details about the Test Banding procedures, A > B > C > D, which was used to group GLOBE countries, see Hanges, Dickson, & Sipe, 2004).

TABLE 19.1

Colombian Society, Cultural Practices ("As Is") and Cultural Values ("Should Be")

(Colombia)	Hofstede (1960/1980) N = 53 countries	GLOBE (1996–1998) N = 61 countries	
	Rank	"As Is" (practices) Score (Rank) Band	"Should Be" (values) Score (Rank) Band
Power (Elitism) Distance	(17)	5.56 (11) A	2.04 (61) E
Institutional Collectivism	–	3.81 (53) C	5.38 (7) A
In-Group (Loyalty) Collectivism	(5)	5.73 (12) A	6.25 (2) A
Uncertainty Avoidance	(20)	3.57 (53) C	4.98 (21) B
Gender Egalitarianism	(11/12)	3.67 (12) A	5.00 (9) A
Assertiveness	–	4.20 (25) A	3.43 (44) B
Performance Orientation	–	3.94 (39) B	6.42 (3) A
Humane Orientation	–	3.72 (46) C	5.61 (14) B
Future Orientation	–	3.27 (53) C	5.68 (25) B

Note. Hofstede's data appear classified in agreement with the position Colombia occupies among the 53 countries reported in 1991 (Hofstede, 1980, 1997). The GLOBE countries were grouped into three or four meaningful groups (A > B > C > D > E) using a statistical procedure (test banding, cf. Hanges, Dickson, & Sipe, 2004). The GLOBE ranking indicates the position occupied by Colombia in comparison with a total of 61 countries (the smaller the rank the higher the dimension value).

Avoidance (20th among 53 nations); whereas, in the latest survey, Colombia is rated as having a medium-high tolerance for ambiguity (Rank 53) but in favor of more Uncertainty Avoidance (Rank 21).

Why has uncertainty increased during the past 25 years in Colombia? This can, in part, be explained as the result of the institutional changes that have transformed the country's economic development model from one based on protecting domestic industry to one based on exporting goods and services, and on the liberalization of commerce. Consequently, nontraditional exports now account for more than half of the country total exports, the outcome, in part, of governmental incentives such as the Vallejo Act. Additional institutional transformations that have played an important role in Colombia's uncertainty profile include the decentralization of political power that began to take place in the 1980s, and that reached its peak when a new, national Constitution was approved in 1991; other changes include: the adoption of a new liberal economic model, new laws governing pensions, health plans, and labor relations, as well as the privatization of public services.

Other factors that have created instability in the country include the following: the arrival of new, illegal capital; the war on drugs; violent crime; powerful guerrilla armies; and the weakness of the government and of the Colombian state in general. All of the aforementioned factors have brought about enormous changes and subsequently greater uncertainty.

Yet another cause for the raise in uncertainty has to do with the performance of the economy and the business sector which, from the beginning of the 1970s has not only grown significantly, but did so in novel ways that have led to the opening up of new areas within the country. In the 25- year period 1972 to 1996, the Colombian economy was the fastest growing in all of Latin America (4.5% on average). This dynamic economic growth has been dominated by new business activities: the exploration, drilling, and distribution of petroleum in new regions; the export of fresh-cut flowers; the production and international distribution of bananas from large farms in the Uraba region; the production and export of primarily marijuana and, then, of coca leaf and cocaine from plantations and laboratories located in remote, jungle regions. This vigorous economic growth has all the trappings of what could be termed a new entrepreneurial phase in Colombian history, one linked to new business ventures and to an outward-looking economy; characterized by new and tenuous ground rules in which rapid economic and institutional transformations require quick decisions, and taking quick advantage of business opportunities—all of which contrast sharply with economically developed societies whose business activities are well established and well on their way to full maturity.

Gender Egalitarianism.   On Gender Egalitarianism, Colombia is positioned as an A country in both practice ("As Is," Rank 12) and ideal terms ("Should Be," Rank 9). The change in values registered between the Hofstede and the GLOBE studies does not come as a surprise. Colombian society was classified by Hofstede as having "masculine" values; that is, employees valued opportunities for high earnings, recognition for good performance, advancement opportunities, and challenging work. The feminine pole carried out by Hofstede listed employee preferences as: a good working relationship with the boss, a cooperative atmosphere at the office, an attractive living area for self and family, and job security.

In the GLOBE study, the Masculine dimension was changed into two different scales: assertiveness and female/male equality. Colombians were described as assertive (dominant, tough, assertive, "As Is" Assertiveness, Rank 25, Band A), but a preference was expressed in favor of a less assertive patterns (Rank 40, Band B). Gender differentiation was classified on the feminine side (Rank 11, Group A), meaning a preference for gender equality. The same preferences—higher equality on the job, equal school opportunities and sports programs— were expressed as desirable for the future. Colombia ranked as 9 on Gender Egalitarianism "Should Be" (Band A).

Oddly enough, neither male nor female managers indicated that gender differentiation was remarkable in Colombia; neither was there a perceptible difference in their answers dealing with sexual equality; furthermore, both women and men expressed leadership concepts in identical terms (Ogliastri, 1996b).

In the majority of countries included in the GLOBE study, a preference for gender equality predominated. Colombia, unlike countries where the role of women is dictated by religion, has been part of the international movement toward achieving gender equality. This is reconfirmed by the large number of managers who have attended coeducational secondary schools, by the growing numbers of women in executive posts (particularly in the financial sector and in government posts), and by the changing attitudes toward equality among university students in recent decades.

In summary, the study confirmed Hofstede's findings on high collectivism and elitism in Colombian society, as described by managers. In spite of a high desire to be able to control unexpected events, Colombian people seem to be less able to reduce uncertainty than it was two decades ago. It has evolved toward gender equality values; the GLOBE managers would prefer as well an average assertiveness pattern. They know that Colombians live for the present, are oriented to achieve, and are not overly sensitive, friendly, tolerant, generous, or concerned, but they would like their society to be more humane and future oriented as well as highly focused toward performance achievement.

The remaining variables in the survey were also classified as about average on the values scale with respondents evidently in favor of creating a social environment that should be more oriented toward the future ("Should Be," Rank 25) and less preoccupied with immediate concerns (more thought given to the future).

Colombian Culture: Nonobtrusive Observations

In addition to the quantitative survey in which nine cultural dimensions were measured, observations were made and nonreactive measurements were taken, in all countries, for these same dimensions. This meant that measurements could be obtained that were independent from the Beta questionnaire. A strong correlation was found for these two measures. A summary of these nonobtrusive observations appears in the following subsections and includes the variables that define Colombian culture in their order of importance: Collectivism, Power Distance, Uncertainty Avoidance, Gender Egalitarianism, Assertiveness, Performance Orientation, Humane Orientation, and Future Orientation.

Collectivism. Unobtrusive research efforts concentrated on determining to what extent a society is oriented toward collectivist values by means of analyzing the family unit, the socialization of children, and sports. The extended family in Colombian society has long been recognized for its distinctive collectivist features: Unmarried or widowed adult children live with their families; elderly parents are not placed in institutions, but rather taken in by one of their children; Colombians learn from childhood to depend on extended family members instead of "making it on their own."

The most important sports in Colombia are soccer, cycling (in teams), and baseball (in the Atlantic coastal region). Individual sports have few adherents. However, Colombian society is not so controlled by family members that parents may arrange marriages, nor is it considered unacceptable for individuals to express nonconformity with the majority. Yet, core social values in Colombia are undeniably collectivist or group oriented in nature.

Power Distance (Elitism). As has been previously clarified, one of Colombian society's key characteristics is the concentration of power in the hands of a closed, powerful elite. It is not difficult to notice that social inequality, and the values that shore it up, is part of daily life; for instance, in cities mansions coexist with shanty towns. Nor is it difficult to notice the privileges enjoyed by the top members of any major business organization; these include lavish offices, special parking lots, fashionable clothing (instead of uniforms), and dining rooms that are reserved for the different ranks among the company's hierarchy. However, there is a trend in corporations for a more egalitarian culture.

A millionaire's household servants are divided into ranks, within just one household, and cemeteries are even classified as being first or second rate. However, restaurants and other public places are not reserved for one specific social caste. It is common in Bogotá to hear the formal prefixes "don" and "doña," or "doctor" and "doctora" in recognition of social and professional status; but these formal genuflexions are not so common in the rest of the country.

The nation's police force can be quite authoritarian; nevertheless, law enforcement is lax, and relations between police officers and the community are very limited. The high figures on the GLOBE dimensions related to elitism in Colombian culture are not surprising, and they are reconfirmed by the social observations garnered on elitism.

Uncertainty Avoidance. Colombia is undoubtedly immersed in improvisation and ambiguity, as can be seen by such behavior as the disobedience to traffic regulations, by the unimportance given to automobile liability insurance (until 1990 liability insurance was nonobligatory), and in most cities, by the lack of organized passenger and driver courtesies at bus stops and on bus rides. Colombians generally arrive late for appointments (half an hour is common) although this custom has become lees acceptable, and there now exists greater pressure toward being punctual, especially among companies and professionals (doctors and dentists). As a rule, Colombians do not plan their vacations ahead of time (unlike members of other societies); at the most, this is done just a few weeks before departure.

Colombian businesses usually have written rules and regulations (e.g., requests for photocopies), but exceptions to the rule, and "last minute" demands are considered equally important. This culture, therefore, tolerates ambiguity which, in turn, has its positive implications including flexibility, open-mindedness, creativity, innovation, reflex capacity, and the ability to handle emergencies. But, this same ambiguity tolerance also has an unattractive side that manifests itself as it does in any poorly planned society where it is not possible to identify fixed rules, and where daily lives are often overwhelmed by chaos.

Gender Egalitarianism.   In general, men have more status than women in Colombia; however, gender is a secondary status factor compared to class or family ties, to income, power, success, skin color, age, or even regional origin. There are four categories into which nonobtrusive observations on gender equality can be divided: the law, social customs, values, and real circumstances.

Monogamy has been the only acceptable marriage contract for both men and women, and there is no judicial distinction between "legitimate" and "illegitimate" children. In legal terms, gender equality has moved forward thanks to the 1991 Constitution. Colombian law punishes sexual harassment and spouse abuse, but it is still not common for such cases to go to court. Divorce laws, which did not exist until the 1970s, ensure equal rights for both spouses. Legal marriage age is the same for both sexes. Women are allowed to join the armed forces, although few do so, and the regulations governing feminine active duty are incomplete, which is beneficial for women in a country where military service is dangerous.

Insofar as social customs are concerned, boys' schools were traditionally considered superior to girls' schools, but this is no longer the case. "Masculine" and "feminine" occupations are still differentiated (nurses, school teachers, psychologists, translators, household servants, housewives, etc., are considered to be "women's work"), the latter being held in less esteem and not as well paid as the former. There are private clubs that still refuse to admit women, and bars where a woman's presence is considered "uncomely"; however, these prejudices are beginning to disappear. Men still pay the bill when a couple is dating, but this custom is also changing among university students since the 1990s.

Gender equality and societal values do not grant a woman greater status because she has a son or because she has a daughter; nevertheless, most men hope to have at least one male heir who will carry on the family name. Most Colombian heroes are men, but even before the dawn of the feminist movement, the heroines of the War of Independence against the Spanish Empire were exalted in Colombian history; and furthermore, women athletes who have earned Olympic medals, or who have set outstanding sports records receive as much news coverage for their achievements as do men. Only 20% of the presidential cabinet are women, a figure that corresponds to the percentage of women presidential candidates who have campaigned since the 1970s—with as yet no woman president being elected. However, a trend for equality in the presidential cabinet is under way. Abortion is common (and illegal); and, if a baby is abandoned or sold shortly after birth, regardless of their sex, it becomes a scandal.

Colombian managers described their nation's culture as one in which gender equality is now the norm. This is a surprising conclusion; however, it should be analyzed in light of the fact that in Colombia, as in many parts of the world, gender equality has come to be considered part of the social ideal, or as part of a new, ideological standard. This is reconfirmed by the Beta survey in which business executives, particularly in Bogotá, expressed their strong support for women at work. Among those interviewed in this segment of Colombian society, the women are graduates of coeducational, bilingual secondary schools and universities; their marriages are often made up of dual-career couples, and both spouses share household and childrearing duties; by doing so, they have placed themselves in the vanguard of changing Colombian social values.

In spite of the fact that gender inequality and discrimination still exist, this author has observed that business executive training programs, in which women made up only 5% of the participants in the early 1970s, now have an enrollment (1990s) that includes 35% women (a proportion similar to the number of women interviewed in the Beta survey).

Assertiveness.   According to homicide statistics and other indicators of violent behavior, Colombia is one of the most aggressive countries in the world. This is, in fact, one of the country's worst problems, as previously mentioned, and it is directly related to political conflict, organized crime, weak government, and social inequality. Aggression is one of their major sociocultural problems. But Assertiveness also has positive undertones for Colombian managers, who are used to soft interpersonal relations at work.

Performance Orientation.   There is a growing tendency in Colombian culture toward Performance Orientation (see Table 19.1), and this can be also observed in four areas: in primary and secondary schools, as well as in colleges and universities; in business organizations; in legal statutes; and in publicly fostered cultural values. Primary and secondary schools often rank students on a monthly basis, and the best students are rewarded at year's end. However, colleges and universities only reward extraordinary achievement (1% of those enrolled), a practice that makes little or no impact (on performance orientation) on the majority of the student body.

Teacher/professor evaluation by the schools is even less common, in part due to respect for authority figures. These evaluations of professors are formal procedures related to scale or promotion; nonetheless, a few universities rely heavily on student evaluations of faculty, which has sometimes brought about a lowering of their respective academic standards. In general, universities are increasing the use of faculty evaluation that focuses on teaching, research, and publishing, and the entire educational system has begun to take steps toward incorporating performance orientation into its agenda.

Many large and medium-size Colombian business organizations, although by no means all of them, evaluate their employees for job performance, which is subsequently used as the basis for promotion and salary increases. This is a standard practice among multinational corporations, but only 50% of Colombian corporations follow suit. Employee rewards, such as prizes and public recognition, are linked almost exclusively to salespeople; whereas promotions are often linked—albeit subtly—not to employee merit, but rather to social status, family ties, and personal connections.

There are very few laws or official initiatives that deal with commercial performance orientation in Colombia, such as tax credits for corporate research and development, on-the-job training programs, or business start-ups. Neither are streets, parks, or avenues named for pioneers of industry, nor for outstanding inventors—this being an honor reserved for those who have achieved political power. Yet, values are changing with regard to the image of business leaders, who are no longer seen as villains but rather as heroes or heroines of industry.

Parents tend to motivate their children toward performance, but the value given to affiliation among Colombian families probably still supersedes performance as a primary goal. Even among the upper middle class, whose members are the most achievement oriented of all, the ideal of successful affiliation is widespread, a fact observed by the author in his teaching in university classes and in executive workshops. Sudarsky (1973) has extensively researched achievement in Colombia, and the results of his studies indicate important variations among the country's different geographical regions and among its social strata over a considerable period of time.

In the final analysis, Colombia can be classified as moderately high on the performance orientation values scale, when placed within an international context; but, the country is clearly on the road toward establishing greater performance values. These conclusions reconfirm Colombia's ranking on Performance Orientation "As Is" in the above-average intermediate Group (B Band), but it is worth noting that it is one of the top three nations that expressed a deep desire toward greater Performance Orientation "Should Be" (A Band), meaning that this variable, among all of those in the GLOBE study, is the one that is undergoing the most significant change.

Humane Orientation.   The traditional Catholic values of charity and resignation to one's destiny have always been part of Colombian culture, but these values are now being questioned by a nation whose majority finds itself face-to-face with an increasingly difficult situation. The GLOBE study's humanitarian indicators were based on Colombian society's treatment of beggars and the homeless, prisoners, physical and mental minorities, children, and the poor.

In Bogotá, beggars and the homeless share the streets with garbage recyclers, street vendors, clowns, mental patients, and "lost souls." Although there are no laws against free vendors in shopping malls, security guards make sure that they do not bother shoppers. There are public and private urban institutions that provide free meals to homeless adults and to children—this is an extension of the philanthropic custom found in Colombia's small towns where many private homes feed the poor once a day. But, Christian charity has not solved the country's social problems, and many citizens oppose giving away food and shelter on the grounds that it leads to even greater poverty and passivity. Terms such as "disposables" or "human garbage" (*desechables*) have been coined and used by many to refer to the nation's homeless and to beggars on the street.

The state of the nation's prisons has become deplorable due to overcrowding and to inhumane living conditions, in spite of the fact that rehabilitation and prison work programs do exist. Colombian law does not permit capital punishment, but prison homicide is common, and many mortal crimes aren't ever solved. Medical attention for prisoners is inadequate, and this has been the cause of recent, bloody uprisings in the nation's penitentiaries.

The treatment of the physical and mentally impaired is yet another indicator of impersonal orientation. Colombia has set up special services, schools, and clinics for this segment of the population, which is often considered as being a progressive step in comparison to the treatment received in the past; however, this special treatment has recently come under fire as being discriminatory and poorly focused toward full integration into society. In response to this criticism, all schools are now enrolling the physically impaired and providing them with special services so as not to exclude them from the general student body. But, Braille is not available in elevators, old buildings and streets do not include wheelchair ramps, national television is not captioned for the hearing impaired, and mental and physical minorities receive no government subsidies, no specific social security, nor are companies required to meet employment quotas for this sector of the population—all of which reveals little official concern for these minorities.

The presence of child paupers and juvenile gangs who live in the streets of the major cities continues to be a pressing national problem. Poverty may be the root of the problem. However, the majority of the population has grown accustomed to this phenomenon, which has not been changed by either public or private efforts to help these impoverished, juvenile citizens. Until now a viable solution for the alleviation of the poverty from which a certain sector of the Colombian population suffers has not been found by sociologists, philanthropists, or international aid organizations.

The legal system differentiates juvenile delinquents from adult criminals, and juvenile courts send lawbreakers to reformatories. Child labor is legal from the age of 14, which is young compared to international standards, and poor urban and rural children often leave school to help their parents. This is not common in the "formal economy" where large companies shun child labor, but it is a frequent practice in the "informal economy," and in family business ventures. Children's rights can hardly be reinforced.

The poor, in general, receive subsidies for public utilities, housing, and university tuition (based on family income), but none of these are sufficient to cover the enormous needs of the nation's poor, many of whom live in extreme poverty.

Colombia is a country at war, and it affects both combatants and the civilian population alike, in war zones. The rebel army, armed drug traffickers, paramilitary groups, and even the national army have been guilty of cruelly violating the Geneva Convention, as well as basic, universal human rights. Colombian society can be classified among the below-average humanitarian cultures—a conclusion supported by the GLOBE survey results about Humane Orientation cultural practices according to which Colombia was rated in the C Band (Rank 46) of 61 countries (see Table 19.1).

Future Orientation.   Colombian society is oriented more toward the present than toward the future, even though it currently emphasizes the need to plan, predict, and sacrifice the here and now for tomorrow. Five observations concerning this cultural value appear next.

First, Colombian culture is impulsive and spontaneous by nature; its members live for the moment and make themselves happy without due thought to life's necessities. This behavioral pattern is passed on from parents to children.

Second, there is a contradiction between the official policy that advocates personal savings and the cultural reality of immediate expenditure. During the past decade, the government has greatly extended coverage for severance pay and pension funds, and there are strong restrictions to immediate consumer expending of such funds.

Third, modern, productive corporations represent a subculture insofar as the need to plan is concerned, this being more the case in the telecommunications sector than in the other two sectors surveyed. This is due to the fact that costly investments in telecommunications technology are justifiable only on a long-term (10 or more years) basis. Market/product research and planning have also become requisites in the financial and food-processing sectors. Competition has reduced profit margins and product feasibility studies take into account 2- to 6- year periods.

Fourth, the country's major universities founded planning departments in the 1960s, oftentimes limited to giving the architectural faculty the responsibility of planning future campus expansion based, obviously, on planning future student enrollment. These plans, however, are not always met, due at times to a lack of planning experience, and at other times to the arrival of new presidents who, in turn, make abrupt changes in plans previously approved. This latter case occurred at the country's most prestigious private university in 1997, and led to a complete failure in predicting student registration, which had previously been based on a 2- to 3- year plan that allowed for adjustments every semester.

The fifth, and final, observation deals with the sale of tickets to important sports events. Tickets go on sale weeks ahead of time, but in reality fans begin to make their purchases only a few days before the event, and it is possible to find tickets available on the same day that the event is scheduled. Consequently, sponsors of such events have begun to offer discounts to those who buy tickets ahead of time—a sales strategy that will, in time, probably become widespread.

Colombian society is largely made up of a population where many basic needs go unmet, and, therefore, embrace a cultural tradition based on instant gratification. Spontaneity is necessary for being authentic in Colombia—the act of living for the here and now, without repressing one's thoughts and feelings. Yet, the Colombian state and large corporations are moving constantly closer to imposing the international tendency toward Future Orientation.

Summary. The nonobtrusive social indicators confirm the results yielded by the GLOBE questionnaire that was used with managerial interviewees. It can be concluded that, in spite of sociocultural tensions and the tendency toward change, Colombian society is characterized by high family and group values but low institutional collectivism; high elitism; high uncertainty (low uncertainty avoidance); high gender equality; high assertiveness; and medium-level performance orientation. There exist, however, contradictions with the tendencies toward favoring a more egalitarian society, high institutional collectivism, and high performance orientation. Colombia strongly favors to keep its family/in-group loyalty values, as well as high gender equality. It is also leading to a more humane and future-oriented society.

Organizational Culture: What It Is and What It Should Be

The GLOBE Alpha questionnaire used in the survey evaluated the responses of 149 midlevel managers who answered items dealing with the same variables described earlier for societal culture (Beta questionnaire); but, in this case, these were specifically related to a business organization (the company where the respondent were employed). Consequently, this sample of managers differ from those surveyed in the previous section on Colombian culture and society. Data collection focused not only on ascertaining what respondents thought about the present state of their business organizations ("As Is" cultural practices), but also what they thought these organizations should become in the future as well ("Should Be" cultural values). The results of this section of the survey are contained in Table 19.2, where data have been divided into three columns corresponding to the three economic sectors studied.

The results broadly coincide with those for cultural values, however, it should be pointed out that there was greater satisfaction expressed where the corporate organization was concerned than with culture and society in general. Not only were the latter two described in terms of diminished expectations, but criticism for both was harsher than it was for a manager's company.

The greatest difference between cultural and organizational results concerned elitist values in Colombian society. The midlevel managers who participated in the study sharply perceived these inequities, as well as the power distance that characterizes Colombian business and society. These

TABLE 19.2
Organization Cultural Practices ("As Is") and Values ("Should Be")

Organizational Culture Dimension	"As Is" (practices)			"Should Be" (values)		
	Finance	Food	Telecom	Finance	Food	Telecom
Institutional Collectivism	3.8	5.0	4.1	5.4	5.4	5.5
In-Group Collectivism	4.4	5.7	4.8	6.3	6.3	6.3
Power (Elitism) Distance	4.4	2.9	3.6	3.1	3.4	3.4
Uncertainty Avoidance	3.4	4.9	4.0	4.3	4.4	4.3
Gender Egalitarianism	3.4	3.5	3.4	4.4	4.9	4.8
Assertiveness	4.3	3.8	3.8	4.0	4.0	4.3
Performance Orientation	3.8	5.0	4.3	6.3	5.6	6.3
Humane Orientation	4.2	5.1	5.3	4.8	5.2	5.3
Future Orientation	4.0	5.3	4.2	6.0	5.9	5.7

managers considered their own companies to be more democratic and less committed to traditional values than to what they considered Colombian society in general to be.[5]

Large Colombian businesses are not a microcosm in the context of the society in which they operate, as shown by the higher level of satisfaction expressed by managers for their respective companies, a level of satisfaction not expressed for their nation's society. In all probability, Colombian companies are more tuned to international cultural and management values. Furthermore, around the world, the average of the managers included in the GLOBE survey favored the values of performance orientation, future orientation, humanitarianism, collectivism, equality, and nonassertiveness. These "universal" managerial values are given fuller expression within Colombian businesses than within society at large, due to the fact that the former make up a subculture whose values are more international. It is also worth pointing out that large business organizations are controlled by management groups who have more alternatives to choose from and greater leeway in acting on decisions that can bring about change in their immediate surroundings—unlike the poorer, underprivileged sectors of Colombian society that are rooted in traditional values. Traditional Colombian values such as family/in-group collectivism and humane orientation are more easily established in the organization than in the society at large. Even though some aspects of this managerial ideal may contradict conventional cultural norms (such as underestimating the patrimonial hierarchy), it is possible for it to prosper within a business organization that bases itself on different values.

---

[5]It is in the food sector where these differences can be seen most clearly, due to the fact, probably, that two of the food processors surveyed actively promote corporate policies and values that shun elitism, carried out intensive managerial development programs, aimed at strategic planning, team leadership, and empowerment. The difference between the food sector results and that of the two other industries may be partially explained by such training. In any event, business managers uniformly expressed their strong desire to have power distance reduced in Colombian society and business.

3. LEADERSHIP IN COLOMBIA

The field of business administration in Colombia has been so dominated by the United States that even the Japanese managerial systems introduced into the country have arrived in English. Colombian executives have a tendency to embrace the latest fashions in managerial systems; foreign gurus in the field are readily accepted, and their works enthusiastically translated—except for terms such as *benchmarking* and *Hoshin kanri*. In the last decade, the following works on leadership have been published in Colombia (initial publication date precedes date of translation): Bennis and Nanus (1985 [1985]); Bennis (1989, 1990), Jaap (1989, 1991), Beckhard and Pritchard (1992, 1993), Badaracco and Ellsworth (1989, 1994), Drucker (1992, 1993), Stumpf and Mullen (1992, 1993), and McFarland, Senn, and Childress (1994, 1996). The following texts became available in Colombia after having been translated in other Spanish-speaking countries: McGregor (1966, 1969), Kotter (1988, 1990a), Vroom and Jago (1988, 1990), DePree (1989, 1993), Covey (1990, 1993), and Kotter (1996, 1997).

Research at the local level has been carried out by Gomez and Dávila, who have described Latin America's contributions and innovations in the field of business administration. The results of their study, based on nine in-depth examinations of successful corporate cases, revealed that outstanding Latin American leadership characteristics included: commitment to the organization—"a giving of one's heart and soul" to the enterprise; followed by charisma, benevolence, paternalism, and intuition (Gomez & Dávila, 1994). Motta (1993) is a successful Brazilian theoretical text translated from Portuguese.

The FES institute on leadership started in 1993 to train Colombian youth on leadership. The business community has also widely accepted outdoor training leadership, as formulated by Matamala (1994) and Mutis (1994), which utilizes know-how imported from the United States and Europe emphasizing leadership that is not centered on the individual alone but rather on the individual and the organization, as well as on empowerment and humanistic and collectivist values.

A large study of Colombian leaders was undertaken by Ogliastri and Dávila (1987). As pointed out earlier, leadership, as practiced by the Colombian ruling class in Colombian society at large, has best been described as closed and elitist. The power structure in Colombia was traditionally intertwined between the public and private sectors, with a power concentration tendency that increased as the economy expanded (Ogliastri & Dávila, 1983).

In contrast with a federalist system of government, the country has a centralized state structure based mainly on the political concepts of President Núñez. More than 100 years ago, he set out to establish a national governing class that would eschew regional factionalism and that would adhere to a conservative political ideology that favored stable government. Once this national governing class came into being, the need for a more regional (federalist) structure became apparent during the 1970s. Another key change that occurred among the nation's leadership was the blurring of the separation between the public and the private sector—the cornerstone of traditional democracies—and a new group of the elite had careers in both the public and the private sectors. These were the real transformational leaders within the elite: Their vision, different from their public and private elite counterparts, was carried out in the 1990s (Ogliastri, 1996).

The most important forerunner of the GLOBE project is Hofstede's study (1980, 1997), which classified Colombians at that time as being highly oriented toward collectivist or group values, highly elitist, living in uncertainty, and predominant in favor of masculine values.

Colombian Leadership: A Study of the Printed News Media

The week of September 1–7, 1996 (when no special events had been programmed that could have distorted research results) was chosen in advance as the period in which to survey six news publications in search of articles that somehow dealt with the subject of leadership in Colombia. According to international research group agreements, three major Colombian newspapers were selected—*El Espectador, El Tiempo, La República*—(the latter dedicated almost exclusively to business news); two news weeklies—*Semana* and *Cambio*—and a weekly business publication—*Portafolio.* As agreed on by participating GLOBE countries, the sports sections and classified advertisements were not evaluated; but all other articles were read in these publications from September 1 to September 7, 1996 (Ogliastri, 1997a).

Any article that dealt with leadership was analyzed in the following manner:

- The subject: who the leader was (i.e. a politician, a business leader, a group or organization, a country, etc.).
- The verb: what he/she/it/they did, what had been done, what could be done, what should be done by the leader/s.
- The adjective: how actions were carried out, how actions were evaluated.

Using this method, key or core paragraphs were selected from 285 articles, and within these chosen paragraphs, verb and adjective phrases that referred to a specific event were underlined. Subsequently, each article was classified under one or two key words, and these were then combined with the underlined phrases in a computer program that allows for constant updating of criteria on grouping and category expansion.

The 285 newspaper and magazine articles and their selected paragraphs were printed out on 56 pages, and once this written information was examined, four important contexts emerged that referred to major socioeconomic problems in Colombia: the ongoing armed conflict that includes guerrilla warfare and narcotics terrorism (20% of the articles); the implantation of a new economic model based on privatization and market liberalization (16%); organized crime related primarily to the production and exportation of narcotics (12%); overwhelming social problems (12%). Other frequently mentioned topics were: debating (13%); negotiating (11%); and planning (8%). And, finally, a small number were classified under "various" (6%).

This initial classification of news articles was based exclusively on context or content; but, subsequently, multiple classifications were made, and more precise categories that took more than just context into account were established. It was then necessary to identify the actions described by the press, as well as how the press itself evaluated Colombian leaders within any given context. This meant cross-classification of some categories, due to the fact that some articles dealt simultaneously with several contexts. For example, articles on the armed conflict often criticized the alliance between guerrilla forces and the peasant growers of coca leaves (an ethical problem) whereas others criticized the violation of human rights among combatants or among the civilian population (a humanitarian problem) and further articles criticized the ineffectiveness of the armed forces and suggested that military activity be increased (a military leadership problem). In general, the articles provided a multifaceted view of a problem which, in turn, contributed to article's being assigned to more than one category (Herrán, 1993).

The military context provided an opportunity to analyze the leadership characteristics of guerrilla leaders, army generals, and police officers on active duty—primarily in confrontation with guerrilla and narcotics organizations—and a few articles dealt with international armed conflicts (i.e., the United States bombed Iraq during that week). In addition to direct physical confrontation, the military context touched on areas such as peace dialogues, peace negotiations, ethics, efficiency, and humanism.

Popularity polls published during September named the special prosecutor of the nation as the most popular public figure in Colombia (just as his predecessor had been upon leaving the post). This preference revealed how concerned Colombians were about the threats to ethical behavior. Indeed, the printed news media emphasized "integrity" as being the most important issue facing Colombian leaders in their efforts to deal with the country's most serious social problems: the exportation of narcotics to the United States by organized crime syndicates; guerrilla forces that financed their illegal activities by carrying out kidnappings or by providing protection services to cocaine producers; and chronic government corruption. The journalistic portrayal of the struggle against organized crime was categorized as an integrity issue as a result of reporters' constant use of terms such as *ethical, honest,* and *legal* when writing on this subject.

Another highly popular public figure was the head of the national police force, who had been successful not only in capturing the principal members of the Cali Drug Cartel (one of whom was killed in a gun battle), but in cleansing the police force itself, and in improving the morale of the nation's police officers. Both of these law enforcement figures were praised for their simplicity, their humanity, their sense of public service, and their equanimity. Their public stances and behavior were perceived as putting them at risk of assassination attempts. Hence, these profiles were categorized as examples of "courage" in the midst of very unfavorable circumstances. The verbs most frequently linked to this context included *to tell the truth, to alert, to criticize, to control, to solve, to manipulate,* and *to negotiate.*

"Competition" in terms of being a leadership characteristic mostly applicable to the business world was also frequently mentioned in press reports. The major competitive challenges cited for the Colombian economy in the 1990s were those of neo-liberal economic policies and the privatization of state-owned enterprises. A successful competitor was often described as one who had a clear-cut plan for future development based on solid research and preparation. In general, protectionist policies were not cited, except those related to joining regional trade blocks; most attitudes were deemed active instead of passive; and hard work and survival tactics were cited as being priorities along with creativity, persistence, and the energetic seeking of successful goals. These terms were consistent with the performance of the Colombian economy, which had been ranked as among the most outstanding in Latin America up to 1997.

The social context referred, in general terms, to those conflicts related to inequality and to the pressing social problems within the country. The government (of Ernesto Samper) came into office pledging to make substantial expenditures on social welfare programs, but was unable to achieve much (in spite of the public deficit), due probably to the many political problems that arose after allegations were made that the president's successful 1994 campaign had been, in part, financed with funds provided by drug traffickers; consequently, one of the government's star cabinet members along with the Samper campaign treasurer have both been imprisoned. The president was judged and acquitted by Congress. Other newspaper and magazine articles in this category made reference to grassroots uprisings, and to the government's reaction to these events in terms of solidarity and humanistic values. Oft-repeated terms in these articles included *justice, ethics, negotiation, violence, service, improvement, love, education, alliance, to encourage, to cooperate,* and *to associate.*

Media reports drew attention to the tendency of Colombian leaders to debate issues, to remedy inequities, and to demand justice based on social and ethical values. These public debates took place on diverse stages: in Congress (political), in the Supreme Court (judicial), and at social and economic forums. The nation's press emphasized that these encounters had been intense and expressed with verbs such as *to democratize, to correct, to compete, to nego-tiate, to control, to judge,* and to pacify, as well as with adjectives like *arbitrary, courageous, honest, legitimate, just, social,* and *military.*

Articles that dealt with negotiations, pacification, reconciliation, solutions and dialogues also contained references to *humanization, criticism, control, commitment, initiative, as well as to the adjectives ethical, courageous,* and *weak.*

Articles that concentrated on planning mentioned verbs like *to alert, to compete, to antic-ipate, to propose,* and *to call,* and the adjectives *opportune* and *visionary.*

In the final analysis, ethical behavior was clearly the most important aspect used in evalu-ating Colombian leaders among the multiple contexts in the articles studied. The second most important leadership characteristic was found to be the ability to improve the current socioe-conomic situation through maximum achievement and success. The ability to negotiate among parties in conflict occupied third place on the list of leadership priorities; fourth place was taken up by characteristics related to social solidarity and to protecting the common inter-ests of Colombian society. The ability to plan with a vision toward the future ranked fifth among leadership qualities, followed by military decisiveness and the use of force to bring about change (Ogliastri & Wittingham, 2000).

Leadership in Colombia: GLOBE Survey

Sample.   The quantitative survey's demographic data for the 302 midlevel managers is as follows: average age, 35; 65% men; 100% residing in Colombia; 99.7% born in the country; 90% classified themselves as Roman Catholics (267 out of 296); 99% spoke Spanish in their parents' home; and 97% spoke this language in the workplace. They had, on an average, 16 years of formal education (equivalent to the time needed to earn a university degree in Colombia, where the average college graduation age is 23) consistent with an average of 12 years full-time work experience, and 7 years experience in executive posts. They had worked an average of 5 years and 3 months in their current positions, and 33% had at one time worked for a multinational corporation. An average of 12.5 people reported to each manager who typically presided over a company section that averaged 24 employees in total. These managers occupied, on average, positions within the corporate hierarchy that were classified two levels away from the highest level and three levels above that of the company's workers.

GLOBE Questionnaire.   Sections 2 and 4 of the GLOBE questionnaires (Alpha and Beta) referred to the characteristics and behavior of "an outstanding leader"; that is to say, a person able to motivate others, and able to influence or to facilitate in others behavior that contributes to achievement and success in a business organization. The questionnaire format requested that each respondent assigns a number, between 1 and 7, to 112 attributes and behaviors, divided into seven categories: 1-greatly inhibits, 2-somewhat inhibits, 3-slightly inhibits, 4-does not influence, 5-contributes slightly, 6-contributes somewhat, or 7-contributes greatly to making a person an outstanding leader.

TABLE 19.3

Scores, Ranks, and Bands for Colombia Based on the 21 GLOBE Leadership Dimensions

Leadership Dimension	Score	Rank	Band
Charismatic I: Visionary	6.36	(4)	A
Performance Orientation	6.39	(5)	A
Collaborative Team	5.90	(5)	A
Team Integrator	6.30	(5)	A
Integrity	6.43	(10)	A
Modesty	5.43	(9)	A
Administratively Competent	6.11	(14)	A
Diplomatic	5.63	(21)	A
Charismatic II: Inspirational	6.34	(13)	B
Charismatic III: Self-Sacrificial	5.21	(15)	B
Conflict Inducer	4.19	(22)	B
Status-Conscious	4.51	(24)	B
Nonparticipative	2.54	(34)	B
Procedural	3.78	(38)	B
Humane	4.56	(42)	B
Decisive	5.52	(53)	B
Autonomous	3.34	(56)	B
Autocratic	2.44	(42)	C
Face Saver	2.50	(44)	C
Self-Centered	1.91	(49)	C
Malevolent	1.59	(48)	D

Based on the total GLOBE sample, leadership attributes were statistically grouped into 21 first-order factors (first-order leadership dimensions) that were consolidated into 6 second-order factors (for more detailed descriptions, see House et al., 2004, and the introduction and concluding chapters of this volume). The raw scores and rankings (the lower the rank, the more important the factor) of each of the 21 leadership dimensions for Colombia appear in Table 19.3. The dimensions are listed in descending order based on Test Bands (last columns).

It is worth noting that in the categories of performance orientation, vision, team integrator, and team collaboration, Colombia ranked among the top 5 of all 61 countries surveyed. Based on the Test Band A categorization, it appears that Colombian managers are convinced that a person who is highly interested in excellence (performance orientation), who organizes teams (team orientation, team collaboration), who clearly indicates where to go (visionary), who is a good administrator, and who leads with integrity, modesty, and diplomacy, possesses the most important assets for being an outstanding leader in their company. On the other end of the spectrum, being malevolent occupied last place on the list of behavioral values and attitudes that contribute to what is deemed essential in an outstanding Colombian business leader. Thus, hostile, dishonest, vindictive, irritable, nondependable, noncooperative, egotistical, and intelligent but cynical, constitute the extreme of least desirable characteristics of a leader.

It is important for a Colombian leader to be charismatic in the sense of being visionary, that is, to be future oriented, to have foresight, to be prepared, and to plan ahead, in a fashion that can be considered intellectually stimulating for the organization. The issue of integrity, meaning an individual who is sincere, who is fair in making decisions and in judging people and events, and who is, furthermore, honest and trustworthy, all of which were considered crucial factors for the success of an outstanding leader was also among the first-ranked behaviors and characteristic. Another important personal trait was that of being modest, self-effacing, and patient.

It may be that the very expressive nature and extreme reactions characteristic of Latin American society contribute to the fact that the diplomacy factor is highly esteemed in the organizational context. It means to be an effective bargainer, and a worldly win-win problem solver. On a final note, the study emphasized the importance of behavioral modes that were judged competent, that boosted organizational efficiency, were orderly, administratively skilled, and organized.

The second-order leadership factors summarize the 21 original factors in the following way: Charismatic/value based (visionary, inspirational, self-sacrifice, integrity, decisive, and performance oriented), Team Oriented leadership (collaborative team orientation, team integrator, diplomatic, malevolent [reverse scored], administratively competent), Participative leadership (nonparticipative [reverse scored] and autocratic [reverse scored]), Self-Protective leadership (self-centered, status-conscious, conflict inducer, face saving, and procedural), Humane Oriented leadership (modesty and humane oriented), and Autonomous (autonomy). Results about the second-order leadership scales confirm the pattern described previously (see Table 19.4). Colombia ranks rather high (5th, Band A) for Team Orientated leadership, and on the three leadership dimensions (Charismatic, Participative, Humane) medium to high (11th, 21st, 25th, all in Band B). The disfavored dimensions for Colombian managers are Autonomous (Rank 56, Band C) and Self-Protective (Rank 35, Band E).

Leadership in Colombia: Case Studies of Successful Organizations

Fourteen Colombian business firms, with reputations for outstanding leadership, were singled out for case studies. Although two of these firms were not, strictly speaking, "Colombian" (both were subsidiaries of multinational corporations), all of their personnel were Colombian nationals, especially those who had been designated as outstanding leaders. "Outstanding" businesses in these cases meant those whose growth and efficiency were higher than that of others in the same sector, and higher than that of Colombian economic indicators in general (Kouzes & Pozner, 1987). Nevertheless, neither do these companies represent the 14 most successful companies in their respective sectors, nor do they represent the most successful in the country as a whole, nor were they chosen through a definite selection process. However, they did share several features: a certain recognition level in business publications; having been mentioned in the qualitative interviews (see the following section); easy access to interview personnel; and they included diverse examples among the heterogeneity of the firms studied.

Fifteen student research aides were assigned in pairs to prepare an in-depth case study on a Colombian business firm. In many of these studies, an attempt was made to amplify the

TABLE 19.4

Leadership in Colombia: Second-Order Leadership Scales

Second-Order Leadership Scales	Score	Rank	Band
Team Oriented	6.07	5	A
Charismatic/Value Based	6.04	11	B
Participative	5.51	21	B
Humane	5.05	25	B
Autonomous	3.34	56	C
Self-Protective	3.36	35	E

analysis of transformational organizational leadership as it had been reported in interviews (see the following section). As a first step in preparing these case studies, Colombian companies recognized for outstanding performance were identified, and members of their executive staff and other personnel (including the leader's secretary) were then interviewed on why they thought their companies were successful. If an interviewee mentioned leadership as among the reasons for the company's success, this topic was then given in-depth treatment. If it was not mentioned, questions were then posed to determine what kind of leadership existed within the organization in terms provided by managers. Finally, the organizational leader was interviewed on specific aspects of his or her career, life, and philosophy, and was then asked to describe his or her actions that had helped to achieve results for the company. After carrying out a minimum of eight interviews at each company, a case study was then written. A number of other well-known leadership cases were also analyzed. The companies studied indepth included six from the financial sector, two from the telecommunications sector, and six from other sectors. These latter six were selected based on the fact that their presidents were considered prominent leaders in the business world.[6]

Once the reports had been written and distributed among the research group, each case was then discussed by the team with leadership being emphasized as the primary topic. As happened in the focus groups, similarities were discovered in the results from among the different sectors, that is, the financial sector, the telecommunications sector, and the six cases from diverse sectors.

In summary, the research results from these three sectors largely coincided. In all three, the primary leadership element discovered among these cases was having an overriding strategic vision for the company, based on a clear, long-range perspective. In second place was a special command of human resources management, particularly the use of extensive training

---

[6]The following is a list of the business firms studied, followed by the names of their researchers (in parentheses) and an asterisk if the case was not collected within the GLOBE project: (a) the financial sector: Colmena Savings Corporation (Pilar Gracia and Layla Spicker), Cáceres & Ferro (Mónica Serna and María Fernanda Ordóñez), Bank of Colombia (Ana María Villodres and Adriana López), Fiduciary Sudameris (Laura Pardo), Las Villas Savings (Jaime Vergara), Solidarity Corporation Corposol (J. Austin & E. Ogliastri, 1996) (*); (b) the telecommunications sector: ATT-NCR Colombia (Claudia Soler and Felipe Gómez), Uisys Colombia (Susana Steiner); (c) other sectors: Reconstructora Comercial (Enrique Ogliastri, 1994b) (*), Transejes (Enrique Ogliastri (*) Corona Tiles (Cristina Otero and Carlos Felipe Betancur), Aces Airline (Ricardo Matamala) (*), Industrial Gabriel (Ricardo Matamala and Jorge Ardila) (*), Group Jom (informal education) (Kenneth Mediwelson). Most of these cases are in the text of Matamala and Ogliastri (1994).

programs outside of the company, joined with the charismatic appeal of the concerned manager, humanistic values in interpersonal relations, contact with personnel, and teamwork. In third place, was an outstanding participatory managerial style characterized by trusting the team and by demanding results. Fourth place was occupied by a confluence of values linked to the social responsibilities of the company, to training programs for employees, and to the integration of the family. And, finally, particularly in the finance and telecommunications sectors, technological innovation was considered essential to the company's success. As is seen later, the qualitative interviews, which were conducted parallel to the case studies, confirm, for the most part, the results on leadership in Colombian businesses obtained in the analysis of these 14 case studies.

Leadership in Colombia: Qualitative Interviews

During the first phase of the qualitative study, a pilot test was conducted on the questionnaires and the methodology to be used. This involved five personal interviews and 27 written reports (Ogliastri, 1994a; Ogliastri & Rodríguez, 1994). The main research consisted of 75 interviews with managers from the three sectors studied, and a focus group set up to review the differences between leaders and managers.

The interviews were based on two semistructured GLOBE questionnaires with open-ended question formats that sought personal responses on experiences and perspectives regarding organizational leadership. Under the direction of the author, 13 senior-year business students (from the University of the Andes) conducted most of the interviews. Each research aide conducted five interviews. Researchers sought out personal acquaintances in a first step toward selecting interviewees described as midlevel business managers in the financial, food-processing, or telecommunications sectors. Due to the heterogeneity, regional origin, and number of interviewers, this part of the study was carried out at random, with no measures taken to identify, or to prevent, possible biases. Forty-six managers from the financial sector were interviewed, 16 from the food-processing sector, 4 from the telecommunications sector, and 6 from other sectors. Three interviews were withdrawn from the research project, due to their very poor quality and incomplete answers. All interviews were tape-recorded and transcribed verbatim, and classified for archival records and computer data analysis (Mishler, 1986).

A focus group, made up of 13 research assistants, later met for 2 hours in an effort to sum up the conclusions reached by research participants (Agar & MacDonald, 1994; Merton, Fiske, & Kendall, 1990; Morgan, 1988, 1993). A psychologist, who conducted focus groups for a marketing and advertising firm, presided over the group meeting in which the following topics were discussed: the definition, according to each research assistant's interviewees, of an outstanding leader and of a normal manager; the differences between the two; descriptions of concrete examples of leadership in action; the names of outstanding leaders; and direct quotes on what had motivated the managers to go beyond the call of duty. Finally, researchers discussed their own methodological approaches in the preparation of final reports. This session was audiotaped and transcribed by the director of the session who later prepared a written report on the focus group.

The core research topic that needed to be absolutely clear in the minds of interviewees was how, as a result of their own experiences, they had come to differentiate a normal, good, or competent manager, who lacked leadership qualities, from a genuine leader capable of producing exceptional results and of transforming a commercial enterprise (Bass, 1985; Kotter, 1990b; Sayless, 1983). This difference between what constitutes a normal manager and what differentiates them from an exceptional leader was quickly and widely accepted by

Colombian interviewees, who needed no extensive explanations by interviewers to clarify this point.[7]

Throughout the research project, results emerged in various stages. The first attempt to arrive at general conclusions was by means of a report based on five interviews that had been carried out by each research assistant. This comparative effort encouraged participants of the validity of their mutually consistent research results, which were later reconfirmed in the focus group meeting, as well as during the content analysis of the interviews themselves.

Thirteen research assistants, who had conducted five interviews each, met to delineate the characteristics of an exceptional leader as deduced from their respective interviews. These leadership characteristics were listed as:

- Works toward goals.
- Works well with people.
- Convinces, motivates, is charismatic, and "has a way with people."
- Inspires, is self-assured, and is recognized by others as being so.
- On the other hand, a normal manager was characterized as someone who:
- Concentrates on daily operations.
- (Ab)uses his or her power.
- Is unable to communicate well.
- Doesn't trust others.
- Is not visionary.
- Seeks individual recognition.

Once further differences between a normal manager and an outstanding leader were clarified, Table 19.5 was prepared.

In the interviews on leadership, questions were posed on actual leadership incidents, many of which had to do with the handling of crisis situations. In these incidents, the leader emerges as the one who is best able to solve a problem through dialogue, negotiation, and mutual understanding; or, as being the person who, in a given situation, makes a decision and convinces others to agree; or who can motivate others to follow specific policies. It was not possible to clarify, however, whether these two modes were caused by different kinds of situations or by different kinds of leaders.

The leaders mentioned in the interviews were almost all Colombians, well-known inside their own companies, but foreigners and historical figures were mentioned as well (i.e., Mother Teresa of Calcutta, Churchill, Bolivar). It should be noted that very few women were cited as "model" leaders. At the same time, interviewees mentioned "negative" leadership as personified by Hitler and Pablo Escobar, or by white-collar criminals, who, according to some interviewees, could not be differentiated from "good leaders" as far as performance and the abstract process of leadership were concerned.

Insofar as the reasons given by interviewees as to what motivated them to work above and beyond that required by their job descriptions, they emphasized in their responses that they

---

[7]Nevertheless, 2 of the interviewees (out of a total of 75) did not accept the difference: One implied that all managers must, by definition, have a natural talent for leadership, whereas the other stated that exceptional leaders were personally unknown. However, an overall methodological problem that did occur during the interview was the tendency of participants to negatively judge "normal" managers while at the same time exaggerating the attributes of the outstanding leader.

TABLE 19.5
Focus Group Results: Differences Between a Leader
and a Manager in Colombia

Leader	Normal Manager
Strategist; has an overall view	Day-to-day detail operator
Long-term vision	Short term vision
Works well with people	Individualistic
Flexible	Inflexible
Ambitious	Standard goals
Looks ahead, anticipates	Constantly in emergencies
Has independent personal power	Personal power based on position

felt their jobs gave them an opportunity for personal growth; that extra effort on their part gave them the authority to set high internal (organizational) standards (not dependent on outside pressure); and that their own outstanding job performance came about as a result of their wanting to test themselves, more often than as having been motivated in terms of a response to a leader's motivation.

As a result of the content analysis carried out on the 72 interviews, three key exceptional leadership elements were identified: outstanding group and individual relations, a vision for the future of the company, and management style. Three complementary aspects were also identified: integrity, innovative action in moments of crisis, and the setting of ambitious goals (described later).

The primary exceptional leadership characteristic, as inferred from the experiences of the 72 interviewees, was taken from the realm of personal relations within the company itself. Leaders described as exceptional were known for being "open" with others; willing to listen; perceptive or understanding; worried about the feelings of others; capable of expressing warmth and friendship; "having a way with people"; and for loyalty to the group. These characteristics were listed alongside charisma, humanistic values, personal magnetism, physical presence, the ability to motivate by example, and the ability to encourage others to follow. Furthermore, excellent communication abilities and the ability to convince people and to move them to make commitments were also pointed out as outstanding leadership characteristics.

The management of personnel by outstanding leaders was described as being based, first of all, on the careful selection of collaborators, knowing how to surround oneself well, and then being able to recognize each individual's limitations and potential. Another aspect of outstanding management style was described as the ability to develop personnel through work assignments, to delegate responsibilities, and to accept others' mistakes as learning experiences. The exceptional leader was profiled as one who communicates well, who makes the company's policies and objectives known throughout the entire organization, and who informs others of the reasons why things are done, and what the problems facing the company are, all in an effort to motivate personnel.

The second most important element that characterizes outstanding leaders in Colombian culture is their ability to have a vision for the future. Visionary leaders were described as "those who know where they are going," as having clear objectives, as being prepared for the future, as being protagonists in their environments, and as having knowledge of how to set priorities and to make opportune decisions. Other facets of extraordinary leaders that were mentioned, included having in-depth knowledge about their specific economic sectors, knowledge that contributed to analyzing problems and finding solutions in an innovative and creative way (innovation as the key to the future), and being able to see things from a different perspective and with greater projection than others do, such as an ability that contributes to bringing about necessary changes. Outstanding leaders are ambitious in defining their long-range strategies; they "dream the impossible"; they are decisive; and they are able to visualize opportunities and to take on challenges with their teams. This latter outstanding leadership characteristic was more sharply profiled in men than in women. Exceptional women leaders seemed to give greater emphasis to interpersonal aspects, to emotions, and to charisma, which are considered as much a part of human relations as they are a part of the management style described later.

The third essential element that identifies an outstanding leader in Colombia is his or her management or administrative style, characterized by the ability to work with groups (teamwork), the ability to foster change in a vigorous and positive manner, the ability to coordinate and integrate the interests of all personnel, and the ability to be strict and demanding but at the same time generous and cognizant that outstanding team members deserve individual recognition. Outstanding organizational leaders in Colombia base their authority on a structure that begins at the bottom of the business: That is to say, they believe in "empowerment," which allows employees to have faith in their own company-orientated achievements. Outstanding leaders are convinced of the capacity of the individuals who work for them, as well as of the same individual's group efforts. Outstanding leaders encourage self-criticism that contributes to improving employee achievement; they consult with, and encourage, the group to make suggestions that facilitate change; and they are able to motivate others to face challenges and to risk making mistakes. This exceptional management style is most apparent during times of crisis, when genuine leaders are put to the test and are forced to prove themselves. It is during these moments when an outstanding leader resorts to persuasion without impositions, thus encouraging others in the organization to aim toward the common good with an enthusiastic attitude that will lead to the solution of the crisis situation.

These three essential elements—human relations, vision for the future, and management style—along with three secondary elements—integrity, innovation in times of crisis, and setting ambitious clear-cut objectives—are what personify outstanding organizational leaders in Colombia.

The definition of personal integrity begins with having an ethical and moral work code, followed by being able to make people feel that what the company is doing is morally and socially correct. Leaders are perceived as having integrity if they are "genuine" and "authentic"; that is to say that they tell the truth and keep their word. An exemplary outstanding Colombian leader is also guided by just moral and social values, and is able to make others believe in his or her sincerity, sense of justice, and consistency in word and deed.

Even in situations that are not deemed critical, an authentic leader seeks new opportunities, takes a stand on important business issues, inspires a positive sense of urgency, generates renovation and radical transformation, changes the status quo, and accepts change in a positive manner.

The final outstanding leadership characteristic listed by the interviewees in Colombia was that of being able to set very high and stimulating objectives, joined with the ability to inspire a sense of responsibility in the fulfillment of these goals.

The qualitative interviews emphasized, time and again, that human relations, vision for the future, and participatory management based on integrity, ambition, and creativity were essential to the makeup of an outstanding organizational leader in Colombia. The results of the study, accumulated through diverse methodologies, appear to point toward the following summary.

4. SUMMARY AND CONCLUSIONS

Organizational leadership has been studied using a variety of research methods and perspectives, and the results appear to be mutually consistent. In specific terms, five of the six elements that characterize the transformational leader in the qualitative interviews also appear among the top factors in the quantitative survey: team orientation, orientation toward outstanding performance, vision, integrity, and participatory management. The other one, innovation, is not a category on the quantitative questionnaire. As can be seen in the comparative Table 19.6, there is a total of eight information sources on transformational leadership characteristics in Colombian culture: three of which were obtained using quantitative methodologies (the GLOBE scales on culture, on the company, and on leadership), one using mixed quantitative and qualitative methodologies (GLOBE questionnaires, which were used to guide observation and nonobtrusive measures), and four using qualitative methodologies (analysis of printed news media, case studies, focus groups, and interviews). This combination of independent methodologies bore fruit in the sense that each part mutually validated the other, meaning that no contradictions were encountered in the overall study results.

Seven Essential Business Leadership Elements in Colombia

The primary organizational leadership element in Colombia seems to reside in the categories that refer to human relations: first of all, within the company itself, followed by team values and family collectivism, considered basic to Colombian culture in general, and, in the rejection of individualism, with preference given to behavioral modes that favor interpersonal relations, teamwork, humane orientation, and social solidarity. These elements were grouped together as the primary factor to emerge from the qualitative interviews on transformational leadership (they were also reconfirmed as the primary factor on the quantitative scales for organizational and social culture) and were placed second among those inferred from the case studies. They were important elements used in analyzing the printed press were among the first leadership qualities listed in the quantitative survey (and Group A of countries).

It is worth mentioning that in Hofstede's study, Colombia, and four other Latin American countries, had the highest appreciation of collectivist values. These results were surprising to many people—and, by differentiating between family and primary group from social collectivist values in the GLOBE study, we have distanced ourselves from Hofstede's more simplified categorization. The Colombian, Nobel Prize–winning novelist, Gabriel García Márquez (1994) sounded the alarm on the growing tendency (among Colombians), "of having become incredulous, abstentionist and ungovernable … (and of pursuing) a lonely individualism in which each one thinks it is possible to be totally self-sufficient." The debate on the group versus the individual in Latin American society has further been brought to the fore by the introduction of Japanese administration systems into this part of the world (Fernández & Ogliastri, 1996; Ogliastri, 1988a).

As is apparent from the narration of personal experiences by managers in the qualitative interviews, there is no doubt as to the importance of group orientation in Colombian culture.

This is manifested in leadership that exalts "group effort," "warm interpersonal relations," and "egalitarian treatment of others," and in "the accessibility of personnel" to the leader.

The second organizational leadership element that was revealed in the Colombian study was performance orientation. Achievement appears as the second most mentioned factor in the press analysis; but performance is classified first in the quantitative leadership questionnaire, in which Colombia ranked among the top four countries in the GLOBE scales on organizational characteristics. To be administratively competent is another key element for a results-oriented manager in Colombia. The value of performance orientation is reinforced by the descriptive results on Colombian culture (expressing a desire for greater performance) and by managers' qualitative interviews. According to managers, the most outstanding performance-orientated leader is one who sets very ambitious goals and who is then very demanding with him or herself and with others in reaching them. Innovative decision making is also mentioned as important in the case studies and in the qualitative interviews. In the classic formulation by McClelland (1961), achievement orientation was linked to innovation and to future orientation—a result of Colombian data research as well. However, in the Colombian study, future orientation was classified as a part of the organizational leadership element described as vision and planning for the future (see later discussion).

The third organizational leadership element is vision for and orientation toward the future, joined with a high desire for uncertainty avoidance and the capacity to reach desired objectives. The ability to be visionary came in first in the case studies; it was the second most frequently mentioned element in the qualitative interviews and (tied) first rank in the quantitative surveys on leadership (among the top five countries in GLOBE). Future orientation appeared among the highly desirable characteristics for Colombian society and business; and the ability to plan for the future occupied fifth place among the essential leadership terms in the survey of the printed press. The word *vision* was part of the vocabulary repeated by managers in the qualitative interviews, in which they recalled having known transformational leaders endowed with a sense of "knowing where they are headed" and able to set priorities and make opportune decisions; who are, furthermore, highly knowledgeable of their respective economic sectors and specific business activities which, therefore, allows them to analyze and solve problems in an innovative and creative manner; they are able to identify new market niches and to focus on situations in such a way that necessary change can be brought about; they are able to define strategies on a long-term basis and in an ambitious manner; they are decidedly "dreamers of the impossible"—able to visualize opportunities and to face challenges jointly with their group. These abilities are required by the increased uncertainty of the Colombian environment. The vision characteristic was more sharply drawn in descriptions of exceptional men than it was among exceptional women, who were described as leaning more toward the interpersonal and emotional aspects of organizational leadership.

The fourth most frequently cited organizational leadership element in the Colombian study was personal integrity. This term led the list of issues discussed in the analysis of the printed news media. Colombia was among the top 10 countries that considered integrity a key leadership factor in the quantitative survey; and it was important (fourth) in the case studies, as well as in the qualitative interviews. This is to be expected in a country beset by violence, drug trafficking, corruption, high crime rates, and a weak government that all contribute to an atmosphere of impunity. Integrity was also a key element in political campaigns. In the specific field of organizational leadership, the qualitative interviews described integrity in a leader as commitment to the truth, to corporate social responsibility, to ethical behavior, and to clearly established values within the organization.

The fifth element considered basic to a definition of outstanding organizational leadership in Colombia was participatory management style. This style was portrayed as being nonelitist and nonautocratic—a style that inspires and stimulates others as a result of a leader's example and close contact with personnel. Participatory management style was listed as the third most important element by managers in the qualitative interview section of the study, and it also placed third in the analysis of case studies. Managers expressed their deep dislike for the stratification and inequities found in Colombian society. Female–male equality was a key attitude and strong desire of the managers in the quantitative survey, ranking the country among Group A of countries. It is worth noting that, among all of the countries surveyed in the GLOBE study, Colombia ranked first (the only country in Group E) in expressing the desire for a less elitist society.

The sixth factor of organizational leadership was the ability to negotiate and to solve conflicts, which appeared in the study of the printed press. In a country plagued by violence and conflict, it is essential to have diplomatic skills: a worldly win/win problem solver and effective bargainer. It was linked to one of the most important abilities of Colombian leaders in the survey: to be modest, self-effacing, and patient.

The seventh factor listed as an organizational leadership characteristic in Colombia was that of inspirational charisma, linked to the classic idea of "personalism" that is found in superior–subordinate relationships in Latin American cultures. This is a fundamental element in the concept of transformational leadership (Bass, 1997). The study stressed the importance of charismatic behavior defined as that which inspires the organization, spreads enthusiasm, stimulates self-sacrifice, provides a vision, builds confidence, is dynamic, motivates, and convinces, and is shown by a leader who asks others to wear the company's colors as he or she does.

Final place on the scale of leadership priorities were the decisive use of power in social problem solving (which appeared in the study of the printed press).

The combination of qualitative and quantitative methodologies in this study led to complementary and noncontradictory results. The categories defined a priori by the international group were not excessively different from those characteristics that emerged from our interviewees' responses.

Managerial Implications

The managerial implications are straightforward. Advice to managers working in Colombia can be summarized as follows. A manager should spend time in establishing personal relationships at work, even including some family outings on weekends. A sound business vision developed with team contributions would have desired motivational effects. The most effective managers set ambitious goals and milestones to guide the path. To have outstanding results authoritarian practices will not do. Leaders must organize the work by teams, give a chance to women managers because they try harder and have the idealistic support of the culture, avoid integrity traps, and have a transparent code of ethics for the organization.

The ideal leadership characteristics, as described by Colombian managers, coincide with those set forth in the classic literature on management (Drucker, 1954, 1964; Likert, 1960; McGregor, 1960)—all refer to group motivation, participation, and management by objectives. These have been the textbooks used in introductory business administration courses included in the curricula of managers interviewed in the survey. This "implicit leadership theory" held to by managers is further substantiated by modern (and modish) concepts that follow the same path: empowerment, strategic planning, and so forth.

TABLE 19.6
Summary and Overlap of Results

Characteristics of Leadership and/or GLOBE Scales	Methods Used (see notes)							
	1	*2*	*3*	*4*	*5*	*6*	*7*	*8*
1 Human relations					2	1		
Family/group collectivism	A (A)	C (A)	A					
Institutional collectivism	C (A)	C (A)	D					
Collaborative team				A				
Team integrator				A				
Social, solidarity								4
Humane orientation	C (B)	C (C)	C					
Team-oriented leadership							A	
Humane leadership							B	
2 Performance orientation	B (A)	D (B)	B	A				2
Ambitious goals						5		
Administratively competent				A				
Innovative decisions					5	6		
3 Vision of future				A	1	2		
Planning								5
Charismatic I: visionary				A				
Orientation to future	C (B)	D (B)	D					
Uncertainty avoidance	C (B)	D (C)	D					
4 Integrity				A	4	4		1
5 Participative					3	3		
Participative leadership							B	
Power distance	A (E)	B (D)	A					
Autocratic				C				
Nonparticipative (reverse scored)			B					
Gender egalitarianism	A (A)	B (C)	B					
6 Negotiating								3
Modesty/patience				A				
Diplomatic				A				
7 Charismatic: inspirational				B			B	
Charismatic: self-sacrificial			B					
8 Power, force								6
Assertiveness	B (B)	B (B)	C					

Note. Column 1: Colombia's positioning (test bands) for GLOBE societal culture practices "As Is" and values ("Should Be," in parentheses); A > B > C > D (Ogliastri et al., 1999). Column 2: Colombia's finance industry positioning (test bands) for GLOBE organizational cultural practices ("As Is">) and values ("Should Be," in parentheses); A > B > C > D. Column 3: Colombia's estimated positioning based on unobtrusive measures (UMQ) and on participant observation (POQ); A > B > C > D. Column 4: Colambia's positioning (test bands) for 21 GLOBE leadership scales (Ogliastri et al., 1999). Column 5: Estimated rank ordering of the five outstanding organizational leadership characteristics found in the 14 case studies on Colombian businesses (Ogliastri, 1997b). Column 6: Estimated rank ordering of leadership characteristics obtained in qualitative interviews (Ogliastri, 1997b). Column 7: Second-order quantitative leadership factors. Column 8: GLOBE media analysis results (Ogliastri & Wittingham, 2000).

The transformational leadership characteristics elucidated in our study were not too different from those included in international managerial literature (especially that from the United States) published during the last few decades—although some differences in emphasis can be found. The most influential author on the subject of management in Colombia observed in 1988 that great leadership could be measured by performance and efficiency; that it consisted, furthermore, of choosing the right collaborators, and of defining missions and goals within a framework of responsibility and integrity (Drucker, 1992, chap. 15). What is most noteworthy about Drucker's conclusions is that they had all been known for some time.

To what, then, can this congruence of Colombian research results with those found in international managerial literature be attributed? The answer lies, in part, in the fact that business administrators (everywhere) have command of a rather standardized professional vocabulary, in part due to the direct influence of the United States in matters of administrative concepts, as well as to the homogeneity of managerial work requirements found in diverse contexts. All of this indicates that sociocultural factors might play a secondary role in the organization of the productive sector with its specific managerial needs.

The managerial profession may be less affected by national cultural norms than it is by internal organizational norms, due in part to the fact that the former is subject to greater variation than is the latter. It is also possible that the growing homogenization in international education, to which many managers nowadays have had access since childhood, has also diminished the impact of national cultural factors in the workplace. In this sense, one can almost be convinced that the postmodern world has become a place shared by several cultures simultaneously—one for home, one for school, and yet another for work. The findings of the present research project are part of a rather long history in the theory of managerial styles, one that asks: "Are we coming to a convergence in our managerial culture that exceeds that found in our national culture?" The first GLOBE volume (House et al., 2004) gave a mixed answer—there are universal leadership concepts and there are culture specific leadership concepts. The other chapters in this second GLOBE volume might help us to answer this question in more depth.

ACKNOWLEDGMENTS

The author acknowledges research support from the University of the Andes, Carlos Rodríguez, María V. Wittingham, Nancy de la Torre, Ada Torres, Juan Carlos Chaparro, and 63 student research assistants. Thanks for critical remarks to Elssy Bonilla, Mauricio Cárdenas, Ricardo Matamala, Jurgen Wiebler, and five anonymous evaluators from GLOBE. (This chapter was written in 1998 and revised in September 2003, and August 2005).

REFERENCES

Agar, M. (1994). *Ethnography manual for leadership study*. Unpublished manuscript.
Agar, M., & MacDonald, J. (1994). Focus groups and ethnography. *Human Organizations, 54*(1), 78–86.
Arrubla, M. (1978). *Síntesis de historia política contemporánea* [Synthesis of contemporary political history]. In M. Arrubla & J. Bejarano (Eds.), *Colombia Hoy*. Bogotá, Colombia: Siglo XXI.
Austin, J., & Ogliastri, E., (1996). *Corposol* (Case N9-796-142). Boston: Harvard Business School.
Badaracco, J., & Ellsworth, R. (1994). *El liderazgo y la lucha por la integridad* [Leadership and the quest for integrity]. Bogotá, Columbia: Norma.
Bailey, J. (1977). Pluralist and corporatist dimensions of interest representation in Colombia. In J. Malloy (Ed.), *Authoritarianism and corporatism in Latin America* (pp. 259–302). Pittsburgh, PA: University of Pittsburgh Press.

Bass, B. (1985). *Leadership and performances beyond expectations.* New York: The Free Press.

Bass, B. (1997). Does the transactional-transformational paradigm transcend organizational and national boundaries? *American Psychologist, 52*(2), 130–139.

Beckhard, R., & Pritchard, W. (1993). *Lo que las empresas deben hacer para lograr una transformación total* [Changing the essence: The art of creating and leading fundamental change in organizations]. Bogotá, Colombia: Norma.

Bennis, W. (1989). *On becoming a leader.* Reading: Addision Wesley.

Bennis, W. (1990). *Why leaders can't lead: The unconscious conspiracy continues.* San Francisco: Jossey-Bass.

Bennis, W. (1990). *Cómo llegar a ser leader* [On becoming a leader]. Bogotá, Colombia: Norma.

Bennis, W., & Nanus, B. (1985). *Leaders: The strategies for taking charge.* New York: Harper & Row.

Covey, S. (1990). *Principle-centered leadership.* New York: Simon & Schuster.

DePree, M. (1989). *Leadership is an art.* New York: Dell.

Drucker, P. (1954). *The practice of management.* New York: Harper.

Drucker, P. (1964). *Managing for results.* New York: Harper.

Drucker, P. (1992). *Managing for the future: The 1990s and beyond.* New York: Truman/Dutton.

Drucker, P. (1993). *Gerencia para el futuro* [Managing for the future]. Bogotá, Colombia: Norma.

Fernández, C., & Ogliastri, E. (1996). ¿Es transferible la administración japonesa? Dos puntos de vista para un debate [Is it possible to transfer Japanese management? Two perspectives for a debate]. *Monografías Administración (Bogotá: Uniandes), 45,* 1–40.

La figura del día [Person of the day]. (1996, May 1). *El Espectador,* p. 3.

García Márquez, G. (1994, July 23). Discurso en la Comisión de Sabios [Speech to the wisemen commision]. *El Tiempo,* p. 23.

Gómez H., & Dávila, C. (1994). Innovation, INTERMAN and International Business in Latin America. *The International Executive, 36*(6), 671–688.

Hanges, P. J., Dickson, M. W., & Sipe, M. T. (2004). Rationale for GLOBE statistical analyses: Societal rankings and test of hypotheses. In R. J. House, P. J. Hanges, M. Javidan, P. Dorfman, &

V. Gupta (Eds.), *Leadership, culture, and organizations: The GLOBE study of 62 societies* (pp. 219–234). Thousand Oaks, CA: Sage.

Hartlyn, J. (1988). *The politics of coalition rule in Colombia.* Cambridge, England: Cambridge University Press.

Herrán, M. T. (1993). Los diálogos de Caracas y Tlaxcala y su cubrimiento por los medios de comunicación [The Caracas and Tlaxcala dialogs: Its coverage by the press]. In I. Orozco (Ed.), *Negociaciones de paz. Los casos de Colombia y el Salvador.* Bogotá, Colombia: CINEP.

Hofstede, G. (1980). *Culture's consequences.* Beverly Hills, CA: Sage.

Hofstede, G. (1997). *Cultures and organizations. The software of the mind.* New York: McGraw- Hill.

Hoskin, G., & Swanson, G. (1974). Political party leadership in Colombia: A spatial analysis. *Comparative Politics, 6*(3), 395–423.

House, R. J., Hanges, P. J., Javidan, M., Dorfman, P. W., Gupta, V., & GLOBE Associates. (2004). *Cultures, leadership, and organizations: The GLOBE study of 62 societies.* Thousand Oaks, CA: Sage.

Jaap, T. (1989). *Enabling leadership.* Aldershot, England: Glower.

Kline, H. (1974). Interest groups in the Colombian Congress: Group consensus in a centralized, patrimonial political system. *Journal of Inter-American Studies and World Affairs, 16*(3), 274–300.

Kotter, J. (1988). *The leadership factor.* New York: The Free Press.

Kotter, J. (1990a). *El factor liderazgo* [The leadership factor]. Madrid, Spain: Díaz de Santos.

Kotter, J. (1990b). *A force for change: How leadership differs from management.* New York: The Free Press.

Kotter, J. (1997). *El líder del cambio* [Leading change]. Mêxico City: McGraw- Hill.

Kouzes, J. M., & Pozner, B. Z. (1987). *The leadership challenge: How to get extraordinary things done in organizations.* San Francisco: Jossey-Bass.

Likert, R. (1960). *New patterns of management.* New York: McGraw-Hill.

Lijphart, A. (1968). Typologies of democratic systems. *Comparative Political Studies, 1*(April), 3–44.

Lijphart, A. (1977). *Democracy in plural societies.* New Haven, CT: Yale University Press.

Matamala, R. (1994, May 9). Liderazgo empresarial [Business leadership]. *Estrategia Económica y Financiera.*

Matamala, R., & Ogliastri, E. (1994). *Empresas de calidad en Colombia. Siete casos* [Quality firms in Colombia]. Unpublished manuscript.

McClelland, D. (1961). *The achieving society.* Princeton, NJ: Van Nostrand.

McGregor, D. (1960). *The human side of enterprise.* New York: McGraw-Hill.

McGregor, D. (1966). *Leadership and motivation.* Cambridge, MA: MIT Press.

Merton, R., Fiske, M., & Kendall, P. L. (1990). *The focused interview.* Glencoe, IL: The Free Press.

Mishler, E. (1986). *Research interviewing: Narrative and context.* Cambridge, England: Cambridge University Press.

Morgan, D. L. (1988). *Focus group as qualitative research.* Newbury Park, CA: Sage.

Morgan, D. (Ed.). (1993). *Successful focus groups: Advancing the state of the art.* Newbury Park, CA: Sage.

Motta, P. R. (1993). *La ciencia y el arte de ser dirigente. Un instrumento indispensable para el desarrollo personal y profesional de actuales y futuros dirigentes* [The art and science of leadership]. Bogotá, Colombia: Tercer Mundo y Uniandes.

Mutis, G. (1994, June 20). Liderazgo colectivo e integral [Collective and integrative leadership]. *Estrategia Económica y Financiera.*

Ogliastri, E. (1976), Estudio comparativo sobre movilidad social inter-generacional en las élite regionales de nueve centros urbanos de Colombia [A comparative study of inter-generational social mobility in eight Colombian cities]. *Revista de Planeación y Desarrollo, VII, 2.*

Ogliastri, E. (1987). En busca de la teoría: Experiencias con el método inductivo de investigación social [In search of theory: Experiences with inductive methods of social research]. *Texto y Contexto, 11.* Bogotá, Colombia: Universidad de los Andes.

Ogliastri, E. (1988). *Gerencia japonesa y círculos de participación. Experiencias en América Latina* [Japanese management and quality circles in Latin America]. Bogotá, Colombia: Norma.

Ogliastri, E. (1989a). Estructura de poder y clases sociales: La democracia oligárquica en Colombia [Power structure and social classes: Oligarchic democracy in Colombia]. *Monografías, 14.* Bogotá: Universidad de los Andes.

Ogliastri, E. (1989b). Liberales conservadores versus conservadores liberales: Faccionalismos trenzados en la estructura de poder en Colombia [Conservative liberals vs. Liberal conservatives: Tangled factions in the power structure of Colombia]. *Monografías, 12.* Bogotá, Colombia: Universidad de los Andes.

Ogliastri, E. (1994a, August 22). El liderazgo en Colombia [Leadership in Colombia]. *Estrategia Económica y Financiera.*

Ogliastri, E. (1994b). Pedro y Gloria [Pedro and Gloria]. Medellin, Colombia: *Revista Universidad EAFIT.*

Ogliastri, E. (1996a). *El liderazgo organizacional en Colombia. Un estudio internacional. Reporte de las investigaciones realizadas entre Enero y Agosto de 1996* [Organizational leadership in Colombia. Research report 1990]. Bogotá, Colombia : Comité de Investigaciones de Administración, Universidad de los Andes.

Ogliastri, E. (1996b). Los polivados, sector público y sector privado en la clase dirigente colombiana al final del Frente Nacional 1972–78 [Polivalents, private and public sector leaders in Colombia 1972–78]. In G. Gónzález & E. Ogliastri (Eds.), *Gerencia pública: ¿Asunto privado?* (pp. 35–96). Bogotá, Colombia: Tercer Mundo.

Ogliastri, E. (1997a, Dec 6). El liderazgo en Colombia [Leadership in Colombia]. Bogotá, Colombia: *Portafolio.*

Ogliastri, E. (1997b). El liderazgo organizacional en Colombia. Un estudio cualitativo [Organizational leadership in Colombia: Qualitative study]. Medellin, Colombia: *Revista Universidad EAFIT, 105.*

Ogliastri, E, & Dávila, C. (1983). Estructura de poder y Desarrollo en once ciudades intermedias de Colombi [Power structure and development in eleven intermediate size Colombian cities]. *Desarrolla y Sociedad, 12,* CEDE, Bogotá.

Ogliastri, E., & Dávila, C. (1987). The articulation of power and business structures: A study of Colombia. In M. Mizruchi & M. Schwartz (Eds.), *Intercorporate relations: Structural analysis of business* (pp. 233–263). Cambridge, England: Cambridge University Press.

Ogliastri, E., & Guerra, E. (1980). Fracciones de clase en la burguesía de ciudades intermedias de Colombia [Class fraction in intermediate cities bourgeoisie in Colombia]. *Revista Mexicana de Sociología, 4* (reprinted in *Monografías de Administracion, 11,* 1–42).

Ogliastri, E., McMillen, C., Altschul, C., Arias, M. E., Bustamante, C., Dávila, C., dela Coletta, et al. (1999). Cultura y liderazgo organizacional en 10 países de América Latina: El estudio GLOBE [Culture and organizational leadership in 10 Latin American countries: The GLOBE study]. *Revista Latino Americana de Administración, 22,* 29–56.

Ogliastri, E., & Rodríguez, C. (1994). *Intercultural study of leadership: Qualitative pilot report of Colombia.* Unpublished manuscript.

Ogliastri, E., & Wittingham, M. (2000). El liderazgo Colombiano: Un estudio de los medios escritos de comunicación [Colombian leadership: A study of printed media]. In Corporación Calidad, *Diálogos sobre Gestión II.* Bogotá, Colombia: Colciencias.

Peeler, J. (1983, October). *The conditions for liberal democracy in Latin America.* Paper presented at the XI International Congress of the Latin American Studies Association, Mexico City.

Peeler, J. (1994). *Constitution building and democracy in Brazil and Colombia.* Paper presented at the American Political Science Association annual meeting, New York.

Sayles, L. R. (1983). *The working leader: The triumph of high performance over conventional management principles.* New York: The Free Press.

Solaun, M. (1980). Colombian politics: Historical characteristics and problems. In R. Hellman, A. Berry, & M. Solaun (Eds.), *Politics of compromise* (pp. 59–83). Piscataway, NJ: Transaction.

Spradley, J. (1979). *The ethnographic interview.* New York: Holt, Rinehart & Winston.

Stumpf, S., & Mullen, T. (1992). *Taking charge: Strategic leadership in the middle game.* Englewood Cliffs, NJ: Prentice-Hall.

Sudarsky, J. (1973). *Motivacion: Individuo y sociedad* [Innovation: Individual and society]. Bogotá, Colombia: Publicaciones Ingenieria Universidad de los Andes.

Thoumi, F. (1994). *Economía política y narcotráfico* [Political economy and drug traffic]. Bogotá, Colombia: Tercer Mundo.

Vroom, V., & Jago, A. (1988). *The new leadership.* New York: Prentice-Hall.

Wilde, A. (1978). Conversations among gentlemen: Oligarchic democracy in Colombia. In Linz & Stepan (Eds.), *The breakdown of democratic regimes: Latin America.* Baltimore: Johns Hopkins University Press.

20

▼▼▼▼▼▼▼

Societal Culture and Leadership in Mexico—A Portrait of Change

Jon P. Howell
New Mexico State University

Jose de la Cerda
ITESO University, Guadalajara, Jalisco, Mexico

Sandra M. Martínez
Widener University School of Business Administration

J. Arnoldo Bautista
*Centro Nacional de Investigación y Desarrollo Tecnológico,
Interior Internado Palmira S/N—Complejo CENIDET,
Col. Palmira, Cuernavaca, Morelos, México*

Juan Ortiz
ITESO University, Guadalajara, Jalisco, Mexico

Leonel Prieto
Texas A&M International University

Peter Dorfman
New Mexico State University

This chapter describes an analysis of societal culture and leadership in Mexico based on data from the GLOBE Project and other relevant sources. Although Mexico is a country with distinct regional cultures, strong unifying socioeconomic and political processes throughout Mexican history have created important cultural features shared by members of Mexican society that make an overall analysis meaningful. These features include a common language, a shared *mestizo* (Spanish/Indian) heritage, and a predominant religion.[1] These important factors are a legacy of Mexico's history—its indigenous past, the early Spanish conquest and colonial period of Mexico, a series of national revolutions, and a complex evolving relationship with the United States. In the later part of the 20th century, Mexicans have struggled to change their economic structure to respond to globalization, and to forge a more democratic society. All these influences and processes have formed the nation and culture that is Mexico today. This chapter attempts to describe this culture and how it explains the image Mexicans currently possess of outstanding leadership.

The chapter begins with a description of the major eras of Mexican history that have influenced its current culture, concluding with a portrait of Mexico today in a state of change. This historical description is designed to highlight the development of Mexican cultural values over time. The most important cultural values emanating from the historical description are then summarized. This is followed by two literature reviews. The first review surveys published academic books and articles from the United States and Mexico describing research on management and leadership in Mexico. The second review provides a media analysis of over 200 articles focusing on leadership in Mexico from five popular publications in Mexico. The methodology of GLOBE research in Mexico is then described.

The empirical results of the research project are then presented. Our approach made use of several information sources to triangulate an accurate picture of what most Mexican citizens view as outstanding leadership. This begins with a description of the results of semistructured interviews and focus groups conducted with Mexican managers and professionals and ethnographic interviews with Mexican *empresarios* (entrepreneur/managers).[2] This is followed by a description of the GLOBE dimensions of national culture in Mexico with comparisons to other GLOBE countries. Then the GLOBE quantitative results on culturally endorsed implicit leadership theories (CLTs) in Mexico are presented and compared with results for other Latin American countries and other GLOBE countries. A short section follows describing the limitations of this study and recommendations for future research. The chapter ends with an integration of the quantitative and qualitative information obtained in the form of traditional and emerging themes for leadership and culture in Mexico.

1. MEXICAN HISTORY AND CULTURE

The cultural roots of leadership in Mexico are deeply imbedded in more than 500 years of history. The following historical description is designed to highlight the development of important societal values and patterns of behavior over time. The description is also designed to demonstrate how leadership has been exercised as Mexican society changed through the years (Cosío Villegas, 1955; Krauze, 1991; Parkes, 1966; Vasconcelos, 1971). This provides a background for an integrative summary of cultural values that are predominant today and influence leadership in organizations in Mexico.

---

[1]Although Mexicans are still predominantly Roman Catholic, significant Protestant populations exist in many regions.

[2]As explained on page xx of this chapter, the term *empresario* in the Mexican context has a broader meaning than the term *entrepreneur,* as currently used in the discipline of entrepreneurship. In Mexico, an *empresario* can refer to both owner-managers (entrepreneurs) as well as corporate managers.

History

Major events in Mexican history are represented by five eras: the indigenous civilizations (before 1520), Spanish conquest and colonization (1520–1810), independence and formation of the nation (1810–1910), consolidating institutions and economic and political transition (1910–2000), and Mexico today (2001).

Indigenous Civilizations.   The early history of the Mexican territory consists of the settlement by several nomadic tribes from the north and subsequent intertribal wars for power and territory. After several hundred years, these tribes evolved into complex civilizations. The Toltecs and the Mayans are examples of these civilizations that dominated the region of Mexico during different eras and made remarkable achievements in the arts and sciences. The Aztecs formed the last and best known of these empires. Theirs was a theocracy headed by an emperor who was treated as a living god. It was forbidden to look him in the face and everyone was required to walk barefoot in his presence. Military, commerce, and religion were strong institutions in the Aztec society.

The Aztec empire was extremely hierarchical. Priests and military generals were at the top of the status hierarchy as part of the noble families. Merchants came next in the status hierarchy, then the peasants who farmed the land, followed by slaves. The Aztecs believed their power came from their gods, who required human sacrifices of prisoners captured in wars, slaves, servants, and even courageous warriors. The Aztecs also imposed heavy tax burdens on many smaller kingdoms in the region. Their ruthlessness caused deep resentment, hatred, and fear among the tribes subject to Aztec rule and within allied tribes.

Spanish Conquest.   Spanish troops led by Hernan Cortés arrived in 1520. Cortés was mistaken for Quetzalcóatl—an Aztec deity whose return was predicted by an Aztec legend. This circumstance led to a series of misjudgments of the Spaniards by the Aztecs. The Spaniards brought several diseases that were unknown to the Indians, such as smallpox, which killed thousands and caused extreme demoralization. Cortés formed alliances with several tribes who opposed Aztec rule. These factors brought about the conquest and destruction of the Aztec Empire. The eventual conquest of northern Mexico was possible later, due in part to the Catholic missionary priests who conquered many of the less organized nomadic tribes with religious strategies.

The era of Spanish conquest and colonialism sought to impose the values of 16th century Roman Catholicism and intellectual repression on indigenous theocratic and militaristic empires—reinforcing a tradition of authoritarianism by leaders. The viceroy was the ruling representative of the Spanish crown in the colony. Among the 62 viceroys who ruled New Spain (Mexico), many were good administrators and a few were outstanding. The first, Don Antonio de Mendoza (1535–1550), achieved order by excellent politics. Luis de Velasco (1550–1564) abolished Indian slavery and initiated other measures to diminish the suffering of the indigenous population. Within the colonial administration, institutions were established to restrain the power of the viceroys and discourage corruption (Meyer, Sherman, & Deeds, 1999). However, these measures were poorly implemented and indigenous populations continued to suffer abuse (Bonfil Batalla, 1987; Horgan, 1984).

The expansion of Catholicism was a key element in the Spanish colonial system. Political and social leadership during the three centuries of colonization was dispersed among the viceroys, the noblemen, and the clergy. Clergymen were essentially part of a royal bureaucracy that dominated the society of New Spain. The archbishop was second only to the viceroy in importance and power. Several thousand priests and members of religious orders became owners of large properties and they answered only to their own clerical courts. Half of the arable land in Mexico may have become property of the clergy. The Catholic Church controlled two thirds of the capital in circulation. It made loans to land owners and acquired mortgages on their estates. The Church sought to replace the worship of pagan gods with Christian images and rituals by exempting converted Indians of all taxes and punishing those who resisted. Parish priests not only represented the Church, but were "agents of the state religion" and "intermediaries between parishioners and higher authorities and between the sacred and the profane" (Taylor, 1996, p. 3). However, besides interpreting and supervising the enforcement of the obligations of their parishioners to the Church and the state, parish priests also interceded to represent the needs of their parishioners to these authorities and were sometimes benefactors. In this way, patterns of control and reciprocal obligations developed between subordinate indigenous and mestizo (mixed Indian and Spanish) populations and their political and religious leaders. These patterns of control and mutual influence evolved into a patronage system and continue to influence present conceptions of effective and desirable leadership among Mexicans.

As in most colonial situations, power was not shared with the indigenous people and, as a rule, indigenous groups were not permitted to benefit from the resources of the colony. Furthermore, Spanish descendants born in the colonies (creoles) were also excluded from some positions of authority and consequently could not benefit, as did their Spanish-born peers, from colonial resources. Nevertheless, it would be incorrect to assume that indigenous groups passively accepted control. On the contrary, they survived, resisted, and accommodated to Spanish rule in complex ways that ethnohistorians and anthropologists are still trying to unravel (Krippner- Martínez, 2001; Taylor, 1996; Wolf, 1966). The threat of violence underlay all social relationships during the colonial period. Although some negotiation and consent took place, power was exercised primarily by agents of the economic and political elite. Military outposts and local militia played key roles in maintaining security (Horgan, 1984). Many historians have regarded the colonial period as a time of cruel imposition of Spanish interests on the welfare of natives with little or no concern for personal rights, needs or cultural values (Bonfil Batalla, 1987). Other scholars, however, suggest that the Spanish tyranny reflects the behaviors during and after the decline of the colonial system in the last decades of the 18th century (J. Krippner- Martínez, personal communication, 2002; Taylor, 1996). The important point is that Spanish conquest and colonialism, with its imposition of Catholicism, reinforced a tradition of authoritarianism and omnipotence by leaders.

Independence and the New Nation. In 1810 the Spanish dominance crumbled in America. A rebellion of mestizos headed by two priests, Miguel Hidalgo and José María Morelos, who invoked the authority of the Church and priesthood, promised revenge on the colonial masters and raised the ideals of an independent nation under a republican rule with a constitution and a congress. Led by Agustín Iturbide, a group of conservative, wealthy creoles, uncomfortable with the liberal ideals espoused by Hidalgo and Morelos, took advantage of the popular insurgency to organize their own struggle for independence from Spain. When the rebellion against Spanish rule was successful, Iturbide took power for himself and became the first emperor of Mexico in 1822 (Meyer et al., 1999). His government was important because it consolidated Mexico's independence. It was shortened, however, because it failed to receive societal and international support and recognition.

The break from Spanish dominance corresponded with the evolution of Mexican *caudillos* or regional governors. These were usually very powerful men, owners of huge estates called haciendas. They imposed their own law within their territories, were expansionist with regard to small landowners and other interests surrounding their property, and relied on bound labor and wielded extreme power over the labor force. As was frequently the case, caudillos became patrons when their leadership was characterized by protective practices toward loyal followers. Krauze (1994) has demonstrated that Mexican leaders have usually invoked moral and religious principles for legitimacy. This patriarchal leadership had its antecedent in the role of missionaries during the spiritual conquest of Mexico, and the role of the church and its padres during the forging of the new nation. Owners of haciendas, or any people in power, had the ecclesiastic right to command people as long as they behaved in a paternalistic manner. The caudillos were sustained not only by their vast properties, but also by their ability to develop patron–client relationships reinforced by deeply rooted notions of legitimacy incorporating religious beliefs and practices (Taylor, 1996; Wolf, 1966). These relationships were sometimes imposed upon people autocratically, under the threat of either death or religious condemnation. Whether emperors, viceroys, presidents, governors, bishops, parish priests, caudillos, or patrones, historical narratives of most Mexican leaders have described an authority based on the intentions of an unassailable supreme figure. Nevertheless, these relationships between dominant and subordinate individuals, as they were enacted on a daily basis in colonial Mexico, were mediated by reciprocal responsibility and negotiation between parties. Indigenous people, and other subordinate groups, did not simply submit to colonial rule, but often negotiated, appropriated, and were accommodating to modify existing patterns of behavior, beliefs, and practices. Taylor and other historians have demonstrated that indigenous and mestizo Mexicans were active participants in changing their own society.

During most of the 19th century, Mexico lived in a state of poverty, turmoil, and constant revolution. There were 50 military governments, two secessions (Texas and Yucatán), seven different congresses, three constitutions, a reform act, and many state constitutions. Several generals from the war for independence became political bosses of their territories, including Guadalupe Victoria, Vicente Guerrero, and Antonio López de Santa Anna. Each of these eventually became president but was unable to consolidate the Republic. Financial affairs were handled poorly, ethnic and social tensions continued, and there was little law enforcement. The military and the clergy, who had the real economic power, opposed genuine reforms. Santa Anna was an extreme example of the corrupt political leadership of this era. He conspired and supported one faction or another, yet he was elected president 11 times between 1832 and 1855 due to his charisma and military stature.

As was true of the rest of the world, socially committed leadership was rare in Mexico during the 19th century. Benito Juárez was an exception. He was an Indian from Oaxaca who built a revolt to establish a more democratic form of government and to stimulate economic development. He sought to abolish the independent powers of the Church (and the generals), to place its wealth in service of the nation, and also to privatize communal indigenous landholdings. Juárez became the first civilian president of Mexico in 1858. His social reforms were interrupted by French intervention, the Maximilian emperor period (1861–1867), followed by the rebellion of Porfirio Diaz.

Porfirio Diaz, a general under Juarez's presidency, consolidated military leadership through continuous reelection for 30 years (1876–1910). He brought peace, order, and economic prosperity through convenient alliances with his former enemies: the landowners, the Church, the generals, and foreign investors. Although Diaz's administration of alliances generated a dynamic economy, only a few Mexicans benefited from the resulting prosperity. Social reform was alien to Diaz's regime and political abuses were frequent. Finally, with differing motivations but united in their desire to remove Diaz from power, several regional movements incorporating diverse social groups coalesced to mount a revolt against Diaz's military dictatorship. Peasants in Morelos and other rural areas, workers in Mexico City and the northern mining economy, and middle-class intellectuals were among the participants in the insurgency. In addition, the very economic changes Diaz initiated had created new social groups that were excluded from the inner circle of power. This was especially the case for the emerging capitalist bourgeoisie of the northern states. After a violent civil war, it was this last group who ultimately emerged from the revolution in control of the country. The end of the revolution did not dispel military leaders from power. With the exception of Francisco Madero, all presidents of the first 50 years of the revolutionary republic were army generals. During Madero's presidency (1911–1913), the realization of his democratic ideals and commitment to social reform were hampered by his inability to unite the different revolutionary groups with sharply conflicting ideas, a weak economy, and his own administration's nepotism. Collusion by Henry Lane Wilson, the U.S. ambassador to Mexico, with leaders of the left and right resulted in a pact to overthrow Madero. Madero was beset by armed revolt from the left, including General Zapata, who believed that Madero was moving too slowly to improve the lot of common Mexicans, as well as insurgents of the right who did not support Madero's democratic agenda (Meyer et al., 1999). Nevertheless, the ideals of liberal democratic revolutionary leaders such as Francisco Madero, and the populist revolutionary military leaders Francisco Villa and Emiliano Zapata, had a lasting effect on the emerging political ideology of future Mexican leaders.

Consolidating Institutions and Economic and Political Transition.   The senseless murder of President Madero in December of 1913 set a tone of continuous betrayal and murder among winning revolutionary leaders that characterized the revolutionary period. Finally, Plutarco Elias Calles, an authoritarian and talented president (1924–1928), found a solution to end the fighting. He helped form a political party called the National Revolutionary Party (PNR), which later became the Revolutionary Institutional Party (PRI). The PRI became a solid structure to support the authority of the national president, and emphasized a political culture of reciprocity within a single-party state. This political party was formed on the basis of a power distribution to leaders of main sectors of society: the military, unions, teachers, the Church, peasant and factory workers, as well as social sectors such as entrepreneurs, intellectuals, and the media. All espoused their commitment to constitutional rule. The PRI maintained control of the government for over 70 years and was effective in consolidating institutions and providing social stability to Mexico through much of the 20th century.

Annual growth rates in gross national product (GNP) of 6% or higher, an increase in real wages, and relatively sound monetary and fiscal policies between 1958 and 1970, often called the stabilizing development period, contributed to social stability. The state provided infrastructure development, tax breaks, and financial support for manufacturers as part of the Import Substitution Industrialization Policies (1930s through early 1960s). After World War II acceptable levels of economic growth were achieved in a closed economy characterized by protective trade policies, government subsidies to industry, and public ownership of enterprises in key sectors. However, by 1970 the capacity of the economy to generate economic growth under the same policies, pursued since the 1930s, was insufficient to meet Mexico's needs. Severe problems, including poorly designed protective tariffs, inefficiently run state-owned companies, and a growing and corrupt government bureaucracy, produced a vicious circle of rising public deficits, accelerating inflation, capital flight, and a mounting foreign debt. Beginning in the late 1960s, in addition to the need for change in the economic structure to ensure growth and prosperity, the political leadership of the PRI also struggled with how to respond to more vocal protest for social change toward greater democracy. Student movements, urban guerillas, increased union autonomy, and increasing discord between the entrepreneurial elite and the government characterized the late 1960s and 1970s.

On the economic front, an entire generation of Mexicans suffered the instability of the sharp devaluations of the peso in 1976, 1982, 1986, and 1994. The first two devaluations coincided with the end of the 6-year terms of Presidents Echeverria and Lopez Portillo. Echeverria's populist policies did not effectively reduce social inequality and his reluctance to impose fiscal reform led to the balance-of-payments crisis of 1976. Lopez Portillo continued to postpone structural economic change and his administration was characterized by excessive spending. The accumulated effects of inappropriate fiscal policy and corrupt government contributed to the problems leading to peso devaluation.

President de la Madrid took office after the devaluation of 1982 during a serious crisis of confidence in the Mexican economy. De la Madrid initiated changes in the economic structure to open the economy to global competition by trade liberalization, privatization, and deregulation of government-run and subsidized firms and industries. During the administration of President de la Madrid, Mexico became a member of the General Agreement on Tariffs and Trade (GATT). The liberalization of the Mexican economy, and the policies of fiscal discipline and austerity, deregulation, and privatization initiated by President De la Madrid, were sustained by the government strategies of his two successors, Carlos Salinas and Ernesto Zedillo. In fact, these three presidents, trained in economics in prestigious U.S. universities, formed the generation of political leadership that radically shifted away from the ideological, political, and economic positions of their predecessors. Nationalistic and populist ideology had dominated political power for 50 years until President De la Madrid took office. These three neo-liberal and technocratic presidents, as they were customarily labeled by their critics and some Mexican intellectuals, not only imposed a new economic policy in Mexico, but completely changed the ideas and discourse that had sustained and dominated political leadership in Mexico for more than half of the 20th century. With their entrance into political leadership, the previous generation of political, unionist, empresarial, and social leaders were replaced by new leaders who introduced concepts such as competitiveness, globalization, technical innovation, and total quality.

Following the administration of President Salinas de Gortari, Ernesto Zedillo took office in December of 1994 to begin his 6-year term. He would be the last in a consecutive line of PRI presidents since 1924. President Salinas continued the liberal reform of the economic structure of Mexico and made Mexico a credible global player in international trade by implementing the North American Free Trade Agreement (NAFTA) and attracting foreign investment to Mexico. However, the end of his term marked the beginning of multiple indictments of widespread corruption, which descredited his administration and personal reputation. When President Zedillo widened the bands on the exchange rate of the peso to more accurately reflect its real value, the value of the peso plummeted as the foreign investors with primarily indirect investments in Mexico withdrew their money. The peso lost 45% of its value and Mexico's foreign reserves were depleted. Facing another economic crisis, Mexicans reflected on the nature and pace of economic reforms and the absence of democratic reforms to accompany economic ones.

During the Zedillo administration it became increasingly evident that political and administrative centralization, corrupt and bureaucratic mismanagement of public resources, resource distribution designed to facilitate political control, and large government subsidies by the PRI government were becoming less useful for maintaining political stability and economic growth. For the first time in a century, open criticism of the president in the press and other media was not suppressed. Three major institutions became leading forces for power redistribution rather than continued political control by the PRI: the Federal Elections Institute (IFE), the Congress, and (to an extent) the Bank of Mexico. The increasing gap between the government's economic and political policies and the demands of key societal actors resulted in a voting population that demanded improved economic performance and political processes. This was reflected in regional electoral triumphs of opposition parties and the political transition that culminated in the presidential election in 2000 of Vicente Fox, a member of the National Action Party (PAN). Fox was very successful in campaigning as a social democrat and offering his political platform as the only hope for deep political change in the country. Replacing the PRI as the party in control became a major pragmatic goal for most Mexican voters, including influential intellectuals, politicians, and many social leaders whose political ideas were otherwise distant from PAN's conservative ideology.

Five years of President Fox's administration have shown that dismantling a self-sustained authoritarian system, replacing inefficient social and economic structures with profound reforms, and bringing about economic prosperity and social justice for a large disadvantaged population was more difficult than Fox anticipated. One of the major failures of this administration is the lack of political expertise to generate enough consensuses for national reforms in three fields: energy, taxes, and labor relations. As Preston and Dillon (2004) recently noted, no one seriously questions the essential vigor of the democracy Mexicans have constructed and the country's peaceful transition to a more equitable power distribution.

The PRI defeat in the 2000 elections and the trend toward democracy and stronger independent institutions does not guarantee the end of old leadership habits. Leadership of caudillos in politics and business is still alive in Latin America, and probably will be for some years. Though certain manifestations of authoritarianism persists in many sectors in Mexico today, a leadership shift has also occurred away from centralized governance toward greater community involvement and open government, more efficient disclosure of corruption at all levels of leadership, and greater social pressure on political power brokers to be far more responsive to the needs of their constituencies.

Current Mexican Society—A Portrait of Change.   Mexico is now predominantly an urban country, almost three fourths of its population lives in cities. Although country life is still important, migration to cities has diminished the size of rural communities. The population in Mexico is approximately 100 million. Fifty percent of Mexicans are younger than 15 years of age, and the age pyramid is changing. In the first two decades of the 21st century, most of the population will be in its working years. The average years of formal education is 8 years and this mean value has increased by almost 2 years each decade. Illiteracy is below 8% and half of this is concentrated in the elderly (Instituto Nacional de Estadística, Geografíae Informática [INEGI], 1990, 1995, 2002). Educated young people should be a major social force for change in the near future.

The structural changes in the Mexican economy initiated by President de la Madrid during the early 1980s, and continued by succeeding presidential administrations, have effectively liberalized trade and opened the economy to foreign investment. Since 1982, Mexico has signed free-trade agreements with countries in North America, Central and South America, the European Union, and several Asia-Pacific countries. Economic reform and international commerce have favorable long-term implications for economic growth. Exports of manufactured goods have steadily increased (INEGI, 2002) and Mexican firms are becoming more competitive. In the short term, however, it has made Mexican firms more vulnerable to international competitors and real wages have declined until very recently. Opening the Mexican economy to global competition has had significant impacts on the business elite's ideas about leadership and organizational practices in many Mexican firms. As documented later in the chapter, some Mexican managers have had to change their leadership behaviors and practices in order to survive.

One of the most important economic developments in recent decades is the establishment of the *maquiladora* industry, which is primarily concentrated along the Mexican border with the United States. Maquiladoras are assembly plants owned and operated by business firms from the United States and other countries that take advantage of the low-wage Mexican labor force and the proximity to the U.S. market. The key concept of the maquiladoras is that components are produced in the United States and other countries, assembled in Mexico, and exported to the United States and elsewhere for distribution with an import tax imposed only on the value added in Mexico. These plants have provided a major industrial economic base for Mexican border cities and have been a major income generator for the Mexican economy. They have also been influential in importing management practices from the United States, Japan, and other countries into Mexican organizations. Quality principles, ISO standards, and autonomous work groups are being used in some Mexican organizations that emphasize increased participation by workers (de la Cerda, 1995). However, because of trade liberalization, maquiladoras have recently lost unique advantages in relation to other Mexican manufacturing concerns. Despite all these social and economic changes, today about 95% of Mexican business firms have fewer than 15 employees, and most are family owned, where traditional leadership practices are used.

The labor force is now predominantly in service and manufacturing industries. Though official unemployment is very low, about 2.5%, underemployment is still a pernicious problem that includes close to one third of the national employed population (INEGI, 2002). The role of women has changed dramatically. More than one third of working-age women are employed and this trend is rapidly increasing. The mean level of education for women is close to that of men, and women are assuming leadership positions in business and politics.

The Catholic religion is still predominant in Mexico (over 90%), but changes in religious affiliation are increasingly common. Hinduism, Buddhism, and other religious practices are no longer unusual and Protestant and other Christian denominations are increasing. This is one of the most significant indicators of social change because Mexicans have always had a strong religious tradition. The Catholic Church has been influential in the politics, government, and society of Mexico for hundreds of years. An increasing number of individuals are choosing to change religion, probably because they are unsatisfied with their socioeconomic and spiritual development and they consider themselves free to choose their spiritual destiny. This change shows the deep transformations occurring in Mexican society.

The election of Vicente Fox from the PAN party is the most prominent indicator of political transformation. Fox campaigned on a platform of social and economic change and well-being (Krauze, 2000). The PAN party also represents the first minority in both branches of National Congress: the Senate and the Representatives Chamber. Three main parties—PAN, PRI, and PRD—share most chairs in both chambers, but no party has a majority in any chamber. Although major changes in political and federal government organizations are expected, all forces for change must surmount traditional structures of power built during more than 70 years of PRI government.

Although unionism is very traditional, unions are no longer completely loyal to the traditional PRI system. Official unions are still powerful and paternalistic, but new labor movements are rising. The structure of unionism in Mexico may be changing. Business and entrepreneurial organizations have supported traditional unionism. They have enjoyed labor stability for decades while strikes and wage demands have been under control. Even though entrepreneurs see labor laws as too paternalistic, they accept their protective orientation in exchange for stability and control. Entrepreneurs are no longer a monolithic group, and political loyalty is not mandatory. Entrepreneurial and professional organizations now operate independently of political or government affiliation.

For many years, large business organizations have existed in Mexico called *grupos empresariales* (or *corporativos*), which are essentially conglomerates. Some grupos originated as domestic business alliances and/or international partnerships that have existed for decades. They engage in the production and distribution of products and services in diverse industries including steel, food, real estate, petrochemicals, telecommunications, finance, agriculture, and publishing. Grupos are historically family owned and operated, but business trends in Mexico since the 1980s have brought about changes in their operations. The ownership of some grupos is no longer concentrated in one or a few families, and in some instances ownership is becoming separate from management. Deregulation of formerly state-owned enterprises allowed some grupos to add significantly to their asset holdings at bargain prices. Many are making extensive use of consultants to improve competitiveness, to link to international production networks, or to take advantage of market niches in the domestic economy. Grupos are among the most powerful economic and political entities in Mexico today.

Other interest groups are also organizing themselves and fighting for their rights. Public education in rural areas began in the 1930s and most of Mexico's population was rural until the latter part of the 20th century. Now that education is widespread and increasing, the potential for influence by various groups is significantly increased. Ethnic groups, social and political movements (such as the Zapatistas in Chiapas), professional groups, intellectual groups, religious groups, women's groups, small-business owners, and some radical groups are examples of the diverse interest groups that make up the pluralistic society that is Mexico today.

The family as a social entity is also changing. As families become urbanized, extended familial identities may be losing their influence. This does not mean that ties with two or three generations are necessarily breaking apart, but that families may not be as demanding of members' loyalty as in the past. Traditional family disintegration is one of the main problems confronting Mexican society. Women have become leaders of many nuclear and mono-parent families because of the economic and psychological support they give when fathers are absent. This is especially the case for thousands of families whose fathers work in the United States as immigrants.

Alduncin (1986) wrote that Mexico is in the middle of two superimposed eras (tradition vs. modernity) and wants to establish itself as a culturally and economically developed country. Permanent changes in Mexican life are likely to come from continued widening of the distribution of power in society, trade liberalization, and major economic progress. These changes are ongoing in Mexico. Many Mexicans are learning new ways of facing life and problems, often different from the passive, fatalistic and dependent modes of the past. But Mexican culture has not changed completely. Many traditions are alive and strong and certain perceptions and values of the Mexican people remain constant. The major cultural values that prevail today and influence leadership in Mexico reflect the country's history as well as the social changes described here.

Culture

The historical evolution of Mexican society provides a frame of reference for describing and understanding important cultural values which are prevalent in Mexico today. These cultural values reflect Mexico's cultural heritage and they strongly affect the behavior of Mexican leaders in business, government, social movements, and many other organizational contexts. Several of these values are related to those identified by GLOBE researchers in the current study, but they are described here as emerging from Mexico's historical development as a nation and a society.

Traditionalism. Traditional societies, like much of Mexico, emphasize family, class, reverence for the past, and ascribed status. Modern societies, such as Sweden or the United States, stress merit, rationality, and progress (Bass, 1990). Men have higher status than women in traditional societies. Time is often viewed with no sense of urgency; punctuality and long-range planning are unimportant (Davis, Ming, & Brosnan, 1986). Traditional societies often accept and respond to autocratic (nonparticipative) leadership. These social characteristics are found in much of Mexico, especially in the less developed and poorer regions in the south and areas that are distant from highly industrialized cities. Paternalism and autocratic behavior by leaders reflect the patterns of authority during the colonial period when power was centralized in representatives of the Spanish monarchy and the Church. These leadership patterns also reflect the post-Colonial periods when the society was dominated by military leaders and a single political party machine. A strong class structure with its ascribed status also emerged from early Indian societies and Spanish dominance. The family has been a safe haven during all the tumultuous periods of Mexican history. Traditional attitudes toward time and the role of women, as well as other traditional practices, are often carried by families and individuals who move from rural regions to the cities. Until recently, families have tended to stay together or closely connected, and the traditional values have been maintained and reinforced in the home. This helps explain why these values continue to be evident in the workplace in small and medium-size organizations, and sometimes in large organizations, where they often conflict with more modern cosmopolitan values.

In-Group Collectivism. A key feature of traditional societies, the family has been a source of nurturance, protection, and support during the Indian, Spanish, and revolutionary eras. Supremacy of the father, sacrifice of the mother, and children who love, obey, and respect their parents characterize the traditional Mexican family.[3] The oldest male (a patriarch) is the head of the traditional extended family in Mexico. Loyalty and abnegation are considered important to satisfy other's needs in the family before one's own needs. This close family structure with a strong father figure and the devotion expected of family members provided the basic model for strict hierarchical organization structures found throughout Mexico. Respect and cooperation with those who are higher in the social hierarchy are expected of all Mexicans. These expectations frequently support the authoritarian and autocratic behaviors often found with Mexican leaders.

Power Distance. Large power differences have always existed in Mexican society; they are expected and respected. Power is desired and exercised by the political strongman

---

[3]Feminists would point out that this is a patriarchal family, though women also gain power as they marry and age. Some abuse and violence occurs within the family.

(*caudillo*), the military leader, and the successful businessman (Foster, 1960). Paz (1981) described the close resemblance between the *macho* male and the Spanish *conquistador.* He believed it was the model for Mexican men with power: feudal lords, hacienda owners, politicians, generals, captains of industry, cardinals, and heads of state, as well as heads of villages, cities, business firms, and families (Drost & Von Glinow, 1998). This model of a powerful leader has advanced the use of authoritarian and paternalistic behaviors by Mexican leaders (Drost & Von Glinow, 1998).

Social Individualism.   The North American concept of individualism includes beliefs in equal opportunity, personal initiative and enterprise, and individual rights (Drost & Von Glinow, 1998). Mexicans, and many other Latin Americans, have a different view of individualism that focuses on personal honor, dignity, and an intrinsic sense of self-worth. For generations, many Mexican people have felt betrayed by the myriad of governments that have exploited them or ignored their needs. This may be one reason that Mexicans often behave individualistically when they are outside their own families. They are frequently highly protective of their "turf" in hierarchical, formal organizations. This type of individualism often discourages democratic processes in organizations and permits individuals to exploit opportunities and to take advantage of others. This cultural trait helps maintain the *caudillo* image of men with power described earlier. One journalist described Latin Americans as having an "inability to become part of the whole, to feel involved in the collective destiny" (Rangle, 1977, p. 208). Octavio Paz (1959) added, "The [Mexican] Revolution has not succeeded in changing our country into a community, or even in offering any hope of doing so" (p. 175). This social individualism is related to a GLOBE cultural dimension entitled Social Collectivism described later in this chapter.

Interpersonal Relationships.   Mexicans developed a pattern of building and maintaining close relationships with others as a strategy for accomplishing things. By building networks of personal interaction, affection, and loyalty within and between organizations, Mexicans developed an indirect way of manipulating their environment. Personal relationships with family and friends take precedence over merit and equity (Bass, 1990). One writer described an example of the strategy as: "If the teacher loves me, I will get an 'A'" (Diaz-Loving, 1999). For people with little political or economic power, social relationships and commitments became paramount in obtaining cooperation or employment in organizations, in signing business or government contracts, and in most aspects of Mexican society. Friendships and personal acquaintances create a network of individuals who can help a person when she or he needs them. This interpersonal strategy for attaining one's goals is often called *personalismo* and is a direct response to individuals with political, economic, or religious power who did not represent the people's interests or meet their needs. The authoritarian traditions of church and state have resulted in laws and regulations being viewed as things to be avoided. Gratification and achievement rely on social individualism and freedom of action that can create lawlessness, but is usually based on effective personal working relationships with the right people (Drost & Von Glinow, 1998).

Summary.   The five eras of Mexican history have been characterized by violence, conflict, accommodation, revolution, and change. Authoritarian leadership, lack of trust in government and the political process, a hierarchical social structure, and enduring poverty have also been present. Today, much of Mexico is rapidly changing—authoritarianism is giving way to more democratic involvement, trust in political leaders and the government is increasing somewhat, and economic progress is creating more opportunity and optimism for the future. In Mexico, these changes are occurring within the context of cultural values that have evolved through 500 years of history, including traditionalism, in-group collectivism, power distance, social individualism, and the importance of interpersonal relations. These values will undoubtedly shape the course of social and economic progress in Mexico during this century.

2. LITERATURE REVIEW ON MANAGERIAL LEADERSHIP IN MEXICO

We conducted a literature review of published academic books and articles that address management and leadership in Mexico. Publications in both the United States and Mexico were included. This literature review continued throughout the project as new material became available.

A media analysis for Mexico was also carried out by scanning five popular publications in Mexico for articles pertaining to leadership in Mexico. This analysis covered two 4-week periods during March, April, and May of 2000. The publications, which were scanned, were one national newspaper (*El Financiero*), two regional newspapers (*Público* and *Mural*), and two national magazines—one of political orientation (*Proceso*) and one business review (*Expansión*). The media sources are independent of one another; they are published in Mexico City and Guadalajara, which are major business centers in Mexico. Their political orientation and target audiences vary, and their circulation is high. Some of these sources occasionally publish applied articles based on management research in other countries, but most of the articles reviewed dealt with trends or changes taking place in organizations in Mexico.

Each of the media publications was scanned to locate articles relevant to leadership in Mexico. More than 200 articles were read. Key phrases were identified in each article that indicated what effective leaders should do or should be like, as well as important leader attributes that fit an accepted pattern of leadership in Mexico. The central verb or adjective of each phrase was identified and used as a code word for this phrase. These code words then represented potential behaviors, actions, or characteristics of effective leaders. Three reviewers participated in this analysis and the key words they abstracted were very consistent across sources and reviewers. The information from the literature review and media analysis was later compared with the quantitative survey results of middle managers using GLOBE questionnaires described later.

Academic Literature

Several cultural characteristics explain a consistent finding by leadership researchers in Mexico—effective leaders in Mexico make extensive use of *supportive/relationship oriented leader behaviors* in influencing their followers (Drost & Von Glinow, 1998; Kras, 1992). Supportive behaviors are effective in Mexico at improving followers' job satisfaction and performance and in reducing followers' role ambiguity (Chemers & Aymen, 1985; Dorfman et al., 1997; Kras, 1994). Although many traditional authoritarian leaders in Mexico are not supportive of their followers, these recent studies show that supportiveness is an important part of *effective* leadership in Mexico today. The efficacy of leaders' supportiveness reflects the importance of interpersonal relations, which require courtesy, respect, and friendliness by leaders. The paternalistic and in-group collectivist orientation in Mexico mean a high value is placed on caring, listening, and understanding (*simpático*), which are hallmarks of supportive leaders.

Another finding in Mexico that is consistent with traditional cultural characteristics is the effectiveness of *directive leadership behavior.* Directive leadership involves focusing on followers' work tasks: how they are completed, who does what, when they must be completed, and the importance of meeting quality and quantity requirements. Directive leader behaviors reflect the traditional autocratic *patrón* model of Mexican history, where the elite leader maintained a sizable social distance from followers who were generally compliant and showed due respect and loyalty to the leader. In the United States and Western Europe, directive leaders are not necessarily autocratic or authoritarian when communicating with followers about their tasks. But with Mexico's cultural traditions, a status-oriented authoritarian style in dealing with followers has been more prevalent (Gutiérrez, 1993; Stephens & Greer, 1995). Mulder (1976) associated this style with a fear of disagreeing with one's superior, resulting in the *"no problema"* syndrome in responding to a superior's instructions (Drost & Von Glinow, 1998). Directive leader behaviors have been shown to improve followers' commitment to the organization and job performance and to reduce role ambiguity in Mexico (Dorfman et al., 1997; Dorfman & Howell, 1988, 1997).

Charismatic leader behaviors also reflect a historical tradition in Mexico. Mexican history is filled with charismatic revolutionary leaders who are continuously honored and celebrated. Political leaders often adopt a historical charismatic leader as a "spiritual" adviser (Riding, 1989). Workers will often rally around an emotional speech by a top manager, rather than a management program that stresses competition with others (Schuler, Jackson, Jackofsky, & Slocum, 1996). Bass (1990) indicated that charismatic leadership would be effective in collectivist cultures and this has been supported in studies of work organizations in Mexico (Dorfman et al., 1997).

Hofstede (1980) found Mexico to be high on his general measure of collectivism. This implies that individualized contingent rewards provided by leaders may not be effective in Mexico. However, control of rewards in organizations reflects a manager's power, and Mexico is also high in power distance. Our cultural description also identified Social Individualism as prevalent in Mexican culture. These factors may explain why leaders' *contingent reward behavior* has produced high worker commitment to the organization in Mexico (Dorfman et al., 1997; Dorfman & Howell, 1997). The cultural mandate not to embarrass or offend others prevents a leader's *contingent punishment behavior* from having any favorable effects on followers in Mexico (Dorfman & Howell, 1997).

Hofstede (1980) also indicated that *participative leadership behavior* was not effective in cultures that were Collectivist and high in Power Distance. The long history of strongly authoritarian military and political leaders in Mexico also does not support a high degree of participation by leaders. Several researchers have found participative leadership behaviors to be ineffective in Mexican organizations (Dorfman et al., 1997; Dorfman & Howell, 1997; Schuler et al., 1996). It should be noted, however, that a more participative leadership style seems to be emerging in the industrial centers of Mexico and along the U.S.–Mexico border. This emphasizes more worker involvement and teamwork than the traditional Mexican leadership approach (Agar, 1998; Lawrence & Yeh, 1995; Pelled & Hill, 1997; Vargas & Johnson, 1993). As Mexican business and other organizations become increasingly internationalized (through trade agreements, *maquiladora* plants, and joint ventures with companies from the United States, Japan, and other countries), this new leadership style may become more prevalent throughout Mexico.

Media Analysis

The 10 most frequently mentioned key words abstracted from the extensive media analysis reflect two persistent leadership themes found in the other data sources for this study (see Table 20.1). The first theme is highly *social oriented* and includes supportive behavior by the leader, such as helping followers and facilitating a feeling of belongingness and harmony. This social theme also includes integrating/conciliative behavior by a leader such as resolving differences, finding common ground, and forming alliances to hold people together in a common cause. This theme clearly supports the importance of positive interpersonal relations (*personalismo*), respect and sensitivity to followers (*simpático*), and collectivism in organizations as described in the Culture section, the interview results, and the research on leadership in Mexico.

The other persistent leadership theme supported by the media analysis is *directive and performance oriented*. This theme includes designing proposals to help achieve goals and change/transform organizations, emphasizing a practical orientation to guide action and achievement, and planning, implementing, and controlling activities to attain effective results. Although the articles seldom associated authoritarian approaches with this leadership concept, this theme does correspond with a strong central leader (*caudillo*) found in the Culture section and the research on directive leadership in Mexico. This theme also reflects the high value placed on Performance Orientation detailed in the GLOBE culture scales measuring societal values in Mexico, as well as the interview results. Both of these data sources are reported later in this chapter.

A newer theme also emerged from the key words abstracted in the media analysis. Although it occurred less often than the two dominant themes already described, it may reflect the newer leadership pattern that is appearing in the industrial centers of Mexico. This theme includes leaders' role in *negotiating and bargaining* to reach agreements, *representing* their followers and organizations to other parties, and creating conditions for and *implementing participation* by followers in decision making. These behaviors imply an outward orientation by leaders to create agreements and conditions where their followers and organizations can thrive. They also indicate a developing shift from the traditionally strong internal leader with passive compliant followers to leaders and followers who work together to solve increasingly complex problems in organizations. This evolving theme supports findings from recent leadership research on participation in Mexico's major industrial regions as well as interview results described later. It also is consistent with the relatively low score on Power Distance obtained on the GLOBE culture scales measuring societal values in Mexico. Although this newer theme may conflict with the second theme of a strong central leader, the presence of both themes in the media shows the ongoing conflict between traditional and cosmopolitan approaches to leadership in Mexican organizations.

3. METHODOLOGY OF GLOBE RESEARCH IN MEXICO

In addition to extensive literature reviews, the GLOBE project in Mexico involved semistructured and ethnographic interviews with managers, focus groups, and questionnaire administration to obtain meaningful data on culture dimensions and leadership processes. Each method is briefly described in this section and results are presented in later sections of this chapter. The different methods yield an interesting web of information that portrays a consistent view of Mexican culture and managerial leadership.

TABLE 20.1
Results of Media Analysis

Action Verbs and Leader Characteristics	Frequency	Rank	Percent
Supporter: Supportive behavior. The leader gives support to the group and gets support from other groups; his or her main role is getting and expanding resources.	144	1	8.1
Integrator/Conciliator: Harmonizing or conciliating behavior. The leader helps people or parties allied for a common purpose. Good leaders find common ground and help to resolve differences. To form alliances is important.	142	2	8.0
Proposing leader: The leader designs proposals to solve problems. Good leaders develop proposals fair to all in solving people problems.	140	3	7.9
Changer: Changing or transforming behavior. The leader guides and produces changes through innovative behavior.	130	4	7.3
Achiever: Achieving behavior. The leader gets good results, reaches goals, is effective and productive. "A man of action."	124	5	6.9
Decision maker & controller: Directive and controlling behavior. The leader makes decisions and gets things done. Good leaders have situations and processes under control.	111	6	6.2
Project leader: Planning behavior. The leaders plan, program, and project new actions. Visioning future solutions. Good leaders look ahead.	96	7	5.4
Negotiator: Bargaining behavior. The leaders know how to negotiate, bargain, and reach agreements.	90	8	5.1
Representative: Representing behavior. The leader represents others (the group to which he or she belongs). Representative behavior is very important under democratic systems. Being a democrat is very good.	81	9	4.5
Participating: Sharing behavior. The leader makes participation possible. Good leaders include people.	69	10	3.8
Improvement leader: Improving behavior. The leader improves operations, increases market or sector share, expands and allows growth of the business.	69	10	3.8
Manager: Being a good administrator. To manage effectively is an important part of a good leader's job.	55	12	3.1
Organizer: Structuring behavior. The leader organizes and structures (or restructures) to get things done. Initiating structure for good performance.	54	13	3.0
Developer: Developing behaviors. The leader is a developer; he or she understands his or her role in development of organizations and people.	53	14	3

(Continued)

TABLE 20.1   (Continued)

Action Verbs and Leader Characteristics	Frequency	Rank	Percent
Strategic leader: Strategic thinking. The leader creates new strategies to compete (win, grow, expand).	50	15	2.8
Risk or challenge taker: Challenging behavior. Good leaders take rational risks, they accept challenges.	49	16	2.7
Informer/Communicator/Dialogue maker: Informative or communicative behavior. Good leaders know how to communicate and dialogue. They know when to inform others.	47	17	2.6
Promoter: Promoting behavior. The leader promotes projects and people. To promote what has to be done is a main part of a leader's job.	37	18	2.1
Recognizer: Good leaders recognize what others do. It is important to give recognition to others.	33	19	1.8
Opportunity maker or taker: Being opportunistic means being in the right place at the right time. Making opportune proposals. Good leaders know when opportunity comes.	31	20	1.7
Process manager: Good leaders manage and control processes.	25	21	1.4
Being responsible: To accept responsibility and comply. Good leaders respond to others.	24	22	1.3
Interesting: Having charisma or an inspiring personality is important to be a good leader. Having a good image.	24	22	1.3
Being objective: Making good judgments.	15	24	0.8
Sharing opinions: Good leaders listen to others' opinions.	13	25	.07
Having persistence: To persist, to insist, to stand up. Good leaders persist.	13	25	0.7
Being competitive: Leaders have to be competitive. Competition enhances good leadership.	13	25	0.7
Being against corruption: Moral behavior and values based leadership are needed to fight corruption.	12	28	0.7
Having initiative: Leaders need initiative to be successful. To initiate actions and projects is part of a good leader's job.	12	28	0.7
Being critical: Accept criticism and being critical is part of democracy. Leaders must be open to mutual criticism and behavior disclosure.	8	29	0.5
Being aggressive: Leaders attack before others do; to be aggressive means to act first.	7	30	0.4
Being healthy: Leaders have to be strong, in good physical shape, healthy.	6	31	0.3
TOTAL	1777		100.0

Interviews and Focus Groups

Semistructured interviews were conducted with Mexican plant managers, midlevel managers and supervisors in the Mexican state of Chihuahua. In these interviews, we sought to learn as much as possible about leadership and organizational practices in Mexico that reflect Mexican culture. We included questions about the importance of leadership in managing Mexican organizations, the styles of leadership that are most effective, and the characteristics, norms and beliefs of Mexican managers.

Focus groups were conducted to further explore the issues that emerged from the literature reviews and semistructured interviews. We conducted focus group sessions with Mexican managers and professionals who were enrolled in classes at New Mexico State University and with managers and technical personnel at the Juárez campus for the Monterrey Technological Institute. Participants were asked to prepare for the sessions by thinking of an outstanding leader and describing the characteristics and behaviors that make this leader effective. We began the sessions by asking for descriptions of specific situations where outstanding leadership was demonstrated.

An ethnographic study of *empresarios* (entrepreneur/managers) was also conducted by Martínez (2000) as part of her dissertation research. The term *empresario* is used broadly in Mexico to refer to owner/managers and corporate managers. This term is not equivalent to the term *entrepreneur,* defined by scholars in the field of entrepreneurship as individuals who identify business opportunities and initiate and manage innovative and competitive firms (Martínez, 2000).[4] The term *emprendador* denotes an entrepreneur. Because of the liberalization of the Mexican economy, Mexican firms must compete globally and *empresarios* increasingly recognize the critical importance of a focus on quality and innovation. Many are implementing this focus in the leadership of their firms.

Martínez interviewed *empresarios* who actively managed their own businesses as well as professional managers providing leadership for Mexican firms. Individuals interviewed for the ethnographic study were an elite group of *empresarios* (defined by a combination of social class, education, and wealth). Throughout the later part of the 20th century, Mexican *empresarios* played an important role in modernization of structures necessary for economic and political development in Mexico (Derossi, 1971; Valdés Ugalde, 1997). Most businesses in Mexico presently either are owned and managed by an entrepreneur/manager, or are family businesses managed by several family members.

In these ethnographic interviews, Martinez sought to gather data, organize concepts, and interpret findings about managerial leadership in Mexico from the point of view of the interviewees. The research process at this stage was inductive, interpretive, and often iterative. Martinez immersed herself in the Mexican culture, conducted the interviews in a semistructured and conversational manner, and then withdrew to reflect on the leadership concepts that emerged and how they related to the current environment in Mexico. She then often returned for a second interview with the same respondent to refine her understanding of the leadership concepts and relationships and to be sure she represented them in a manner consistent with "native" concepts and construction of reality of the informants.

---

[4]By adopting this distinction between a business owner-manager and an individual who identifies a business opportunity then initiates and manages a dynamic business, Mexican business leaders, consultants, and academicians have begun to use the term *emprendador* to denote the later, more restricted definition. This distinction places value and emphasis on the entrepreneurial behavior that is associated with economic growth (Martínez, 2000).

Thirty-three *empresarios* were interviewed in Mexico City (in central Mexico) and Ciudad Juárez (on the U.S. border). Both areas are major centers of business activity for the country. The business sectors represented were varied. Five women participated; the interviews were conducted in Spanish and were audiotaped. They were transcribed and subsequently analyzed using QSR NUD*IST (Version 3), a software program designed to support qualitative research.

Survey Questionnaires

The quantitative survey data on GLOBE dimensions of national culture and leadership dimensions were gathered from 152 middle managers in the financial services and food-processing industries (73 were from financial services and 79 from food processing). Nine organizations were sampled in financial services in northern Mexico, and six organizations in food processing were sampled in Mexico City. All of the organizations sampled were branches of large domestic Mexican business organizations and they were not affiliated with transnational corporations from other countries. The size of the branch organizations varied from 25 to several hundred employees. Both of the geographic regions represented are major centers of business activity in Mexico. There were 78 male and 74 female respondents and their ages ranged from 22 to 58, with an average age of 36.

Economic activity increased in Mexico during the early 1990s due to favorable government policies and NAFTA. High economic expectations created a surge of business start-ups and bank loans. However, a peso devaluation in 1994 prompted a severe financial crisis, which was compounded by poor management practices in the banking industry. Swift financial support by the U.S. government, the International Monetary Fund, and the World Bank provided some stability for the Mexican economy. In 1995, the Mexican government activated a controversial FOBAPROA (a government fund to protect savings). Although this program and the international financial support provided some stability, there was still uncertainty and considerable adjustment occurring in the economy. The GLOBE surveys were administered in 1995 during this period. Nine dimensions of culture were investigated using quantitative measures in all of the countries included in the GLOBE research project. These dimensions are based on earlier cross-cultural research by Hofstede (1980), Hofstede and Bond (1988), Triandis (1995), and McClelland (1961). The nine cultural dimensions are: Performance Orientation, Future Orientation, Assertiveness, Institutional Collectivism, Gender Egalitarianism, Humane Orientation, Power Distance, In-Group Collectivism, and Uncertainty Avoidance. Each of these is defined in the following sections along with the scores for Mexico from the GLOBE quantitative measures. Two types of measures were used for each cultural dimension. The institutional cultural practices in a country were measured by "As Is" (society practices) questions, indicating the respondents' perception of the current state of a cultural dimension in their society. Respondents' desired levels of emphasis on each cultural dimension in their society were measured by "Should Be" (society values) questions. These questions indicated how much the respondent believed a cultural dimension should be emphasized in the policies and practices of their institutions. Seven-point Likert scales were used throughout the GLOBE research.

Additional GLOBE questionnaire items were developed to assess the degree to which different leader characteristics and behaviors facilitate or inhibit "outstanding leadership." These items were carefully validated in two pilot studies of white-collar workers and managers in over 40 countries and in Phase 2 of the main GLOBE project with middle managers in 61 countries. The same sample of middle managers that responded to the culture scales was used for the leadership scales. The rating scales used in the GLOBE surveys indicate the degree that a leadership factor contributes to or inhibits a person from being an outstanding leader. A rating of 4 on this scale means the factor has no impact on whether a person is an outstanding leader. Ratings above 4 indicate a factor contributes to being an outstanding leader and ratings below 4 indicate a factor inhibits a person from being an outstanding leader. The development and validation of GLOBE scales used to gather this survey data were described in House et al. (1999). More information on these scales and examples of questionnaire items is contained in the first chapter of this volume.

Analysis Strategy

The semistructured and ethnographic interviews and focus group discussions were audio-recorded, transcribed, and analyzed for major themes expressed by the participants. The themes that were identified addressed effective leadership and organizational practices in Mexico as well as important cultural beliefs and values that influence leadership processes in Mexican organizations.

The survey questionnaire data on GLOBE culture dimensions in Mexico are summarized later in Table 20.2 by reporting mean scores on each dimension for Mexico versus all GLOBE countries. These data are reported separately for "As Is" (society practices) and "Should Be" (society values) culture scores as well as the difference on each culture dimension between the "Should Be" and "As Is" scores. The groups (A through C) reported in Table 20.2 indicate the relative score (rank) for Mexico on each specific culture dimension in relation to other countries (see footnote to Table 20.2).

The survey questionnaire data on GLOBE leadership dimensions were factor analyzed resulting in six second-order leadership factors. Mexico's mean score on each of these leadership factors is reported later in Table 20.4. Groups are also reported for the leadership factors in Table 20.4, indicating the relative score (rank) for Mexico on each specific leadership factor in relation to other countries (see footnote to Table 20.4). These mean scores for Mexico, all Latin American GLOBE countries, and all GLOBE countries are also presented in graphic form to facilitate comparison and interpretation.

4. RESULTS

Semistructured Interviews and Focus Groups

The semistructured interviews were the first phase of empirical qualitative research carried out in Mexico. They yielded several initial findings that were further explored in the focus groups. The interviews showed that although an authoritarian leadership style has traditionally been accepted by Mexican workers, a heavy-handed approach that emphasizes threats and punishment is not considered effective. Mexican workers do not approve of leaders who are rude or who offend or embarrass followers in public. In order to be accepted, *leaders must respect their followers'* pride and customs.

There was some indication of a persistent Social Darwinist belief among those interviewed that leaders are more competent and deserving than followers. Managers who request subordinates' input prior to making a decision may be viewed as weak. Consequently, some managers feel little need to share information and objectives with their followers. Subordinates may often be intimidated by status differences and become reluctant to discuss problems with superiors because of the cultural norm of avoiding interpersonal conflict. This may be most common at lower organizational levels or where there is a large difference in the status levels of the leader and employee. These behavioral tendencies indicate a strong belief in *high Power Distance* in Mexican organizations.

A key cultural theme in the focus groups in Mexico was the importance of maintaining *good interpersonal relations.* Outstanding Mexican leadership was characterized by terms like *trust, respect,* and *sensitivity.* Gaining trust, treating people as human beings, and maintaining courtesy and respect pervaded the discussions. The Mexican expression *simpático* describes this critical aspect of Mexican leadership. *Simpático* reflects the ability and willingness to trust people with a special sensitivity to their dignity and worth as individuals. It involves demonstrating respect and empathy to bring out the uniqueness and special characteristics of each person. This aspect of Mexican leadership is often linked with terms such as *agradable* (nice), *comprensivo* (understanding), and *sencillo* (easy to get along with). Mexican leaders take time to learn something about their subordinates' personal lives and inquire with sincere interest about their families. A manager demonstrated *simpático* by visiting a subordinate's home to see his wife and their new baby, showing his respect for the importance of family in Mexican culture. This concern for *simpático* and pleasant interpersonal relations reinforced the essential respect for followers' pride and customs identified in the interviews.

Another major theme in the focus groups was a type of *collective problem solving* that only partially resembled participative leadership as practiced in North America and Western Europe. One discussant described this process by saying that managers were expected to design strategies, develop proposals, and offer suggestions that are then discussed by subordinates who are expected to carry them out. We suspect that acting on subordinates' suggestions may not be as important as in the United States. In contrast to the norm in the United States and Europe, interacting with subordinates to solve problems is often done in an apparent chaotic but highly meaningful manner in Mexico. A manager may deal with more than one person and problem at the same time and in the same room. Here the leader demonstrates control over complex situations, using subtle and indirect means to address each individual's suggestions and concerns. A key point is that all individuals involved must believe they can be involved in problem solving.

A final theme that emerged in the focus groups was a wide agreement that high-level leaders used their "persona" to command allegiance. The managers who were described as examples of this tendency in Mexico were clearly very charismatic individuals who manifested their *charisma* by a combination of paternalistic directiveness, elements of male *machismo,* as well as respect and sensitivity for followers (*simpático*). This theme indicates the salience of charisma as an element of outstanding leadership in Mexico.

In summary, the semistructured interviews and focus groups identified the following leadership themes as important in Mexico: respect for followers and good interpersonal relations, high power distance between leaders and followers, and personal charismatic leadership with a unique type of collective problem solving. All but the last theme support findings reported earlier from the historical analysis and/or the literature reviews.

Ethnographic Interviews

In her ethnographic analysis of the interviews she conducted with Mexican *empresarios,* Martínez (2000) identified four themes that either directly relate to the results of the GLOBE analysis or have relevance for its interpretation. The first theme is the *importance of the family* in Mexican culture and "the replication of its structure, system and values within the entrepreneur's firm, especially the patriarchal model" (p. 84). Kinship has played a critical role in Mexican society throughout its history. Most Mexican firms are still owned and controlled by families. Many Mexicans secure financial capital from family members, use the influence of their families to launch business ventures, and choose family members as partners, employees, and/or to serve as members of the board of directors. "Leadership attributes and behavior among Mexican *empresarios* are usually described by their relationship to the traditional patriarchal model" (p. 100). For instance, a small traditional firm of 60 employees in Mexico City manufactures and distributes children's board games and is controlled by the 89-year-old patriarch-founder who is an autocratic leader. Although unable to come to the office daily because of poor health, he makes the decisions regarding raises for union workers, product lines, and even what color to paint the office. This behavior continues even though his son, who manages the daily business, is a very able man in his 60s and has worked in the business since he was 12 years old. The son finds it difficult to argue with the patriarch who has achieved and sustained success in the business.

"The entrepreneurs associated with larger businesses expressed a leadership style which seemed to negotiate a path between the forces of globalization and modernization … and the former traditional emphasis on family and personal relationships …" (Martínez, 2000, p. 101). What is interesting is the persistence of the influence of one or more elements of the family model within the newly reorganized and more competitive Mexican firms, whether they are controlled by the family or not. A CEO and major shareholder of a dynamic medium-size telecommunications firm spoke of "rewarding employees in a manner that advances their patrimonial interests, achieving a better life and a higher standard of living for their family" (pp. 91–92). It is noteworthy that he describes and designs his reward system in terms of the family. The very high scores on the GLOBE In-Group Collectivism cultural practices dimension are consistent with Martiníez's findings and her description of the theme related to the importance of the family and the patriarchal model.

The second theme described in the ethnographic study, which could be viewed as a subtheme of the first, is the *importance of personal relationships*. "This focus on personal relationships creates a distinctive humanistic belief system that governs employment. That is, in the relationship between employer and employee, the respect, concern, and long-term employment offered by the employer is exchanged for respect and loyalty on the part of the employee" (Martínez, 2000, p. 85). This same theme was also found in the semi-structured interviews. However, in traditional Mexican business organizations, Mexican entrepreneurs have not always treated employees well.

Within this personal and often paternal relationship, the employer often offers protection and assistance in activities outside the strict boundaries of the organization. Many of the entrepreneurs mentioned a commitment to the growth and development of their employees. One *empresario* "believes that employees come to the firm with their youth, their enthusiasm and their interest and they should not be returned to society as human 'rags'—tired, frustrated and feeling old. An employee should be given the opportunity to feel they have fulfilled an obligation to their families and to Mexico by means of their work" (Martínez, 2000, pp. 116–117). A specific GLOBE cultural dimension is relevant to this theme of personal relationships—Humane Orientation. Though Mexico was only average on the Humane Orientation cultural practices dimension ("As Is"), like most countries in GLOBE, Mexicans desire somewhat more Humane Orientation for their society ("Should Be"). Most likely, scores for the Humane Orientation dimension would be higher in Mexico if the construct reflected the importance of respect and concern for those personal relationships within the family.

Both themes just discussed describe the influence on leadership and organizational behavior of the traditional patterns of organizing that have characterized Mexican society. The third theme Martínez identified in her ethnographic study was the *influence and proximity of the United States* as the major source of managerial models and practices, capital, as well as the primary market and competitor. In general, Mexican *empresarios* admire the success of U.S. businesses and wish to emulate practices and models to improve their own performance and competitiveness. Managers are beginning to recognize the importance of motivation and the impact of the leader's behavior on the organization. Furthermore, *empresarios* are now forced to focus on the quality of their products and services. This aspect of productivity and service was not a major consideration before the Mexican economy was liberalized and markets opened to global competition (Martínez, 2000).

The fourth theme is the preoccupation of the entrepreneur/manager with the *institutionalization of their firms. Empresarios* who participated in the ethnographic study spoke of the need for "institutionalization," which is a term they use to describe the establishment of systematic managerial processes to ensure productivity, consistency of quality, and the ability to compete. *Empresarios* view institutionalization as a means to overcome the weaknesses of the family firm, such as hiring based on criteria that are not job related. Institutionalization emphasizes planning and development by which managers can share information and seek support for decisions within the firm, especially among subordinates.

In summary, Martínez (2000) identified several overall leadership themes for *empresarios* in Mexico: the importance of the family and the patriarchal model, the value of personal relationships between managers and employees, and the influence of the United States on Mexican organizations, which is often shown through the institutionalization of modern management practices originating in the United States. The first two themes reflect those identified previously from other data sources. The final theme may partially reflect the last theme that emerged from the media analysis, describing new roles for organizational leaders in today's organizations in Mexico.

Globe Dimensions of National Culture

Both "As Is" (society practices) and "Should Be" (society values) scores on the nine cultural dimensions are reported in the following sections, along with the differences between these two scores ("Should Be"–"As Is"). These differences indicate the directions that respondents believe their country should be changing regarding the GLOBE cultural dimensions. Table 20.2 summarizes these quantitative scores for the GLOBE cultural dimensions. We also include observations and insights in this section from the qualitative portion of the GLOBE project in Mexico, regarding norms and practices that further elucidate each of the cultural dimensions in Mexico.

Performance Orientation

Performance Orientation is the degree to which a society encourages and rewards group members for performance improvement and excellence. Mexico's "As Is" score on Performance Orientation is medium (4.10 on a 7-point scale). Its score is near the middle of three groups on the distribution of all GLOBE country scores on this culture dimension and its rank was 32 out of 61 countries. Mexico's "Should Be" score on Performance Orientation is

TABLE 20.2
Mexico Means for GLOBE Societal Culture Dimensions

| | Society "As Is" | | | |
Culture Dimensions	Mean for Mexico	Mean Across All Countries	Group[a]	Rank
Performance Orientation	4.10	4.10	B	32
Future Orientation	3.87	3.84	B	26
Assertiveness	4.45	4.15	A	16
Institutional Collectivism	4.06	4.27	B	38
Gender Egalitarianism	3.64	3.37	A	16
Humane Orientation	3.98	4.08	C	34
Power Distance	5.22	5.17	B	30
In-Group Collectivism	5.71	5.13	A	12
Uncertainty Avoidance	4.18	4.16	B	26

| | Society "Should Be" | | | | |
Culture Dimensions	Mean for Mexico	Mean Across All Countries	Group[a]	Rank	Difference ("Should Be"– "As Is")
Performance Orientation	6.16	5.94	B	14	2.06
Future Orientation	5.86	5.4	A	13	1.99
Assertiveness	3.79	3.83	B	27	−0.66
Institutional Collectivism	4.92	4.73	B	23	0.86
Gender Egalitarianism	4.73	4.51	A	24	1.09
Humane Orientation	5.10	5.42	C	55	1.12
Power Distance	2.85	2.75	C	19	−2.37
In-Group Collectivism	5.95	5.66	B	14	0.24
Uncertainty Avoidance	5.26	4.62	A	9	1.08

[a]Groups A through C indicate the relative score (and rank) for Mexico on the specific culture dimension in relation to other countries. The groups were formed using the following "banding" procedures (cf. House et al., 2004). This procedure uses the mean score on each culture dimension along with the standard error of estimate (a measure of dispersion) from the total data set to calculate "bands" of similarly rated countries. The number of bands (groups) for each culture dimension depends on the amount of variance (standard error) for each factor. There are significant differences between groups but no significant differences within each group. "A" indicates highest country ranking where "C" indicates next-to-lowest country ranking for Mexico.

high (6.16), near the top of the second group on the distribution for all GLOBE countries and ranked 14 out of 61 GLOBE countries on this culture dimension. Most GLOBE countries scored highly on the "Should Be" scale for Performance Orientation and Mexico was no exception. The difference between the "Should Be" and "As Is" scores on Performance Orientation was strikingly large (2.06). Clearly, Mexican respondents saw a strong need to encourage more achievement and excellence in their organizations. This may be a reaction to a sentiment expressed in some ethnographic interviews that Mexicans in the past have had trouble organizing and achieving success.

Future Orientation

Future Orientation is the degree to which individuals in a society engage in future-oriented behaviors such as planning, investing in the future, and delaying gratification. Mexico's "As Is" score on Future Orientation is medium (3.87). Its score is second out of four groups (next to highest) on the distribution of all "As Is" GLOBE country scores on this dimension, and ranks 26 out of 61 countries. Riding (1989) and Ramos (1976) described Mexicans as viewing the future with fatalism, so planning seems unnatural. Ardila (1979) also described an emphasis on the present or "losing future perspective" as part of a poverty psychology in Mexico. However, the spreading economic and social development in Mexico may be encouraging more emphasis on Future Orientation (Sotelo Valencia, 1999). Mexico's "Should Be" score on this dimension is high (5.86). Its score is in the top group in the distribution of all "Should Be" scores on the GLOBE cultural dimensions and its rank was 13 out of 61 countries. The difference between the "Should Be" and "As Is" scores on Future Orientation was quite large (1.99), indicating that Mexican respondents perceived the need for much more future- oriented behavior by individuals than currently exists. Until recently, many industries enjoyed a monopoly or were protected from competition by trade regulations. In these situations, there was little motivation to plan. As the economy becomes more open, perception of a need for more Future Orientation can be seen in the increasing number of public and private organizations in Mexico that are developing strategic plans including a vision, mission statement, and overall objectives. Increasing international influences on the Mexican economy and society may be slowly changing the views of Mexican citizens regarding the future of their society.

Assertiveness

Assertiveness is the degree to which individuals in a society are assertive, aggressive, and confrontational in social relationships. The GLOBE scale includes descriptors such as "dominant" and "tough" to describe Assertiveness. Mexico's "As Is" score on Assertiveness is high (4.45). It is in the top group on the distribution of all country Assertiveness scores and it ranked 16 out of 61 countries. This score may seem surprising until one considers that the assertive items on the GLOBE scale reflect a strongly dominant male orientation (machismo), which is traditional in Mexican society. Mexico's "Should Be" score on Assertiveness is medium (3.79). It is in the middle group and ranks 27. The difference between "Should Be" and "As Is" scores on Assertiveness was negative, but not large (–0.66). This indicates the Mexican respondents may see a slight need to decrease their degree of Assertiveness.

Institutional Collectivism

Institutional Collectivism indicates the extent that a society's organizational and institutional norms and practices encourage and reward collective action and collective distribution of resources. The "As Is" score for Mexico on institutional Collectivism was medium (4.06). Its score was in the second group (of four) in the distribution of all GLOBE country scores and its rank was low (38) in comparison to other countries. Riding (1989) stated that Mexican men often feel little solidarity with society outside their own family and that community approaches to shared problems are rare. This may reflect their disappointment and frustration with most society-wide institutions, especially those related to government. It should be noted here that Mexico was high in In-Group Collectivism, which indicates identification and loyalty to one's family and organizations. In-Group Collectivism is prominent in Mexican society and is described later in this section. Mexico's "Should Be" score on Institutional Collectivism was medium-high (4.92). Its rank was 23 in the distribution of all country scores, placing it near the top of the second group of scores. The difference between "Should Be" and "As Is" scores was not large (0.86). This indicates that Mexican respondents might like slightly more collectivism in their institutions. Both "As Is" and "Should Be" scores are consistent with the increasing activities of diverse interest groups in Mexican society.

Gender Egalitarianism

Gender Egalitarianism indicates the extent that a society minimizes gender role differences. A score of 4 on this scale indicates Gender Egalitarianism, scores higher than 4 indicate greater female orientation, and scores lower than 4 indicate greater male orientation. The "As Is" score for Mexico for Gender Egalitarianism is medium (3.64), it is in the first of three groups on the distribution of all country scores on this dimension, and ranks 16 out of 61 countries. Mexico's "As Is" score reflects a slight male orientation, but its rank and grouping place it high in contrast to other GLOBE countries. Mexico's "Should Be" score on this dimension is medium-high (4.73), it is in the top group on the all country distribution, and its rank is 24 out of 61 countries. The difference between "Should Be" and "As Is" scores on this dimension is 1.09, indicating some desire by Mexican respondents for more female orientation in their society. As noted earlier, women are increasingly becoming leaders in business but their participation in politics is still very limited. Female entrepreneurs in Mexico believe that attitudes of machismo still represent a major obstacle to the growth and development of their businesses (Zabludovsky, 1998).

Humane Orientation

Humane Orientation reflects the degree to which a society encourages and rewards individuals for being fair, altruistic, friendly, generous, caring, and kind to others. The "As Is" score in Mexico for Humane Orientation is medium (3.98) and in the third of four groups on the distribution of all country scores for this dimension. It ranks 34 out of 61 countries. Mexico's "Should Be" score on this dimension is medium-high (5.10). It is also in the third of five groups on the distribution of all country scores, but its rank is fairly low at 55 out of 61 countries. Most GLOBE respondents indicated that their society should emphasize much more Humane Orientation resulting in even higher "Should Be" scores than in Mexico. The difference between "Should Be" and "As Is" scores on this dimension is 1.12, indicating Mexicans also desire more Humane Orientation for their society. Humane Orientation relates closely to the importance of maintaining pleasant interpersonal relations, which is a major leadership theme that emerged from the focus groups and interviews.

Power Distance

Power Distance is the degree to which members of a society accept unequal distributions of power in their institutions and society in general. The "As Is" score in Mexico for Power

Distance is fairly high (5.22) and is near the top of the second of four groups on the distribution of all GLOBE country scores. Its rank is 30 out of 61 countries. Mexicans are the product of two cultures that emphasized authoritarianism and omnipotence by leaders—the indigenous theocratic and militaristic Aztecs, and the Spanish conquerors who imposed a highly centralized colonial government and Catholicism, as well as their language (Riding, 1989). The Power Distance score for Mexico is reflected in Mexican workers' respect for formal authority as shown by hierarchical position. Status and titles are crucial throughout society. Power and authority have traditionally resided at the top of organizations. Workers expect managers to provide direction, make final decisions, and draw clear status lines between managers and workers. One coauthor was a staff member in a non-PRI state government for several years. In the governor's meetings with his ministers, not one minister ever openly disagreed with the governor's opinions. Centralized decision making is also the norm in large Mexican business organizations (grupos), where individual families often control many companies.

Mexico's "Should Be" score on Power Distance was considerably lower (2.85) than the "As Is" score (this was true for many GLOBE countries). The "Should Be" score for Mexico was in the third of five groups on the distribution of all GLOBE country scores for this dimension, and it ranked 19 out of 61 countries. The difference between the "Should Be" score and "As Is" score on this dimension for Mexico was –2.37. This indicates that Mexicans desire much less Power Distance in their society, as do most of the respondents throughout the GLOBE countries that were studied. This desire among Mexicans may reflect a gradual increase in the education of the Mexican workforce, the desire for a "fairer" society where they can influence their future, and the use of Western management methods such as Total Quality Management and self-managed work teams. These techniques require more lateral communication and interaction, as well as initiative and self-leadership by workers. Many Mexicans may see the need for change in their managers' views of power and authority in order to compete in a global economy. These changes are most likely to occur in industries utilizing more advanced technologies that require a highly educated workforce. When the non-PRI governor's party (described earlier) eventually lost power, several ministers, who had never disagreed with their governor, stated that a more open expression of their real opinions may have prevented the loss. They vowed to reduce the Power Distance and state their opinions in their next political experience.

In-Group Collectivism

In-Group Collectivism is the extent to which individuals express pride, loyalty, and cohesiveness in their organizations and families. The "As Is" score for Mexico on In-Group Collectivism is high (5.71), and the highest of three groups on the all country distribution for this dimension. It ranks 12 out of 61 GLOBE countries. Díaz-Loving (1999) indicated that the extended family is the principal safe haven in Mexican society where emotions can be shown without risk, unquestioned loyalty is guaranteed, and customs are maintained. A large personal network of family and friends is the primary source of support for Mexicans, as well as other Latin Americans. Rather than depending on public institutions and resources, Mexicans develop intimate support systems by marriage, coparenting, and patron–client relationships (Wolf, 1966; Wolf & Hansen, 1972). Because of the importance of the extended family, staying close to roots and home has been highly valued. As one participant in the focus groups stated: "We grow up … and we continue to depend on our parents. … There is a feeling of unity, of love that exists until you cease to exist." Mexico's "Should Be" score on

In-Group Collectivism was high (5.95), placing it at the top of the second group of the all-country distribution. Mexico ranks 14 on the "Should Be" scores for this dimension. The difference between the "Should Be" and "As Is" scores for this dimension is 0.24, indicating that Mexican respondents are content with the high level of In-Group Collectivism displayed in their culture. Although increasing numbers of Mexican managers recognize the need for less hierarchical and patriarchal patterns of authority in order to compete successfully in the global market place, they continue to honor the importance of the family. These managers believe that these values contribute to cohesion and productivity within their organizations (Martínez, 2000).

Uncertainty Avoidance

Uncertainty Avoidance is the extent to which individuals in a society seek to alleviate the unpredictability of future events by relying on social norms, rituals, and bureaucratic procedures. The "As Is" score for Mexico on this dimension is medium (4.18) and it is in the second of four groups in the distribution of all country scores on this dimension. It ranks 26 out of 61 countries. The "Should Be" score for Mexico on Uncertainty Avoidance is high (5.26), in the top group on the all country distribution, and ranking 9 out of 61 countries. The difference between the "Should Be" and "As Is" scores for this dimension is 1.08. It appears that Mexicans believe their institutions should engage in somewhat more normative and bureaucratic control to avoid the unpredictability of future events. Mexican managers and entrepreneurs deal with great uncertainty in their economic environment: lack of available credit; fluctuating interest and inflation rates; volatile currency values; and the radical changes in the economic structure that have been implemented during the past 20 years. Successful Mexican entrepreneurs and managers have learned to be flexible, respond quickly, and improvise in order to survive. Mexican workers do value job security and may have a slight preference for close supervision rather than working on their own, although this preference may also reflect their lack of power and other conditions for working independently.

Summary of GLOBE Culture Dimensions

The Mexican scores on the GLOBE dimensions portray a society with an interesting cultural configuration that has several noteworthy elements. A few dimensions stood out in comparison to other societal cultures. Particularly striking is the very high "As Is" score and rank for In-Group Collectivism, which is consistent with the importance of the family in Mexican life. In comparison to other countries, the "As Is" score for the Assertiveness dimension is also high. These cultural dimensions reflect traditional values and beliefs in Mexican society—the importance of family within a male-oriented society. Somewhat to our surprise, the "As Is" score on Gender Egalitarianism for Mexico was in the top country grouping, but still reflects a slight male orientation for the societal culture. In contrast to the "As Is" scores, which reflect cultural practice, the "Should Be" scores reflect cultural values. When considering these "Should Be" scores, it is apparent that the high In-Group Collectivism in the "As Is" score continues to be viewed favorably as respondents indicated no desire to change or alter the importance of this dimension. In contrast, there was a significant desire by respondents to reduce levels of Power Distance, but increase the level of Gender Egalitarianism. The "Should Be" scores also showed a desire for appreciably more Performance Orientation, Future Orientation, and Uncertainty Avoidance in Mexican society and organizations. These desires reflect recognition of the importance of planning and preparing for high performance and rapid change in organizations if Mexico is to be successful in its continued development and internationalization of its economy. The increased desire for practices to reduce uncertainty reflects Mexicans' concerns for the lack of economic stability of their country in recent years.

Culturally Endorsed Implicit Leadership Theories

A central question investigated in the GLOBE project is the extent to which specific leader characteristics and behaviors are universally endorsed in all cultures as aspects of outstanding leadership, and the extent to which other characteristics and behaviors are attributed to outstanding leaders only in certain countries or cultures (House et al., 1999). Considerable research evidence exists showing that individuals develop implicit leadership theories or prototypes about the characteristics and behaviors they believe differentiate leaders from nonleaders, effective from ineffective leaders, and moral from evil leaders (Lord & Maher, 1991). A follower's implicit leadership theory affects how she or he reacts to a leader and leaders are more influential with followers when their perceived characteristics and behavior match the implicit leadership theories of followers (Hanges, Braverman, & Renstch, 1991; Hanges et al., 1997; Lord & Maher, 1991).

Implicit leadership theories have been shown to be related to specific dimensions of national culture (House et al., 1999). Because these cultural dimensions vary across countries, this implies that implicit leadership theories will also vary. *Culturally endorsed implicit leadership theories* (CLTs) represent the varying configurations of leader characteristics and behaviors that comprise predominant implicit leadership theories in different countries and cultures. A major hypothesis of the GLOBE project (to be tested in the next phase) is that when a leader's characteristics and behaviors are congruent with his or her CLT, the leader will be highly effective within his or her own culture (House et al., 1999, 2004).

GLOBE Leadership Dimensions and CLTs

Existing leadership theory and factor analysis of the GLOBE leadership questionnaires resulted in 21 first-order factors and 6 second-order factors, which comprise the elements of CLTs investigated in GLOBE. These first- and second-order factors are described in Table 20.3 and the quantitative results for Mexico from the 61-country survey are shown in Table 20.4.

The second-order leadership factors, which are called Global Leadership Dimensions, are (1) Charismatic/Value-Based, (2) Team Oriented, (3) Self-Protective, (4) Participative, (5) Humane, and (6) Autonomous. As explained in the first footnote for Table 20.4, the GLOBE country scores on each Leadership Dimension were placed in several groups that ranged from the highest scores on this dimension to the lowest scores. The first group (A) represents the countries with the highest scores, the second group (B) the next highest, and so on. The number of groups for each dimension depends on the amount of variability within each dimension.

Charismatic/Value-Based and *Team-Oriented leadership* were strongly endorsed as facilitating outstanding leadership in Mexico. However, these two factors were also strongly endorsed in most GLOBE countries. This resulted in Mexico's score on Charismatic/Value-Based leadership (5.66) being in the fourth (D) group out of eight groups on the distribution of all GLOBE country scores on this factor. It ranked 47 out of 61 countries (see Table 20.4).

TABLE 20.3
Culturally Endorsed Implicit Leadership Dimensions (GLOBE Study)

Leadership Dimensions	Questionnaire Items
Charismatic/Value-Based	
Visionary	Visionary, foresight, anticipatory, prepared, intellectually stimulating, future oriented, plans ahead, inspirational
Inspirational	Enthusiastic, positive, encouraging, morale booster, motive arouser, confidence builder, dynamic, motivational
Self-Sacrificial	Risk taker, self-sacrificial, convincing
Integrity	Honest, sincere, just, trustworthy
Decisive	Willful, decisive, logical, intuitive
Performance Oriented	Improvement, excellence, and performance oriented
Team Oriented	
Collaborative Orientation	Group oriented, collaborative, loyal, consultative, mediator, fraternal
Team Integrator	Clear, integrator, not subdued, informed, communicative, coordinator, team builder
Diplomatic	Diplomatic, worldly, win/win problem solver, effective bargainer
Malevolent (reverse scored)	Irritable, vindictive, egoistic, noncooperative, cynical, hostile, dishonest, nondependable, not intelligent
Administratively Competent	Orderly, administratively skilled, organized, good administrator
Self-Protective	
Self-Centered	Self-interested, nonparticipative, loner, asocial
Status-Consciousness	Status-conscious, class-conscious
Conflict Inducer	Intragroup competitor, secretive, normative
Face Saver	Indirect, avoids negatives, evasive
Procedural	Ritualistic, formal, habitual, cautious, procedural
Participative	
Autocratic (reverse scored)	Autocratic, dictatorial, bossy, elitist, ruler, domineering
Nonparticipative (reverse scored)	Individually oriented, nonegalitarian, micro manager, nondelegator
Humane	
Humane Orientation	Generous, compassionate
Modesty	Modest, self-effacing, patient
Autonomous	Individualistic, independent, autonomous, unique

Note. Second-order factors are in bold letters; first-order factors are grouped under the appropriate second-order factor. *Source:* Adapted From House et al. (1999). Copyright 1999 by JAI Press. Adapted by permission.

TABLE 20.4
Mean, Grouping, and Rank on First- and Second-Order CLT Leadership Factors for Mexico

Leadership Factor	Mean	Group[a]	Rank
Charismatic/Value-Based	5.66	D	47
Visionary	5.78	C	50
Inspirational	5.91	C	46
Self-Sacrificial	4.80	B	46
Integrity	5.77	C	48
Decisive	5.54	B	52
Performance Oriented	6.14	B	25
Team Oriented	5.74	B	38
Collaborative Oriented	5.85	B	35
Team Integrator	5.54	B	27
Diplomatic	5.55	A	31
Malevolent (reverse scored)	2.09 (5.91)	B	11
Administratively Competent	5.92	B	23
Self-Protective	3.86	C	11
Self-Centered	2.52	B	11
Status Consciousness	4.64	B	18
Conflict Inducer	4.27	B	17
Face Saver	3.34	B	15
Procedural	4.48	A	8
Participative	4.64	F	59
Autocratic (reverse scored)	3.35 (4.65)	B	4
Nonparticipative (reverse scored)	3.38 (4.62)	A	5
Humane	4.72	C	41
Humane Orientation	4.72	B	33
Modesty	4.74	B	44
Autonomous[b]	3.86	B	31

[a]The first group (A) represents the highest scores, the second group (B) the next highest, and so on. The groups were formed using the following "banding" procedure. This procedure uses the mean score on each Leadership Dimension along with the standard error of estimate (a measure of dispersion) from the total data set to calculate "bands" of similarly rated countries. The number of bands (groups) for each leadership factor depends on the amount of variance (standard error) for each factor. There are significant differences between groups, but no significant differences within each group.
[b]The autonomous second-order leadership factor was composed of a single first-order factor with the same name.

The first-order factor labeled Performance Oriented produced the highest score in Mexico of the six first-order factors that comprise Charismatic/Value-Based leadership. The score for Mexico on the Performance Oriented factor was 6.14 and it ranked 25 in comparison to other GLOBE country scores. Inspirational (5.91), Visionary (5.78), and Integrity (5.77) also produced medium-high ratings as first-order factors of Charismatic/Value-Based leadership. As noted earlier, Mexicans continuously honor and celebrate their charismatic revolutionary leaders, and current leaders may adopt a historical charismatic leader as a "spiritual" adviser.

Guerilla leader "Marcos" of the Zapatista Army for National Liberation recently declared that Francisco Villa and Emiliano Zapata were his spiritual advisers (García, 2001).

Mexico's score on *Team-Oriented leadership* was 5.74, the second (B) group of five groups in the distribution of all GLOBE country scores on this factor. Its rank was 38 out of 61 countries. Three first-order factors that comprise Team Oriented leadership resulted in medium-high scores in Mexico. Administratively competent (5.92), Nonmalevolent (5.91), and Team Integrator (5.54) were rated as important for outstanding leadership. Mexican respondents clearly believe in the importance of Charismatic/Value-Based and Team Oriented leadership, although there are many countries in the GLOBE sample that rate these leadership dimensions even higher in importance.

Humane and *Participative leadership* were rated slightly above the midpoint ("has no impact") in terms of their importance for outstanding leadership. Humane (4.72) was in the third (C) of five groups on the distribution of all country scores, ranking 41 out of 61 countries. Participative (4.64) was in the sixth (F) of six groups and ranked 59 out of 61 countries. All of the first-order factors in these two leadership dimensions produced scores near the scale midpoints in Mexico. Though Mexicans view a humane orientation and participative approach as barely positive contributors to outstanding leadership, the relatively low score on participative leadership was striking, but not surprising. Dorfman et al. (1997) recently noted that in many parts of Mexico, the "authoritarian tradition … still resists incursions of western liberalism, including seeking input from all levels for decision making. Participative leadership, as practiced in Western Europe and North America, requires individualistic followers, trusting relationships between managers and followers and a firm structure for participation" (p. 242). These conditions are not generally found in Mexican organizations. Prior research has shown that Mexican workers do not respond well to participative approaches by their managerial leaders (Dorfman et al., 1997), although the media analysis showed that some Mexican managers may adopt participative approaches in order to compete in the global economy.

An example showing the ineffectiveness of participative leadership in a rural area of Mexico was provided by one of our coauthors, who had the responsibility of creating a group of agricultural extension experts to operate agriculture support programs that represented about $44 million. At first, he chose a participative and humane-oriented leader who behaved democratically with a strong interest in his followers' welfare. The results were not impressive. The group failed to develop a sense of being a team. The humane behavior by the leader was not appreciated, and the participative behavior was considered either to be a weakness or lack of knowledge. The programs were primarily labeled as failures or mistakes and much conflict developed among the group members. One year later, he decided to let the group choose a new leader. This new person met the profile of a charismatic and team-oriented leader. He was already known to be competent and trustworthy, but he was also visionary and enthusiastic. He used a directive approach by requiring followers to collaborate and integrate their efforts to reach overall program goals. Within 1 month, team performance improved significantly. Members became proud to belong to the team. Technological advances were implemented, new resources were located, and team efficiency reached a new high.

Self-Protective and *Autonomous* were global leadership dimensions that resulted in scores slightly below the scale midpoints. Self-Protective (3.86) was in the third (C) of nine groups on the distribution and ranked 11 out of 61 countries. Several writers state that formal, and sometimes obscure, language is a prime strategy for self-protection for Mexicans (Paz, 1959; Ramos, 1976). It allows them to protect their emotions, avoid confrontations, and be conciliatory in a society that often functions through relationships of power. By being ambiguous in their directives, managers can avoid accountability. Like the oracle at Delphi where intermediaries were employed to interpret the meaning of what was said, the manager can then blame the interpreter rather than take responsibility for being wrong (Martínez, 2000). However, this does not promote direct and efficient communication required for competitive firms. Autonomous (3.86) was in the second (B) of four groups and ranked 31 out of 61 countries. It appears that Mexicans do not reject self-protective behaviors by outstanding leaders to the same degree as workers in most other GLOBE countries.

Non-GLOBE Leadership Dimension

Strong paternalistic attitudes in Mexico contribute to employees' expectations of job security and to be looked after by their manager as a person, not only as an employee (Dorfman & Howell, 1983). Although salaries are usually low, there is often greater institutional bureaucratic protection in Latin organizations in comparison to organizations in English-speaking countries. Mexican companies have a significant legal responsibility for the welfare of their workers. Having a job is considered a social right in Mexico. Workers in large organizations often expect to be treated as part of the extended family of their boss, to be taken care of with courtesy and friendliness. Large employers are expected to provide food baskets and medical care for workers and their families. Organizations often celebrate numerous holidays and throw parties for various events. Many of these expectations are contained in collective bargaining agreements. Managers and supervisors usually maintain a social distance from followers, and command respect and loyalty in the image of a *patrón* or father figure (Teagarden, Butler, Von Gilnow, 1992). The roots of paternalism in organizations lie in the strong patriarchal nature of most Mexican families and are embedded in the society itself.

Mexico Versus Other Latin American and GLOBE Countries

Figure 20.1 presents a summary profile of GLOBE implicit leadership theory dimensions for Mexico, all Latin American countries, and all countries in the GLOBE sample. The vertical scale in Fig. 20.1 is taken directly from the GLOBE rating scales used in the surveys of middle managers for all the CLT leadership scales. As noted earlier, it measures the degree that a leadership factor is perceived to contribute to or inhibit a person from being an outstanding leader. All ratings presented in Fig 20.1 are raw scores.

Charismatic/Value-Based and Team-Oriented leadership are the major contributors to Mexican's CLTs for outstanding leadership, although the score for Charismatic/Value- Based is slightly lower than the average for Latin America. Participative and Humane also contribute a minor amount to the CLTs for Mexico although the participation score appears lower in Mexico than in other Latin American and all GLOBE countries. Mexico's scores on Autonomous and Self-Protective show that these factors have little if any perceived impact on Mexican's CLTs for outstanding leadership. Figure 20.1 also shows that Mexicans do not believe these last two factors inhibit outstanding leadership to the same extent as respondents in other countries. Mexico's history and culture may have created a milieu that encourages acceptance of leaders who are self-protective and autonomous in their behavior.

Each country in the GLOBE project has been placed in 1 of 10 "country clusters" based on extensive anthropological data. Discriminant function analysis of country scores on the GLOBE culture dimensions was used to validate the placement of each country within a

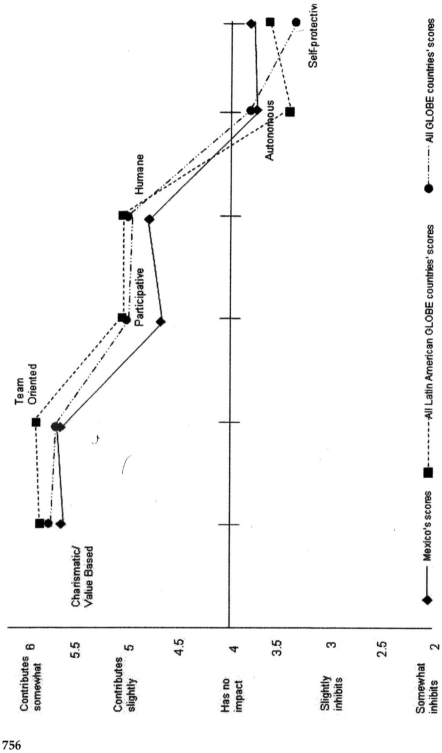

Figure 20.1 CLT leadership factors for Mexico and all Latin American countries.

country cluster. The country clusters are Eastern Europe, Latin Europe, Germanic Europe, Nordic Europe, Sub-Sahara Africa, Confucian Asia, Southern Asia, Latin America, Middle East, and Anglo. Mexico has been placed in the Latin America cluster. GLOBE researchers have also analyzed the CLT leadership factor dimensions for each country and cluster after adjusting the scores for response biases that vary with different countries. That is, respondents in some countries simply gave higher ratings on the GLOBE survey questionnaires than did respondents in other countries. Respondents in other countries avoid the use of extreme scores. By adjusting the scores (standardizing each score with regard to each respondent's other scores on the comprehensive GLOBE surveys), these response biases are removed. In addition, the adjusted scores indicate the *relative importance* of each CLT dimension in comparison to other CLT dimensions in a given country.

The relative (adjusted) scores in Mexico and other Latin American countries show that *team-oriented* leadership is especially important. *Self-protective* leadership was not viewed as negatively as in other country clusters, and *autonomous* leadership was rated lower (less desirable) than in other country clusters.

5. LIMITATIONS OF THE GLOBE PROJECT AND FUTURE RESEARCH

In a country as large and diverse as Mexico, we could not expect to capture all the regional cultural influences that are likely to affect leadership prototypes in the country. We sampled 152 managers in two industries and in two different regions of Mexico. Both regions have very active business communities, although one region borders the United States and may reflect a stronger management influence from its northern neighbor. Other regional variations in culture and leadership probably occur and recent research shows that managers in Mexico must be sensitive to regional culture in order to be effective (Howell, Romero, Dorfman, & Paul, 2003).

We included researchers from both the United States and Mexico on this project to try to provide separate perspectives. However, the strong influence of U.S. management practices in Mexico and the fact that four of the authors were educated in the United States may provide some bias to our conclusions.

The survey questionnaires that elicited data for the culturally endorsed implicit leadership theories asked respondents to describe "outstanding leaders" in their country. There may be a bias in this method that results in omitting descriptions of less charismatic leaders who do not necessarily "stand out" but are nevertheless very effective. This could be one reason that Charismatic/Value-Based leadership is endorsed as a major part of the CLTs for nearly all the GLOBE countries.

Finally, the quantitative research reported in this chapter deals with perceptions of culture and prototypes (CLTs) of outstanding leaders in Mexico. This research does not directly address the effectiveness of these leaders. GLOBE research is now under way that explores the fit between the actual behavior of Mexican leaders and these prototypes. This research focuses on CEOs in each country and should provide evidence regarding the effectiveness of leaders whose behavior fits their countries culturally endorsed implicit leadership theory. This is clearly the necessary "next step" in making the GLOBE findings most useful for managerial leadership in Mexico. Another useful extension of this research would be to gather data on CLTs from nonmanagerial workers in Mexico and to compare these findings with those reported here.

6. INTEGRATION

The variety of information and data gathered for the GLOBE research project have helped to identify several themes that characterize Mexican culture and the leadership styles that reflect these themes. Some of the themes and leadership styles are traditional and directly reflect Mexican history and the type of leadership that has been common during this history. Other themes and leadership styles are emerging as Mexico is becoming highly involved in international business activities through *maquiladora* operations, joint ventures, Mexican multinational corporations, international agreements (such as the NAFTA) and membership in the World Trade Organization. The material presented in this chapter is integrated in this section by describing these cultural themes and what they imply for effective leadership in Mexico. These themes should be recognized and understood by expatriate individuals working in Mexico.

Traditional Themes

A dominating orientation (*Assertiveness*) and the Mexican tendency to accept that power is distributed unequally in society and its institutions (*Power Distance*) were clear in the GLOBE quantitative measures of societal culture. This tendency reflects the hierarchical power wielded by theocratic, autocratic, and militaristic rulers throughout much of Mexican history. These leaders were often oppressive, but sometimes highly charismatic. Assertiveness and power distance are consistent with the effectiveness of *directive leadership* found in empirical studies of leadership in Mexico cited earlier. These leaders may also be somewhat *autonomous* and *self-protective* in their leadership styles. This was shown in the GLOBE CLT data indicating that Mexicans accept self-protective behavior by leaders more so than individuals in most other GLOBE countries. This autonomy and self-protective behavior may be essential for survival when high-level leaders hold absolute power. This concern still lives as Mexicans expressed a need for even more *uncertainty avoidance* in their institutions (shown in the GLOBE culture measures) to protect themselves against unforeseeable events.

High assertiveness and power distance are also consistent with the importance of *Charismatic/Value-Based* leadership found in the GLOBE data and the focus group discussions, although this leadership factor was not endorsed as strongly as in most GLOBE countries or other Latin American countries. Charismatic leadership in Mexico has traditionally been represented by a strongly directive and masculine (*machismo*) image of a leader. But the strongest element of charismatic leadership in Mexico from the GLOBE data was a concern for performance orientation. This showed that Mexicans expect their leaders to strongly emphasize excellence and continuous improvement in their organizations. Because the traditional Mexican family has often expected loyalty and abnegation by children, this may have made many Mexicans willing followers of powerful charismatic and directive leaders. The willingness to accept power differences may also influence the effectiveness of a *leader's contingent reward behavior* in Mexico, as powerful leaders are expected to bestow rewards on favored followers. It appears that the high power distance of Mexican culture is pervasive in its influence on a Mexican's perception of the characteristics of outstanding leaders.

The importance of the family in Mexican culture is shown by high levels of *In-Group Collectivism* in the quantitative GLOBE data, as well as in the interviews and the literature on Mexican history and culture. Contemporary Mexican society, like others in Latin America, emerged from a complex tradition of agrarian life with domination by oppressive rulers, many of whom had little concern for the care and nurturance of the common people. Kinship has played a critical role in survival as Mexicans turned to their families for a safe haven and support throughout their lives. The same patterns of affiliation and support are also established and maintained in work organizations as Mexicans develop trusting relationships with coworkers and business associates to help them achieve their goals. The supremacy of the father in Mexican families is replicated in work organizations by *patriarchal leadership patterns* in family-owned businesses, which are extremely common in Mexico. Numerous large Mexican business groups, known as *grupos,* have evolved from and operate based on strong family ties and traditions. The family structure is also found in the high level of *paternalism* demonstrated by leaders toward workers by providing food baskets, cafeterias, medical care, transportation, loans, numerous holidays, as well as personal care and concern for individuals apart from their organizational roles (although salaries often remain at low levels). The importance of *supportive leadership* behaviors in Mexican work organizations has been shown in published empirical research and probably reflects the traditional paternalistic tendencies of Mexican leaders. These leadership patterns emerged repeatedly in the interview data, focus groups, and published leadership research. Family membership, structure, and role requirements have a major influence on the self-concept of most Mexicans and this carries into their conception of an outstanding leader.

Mexicans typically emphasize developing and maintaining *pleasant social/interpersonal relations* with people they interact with, including their business associates, coworkers, and followers. This emerged repeatedly in the interviews as well as the literature on Mexican social customs. Treating people with courtesy and respect and developing trust are dominant guidelines in Mexico for interpersonal relations. The *simpático* shown by Mexican leaders who demonstrate acute sensitivity to the dignity and worth of individuals by displaying empathy and respect demonstrates the importance placed on interpersonal relations in Mexico. This is also shown by the value placed on *personal networks* in business dealings. Mexican executives prefer to conduct business with people they know and trust. The first question a person often asks when dealing with an organization is: "Do I know someone there, or do I have a friend or acquaintance who may know someone in that organization?" Business leaders often emphasize trust and friendship networks more than costs and profits. Manipulating the social environment to control personal and organizational achievements requires interpersonal sensitivity, skill, and a belief in the efficacy of personal networks. Positive interpersonal relations are a cardinal element in the Mexicans' view of an effective leader.

Emerging Themes

A corollary of the high assertiveness (tough and dominating) and high power distance of traditional Mexican culture is that individuals with little formal power have had very little influence and involvement in determining organizational policies and practices. This was shown in the GLOBE CLT data where *participative leadership* approaches were rated only slightly above "no impact" in terms of their contribution to outstanding leadership in Mexico. Mexico ranked 59 out of 61 GLOBE countries in importance placed on participative leadership. This assessment of participation in Mexican organizations was supported in the semistructured interviews and in the published empirical research on leadership in Mexico. Studies show that participative leadership has generally had little impact on followers' attitudes and performance in Mexico.

This traditional view of participation may be changing. In several industrial centers, including the urban border area shared with the United States, there is an increased interest in participative management approaches. This corresponds with the increasing numbers of joint ventures and *maquiladora* operations in Mexico, where popular international management styles are being tried with some apparent success. This was evident in the media analysis and the focus group discussions. A type of participative involvement was discussed, which differs from approaches that are popular in the United States and Europe, but may be similar to that found in Asian countries (which are often high in power distance). With this approach, leaders were expected to make decisions and design strategies, which they then discussed with followers who would eventually carry them out. There is an active give-and-take between leaders and followers regarding how decisions and strategies are implemented. These discussions may jump from one issue to another, but the skillful leader can apparently manage multiple discussions at one time. The key point of these discussions was that all individuals who were involved had an opportunity to make an input for discussion. Leaders who obtain follower input in this manner represent a significant change from the strongly centralized autocratic approaches that have been traditional in Mexico. Once this input is made and discussed, followers may be less concerned that their ideas are implemented than in the United States. One *empresario* gathers information from all his production and administrative staff before he makes a decision. He stated: "I have the last word, but apart from that, we work together in the battle to improve the quality of our product" (Martínez, 2000, p. 106). The increasing popularity of participative approaches may also be indicated by the GLOBE culture data showing that Mexicans believe there should be much less emphasis on power distance in their society. We expect the changing portrait of Mexican society and organizations to include more participative leadership of some type in the 21st century.

Current societal trends in Mexico indicate increasing involvement of different groups to influence government policies and practices. The increasing importance of collective/team efforts inside Mexican organizations may be indicated by the high score for *team-oriented leadership* in the GLOBE CLT data. Team Oriented leadership was rated the highest of the CLT leadership factors that contributed to outstanding leadership in Mexico. This factor includes being diplomatic, collaborative, integrative, and administratively competent. It should be noted that both directive and participative leadership approaches can be important in producing team effectiveness. Directive leadership is often useful early in a team's development, whereas participation becomes effective later on. A team orientation shows recognition of the importance of collective effort to compete in Mexico's changing economy and may be an organizational extension of family collectivism in Mexico.

GLOBE respondents expressed a strong desire for more *performance orientation and future orientation* in their institutions and organizations. This probably reflects the many changes occurring in Mexican society as Mexico becomes an increasingly important member of the international business community. Mexicans recognize the importance of emphasizing planning and performance in order to compete successfully in international markets. This includes recognition of the value of new technologies as armor in the competitive arenas they face. The institutionalization of current management processes and programs (such as Total Quality Management) is becoming an important trend in many Mexican organizations. The "*mañana* culture," often attributed to Mexico by outsiders, is inconsistent with a growing achievement orientation in Mexico.

The GLOBE culture data showed some desire for a *stronger Humane Orientation and Gender Egalitarianism* in Mexican society. This surely reflects a long-term desire among Mexicans for more opportunity, self-development, and control of their lives. It may also reflect the increasing internationalization of the business community and the recognition that all of Mexico's human resources must be nurtured and developed in order to be competitive. The increasing importance of leaders developing followers' potential was evident in the ethnographic interviews and probably signals a move toward less *machismo* in Mexican leadership styles.

Summary

In summary, the following themes and leadership styles should be carefully considered by expatriate managers, others working in Mexico, or those working with Mexican organizations. Historical cultural values in Mexico (such as traditionalism, assertiveness, and high Power Distance) have resulted in society viewing outstanding leaders as highly directive, charismatic, rewarding, and autocratic, and sometimes autonomous and self-protective. These leaders are also often patriarchal, paternalistic, and supportive of followers (reflecting high In-Group Collectivism) and they emphasize maintaining pleasant interpersonal relations (another important cultural value) through showing respect and empathy (*simpático*) for others. These leaders often seek to attain objectives through social influence and personal networks. Evolving cultural changes point to increases in Participative and Team Oriented leadership styles in Mexico. A stronger leadership focus on Performance and Future Orientation is also indicated as well as some added concern for creating more Humane and Gender Egalitarian organizations. These emerging leadership trends undoubtedly reflect the internationalization of business in Mexico and its anticipated major role in the highly competitive world economy of the 21st century.

ACKNOWLEDGMENTS

We would like to thank James Krippner-Martinez and two anonymous reviewers for their insightful feedback during the development of this chapter. Sandra M. Martinez's research was supported by a National Security Education Program Doctoral Fellowship.

REFERENCES

Agar, M. (1998). *Ethnography manual for leadership study.* Working Paper. Takoma Park, MD.

Alduncin, A. E. (1986). *Los valores de los Mexicanos* [The values of the Mexican people]. México City: Banamex, Fomento Cultural Banamex.

Ardila, R. (1979). Psicología social de la pobreza [The social psychology of poverty]. In J. O. Whittaker (Ed.), *La psicología social en el mundo de hoy* (pp. 399–418). México City: Editorial Trillas.

Bass, B. M. (1990). *Bass and Stogdill's handbook of leadership* (3rd ed.). New York: The Free Press.

Bonfil Batalla, G. (1987). *México profundo: Una civilización negada* [Rural Mexico: Reclaiming a civilization]. México City: CIESAS-SEP.

Chemers, M. M., & Aymen, R. (1985). Leadership orientation as a moderator of the relationship between job performance and job satisfaction of Mexican managers. *Personality and Social Psychology Bulletin, 11*(4), 359–367.

Cosío Villegas, D. (1955). *Historia moderna de México* [Modern history of Mexico] (2nd ed.). México City: Editorial Hermes.

Davis, J. H., Ming, L. W., & Brosnan, T. F. (1986). *The Farmer–Richman model: A bibliographic essay emphasizing applicability to Singapore and Indonesia.* Paper presented at the meeting of the Academy of Management, Chicago.

de la Cerda Gastélum, J. (1995). *Los laberintos del mejoramiento* [The labyrinths of advancement]. México City: Editorial Iberoamérica.

Derossi, F. (1971). *The Mexican entrepreneur.* Paris: Organization for Economic Cooperation and Development.

Díaz-Loving, R. (1999). The indigenisation of psychology: Birth of a new science or rekindling of an old one? *Applied Psychology: An International Review, 48,* 433–449.

Dorfman, P. W., & Howell, J. P. (1983). *Management practices and personnel policies of the maquiladoras—a cooperative manufacturing effort between the United States and México.* Las Cruces, NM: New Mexico State University, Bureau of Business Research.

Dorfman, P. W., & Howell, J. P. (1988). Dimensions of national culture and effective leadership patterns: Hofstede revisited. *Advances in International Comparative Management, 3,* 127–150.

Dorfman, P. W., & Howell, J. P. (1997). Managerial leadership in the United States and México: Distant neighbors or close cousins? In S. K. Granrose & S. Oskamp (Eds.), *Cross-cultural work groups* (pp. 234–264). Thousand Oaks, CA: Sage.

Dorfman, P., Howell, J., Hibino, S., Lee, J., Tate, U., & Bautista, A. (1997). Leadership in western and Asian countries: Commonalities and differences in effective leadership processes across cultures. *Leadership Quarterly, 8,* 233–274.

Drost, E., & Von Glinow, M.A. (1998). Leadership behavior in Mexico: Etic philosophies—emic practices. In T. A. Scandura & M. G. Serapio (Eds.), *Research in International Business and International Relations, 7,* 3–29.

Foster, G. (1960). *Culture and conquest: American's Spanish heritage.* Chicago: Quadrangle Books.

García, J. S. (2001). La entrevista insólita [The unusual interview]. *Proceso, 1271*(March 11), 11–16.

Gutiérrez, S. (1993). Can you make it in México? *Financial Executive, 9*(2), 20–23.

Hanges, P. J., Braverman, E. P., & Rentsch, J. R. (1991). Changes in raters' impressions of subordinates: A catastrophe model. *Journal of Applied Psychology, 76,* 878–888.

Hanges, P. J., Lord, R. G., Day, D. V., Sipe, W. P., Smith, W. C., & Brown, D. J. (1997*). Leadership and gender bias: Dynamic measures and nonlinear modeling.* Symposium presented at the Twelfth Annual Conference of the Society of Industrial and Organizational Psychology, St. Louis, MO.

Hofstede, G. (1980). *Culture's consequences: International differences in work-related values.* Beverly Hills, CA: Sage.

Hofstede, G., & Bond, M. H. (1988). The Confucius connection: From cultural roots to economic growth. *Organizational Dynamics, 16,* 4–21.

Horgan, P. (1984). *Great river: The Rio Grande in North American history* (4th ed.). Hanover, NH: Wesleyan University Press.

House, R. J., Hanges, P. J., Javidan, M., Dorfman, P. W., Gupta, V.,& GLOBE Associates. (2004). *Cultures, leadership, and organizations: The GLOBE study of 62 societies.* Thousand Oaks, CA: Sage.

House, R., Hanges, P., Ruiz-Quintanilla, S. A., Dorfman, P., Javidan, M., Dickson, M., et al. (1999). Cultural influences on leadership and organizations—Project GLOBE. *Advances in Global Leadership, 1,* 171–233.

Howell, J. P., Romero, E. J., Dorfman, P. W., & Paul, J. (2003). Effective leadership in the Mexican maquiladora: Challenging common expectations. *Journal of International Management, 9,* 51–73.

Instituto Nacional de Estadística, Geografía e Informática. (1990). *Censo de población y vivienda* [Census of population and housing]. Aguascalientes, México: Author.

Instituto Nacional de Estadística, Geografía e Informática. (1995).*Censo de población y vivienda* [Census of population and housing]. Aguascalientes, México: Author.

Instituto Nacional de Estadística, Geografía e Informática. (2002).*Censo de población y vivienda* [Census of population and housing]. Aguascalientes, México: Author.

Kras, E. S. (1994). *Modernizing Mexican management style.* Las Cruces, NM: Editts Publishing.

Krauze, E. (1991). *Biografía del poder* [A biography of power]. México City: Fondo de Cultura Económica.

Krauze, E. (1994). *Siglo de Caudillos: Biografía política de México 1810–1910* [A century of caudillos: Political biography of Mexico 1810–1910]. México: Tusquets.

Krauze, E. (2000, July 17). A new era. *Time,* 16–18.

Krippner-Martínez, J. (2001). *Rereading the Conquest: Power, politics, and the history of early colonial Michoacán, México, 1521–1565.* University Park: Pennsylvania State University Press.

Lawrence, J., & Yeh, R. (1995). On the use and effectiveness of employee involvement in México. *Journal of International Management,* 1(4), 389–416.

Lord, R., & Maher, K. J. (1991). *Leadership and information processing: Linking perceptions and performance.* Boston: Unwin-Everyman.

Martínez, S. M. (2000). An ethnographic study of the Mexican entrepreneur: A configuration of themes and roles impacting managerial leadership in an emerging economy. *Dissertation Abstracts International, 63*(01A).

McClelland, D. C. (1961). *The achieving society.* Princeton, NJ: Van Nostrand.

Meyer, M. C., Sherman, W. L., & Deeds, S. M. (1999). *The course of Mexican history* (6th ed.). New York: Oxford University Press.

Mulder, M. (1976). Reductions of power differences in practice: The power instance reduction theory and its application. In G. Hofstede & M. S. Kassen (Eds.), *European contributions to organization theory* (pp. 79–94). Assen, Netherlands: Van Gorcum.

Parkes, H. B. (1966). *A history of México* (3rd ed.). Boston: Houghton Mifflin.

Paz, O. (1959). *El laberinto de la soledad* [The labyrinth of solitutde]. México City: Fondo de Cultura Económica.

Paz, O. (1981). *El ogro filantrópico* [The philanthropist ogre]. México City: Joaquin Mortiz.

Pelled, L. H., & Hill, K. D. (1997). Participative management in northern Mexico: A study of maquiladoras. *The International Journal of Human Resource Management, 8*(3), 197–212.

Preston, J., & Dillon, S. (2004). *Opening Mexico: The making of a democracy.* New York: Farrar, Straus & Giroux.

Ramos, S. (1976). *El perfil del hombre y la cultura en México* [An outline of Mexico's people and culture]. México City: Austral.

Rangle, C. (1977). *The Latin Americans: Their love–hate relationship with the United States.* New York: Harcourt Brace.

Riding, A. (1989). *Distant neighbors.* New York: Vintage.

Schuler, R., Jackson, S., Jackofsky, E., & Slocum, J., Jr. (1996, May–June). Managing human resources in Mexico: A cultural understanding. *Business Horizons,* pp. 55–61.

Sotelo Valencia, A. (1999). *Globalización y precariedad del trabajo en México* [Job globalization and insecurity in Mexico]. México City: El Caballito.

Stephens, G. K., & Greer, C. R. (1995). Doing business in Mexico: Understanding cultural differences. *Organizational Dynamics, 24,* 39–55.

Taylor, W. B. (1996). *Magistrates of the sacred: Priests and parishioners in eighteenth-century Mexico.* Stanford, CA: Stanford University Press.

Teagarden, M. B., Butler, M. C., & Von Glinow, M. A. (1992). Mexico's maquiladora industry: Where strategic human resource management makes a difference. *Organizational Dynamics, 20*(3), 34–47.

Triandis, H. C. (1995). *Individualism and collectivism.* Boulder, CO: Westview Press.

Valdés Ugalde, F. (1997). *Autonomía y legitimidad: Los empresarios, la política, y el estado en México* [Autonomy and legitimacy: Entrepreneurs, politics and the Mexican state]. México City, Mexico: Siglo Veintiuno Editores.

Vargas, G.A., & Johnson, T. W. (1993). An analysis of operational experience in the U.S./Mexico production sharing (maquiladora) program. *Journal of Operations Management, 11,* 17–34.

Vasconcelos, J. (1971). *Breve historia de México* [Brief history of Mexico]. México City: Editorial Continental.

Wolf, E. R. (1966). Kinship, friendship, and patron–client relations in complex societies. In M. Banton (Ed.), *The social anthropology of complex societies* (pp. 1–22). New York: Praeger.

Wolf, E. R., & Hansen, E. C. (1972). *The human condition in Latin America.* New York: Oxford University Press.

Zabludovsky, G. (1998). *Women business owners in Mexico: An emerging economic force.* Silver Springs, MD: National Foundation for Women Business Owners, USA.

VI

EASTERN EUROPE CLUSTER

The Eastern Europe cluster in the GLOBE Research Program consisted of Albania, Georgia, Greece, Hungary, Kazakhstan, Poland, Russia, and Slovenia. Only two of these countries, Greece and Russia, are represented in this volume.

The Eastern Europe cluster scored high on Assertiveness, Gender Egalitarianism, and In-Group Collectivism. Its scores on Humane Orientation, Institutional Collectivism, and Power Distance were in the middle range. It scored low on Future Orientation, Performance Orientation, and Uncertainty Avoidance (House et al., 2004).

An outstanding leader in Eastern Europe would be one who combines Team Oriented leadership with Charismatic/Value Oriented leadership, displays fairly high levels of Autonomous leadership, and is also capable of Self-Protective behaviors. The range of variation between the countries of the cluster is quite varied, for example, slightly positive and strong positive endorsement of Participative leadership, to neutral to positive endorsement of Humane Orientation leadership.

There are strong differences between Greece and Russia, the countries represented in this volume. However, high Power Distance and high Family and Group Collectivism seem to be characteristic of this cluster. Most of the countries in this cluster faced significant challenges in the recent past during the transition from communism to market-based economies (Bakacsi, 2002).

REFERENCES

Bakacsi, G., Sandor, T., Andras, K., & Viktor, I. (2002). Eastern European cluster: tradition and transition. *Journal of World Business, 37,* 69–80.

House, R. J., Hanges, P. J., Javidan, M., Dorfman, P. W., Gupta, V., & GLOBE Associates. (2004). *Culture, leadership, and organizations: The GLOBE study of 62 societies.* Thousand Oaks, CA: Sage.

21

▼▼▼▼▼▼▼

Greece: From Ancient Myths to Modern Realities

Nancy Papalexandris
Athens University of Economics and Business,
Athens, Greece

Study Aims and Objectives

Every researcher looking into organizations comes across two main realities that keep recurring all the time: first, the fact that societal culture has a very strong influence on the way firms and their members are operating and, second, that managerial practices, which are normally perceived as reasonable, fair, and worth following, cannot be implemented unless the appropriate organizational culture and leadership style exists.

GLOBE's main objective, to identify the effects of societal culture on leadership, organizational practices, and values, is (cf. House et al., 2004), therefore, a most desirable subject for exploration among Greek organizations.

In view of the aforementioned, this chapter focuses on the following objectives:

- First, to help the reader understand modern Greek reality by shedding light on historical aspects of the country, as well as political, economic, and sociocultural elements, and the influence they have on people's social values and personality characteristics.
- Second, to present and discuss the results from the GLOBE study in Greece on perceived and preferred cultural dimensions, as revealed from the empirical research among respondents in the telecommunications and finance sectors.
- Third, to describe and interpret results from the GLOBE study in Greece on leadership and its most desirable attributes, combined with information provided by focus groups and media analysis.

Much about modern Greek reality is deeply rooted in ancient tradition and practice, which was often expressed allegorically in mythology. Are Odysseus's inventiveness, Zeus's power, and Athena's wisdom among the main characteristics Greeks are looking for in their leaders? To what extent does a modern country, strongly oriented toward the future, remain rooted in

TABLE 21.1
Characteristics of Firms in the Sample

Sector	Organization	Ownership	Size of Firms	No. of Respondents
Finance	Bank A	State owned	Large	42
	Bank B	State owned	Large	37
	Bank C	Private Greek	Large	27
	Bank D	Private foreign owned	Medium	32
	Total			138
Telecommunications	Organization of Public Telecommunication Services	State owned	Large	34
	Telecommunication Equipment	Private Greek	Large	24
	Software House	Private Greek	Medium	10
	Cellular Phones	Foreign Subsidiary	Large	15
	Cellular Phones	Foreign Subsidiary	Medium	4
	Software & Multimedia Lab	Private Greek	Small	10
	Total			97
Total				**235**

and draw from its past? I hope that by reading through this chapter, based largely on existing information and interpretations of GLOBE findings, the reader will gain an insight into a country often considered as indecipherable while presenting an integrated and meaningful paradigm, unique in its combination of diverse elements.

Design and Methodology

Greece participated in the GLOBE study from the initial phase, with the sorting of questions and pilot testing of the initial questionnaires, through to the finalized version of the GLOBE questionnaire, which was completed by 235 Greek middle managers (see Table 21.1). The mean age of respondents was 37 years and all of them had at least one level of subordinates. In both sectors, finance and telecommunications, questionnaires were gathered in 1996.

Furthermore, two focus groups were conducted. The first took place in spring 1995, prior to the gathering of the questionnaires, among junior middle managers attending a training seminar in the banking sector that centered on the differences between managers and leaders. The second took place at the beginning of 1996 among employed adult students of an engineering background attending a part-time executive MBA course. Participants were asked to select and comment on their preferred leaders, from the historical/political and business perspective. A media analysis was also conducted on articles describing outstanding business leaders, as well as a factor analysis of the results from the leadership part of the GLOBE questionnaires.

All the preceding, combined with the author's knowledge and experience of her country and existing relevant literature from previous research, have served as the basis for this chapter.

1. THE GREEK ENVIRONMENT

Historical Background

Situated geographically in the southeastern part of Europe and close to Africa and Asia, Greece has a history that cannot be covered in just a few pages. Despite its small size, Greece has played an important role in world history, mainly through its contribution to civilization. The most important period of Greek history is the Classical period (sixth to fourth century BC). Classical Greece is known throughout the world for its development of the arts, the birth of democracy, and the creation and implementation of great institutions such as the Olympic Games. However, the first noteworthy civilizations appear long before that, in the Bronze Age around 3000 BC. These civilizations can be divided into the Cycladic, the Minoan, and the Mycenean. During the Cycladic Civilization, Santorini and other islands of the Aegean Sea became centers of trade due to their location and natural resources. The Minoan Civilization developed in Crete, where one can admire today important remains of its architectural and artistic achievements. The Mycenean Civilization developed in the Peloponese and its dis-covery helps us understand the epic works, *The Iliad* and *The Odyssey,* written by the great poet Homer, which have most probably been drawn from this era. These early civilizations gradually declined and it is later, during the classical times, that civilization reaches its peak.

During the Classical period (sixth to fourth century BC), Greece was organized into city-states, which were independent and self-governed. The greatest of these city-states were Athens, Sparta, Thebes, and Corinth. During this period, the Greeks colonized many locations in Asia Minor and in the Mediterranean where they developed commerce. In addition, they blossomed culturally and artistically. During the fifth century BC, democracy, the form of government that was 25 centuries later to prevail throughout most of the world was born in Athens. At the same time, the different areas of Greece started to develop bonds through different common celebrations. The most important of these were: (a) the Olympic Games, which took place every 4 years and during which all hostilities between city-states would stop, and (b) the Amphiktyonies, meetings that took place in Delphi or Delos where city-states would discuss common problems and try to solve differences.

At the beginning of the fifth century BC, the Persian Empire, in its attempt to expand to the west, attacked Greece and threatened its independence with a strong army outnumbering by far the forces of Greece. The Persian attack was finally rebuffed after a series of battles in Marathon, Thermopylae, and Plataea, and the sea battle at Salamis. These battles are still alive in the minds of modern Greeks as proof of spirit and bravery. The names of their hero figures, such as Aristides, Miltiadis, Themistocles, and Lykourgos, are quite common birth names among modern Greeks. The most important outcome of the war was the fact that the Greek city-states united for the first time against the common enemy.

The fifth century is known for Athens as the Golden Era of Pericles. During his rule, the Acropolis and the famous temple of Parthenon, dedicated to Athena, Goddess of Wisdom, was built. Pericles made Athens the military, political, and artistic capital of the Ancient Greek world. Unfortunately, peace did not last long. A series of wars between Athens and Sparta, known as the Peloponnesian Wars, broke out and lasted for 27 years. This gave a weakening blow to the unity of the Greeks and led to a decline of both powerful cities, Athens and Sparta.

Soon another great power, Macedonia, emerged. From his headquarters in Vergina, close to Thessaloniki, King Philip and his son Alexander the Great succeeded in uniting continental Greece and began a great campaign in the East, with the purpose of spreading civilization. A huge amount of territory was conquered with Alexander reaching as far as India. He created a huge empire, which could not survive intact after his death (323 BC). His heirs divided the lands but his spirit survived for many centuries. He succeeded in spreading Greek civilization and he is perhaps the only invader in history who won the hearts of the people he conquered. The period until the third century was marked by the presence of many great historians, writers, philosophers and scientists, such as Thoucydides, Xenophon, Socrates, Plato, and Aristotle, who lived and produced immortal works. At the same time, the tragic poets Aeschylus, Eurypides, and Sophocles wrote, among others, the world-known tragedies *Antigone, Electra,* and *Medea.*

After the fall of the Macedonian Empire, the Romans became the new great power and moved to Greece. It was during this time that Christianity was born, which soon became the main religion of the Greeks. The gradual weakening of the Roman Empire led to its division into eastern and western parts and, thus, to the creation of the Byzantine Empire in the eastern part, with Constantinople as its capital (323 AD).

The new capital got its name from its founder, Constantine the Great, who was a great supporter of Christianity and decided to create a new empire independent of the Roman influence. The Byzantine Empire was Greek in character, with Christianity as its main religion. All of the strength of the empire was concentrated in Constantinople where Greek language and culture reigned. Constantinople was to become one of the great world capitals with vast wealth and beauty, the chief city of the Western world until the 11th century AD.

Economically and politically strong, Byzantium repelled the attacks of its numerous invaders. In the sixth century AD, under the great Emperor Justinian, Byzantium reached its peak. He wrote "The Roman Civic Law," a monumental piece of work, and fought to strengthen the borders of his empire and to spread Christianity. The followers of Justinian tried to keep control over the territories of the empire but it was extremely difficult, because at the same time the Arabs were threatening Byzantium with their emerging power. In Mecca, Mohamed created the new religion of Islam and fought against Byzantium with great fervor. Byzantium was then attacked by the Ottoman Sultans. Many territories were lost, as well as control over the areas that held the best soldiers and greatest incomes.

Western European forces organized eight crusades to free the Holy Land but also to take advantage of Eastern wealth. During one of the Crusades, Constantinople was seized. These wars resulted in the weakening of the Byzantine Empire and led to its eventual downfall. The Ottomans seized one city after the other in Northern Greece and the Balkans. Then they attacked Constantinople. On May 29, 1453, Mohammed the Second conquered the "queen of cities," 1,129 years after it had been built by Constantine the Great and after having survived 20 sieges.

The fall of Constantinople is a tragic moment in Greek history as it marked the beginning of four centuries of slavery. The conquering forces of the Ottoman Empire were prepared neither to continue, nor to assimilate, into the existing civilization. The entire East fell back into the dark Middle Ages. This was a deep wound for Hellenism. However, Greek people, humbled and enslaved, kept their faith strong for their future independence during the four centuries of occupation that followed.

This was a period of great suffering for Greece, especially at a time when other Europeans were developing and experiencing the Renaissance, having successfully confronted Turkish invasion, which managed to reach the outskirts of Vienna. The main consequences of occupation were the destruction of Greek culture, a reduction in the population because of slaughter, kidnapping of children, forced conversion to Islam, and a weakening of the economy due to the burden of harsh taxation.

An important role in the emancipation from Ottoman rule was played by the educated Greeks of diaspora, who had studied in Europe and supported Greece by making its cause known throughout Europe. Led by Adamantios Korais and Regas Feraios, they were the pioneers in creating a supportive movement for the liberation of Greece. At the beginning of the 19th century, a secret society, "Filiki Etairia," was founded in Odyssos, to which many Greeks contributed money and became members. The society took the lead in planning the country's struggle for independence against the Ottoman Empire, which began on March 25, 1821, in the monastery of St. Lavra in the Peloponnese.

The revolution quickly spread throughout Greece and bloody battles started with the Ottomans. The first great victories in Tripoli, Valtetsi, Gravia, and Vasilika raised the morale of the Greeks. At the same time, skilled Greek sailors succeeded in naval victories against the Ottoman navy. With the passing of time, Greece started to hope for the help of the great European powers, which at the beginning were against the country's struggle for independence. The change in European policy followed the change in public opinion, in both Europe and the United States, which was in favor of Greek independence.

The year 1825 was the most decisive; Greece's limited resources were weakening, whereas the Ottomans were reorganizing and accepting reinforcements from Ibrahim in Egypt. Ibrahim seized all of the Peloponnese and, with the help of Kioutachis, he conquered Messolongi where Lord Byron, the British poet, a strong supporter of the Greek cause, fought and lost his life. The descriptions and accounts of the heroic exodus at the end of the siege of Messolongi moved the world and greatly increased feelings of philhellenism. Following the sea battle of Navarino in October 1827, where the naval forces of England, France, and Russia defeated the navies of Turkey and Egypt, Greece was declared an independent country, occupying only a small part of its present territory.

In 1828, Ioannis Kapodistrias, a former foreign minister of Russia, became the first governor of the country with the blessing of the other European countries. He undertook the reorganization of the state. At the same time, the Russo-Turkish war broke out, which led to the defeat of the Turks. In 1832, Prince Otto, a Bavarian prince, became the King of Greece, following an agreement among the great European powers.

There followed a period in which the Greeks were able to liberate part of Thessaly. In 1863, George, a Danish prince, was declared King of Greece. In addition, the Ionian Islands were returned to Greece by the British. In 1866, revolution broke out in Crete, which was still under Turkish rule, for union with Greece. Following victorious battles, Crete was granted self-rule and the use of the Greek language. Finally, with the Treaty of Berlin in 1878, the Turks conceded Epirus and the rest of Thessaly to Greece.

In the meanwhile, a new enemy had appeared in the north, the Bulgarians, who wanted to take control of Macedonia (1890). Following great battles the Greeks expelled the Bulgarians. At the same time, in 1908, the Cretans repelled the Turkish army and declared Crete's unification with Greece.

The Balkan countries united against Turkey and the first Balkan war broke out in 1912–1913. The war had positive results for Greece because Thessaloniki was liberated, and the Balkan countries also largely achieved their goals. However, the Bulgarians and the Serbians had agreed to divide among themselves land that was Greek. The result was the

Second Balkan War between the Greeks and the Bulgarians. When the war was over, Greece had doubled its territory but many Greek lands were not liberated, such as the Dodecanese Islands and Northern Epirus.

In 1914, the First World War broke out in Europe. Greece found itself on the side of the Triple Entente (France, England, and Russia), fighting against Germany, Turkey, and Austria. Greece first engaged in fighting on the Balkan front against the Turks and the Bulgarians. This war led to the defeat of the central axis powers. In 1919, with the signing of the Treaty of Neilly, Bulgaria handed over Eastern Macedonia and Western Thrace to the Greeks. Then in 1920, with the signing of the Treaty of Sevres, the Turks had to render Eastern Thrace and the islands of Imvros, Tenedos, and Smyrna to Greece. The Greek government, under Eleftherios Venizelos, the prime minister, wanted this treaty enforced, but the Turks refused. For this reason, the Asia Minor campaign began. Greek troops were defeated and the result was the destruction and uprooting of 1.6 million Greeks from Eastern Thrace and the coast of Asia Minor, as well as the loss of these territories. With the influx of refugees amounting to an extra one third of the country's population, the impoverished, weakened, and defeated Greek state entered a period of political instability, which led to the dictatorship of Metaxas on August 4, 1936. On October 28, 1940, when Mussolini attacked, Greece refused to surrender, thus entering the Second World War, which was catastrophic for the country as Greece suffered 1 million victims (the highest percentage of casualties for any country involved in World War II).

The siege against Greece lasted 216 days, from October 28, 1940, to May 31, 1941. Of those 216 days, 160 constituted the period of resistance by Greece to the invasion of the Italians in the mountains of North Epirus, 25 days constituted the period of the resistance by the Greek army to the Germans in Northern Macedonia, and 31 days constituted the period of the resistance in Crete. This shocked the world, which did not expect such bravery at a time when other, larger countries did not resist or were defeated in just a few days. It is at that time when Winston Churchill, Prime Minister of Great Britain, said: "From now on, we will say not that Greeks fight like heroes but that heroes fight like Greeks." Although the country was eventually conquered, this resistance forced Hitler to delay his expedition to Russia. This delay contributed largely to Hitler's defeat due to the Russian winter, which his troops were unable to face.

The next 4 years were very difficult for Greece. People suffered, there was no freedom at all, and every family experienced loss as thousands died from famine. Despite these difficult conditions, the National Resistance was organized. It created many problems for the Germans during their occupation of Greece. The climax was the explosion of the Bridge of Gorgopotamos, which blocked the import of German provisions into Northern Africa for many weeks and hence contributed to Rommel's defeat. On October 12, 1944, the Germans, retreating on a number of fronts, left Greece. This was not, however, the end of the difficulties for the country.

Immediately after the end of the Second World War, a civil war broke out in Greece between pro-Russian forces wishing to establish a communist regime and the pro-Western government forces. This lasted for 5 years. At the end, Greece found itself deeply wounded, both physically and in terms of morale. The visible losses were 80,000 dead and 700,000 left homeless. But the most substantial consequence was the ideological, political, and cultural gap that divided the people. However, most of the Greeks, sensing the dangerous direction into which their country was heading, started on a path toward reconciliation and healing.

During the first period after the civil war, Greece joined NATO and with the support of the Americans, Greece took back the Islands of the Dodecanese but not Northern Epirus or Cyprus. The Cypriots, with Archbishop Makarios as their leader, started a fight for independence, demanding their union with Greece. Cyprus became an independent free state with Britain, Greece, and Turkey as guaranteeing powers. In 1967, democracy was abolished in Greece and a military regime under George Papadopoulos was established, which eventually abolished the monarchy. In 1974, just before the end of the dictatorship, a short-lived military coup threatening to unite Cyprus with Greece provoked a response from Turkey that was far beyond what could be reasonably expected and ended with the occupation of a large section of Northern Cyprus. This part is controlled by the Turks even today, despite various resolutions passed by the United Nations (UN). Information about 2,000 missing Cypriots has been withheld ever since.

In July 1974, following the fall of the dictatorship, Konstantine Karamanlis became for the third time the prime minister of Greece. Under his presidency, on January 1, 1981, Greece became the 10th member of the European Economic Union. In June 2000, the country was admitted into the European Monetary Union and the Euro Zone, effective from January 1, 2001. One year later, on January 1, 2002, Greece changed its traditional currency, the drachma for the euro. Despite its size, Greece is a nation with a great, yet tragic, history that has seen its existence threatened several times. Due to this, its heroes are mostly respected for their achievements in preserving Greek national entity and Greeks seem to draw strength from their example. They take pride in the fact that their culture is known throughout the world. They believe that their civilization and tradition has still a great deal to offer to humanity. However, there is a common feeling that modern Greece, being a small country, cannot live up to its desired image and this leads to disappointment, wounding national pride among Greeks, especially whenever their national rights are not respected.

The Political Situation in Greece

Ancient Greece is the place where democracy was born. Although modern Greece has seen its democracy suffer at times, it has survived two world wars, a civil war immediately after World War II, and various military coups and dictators. Over the last 30 years the state of politics is characterized by an impressive stability and the presidential parliamentary democracy functions smoothly. From 1974, when the military dictatorship fell, Greece has enjoyed its most peaceful and creative period of the 20th century. As the name of the government suggests, the power is shared between the cabinet and the Parliament, which are elected by the people, and the president who is elected by the Parliament.

Internally, the legislative body revolves around two political axes: the center left and the center right. The two main parties, which represent these two sides, the Panhellenic Socialist Party (PASOK) and New Democracy respectively, have had clear differences in their policies for many years. Today, the differences between the two largest parties are small and there are no serious differences as far as the basic choices and the future direction of the country are concerned. Among the most important goals shared by both parties are the decrease in size of the public sector, the curbing of public spending, the improvement in productivity and competitiveness of the economy, the privatization of state-owned businesses, the implementation of large public works for the country's infrastructure, and the continuing integration of Greece into the European Union (EU).

Greek politics appear to be entering a phase of maturity after the departure from the political scene (and from life) of Konstantine Karamanlis and Andreas Papandreou. These were the personalities who ruled public life from the 1950s to the 1990s. After the departure of these "charismatic" politicians, the new party leaders have acted with moderation and realism. Many spoke about the end of politics, as we knew them, meaning that politics have lost their glory and mythic dimensions, which the leaders of the past had given them. Things are not exactly that way, of course. The truth is that having entered the 21st century, the interest is shifting away from European capitals, including Athens, toward Brussels, which represents the center of EU activity. The economic and monetary unification of Europe has forced the Greek political parties to rethink their goals, with Greek foreign policy, in particular, keeping a strong European orientation.

The main issue in Greek foreign affairs is its proximity to Turkey. In August and September 1999, following the catastrophic earthquakes, which hit both Turkey and Greece, the two countries have become closer offering humanitarian assistance to each other. It appears that this was the beginning for easing tension and solving long-standing political problems, such as the most serious issue facing Greek–Turkish relations, the Cyprus problem. Over the past 30 years, after military invasion by Turkey on the island, the northern part of Cyprus is under occupation, and the island is divided into two parts with the two communities, Greek-Cypriot, and Turkish-Cypriot, living separately.

In December 2002, a plan for the unification of the island by the secretary general of the UN was submitted as a basis for negotiations to solve the long- lasting problems. Although this plan was not accepted by inhabitants in both communities, negotiations are continuing. Cyprus has been accepted as a new member to the enlarged EU in 2004 and since 2003, inhabitants of both parts can visit the other part of the island.

Greek diplomatic relations with the Balkan states are especially friendly and are based on the premise of being good neighbors, providing support when necessary. Greece has always been supportive toward the Balkans whenever they are facing political or economic problems and has received over the last decade more than 1 million economic refugees from Balkan countries, who now live and work in Greece.

The Greek Economy

The spectacular improvements in the macroeconomic indicators, the change in the mentality of the public sector and of business, as well as the opening of new export routes to Eastern Europe and Asia, are the most important achievements in the Greek economy during the last years. International organizations, like the UN, the Organization for Economic Cooperation and Development (OECD), and the International Bank, have ranked Greece as a developed economy, however not among the most economically advanced nations. Greece does not possess a developed heavy industry or a high-tech industrial base. Food, beverages, and textiles constitute the largest portion of manufacturing. It is clear that Greek industry is oriented toward producing goods, which are labor intensive rather than innovative and high-tech. Most economists rightly believe that the main structural problem in the Greek economy stems from the large, slow, and low-performing public sector. The 320,000 public-sector employees are equal to the number of workers in industry but their work is of less value when compared to what they offer the economy.

The large public sector with its heavy bureaucracy and inefficiency receives constant criticism (Papalexandris & Bourantas, 1993). However, its overstaffing has a cultural explanation. The 19th-century Greek state lacked any effective development policy and merely acted as an employment agency for peasants, who had left the countryside in search for work in the cities (Mouzelis, 1978). This was accomplished through a large clientelistic network, under the patronage of highly personalized political parties and using a practice commonly known as *rousfeti*. This is a word of Arab origin, which means personal favor to supporters and differs from bribery (Broome, 1996).

TABLE 21.2
Structure of the Greek Economy

Sector	Share in Employment	Share of GDP
Agricultural Sector	16.0%	8.2%
Manufacturing Sector	22.8%	22.3%
Services Sector	61.2%	69.5%

Note. From OECD (2002).

Rousfeti often serves to surpass bureaucratic formalities and serves to connect individuals thus offsetting insecurity. Although today staffing in the public sector is strictly limited to objective types of entry procedures, personal relations are still important in dealing with the state, whereas political affiliations influence staffing decisions for higher positions.

Apart from the peculiarities of the public sector, careful study of the structure of the Greek economy shows another important structural problem: until recently, the orientation of the Greek economy toward the production of low-value goods. Greece produced and exported mainly food and cheap garments, whereas it imported cars, industrial equipment, computers, electrical appliances, and other similar items.

The country exhibited a level of consumption that was greater than its production. This was translated to deficit in the trade balance. For years this has caused a devaluation of the currency and an inflationary trend. For the past years, this situation has been changing for the better and has resulted in Greece joining the European Monetary Union. Investment in technology and economic austerity measures applied since 1996 have yielded their fruits, improving the picture of the economy. The Greek economy has expanded continuously since 1993, with growth particularly strong and averaging almost 4% during the 5-year period starting in 1997, exceeding that of the EU by more than 1% (OECD, 2002). Today, inflation is at 3%, the government debt ratio has fallen by 11% from 1996 to 2002, interest rates have fallen substantially, and public and private investments have shown a steady increase since 1996. However, despite improvements in the Greek economy, serious structural problems continue to exist. One of these is the distribution of employment among the various sectors, with a high percentage employed in agriculture (Table 21.2).

In agriculture, the fragmentation of land due to the mountainous regions occupying five sixths of Greece's surface, the lack of infrastructure, and limited scientific support held back agricultural production. It is hoped that all this may be remedied with modern technology, leading to significant improvements in the future. Manufacturing, after some years of stagnation in the 1980s, is now showing some spectacular developments in construction, shipbuilding, and telecommunications infrastructure. In the service sector, some worthwhile developments can be seen in the area of tourism, shipping, telecommunications, and finance, with banks and insurance companies showing continuous growth, offering new modern products and investing in technological equipment and automation. Tourism and shipping have traditionally been, and continue to be, important sources of revenue for Greece. Today, Greece is among the most attractive world destinations, offering luxurious hotels, a rich culture and tradition, sea and mountain resorts, exhibition and conference centers, recreation areas, ski centers, modern marinas, paths for hiking, and other tourist attractions. For many years, Greece has been the world's leading power in shipping. Today, due to the legal framework, many Greek ships have changed into convenience flags. Yet, there has been an economic recovery in the passenger- and cruise-ship sectors and the Greek fleet is renovated with ships, which are distinguished for their luxury and safety.

To sum up, despite structural problems, continuous change and improvement is taking place in the Greek economy. The extensive privatization, the improvements in the infrastructure of transportation, energy, communication, the environment, and education, the improvement in the macroeconomic indices, and the increase in private investments show that the country is progressing toward its central goal, which is to have equal standing among other advanced countries in the EU.

The Banking Sector

In Greece, over the last few decades banks have played an important role in the development of the country's economy. Two semistate banks, Emporiki and Ioniki, and two private banks, Alpha Bank and Barclays, were included in the sample with the purpose of conducting intersector comparisons. (Since the completion of the study, the ownership of Ioniki and Barclays has changed.)

For the past few years, the reorganization of the Greek banking sector, following the trend toward mergers that was already well under way in the international market, has become an important issue. The multifaceted Greek banking system, consisting of many small and medium-size banks, both Greek and foreign on the one hand and some large state banks on the other, has undergone serious changes.

The number of state- and semi-state-controlled banks has been reduced since 1995. The market share of state-controlled banks in total assets of commercial banks fell from 60% in 1995 to approximately 40% in 2001. This is due to the process of consolidation and privatization, which led to larger financial groups and to a higher degree of concentration in the Greek banking sector. The share in total assets of the banking sector for the five biggest banks increased from 58% in 1995 to around 66% in 2001.

Rapid credit expansion has offset losses from narrowing interest margins, and bank profitability has improved substantially in recent years, comparing very favorably with a number of other EU countries. This is so in spite of comparatively high operating expenses and provisions on loans. Altogether, the financial strength of the Greek banking system has improved after the liberalization of the sector. Consolidation and privatization have created larger and more cost-conscious financial groups, and banks have expanded into new financial services. Bank capitalization has improved substantially in recent years and most Greek banks are reported to satisfy the minimum capital adequacy ratio, even after the strong decline in stock prices since the second half of 1999.

Today, there are two great banking conglomerates, both of which are controlled by the state. One is the National Bank of Greece, with many branches all over the country. For the last few years, the National Bank has experienced developments, which have established it as one of the most reputable banks in Europe. The other state bank is the Agricultural Bank, which serves the specific needs of the people in rural areas. Also belonging to the semistate sector is the Emporiki Bank. In the private sector, there are three major banks: Alpha Bank (which has now absorbed Ioniki), EFG Eurobank Ergasias, and the Bank of Piraeus. Over the last few years, the important moves in the banking map have included a number of mergers and acquisitions, as well as the creation of a few smaller specialized banks. At the same time, banks constantly add new products and increase the range of services offered to their customers.

In view of this wave of developments, especially of mergers and acquisitions, the exploration of values and attitudes in the banking sector through GLOBE can be useful for purposes of organizational culture, integration, and leadership.

The Telecommunication Sector

In recent years, drastic changes occurred in the field of telecommunications. Until 1992, there was only one state-owned company, OTE (Organization of Telecommunication of Greece), providing conventional phone services. Today OTE continues to provide a standard (conventional) phone service in Greece, but in 1995 its stock went public in the Athens, London, and New York Stock Exchanges, meaning that now 35% of the company is owned by private investors. As a result of the deregulation of the Greek telecommunications market on January 1, 2001, OTE ceased to be a monopoly and has since been operating in a more competitive environment, as more companies provide the same type of services.

Mobile-phone services started in 1992 with two enterprises, Telestet and Panafon. A little later Cosmote, a subsidiary of OTE, joined the market. Today, Panafon has changed its name to to Vodafone, because it belongs to the Vodafone group, and another company Q-Telecom has entered the market. Telecommunications is not only a dynamic, rapidly developing branch of the Greek economy, but a sector in which the country has shown real technological progress and in which Greece parallels international development, having surpassed every forecast made by economic policymakers.

The most interesting statistic, however, is the number of people who have mobile phones. Today cellular-phones exceed in numbers the total Greek population! The great jump came in 1997 when mobile-phone subscribers increased by 87%, which ranked the Greek mobile-phone market as the fourth most developed in Europe, according to statistics published by Mobile Communications International.

The impressive development of the Greek market is based mainly on three factors:

- The variety of products that subscriber mobile phones offer. At this time, every subscriber can choose from various packages according to his or her needs.
- The fact that most Greek businesspeople spend a lot of time out of the office, and for this reason, they need a phone, especially because major Greek cities are large and have serious traffic problems.
- The cultural characteristics of Greeks, who are very fond of going out, have a strong social life, and like to communicate with friends at all times. Therefore phones are used not only for business but also for social purposes.

In the present study respondents were taken from OTE, Telestet, and Panafon, as well as from other companies all falling within the wider classification of telecommunications, such as production of telecommunication equipment and production of software and multimedia applications. The common characteristic of all companies is that both in 1996 when the sample was taken, as well as today, they operate in a dynamic changing and demanding environment.

2. SOCIETAL CULTURE AND THE GLOBE STUDY

Before presenting and interpreting the GLOBE findings on societal culture, some major characteristics of Greek culture are introduced as background information.

Social Values and Patterns of Social Behavior

The great Cretan writer Nikos Kazantzakis refers to "the two great currents which constitute the double-born soul of Greece" (Kazantzakis, 1966, pp. 167–168). By this duality he meant the complex mixture of character constituents that have resulted from Greece's location between East and West and from the combination of classical with modern elements in the Greek national character.

The four centuries of Ottoman rule imparted to Greek institutions a structure radically different from what is the norm of the West. An important feature was the astonishing tenacity of the Greeks in maintaining their ethnic identity through long-lasting foreign dominations. A strong contributory factor in this respect was undoubtedly the importance of religion, the strength of the family institution, and the love of independence.

Importance of Religion.   Religion is closely linked with Greek nationality as 97% of Greek nationals are reported to be Greek Orthodox Christians. The Orthodox clergy has played a major role in the revolution for independence and in preserving Greek language, culture, and tradition through centuries of foreign occupation. Links between the Greek Orthodox Church and Greek tradition are believed to be very deeply rooted, dating from the time when the Roman Empire was divided into its eastern and western halves in 395 AD and the Byzantine Empire was established in the eastern part, with Greek as its official language (Armstrong & Markus, 1960). The church with its many scholars, some living in monasteries, played an important role in preserving ancient Greek culture and philosophy. It is believed that the Renaissance in Europe profited by the Byzantine thinkers, mostly associated with the church, who brought ancient Greek works to Europe following the fall of Constantinople in 1453 (Campbell & Sherrard, 1968). Today, important events in a person's life, such as baptism and marriage, are usually celebrated in churches. Also, people celebrate their saint's day (name day) more than their birthday. Indeed, many religious feasts to honor saints involve music, drinking, and dancing, thus acting as occasions for social gathering and reinforcement of social ties.

Strength of the Family Institution.   The family institution in Greece has been the social entity that protected its members against unfavorable or hostile elements. In the Ottoman period, it was the head of the patriarchal family who alone dealt with the Turkish overlords when this was necessary. In the majority of Greek families, parents still strive to the maximum of their ability to provide their sons and daughters with property and education, to secure employment for them, or to start a business, hence the large numbers of small family-owned firms.

Most large firms in Greece have started as family firms and, for many years, these larger firms have functioned as large patriarchal organizations, where members of the workforce and staff depended on the benevolence of the owner for their well-being. Although this tendency still somehow exists today, increased company size, social awareness, and questioning of authority make it necessary to find new means for securing cooperation and weakening antagonism, a characteristic often shown in both industrial and peer relations within firms ("Greece—Industrial Relations," 1998).

Love of Independence.   Love of independence, the need to express freely and support one's opinion, is a strong characteristic of Greek society. This often results in strong arguments, as each person feels that only his or her views are correct and cannot be easily convinced to modify them. Skouras believes that this is evidence of an "inflated ego," often resulting in a form of antagonism between members of society.[1] Although Greek society shows elements of collectivism, individualism, a tendency to mistrust, difficulties in sharing or combining efforts for a common goal, and constant verbal conflict over facts and ideas are very frequent. One of the most common sources of conflict in most social situations is the argument over politics, because almost every person has a strong opinion on almost every issue and strongly fights to support his or her views. According to an American study of a small Greek village "where perpetual struggle, principally outside the family, is a part of life," the ultimate aim of this struggle appears to be the assertion of individual identity (Friedl, 1962, p. 83). Individualism often stands as a barrier when it comes to delegating authority or collaborating in teams. However, all of the aforementioned is offset by an important feature that acts as a moderator of in-group conflict, namely *philotimo*. There is no equivalent for this word in English; literally translated, it means love of honor and, as a concept, it implies a self-imposed code of conduct based on trust and fairness. *Philotimo* often helps in overcoming difficulties and encouraging cooperation between workers or staff, which no rule or order could impose. It also means that, if treated "properly," an employee will give more than what is normally expected in order to please his or her employers, "properly" meaning being respected, praised, and shown concern with regard to personal matters. As Triandis (1972) indicates, a person who is considered *philotimos* behaves toward members of his or her in-group in a way that is "polite, virtuous, reliable, proud, truthful, generous, self-sacrificing, tactful, respectful and grateful" (p. 308).

A strong belief in independence makes those who work in the private sector willing to work for themselves. The phrase "I want to be my own boss" is commonly heard among young people who, after working for a few years as employees, start their own small business. About half of the labor force is self-employed and 90% of Greek firms have fewer than 10 workers (Papalexandris, 1997).

Overall, the readiness of Greeks to engage in entrepreneurial activities is further strengthened by the considerable degree of social mobility in Greece. With no line of separation between classes, there is high expectation and much opportunity for success. There is no limit to the opportunities for people to advance and Greeks tend to compete fiercely to grasp these opportunities before anyone else does. This explains also the preference for ventures that allow a high margin of profit (trade, shipping) and the willingness to seek opportunities abroad (Papalexandris, 1995).

The desire to advance socially and secure social recognition, together with the love for learning and self-fulfillment, also explain the great value Greeks attach to higher education, which was traditionally a prerequisite for success, social status, and economic prosperity (Dimaki, 1974). Higher education in Greek universities is free for those who can pass the national admission exam. However, the number of candidates exceeds the available places for admission and, for students who are not admitted to the Greek universities, the Greek family is ready to sacrifice important sums of money for their education, either abroad or in private colleges in Greece. Also, it is quite common for the family to finance children's postgraduate studies abroad. In general, Greek independence is balanced by collectivism in many other domains, such as personal relations, family, and even employee–employer relationships.

---

[1]Written communication by Prof. T. Skouras, Athens University of Economics and Business, who acted as one of the referees for this chapter.

TABLE 21.3
GLOBE Results on Greek Societal Culture

Culture Dimensions	Society "As Is"			Society "Should Be"			Differenced "Should Be"– "As Is"
	Mean[a]	Band[b]	Rank[c]	Mean[a]	Band[b]	Rank[c]	
Performance Orientation	3.20	C	61	5.81	C	40	2.61
Future Orientation	3.40	C	51	5.19	B	48	1.79
Assertiveness	4.58	A	9	2.96	C	57	−1.62
Institutional Collectivism I	3.25	D	61	5.40	A	5	2.15
In-Group Collectivism II	5.27	B	35	5.46	B	41	0.19
Gender Egalitarianism	3.48	A	27	4.89	A	15	1.41
Humane Orientation	3.34	D	59	5.23	B	48	1.89
Power Distance	5.40	A	21	2.39	D	52	−3.01
Uncertainty Avoidance	3.39	D	57	5.09	A	17	1.70

[a]Country mean score on a 7-point Likert-type scale. [b]Bands A > B > C > D are determined by calculating the grand mean and standard deviations across all society "As Is" and "Should Be" scales respectively for the GLOBE sample of countries. These means and standard deviations are used to calculate low, medium, and high bands of countries (GLOBE standard procedure, cf. Hanges, Dickson, & Sipe, 2004). [c]The rank order for Greece relative to the 61 countries. [d]Absolute difference between the "Should Be" and "As Is" scores.

Against this overall country background, results obtained from the GLOBE study on societal culture are interpreted in the next section.

GLOBE Results on Perceived and Desired Dimensions

Results from GLOBE on the societal level of culture in Greece are presented in Table 21.3. This table shows the mean scores and ranks of the various dimensions of culture, as respondents believe that they currently exist and should be, as well as the differences between them.

Societal cultural differences between practices, "As Is" responses, and values, "Should Be" responses, are interpreted here in a similar way as Bourantas, Anagnosteli, Mantes, and Kefalas (1990) have argued for organizational culture. They consider the discrepancy between organizational practices as perceived by managers ("As Is") and their personally preferred culture or values ("Should Be") to indicate a desire for change within organizations.

Performance Orientation.   Performance Orientation refers to the degree to which the society encourages and rewards individuals and groups for high performance. In this section, Greece has an especially low "As Is" score of 3.20 (with the maximum being 7.00), ranking it last among 61 countries. On the "Should Be" dimension, Greece's score of 5.81 ranks on the 40th position. There is a substantial gap between what is happening now ("As Is") and what should be happening ("Should Be"), although both are low in relation to the other cultures studied.

Middle managers perceive the recognition granted to high performance in their society to be low, whereas they believe this should be much higher. A number of explanations can be offered here:

- Greek managers seem to resent ("Should Be") the perceived general tendency ("As Is") toward mistrusting those who achieve individual goals and reach high levels of success. This seems similar to the "tall poppy" syndrome reported in Australia (chap. 9, this volume). The "tall poppy" syndrome refers to a dislike of those who excel and are above others, especially when success leads to arrogance. Thus, although Greeks strive for achievement, they often refuse recognition to those performing well. Contrary to this they very often think of themselves as victims of this lack of recognition, having a feeling of being betrayed by society in general.
- More straightforwardly, the results may also indicate that Greek managers want their society to become more performance oriented.
- Results may also reflect the general tendency of most Greeks for self-criticism, which stems to a large extent from a high need for progress and excellence, which everyone would like to see but, due to the lack of infrastructure or the general framework, finds difficult to achieve. The drive and desire for excellence among Greek managers can be seen in the high achievements of overseas Greeks, for example, in the United States, who "work within a system that encourages and supports individual initiative" (Broome, 1996, p. 96).

Over the last few years, as shown by economic figures things have started to change in certain segments of the economy. The concepts of productivity and free trade, already prominent in the private sector, are entering in the public sector while, at the same time, there are more professional managers with scientific background offering their services in various posts in organizations controlled by the state. At the same time, competition is causing a change in the philosophy of management and is forcing companies to make constant improvements in order to attain better results. Thus, it seems likely that overall the Greek management shows more acceptance of performance orientation and sees higher value in recognizing high achievements publicly.

Future Orientation. Future Orientation is defined as the extent to which a society encourages its members to plan for the future and to take long-term perspectives. Greece's "As Is" score (3.40) positions low (Rank = 51, Band C) among the 61 GLOBE countries. The "Should Be" score (5.19) ranks on the 48th position, which differs somewhat from the perceived Future Orientation because it puts Greece in Band B.

It seems that Greece follows the general tendency of all countries in the GLOBE study by showing a desire for more Future Orientation. However, the Greek culture has always been characterized by its "here and now" attitude, mainly due to the environmental instability, wars, and the resulting insecurity. What is missing is the sense of belief in the future and the systematic approach to a long-term program that will look ahead and prepare action plans to meet future needs. It seems that wars, threats, and various calamities that Greeks have faced over the years make them reluctant to plan too far ahead. To this, should be added the frequent changes in legislation, practiced over the past years by the state, and the general mistrust about what lies ahead, possibly due to the country's geopolitical position. According to Broome (1996), the Greek approach to time is considerably different from that found in the United States or Western Europe. There is little advance planning unless it is imposed from the outside. On a personal level, if you ask a Greek what he or she will do over the next few years, you may receive the following answer "Who knows? I may not even be alive then."

Until recently this phenomenon could be observed at all levels of Greek culture, with politicians and businesspeople in the forefront. As a result, the talent for business and the intelligence, which distinguish Greeks, was rather channeled to short-term plans. Trade has been a preferred activity over manufacturing and short-term profit was more appealing than long-term investment (Alexander, 1968). Over the last few years, there have been efforts in large Greek organizations to implement strategic planning and to get ready to anticipate and face the future, by building alternative solutions for unpredictable changes. Thus, many Greek firms have invested abroad, in both Eastern and Western countries, hoping for long-term benefits. This is largely due to globalization and the competition faced by the operation of multinational firms in Greece. Furthermore, because Greece is a member of the EU (and recently joined the European currency), detailed planning ahead of time, in order to participate in projects and get access to available funds, is necessary. This forces state administration to adjust their practices and become more future oriented. It is worth noting that Greeks are among the most pro-European of all EU country nationals—a clear indication that despite their unwillingness to engage in routine planning, they look to the future with hope.

Assertiveness.   This dimension refers to the degree to which members of the society are encouraged to be tough, dominant, and aggressive. Greece positions 9th (Band A) in the "As Is" and 57th (Band C) in the "Should Be" ranking. The apparent difference in ranking is very high. Apparently, the respondents see the Greek society to be very high on dominance and toughness and seem not satisfied by that.

Greece has been involved in several wars over the years, either in response to a foreign invasion or in order to liberate occupied territories. This has led people to act in a confrontational and aggressive way, mostly to safeguard their rights. However, people believe in the Christian spirit of loving peace and the motto of "Love thy neighbor as thyself," which is something strongly encouraged by parents and teachers in childrearing. Among schoolchildren, it is not the person who shows aggression who is most respected, but rather, the child who can help schoolmates in meeting difficult assignments and teachers' requirements or the child who will defend verbally his or her classmate to the teacher, even if the latter is a wrongdoer.

In the organizational setting, competition and the need for efficiency make aggressive behavior an everyday practice. However, back-stabbing or judging strictly your colleagues or subordinates is not encouraged whereas solidarity is well desired. This shows that most people resent the perceived aggression and long for a less confrontational environment.

As Broome (1996) describes, in order to motivate employees to put extra effort into a project, it is necessary to appeal to their *philotimo* or "love of honor" by showing trust in their abilities, kindness, and concern about their personal problems. The allowance of non-work-related activity on the job, and the time often spent by managers in order to learn about their employees' family concerns and problems, can create more loyalty and a sense of obligation, thus leading to higher degrees of productivity whenever needed. Kindness and concern about people rather than about products will bring much better results, because keeping to the norms and being tough and strict can create an adversarial relationship with very negative results. It appears that less aggression is what all countries participating in the GLOBE study around the world desire and Greece, despite the perceived practices, is among the countries with a strong desire for lower levels of aggression.

Institutional Collectivism.   Institutional Collectivism refers to the extent to which a society encourages and rewards collective action. Here, the Greek society has a very low score (3.25) and is in the 61st position (Band D). The "Should Be" score is very high, 5.40, which places Greece 5th among all 61 countries (Band A). This difference is the highest of all nine GLOBE dimensions for Greece.

Although respondents perceive Greek society as high on individualism, it would not be wise to characterize Greek culture as such, based on these findings. The gap indicated by the results of this dimension brings forward the wish to return to older times, when concern for others was more important than individual success. Greeks have learned to take initiative, and have a strong entrepreneurial spirit. However, they do not easily work well with others, especially in organizational settings. It is common for those in position of power to take all the responsibility and delegate only to a limited extent, because their subordinates are neither trained nor encouraged to work in teams. Team spirit is reached only in cases of emergency. In Greek history, there are instances where prominent Greeks have overcome their differences joining together when important decisions had to be reached. However, it seems that once the danger was over, the need to act as a team faded and individuality prevailed again.

An important characteristic in Greek societal culture is the distinction between in-group and out-group, which affects significantly the ways in which Greeks relate to others (Triandis, 1972). The in-group usually includes family, relatives, and friends and there is a lot of protection, trust, support, and cooperation between its members. The out-group is often viewed with hostility and relations with out-group members are often characterized by suspicion and mistrust. According to Doumanis (1983), in traditional Greek communities social relationships were polarized, being either positive or negative with no room or neutral gradation in between the two. This explains the lack of cooperation between management and employees or between state officials belonging to different political parties. However, any stranger or foreigner is a potential in-group member and receives excellent treatment because of the emphasis tradition places on *philoxenia* or friendliness to strangers.

As Herzfeld (1987) observed, one finds in the mosaic of Greek culture a mixture of the traditional and modern that cannot easily be separated. Although the largest percentage of the Greek population lives in urban centers, such as Athens, Thessaloniki, and Patras, most Greeks have their roots in the rural communities. Thus, although leading the life of a modern city dweller with fast and busy schedules and little time for team spirit and collectivism, they identify with their own or their parents' village community and long for the type of institutional collectivism that prevailed there. The first thing two Greek strangers do when they first meet is try to find out their place of origin. If they happen to come from the same geographical area or happen to know someone from each other's area, this can form enough of a basis for cordial social relations. Strong or influential members of a village, who have "made it" in large cities, often become a source of jobs or contacts that lead to employment and it is still common to find in large organizations high percentages of employees coming from the same province that happened to be the owner's or the top manager's province.

The "Should Be" results of GLOBE confirm the research, which was carried out in Greece by Hofstede 15 years ago (Hofstede, 1991). Greece was among the countries showing a strong desire for collectivism. This was apparently due to the fact that respondents in Hofstede's research, all belonging to the same firm, felt as members of the in-group that they had developed solidarity among themselves. The "Should Be" Collectivism scale also reflects the critical attitude toward antagonism and distrust often evident in Greek society.

On the societal level, as a great portion of the population has moved to the cities and relationships have become more impersonal, Collectivism even at the inner group is perceived as low although it is highly desirable among respondents. As we can see in the study, the coefficient on what the situation "Should Be" is especially high and places Greece at Rank 5 in this dimension. Therefore, Greeks seem both to miss Collectivism and to realize that they have to work together in order to be successful as Europeans and develop team spirit if they want to develop as a country. It is therefore the task of top managers to transform the organization into a big extended family, in order to make their people feel as members of the inner group and achieve the results of teamwork. In fact, most executive training in modern Greek firms today aim at improving teamwork and systematic efforts have already brought promising results, as expressed by many consultants working in that field (Broome, 1996).

In-Group Collectivism. This dimension describes the degree to which individuals express pride, loyalty, and interdependence in their families. On the "As Is" dimension, Greece shows a medium to high score of 5.27 and ranks 35 among the GLOBE countries (Band B). The rank Greece holds in the "Should Be" score is 42 (Band B). The difference between the current and desired state of affairs is negligible (0.19). It seems that on the issue of family pride, respondents feel that the Greek society is on the right track.

The bond of family has an unbreakable connection to the development of Greek society. Throughout the tradition of centuries and with the passing of different forms of family, from the patriarchal family found in continental Greece to the matriarchal family found in the Greek islands, the family bond has constituted the first and strongest societal group through which individuals develop their personal identity.

In-Group Collectivism is expressed in the form of most small to medium-size Greek businesses of the past decades. The majority of these businesses preserve their family character throughout their life and, very often, the motivation for establishing them stems from the need to create a safe working environment for members of the family. There are many examples of companies in Greece that have developed while preserving their family nature. These companies face the serious problem of transition, for example, when the founder grows and when some other member of the family taking over is not necessarily able to keep the business alive.

Note that the Greek family includes not only parents and children. The elderly are always included as well as aunts, uncles, cousins, nephews, and nieces, and relationships with in-laws are also important. Younger members of the family enjoy a high degree of support from the family and older members enjoy in turn a lot of care in their late years. It is very common for mothers of young children to spend evening hours tutoring their children and for grandmothers to baby-sit for their grandchildren, while their daughters or daughters-in-law are out at work. Also, in times of illness, there are always family members who will take a turn at the sick person's bedside. Perhaps the support provided by the family partly explains the facts that Greece has the longest mean life expectancy in Europe, the lowest suicide rate in Europe, and a very low percentage of children born outside marriage.

The family in Greece manages to replace the gap in organized state services in the area of education, health, day-care centers for children, and care for the elderly. At the same time, it serves as a means to control behavior of its members. As described by Gage (1987) in a discussion he had with a criminal lawyer, the latter had told him that almost all his clients involved in a crime were more concerned about their family's reaction than about their judge's verdict.

In conclusion, we must mention the fact that the family bond has been going through a difficult period throughout the world and this has inevitably touched Greece. The relationship between family members is becoming detached, divorce rate is increasing, and this phenomenon is especially important for the Greek society, if we take into account that the Greek society is largely supported by and draws its strength from the family institution.

Gender Egalitarianism. This dimension measures the extent to which role differences between the different gender are minimized. Greek society scores comparatively high on this dimension (3.48, 27th, Band A), although restrictions placed on women, due to their dual role in work and family settings, are commonly evident (Papalexandris & Bourantas, 1991). With its "Should Be" score of 4.89, Greece ranks 15th among other GLOBE countries and again in Band A.

One would expect less Gender Egalitarianism because the Greek society held until recently a traditional and more inflexible position regarding the independence of women and their involvement in important aspects of economic and political life. However, anthropologists have argued that the Greek society affords Greek women a lot of power at home, and it is true that women have held a most important place in communities where men were absent for long periods of time, due to emigration, work at sea, or wars. Traditionally in the presence of men, women were expected to serve and make men feel like masters in the home. Young women would often marry according to their parents' will and they would gain status after bearing children, whereas the mother-in-law was a most important figure in rural communities.

Ethnographer Irvin Sanders (1962), who studied rural parts of Greece in the early 1960s, reported that when he asked a villager how many children he had, he replied "two children and one girl," referring to the preference for sons. As fathers needed to provide daughters with *prika* or dowry in order for them to get married, daughters were often considered as financial burdens. Today, the dowry system does not exist and equal treatment is given to both male and female children, who share the overprotectiveness and financial sacrifices of their parents and are strongly encouraged to study and make progress in their lives.

Although the presence of women in top levels of the hierarchy is still limited, according to Dubisch (1986), most of the power of Greek women remains out of public display. Women have demonstrated that they can play an important role within Greek society as professionals, academics, and executives, in both the public and the private sectors. Women outnumber men gaining entrance to universities, women managers have been very successful in the services sector and, over the next few years, trends show that they will be an important part of the business world. Still, the largest proportion of responsibility with respect to childrearing and housework is carried out by women, who seem to manage particularly well in most cases, largely due to the support of the extended family (parents and close relatives) still prevailing in Greece.

Humane Orientation.   Humane Orientation is defined as the effort and practices that a society shows in support of human beings including caring, generosity, concern, and friendliness. Greek society scores 3.34, which positions it very low (59th, Band D) among the 61 GLOBE countries. The "Should Be" score is 5.23 and puts Greece on 48th position in Band B. The difference can be interpreted such that the respondents feel that in the Greek society there should be more generosity, concern, and friendliness among people.

One must however look closer at the Greek society in order to understand the respondents' views. A person not familiar with Greek culture may gain the impression that Greek society is actually low on Humane Orientation. The fact is that it is much lower than what respondents would like it to be and this high desire for humanism is deeply rooted in Greek traditional values, which respondents see as being threatened in an era of commercialization and cut-throat competition.

One of the most well-known traditional Greek values has been the offer of *philoxenia* or hospitality. According to Fermor (1958), *philoxenia* is based on a genuine and deep-seated kindness, the feeling of pity and charity toward a stranger who is far from home, as in ancient Greek the word *xenos* means both stranger and guest. Greek hospitality especially in smaller communities is one of the reasons that many tourists keep coming back to Greece. The visiting foreigner or the newly met person is considered a potential friend until he or she proves the opposite.

Of course, this contradicts the already mentioned antagonism and distrust often shown by Greeks. The explanation can be found in the distinction between in-group and out-group described by Triandis (1972). In spite of the apparent contradiction, the independence and individualism of Greeks coincide with the strong loyalty and even sacrifice for the in-group or for appropriate others. According to Hart (1992), who studied rural Greece, individuality is admired whereas autonomy, which disregards needs of family or community, is condemned.

As Broome (1996) describes, closely related to hospitality is generosity, or the overwhelming spirit of giving that accompanies true friendship in Greece. A person may make real sacrifices to help a friend in need. However, if something goes wrong in the relationship or the person joins a conflicting interest group, the situation may change drastically and strong antagonism may develop.

An example from the recent past shows the difference between Greek culture and the West in Humane Orientation. In 1993, during the campaign for parliamentary election, one of the two major candidates was in bad health and apparently unable to rule the country as before. The opposite party, following advice by foreign consultants, used this as an argument against their opponent. Contrary to what foreign advisers had believed, the weak candidate did not lose any of his supporters, who felt very sympathetic toward him, and he finally won the election.

It is true that Greeks of all social levels have traditionally been humanitarian and supportive toward their fellow men. It is still common for poor people to survive on neighbors' support, and charity donations are very common, even from people with limited financial means. Almost all major educational institutions, hospitals, and public buildings owe their existence to donations from diaspora Greeks and there is a widespread tradition to help the needy around the world. Greece at present supports 1.5 million economic immigrants from poor neighboring countries and also helps those from the Third World ones. At the same time, the state is expected to contribute to its citizens' welfare, something that it cannot do to a satisfactory degree, thus creating dissatisfaction and unrest. In general, people fear that the impersonal nature of life in urban centers will deprive them of their cultural qualities of caring for each other. It is a fact that, over the last few years, with increasing population and alienation in large towns, people feel uneasy. Not knowing your neighbor and not being able to know whether or not to trust him or her is something against traditional values. We believe that this change is reflected in the low score perceived in Humane Orientation. Furthermore, in work settings the need to increase competitiveness seems to threaten existing employee-friendly practices, tenure, and supportive labor measures and this is something people resent in general.

Overall, one may conclude that, as in the general GLOBE results, Greek respondents show a great desire for a stronger Humane Orientation and this desire makes them see the present situation as worse than what an outsider or an objective observer would perceive it to be. Thus, higher expectations and a longing for what is universally considered good is evident across respondents and explains the gap between the "As Is" and the "Should Be" findings.

Power Distance.   This dimension describes the extent to which a society accepts and endorses authority, power differences, and status privileges. Greece has a comparatively high "As Is" score of 5.40 (21st, Band A) and a very low "Should Be" score of 2.39 (52nd, Band D). According to Hofstede (1991), a large Power Distance coincides with might prevailing over right—the powerful having privileges and the ability to use force over subordinates. This is something found for powerful people (influential in politics, the media, or business) in countries all over the world, which most respondents consider as undesirable and unfair. A person who is not familiar with Greek society may conclude from the Greek "As Is" score that it is a hierarchical society, where the ordinary people's opinions are not considered and where ordinary people are kept at a distance from the powerful. However this is not the case. Greek people have the tendency to challenge, question, and criticize authority and react fiercely whenever they feel that their rights are violated. In fact, industrial relations have traditionally been a difficult area for large firms and union leaders fought strongly whenever their views were not taken into consideration. So, it might well be that the "As Is" Power Distance is perceived to be comparatively high; however, it is believed that due to the desire of Greeks for a more egalitarian and participatory society, the "Should Be" scores for Power Distance are extremely low. Holden (1972) states in his book on Greeks, that they are indeed not only natural participators but compulsive egalitarians: Rank, class, or status mean little to them. According to Broome (1996), Greeks are not the least intimidated by status or hierarchy and they believe they have the solution to all company or state problems. Every individual has a strong opinion about how things should be done and doesn't hesitate to let that opinion be known.

Today, the tendency toward globalization requires the involvement of the individual and his or her conscious participation in the common vision. Greek management is still characterized to a large extent by formal relationships, which no one approves of and everyone questions. A different type of employee involvement is evident in some modern organizations and the perspective of spreading this to other organizations and institutions of Greek society is highly desirable and strongly demanded.

Uncertainty Avoidance. This dimension refers to practices adopted and encouraged within the framework of a society in order to avoid the uncertainty existing among its members, often at the expense of experimentation and in favor of strict rules and strong legislation. Greece scores 3.39 (57th, Band D) on the "As Is" dimension and 5.09 (17th, Band A) on the "Should Be" dimension,

Respondents perceive a very low level of Uncertainty Avoidance in their society and desire it to be substantially higher. Greece seems to lack preventive measures for coping with critical situations (wood fires, floods, road accidents, crimes, etc.). The Greek state has been often accused for improvisation in solving problems and a lack of planning for facing emergency situations, which cause panic and are met with great difficulty and often without success.

The results for Uncertainty Avoidance match the results for Future Orientation. Many in the Greek society seem reluctant to plan ahead, because they feel uncertain about the future and there is a common attitude of "who knows what lies ahead?" According to Hofstede (1991), Greece showed high ranking in the Uncertainty Avoidance index. This is only in agreement with the GLOBE "Should Be" score for Greece. Individuals in High Uncertainty Avoidance cultures are more anxious and also more expressive, where people appear busy, emotional, aggressive, and active. This description coincides with the impression one gets from watching Greeks. Greeks tend to react to uncertainty and unpleasant situations with sociability. Talking, eating, drinking, dancing, discussing the world's problems, and telling jokes seem to provide a release from tension and anxiety. In order to fight uncertainty, Greeks were and are still attracted to state jobs, which in the past offered tenure and are still considered as more secure. Thus, voters exercised great pressure on politicians to obtain them. Although the heavily staffed state sector allows little room for such practices any longer, political parties have for many years secured votes in exchange for the certainty offered by a tenured job in the state sector.

Hofstede (1991) also found that countries with high Uncertainty Avoidance, in an attempt to moderate uncertainty, have a complicated system of laws and rules as citizens show mistrust for their country's institutions. This is true for Greece, where the complicated legal framework, lending itself to various, often unexpected interpretations is something that, although designed to fight uncertainty, adds to the general feeling of uncertainty together with constant mistrust about state institutions. Here we must notice that our respondents were mostly managers in secure jobs, so they would welcome lower levels of uncertainty. At the same time, risk taking, innovation, and experimentation are common among a considerable number of businesspeople, who choose to engage in entrepreneurial activities. This comes as no surprise if one takes into consideration Hofstede's distinction between Uncertainty Avoidance and risk avoidance. Many entrepreneurial firms are created at high risk, mostly to satisfy the individualism of their founders, but also because people who have a high motive to assume entrepreneurial risk have in fact high levels of tolerance to uncertainty. Research among people employed in the state sector when compared to those employed in less secure, more demanding jobs, has shown that people attracted to more secure jobs, as is the case with most of our respondents, have different personality traits and somehow higher security needs (Bourantas & Papalexandris, 1999).

It seems that for Greece, the high score of perceived Uncertainty Avoidance does not hinder large parts of the population from engaging in entrepreneurial activity. Greece has the highest percentage of entrepreneurs within the EU (Papalexandris, 1997). Broome (1996) believes a lot of safeguards against uncertainty are provided by the extended family and friends/members of the in-group. Insecurity caused by the societal environment and the lack of infrastructure can be met by establishing personal connections, and Greeks invest a lot of time and effort in that direction.

Summary of Findings on Societal Culture

Summarizing the findings, we can conclude the following about perceptions of societal culture by our respondents.

- They are not satisfied with the performance orientation of their society.
- They wish that things should be planned more carefully.
- They are not satisfied with the high levels of assertiveness shown.
- They show a longing for more collective ways of life that was the rule in the past but is now threatened by rapid urbanization and modern ways of life.
- They value family life and gender equality.
- They also long for a more caring society, which was the rule in the past.
- They resent power distance, which they perceive as high.
- Finally, they perceive their society as highly uncertain and would like this situation to improve.

These general findings are discussed in combination with results on leadership at the end of the following section of this chapter.

3. GLOBE AND LEADERSHIP

Literature Review on Leadership in Greece

The word *leadership,* literally translated as "igesia" in Greek, is a word usually used to describe the top-rank officials in large institutions such as the army, ministries, or political parties. Only during recent years, and after extensive use in executive seminars and business courses, has the term acquired the meaning it has in the English language.

On the contrary, the term *leader,* when used alone as a noun, for example, "he is a leader," refers to the person who has some kind of special quality or charisma to guide people, whereas when used in combination with another word, for example, "the leader of the party," simply refers to the person who is on top of the hierarchy.

The distinction between leaders and managers is somewhat difficult for those not having studied management. In fact, there is no corresponding translation for *manager* in Greek language. For higher levels, the word most often used is *diefthintis,* meaning director. Indeed, many managers still carry out their jobs in a more directive and controlling approach than is commonly found in Western companies. Research in the mid-1960s showed that autocratic management was a consequence of the family structure and the lack of separation between ownership and management (Alexander, 1968).

Today, even in family-owned companies, which could be characterized as patriarchal, very rarely does the directive style mean harsh treatment to employees. According to Broome (1996), the successful Greek manager is expected to take care of employee needs as they arise, showing an interest in their family problems, because for most Greeks, the family is more important than work. The personal relationship with employees and the ability of the manager to develop and maintain personal connections with both subordinates and colleagues is often what distinguishes a leader from a manager, especially at the middle levels of hierarchy.

As already mentioned, very important at this level is the ability of the leader to appeal to the *philotimo* or "love of honor" of his or her employees and create conditions that allow employees to show their creativity, diligence, and dexterity, while creating a system that encourages and supports individual initiative. One must take into account that Greeks are very hard-working people, when the situation requires it, and it is the personal quality of diligence, not work itself that is important (Lee, 1959). Meaningless and routine work is viewed with disdain and this explains the low productivity of the public sector, which is nevertheless sought by employees because it offers job security. Yet many people, showing lower productivity in lower paid jobs of the public sector, will take an extra job to support their family. Recent statistics have shown that Greeks work the longest working hours per year in the EU. (International Labour Organizaton [ILO], 2003).

Very important is the ability to treat each employee as a person. As stated by Broome (1996), "In Greece you must manage persons, not personnel." As already mentioned, Greeks are both very individualistic and independent. According to Fermor (1958, 1966), an English author who fought in Greece during World War II and has studied Greek culture extensively, "Every Greek may be said to comprise a one-man splinter-group"; in fact, the Greek word for person, *atomo,* comes from the word that was believed by ancient Greek scientists to be the indivisible unit of the universe. In the work environment, employees are always inclined to fight against perceived limitations on their personal freedom, independence, and individual rights.

In view of all this, being granted the attribute "leader" in a Greek organization is not a simple task but a great achievement. Greeks do not like to be told what to do without proper explanations. They dislike orders and are not at all intimidated by status. They face difficulties in cooperating and are very quick to question authority and mistrust superiors. Therefore, only the person who can win approval, encourage teamwork, and be recognized as superior due to his or her qualities, skills, fairness, and integrity, can be characterized as a leader. Such a person can achieve levels of performance from his or her group that far excel what would be considered as normal by international standards.

This overall picture of Greek leadership is further analyzed with the help of data from media analysis, focus groups findings, and factor analysis of leadership results from GLOBE.

Media Analysis

In this section, we examine the concept of leadership and the special practices, which are considered as characteristic of a successful manager/leader according to media analysis. For the needs of GLOBE, we carried out media analysis in a series of magazines and newspapers with economic contents.

The magazines used have permanent columns on leaders, who are selected due to their success and their contribution to the high performance of their firm. These media were *Economicos Tachydromos, Epilogi, Industrial Review, Capital,* and *Know How.* The newspapers were *Naftemboriki, To Vima,* and *Express.* The 2-month period covered by the study commenced January 1, 1998 and ended March 1, 1998. The main objective was the identification and collection of expressions assigning characteristics to well-known managers/leaders, in order to arrive at the ideal profile according to the media.

At this point, we must stress the difficulty we faced in identifying leadership characteristics among persons described. The Greek press gives special emphasis to what top managers, both professionals and entrepreneurs, have done. Therefore, the classic presentation of top managers starts with their studies and continues with the field they have chosen and how they have developed in their career or in their business. This presentation is given without any special mention to their personality, behavior, and practices, which contributed to their success. Thus, no valuable information on leadership qualities of managers could be drawn. In some cases, where special reports were made on important business personalities, the qualities mentioned were that they were self-made or were able to take over and expand a small family business. The ability to overcome obstacles of the external environment and to identify new business opportunities was also stressed. Entrepreneurial ability was considered important for top managers and, if they had succeeded in staying for many years in business, this was also attributed to their humanistic feelings and supportive behavior to their employees, which had secured their loyalty and commitment.

Apart from these top managers making the headlines, the list of managers' characteristics according to the articles is presented in Table 21.4.

From the 150 top-managers that were in the analysis, every one was characterized by more than one adjective. As we can see from the result of the research, the basic characteristic of the successful Greek manager is experience: 30.14% referred to the experience of the managers. Other characteristics that were mentioned were intelligence and decisiveness, innovation, administrative ability, risk taking, and the ability to inspire.

Most important for the overall understanding of Greek leadership are the results from the two focus groups, which follow.

TABLE 21.4
Media Analysis Results

Characteristics	Rank	Number of Times Mentioned	Percentage %
Experienced	1	88	30.14
Intelligent	2	27	9.25
Decisive	3	25	8.56
Innovative	4	19	6.51
Good administrator	5	18	6.16
Risk taker	6	14	4.76
Inspirational	7	11	3.73
Enthusiastic	8	9	3.08
Forecaster	8	9	3.08
Independent	8	9	3.08
Cooperative	11	7	2.40
Encouraging	12	6	2.05
Sincere	12	6	2.05
Problem solver	14	5	1.71
Improver	15	4	1.37
Positive	15	4	1.37
Well-prepared	15	4	1.37
Fair	18	3	1.03
Diplomatic	18	3	1.03
Unifier	18	3	1.03
Mind stimulator	18	3	1.03
Unique	18	3	1.03
Calm	23	2	0.68
Clear, concrete	23	2	0.68
Consultative	23	2	0.68
Orderly	23	2	0.68
Mediator	23	2	0.68
Morale booster	28	1	0.34
Formal	28	1	0.34
Total		**292**	**100 %**

Focus Groups on Leadership

Here, we present the results of two focus groups. The first was conducted among executives attending an executive part-time MBA program and working mostly as mechanical and electrical engineers. The discussion aimed at selecting the most important leader from both the historical/political and the organizational perspective. The second was conducted in a Greek semistate bank. The discussion covered the respondents' perception of characteristics possessed by a manager versus those of a leader.

First Focus Group.   The two persons selected as outstanding leaders were E. Venizelos, a political leader, and A. Onassis, a business leader.

Eleftherios Venizelos is considered the principal political leader of modern Greece. As the country's prime minister at the beginning of the 20th century, he had the vision to liberate all parts of Greece, which were still under Turkish occupation. He won victoriously the two Balkan wars and started the Asia Minor expedition counting on the support of Western allies. When the latter withdrew their support, the Greek army were defeated; consequently Greece was forced to accept 1.6 million Greek refugees from the coast of Asia Minor. Yet his political insight, diplomatic talent, ability to mobilize his people, and commitment to the vision of freedom for the homeland have won him perhaps the top position among political leaders of modern Greece.

Aristotelis Onassis was born at the beginning of the century in Smyrna situated in Asia Minor. After the loss of Asia Minor, he was forced to emigrate and subsequently started his business ventures trading tobacco in Argentina. He soon developed a fleet of whalers, which he then turned into cargo ships and later into tankers of very large tonnage. In 1956, when the Suez Canal was blocked, he was able to carry oil fast, by transporting it around Africa with his huge oil tankers, and this made him a billionaire. His legendary affair with the famous opera singer Maria Callas and his marriage with Jackie, the widow of U.S. President John Kennedy, occupied the headlines for many years. He was the founder of the Greek airliner Olympic Airways and left a huge fortune after his death, including a large medical center in Athens, a scholarship foundation for students in higher education, and the Onassis world prizes for people showing outstanding achievements in the area of humanities, arts, and sciences. His intelligence, business intuition, global awareness, risk taking, ability to adapt and take advantage of unexpected events, together with his love for the homeland, place him at the top of business leaders in the eyes of Greeks and have won him also a position among the best known business leaders of the world.

In general we can conclude that charismatic leaders receive high recognition in Greece and this happens in general after their death, as the tendency to criticize and find faults with others stands in the way. Some unobtrusive measures such as statues, street names, banknotes, and monuments all point to the heroic figures of the past. These are leaders who inspired their people in the struggle for independence, political or state leaders and scientists with international reputation. Businesspeople are less represented although there is much oral conversation surrounding those who started with poor means and made it to the top.

Second Focus Group.   All the participants agreed that there are important differences between a manager who tries to carry out his or her duties correctly and a leader who creates a team, prepares its members for action, and gets them all to work together. The differences, which were stressed, are presented in Table 21.5.

The conclusions reached from this focus group describe the leader as someone with vision, inspiration, and the ability to be persuasive. He or she is a person who can motivate others and present new ideas, which can be materialized. The leader is thought to be a charismatic person with a strong personality, who is able to win the acceptance not only of his or her subordinates but also of his or her superiors.

TABLE 21.5
Differences Between Managers and Leaders

Manager	Leader
• Puts emphasis on results.	• Puts emphasis on results and on people.
• Plans, organizes, and controls the different branches.	• Gets results through the trust she or he has won.
• Assigns tasks and directs in the best possible way.	• Motivates his or her team to do their work in the best possible way.
• Assigns power and responsibilities.	• Motivates not by giving orders but by persuading his or her employees.
• Dictates his or her will by giving orders.	• Persuades by giving example to others.
• Does not have the ability of the leader to stimulate his or her team.	• Creates the ideal environment and climate in order to motivate his or her people.
• Acts as the conductor who directs an orchestra with his or her wand.	• Differentiated from the other members of the team by his or her ability to help in the work.
• It is possible that she or he is good at his or her job without being a leader, like a good basketball player who does not necessarily make a good coach.	• Is the conductor but communicates with the orchestra without using the wand.
• His or her opinion dominates.	• Gains the admiration of those around him or her.
• Functions within already existing limits.	• Has vision.
• Takes initiatives and has ideas that cannot always be applied because she or he cannot get the rest of the team to collaborate.	• His or her opinion does not dominate.
• Attributes importance to bureaucratic details.	• Offers new ideas at difficult moments.
• Pays special attention to scheduling and control.	• Has the ability to persuade, to impress and influence others to accept his or her ideas.
• Not necessarily flexible and multifaceted and often avoids risk.	• Psychologically supports his or her team.
• Can use threats such as firing.	• Able to transform unproductive teams into successful, productive ones, making them realize that this is the correct way to work.
	• Often insubordinate, going against the rules and taking risks.
	• Talented and with a strong personality that helps him or her lead others, spread his or her vision and create enthusiasm.

GLOBE Results on Leadership

GLOBE used 21 leadership dimensions derived from a factor analysis of the entire GLOBE sample (see Table 21.6). Respondents were asked to give a score on a 7-point scale declaring the extent to which each of 112 leadership characteristics is hindering or contributing to effective leadership.

Among positive dimensions, diplomacy ranks the highest among Greek respondents, something quite expected because the ability to negotiate, to find a balance between opposite trends, to survive in changing circumstances, and to take advantage of unexpected events requires a great deal of "diplomatic" skills, which business leaders must by all means possess.

TABLE 21.6

Country Mean Scores for Leadership Dimensions and Subdimensions

Dimensions *Subdimensions*	*Mean Score*	*Rank*
I. Charismatic	*6.01*	*13*
1. Performance Orientation	5.82	48
2. Visionary	6.19	24
3. Inspirational	6.25	25
4. Integrity	6.27	20
5. Self-Sacrificial	5.42	10
6. Decisive	6.18	9
II. Team Oriented	*6.12*	*3*
7. Team Integrator	5.76	10
8. Collaborative Team Oriented	6.19	12
9. Administratively Competent	6.18	8
10. Diplomatic	6.01	2
11. Malevolent (reverse score)	1.55	53
III. Self-Protective	*3.49*	*29*
12. Self-Centered	2.10	31
13. Status-Conscious	5.12	10
14. Conflict Inducer	3.62	47
15. Face Saver	3.05	23
16. Procedural	3.74	40
IV. Participative	*5.81*	*10*
17. Autocratic (reverse score)	2.14	51
18. Nonparticipative (reverse score)	2.25	52
V. Humane	*5.16*	*18*
19. Humane	5.02	22
20. Modesty	5.28	20
VI. Autonomous	*3.98*	*22*
21. Autonomous	3.98	23

The other three dimensions ranking high in the Greek sample describe a leader as administratively competent, decisive, self-sacrificial, and a team integrator. In all the aforementioned dimensions, Greece ranks among the first 10 countries in the sample of 61 countries participating in GLOBE. Greece also ranks high in the dimensions of collaborative team orientation, integrity, modesty, and humane orientation. The only dimension in which Greece shows a low position (48th out of 61 countries) is that of performance orientation, even though the score is 5.82 on a 7-point scale. Greek leadership is perceived to be lacking in this dimension, something already found at the societal culture level.

Greek leadership ranks low in the malevolent behavior, as well as in nonparticipative, auto-cratic, conflict inducer, and procedural behavior. However, relatively high scores appear in status consciousness, self-centered, and autonomous behavior. These dimensions have largely to do with a leader's "ego."

Factor Analysis on GLOBE Results for Greece.[2] Regarding leadership factors derived from the second-order factor analysis of the 21 first-order factors, Greek leadership ranks highly, such as in Team Orientation (3rd position), Participative (10th position),and Charismatic leadership (13th). In the remaining three factors, Humane Orientation, Autonomous, and Self-Protective Leadership, Greece ranks in the midrange, at the 18th, 22nd, and 29th position, respectively. Overall, very encouraging is the emphasis given to par-ticipative and collaborative leadership behavior, which seems to gain ground in modern com-panies and is the only way for offsetting strong individualism in the work environment.

The next step in the exploration of Greek leadership was to conduct a second-order factor analysis, in order to arrive at distinguishable types of leadership concepts. Six factors that explain approximately 50% of the variance were identified. They serve as basic indicators of Greek leadership concepts. Between sectors (finance and telecommunications) no differences in factor structure are apparent. In Table 21.7, the rotated factor matrix of the total Greek sam-ple is shown. Only variables with loadings higher than 0.30 are included under the factor in which they showed the highest value—provided they had a difference of at least 0.10 to the next highest loading.

According to the results of this analysis, we can characterize the six factors observed as described in Table 21.8. In Factor 1, we have at first the ideal charismatic leadership charac-teristics that were found as most desirable in both the media analysis and the focus groups. A charismatic leader in Greece is a morale booster and has vision, intuition, intelligence, and dynamism. These characteristics are held by the two prominent political and business per-sonalities the first focus group identified as outstanding leaders. In Factors 2 and 3, two types of negatively valued leadership profiles are obtained. Whereas Factor 2 denotes ruthless and tyrannical attributes, Factor 3 comprises dictatorial, elitist, self-centered, and individually ori-ented attributes. The remaining three factors all denote positive characteristics at least to some extent. Factor 4 describes human-oriented, supportive, generous and, generally speaking, low-profile leadership that is carefully following procedures. Here we can think of a leader that treats his or her employees fairly, combining a just and cautious behavior with kindness

[2]The GLOBE scales were designed to measure organizational- or societal-level variability (Hanges, Dickson, & Sipe, 2004). The scales were *not* intended to meaningfully differentiate among individuals within a particular soci-ety. However, even though the scales were not constructed to provide such information, in some cases it is interest-ing to assess whether similar factors differentiate individuals within a society. Country-specific factor analysis is intended as an exploration of the themes captured by GLOBE in a new domain, that is, individual differences within a society. It should be noted that, because of the within-society restriction of the GLOBE scales true-score variabil-ity (which was based on between-society differences), the loadings of the GLOBE scale's items on within-society factors should be lower than between societies (cf. Hanges, Dickson, & Sipe, 2004). Furthermore, one should not interpret the within- society factor analyses as replications of the GLOBE factor structure. And the absence of a GLOBE factor within a society should not be automatically interpreted as the factor being irrelevant to the people in that country. Rather, a factor may fail to emerge within a society even when that theme is extremely critical because there was no variability in how the individuals from a single society rated the items (e.g., they all rated the items a 7). Factor analysis requires variability and so a factor could fail to emerge because it is extremely critical or com-pletely irrelevant to the people within a society.

TABLE 21.7
Rotated Factor Matrix

	FACTOR					
	1	2	3	4	5	6
Morale Booster	.644					
Intuitive	.637					
Dynamic	.561					
Team Builder	.561					
Willful	.546					
Encouraging	.543					
Visionary	.520					
Confidence Builder	.498					
Asocial	−.493					
Hostile	−.482					
Win-Win Problem Solver	.472					
Clear	.472					
Decisive	.464					
Communicative	.461					
Collaborative	.459					
Calm	.452					
Integrator	.452					
Prepared	.400					
Convincing	.378					
Enthusiastic	.366					
Ambitious	.366					
Performance Oriented	.362					
Loner	−.339					
Intellectually Stimulating	.322					
Dependable	.311					
Sincere		−.680				
Inspirational		−.638				
Tyrannical		.625				
Self-Interested		.619				
Trustworthy		−.585				
Just		−.561				
Egocentric		.527				
Vindictive		.505				
Nonexplicit		.489				
Secretive		.482				
Improvement Orientated		−.470				
Positive		−.466				
Ruthless		.466				
Bossy		.454				
Provocateur		.436				
Evasive		.409				
Irritable		.350				

(Continued)

TABLE 21.7 (Continued)

	1	2	3	4	5	6
				FACTOR		
Ruler			.612			
Elitist			.532			
Egotistical			.463			
Nonegalitarian			.448			
Dictatorial			.443			
Domineering			.417			
Cynical			.404			
Individually Oriented			.365			
Cunning			.355			
Micromanager			.352			
Autonomous			.333			
Honest				.540		
Compassionate				.512		
Fraternal				.474		
Cautious				.470		
Class-Conscious				.464		
Modest				.464		
Patient				.445		
Procedural				.436		
Tender				.432		
Formal				.432		
Generous				.405		
Group Oriented				.378		
Logical				.365		
Self-Sacrificial				.365		
Self-Effacing				.330		
Loyal				.326		
Foresight					.748	
Plans Ahead					.711	
Motive Arouser					.595	
Able to Anticipate					.585	
Status-Conscious					.341	
Avoids Negatives					−.315	
Administratively Skilled						.480
Orderly						.458
Excellence Oriented						.433
Good Administrator						.428
Intragroup Conflict Avoider						.412
Intelligent						.397

Note. Extraction method: maximum likelihood. Rotation method: Varimax with Kaiser normalization.

TABLE 21.8
Description of Factors

Factor	Leadership Characterization
1	Charismatic/Ideal Leader
2	Ruthless-Tyrannical Leader
3	Egotistical-Elitist
4	Honest-Compassionate-Fraternal
5	Careful Planner
6	Administratively Skilled

and attention to employee needs. Factor 5 describes leadership attributes of planning ahead, foresight, and anticipating changes, which overall denotes future orientation. Factor 6 describes administrative skill, excellence orientation, intelligence, and reducing intragroup conflict.

Experience, one leadership characteristic very frequently met in the media analysis, is not included in the dimensions of the GLOBE study because it was not included in the 112 leader descriptions in the questionnaire. For Greek management, it means experience in dealing with management problems, external threats, and opportunities, having served for many years in a leading position, and having good knowledge of the Greek business environment.

At this point, we may conclude that the six leadership dimensions that resulted from the factor analysis seem to cover to a large extent Greek reality as already described, with most characteristics, however, loading as in the case of GLOBE's international results on the first factor, that of the ideal, charismatic leader.

4. CONCLUSIONS

Leadership and Societal Culture

The picture that emerged from the research on leadership is quite consistent with results from societal culture. A society where longing for collectivism, family values, and humane orientation is high normally respects leaders who treat employees fairly, are good team integrators, have integrity, are not tough, can raise morale, but are at the same time kind and pay attention to employee needs.

Concurrently, a society perceived as high in uncertainty values diplomacy, experience, administrative competence, and performance orientation, but they are also perceived as missing. Low-profile, modest leaders are also accepted because power distance is perceived as high and is not accepted in general. Charismatic leadership is also recognized in a society that values achievements of the past and is full of stories about heroic figures. In addition to the aforementioned, all the negative dimensions of leadership, such as autocratic, nonparticipative, or malevolent behavior, are strongly resented as could be expected and as found from the evidence across all countries in the GLOBE study.

Implications for Foreign Managers Working in Greece

Societal patterns of behavior influence the Greek work environment and leadership concepts. The foreign manager/leader in Greece should remember that leadership means:

- To spend a lot of time with members of his or her group.
- To spend time on establishing personal connections with peers and subordinates, as good human relations will speed up operations and improve communications and overall performance.
- To use a participative leadership style, listening to suggestions and inviting comments from employees.
- To avoid criticizing everyday reality as Greeks are eager to criticize their society but reluctant to listen to others doing so.
- To not expect much formality and attention to detail, making sure to constantly insist on deadlines if she or he wishes to keep a time schedule.
- To keep a firm position after reaching a well-informed decision and make clear that although the leader considers others' opinions, the responsibility rests with the leader.

Limitations and Suggestions for Further Research

This study of Greek societal culture and leadership is only a first step into what could become an in-depth survey of contemporary Greek societal and organizational culture. In order to have a full picture of the existing situation, a much larger sample would be necessary as well as subsamples of employees from different educational and employment backgrounds.

Despite those limitations, future research into the organizational settings of various organizations, in both the public and private sector, could pinpoint at particular differences and help leaders adjust their style accordingly. Something worth trying could also be a repetition of the survey so that differences that occurred since the GLOBE data were gathered could provide valuable information on changes over time.

Epilogue

Many cultural anthropologists and sociologists have stressed the duality and the various elements comprising the Greek mosaic. In his excellent book on Greece, Broome (1996) mentions several of these contradicting dualities. Some of them are:

- The geographical location between East and West and the simultaneous proximity with both sides.
- The orientation toward the past as a source of strength for heading into the future.
- The tendency to leave Greece for distant lands combined with the great tenacity in keeping ethnic identity.
- The common critical and pessimistic attitude with the great desire to enjoy life and engage in social activity.
- The urbanization of the Greek population combined with love for the place of native birth, with which most people keep close ties.
- The persistence of the traditional family institution and the independence young women enjoy lately.
- The close link with a religion that, although close to old tradition and early rituals, is full of feasts, music, and dancing and offers an informal atmosphere to members of its community.
- The love and support granted to members of the inner group and the rivalry and antagonism shown to out-group members.
- The resistance to imposed behavior and the voluntary self-sacrifice, when appeal to a person's philotimo is made by someone perceived as fair, friendly, and trustworthy.

- The fear of the unknown and the need to challenge the future by being venturesome, traveling abroad, and exploring new lands.
- The love of friendship and close ties and the enjoyment in engaging in continuous argument over political issues, constant criticism, and debate over facts and views.
- Flexibility as shown by the adoption of modern lifestyles and rigidity as shown by keeping family and religious traditions.

Perhaps the following statement, written by Holden (1972), best describes these characteristics of Greek culture:

> Greek identity as a whole is best seen as a constant oscillation between just such opposites as these. The spirit and the flesh, ideal and reality, triumph and despair—you name them and the Greeks suffer or enjoy them as the constant poles of their being, swinging repeatedly from one to the other and back again, often contriving to embrace both poles simultaneously but above all, never reconciled, never contented, never still. This perennial sense of tension between diametrically opposed forces is the essence of their existence-the one absolutely consistent feature of their identity since Greek history began. In the phrase of the Cretan novelist, Kazantzakis, they are double-borne souls. (pp. 27–28)

Although these remarks appear impressionistic and cannot be directly supported by the quantitative findings of this study, the author of this chapter believes that they reflect the cultural environment of Greece and could serve as guidelines for anyone wishing to work and live there. Managers and people of foreign origin should remember that Greece is a country with a complex past history where ancient myths blend with modern reality. This has led to a vast and diversified pool of values, attitudes, and behavioral patterns, from which individuals draw to form their own character and personality. Herzfeld (1985, 1987), an anthropologist who has conducted several ethnographic studies in Rhodes and Crete, describes Greece "as a country that falls disconcertingly between the exotic and the familiar." One can find traditional attitudes as expressed by the Orthodox Church along with the spirit of exploration expressed by Odysseus; the thunder power of Zeus blending with humane, egalitarian behavior; Athena's wisdom going hand in hand with haphazard, ad hoc solutions; and people longing for strong collectivism while sticking to their individualism. One may find people strongly desiring and considering appropriate for society what they themselves would be reluctant to practice, while also having high unrealistic expectations and tending to blame others or society for not being able to fulfill them. All this explains the strong gaps found between the "As Is" and "Should Be" GLOBE dimensions in societal culture.

To the modern world, Greece means classical antiquity, pictures of the sea, the sun, and the Greek islands, and Zorba, the famous Greek movie character, dancing and expressing his joy of life. In reality, it is all of these. It is a warm, sociable, vivid, argumentative society with people who can show high levels of performance, friendliness, collectivism, and support to each other as well as low motivation to achieve, antagonism, and strong individualism, depending on the circumstances. Being an effective leader in Greece can be both very challenging as one develops flexibility and deeper understanding of the appropriate characteristics and very difficult if one ignores them.

In Greece, as in any other part of the world, the leader-to-be can be compared to an explorer in social reality who sets off to find out about his or her peers, employees, and superiors, while also learning about him or herself. Because to "now thyself," according to ancient

Greek philosophers, was the optimum achievement. And there is no better way for becoming a leader than through self-knowledge and knowledge of your people, who can serve as a mirror glass where you can observe unknown parts of yourself.

Having arrived at the end of this short description of societal culture and leadership in Greece, I wish to thank Bob House, his scientific team, and all GLOBE contributors for providing me with the stimulus to look again with a fresh eye into my country and gain deeper insight into my past and present.

REFERENCES

Alexander, A. (1968). *Greek industrialists* (Research monograph series). Athens: Center of Planning and Economic Research.

Armstrong, A., & Markus, R. (1960). *Christian faith and Greek philosophy.* London: Darton, Longman, & Todd.

Bourantas, D., Anagnosteli, G., Mantes, G., & Kefalas, A. (1990). Culture gap in Greek management. *Organization Studies, 11*(2), 261–283.

Bourantas, D., & Papalexandris, N. (1999). Personality traits discriminating employees in public and in private sector organization. *International Journal of Human Resource Management, 10*(5), 858–869.

Broome, B. J. (1996). *Exploring the Greek mosaic: A guide to intercultural communication in Greece.* Yarmouth, ME: Intercultural Press.

Campbell, J., & Sherrard, P. (1968). *Modern Greece.* London: Benn.

Dimaki, J. (1974). *Towards Greek sociology of education* (2 volumes). Athens: National Center of Social Studies.

Doumanis, M. (1983). *Mothering in Greece: From collectivism to individualism.* London: Academic Press.

Dubisch, J. (1986). *Gender and power in rural Greece.* Princeton, NJ: Princeton University Press.

Fermor, P. L. (1958). *Mani: Travels in the southern Peloponnese.* London: Penguin.

Fermor, P. L. (1966). *Roumeli: Travels in northern Greece.* London: Penguin.

Friedl, E. (1962). *Vasilika: A village in modern Greece.* New York: Holt, Rinehart & Winston.

Gage, N. (1987). *Hellas: A portrait of Greece.* Athens: Efstathiadis Group.

Greece—Industrial Relations Background. (1998, August). *European Industrial Relations Review, 295,* 28–32.

Hanges, P. J., Dickson, M. W., & Sipe, M. T. (2004). Rational for GLOBE statistical analysis, societal ranking and test of hypotheses. In R. J. House, P. J. Hanges, M. Javidan, P. Dorfman, & V. Gupta (Eds.), *Leadership, culture, and organizations: The GLOBE study of 62 societies* (pp. 219–234). Thousand Oaks, CA: Sage.

Hart, L. (1992). *Time, religion and social experience in rural Greece.* Lanham, MD: Rowman & Littlefield.

Herzfeld, M. (1987). *Anthropology through the looking-glass.* Cambridge, England: Cambridge University Press.

Hofstede, D. (1991). *Cultures and organizations.* London: Harper-Collins Business.

Holden, D. (1972). *Greece without columns: The making of the modern Greeks.* Philadelphia: Lippincott.

House, R. J., Hanges, P. J., Javidan, M., Dorfman, P. W., Gupta, V.. & Globe Associates. (2004). *Culture, leadership, and organizations: The GLOBE study of 62 societies.* Thousand Oaks, CA: Sage.

International Labour Organization. (2003). *Key indicators of the labour market.* Retrieved January 9, 2005 from http://www.ilo.org/public/english/employment/strat/kilm/index.htm

Kazantzakis, N. (1966). *Travels in Greece.* Oxford, England: Bruno Cassirer.

Lee, D. (1959). *Freedom and culture.* Washington, DC, American University.

Mouzelis, N. (1978, July). *Modern Greece: Facets of underdevelopment.* London: Macmillan.

Organization for Economic Cooperation and Development. (2002). Greece. *OECD Economic Surveys.*

Papalexandris, N. (1995). Greece. In I. Brunstein (Ed.), *Human resource management in Western Europe* (pp. 113–134). Berlin: de Gruyter.

Papalexandris, N. (1997, November). *Issues and prospects of internationalization among Greek SME's.* Paper presented at the 24th International Small Business Congress, Taipei, Taiwan.

Papalexandris, N., & Bourantas, D. (1991). Attitudes towards women as managers: The case of Greece. *International Journal of Human Resource Management 2*(2), 133–148.

Papalexandris, N., & Bourantas, D. (1993). Differences in leadership behavior and influence between public and private organizations in Greece. *International Journal of Human Resource Management, 4*(4), 859–871.

Sanders, I. (1962). *Rainbow in the rock: The people of rural Greece.* Cambridge, MA: Harvard University Press.

Skouras, T. S. (1992). *The Greek economy: Economic policies for the 1990s.* London. Macmillan.

Triandis, H. (1972). *The analysis of subjective culture.* New York: Wiley.

22

▼▼▼▼▼▼▼

Leadership and Culture in Russia:
The Case of Transitional Economy

Mikhail V. Grachev
Western Illinois University

Nikolai G. Rogovsky
Management Consultant, Geneva, Switzerland

Boris V. Rakitski
Institute of Problems and Perspectives of the Country, Moscow, Russia

Countries of the former communist bloc adjust to global factors and conditions of socioeconomic development in parallel to their revolutionary efforts to substitute the totalitarian system of the past with democracy and the free market. Although the level of success of such a transition varies among different countries, Russia with no doubt is overcoming the most substantial change in macro- and microeconomic systems, in political structure, and in cultural norms and behaviors in the society. This makes it important to understand the current developments in Russia within the global context, and at the same time explain the factors that determine cultural configuration and effective leadership in transitional economy.

In the late 1990s, when the major GLOBE data collection was conducted, one could see Russia among visible global players, still on top in military expenditure of 12.3% in gross domestic product (GDP), with the largest territory covering 11 time zones. Economic transition in 1990–1998 resulted in deep crisis with an annual decline of GDP amounting to 7%, in addition to an annual decline in gross domestic investment of 13.7%. According to 1998 data, Russia comprised 146.9 million people, with the country having low indicators of life expectancy of 67 years. The unemployment rate was high at 13.3% even with high indicators of female economic activity (80.8%).

In the early 2000s, after the deep economic crisis in the previous decade, there are strong indications of revitalization and purification of the economy. Obsolete industries shrink. New advanced industries emerge at an incredible pace. Legislation is under construction. There are visible signs of openness of Russia to the global business community, and indications for civilized business practices.

The critical mass of people who act as entrepreneurs and as real business leaders is growing. A shift in management paradigm and organizational techniques is visible everywhere—in traditional mining and machine-building industries fighting for survival, in new fast-growing telecommunication, construction, business services, and trade. The business community has begun to understand that cultural variables (at both organizational and national levels) and certain leadership styles and behaviors could be the sources of competitive advantage. Multinational corporations transfer leadership skills and management know-how to Russia. Local managers and entrepreneurs seek compatibility in organizational methods and language of business with their foreign partners.

The period when the main GLOBE research was conducted coincided with the time of radical change in all spheres of economic and social life, such as property, financial system, or labor legislation. Mikhail Gorbachev's words about "chaos in the minds" adequately described the "mental model" of many Russians at that time. This is why the historic overview of Russian business culture and leadership at large should be combined with the specific analysis of transitional effects on culture and leadership. This chapter is guided by these current changes, and describes the culture specific characteristics of Russia with special focus on business culture and leadership in *a transitional economy*. GLOBE methodology and techniques help to understand that in contemporary Russia: (a) Instead of Soviet universalism of the past we find a fragmented managerial corps and cultural clusters; (b) types and characteristics of business culture are marginal when compared to the other countries, and Russian management does not fit easily into internationally recognized practices; (c) the profile of an effective business leader in Russia absorbs historical features of a nation, heritage of totalitarian system, and peculiarities of society-in-transition, and (d) there is a visible shift in public attention to business leadership with the media playing an important role in re-creating this leadership profile.

The chapter develops an interpretation of empirical data collected through Global Leadership and Organizational Behavior Effectiveness (GLOBE) Research Project. These data are based on the survey of 450 Russian managers in banking and finance, telecommunication, and food processing industries. Sampling from middle managers permitted GLOBE researchers to generalize the subculture of middle managers in the countries and the three industries studied, and increased the internal validity of the study by ensuring the homogeneity of the sample. But the design of the GLOBE project, in particular, through the combination of anthropological and psychological/behavioral traditions of culture assessment, broader range of variables not often considered in cross-cultural theories, and integrated theory of leadership, increased the generalizability of these findings beyond the culture of middle managers alone (den Hartog, House, Hanges, Ruiz-Quintanilla, & Dorfman, Lindell et al., 1999 House, Hanges, Javidan et al., 2004; House, Hanges, Ruiz-Quintanilla et al., 1999; House, Wright, & Aditya, 1997). The following chapter summarizes the main streams of research on the societal cultural and leadership profile in Russia; explores the history and logic of the development of Russian cultures; and focuses on GLOBE results and their interpretation by analyzing the data from prepilot study, focused interviews, GLOBE survey, and media analysis. The basic conclusions about the impact of culture on leadership in Russia are then finally summarized at the end.

1. RESEARCH ON THE CULTURAL PROFILE OF RUSSIAN BUSINESS AND MANAGEMENT

There is an extensive historiography on the roots of business values and behaviors related to the *pre-Revolutionary period* within Russia, such as memoirs of traders (*kuptsi*), books by Russian historians (Karamzin, 1892; Klyuchevski, 1904; Soloviev, 1913), business records, documents, and papers on the industrial development of the late 19th and early 20th centuries. However, during the *Soviet period* the phenomenon of business values and behaviors received limited attention in the USSR. The state was the only employer legally capable of exploiting economic freedom. The Communist Party had monopolized responsibility for moral judgments and created standards by manufacturing economic "heroes," such as politically loyal directors of state-owned enterprises or Party *nomenklature* leaders.

In the West, Sovietologists focused on entrepreneurship in Imperial Russia: the rise of Muskovy business activity in the 16th/17th centuries, cultural economic determinants of Russian business in the 19th and early 20th centuries, and the role of foreign businesses influencing Russian economy. They also gave insight relevant to business activity in the USSR such as the state's domination of the economy, the pseudo-entrepreneurial role of the Party, central planning as a determinant of Soviet economy, and the transfer of risk of entrepreneurship from the individual to the state (Berliner, 1976; Blackwell, 1994; Guroff & Carstensen, 1983; Owen, 1981).

In the *post-Socialist period,* a discussion started in Russia on the rebirth of entrepreneurship and on diversity of its cultural characteristics (Kuzmichev & Petrov, 1993; Shikhirev, 2000). Particular attention was paid to characteristics of Russian society influenced by: (a) traditional features of pre-Revolutionary Russia; (b) totalitarian heritage of the 20th century, and (c) the radical revolution in the economy and values in the 1990s transitional period.

Western academics gained access to Russian data and provided insights on, and international comparisons of, organizational practices and business ethics (de Vries, 2000; Fey & Beamish, 2001; Michailova, 2000; Puffer, 1992, 1994). These research activities were strengthened through interaction with Russian scholars (Ageev, Gratchev, & Hisrich, 1995; Anderson & Shikhirev, 1994; Hisrich & Gratchev, 1993, 1997; Puffer, McCarthy, & Naumov, 1997, 2000; Rogovsky, Bertocci, & Gratchev, 1997). Detailed case studies developed in the 1990s helped scholars to better understand the changing business practices in the Russian transitional economy.

Recent research initiatives successfully applied advanced Hofstede-type cross-cultural tools integrating the Russian data into the stream of *comparative management* studies (Gratchev, 2001; Naumov, 1996; Naumov & Puffer, 2000), and evaluated it in the context of Eastern European cluster, with its distinctive cultural practices (Bakacsi, Takacs, Karacsonyi, & Imrek, 2002).

2. GENESIS OF RUSSIAN BUSINESS CULTURE AND LEADERSHIP

Based on a literature overview, relating to the different periods of the nation's history, general features of business culture and leadership can be determined. They refer to aggregate characteristics of culture, the entrepreneurial potential of Russian people, their continuous fight against monopolism, and the search for effective principles of business management.

The Fundamental Characteristics

Russian culture is rich in contradictions, spiritual, and sustainable. With Russian contribution to the human civilization, it is seen as an important factor for global development. Being holistic and influential, Slavic-Orthodox culture is treated as one of few global cultures (Huntington, 1993). Historically developed characteristics of Russian culture are rooted in Slavic history, Orthodox religion, specific features of natural environmental, and unique social capital.

While Russia was growing through the centuries, its leaders were traditionally associated with the State, religion, or military. The first independent Slavonic state—Kievan Rus—was founded in 862 with the capital in Kiev. Later the center of gravity had shifted to the cities of Novgorod and Vladimir. Being subjugated by the Tatars, the Russian development was seriously stunned from the 13th through 15th centuries until in 1480 Muscovy (Moscow State) succeeded in uniting all the Russian states. After liberalization from the Tatars, Muskovy strengthened as the dominant principality, and Russian Tzars such as Ivan the Great (ruled in 1462–1505) and Boris Godunov (1598–1605) became respected historic figures. The Russian Orthodox Church was a great influence in society, and several spiritual leaders were deified and highly respected (such as St. Sergii of Radonezh).

Russian history was marked by repeated attempts to catch up with the West economically, politically, and culturally. At the same time the country's leaders pursued imperial ambitions to the south and east (Caucasus, Central Asia, Siberia, and Far East). Peter the Great (1696–1725) started "Westernization" by autocratic and barbarian means, proclaiming Russia as empire in 1721, and constructing St. Petersburg as its new capital. He was also an admired military leader, leading Russia to victories in several wars. The imperial gains were later consolidated by Catherine the Great (1762–1796).

Through the centuries Russia absorbed the basic values of both the West and the East—reason and inspiration. It served as a bridge between Western and Eastern cultural traditions, with a certain psychological dependence on both. These characteristics attracted much attention from the 18th century to early 20th century. According to one of the best Russian historians of the 19th century, V. Kluchevski, the national character combined, among others, such qualities as the habit of patient struggle against misfortunes and hardships, the ability to concentrate efforts, and the ability to cooperate within large geographic space (Kluchevski, 1904). The other famous intellectual, P. Chaadaev, defined contradictive Russian national character by such features as brutality and inclination to violence, impersonal collectivism, messianic, internal freedom, kindness, humanism, gentleness, and the search for truth (Chaadaev, 1991).

But in the 20th century under Communism these Russian characteristics were enforced by the specific Soviet (totalitarian) traits, such as the perception of the environment as hostile and dangerous, society's supremacy over the individual's goals, and a relativistic view of the morality with acceptance of double standards in life. One feature should be underlined. As D. Mikheev explains, "Real courage and cowardice can be measured only in the face of obvious, not just perceived, dangers. In these circumstances, Russians are anything but cowards" (Mikheyev, 1987, pp. 521–522).

Entrepreneurial Potential and the Fight Against Monopolism

In Imperial Russia, in the Soviet Union, and in post-Socialist Russia, one can see a vast amount of entrepreneurial potential. In the medieval Russian cities of Kiev and Novgorod, not only did merchants and artisans have political power and substantial wealth, but almost everyone above the lowest level of peasantry was engaged in one type of enterprise or another. In Imperial Russia, there was a substantial supply of entrepreneurial energy from both within and outside the business enterprise.

Entrepreneurs in the time of Peter the Great were traders who had created Europe's strongest military-industrial complex for Imperial Russia. The economic liberalism of Catherine the Great, in the late 18th century, had attracted the highest-ranking Russian nobles to entrepreneurial activities. After defeating Napoleon in 1812–1815 Russia was recognized as the great power, despite lagging behind the West institutionally and economically. The autocratic state was based on the predominantly agrarian economy and a feudal serf system.

The Industrial Revolution (which started in Russia half a century later than it had started in England) brought to Russia the real spirit of private entrepreneurship. The economic reform of 1861 gave freedom to peasants and activated different social groups. Industrial policy led to the "railway fever," and created favorable conditions for development of banking capital to be added to existing industrial capital. Talented Russian businessmen S. Morozov, L. Knopp, P. Ryabushinski, and others became founders of successful business empires in Russia and introduced many organizational innovations.

A vigorous level of entrepreneurial response existed even within the Soviet command system. There is a certain positive Russian entrepreneurial heritage, including courageous behaviors, great technical projects, and charitable traditions. However Russian history has been a continuous fight against monopolism. In contrast to the West:

> [Russia] appears to have largely retained, even in periods of rapid industrial expansion, an autocratic or patrimonial system (single-centered) which has sharply limited the autonomy of economic units in the use and disposal of resources, and which has preserved for those in political control the right, if only de jure, to determine the pace and pattern of economic development. (Guroff & Carstensen, 1983, p. 347)

The feature of pre-Revolution and Soviet societies—noneconomic domination of a small group of elite aristocracy or Party nomenclature over economic development—directly influenced economic policy (imperial foreign and oppressive domestic economic policy and the creation of the military-industrial complex), ownership (the state as the owner and employer, restriction of other ownership forms), institutions (legislation hostile to business, bureaucratization, and the standardization of structures and decisions), and culture (state paternalism and lack of personal responsibility and initiative).

In the Soviet era, the overwhelming majority of resources were under the control of a small group of monopolistic or oligopolistic coalitions.[1] The needs of the society were sacrificed for the sake of stability and the expansion of these coalitions. Their influence on political leadership secured decision making by the suppression of competition and by channeling public opinion. In general, their domination resulted in a 20 to 25-year delay in undertaking the required structural changes, causing Russia to lag behind international standards of quality of life.

---

[1]This phenomenon existed not only in the military-industrial complex, but also in such industrial areas as construction, mining, trade, and power engineering. For example, in the mid-1980s in the USSR one could identify only two main retail networks, one airline company, one oil-extraction ministerial monopoly, and nine ministerial conglomerates in defense industries.

In President Yeltsin's era (1991–2000), the question of the role of the state and large corporations in economic development became critical. Russia's economy was run by a small number of financial-industrial groups, arguably more powerful than the state. The oligarchs—leaders of industrial and financial empires, such as M. Khodorkovsky, V. Potanin, or R. Abramovich—displayed the new model for leadership in the Russian economy. The future of the country became largely dependent on the relationships between these major economic players and the government.

In the transitional economy under President Putin (2000–current), when the period of selling state property ("privatization stage") and rapid accumulation of capital is over, the discussions about the future of Russian business focus on interaction between large corporations and small businesses, on the role of the government in supporting large businesses, and on corporate governance. At this stage the main task for business is to manage capital effectively.

Three main assumptions help to understand the process of re-creating the Russian corporation in the early 2000s. First, the leaders of the large industrial corporations are interested in effective business and organizational development. They seek new ways to move from conglomerates of financially loosely linked entities to diversified corporations—whether with related or unrelated businesses.[2] This reflects the new stage in development of management mentality of the Russian business leaders, and the process of building the critical mass of people able and willing to manage their businesses effectively, in a "modern" civilized way. Second, many business leaders resist the current government actions to reprivatize the Russian economy. They consider that the government may not have a clear strategy to support the development of private business enterprises. Third, currently there is no visible stakeholders' influence on corporate design and development. There is no indication of any constructive dialogue between business and its stakeholders (unions, in particular) in the nearest future. The Russian corporations are displaying a unique, yet not clear national identity.[3]

Leadership Diversity

The multifaceted kaleidoscope culture of the current transitional society is different from the homogenous Soviet culture. Business leaders and managers in Russia are motivated by one, or a combination of the following business philosophies: *bureaucratic,* based on active initiatives but under state-run bureaucratic supervision; *pragmatic,* based on maximum profitability on a technocratic basis; *predatory,* based on the search for success through tough suppression of rivals including Mafia connections, growth by any means, cheating on partners, and consumers and the state; and *socially responsible,* based on linking business to the promotion of national interests, the resolution of social problems, and universal human values and beliefs.

---

[2]In May 1998, representatives of large financial-industrial groups (FIG), questioned by the European Bank for Reconstruction and Development (EBRD), ranked lack of finance and lack of competitive advantage among their most critical problems in business and organizational development. According to EBRD experts, however, the main FIG problems were structural weaknesses, poor corporate management, low cost-effectiveness, and the unclear role of the financial institution.

[3]The managing director of the International Monetary Fund, Michael Camdessus, in spring 1998 personally warned Russian President Yeltsin about the dangers of Asian-like "incestuous relationships between banking, government and corporate sectors" in Russia, comparing a growing oligarchy with the Asian system of *chaebols,* which are closed, family-controlled conglomerates with secret ties to banks and government officials (April 1998 press conference at the U.S.–Russia Business Council and at the National Press Club in Washington, DC).

The current transitional economy makes the carriers of those business philosophies very diverse, with a variety of economic and political interests. In the literature, a number of similar typologies exist to differentiate these carriers. Although they often do not go far beyond informal observations, they help to better explain the diversity of the Russian management community.

One such typology identifies the Old Guard, the New Wave, and the International Corps by linking their roots to the stages of Russian business history (Ageev et al., 1995). The first group, the Old Guard, consists of those who proved their talents in the past as leaders of large-scale projects, such as technological innovations in the space or defense industries. They exploit their access to key decision-making points and information, and use bureaucratic connections and control over resources. These people keep the leading positions in the large industrial corporations, or in the internationally competitive sectors of the economy (such as oil-and-gas, space, aviation, and shipbuilding). The second group, the New Wave of managers, initiated by economic reform, follows a different road to economic independence. They are former shadow-economy entrepreneurs, Young Communist League functionaries, or military officers who successfully transformed into businessmen. A large proportion of this group comprises young people, hungry for success and business education. The other part of this group can be called Unwilling Entrepreneurs. They are forced to take initiatives due to fear of unemployment and are involved primarily in small-scale trade transactions. Finally, there is a growing influence of the International Corps—Russian managers of multinational companies and representatives of the Russian diaspora, who strengthen economic ties with Russian business.

A similar system of categorizing Russian business leaders is suggested by M. de Vries (de Vries, 2000, pp. 71–72). He identifies two groups separated by a substantial generation gap. The administrators and bureaucrats who used to supervise the Soviet economy in the past make up one such group. However this group is not homogeneous. One subgroup consists of the present business elite, well connected and retaining privileged positions. The other subgroup among the older generation is focused on self-preservation, making superficial adjustments to maintain their status, but often giving lip service to the new economy. In the second group, de Vries places young, enthusiastic, talented people who recognize the opportunities of the new open society. This group also includes former black-marketers turning to legitimized business and children of Party nomenclature.

These categories indicate that typical carriers of management philosophies depend on their past history and practices, that generation gaps differentiate certain groups of business people, and that there are different combinations of basic business philosophies in society.

3. GLOBE DATA COLLECTION

The main body of GLOBE quantitative data was generated in 1995–1998 with additional data collected from media analysis in 2001. In order to create the cultural and leadership profile of Russia, Country Co-Investigators (CCIs) analyzed information accumulated through a pilot study, focused group interviews, the GLOBE survey of managers in the telecommunication, food-processing, and banking industries, and media research.

Pilot Study

In the 1994 pilot study, Russian CCIs surveyed 127 managers and entrepreneurs using the simplified design with questions linked to the GLOBE societal culture dimensions. The respondents represented key areas of the Russian economy: state-owned enterprises (5%), joint-stock companies (28%), limited partnerships (35%), individual businessmen (26%), and joint-ventures (6%). They did their business in manufacturing (31%), extraction industries (2%), agribusiness (3%), trade (20%), construction (4%), business services (30%), and communications (10%). The results of the pilot survey provided preliminary ideas for a generic profile of Russian culture.

Focus Group Interviews

Focus group interviews were designed along the GLOBE guidelines to provide a preliminary generic profile of leadership in Russia. Because the authors were aware of tremendous differences between various groups of managers/entrepreneurs, they targeted two groups. The first group of five managers/entrepreneurs represented those with experience in the Soviet economy and contemporary business organizations. They were mature people between the ages of 38 to 51 years, from the machine-building, construction, and publishing industries. The second group of three managers/entrepreneurs represented new businessmen aged between 22 and 36 years, who had started businesses only 1 to 3 years ago in such industries as telecommunications and wholesale trade. All respondents represented businesses in Moscow or in the Greater Moscow Region. This approach helped CCIs to understand leadership similarities shared by managers of Russia, and also uncover the differences in attitudes toward leadership, expressed by representatives of these two groups. The interviews, conducted in an informal atmosphere, were recorded and analyzed.

The Main GLOBE Study

When Russian CCIs were distributing GLOBE questionnaires and interacting with respondents, they faced a number of country-specific problems. First, not all the questions designed in the West were perfectly clear to those surveyed. In a few cases, the authors had to explain to those managers trained in the Soviet era basic conceptual management ideas in order to facilitate adequate response. Market-oriented human resource management was an example. Second, the culture of interviewing people had not been appreciated in the former Soviet era. Historically, people were suspicious about any unofficial attempts to learn about their views and assessments. Those interviewed were somewhat hesitant to give honest answers to some questions, especially those related to the profile of their organization and to personal data on employment and education. Third, motivation to contribute to GLOBE was low, with no visible quick benefits to respondents who complained about spending a lot of time on answering the questions. Fourth, in the turbulent economic environment of the 1990s it was hardly possible to access few organizations with deep and detailed research, and Russian CCIs had to look for creative solutions to accessing such a large number of managers from three industries. Industry-related data and statistics in a recently privatized economy were also not adequate. All these factors had added additional difficulties to the data collection. This explains why the CCIs could not effectively create the database for the organizational-level research.

The main GLOBE data were received from 450 managers in food processing, telecommunication, and banking/finance—150 managers in each industry. In order to access this large group, the authors targeted nationally recognized management training and development centers. In Moscow, respondents from banking and finance were accessed through a training and development center under the Ministry of Finance. The Academy of National Economy under the government of the Russian Federation helped with accessing managers in the food-processing industry. In St. Petersburg, the authors surveyed participants in management development programs at the Ministry of Communication's Training and Development Institute. The surveys were administered in two of the largest cities in Russia, but the trainees had come from different parts of the country—Far East, Siberia, the Urals, Southern and Northern Russia, and large cities of the Central Region.

Based on the data collected, the authors aggregated responses to demographic questions of the survey and designed the profile of the sample. The average age of respondents was 38.8 years, and the gender composition of the sample was 61.7% men and 38.3% women.

The questions related to citizenship and nationality in a transitional country that had just changed its name, anthem, and flag, and were often considered as ambiguous. Some people differentiated Russia and the USSR, whereas others did not: 96% had named the USSR and Russia as the place of birth, but Georgia and Ukraine (which were a part of the USSR in the past) were mentioned by only 2% of respondents accordingly. The average number of years that respondents had lived in Russia was 37.9. Out of the whole sample, three respondents had lived outside Russia for more than 1 year. Ethnic composition of the sample was very diverse: Russians 69%, Ukrainians 10%, Tatars 5%; other nationalities' percentage was under 2%, such as Kalmyk, Khakas, Georgians, Mordva, Belarus, Karel, Buryat, and German. Previously, in the USSR, the Jews were formally considered a nationality, and so 4% of the respondents mentioned being a Jew in answer to the nationality question. With regard to faith, believers accounted for 25%, out of which 22% considered themselves as Christians (including those of the Russian Orthodox Church) and 3% as Buddhists. When asked about their families, all of them reported that their fathers and mothers were born in the USSR. However, out of the whole sample 10% indicated that the Ukrainian language was spoken in the family, 1% German and 1% Hebrew.

The average employment profile of managers consists of: number of years employed 16.8 years, management experience 7.4 years, and employment in their current organization 8.6 years. Members of professional organizations totaled 40%, whereas 15% were actively involved in trade and industry associations. Respondents working for multinational corporations amounted to 5%.

Managers surveyed as to function were employed in production and engineering (42%), administration (28%), sales and marketing (15%), human resource management (8%), research and development (5%); the remaining 2% were in planning and other functions. The average number of subordinates reporting to those managers surveyed was 15.4, with the average number of administrative layers between them and the CEO being 2.1, and layers below 2.9. The average number of people employed in the organizations was 1,378. The use of one language, by managers, in their work was 83%, with 15% representing the use of two languages and 2% using three.

Educational levels for respondents were very high—total number of years in education was 15.5. The university/college background revealed that 61% was technical and 39% in economics, planning, and finance. However, in the food industry and telecommunications the number of technical graduates was even higher. Respondents that had received some training in Western management concepts and techniques amounted to 12% overall.

4. CULTURE PROFILES FROM THE PILOT STUDY

The pilot study helped to sketch a rough picture of Russian societal culture as perceived by managers, which is explored later, in detail, through GLOBE questionnaires. When asked about future versus present orientation, fewer respondents (44%) preferred future orientation versus present (56%). It was considered as the "positive surprise" for the people in the economy under hyperinflation and with strong demand for short-term return on investments. Respondents that relied more on power and authority accounted for 62%, as opposed to 38% who relied on consensus and team building. Few respondents (17%) preferred impersonal versus personal approach (83%) in dealing with people. However, the majority of respondents mentioned they lacked skills in human resources management. Most of the respondents were willing to accept the idea of establishing order and following the rules (69%), rather than exploiting the benefits of uncertainty (31%); adding to this are the entrepreneurs who need stability in the rules of the game in order to do business effectively. Political shifts, poor legislation, and rapid changes in the laws were treated as strong limitations for business leadership. It was a surprise to Russian CCIs to see how many entrepreneurs/managers (64%) preferred the individualistic versus collectivist approach, if one takes into consideration past history and the indoctrination of collectivist-socialist ideology in the former USSR. Also when asked to assess assertiveness, 52% preferred assertive to nonassertive behavior.

Based on this survey, the authors had summarized respondents' reactions to societal issues in a transitional economy as more present oriented, with modest assertive and individualistic behavior, but seeking more order and relying on personal approach in management.

5. GLOBE SCALES: SOCIETAL CULTURE RESULTS AND INTERPRETATION

The main results are based on societal culture profiles generated from the main study's GLOBE questionnaires. Figure 22.1 summarizes quantitative findings that lead to the most important conclusions. Here we review the data along each GLOBE dimension and then discuss the content of these findings and interrelations among the main results. Table 22.1 contains quantitative data. We make important observations of these results: Some dimensions display agreement between perceptions of Russian societal culture "As Is" and "Should Be," namely, Institutional Collectivism, In-Group Collectivism, Egalitarianism, and Assertiveness, whereas others display marked differences between perceptions of the Russian societal culture ("As Is") and respective cultural values ("Should Be"), namely, Power Distance, Performance Orientation, Future Orientation, Uncertainty Avoidance, and Humane Orientation. We now examine the results in the order mentioned here.

Institutional Collectivism is the degree to which cultural norms and practices encourage and reward collective distribution of resources and collective action. On Institutional Collectivism "As Is" Russia scores 4.50, which equates to Rank 17 (out of 61 GLOBE countries) within Band B (i.e. second-highest group of countries on that dimension). The societal culture, as it is perceived by the respondents, reflects traditional collectivistic practices rooted in historic traditions and Socialist indoctrination. At the same time, the "Should Be" score (3.89) reflects the cultural values endorsed by the responding managers, which place Russia much lower, at the end of the spectrum (Rank 60, Band D). The marked difference between "As Is" and "Should Be" scores is in line with the notion of a decline of traditional collectivistic values, which we attribute to the aforementioned process of fragmentation of the Russian society.

In-Group Collectivism is the degree to which individuals are encouraged in a society to express pride, loyalty, and cohesiveness in groups, organizations, or families. In-Group Collectivism "As Is" is relatively high (5.63, Rank 17), which places Russia in the leading

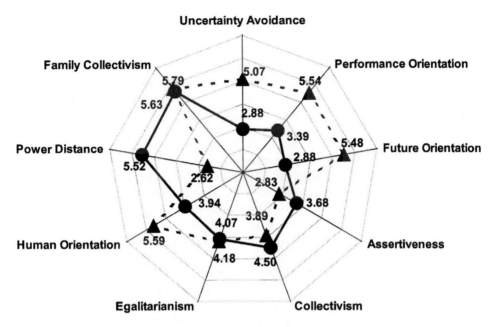

Figure 22.1.   Societal culture scales for Russia (circles– "As Is"; triangles–"Should Be").

TABLE 22.1
GLOBE Societal Culture Scores for Russia

	"As Is" Score[a]	Rank[c] (Band)[b]	"Should Be" Score	Rank[c] (Band)[b]
Institutional Collectivism	4.50	17 (B)	3.89	60 (D)
In-Group Collectivism	5.63	17 (A)	5.79	20 (B)
Gender Egalitarianism	4.07	2 (A)	4.18	49 (B)
Assertiveness	3.68	54 (B)	2.83	59 (C)
Power Distance	5.52	14 (A)	2.62	40 (C)
Performance Orientation	3.39	59 (C)	5.54	55 (D)
Future Orientation	2.88	61 (D)	5.48	34 (B)
Uncertainty Avoidance	2.88	61 (D)	5.07	18 (A)
Humane Orientation	3.94	37 (C)	5.59	18 (B)

[a]Country mean score on a 7-point Likert-type scale. [b]Band letters A–D indicating meaningful country bands for the scales A > B > C > D; the band widths are equal to 2*SD. [c]The rank orders for Russia relative to the 61 GLOBE countries.

group of countries on this dimension (Band A). Although the "Should Be" scores are still high (5.79, Rank 20), Russia ranks slightly lower (Rank 20, Band B).

Russia is stereotyped as a collectivistic culture. However, the GLOBE data necessitate a closer inspection, because on both collectivism dimensions, the cultural values ("Should Be") scores are lower than the respective "As Is" scores for culture perceptions. Historically, Russians lived on large open spaces and were forced by (a relatively hostile) nature to work together. An agrarian country for centuries, with low geographic mobility of peasants within the serf system, Russia was known for collective agricultural practices. The Russian Orthodox Church supported strong family ties and mutual support. The social framework did not permit a high level of individual freedom, and there were quite a few limitations to express individual competitiveness (winning was not always appreciated). In many cases, Russian collectivism was formal, prescribed by the social institutions.

Economic reforms of the second half of the 19th century and early 20th century started the process of destroying the collectivist traditions cultivated by the church and agrarian social system. However, the higher level of individual freedom (migration, developing labor market, access to education, democratic trends) after the Revolution was replaced with politicized artificial loyalty and obedience to the Communist Party, which controlled behavior and enforced people's conformity through total surveillance and purges. The Party also took responsibility for substituting family and natural group loyalty, with loyalty to the political system and to the State.

However, collectivist behavior was important in periods of high danger, such as the fight for national survival during the Second World War. In the early 1990s, when the struggle for survival in economic turmoil made mutual support important, some more reflections of collectivism became visible, especially among socially excluded groups. More contemporarily, indoctrination of Westernized behavior through media and the official doctrine of entrepreneurship are now pushing the country along the road of higher individualism and social fragmentation. That is why in current Russia striking contradictions between highly individualistic behavior and low social responsibility on the one side, with active networking for survival—often exploited by criminal structures—on the other side, are evident. From the trend toward less collectivistic cultural values on both dimensions, it is clear that Russia is inclined to transform itself into a more individualistic society.

Gender Egalitarianism is the extent to which an organization or society minimize gender role differences. The "As Is" (4.07) and "Should Be" (4.18) scores for Russia are quite similar, thus displaying relatively low concern of respondents with the difference between cultural values and practices in this case. In comparison to all 61 GLOBE countries, which show a clear trend from comparatively low perceived Gender Egalitarianism toward a much higher valued Gender Egalitarianism, in Russia, the current cultural practices are perceived as already highly Egalitarian (Rank 2, Band A), whereas the respective cultural value ("Should Be") ranks considerably lower (Rank 49, Band B).

There are interesting historic interpretations of Gender Egalitarianism in Russia. In medieval times, the roles of Russian men and women were clearly defined and separated from each other. Men were responsible for activities outside the home (hunter, agrarian, spokesperson for the family), whereas women took care of internal home affairs. But with the increased influence of the state (and later, the communist system) on the social environment, the individual's control of this environment declined, and, as a result, the gender-defined social roles were changing. During the Soviet period, Joseph Stalin's repressions and the Second World War severely decreased the male population and enabled women to take over various traditional men's activities in such industries as textiles, education, and health care, turning them into women's professions. The state facilitated equal access of men and women to education and social benefits, and the Party controlled the "right" balance of men and women in the political and government bodies.

In the transitional 1990s, the country was backsliding from the Soviet era. The gap between men and women in employment structure somewhat increased: In 1990, 37 million men and 38 million women were involved in economic activity versus 39 million and 33 million respectively in 1995, prior to the GLOBE data collection. Compared with the upward trend in value orientation, expressed by respondents from other surveyed countries, Russian managers are not much concerned with strengthening Gender Egalitarianism. This seems to reflect the patrimonial system of traditional Russian society, only superficially moderated in the Soviet period (Izyumov & Razumnova, 2000). The Russian managers, unlike their peers in other countries, do not express willingness to increase or change the role of women in organizations, and in society as a whole.

Assertiveness is the degree to which individuals are encouraged within a society to be assertive, confrontational, and aggressive in social relationships. The "As Is" score is 3.68, placing Russian societal culture on a low position (Rank 54, Band B), and the "Should Be" score 2.83 is also low (Rank 59, Band C). In the medieval times, the roles were clearly divided by gender. Masculine type of culture was reflected by male-headed households, and publicly by the role of the tzar (with few historic exceptions, such as Catherine the Great). Western influences (French in particular) in the 18th and 19th centuries added some feminine characteristics to the *noble strata* of the society. Through active interaction with the French establishment, and acceptance of the French language by the aristocracy as its second (occasionally even the first) language, and the French literature and arts, higher respect for women and romanticism were transferred to the Emperor's court. In the decades of Communist rule, elements of feminine culture were indoctrinated by promoting official policy of caring for people (especially for children), education, and full employment.

The current transitional society demands more assertive behavior, with tough measures to survive and transform businesses, and society at large. However, the heritage of caring for other people and social assistance limits such assertive behavior for many managers. Also, interpersonal networks (family ties, nepotism, Mafia structures) and collective obligations often suggest forms that are different from open and direct assertive management.

Power Distance is the degree to which members of a society expect and agree that power should be unequally shared. For Russia, the gap between "As Is" and "Should Be" scores is substantial. Over and above the common trend among GLOBE countries toward lower Power Distance "Should Be," Power Distance "As Is" in Russia ranks very high (5.52, Rank 14, Band A), whereas Power Distance "Should Be" ranks substantially lower (2.62, Rank 41, Band C).

Again, in the past, Russia has experienced serious changes in behaviors and values related to Power Distance. The pre-Revolutionary period formalized social status stratification, with the system of serfdom that had existed until the mid-19th century, the weak middle class, strong centralization of power in the hands of the state, and lack of democratic traditions. This trend continued in the Stalin era, with the Party hierarchy as the power stratification framework. That system suppressed people's independent behavior by all means of control. The tradition of respect for authority and privileges is still strong in contemporary Russian society. Current common belief in democratic reforms (as expressed by GLOBE respondents) may eliminate political power over economic behavior, and give society a higher level of economic freedom and competition. The opportunities for people today are increasingly linked to education, skills, and experience, rather than political connections. This, in turn, may modify the behavior of people toward more democratic management styles and social norms. But this option, to a great extent, depends on Russia's overall ability to balance democracy with establishing order in society.

Performance Orientation is the extent to which a society encourages or rewards group members for performance and excellence. In the Russian case, quite poor Performance Orientation is reported with the "As Is" score of 3.39 (Rank 59, Band C). Though Performance Orientation "Should Be" scores high (5.54) in comparison to the "As Is" score within Russia, in comparison to the 61 GLOBE countries, the Performance Orientation "Should Be" scores position Russia still at the lower end of the distribution (Rank 55, Band D). In the Soviet era, enterprise managers de-emphasized the need to exceed the planned indicators delegated from above. Managers and factory directors were not rewarded for high results that did not fit the state-designed economic plans, nor had they additional resources for unplanned initiatives. Legitimized achievements were not recognized by monetary means (there were official ceilings for salaries), but in this case managers were awarded symbolically or with higher status in *nomenklatura* hierarchy. In the other domains of human activity, the state rewarded those high achievements in science, sports, and the arts that were blessed by the Party and official propaganda. During mass privatization in the 1990s, many managers of large enterprises made their fortunes, not by improving enterprise performance, but by capitalizing on management buyout schemes. Successful performance results could be achieved by ignoring ethical standards and rules of morality, thus making Performance Orientation a contradictory weapon in competition. The small business (still underdeveloped), however, provides selected examples of high Performance Orientation with socially responsible managerial behavior (Hisrich, Gratchev, Bolshakov, Popov, & Ilyin, 1996).

Future Orientation is the degree to which individuals in organizations or society engage in future-oriented behaviors such as planning, investing in the future, and delaying gratification. This dimension is important to better understand the social side of the economy-in-transition. It presents striking differences in the assessment of cultural practices versus cultural values by the respondents. The "As Is" score (2.88) is extremely low (Rank 61, Band D). As in the case of Performance Orientation, the Russian managers believe that economic stabilization is contingent on changes in value orientation—at least when "As Is" (2.88) and "Should Be" (5.48) Future Orientation scores are compared within Russia. In contrast, the Future Orientation "Should Be" score (5.48) positions Russia not at the lower end of the distribution, as was the case for Performance Orientation "Should Be," but at a midrange level (Rank 34, Band B). After decades of strong beliefs in a better life under Communism and a national long-term planning system, in the 1990s Russia has transformed into a society with at least limited Future Orientation. The continuous government reshuffling, changes in legislation, and political instability added to this enormously. People and businesses in the mid- and late 1990s did not rely on savings, quickly transferring inflated rubles into hard currencies or spending money above all reasonable limits. The signs of economic stabilization in 2000–2006 are still coupled with mass suspicion of authorities and their promises about positive future changes. However, the managers we interviewed in focus groups expressed a strong belief in values related to stability in the economy and society, which enables them to think and act strategically. This leads to a more optimistic conclusion about the potential economic development of Russia and the predictability of its businesses, which seems to be reflected in the midrange (rather than low) positioning of Future Orientation "Should Be."

Uncertainty Avoidance is the extent to which members of a society strive to avoid uncertainty by relying on social norms, rituals, and bureaucratic practices to alleviate the unpredictability of future events. With an "As Is" score of 2.88, Russia ranks lowest among all GLOBE countries (Rank 61, Band D) on Uncertainty Avoidance practices. This could be interpreted as "uncertainty acceptance" in the transitional economy. To a certain extent, this indicates the entrepreneurial and risk-oriented behavior of Russian managers. At the same time, managers' responses to the "Should Be" questions relating to Uncertainty Avoidance show a large gap between reality, on the one hand, and values and expectations on the other. The "Should Be" score of 5.07 (Rank 18, Band A) positions Russia among the countries with a clear value preference for Uncertainty Avoidance. That may indicate a still existing preference for a planning system among Russian managers, which they feel comfortable with, or an increased need for security and direction in times of transition where uncertainty is particularly high.

In the 1990s, most of the population lost a clear sense of direction in the new fragmented and uncertain environment. Realities of the past that provided security and supported tolerance of uncertainty (respect for age, tradition, rule orientation, social order) are no longer valid. In the current situation, managers quickly and creatively adjust to rapidly changing situations in the environment. This demands specific traits for quick reaction, multiscenario thinking, networking, and sharing risk. Many Russian managers and entrepreneurs work successfully in networks, relying not only on formal agreements, but on friendship and social interaction as well.

Humane Orientation is the degree to which individuals in organizations or societies encourage and reward individuals for being fair, friendly, generous, caring, and kind to others. The relations between the current behavior and the values of the Russian managers look encouraging for the prospects of the country. Whereas the "As Is" score of 3.94 positions Russia on Rank 37 (Band C), the "Should Be" score is high, 5.59 (Rank 18, Band B), and positions Russia among the countries with strong endorsement of humane-oriented values. Transitional Russia can be characterized by the absence of social norms and laws that protect the less fortunate. There is much unfairness and corruption in business, and ethical norms and morality are not highly respected in business or in society at large. Much of the current behavior in the economy is quite exploitative, and much wealth is concentrated in the hands of very few. Poverty and social exclusion in Russia today are widespread. Suspicion and mistrust are more a rule than an exception. At the organizational level, welfare and social benefits are often neglected. Humane Orientation "Should Be" is usually inversely related to the frequency and severity of aggressiveness and hostile actions ("As Is") within cultures, which is evident in contemporary Russia, with its multiple ethnic and industrial conflicts.

To summarize, GLOBE indicators and rankings for Russia seem to reflect the realities of painful economic transformation and current "mental models" of "doing business" in Russia. Our research had positioned Russia as having an *extreme* "As Is" profile when compared to the other countries on the GLOBE dimensions: very low in Uncertainty Avoidance, Future Orientation, Performance Orientation, and Humane Orientation, and very high on Power Distance. An extremely low Uncertainty Avoidance score and rank could be considered favorable for entrepreneurship activities unless one links it to a very low Future Orientation. That can be interpreted as a lack of vision in management and entrepreneurship, as the primary focus is on survival and short-term business development. Low Performance Orientation makes it difficult to encourage managers to focus on continuous improvement and learning. Low ranking on Humane Orientation raises doubts about long-term investments in human resources. High Power Distance scores explain the tough bureaucratic measures in crisis management and in restructuring enterprises and industries.

An analysis of societal culture trends, evident in discrepancies between "As Is" and "Should Be" scores, makes further interpretations possible. In particular, the discrepancies found display deficits in, and preference for, humanistic, ethical, and democratic practices. No discrepancies were found, for example, for In-Group Collectivism, which is strongly linked to historical cultural roots of collectivism. Also for Gender Egalitarianism, no discrepancies between relatively high "As Is" and "Should Be" scores were found. However, when compared to the overall trend among the other GLOBE countries, a dramatic decline in Gender Egalitarian values is evident ("As Is" Rank 2 vs. "Should Be" Rank 49).

6. LEADERSHIP PROFILE IN FOCUS GROUP INTERVIEWS

In focused group interviews, participants talked about characteristics of leadership and leaders in Russia. They suggested that leaders should be defined differently in society on the one hand, and in the economy on the other.

According to the interviewees, the definition of leadership in general should be based on stereotypes of heroes, developed in history, as well as indoctrinated by official propaganda. Leaders were associated with national success, great achievements, and heroism, inspiring people with personal ability, creativity, courage, and risk taking. The effectiveness of leaders was judged by interviewees via results and success. More often, strong leaders were valued in the history of the state (Tzar Peter the Great; Dictator Joseph Stalin), in large-scale national projects (physicists I. Kurchatov and A. Sakharov in nuclear industry, engineer S. Korolev in space exploration). Both groups of respondents shared these views.

In the economy, however, leadership was viewed differently by representatives of Group 1 and Group 2, and without consensus. In the Soviet economy, the responsibility of factory manager was the implementation of the plan: meeting previously indicated targets. Extraordinary results in productivity, innovations that did not fit the "planning system" were the factors of unbalance and were not appreciated. The state used propaganda to create an image of those leaders who were productive, loyal to the Communist Party, and channeled officially recognized values.

Representatives of the first group defined leadership in the economy as the ability to represent and share technical skills and expertise. Few remarks were made about managers' professionalism and to deal with people effectively. The representatives of the first group thought that the most important job of the manager was to follow the already established norms and principles. The second group, consisting of younger aggressive entrepreneurs, with practically no experience in the old Soviet system, was more definite on leadership qualities such as creating new companies, new businesses, and in general, taking risk and inspiring others to follow them. The interviewed managers/entrepreneurs of this group showed themselves as not just administrators but also "creators of organizational culture."

One interesting comment related to charitable traditions of Russian entrepreneurs. People from both groups appreciated the charitable activities of the pre-Revolutionary industrialists (S. Morozov & P. Ryabushinski) who donated resources to hospitals, theaters, and museums, and preserved Russian arts and culture.

In general, discussion with the Russian managers/entrepreneurs indicated their strong interest in leadership qualities, and consequently in leadership development. The issues of special interest were related to the nature of leaders: whether leaders are those with naturally developed features, or those who have leadership qualities, based on focused individual work, individual training. It became clear that most of those interviewed agree that one can develop these qualities.

Though displaying different interpretations of leadership, the interviewees had raised the following critical issues. First, leadership is the *reality* of every society. It is based on the freely released diverse human activity. At a certain historic moment it becomes the focus of special attention, when it can be purposefully accumulated and developed, thus making leadership one of management's strategic resources. Second, leadership is a *practical,* social phenomenon, which can be found in various social fabrics (individual, collective, culture, and politics). Leadership includes the ability to catalyze practical reaction to the factors of socioeconomic development. This is "the first social move" to one of the possible options (scenarios) of getting into the future. In other words, leadership creates something new, nonstandard—in the practical form (precedent) by involving others into its activity. Third, leadership also is an *organizational* phenomenon, and here respondents agreed with GLOBE's definition of leadership as "the ability of an individual to influence, motivate, and enable others to contribute toward the effectiveness and success of the organization of which they are members." Fourth, leadership is also *interdependent with society,* and only those leaders who comply with the social capital of their nation are able to absorb and distribute the advanced international experience, without possible dangerous side effects. If a society is unable to generate mass motivation, it may create leaders who will move the society away from the road of ethical development. Social partnership, degree of corporate citizenship, and social responsibilities depend on the moral potential of leadership. At the same time, the discussants concluded that society is responsible for facilitating healthy leadership, for providing the appropriate level of freedom and reasonable tolerance to unexpected and unusual behaviors.

7. GLOBE SCALES: LEADERSHIP RESULTS AND INTERPRETATION

The scores of the overall profile of Russian leaders according to globally endorsed implicit leadership theory dimensions (Charismatic, Team Oriented, Participative, Humane, Self-Protective, Autonomous) are displayed in Figure 22.2. In Table 22.2, the scores for the 21 first-order leadership dimensions are described together with Russia's positioning relative to the 61 GLOBE countries (Ranks) and the country groupings (Bands) on each dimension.

Charismatic/Value-Based Orientation

Aggregate indicators for universal positive leader attributes summarized in Charismatic/Value- Based leadership dimensions are relatively low for Russia (5.66, Rank 47, Band D). The first-order dimensions for Charismatic/Value-Based leadership display Visionary (6.07) as the most important dimension in considering effective leadership in Russia. In the range for factors slightly contributing to effective leadership, we find the following first-order dimensions: Performance Oriented (5.92), Inspirational (5.93), Decisive (5.95), and Integrator (5.19). Self- Sacrifice (4.28) has no impact on outstanding leadership. Comparing these factors for Russia to the other countries, one can consider the Russian profile in Band A on the Decisive dimension, in Band B on Visionary, Performance Orientation, and Integrity, and in Band C on Self-Sacrificial.

Team Orientation

Second-order scales for Team Oriented leadership do not provide us with an optimistic assessment of Russia's leadership profile as well. The Team Orientation country score is 5.63 (Rank 46, Band C). The first-order scales provide us with the following data. Whereas Administrative Competence is the factor most contributing to effective leadership in Russia (6.01), the other global dimensions present, only somewhat contributing to this leadership are:

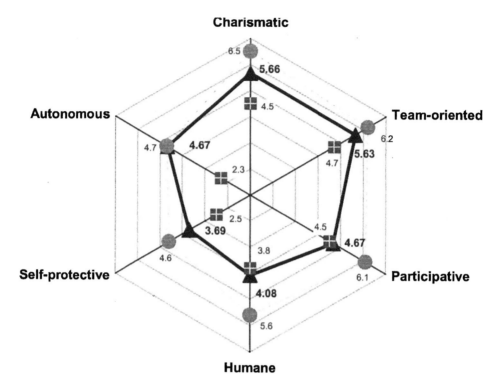

Figure 22.2.   Global culturally endorsed implicit leadership (CLT) scores for Russia (circles–maximum mean, squares–minimum mean within 62 countries).

Team-Oriented (5.68), Team Integrator (5.19), Diplomatic (5.35), and Malevolent (2.02, reverse score). In the all country benchmarking, Russia is among the countries with high indicators for Administratively Competent (Band A), whereas the critical factors such as Team Orientation and Malevolence place it only into Band C. On the other two dimensions Diplomatic and Team Integrator, Russia is placed in Band B.

Humane Orientation

The dimension that nearly universally contributes to effective leadership is Humane Orientation, and by Russian managers it is perceived to have only limited impact on outstanding leadership (4.08, Rank 60, Band D). The first-order dimensions related to the second-order Humane Orientation are Modesty (4.25), which in the Russian case slightly facilitates effective leadership, and Humane Orientation (3.91), which slightly inhibits people being perceived as outstanding leaders.

Participative Orientation

On Participative Orientation in leadership perception, Russia scores comparatively low (4.67, Rank 58, Band D) with the two reverse-scored first-order dimensions, Autocratic (3.86, Rank 1, Band A) and Nonparticipative (2.82, Rank 23, Band A), ranking very high and medium respectively.

TABLE 22.2
GLOBE First-Order Leadership Dimension Scores for Russia

Dimensions Subdimensions	Country Score	GLOBE Rank (Band)
Charismatic/Value Based	**5.66**	**47 (D)**
Visionary	6.07	35 (B)
Inspirational	5.93	42 (D)
Self-Sacrificial	4.28	58 (C)
Integrity	5.19	50 (B)
Decisive	5.95	26 (A)
Performance Orientation	5.92	45 (B)
Team Oriented	**5.63**	**46 (C)**
Collaborative Team Oriented	5.68	52 (C)
Team Integrator	5.19	45 (B)
Diplomatic	5.01	43 (B)
Malevolent (Recoded)	2.02	14 (A)
Administratively Competent	6.01	19 (A)
Self-Protective	**3.69**	**17 (D)**
Self-Centered	2.48	13 (B)
Status Consciousness	5.06	12 (B)
Conflict Inducer	4.43	14 (B)
Face Saver	3.40	13 (C)
Procedural	3.21	53 (D)
Participative	**4.67**	**58 (D)**
Autocratic (Recoded)	3.86	1 (A)
Nonparticipative (Recoded)	2.82	23 (B)
Humane	**4.08**	**60 (D)**
Modesty	4.25	60 (C)
Humane	3.91	57 (C)
Autonomous	**4.63**	**1 (A)**

Autonomous

In relation to all GLOBE countries, Autonomous leadership seems to be strongly endorsed in Russian culture (4.63, Rank 1, Band A). It is based on such characteristics as individualism, independence, uniqueness, and being autonomous.

Self-Protective

Self-Protective leadership perceptions (3.69, Rank 17, Band A) slightly inhibit outstanding leadership in Russia. This is based on a profile or some positive impact of the dimension Status-Conscious (5.06) and Conflict Inducer (4.43), counterset by negative impacts of the dimensions Self-Centered (2.48), Face Saver (3.4), and Procedural (3.21). Relative to the 61 GLOBE countries, Russia positions itself in Band B on such dimensions as Status-Conscious, Self- Centered, and Conflict Inducer, in Band C for Face Saver, and in Band D for Procedural. With a very low score on the Procedural dimension, it indicates that being procedural is likely to be a greater inhibitor of effective leadership in Russia than in most countries included in the GLOBE sample.

The Profile of Effective Leadership

In terms of GLOBE dimensions, Russia displays a clear picture of what makes effective leadership in a transitional economy. The most important within-country attributes are Visionary and Administrative Competency. They are followed by being Decisive, Performance Orientated, and Inspirational. Also Integrity, Team Integration, Collaborative, and Diplomatic are considered to contribute somewhat to outstanding leadership. At the same time such dimensions as Self- Sacrifice, Modesty and Humane Orientation, Status Consciousness, and Conflict Inducer do not make a difference; that is, if they are perceived, they do not subtract from being perceived as an outstanding leader for other reasons. These findings display the *profile* of an administratively competent manager, capable of making serious decisions and inspiring his or her followers to meet performance targets. Only to a certain extent is there positive reliance on diplomacy and collaborative moves. Humane Orientation and modesty in personal behavior seem neutral to perceptions of outstanding leadership, as is the case for face-saving behavior. However, that can mean that a positive perception of a leader (for other reasons) would not be negatively affected by a leader who shows either face-saving behavior and/or low humane orientation. Status does not seem important to the modern Russian business leader.

The GLOBE results suggest that universal positive leader attributes such as Charismatic/Value Based leadership and Team Oriented leadership are considered as contributors to outstanding leadership in Russia. However the level of such contribution is much lower than in most of the other countries. The other two dimensions that nearly universally contribute to leadership—Participative and Humane Orientation—have only limited impact in Russia. Universal negative leader attributes such as Self-Protective and Autonomous seem also less relevant to the implicit leadership theories endorsed in Russia. Summarizing these findings, one may consider Russia as marginal in finding the ways for effective leadership concepts and practices within the global framework.

The authors however are far from taking a morbid point of view that Russia will never catch up with the others, even in the attitude toward leaders. Young people are more individualistic and creative. Moreover, they are ready to express their own ideas and to defend their own principles. It's very unlikely that today's youngsters will blindly obey a leader, no matter who he or she is. The authors had some other positive discoveries, noticing the growing interest in Future Orientation and in moral values. While the country is going through transition in the market and in its democracy, it's very hard to work out an exact definition of the Russian country-specific leadership. The situation in the economy and social sphere is changing rapidly, and the psychology of the Russian businesspeople is not an exception.

TABLE 22.3
Media Sources for Analysis

Media Source	1996	2001	Circulation	Number of Pages
Izvestiya	X	X	556,284 (1996) 234,500 (2001)	6 (1996) 12 (2001)
Argumenty I Fakty	X	X	3,360 000 (1996) 2,921 170 (2001)	24 (1996) 20 (2001)
Moskovsky Komsomoletz	X		868,523	8
Nezavisimaya Gazeta	X		48,000	16
Kommersant-Daily	X		400,000	12–18
Komsomolskaya Pravda		X	765,000	24
Trud		X	612,850	8

8. LEADERSHIP EXPRESSED IN MEDIA

Media analysis was carried out as part of the GLOBE project with a view to reveal public opinion toward leaders and leadership in Russia. The authors' main task was to determine how the media portrays leaders and the phenomenon of leadership, and then to compare the results to the other GLOBE findings for Russia.

For the media analysis two periods from November 26 to December 2, 1996 and from July 30 to August 6, 2001, were chosen. Within these periods there were neither significant political events, nor holidays that could somehow influence the content of the media publications. Thus, the information published in the studied newspapers was quite generic.

Russian newspapers are the second-largest source of information for the public, after television. In recent years, however, there was a certain decline in the reading audience as compared statistically to the 1980s. This is the result of growing social and political apathy in the late 1990s. It also reflects the fact that many people are concerned with their survival rather than with national events they can not control. Also, there is a widespread belief that the media is increasingly controlled by tycoons and by the Kremlin administration, and as a result, is less objective, serving populist interests of a narrow group. Five leading nationally distributed newspapers were selected for the analysis (see Table 22.3).

Izvestiya is a daily newspaper that provides in-depth analyses of national and international economy and politics, comments on events in sports and cultural life, and presents interviews with well-known politicians and businesspeople. Its readers are mostly middle-aged people with higher education, many of them civil servants. *Argumenty I Fakty,* a weekly newspaper with the largest circulation in Russia, offers its readers a wide range of information in practically all possible areas: from political news to UFOs. The newspaper is oriented on mass readership of all ages and occupations. Moreover, it is one of the few relatively independent newspapers, respected by representatives of different, sometimes even extremely opposite political groups. *Moskovsky Komsomoletz,* a popular daily newspaper, absorbs scandals, sensations, piquant details of the personal life of politicians, and compromising data about well-known people. However, this newspaper has a considerable influence on many people; it is popular and may form public opinion on an event or a person. *Nezavisimaya Gazeta,* with the smallest circulation of all those sampled, is considered one of the best informed and most reliable newspapers, targeting the intellectually elite segment of the market. *Kommersant-Daily* was among the first newspapers in democratic Russia to be differentiated as a business daily. Though it publishes news and opinions on politics, arts, and international affairs, business focus is still dominating in this newspaper. One can get the latest market trends, CEO's opinions, and stories of mergers and acquisitions, among others. *Komsomolskaya Pravda,* originally targeting a younger population, now is considered a well-informed and analytical newspaper with a broad customer base. *Trud,* the former trade union daily, currently is among the most popular newspapers for the general public, trying to distance itself from union-oriented papers and position itself as well-informed, enjoyable reading.

Altogether 217 articles and editorials were identified that could be referred to as dealing with issues leadership in various spheres of life: economics, politics, sports, culture, and daily events. Among all the articles selected for media analysis 162 articles (75%) focused on Russian leaders and 55 articles (25%) commented on leaders from foreign countries.

At the first stage the articles were sorted according to the spheres of the leaders' activity: politics, business, sport, arts and show business, others.

The structures of the "foreign" and "Russian" sets were different (see Table 22.4). In the "foreign" set, the interest in political leaders was the highest with 22 articles (40% of the "foreign" sample); business leaders were mentioned in 16 articles (29%), in show business 7 articles (13%), and in sports also 7 articles (13%). In the "Russian" set, the highest interest was expressed in political leaders, consisting of more than half of the sample and totaling 82 articles (51% of the "Russian" set), business leaders were described in 25 articles (16%), in sports 10 articles (6%), arts and show business 30 articles (18%) and other areas 15 articles (9%). These findings present a moderate interest by the Russian media of leaders in business when compared to the other groups of leaders. Also political leadership, both international and domestic, is a visible priority for Russian newspapers.

The next step filtered the articles and assessed the kind of leadership issues they had discussed. At this stage, in the "Russian" set, the authors excluded interviews (as not impartial because one can hardly speak impartially about him or herself) and simply informative articles (as not allowing any idea of media attitude to the personality of leaders). Finally, out of 162 articles that had mentioned leaders in Russia, 130 (80%) remained for the linguistic analysis.

The words and word combinations ("typical phrases") were sorted according to GLOBE media analysis guidelines and grouped by category of descriptions of leaders and leadership (Table 22.5). We identified the frequency with which these categories were mentioned. These frequencies displayed relative importance of different categories.

The most important trait of a leader expressed by media was *image* with a frequency of 25 (13% of all phrases and expressions). That was not a surprise as creating an image is one of the main tasks of media itself and is the means for the newspapers to communicate the effective and outstanding leadership. The next four characteristics were *facilitate* and *action* with frequencies of 22 and 21 respectively (11% each), *knowledge* with a frequency of 19 (10%), and *energy* with a frequency of 17 (9%). This result corresponds with the GLOBE leadership profile of a manager oriented on decision making with a capability to inspire the followers.

The *communication* trait was somewhat less visible with a frequency of 15 (8%) and corresponded with moderate team orientation in a leadership profile. Moderate frequencies of 7 and 6 (4% and 3%) were displayed for *change* and *survive* traits that might be important to the current transitional economy.

TABLE 22.4
The Composition of the Sets of Articles (1996/2001)

Areas of Interest Leaders	Russian Leaders Number of Articles (1996 + 2001 = Total)	Russian Leaders (%)	Foreign Leaders Number of Articles (1996 + 2001 = Total)	Foreign (%)
Politics	48 + 34 = **82**	51	7 + 15 = **22**	40
Business	10 + 15 = **25**	16	12 + 4 = **16**	29
Sport	5 + 5 = **10**	6	3 + 4 = **7**	13
Arts and ShowBusiness	3 + 27 = **30**	18	5 + 2 = **7**	13
Others	8 + 7 = **15**	9	0 + 3 = **3**	5
Total	74 + 88 = **162**	100	27 + 28 = **55**	100

Not only those traits mentioned most frequently, but also those less frequent ones, were reviewed by the authors. Characteristics that should be important for Value-Based Charismatic leadership were not visible in the media analysis. *Charisma, vision, and creativity* were mentioned less than five times (under 2%) and *role model* of a leader only five times (3%). These results correspond with the marginal acceptance of such a Charismatic leadership in Russia as discussed in the previous section. It is worth mentioning that the *weakness* and *fault* items were both rare with each trait having a frequency of 3 (1.5%), which can bring us to the conclusion that in a non-Face Saving society, media designs more of a positive image of a leader than the reality actually is.

Based on linguistic analysis, we can construct the following typical *media leadership profile.* A Russian leader has a rich image linked to his or her success, competencies, and social and professional recognition. He or she displays the action-oriented and energetic behavior of a facilitator with entrepreneurial competencies. In particular, he or she is "full of unprecedented intervention," "acts with no hesitations" as a "real fighter," and "hard-working, restless, and enduring." He or she is somewhat capable of controlling the situation, can facilitate change in the organization, and can survive in a turbulent environment. At the same time the media profile does not consider him or her to be a charismatic leader with clear systemic vision and cultural sensitivity.

9. CONCLUSIONS

The radical transformation in Russia in the 1990s and the first years of the 21st century has set the stage for transition toward a democratic civil society. In the economy, the market is substituting a previous monopolistic and ideology-dominated system. Combined with these two trends is the cultural change, when values, norms of behavior, and artifacts are reassessed, renewed, created, or removed.

Culture and leadership in contemporary Russia are rooted in three groups of factors: *first,* traditional and historically developed cultural features of Russian society; *second,* the influence of a totalitarian heritage of the twentieth century; and *third,* the radical revolution in culture

TABLE 22.5

Leadership Characteristics Displayed in Russian Media

Category	N (1996)	N (2001)	Total	Typical phrases
Image	13	12	25	has a modest way of life; image of professional; the most popular; the most patient and stable; in style of a man who always says I don't know; not ordinary man; unbelievably modest; one of the richest men of the country; I'm self-sufficient; old charming manners; extremely ambitious; the thing in itself; round, bumpy, smell like buns; successful business; was very successful in start-up; representative of large Russian business; famous economist; well-known expert; economic brains; a person you should trust; recognized expert in international finance and investments; extraordinary financial leader; elite of Russian business; respected.
Facilitate	16	6	22	able to attract people; moderate, bright, clear minded; can help; can solve; will try to settle disputes; was more concrete; gave his support to all; power methods; has an entrepreneurial talent; flexible and compliant; expressed maximum loyalty; beloved man; doesn't worry; can concentrate; accumulate seriously; attractive, working man; calm smile; natural liberality; advice and support; supervised the project to its implementation; facilitator; made it possible; organized training the other people.
Action	13	8	21	active and fruitful cooperation; actively urged; acted self-sacrificing; actively gesticulated; shot while arguing; offended Catholic Church; got everybody out; storm and rush; variety of started businesses; hurry in search; well-trained aggression; impudence is good and fruitful not only in war actions; promise; business activity; started in new position; brainstorming; worked on a project; start-up initiative; restructuring.
Knowledge	11	8	19	a man with great organizational potential; put in all they learned successfully; soft intelligence; awarded with diplomas; his career was impetuous; did a lot in the term when the others can only learn the basics; has got master's degree; respected professional; qualities of a leader; highly professional conversation; with knowledge of facts; experienced; has strong abilities, managerial experience, deserved authority and confidence; experience in working in international markets; has 30 years of experience as director; has extraordinary capabilities; bachelor; master of business administration; topic of the dissertation; accumulated experience and knowledge; PhD in law.

(*Continued*)

TABLE 22.5 (Continued)

Category	N (1996)	N (2001)	Total	Typical phrases
Energy	9	8	17	at work from 9 to 9; stays longer than anyone else; high energy; has done a hard work: resisted furiously; inspired by energy; his way was hard and he went to his goal through heavy fighting; behaved courageously: very strong, that's the wife who is the engine of this couple; sources for quick success; was not job hopper, rather energetically climbed the career ladder; was courageous to propose; he is brave as expert; business activity; 1 year was enough for breakthrough.
Communicate	11	4	15	the man who can not work in team; joked and peppered his speech with phraseologisms; soft voice; active and fruitful cooperation; read from my lips; try not to aggravate relationships; the best propagandist; understood each other; easily communicates; let's keep together; doesn't speak a lot; never keeps his friends and colleagues with whom he had a business; talks a lot; involved in international business and broad economic ties; easy going; uses simple language; relies on cooperation.
Direct or Direction	9	2	11	recommended; suggested; gave advise; was able to convince; enjoy planning; against war; competition- yes; don't take into consideration existing rules and customs if they are the obstacles on the way up; growing leader; makes principle statements; follows clear and simple ideology.
Obligation	8	2	10	personally make decisions and personally take responsibility; didn't leave his stand but for order obligation promised help; no partner betrayed him, although they were under terrible pressure; set a high value on his position; pass responsibility to somebody else; he always kept his point of view; easily does unauthorized things; never goes against the will of the people; is responsible for financial and economic issues; always kept his promises.
Objective	7	0	7	has confidence; has come to bring everything in order; will be as in Europe; he's sure he'll win; all his actions are aimed at an external effect; I looked for morality everywhere; doesn't intend to sit on two chairs.
Control	4	3	7	mighty governor; as general commands; solid capital, good power; the most influential; can manage all the assets of the company; tries to have the process under control; full control.

(*Continued*)

TABLE 22.5 *(Continued)*

Category	N (1996)	N (2001)	Total	Typical phrases
Change	3	4	7	decided to reconstruct; decided to reconstruct according to the rules of science; I know what I want to change; transformational leadership; restructuring; changing the organization; change master.
Survive	3	3	6	survivor; had enough energy to resist; life is a series of strikes that we should survive at any cost; learned to protect himself; was not confused with the competitors' moves; quickly avoided confrontation.
Role Model	3	2	5	model; with care of a wolf; exemplary model; entrepreneurial talent that was awarded by life, business and recognition; a long-term leader of a large corporation for 30 years.
Creativity	2	2	4	unique creativity; full of ideas; could creatively apply his potential; multiple hobbies.
Charisma	2	2	4	charismatically popular; uncharismatic; man capable to create a successful business for 10 years; one of the most influential oil businessmen in the country.
Weakness	2	1	3	terrible when angry; chef's expression wasn't quite correct; he looked upset and didn't know what to do; failed only once.
Faults	1	2	3	was several times prosecuted; blamed for money laundering; criminal sources for capitals.
Culture	2	0	2	begin to use classical phrases; fond of ritual African religions.
Vision	1	1	2	estimated the situation correctly at once; made the company one of the leading businesses.
System	1	1	2	wanted to bring everything in order; multidimensional approach.

and leadership in the 1990s transitional period. All three were considered as substantial for interpretation of the GLOBE findings and for comparing Russian profile to the other countries.

GLOBE research positioned Russia very low in Uncertainty Avoidance, Future Orientation, Performance Orientation, and Humane Orientation, but very high on Power Distance. Whereas Institutional and In-group Collectivism, Egalitarianism, and Assertiveness dimensions displayed some agreement between the "As Is" and "Should Be" scores, dimensions such as Power Distance, Performance Orientation, Future Orientation, Uncertainty Avoidance, and Humane Orientation—primarily linked to the current economic and social transformation—showed the visible gap between the "As Is" and "Should Be" scores.

The profile of an effective business leader in Russia is based on administrative competence and the capability of serious decision making. He or she is able to motivate followers in order to meet performance targets, work in teams, and integrate efforts. However, there is no serious caring about humane motivation and modesty in personal behavior. Universal characteristics such as Charismatic/Value Based leadership and Team Oriented leadership are considered as contributors to outstanding leadership in Russia, however at a lower level when compared to most of the other countries. Participative and Humane Orientation have only limited impact in Russia. Attributes such as Self-Protective and Autonomous are also not very important.

Media analysis to a certain extent supports the findings based on the GLOBE survey. Media create the leadership profile that is focused on personal success and recognition. The Russian leader is action oriented and energetic, being capable of controlling the situation, facilitating change in the organization, and surviving in a transitional society. However, media analysis does not consider him or her as a charismatic leader and visionary.

This chapter has shed light on the state and current transformation of culture and leadership in Russia. The findings presented here seem to have quite important implications for both researchers and practitioners. The GLOBE project is one of the first attempts to collect a research-oriented Russian data set by using internationally recognized and reliable research methods, to provide cross-cultural comparisons among 61 nations.

As the current Russian economic situation is becoming more and more predictable, the GLOBE findings convey certain optimism. Russia's competitiveness at both national and corporate levels could be based on advantageous characteristics of Russian managers, mentioned in this study, such as the courage and ability to launch large-scale projects, decisiveness, the ability to make decisions and assume responsibility, and the ability to quickly react and operate in an unstable environment. Cultural transformation related to Future Orientation and healthy individualism also looks promising.

Certain current societal trends, however, lead the authors to more cautious predictions. In particular, in the 2000s there is a visible rapid increase in Power Distance. Russian President Putin and his administration redesign the relations between the government and oligarchs, and strengthen the vertical power structure. It is obvious that Russia is moving toward its traditional center-oriented model, where even the richest oligarch is nothing but a serf to the centralized state. Indications of the widening gap between the rich and the poor, numerous signs of status (VIP, exclusive arrangements for the elite) on the one hand, and visible social exclusion, on the other, are the facts of Russian life. This is also true about the widening gap between the wealthy regions (Moscow and St. Petersburg, rich oil-and-gas Tyumen) and the other parts of the country.

Considerations for Foreign Managers in Russia

This chapter described a number of characteristics that Russian managers believe their leaders should possess. Foreign managers, working in Russia, should be aware of these expectations and make sure that their own skills and abilities reflect a desirable leadership profile, as described in this chapter. We are certainly not suggesting, however, that foreign managers should get rid of their characteristics, highly valued in their own cultures, but not necessarily in Russia. The best expatriate managers should not try to "play a role," but should rather enrich themselves through cultural learning. Such learning will help foreign managers to benefit from cultural synergies and to be successful in Russia. We therefore advise foreign managers to be open-minded and nonjudgmental when dealing with the Russian managers.

As we have tried to show in this chapter, present-day Russian business culture is rather unstable, and the business environment is still volatile. That's what any foreign manager should expect. However, foreign managers should not assume that Russian business culture does not exist at all, and that they are free to establish their own "rules of the game." Russian business culture is increasingly becoming more predictable and transparent. This evolutionary process is influenced by both increased self-awareness about the business cultures of pre-revolutionary and Soviet periods of Russian history, and emulation of the Western managerial principles, policies, and practices.

ACKNOWLEDGMENTS

The authors acknowledge the contribution of GLOBE Research Assistants Mariya Bobina, Mariya Frolova, and Sergei Yurkov in data collection and in preparing this manuscript for publication.

REFERENCES

Ageev, A., Gratchev M., & Hisrich, R. (1995). Entrepreneurship in the Soviet Union and Post- Socialist Russia, *Small Business Economics, 7*(5), 365–376.

Anderson, D., & Shikhirev, P. (1994). *Akuli I delfini.* [Sharks and dolphins]. Moscow: Delo.

Bakacsi, G., Takacs, S., Karacsonyi, A., & Imrek, V. (2002). Eastern European cluster: Tradition and transition. *Journal of World Business, 37,* 69–80.

Berliner, J. (1976). *The innovation decision in the Soviet industry.* Cambridge, MA: MIT Press.

Blackwell, W. (1994). *The industrialization of Russia: A historical perspective.* Arlington Heights, IL: H. Davidson.

Chaadaev, P. (1991). *Philosophical works of Peter Chaadaev.* Boston: Kluwer Academic.

de Vries, M. (2000). J Journey into the "Wild East": Leadership style and organizational practices in Russia. *Organizational Dynamics, 28*(4), 67–81.

den Hartog, D., House, R., Hanges, P., Ruiz-Quintanilla, S., Dorfman, P., Lindell, M., et al. (1999). Culture specific and cross-culturally generalizable implicit leadership theories: Are attributes of charismatic/transormational leadership universally endorsed? *Leadership Quarterly, 10*(2), 219–256.

Fey, C., & Beamish, P. (2000). Joint venture conflict: The case of Russian international joint ventures. *International Business Review, 9,* 139–162.

Fey, C., & Bjorkman, I. (2001). The effect of human resource management practices on MNC subsidiary performance in Russia. *Journal of International Business Studies, 32*(1), 59–75.

Gratchev, M. (2001, October). Making the most of cultural differences. *Harvard Business Review,* 28–30.

Guroff, G., & Carstensen, F. (1983). *Entrepreneurship in imperial Russia and the Soviet Union.* Princeton, NJ: Princeton University Press

Hisrich, R., & Gratchev, M. (1993). The Russian entrepreneur. *Journal of Business Venturing, 8*(6), 487–498.

Hisrich, R., & Gratchev, M. (1997). Russian vs. American entrepreneurs: Where are the ethics? In P. Reynolds (Ed.), *Frontiers of entrepreneurship research* (pp. 256–257). Boston: Babson College.

Hisrich, R., Gratchev, M., Bolshakov, Z., Popov, D., & Ilyin, A. (1996). DOKA Corporation: The case of Russian high-tech company. In R. Hisrich (Ed.), *Cases in international entrepreneurship* (pp. 287–302). Chicago: Irwin.

House, R. J., Hanges, P. J., Javidan, M., Dorfman, P. W., Gupta, V., & Globe Associates. (2004). *Culture, leadership, and organizations: The GLOBE study of 62 societies.* Thousand Oaks, CA: Sage.

House, R., Hanges, P., Ruiz-Quintanilla, S., Dorfman, P., Javidan, M., Dickson, M., et al. (1999). Cultural influences on leadership and organizations: Project GLOBE. In W. Mobley, M. Gessner, & V. Arnold (Eds.), *Advances in global leadership* (pp. 171–233). Stamford, CT: JAI.

House, R. , Wright, N., & Aditya, R. (1997). Cross-cultural research on organizational leadership: A critical analysis and a proposed theory. In P. C. Early & M. Erez (Eds.), *New perspectives on international industrial/organizational psychology.* San Francisco: Lexington Press.

Huntington, S. (1993). The clash of civilizations? *Foreign Affairs, 72*(3), 22–49.

Izyumov, A., & Razumnova, I. (2000). Women entrepreneurs in Russia: Learning to survive the market. *Journal of Developmental Entrepreneurship, 5*(1), 1–20.

Karamzin, N. (1892) *Istoriia gosudarstva Rossiiskago* [History of the Russian state]. St. Petersburg, Russia: Izd. Evg. Evdokimova.

Kluchevskii, V. (1904). *Kurs Russkoi istorii* [The course in Russian history] Moscow: Sinodalnaya Tipografiya.

Kluckhohn, F., & Strodtbeck, F. (1961). Variations in value orientation. New York: HarperCollins.

Kuzmichev, A., & Petrov, R. (1993) *Russkie millionshiki* [Russian millionaires]. Moscow: Vlados/Foros.

Michailova, S. (2000) Contrasts in culture: Russian and Western perspectives on organizational change. *The Academy of Management Executive, 14*(4), 99–112.

Mikheyev, D. (1987) The Soviet mentality. *Political Psychology, 8*(4), 491–523.

Naumov, A. (1996). Hofstedovo Izmerenie Rossii [Hofstede's dimension of Russia]. *Menedzhment, 3,* 70–103.

Naumov, A., & Puffer, S. (2000) Measuring Russian culture using Hofstede's dimensions. *Applied Psychology: An International Review, 49*(4), 709–718.

Owen, T. (1981). *Capitalism and politics in Russia: A social history of Moscow merchants, 1855–1905.* New York: Cambridge University Press.

Puffer, S. (Ed.). (1992). *The Russian management revolution: Preparing managers for the market economy.* Armonk, NY: M. E. Sharpe.

Puffer, S. (1994). Understanding the bear: A portrait of Russian business leaders. *Academy of Management Executive, 8*(1), 41–54.

Puffer, S., McCarthy, D., & Naumov, A. (1997). Russian managers' beliefs about work: Beyond the stereotypes. *Journal of World Business, 32*(3), 258–276.

Puffer, S., McCarthy, D., & Naumov, A. (2000). *The Russian capitalist experiment: From state-owned organizations to entrepreneurships.* Cheltenham, England: Edward Elgar.

Rogovsky, N., Bertocci, C., & Gratchev, M. (1997). *Social exclusion and business initiatives in the economies in transition: The case of Russia.* Copenhagen: Danish National Institute of Social Research.

Shikhirev, P. (2000). *Vvedenie v Rossiiskuyu Delovuyu Kul'turu* [Introduction to Russian business culture]. Moscow: Novosti.

Soloviev, V. (1913). *Sobranie sotchinenii* [Collection of works]. St. Petersburg, Russia: Prosveshenie.

VII

MIDDLE EAST CLUSTER

The Middle East cluster in the GLOBE Research Program consisted of Egypt, Kuwait, Morocco, Qatar, and Turkey. The last one, Turkey, is the only country represented in this volume.

In-Group Collectivism is the only societal culture dimension on which the Middle East cluster scored high. It was in the medium range for Assertiveness, Humane Orientation, Institutional Collectivism, Performance Orientation, and Power Distance. Its scores on Future Orientation, Gender Egalitarianism, and Uncertainty Avoidance were in the low range (House et al., 2004).

Although there is considerable between-country variation for the preferred leadership, Charismatic/Value Based leadership and Team Oriented leadership are considered to be contributing positively to outstanding leadership. Humane Oriented leadership is seen as either contributing or neutral to outstanding leadership. Autonomous leadership covers the entire range, from contributing to neutral to inhibiting outstanding leadership. Self Protective leadership is considered either neutral to or inhibiting outstanding leadership. There seems to be medium endorsement of Participative leadership across all countries in the Middle East cluster.

There are several commonalities running through these countries such as religion (Islam), and some geographical features such as the Nile River and the Sahara desert. The commonalities also result from their historic, religious, and sociocultural characteristics and are reflected in their social norms and practices (Kabasakal & Bodus, 2002).

REFERENCES

House, R. J., Hanges, P. J., Javidan, M., Dorfman, P. W., Gupta, V., & GLOBE Associates. (2004). *Culture, leadership, and organizations: The GLOBE study of 62 societies.* Thousand Oaks, CA: Sage.

Kabasakal, H., & Bodur, M. (2002). Arabic cluster: A bridge between East and West. *Journal of World Business, 37,* 40–54.

23

Leadership and Culture in Turkey: A Multifaceted Phenomenon

Hayat Kabasakal
Muzaffer Bodur
Bogaziçi University, Istanbul, Turkey

The Turkish Republic is situated mainly in Western Asia and partly in Southeastern Europe. Its geographical location over two continents serves as a bridge between East and West culturally, economically, and politically. The country is bordered in the east by Georgia, Armenia, and Iran, in the south by Iraq and Syria, and in the west by Greece and Bulgaria. Inland Turkey is 297,000 square miles and is surrounded by the Mediterranean Sea in the south, the Aegean in the west, and the Black Sea in the north.

Population is estimated to be approximately 68 million. Nearly 64.7% of the Turkish population lives in urban areas where the major cities are Istanbul, Ankara (the capital), Izmir, Adana, Antalya, Bursa, and Konya. Life expectancy is 69.5 years of age, and infant mortality per 1000 is reported as 39 for the second quarter of 2001 (http://www.dpt.gov.tr).

The official language is Turkish, spoken by 90% of the population; followed by 7% Kurdish, which is spoken mainly in the southeast. Though Islam is the religion of 99% of the population, the Turkish Republic is a secular state (Appendix: Statistical Profile of the GLOBE Society Sample). It was estimated that in 1986 there were approximately 100,000 Christians and in 1996 there were approximately 25,000 Jews in Turkey (*The Europa World Year Book*, 1996).

At the threshold of the 21st century, in view of the recent developments in Central and North Asia, Eastern Europe, and the Middle East, Turkey is faced with the challenges of sustaining a Western economic and political ideology. With continuing economic liberalization, industrialization take-off, and a highly favorable geographical location, Turkey is a promising country for foreign investments and international trade prospects.

Turkey is a democratic and secular state formed in 1923 upon the demise of the Ottoman Empire and after a war of liberation against foreign powers, which occupied the country at the end of World War I. The early years of the Republic were characterized by vast economic and social reforms. With the decline of the Empire, many Muslim groups living in former Turkish territories in Southeastern Europe and around the Northern Black Sea migrated to the home country. At that time these migrations created a subculture that had a Western orientation, which still prevails today. Currently, Turkish culture may be characterized as having elements of modernity, tradition, and Islam. With the worldwide globalization trends, new lifestyles are being created, especially among the younger population. On the other hand, the rise of the Islamist movement in the country is leading to a new subculture. The subculture that identifies itself with Islamism includes not only the aspiring middle class of the towns, but also some university students and young professionals of the middle class, owners of small- to medium-size firms, and the lower socioeconomic groups of the metropolises.

Turkey has been moving closer to Europe by entering into a Custom Union with European Union (EU) countries with the intention of becoming a full member in the near future. At the Helsinki meeting held in 1999, Turkey was officially recognized as a candidate state on equal footing with the other candidate states. According to the Accession Partnership, Turkey participated in meetings with the EU states in 2004 and was accepted to start the accession process in the later part of 2005 (cf. EU enlargement, 2005). On the other hand, the recent restructuring of the former Soviet states (Azerbaijan, Kazakhstan, Krgyzstan, Uzbekistan, and Turkmenistan) is also offering many opportunities economically and culturally. In addition, the proponents of the Islamist movement claim that Turkey should initiate closer ties with the Islamic countries. Thus, a multiplicity of ideologies is seen that is leading to a culture that has a mixture of traditional, modern, and Islamic values, and an Eastern and Western orientation at all layers of society and organizations.

This chapter describes the unique aspects of society, organizations, and leaders in Turkish culture with the objective of providing insights and drawing implications for culture specific leadership and organizational practices. After an overview of the Turkish history, politics, economy, and society, the chapter proceeds with a description of the methodology used for generating the qualitative and quantitative GLOBE data, followed by presentation and discussion of GLOBE dimension findings at societal, organizational, and leader levels.

1. AN OVERVIEW OF TURKEY: HISTORICAL, ECONOMIC, POLITICAL, AND SOCIETAL PERSPECTIVES

A Historical Perspective and the Legal System

The Turkish legal structure is organized along Western lines. Westernization of the laws can be traced back to the latter periods of the Ottoman Empire, specifically to the period after the proclamation of the Edict of Reorganization (Tanzimat Fermani) in 1839. In the period from 1839 until the establishment of the Republic, the old Islamic laws and institutions were basically maintained, although some Western statutes were adopted from Europe (Güriz, 1987).

With the defeat of the Ottoman Empire in World War I, the Ottoman government in Istanbul collapsed and armies of the Allies occupied the country. A parallel government was developed in Anatolia by the nationalists who had resisted the armed forces of the Allies; the leader of the nationalists was Mustafa Kemal. The Independence War ended with the establishment of the Turkish Republic in 1923. The 1924 constitution proposed a "majoritarian" system, rather than a system of checks and balances (Özbudun, 1987). In both the single-party (1924–1946) and the multiparty (1946–1960) years of the constitution, the "executive" dominated the Assembly. During this period, the Turkish political system witnessed the authoritarian leadership of party leaders and the obedience of the parliamentarians to party decisions.

The authoritarian measures taken by the government in the 1950s created unrest in society, and on May 27, 1960, Turkish armed forces overthrew the Menderes government. In 1961, a new Constitution was prepared that represented a reaction to the 1924 Constitution. This new Constitution proposed a pluralistic, rather than a majoritarian system of democracy. After a decade of stability, the second military takeover took place in 1972. The second half of the 1970s was characterized by considerable political instability. With the succession of weak coalition governments, terrorism and political polarization became widespread. Turkish armed forces intervened in the political system for the third time on September 12, 1980. In 1982, a new constitution was prepared that was a reaction to the earlier one in 1961. The political crisis of the 1970s was attributed to the "excessive permissiveness" of the 1961 Constitution and to the weaknesses of the executive branch. The underlying objective of the 1982 Constitution was to establish both a strong state and a strong execution.

The Turkish legal system was Westernized by some radical reforms after the proclamation of the Republic in 1923. The radical reforms in legal matters paralleled other social reforms in all facets of life. Both in the field of private law and in the sphere of public law, Western codes were adopted. Though societal requirements for order and consistency are spelled out by rules and laws, in many cases, some of them are overridden by religious laws and traditions. Written laws prepared under the influence of Western laws, mainly in the early years of the Republic, represent a need for Westernization of the country and breaking the ties with the past, which represent the religious state. However, we often see a dual structure and mixed applications in society. Some parts of society that aspire for Westernization adhere to the rules and laws of the formal ideology and state (named as Kemalist ideology to represent the ideals and vision of Kemal Atatürk), whereas other subcultures in society, mainly the rural and lower socioeconomic groups in the urban areas, prefer to rely on the traditions.

Economic Environment and Business Structure

At the macro level, the Turkish economic environment, strengthened by the government's neo-liberalization measures since the early 1980s, demonstrates a commitment for growth. The Turkish economy grew at a rate of 4.2% in the period 1990–1998 (Appendix: Statistical Profile of the GLOBE Society Sample). However the neo-liberalization process has intensified the income inequalities (Önis, 1997) and as can be seen from the Statistical Profile of the GLOBE Society Sample, Turkey with a Gini Index of 41.5 stands among the countries with a highly unequal distribution of income. Nearly 65% of the GLOBE sample countries have a more equal income distribution than Turkey.

In 2001, Turkey's gross national product (GNP) was estimated to be U.S.$ 147,062 million, equivalent to $2,143 per person. Agriculture (including forestry and fishing) contributed 12.9% to GDP and industry (including mining, manufacturing, construction, and power) contributed 30.4% to GDP (http://www.dpt.gov.tr/dptweb/esg/esg-i.html). According to 2002 second-quarter figures, about 35% of the employed population worked in agriculture, and 18.7% in industry (http://www.die.gov.tr). Turkey was experiencing high inflation rates, over 30% per year and political instability between the mid-1980s and early 2000s (http://www.tcmb.gov.tr), yet in the 2000s inflation rates have been taken under control to around 10 per cent and political stability was achieved to a significant degree with a single-party government. Economic and political stability together with high economic growth rates have created a favorable economic environment for business. On the other hand, there exist large differences in economic development between western and eastern Turkey. The eastern part of the country is rural and much more traditional whereas the western region is industrialized, more urban, and Westernized.

State (Inter)dependence of Business.   Business life in Turkey is dominated by private business groups and state economic enterprises. Since the inception of multiparty rule in 1946, a period of economic liberalization followed leading to a mixed economy, yet the state has been an important institution in shaping the business structure in Turkey. Historically, there was no capitalist class at the end of the Ottoman Empire. When the Republic of Turkey was founded, there was virtually no industry and a weak infrastructure. Due to the economic concessions made to foreign powers during the last years of the Ottoman Empire and the war of liberation, there was suspicion of foreign investment; this coupled with the prevailing economic ideology of the time led to the state becoming the main actor.

Turkish private companies remain highly dependent on the state for financial incentives and the state often intervenes with frequent and unpredictable policy changes, which introduce uncertainties in business life (Bugra, 1990). Although there has been significant liberalization in many areas, such as the finance sector, international trade, and some privatization of state economic enterprises, the state still remains the key actor in the economy, as well as the distributor of resources in the second half of the 1990s and early 2000s. In their study of Danish investments in Turkey, Bodur and Madsen (1993) conclude that personal contacts with influential government officials become important in finalizing decisions.

The Political System and Religious Ideology

The Turkish Republic was founded in 1923 after which several reforms in social, political, economic, and legal systems were undertaken. The first president of the Republic was Mustafa Kemal Atatürk, whose principles for reform, such as nationalism, secularism, and statism, have come to be called Kemalism. The basis of the Kemalist ideology was to transform the society into a Western and secular structure.

In the Turkish political system, the legislative power is vested in the Turkish Grand National Assembly, whose members are elected for a 5-year term. The party leader with the highest number of parliamentarians is assigned by the president as the prime minister. The president is elected by the parliament for a 7-year term.

Political life has been frequently interrupted by military coups or interventions whenever political crises developed. The military has played a unique role in Turkey over the last 40 years. Though Turkey has had three military coups, each time the military has relinquished power fairly quickly and on its own accord. After a short period of restructuring, the military typically hands over the system to the political parties and restarts democracy. Furthermore, the military remains the most trustworthy institution according to the public polls (Ergüder, Y. Esmer, & Kalaycioglu, 1991; Esmer, 1999) and the Turkish people seem to be most satisfied with the services of the military (Adaman, Çarkoglu, & Senatalar, 2001).

The 1990s and early 2000s were an era of coalition governments with very short life spans. Elections conducted in 2002 yielded a single-party government, which provided political stability after a long period of instability. In parallel, Turkish society has been experiencing the simultaneous influence of secularism and Islamism. The rise of Islamism can be perceived as a product of the frustration of the promises of Western modernization and represents a critique of modernism (Gülalp, 1995). In this respect, Islamism can be interpreted more as an opposition to modernism, rather than as traditionalism. On the other hand, a majority of

Turkish society has fragmented political ideologies, ranging from strong commitment to Kemalism to moderate rightist traditional manifestations.

Perspectives on the Social System

Education.   There has been a great increase in the literacy rates during the Republican era, though room for improvement remains. The 1990 statistics for the population aged 6 years and above indicate that 46.1% were primary school graduates, 7.6% junior high school, 7.8% high school, and 3.0% were university graduates, adding to 64.5% (State Planning Organization, 1995, p.12). In 1999, the literacy rates for males and females were 93.2% and 75.9%, respectively (*Human Development Report 2001: Turkey,* 2001).

Primary school is legally mandatory, which in 1996 increased to 8 years. The average rate of adult literacy was 84% in 1999. In Turkey, public education is essentially free at all levels including the universities.

Human Development.   Turkey's human development practices continuously improved during the 1990–1998 period. Based on the Human Development Index (HDI) Rank of 82 with a value of 0.735 for 1999, Turkey stands among the medium human development countries (*Human Development Report: Turkey,* 2001). A majority of Turkey's population (51%) live in provinces that have high human development indices, 47.1% in those with medium, and 1.9% in those with low (*Human Development Report 1996: Turkey,* 1996).

2. METHODOLOGY

Qualitative and Quantitative Data

The country analysis is based on both qualitative and quantitative data. The following data sources were used.

Focus-Groups and In-Depth Interviews.   Two focus group interviews were conducted; one consisted of five individuals and the other of seven. All participants had full-time work experience as middle-level managers, supervisory-level managers, or office workers. In-depth interviews were carried out with six middle-level managers from the financial and food-processing sectors. We conducted the focus groups and in-depth interviews in autumn 1994. After a preliminary analysis of the interviews and survey results, two more in-depth interviews were conducted to validate the findings. All interviews were recorded on tape and later transcribed verbatim. The transcribed data served as the basis for ethnographic analysis.

Media Analysis.   This analysis had the purpose of analyzing news published in the printed media for identifying leadership patterns in the Turkish context. We collected the data during April 4-19, 1996. Five separately printed media, which consisted of three daily newspapers (*Milliyet, Türkiye,* and *Dünya*) and two weekly periodicals (*Nokta* and *Ekonomist*), were used as the database.

A Survey of Middle-Level Managers.   Two types of self-administered questionnaires were conducted with 323 middle-level managers employed in 23 firms, 150 employed in the financial sector and 173 in the food-processing sector. The data were collected in autumn 1995. The mean age of the sample was 35.2 years, they averaged 14 years of formal education, 71.5% were male, and the remaining 28.5% were female. On average they had 14.4 years of work experience, 11.2 years of managerial experience, and 6.7 years of tenure with their present organization.

Organizational Demography Questionnaires.   A total of six companies were selected out of the 23 companies covered in the survey. Those six companies with the highest representations in the survey were selected for the organizational demography study. Three of these companies were from the financial and three were from the food-processing sectors.

Participant Observation and Unobtrusive Measurement Questions.   The participant observation questionnaire included 101 questions, and the unobtrusive measurement questionnaire had 38 questions about the societal dimensions of culture. These questionnaires were completed by the researchers and were based on their own knowledge and expert opinion about the values, structures, and institutions prevalent in society.

Industry Analysis.   Industry analysis included a review and ethnographic analysis of routinely printed media, in- house newsletters or magazines that cater to managers in that industry, trade association newsletters, publications on industry structure, and sector-based reports.

Ethnogenic Analysis of Major Political and Industry Leaders.   Leader autobiographies, biographies, historical diaries, and news published upon their death were reviewed with the purpose of evaluating leadership patterns, the position attributed to business and political leaders throughout history within a societal and institutional context.

Further methodological parameters of the GLOBE study are set out in House et al. (1999, 2004).

3. TURKISH SOCIETY AND GLOBE DIMENSIONS

In this section, the results of the survey conducted with 323 middle-level managers from the financial and food-processing sectors are presented. This section of the questionnaire probed about the beliefs of the respondents with respect to "how are" the current norms, values, and practices and "how they should be" in their society. In both sections of the questionnaire, a series of 7-point Likert scale statements were given to the respondents. The items were categorized into nine dimensions. Table 23.1 portrays the societal "As Is" and "Should Be" scores.

"As Is" scores reveal that Turkish society is viewed as having practices that are high in In-group Collectivism (M = 5.88, Rank 5), Power Distance (M = 5.57, Rank 10), and Assertiveness (M = 4.53, Rank 12). All three of these dimensions have high absolute scores and belong to Band A. In terms of societal practices regarding Uncertainty Avoidance (M = 3.63, Rank 49), Humane Orientation (M = 3.94, Rank 37), and Future Orientation (M = 3.74, Rank 36), Turkey has low absolute and relative scores. All three of these dimensions belong to Band C. Turkey's Gender Egalitarianism "As Is" score is low in absolute scale (M = 2.89) and it Ranks 56th; however it stands in Band B, implying that most cultures in the GLOBE sample have practices representing gender inequality. In Performance Orientation (M = 3.83, Rank 45), Turkey

TABLE 23.1
Country Means for Societal Culture Dimensions

Culture	Society "As Is"			Society "Should Be"			Difference[d]
Dimensions	Mean[a]	Band[b]	Rank[c]	Mean[a]	Band[b]	Rank[c]	"Should Be"–"As Is"
Performance Orientation	3.83	B	45	5.39	D	58	1.56
Future Orientation	3.74	C	36	5.83	A	16	2.09
Assertiveness	4.53	A	12	2.66	C	61	−1.87
Institutional Collectivism	4.03	B	41	5.26	A	10	1.23
In-Group Collectivism	5.88	A	5	5.77	B	22	−0.11
Gender Egalitarianism	2.89	B	56	4.50	B	37	1.61
Humane Orientation	3.94	C	37	5.52	B	25	1.58
Power Distance	5.57	A	10	2.41	D	51	−3.16
Uncertainty Avoidance	3.63	C	49	4.67	B	32	1.04

[a]Country mean score on a 7-point Likert-type scale. [b]Band letters A–D indicating meaningful country bands for the scales A > B > C (>D); see Hanges, Dickson, & Sipe (2004). [c]The ranking for Turkey relative to the 61 GLOBE countries. [d]Difference: "As Is" score minus "Should Be" score.

has a low absolute score, yet it has a moderate relative standing, falling into Band B. In terms of Institutional Collectivism ($M = 4.03$, Rank 41), Turkish society is moderate both in absolute and relative scale scores, with a standing in Band B.

Looking at the societal values ("Should Be" scores), it can be seen that Turkey has high absolute and relative scale scores in Future Orientation ($M = 5.83$, Rank 16) and Institutional Collectivism ($M = 5.26$, Rank 10). In these two dimensions, Turkish society stands in Band A. In terms of Power Distance ($M = 2.41$, Rank 51) and Assertiveness ($M = 2.66$, Rank 61), Turkey has low scores in both absolute and relative terms. In Power Distance, Turkish society has a standing in Band D and in Assertiveness it is in Band C. In the rest of the societal values, Turkish society has high absolute scores, yet in terms of relative standing with respect to GLOBE countries, it has a moderate or a low standing. In In-Group Collectivism ($M = 5.77$, Rank 24), Humane Orientation ($M = 5.52$, Rank 25), Uncertainty Avoidance ($M = 4.67$, Rank 32), and Gender Egalitarianism ($M = 4.50$, Rank 37), Turkey has high absolute and moderate relative scores. In Performance Orientation ($M = 5.39$, Rank 58), though Turkey has a high absolute score, its low Ranking and standing in Band D places it in a low relative place.

The last column of Table 23.1 shows the differences between societal values and practices. The highest absolute difference between "Should Be" and "As Is" scores is in Power Distance (−3.16), followed by Future Orientation (2.09), which suggest that Turkish society desires substantially lower levels of Power Distance and higher levels of Future Orientation. In addition, Turkish society aspires for moderately more Gender Egalitarianism (1.61), Humane Orientation (1.58), Performance Orientation (1.56), Institutional Collectivism (1.23), and Uncertainty Avoidance (1.04). On the other hand, society desires a moderately lower level of

Assertiveness (−1.87). In terms of In-Group Collectivism, the difference between societal values and practices is negligible (-0.11), indicating that societal practices match aspirations.

In light of findings on societal GLOBE dimensions, the next sections focus on each dimension separately, integrating it with the society's historical, social, and economic characteristics. These discussions lead to interpretations of findings on organizational culture and leadership dimensions.

Performance Orientation

Performance Orientation describes the degree to which society encourages people to continuously improve performance and rewards performance effectiveness and achievements. Turkey's "As Is" score in Performance Orientation is low in absolute terms ($M = 3.83$). It Ranks 45th among GLOBE countries and it stands in Band B, placing it in a moderate relative standing. In absolute terms, the "Should Be" score in Performance Orientation ($M = 5.39$) is higher than the "As Is" score, yet its ranking (58th) and standing in Band D puts it in a low relative place among GLOBE societies. This finding suggests that cultures around the world aspire for very high levels of Performance Orientation and Turkey's high score in absolute terms stands to be relatively low compared to other societies.

In general, "As Is" and "Should Be" scores in Performance Orientation point to the fact that Turkish society is not characterized by high performance orientation. The general indicators point to rather low levels of economic productivity, foreign direct investments, and competitive strength in the global arena (Uluslararasi Dogrudan Yatirimlar ve Türkiye, 2002). Beginning with the 1990s, the Turkish public sector increasingly borrowed money from internal and external sources to compensate for the budget deficit, instead of creating resources by increased productivity and better allocation of expenses. Parallel with low Performance Orientation scores, Turkey's investment in research and development is rather low. Only 0.45% of gross domestic product (GDP) is allocated to research and development, whereas this figure is 2.7% to 3.9% in most developed nations of the world. A comparative study shows that Turkey ranks 39th in research and development investments and 40th in size of research and development personnel among 47 nations (Institute for Management Development, 1999).

In general, there is a moderate level of emphasis on education in Turkish society. Primary school education is mandatory and it was increased from 5 to 8 years in 1996. Students at universities are encouraged to study at a moderate level, yet at graduation, universities honor students with the highest grades by awarding plaques. Public education is free at all levels, including the university education. The emphasis on education has created a sizable group of well-educated professionals in the labor market. The existence of a skilled and highly educated workforce was found to be one of the major strengths of Turkey in attracting foreign direct investments (Uluslararasi Dogrudan Yatirimlar ve Türkiye, 2002).

Compared with the public sector, the private sector has a higher Performance Orientation. Most private organizations take performance-oriented measures and invest in training and development. In a study conducted with 307 private Turkish companies, it was found that 81% conducted performance appraisals and 82% had training and development programs (Arthur Andersen, 2000). On the other hand, the percentage of companies that applied career planning dropped to 42% and the organizations were quite reluctant to tie performance appraisal results to pay, salary decisions, or career planning. This finding indicates that variables other than performance are taken into account as rewarding mechanisms, which supports Turkey's mediocre GLOBE Performance Orientation scores.

Future Orientation

Future Orientation measures the extent to which society values and practices planning and investment, as opposed to focusing on current problems and the present. The "As Is" Future Orientation score shows that Turkish society is characterized by a low absolute ($M = 3.74$) and relative standing (Rank 36, Band C) in terms of future-oriented practices. On the other hand, compared to the "As Is" score, the "Should Be" Future Orientation score ($M = 5.83$, Rank 16, Band A) is substantially higher both in terms of absolute and relative values.

The low level of "As Is" Future Orientation score in both absolute and relative scale reflect the fact that people accept status quo and take life events as they occur rather than planning for the future. Societal practices that encourage and reward accepting the status quo can at least partly be explained by the Islam religion (H. Kabasakal & Bodur, 2002; H. Kabasakal & Dastmalchian, 2001). Turkish society is 99% Muslim, which is one of the highest population ratios in the world, in terms of religious homogeneity. The concept of "fate" in Islam can be considered to be a factor that is associated with accepting life events and the status quo. According to *amentu* in studies of Islam, believing in fate is among the basic principles of faith in God (Ilmihal I, 1999). Many verses of the Koran openly indicate that all deeds that happened in the past and that will occur in the future are prearranged and within God's preordaining. Although the concept of fate in Islam is very complicated and there are some verses in Koran that focus on the importance of individual responsibility and choice of action in people's lives, interpretations of Islam mostly create a passive attitude toward the future because all conduct is perceived to come from God.

Low levels of future-oriented practices are currently perceived as lack of effective plans for the cities on the part of municipalities, as most cities grow in an unplanned and haphazard manner. Though most of Turkey is in a high-risk area in terms of earthquakes, public offices and individuals in the high-risk areas are found to avoid mitigation and planning activities (Iseri, Inelmen, Kabasakal, & Akarun, 2002). Part of the reason for avoiding mitigation and planning is attributed to fatalism because one third of the participants that responded to in-depth interviews indicated that they do not feel they can do anything to prepare themselves for a future earthquake and close to two thirds expected fate or luck to play a role in their future survival (Fisek, Müderrisoglu, Yeniçeri, & Özkarar, 2001).

As opposed to the low level of Future Orientation in societal practices, Turkish society is characterized by high aspirations for planning. People believe that activities should be planned and they should live for the future. As an indication of the high value attributed to planning, both the 1961 and 1982 Constitutions have articles on "planning." According to the Constitutions, the planning of economic, social, and cultural development and the efficient use of national resources on the basis of detailed analysis and the establishment of the necessary organization for this purpose is the duty of the state. The State Planning Organization, as established by the 1961 Constitution, is the highest body responsible for planning and directly reports to the prime minister. Although the importance attributed to planning is evident in the Turkish Constitution, in recent years the plans that are formulated by the State Planning Organization are mostly bypassed by the governments.

Similarly, many large organizations have planning departments and staff responsible for planning. They formulate vision and mission statements and conduct strategic planning. On the other hand, most of the time plans are not applied in practice and companies focus mainly on solving current problems. One of the reasons that can be cited for focusing on the present is the fact that Turkey has been experiencing political and economic instability and high inflation rates in the last two decades. Economic instability and high levels of inflation, coupled with political instability make planning very difficult for companies. Unavoidably, the decision makers focus on the short term; sometimes even yearly plans become difficult. Because predicting the future is almost impossible, speculative activities decided by the company owners gain importance, which reflects the relatively low levels of Future Orientation "As Is" scores that were obtained by the quantitative findings of the GLOBE scales. Furthermore, given the fact that there is high dependence on the state, owners of large companies and conglomerates decide on the direction of the companies based on advice and guidance of politicians and top state officials. In a study of Danish investments in Turkey, Danish investors pointed to the contributions of Turkish partners in establishing relationships with government officials and the importance of such contacts on company decisions (Bodur & Madsen, 1993).

Assertiveness

Assertiveness describes the extent to which people in society are dominant and tough, as opposed to soft and tender. The "As Is" Mean score for Turkish society is high in both absolute and relative scale ($M = 4.53$, Rank 12, Band A). On the other hand, the "Should Be" Assertiveness score of Turkish society is low in terms of its absolute value and relative place; indeed it has the lowest score among other GLOBE societies in this cultural dimension ($M = 2.66$, Rank 61, Band C). Whereas Turkish society is characterized by high levels of dominance and toughness, people in society aspire for tender and nonassertive relationships.

The "Masculinity/Femininity" dimension in Hofstede's (1980, 2001) research has some overlaps with the GLOBE Assertiveness dimension. According to Hofstede, in masculine cultures, men are supposed to be assertive, tough, and focus on material success, whereas women are supposed to be more modest and tender. In feminine societies, both men and women are supposed to be modest and tender. In Hofstede's work (1980), Turkey was found to be in the middle of the Masculinity/Femininity scale, tilting toward the femininity side, and when the values were controlled for the percentage of women among the respondents, Turkey was placed more on the masculinity side (Hofstede, 2001). Compared with Hofstede's study, GLOBE findings point to the fact that Turkish society has become a substantially more assertive society in the last two decades.

Starting in the late 1970s, high levels of political instability, high inflation and unemployment rates, and massive migration to urban areas have created an uncertain environment and made survival difficult for members of society. Given the difficulties and uncertainties in the socioeconomic environment, relationships turned out to be tough and assertive in many facets of life.

In general, at all education levels, student–teacher relations are based on teacher assertiveness. The relation is characterized by assertiveness and dominance of the teachers rather than tenderness and students are usually afraid of being scolded by their teachers. There is also strong assertiveness in the family, mainly on the part of the men, who are mostly dominant and authoritarian toward their wives and children. In addition, mothers-in-law practice dominance over their daughters-in-law after their sons get married.

The assertive and authoritarian practices in society can be observed in task-related contexts as well. Government officials usually act in a very authoritarian and assertive manner toward the citizens in public work, including the police stations, courts, and other bureaucratic processes. Private-sector organizations are also characterized by authoritarian relationships between supervisors and subordinates, with supervisors typically having a dominant style in their work relationships.

Members of Turkish society seem to be very dissatisfied with the aggressive and assertive practices they face in everyday life. They aspire for a society where relationships are tender and soft. Turkish society desires one of the least assertive cultures compared to other GLOBE societies.

Institutional Collectivism

Institutional Collectivism measures the extent to which society encourages and rewards collective work and group solidarity in societal and institutional settings. Turkish society is found to have a moderate "As Is" score in Institutional Collectivism in both absolute and relative standing ($M = 4.03$, Rank 41, Band B). The Institutional Collectivism "Should Be" score ($M = 5.26$, Rank 10, Band A) points to the fact that Turkish people desire for high levels of societal and Institutional Collectivism.

Previous studies revealed somewhat similar findings about the level of collectivism in Turkish society. In Hofstede's (1980) study, Turkey was found to be more on the collectivist side of the individualism–collectivism index, however not among the most collectivist societies included in the sample. In Hofstede's work, individualism stands for a society in which the ties between individuals are loose and collectivism stands for a society in which people are integrated into strong, cohesive in-groups. Similarly, Göregenli (1997) found Turkey to exhibit collectivist patterns in some areas, but not display all of the characteristics of a collectivist orientation. According to Göregenli's study, when institutional settings are considered, relationships with coworkers were found to be individualistic in consideration of implications of one's own decisions and actions for others, sharing of material resources, susceptibility to social influence, and feeling of involvement in others' lives. However, collectivist tendencies in institutional settings prevailed in the areas of self-presentation and face work, and sharing of outcomes with coworkers.

Although in general the Turkish society has moderate scores on GLOBE Institutional Collectivism, Turkish society has a strong sense of nationalism and national pride, which can be seen historically as well as in current times. The Turkish Independence War (1919–1923) that was won after the World War I against a coalition of nations that invaded the country is a dramatic example of national unity and solidarity that was portrayed among members of society. Turkish people show great respect for the Turkish flag and national anthem in ceremonies. Winning as a nation in international sports activities has become a very important event, one that is nationally celebrated.

On the other hand, Turkish society seems to exhibit relatively lower levels of collectivism in terms of joining institutions that are formed for different purposes. In general, members of society refrain from joining NGOs (nongovernmental organizations) and CBOs (community-based organizations) (Kabasakal, Akarun, Iseri, & Inelmen, 2001). The general low level of trust in society may be a factor in people's refraining from joining institutions and forming solidarity in institutional frameworks. Data collected from Turkey for the World Values Survey in 1990 and 1997 point to the fact that Turkish people in general have very low levels of trust in other people (Ergüder et al., 1991; Y. Esmer, 1999). In 1990 and 1997, 10% and 6.5% of the respondents, respectively, indicated that in general most people are trustable. In relative standing among the 43 countries that participated in the World Values Survey, Turkey has one of the lowest scores in trusting others. The finding that Turkish people generally have low levels of trust in others may be a significant factor in reducing the level of group solidarity and association with others in teamwork in institutional settings. Fukuyama (1995) ties trust levels in society to forming associations and in this sense low levels of trust in Turkish society may be considered to be a variable that hinders forming partnerships in the private sector as well. The Turkish private sector is dominated by family firms and even the large business groups are owned by families, rather than partnerships with others who may bring different expertise and resources to an organization. Despite this, Turkish people strongly believe in the value of Institutional Collectivism as reflected in the high GLOBE "Should Be" score for Institutional Collectivism.

In-Group Collectivism

In-Group Collectivism describes the degree of collectivism and solidarity among in-group members, particularly in families or organizations. Turkish society is characterized by high levels of In-Group Collectivism in societal practices and has one of the highest "As Is" scores among the GLOBE societies ($M = 5.88$, Rank 5, Band A). Aspirations of people match societal practices, given the finding that the "Should Be" score ($M = 5.77$, Rank 22, Band B) is very close to the "As Is" score.

Family stands at the center of life in Turkish society and people have a high trust of family members (Ergüder et al., 1991; Kagitçibasi, 1982b). The verses of the Koran and interpretations of the Islam religion reinforce the importance of family. Mutual trust within the family is the rule in both rural and urban families. In their socialization, children are taught to support and help their family members rather than to be self-reliant or fending for oneself. In Turkish society there is commonly an interdependent relationship between the children and the family. As a part of this interdependence, the family is always available to support the children when needed. In turn, children, particularly the male children, are expected to provide material and social support to their parents in old age (Kagitçibasi, 1982b). Older brothers are expected to finance the younger siblings' education and costs incurred at marriage. It is common practice that the older members of families arrange marriages for the younger family members and important personal problems are solved by seeking help from the family.

In addition to the family, other in-group relationships also bear a great significance and carry a highly collectivist nature. Among the network of interdependent relationships, belonging to the same school or region plays an important role (Kiray, 1997). For example, when people migrate to urban areas, they usually find employment and housing by the help of their associates who migrated from the same region to the cities before themselves.

Göregenli (1997) found strongly collectivist tendencies in Turkish society in relationships with in-groups, including spouse, mother, siblings, and friends in many categories, such as self- presentation and face work, sharing of outcomes, sharing of nonmaterial resources, consideration of implications of one's own decision and actions for other people, and sharing of material resources. More individualistic tendencies were apparent in relationships with in-groups in the area of susceptibility to social influence.

Most organizations in the Turkish economy are family-owned enterprises. Family members, rather than professionals, constitute the top management of many large business groups. Although the domination of family members, rather than professionals, in management can partly be explained by state–business relationships, it can also be explained by high In-Group Collectivism that is prevalent in Turkish society. In addition to kinship and family ties, belonging to the same school or region also plays a role in employment decisions. For example, it is common practice in Turkish organizations that people who attended the same school are frequently employed in the same management and professional groups. In summary, Turkish people have a strong commitment to their relationships in a network of close interdependent relationships.

Gender Egalitarianism

Gender Egalitarianism measures the extent to which gender differences and discrimination against females in society is minimized. The Gender Egalitarianism "As Is" score for Turkish society is low in absolute terms (M= 2.89) and its relative standing among GLOBE societies is also not high (Rank 56, Band B). When one looks at the "Should Be" score, it can be seen that there is a desire for more Gender Egalitarianism (M = 4.50, Rank 37, Band B), placing Turkish society in a moderate place in comparative terms.

When the Republic of Turkey was established in 1923, a series of reforms were undertaken that aimed at incorporating Westernization and modernization into society. Women were assigned an important part in this modernization project and their progress was perceived as a measure of reaching modernity (Arat, 1999). Although these reforms achieved a significant amount of success in areas such as legal rights, increasing the level of literacy, and education, the patriarchal Middle Eastern practices still exist in society.

In general, the social differences between women and men lie primarily in the area of what they are expected to "do." More specifically, women are expected to engage in activities that are inside the house or the organization, basically in support roles. Alternatively, men engage in activities that require relationships with the outside. In another perspective, women are more in support activities, whereas men are more in positions of power and decision making. Beyond the differences in what they are expected to do, few sex role stereotypes exist. In a study of sex role stereotypes, high school students of both sexes judged the desirability of personality characteristics for women and men (Gürbüz, 1988). Accordingly, the six socially desirable characteristics, "ambitious," "analytical," "forceful," "rash," "insists on one's rights," "enterprising," and three socially undesirable characteristics, "dominant," "jealous," and "autonomous" were all identified as masculine traits. Four socially desirable characteristics, "loves children," "dependent," "elegant," and "thrifty," and five socially undesirable characteristics, "submissive," "cowardly," "weak," "insecure," and "naive" were identified as feminine. It can be seen from the results of this study that femininity is associated with more negative and passive attributes than masculinity, which is in line with low Gender Egalitarianism that is obtained by the GLOBE scales.

Parallel with the low Gender Egalitarianism scores of the GLOBE study, the HDI score of men is 0.824, whereas women have a much lower HDI value, that is, 0.648. In 1998, Turkey's Gender Development Index (GDI) was 0.726, standing in the last one third of the GLOBE societies in terms of gender development (Appendix: Statistical Profile of the GLOBE Society Sample). Hofstede's (1980, 2001) study placed Turkey in the middle of the Masculinity–Femininity index. On the other hand, results of a cross-cultural study shows that there is a huge variation between the intrafamily status of Turkish women in rural settings and urban women in professional/managerial occupations (Kagitçibasi, 1982a). Such wide variation was not found in the other eight countries where the same study was conducted.

Dual structure of women in Turkish society is also observed in the employment and labor market. Women with rural and lower socioeconomic origins are employed mainly in the agricultural sector as unpaid family workers and their representation in the paid urban force is quite low, with a concentration in low-paying and low-status jobs (H. Kabasakal, Aycan, & Karakas, 2004; Özar, 1994; Özbay, 1994). In 1999, only 15.8% of the urban workforce was female (State Institute of Statistics, 1999). On the other hand, women with middle or upper socioeconomic backgrounds have very high percentages in highly prestigious professions. In the 1990s and early 2000s Turkish women constituted 35% of academics, 60% of pharmacists, 19% of physicians, 30% of dentists, and 34 % of lawyers (Acar, 1991; Gürüz, 2001; Koray, 1991). Despite the high ratios of women in many prestigious professions, women's representation in managerial and executive positions ranges between 3% and 4% in the private sector (H. Kabasakal, 1998; H. Kabasakal, Boyacigiller, & Erden, 1994) and only 4% of the Turkish parliament was composed of women in 1999 (General Directorate, 2001). These statistics show that women's representation in positions that require the use of executive and political power is very restricted, although in general they may have high ratios in highly professional and technical jobs.

A nationwide study conducted in 1987 points to a large wage gap between men and women, where women received as much as 60% of men's wages (Tan, Ecevit, & Üsür, 2000). It is interesting to note that the wage gap decreased as the education levels of employees increased. Women directors, entrepreneurs, and managers earned as much (95.6%) as their male colleagues in the public sector. Although comparably lower, female managers' wages are 84% of male managers in the private sector (State Planning Organization, 2000). These statistics support the interpretation that there is a dual structure in the status of women, based on their socioeconomic backgrounds.

Despite the significant attempts at improving the status of women in the Republic of Turkey, the reforms have achieved limited success among rural and lower socioeconomic groups within society. Significant, success was achieved in legal, education, and employment-related areas for women in urban, middle, and upper socioeconomic groups, yet some conflicting and traditional roles are simultaneously present in Turkish society as part of the Middle Eastern culture and Islamic ideology (Topaloglu, 1983). These traditional roles promote segregation of gender roles, the role of women as mothers and wives, and some passive traits that are considered to be feminine.

Humane Orientation

Humane Orientation refers to the degree to which people in society are concerned, sensitive, and generous to each other. Turkey has low absolute and relative "As Is" Humane Orientation scores (M = 3.94, Rank 37, Band C). On the other hand, as reflected in "Should Be" scores, aspirations of Turkish respondents for a humane-oriented society are high in absolute terms and moderate in comparative terms (M = 5.52, Rank 25, Band B).

In Turkey, the family and in-groups take care of many problems of individuals. Given the prevailing social structure where individuals are surrounded by an interdependent network of close relationships, individuals get help and assistance from their close circle. People receive both material and psychological support, even without asking for it. The family, neighbors, and school friends offer help and arrange the conditions for those individuals who are in need of it in both rural and urban areas and, among all classes (Duben, 1982). Contrary to this, the general tendency to help and act in a generous, friendly manner to others who are outside the close network is relatively low.

Mead (1994) argues that patronage relationships foster in environments where welfare services are weak or nonexistent. In Turkey, there is not a well-developed social security and welfare system and many institutions that would serve the well-being of individuals are quite weak. Instead, informal relationships, including patronage relationships take care of the welfare of individuals. Although in patronage relationships, resources are offered to members of the network and nonmembers are denied (Mead, 1994). In line with this proposition, in Turkey, help and assistance is offered selectively in an informal network, rather than as a general commodity.

As part of the patronage relationships, paternalistic leaders in Turkish organizations look after the well-being of their employees in many personal matters (Aycan et al., 2000; Dilber, 1967). In addition, many parliamentarians spend a significant amount of their time resolving the personal problems of their voters, such as finding jobs and hospital places and solving their bureaucratic problems. Thus, paternalistic leaders in Turkish society provide help and assistance to their followers in many facets of life, like a father would.

Power Distance

Power Distance measures the extent to which members of society expect power and influence to be distributed equally in that society. Turkey has high "As Is" Power Distance scores in both absolute and relative scale ($M = 5.57$, Rank 10, Band A). As opposed to the high Power Distance practices, the "Should Be" scores indicate that people aspire for a low Power Distance society in absolute and relative terms ($M = 2.41$, Rank 51, Band D).

GLOBE's finding that practices in Turkish society represent hierarchical relationships are in line with previous cross-cultural studies (Hofstede, 1980, 2001; Schwartz, 1994; Trompenaars & Hampden-Turner, 1998). Hofstede's study indicated that in high–Power Distance societies like Turkey, employees are afraid to express disagreement with their managers. Parallel with Hofstede's definition of high–Power Distance cultures, Turkish managers in general expect obedience from their employees and employees are quite reluctant to declare their disagreements with their managers. Trompenaars and Hampden-Turner's study showed that Turkish companies have the steepest hierarchy among companies of 38 nations. Trompenaars and Hampden-Turner indicated that the familial cultures like the Turkish society have steep hierarchies in their organizations. In such societies, leaders get their power and confidence from their followers and from the obedience of followers to the leaders, like in father–child relationships. In a cross-cultural study conducted by Schwartz (1994), Turkey was found to be among the most hierarchical societies, ranking 6th among 38 cultures in terms of preferring high Power Distance, influence, and authority.

Previous studies together with GLOBE's findings show that Turkish society is characterized by the centralization of authority and influence. Power and resource allocation is based on hierarchy rather than an egalitarian distribution. There is a large social distance among groups that belong to different strata in society and organizations. Vast differences in socioeconomic status of classes are manifested at both societal and organizational levels.

In most business organizations, the amount of office space is generally allocated according to the status of the employees/managers, rather than the requirements of the work to be done. Usually at places of work, titles are listed on the doors of the offices. Titles are generally used when addressing others who are not intimate friends. In business organizations, some eating places and parking spaces are separated according to the status of the employees. In addition, privileges such as health insurance, housing, and cars are all allocated on a hierarchical basis.

The way people address each other in society reflects status differences. Individuals are addressed differently: (a) with different pronouns, and (b) with their first names or the use of sir/madam beforehand, based on status differences. Lower-status people are addressed by their first name, whereas for higher-status people madam or sir is added. Wealthy families generally have three or more domestic servants. Even middle-income groups would have a domestic servant in their houses.

Wealthy people generally have more political influence in the country. The Turkish Businessmen's and Industrialists' Association includes only very wealthy owners and few professional managers; this association frequently prepares reports on social, political, and economic affairs. In addition, in the eastern and southeastern regions of Turkey, the wealthy individuals who are also the patrons are usually elected as parliamentarians and have political power in the sense that they influence their followers' votes.

Uncertainty Avoidance

Uncertainty Avoidance is the extent to which society emphasizes orderliness, structure, and rules in order to reduce unpredictability and uncertainty. Turkish society has low absolute and relative "As Is" scores in GLOBE's Uncertainty Avoidance scale ($M = 3.63$, Rank 49, Band C). It seems like society can tolerate unpredictability and uncertainty to a significant extent. On the other hand, the respondents aspired for more predictability as reflected in moderate "Should Be" scores in absolute and relative terms ($M = 4.67$; Rank 32, Band B).

Hofstede (1980, 2001) classified Turkey as being a high–Uncertainty Avoidance culture, yet it seems like society has become more tolerant of uncertainty over time. Hofstede (2001) reported significant correlations between rule orientation and employment stability, indicating that both factors serve as uncertainty reduction mechanisms. Turkey experienced extensive political and economic instability during 1980s and 1990s. Turkey was governed by coalitions that have had short durations and experienced significant economic instability, as reflected in high inflation and unemployment rates. A study conducted with 216 Turkish manufacturing companies showed that more than half of the companies in the sample reduced their production capacity and 30% laid off workers during the period 1998–1999 (Eren, Bildirici, & Firat, 2000). Furthermore, employees who were laid off were from all levels, covering a range of unskilled workers to top management. The period of instability has reduced rule orientation in organizations and society at large in an effort to produce more organic and flexible survival techniques in the highly uncertain environment.

Political instability, high levels of inflation and unemployment rates, existence of a large informal sector, and frequent lay-offs in the Turkish business world and economy created flexible forms of coping mechanisms with the turbulent and uncertain conditions on the part of individuals and organizations. The Adaman et al. (2001) study conducted among 3,021 individuals shows that people in Turkish society frequently consider giving money or presents to public officers to receive service even for some cases that may be their legal right. It can be argued that Turkish people have developed crude survival techniques in order to survive in the unfavorable and uncertain conditions that were experienced in the last few decades, rather than focusing on orderliness and rules as reflected in GLOBE's low Uncertainty Avoidance "As Is" scores. On the other hand, Turkish people aspire for a more orderly and predictable environment.

4. LEADERSHIP IN TURKEY

Kemal Atatürk is the most effective leader that has emerged in Turkish society. He was the leader in the Independence War, the establishment of the Republic, and many reforms that aimed at the development, modernization, and Westernization of society. He is known for his action and change orientation, decisiveness in the vision he provided to society, inspiration, and belief in Turkish people. He consistently pointed to the need for Westernization and modernization, took radical actions in this direction, and continuously increased the morale of society and inspired the public. He had injected self-confidence and hope into individuals and constantly repeated his belief in the capabilities of the Turkish people.

Apart from Atatürk, Turkey has produced very few well-known leaders. Although they are still not completely accepted as effective leaders by the entire public, those political leaders who have had large groups of loyal followers are Inönü, Menderes, Demirel, Ecevit, Özal, and Erbakan. Though all of them are known for providing vision to society, these political leaders have two distinct approaches. One type such as, Menderes, Özal, and Erbakan, are the more action- and change-oriented leaders, whereas the second type, Inönü, Demirel, and Ecevit, can be identified more as pro status quo, yet administratively skilled. Change oriented leaders are often criticized for going against the status quo, but at the same time praised for initiating change.

Koç, Sabanci, and Eczacibasi are among the few industrial leaders who are well known by the public at large and particularly acknowledged for their contributions to the national economy by creating employment opportunities. They are not known to be high risk takers, but created their wealth and business groups through intensive relations with the state (Bugra, 1987). They also engaged in a variety of cultural activities that are targeted toward contributing to the welfare of society, such as sponsoring festivals, building schools, universities, hospitals, and providing scholarships to a large number of students. In their speeches, they often emphasized their motivation to contribute to the welfare of society, rather than to their business success. Thus, focus of industrial leadership revolves around input in to the national economy and well-being of society, rather than market success, innovation, and managerial effectiveness.

Leaders in Turkish society are on the one hand viewed with skepticism, their integrity is often questioned, and their source of power is discussed by the common public; whereas on the other hand, they are appraised by their fellow followers as supreme idols. In general, attitudes toward political leaders are more negative compared to business, sports, and arts leaders.

Political and industrial leaders portray a combination of an autocratic, paternalistic, and consultative leadership style. In a study conducted by T. Esmer (1997) among 4,824 individuals residing in a variety of geographic locations in Turkey, working respondents were asked to evaluate the styles of managers with whom they were familiar, together with their preferred management styles. Responses show that the most dominant management style was authoritarian (53%), followed by paternalistic (25%), consultative (13.6%), and democratic (8.5%). The most preferred style was consultative (35.2%), followed by paternalistic (28.9%), democratic (25.6%), and authoritarian (10.3%).

Paternalistic leaders tend to emerge in cultures that do not restrict the manager's status in the workplace. They flourish in societies where managers are provided with status in other areas of life (Laurent, 1983). Turkey can be characterized as a society that does not restrict the status of its managers and leaders only to the workplace but also provides them with a large area of freedom and responsibility.

Qualitative Studies on Leadership in Turkey

Semantic Interpretations of Leadership Concept. This section includes semantic interpretation of the concept of leadership in Turkish culture. For this purpose, managers who participated in the focus groups and in-depth interviews were asked to describe the concept of leadership, the concept of management, and behavior/traits of ideal leaders. Narrative texts from interviews and focus groups have been transcribed verbatim from recorded tapes and were subjected to ethnographic analysis.

An ethnographic analysis of focus group and in-depth interviews revealed that leadership as a concept is viewed as superior to management. Respondents indicated that whereas management is learned through education and experience, leadership is innate and inborn. Leadership is perceived to be about sensing the opportunities that come with change, involving innovation and creativity, having vision, and keeping the group together around a common task or goal. On the other hand, management is perceived to be a less ambitious task, routine, technical, and adhering to rules and regulations. Leadership incorporates emotions and subjectivity, whereas management is thought to be rational and objective. In general, management is portrayed as somewhat inferior to leadership and expectations from a manager are less demanding than those from a leader. Respondents indicated that a manager needs to be consistent in behavior and thinking and needs to take the same actions under similar conditions, whereas, a leader's behavior can be less predictable. Both managers and leaders have to motivate; but in management motivation is attained through rewards and punishment whereas in leadership, the leader finds innovative rewards to motivate.

Turkish respondents indicated that they do not know any leader in their own organization, sector, or in society who fits their definition of an ideal leader. Their image of an ideal leader carries the attributes that have come out to be important in the quantitative analysis of GLOBE leadership attributes, such as decisive, visionary, team integrator, collaborative, team oriented, inspirational, of integrity, diplomatic, and administratively competent. In addition, action-oriented/assertive leadership came out as an important dimension in the perceptions of respondents. Though paternalistic leadership is frequently described as a desired style, there were also autocratic, consultative, and even democratic descriptions of outstanding leaders. The most frequently mentioned behaviors and traits of an ideal leader are categorized as follows:

- *Decisive:* does not give in about own ideas in case of conflict, decides fast without hesitation, implements decisions with confidence, pursues own objectives and goals even if they are contradictory, and asks for opinions but makes the decisions themselves.
- *Visionary:* recognizes that the world is changing and senses the opportunities that come with change; is imaginative, anticipating, and creative; has vision; encourages innovations and new ideas; balances rationality with emotions in the decision process; is not too scientific or rational; is after a dream that may never come true; is flexible-minded; evaluates from multiple perspectives; gives importance to the subjective and qualitative side of the decisions; does not like to work with detailed and routine things; likes to deal with more general conceptual overviews; interprets rules and regulations with a flexible mind; behaves and thinks in extremes; is ahead of others in recognizing what should be the goals and how to achieve them; his or her objectives have repercussions on society; and is curious.
- *Team Integrator:* communicates and shares information; creates an environment where people can tell their ideas to each other openly; is able to share, is accessible to followers, is empathetic, and is good in human relations; listens to people and asks people's opinions to make them feel part of the group.
- *Collaborative Team-Oriented:* puts forward his or her own ambitions, ideas, and benefits, but would not go against the benefit of the group; encourages participation; instills corporate/team culture to followers; seeks acceptance and tries to increase acceptance of

decisions; listens and really takes into account the ideas of people who do not carry the legitimacy/formal position/status to speak out publicly; seriously takes into account all spoken ideas or at least seems to do so; and has to keep people in extremes equally happy in a manipulative way.

- *Inspirational:* tolerates failure and gets people to overcome their fear of it; gives room for people to fail and learn from mistakes; gives as much independence to people as possible by delegating; develops people, increases their commitment and development; makes people feel secure under conditions of change and uncertainty; gives credit to followers; empowers followers by viewing them as colleagues, not as subordinates, seeing them as a resource, letting them decide, showing respect, providing recognition, and recognizing their potential; and is dynamic.
- *Paternalistic:* is able to say "no" in the right place if the task requires it even if people are hurt; shows/directs people about what needs to be done; is concerned with the private problems of followers; would take the initiative in deciding for the employees with regard to their problems; attends social events such as wedding ceremonies of employees' children; would act like one of the employees at social events; creates a family-like atmosphere in the organization.
- *Action oriented and assertive:* is assertive and ambitious; has an aggressive approach to life; is aggressive in a controlled way; is not necessarily well-educated; is intelligent, dynamic, and ambitious; speaks well; likes to take challenges; uses body language and nonverbal communication; shakes hands frequently and has direct eye contact; when they die, common cause may fade away; are recalled by their names rather than ideas; has a hands-on approach to solving problems; is a go-getter.
- *Integrity:* is a person whom people can trust; tells the truth; is trustworthy and is believable; always meets promises; and is fair.
- *Nonprocedural:* avoids bureaucracy, challenges status quo, and is a risk taker.
- *Diplomatic:* is skillful in convincing others; rewards and punishes by nonmonetary means.
- *Equanimity:* is mentally and emotionally mature, does not compete with anyone, is not afraid of working with people better than themselves, is sensitive and has cultural awareness, does not criticize publicly.
- *Administratively competent:* in delegating tasks does not interfere until there is a mistake; knows what is going on around them, what is taking place; does not learn it from others.
- *Self-confident and development oriented:* is open to self-development, is open to criticism, receives feedback, is self-confident, and accepts own mistakes.
- *Outlier:* need not be always ethical, is lonely, has few good friends, and lacks an established family.

Leadership Types. Data obtained from focus groups and in-depth interviews maybe interpreted and summarized in terms of various leadership styles. Three types of leadership styles are dominantly observed in Turkish society: autocratic, paternalistic, and consultative leadership.

Autocratic Leaders: Respondents indicated that autocratic leadership is frequently observed in Turkish society. Autocratic leaders try to make all the decisions, execute important tasks themselves, and only let others apply the decisions. They may override the defined area of freedom of individuals and impose their own preferences. An autocratic leader says "no" for all things that do not pass such approval. They are afraid of working with people better than themselves. These leaders most often do not take into account the ideas of people who are in lower positions—not as a punishment for a particular mistake but as a common practice. For punishment in a particular case, they scold, criticize publicly, and downplay the individual—this is very frequently used. Respondents in general had negative feelings toward autocratic leaders and perceived them as having adverse effects on the motivation of their followers.

Paternalistic Leaders: Paternalistic leadership is often practiced in Turkish society. This type of leadership is fairly similar to autocratic leadership, except that in paternalism, the leader is like a father and takes care of the followers like a parent would. In the paternalistic exchange between the leader and the followers, the leader provides a holistic concern for the followers and their families in return for unquestioned obedience and loyalty on the part of the followers. For example, a respondent indicated that the general manager of the company accompanied a worker's child who was receiving cancer treatment in England because the family did not speak English. As part of being a parent, the leader may sometimes make decisions for the employees in place of asking them their own decisions and preferences.

In the paternalistic relationship, employees may be punished by the leader if they act independently. Employees who work for paternalistic leaders would be expected to be totally committed and loyal to their leaders. Respondents indicated that most people who work for paternalistic leaders would not leave their organizations for better payment or promotion opportunities. Also as part of the paternalistic role, the leader would fulfill social roles, such as attending the wedding ceremonies of the employees and their children, sharing the same table with them at department dinners, dancing with the employees of the department at a celebration party, being a team member at the company tournaments, or having a vacation with the families of the whole staff for a week. While fulfilling such social roles, the leaders in a way diminish the social distance between themselves and the followers and act like a father. At work, the social distance would creep up.

Paternalistic leaders are often looked on positively because of their fatherly concern for the followers and their attempt to create a family-like atmosphere. The dark side of paternalistic leadership is cited as its possibility to turn into nepotism and providing resources to only a loyal group of followers, while excluding others.

Consultative Leaders: Respondents indicated that among Turkish leaders consultative behavior is observed to some extent. Consultative leaders tend to make decisions after they listen to their followers. They create an environment where people can speak about their ideas openly, within a framework, and avoid an environment where people only try to apply the instructions given to them. Respondents did not indicate that consultative leaders use consensual decision making, but they would ask for people's ideas and then make the decision themselves.

In the Turkish context, listening to subordinates' ideas was not used mainly to increase quality of the decisions, but rather as a strategy for making people feel good. Leaders used consultation either to make people feel they had an input to the decisions or to create a team spirit where people felt as part of the group. Leaders often had a small circle of close colleagues, a nucleus, in which a real contribution to decisions was possible. Often the nucleus included people who were similar to the leader in terms of their socioeconomic background. The rest would be consulted mainly to create positive feelings, such as to create a feeling of team spirit or to make them feel valued. In general there are positive reactions to consultative leaders who ask people's ideas to make them feel good or to create a team spirit. Given the large Power Distance and social differences in society, employees do not negatively react to the fact that the leader makes the decisions alone or in a small group of close colleagues. On the other hand, those people who perceive themselves as equals to the nucleus, in terms of their socioeconomic background or skills, would react negatively if they were omitted from the nucleus.

Leadership as Reflected in the Media.   An ethnographic analysis of leadership patterns as reflected in the Turkish printed media revealed that a great majority (95%) of the news about leadership focused on political leaders. A smaller percentage was about managers/owners in large organizations, followed by women leaders, sports leaders, and arts leaders. This finding portrays high Power Distance prevalent in society as well as the centrality of the state in people's lives.

Almost all of the articles included news about the interaction of the leader with a situation, with the focus being on the intersection or interrelationship, rather than on the leader. Very little news focused on attributes of the leaders. Thus, it was not possible to identify verbs and adjectives relevant to leadership. It was possible to describe leadership within a context, in relation to other people or issues. This picture clearly demonstrates the high In-Group Collectivism in Turkish society where the focus is not on individual attributes/actions of the leader but on interdependencies and interrelationships between leaders and other people.

A striking finding of the media analysis about leaders was that success stories or accomplishments of leaders were almost nonexistent. This finding is in line with the relatively low levels of Performance Orientation as well as the highly collectivist nature of society. It also reflects skepticism and negative experiences with leaders.

Skepticism and negative experiences were most apparent in the case of political leaders. The media was full of news about criticisms for nepotism, transgressions, and questions about whether the leaders would be able to pursue the interests of the general public. There were many pressures on the leaders, including complaints and protests or personality-based accusations from other leaders. There was also an enormous demand on the leaders to supply resources to organized groups. Such expectations of a leader being a supplier of resources are in line with the paternalistic leader model that is prevalent in society. The role of paternalistic leadership includes supplying the demands of the followers and groups. Although the leader is expected to find the needed resources, there is great skepticism toward the leaders who have the power to supply these resources and they are widely criticized for nepotism.

Whereas skepticism and negative reactions toward political leaders are common among the opponents and the disenchanted public, the followers and the close circle of the leaders demonstrate unquestioned loyalty to their leaders. Such interaction is part of a paternalistic leadership model where the followers are expected to be devoted to their leaders in exchange for the resources and holistic concern that the leader provides. There is frequent news about the loyalty of the followers to their leaders. If the leaders ignored their paternalistic duties to their close circle, the followers would criticize or leave them. In other words, when paternalism transforms into autocratic leadership, the leaders would be criticized for lack of concern for their followers and lose their loyalty.

Paternalistic leadership and loyalty to the elderly is often praised in the case of arts leaders as well. More established and famous artists are praised for helping the young artists, whereas the young ones seem to be devoted to their mentors. In addition, there was frequent news that praised the artists who visited and helped out elderly artists. This behavior on the part of artists is in line with the strong In-Group Collectivism in Turkish society.

As with the lack of success stories, there was very little news about the vision of political leaders. This finding reflects the relatively low level of Future Orientation that prevails in society. Only in the instances of relationships with other nations was there news about a leader's vision. Leaders were also frequently criticized for making exaggerated promises and having an unrealistic vision. It seems that only in the case of a proposed national policy of foreign relations that the leaders were not criticized severely. Not criticizing national policies regarding foreign relations is in line with the strong nationalism that resides in Turkish society. Though it is acceptable to criticize the leaders in terms of internal affairs, when it comes to relations concerning other nations, the issue becomes very sensitive in society.

Although there was not much news about the successes or visions of the political leaders, they were frequently seen in symbolic roles. They were portrayed mostly receiving or giving plaques and making speeches at ceremonies or commemorations. It seems as if an important aspect of leadership in Turkish society is to fulfill a symbolic role. Political leaders are criticized for almost everything, except for their symbolic roles.

A symbolic role seems to be an important aspect of leadership for managers/owners of large corporations, including women leaders. Leaders are frequently shown as chairing conferences. Almost all the news about women leaders involved their symbolic role, chairing international conferences on the one hand and wearing headscarves on religious occasions on the other. Much of the ideological debates between the Westernization and Islamization of society focuses on the role of women in society. Thus, a woman leader's image has an ideological connotation. For this purpose, news about women leaders concentrates on their images rather than their performance or other roles. Chairing international conferences would have the connotation of Westernization, whereas a focus on wearing a headscarf would indicate that traditions or Islamization in society are not ignored. Finally, a role of sister or mother is frequently emphasized by women leaders and takes place in the media because these roles are commonly accepted for women.

Managers/owners of large corporations often contact representatives of the state to demand resources or incentives for their sectors. There was more news in the media about state orientation of private enterprises than their market orientation, which is a reflection of the low level of Performance Orientation. Such news is also an indicator of the centrality of the state in the lives of private companies. The state is commonly referred to as the "father," indicating its role as supplier of incentives and resources. One way to approach the government and the state is to be elected to the boards of chambers and unions. Therefore managers and owners of private companies seek representations on the boards of such institutions and there was frequent news about board members visiting political leaders.

Compared to political leaders, managers/owners of large organizations are portrayed more often as having vision. Some of this vision includes plans about their market orientation, such as plans for new investments or exports. In addition, future plans of managers/owners frequently included professionalization of the corporation given that most organizations, including the large business groups, are run by family members in Turkey.

A common criticism of political, sports, and arts leaders is the flamboyant style of either themselves or their family members. It would appear that leaders are expected to have more modest private lives and not to engage in extravagant lifestyles, such as driving expensive cars or going to flashy restaurants and bars.

Private-sector leaders as well as arts leaders are frequently shown as engaging in socially responsible acts, such as helping charity organizations or sponsoring cultural activities. These leaders and politicians frequently mention that they are conducting such activities for the good of society and the nation. Leaders of the private sector often indicate that the incentives they get or their investments are all for the benefit of the nation, such as increasing employment opportunities and export potential. They are careful not to mention to outsiders about the profitability of the company as their target. In the Turkish context, it looks better for a leader to prioritize national benefits in the speeches made to the public.

Leaders as Reflected From Company Newsletters.   Newsletters of companies that were included in the sample were analyzed in order to understand how leadership is portrayed in the financial services and food-processing companies in Turkey. In general, the opinion of leaders from company newsletters was found to be similar to media reflections. In the newsletters of companies in the finance and food-processing sectors, there were no individual success stories and no project, change, or achievement was attributed to any one person.

Analysis of company newsletters portrayed a strong collectivist orientation with the emphasis on "the company being like a family" and the nonexistence of individual accomplishments. Furthermore, the collectivist orientation is manifested with the need for achieving the "nation's" well-being. The speech by the owner of a large food-processing company on the anniversary of its establishment reflected such collectivist achievement orientation: "The root of our success lies in disciplined work, integrity, love of the nation and its people. We are a family. We will never be similar to those who only want for themselves. We will always put the benefit of the national economy and the society in the forefront; we will grow with Turkey." He also announced how much tax was paid as an indication of focus on societal contribution.

The leaders of the companies were basically presented in a symbolic role, such as cutting a cake, making an opening speech for a commemoration, or giving a plaque. They are also presented while making speeches on some concepts from the Western literature, such as professionalization, total quality management, and importance of human resources management, which reflected the importance of Westernization, knowledge, and administrative skills for leadership.

Leaders As Reflected in Leader Autobiographies, Biographies, and News About Them. Autobiographies, biographies, and news about political and industrial leaders were analyzed with the purpose of finding out how leadership is presented in the Turkish context. Based on these analyses, several themes about leadership emerged: Leadership involved a collective-achievement orientation, state-oriented vision, being of integrity, good administrator, emotionality, one-man show, and a symbolic role.

Collective-Achievement Orientation: Similar to the findings in media and newsletter analyses, leaders were not presented with personal success stories. Business leaders were portrayed as if they have not achieved anything through their own ability. Koç, a prominent industrial leader, mentioned in his autobiography that he owes his success to God, the country, the cooperation of work friends, and his own love of working (Koç, 1973).

The need for collective achievement, which is embodied in serving one's community and nation, emerges frequently. The ideas of industrial leaders about the country, state ideology, and political and economic problems are in the forefront, rather than their business accomplishments. Eczacibasi, who is another prominent industrial leader, wrote in his autobiography that an industrial institution's main aim is to contribute to the economic and social development of the nation. (Eczacibasi, 1982). The writings in the media about Koç and Eczacibasi upon their death also focused on their contributions toward society and the nation rather than their entrepreneurial or managerial success. A newspaper article written about Koç on the first anniversary of his death indicated that his value was derived from predominantly two factors (Güngör, 1997): (a) He had lived through many of the significant stages of the Turkish Republic, such as the military coups and the years where it passed to a liberal market economy, and (b) he loved his country to the extent that he was interested in major issues about it, for example, the traffic problem.

State-Oriented Vision: When we analyzed the entrepreneurial activities of leading businesspeople, we observed the combination of a state-oriented vision with a Western, international focus (Eczacibasi, 1982, 1994; Koç, 1973; Sabanci, 1985). State-oriented vision parallels and even requires an autocratic leadership approach. Many of the entrepreneurial and trade accomplishments are achieved through personal contacts with the state, which is not a function that is delegated to professionals.

In the case of the networks of small and medium-size enterprises, which has an Islamic orientation, initial market-oriented vision is transformed into a state-oriented and partially dependent structure. Through such structures, these networks also attempt to get resources from the central and local governments.

Integrity: Another theme that emerged in the news about leaders and in the autobiographies or biographies was the integrity of leaders. The same attribute was frequently mentioned in the focus groups and in-depth interviews. Industrial leaders in their speeches often cite integrity at work as an important personality trait and advise their followers to be honest and trustworthy.

One of the means of earning integrity seems to be by showing a preference for a modest lifestyle. Some industrial as well as political leaders advise and live a modest lifestyle, which is reflected by economizing such as driving nonluxurious cars, avoiding unnecessary expenditures and flamboyant lifestyles, and presenting a socially responsible image. They invest in social-welfare activities, such as charity organizations that involve the poor and disabled.

Good Administrator: In the review of autobiographies, biographies, and news about leaders, an important trait seems to be their administrative skills and having a comprehensive knowledge in their field. In the organizational culture context, this attribute of a leader is reported as a requisite for an outstanding leader. Furthermore, the leader has to have a thorough comprehension and knowledge of the legal system, which is mostly adapted from Western codes and statutes. Thus a leader who knows the procedures and practices them is also perceived as a professional administrator with a Western outlook.

Emotionality: Similar to the findings of the focus groups and in-depth interviews, leaders are often reflected as freely displaying their emotions. In the biographies of Atatürk and autobiography of Inönü, who were the two most influential political leaders during the establishment and early years of the Republic, we frequently observe the emotional sides of the two leaders (Atay, 1980; Inönü, 1985, 1987).

It is quite common to observe emotional attributes among contemporary leaders in Turkish society. Political, religious, military, and arts leaders were often seen in the printed media and on television crying because they were full of emotion in situations such as watching a national play at the military school or listening to the national anthem. This observation parallels semantic interpretation of leadership in focus groups and in-depth interviews where respondents differentiated leaders as emotional and managers as rational.

One-Man Show and Leader as a Symbol: Analysis of writings on leadership portrayed the prevalence of strong leadership historically, as well as in contemporary Turkey. Leadership in political, industrial, and other areas are exhibited as a one-man show, where the leader as the single person has immense power and takes on the role of representing the whole institution.

The roots of strong leadership in Turkish society go back to the early Republican era (1923–1946) when there was in existence a single-party rule (Atay, 1980; M. Kabasakal, 1991). Analyses of leadership as portrayed in these books showed that all the power was concentrated in the hands of the party leader. The leader was the natural head of all major party institutions.

Turkish society historically provided its leaders with huge power and expected them to exhibit strong leadership. Strong leadership goes hand in hand with the symbolic role of leaders, who are heads of most activities and publicly are the sole representatives of their institutions.

A similar picture prevails in the case of founders of private-sector companies, such as Koç and Eczacibasi, who stayed as the leader of large business groups until they died. It can be stated that industrial leaders also fulfill a symbolic role and represent their institutions in public appearance and chair many organizations. When the founder of a company dies, often a close family member, a son or son-in-law, comes to power.

The Quantitative Study of Leadership in Turkey

Findings. In order to induce a profile of preferred leadership attributes and behaviors, Turkish managers were asked to rate a set of 112 behaviors and characteristics, on a scale ranging from 1 = greatly inhibits a person from being an outstanding leader to 7 = contributes greatly to a person being an outstanding leader. Based on these items, 21 leadership subdimensions were formed, which were further reduced to 6 dimensions (House et al., 1999, 2004). Table 23.2 presents the absolute scores and relative ratings for leader behaviors and attributes.

When outstanding leader attributes in the six dimensions are analyzed, the highest absolute score and relative standing among GLOBE countries is achieved in the Team Oriented dimension (M = 6.01, Rank 7, Band A). Charismatic attributes were rated highly in absolute scale, yet its relative standing is rather low (M = 5.95, Rank 23, Band C). Participative leadership is perceived to be contributing to outstanding leadership at a mediocre level, and it has a low relative standing (M = 5.09, Rank 42, Band D). Humane-oriented leadership has mediocre absolute and relative scores (M = 4.90, Rank 29, Band B). Autonomous (M = 3.83, Rank 34, Band B) and Self-Protective (M = 3.57, Rank 26, Band E) attributes are perceived to slightly inhibit outstanding leadership, and their relative ranking is medium and low, respectively.

When the subdimensions that form the six dimensions are analyzed in terms of relative ratings, the highest ranking leadership characteristics for Turkey were Decisive (2nd), Team Integrator (6th), Autocratic (8th), Diplomatic (10th), Administratively Competent (10th), Visionary (13th), Status-Conscious (14th), and Collaborative Team Oriented (15th); all dimensions fell within the first quartile among 61 cultures. Relative standings show that the lowest ranking leadership attributes for the Turkish sample are Performance Orientation (46th) and Self-Centered (48th), both rankings being in the last quartile.

Although the high relative and absolute ratings for outstanding leadership attributes were fairly similar to each other, there were some differences between the two analyses. According to the absolute scores, leadership attributes that were rated as contributing most to outstanding leadership were Decisive (6.29), Team Integrator (6.28), Visionary (6.25), Integrity (6.16), Administratively Competent (6.13), and Inspirational (6.08), all having mean values above 6. The lowest absolute scores were obtained for Malevolent (1.76) and Self-Centered (1.93), both perceived as greatly hindering a person from becoming an outstanding leader.

An analysis of leadership characteristics that had the highest ratings in both the relative and absolute scores indicated that Decisive, Team Integrator, Administratively Competent,

TABLE 23.2
Country Mean Scores for Leadership Dimensions and Subdimensions

Dimensions Subdimensions	Mean	Band	Rank
Charismatic	5.95	C	23
Performance Orientation	5.91		46
Visionary	6.25		13
Inspirational	6.08		38
Integrity	6.16		27
Self-Sacrificial	5.03		29
Decisive	6.29		2
Team Oriented	6.01	A	7
Team Integrator	6.28		6
Collaborative Team Oriented	5.70		15
Administratively Competent	6.13		10
Diplomatic	5.74		10
Malevolent	1.76		31
Self-Protective	3.57	E	26
Self-Centered	1.93		48
Status-Conscious	4.91		14
Conflict Inducer	4.17		23
Face Saver	2.99		27
Procedural	4.02		25
Participative	5.09	D	42
Autocratic (reverse coded)	3.22		8
Nonparticipative (reverse coded)	2.62		31
Humane	4.90	B	29
Humane	5.02		22
Modesty	4.82		40
Autonomous			
Autonomous	3.83	B	34

and Visionary come out to be common in both ratings. These attributes indicate a culturally endorsed theory of leadership where the leaders are expected to be competent in decision-making and executive functions, and carry these attributes with integrity. In terms of decision-making abilities, outstanding leaders are perceived as decisive and visionary. Most important, they are perceived as decisive, rational, persistent, quick, with no hesitation, and intuitive. They are also expected to provide a strong vision to their followers, plan ahead, have foresight, have goals and ideas for the future, make plans and take action related to their vision, be ready for future events, make realistic forecasts, and inspire the values, beliefs, and behaviors of followers.

In terms of their executive abilities, outstanding leaders are perceived as team integrators and competent administrators. As a team integrator, they are open to communication, are clearly understood by the followers, are informed about issues, create an environment where the team members work together, integrate the activities and people together, unify the efforts of people in the team, and create a team spirit. As part of administrative skills, most important they are perceived as being able to coordinate and control the activities of a large number of people and manage complex office activities and systems. Furthermore, they are expected to be trustworthy, honest, and just.

An analysis of both relative and absolute scores shows that self-centered behaviors greatly hinder outstanding leadership. This finding is in line with the high In-Group Collectivism that is prevalent in Turkish society.

5. ORGANIZATIONAL CULTURE AND LEADERSHIP IN THE FINANCIAL SERVICES AND FOOD-PROCESSING SECTORS

As mentioned in the section on methodology, the data on organizational culture dimensions were collected from middle managers working in 9 financial services and 14 food-processing companies. Presentation of the findings on organizational culture dimensions is preceded by a short description of the two sectors.

The Turkish Financial Services Sector

Banking Sector. The banking sector in Turkey is characterized by an oligopolistic structure. The largest five banks in the sector hold more than 50% of the market. The dominant form is "state- owned" and "business group" banks, which are owned by diversified large corporations. Although this oligopolistic structure continues in the 2000s, the banking sector in Turkey experienced a radical change in the early 1980s. The pre-1980 period was characterized by a tightly administered system with extensive state intervention (Öncü & Gökçe, 1991). With the deregulation policies, the post- 1980 period was identified by a significant shift toward liberalization. The changes that were realized in the post-1980 period led to increased competitive uncertainty in the banking sector. As a result of these changes, the sector has become dynamic and open to innovative applications. During the last decade, the number of local firms decreased from 49 in 1992 to 39 in 2002 and foreign banks decreased from 20 to 18 in the same period (*Bankalarimiz 1992,* 1993; http://www.tbb.org.tr). Starting with the late 1990s, the smaller banks in the sector either were acquired by larger foreign and local banks or those with performance problems were forced to be under the custody of a semiformal auditing council, which led to a gradual decrease in the number of banks operating in Turkey.

Insurance Sector. The oligopolistic structure of the insurance sector was changed in 1987 via modifications in the laws. New company start-ups have become possible with these changes. Furthermore, in 1990, there were further moves toward liberalization of the sector by deregulation of the premiums. In 1994, there were 37 local and 15 foreign firms in this sector, and in 2000 the number of local firms increased to 59, with foreign firms decreasing to five (Ergenekon, 1995; http://www.treasury.gov.tr). Whereas the number of foreign firms was larger than the number of local firms before the 1960s, the trend has been reversed since the 1970s. Although the number of local companies has been increasing at a very fast rate since 1987, insurance premiums per person are still quite small, ranking 53rd in the world in 1992. The low rate of insurance premiums in Turkey may be related to the relatively low levels of Future Orientation that is prevalent in Turkish society, which may be shaped by Islamic values. In 1979, the state official responsible for Islamic Affairs declared that according to the

TABLE 23.3

Country Mean Scores for Organizational Culture Dimensions

Organizational Culture	Finance			Food		
Dimensions	"As Is"[a]	"Should Be"[a]	Difference[b]	"As Is"[a]	"Should Be"[a]	Difference[b]
Performance Orientation	4.15	6.06	1.91	3.91	5.80	1.89
Assertiveness	4.07	5.04	0.97	4.27	4.82	0.55
Future Orientation	4.25	5.98	1.73	3.98	5.77	1.79
Gender Egalitarianism	3.92	4.40	0.48	2.63	4.10	1.47
Humane Orientation	3.79	4.80	1.01	4.15	4.91	0.76
Institutional Collectivism	4.16	5.13	0.97	4.27	5.16	0.89
Power Distance	4.17	3.92	−0.25	4.70	4.17	−0.53
In-Group Collectivism	4.62	6.01	1.39	4.82	6.18	1.36
Uncertainty Avoidance	3.76	4.50	0.74	3.63	4.30	0.67

[a]Country mean score on a 7-point Likert scale. [b]Difference: "As Is" score minus "Should Be" score.

laws of Islam, contracts that are based on hypothetical arrangements or assumptions would not be valid, and thus insurance contracts are not accepted in Islam. On the other hand, beginning in the 1990s, a general increase in awareness about the opportunities brought about by insurance is reflected by the increase in insurance purchases made by the public.

The Turkish Food-Processing Sector

Food processing is one of the major industries in the country, dominated by local firms. The basic categories in the industry are: frozen vegetables and fruit, meat and dairy products, sugar and sweet products, vegetable oil, canned products, and fruit juice. Turkey is a major exporter of processed food. The sector includes a large variety of firms, ranging from small and technologically less advanced firms to those much larger and more technologically advanced. In some categories, such as sugar and dairy products, there are large state-owned institutions.

Organizational Culture in the Two Sectors

Findings.   The survey administered to Turkish managers probed about the beliefs of the respondents with respect to "how are" the current practices and "how they should be" in their work organizations. The same nine culture dimensions that were used in measuring societal culture were used in assessing organizational culture. The GLOBE study proposes that organizational culture has a strong impact on leader behaviors. Thus, it is important to study organizational culture as it is shaped by the immediate task environment and is more proximate to managers and employees. Table 23.3 illustrates the culture dimensions on "As Is" and "Should Be" for the food-processing and finance sectors.

On average, the beliefs of Turkish middle-level managers regarding "how their organizations are" do not show a strong tendency for the organizational culture dimensions. Whereas the intensity of measures on "As Is" dimensions lie near the midpoint of the scale, the highest mean response is attributed to In-Group Collectivism in both the finance and food-processing sectors. The lowest "As Is" score is achieved in Gender Egalitarianism in the food-processing sector, whereas this dimension has a moderate absolute score in the finance sector. In-Group Collectivism dimension also received high absolute "Should Be" scores in both sectors, indicating that In-Group Collectivism is a distinctive characteristic of Turkish organizations in line with high In-Group Collectivism that is prevalent in societal culture at large. Compared to other culture dimensions, Gender Egalitarianism and Power Distance have relatively lower "Should Be" scores in both sectors, although they are moderate scores in absolute scale.

When "As Is" and "Should Be" scores of organizational culture dimensions are compared, it is seen that middle managers have higher "Should Be" scores in most dimensions. The highest difference is achieved in Performance Orientation (1.91 finance; 1.89 food processing), followed by Future Orientation (1.73 finance; 1.79 food processing) and In-Group Collectivism (1.39 finance; 1.36 food processing). Turkish managers in both sectors aspired for substantially higher levels of achievement, planning, and in-group loyalty in their organizations. Turkish managers also aspired for more Humane Orientation (1.01 finance; 0.76 food processing), Institutional Collectivism (0.97 finance; 0.89 food processing), Assertiveness (0.97 in finance; 0.55 in food processing), Uncertainty Avoidance (0.74 finance and 0.67 food processing), and Gender Egalitarianism (0.48 finance; 1.47 food processing). On the other hand, managers indicated that they would prefer slightly lower levels of Power Distance (–0.25 finance; –0.53 food processing).

In-Group Collectivism, which reflects in-group interdependence and organizational loyalty, received relatively high scores in both "As Is" and As "Should Be" scales for the two sectors, when compared with the scores in other culture dimensions (financial services "As Is" $M = 4.62$, "Should Be" $M = 6.01$; food processing "As Is" $M = 4.82$, "Should Be" $M = 6.18$). Whereas organizational practices reflected medium absolute scores in the In-Group Collectivism dimension, preferences of middle managers were high in absolute terms. This finding is in line with the qualitative findings of a previously conducted study, where respondents were asked to list the dominant practices and norms in their organizations (Pasa, Kabasakal, & Bodur, 2001). An analysis of the listed items by referees indicated that the most frequently mentioned practices and norms reflected the dominance of In-Group Collectivism and the importance of loyalty between leader and followers in Turkish organizations. The importance of loyalty in leader–follower relations is in line with the paternalistic culture that is prevalent in Turkish organizations (Aycan et al., 2000). Both the financial services and food-processing companies have medium Institutional Collectivism "As Is" scores and the scores in "Should Be" are high in absolute terms (financial services "As Is" $M = 4.16$, "Should Be" $M = 5.13$; food processing "As Is" $M = 4.27$, "Should Be" $M = 5.16$).

Organizational culture in both sectors is characterized by practices that represent medium levels of cohesiveness and use of collective rewards. Turkish middle managers indicated that they would prefer their organizations to be more cohesive and use collective rewards in motivating their employees as reflected in the high "Should Be" Institutional Collectivism scores.

When Performance Orientation scores of the finance and food-processing sectors are compared, it is seen that the financial services sector has higher "As Is" and "Should Be" scores (finance "As Is" $M = 4.15$, "Should Be" $M = 6.06$; food processing "As Is" $M = 3.91$, "Should Be" $M = 5.80$). The same pattern is observed for the Future Orientation dimension (financial services "As Is" $M = 4.25$, "Should Be" $M = 5.98$; food processing "As Is" $M = 3.98$, "Should Be" $M = 5.77$), whereas the financial services sector has higher scores in "As Is" and "Should Be," compared to the food-processing sector. These findings show that the financial services sector in Turkey has moderate absolute "As Is" scores in the Performance Orientation and Future Orientation dimensions and managers in this sector aspire for substantially higher levels of achievement and planning in their organizations. The food-processing sector has lower absolute scores in practices and values achievement and Future Orientation compared to the financial services sector.

The relatively lower levels of Performance and Future Orientations in the food-processing sector could be due to the high competitive advantage of the sector deriving from low costs of input. The food-processing sector in Turkey employs unskilled labor with lower wages compared to most developed nations. Furthermore, due to the large arable land in the country and the favorable climatic conditions, the food-processing sector enjoys a large variety of high-quality agricultural inputs at low costs. These low costs of input make the Turkish food-processing companies competitive in the international markets and Turkey has become a major exporter of processed food. Thus, it can be proposed that the food-processing companies in the country are competitive despite their mediocre Performance and Future Orientation practices. However, middle managers in the sector are aware that in order to continue with their position in the world markets, they should be more excellence oriented and make plans and investment into the future.

The financial services sector lacks many of the advantages of the food-processing companies and they focus more on Performance and Future Orientation. Financial services organizations use more skilled employees and are more dependent on their human resources in order to stay competitive. The input and ideas of employees at lower levels of the hierarchy are more important for the financial services organizations compared to the food-processing sector. The importance of participation and input of lower levels is reflected in the relatively lower levels of Power Distance in the financial services sector compared to food processing (financial services "As Is" $M = 4.17$, "Should Be" $M = 3.92$; food processing "As Is" $M = 4.70$, "Should Be" $M = 4.17$). These figures show that the financial services organizations have lower Power Distance scores and their managers furthermore aspire for less hierarchy compared to managers in the food-processing organizations. Despite this, managers in both sectors aspire for lower Power Distance, indicating their desire for less hierarchy and more egalitarian distribution of power and authority in their organizations. Decentralization and less hierarchical structures are perceived as mechanisms of competing in the more dynamic and competitive environments that organizations are currently facing.

Gender Egalitarianism scores in the two sectors show that the financial services organizations are more egalitarian than their food-processing counterparts (financial services "As Is" $M = 3.92$, "Should Be" $M = 4.40$; food processing "As Is" $M = 2.63$, "Should Be" $M = 4.10$). Turkish food-processing organizations have low absolute "As Is" Gender Egalitarianism scores, whereas the financial services sector has more mediocre scores. In both sectors, middle managers aspire for more Gender Egalitarianism, although managers in the finance sector perceive a greater need for it.

The Turkish financial services sector is characterized by employing a high percentage of women. A study conducted in 64 financial services companies indicated that women constituted 43% of all employees (H. Kabasakal et al., 1994). On the other hand, several studies show that the manufacturing sector in general employs substantially lower levels of women labor (Özbasar & Aksan, 1976; Tabak, 1989). Furthermore, these studies pointed to the fact that representation of women in managerial positions dropped significantly as one moved to managerial positions in all sectors. In general, women constituted only 3% to 4% of executive positions in the Turkish context (H. Kabasakal, Aycan, & Karakas, 2004). That is why the middle managers in both the financial services and food-processing companies indicated that their organizations need to become more Gender Egalitarian places. The need for greater Gender Egalitarianism is more evident in the financial services organizations given their higher dependence on their human resources for keeping their competitive position in the market.

Organizations in both sectors have medium levels of Assertiveness and managers aspire for more than what is apparent at present (financial services "As Is" $M = 4.07$, "Should Be" $M = 5.04$; food processing "As Is" $M = 4.27$, "Should Be" $M = 4.82$). The food-processing companies have slightly more assertive and dominant practices compared to the financial services companies, yet their aspirations regarding Assertiveness is lower than the aspirations in the finance sector.

Managers in both financial services and food-processing organizations aspire for higher levels of Humane Orientation (financial services "As Is" $M = 3.79$, "Should Be" $M = 4.80$; food processing "As Is" $M = 4.15$, "Should Be" $M = 4.91$.) In general, the food-processing organizations are more humane compared to the financial services sector. Managers in both sectors think that their organizational culture needs to become more nurturing and generous.

Organizations in both sectors have low absolute "As Is" Uncertainty Avoidance scores and aspire for medium levels of this cultural dimension (financial services "As Is" $M = 3.76$, "Should Be" $M = 4.50$; food processing "As Is" $M = 3.63$, "Should Be" $M = 4.30$). Organizational cultures in both sectors display rather low levels of rule orientation, orderliness, and consistency. Managers would like their organizations to have medium levels of Uncertainty Avoidance and be somewhat more rule oriented and orderly in their operations.

In summary, there are more differences between the "As Is" scores of the two sectors, although they are similar in terms of desired cultural attributes, indicating that the "task performed" influences organizational cultures. In general, managers prefer to work in similar types of organizational cultures. However, when it comes to comparing their existing organizational practices, the managers in the two sectors indicate dissimilarities. Organizational demographic analysis that is based on responses obtained from top managers of six companies in both sectors might indicate the sources of differences in the cultures of the two industries.

Results of the organizational demography questionnaires show that the food sector is at a steady growth stage whereas the finance sector is accelerating. Consequently, the companies in the finance sector experience a greater amount of change in terms of their markets (4.2 vs. 3.4), financial structures (4.3 vs. 3.3), internal organizational processes (4.3 vs. 3.4), executive personnel (4.0 vs. 3.2), divestments (3.0 vs. 2.4), acquisitions (4.0 vs.3.7), and products (4.5 vs. 3.2) (1 = very little change; 2 = changed somewhat; 3 = changed a.moderate amount; 4 = substantial change, 5 = changed a great deal). The greater amount of change also necessitates more planning on the part of personnel in finance organizations. Whereas the perceptions of managers in the two sectors regarding the intensity of marketing competition was very similar ($M = 5.4$ in both sectors; 1 = virtually no competition, 7 = extremely intense competition), finance managers indicated that the market for their organizations was more unpredictable ($M = 4.8$) compared to the market for food-processing organizations ($M = 4.4$) (1 = very predictable and very easy to forecast, 7 = very unpredictable and very hard to anticipate).

In terms of changes in government regulations and political environments, although managers in both sectors evaluated the external environment as very unpredictable, finance managers indicated greater unpredictability. In addition, finance managers indicated that competition for purchases or inputs (raw materials, parts, or equipment in the case of manufacturers, cash with respect to financial service firms) and for technical manpower such as engineers, accountants, or programmers were extremely intense, whereas managers in food-processing organizations perceived the intensity of competition as moderate.

The accelerated growth stage of the sector, the greater amount of change in the operations of the organizations, the unpredictability of the market, and the unpredictability of the likely changes in regulations and political environment all necessitate more planning and future

TABLE 23.4

Comparison of the Organizational Mean Scores for Leadership Attributes in the Financial Services and Food-Processing Sectors: Turkey

	Finance		Food	
Characteristics	Mean	Within-Country Rank	Mean	Within-County Rank
Decisive	6.33	1	6.34	3
Team Integrator	6.31	2	6.36	2
Visionary	6.22	3	6.30	4
Integrity	6.15	4	6.40	1
Administrative Competent	6.10	5	6.27	5
Inspirational	6.09	6	6.12	6
Performance Oriented	5.88	7	5.76	9
Diplomatic	5.84	8	5.83	8
Collaborative Team Oriented	5.65	9	5.98	7
Humane Oriented	5.02	10	4.98	13
Self-Sacrificial	4.90	11	5.20	10
Modesty	4.78	12	5.03	11
Status-Conscious	4.73	13	4.98	13
Conflict Inducer	4.09	14	4.29	14
Procedural	3.89	15	4.15	15
Autonomous	3.65	16	3.90	16
Autocratic	3.15	17	3.24	18
Face Saver	2.93	18	3.28	17
Nonparticipative	2.47	19	2.71	19
Self-Centered	1.91	20	1.94	20
Malevolent	1.75	21	1.67	21

focus on the part of personnel in the finance sector, compared to those in the food-processing industry. Furthermore, the greater amount of organizational change and unpredictability in the external environment of the finance sector seems to create high stress and thus less friendly, less sensitive, and less concerned relationships among the employees, resulting in less Humane Orientation in the organizational culture. In addition, the fact that the food-processing companies are producing tangible products, which are directly related to the health of people, might create a more humane organizational culture.

Leadership in the Two Sectors. In order to analyze organizational leadership, Turkish middle managers employed in the financial services and food-processing sectors rated 112 leadership attributes in terms of their contribution to outstanding leadership on a 7-point Likert scale. Based on these items, 21 leadership subdimensions were formed. Table 23.4 reports the perceptions of Turkish managers in the two sectors regarding the contribution of these attributes to outstanding leadership.

Analysis of leadership attributes based on the two sectors indicates that the Charismatic/Value Based dimension of leadership is endorsed in both. Most subdimensions of charismatic/value-based leadership, including decisive, visionary, integrity, and inspirational, were perceived to be important contributors to outstanding leadership in both sectors.

Among the charismatic/value- based characteristics, the highest mean is attributed to integrity ($M = 6.40$) in the food-processing sector, whereas the mean of this attribute is slightly lower in the financial services sector ($M = 6.15$). Given the fact that the food-processing organizations are producing outputs that are directly related to the health of people and that the press has been providing large space and attention to the relationship between food products and health in the recent years, integrity is attributed the utmost importance in the food-processing sector. Leadership in the food-processing sector is particularly expected to include honesty, sincerity, justice, and trustworthiness.

In the financial services sector, the highest mean is attributed to decisive leadership qualities ($M = 6.33$) and this characteristic also received very high in importance in the food-processing sector ($M = 6.34$). Other characteristics of charismatic/value-based leadership, including visionary (financial services M = 6.22, food processing $M = 6.30$) and inspirational (financial services $M = 6.09$, food processing $M = 6.12$), are attributed high importance in both sectors, followed by a slightly lower importance attributed to performance orientation (financial services $M = 5.88$, food processing $M = 5.76$). In both sectors, managers perceived the importance of performance orientation to be slightly lower compared to other characteristics of charismatic/value-based leadership. It can be proposed that the importance of performance orientation as a leadership attribute would increase as competition in the sectors increased in the future. The self-sacrificial aspect of the charismatic/value-based leadership was not perceived to carry high significance in both sectors and the managers attributed slightly more importance to self-sacrifice in the food-processing organizations ($M = 5.20$) compared to the finance organizations ($M = 4.90$), with an important ranking of 10th and 11th, respectively. It seems like managers in both sectors do not perceive self-sacrifice by risk-taking and convincing behavior to be among the most important characteristics contributing to outstanding leadership.

The Team Orientation dimension is attributed as being of high importance as a leadership quality by Turkish managers working in the two sectors. The team integrator subdimension received the second-highest importance in both the financial services ($M = 6.31$) and food-processing ($M = 6.36$) organizations. It can be proposed that team integrator qualities of team builder, integrator, coordinator, informed, and clear are in line with the In-Group Collectivism that is dominant in Turkish culture and organizations. An outstanding leader in the Turkish context is expected to keep the team together by serving as an integrator and coordinator, providing the required information, and communicating in a clear way with the followers. In addition, the administratively competent characteristic (financial services $M = 6.10$ and food processing $M = 6.27$) received the ranking of 5th most important in both sectors, with very high absolute values. Outstanding leaders in both sectors are expected to be orderly, administratively skilled, and organized. The diplomatic (financial services $M = 5.84$ and food processing $M = 5.83$) and Collaborative Team Oriented (financial services $M = 5.65$ and food processing $M = 5.98$) dimensions were attributed slightly lower importance compared to the other characteristics of the Team Orientation dimension.

Humane-oriented characteristics are perceived to contribute slightly toward outstanding leadership in both the financial services and food-processing sectors. Managers in both value generous and compassionate qualities, as well as modest, calm, and patient behaviors—all of which contribute to outstanding leadership. These leadership qualities received medium importance as they were in Ranks 10 to 13 in the two sectors.

The Self-Protective dimension of leadership was perceived to impede outstanding leadership in the Turkish organizations in both sectors. Among the self-protective characteristics, procedural, face-saver, and self-centered attributes were particularly perceived as negative leadership qualities. Leaders are not expected to be procedural and they need to eliminate bureaucratic, ritualistic, formal, habitual, and cautious behavior. Furthermore, face-saving qualities are perceived negatively and leaders are expected to eliminate indirect and evasive behavior. In addition, self-centered behaviors, including serving self-interest, asocial, and loner attributes are perceived negatively.

Turkish managers in the financial services and food-processing industries perceived nonparticipative and autonomous characteristics as impeding outstanding leadership to a great extent. Leaders are expected to evade domineering, bossy, autocratic, and elitist behaviors for effective leadership. Furthermore, they need to eliminate micromanagement and non-delegation attributes. Finally, autonomous leadership, including individualistic, independent, and unique behaviors are perceived to impede outstanding leadership in the financial services and food- processing sectors.

6. CONCLUSIONS

Given its geographic location as a bridge between Europe and Asia, its state ideology that aims at modernization and Westernization, predominance of Islam among most members of society, and its historical roots in the Middle East, Asia, and Europe, Turkish society is characterized by the contrasts and combinations of East and West, having elements of modernity, traditionalism, and Islamism. The GLOBE study conducted in Turkey attempts to describe, explore, and explain the interrelationships between the contextual elements of Turkish society and its societal and organizational culture. Furthermore, it attempts to analyze the impact of contextual and cultural elements on existing leadership patterns and behaviors in Turkish society. For this purpose, various methodologies, including quantitative and qualitative studies, were employed to understand cultural and leadership patterns.

Limitations

A limitation of the study is that the data were collected from companies with specific demographics and may not be considered to be representative of all types of firms in Turkey. The sample included private companies in food-processing and financial services sectors, which are the major large/medium-size firms in these sectors and situated in the western part of the country. Given that economic activity is significantly focused in the western, more developed regions of Turkey, researchers chose to collect data from firms that are densely populated in this region. All 23 companies that are included in the sample are located in western Turkey and thus may reflect specific regional values and practices. Furthermore, the sample is not representative of other types of companies, like small and publicly owned firms.

Future Research

In order to overcome the methodological limitations, future research can focus on collecting data from firms carrying a wider array of demographic characteristics. A more representative sample would include companies of a variety of sizes and ownership, and located in eastern and less developed parts of the country.

The qualitative part of the study has revealed some culture specific leadership attributes, including paternalism, emotional, consulting, or collective-achievement orientation. These are worth investigating further. Future research can test the prevalence of these culture-specific attributes in terms of their contribution to outstanding leadership in a large sample of Turkish respondents and in other cultural contexts.

Summary and Discussion

In terms of the GLOBE societal "As Is" dimensions, Turkey has absolute and relative high scores in terms of In-Group Collectivism, Power Distance, and Assertiveness, whereas it has lower scores in Gender Egalitarianism, Uncertainty Avoidance, Performance Orientation, Humane Orientation, and Future Orientation. In terms of the societal "Should Be" scales, Turkey is found to have high absolute and relative scores in Future Orientation, Institutional and In-Group Collectivism, Humane Orientation, and Uncertainty Avoidance, and has lower scores in Performance Orientation, Assertiveness, Power Distance, and Gender Egalitarianism.

A comparison of the societal "As Is" with the "Should Be" dimensions indicate that the respondents prefer to have higher levels of Future Orientation, Performance Orientation, Gender Egalitarianism, Humane Orientation, Institutional Collectivism, and Uncertainty Avoidance, whereas they would like to have lower levels of Power Distance and Assertiveness. The preferred level of In-Group Collectivism is as high as the actual level in Turkish society.

GLOBE societal dimension findings strongly match the major characteristics of Turkish society. Turkish society is indeed high in In-Group Collectivism, where group solidarity among members is both valued and practiced. Part of this solidarity stems from the role family plays in people's lives. Strong ties among the family members create a nurturing and trustworthy environment for the individuals. Islamic ideology and verses of the Koran reinforce the importance of family and patriarchal relationships inside. Family is always available to give support, advice, and direction whenever members face important personal problems. Another manifestation of In-Group Collectivism is observed when people migrate from rural to urban areas. Coming from the same region or kinship ties create a strong interdependent network of relationships, where migrants are drawn into a nucleus of close ties and are given a hand in finding jobs and dwellings.

The strong network of interdependent relationships in Turkish society reduces the importance attributed to Future Orientation as individuals feel secure about their futures because the network would always provide the assistance and help that may be needed in the future. The low scores in GLOBE's Future Orientation dimension in Turkish society can also be explained by interpretations of Islam that promote fatalism.

In the context of GLOBE societal dimensions, Turkey is characterized as an assertive and high–power distance society. In the Turkish context, assertive and dominant relationships prevail in the education system, family, and public at large. In these contexts, assertive and authoritarian practices are common in teacher–student, husband–wife, mother in-law–daughter in-law, and government official–citizen relationships. As GLOBE findings reveal, Turkish people are unsatisfied with the level of assertiveness in society and aspire for more tender relations. In addition, Turkish society's high–power distance characteristics go hand in hand with the centralization of authority and influence. Power and resource allocation is based on hierarchy and there is a large social distance among different socioeconomic groups in society. The way people address each other also reflects the social status of individuals. On the contrary, Turkish people desire a culture that is substantially less hierarchical.

Turkish organizations, similar to society, are workplaces where in-group ties and network of interdependent relationships are both practiced and valued. Although at the organizational setting Turkish managers aspire for more performance orientation and planning, collectivism at institutional and in-group dimensions receive higher standings. As a manifestation of in-group collectivism, family members usually constitute the top-management team and board of directors in companies. Family members are trusted more than professionals in running the business and with the relations with state officials in the state-interdependent context of Turkey. In addition to family members, other in-groups, including the same school or region, serve as a basis of trust in organizations and business relationships.

An emerging profile of leadership in Turkey based on the absolute and relative scores of the GLOBE leadership attributes show that outstanding leaders are perceived to be decisive, team integrators, diplomatic, administratively competent, visionary, of integrity, and collaborative team oriented. These attributes and behaviors reflect that charismatic and team-oriented leadership is highly valued by Turkish managers, whereas self-protective, autonomous, and nonparticipative leadership attributes are perceived to inhibit outstanding leadership.

A series of qualitative analyses were conducted in order to explore the culture-specific leadership attributes and patterns in the Turkish context. The qualities of paternalistic, consultative, collective achievement-oriented, hands-on, and action-oriented types of leadership are regarded as positive characteristics in Turkish society.

Paternalistic leadership in Turkey (Aycan et al., 2000; Dilber, 1967) is associated with the prevailing patronage relationships and high in-group collectivism, where the leaders are expected to take a holistic concern for their followers and their families. A paternalistic leader acts in an authoritarian manner like a father would, even making decisions for their followers when necessary, which goes hand in hand with dominant and assertive practices in Turkish society. Furthermore, there is a high societal distance between the leaders and followers in the paternalistic relationship. The highly valued leadership attribute of hands-on, action orientation coincides with the assertive and high–power distance practices that are prevalent in Turkish society. In addition, qualitative data show that consultative leaders are perceived positively because consultation is used as a mechanism to make people feel important and valued in making decisions, make them feel part of the group, and increase their commitment, rather than for obtaining consensus. Leaders often make decisions by taking the input of a small nucleus of close associates, whereas consulting people in general is used more for the purpose of creating group loyalty. Thus, consultation in the Turkish context goes hand in hand with high in-group collectivism.

Practical Implications

Given the importance of acquaintances and close personal relationships in societal and organizational contexts, managers in Turkey should spend time on developing personal trust before going into business. This becomes paramount in both international and local contexts. Implications of this business setting for international companies planning to enter into Turkish markets are various. A joint venture type of entry mode would require a great deal of time for relationship development. In the negotiation process of international business, potential foreign partners need to demonstrate their capabilities and competencies in building trust by spending time on socialization and activities that even include their families.

Altogether, when the universal and culture-specific manifestations of outstanding leadership attributes are taken into consideration, leaders and managers in the Turkish context should act without hesitation, be knowledgeable about the topics and what is going on around them, be a go-getter, keep things under control, yet be concerned about the private and organizational problems of followers, and make them feel important and part of the group by consultation and integrating them into activities. An outstanding leader has integrity and, together with their family members, should pursue a modest lifestyle by avoiding luxurious consumption and flamboyant practices. Additionally, an outstanding leader should not be self-centered or autonomous, and thus present achievements as collective accomplishments or as contributions to the nation and well-being of society.

Leadership in Turkish society is a multifaceted phenomenon. A societal culture that is characterized with high In-Group Collectivism, Power Distance, and Assertiveness expects its leaders to enhance team integration and inspire togetherness in unique ways. Kozan and Ergin (1998) point to the importance of the mediation role that leaders and managers play in Turkish society, where leaders are expected to intrude into conflict resolutions in order to preserve peace and group solidarity. Thus, effective Turkish leaders develop mediation skills that "give face" to both parties and keep the group together at peace. The integrity of the leaders enables them to exercise power, which further builds on their symbolic and supreme roles. Assertiveness as a cultural trait implies that leaders who are decisive and hands-on, who can offer solutions to problems with new ideas, and who satisfy their followers' needs in a paternalistic way are the ones who can maintain their status.

Leadership in Turkish society is a paradoxical concept. Leaders on the one hand are granted with supreme status and power, and on the other, there is great skepticism and suspicion about them. This duality about the position of leaders stems from the competing values and practices that are simultaneously present in Turkish society. Turkey carries Eastern and Western values, traditional and modern practices, religious and secular ideologies at the same time, which create conflicting expectations from leaders. Leaders are expected to maintain in-group solidarity and behave in a paternalistic style, yet at the same time encourage performance and improvement in their organizations. There is a push in Turkey away from paternalism with the criticism of leading to nepotism and inefficiencies. Leaders in Turkish society and organizations face the dilemma of managing this duality between expectations of efficiency and performance and the more traditional hierarchical, assertive, and paternalistic values. Because Turkish society values performance, planning, and more egalitarian distribution of authority and resources, together with collectivistic tendencies, the ideal leader will be a person who is able to initiate change and provide vision and performance excellence by keeping group solidarity and at the same time avoiding nepotism.

ACKNOWLEDGMENTS

We would like to thank Hakan Özçelik, Tolga Akçura, and Çigdem Arsiray for their assistance in data collection phase of the study.

REFERENCES

Acar, F. (1991). Women in academic science careers in Turkey. In V. Stolte-Heiskanen, F. Acar, N. Ananiveva, D. Guadart, & and R. Fürst-Dilic (Eds.), *Women in science: Token women or gender equality* (pp. 147–171). New York: St. Martin's Press.

Adaman, F., Çarkoglu, A., & Senatalar, B. (2001). *Hanehalki gözünden Türkiye'de yolsuzlugun nedenleri ve önlenmesine iliskin öneriler* [The reasons for unethical conduct and propositions for eliminating them: Perspectives of the households]. TESEV Publications 24. Istanbul, Turkey: Acar Matbaacilik.

Arat, Z. (1999). *Deconstructing images of the Turkish women.* New York: Palgrave.

Arthur Andersen. (2000). *Human resources research while approaching 2001.* Istanbul, Turkey: Sabah Yayincilik.

Atay, F. R. (1980). Çankaya. Istanbul, Turkey: Sean Matbaasi.

Aycan, Z., Kanungo, R. N., Mendonca, M., Yu, K., Deller, J., Stahl, G. et al. (2000). Impact of culture on human resource management practices: A 10-country comparison. *Applied Psychology: An International Review, 49*(1), 192–221.

Bankalarimiz 1992. (1993). Ankara, Turkey: Rekmay Ltd. St.

Bodur, M., & Madsen, T. K. (1993). Danish foreign direct investments in Turkey. *European Business Review, 93*(5), 28–44.

Bugra, A. (1987). The late coming tycoons of Turkey. *Journal of Economics and Administrative Studies, 1*(1), 143–155.

Bugra, A. (1990). The Turkish holding company as a social institution. *Journal of Economics and Administrative Studies, 4*(1), 35–51.

Dilber, M. (1967). *Management in the Turkish private sector industry.* Ann Arbor, MI: University Microfilms Inc.

Duben, A. (1982). The significance of family and kinship in urban Turkey. In Ç. Kagitçibasi (Ed.), *Sex roles, family and community in Turkey* (pp. 73–100). Bloomington: Indiana University Turksih Studies.

Eczacibasi, N. F (1982). *Kusaktan kusaga* [From generation to generation]. Istanbul, Turkey: Agaoglu Yayinevi.

Eczacibasi, N. F. (1994). *Izlenimler, umutlar* [Observations, hopes]. Istanbul, Turkey: Tur Matbaacilik.

Eren, E., Bildirici, M. E., & Firat, U. (2000). *Türkiye'de 1998–1999 krizinde yónetici davranislari* [Managerial behavior during the 1998–1999 crisis]. Istanbul Chamber of Industry Publications. Istanbul, Turkey: Avciol Basin Yayin.

Ergenekon, C. (1995). *Sigorta sektórü* [The insurance sector]. Report Prepared for the Istanbul Securities Exchange Market, Sectorial Research Series, No. 5, Istanbul, Turkey.

Ergüder, Ü., Esmer, Y., & Kalaycioglu, E. (1991). *Türk toplumunun degerleri* [Values of Turkish society]. Report Prepared for TÜSIAD, No. TÜSIAD- T/91, 6145, Istanbul, Turkey.

Esmer, T. (1997, July 27). Türk kültürünün ózellikleri (Characteristics of Turkish culture). *Radikal,* p. 5.

Esmer, Y. (1999). *Devrim, evrim, statüko: Türkiye'de sosyal, siyasal, ekonomik degerler* [Revolution, evolution, status quo: Social, political, and economic values in Turkey]. Report Prepared for TESEV. Istanbul, Turkey: Acar Matbaacilik.

EU enlargement. (2005). Retrieved August 2005, from http://www.europa.eu.int/comm/enlargement /turkey/eurelations.htm

Fisek, G. O., Müderrisoglu, S., Yeniçeri, N., & Özkarar, G. (2001). *Integrated decision support system for disaster management in Turkey: Pilot study results of the psychological module.* CENDIM (Center for Disaster Management) Report, Bogaziçi University, Istanbul, Turkey.

Fukuyama, F. (1995). *Trust.* London: Penguin.

General Directorate of Women's Status and Problems. (2001). *Türkiye'de kadin* [Women in Turkey]. Ankara, Turkey: Author.

Göregenli, M. (1997). Individualist-collectivist tendencies in a Turkish sample. *Journal of Cross-Cultural Psychology, 28*(6), 787–794.

Gülalp, H. 1995. The crisis of westernization in Turkey: Islamism versus nationalism. *Innovation, 8*(2), 175–182.

Güngör, Z. (1997, February 25). O bir üniversiteydi [He was a university]. *Milliyet,* p. 6.

Gürbüz, E. (1988). *A measurement of sex-trait stereotypes.* Unpublished master's thesis, Bogaziçi University, Istanbul, Turkey.

Güriz, A. (1987). Sources of Turkish law. In T. Ansay & D. Wallace, Jr. (Eds.), *Introduction to Turkish law* (pp. 1–22). Deventer, Netherlands: Kluwer Law & Taxation

Gürüz, K. (2001). *Dünyada ve Türkiye'de yüksekógretim: Tarihçe ve bugünkü sevk ve idare sistemleri* [Higher education in Turkey and the world: History and administration systems]. Ankara, Turkey: ÖSYM.

Hanges, P. J., Dickson, M. W., & Sipe, M. T. (2004). Rationale for GLOBE statistical analyses: Societal rankings and test of hypotheses. In R. J. House, P. J. Hanges, M. Javidan, P. Dorfman, & V. Gupta

(Eds.), *Leadership, culture, and organizations: The GLOBE study of 62 societies* (pp. 219–234). Thousand Oaks, CA: Sage.

Hofstede, G. (1980). *Culture's consequences: International differences in work-related values.* Beverly Hills, CA: Sage.

Hofstede, G. (2001). *Culture's consequences: Comparing values, behaviors, institutions, and organizations across nations.* Thousand Oaks, CA: Sage.

House, R. J., Hanges, P. J., Javidan, M., Dorfman, P. W., Gupta, V., & GLOBE Associates. (2004). *Cultures, leadership, and organizations: The GLOBE study of 62 societies.* Thousand Oaks, CA: Sage.

House, R. J., Hanges, P. J., Ruiz-Quintanilla, S. A., Dorfman, P. W., Javidan, M., Dickson, M., et al. (1999). Cultural influences on leadership and organizations: Project GLOBE. In W. H. Mobley, M. J. Gessner, & V. Arnold (Eds.), *Advances in global leadership* (Vol. 1, pp. 171–233). Stamford, CT: JAI.

Human Development Report 1996: Turkey. (1996). Report prepared for the United Nations Development Program (UNDP), Ankara, Turkey.

Human Development Report 2001: Turkey. (2001). Report prepared for the United Nations Development Program (UNDP), Ankara, Turkey.

Ilmihal I. (1999). *Ilmihal I: Iman ve ibadetler* [Faith and worship]. Istanbul, Turkey: Divantas.

Inönü, I. (1985). *Hatiralar 1* [Memories 1]. Ankara, Turkey: Bilgi Yayinlari.

Inönü, I. (1987). *Hatiralar 2* [Memories 2]. Ankara, Turkey: Bilgi Yayinlari.

Institute for Management Developments. (1999). *The world competitiveness yearbook.* Lausanne, Switzerland: Author.

Iseri, A., Inelmen, K., Kabasakal, H., & Akarun, L. (2002). *An investigation of low levels of participation in CBOs and NGOs for disaster preparedness and mitigation: The case of Mimarsinan-Istanbul.* Report prepared for CENDIM (Center for Disaster Management), Bogaziçi University, Instanbul, Turkey.

Kabasakal, H. (1998). A profile of top women managers in Turkey. In Z. Arat (Ed.), *Deconstructing images of the Turkish women* (pp. 271–290). New York: St. Martin's Press.

Kabasakal, H., Akarun, L., Iseri, A., & Inelmen, K. (2001). *Community involvement in disaster management: Gayrettepe field research.* Paper presented at the Workshop on Urban Risk Management for Natural Disasters, Istanbul, Turkey.

Kabasakal, H., Aycan, Z., & Karakas, F. (2004). Women in management in Turkey. In M. Davidson & R. J. Burke (Eds.), *Women in management worldwide* (pp. 273–293). Aldershot, England : Ashgate.

Kabasakal, H., & Bodur, M. (2002). Arabic cluster: A bridge between east and west. *Journal of World Business, 37,* 40–54.

Kabasakal, H., Boyacigiller, N., & Erden, D. (1994). Organizational characteristics as correlates of women in middle and top management. *Bogaziçi Journal: Review of Social, Economic, and Administrative Studies, 8*(1–2), 45–62.

Kabasakal, H., & Dastmalchian, A. (2001). Introduction to the symposium on leadership and culture in the Middle East. *Applied Psychology: An International Review, 50*(4), 479–488.

Kabasakal, M. (1991). *Türkiye'de siyasal parti örgütlenmesi: 1908–1960* (The organization of political parties in Turkey: 1908–1960). Istanbul, Turkey: Tekin Yayinevi.

Kagitçibasi, Ç. (1982a). *The changing value of children in Turkey.* Papers of the East-West Population Institute, No. 60, East-West Center, Honolulu, HI.

Kagitçibasi, Ç. (1982b). Sex roles, value of children, and fertility. In Ç, Kagitçibasi (Ed.), *Sex roles, family and community in Turkey* (pp. 251–180). Bloomington: Indiana University TurkishStudies.

Kiray, M. (1997). Abandonment of land and transformation to urban life. *Human Development Report.* Ankara, Turkey: United Nations Development Programme.

Koç, V. (1973). *Hayat hikayem* [The story of my life]. Istanbul, Turkey: Apa Ofset Basimevi.

Koray, M. (1991). *Günümüzdeki yaklasimlar isiginda kadin ve siyaset* [Women and politics in the light of current approaches]. Türkiye Sosyal Ekonomik Arastirmalar Vakfi.

Kozan, K. M., & Ergin, C. (1998). Preference for third party help in conflict management in the United States and Turkey. *Journal of Cross-Cultural Psychology, 29*(4), 525–539.

Laurent, A. (1983). The cultural diversity of western conceptions of management. *International Studies of Management and Organization, 13*(1–2), 75–96.

Mead, R. (1994). *International management: Cross cultural dimensions.* Cambridge, MA: Blackwell.

Öncü, A., & Gókçe, D. (1991). Macro-politics of de-regulation and micro-politics of banks. In M. Heper (Ed.), *Strong state and economic interest groups: The post- 1980 Turkish experience* (pp. 99–117). Berlin: de Gruyter.

Önis, Z. (1997, July). *The political economy of Islamic resurgence in Turkey: The rise of the Welfare Party in perspective.* Paper presented at the BRISMES International Conference on Middle Eastern Studies, Oxford, England.

Özar, S. (1994). Some observations on the position of women in the labour market in the development process of Turkey. *Bogaziçi Journal: Review of Social, Economic and Administrative Studies, 8*(1–2), 21–43.

Özbasar, S., & Aksan, Z. (1976). Isletmelerimizde beseri kaynaklarin ózellikleri ve yónetimi [Characteristics and management of human resources in organizations]. *Yónetim, 2,* 97–116.

Özbay, F. (1994). Women's labor in rural and urban settings. *Bogaziçi Journal: Review of Social, Economic, and Administrative Studies, 8*(1–2), 5–19.

Özbudun, E. (1987). Constitutional law. In T. Ansay & D. Wallace, Jr. (Eds.), *Introduction to Turkish law* (pp. 23–60). Deventer, Netherlands: Kluwer Law & Taxation.

Pasa, S. F., Kabasakal, H., & Bodur, M. (2001). Society, organizations, and leadership in Turkey. *Applied Psychology: An International Review, 50*(4), 559–589.

Sabanci, S. (1985). *Iste hayatim* [This is my life]. Istanbul, Turkey: Aksoy Matbaacilik.

Schwartz, S. H. (1994). Beyond individualism/collectivism: New cultural dimensions of values. In U. Kim, H. C. Triandis, Ç. Kagitçibasi, S. C. Choi, & G. Yoon (Eds.), *Individualism and collectivism: Theory, methods, and applications* (pp. 85–119). Thousand Oaks, CA: Sage.

State Institute of Statistics. (1999). *Household labor force survey 1989–1999.* Ankara, Turkey: Author.

State Institute of Statistics. (2001). *Statistical yearbook of Turkey, 2001.* Ankara, Turkey: Author.

State Planning Organization. (1995). *Seventh five-year development plan, 1996–2000.* Ankara, Turkey: Author.

State Planning Organization. (2000). *Eighth five-year development plan, 2000–2005.* Ankara, Turkey: Author.

Tabak, F. (1989). *Women top managers in different types and sizes of industry in Turkey.* Unpublished master's thesis, Bogaziçi University, Istanbul, Turkey.

Tan, M. G., Ecevit, Y., & Üsür, S. S. (2000). Kadin-erkek esitligine dogru yürüyüs: Egitim, çalisma yasami ve siyaset [Approaching gender equality: Education, work life, and politics]. Istanbul, Turkey: TÜSIAD.

The Europa World Year Book 1996 (Vol. 2). (1996). London: Europa Publications Limited.

Topaloglu, B. (1983). *Women in Islam.* Istanbul, Turkey: Yagmur Yayinevi.

Trompenaars, F., & Hampden-Turner, C. (1998). *Riding the waves of culture* (2nd ed.). New York: McGraw-Hill.

Uluslararasi dogrudan yatirimlar ve Türkiye. (2002). [Foreign direct investments and Turkey]. Istanbul Chamber of Industry Publication. Istanbul, Turkey: Boyut Matbaacilik.

http://www.dpt.gov.tr/dptweb/esg/esg.i.html. Retrieved May 2004.

http://www.die.gov.tr. Retrieved April 2004.

http://www.dpt.gov.tr. Retrieved April 2004.

http://www.tcmb.gov.tr. Retrieved April 2004.

http://www.tbb.gov.tr. Retrieved April 2004.

http://www.treasury.gov.tr. Retrieved April 2004.

VIII

CONFUCIAN ASIA CLUSTER

The Confucian Asia cluster in the GLOBE Research Program consisted of China, Hong Kong, Japan, Singapore, South Korea, and Taiwan. Three of these countries, China, Hong Kong, and Singapore, are represented in this volume.

The Confucian Asia cluster scored high on In-Group Collectivism, Institutional Collectivism, and Performance Orientation. The remaining dimensions of societal culture, namely, Assertiveness, Future Orientation, Gender Egalitarianism, Humane Orientation, Power Distance, and Uncertainty Avoidance were in the midrange. It was not in the low-score range of any of the societal culture dimensions. (House et al., 2004).

The most strongly endorsed leadership dimensions in this cluster were Charismatic/Value Based and Team Orientated. Humane Oriented leadership and Participative leadership were also positively endorsed. Self-Protective leadership, though seen as neutral or inhibiting outstanding leadership, is the highest among all the clusters.

The theme running across this cluster is the strong influence of Confucian ideology and the influence of the Chinese civilization. Some of the distinctive Confucian teachings—such as the emphasis on learning through a hierarchical and family-modeled institution; teaching principles such as diligence, self-sacrifice, and delayed gratification—seem to be reflected in the societal norms and practices of this cluster. Singapore and China seem to be two distinct countries, possibly because of the colonial past of Singapore, and political developments in both China and Singapore.

REFERENCES

House, R. J., Hanges, P. J., Javidan, M., Dorfman, P. W., Gupta, V., & GLOBE Associates. (2004). *Culture, leadership, and organizations: The GLOBE study of 62 societies.* Thousand Oaks, CA: Sage.

24

Chinese Culture and Leadership

Ping Ping Fu
The Chinese University of Hong Kong, Hong Kong

Rongxian Wu
Suzhou University, Suzhou, China

Yongkang Yang
Jun Ye
Fudan University, Shanghai, China

Preface

As authors of the chapter on the Chinese GLOBE findings, we would like to make it clear that ours is, by no means, a comprehensive reflection of what the topic might suggest. Try as we possibly can, there is just no way we could do any justice to the topic within the space given and with the knowledge we have as individuals. Although the general information applies to the rest of the country, the quantitative information gathered for the analyses was from Shanghai only. The data for the project were collected in Shanghai, where the focus group interviews were conducted. For that reason, we would like to warn our readers against any incorrect impression that the Chinese are homogeneous among themselves, bearing only the characteristics described in the chapter. What is presented should be used as a useful reference for getting to know the culture and leadership in China, rather than an overview of the topic in the country.

1. INTRODUCTION

The opening of the People's Republic of China (PRC) to the rest of the world has changed the world's economic landscape (Tsui & Lau, 2002). The steady economic growth in the past few years, together with WTO (World Trade Organization) membership, has aroused an increasing interest in Chinese organizations in the business world. Chinese culture and leadership has also become an interesting topic, even to the general public. In this chapter, we use the Chinese GLOBE data as our empirical support and briefly introduce the societal culture in China and its leadership. The first part discusses societal culture, starting with a brief introduction about Confucianism, which forms the roots of the Chinese societal culture, followed by a brief introduction of the Chinese history, culture, contemporary economics, and politics. We refer to it as a brief introduction because China is such a large country with such a long history, that anything written within such a limited space can only be viewed as such. Following this, we present the results from the GLOBE project about Chinese societal culture and organizational culture. We end the first part with a summary and integration of the findings.

The second part focuses on leadership in China. We start with a brief introduction about leadership in China, and use the stories of three historical leaders to show the persistent influence of Confucianism. The results of three focus group interviews are then presented to show that many of the desired attributes and behaviors of the contemporary leaders are still similar to those that have been historically respected. The connection clearly shows the influence of Confucianism, but at the same time, there is an obvious influence from Communist ideologies and Western management philosophies. Finally, we present the results from the GLOBE leadership survey to demonstrate the empirical evidence about the desirable leadership attributes and behaviors in China. The chapter ends with a summary of the findings in leadership and discussion of the implications of the findings.

2. CONFUCIANISM: ROOTS OF CHINESE CULTURE

Of all the ideologies that influenced the thinking and life of traditional and agricultural China, Confucianism should account for the most. Over a century ago, an American missionary in China observed: "Confucianism is the base, and all Chinese are Confucianists, as all English are Saxons" (Smith, 1894, p. 295). In fact, since the Song Dynasty (960–1126), Confucianism has exerted such an enormous influence on Chinese history that the word *Confucianism* is almost synonymous with the words *"Chinese traditional culture"* (Li, 1986). Therefore, in order to understand Chinese culture, one must first understand Confucianism.

Confucianism was founded by Kong Fuzi (551–479 BC), who was later called Confucius by the Jesuit missionaries (all the Chinese names in this chapter are written according to the pronunciation of the standard Chinese). Confucius died almost a decade before the birth of the ancient Greek philosopher Socrates (469–399 BC). However, the basis of the Confucian ideology were laid by the ceremonies and rituals established by Zhou Gong, brother of Emperor Wu of the *Shang* Kingdom. Zhou Gong, and others, enforced order and status among people at the start of the Zhou Dynasty, almost 300 years before Kong Fuzi was born. Confucius led his disciples to disseminate the rituals and ceremonies from the Zhou Dynasty and organized them in books. But it was in the Han Dynasty, more than 300 years after his death, when Confucian philosophy was officially accepted.

In 134 AD, Dong Zhongsu, a famous Confucian scholar, proposed the banning of all schools of thought except the Confucian school. Emperor Shun accepted Dong's proposal and government officers were then selected from among Confucius's disciples. Ever since then, Chinese culture has almost exclusively been identified with Confucianism. Even though Buddhism and Taoism were other two major schools of thought, and filled the needs of popular imagination and a popular religion, it is Confucianism that has continuously influenced the Chinese people and formed the Chinese culture (Li, 1986).

Although the "five constant virtues: benevolence (*ren*), righteousness (*yi*), propriety (*li*), wisdom (*zhi*), and fidelity (*xin*)" in Confucianism are the guidelines for behaviors, ideologically there are four major virtues in Confucianism: class system, obedience, doctrine of the mean, and *renqing*.

The class system refers to maintaining the ancient rituals and proper ordering of positions in society. According to Confucius, a person's social status, no matter how high or low, was given at birth and in the order specified by the five cardinal relationships ("wu lun"; Yang, 1993; cited in Farh & Cheng, 1999, p. 99). "By affirming and embracing patriarchy as the organizing principle of society, China's imperial rulers solidified their absolute authority over their subjects as well" (Farh & Cheng, 2000, p. 103).

The four virtues are closely connected to each other. The observance of orders would not have been possible without obedience, the next major virtue, which is also embedded in the order of the hierarchical relationship. Of the five cardinal relationships, three of them (father–son, husband–wife, and brother–brother) explicitly address social relations within the family (Tom, 1989). Because wisdom gained in a long life experience comes with old age, obedience is essentially the doctrine of filial piety in the family. Therefore, the eldest male possessed absolute authority, and all others were expected to be absolutely obedient and loyal to the family head. In ancient China, a country was perceived as a large family with the emperor as the head, so all countrymen were the children, and were expected to obey the emperor as their own parent (Yu, Cheng, & Chen, 1999). Therefore, we can say that the virtue of obedience is the cultural root of paternalistic leadership found in many overseas Chinese enterprises (Farh & Cheng, 2000).

Despite the orders and the expectations of obedience, however, there are always conflicts. When conflicts occur, doctrine of the mean (avoiding extremes, also translated as moderation) is the principle to handle them. Confucius believed that any extreme ideas would lead people astray and create disorder in society, and therefore urged people to control their emotions and refrain from desires in order not to lose insightfulness and the ability to remain obedient to one's superiors under all circumstances.

The last virtue, *renqing*, refers to being kind, benevolent, righteous, or respecting the feelings of other people. According to Confucianism, *renqing* is an internalized moral virtue that is more powerful than laws, because laws can force people to obey temporarily, but only moral virtues can teach people to have a sense of shame, which will then prevent them from doing bad things at any time, and urge them to be kind and righteous.

Chinese historian Li Zehou pointed out (1986) that Confucianism's domination of Chinese traditional culture is by no means accidental. Compared to numerous other schools of thought, Confucianism is more deeply related to ancient Chinese economic traditions and family legal practices. Active enforcement of Confucius ideologies can be seen in the socialization, education, and daily living practices.

3. CHINA: HISTORY, ECONOMY, POLITICS, AND CULTURE

China is situated in the eastern part of Asia, on the west coast of the Pacific Ocean. It has a total land area of 9.6 million square kilometers, next only to Canada. From north to south, it measures some 5,500 kilometers, stretching from the central line of the Heilong River, north of the town of Mohe, to the Zengmu Reef at the southernmost tip of the Nansha Islands. From west to east, the territory of China extends about 5,200 kilometers from the Pamirs to the confluence of the Heilong and Wusuli rivers.

China's land border is 22,800 kilometers long. The nation is bordered by Korea in the east; Mongolia in the north; Russia in the northeast; Kazakhstan, Kirghizia and Tadzhikistan in the northwest; Afghanistan, Pakistan, India, Nepal, Sikkim, and Bhutan in the west and southwest; and Myanmar, Laos, and Vietnam in the south. Across the seas to the east and southeast are the Republic of Korea, Japan, the Philippines, Brunei, Malaysia, and Indonesia.

The Chinese mainland is flanked by the Bohai, the Huanghai (Yellow Sea), and the East China and South China seas in the east and south. The territorial waters of the People's Republic of China extend 12 nautical miles out from the base line drawn where China's land territories and interior waters border the sea. More than 5,000 islands are scattered over China's vast territorial seas.

The coast of the mainland, 18,000 kilometers long, is dotted with excellent harbors and ports, the most famous of them, from north to south, being Dalian, Qinhuangdao, Tianjin, Yantai, Qingdao, Lianyungang, Nantong, Shanghai, Ningbo, Wenzhou, Fuzhou, Xiamen, Guangzhou, Zhanjiang, and Beihai. Among them Shanghai is the largest city in China with a population of 13.56 million and well-developed industry, commerce, finance, and ocean transportation (information from the materials prepared by the Chinese Embassy to the United States).

History

With records showing the establishment of the *Xia* Dynasty in the 21st century BC, China has a written history of over 4,000 years. The history of China is usually divided into four major epochs: ancient times (from antiquity to 1840 AD), modern period (1840–1919), new democratic revolution (1919–1949), and the People's Republic of China(1949–).

Ancient China was fairly well developed in both economy and culture. During the apex of the Chinese feudal society, the *Han* and *Tang* dynasties (agriculture, handicrafts, weaving, and shipbuilding) were advanced. Transportation by both land and water was made possible; extensive economic and cultural relations were established with Japan, Korea, India, Persia, and Arabia. Ancient China was also home of the four major creations, papermaking, printing, gunpowder, and the compass, which exerted an enormously profound influence on the history of mankind. Influential thinkers such as Confucius, Lao Zi, and Sun Zi (the author of *The Art of War*) all lived in ancient China.

The Opium War (1840) was a turning point in Chinese history. The Treaty of Nanking with Britain signed by the corrupt *Qing* court in 1842 resulted in bartering away China's national sovereignty, and marked the reduction of China to a semicolonial, semifeudal country. The situation remained till the Revolution of 1911, when Dr. Sun Yat-sen led the bourgeois democratic revolution, which ended the rule of the *Qing* Dynasty, and founded the provisional government of the Republic of China, thus putting an end to the monarchy that had existed for 2,000 years.

The May Movement against imperialism and feudalism took place in 1919. Two years later, with the help of the former Soviet Union, the Chinese Communist Party held its first National Congress and founded the Communist Party of China. After almost three decades of hard struggle, including civil wars against the Kuomintang headed by Chiang Kai-shek, and the war of resistance against Japan following the first Party Congress, the Chinese

Communist Party, led by the late Mao Zedong, proclaimed the founding of the People's Republic of China on October 1, 1949.

For the next three decades, following the economic recovery in the first three years (1950–1952), China underwent several major political movements, including the socialist transformation (1953–1956), large-scale socialist construction (1957–1966), and finally the Cultural Revolution, which lasted for 10 years from 1966 to 1976. The Cultural Revolution brought great calamity to the country and the people, causing the most serious setbacks and most damaging losses since the founding of the People's Republic of China.

Economy

The Cultural Revolution left the Chinese economy on the verge of collapse. Fortunately, the Party held its historical Third Plenary Session of the Eleventh Congress in 1978 and decided to open up the country to the outside world and started the economic reform. Ever since then, the country has not engaged in any large-scope political movements but instead has focused on building a socialist modernization with Chinese characteristics. Prior to the reform, the Chinese economic system had the following four main characteristics:

1. *State ownership:* Because state ownership was required by state socialism, all major industrial enterprises were owned by the state. There were many privately owned small businesses when the new China was first established, but they were all eliminated during the 3-year "Socialist Transformation" movement launched in 1956. In the two decades that followed, private ownership was virtually non-existent. Family-owned businesses were also collectivised and transformed into collectively owned types of businesses in order to sustain their existence. By 1984, about 70% of the industries were state owned, and 30% collectively owned. Therefore, until the reform, state enterprises were the backbone of China's business industry.
2. *Central planning:* Together with socialism, the Chinese government also copied the highly centralized planned economic system that the former Soviet Union established in the early stage of its industrialization. Under the central planning system, there is an institutional framework with the State Council at the top and several state commissions underneath it. The two most important economic administrative commissions were the State Planning Commission (SPC), established in 1952 and responsible for long-term plans, and the State Economic Commission (SEC), established in 1956 and in charge of annual operational plans. Established in the same year was the General Bureau for the Supply of Raw Materials, which allocated resources and materials, and the State Technology Commission, which was created to plan long-term technical development.
3. *Local government involvement:* It would have been impossible for China to implement the central planning system without the agencies at various levels. The structure of the local government and their functions usually corresponded to that of the central government and embraced the local planning and economic commissions and industrial and functional bureaus. Organizations were also categorized into provincial, municipal, or county level, and were controlled by the government agencies correspondingly.
4. *Dominance of the Chinese Communist Party:* The relationship between the Central Government and central Chinese Communist Party Committee is displayed in Figure 24.1. As can be seen, the Communist Party committee exists at every level and was,

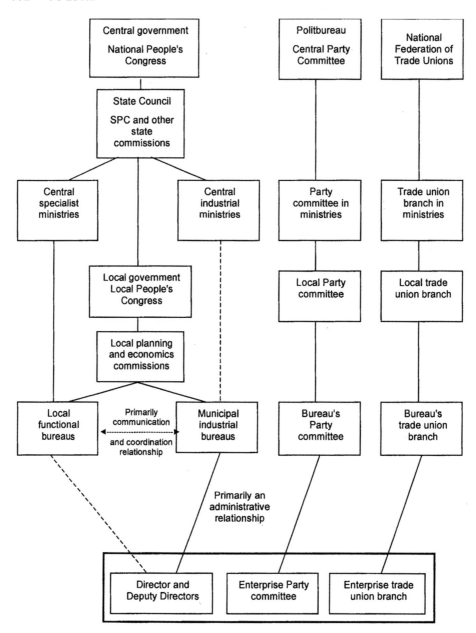

Figure 24.1.   Industrial governance in the Chinese urban industrial sector. From Lu (1996).
Copyright 1996 by Macmillan. Adapted by permission.

and still is in many organizations, part of the decision-making body. Party committees
or general branches (depending on the size of the enterprise), headed by the Party
secretary, issued directives and commands, supervised individual Party members and
other non-Party staff, determined personnel issues (within the organization), and
organized political educational programmes.

The rapid economic development over two and a half decades has lifted millions out of poverty and seen China emerging increasingly prosperous and confident. With China's entering into the WTO in 2001, "past speculations about China as a world economic power in the 21st century have become a reality few would dispute anymore" (Tsui & Lau, 2002). However, the rapid pace of change has not been without its costs. According to China Briefing (http://www.asiasociety.org), a growing economic gap has opened up between the prosperous coastal regions of the east and the poverty-stricken western hinterland. Even within the more prosperous regions, economic inequality is becoming more pronounced. Unemployment is also rising. All these problems, fortunately, have been put on the agenda of the ruling Party, and the development of the country's west is already under way.

Politics

Under China's socialist political and economic system, the government was explicitly responsible for planning and managing the national economic. A major portion of the governmental apparatus was devoted to managing the economy; all but a few of the more than 10 ministries, commissions, administrations, bureaus, academies, and corporations under the State Council were concerned with economic matters (see The State Council, Chap. 10).

Under the old system, economic policies and decisions adopted by the National People's Congress and the State Council were passed on to the economic organizations under the State Council, which incorporated them into the plans for the various sectors of the economy. Each of the economic organizations under the State Council directed the units under its jurisdiction through subordinate offices at the provincial and local levels. A major objective of the reform was to reduce the use of direct controls and to increase the role of indirect economic levers. By 1987, the majority of state-owned industrial enterprises, which were managed at the provincial level or below, were partially regulated by a combination of specific allocations and indirect controls, and the planned economy is shifting increasingly to the market-oriented economy.

Starr (1997), author of a guidebook on China, wrote:

China's political system has three branches—a legislature, an executive branch, and a judiciary—but in practice there are really two, since the Chinese judiciary functions more as a department of the executive than it does as an independent check on the other two arms of the government. Similarly, the legislature has only very recently come to see itself as a potential check on the operations of the executive branch and the judiciary. The branches are not equal partners, and there is no provision in the Chinese constitution for checks and balances to maintain equality. (p. 60)

The constitution itself, the fifth since the People's Republic of China was founded in 1949, is "probably best understood as a mission statement or policy platform with a finite duration" (Starr, 1997, p. 60) rather than laws for regulating behaviors.

Culture

Because culture is the major theme of the chapter, it is discussed in more detail. We mentioned earlier that Confucianism is the root of the Chinese culture. As such, many of the Chinese cultural characteristics are related to the four virtues discussed previously. To a certain extent, we can say that the Chinese society is structured around webs of social relationships (Bian, 1994), and Chinese people all live in an invisible network of *guanxi* (relationships or ties). When dealing with relationships, one has to be careful with *renqing* (individually internalized sense of moral responsibility) and *mianzi* (face). All these can be viewed as major Chinese cultural characteristics and have deep roots in Confucianism.

Guanxi.   The Chinese term is used in this chapter instead of the word *relationship,* because *guanxi* has a much more involved connotation than the latter. "*Guanxi* ties people together according to the specific relationship between these people" (Hui & Graen, 1997, p. 454). A survey of Chinese citizens conducted a few years ago showed that 92% affirmed the importance of *guanxi* in their daily lives, and 72% preferred to use *guanxi* connections over normal bureaucratic channels to advance personal interests and solve problems (Yeung & Tung, 1996). Western business people who have done some business with China also know that companies wanting to get in on the ground floor in China need *guanxi* in addition to planning, funding, and a good product (Murphy, 1996).

The reason *guanxi* is so important is because China is a country "ruled by people" (*ren zhi*) not by law, and the predefined nature of *guanxi* dictates the behavior. The notion of rule by people can be seen as a result of the belief in morality as defined under Confucianism. According to Confucius, governance by ethics (*li zhi*) is preferred over governance by law (*fa zhi*), and people follow ethics, making China ruled by people. The reliance on people rather than law would naturally promote the practice of *guanxi,* because an individual (rather than institutional authority) defines what is permissible in a given context at a particular time. Even the central government deals with provincial and municipal governments by means of myriad of ad hoc agreements made after complex bargaining negotiations. As Lee Kuan Yew, former premier of the Republic of Singapore, put it, the Chinese use *guanxi* "to make up for the lack of the rule of law and transparency in rules and regulations" (Yeung & Tung, 1996, p. 56). To some extent, it is correct to say that without *guanxi,* nothing happens in China (Murphy, 1996).

Renqing and Mianzi.   We explained earlier that the notion of *renqing* is one of the Confucius virtues, and *mianzi* is almost inseparable from *renqing.* Generally speaking, *renqing* indicates the emotional responses of an individual confronting the various situations of daily life (Hwang, 1987). Individuals are expected to control their anger, hatred, and desire, because the notion of *renqing* is reciprocal and a person is believed to be treated however the person treats others. Also, if the person lets his or her emotions take over, she or he will cause the other to lose "face." Over a hundred years ago, Arthur Smith pointed out that in China the word *face* does not signify simply the front part of the head, but is "literally a compound noun of multitude, with more meanings than we shall be able to describe, or perhaps to comprehend" (Smith, 1894, p. 16).

There is a Chinese saying that "*mianze* is like the bark of a tree; without which, the tree dies." People who have lost *mianzi* in Confucian societies are more than social outcasts. A loss of *mianzi* brings shame not only to the individuals, but also to their family members, leaving them unable to function in society (Yeung & Tung, 1996). In Chinese history, there are people who have actually killed themselves in order to save face. A district magistrate in the Ming Dynasty, as a special favor, was allowed to be beheaded in his robes of office in order to save face (Smith, 1894).

Swaak (1995, p. 43) pointed out that the Chinese value the notion of *mianzi* because it allows them to maintain their esteem and personal dignity. It is a difficult value to comprehend for people who believe in being direct and open. But in China, you can cause someone to lose *mianzi,* esteem, or personal dignity by saying exactly what you mean or feel. In turn, the person who has lost *mianzi* may—indirectly—make you lose *mianzi* without you knowing it.

This is because Confucianism provides a prescribed response to most situations and individuals are judged by the way they use these prescribed patterns of behavior when dealing with other people. So long as the person conforms to the expected behaviors this person's face is maintained. The loss of *mianzi* occurs when the prescribed expectations are not met. This is still true to this day. For example, friends are expected to help each other out in times of difficulty. If Person A asks his friend, Person B, for help and Person B cannot or does not give the help, then Person B is not giving Person the face, and Person A would feel that he lost his face.

The concept of *mianzi* is especially intriguing because it also involves the influence of other cultural notions. For example, the Chinese vastly prefer consensus to a simple majority rule when making a decision. If people have different views about a decision, they will keep pushing the decision to higher authorities until a unanimous consensus is reached, so that people whose opinions were rejected by peers would not lose face. Here the concern for *mianzi* is mixed with the belief in high power distance. It is that belief that makes succumbing to the higher authority easier than agreeing with peers. In addition to *guanxi, renqing. and mianzi,* another much-emphasized phenomenon in Chinese culture is the notion of political morality, which too is historically rooted in Confucianism.

Political Morality. Throughout China's history, political thought has been one of the essential branches of literature. Moral forces are the means by which "this incomputable mass of human beings, dwelling on the Chinese plains from the dawn of history has until now, been controlled," and made itself "an exception to the universal law of the decay and death of nations" (Smith, 1894, p. 287). Unlike in the West, where the source of morality is the individual conscience, in China morality fixes social norms as well as individual codes of behavior, and in doing so it plays the role that religion does in the West (Tom, 1989).

For Confucius, morality and government were so closely related that it was scarcely possible to think about them separately. According to Confucius: *"Lead the people with governmental measures and regulate them with laws and punishment, and they will avoid wrongdoing but will have no sense of honor and shame. Lead them with virtue and regulate them by the rules of propriety, and they will have a sense of shame and, moreover, set themselves right"* (Confucius, 1992, 2:3).

Throughout Chinese history, political thought has been one of the essential branches of literature. The extensive coverage in the media on various types of meetings is good evidence. In ancient China, emperors and government officers were also scholars. The late Chairman Mao Zedong himself wrote poems and studied calligraphy. In fact, the construction of political morality is one of the three tasks of the Communist Party, and weekly meetings to discuss moral issues are routine in all types of organizations everywhere in China. Often the deputy president or director in an organization is specialized in handling the work of political morality. These people are expected to act somewhat like fathers in churches or clinical psychologists (even though they are not trained as such), listening to people's problems and providing advice when they can, but often they are also expected to find the necessary resources and help solve practical problems.

Summary

The preceding section has provided a very brief overview of China's history, economy, politics, and culture. In particular, it talks about the few characteristics that have made the Chinese culture "unique" and somewhat "difficult" for Western people to understand.

Although the past two decades' rapid development has dramatically turned China from a poverty-driven country to a new rising economic power, China itself has remained "unchanged" (Chine, 1999, p. 34) in many ways, and the state paternalism is still a dominant feature of China's business environment. According to Child and Tse (2001), "so long as China retains its one-party system, this feature is likely to persist" (p. 17). Chinese people, on the other hand, are still largely clinging to the traditional values (see Goldman, 1994; Ralston, Egri, Stewart, Terpstra, & Yu, 1999; Ralston, Gustafson, Terpstra, & Holt, 1995; Ralston et al., 1993) and "Confucianism is now again at the core of the national essence that is being rediscovered, reinvented, and re-embraced today" (*People's Daily,* 1994).

However, Chinese business leaders, living and working under the Chinese Communist Party, are also exposed to communist ideology, which discourages autocratic and dictatorial leadership. Leaders are encouraged to show concerns for their followers, respect them, and are expected to sacrifice themselves for their followers. Furthermore, the country has been going through an unprecedented influence of Western management philosophies (Chen, 1995). Naturally, in addition to the Confucius values, the influence of Communist and Western managerial values would also be obvious. In the following section, we present the Chinese results of the GLOBE societal cultural survey, which show the influence of the multiple values we stated previously.

4. GLOBE FINDINGS ABOUT CHINESE SOCIETAL CULTURE

The Chinese data of the GLOBE Project were collected in Shanghai, which is the largest industrial city in China. Shanghai was selected as the research site because of its rapid development and strategic position in China. With a population of 13 million people, a well-developed infrastructure for utilities, communications, and all forms of commercial transportations, and a political climate conducive to foreign investment (Fung, Yan & Nin, 1992), Shanghai serves as an ideal environment to investigate changes in values and implications of such changes in managerial practices. Whether development in Shanghai can be generalized and extended to the rest of China is an unresolved question, but there is a strong case for similar patterns of economic development and increased foreign investment throughout China's urban centers and coastal port cities (Ralston et al., 1995).

A total of 158 responses were collected from middle managers working in the finance industry (77) and food industry (81).[1] Table 24.1 presents China's mean scores on each of the cultural dimensions "As Is" (the perceived practices in society) and "Should Be" (how the society should be in an ideal situation). Next to the mean scores are the rankings of the scores in reference to the other scores by the 61 participating countries (for the purpose of the research, regions like Hong Kong are also referred to as countries). Also presented in Table 24.1 are the absolute differences between the "As Is" score and the "Should Be" score, the highest and lowest mean scores on each of the dimensions.

Performance Orientation.   Performance Orientation refers to the degree to which a society encourages and rewards group members for performance improvement and achievement of excellence. According to House, Javidan, Hanges, and Dorfman (2002) and House et al.

---

[1]The detailed information on the sample is missing because the demographic data of the project was lost in the mailing process.

TABLE 24.1
Results of GLOBE Societal Value Survey

Cultural Dimension	Mean	Rank[a]	Absolute[b] Difference	Band[c]	Highest Score	Lowest Score
Performance Orientation						
"As Is"	4.45	13	1.22	A	4.94	3.20
"Should Be"	5.67	50		C	6.58	4.92
Future Orientation						
"As Is"	3.75	34	0.98	C	5.07	2.88
"Should Be"	4.73	60		C	6.20	4.33
Assertiveness						
"As Is"	3.76	51	1.68	B	4.89	3.38
"Should Be"	5.44	2		A	5.56	2.66
Institutional Collectivism						
"As Is"	4.77	7	0.21	A	5.22	3.25
"Should Be"	4.56	9		B	5.65	3.83
In-Group Collectivism						
"As Is"	5.80	9	0.71	A	6.36	3.53
"Should Be"	5.09	58		C	6.52	4.94
Gender Egalitarianism						
"As Is"	3.05	48	0.63	B	4.08	2.50
"Should Be"	3.68	58		C	5.17	3.18
Uncertainty Avoidance						
"As Is"	4.94	10	0.34	A	5.37	2.88
"Should Be"	5.28	9		A	5.61	3.16
Power Distance						
"As Is"	5.04	41	1.94	B	5.80	3.89
"Should Be"	3.10	12		B	3.65	2.04
Humane Orientation						
"As Is"	4.36	17	0.96	B	5.23	3.18
"Should Be"	5.32	39		C	6.09	4.49

[a]The rank order for China relative to the 61 societies. [b]Absolute difference between the "As Is" and "Should Be" scores. [c]Letters A to D represent statistically different clusters of countries (Bands) with A > B > C > D (cf. Hanges, Dickson, & Sipe, 2004).

(2004), GLOBE's Performance Orientation is similar to Hofstede and Bond's (1988) Confucian work dynamism, which focuses on social hierarchy, protecting the status quo, and personal virtue. The Chinese score was among the higher ranking countries on "As Is" (4.45, Rank 13), which is supportive of the traditional Chinese culture in which hard work and diligence were highly praised and appreciated. When describing the same value as how it "Should Be," the average scores among other countries are much higher than those on "As Is." The Chinese score was also higher than its score on "As Is" (5.67 vs. 4.45). However, the score was much lower compared to those of other countries (ranked 50th out of 61 compared to the 13th out of 61 on "As Is").

Like China, the scores of Singapore, Hong Kong, and Taiwan on Performance Orientation "As Is" were among the highest ranking countries (2, 3, and 8, respectively) and their scores on Performance Orientation "Should Be" were higher than their scores on "As Is," but their respective rankings are also much lower compared to their rankings on "As Is" (48, 52, and 46, respectively). In other words, the discrepancies between the "As Is" and "Should Be" scores for the four Chinese-speaking societies are all low. To find out the more accurate explanation to the reason will require much more investigation, but a couple of possible reasons might be: (a) the tendency for the Chinese people to score toward the mean as a result of the influence by the "doctrine of the mean" (although no response bias has been identified for the Chinese sample for this dimensions; Javidan, 2004, p. 250); (b) the Chinese people think good performance is already highly encouraged, (c) the Chinese, being more collectivistic, may not like extreme emphasis on encouraging individual performances.

Future Orientation.   The Future Orientation dimension in the GLOBE instrument measures values and beliefs pertaining to long-term orientation (e.g., delaying gratification, planning, and investing in the future). The results showed that Chinese managers' score on Future Orientation "As Is" (3.75) ranked about the middle (34) among the 61 countries; whereas their score on Future Orientation "Should Be" (4.73) ranked 60, which is next to the lowest among the 61 countries. Hofstede (1993) pointed out that Chinese culture is long-term oriented. China is a farming country, and for farmers, planning long-term means to save as much as you can and thriftiness was a virtue cherished in the traditional agricultural society that forms the backbone of China (Cheung et al., 1996). But the GLOBE items on this dimension do not capture thrift or saving. If we look at the dimension as emphasizing on conscientiously planning for the future, this might be a reason for the low score.

Unlike most religious societies, the Chinese society does not have a dominant religion, but it was exposed to multiple schools of thought in ancient times and people have the habit of using often seemingly contradictory principles to rationalize their thinking when necessary. Whereas Confucianism encouraged people to be thrifty and to think long-term, the founder of Taoism, Lao Zi, opined that the cosmos is uncertain, and therefore we had better leave things alone, letting things take their natural course. To him, planning is both unnecessary and against nature.

Another possible reason might be due to the high level of uncertainties caused by the too many changes in China. Take the saving habit, for example. Chinese people used to put into the bank every single penny they could spare. But now that the government has dropped the interest rate to such a low level in order to stimulate expenditure there is no incentive to save anymore. Therefore, it may be safe to say that the current situation in China discourages people to think long-term. As Cherry Li, a middle-level manager in a U.S.-owned Chinese company who was getting on-the-job training in the U.S. said: *"Americans pay a lot of attention to individual development. They have 'road maps' for individuals and try to lay ahead where you are going to be in the next five years. We Chinese don't do that at all. We watch our steps as we walk along. How can we plan ahead when we don't even know which company we'll be working for in the next five years?"* (Li, 1997, personal communication). It is suggested that further research is required in order to decipher the real reason.

Assertiveness.   Assertiveness measures the degree to which individuals in a society are assertive, dominant, and aggressive in social relationships. China has traditionally been a male-dominant society. Until modern times, men in China were always superior to women.

Being a woman in China meant being a servant to the men in their lives—"first father, then husband, then son"—and there has been a long-standing prejudice against females in China although literature relevant to masculinity ideology in China is quite sparse (Levant, Wu, & Fischer, 1996). In fact, even to this day, traditional masculinity ideology is still endorsed highly as shown in the Levant et al. study. Masculine behaviors such as assertiveness, dominance, and aggression should therefore be highly acceptable in China.

In fact, a number of studies, which included the United States, Hong Kong, China, and Taiwan, found Chinese more masculine and assertive than Americans (Schmit & Yeh, 1992; Shermerhorn & Bond, 1991). However, literature on unique Chinese cultural concepts such as *mianzi* (face; maintaining the respect of others as well as to respect others), *renqing* (being kind or respecting the feelings of other people), and *guanxi* (relatedness or connections among individuals) strongly indicate otherwise. These terms distinguish the Chinese from other cultures (Bond, 1991). They constrain the behaviors of Chinese individuals and discourage them from behaving assertively. The conflict of interests may explain the large discrepancy between China's two scores on assertiveness "As Is" (3.76) and "Should Be" (5.44). The respective "As Is" ranking (51 out of 61) indicates that the respondents did not think Chinese society encouraged individuals to be assertive. However, the Chinese score on how society should value such behavior ranked 2nd highest among the 61 scores, showing that Chinese managers have a much stronger desire for the society to value assertive behavior in comparison to others. An accurate explanation of the discrepancy between the two scores requires further study, but a plausible reason that the current Chinese society has a lower level of assertiveness than many other societies could be because Chinese managers are still influenced by their concerns for notions such as *renqing* (emotional responses), *guanxi* (relations or ties), and *mianzi* (face), whereas their strong aspirations for such behavior could be due to the fact that rapid changes in society created an extremely high level of uncertainty, urging Chinese people to become increasingly aggressive in order to protect themselves.

Institutional Collectivism. This scale measures the degree to which individuals are encouraged by societal institutions to be integrated into broader entities, such as the extended family, the firm, or the village. For centuries, the individual as an end in itself was de-emphasized in Chinese society. Instead, the network of obligations and responsibilities as a group member of the society was emphasized (Chew & Putti, 1995). As Michael Bond (1991) described it: "Chinese think of themselves using more group-related concepts (such as attentive to others) than Americans do; and they see their ideal 'self' as being closer to their social (or interpersonal) self than Westerners do" (p. 34). Based on these traditional values, it would be natural for one to expect China to score relatively higher on this dimension.

Consistent with the assumption, the Chinese score on Institutional Collectivism "As Is" (4.77) was among the highest, ranking 7th among the 61 countries, meaning Chinese society is very collectivistic. The Chinese score on Institutional Collectivism "Should Be" (4.56), however, is slightly lower compared to the "As Is" score. Although it ranked in the middle (36 among the 61 countries), the absolute difference between the two scores was very minimal (0.21). The relative discrepancy to other countries may be the result of the changes taking place in China, especially within the business context, which is particularly likely to be picked up by sampling from a managerial population. Like many other Chinese cultural ideologies that are being threatened by the acceptance of Western views, the collectivistic orientation, too, is being *challenged.* For example, the extremely egalitarian practices that were derived from the collectivistic orientation and that were preached in China for decades are now *often* being rejected and replaced by more equitable standards (Chen, 1995). Individual contributions are now being acknowledged and rewarded. However, overall, people's values in collectivism are still quite consistent with the traditional values.

In-Group Collectivism.   The second collectivism, labeled *In-Group Collectivism,* measures the degree to which members of a society take pride in membership in small groups such as their family and circle of close friends, and the organizations and units in which they are employed. Like its scores on the Institutional Collectivism dimension, Chinese scores on In-Group Collectivism "As Is" (5.80, ranked 9th) were slightly higher than the scores on family cohesiveness "Should Be" (5.09, ranked 58th). The absolute difference between the two scores is bigger than that for Institutional Collectivism. However, the reasons for the discrepancy are similar to the ones discussed previously. The concept of family has always been important to the Chinese people. Pursuit of individual interests at the sacrifice of families has always been discouraged. In China, altruism and loyalty, loyalty to parents at home and to bosses at work, are values that the society tries very hard to instill in children. A close parent–children relationship is a virtue that is widely respected and valued. "Chinese parents take great interest in their children throughout their lives, and their children, imbued with the doctrine of filial piety, are constantly reminded of their filial duty towards their parents" (Chao, 1983, p. 72). Most Chinese children live with their parents until they get married. Very often even after they get married, if they do not have a place to live, they continue to live with their parents. In many rural areas, new extensions are made to the house when male children get married. The tradition that all children live under the same roof is still kept there. So the current practice reflects the lingering influence of the traditional values.

The reforms, nevertheless, have forced the Chinese to take care of themselves. A study that compared values held by Chinese managers before and after the Tian An Men Square incident in 1989 found a growing spirit of "Chinese-style" individualism, which is "tempered by cultural relationships and centralized controls, yet compatible with Western values" (Ralston et al., 1995, p. 15). Young people are becoming increasingly independent. They move away from their parents as soon as they can. At work, they are no longer constrained to the organization, and therefore can "afford" not to be loyal to their employers. The increasing divorce rate and the one-child-per-family policy also make it impossible to maintain some of the traditional values of a family. That is probably a good reason explaining why the Chinese score on In-Group Collectivism "Should Be" is much lower than its score on In-Group Collectivism "As Is."

Gender Egalitarianism.   Gender Egalitarianism refers to the extent to which a society minimizes gender role differences. It measures the level of stereotype held by a society that favors one gender over the other (House et al., 2002). A lower score favors male-oriented behaviors, a middle score means egalitarian values, and a higher score favors female-oriented behaviors. Chinese scores on both Gender Egalitarianism "As Is" (3.05) and "Should Be" (3.68) are low, indicating that the society favors men more (ranking 48th among scores on "As Is" and 58th on "Should Be"). In fact, the two means are also very close to each other. There are historical reasons for such obvious favor for the men.

In China, despite all the economic advances, the majority of the population is still poor and a large proportion still depends heavily on farming and on men for labor. In these places, women are still discouraged in education or employment except as *"wet nurses, maids, or cooks"* (Chia, Moore, Lam, Chuang, & Cheng, 1994, p. 25). Women still lag behind men in terms of salary, job benefits, and job privileges (Eaton, 1998; Shaffer, Joplin, Bell, Lau, & Oguz, 2000).

Gender Egalitarianism may not happen until China becomes more economically developed. People in rural areas may still have to rely on men for heavy manual labor, and it will be hard for the Chinese to treat the two genders equally when one is, in practice, more useful than the other. Until the majority of the population is liberated from the land and women become more independent, the bias in favor of men will remain.

Uncertainty Avoidance.   Uncertainty Avoidance indicates the extent to which people seek orderliness, consistency, structure to cover situations in their daily lives, try to avoid uncertain and ambiguous situations by reliance on social norms and procedures and belief in absolute truths and the attainment of expertise (House et al., 2002; 2004). As can be seen in Table 24.1, China's two scores on Uncertainty Avoidance are fairly consistent between "As Is" (4.94) and "Should Be" (5.28), ranking 10th and 9th, respectively.

The high Chinese scores are consistent with the traditional Chinese value of order. Starting with Confucius, who thought the "Golden Age is in the past" (Smith, 1894, p. 115), the Chinese seek peace and security by clinging to the past. Under that kind of mind-set and being exclusively shut off from the rest of the world, the Chinese people's creativity withered like flowers deprived of sunshine and water. For centuries, Chinese people were comfortable and felt secure only when they "played-it-safe." It may sound bizarre to Westerners, actually ridiculous even to us Chinese now, but it was unfortunately true that during the 1960s and 1970s people in China were led to seek "unity and order" to such a degree that they would run their businesses the same way year after year without change, maintaining the same structure, the same products, the same everything. They even wore clothes in the same uniform color, making the country either "a sea of blue" or "a sea of green." Therefore, if one understands the long history and the traditional values of order, one should have no problem understanding why the current Chinese society has such a high intolerance for uncertainty.

The Chinese's strong desire to see more order in society, as reflected in their high score on "Should Be," reflects the anxiety caused by the unprecedented changes going on in China. It is true that all Chinese people enjoy the better living they have now and welcome change in that sense, but many of them are worried about the loss of "order," therefore longing for more rules and regulations to reduce uncertainties.

Power Distance.   Power Distance measures the extent to which a culture accepts inequalities between various groups within a culture such as social classes and organizational hierarchy (House et al., 2002). The two Chinese scores on Power Distance "As Is" (5.04) and "Should Be" (3.10) showed the largest discrepancy among the nine pairs of scores. In fact, scores of all countries on "Should Be" were lower than "As Is," showing a common desire that people in all these countries aspire for more equality than they currently have. The relatively higher ranked Chinese "Should Be" score (12th) compared to "As Is" (41st) among the 61 countries may indicate that, compared to managers from other countries, the Chinese managers demonstrate a higher level of tolerance for inequality of power in society. The discrepancy between China's two scores may be viewed as an indicator of the existing two forces: while the internal forces from the still highly-respected traditional values are pulling the Chinese business leaders away from becoming competitive, the external pressures form an opposite force, pushing these leaders toward becoming increasingly competitive.

The influence of Western democracy in recent years has made the younger Chinese strive for equality in power. More and more, they break away from the traditional norms that restricted their behaviors, such as absolute respect for the senior and obedience. The reformed system has also made it possible for them to do many things they could not, or dared not, do before. For example, they can quit their jobs for better opportunities now. They can look for jobs themselves instead of having to be assigned by the government. They no longer have to work in places where they were born, but can work thousands of miles away from home without being punished. So the score on "As Is" was surprisingly lower than previous studies have reported.

Nevertheless, the influence of traditional values can still be observed among middle managers. As stated earlier in the chapter, in ancient China, people were born with status and it was a virtue for subordinates to show respect for their superiors. Until the early 1980s, it was "dangerous and self-destructive to struggle openly against persons whose authority over one is broadly approved" (Bond, 1991, p. 35). The reforms have changed people's behaviors on the surface, but deep inside, their values, which were formed at an early stage in life, are still there. Even now, people holding official titles *are still* addressed formally and deferentially in China. Social rights and privileges are still closely tied to one's status. The higher Chinese score on Power Distance "Should Be" may indicate the lingering influence of traditional values for hierarchical power and order.

Humane Orientation. Humane Orientation measures the degree to which a society encourages and rewards individuals for being fair, altruistic, generous, caring, and kind to others (House et al., 2002). Being humane is consistent with the Confucian principles of moderation and human heartedness. The GLOBE results show that Chinese participants scored among the higher ranking countries on Humane Orientation "As Is" (4.36, rank 17) but China's score dropped much lower when describing how much they thought Humane Orientation "Should Be" (5.32) valued by their society (rank 39). This result shows another paradoxical situation: Because the notion of humane is closely related to ren (benevolent, kind), one of the "five constant virtues," so people are expected to be kind and humane, and yet the future values as perceived by middle managers seem to push the Chinese culture away from that.

Traditionally, the Chinese people think it is more important to maintain a harmonious environment than to get a job done on time. A person high on Humane Orientation would be described as having a strong sense of *renqing* in China, which implies an *"implicit set of rules"* that involve reciprocation in the form of money, goods, information, status, service, and affection (Cheung et al., 1996). Under these rules, two basic kinds of social behavior are expected: (a) ordinarily, one should keep in contact with acquaintances in one's social network, exchanging gifts, greetings, or visitations with them from time to time, and (b) when a member of one's network gets into trouble or faces a difficult situation, one should sympathize, offer help, and "do a *renqing*" for that person (Hwang, 1987, p. 954). All those expectations urge Chinese individuals to be kind and considerate to others.

However, the society is going through so much change and the ways in which things used to get done are all being reformed, creating an extreme amount of uncertainties. Many traditional values are also being challenged by realities and people there find it increasingly important to be assertive and aggressive in order to survive. Therefore, the notion of being kind and maintaining harmony with others is not as important as it used to be. Maybe that is why the score on Humane Orientation "Should Be" dropped so much from the "As Is" score.

Summary

From the preceding discussion, we can see that the current Chinese culture still heavily reflects the influence of Confucianism ideologies. However, there seem to be historical as well as contemporary reasons for current Chinese society to be so intolerant of uncertainties, relatively more collectivistic oriented, more humane, and comparatively unassertive and still favor men more than women. We compared data from the food industry and the finance industry, but the results showed that none of the pairs of scores differed significantly, indicating the representativeness of the views on the societal values.

How do these values affect leadership behaviors? What are the implications of this profile for leadership in Chinese society? The GLOBE project studied the effect of cultural values on effectiveness of leadership behaviors. In the following sections, we first give a general overview of leadership in China. We then tell stories of two royal ministers and one more recent leader, the first premier of the new China, to show the permanence of the Chinese culture and its persistent influence on its leaders over the thousands of years.

5. LEADERSHIP IN CHINA

The idea of business leadership is a new product of the economic reform that started about 20 years ago. The view of leadership as a science did not exist previously. This is due largely to the planned economic system prevalent in prereform China. When the new China was founded in 1949, the Chinese Communist Party (CCP) adopted state socialism. In doing so, the Chinese government followed the central ideological tenet of socialism, which emphasized collective ownership and identity. Under that system, the state and the Party were supposed to represent the interests of the working class as a general collective, thus legitimizing the hierarchical control of organizations. Business enterprises followed the plans set up by the planners. Their objectives were to do nothing but to fulfill or exceed the quota the government established. They paid part of their profits, rather than tax, to the government. So there was not much for the leaders to do at the organizational level in terms of leadership so long as their businesses fulfilled the production quota (Fu & Wu, 2000).

Figure 24.1 describes the relationships among *dan wei* (organizations) at various levels. As can be seen in the figure, all organizations in China were under different industrial bureaus or government agencies under the central government. Each industry had a ministry at the top overseeing the overall performance of all the factories under its auspices. For example, the Capital Steel Complex belonged to the Ministry of Metallurgy. Yanshan Petrochemical Factory belonged to the Ministry of Chemistry. Leaders in business organizations were also administratively parallel to department leaders in government agencies. For example, leaders in large state-level enterprises could be ministry-level or deputy ministry-level leaders. Such comparability made it possible for the personnel system to operate the way it did.

The reform in China terminated the planned economic system and instilled a market economy with socialist characteristics in the country. The past two decades have pushed China's metamorphosis into a hybrid economic system with many forms of corporate governance and economic control (ownership): state-owned companies, collectives, township and village enterprises, joint ventures, solely foreign-owned enterprises, private and individual enterprises. The Chinese central government has been trying very hard to separate government from business practices so that businesses can follow the rules under the market economy. State-owned companies have lost their reliable support, having to become economically independent entities, which must find ways to survive by themselves. As a result, the term *leadership* in China has gained meaning and substance. Leaders who used to be followers of orders from the central authorities found themselves having to be accountable and to lead in order to keep their companies going (Fu & Wu, 2000).

The pressure to transition from managers into leaders has brought new challenges to the business leaders and has also changed people's expectations in leaders as well. However, many of the qualities that Chinese people expect to see in their leaders are surprisingly similar to what well-respected leaders throughout history displayed. In the following section, we introduce three Chinese leaders who lived in a period of 1,500 years to illustrate our point.

Stories of Three Leaders

Famous leaders in China are like stars in the sky, which are bright and visible, but too many to count. The three leaders we chose lived in different times but shared very similar characteristics and have been very well respected to this day. The two royal ministers are compared to today's business leaders because there were no parallel business organizations then, and they were responsible for decision making in the sense contemporary business leaders do, according to *Managing Crises in Northern Song Dynasty* (Wang, 1998). The information about the two ministers is taken from *Biographies of Famous Chinese Generals* (1987).

Zhu-Ge Liang of the Eastern Han Dynasty. Zhu-Ge Liang (181–234), minister of the *Shu* kingdom of the Eastern Han Dynasty, has been a role model for generation after generation. The Han Dynasty was the period in Chinese history that witnessed the most fighting among the warlords. Zhu-Ge lost his parents when very young and lived a secluded life in his early days, studying war strategies by reading all sorts of books. At an early age, he was already known for his extreme intelligence and broad knowledge. As a result, Liu Bei, who was an offspring of a royal family and later became the ruler of the kingdom, went to Zhe-Ge three times in person to invite him to come out of seclusion and be his adviser. Touched by Liu's sincerity, Zhu-Ge eventually did so, determined to fight with Liu Bei to restore the lost kingdom.

Zhu-Ge's life can be divided into two parts. In the first part, he led the army fighting for the establishment of the Shu Kingdom, and in the second part, he did all he could to enable the most incapable son of Liu Bei to rule the country after Liu died. During the last few years of his life, he continued leading armies to attack the neighboring *Wei* Kingdom even though all his attempts failed. He fought endlessly, knowing he would not succeed. He wrote down his reasons for these attacks, explaining to the incapable son of the late emperor that what he did was to protect the Kingdom of *Shu* from being destroyed by the powerful *Wei*. Although Zhu-Ge is regarded as a legalist rather than a Confucian, his efforts were surprisingly similar to those of Confucius, who kept leading his students touring around the country, trying to persuade the rulers to adopt the ceremonies of the Zhou dynasty, knowing they would not listen. Because of his unyielding determination, despite *many failures,* Zhu-Ge has been remembered as an extremely intelligent man, as well as a faithful and devoted minister. His quote *"ju gong jing cui, si er hou yi"* (I have no regret when I die if I did all I could possibly do) has been greatly respected and is still frequently cited. Modern people use the saying to encourage the self-sacrificing and hard-working spirit. The Communist Party also uses Zhu-Ge's saying to encourage its members to be devoted and faithful.

Sima of the Song Dynasty. Sima Guang (1019–1086) was also a famous minister. Besides being an administrative officer, he was a thinker, a literary man, and a historian. Sima Guang is known for his broad knowledge and hard-working spirit. He started reading classics at 6 and received a very restrictive family education. To this day, Chinese people still read stories about him using a round piece of wood as a pillow to prevent himself from sleeping too deeply. Because of the pillow, Sima Guang would easily wake up when turning his body around at night and would continue reading. His hard-working spirit made him a local government officer at the age of 20 and an officer of the central government at 27.

A faithful believer of Confucianism, Sima Guang was always honest and straightforward with his opinions. Politically, he advocated cultivating people with ceremonies and rituals and being merciful to them. He was determined to build an ideal Confucian society by reducing or eliminating taxes, cutting down government expenses, and establishing special storehouses to provide aid to people in bad years. Sima Guang was such a firm believer of Confucian doctrines and had such a stubborn personality that he stepped down twice from his positions when he could not pursue his ideals. After leaving his official position the second time, Sima Guang concentrated on writing the "Conclusions on Reading the Mirror of History," in which he elaborated a theory of social evolution, exalted national heroes and denounced traitors in all ages, and dissected the failings of bureaucratic society. In 1085, one year before his death, he became a minister once again and reversed all the reforms made by another reformist. He was a genuine Confucian scholar and fought hard till death stopped him. When cleaning up his effects, his family members found unfinished papers that he was writing to report to the emperor. People compared him to Zhu-Ge Liang for his selfless devotion and hard-working spirit. Like Zhu-Ge, Sima was also highly respected for maintaining the Confucian ideology and has been regarded as a good model for standing up for his conviction and fighting for his beliefs at all costs. His case also shows that true loyalty is not manifested by complete obedience to emperors or masters, but by standing firm for righteousness, which is an essential part of the Confucius virtues.

Zhou Enlai of Modern China. Very few Westerners may know Zhu-Ge Liang or Sima Guang, but many have heard the name of Zhou Enlai. The former Secretary of State Henry Kissinger, who found Zhou *"one of the two or three most impressive men"* he had ever met, called him "urbane, infinitely patient, extraordinarily intelligent, subtle" (Wilson, 1984, p.17).

To the 1.2 billion Chinese, Zhou was their "beloved Premier." For 27 years, Zhou was the only premier of the nation. He understood people's problems and sympathized with their painful plight. People adored him, simply loved him. January 8, 1976, the day he died, seized the nation with grief. The mourning for him spread all over the country, with his pictures hung on walls, in the streets, and in the homes of millions. In the few days that followed, people everywhere sang songs and recited poems in tribute to his memory and to express their love for him. The singers' tears flowed as they sang; so did the listeners'. Zhou touched the masses to the extent of a spontaneous show of love and affection.

Why would an individual have such an enormous power to capture the heart of billions? To put it simply, Zhou was everything the Chinese people worship. He was "gentle, honest and uncomplicated" to the people (Chang, 1984, p. 41). He was "loyal, selfless, open and straightforward, modest and prudent" (Deng, 1976, p. 1) to his comrades-in-arms in the central Chinese government. In the classical Chinese tradition, he would have been called a "perfect man" because he conformed to the expected behaviors. Although by classical Confucian standards, Zhou would not be considered a good Confucian because he did not stand up for what is right, but his life exemplified many of the fine qualities advocated by Confucianism and praised in history over the thousands of years.

Zhou was a pragmatic communist who was determined irrevocably by both broad conviction and current expediency to give his full loyalty to the Party and its policies in spite of his personal reservations. He did the best he could in terms of damage control, exercising the doctrine of the mean. At an early age, he had proven himself a leader of tact, reconciliation, personal integrity, and self-assurance. He retained a popular respect throughout his entire career as a Chinese statesman from 1927 to his death in 1976 and became "China's man for all seasons, a complex, charming, and intelligent character, who embodies many of the contradictions of an ancient land in rapid transition" (Dittmer, 1978, p. 459).

Summary. Brief as these vignettes are, they gave a general picture of the three men who lived in a period of almost 1,500 years. Admittedly, the descriptions tend to oversimplify the historical events and the interpretation of their leadership behaviors probably should not be as straightforward as depicted in the chapter. They are not meant to represent all generals/premiers in Chinese history. However, for the purpose of this chapter, they are to show the uninterrupted influence of Confucius values and some of the qualities they shared despite of the different times they lived.

All three individuals were highly intelligent people, studied hard, and were known as well-learned men. They firmly followed their beliefs and were all extremely loyal to their superiors. They all conformed to Confucian's "five constant virtues." Their behaviors were consistent throughout their lives and they were well respected by their peers, and by people who survived them. Surprisingly, the qualities these three people displayed are still very much those that the Chinese people respect in current China despite all the material changes that have taken place in the country as shown in the later sections.

In the following sections, we introduce the results of three focus group interviews with some middle managers in Shanghai to show that many of the desired qualities have remained unchanged although some are different as a result of the reform. We then introduce the results from the Chinese GLOBE project to provide some quantitative support for the findings from the interviews.

Results of Focus Group Interviews

Three focus group interviews were conducted with managers from the same or similar organizations in Shanghai where the questionnaire survey data were collected in the spring of 1997. The focus group interviews were conducted to explore qualitatively, the desired leadership attributes and behaviors and to find out what kinds of values influence the thinking and behavior of business leadership in China. The first group consisted of 7 managers from 7 different organizations including heavy industry, service, and government agencies. The second group consisted of 12 managers from 12 companies under a large service-oriented corporation. The corporation started 10 years ago and has become one of the four largest corporations in the industry since the company was publicly traded in 1992. The third group consisted of 6 managers from a food-manufacturing corporation. The majority of the participants were middle managers; a few were higher-level managers. Of the 25 people, 6 were women, and the rest were male managers, with an average age of 40 years.

The interviewees' answers to the focal question, "What are the qualities of your ideal leader?", were all recorded and transcribed. The most emphasized was the quality of the leader, including honesty, trustworthiness, and integrity. Interviewees unanimously agreed that without a high level of integrity no leader can hope to establish high level of credibility, and without credibility no leader can hope to be effective. The following summarized a few other major characteristics people described during the interviews.

A Good Leader Knows How to Balance Between Being Conservative and Aggressive. Conservative and aggressive sound opposite to each other because aggressiveness is highly discouraged: It is against the essential Confucian ideologies, and yet to be effective in the increasingly competitive business world, business leaders have to be aggressive. Leaders had to be conservative under the planned economy, because "At that time if you followed the orders and did what you were told to do, you would be a good leader." But nowadays, one also needs to be assertive because "you have to take the responsibility and make sure that the market accepts the products your people make." According to the focus group respondents, however, a balance between the two is necessary because the Chinese are "crossing the water by feeling out the way." There is no precedence to most of the things the Chinese are doing; therefore, "you have to be conservative while being assertive."

One example given was a 50-year-old Party secretary and director:

> He is constantly looking for new ideas to surpass himself. He established the largest Real Estate Corporation Ltd. in Shanghai when the stock market was just starting. He has just bought a processing company to increase funding. His actions are often big and aggressive, but he also appears very conservative and assured to you because he periodically talks about his ideas and the company status at meetings to make you understand what he is doing and what the company needs to do next.

The balance between two seemingly contradictory values may be consistent with the large discrepancy between Assertiveness "As Is" and "Should Be" in the value survey we discussed earlier.

A Good Leader Must Have a Vision, Must Be Able to Look Far Ahead. The term *visionary leadership* is new in the Chinese vocabulary according to the result of a media analysis that compared desired leadership attributes in two national newspapers over 20 years (Fu & Tsui, 2003). Confucians certainly would not emphasize visionary because emperors were the only real decision makers. And under the planned economy, the hierarchical power structure also made it impossible for managers to have a vision. But now things are different. One of the interviewees used one of his former bosses as an example to illustrate the difference in expectations:

> He was regarded as a good leader back then. He used to do everything he asked his subordinates to do and set a good example using his own behaviors. One time, a factory leader asked a molder in the department to do a job, and the molder refused. But when the department head asked him to do it, he happily did it. Why? Because the worker respected his immediate boss and was willing to "give him face." But such a leader now will not be good enough, because you need to look beyond what your workers can see in order to remain competitive, you should know where the department is heading.

The example shows that even though managers still relate compliance to the notion of face, being able to lead is obviously considered more important than to win followers' compliance.

Another example showed how being visionary is recognized. One of the subdivisions under the Municipal Economic Commission is in the oil business and has been very successful for the past few years. Two years ago, Mr. Wang was named the director of the division. As soon as he got there, he foresaw the increasing competition as a result of the growing automobile market and decided to build 20 additional gas stations every year. The goals for the past 2 years were both successfully fulfilled. That year, the division fulfilled their annual target in the first 5 months. Such a leader in the old days would very likely be regarded as "discontented with his lot," but now he is hailed as an outstanding leader.

A Good Leader Must Be Open to New Ideas and Constantly Try to Improve Himself. This quality should not be viewed as a new one, because one of the things that Confucius repeatedly asked his disciples to do was to "take great pains in learning." However, in the past several decades, only learning Marxism and Mao Zedong thought was encouraged. Learning a trade was discouraged. Now all managers have to learn managerial skills because, "The new structure of the economy forces you to have a brain of your own. You have to manage the followers, not just to make them do what your leaders told them to do." Almost all the leaders whom the participants talked about have obtained an MBA degree while working full-time. A female manager said her boss had a "really broad interest" and he reads "all sorts of things" and "gets his ideas from different sources." A male manager from the steel complex said his superior had gone to Australia for 6 months to learn English in order to "read and appreciate Western management ideas better."

Several interviewees from the same corporation said their general manager kept a very close relationship with his friends working in different companies from whom he found out what his competitors were up to. "Nothing can beat such *guanxi* when it comes to information," they said. The general manager also requires employees in the company to work 5 days and studying 1 day every week ("5+1" schedule). All middle-level managers in the corporation are rotated every 6 months to receive systematic training in management, thus all the middle managers "who are still 'lambs' now can all be turned into 'lions' so they could be better leaders."

A Good Leader Must Initiate Change and Be Determined to Carry Out the Change. As was reflected in the media analyses (Fu & Tsui, 2003), change orientation was also said to be one of the most important leadership qualities. According to the participants, nobody now trusts leaders who have "the head of a tiger, but the tail of a snake" (people who make lots of empty promises without carrying through them). A female manager, who happened to be a personal friend of a CEO and knew how much pressure he went through for each of his new ideas, said "People give him a lot of respect and admiration after he succeeds. But most of them shy away when he needed the support and understanding most." Therefore, good leaders not only have the ideas to change, but should also be very determined to carry out their ideas.

A Good Leader Must be Humane. As reflected in GLOBE societal value survey and media analyses, which found being humane an important leadership quality (Fu & Tsui, 2003), the quality of being humane was also viewed as important by the interviewees. In fact, good business leaders are described as "Confucius businessman," because the word *Confucius* indicates benevolence or kindness, but the image of a businessman used to be regarded as bad, someone who was most concerned with money and had no sense of *renqing,* thus being a "Confucius businessman" means to be humane while being profit oriented.

In one company, there is a policy that forbids coaches from accepting any forms of bribes in the company's driving school. Once, one of the coaches accepted a packet of cigarettes, thinking that was not a big deal. But he was fired according to the rule. A few weeks later, the person came back to the company, asking his former employer to let him come back because he could not find a job anywhere else that could pay him as much. The company did not take him back because that would be against the rule. However, they called around and introduced him to another company. "We wanted to be humane to him because we know he needed the money he had been making but we also did not want to violate the rules," an interviewee said, adding: "We are Chinese. *Renqing* is a big thing to us."

Other interviewees offered more examples. One said that his boss would go to the hospital if he heard of someone in the company being hospitalized if he could find the time, or send someone else to go on his behalf if he could not find the time: "Even when family members are sick or have an accident, he would ask people in his office to show concerns and to help in ways the company can." Another respondent said that his boss "would make sure that he call[ed] on their families when some employees go on business trips just to check and see if everything is OK and offer them help if needed." These behaviors were consistent with Confucius virtue of *renqing* (benevolence, righteousness). One of Confucius's favorite sayings was: "The character of a ruler is like wind and that of the people is like grass. In whatever direction the wind blows, the grass always bends" (Confucius, 12:19).

A Good Leader Knows What Works for the Chinese While Learning From the West. Since the reform, the Chinese Communist Party, which had been emphasizing ideological construction till the reform, has been urging the whole country to learn Western managerial philosophies in order to speed up its modernization (Fu & Tsui, 2003). Textbooks published by Harvard Business School, management cases, and translated books on successful Western businesspeople are everywhere. However, all our interviewees pointed out that "what works for the Americans or the Germans may not work as well or may not work at all, for the Chinese." China has a unique history and culture; to succeed, "China's reforms must have Chinese features," they said. They gave many examples to explain what they meant by "Chinese features."

One interviewee said most of the employees in his company were researchers and used to be very self-centered and opinionated. All of them were good at what they were doing, but they were not very good collaborators. To get them to cooperate with each other, his boss visited those people one by one after work and had long talks with them in their homes. He also invited them to have dinner together on a weekly basis to give them the opportunity to get to know each other. "These ways may not be written anywhere in Western management books, but they surely worked with this group of people," he said.

"My boss knows how to touch people's hearts," he said. "Westerners use job descriptions to tell workers what they are expected to do and reward people accordingly, but those kinds of things don't work very well here." He gave an example to illustrate that. One of the senior researchers was living in a one-bedroom apartment because his research projects failed to get any of the prizes, which were necessary to get bigger living spaces according to the company policy. However, his projects were of great value. When the company built another apartment building, the manager gave the senior researcher a three-bedroom apartment. But the researcher's wife did not want to move because she did not like the location. He went to the researcher's home to talk to the wife in person and also talked to her several times on the phone, explaining to her why he thought they should take the bigger apartment. Finally, the couple accepted it and the researcher, even though 70 years old now, is still producing new product designs.

Another interviewee said: "Chinese people 'jiang *renqing*' (value *renqing*)," which implies reciprocity; "if you touch their heart, they will for sure devote themselves to you." Still another participant said: "Rules and policies can make people work hard, but can never win their hearts."

Summary.   The interview results show clear connections between the profile of Chinese society generated from the GLOBE cultural survey and the desired leadership attributes and behaviors. For example, the high degree of uncertainty avoidance, as well as the desire for the society to encourage more assertive behaviors can be seen in the emphasis on the balance between conservatism and aggressiveness. The results also show that whereas the influence of the traditional values, which consist of class system (social hierarchical order), obedience, doctrine of the mean, and *renqing,* have been the most deep-rooted, the influences of Communist ideologies, which advocate values such as action orientation, confidence, and determination, and Western management philosophies, which promote aggressiveness, ambitiousness, and competency, are also obvious (Fu & Tsui, 2003).

The connections between the societal value survey results and the findings from the qualitative data are further supported by the quantitative results from the GLOBE leadership survey, which are presented in the following section.

Results of GLOBE Leadership Survey

The GLOBE leadership questionnaire survey was conducted along with the societal value survey. The same group of respondents completed the survey. We compared the responses by managers from the two industries, using independent sample *t* tests. Because there were no significant differences, we combined the two groups of answers in our analyses. The results of the survey are presented in Table 24.2. The table shows the average score by the Chinese managers on each of the 21 first-order and each of the 6 second-order (bold letters in Table 24.2) leadership dimensions (Dorfman, Hanges, & Brodbeck, 2004; for definitions, see also the introductory and concluding chapters in this volume), as well as the ranks of those scores among the 61 participating countries. It also shows the highest and the lowest country scores on each of the scales.

The GLOBE leadership dimensions are summary indexes of the characteristics, skills, and abilities (cf. Dorfman et al., 2004, p. 675) that are perceived to inhibit outstanding leadership (greatly = 7, somewhat = 6, slightly = 5), have no impact (4), or contribute to outstanding leadership (slightly = 5, somewhat = 6, greatly = 7).

On one hand, the table shows that compared to managers in other countries, Chinese managers are less likely to perceive Face Saving (3.97, ranked 4th) to have a negative impact on a person being an outstanding leader than managers in most of the other countries. Similarly, Nonparticipative leadership (3.24) is perceived to only slightly inhibit a person from being an outstanding leader (Rank 8). These relatively more positive views about face-saving and nonparticipative attributes of leaders could be due to the fact that Chinese are discouraged to take extreme views on any matter (e.g., none of the Chinese scores on the 21 first-order scales is below 2 or above 6 on the scale from 1 to 7). However, as was described earlier about societal culture dimensions, there was no indication of response bias to result in distorted values for China.

On the other hand, Chinese managers seem to place particular positive emphasis on Humane Orientation (5.40, Rank 6), which corresponds with the societal cultural emphasis on personal dignity (*mianzi*).

The highest scores within China were on subscales such as Integrity (5.98), Inspirational (5.92), Administratively Competent (5.88), and Visionary (5.85). These findings suggest that, despite comparatively low scores (the second-order dimension of Charismatic Leadership ranks 54), among the 61 GLOBE countries, the universally endorsed charismatic value-based leadership (cf. Dorfman et al., 2004) is also relatively strongly espoused within the Chinese

TABLE 24.2
Chinese Results of GLOBE Leadership Survey

Leadership Dimensions	Mean	Rank	Highest Score	Lowest Score
Self-Protective Leadership	3.80	14	4.62	2.55
Self-Centered	2.22	23	6.20	1.55
Status Conscious	4.47	25	5.93	3.00
Conflict Inducer	4.40	14	5.01	3.09
Face Saver	3.97	4	4.63	2.05
Procedural	3.94	28	5.12	2.82
Humane Leadership	5.19	16	5.75	3.82
Humane	5.40	6	5.68	2.23
Modesty	5.03	32	5.86	4.14
Autonomous Leadership	4.07	18	4.63	2.27
Participative Leadership	5.04	44	6.09	4.50
Autocratic (reverse scored)	2.66	27	3.86	1.89
Nonparticipative (reverse scored)	3.24	8	3.61	1.86
Team-Oriented Leadership	5.57	51	6.21	4.74
Team Integrator	5.71	14	6.09	4.42
Collaborative Team Oriented	5.36	57	6.43	4.10
Administrative Competent	5.88	26	6.42	4.53
Diplomatic	5.05	58	6.05	4.49
Malevolent (reverse scored)	2.04	12	2.67	1.33
Charismatic Leadership	5.56	54	6.46	4.51
Performance Orientation	5.64	56	6.64	4.51
Visionary	5.85	48	6.50	4.62
Inspirational	5.92	45	6.63	5.04
Integrity	5.98	43	6.79	4.72
Self-Sacrificial	4.70	51	5.99	3.98
Decisive	5.29	57	6.37	3.62

sample, when compared to the scores of the other leadership dimensions for China. This is consistent with the results of a recently completed media analyses (Fu & Tsui, 2003).

The other dimension that received relatively high scores within China was Team-Oriented leadership, the subscales of which include Team Integrator (5.71), Administratively Competent (5.88), and Collaborative Team Orientation (5.36), indicating that Chinese managers consider various facets of team-oriented leadership (blended with administrative skills) to be important facilitators of outstanding leadership. Such findings are also consistent with the results of another recent study by Fu and associates on the top-management teams in Chinese high-tech firms (see Fu et al., 2002), which shows that there is a tendency for high-tech firms to rely on a team of leaders rather than a single leader. Furthermore, it seems that the dual identity (see later) of many business leaders, who tend to be also members of the Communist Party, left its trace in relatively high scores for Administrative Competency.

The subscales that received the lowest scores included Autocratic (2.66, Rank 27), Self-Centered (2.22, Rank 23), and Malevolent (2.04, Rank 12), showing that Chinese managers regard these factors as clear inhibitors of outstanding leadership. The inhibiting self-protective leadership style, also universally endorsed among GLOBE countries, is obviously also not accepted by Chinese managers. However, China's comparatively high score on the second-order

Self-protective leadership dimension (3.80, Rank 14), which comprises some of the afore-mentioned and further subscales (e.g., Status-conscious, 4.47; Conflict Inducer, 4.40; see Table 24.2), is comparatively high within the 61 GLOBE countries. Its score is near 4.00, which marks the scales' center (no impact on outstanding leadership).

Additional Chinese Characteristics

The profile of the Chinese leadership presented by the scores on the GLOBE leadership dimensions is quite consistent with the findings of other empirical research. In fact, due to the small N for the study, the first author used the GLOBE instrument and collected data from more than 400 middle managers in the US and China, respectively, and then from another over 400 Chinese only sample in a different study. The results were all consistent with those presented here. However, there are a couple of additional features about Chinese leadership that were not evaluated in the GLOBE leadership survey and yet will help our readers better understand Chinese business leaders.

Dual Identity.   This may not be a historical heritage, but this is definitely an emic (i.e., culture-specific) Chinese feature for now: Almost all business leaders are, at the same time, Communist Party members. The leaders who participated in our focus group interviews were all Party members. Some of them held leading positions in the Party committee as well, therefore having dual identities. In fact, the most important difference between the American and the Chinese political systems may concern the political parties. In the United States, the Democratic and the Republican parties compete with each other, but in China, the only ruling party is the Chinese Communist Party (CCP), and all the other parties have to work collaboratively with the ruling Party.

A selective organization, the Party recruits its members on the basis of their suitability for leadership in its political life or for role models for their coworkers. One in every 22 Chinese now is a Party member, for a total membership of about 57 million in 1997 (Fu & Wu, 2000). Functioning somewhat like a board of directors for the country, the CCP defines its function as that of making all the critical decisions, which the government must then carry out. Unlike a board of directors, however, the CCP has created an organizational structure operating in parallel to that of the government bureaucracy, so that Party members oversee the work of the bureaucrats at every level (Starr, 1997): *"[Communists] must be modest and prudent, restrain themselves from any presumption and any precipitation, be capable of practicing self-criticism and have the courage to correct inadequacies and errors in their work. In any case, they should not hide their errors, take all the credit for themselves and lay all the blame on others"* (Mao, cited in Bouc, 1977, p. 199). Being Communist Party members, organizational leaders all have to abide by rules stipulated by the Party and all have to contribute to the construction of the Party ideology. They have to meet at least once a week as a Party committee to reflect on what happened during the week and to study the works of Party leaders or documents issued by the Central Committee. As Party members, they are also expected to be role models for their followers, working hard and serving the people whole-heartedly. Those who hold both Party leadership and managerial positions are expected to lead in morality cultivation.

Paternalism.   Paternalistic is another feature of the Chinese leaders. Confucius extended the family structure to organizations and made government leaders "heads of families." As a result, some researchers explicitly call Asian leadership "headship" to distinguish it from Western leadership (e.g., Holloman, 1986). Traditionally, in Chinese contexts, a person was born into a headship position and was thereby expected to display leadership by virtue of that background and position: This is the reverse of the situation in the West where people show leadership capabilities or qualities before becoming a leader. Although leaders are no longer explicitly "heads of families," expectations for fatherly roles are still visible; therefore it is suggested that leadership in China is still somewhat paternalistic. This leadership concept is well in line with the Chinese societal cultural perceptions and values of low Gender Egalitarianism as was discussed previously.

Weber (1951) expressed the foundation for the paternalistic feature when he characterized the form of domination prevalent in the Chinese context as patrimonial, and linked it to the patriarchal traditions whereby absolute power is invested in the male head of the household. Bond and Hwang (1986) argued that Chinese leadership is modeled on this father's role as household head, and Bond (1991) explicitly stated that "The effective model for leadership systems like the Chinese is thus the wise and loving father" (p. 453). In fact, the whole country was considered as a huge family with the late Chairman Mao being the "father." Organizations were also viewed as families; the top leader of an organization was regarded as the head of the family. Therefore, it was only natural that members in the organization expect themselves to be taken care of once they joined the organization.

This feature is still obvious in today's media, even though not as strong as it used to be. You can still read descriptions such as so-and-so cares for the young workers "like his own children," or a leader sacrifices his "small family's interests for the bigger family" (the organization). The purpose of these various formulations is also to make employees feel that the organization they work for is like a big family for them. For example, a factory leader in Shanghai heard that young employees in his factory were having difficulties finding lovers. He found another factory in town whose majority workforce were female and organized parties for the workers in the two factories and also purposely let his young employees who were still single work day shifts only so "they can go out dating" in the evening.

Integration, Limitations, and Future Research

If you remember the stories of the three leaders we discussed earlier, you would probably agree that despite the lapse of time, many of the qualities people look for in good leaders in China now remain surprisingly unchanged from earlier times. Qualities such as hard-working, knowledgeable, and capable all conform to the expected behaviors under Confucianism and are still well respected. Most of the leaders' qualities mentioned by the participants, such as humane, aggressive, change-oriented, and eager to learn, are similar to those covered in the media (Fu & Tsui, 2003).

Qualities such as visionary, aggressive, anxious to learn, and humane, which were unanimously pointed out as the most important in the interviews, are also most frequently mentioned attributes in the printed media (Fu & Tsui, 2003). But in addition to those, a few other characteristics such as problem solving, devoted, and hard-working, which were also among the frequently mentioned in stories on leaders in the printed media, were not mentioned by the interviewees.

The interviewees shared most of the media opinions, but differed on a few. Where they could not agree with each other actually reflects the differences caused by emphases on different values. For example, managers from one large corporation, who were mostly in their late 40s and early 50s, all thought that management should be accomplished by a group of people, because one individual person could not have all the favorable qualities. However, one participant explicitly pointed out that leadership should be individualized. She was a few years younger than most of the participants and received her MBA in the United States. She argued that group leadership was irresponsible, because when a group made a decision, individuals tended to just go along with it rather than voice their real opinions.

Another group of participants pointed out that many of the traditional values, such as hard-working and setting up role models, were still necessary even though they alone no longer made leaders effective. However, the female participant argued that those were not important qualities and did not, and should not, affect the effectiveness of a leader. It was hard to judge whose view is more representative. More research is necessary to qualitatively examine whether age serves as an intervening factor on choice of leadership styles.

The inability to reach any conclusion due to limited sample size was an obvious limitation of our study. Due to this limitation, there were several other unresolved differences. For example, in the current printed media, one can still read descriptions of leaders such as "on his calendar, there are no holidays or weekends"; "He stayed with his workers, feeling guilty that he could not be with his dying mother"; or "He stayed in cheap hotels, eating instant noodles." However, most participants in our focus group interviews explicitly pointed out that "qualities such as frugality, not caring for home" were not necessarily good qualities; at least they were not the most important ones to make good leaders. This shows that the Chinese government is still trying to use those traditional values to influence its leaders, but the leaders seem to be more interested in keeping up with the fast-growing trend of using the West as the model and trying to keep up with the rest of the world. In fact, due to the small N for the study, for the first author used the GLOBE instrument and collected data from over 400 middle managers in US and China respectively, and then from another over 400 Chinese only sample in a different study.

6. CONCLUSIONS

"Deep cultural undercurrents structure life in subtle but highly consistent ways that are not consciously formulated. Like the invisible jet streams in the skies that determine the course of a storm, these currents shape our lives; yet their influence is only beginning to be identified" (Hall, 1981, p. 12). It is interesting to notice that the analogy Hall made in the preceding quote is very similar to the one American missionary Arthur Smith gave over a century before in his book on Chinese characteristics: "The Confucian Classics are the chart by which the rulers of China have endeavored to navigate the ship of state." Confucianism has affected the Chinese people for thousands of years. In fact, Confucianism, as a system of thought, is "among the most remarkable intellectual achievements of the race" (Smith, 1894, p. 287). It has navigated the Chinese craft into waters they have sailed and is still steering the ship of state. Indeed, as Dr. Williams (quoted by Smith) said: "It would be hard to overestimate the influence of Confucius in his ideal princely scholar, and the power for good over his race which this conception has ever since exerted" (p. 287).

Chinese society is going through unprecedented changes. Though traditional values are still highly respected, and constantly pull back Chinese organizational leaders and urge them to conform to the traditional values, their internal desires to become competitive and the external pressure to do so are all pushing them toward modern Western ideologies, encouraging them to challenge the norms. In its endeavor to modernize itself, China has absorbed much of the Western influences. However, the influence of Confucianism still exists. The doctrine that the virtuous and the able should be the rulers, and that their rule must be based on virtue, the comprehensive philosophy of the five relations of men to each other, and the doctrine that no one should do to another what he would not have done to himself are still deeply embedded in the Chinese thought. At the same time, the influence of communist ideologies and the rising influence of Western philosophies are also very prominent.

It is true that there are many problems in China: aging, corruption, company downsizing, pollution, poor efficiency, to name just a few. However, China is also full of hope. Despite the Asian financial crisis and the SARS epidemic, China's economy has been growing steadily. In the past 20 years, its gross domestic product (GDP) has increased more than 10-fold (Ahlstrom, Bruton, & Lui, 2000), and its economic growth has been sustained at 8% every year according to the data released by International Monetary Fund (IMF). "Despite the dim economic report, China looks robust compared to the shrinking economies of many Asian countries, economists said." (AFP, 1998).

Even though made over three decades ago, Zhou Enlai's prediction still applies: *"I can predict China's future is bright and colorful; a few clouds will in the end be driven away by thunder and lightning; and the raindrops under the bright sunshine will reflect our fatherland in more beautiful colors. What follows will be the discharging beauty of competing flowers by the hundreds, and it will be the springtime for all mankind. Let this prediction be my last parting words" (Chang, 1984, p. 167).* Epstein, an American journalist who went to China in the 1920s and later became a Chinese citizen, wrote:

> *China is the fastest developing country in the world, with one fifth of the world's population. ...*
> *Of course, she still has a long way to go. Alongside the positive effects of reform and opening to the outside world, there is garbage, meaning corruption and inflow of old world values. But China is neither going all out for privatization—a la Russia—nor going to be partitioned like the Soviet Union. Nor is China preparing to be the next big expansionist conqueror as some like to depict her. In the world, China is a positive presence, and likely to be more so in the coming century. (Epstein, 1998, p. 23)*

The bright future of China makes it necessary and useful to study and understand Chinese culture and its influence on its business leaders. We tried to present some basic information in the previous pages and hope it will help our readers understand the influence of cultural values on Chinese business leaders. But we know we have only barely touched those "cultural undercurrents." Maybe together we can continue the exploration of the cultural undercurrents that shape the thinking and behavior of the people in this ancient land, and gain a good understanding of the traditional values that have lasted for thousands of years. Such an understanding will be beneficial to us all in our endeavor to *make* this world a better place to live in.

ACKNOWLEDGMENTS

We would like to acknowledge the contributions made by Fudan doctoral student Zhou Jian and other project team members in the collection and analyses of the data. We would also like to thank the comments from our anonymous reviewers, which have made the chapter more informative and readable.

REFERENCES

AFP. (1998, July 19). *News from China.*

Ahlstrom, D., Bruton, G. D., & Lui, S. S. Y. (2000). Navigating China's changing economy: Strategies for private firms. *Business Horizons, 43,* 5–15.

Bian, Y. (1994). *Guanxi and the allocation of urban jobs.* Albany: State University of New York Press.

Biographies on Famous Chinese Generals. (1987). Guangzhou, China: Nanfang Publishing House.

Bond, M. H. (1991). *Beyond the Chinese face.* Hong Kong: Oxford University Press.

Bond, M. H., & Hwang, K. K. (1986). *The social psychology of Chinese people* (pp. 213–266). Hong Kong: Oxford University Press.

Bouc, A. (1977). *Mao Tse-Tung: A guide to his thought.* New York: St. Martin's Press.

Chang, D. W. (1984). *Zhou Enlai and Deng Xiaoping in the Chinese leadership succession crisis.* New York: University Press of America.

Chao, P. (1983). *Chinese kinship.* London: Kegan Paul International.

Chen, M. (1995). *Asian management systems: Chinese, Japanese and Korean styles of business.* New York: Routledge.

Cheung, F. M., Leung, K., Fan, R. M., Song, W. Z., Zhang, J. X., & Zhang, J. P. (1996). Development of the Chinese personality assessment inventory. *Journal of Cross-Cultural Psychology, 27*(2), 181–199.

Chew, I. K., & Putti, J. (1995). Relationship on work-related values of Singaporean and Japanese managers in Singapore. *Human-Relations, 48*(10), 1149–1170.

Chia, R. C., Moore, J. L., Lam, K. N., Chuang, C. J., & Cheng, B. S. (1994). Cultural differences in gender role attitudes between Chinese and American students. *Sex Roles, 33,* 23–30.

Child, J., & Tse, D. K. (2001). China's transition and its implications for international business. *Journal of International Business Studies, 32*(1), 5–21.

Chine, F. (1999). Has China changed? *Far Eastern Economic Review, 162,* 33–34.

Confucius. (1992). *The Analects.* (D. C. Lau, Trans.) Hong Kong: Chinese University Press.

Deng, X. P. (1976, January 15). Speech at Zhou Enlai's memorial ceremony. *People's Daily.*

Dittmer, L. (1978). Zhou Enlai and Chinese politics. In E. Feit (Ed.), *Government and Leaders: A Comparative Approach to Politics.* Boston: Houghton-Mifflin.

Dorfman, P., Hanges, P. J., & Brodbeck, F. C. (2004). Leadership and cultural variation: The identification of culturally endorsed leadership profiles. In R. J. House, P. J. Hanges, M. Javidan, P. Dorfman, & V. Gupta (Eds.), *Leadership, culture, and organizations: The GLOBE study of 62 societies* (pp. 669–719). Thousand Oaks, CA: Sage.

Eaton, J. S. (1998). Gender issues in transitional China. *Multicultural Education, 6*(2), 32–36.

Epstein, I. (1998). Letter from Beijing. *US–China Review, 22*(1), 23.

Farh, J. L., & Cheng, B. S. (1999). A cultural analysis of paternalistic leadership in Chinese organizations. In J. T. Li, A. S. Tsui, & E. Weldon (Eds.), *Management and organizations in China: Current issues and future research directions* (pp. 84–127). London: Macmillan.

Farh, J. L., & Cheng, B. S. (2000). A cultural analysis of paternalistic leadership in Chinese organizations. In J. T. Li, A. S. Tsui, & E. Weldon (Eds.), *Management and organizations in China: Current issues and future research directions* (pp. 84–127). London: Macmillan.

Fu, P. P., & Tsui, A. (2003). Utilizing media to understand desired leadership attributes in the People's Republic of China. *Asia Pacific Journal of Management, 20*(4), 423–446.

Fu, P. P., & Wu, W. K. (2000). Management and leadership in Chinese organizations: Change and development in the past two decades. In C. M. Lau & J. F. Shen (Eds.), *China Review 2000* (pp. 381–404). Hong Kong: Chinese University Press.

Fung, K., Yan, Z., & Nin, Y. (1992). Shanghai: China's world city. In Y. Yeung & X. Hu (Eds.), *China's coastal cities: Catalysts for modernization* (pp. 124–152). Honolulu: University of Hawaii Press.

Goldman, M. (1994). *Sowing the seeds of democracy in China.* Cambridge, MA: Harvard University Press.

Hall, E. T. (1981). *Beyond culture.* New York: Bantam.

Hanges, P. J., Dickson, M. W., & Sipe, M. T. (2004). In R. J. House, P. J. Hanges, M. Javidan, P. Dorfman, & V. Gupta (Eds.), *Leadership, culture, and organizations: The GLOBE study of 62 societies* (pp. 219–234). Thousand Oaks, CA: Sage.

Hofstede, G. (1993). Cultural constraints in management theories. *Academy of Management Executive, 7,* 81–90.

Hofstede, G., & Bond, M. H. (1988). The Confucius connection: From cultural roots to economic growth. *Organizational Dynamics, 16*(4), 5–21.

Holloman, C. R. (1986). "Headership" vs. "leadership." *Business and Economic Review, 32*(2), 35–37.

House, R. J., Hanges, P. J., Javidan, M., Dorfman, P. W., Gupta, V. & GLOBE Associates. (2004). *Cultures, leadership, and organizations: The GLOBE study of 62 societies.* Thousand Oaks, CA: Sage.

House, R., Javidan, M., Hanges, P., & Dorfman, P. (2002). Understanding cultures and implicit leadership theories across the globe: An introduction to Project GLOBE. *Journal of World Business, 37,* 3–10.

Hui, C., & Graen, G. (1997). Guanxi and professional leadership in contemporary Sino- American joint ventures in mainland China. *Leadership Quarterly, 8*(4), 451–465.

Hwang, K. K. (1987). Face and favor: The Chinese power game. *American Journal of Sociology, 92,* 944–974.

Javidan, M. (2004). Performance orientation. In R. J. House, P. J. Hanges, M. Javidan, P. W. Dorfman, V. Gupta, & GLOBE Associates. (2004). *Cultures, leadership, and organizations: The GLOBE study of 62 societies* (pp. 239–281). Thousand Oaks, CA: Sage.

Levant, R. F., Wu, R. X., & Fischer, J. (1996). Masculinity ideology: A comparison between U.S. and Chinese Young men and women. *Journal of Gender, Culture, and Health, 1*(3).

Li, Z. H. (1986). *On history of ancient Chinese thought.* Beijing: People's Publishing House.

Lu, Y. (1996). *Management decision-making in Chinese enterprises.* London: Macmillan.

Murphy, I. P. (1996). It takes *guanxi* to do business in China. *Marketing News, 30*(22), 12.

Ralston, D. A., Egri, C. P., Stewart, R. H., Terpstra, R. H., & Yu, K. C. (1999). Doing business in the 21 century with the new generation of Chinese managers: A study of generational shift in work values in China. *Journal of International Business Studies, 30*(2), 415–428.

Ralston, D. A., Gustafson, D. J., Terpstra, R. H., & Holt, D. H. (1995). Pre–post Tiananmen Square: Changing values of Chinese managers. *Asia Pacific Journal of Management, 12,* 1–20.

Ralston, D. A., Gustafson, D. J., Terpstra, R. H., Holt, D. H., Cheung, F. M., & Ribbens, B. A. (1993). The impact of managerial values on decision-making behavior: A comparison of the United States and Hong Kong. *Asia Pacific Journal of Management, 10*(1), 21–37.

Schmidt, S. M., & Yeh, R. H. (1992). The structure of leader influence: A cross national comparison. *Journal of Cross-Cultural Psychology, 23*(2), 251–262.

Schermerhorn, J. E., Jr., & Bond, M. H. (1991). Upward and downward influence tactics in managerial networks: A comparative study of Hong Kong Chinese and Americans. *Asia Pacific Journal of Management, 8*(2), 147–158.

Shaffer, M. A., Joplin, J. R. W., Bell, M. P., Lau, T., & Oguz, C. (2000). Gender discrimination and job-related outcomes: A cross-cultural comparison of working women in the United States and China. *Journal of Vocational Behavior, 57*(4), 395–427.

Smith, S. H. (1894). *Chinese characteristics.* New York: Fleming H. Revell.

Starr, J. B. (1997). *Understanding China: A guide to China's economy, history, and political structure.* New York: Hill & Wang.

Swaak, R. A. (1995). The role of Human Resources in China. *Compensation and Benefits Review, 27*(5), 39–46.

Tom, K. S. (1989). *Echoes from old China: Life, legends and lore of the middle kingdom.* Honolulu: Hawaii Chinese History Center.

Tsui, A. S., & Lau, C.-M. (2002). Research on the management of enterprises in the People's Republic of China: Current status and future directions. In A. S. Tsui & C.-M. Lau (Eds.), *The management of enterprises in the People's Republic of China* (pp. 1–27). Boston: Kluwer Academic.

Wang, Y. F. (1998). *Managing crises in Northern Song Dynasty.* China: Yuanfang Publishing House.

Weber, M. (1951). *The religion of China: Confucianism and Taoism.* Glencoe, IL: The Free Press.

Wilson, D. (1984). *Chou: The Story of Zhou Enlai (1898–1976).* London: Hutchinson.

Yeung, I. Y. M., & Tung, R. L. (1996). Achieving business success in Confucian societies: The importance of guanxi (connections). *Organizational Dynamics, 25*(2), 54–66.

Yu, K. C., Cheng, W. W., & Chen, W. Z. (1999). *Human resource management.* Dalian, China: Dalian University of Science and Technology.

25

▼▼▼▼▼▼▼

Culture and Leadership in Hong Kong

Irene Hau-siu Chow
The Chinese University of Hong Kong

Hong Kong was known to the world as "pearl of the orient." Now it repositions itself as "Asia's world city" and a gateway to China. Hong Kong is a major hub of Asia and is one of the world's largest trading economies. This tiny city plays an important role in the global market. Over the past two decades, the Hong Kong economy has tripled with per capita gross domestic product (GDP) more than doubling. Over 60% of the FORTUNE Global 500 companies have a presence in Hong Kong. One of the critical success factors was the founder's paternalistic leadership style and risk-taking behavior. Hong Kong has been under British rule for 150 years and on July 1, 1997, it was returned to China. What makes Hong Kong unique is the combination of Chinese culture and British bureaucracy.

Culture plays a strong influence in organizational practices and leadership behaviors. Hofstede and Bond (1988) suggest that differences in power distance and individualism determine the type of leadership most likely to be effective and differences in uncertainty avoidance affect people's motivation. Leadership perceptions in a society are unique and to a certain extent very likely to be influenced by culture and other contextual variables, such as beliefs, values, and needs as well as political, and socialcultural factors. The leadership perceptions associated with the GLOBE factors differed in ways that could be better understood within specific social and cultural environments.

The purpose of this study aims to identify the unique societal and organizational cultures and leadership perceptions quantitatively and qualitatively by using both qualitative and quantitative measures. This chapter begins with a historical overview, as well as the economic, political, and sociocultural background. It describes unique aspects of the Hong Kong culture and provides a better understanding of how culture influences organizational and leadership practices. In the following section, the societal culture, Confucian philosophy, and the political and economic systems that may have significant effects on values of Hong Kong Chinese managers are described. Included in the study are survey results from 171 middle managers from two industries, telecommunications and financial services. Next, the organizational culture of the two industries is examined. Cultural practices at the organizational level are compared with the societal culture. Following this, the leadership perceptions in Hong Kong are explored. The quantitative data relevant to these cultures are interpreted in relation to the qualitative findings and both theoretical and practical implication are discussed. The chapter concludes with a summary of findings and their implications and future research directions are provided.

1. HISTORICAL OVERVIEW OF THE SOCIETY AND CULTURE IN HONG KONG

As a result of Opium War in 1839, the British seized the deserted rocky island of Hong Kong. The tip of Kowloon was ceded in 1860 under the Convention of Peking. In 1898, the New Territories were ceded under a 99-year lease. China refused to recognize any of the three unequal treaties regarding Hong Kong and insisted on its full return. After the lease ended, Hong Kong was reverted back to China. It was the first-ever return of a prosperous, free-market economy to communist rule.

Hong Kong is located in southern mainland China and is largely populated by Cantonese from Guangdong province who adhere to tradition cultural patterns. The total land area covers 1,078 sq. km., with a population of 6.8 million. It was under British rule for 150 years so its political, educational, and legal systems, to a certain extent, reflect the British influence. Long before the reunification with China, Hong Kong was well integrated with China economically.

On July 1, 1997, Hong Kong was returned to China under the "one country, two systems" principle. Hong Kong could retain its own economic, legal, and social systems that were drastically different from Communist China. The concept of "Hong Kong people ruling Hong Kong" with a high degree of autonomy assured the Hong Kong people that China would not interfere the territory's domestic affairs or seek to change its lifestyle. Hong Kong's success was attributed to an independent judiciary, a free system of press, creativity of its people, and the entrepreneurial spirit (Davies, 1996). The rapid economic development in Hong Kong and Taiwan has been attributed to the entrepreneurial spirit of the founders of many small and medium-size firms (Redding, 1990). These enterprises were flexible in adapting to the fast-changing environments. One of the critical success factors for performance was the founder's paternalistic leadership style and risk-taking behavior.

Economic and Political Background

Economic transformations of Hong Kong in the past few decades have greatly been influenced by political and economic developments in the mainland China. Starting from the 1950s, Hong Kong experienced rapid economic growth and developed a labor-intensive manufacturing industry dominated by textiles and electronics. The Hong Kong economy has gone through another dramatic structural change following China's decision to embark on economic reforms and open up to trading in 1979. Manufacturers in Hong Kong took advantage of China's open-door policies by relocating to the mainland. By shifting their labor-intensive manufacturing processes across the border, Hong Kong manufacturers were able to keep their production costs down and their products very price competitive in international markets. At the same time it offered great opportunities for expansion of production and outsourcing capacity. Since the 1980s, Hong Kong has transformed into a service economy and financial center, capitalizing on its vital links with offshore production and the rapid economic growth in the mainland. Eighty-four percent of the workforce was engaged in the service sector, employing nine times as many workers as manufacturing sector. At the macro level, Hong Kong had the highest per capita GDP but in the last few years recorded the lowest economic growth among the Chinese societies, that is, Singapore, Taiwan, and China. GDP per capita in 1997 was U.S.$26,610. Hong Kong is the freest economy in the world, according to the Heritage Foundation. In terms of world competitiveness, Hong Kong ranked third, just after United States and Singapore, but ahead of Taiwan and China (International Institute for Management Development [IMD], 1998).

The economic development of Hong Kong was spectacular, measured in material terms. In 1960, the average per capita income was 28% of that in Great Britain; by 1996, it had risen to 137% of that in Britain (Information Service Department, Hong Kong Government, 1997). Now Hong Kong is a major hub of Asia—it is the world's 10th-largest trading economy (equivalent to about a fifth of China's GDP), the fifth-largest banking center and foreign-exchange market, and the busiest container port. Foreign investments in Hong Kong total around $100 billion. It is a remarkable success story. The economic miracle took place in just the last three decades. Within a generation the average living standards rose from Third World levels to levels exceeding those in some of the Western European countries, including the UK. After 5 years under the Chinese rule, the rosy economic environment has changed.

During China's modernization process, Hong Kong acted as a major source of management expertise and business skills. Starting from the mid-1980s, over 52,000 Hong Kong residents were working in China, most of them professionals and managerial staff. They brought in experience and expertise regarding business operation in mainland and thereby helped Hong Kong to establish close relations with the mainland. At the same time, about the same number of people from the mainland worked in China-funded companies in Hong Kong. In the late 1980s and early 1990s, about 1% of the Hong Kong professional and experienced businesspeople left Hong Kong and immigrated to other countries because of the anxiety about Hong Kong's reversion to China. The emerging dynamic economies and growth potential attracted a large number of overseas Chinese businesspeople to return to Hong Kong to take the advantage of the opportunities. These returnees contributed positively with a broader international perspective. The influx of professionals from outside Hong Kong served Hong Kong well, boosting its efficiency and economic vitality.

The Basic Law has granted Hong Kong residents the freedom of religion. The church provides a high percentage of health care (20%), education (40%), and social welfare (60%) in Hong Kong (Kwok, 2000, p. 102). In education, the Roman Catholic Church is running all kinds of schools including kindergartens, primary and high schools, and adult education.

On the political side, Hong Kong was described as "undemocratic and unrepresentative, executive led, and based on a colonial form of constitution." The last governor, Chris Patten, brought in political reforms. It was criticized as too little too late by the democratic, and condemned by the Chinese government. The legislature was elected under the democratic reform of Patten, and Beijing ordered it to be disbanded as of July 1, 1997, replacing it with a Provisional Legislature that would rubber-stamp China's dictates. After the handover, the Legislative Council was immediately replaced by the Provisional Legislative Council. Elections in May 1998 were far more restricted, with 20 directly elected legislators (one third) representing geographic constituencies. Several provisions of the British-introduced Bill of Rights were scrapped. The reinterpretation of the basic law concerning the right of abode ruling for mainland-born children of Hong Kong permanent residence and the legislation of the controversial Article 23 that prohibits succession, subversion, and the theft of state secrets, undermined the society's confidence in the legal system. The majority of the Hong Kong people are willing to sacrifice their political participation in order to retain economic vitality. Even if Hong Kong were to become like Shenzhen in terms of freedom, human rights, and legal systems, the people would still be expected to consider it tolerable.

The sentiment toward China's 1997 embrace is much more ambiguous and complex. It is a mixture of happiness over Britain's departure and anxiety over what could happen under Chinese rulers who ordered the army attack on Beijing in 1989. After the handover, there has been little sign of direct interfering from the central government in Beijing with the day-to-day running of the Special Administrative Region (SAR). The key members of the government under British rule were retained after 1997, in an effort to bolster confidence about Hong Kong's future autonomy in the run-up of the handover. The conditions largely remain unchanged in the initial posthandover period. After the territory reverted to Chinese sovereignty, the political and economic environments were expected to deteriorate, with a forecast that the business environment score would fall from 8.71 for 1994–1998 to 8.24 for 1999–2003 (Economist Intelligence Unit, 1998). China's resumption of sovereignty over the territory would have an adverse affect on both political stability and effectiveness. The economic downturn, together with the legitimacy deficiency of the government is likely to reduce political effectiveness. The regional economic problem has worsened the macroeconomic environment and the city's competitive edge continues to erode. Hong Kong has lost its top position on the global ranking, falling to 12th among the 60 countries covered by the EIU's Country Forecasts. However, Hong Kong will remain to be an outward-looking, international city.

During the 5 years under Chinese rule, Hong Kong suffered from both internal economic structuring and the external Asian financial crisis that resulted in a region economic downturn. The trade-dependent Hong Kong was severely hit and ran into recession in 1998, one of the worst recessions and the most difficult times. When the Internet era faded, the economy went into recession again. Hong Kong has encountered a double-dip recession within the last 4 years. Unemployment rose to 7.8% in mid-2002 and further up to 8.7% after the hard hit by the Severe Acute Respiratory Syndrome (SARS) crisis on the economy. Hong Kong has been experiencing mild deflation for 4 consecutive years. The consumer price index dropped a total of 13% during the same period. The average GDP recorded a negative figure (–0.2%) from 1997 to 2001. The prolonged adjustment period created a sense of frustration and pessimism among the people in Hong Kong. A survey conducted by the Hong Kong General Chamber of Commerce revealed concerns looming over the city's economic competitiveness and frustration with the local government. Their worries ranged from high property and labor costs to declining educational standards and air pollution (Wonacott, 2000).

Despite of all this, Hong Kong is still considered as one of the best business hubs in Asia. Hong Kong's business environment is relatively attractive because of its low tax rates, a stable political environment, the absence of trade barriers, and exchange controls.

2. SOCIETAL CULTURE OF HONG KONG

Confucian and Chinese Culture

Hong Kong is a place where the East meets the West. It offers a cosmopolitan culture that reflects the native Chinese culture and the British colonial influence. The Hong Kong people have adopted Western ideas in order to achieve commercial success. Despite the strong British influence, Hong Kong still keeps much of its Chinese cultural tradition. The emphasis placed on certain Confucian values, such as filial piety and harmony, may reflect the lingering influence of traditional Chinese culture. The governors were all British, and all of them were appointed at the Crown's will. The British national flag and portrait of the Queen of England were over most of the government buildings. Yet the majority of the people of

Chinese descent in Hong Kong do not identify with the British. A century and half of British presence have left remarkably little impression on the Chinese population of Hong Kong, who never identified with the colonial rulers. Although living under a colonial regime and experiencing low social and political participation, the majority of the Hong Kong people identify themselves as "Hongkongese" rather than Chinese. They are proud of their identity and maintain a sense of belonging to Hong Kong. Over half of the population came from China and settled for quick money. Living "on borrowed time, in borrowed place" (Hughes, 1968), people in Hong Kong tend to develop a very short-term orientation, with a preference for short- term measures and quick profit.

The Chinese have historically been dominated by respect for a hierarchy of authority, which can be traced back to the Confucian value of loyalty between sovereign and ministry (Von Glinow & Teagarden, 1988). Chinese cultural traits attributable to an upbringing in the Confucian tradition are: (a) socialization within the family, (b) a tendency to help the group, (c) a sense of hierarchy, and (d) a sense of complementary relations (Kahn, 1979). Confucianism is a Chinese social philosophy and set of moral guidelines. Confucian values emphasize the importance of education, obedience to authority, interpersonal harmony, loyalty to the family, kinship affiliation, and individual responsibility (Hofstede & Bond, 1988; Yeh, 1989). When there is conflict between loyalty and filial piety, the Chinese tend to show loyalty only to the family. The deeply rooted cultural values of Confucianism still guide individual actions and attitudes (Adler, Docktor, & Redding, 1986; Shenkar & Ronen, 1987; Tung, 1981). Hong Kong residents have been brought up with the virtues of Chinese culture as well as the instinctively Chinese values such as humility, patience, persistence, and working hard. They also appreciate the Western traits such as creativity, aggressiveness, and directness that often get things done. Hong Kong people are pragmatic enough to preserve the virtues of Chinese culture while at the same time assimilating the knowledge and experiences of the West.

The people of Hong Kong have long lacked a common identity. Over half of the population has successfully escaped the communist rule and settled in Hong Kong with a refugee mentality. The recent new immigrants or new arrivals from mainland are in a poor economic situation and in need of financial assistance to integrate into the community. Some better-off people migrated to foreign countries, mainly Canada and Australia, to secure a foreign passport and then returned to Hong Kong. These overseas returnees have evolved into a curious hybrid of Eastern and Western culture with a different identity.

Others may not consider Hong Kong as their permanent home. Living in a "borrowed place, borrowed time," there is a limited sense of belonging. Facing the identity crisis, the chief executive, Tung Chee-hwa, shared his vision in governing Hong Kong in the following way:

> Trust, love and respect for our family and our elders, integrity, honesty and loyalty towards all, commitment to education and strong desire to strive to improve and advance oneself, a belief in order and stability, an emphasis on obligations to the community rather than rights of the individual; a preference for consultation rather than open confrontation. These are some of the share values which make our society more cohesive. Together with a strong identity, they will provide us with clarity of direction and unity of purpose. (Howlett, 1998, p. 2)

3. METHODOLOGY

In this study, both qualitative and quantitative methods were used to collect the data. Three themes were addressed by the GLOBE questionnaire (House et al., 1999, 2004): (a) perceptions

TABLE 25.1

Sample Characteristics

Sample Size: N = 171	Mean	Std.Dev.
Age	35.67	9.06
Years of formal education	17.54	13.09
Years staying in Hong Kong	31.64	12.32
Years of full-time work experience	14.11	11.36
Years as manager	9.96	21.47
Years with current employer	7.98	9.61
Gender	Male n = 102 (60%)	Female n = 6 9 (40%)
Work for an MNC	Yes n = 92 (54%)	No n = 79 (46%)
Member of a professional association	Yes n = 31 (18%)	No n = 139 (82%)

about effective leadership, (b) societal cultural practices and values as perceived ("As Is") and as desired ("Should Be"), and (c) organizational cultural practices and values as perceived ("As Is") and as desired ("Should Be"). The sample of respondents comprises altogether $N = 171$ middle managers in the telecommunications and financial services sectors. The sample characteristics are described in Table 25.1.

The qualitative research methods include interviews, unobtrusive measures, and content analysis of narratives, for example, media, literature, and archival records. These methods provide a rich description of the specific societal culture and leadership perceptions that are endorsed in Hong Kong. The culture-specific characteristics are also discussed in terms of how they influence leadership perceptions.

Results of the Quantitative Study of Societal Culture in Hong Kong

Results of the quantitative analysis are presented in Table 25.2. It contains Hong Kong's country score (mean score of all respondents) and its ranking among the 61 countries that participated in the GLOBE research program for the nine societal culture "As Is" and "Should Be" scales. The highest mean scores obtained by Hong Kong were on In-Group Collectivism (5.32) and Power Distance (4.96), followed by Performance Orientation (4.80). Relatively low scores were measured for Humane Orientation (3.90) and Future Orientation (4. 03) at the society level. A comparatively low score for Institutional Collectivism indicates that Hong Kong is individualistic in its societal culture. When comparing the within-country scores of In-Group Collectivism (5.32) and Institutional Collectivism (4.13) a discrepancy becomes apparent. It seems to reflect that Hong Kong Chinese individuals are more collectively oriented to their family but they are more individualistic oriented within their society. Despite the importance that Hong Kong Chinese respondents placed on family cohesiveness, the score is significantly lower than that of other Chinese communities (e.g., 4.77 for China, 4.59 for Taiwan).

It is worth noting that Hong Kong society ranked 3rd in Performance Orientation, 5th in Assertiveness, and 28th in Gender Egalitarianism among the 61 GLOBE countries and regions included in the study.

TABLE 25.2
Results of the Nine GLOBE Cultural Dimensions at the Societal Level

Culture Dimension	"As Is"		"Should Be"	
	HongKong Mean score[a]	Rank[b]	HongKong Mean score[a]	Rank[b]
Assertiveness	4.67	5	4.81	5
Future Orientation	4.03	21	5.50	33
Gender Egalitarianism	3.47	28	4.33	41
Humane Orientation	3.90	41	5.32	38
In-Group Collectivism	5.32	33	5.11	57
Institutional Collectivism	4.13	34	4.43	41
Performance Orientation	4.80	3	5.64	52
Power Distance	4.96	43	3.24	5
Uncertainty Avoidance	4.32	21	4.63	38

[a]7-point Likert scale. [b]The rank order is relative to the 61 GLOBE countries.

Value or "Should Be" items describe the respondent's perception of what people claim to want or desire for themselves. For the "Should Be" score, there appears to be a clear preference for higher level of Performance Orientation (5.64), and Future Orientation (5.50), followed by Humane Orientation (5.32). It should be noted that all of the "Should Be" scores were higher than the "As Is" scores, with the exception of Power Distance. In fact, Power Distance was the lowest (3.24) in the nine "Should Be" dimensions. This indicates that the Chinese respondents desire to have a lower power distance society. In comparing the "As Is" scores with "Should Be" scores, there were significant differences. In general, the "Should Be" scores are higher than the "As Is" scores in most of the cultural dimensions, except for Power Distance. This may reflect the social desirability, or something people want to have. The discrepancies between the "As Is" and "Should Be" scores can be interpreted to indicate the desired direction for societal change.

Hong Kong ranked third in Performance Orientation ("As Is"), however the respective "Should Be" ranking dropped tremendously to 52. Conversely, Power Distance "As Is" (4.96) ranks 43rd and Power Distance "Should Be" (3.24) ranks 5th highest among the 61 GLOBE countries.

Other scales that attract attention are Gender Egalitarianism and Humane Orientation. A moderate level of Gender Egalitarianism "As Is" (3.47) is evident and the respective "Should Be" score indicates a desire for higher levels of Gender Egalitarianism (4.33). The Hong Kong society is not considered as a very humane society as indicated by a low-ranked "As Is" Humane Orientation score (3.90, Rank 41). In line with the worldwide trend, the respective "Should Be" score is considerably higher (5.32, Rank 38), which makes it a desirable cultural value in Hong Kong's society. A similar trend is apparent for Future Orientation "As Is" (4.03, Rank 21) and "Should Be" (5.50, Rank 33). Interestingly, In-Group Collectivism, which received the highest "As Is" from middle managers in Hong Kong, received a much lower "Should Be" score (5.11), which positions Hong Kong among the lower end of all 61 GLOBE countries (Rank 57). The high ratings for Assertiveness remained about the same for both dimensions, "As Is" (4.67, Rank 5) and "Should Be" (4.81, Rank 5).

Results of the Qualitative Study of Societal Culture of Hong Kong

This section describes the Hong Kong societal culture based on unobtrusive indicators and archival data.

Uncertainty Avoidance.   Hong Kong is characterized as a free-market capitalist economy. Being a laissez-faire economy, the government provides few tax incentives for new businesses. Unlike the economic development of Taiwan, Singapore, and South Korea, the Hong Kong government adopts the "positive nonintervention" philosophy. Such a hands-off, laissez-faire culture greatly enhances entrepreneurial activities. This can be reflected by a large proportion of entrepreneurial firms and high rate of new business start-ups. Greater industrialization also encourages individual initiatives, and Hong Kong is known for having a large number of risk-taking entrepreneurs and a general speculative attitude among its people. Hong Kong people are more speculative than other capitalistic societies and are more prone to take calculated risks. They recognize and acknowledge the significant rewards that may result from taking risks to start a new business (McGrath, MacMillan, Yang, & Tasi, 1992). Terpstra, Ralston, and Bazen (1993) found that U.S. managers and Hong Kong managers have no significant difference in risk-taking propensity. On the other hand, the relatively low expenditures for research and development and reluctance to invest in high-tech industry reflect the mentality of uncertainty avoidance. Without government subsidy, investors are simply not willing to bear the risk of failure in high-tech industry.

Power Distance.   A person's influence is based primarily on one's ability and contribution to society. Hong Kong Chinese are more confined by social classes and organizational hierarchy. People in positions of power tend to increase their social distance from less powerful individuals and so power is concentrated at the top. Followers are expected to obey their leaders without questioning.

Hong Kong is a social class–conscious society and its people are endlessly chasing money. Wage differential is high with great discrepancy in wealth distributions. Every year the media identifies the wealthiest and the most powerful families in the Hong Kong. Most of them make their fortune in the property industry. These wealthy families generally have more domestic servants, luxury houses, and expensive cars. Anything that reflects class, status, and power distance is welcome. The dressing code also reflects one's status with managers tending to dress formally. Graduating students are also ranked and classified into different class of honors degree according to their academic records.

Power stratification can also be reflected in the number of hierarchical levels in a particular organization, status-relevant occupational and honary titles, and size of office. The amount of office space is generally allocated according to the status rather than the requirements of the work to be done. It is viewed as a privilege. The way people address each other in society reflects status differences. In Hong Kong, management practices in small and medium-size organizations are often based on kinship relationships and involve obedience to elders, based on deference to the wisdom of experience.

There were very few historical heroes or leaders in Hong Kong. The main streets and buildings were named after the Royal Family of England. The Royal Crest was found on most of the government buildings and post boxes before the 1997 handover. The governors were appointed by the Crown in England. Local people believed that the governor served the interest of England rather than the interest of the Hong Kong people. There is an absence of public symbols that attest to the greatness of national leaders.

Institutional Collectivism.   Hofstede and others describe Hong Kong as a moderately collective-oriented society, with individuals belonging to a set of different and overlapping social networks. Contrary to Hofstede's (1980) findings two decades previously, Hong Kong society seems to be more individualistic now. In a large social survey conducted in Hong Kong, the conception of happiness is very personal and individualistic and good health and money were the major concerns. In a densely populated city-state, the majority of the people lives in crowded high-rise buildings. They are only concerned with their private life and seldom socialize with their neighbors.

In-Group Collectivism.   In a family- and relationship-oriented society, in-group collectivism becomes more important. Aging parents generally live at home with their children and children live at home with their parents until they are married. Parents take pride in the accomplishments of their children.

Because of the space constraint, the prevalence of extended families is increasingly more difficult. A more affluent society can afford to have better accommodation for the nuclear family. The share of the nuclear family increased from 54% in 1981 to 63.6% in 2000. Married children with their own children will no longer live with their parents; however, they will get together for dinner at least once a week or several times a month. Members of the extended family stay nearby to offer help. It is also a common practice to have communal dishes, which are shared by all family members. It is the government policy to encourage households living with aged parents. Commitment to live and take care of aged parents will be given high priority in the allotment of government-subsidized public housing for low-income families. Despite the growing incidence of family conflicts and rise in divorce rate, survey results show that the highest satisfaction is consistently found in the domain of family life (Lee, 1992).

Gender Egalitarianism.   In most Chinese societies, the traditional family remains patrimonial (absolute power is vested in the male head of the household). Male children are preferred to carry the family name. The patriarch would be the ruler and leader of the household, making all-important decisions and dictating his wishes. He would enjoy the highest status in the family, and the domestic burdens would fall on to his wife. Husbands are masters of the households and wives are expected to submit to their authority. Despite the centrality of family in Chinese societies, the importance of love and marriage is given a relatively low significance (Lee, 1992). In Hong Kong, as far as the gender aspect of family life was concerned, there was evidence of a strong departure from the male-centered gender-unequal family. The Hong Kong families were far more gender-equal than commonly assumed. In a large social survey, the majority of the respondents disagreed that "women should put family before everything else and even give up work if there is the need." It can be argued that in Hong Kong people are pragmatic enough to see the advantage of having a second paycheck (Lee, 1992, p. 14).

In the education system, there is a tendency for male students to enroll in mathematics and the hard science, and for female students to enroll in the arts. This is quite a universal phenomenon. Requiring the female students to take courses in needlework and domestic science and male students to take courses in wood and metal work reinforces the gender roles. The gender role is also implicitly reflected in the content of textbooks in junior high school (Shamdasani, 2002). Content analysis of Chinese history textbooks in Hong Kong revealed more than 2,900 episodes on gender roles. Out of these episodes, only 99 described the female role, just 1 out of 30. In most cases, women were described as housewives, sex slaves, concubines, and so on. The female roles were seriously downgraded whereas the men were projected to have attained high levels of achievement and made significant contributions to the country. One may question that there were very limited female role models in traditional Chinese history. More recently, in a survey of integrated social studies that included more than 10,000 lines of text and more than 250 pictures, the frequency of men appearing in text and pictures compared with women was found to be more than double. The image of the man is projected to be more important and professional than the woman. Women are shown to take more responsibility related to homemaking and child caring.

In the workplace, the involvement of women in the labor force has been rising. Female labor force participation rate was 51.1% in 2001. As more and more women join the workforce, together with the equal opportunity in both the educational system and the workplace, women have a better chance to move into the managerial and professional occupations. There is a high proportion of women represented in the senior civil service and the private sector. In 1999, one third of the civil servants were female (Civil Service Personnel Statistics, 1999). In the directorate grade, 24% are female and in public office, females represented 11.5% and 16.7% in the Executive Council and Legislative Council membership, respectively (Department of Census and Statistics, Hong Kong Government, 2001).

Ngo (2000) investigated the trends in occupational segregation by gender in Hong Kong. Antidiscrimination legislation regarding women's employment has been enacted only recently. Education and job opportunities have been available for women in Hong Kong, owing largely to prosperous economic conditions; for instance, female labor force participation rate was 51.1% in 2001. In the past 15 years, the female labor force increased by 45%, compared to 14% of their male counterparts. However, women predominantly work in jobs that have lower status and lower income such as clerical (72.5%), sales, and personal services (45%). Rising levels of educational attainment qualifies young women to enter a broad range of jobs. There is an increase in women's representation in managerial/administrative (25%) and professional (32.7%) occupations (Department of Census and Statistics, Hong Kong Government, 2001).

The restructuring of the Hong Kong economy has changed occupational sex segregation due to two major forces. First, Hong Kong has undergone a process of "occupational upgrading," which is characterized by an increased share of higher status administrative, professional occupations in the labor market. The growth of managerial and professional jobs over the last decade has facilitated women's entry into these prestigious jobs, which have been traditionally dominated by men. Second, the middle-aged, less-educated women who lost their jobs in the manufacturing sector have also possibly sought employment in low-skill service occupations. Only the skilled and craft male workers remained in their original job positions. The blue-collar occupations have become more sex segregated.

Assertiveness.   It measures the extent to which a society is assertive, dominant, and tough in social relationships. A previous study by Schermerhorn and Bond (1991) found that Hong Kong Chinese are more masculine and assertive than Americans. However, the Chinese cultural concept indicated otherwise. In a society where strong emphasis is placed on harmony and face saving, confrontations are avoided. Tung Chee-hwa, the chief executive of Hong Kong Special Administrative Region, "strongly believes in greater harmony, less hostility, less unnecessary quarreling, but more rational discussion" (www.Info.gov.hk/gia/General2000/0/111011 40.htm). After all, "quiet negotiation does not mean weakness."

Future Orientation.   Chinese in general are often described to have a long-term orientation (Hofstede & Bond, 1988). Future orientation and future investments of enterprises in

Hong Kong ranked number 7 and 10 respectively (IMD, 1997). As for attitudes toward the future, Hong Kong people do not have much confidence in the territory's future. A significant and expanding percentage of graduates in the professional fields, such as engineering and computer science, opt for jobs in the financial sector, or in the business field, instead of trainee posts in engineering or manufacturing industries. Young people are reluctant to engage in long-term planning and long-term investment in improving their qualifications. Living in a "borrowed time, borrowed place," people in Hong Kong tend to focus on the short term. There is a saying that "Hong Kong is a place where you can have an idea at nine, incorporated by noon, and have your profits by six." Investors with long-term objectives are skeptical about Hong Kong's future and tended to engage in short- or medium-term investment only. The economic downturn in the past few years further deteriorates entrepreneurs' investment confidence.

Investment in research and development is another indicator of future orientation. Hong Kong manufacturers do not have a tradition of innovation. Many of them started their business as original-equipment manufacturers (Chua et al., 2002) and very few of them are willing to spend resources on research and development. According to a report written by researchers from Massachusetts Institute of Technology (Berger & Lester, 1997), the proportion of research and development was estimated to be 0.1% of GDP, compared with 2.4% in the United States and 2.9% in Japan. Only 1% of the total number of patents granted in Hong Kong originated from a proprietor from Hong Kong (Department of Census and Statistics, Hong Kong Government, 2003). The SAR government proposed to increase spending on research and development and upgrade technology. The infringement of intellectual-property rights in Hong Kong and China is so widespread that without proper intellectual-property protection, being innovative to improve performance is not substantially rewarded.

Performance Orientation.   Hong Kong is still strong in business and was ranked third in the world in terms of competitiveness for a short period. Unfortunately, its ranking dropped to 7th in 1999, and further down to 14th in 2000. Management efficiency and entrepreneurship ranked second.

Though work is of utmost importance in life, high priority is placed on performance orientation. The support of competitiveness as indicated by working hard, tenacity, or loyalty ranked on top of the world (IMD, 2000). The average number of working hours per year was 2,500.

In a high performance- or achievement-oriented society, students are encouraged to strive for continuously improved performance. At the age of 12 students are assessed by Academic Aptitude Tests and get a secondary-school place according to the banding of 1 to 5. Students attending Band 1 schools are labeled as high achievers. The Academic Aptitude Tests were abolished and the branding was reduced to 3 to avoid a labeling effect. Good academic records are still very much emphasized. There is a strong tendency to chase credentials in the form of certificates, diplomas, and university degrees. Both parents and the government are willing to invest in human capital and education.

Hong Kong is far closer to Western-style management than most other Asian nations. People in the former British colony, with a weak political and national identity, developed a pragmatic orientation that emphasizes survival and growth by pursuing material gains. They tend to be more result and performance oriented. Hard work and good performance are always valued by employers. Hong Kong's workforce has been maintaining its efficiency and high spirits very well. They are very dedicated to their work and they derive considerable job satisfaction alongside financial rewards.

Hong Kong is a place full of opportunities with a high degree of social openness. Wealth is considered as an important criterion to determine one's social status. It is generally accepted that to become rich is glorious. The entrepreneurial spirit among the Hong Kong people has remained strong. The culture encourages people to be their own boss and entrepreneurs and those who have become wealthy by setting up businesses are respected and admired in the society. The self made billionaires, *taipans,* are glorified for their wealth-creating ability. Major rewards are based on performance effectiveness and the use of a formal performance appraisal system is a common practice.

Humane Orientation. Renqing, the affect and care components of the relationship (*Guanxi*), is particularly important in the Chinese society. Results from Chinese Culture Connection (1987) found no difference between the United States and Hong Kong on this dimension. Ralston, Gustafson, Elsass, Cheung, and Terpstra (1993) found that U.S. managers are more concerned with getting jobs done whereas the Chinese managers were more concerned with maintaining a harmonious environment.

Treatment of the poor and the less fortunate reflects the society's humane orientation. Direct government spending is about 21% of national income in Hong Kong, despite the forecasted budget deficit of HK$36.5 billion for the year 2000 (2.8% GDP). During the period of economic downturn (coupled with demands for greater social expenditure) the total public expenditure increased by 4.3%. The largest share of spending is on education (19% of the total expenditures), amounting to HK$55.2 billion, and the greatest increase in spending is on social welfare, which has risen to 13.7%. Despite all these efforts, Hong Kong residents still consider this to be not enough. Another indicator of increasing humane orientation is that human rights organizations are gaining a bigger voice and are becoming more visible in Hong Kong society. The Hong Kong –style protest (display of public indignation) is seen as tame by Western standards.

Overall Profile of Societal Culture of Hong Kong

An overall profile of the societal culture of Hong Kong based on a combination of the findings of both the quantitative and qualitative studies can be summarized as follows.

The findings of the GLOBE study presented in this chapter reflect the changes in societal culture during the last decade, particularly after Hong Kong was returned to China. The societal culture is described as high in Power Distance and Performance Orientation. In contrast, Hong Kong society is relatively low in Institutional Collectivism, Future Orientation, and Humane Orientation. One of the most striking observations is the medium to low score on In-Group Collectivism. Family business is overwhelmingly the dominant form in Hong Kong. The major characteristics of small family business are centralized, paternalistic, and nepotistic in nature that rely on personal networks for external linkage. The dependence, conformity, and Lau's (1982) depiction of "utiliarianistic familism" are the most prevailing societal values of Hong Kong. The key success factors are adaptability and flexibility in response to the rapidly changing demand of their clients and markets. The laissez-faire policy and free market provide the opportunities for entrepreneurial spirit to flourish. The people of Hong Kong are pragmatic and materialistic, with short-term orientation.

In terms of values at the societal level, it is interesting to note that Hong Kong scored lower in several cultural dimensions (Power Distance, Institutional Collectivism) than the other three Chinese societies (PRC, Taiwan, and Singapore). In contrast, Hong Kong people are more individualistic in societal cultural practices and values than citizens in other Chinese societies. In-Group Collectivism was considered as the most important cultural dimension in Hong Kong, yet the score was still lower than the other three Chinese societies. And, the Hong Kong society seems to prefer a more assertive pattern of behavior. Hong Kong women are no longer subordinated to men and confined to domestic work as in traditional Chinese society and women are more readily accepted in the business world due to Hong Kong's long exposure to the more egalitarian Western view. Hong Kong scored higher in Gender Egalitarianism than other Chinese communities (e.g., Taiwan, PRC) as indicated by a medium score in the Gender Egalitarianism scale. To a certain extent, this may be due to the prolonged Western influence. The preference for higher female orientation (high equality on the top positions, employment opportunity, education, etc.) was expressed as desirable for the future.

Hong Kong is still struggling with uncertainty and economic downturn after its return to Chinese sovereignty and it is attempting to regain its competitiveness. Emphasis should be placed on Future Orientation and Performance Orientation. It is the pervasive anxiety about the future that releases the boundless energy of the community. The anxiety also spurs self-employment and entrepreneurship. Unfortunately, there is increasing evidence on the erosion of entrepreneurial values and increasing risk aversion as well as reliance on government support. Currently Hong Kong has one of the lowest entrepreneurial participation rates in the world because of deteriorating business sentiment (Chua et al., 2002). Just like Singapore and other welfare states, Hong Kong people have fewer incentives to start a business because their basic needs are being well taken care of with subsidized public housing, an inexpensive public health system, and increased welfare spending. All these have affected their motivation to work hard to meet their own needs. Other developments of cultural and social norms, such as rising professionalism and higher living standards, are unlikely to nurture entrepreneurial spirit. Following the breakdown of the "Hong Kong economic miracle" and the difficult time encountered after its return to China, consumer confidence was relatively pessimistic about the future regarding employment, the economy, regular income, stock market performance, and quality of life. According to Master Card International's biannual survey around the Pacific region, Hong Kong's score was 21.3 based on a scale of 100, second to last in the 13 markets studied (V. Yu, 2003).

According to IMD's (2000) world competitiveness survey, Hong Kong scored 6 on a 10-point (most satisfied) scale in overall life satisfaction. The average number of weekly work hours was 50, the highest, whereas job autonomy was only 2.2, the lowest among all the countries surveyed. Work was under a great deal of pressure. Satisfaction with the relationship with supervisor was 4.9, also the lowest on a 7-point scale. Subordinates do not think their superiors are weak in abilities or poor in work attitudes, but they are weak in management communication skills and too results oriented, creating too much pressure for staff. Hong Kong employees are much less satisfied with their jobs and the management practices of the firms than their European counterparts (Leung, 2002).

4. ORGANIZATIONAL CULTURE IN HONG KONG

Organizational culture is obtained by using GLOBE questionnaires surveys from respondents in the telecommunications and financial services sectors. A brief history of both sectors in Hong Kong is provided in the Appendix. The results obtained from the GLOBE study are presented together with the societal value for comparison.

TABLE 25.3

Organizational Culture for the Telecommunications and Financial Industry

Culture Dimension	"As Is"		"Should Be"	
	Telecom	Financial	Financial	Telecom
Assertiveness	4.77	4.60	4.93	4.72
Future Orientation	4.08	3.98	5.29	5.67
Gender Egalitarianism	3.51	3.43	4.41	4.31
Humane Orientation	3.84	3.95	5.31	5.34
Performance Orientation	4.79	4.80	5.61	5.67
In-Group Collectivism	5.24	5.39	4.92	5.26
Institutional Collectivism	4.17	4.09	4.52	4.36
Power Distance	4.87	5.03	3.22	3.26
Uncertainty Avoidance	4.45	4.21	4.57	4.68

The results of organizational culture in telecommunications and financial industries are presented in Table 25.3. It should be noted that there is no significant difference between the two industries in both "As Is" and "Should Be" scores. The scores for In-Group Collectivism are the highest among all cultural dimensions in both industries. The importance of In-Group Collectivism remained high at the organizational level. Gender Egalitarianism and Humane Orientation scored around the midpoint on a 7-point scale in both industries. It implies that Gender Egalitarianism is pretty much achieved in organizations. Power Distance is also high in these two industries. It is desirable to have lower Power Distance in an organization as indicated in the way it "Should Be." Future Orientation is not practiced as it is now but is highly desirable. Assertiveness, Institutional Collectivism, Future Orientation, Humane Orientation, and Performance Orientation all received higher scores for the way it "Should Be" than the way it is. It highlights room for improvement in these dimensions.

In terms of "As Is," the organizational-level culture of both the telecommunications and financial sectors followed more or less the same pattern as the societal level. In general, there was a consistent pattern on these cultural dimensions on both the societal and organizational level. For example, Gender Egalitarianism received a similar score at the societal level and the organizational level. The medium scores around 3.5 at the organizational level implied a preference for gender equality. Assertiveness remained high at the organization level in both "As Is" and "Should Be" scores. Assertive behaviors are considered important in organizations. Future Orientation ("As Is") is highly desirable but did not receive the same level of attention at the organizational level, with a lower score in both industries. Humane Orientation scored low at both the societal and organizational level. Facing the financial pressure of downsizing and salary cuts, organizations were not doing enough to take care of their employees. At the societal level, In-Group Collectivism received the highest score (5.32), and it remained very important at the organizational level, but was slightly less desirable in the telecommunications industry. Power Distance was less desirable, even more so at the organizational level than the societal level, and value placed on the way it "Should Be." In comparison with the society-level values, the score of Uncertainty Avoidance is lower at the organizational level for both "As Is" and "Should Be." Even though the organizations surveyed are not family-owned business, the organizational culture is characterized by family control and personal authority.

5. LEADERSHIP IN HONG KONG

Until 1994, all the top posts in the public administration were held by British expatriates. In the private sector, top-management positions in traditional *Hongs* (trading houses or conglomerates) are held primarily by British and Anglo-Saxons. There is a marked difference in the culture and leadership before and after the reunification with China. Up to the 1980s, the Hong Kong business community was dominated by a few large Hongs, such as The Hong Kong Bank, Jardine, Matheson & Company, and The Swire Group. These British Hongs monopolized the market and played a leading role in the domestic economy. The operations of these Hongs have had a significant influence on culture and leadership style, the typical Western style. Since the reunification, the China-controlled firms have gained importance and started exerting more powerful influence on the Hong Kong economy. The new dominant organizations in Hong Kong are headed by Chinese *taipans*. It is estimated that the market value of the listed companies controlled by Chinese capital in Hong Kong amounts to about 55% of the gross value of the Hong Kong Stock Exchange (Liu, 1997, p. 136). When Patten's proposed reform was attacked by China, Hong Kong business leaders were less enthusiastic about his reforms. Some prominent businesspeople and probusiness voices endorsed the idea of "democratizing" the Legislative Council. Tycoon Li Ka-shing threatened to pull out a $10 billion project simply because he was worried about the political climate (criticism from political parties). Business leaders also complained that the business community's influence was being diluted by increasingly powerful elected politicians (*South China Morning Post,* December 23, 1998, p. 1), which has generated the irrepressible energy propelling Hong Kong to its economic prosperity (S. L. Wong, 1997).

Review of Prior Research and Literature on Leadership in Hong Kong

Westwood and Chan (1992) tried to distinguish leadership and headship in the Chinese context. Leadership is related to individual qualities or behaviors. The person who is the head of an organization may achieve that status through some means outside of the leader-led relationship (e.g., inheritance or ownership). Headship is viewed as being imposed on the followers. This is particularly true in the family-owned business. A Chinese businessman's headship of an enterprise will be accepted and his rights as owner will not be challenged.

Westwood and Chan's (1992) study of headship of Chinese-owned organizations found Chinese entrepreneurs to be very autocratic. They believed that their rights as owner should not be challenged. Silin (1976) argued that Chinese leaders, in order to protect their organizational status, would withhold information and power from their subordinates. Only when it was necessary would Chinese supervisors release this information and power so that subordinates would remain dependent to their leaders. Silin found that the vertical hierarchy in Chinese organizations facilitates control and did not give much room for subordinates' initiative. Chinese supervisors also regularly played down or denied the contributions of subordinates so that their own position could be strengthened (Redding & Wong, 1986, p. 288). Coaching subordinates to encourage intellectual exploration would go against the supervisors' wishes. Smith, Misumi, Tayeb, Paterson, and Bond (1989) studied the leadership style of Hong Kong using Misumi's PM (performance–Maintenance) leadership theory, which is parallel to Ohio State's study of initiating structure and consideration. The maintenance supervisor's distinctive behaviors include discussing a subordinate's personal difficulties, spending time together socially both at work and after hours, and talking about work problems. In addition to all these behaviors, the performance leader engages in more frequent

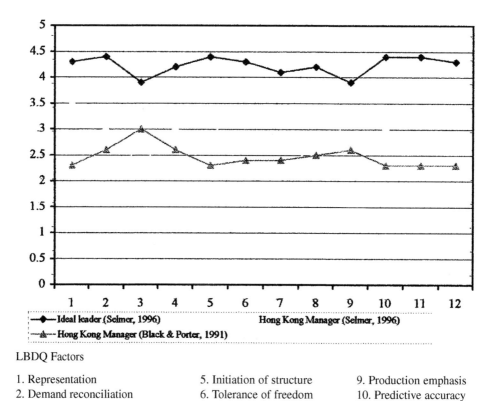

LBDQ Factors

1. Representation
2. Demand reconciliation
3. Tolerance of uncertainty
4. Persuasiveness

5. Initiation of structure
6. Tolerance of freedom
7. Role assumption
8. Consideration

9. Production emphasis
10. Predictive accuracy
11 Integration
12. Superior orientation

Figure 25.1.   LBDQ—Ideal leader versus Hong Kong manager.

meetings with subordinates, discussion on career plans, and communication with other work groups. The distinction between P and M is not clear-cut. The maintenance leader is best exemplified by the tactfulness employed in resolving personal difficulties in an indirect manner, whereas the performance leader encourages cooperative work behaviors.

Selmer (1996) studied Hong Kong managers using the Leadership Behavior Description Questionnaire (LBDQ–XII). The ideal leader is expected by subordinates to be high on "prediction accuracy," and "integration," low on "tolerance of uncertainty," "role assumption," and "production emphasis." The scores for the ideal leader are consistently higher than actual Hong Kong managers in all 12 leadership behavior factors. In another study, Black and Porter (1991) found none of the 12 dimensions of managerial behaviors were related to performance as measured by the LBDQ among Hong Kong Chinese managers. The comparison of results from these two studies is provided in Figure 25.1. It should be noted that Black and Porter's study recorded consistently lower scores on these factors except for "tolerance of uncertainty" and "consideration."

Okechuku and Man (1991) compared the managerial traits in Canada and Hong Kong and concluded that the role of manager in the Hong Kong context is different from Canada as power concentration reduces discretion and increases dependence. Compliance inhibits initiatives from subordinates. From a Confucian perspective, a leader should be a morally superior person and should behave in ways that conform to the key virtues of consideration and human-heartedness and should follow the rules of propriety. Relationships may be unequal but they are also reciprocal and contain mutual obligations. Owner managers expect loyalty and obedience from their subordinates, and they must also reciprocate by taking care of and nurturing their subordinates. Paternalism is the kind of generally well-known management style in Hong Kong (Westwood & Chan, 1992). Paternalism combines discipline and authority with fatherly concern and benevolence. The leader must show paternal qualities of care, concern, and protection of subordinates. Managers who are high on both initiating structure and consideration are effective.

Results of the Quantitative Study on Leadership in Hong Kong

The quantitative data on leadership attributes were collected from 171 middle-level managers in the telecommunications and financial services sectors. The sample characteristics are given in Table 25.1. All of the sample were ethnic Chinese working in local companies. The average age of the participants was 35.7 years old, ranging from 21 to 55. They had an average of 17.5 years of formal education. Sixty percent of the respondents were male and had an average of more than 14 years of full-time work experience and 10 years as a manager. The respondents had worked for their current employer for an average of 8 years. About half of the participants have worked for a multinational corporation and 18% of them belong to professional associations or networks. The average time that the respondents have lived in Hong Kong was 31.6 years and they have lived in two to three foreign countries for longer than a 1-year period.

The questionnaire aims to identify the characteristics and behaviors of a leader who is perceived to be outstanding. GLOBE defines a leader as a person who is able to motivate others and influence or facilitate in others behavior that contributes to the achievement and the success in a business organization. The questionnaire items consisted of behavioral and trait descriptors (e.g., autocratic, benevolent, nurturing, visionary). There were 112 attributes and behaviors to be rated on a 7-point Liekert scale that ranges from greatly inhibits (1) to contributes greatly (7) to making a person an outstanding leader. Based on the total GLOBE sample, a series of exploratory factor analyses and internal consistency analyses were conducted resulting in 21 leadership prototypicality dimensions. The Cronbach alphas of these scales range from .83 to .98 and within-group correlation range from .78 to .97. All scales demonstrated significant and nontrivial within-country response agreement, between-culture differences, and respectable interitem reliabilities (cf. House et al., 1999, 2004). The country scores together with the ranking of Hong Kong among the 61 countries on leadership prototypicality are presented in Table 25.4.

The implicit theory of leadership among Hong Kong managers favors behaviors and attitudes that include inspirational, performance orientation, decisive, visionary, team integrator, integrity, administrative competent, diplomatic, collaborative, self-sacrificial, and modesty. All the dimensions received a score above 5 on a 7-point scale. On the other end of the spectrum, procedural, autocratic, nonparticipative, self-centered, and malevolent are perceived as the least desirable characteristics of a leader. These attributes are viewed as ineffective or impediments to outstanding leadership. Procedural and face saving will slightly inhibit a person from being an outstanding leader and these attributes are seldom found in the media reports (see later discussion). The ranking of Hong Kong's scores among the 61 countries help to further refine the picture. On the one hand, malevolent, autocratic, nonparticipative,

TABLE 25.4

The Average Score and Ranking of GLOBE Leadership Scale for Hong Kong

Leadership Dimension	Hong Kong	
	Mean	*Rank*
Charismatic Inspirational	5.85	48
Performance Orientation	5.82	48
Charismatic Visionary	5.76	51
Collaborative Team Oriented	5.76	40
Integrity	5.73	49
Administratively Competent	5.71	37
Diplomatic	5.60	23
Decisive	5.57	40
Team Integrator	5.28	45
Charismatic—Self-Sacrificial	5.13	21
Modesty	5.00	33
Humane	4.77	31
Autonomous	4.38	8
Conflict Inducer	4.34	15
Status-Consciousness	4.31	33
Procedural	3.83	36
Malevolent	3.34	4
Autocratic	3.27	5
Face Saver	3.14	21
Nonparticipative	3.02	13
Self-Centered	2.63	9

and self-centered attributes were perceived to inhibit a person from being an outstanding leader by Hong Kong managers. On the other hand, the rankings for Hong Kong relative to all 61 GLOBE countries are comparatively high. For example, self-centered scored 2.63, the lowest among all dimensions within Hong Kong, but it ranked high (9th) in comparison to all GLOBE countries. Or, malevolent scored 3.34, yet it ranked fourth among the 61 countries. This indicates that Hong Kong managers perceive these attributes to be less inhibitory to effective leadership than managers in most of the other GLOBE countries do.

In contrast, Hong Kong managers perceive inspiration, performance orientation, visionary, and integrity to most strongly facilitate effective leadership in comparison to the other leadership dimensions. But the relative ranking of Hong Kong on these leadership attributes when compared to all 61 countries is relatively low. In particular, visionary and integrity are two of the vital characteristics of value-based leadership. In this respect, Hong Kong ranks only 51 and 49, respectively, in the GLOBE sample. Overall, these results seem to suggest that Hong Kong business leaders are not perceived very favorably compared with leaders in other countries included in the GLOBE study. However, this may be due to the fact that in Asian cultures, including Hong Kong, respondents tend to avoid the extreme ends of a scale and prefer the midrange responses (Adler, Campbell, & Laurent, 1989; Bond & Hwang, 1986; Hofstede, 1980). GLOBE controlled for response bias (House et al., 2004) and found that a substantial level of agreement existed between the "corrected" and "uncorrected" leadership scales

TABLE 25.5
Second-Order Leadership Scales

Leadership Dimensions	Mean	Rank
Charismatic/Value-based:	5.68	47
Visionary, Inspirational, Self-sacrifice, Integrity, Decisive, and Performance orientation		
Team Oriented:	5.58	50
Collaborative team orientation, Team integrator, Malevolent, Diplomatic Administratively competent, Diplomatic		
Humane:	4.89	31
Humane orientation, Modesty		
Participative:	4.86	54
Autocratic, Nonparticipative (reverse scored)		
Autonomous	4.38	7
Self-Protective:	3.67	18
Self-centered, Face saver, Status-consciousness, Procedural, Conflict inducer		

(range of correlations: .85 to .99, average correlation: .94). This implies that cultural-response bias plays a small role in the GLOBE leadership scales.

Compared with China, Taiwan, and Singapore, the GLOBE data showed no significant difference in administrative competence and nonparticipative behavior among all four Chinese societies. Compared to the scores of other Chinese economies in the GLOBE study, Hong Kong leaders rank high in terms of autonomous and autocratic leadership attributes. Differentiating from their counterparts in other Chinese societies, Hong Kong people try to solve problems by themselves without seeking help from others. Seeking help from others means an obligation people owe to friends, with an expectation to return the favor in the future. The mentality of "to achieve self-renewal with one's own effort" is strongly held. Compared with other Chinese societies, Hong Kong scored lowest in relation to modesty, face saving, integrity, and administratively competent. On the surface, this profile appears to be consistent with the portraits of Hong Kong managers described in the literature. There were, however, some contradictory results in team-oriented leadership. People in Hong Kong are very individualistic. They show solidarity only to protect their own interests.

Based on the 21 primary leadership factors, the second-order factor analysis yielded six dimensions (House et al., 1999, 2004) which are presented in Table 25.5. Hong Kong leaders received the score of 5.66 and 6.58 for charismatic and team-oriented leadership, respectively. It implies that value-based leadership is complemented with collaborative team-oriented attributes. Humane and participative leadership received medium scores of 4.89 and 4.86, respectively. Only autonomous and self-protective scored below 4.5. Self-protective is the least desirable attribute for outstanding leaders, with a score of 3.67. More discussion of these factors is given as follows.

Charismatic/Value Based. Items loaded in this factor are visionary, inspirational, self-sacrificial, integrity, decisive, and performance. Hong Kong managers live through an increasingly uncertain environment; a clear vision is critical for leaders during the transitional period. They are inspirational, performance oriented, decisive, and visionary.

Team Oriented.   Items include collaborative team orientation, team integrator, modesty, diplomatic, malevolent, and administratively competent. In a moderately collective society, dominant leaders form alliance to protect their interests. They also need the support from the masses. This is the only scale that showed no significant difference among the four Chinese economies. Hong Kong people seem to be very individualistic in the workplace. Yet they are very cohesive to their family and friends.

Humane Orientation.   Consistent with the paternalistic style of management in the Chinese society, leaders show their command and authority together with the care and concern. Hong Kong ranked in the middle among the 61 countries in humane orientation and modesty. Hong Kong received the lowest score among the four Chinese communities on this dimension, possibly indicating that Hong Kong managers perceive personal care of the well-being of followers to be less important for effective leadership.

Participative.   Hong Kong ranks 54th on this scale. Hong Kong managers perceive autocratic and nonparticipative attributes to inhibit effective leadership less strongly than most of the other managers in the GLOBE sample do. This can be confirmed in both the literature and the interviews (see later discussion). Participation is not necessarily effective in Hong Kong. Redding and Richardson (1986) found no apparent connection between participative attitudes and productivity in their study of Hong Kong managers. Empowerment is still not well accepted in Hong Kong because of the deep-rooted belief in the Confucian analects of filial piety and the unquestioning obedience expected from the subordinates. Leaders should be respected, obeyed, and not questioned.

Autonomous.   Hong Kong ranks 7th with a score of 4.38 on autonomous leadership. The desire for autonomy and self-reliance in matters relating to work is very persistent in Hong Kong. This is consistent with the Hong Kong government's "positive nonintervention" policy. Hong Kong's success, compared with Asia's newly industrialized economies, Singapore, Taiwan, and Korea, to a large extent depends on the freedom and entrepreneurship spirit. In the case of economic downturn and rising unemployment situation, the typical response of the Hong Kong resident was not to press for government assistance or unemployment benefits. Instead, they were planning to upgrade their qualification and considering the possibility of starting their own businesses. It is apparently there is a burning desire for autonomy.

Self-Protective.   Self-centered, face saver, status-consciousness, procedural (or bureaucratic), and conflict inducer were believed to slightly impede making a person an outstanding leader. Self-serving, greedy, and exploitative were seen as some of the negative attributes of leadership. Pursuit of one's own interest projects a negative image of selfishness.

Results of the Qualitative Studies on Leadership in Hong Kong

In addition to the quantitative survey results, the qualitative analysis yields rich information that is important to identify the culture-specific aspect of leadership behaviors. The following description is based on data that were collected from 30 branch managers and bank officers attending a part-time course from a large local bank. The participants were asked to select their preferred leaders and describe leader attributes and behaviors that enhance outstanding leader performance. An interview was conducted with a professor who taught the graduate-level leadership course. The interview lasted for an hour and the purpose was to identify the beliefs held about how leaders behave and what is expected of them. Secondary sources also include analysis of media coverage of leaders and biographies.

In the interview with a professor teaching the leadership course to Executive MBA participants, he supported the idea that:

> Headship and ownership of Chinese entrepreneurs will affect the leadership style of Hong Kong managers. Their background and low mobility in the organization makes a difference. Unlike other large companies in the Western countries, the tenure of CEO is about five years; Chinese owners/managers stay in their organizations for life. The Hong Kong people are very pragmatic. They talk about vision, but only a few are able to put it into practice.

Characteristics and Behaviors of an Outstanding Leader.   The findings based on the content analysis of the data collected from branch managers and bank officers regarding their perception of leader are listed in Table 25.6. The content analysis centered on the differences between outstanding leaders and effective managers. The most common description of an outstanding leader is charming, confident, and decisive, with foresight and strong gut feelings. Good communication, trust, reputation, and a desire to lead are considered important components of leadership. To be seen as an outstanding leader, respondents also indicate that charisma, providing a role model, and setting direction are important. Other items endorsed include risk taking, sacrifice, and long-term/future orientation. Effective managers are seen to be persistent, knowledgeable, sensitive, responsive, hard-working, and responsible. They are experienced, skillful enough to carry out the required work efficiently, and follow through on procedures. They rely on position power and authority but also try to maintain harmony. A consensus approach is preferred to an adversarial style.

Media Analysis on Public Image of Leaders.   One way to understand leadership is through leadership image projected in the mass media. Media analysis was conducted on articles describing outstanding leaders as well as content analysis of recruitment advertisements for managerial and professional positions. An attempt was made to carry out an analysis of the media reports on leadership behavior in two time periods, 1 week in June 1997 (16th to 22nd) from the *Ming Pao* (one of the well-respected comprehensive daily Chinese newspapers) before the 1997 handover, and the first week in February (1st to 6th) 1998 (before the Chinese New Year) from the *Hong Kong Economic Journal.* During each time period, articles pertaining to leadership were content analyzed. In the first period, 82 articles were selected with 205 extracts. In the second period, 127 articles were identified with 347 extracts for further analysis.

In the first period, the major focus was on the change of leadership during the transitional period. On June 23, *Time* magazine identified the 25 most influential leaders from different sectors in the new Hong Kong. Though the leaders differ from each other in terms of social background, educational level, and professional qualifications, the public image from the media exhibits a common characteristic: high achievement motivation. Leaders are glorified for their ability to get rich and for being successful and results-oriented. A number of these successful business tycoons came from a humble background. They are very dedicated and hard-working. They deeply believe in maintaining credibility and trust in their working relationships.

The media analysis confirmed several of the themes identified through the discussion with bank managers. These features are relevant and, to some extent, consistent with some of the

TABLE 25.6

Content Analysis Results of Narratives from Bank Managers and Officers

Category	Effective Managers	Outstanding Leaders
Skills	Communication	Interpersonal skills
	Strategy formulation	Attention to details
	Resolve conflict	Delegate
	Problem solver	Risking taking
	Blend of rights and duties	Emphasis on leading role
	Enabling process flexible	Aligning people
	Tactics	Autonomy
	Negotiate	Empowered
	Instruction	Human relations
	Express opinion	Consultative
	Involvement	Capture the opportunities
	Contingent reward	Articulate
	Compromise	
	Flexible tactics	
	Take precaution	
Personality	Hard working	Charismatic
	Smart	Coach
	Loyal	Active
	Good temper	Intelligence
	Kind	Tremendous memory
	Considerate	Maturity
	Team	Role model
	Stable	Good exemplar
		Calm
		Sensitive
		Genius
		Open-minded
Abilities	Experience	Set direction
	Carry out required work	Shaping ideas
	Follow the rules, procedures, direction	New ideas
	Handling routine	Intuitive
	Operating efficiency	Enthusiastic
	Analytical	Independence
	Team work	Flexibility
	Task oriented	Darling and resolution
	Meeting deadline	
	Completion schedules	
	Execute the stated policy	
	Closely monitor progress	
Values	Responsible	Innovative
	Tolerate	Imaginative
	Goodwill	Long-term/future orientation
	Goals arise out of necessity rather than	Ideal
	desires	Objective
	Harmony	Responsive
	Accomplishment	Pervasive
	Persistence	Aggressive
	Tough-mindedness	Long-term goals

(*Continued*)

TABLE 25.6   (Continued)

Category	Effective Managers	Outstanding Leaders
	Reputation	Heroism
	Good temper	Inspiring
	Balance	Ambition
	Creative	Challenge
		Reputation
		Trust
		Devoted
		Achievement
		Drive
		Motivation
		Courage
		Respect
		Tough attitude
		Reputation
		Considerate
		Affectionate
Behaviors	Efficient	Sacrifice
	Productivity	Cooperative
	Coercive power	Team
	Appointed	Encouragement
	Involvement	Appreciate
	Assist	Strategic
	Coordinate	Influential
	Position power and authority	

core dimensions of the GLOBE study. The effective leaders as portrayed in the media are summarized in Table 25.7. The media image of a leader is of a person with high achievement orientation and a strong desire for success. They continuously aim for the best. Similarly, administrative competence, experience, and expertise are highly valued. Some elements of the value-based leadership are also present. They may not be regarded as visionary leaders. However, they serve as a role model and lead by example. Operating under a competitive environment, outstanding leaders tend to develop a strategic orientation. They are forward looking, with accurate business judgment. The characteristics most frequently mentioned in the media reports are how leaders seize opportunities and become wealthy, followed by turning around a failing business. Hong Kong leaders are very opportunistic. Paternalistic leadership style is a common practice. Leaders are portrayed as benevolent and caring. They treat their longtime employees and business partners generously. Leaders are also seen as less autonomous and independent and are described as decisive and determined, with little evidence of participative and face saving. "Face" is important in the Chinese society. The importance of "face" to the Chinese is similar to the bark of the tree. But "face" has to be earned. When a person is successful, he or she will be given "face." It is akin to honor and glory.

There are not many saint like historical heroes or leaders in the Hong Kong community. One can hardly find a local leadership figure in stamps, banknotes, or statues. However, there are more prevalent business leaders as indicated by an analysis of magazine articles from major

TABLE 25.7
Media Analysis on Public Image of Leaders

ADMINISTRATIVE COMPETENCE

Expertise, competence, educated, talented, experience, global mind-set, professional knowledge, potential

CHARISMATIC/VALUE-BASED

Confidence, long-term objective, long-term consideration, long-term planning, personal image, vision, favorable impression, dignity, charisma, value and expectation, role model, mission, ideal, influential, recognition, appraise, principle, standing out from the crowd

INSPIRATIONAL

Commitment, moral support, moral responsibility, assertive, ambitious, strong will, aggressive, political wisdom, courage

INTEGRITY

Justice, trustworthy, enthusiastic, fair, truth, honest upright, no prejudge, equal opportunity, credibility, frank

PERFORMANCE ORIENTATION

Reward outstanding performance, profit oriented, improvement, lesson learnt, try the best, merit, emphasis efficiency, contribution, distinguished achievement, management objectives

HUMANE ORIENTATION

Help employees, fighting for right and benefits, friendly, social contract, talkative, sociable, approacable, help the less fortunate, easy to get along with, compassionate, attention to the needs of employees, considerate, generous, supportive, contact, understanding, expressive, humble, sense of humor

TEAM ORIENTATION

Coalition, partnership, collaborate and support, coordination, cooperative, harmony, support from the mass, resolve the differences, consultative rather than fighting/struggling, daring and resolution, communication, public opinion

PARTICIPATIVE

Consult, delegation, consensus, democratic, autocratic, develop talent, constructive suggestion

AUTONOMUS

Independent, independent assessment, empower, freedom, remain mutual, mutual respect, cool-minded, calm

NARCISSISTIC (SELF-PROTECTIVE)

Self-discipline, avoid conflict, role conflict, preaches what he says, authority, arouse emotional conflict, sacrifice, power, self-restraint, status, self-interest, isolated, strong personality, show extreme forbearance, control emotional/feeling

DECISIVE

Solve problem, objectivity, determined, reasonable, clear message, investigate, viewpoint, rational, prepared, detailed investigation, logical, information dissemination, listen to opinion, criticism, persistence, open-minded, carefully conceived, well thought, broad-minded, seek true from fact, judgment, handling the dilemma, stand firm

(Continued)

TABLE 25.7 (Continued)

STRATEGIC ORIENTATION

Advantage, adaptive, flexible, capture the opportunity, competitive, innovative, risk taking, future oriented, invention, curiosity, handling crisis, conservative, optimistic, goals, legal principles, turn threat into opportunity, correct judgment

DUTY AND RESPONSIBILITY

Responsible, resourceful, provide resources, cautious, devoted to one's duty, how perilous it is, duty-bound, no passing the buck, intervention, innovative operative concepts, down to earth, know one's place, take protective measure in advance, attention to details, face the consequence, practical, correct, action oriented, monitor, admit mistake, passive, play politic, successor, stress on traditional culture, selfless, appeal for higher authority, tolerate, workaholic, active, pragmatic, simplicity, simply life, try the best, stress, worry, coercive, uneasy

PROCEDURAL

Rule of law, rigorous, monitoring mechanism, follow the rules and regulations, manipulation, order and procedure

---

periodicals. "Men of the Decade" were chosen for their contributions to Hong Kong by *Hong Kong Business,* a monthly magazine. Among them was Tung Chee-Hwa, the first chief executive of the Hong Kong SAR of China. Gordon Wu was chosen twice within 4 years for his visionary investment in infrastructure projects in China and Asia. Larry Yung, a red capitalist, stepped into the spotlight for his successful steering of the China-backed conglomerate, CITIC Pacific Ltd., within a short period. These men have proven themselves to be visionaries.

Mr. Tung Chee-hwa, a former shipping magnate and the first chief executive of Hong Kong SAR, is now serving his second term in office, running until 2007. He was born in Shanghai, raised in Hong Kong, educated in Britain, and trained in the United States. Throughout his career he has gained the trust of the Chinese authorities. Evidence of this was shown when Tung's failing business was bailed out by China in the early 1980s. Intensely patriotic and instinctively conservative, he was very reluctant to take the position of chief executive. He did so out of a sense of patriotism and responsibility rather than ambition. Mr. Tung was portrayed as a puppet of Beijing by the foreign media. His background in business seems to have left him ill-equipped to meet the demands of modern politics, especially in handling the media as indicated by his deteriorating popularity (ratings fell from 89% in October 1997 to 56% in August 1998). Steven Vines, former foreign correspondent for the *Independent* and founding editor of the *Eastern Express,* described the new chief executive hand-picked by China in this way:

> Tung Chee-hwa embodies almost everything the new sovereign power expects of a leader. He is conservative and cautious. He shares the views of China's leaders about the need to preserve order. He is suspicious of representative government. He is instinctively authoritarian and he is intensively patriotic. Unlike most senior cadres in Peking, he is also rather affable and has a knack of not making personal enemies. (Vines, 1998, p. 77)

Tung Chee-hwa outlined his vision when addressing the people of Hong Kong on the first day of Chinese rule: "I see an economy that is one of the most important in the world. Hong Kong will be the most important trade, transportation, communication, education and entertainment center in Asia." Hoping that to inspire the trust and confidence of the community, the slogan, "Government cares about the people," revealed his typical paternalistic style of leadership.

During his 5 years in office, Mr. Tung did not show strong leadership. Property prices fell 65%; the stock market lost more than one third of its value; unemployment soared; and there was a record high budget deficit. There was no relief for the growing number of unemployment. The performance of the government was not inspiring and the people's trust in the government has been declining. The dramatic changes in Hong Kong's economy began to reverberate throughout the society. In June 1998, 1 year after the turnover, Hong Kong saw a steady economic decline. Satisfaction with life in Hong Kong had plummeted to a record low never seen in the 1990s (Hong Kong Transition Project, 1999, 2002).

Tung was reelected by an electoral committee made up of China's supporters in spite of his unpopularity. He initiated some changes to improve the government's accountability to the public. The ministerial system was introduced to replace top civil servants. In his policy address for his second term, the main theme was "revitalizing our economy" through economic restructuring, forging closer economic co-operation with the mainland, and eliminating the fiscal deficit. But his policy address did not bolster the confidence of Hong Kong's citizens. The opinion survey conducted by the University of Hong Kong revealed that half of the respondents were not satisfied with the policy address. The approval rating for the chief executive dropped to a record low of 46.9 points out of 100. The disappointment was partly due to the lack of initiatives of the new team of ministers.

Leaders are viewed as heroes who come forward at a time of crisis to resolve a problem. With the lack of confidence in the chief executive and his administration, Hong Kong's world-class civil service could be ruined by the poor performance in handling the posthandover crisis. This may reflect a general downplay of leadership quality in the public sector due to premature promotion during the transitional period and the team-based orientation. This has created a tendency to devalue the perception of leaders.

In the business circle, Li Ka-shing, nicknamed "superman," represents the new generation of Chinese *taipans,* coming from a rice field in China and ending up as Hong Kong's richest man. He has a slice of virtually every profitable pie in Hong Kong. Li is among the global power elite and ranked the world's wealthiest person by *Forbes* magazine. His net worth was estimated to be $11 billion (Tanzer, 1997). He began by making plastic flowers for a living and now controls property, utilities, retailing, telecommunications, and infrastructure companies. In 1979, he acquired a controlling stake and became the first Chinese to win control of a large British trading conglomerate, Hutchison Whampoa. He is the most admired and influential person in Hong Kong and *Asiaweek* (May 2000) ranked him as the most powerful person in Asia.

Li Ka-shing is also very successful in grooming his two sons, Victor and Richard, for the new generation of high-flying Hong Kong entrepreneurs. The elder son, awarded young leader of the year 1997, is the successor of the family's flagship Cheung Kong (Holdings) and the younger son, Richard, is also a rising star in the corporate world. Richard, at the age of 30, was the deputy chairman of Hutchison Whampoa, a company capitalized at $270.2 billion, the second-largest company in Hong Kong. In 1990, he founded Star TV, Asia's first pan- Asia satellite television network operating in more than 50 countries across the continent. Subsequently it was sold to Rupert Murdoch at approximately six times what was invested in it. Richard, currently CEO and chairman of Pacific Century Cyberworks, built his company by taking over the formerly British-controlled Cable and Wireless Hong Kong Telecom.

Gordon Wu is a different type of entrepreneur with a vision of constructing the largest and most significant infrastructure for the development of China. Often referred to as a visionary, he is prone to dreaming big dreams. After graduating from Princeton University in 1958, he returned to Hong Kong to start his career. His company, Hopewell, was set up in 1969. After a decade of dealing with eight governments, problems with the ministers of transport, and cancellation of mass transit in Thailand, Sir Gordon still thinks about Hopewell's vigorous infrastructure plans in the Pearl River Delta.

Beijing has been cultivating numerous pro-China leaders with the new elite group embracing a pro-Beijing, patriotic view. Larry Yung is the founder and chairman of CITIC Pacific, the Hong Kong–listed subsidiary of China's premier state-owned investment conglomerate. It is China's most powerful conglomerate in Hong Kong and its empire spans property, aviation, telecommunications, and civil works. Larry, son of PRC Vice President Rong Yiren, has already established himself into the traditional power elite by becoming a steward of the Hong Kong Jockey Club. He helped raise China's equity stake in major Hong Kong institutions such as Swire Group's Cathay Pacific Airways and the electric power utility China Light and Power.

In Hong Kong, political leaders are often found in comic strips that are prohibited in Singapore and China. The majority of the people remains largely apolitical due to there being no strong and powerful leader on the political scene. Political leadership refers to those individuals who either directly or indirectly exercise influence and/or control over the process of governmental decision making. In Hong Kong, the process of decolonization is complicated by the fact that the state is to be reverted back to a communist system that is fundamentally incompatible with its capitalist system. Political leaders have to accommodate the conflicting claims and pressure from Hong Kong, China, and Britain in the transition to 1997. During the transition period, an atmosphere of uneasiness and mutual skepticism and distrust overshadowed the relationship between Hong Kong and China. Every Chinese policy on Hong Kong was seen as an attempt to exercise greater control over the territory. Any consensus reached between Britain and China was seen as a British betrayal of Hong Kong's interests. Beijing saw some of the political leaders as confrontational and radical. Since the return of Hong Kong to China, public demonstrations are part of the daily life in Hong Kong. China worried that Hong Kong would be potentially become subversively anti-China. The Article 23 (the proposed national security law to legislate against subversion) controversy will undermine the confidence in Hong Kong if the issue is mishandled.

The introduction of electoral politics had a significant impact on the evolving political leadership in Hong Kong. The Democratic Party and grassroots leaders were introduced into the Legislation Council. They would fight for Hong Kong's interests and occasionally condemn the autocracy of the Chinese leadership. However, the dominance of the elite was continued through political appointment. The leadership style of the Chinese officials was very imposing and dominating. After the handover, the pro-China figures enjoyed better access to and acceptance by the Chinese officials.

In Hong Kong, the Leader of the Year is elected annually by a group of prominent judges. The *Hong Kong Standard* (a local English newspaper) printed an eight-page special on the event. The profile of the award winner will shed some light into the characteristics of an outstanding leader. Victor Fung was honored Leader of the Year 1999 by a panel of nine judges. Dr. Fung was Chairman of the Hong Kong Trade Development Council, the statutory body responsible for the promotion of Hong Kong's external trade and member of Hong Kong SAR Chief Executive's Commission on Strategic Development. Currently he chairs the Airport Authority Management Board. He wears many hats in public positions. Born and raised in Hong Kong, Dr. Fung holds bachelor's and master's degrees in electronic engineering from the Massachusetts Institute of Technology and a doctorate in business economics from Harvard University. He was a professor at Harvard Business School before returning to Hong Kong. Victor is the chairman of the Li and Fung Group, a leading Hong Kong–based regional trading company. In 1995, Dr. Fung was voted businessman of the year under the Hong Kong Business Awards Scheme for his success as an entrepreneur and for his contribution to Hong Kong's economic development. He is one of the most influential people in Hong Kong. He has featured in more than 200 media interviews. The criteria for being elected include reaching out to society, contribution to society's well-being, not just in his own discipline, having a compassion and empathy, and voluntarily contributing time, effort and money for the well-being and betterment of Hong Kong society. Dr. Lawrence Wong, chairman of the panel of judges, described Dr. Fung as an "achiever [who] points [the] way with compassion." He gave further comments on being a leader:

> A leader is a little like a priest, an evangelist. You have to preach, you have to convince your people. … The most important quality of a leader is the ability to manage change. … A good leader must have vision so he can lead the organization to respond and adapt to external change. … You have to be a coach, on top of that you have to be cheerleader and sometimes you have to be a little bit of a godfather. (Leader of the Year, 1999).

Media analysis also included an analysis across 63 pages of the *Classified Post,* a total of 1,127 recruitment advertisements in the *South China Morning Post* (a highly regarded English newspaper in Hong Kong and the region) on March 6, 1996 (a peak recruitment season of the year). The content analysis of recruitment advertisements for managerial or professional positions provides the attributes of the person they are seeking. The qualifications and attributes required for senior management are summarized in Table 25.8. It can be seen that in addition to educational qualifications, technical skills, and relevant experience, interpersonal skills, communication, and personal attributes, such as energetic, motivated, dedicated and confidence, are also considered important.

Overall Profile of Leadership in Hong Kong

The leadership profile emerges from the quantitative and qualitative data emphasizes on results, decisiveness, and competence. Through aspiration and vision are important, Hong Kong leaders are rather pragmatic, focusing more on results and performance. They place high traditional values on the virtue of being industrious as well as being frugal (England, 1989, p. 40). In a materialistic and social class–conscious society, leaders are glorified for the ability to get rich and be successful. There is strong desire for success. Business leaders are very opportunistic and seize every opportunity to become affluent. They are the wealthiest and the most powerful people within society.

With wide exposure to Western culture, Hong Kong Chinese remain Sino-centric, regarding themselves as modern without losing their "Chineseness" (Bond & King, 1985). Indigenous leadership styles and work values include relationships, harmony, order, and discipline. As a group, the Chinese are higher than Western groups on various measures of authoritarianism (Bond, 1991). Several empirical studies have shown that Chinese also scored higher on power stratification when compared with the United States (Cragin, 1986; Ralston, Gustafson,

TABLE 25.8
Qualifications and Attributes in Recruitment Ads

- Professional qualifications
- Degree holder of reputable university, MBA
- Work experience
- High level of commercial awareness
- Forward thinking
- High proficiency in English, Mandarin, and Cantonese
- Good communication and analytical skills
- Cross-cultural sensitivity
- Extensive travel within the Greater China region
- Knowledge in PC, computer software
- Familiar with Internet and IT, Web- and media-related experience
- Ability to critically evaluate issues and solve problems
- Ability to organize and lead
- Ability to work in fast-paced and busy environment
- Ability to develop strong customer relationships
- Commitment to working with team, good team player
- Excellent interpersonal skills
- Hard working
- Driven, result-oriented, and strategically minded
- Highly energetic
- Motivated individual
- Mature, dynamic, proactive, business oriented, confidence
- Independent
- Reliable and dedicated, cool, calm under pressure, meeting deadline
- Positive and pleasant personality
- Creative, innovative
- Ideas people, a lot of initiative, energy, patience, and tolerance

Terpstra, et al., 1993b). The leadership style is substantially influenced by Confucian values on order and compliance and acceptance of authority, resulting in a predominantly autocratic manner. High power distance creates hierarchical structure, conformance, and dependence. Subordinates have little discretion and initiative and are seldom consulted before decisions are made. They simply obey their leaders without questioning. Managers are reluctant to share information with subordinates and are averse to a participative system. In a relationship-oriented society, leaders need to maintain harmony, order, and discipline. In addition, leaders are expected to be sensitive to the needs of subordinates and uphold a high moral standard.

To summarize, leadership style appears to be culture specific. The predominant leadership style is paternalistic and benevolent autocratic. Leaders are expected to be nurturing, considerate, and sympathetic in exchange for unquestioning loyalty, dedication, and compliance from subordinates.

6. MANIFESTATIONS OF LEADERSHIP AND CULTURE IN HONG KONG

The Chinese society is governed by *guanxi*. The *guanxi* relational network is defined by "five cardinal relationships," or in Chinese *wu-lun*, that is, master–servant, father–son, husband–wife, elder–young siblings, and friends–friends. These five relationships give order and stability to the social system and offer the role-context requirements for individuals in the five fundamental relationships of life. It ties people together according the specific relationship between people. The unique Chinese culture on the preset fundamental relationships determines the order of social hierarchy. *Wu-lun* and *guanxi* networks can be used to explain these societal dimensions of Collectivism, Gender Egalitarianism, and Power Distance.

Family occupies the central position within the nested *guanxi* relationships. Such relationships will be extended to distant relatives, friends, and new acquaintances. Chinese are expected to have different role obligations within the network in comparison to close and distant *guanxi* networks. *Guanxi* defines who is a member of the close inner circle and who is a member of distant outside groups. This is analogous to the in-group and out-group differentiation in the social-psychological literature. That is why family cohesiveness remains important.

Hong Kong people seem to be very individualistic in the workplace and society, yet family solidarity is strong. The collectivism in the Chinese culture is actually family network group–specific. In the Chinese society, developing a close parent–child relationship is a virtue that is widely respected and valued. Children are taught to be obedient, conforming, and dependent. They are often reminded of the bounded filial duty toward their parents. There are close bonds, loyalties, and a strong sense of duty associated with the family network.

Family business orientation remains strong in Hong Kong. Owners-managers thrive on being involved in every aspect of their business. A leader has the authority to rule and lead the organization as well as the responsibility to provide and protect (Bond, 1991). Leaders need to show their command and authority as well as their caring and consideration. This is a typical paternalistic or benevolent authoritative style. The Chinese style of leadership tends to exert tight control as the owner of the organization has absolute power. The authority figure should not be challenged. There is little discussion on empowerment and decentralization in the media. In such a highly personal management, ability to inspire is less important. In a typical Chinese family business, the inner circle of the top-management team is reserved for family members only. The owner-manager will prepare and arrange for the next generation to be the successors. There is less concern about developing subordinates and potential successors outside the family members.

Hong Kong people are pragmatic enough to preserve the virtue of Chinese values and at the same time absorb the knowledge and experience of the West. The deep-rooted Confucian values, such as humility, patience, and persistence, still guide individual actions and attitudes. The Confucian values emphasize modest, humble, and harmonious relationships. The notions of "face" and mutual respect also constrain the behavior of Chinese individuals and discourage them from being assertive. Respect for hierarchy also creates social-class consciousness. Wealth is considered as an important criterion to determining one's social status. In comparison, Hong Kong people are more materialistic. Leaders make accurate business judgment by capturing every opportunity to create wealth. They are glorified for their ability to get rich.

High levels of work motivation exhibited by the Chinese as a group have been explained by culture-based work values and strongly held cultural traditions and beliefs tied to Confucianism such as working hard, self-control, frugality, and willingness to adapt (Chinese Culture Connection, 1987). In work organizations, individual contributions are rewarded. Individuals work hard to achieve personal success, however individual achievement was only encouraged if it would not harm others and would lead to group success (A. B. Yu, 1996). Hong Kong people maintain a strong work ethic as a result of the cultural heritage of working hard, dedication, and uncritical abdication of responsibility to higher authority. Thus employees in general suffer and work under stress from their demanding bosses.

Implications for Foreign Managers Doing Business in Hong Kong

Hong Kong, as a gateway to China, provides great opportunities for multinational business. The findings in this study offer some important implications for foreign managers doing business in Hong Kong or dealing with managers from Hong Kong. For multinational firms, it is necessary to pay more attention to the cultural differences and the unique leadership characteristics. As Project GLOBE (House et al., 1999) has pinpointed, multinational firms need to pay attention not only to basic cultural differences between their home country and the host country, but also to the subcultural differences between different societies that share the same language, religion, and ethnic traditions, and leadership styles (e.g., China, Hong Kong, Singapore, and Taiwan). Even for an ethnic Chinese manager, it is still necessary to understand the cultural difference in other Chinese societies. Hong Kong managers behave differently than their counterparts in China and Taiwan. An effective leadership style from one Chinese society may not be effective or even applicable to other Chinese societies. This has special implications for multinational companies in managing their global workforce. Developing cultural awareness and sensitivity is an important starting point. Globalization and standardization may be a cost-effective way to handle global business, however the universal approach in applying headquarter policies to foreign subsidiaries is not necessary the best way to do business. Cultural differences should be taken into consideration. Paying attention to cultural differences and the unique leadership perceptions by detailed investigation of the determinants for managing in a global context can pay dividends. Research findings support the idea that local differences should be contextualized rather than minimized (N. Wong, 2000). Knowledge of global, regional, and subcultural differences enables practitioners to formulate their human resources (HR) policies and strategies accordingly. In addition to technical knowledge, soft skills such as relational/interpersonal skills are important in the relationship-oriented Chinese society.

Another implication is preparation for international assignments such as selecting and training expatriates and developing skills in coping with the growing need for global management. It helps international assignees adapt to a new and different environment outside their country. Expatriates should be aware of the cultural differences and develop skills in handling employees and customer needs more effectively. Without understanding the national culture, multinational firms may make mistakes in selecting and training their staff, in marketing and promoting their products, or in making short-term and long-term investments. The costs of sending expatriates overseas are very high both directly (salary and allowances) and indirectly (damaged reputation, career prospects, relationship with clients, etc.). Thus becoming familiar with local culture and leadership behavior is critical in selecting local partners, locating and retaining staff, as well as establishing HR policies and practices.

Hong Kong is playing a vital role in the international arena; however, the traditional Chinese family business features, like cronyism and nepotism, which coexist with international business practices, may have been difficult for some Westerners to understand. Chinese family business is rooted in Chinese values, and has a strong sense of Chinese tradition. The traditional Chinese view tends to treat employees as family members. Employers expect loyalty from employees and reward their diligence. It is not a good practice to retrench an employee. If one doesn't succeed, it is not necessary to get rid of him or her right away. The person will be given a chance to move around if poor results are a consequence of something other than their efforts.

Harmony is crucial in societal and corporate culture. This can be achieved by avoiding extreme behavior. Situations such as direct confrontation that could lead to loss of "face" or shame should be avoided. Western managerial techniques that are built heavily on individualistic assumptions may not be effective. Aggressive bargaining is not practiced in a collective and high–power distance society. Employees are not supposed to challenge the decisions on compensation and leaders will assure workers they can get what they are promised in exchange for their loyalty and efforts. Contingent reward seems to be a very powerful tool to motivate subordinates. Hong Kong business leaders are more transactional and this tends to be instrumental.

All in all, multinational corporate managers doing business in Hong Kong need to be aware of the effectiveness of managerial practices that are embedded in different institutional contexts, and take into account those specific cultural dimensions that are manifested in Hong Kong. The present study provides managers in international business some universal valid behaviors as well as allowances for comparison and contrast in culture-specific behaviors.

Limitations and Future Research Directions

The present study utilizes both quantitative comparative and qualitative culture-specific measures to draw an altogether richer picture of Hong Kong's societal, organizational, and leadership culture. Triangulation research methods from multiple sources of data such as questionnaire surveys, interview, media analysis, and archival data were used to cross-validate the research findings. The quantitative data were interpreted with qualitative data. No matter how vigorous the research design is, limitations are unavoidable. Some limitations of the present study and possible directions for future research are suggested.

The sample was restricted to middle managers from the telecommunications and financial services sectors and this limits the generalizability of the findings. These two industries are the most important business sectors in the Hong Kong economy. Generalizing the results to other industries should be approached with caution. As such, future research should include respondents from different industries and economic sectors to extend the generalizability of the results.

This study suggests many avenues and promising directions for future research. Longitudinal studies and more in-depth case analyses are needed to provide insight into how outstanding leaders respond to environmental changes. Equally important, the present study focuses on the embedded cultural environment and its impact on leadership behaviors. Future research could investigate the causal relationships on antecedents, leadership behaviors, and performance measures.

7. CONCLUSIONS

The present study identified the effects of societal and organizational culture on leadership behaviors and practices in Hong Kong. The findings of the GLOBE study presented in this chapter reflect the changes in societal culture and leadership during the last decade, particularly after Hong Kong was returned to China. The leadership behaviors that emerge from the quantitative data are consistent with the qualitative study and the cultural dimensions.

Consistent with the universally endorsed leadership attributes, the GLOBE results for leadership dimensions in Hong Kong indicated that effective leaders were seen to be inspirational, of high integrity and vision, as well as being decisive and performance oriented. These were considered crucial factors for success of an outstanding leader.

A few key exceptional leadership elements include being hard-working, results-oriented, and highly adaptive. In general, outstanding leaders are expected to be the role model, have high moral standards, have integrity, and maintain good interpersonal relations. In addition, demonstrated competences to solve critical problems, plan, and communicate are of vital importance. The Confucian values, to coincide with the culturally endorsed leader attributes, place great emphasis on integrity, dependability, trustworthiness, and honesty.

In a high–power distance environment, leaders can carry out positive actions for the entire organization more easily and generally receive fewer challenges. Major decisions are made and carried out in a top-down manner. Charisma is considered as the respect subordinates have for their leaders, who have the power and authority to allocate resources at their own will. Contingent reward is explicit in Hong Kong, and in this respect it is necessary to provide appropriate rewards and incentives for the desirable outcomes. As such, Hong Kong managers are perceived to be more transactional than transformational.

Hong Kong people are pragmatic and realistic. The ability to earn money and create wealth is very important. They hold a down-to-earth view of leadership that concerns performance rather than charisma and responsibility, not just privilege. To this end, there is a strong belief in maintaining harmony. The virtues described in biographies on leadership characteristics, such as courage, authenticity, integrity, vision, passion, conviction, and competence, are not necessarily found in real situations. Leaders can be unwilling to listen to or share information with others, and lead by using power, manipulation, and coercion. Seldom do they inspire trust and confidence in their followers, who in turn are encouraged to serve, sacrifice, and comply. Empowerment and granting ample authority to their subordinates is not very likely to happen in Hong Kong organizations. Employees expect to be treated with dignity and respect, and to participate only in decisions that affect their work life.

Hong Kong is an ideal place where the Western system had been successfully transplanted to Chinese society. Hong Kong people are more individualistic than the other three Chinese societies studied in GLOBE. The Chinese society pays attention to education and knowledge and wisdom are regarded as important virtues. The new generation of leaders are better educated with many of them receiving their education in Western countries. Their management styles represent a blend of Confucian and Western philosophy. They are willing to expend a portion of their effort toward work- or career-oriented activities and improve the individual well-being by enlarging one's personal resources, for example, social ties, education, and professional qualifications. This type of orientation will serve to enhance the career- or work-oriented performance of the Hong Kong Chinese.

REFERENCES

Adler, N. J., Campbell, N., & Laurent, A. (1989). In search of appropriate methodology: From outside the People's Republic of China looking in. *Journal of International Business Studies, 70*(1), 61–74.

Adler, N, J., Docktor, R., & Redding, S. G. (1986). From the Atlantic to the Pacific century: Cross-cultural management revisited. *Journal of Management, 12,* 295–318.

Berger, S., & Lester, R. K. (Eds.). (1997). *Made by Hong Kong.* Hong Kong: Oxford University Press.

Black, J. S., & Porter, L. W. (1991). Managerial behaviors and job performance: A successful manager in Los Angeles may not succeed in Hong Kong. *Journal of International Business Studies, 22*(1), 99–113.

Bond, M. H. (1991). *Beyond the Chinese face: Insights from psychology.* Hong Kong: Oxford University Press.

Bond, M. H. & Hwang, K. (1986). The social psychology of Chinese people. In M. H. Bond (Ed.), *The psychology of the Chinese people* (pp. 213–266). Hong Kong: Oxford University Press.

Bond, M. H., & King, A. Y. C. (1985). Coping with the threat of Westernization in Hong Kong. *International Journal of Intercultural Relations, 9,* 351–364.

Chinese Culture Connection. (1987). Chinese values and the search for culture-free dimensions of culture. *Journal of Cross-Cultural Psychology, 18,* 143–164.

Chua, B., Thomas, H., Au, K., Ahlstrom, D., Law, C., Makino, S., et al. (2002). *Global entrepreneurship monitor: Hong Kong.* Hong Kong: Chinese University of Hong Kong.

Civil Service Personnel Statistics. (1999). *Hong Kong.* Hong Kong: Civil Service Branch, Government Secretariat.

Cragin, J. P. (1986). Management technology absorption in China. In S. R. Clegg, D. C. Dunphy, & S. G. Redding (Eds.), *The enterprise and management in East Asia* (pp. 327–340). Hong Kong: Centre of Asian Studies.

Davies, K. (1996). *Hong Kong after 1997* (Research Report). London: Economist Intelligence Unit.

Department of Census and Statistics, Hong Kong Government. (1999, March). *Hong Kong Monthly Digest of Statistics.* Hong Kong: Author.

Department of Census and Statistics, Hong Kong Government. (2000, March). *Hong Kong Monthly Digest of Statistics.* Hong Kong: Author.

Department of Census and Statistics, Hong Kong Government. (2003, January). *Hong Kong Monthly Digest of Statistics.* Hong Kong: Author.

The Economist Intelligence Unit. *Hong Kong, Country Forecast, 1998.* London: Author.

England, J. (1989). *Industrial relations and law in Hong Kong* (2nd ed.). Hong Kong: Oxford University Press.

Hofstede, G. (1980). *Culture's consequences: International differences in work-related values.* Beverly Hills, CA: Sage.

Hofstede, G., & Bond, M. H. (1988). The Confucius connection: From cultural roots to economic growth. *Organization Dynamics, 16,* 5–21.

Hong Kong Transition Project. Retrieved 2007, from http://www.hkbu.edu.hk/~hktp

House, R. J., Hanges, P. J., Ruiz-Quintanilla, S. A., Dorfman, P. W., Javidan, M., Dickson, M. W., et al. (1999). Cultural influences on leadership and organizations: Project GLOBE. In M. H. Mobley, M. J. Gessner, & V. Armold (Eds.), *Advances in global leadership* (Vol. 1, pp. 171–233). Stamford, CT: JAI.

House, R. J., Hanges, P. J., Javidan, M., Dorfman, P. W., Gupta, V., & GLOBE Associates. (2004). *Cultures, leadership, and organizations: The GLOBE study of 62 societies.* Thousand Oaks, CA: Sage.

Howlctt, B. (Ed.). (1998). *Hong Kong: A new era.* Hong Kong: Information Service Department, Hong Kong SAR Government.

Hughes, R. (1968). *Hong Kong: A borrowed place—borrowed time.* London: Andre Deutsch.

Information Service Department, Hong Kong Government. (1997). *Hong Kong.* Hong Kong: Author.

Information Service Department, Hong Kong Government. (1998). *Hong Kong.* Hong Kong: Author.

Information Service Department, Hong Kong Government. (2000). *Hong Kong.* Hong Kong: Author.

International Institute for Management Development. (1997). *The world competitiveness yearbook.* Lausanne, Switzerland: Author.

International Institute for Management Development. (1998). *The world competitiveness yearbook.* Lausanne, Switzerland: Author.

International Institute for Management Development. (2000). *The world competitiveness yearbook.* Lausanne, Switzerland: Author.

Kahn, H. (1979). *World economic development: 1979 and beyond.* London: Croom Helm.

Kwok, N. W. (2000). *Hong Kong after 1997: The first 1000 days.* Hong Kong: Asian Human Rights Commission.

Lau, S. (1982). *Society and politics in Hong Kong.* Hong Kong: Chinese University Press.

Leader of the year. (1999, February 5). *Hong Kong Standard,* p. 1.

Lee, M. K. (1992). Family and gender issues. In Lau Siu-kai et. al. (Eds.), *Indicators of social development: Hong Kong 1990* (pp. 1–131). Hong Kong: Hong Kong Institute of Asia- Pacific Studies, Chinese University of Hong Kong.

Leung, K. (2002). *Survey on quality of work life of Hong Kong employees.* Paper presented at the 2002 annual conference of the Hong Kong Psychological Society, Hong Kong.

Liu, S. (1997). *An outline history of Hong Kong.* Beijing: Foreign Languages Press.

McGrath, R., MacMillan, R. I., Yang, E., & Tsai, W. (1992). Does culture endure, or is it malleable? Issues for entrepreneurial economic development. *Journal of Business Venturing, 7,* 441–458.

Ngo, H. Y. (2000). Trends in occupational sex segregation in Hong Kong. *International Journal of Human Resource Management, 11*(2), 251–263.

Office of the Telecommunications Authority. (1997/1998). *Trading Fund Report 1997/98.* Hong Kong: Author.

Okechuku, C., & Man, V. Y. W. (1991). Comparison of managerial traits in Canada and Hong Kong. *Asia Pacific Journal of Management, 8*(2), 223–235.

Ralston, D., Gustafson, D., Elsass, P., Cheung, F., & Terpstra, R. (1993). Differences in managerial values: A study of U.S. Hong Kong and PRC managers. *Journal of International Business Studies, 24*(2), 249–275.

Ralston, D., Gustafson, D., and Terpstra, R., Holt, D. H., Cheung, F., & Ribbens, B. A. (1993). The impact of managerial values on decision-making behavior: A comparison of the United States and Hong Kong. *Asia Pacific Journal of Management, 10,* 21–37.

Redding, S. G. (1990). *The spirit of Chinese capitalism.* Berlin: de Gruyter.

Redding, S. G., & Richardson, S. (1986). Participative management and its varying relevance in Hong Kong and Singapore. *Asia Pacific Journal of Management, 3*(2), 76–98.

Redding, S. G., & Wong, G. Y. Y. (1986). The psychology of Chinese organizational behavior. In M. H. Bond (Ed.), *The hand book of Chinese psychology* (pp. 267–295). Hong Kong: Oxford University Press.

Saranow, J. (2001, November). Hong Kong residents use Web to access government data: City leads Asia in utilization of online service. *Asian Wall Street Journal.*

Schermerhorn, J. E., Jr., & Bond, M. H. (1991). Upward and downward influence tactics in managerial networks: A comparative study of Hong Kong Chinese and Americans. *Asia Pacific Journal of Management, 8*(2), 147–158.

Selmer, J. (1996). Expatriate or local bosses? HCN subordinates preferences in leadership behavior. *The International Journal of Human Resources Management, 7*(1), 165–178.

Shamdassani, R. (2002, January 27). School pupils still presented with images of women in outdated domestic roles, study shows. *Sunday Morning Post.*

Shenkar, O., & Ronen R. (1987). Structure and importance of work goals among managers in PRC. *Academy of Management Journal, 29*(1), 9–14.

Silin, R. (1976). *Leadership and values.* Cambridge, MA: Harvard University Press.

Smith, P. B., Misumi, J., Tayeb, M. H., Paterson, M., & Bond, M. H. (1989). On the generality of leadership style across cultures. *Journal of Occupational Psychology, 62,* 97–110.

Tanzer, A. (1997). The global power elite. *Forbes, 160*(2), 98.

Terpstra, R. H., Ralston, D. A., & Bazen, S. (1993). Cultural influences on the risk taking propensity of United States and Hong Kong managers. *International Journal of Management, 10,* 183–193.

Tung, R. L. (1981). Patterns of motivation in Chinese industrial enterprises. *Academy of Management Review, 6*(3), 481–489.

Vines, S. (1998). *Hong Kong: China's new colony.* London: Aurum Press.

von Glinow, M. A., & Teagarden, M. B. (1988). The transfer of human resource management technology in Sino-U.S. cooperative ventures: Problems and solutions. *Human Resource Management, 27,* 201–229.

Westwood, R. I., & Chan, A. (1992). Headship and leadership. In R. I. Westwood (Ed.), *Organizational behavior: Southeast Asia perspectives* (pp. 118–143). Singapore: Longman Group (Far East).

Wonacott, P. (2000, December 13). Hong Kong survey reveals concerns. *The Asian Wall Street Journal.*

Wong, N. (2000). Mark your calendar! Important tasks for International HR. *Workforce, 4,* 72–74.

Wong, S. L. (1997). Hong Kong: Past, present, future. In S.-K. Lau et. al. (Eds.), *Indicators of social development: Hong Kong 1995.* Hong Kong: Institute of Asia Pacific Studies, Chinese University of Hong Kong.

Yeh, R. S. (1989). On Hofstede's treatment of Chinese and Japanese values. *Asian Pacific Journal of Management, 6*(1), 129–160.

Yu, A. B. (1996). Ultimate life concerns, self, and Chinese achievement motivation. In M. Bond (Ed.), *The handbook of Chinese psychology* (pp. 227–246). Hong Kong: Oxford University Press.

Yu, V. (2003, January 30). Hong Kong's consumer confidence lags as mainland's surges. *South China Morning Post,* p. 1.

Appendix

Overview of Financial and Telecommunications Industries

The two industries included in this project were telecommunications and financial services. Both these industries play a vital role in the Hong Kong economy. The financial sector is the single largest sector and telecommunications is one of the fast-growing sectors in Hong Kong.

In 2000, financing, insurance, real estate and business services contributed 23.2%, the second-largest contribution to the gross domestic product (GDP). The share of transport, storage, and communications in the GDP was 10.3%. Regarding the contribution to total employment, the service sector as a whole accounted for about 79% in 2000. Within this total, financing, insurance, real estate, and business services accounted for 13%, whereas transport, storage, and communications accounted for 11.3% (Department of Census and Statistics, Hong Kong Government, 2000).

Telecommunications Industry

Hong Kong has a world-class telecommunications infrastructure that is an important factor in Hong Kong's success as a leading business and financial center. The infrastructure comprises fixed-line telephone companies, mobile-phone services, paging operators, and over 170 value-added service providers offering a wide range of services including facsimile, data communication, Internet access, and so on. Hong Kong serves as Asia's telecommunications hub. Hong Kong is among the world's top-ranked in terms of using video cameras, mobile phones, and the Internet. Hong Kong maintains the highest telecommunications penetration and usage rates in the world as is evident by the portable phone–toting executives conducting business while they eat, drive, and walk. Hong Kong has one of the most modern telecommunications systems in the world.

Since 1925, domestic telephone services in Hong Kong have been provided exclusively by Hong Kong Telephone Co., Ltd. Its franchise expired in 1995. Cable Wireless (Hong Kong) Ltd. has had the exclusive right to handle Hong Kong's international communications services since 1981. The government's policy on telecommunications is to encourage the competitive provision of telecommunications services. Competition is viewed as a mechanism that fosters economic and efficient supply of services and that disciplines supplier behavior such that prices to consumers are fair and reasonable (Office of the Telecommunications Authority, 1997/1998). In order to satisfy demands within the telecommunications industry for greater participation, the industry was deregulated. The deregulation of the telecommunications industry has progressed steadily, with the result of increasing level of competition in the market. Increased competition in telecom forces prices down.

One half of the Hong Kong households installed a PC at home. The penetration of the Internet at home was 73.3% (Department of Census and Statistics, Hong Kong Government, 2003), one of the highest Internet household penetration rates in Asia. Thirty-one percent of

Hong Kong's population has used the Internet to access government information (Saranow, 2001). It leads the rest of Asia in using Internet for accessing information but not for doing business like online transactions. The prevalent use of e-government services is due to the territory's high Internet usage and educated population.

Finance Industry

Hong Kong has emerged as an important international banking and financial center. Eighty-five of the world's top 100 banks are present in Hong Kong. The 6,957 financial institutions employed a total of 127,012 employees (Department of Census and Statistics, Hong Kong Government, 1999). The banking industry in Hong Kong is operating under fierce competition. As a snapshot of the competitive environment, there are 367 authorized financial institutions with 1,485 branches in a small city-state with 6.8 million people. As of April 1998, there were 177 banks; 31 are locally incorporated and the rest are incorporated outside Hong Kong. Hong Kong is thus an important regional financial center. The stock market capitalization ranked 7 in the world, with U.S.$7,449.4 billion. According to the International Institute for Management Development's world competitiveness report (2000), access to local capital market and availability of capital market ranked number two in the world.

26

▼▼▼▼▼▼▼

Culture and Leadership in Singapore: Combination of the East and the West

Ji Li
Hong Kong Baptist University

Phyllisis M. Ngin
National University of Singapore

Albert C. Y. Teo
National University of Singapore

As a newly industrialized economy in Southeast Asia, Singapore stands out as a unique country in terms of culture and leadership style. This uniqueness can be attributed to the influences of both the East and West. In this chapter, we examine Singapore's unique culture based on the results of our recent study, which is a part of the GLOBE research effort. To better understand the results, we first provide a brief discussion regarding Singapore's cultural heritage, and then discuss the environmental factors that have influenced the country's culture and leadership style in recent years. After that, we review past research on leadership style in Singapore. Finally, we report on the findings of our studies and discuss their implications.

1. CULTURAL HERITAGE OF SINGAPORE

Background

At one time, Singapore was a British Crown colony, founded by Sir Stamford Raffles in 1819. It suffered Japanese occupation during World War II and was granted internal self-government status by Britain in 1959. After briefly entering into a federation with Malaysia in 1963, lasting until 1965, Singapore has since existed as an independent country. It has been under the uninterrupted leadership of the People's Action Party, specifically the party's stalwart, Lee Kuan Yew, since 1959.

According to the latest estimates, ethnic Chinese account for 77% of Singapore's population of 3 million and have control over 81% of Singapore's listed companies in terms of market capitalization (see, e.g., C. Tan & Torrington, 1998, p. 471). Over 40% of Singapore's ethnic Chinese can trace their ancestral roots to the Fujian Province, and another 40% to the Guangdong Province. In terms of dialect background, 40% of the Chinese in Singapore are Hokkien, 18% Cantonese, 23% Teochew, 9% are Hakka, 7% Hainanese, and the remainder comprise an assortment of other dialect groups. In terms of language preference, around 20% of the Singaporean Chinese speak English as their preferred language. These tend to be the political, bureaucratic, and professional elite. A further 65% speak English adequately, but prefer to speak in Mandarin or other dialects. The remaining 15% either cannot speak English at all or speak it very poorly (East Asia Analytical Unit, 1995, p. 240).

The Chinese junk traders of the Fujian and Guangdong Provinces had been active in dealing with Southeast Asian countries for several centuries before the actual founding of Singapore. The first arrivals of Chinese to Singapore are known to have come from Malacca. These Malacca-born Chinese were originally attracted to Singapore's free-port status. Chinese emigration to Singapore was largely based on economic pursuits and was an unorganized, individual process, unaided by government although there were instances of indentured labor. Commerce and trade formed the primary basis of business activity among the Singapore Chinese. However, the earlier Singapore economy also needed the knowledge of the English and Malay that had been gained by the earlier Chinese merchants and traders who had arrived from Malacca. These Malacca-born Chinese also knew the habits and commercial procedures of both the European merchants and the natives. They showed great skill and perseverance in their methods of bargaining and haggling over business transactions with the natives, a procedure considered as being demeaning by the European merchants (Selmer, 1997). Finally, the establishment of Singapore as a free port provided traders with an environment to match the motivation and skills of these Singapore Chinese. As Cheng (1985) pointed out:

> In a colonial laissez faire economy based on trade, the Chinese realized that the effective avenue of upward mobility lay in petty trade. This accounts in part for the strong desire of the Chinese to be their own masters in business. The easy entry into petty trade provided the individual Chinese entrepreneur a chance to exercise his talent. It is through petty trade that skills were developed and more capital was accumulated. (p. 102)

Because the ethnic Chinese are the majority population in Singapore, Chinese cultural values have great influence over the culture and leadership styles adopted there. This is especially true in recent years with the emphasis that has been placed on Confucianism by the Singapore government. In the rest of this section, we provide a brief review of Chinese cultural values and discuss their influences on Singapore today.

Chinese Cultural Value and Its Influences

It is easy to see the influences of Chinese cultural value in Singapore today. In other words, notwithstanding the strong influence of the British and other cultures in Southeast Asia, Singapore still manages to maintain much of its Chinese cultural tradition. This is because the majority of Singaporeans come from traditional Chinese family backgrounds, rather than Peranakan backgrounds. For instance, Chinese family and clan associations are prevalent in Singapore. These associations often hold valuable real estate, and function to provide mutual help, loans, and scholarships for the children of its members (Cheng, 1990). Leadership among the Chinese is reflected in the role of clan associations. Nearly all of the traditional Chinese associations have been initiated, controlled, and led by wealthy businesspeople who accordingly have enjoyed high social status and prestige as leaders. This indicates that wealth has always been a very important variable in determining one's social position, particularly during the colonial era. Furthermore, with leadership's link to the association, the association has been turned into an institutional base for those who aspire to become dialect or community leaders. Over the years, a strong conviction about the association leader has been developed among the Chinese; a leader is required to be public spirited, generous, and willing to serve.

An example of a successful clan association is the Ngee Ann Kongsi. It was founded in the 20th century by 12 families who paid $175 for 75 acres of land alongside what is now Singapore's (City) Orchard Road, a major shopping and tourist precinct. The Kongsi subsequently developed Ngee Ann City, Singapore's largest shopping mall, in a joint venture with a Japanese department store. Net revenues from such projects enable clan associations to continue funding schools and other charitable works (Kraar, 1971).

To promote greater coordination and mutual assistance among clan associations, an umbrella organization, the Singapore Federation of Chinese Clan Associations (SFCCA), was formed in 1986. The objectives of the SFCCA, listed next, reflect the determination of Singapore Chinese to maintain their cultural heritage:

- To promote, foster, and encourage better and closer relationship, coordination, cooperation, and understanding among the various Chinese clan associations in Singapore.
- To promote, organize, or finance educational, cultural, social, and other activities for greater awareness, understanding, and appreciation of the Chinese language, culture, and traditions.
- To encourage, finance, or undertake research related to the Chinese language, culture, and traditions.
- To promote better relationships, understanding, and cooperation between the SFCCA and other organizations in the public and private sectors.
- To organize, participate, or help in community and welfare services.
- To promote and protect the interests and welfare of its members.
- To do all such other things as are incidental or conducive to the aforementioned objectives.

It should be pointed out that the Chinese cultural values in Singapore differ, in some aspects, from those values in mainland China. For example, the traditional Chinese culture reflected heavily on the philosophy of Confucius, which emphasized the importance of farming rather than business. Businesspeople were considered the lowest in the social hierarchy, below officials (intellectuals), farmers, and workers (Creel, 1953). The early Chinese cultural value in Singapore, on the other hand, valued entrepreneurs' spirit and encouraged the setting up of businesses, especially family-run businesses (e.g., Godley, 1981; Hicks, 1993). These differences can be attributed to the history of the ethnic Chinese in Singapore. As it was mentioned earlier, some of the Chinese came to Singapore as traders, and some were brought into Singapore in the 19th century as indentured labor. After paying off their bonds, many of these laborers also set up their own businesses. With the development of the Malay Peninsula as a major tin- and rubber-producing region at the beginning of the 20th century, a major business activity of these Chinese became that of purchasing goods from Malaysia and Indonesia, and then selling them to European or American importers. An outcome of this trading activity was the development of the "traders' mentality" (i.e., a preference for short-term measures and quick profits), which is acknowledged to still persist in Singapore society today (Cheong, 1991).

Finally, we should note that an important part of Singapore's cultural heritage is the culture of the Straits Chinese or Peranakans. Peranakans are a distinct ethnic group peculiar to Singapore and parts of Malaysia, who can trace their ancestry to both ethnic Chinese and Malays. Their unique culture is an eclecticism of Chinese, Malay, and English cultural elements. Many of Singapore's first-generation political leaders came from this British-educated Peranakan elite (including the country's most influential leader, Lee Kuan Yew, ex-Deputy Prime Minister Goh Keng Swee, and ex-Cabinet Minister Lim Kim San). Along with the British during the colonial period, these first-generation leaders formed many of the institutions that made Singapore what it is today (East Asia Analytical Unit, 1995). For example, these leaders built a British-style public administration (albeit with increasing Confucian characteristics in recent years) rather than a traditional Chinese structure.

In summary, the cultural heritage of Singapore reflects values of both the East and the West. This heritage has had a strong influence on the formation of the country's culture and leadership style. Further discussion on this issue is provided in other parts of this chapter.

2. ENVIRONMENTAL FACTORS INFLUENCING CULTURAL VALUES AND LEADERSHIP IN SINGAPORE

In this section, we focus on two environmental factors that have had a major effect on the development of culture and leadership style in Singapore. One factor is the presence of a large number of foreign firms; the other is the heavy involvement of the government in all aspects of the country's social life.

Role of Foreign Firms in Singapore

One important environmental factor in Singapore is the preeminence of foreign firms in the country's economy. In this island nation comprising only 650 square km in territory, the industrialization process began in the early 1960s with an import substituting thrust. This thrust was intensified during the 2-year federation with Malaysia. However, by the late 1960s, it was apparent that the import substitution strategy (greatly limited by the small size of the domestic market) was not working (Cheong, 1991).

The Singapore government then decided to shift to an export-oriented focus. Specifically, the government implemented trade liberalization policies and introduced export subsidies to equalize incentives across different activities and to ensure that domestic producers competed on equal terms with foreign firms. Additional export promotion measures, such as the development of overseas marketing services, were also undertaken by the government (Tay, 1986). Most import duties had been set at 5% since 1981, and in 1988 the last quota (on air conditioners) was removed, making Singapore practically a free-trade economy.

The government also changed its foreign investment policies to encourage foreign direct investment (FDI). For example, tax incentives to encourage FDI were introduced in 1967 and extended later. This encouragement of foreign investment, particularly that of multinational corporations (MNCs), enabled Singapore to combine local productive factors with foreign technical and managerial know-how, and to overcome local producers' lack of knowledge or information about world markets.

The shift in trade and foreign investment policies in Singapore was accompanied by labor law revisions, introduced with the explicit intent of enhancing the attractiveness of Singapore to foreign investors. Legislation enacted in 1969 lengthened the standard workweek; reduced the number of holidays; placed various restrictions on the payment of retirement benefits, paid leave, overtime, and bonuses; limited unions' ability to represent managerial or executive employees; exempted promotions, transfers, firings, and work assignments from collective bargaining; and lengthened the minimum and maximum durations of labor contracts (Haggard, 1990).

Over the years, the presence of foreign companies in the Singapore economy has steadily increased. This is especially true in manufacturing, where foreign firms regularly account for more than 80% of net investment. By 1984, for instance, foreign companies (defined as firms with more than 50% foreign equity) produced 71% of Singapore's total output, and accounted for 63% of value added and 82% of manufactured exports (A. T. Koh, 1987). Other sectors of the Singapore economy, such as finance and banking, are similarly dominated by foreign firms (East Asia Analytical Unit, 1995).

The operations of these foreign firms in Singapore have had a major effect on the country's culture and leadership style. Most of these MNCs come from the Organization of Economic Cooperation and Development (OECD) countries, particularly the United States,

Japan, and the European Union. As each MNC is given a free hand in developing its management system, Singapore has acquired a wide selection of advanced management systems, developed and tested in different parts of the world. For instance, American management systems and Japanese corporate philosophies have been effectively implemented in the Singapore context (Tan & Torrington, 1998).

According to Cheong (1991), a typical American subsidiary in Singapore usually prepares a long- term plan for about a 3- to 5-years duration. The planning process involves all levels of managerial, technical, and supervisory personnel. The plans are generally concentrated in the areas of products, pricing, personnel selection and development, salary standards, and plant investment. American subsidiaries in Singapore typically pay good wages to their local employees and give them sufficient training and business exposure so that they can assume very senior management positions. The chief executive officers (CEOs) of Hewlett Packard and National Semiconductor, for example, are local employees, trained and promoted from within their respective organizations. In general, the manpower management policies in a typical American subsidiary in Singapore are fairly well structured. Human resource management techniques, such as job evaluation, promotion criteria for managerial and technical personnel, and training programs, are frequently employed. The training grants provided by the government- administered Skills Development Fund (SDF) have enabled the American companies to have long-term training programs for the development of their employees.

As for the Japanese companies, they have promoted the value of teamwork or Japanese-style collectivism by setting up Quality Circles (QCs). Surveys done by the National Productivity Board show that QCs have improved teamwork both among workers and between workers and management. The activities of QCs also help increase employee morale and change the leadership style in Singapore from autocratic to more participative. Moreover, the subsidiaries of Japanese MNCs also encourage a leadership style that helps promote harmonious labor–management relations. This style is often characterized by management spending more time with the local staff, especially after office hours, through company dinners or after-dinner visits to bars and pubs.

Effects of Heavy Government Involvement

Another important characteristic in the environment of Singapore is the heavy involvement of the government in the economy and other aspects of social life. This heavy government involvement makes Singapore different from other Chinese communities with a similar economic development, such as Hong Kong and Taiwan. For instance, only in Singapore can one see such powerful government organizations as the Economic Development Board (EDB) and the Trade Development Board (TDB). The government has either direct or indirect control over all the major local banks. For example, the largest local bank, the Development Bank of Singapore (DBS), is a well-known government-linked bank.

This issue is best discussed and understood by doing a comparison of Singapore with another country such as Hong Kong. Both entities are island cities, with ethnic Chinese representing the majority of their society. Both cities also share historic similarities. They were both former British colonies and were occupied by the Japanese during World War II. Additionally, the two cities possess similar levels of technological and economical development. Nevertheless, these two Chinese communities differ immensely in governance, specifically with regard to government involvement in business and other aspects of social life.

In Hong Kong, the government has always adopted a laissez-faire approach to the economy (see, e.g., East Asia Analytical Unit, 1995). There also exists a very low level of government control and involvement in business. Government policies have created an environment that thus allows the survival of a substantial number of small and medium-size firms in Hong Kong's manufacturing industry (East Asia Analytical Unit, 1995). The small size of the firms and the free-market environment favor risk taking and entrepreneurship. In Singapore, on the other hand, there has been heavy government involvement in business since the country's independence. For example, the Singapore government often gets involved in the mergers of local companies, including taxi companies, high-tech firms, or banks. Consequently, the Singapore economy is now dominated by two groups of large companies: the MNCs, of which there are some 7,000 in the country, and the government-linked companies, which have penetrated almost all industries in Singapore, from taxi operations to newspaper publication.

The Singapore government not only maintains a heavy economic presence, but also makes individuals in the country much more dependent on the government, compared to Hong Kong. For example, the people in Singapore depend on the government for housing, low-cost medical service, and pension (i.e., the Central Provident Fund). This dependence has become so significant that, in recent years, even the Singapore government leaders have begun to worry. Recently, a senior government official referred to Singaporeans as "flowers in a greenhouse," who are unable to survive without the greenhouse (*Lianhe Zaobao,* July 8, 1997, p. 11).

One direct consequence of this heavy government involvement is an increase in Uncertainty Avoidance, a cultural value first identified by Hofstede (1980). When Hofstede studied the cultures in Asian countries in the 1970s, he found that all Chinese communities included in his study (such as Hong Kong, Singapore, and Taiwan) had low Uncertainty Avoidance (UA) values. Hofstede and Bond (1988, p. 17) subsequently linked this low UA to what they called East Asian entrepreneurship. Similar findings have been obtained by other studies using historical data and observations (e.g., Godley, 1981). This explains why, historically, there was little need for any government to encourage entrepreneurial activity among ethnic Chinese.

Interestingly, in the 1990s, the Singapore government had to make great efforts to encourage entrepreneurship in the country. In fact, as early as 1986, the government had already detected the decline of entrepreneurship in Singapore society. That year, a special government committee, headed by Lee Hsien Loong, then minister of state for defense and trade & industry and currently deputy prime minister, was formed to study this decline. In its report to the government, the committee pointed out that: *"Entrepreneurship has historically been a key ingredient in the economic success story of Singapore. As Singapore progressed from its entrepot role to that of a low cost export oriented assembly centre, and recently to that of a high tech manufacturing and services centre, the significance and impact of local entrepreneurship in the private sector gradually declined in relative terms"* (Lee, 1985, p. 1).

In the report, the committee attributed the decline of entrepreneurship in Singapore mainly as a result of economic and technological development. In doing so, the committee failed to consider an important fact: High-tech manufacturing, service industries, and/or socioeconomic development have not led to less entrepreneurship in other societies. For instance, Hong Kong and Taiwan, which have similar conditions to those in Singapore, have shown no decline in entrepreneurship. Neither has the United States, with its highly developed high-tech and service industries. Having failed to understand the real cause of declining entrepreneurship in Singapore, this committee could not really propose effective measures to address the issue. As a result, lack of entrepreneurship remained a problem in Singapore's economic development.

In the early 1990s, while Hong Kong and Taiwanese firms aggressively invested in China and other Asian emerging markets, Singapore firms remained reluctant to venture abroad, suggesting little improvement in entrepreneurial spirit. In response, the Singapore government formed another special committee in 1993 aimed at studying how Singapore enterprises can be promoted overseas (Ministry of Finance, 1993). In its report to the government, the committee commented:

> As we seek to encourage Singapore companies to venture abroad, the local enterprise sector takes on a greater significance as we need to depend on our home grown enterprises, and our home grown entrepreneurs to lead the way. But some have argued that our companies are not sufficiently well developed to compete abroad, as compared to those from the developed countries, or Hong Kong and Taiwan, and that Singaporeans are generally risk averse, preferring to take safe professional and managerial jobs rather than to strike out on their own. (Ministry of Finance, 1993, p. 31)

Once again, the committee failed to identify the root of the problem. In explaining the lack of entrepreneurial spirit in Singapore, the committee simply said that:

> Economic success has brought about even higher expectations of success, but it has also brought the expectation that progress and growth is assured. It has brought about a desire for more possessions, but also a reluctance to risk what we already have. There also appears to be a common perception amongst younger Singaporeans that to be successful, it is only necessary to do well in school, graduate with a good degree or diploma, and then join a large local or foreign company to get onto the escalator of stable jobs, ever growing wages, and good future prospects. We need to correct this misconception. (Ministry of Finance, 1993, p. 34)

Without identifying the real cause of declining entrepreneurial spirit, the Singapore government has made little progress in encouraging entrepreneurship. Recent empirical observation and academic research support this assertion. For example, Yeo's (1997) research showed that, among managers in manufacturing industries, those from Singapore have significantly higher Uncertainty Avoidance scores compared to their counterparts in Hong Kong and Taiwan. More significantly, studies on the actual behavior of Singapore firms also showed a strong risk avoidance tendency. A recent study conducted by the Singapore Chartered Institute of Marketing (C. Tan, 1997), which examined over 150 companies, found that local Singapore firms are reluctant to invest in other countries even though limited local markets and resources constitute serious impediments to a firms survival and growth. The study also found that only 40% of local firms in Singapore have plans to expand to other countries in Asia the following year. This low percentage contrasts with the 70% of Western MNCs with regional headquarters in Singapore, and the 80% of MNCs from other Asian countries with regional headquarters in Singapore.

Among Singapore firms that do conduct business in foreign markets, they tend to adopt a different approach than their Hong Kong and Taiwanese counterparts. In China, for example, whereas the firms from Hong Kong and Taiwan rely mainly on their kinship and friendship networks in China, the majority of Singapore firms rely on the networks built by the government. In other words, regardless of business opportunities, Singapore investors prefer to go into those Chinese cities where their government has already established relations with the local governments. The reason is that this approach involves lower risks. As a group of Australian government researchers observed:

> Despite 80% of Singapore's Chinese having ancestral origins in either Guangdong or Fujian Provinces, only 24.1% of recently announced projects are in either province. Very few Singaporeans have ancestral origins in Jiangsu or Hebei Provinces and yet 45.1% of recent projects are there. Thus, Singapore might well be a "gateway to China" for Western investors, but the means of access will usually not be traditional Chinese networks. (East Asia Analytical Unit, 1995, p. 240)

Singapore government officials are aware of this problem and have expressed their concern. For example, some government officials such as Ow Chin Hock, the secretary of state for foreign affairs, have argued that Singaporeans should learn from Hong Kong and Taiwanese entrepreneurs and adopt a more aggressive and higher risk-taking strategy in their foreign ventures. His views were published in a major Singapore newspaper, *Lianhe Zaobao* (July 8, 1997, p. 11). These views highlight a prevalent mind-set that pervades much of Singapore society today: *kiasuism,* the fear of failure or of losing out to others. Kiasuism is derived from the word, *kiasu,* in the Hokkien dialect (which is equivalent to the term pa(4) shu(1) in the Mandarin dialect). According to Singapore government officials, the negative consequence of *kiasuism* is the lack of creativity and entrepreneurial spirit among Singaporeans. In fact, there has been support among empirical studies for a partial relationship between government involvement and the level of Uncertainty Avoidance in any society. According to the data collected by Hofstede (1980), among industrialized countries, societies with high degrees of government involvement in the economy and with well-developed social welfare systems (e.g., France and North European countries) tend to register high values of Uncertainty Avoidance. On the other hand, societies with low levels of government involvement in the economy and with less developed social welfare systems (e.g., the United States) generally have low Uncertainty Avoidance scores. Thus, if a government adopts extensive social welfare policies, people in that society will enjoy a high level of certainty from childhood, and will grow up feeling less comfortable with uncertainty and risk. As a result, the culture in that society will move toward the direction of high Uncertainty Avoidance.

In summary, the cultural values and leadership style in Singapore can be influenced by many environmental factors. Among them, two factors, according to past research and empirical observations, may have the most important effect. One of these two factors is the influence

TABLE 26.1

Ranks and Scores of Societal Cultural Dimensions In Singapore

Dimension	"As Is"		"Should Be"	
	Rank	Score	Rank	Score
Future Orientation	1	5.07	22	5.51
Performance Orientation	2	4.90	48	5.72
Uncertainty Avoidance	3	5.31	46	4.22
Institutional Collectivism	4	4.90	37	4.55
Gender Egalitarianism	11	3.70	36	4.51
In-Group Collectivism	17	5.64	40	5.50
Assertiveness	28	4.17	12	4.41
Power Distance	42	4.99	14	3.04
Human Orientation	55	3.49	3	5.79

Note. Dimensions are listed from highest to lowest "As Is" rank (out of 61 GLOBE countries).

of Western MNEs operating in Singapore; the other is the influence of the Singapore government since the independence of the country. In the rest of this chapter, we report on the GLOBE studies about societal cultural practices, values, and leadership style in Singapore.

3. RESEARCH FINDINGS ON SOCIETAL CULTURE IN SINGAPORE

In this section, we report the results of the GLOBE questionnaire survey (cf. House et al., 2004), which was used to evaluate societal culture practices ("As Is") and values ("Should Be") in Singapore. GLOBE results about leadership concepts held in Singapore are reported in the next section.

Respondents.   The respondents were middle managers working in two Singapore industries: the food industry and the finance and banking industry. After reading a letter inviting them to take part in this study, 217 managers (i.e., 113 women and 104 men) agreed to participate. Eighty-three managers responded to the GLOBE questionnaire dealing with societal culture; the remaining 134 managers (58 and 76 managers from the food and banking industries, respectively) responded to the GLOBE questionnaire about organizational culture.

All the subjects who participated in this study were ethnic Chinese. The mean age of these managers was 36 years. On average, they had about 16 years of work experience and 11 years of management experience. The average number of subordinates for each manager was 23 persons, indicating that they were mainly middle managers.

Results

Table 26.1 reports the cultural values in Singapore's society and their rankings among the 61 countries sampled in the GLOBE project.

Uncertainty Avoidance.   On "what things are" of this cultural dimension, Singapore is ranked third (see Table 26.1, "As Is" section) among 61 countries sampled. Its score on this dimension is lower than only two of those north European countries, Switzerland and

Sweden. In fact, among the top eight countries on this dimension, Singapore is the only Asian society. All the others are north or west European countries (i.e., Switzerland, Sweden, Denmark, Germany, Finland, and Austria), which typically have the best social welfare and security systems in the world. Therefore, on this particular dimension of societal culture, Singapore seems to have become very similar to these European "welfare" states. This finding seems to support our argument that the more a government gets involved in the social lives of its citizens, and the better this government takes care of its citizens, the higher the societal value of Uncertainty Avoidance. As for the other Chinese societies, China's higher rank of 9, compared with the lower ranks for Hong Kong and Taiwan (ranks of 20 and 19, respectively), is also consistent with this argument.

However, on the "Should Be" of this cultural dimension, the score from Singapore is much lower. This seems to reflect the effect of education campaigns by the Singapore government in recent years. As was suggested earlier, the Singapore government has been making great efforts recently to encourage people to go regional/international, to overcome the psychology of fearing failure, and to learn from successful entrepreneurs at home and abroad. Therefore, Singapore managers seem to agree that the culture in their society should have less Uncertainty Avoidance.

Gender Egalitarianism.   For the societal cultural practices ("As Is") on this cultural dimension, Singapore (Score 3.70, Rank 11, see Table 26.1) is much less male dominated than Hong Kong (Rank 40), China (Rank 58), and Taiwan (Rank 52). On the dimension of "Should Be," Singapore managers Score 4.51 (Rank 36), which is still higher than their counterparts indicate in China (Rank 58) or Taiwan (52). Knowing that in the GLOBE sample of 61 countries, the overall trend is toward more Gender Egalitarianism "Should Be," it would be interesting to investigate why Singapore managers' societal cultural values in terms of Gender Egalitarianism score go up (from 3.70 to 4.51) but in terms of the worldwide ranking it goes down (from Rank 11 to Rank 36).

Future Orientation.   The Future Orientation score given by the Singapore respondents shows that the current societal culture in Singapore is very future oriented (Rank 1). This high score can at least partially be attributed to the Singapore government's practice of making "unpopular" but far-sighted decisions. However, it is interesting to note that, on the dimension's "Should Be," Singapore's score was lower (Rank 22). This lower score seems to suggest that the Singapore respondents may want to see less Future Orientation in their societal culture.

Power Distance.   Again, on this cultural value, Singapore (Rank 42) is very similar to Hong Kong (Rank 43). Interestingly, in respect to this dimension of culture, all four Chinese communities are very similar, with China ranking 41 and Taiwan ranking 32. However, on the "Should Be" dimension all four Chinese communities show similar desires to have less power stratification in their societal culture, which is also apparent in nearly all 61 GLOBE countries.

Institutional Collectivism.   On the dimension of Institutional Collectivism, Singapore is ranked fourth, while Japan is third and China is seventh. In contrast, Hong Kong, Taiwan, and the United States are ranked lower. These observations are consistent with recent findings by other researchers. In the case of Singapore, the government has been instrumental in cultivating a greater degree of collectivism. For example, Singapore's prime minister, Goh Chok Tong, recently urged young Singaporeans to turn away from Western materialism and Western-styled democracy (see, e.g., "Singapore: West-Bashing," 1994), which are closely related to Western individualism. Recent studies confirm that a high collectivistic value does exist among Singaporeans (e.g., Chew & Putti, 1995; Yeo, 1997). In fact, Chew and Putti's study found that Singapore managers value collectivism even more than their Japanese counterparts. In contrast, the societal cultures in Hong Kong and Taiwan seem to be moving toward the direction of Western individualism (e.g., McGrath, MacMillan, Yang, & Tsai, 1992; Westwood & Posner, 1997; Yang, 1986, 1991; Yeh, 1988; Yeh & Lawrence, 1995; Yeo, 1997). Finally, on the "Should Be" Institutional Collectivism dimension, Singaporean's do show a desire to have less collectivism (Rank 37) or more individualism. This seems to be consistent with the fact that many Western-educated Singapore professionals emigrated to the West in recent years. Many middle managers included in the study were also young professionals who received their education in the West. Therefore, they show the same tendency to prefer less collectivism.

Humane Orientation. Singapore's score on "As Is" of this cultural value was very low among the other countries included in this study (Rank 55). Singapore's score is also lower than the scores of other Chinese communities. This seems to reflect some of the dimensions of reality in Singapore society today. Compared with the majority of countries in the world, Singapore society has a high degree of control on individual behaviors. Moreover, many rules adopted by British colonists, such as punishment with a cane, remain unchanged.

On the other hand, with a very high score in "Should Be" (Rank 3), respondents indicated that Humane Orientation should be much higher in its culture. This is consistent with the situations in other Chinese communities. We believe that this desire to have more Humane Orientation also reflects the influence of modern civilization from the West.

Performance Orientation. On the dimension of "As Is," Singapore's score on Performance Orientation is high, ranking second among all of the countries tested in the GLOBE project. Here again, Singapore and Hong Kong had very similar scores whereas China and Taiwan had lower ones.

These scores seem to indicate that the society in Singapore stressed performance or achievements as much as that in Hong Kong. However, stressing performance or achievement might not mean risk taking. According to the scores on both Uncertainty Avoidance and Performance Orientation, it seems arguable that the Singapore culture stresses performance but not risk taking.

On the other hand, the culture in Hong Kong stresses Performance Orientation as well as risk taking. On the "Should Be" dimension, the absolute score from Singapore in respect of Performance Orientation is even higher (5.72). However, the score ranks only 48th among all of the GLOBE countries tested. Almost all of the countries seem to believe that there should be more Performance Orientation in their societal cultures. This is also true for Singapore although the "Should Be" score is comparatively low.

In-Group Collectivism. Whereas institutional collectivism refers to the degree to which individuals are encouraged by societal institutions to be integrated into broader entities (e.g. the government), In-Group Collectivism refers to the extent to which members of a society take pride in membership in small groups such as their family and circle of close friends, and the organizations and units in which they are employed. Singapore's score (Rank 17) on this value is the second highest among the four Chinese communities. Several studies have found that as Hong Kong, Singapore, and Taiwan become industrialized, the traditional Chinese family value is decreasing in these societies (e.g., Westwood & Posner, 1997; Yang, 1986, 1991; Yeh, 1988; Yeo, 1997). Singapore's score on this cultural value may be higher than those from other Chinese societies due to the efforts by the Singapore government to cultivate family value and Confucian philosophy in recent years. For example, in 1999, the Singapore government launched the Singapore 21 Committee with a purpose to strengthen the "heartware" of Singapore in the 21st century. "Heartware" refers to the intangibles of society such as social cohesion, political stability, and the collective will, values, and attitudes of a people (cf., "Co-opt People," 1999). After talking to 6,000 Singaporeans from all walks of life, to help the country navigate the challenges of the new millennium, five key ideas evolved that form a vision for the future. One of these ideas is the importance of the family; that is, "Strong families are our foundation."

However, in terms of "Should Be," middle managers from all four Chinese communities seem to prefer less In-Group Collectivism (Rank 40). This seems to be the result of fast economic development and the improvement of living standards in these societies.

Interestingly, this value in the United States and Japan seems to be changing in the opposite direction. Although these two developed societies reported low scores on "As Is," the managers from these countries indicated that they prefer more In-Group Collectivism in their culture.

In summary, in terms of societal culture, Singapore has been influenced by values from both the East and the West. Specifically, compared with other cultures in the "As Is" part of the testing, the Singapore subjects have been found to have high scores on the dimensions of Uncertainty Avoidance and Future Individualism/Collectivism, and low scores on the dimension of Humane Orientation. Also, the Singapore respondents are often similar to their counterparts from Hong Kong on such dimensions as gender differentiation and others. On the other hand, compared with other cultures in the "Should Be" part of the testing, the Singapore respondents score high on only one dimension, that is, Humane Orientation (Rank 3), and medium to high on Power Distance "Should Be" (Rank 13), Assertiveness "Should Be" (Rank 14), and Future Orientation "Should Be" (Rank 22).

As a follow-up study, it would be interesting to examine the process in which these influences have taken place and to explain why certain values have become more salient/less salient. It seems that the two environmental factors that we mentioned earlier (i.e., the dominance of Western MNCs in Singapore's economy and the heavy involvement of the Singapore government in all aspects of social life) have much to do with the direction of malleability of societal culture in Singapore.

4. RESEARCH FINDINGS ON LEADERSHIP STYLE IN SINGAPORE

In this section, we discuss leadership research in Singapore and report the results of three studies, (a) focus group interviews, (b) media analysis, and (c) the GLOBE questionnaire study, each of which is focused on leadership style in Singapore. These studies were conducted during the period of 1994–1996.

Past Research

Influenced by the same cultural heritage and environmental factors, one can also observe a process of malleability in Singapore's leadership style. Some earlier studies suggested that management practices among the local Chinese companies were poorly developed, and that the traditional leadership style could best be characterized as paternalistic autocratic (see, e.g., Cheong, 1991). In other words, traditional Singapore managers or leaders typically made decisions promptly, ordered their subordinates to take certain actions (without sufficiently explaining the rationale behind those actions), and expected their subordinates to comply regardless of the correctness of those actions. Although these traditional Singapore leaders showed little respect for the opinions of their subordinates, they tried hard to make all their employees feel that they were members of a large extended family. Not surprisingly, these leaders could be found visiting employees or their family members when they were ill, and often subsidizing their medical expenses (Cheong, 1991).

According to Hofstede (1980), such a paternalistic autocratic leadership style tends to be favored in all large–Power Distance societies in Asia (Hofstede, 1980). Some other researchers have tried to explain this observation in the context of Singapore. For instance, it has been argued that the large Power Distance in Singapore's culture could be attributed to the autocratic rule of British and Japanese governors before the independence of Singapore (Yeh, 1988).

Following the influx of direct foreign investment into Singapore in the 1970s, more advanced management practices were gradually introduced. With American, Japanese, German, French, and British MNCs being the major investors in Singapore, new cultural values and leadership styles were introduced to Singaporeans. These new styles and practices subsequently influenced the behaviors of local managers or leaders.

Several studies reflect the changes in leadership style in Singapore over the recent years. For example, Chew and Putti (1995) interviewed Chinese managers in Singapore firms and found that these managers "generally emphasize the total welfare of their staff by understanding as well as explaining to and cultivating their staff" (p. 1167). These managers preferred talking to their subordinates and maintained a "relatively small Power Distance" (p. 1167). A study by Koh, W. L. Steers, and Terborg (1995) examined transformational leadership in Singapore schools, and concluded that the transformational leadership style of school managers predicted the satisfaction of their subordinates (i.e., the teachers).

In spite of the aforementioned studies, our understanding of culture and leadership style in Singapore is still not sufficient. Several issues need to be addressed further. First, past study results often contradict each other. It is hard to decide which result is more reliable and defendable. For example, some studies indicated that the societal culture in Singapore is characterized by low Uncertainty Avoidance, but some suggested that the Singapore society emphasizes high Uncertainty Avoidance (Yeo, 1997). The same is true on the issue of paternalism. Whereas some authors suggested that the leadership style in Singapore could be characterized as paternalistic autocratic (e.g., Cheong, 1991), others may imply that, in recent years, the employer–employee relationship is becoming more business like than family oriented (e.g., Yeo, 1997). Second, past research relied on questionnaire survey only. Other research methods, such as focus group interviews and media analysis, have never been adopted in studying cultural and leadership issues in Singapore. It is still not clear whether the results from studies with different methods can converge. Finally, few empirical studies tested culture together with leadership styles at both the societal and the organizational level. It remains a question as to whether and how cultures influence leadership styles in a society. To address these issues, we conducted, as part of the GLOBE research project, empirical studies on culture and leadership styles in two main industries in Singapore (food processing and financial services). Our results show some interesting consistencies with the results of past research as reported previously. In the following sections, we first report on the results of the media analyses and focus group interviews in the first part of the research methods portion of the chapter. We follow that with a report on the results of a large-scale questionnaire survey.

Study 1: Focus Group Interviews

From 1994 to 1997, we conducted four focus group interviews with middle managers from both the banking and food industry sectors in Singapore. The purpose of these interviews was to identify the cultural values and preferred leadership styles among managers and leaders. In total, 21 participants took part in these interviews: 9 were female managers; those remaining were male managers. The average age of participants was 32 years, average work experience 13 years, and finally, their average education was 11 years.

We asked all participants to respond to two questions: (a) What are the qualities of a capable leader? And (b) What are the qualities of an outstanding leader? Following is a summary of their opinions.

The Quality of a Capable Leader.   There are different opinions on what should be the quality of a capable leader. When asked to provide an example about a capable leader, the majority of the participants seemed to agree that some of the business leaders in Singapore, such as some well-known bankers or leaders in the subjects' own corporations, could be seen as capable leaders. The qualities of these leaders were mainly hardworking, knowing how to identify and capitalize on opportunities, and overcoming great difficulties to achieve great successes in their businesses. Interestingly, no female business leader was mentioned by the subjects in these interviews.

Some of the participants mentioned student leaders whom they had remembered in their high schools or universities. The qualities of these leaders, according to participants, were the knowing of how to organize people in activities, and being able to overcome difficulties and, get things done.

One participant considered the former Chinese premier, Zhou Enlai, as a capable leader; the major quality of this leader being said to be "the ability to get things done." The participant did however obtain her information mainly from books and newspapers.. It should be pointed out that no Western leaders were mentioned in these interviews; neither were any military leaders, be they from the West or the East.

The Quality of Outstanding Leaders.   The majority of the participants in the interviews believed that the founder and leader of the Republic of Singapore, Lee Kuan Yew, should be considered as an outstanding leader. The qualities of an outstanding leader, according to these participants, included being visionary, making unpopular but farsighted decisions, and overcoming great difficulties to achieve success. Two of the participants pointed out that they themselves did not favor or support some of the decisions made by Lee Kuan Yew in the past. Some even believed that he had previously being doing something wrong against the interests of the Chinese community in Singapore. However, seeing the success of Singapore in the past decades, these subjects now believed that Lee Kuan Yew was in fact doing the right thing.

It is interesting to note that none of the participants, in spite of their ethnic Chinese background, discussed the moral quality of the leaders. Confucian philosophy stresses the moral quality of a leader. If these Chinese participants are heavily influenced by Confucianism, they should have more or less discussed the moral quality of the leaders in the interviews. The fact that moral quality was not even mentioned seems to suggest that the

Singapore middle managers are less influenced by traditional Chinese values, such as those from Confucianism.

Study 2: Media Analysis

In this report, we discuss the media analysis in three parts: (a) the selection of the media; (b) the coding of stories, and (c) results and implications.

Selection of the Media.   We selected three printed media sources for this analysis. One is the largest local English newspaper in terms of circulation, the *Strait Times.* Another is a government publication by Singapore's Information Ministry, the *Singapore Bulletin.* Finally, the third publication is a magazine targeting the business community, the *Singapore Business Review.* Considering the fact that Singapore is a small country with less than 4 million people and few newspapers and magazines, we believed that the number of publications included in this media analysis was sufficient.

Two time periods of the newspaper were selected. One was between mid-October and mid-November 1998. The other was between mid-December and mid-January 1999. For the newspaper in these two periods, we covered all the major sections including politics, foreign affairs, economy, sports, and society.

For the magazines, we covered eight issues from February to September 1998. These issues were read from cover to cover to identify stories about leaders' behavior and activities.

The Coding of Stories.   An instrument for data coding was developed based on the GLOBE pilot leadership survey and the methods described in the Australian and Indian GLOBE chapters (chaps. 9 and 27, this volume). Specifically, this instrument consisted of 50 dimensions of leader behaviors or activities, such as "aggressive," "objective," or "live a simple life." Among these 50 dimensions, 16 were from the GLOBE pilot leadership survey (cf. Hanges & Dickson, 2004, p. 127). Others were developed based on the findings of the two pilot studies mentioned previously.

Two student research assistants (research students at Master level) were employed to code the stories from the aforementioned publications. Training was provided by asking the research assistants to practice coding several sample stories together with the first author of this chapter. For example, if a leader in a story was reported to get things done effectively, the activity would be coded as "capable." If a leader was proposing reform or changes, the coding would be "change oriented." Finally, if a leader was praised for doing or proposing something because of a certain value, we would code the leader's behavior as "value driven."

After the training, we requested the research assistants read stories in the three publications together, and code all the discussions about leaders' activities and behaviors. If there was any disagreement, these research assistants would first discuss the discrepancy and then reach a consensus between them. The first author of this article would get involved if these student assistants could not reach an agreement on a certain coding decision.

Results of Media Analysis.   In total, 57 stories about leaders' behavior or activities were found. Out of these stories, 29 of them were about business leaders (50%), 18 of them were about political leaders (32%), and the rest were about leaders in other areas, such as leaders in the military or in sports (18%).

Table 26.2 presents the information about the characteristics of these Singapore leaders. The most frequently praised characteristics of the leaders are, visionary (51 times), confident

TABLE 26.2
Results of Media Analysis

Leadership Characteristics	Rank	No. of Times Raised	Percentage
Visionary	1	51	13.08
Confident	2	45	11.54
Objective	3	35	8.97
Considerate	4	27	6.92
Capable (competent)	5	24	6.15
Change oriented	6	23	5.90
Open to learning	7	20	5.13
Understanding	8	18	4.62
Competitive	9	18	4.62
Charismatic	10	15	3.85
Dependable	11	15	3.85
Cooperative	12	10	2.56
Decisive/Value-driven	13	9	2* 2.31
Face saving	15	8	2.05
Determined/Inspirational	16	7	2* 1.79
Directive/Energetic/Entrepreneurial	18	6	3* 1.54
Self-Sacrificing	21	5	1.28
Humane	22	4	1.03
Impartial	23	4	1.03
Live a life sample/Modest / Self-Observed/Collectivistic	24	3	4* 1.03
Relying on followers/Relationship oriented/Democratic	28	2	3* 0.51
Procedural/Diplomatic	31	1	2* 0.26
Autocratic/Aggressive/Status-conscious/Bureaucratic/Devoted/ Action-oriented/Performance-oriented/Control-oriented/Individualistic	33–39	0	8* 0.00

(45 times), objective (35 times), considerate (25 times), capable (competent) (24 times), change oriented (23 times), and open to learning (20 times).

The results of this media analysis are largely consistent with the focus group analysis. Some of the most praised characteristics of leaders, such as being visionary, are mentioned by the middle managers in the focus group interviews as the most important ones for outstanding leaders. However, it is interesting to note that many behaviors that commonly exist among Asian leaders, such as autocratic, bureaucratic, and face saving, were not even mentioned in this media analysis. This seems to suggest that there are differences between the behaviors encouraged by the media and those actually practiced by the Singapore leaders. Also, it should be pointed out that Singapore media seldom publish anything that is inconsistent with the policies or ideas of the Singapore government. Therefore, the results of the media analysis can be seen as a reflection of the government policies in Singapore.

To summarize, among the Singapore participants, the qualities of capable leaders were said to be hardworking, knowing how to identify and taking advantage of opportunities, and

TABLE 26.3
Comparison of All Countries From the Confucian Asian Cluster

Leadership Dimensions	Confucian Asian Cluster					
	Singapore	China	Hong Kong	Japan	Korea South	Taiwan
Charismatic	5.95 >	5.56	5.66	5.49	5.53	5.58
Team Oriented	5.76	5.57	5.58	5.56	5.52	5.69
Participative	5.30 >	5.04	4.86	5.07	4.92	4.73
Humane	5.24	5.19	4.89	4.68	4.87	5.35
Autonomous	3.87	4.07	4.38	3.67	4.21	4.01
Self-Protective	3.31 <	3.80	3.67	3.60	3.67	4.38

Note. Compared to the other countries from the Confucian Asian cluster, Singapore scores more similar to Western country clusters (e.g., Anglo, Germanic, Nordic), that is, higher on Charismatic and Participative Leadership and lower on Self-Protective leadership.

overcoming great difficulties to achieve great successes in their businesses. On the other hand, the qualities of an outstanding leader, according to these participants, included being visionary, making unpopular but farsighted decisions, and overcoming great difficulties to achieve success. The media analysis suggested that, among some of the major Singapore's news media, at least the major English news media, the most frequently mentioned characteristics of good leaders include visionary, confident, objective, considerate, capable (competent), change oriented, and open to learning.

Study 3: GLOBE Questionnaire Survey

In Table 26.3, Singapore's scores on the second-order GLOBE leadership dimensions are compared to five countries (China, Hong Kong, Japan, South Korea, and Taiwan), which also belong to the Confucian Asian cluster (cf. Dorfman, Hanges, & Brodbeck, 2004). Compared to these countries, Singapore scores more similar to "Western" country clusters like Anglo, Germanic, or Nordic, than to the countries in the Confucian Asian cluster. In particular, Singapore scores higher on Charismatic and Participative Leadership and lower on Self- Protective leadership than the other Confucian Asian countries. On the other hand, Singapore scores high on Team Oriented and Humane Leadership, which is typical for the Confucian Asian but also for the Southern Asian cluster. This supports our argument that the cultural values and leadership style in Singapore are influenced by both the East and the West.

A more detailed view is given in Table 26.4 which shows the scores and ranks of the 21 first- order and the 6 second-order GLOBE leadership dimensions for Singapore, together with highest and lowest country scores in the GLOBE sample of 61 countries.

It is interesting to note in Table 26.4 that, on several dimensions related to Confucian cultural values, the scores from Singapore managers ranked high. Specifically, on the dimension Self-Sacrificial, Singapore ranked 11, which is consistent with empirical observations in recent years. For example, since the 1998 financial crisis, the governments in both Hong Kong and Singapore have faced some financial difficulties and needed to cut the salaries of its employees. In Hong Kong, there has been fierce resistance among government employees recently against cuts to their incomes or benefits, which is necessary to control the government's

TABLE 26.4
Scores and Ranks of the 21 First-Order and the 6 Second-Order
GLOBE Leadership Dimensions

Second-Order Leadership Dimensions First-Order Leadership	Score	Rank	Highest Score	Lowest Score
Charismatic Leadership	5.95	23	6.46	4.51
Performance Orientation	6.11	26	6.64	4.51
Visionary	6.17	25	6.50	4.62
Inspirational	6.09	37	6.63	5.04
Integrity	6.15	28	6.79	4.72
Self-Sacrificial	5.39	11	5.99	3.98
Decisive	5.85	32	6.37	3.62
Team-Oriented Leadership	5.76	34	6.21	4.74
Team Integrator	5.41	38	6.09	4.42
Collaborative Team Oriented	5.94	33	6.43	4.10
Administratively Competent	5.71	37	6.42	4.53
Diplomatic	5.58	27	6.05	4.49
Malevolent (reverse scored)	1.83	21	2.67	1.33
Participative Leadership	5.30	32	6.09	4.50
Autocratic (reverse scored)	2.73	25	3.86	1.89
Nonparticipative (reverse scored)	2.68	28	3.61	1.86
Humane Leadership	5.24	10	5.75	3.82
Humane	5.10	17	5.68	2.23
Modesty	5.35	13	5.86	4.14
Autonomous Leadership	3.87	30	4.63	2.27
Self-Protective Leadership	3.31	40	4.62	2.55
Self-Centered	2.05	37	6.20	1.55
Status-Conscious	3.78	46	5.93	3.00
Conflict Inducer	3.64	46	5.01	3.09
Face Saver	3.19	11	4.63	2.05
Procedural	3.81	37	5.12	2.82

Note. Leadership scores where compared across industries (food, finance) within Singapore. Only one significant result out of 21 comparisons was obtained, which equals chance probability.

huge financial deficits. Similar resistance has never occurred in Singapore, even when the Singapore government actually asked its people to make a greater sacrifice for the long-term interests of their society. Here the explanation can be that, influenced by the Confucian cultural values, which see the society as one family, Singapore managers are more willing to make self-sacrifice for their society. On the other hand, influenced by a societal culture with more Western individualistic value, Hong Kong managers are less willing to make personal sacrifice.

Similarly, on such items as Humane leadership and Face Saver, one can also see the heavy influences of Confucian cultural values in Singapore. Singapore manager ranked high on these dimensions, whereas other East Asian societies with less Confucian influences today, such as the case of Hong Kong, ranked lower on these dimensions.

5. CONCLUDING DISCUSSION

In this chapter, we have shown that the cultural values and leadership style in Singapore can be seen as a combination of the East and the West. To understand the culture in this country, one needs to consider the interactions of various environmental factors, especially the significant role of foreign MNCs in the country and the heavy involvement of the government in social life. All of these have important implications for future research. Take the involvement of government as an example. Past research has largely attributed cultural change to such factors as technological revolution and socioeconomic development, and pays insufficient attention to the role of government in this process. On the other hand, in a society heavily influenced by Confucian cultural value, such as Singapore, the role of government in shaping and changing the societal and organizational cultures seems to be very significant. Although the dominant view today suggests that government policies reflect societal cultures (e.g., Hofstede, 1980), the cases of Singapore and other Chinese societies in East Asia often suggest a reverse notion. This is especially true in those societies where Western-style democracy does not exist. In such societies, governments do not necessarily reflect majority opinion or societal culture when generating policy. Instead, it may be the societal and organizational cultures that are more often influenced by the government policy (cf. Li & Karakowsky, 2002). Therefore, a contingency approach regarding the relationship between cultures and government policies may be more useful for future study.

Also, consistent with past research findings, Singapore's societal culture has been observed to have a greater effect than specific organizational cultures on individual Singaporeans' perceptions and attitudes about leadership. This finding is in line with the results from an analysis across all 61 GLOBE countries showing that societal culture is a much stronger predictor of organizational cultural practices than is industry sector (Brodbeck, Hanges, Dickson, Gupta, & Dorfman, 2004).

Limitations and Implications for Future Research

The culture in Singapore seems to have changed dramatically over the years, making it inappropriate to label its societal culture as Chinese or Asian. This finding is important for both researchers and practitioners. For researchers, it suggests the need to deal with the issues of cross-cultural management within a more dynamic, more comprehensive, and more timely approach. First, cross-cultural management issues need to be addressed not only from the dominant perspective of cross-cultural research that treats culture as a constant and independent variable (e.g., Hofstede, 1980), but also from a dynamic perspective that examines culture as a dependent variable that can be influenced by other environmental factors. This approach will improve our understanding of cultural differences and their consequences. Researchers who continue to employ a broad and static definition of Asian culture, for example, may find it difficult to explain important differences in individual and organizational behaviors that continue to emerge across different Asian societies. To effectively conduct cross-cultural studies in modern societies, we need to adopt a more dynamic approach.

Second, we argue for a more comprehensive approach to examine the nature of culture, its antecedents, and the processes of change, and not merely the differences and consequences of culture. Whereas past research has often attributed cultural change to technological revolution and socioeconomic development, the cultural changes noted in this study and some other recent studies on culture (e.g., Ralston Gustafson, Cheung, & Tarpstra, 1993) suggest more complex processes are at play. With comparable levels of economic and technological development in many modern societies (e.g., the development of information technology), the effects of other antecedents, such as government policy, may act as much more significant roles. Consequently, examining cultural values and their effects should entail a more comprehensive approach that considers additional factors as well as the interactions among these factors.

Finally, we also need a more timely approach to cross-cultural research. Because the elements of cultural value may change rapidly, cross-cultural research faces a new challenge—outdated data. Many studies currently published may actually be reporting on data collected many years ago. This can be seen as a common limitation of these studies, including our studies reported in this chapter. On the other hand, the increasing level of influence exerted by foreign sources, for example, may call into question the accuracy of such data. Specifically, with globalization, greater interactions among modern societies and the rapid development of communication technology are increasing the level of access to foreign cultures, which, in turn, will accelerate and magnify the influence of foreign cultures on cultural values in a given society. This will create difficulty for researchers studying cultural differences and their consequences. For example, the research data collected not long ago may soon become obsolete or irrelevant because of partial changes to some elements of culture in a society. A study conducted today may show that Taiwan manifests a high Power Distance in societal culture, whereas a study conducted in 3 years' time may show that Taiwan possesses a low Power Distance culture. Therefore, for cross-cultural management studies conducted in modern societies, we need to adopt a more timely approach. For example, more frequent measurements may be needed in those societies where rapid political, social, technological, or economic changes are taking place.

In addition to the limitations that we have already mentioned, another major restriction of this study is its relatively small sample size. Because of the difficulty in collecting data from middle mangers in Singapore, we could not obtain a larger sample. Therefore, we had to adopt a practical anthropological approach toward an understanding of cultural values and leadership in Singapore. Yet this approach limits the generalization of the conclusion to the nation. It also prevents us from conducting a more powerful study in our empirical testing, such as the testing of cultural differences between the two types of industrial organizations in Singapore. Future study should commit more resources to data collection in order to obtain a larger sample size. With a large sample size, more power data analyses can be conducted and more significant findings may be obtained.

Still another limitation of this study is its failure in obtaining more information about the consequences of the cultural values in Singapore. Future study should test more dependent variables that may be influenced by the cultural values, especially those dependent variables measuring individual and organizational performance in Singapore. With more such dependent variables, more interesting findings for both researchers and practitioners may be found.

Practical Implications

Our findings also have some practical implications for mangers or leaders within international business. As our data suggested, there exist significant differences even among East Asian Chinese societies. Accordingly, managers or leaders of international business need to pay more attention to the difference in cultural values and the factors that have caused the partial changes. As Huo and Randall (1991) have argued, multinational firms need to pay attention not only to basic cultural differences between their home country (e.g., the United

States) and the host country (e.g., China), but also to differences between different societies that share the same language, religion, and ethnic traditions (e.g., Singapore compared to Hong Kong and Taiwan). This is also true for ethnic Asian managers from an Asian society, such as Singapore. Even for an ethnic Asian manager, it is still necessary to understand cultural changes that have taken place in other Chinese societies. Experience from one Chinese society may not be applicable to other Chinese societies. A successful business policy in Hong Kong may not work well in Singapore; and a successful manager who works well in Taiwan may not work well in China (e.g., Li, Lam, & Qian, 2001). Without an awareness of the differences caused by cultural change and the consequences that follow, multinational firms will risk failure in any attempts to generate effective strategies in areas such as selection and training, marketing and promotion, and business investment.

REFERENCES

Brodbeck, F. C., Hanges, P. J., Dickson., M. W., Gupta, V., & Dorfman, P. W. (2004). Comparative influence of industry and societal culture on organizational cultural practices. In R. J. House, P. J. Hanges, M. Javidan, P. Dorfman, & V. Gupta (Eds.), *Leadership, culture, and organizations: The GLOBE study of 62 societies* (pp. 654–668). Thousand Oaks, CA: Sage.

Cheng, L. K. (1990, April). Reflections on the changing roles of Chinese clan associations in Singapore. *Asian Culture*, pp. 38–49.

Cheong, W. K. (1991). The style of managing in a multicultural society—Singapore. In J. M. Putti (Eds.), *Management, Asian context* (pp. 258–283). Singapore: Superskill Graphics.

Chew, I. K. H., & Putti, J. (1995). Relationship on work-related values of Singaporean and Japanese managers in Singapore. *Human Relations, 48*(10), 1149–1170.

Co-opt people, ideas at all levels, urges BG Lee. (1999). *Singapore Bulletin, 27*(4), p.2.

Creel, H. G. (1953). *Chinese thought, from Confucius to Mao Tse-tung.* Chicago: University of Chicago Press.

Dorfman, P., Hanges, P. J., & Brodbeck, F. C. (2004). Leadership and cultural variation: The identification of culturally endorsed leadership profiles. In R. J. House, P. J. Hanges, M. Javidan, P. Dorfman, & V. Gupta (Eds.), *Leadership, culture, and organizations: The GLOBE study of 62 societies* (pp. 669–719). Thousand Oaks, CA: Sage.

East Asia Analytical Unit (Dept. of Foreign Affairs and Trade, Australia). (1995). *Singapore's investment in China.* In Overseas Chinese business networks in China (pp. 19–33). Canberra, Australia: AGPA Press.

"Singapore: West-bashing." (1994, April 27). *The Economist,* pp. 28–29.

Godley, M. (1981). *The Mandarin-capitalists from Nanyang: Overseas Chinese enterprise in the Modernisation of China 1893–1911.* Cambridge, England: Cambridge University Press.

Haggard, S. (1990). *Pathways from the periphery: The politics of growth in the newly industrializing countries.* Ithaca, NY: Cornell University Press.

Hanges, P. J., & Dickson, M. W. (2004). In R. J. House, P. J. Hanges, M. Javidan, P. Dorfman, & V. Gupta (Eds.), *Leadership, culture, and organizations: The GLOBE study of 62 societies* (pp. 122–151). Thousand Oaks, CA: Sage.

Hicks, G. L. (1993). *Overseas Chinese remittances from South East Asia 1910–1940.* Singapore: Selected Books.

Hofstede, G. (1980). *Cultural consequences: International differences in work-related values.* Beverly Hills, CA: Sage.

Hofstede, G., & Bond, M. H. (1988). The Confucius connection: From cultural roots to economic growth. *Organization Dynamics, 16,* 178–190.

House, R. J., Hanges, P. J., Javidan, M., Dorfman, P. W., Gupta, V., & Globe Associates. (2004). *Culture, leadership, and organizations: The GLOBE study of 62 societies.* Thousand Oaks, CA: Sage.

Huo, Y. P., & Randall, D. M. (1991). Exploring subcultural differences in Hofstede's value survey: The case of the Chinese. *Asia Pacific Journal of Management, 8*(2),159–173.

Koh, A. T. (1987). Linkage and the international environment. In L. B. Krause, K. A. Fee, & L. T. Yuan (Eds.), *The Singapore economy reconsidered* (pp. 318–343). Singapore: Institute for Southeast Asian Studies.

Koh, W. L., Steers, R. M., & Terborg, J. R. (1995). The effects of transformational leadership on teacher attitudes and student performance in Singapore. *Journal of Organizational Behavior, 16*(4), 319–333.

Kraar, L. (1971, March). The wealth and power of the overseas Chinese. *Fortune.*

Lee, S. L. (1985). *Documents of a special government committee.* Singapore: Singapore Press.

Li, J., & Karakowshy, L. (2002). Cultural malleability in an East Asian context: An illustration of the relationship between government policy, national culture and firm behaviour. *Administration and Society. 34*(2), 176–188.

Li, J., Lam, K., & Qian, G. (2001). Does culture affect behaviour and performance of firms: The case of joint venture in China. *Journal of International Business Studies, 32*(1), 115–131.

McGrath, R. G., MacMillan, I. C., Yang, E. A., & Tsai, W. T. (1992). Does culture endure, or is it malleable? Issues for entrepreneurial economic development. *Journal of Business Venturing, 7,* 441–458.

Ministry of Finance. (1993). *Report of a task-force from the Ministry of Finance.* Singapore: Singapore Press.

Ralston, D. A., Gustafson, D. J., Cheung, F. M., & Terpstra, R. H. (1993). Differences in managerial values: A study of U.S., Hong Kong and PRC managers. *Journal of International Business Studies. 24*(2), 249–275.

Selmer, J. (1997). *Vikings and dragons.* Hong Kong: Baptist University.

Tan, C. (1997, January 7). Local firms are not too keen to go regional. *The Business Times,* p.2.

Tan, C., & Torrington, D. (1998). *Human resource management for southeast Asia and Hong Kong* (2nd ed.). Singapore: Prentice-Hall.

Tay, B. N. (1986). The structure and causes of manufacturing sector protection in Singapore. In C. Findlay & R. Garnaut (Eds.), *The political economy of manufacturing protection: Experiences of Asia and Australia* (pp. 83–103). Sydney, Australia: Allen & Unwin.

Westwood, R. I., & Posner, B. Z. (1997). Managerial values across cultures: Australia, Hong Kong and the United States. *Asia Pacific Journal of Management, 14,* 31–66.

Yang, K. S. (1986). Chinese personality and its change. In M. H. Bond (Ed.), *The psychology of the Chinese people* (pp. 106–170). Oxford, England: Oxford University Press.

Yang, K. S. (1991, July). *Will traditional and modern values co-exist?* Paper presented at the International Conference on Values in Chinese Societies: Retrospect and Prospect. Taiwan: Taipei.

Yeh, R. S. (1988). Values of American, Japanese and Taiwanese managers in Taiwan: A test of Hofstede's Framework. *Academy of Management Best Papers Proceedings,* pp. 106–110.

Yeh, R. S., & Lawrence, J. (1995). Individualism and Confucian dynamism: A note on Hofstede's cultural root to economic growth. *Journal of International Business Studies, 3,* 655–669.

Yeo, H. P. (1997*). Fit of culture in Asian emerging markets: An empirical study of Singapore manufacturing firms* (Research Paper). Singapore: National University of Singapore.

IX
▼▼▼▼▼▼▼

SOUTHERN ASIA CLUSTER

The Southern Asia cluster in the GLOBE Research Program consisted of India, Indonesia, Iran, Malaysia, Philippines, and Thailand. India is the only country from this cluster represented in this volume.

The Southern Asia cluster is among the high scores on Humane Orientation, and In-Group Collectivism. Its scores on Assertiveness, Future Orientation, Gender Egalitarianism, Institutional Collectivism, Performance Orientation, Power Distance, and Uncertainty Avoidance are in the midrange (House et al., 2004).

Charismatic/Value Based leadership and Team Oriented leadership are seen to be contributing the most to the outstanding leadership in this cluster. Participative leadership and Humane Oriented leadership are viewed positively. Autonomous leadership and Self-Protective leadership are reported to be neutral toward outstanding leadership in this cluster.

One of the distinct features of this cluster is the assimilation of foreign cultures, often those of the conquerors, with the result that people of widely different beliefs have coexisted peacefully in the countries of this cluster (Levi-Strauss, 1951). Peaceful coexistence of people of different religions, different ethnic groups, and so on, is thus, quite common in this cluster. Commenting on the existence of places of worship of different religions next to each other, Levi-Strauss has observed that "complementary forms of faith seem irreconcilable yet they co-exist peaceably."

REFERENCES

House, R. J., Hanges, P. J., Javidan, M., Dorfman, P. W., Gupta, V., & GLOBE Associates. (2004). *Culture, leadership, and organizations: The GLOBE study of 62 societies.* Thousand Oaks, CA: Sage.
Levi-Strauss, C. (1951). Foreword to documents on South Asia. *International Social Science Bulletin, III*(4).

27

▼▼▼▼▼▼▼

India: Diversity and Complexity in Action

Jagdeep S. Chhokar
Indian Institute of Management, Ahmedabad, India

India is a country of great diversity. There are substantial regional, linguistic, cultural, and religious variations across the country. Given the wide range of variation, it should be impossible to generalize not only about the society, organizations, and leaders in India, but also about organizational and leadership practices in Indian organizations. There is, however, hope because:

> In spite of the fact that the languages of India are many, and there are well marked differences between one regional culture and another, yet there is an over-all unity of design which makes them all members of one family. This stems primarily from the economic and social organization of the country and extends to commonness of intellectual and emotional attachments and obligations. The details might vary from place to place, and from one caste to another, yet the sameness of the traditions on which all of them have been reared cannot be overlooked. (Bose, 1967, p. 9)

It is in this spirit that this chapter reports the India-specific findings of the GLOBE Research Project. The following section attempts to describe the evolution of India's society and culture, concluding with a description of the current situation. It is followed by a brief description of leadership in India. The methodology of GLOBE research in India is described next, followed by presentation of the results of the qualitative and quantitative analyses. A brief note containing some basic information on India can be found in Appendix A.

1. SOCIETY AND CULTURE IN INDIA

Any attempt at describing society and culture in India must begin with three assertions. One, though the political entity that is today known as India formally came into being only 50 years ago, the broader region that has been the cradle for what is called Indian culture, society, and civilization, has long been a loose, informal confederation joined by an indefinable similarity of social and cultural customs and practices. It is therefore more accurate to refer to it as a cultural unit rather than a political entity. Two, the physical boundaries of this cultural unit have differed during various periods of history. The boundaries were almost never *identical* to what the boundaries of today's India are. The cultural unit in terms of geographical area was almost always larger than what India is today. Lastly, India as it exists today is a composite of multiple influences in a civilization that has continued to evolve for more than 5,000 years. What may be termed as the culture of India today is the outcome of, or merely the current stage in, a process of evolution of a continually living and changing culture. What follows is a brief, somewhat inadequate description of the origins and evolution of Indian culture, because any attempt at capturing the mosaic of Indian culture in a few pages is bound to be inadequate.

The social and cultural roots of India are shrouded in antiquity. Archaeological excavations of the Indus Valley civilization at several locations, of which Harappa and Mohenjo Daro are the best known, attest to a highly developed civilization in the third millennium BC (Basham, 1954/1967).

> I shall not now speak of the knowledge of the Hindus ... of their subtle discoveries in the science of astronomy—discoveries even more ingenious than those of the Greeks and Babylonians—of their rational system of mathematics, or of their method of calculation which no words can praise strongly enough—I mean the system using nine symbols. If these things were known by people who think that they alone have mastered the science because they speak Greek they would perhaps be convinced, though a little late in the day, that other folk, not only Greeks but also men of a different tongue, know something as well as they. (Sebokht, AD 662; quoted in Basham, 1954/1967, p. xi).

The study of ancient Indian civilization in the Western scientific mode began in the mid-1700s during the British period. However, India had a long tradition of oral history. Indian folklore is full of kings and noblemen of all shades—good, brave, wise to bad, cowardly, and foolish. A constant refrain in folklore is the presence of sages, seers, and saints who renounced the material world, and practiced and propagated spiritualism. Though agriculture was the predominant occupation, other activities such as trade and commerce, art (e.g., Ajanta cave paintings), architecture (temples), performing arts (classical dance forms), music, poetry, education (e.g., Taxsila and Nalanda Universities[1]), science (particularly astronomy), urban planning and design (Indus Valley cities), and religion also thrived.

Basham (1954/1967) claims that Indian history emerged from "legend and dubious tradition" in the sixth century BC, and what emerged was a society highly developed materially, intellectually, and spiritually. It was also characterized by a great sense of fairness in social and civic relations. *"In no other early civilization were slaves so few in number, and in no other ancient law book are their rights so well protected as in the Arthasastra. No other ancient lawgiver proclaimed such noble ideals of fair play in battle as did Manu.... The most striking feature of ancient India's civilization is its humanity"* (Basham, 1954/1967, p. 8).

Basham stresses the "secular literature, sculpture, and painting" of the time and points out that the "people enjoyed life, passionately delighting both in the things of the senses and the

---

[1]Taxsila flourished as a large center of learning around 550–500 BC in the northwestern part of India and attracted scholars and students from far and wide. Nalanda was set up in third century AD as a Buddhist monastery in Bihar. It "did not confine itself to training Buddhist novices, but also taught the Vedas, Hindu philosophy, logic, grammar and medicine. ... The student population was not confined to the Buddhist order, but ... candidates of other faiths who succeeded in passing a strict oral examination were [also] admitted.... It provided free training for no less than 10,000 students" (Basham, 1954/1967, p. 166).

things of the spirit" (p. 9). He describes ancient India as "a cheerful land, whose people, each finding a niche in a complex and slowly evolving social system, reached a higher level of kindliness and gentleness in their mutual relationship than any other nation in antiquity" (p. 9). The collectivist and humane nature of Indian society can thus possibly be traced back to these ancient roots.

The predominant political system was of kings ruling their individual territories. Though kings were originally elected, the system soon became one of succession based on heredity, with the king being succeeded by the eldest son. Women were excluded from succession though there were a few exceptions. The equivalent of modern-day councils of ministers and state assemblies often existed, but the authority and responsibility for governance rested almost exclusively with the king. Nehru (1985) describes the king in ancient India as an "autocratic monarch" who most of the time functioned within established conventions. This possibly contributes to the fairly widespread preference for "strong" leadership in India even today.

The culture of ancient India was continuously modified by a series of invasions, the last one being the British, which ended in 1947. These began about 2000 BC with what has come to be called the Aryan invasion. "The Aryan invasion of India was not a single concerted action, but one covering centuries and involving many tribes, perhaps not all of the same race and language" (Basham, 1954/1967, p. 30). The native people of India were peace-loving agriculturalists, and did not offer much resistance to the invading tribes. All these tribes got assimilated and absorbed in to the native population in a thorough mix. The system of a king being the head of a tribe that occupied a demarcated geographical area continued. This was also the period when the well-known spiritual texts, the *Vedas* and the *Upanishads,* were composed, and to which the popular epics, the *Mahabharata* and the *Ramayana,* are attributed. The sixth century BC saw the advent of Buddhism and Jainism as separate religions. Buddha himself was a prince who renounced the material world for the spiritual. India was invaded by the famous Greek general, Alexander of Macedon (also called Alexander the Great) in 326 BC, who left behind garrisons, and appointed satraps to govern the conquered territories. However revolts in Indian provinces and the death of Alexander in 323 BC lessened the Greek control, and the last of Alexander's generals, Eudamus, left the Indian northwest in 317 BC.

The first major Muslim invasion of India was by the Turkish chieftain Mahmud, who had established a powerful kingdom at Gazni in Afghanistan. Mahmud of Gazni conducted 17 raids on northwestern India between 1001 and 1027 AD. These were essentially pillaging raids and Mahmud did not stay to reign. Mahmud died in 1030 AD, and the next important invasion was that by Shahab-ud-din Ghuri, another Afghan, who conquered Delhi in 1192 AD. Such periodic incursions continued until the beginning of the Mughal Empire in India when Babar, a Turco-Mongol and a prince of the Timurid line in central Asia, occupied Delhi in 1526. The Mughal Empire lasted for about 200 years and its decline started with the death of Aurangzeb in 1707. After a period of strife and struggle, the British Empire began its reign in 1757 when Robert Clive won the battle of Plassey in Bengal.[2] There were, however, other smaller invasions that had taken place in between. Following a visit by Vasco de Gama to Calicut, on the western coast of south India, the Portuguese set up a colony in Goa in the early

---

[2]Unlike the earlier invasions, the British Empire had its roots in traditional Indian hospitality. A local ruler in one of the eastern provinces allowed a British trading post to be set up in his kingdom. This trading post grew into the East India Company. Over time, the protection of commercial interests evolved into the British taking complete control of governance over the area.

1500s. British rule ended with the independence of India in 1947 and the present Republic of India was proclaimed in 1950 with the adoption of a new constitution.

Throughout these long periods of domination, by the Mughals and the British, the political structure in the region remained more or less the same. There were territories directly administered by the conquerors, along with a large number of local "princely" states that had individual and varying relationships with a major ruling administration. Some were semi-autonomous and were formal protectorates of the ruling administration; some were quite independent and had a friendly relationship, whereas others maintained an independent and antagonistic relationship. Most of the invaders, except the Greeks and the British, stayed on in India, and in some ways got absorbed and assimilated in to the local indigenous social and cultural milieu, also influencing and changing it in the process. The British period, for example, resulted in a new group referred to as "Anglo-Indians" consisting of the offspring from the marriages between the British and native Indians, which continues to exist as an integral part of Indian society even today. Intermarriages among the invaders-turned-local-rulers and the indigenous nobility, though not frequent, did take place from time to time. There were long, almost continuous periods of ferment when India reacted to these new situations subconsciously, absorbing the new foreign elements into itself, and herself changing in the process. These influences percolated all aspects of culture including language, religion, and traditions, and resulted in a situation where the different groups coexisted in mutual harmony despite the differences of language and religion.

Caste System

One of the most widely known and commented upon features of Indian society is the caste system. The origin of this particular usage of the term *caste* is traced by Basham (1954/1967) to the 16th century when the Portuguese came to India and "found the Hindu community divided into many separate groups which they [the Portuguese] called *castas,* meaning tribes, clans or families" (p. 149). The well-known four fold classification—*Brahmins, Kshatriyas, Vaisyas,* and *Sudras*—in descending order of social status, is believed to have been first enunciated by the ancient law giver Manu some time in the Vedic period (1500–1000 BC). These four are the *varnas,* aggregated macro groupings, which were further divided into a myriad castes and subcastes. Each *varna,* caste, and subcaste had an internal hierarchical social order. The distinctions between adjacent hierarchical levels both between and within a *varna,* caste, and subcaste were somewhat blurred, particularly at the boundaries.

Caste is often "defined as a system of groups within the class which are normally endogamous (marriage being legitimate only within the group), commensal (food to be received from and eaten only in the presence of members of the same or higher group), and craft-exclusive (each man to live by the trade or profession of his own group, and not take up that of another)" (Basham, 1954/1967, p. 149). Though the origins and rationale of the caste system are obscure, it gradually evolved into a social as well as economic structuring of society. Originally a feature of Hindu society, the influence of caste often transcended religion, and most non-Hindu religions in India developed their own versions of something like a caste system. Though it is the maladies of the caste system that attract the most comment today, there is also a view that maintains that the caste system served a useful purpose in society. It is claimed that the system provided "economic security in spite of obvious inequalities; and this security was guaranteed both by law and by custom" (Bose, 1967, p. 221).

The complementary noncompetitiveness was not confined to occupations; it also extended to the use of natural resources. Some recent analyses and interpretations of the workings of traditional Indian villages maintain that these were sustainable societies consisting of various castes. Each caste was dependent on a different component of the natural resource base for their primary economic activity. *"Caste groups tended to pursue a relatively specialized and hereditary mode of subsistence. With their overlapping distributions and occupational specializations, the different caste groups were linked together in a web of mutually supportive relationships. This is not to say that caste society was at all egalitarian. It was in fact a sharply stratified society" (Gadgil & Guha, 1992, p. 93).*

Though most descriptions portray the caste system as a rigid hierarchy, its actual practice appeared to have had at least some scope for changes. Basham (1954/1967) maintains that "castes rise and fall in the social scale, and old castes die out and new ones are formed" (p. 149). Srinivas (1966) referred to the concept of "sanskritisation" to denote attempts of lower castes to raise their status in society. The continued, though dynamic, existence of the caste system is one of the major sources of the high power distance index for India found in Hofstede's (1980) studies.

The caste system, being the basis of social and economic structuring of society, has obviously influenced the practice of leadership in India over the centuries. The ability to lead in wars with other states being a major requirement to defend a state, warrior-kings belonging to the martial group, *Kshatriya,* were very common. The kings were however often guided by the high priest, who belonged to the highest group, *Brahmin,* and had an exalted position in the king's court. Business, trading, and commerce, not being considered very noble activities, were left to the third level, *Vaisya.* These patterns of leadership continued until very recently, and can be seen in operation even today. A lot of social and political leaders have been from the so-called higher castes, whereas a number of business leaders continue to be from the lower castes. There has however been a distinct though gradual shift in political leadership with more leaders from the lower castes emerging, possibly as a result of the universal franchise system introduced since independence.

The Current Situation

The evolution of Indian society and culture has continued its course along with the march of time. The current situation is captured well by the *People of India,* a large-scale ethnographic project undertaken by the Anthropological Survey of India from 1985 to 1992 (Singh, 1992). It was found that "caste has weakened to some extent in recent years in terms of its adherence to hereditary occupation and norms of purity and pollution. It has also acquired new strength in a political sense as a constituency and as a vote bank" (p. 24).

The survey found that about 75% of the 4635 communities studied followed Hinduism, 12% followed Islam, 7% Christianity, 2.5% Sikhism; 2% each, Jainism and Buddhism; and about 0.2% for both Judaism and Zoroastrianism. An interesting finding was that as many as 393 communities comprised followers of two religions, and 16 had followers of as many as three religions. Linguistically, the survey identified a total of 325 languages belonging to 12 different language families. Apart from the languages, 24 different scripts were found to be in use. The incidence of bilingualism was found to be as high as 65.51% in terms of the number of communities.

The change in the rigidity and influence of the caste system also continues. The emerging national identity seems to coexist with the castes and communities acquiring clearly identifiable political identities:

Social progress since independence has served to heighten the awareness of cultural pluralism. ... There is an all pervasive sense of "Indianness" often elusive and indefinable but ever present as noted by colonial ethnographers. Risely, for example, in 1891 spoke of an "equally mysterious thing called national character" and that "beneath the manifold diversity of physical and social type, language, custom and religion there is an Indian character, a general Indian personality which we cannot resolve into its component elements" (Singh, 1992, pp. 102–104).

The ferment in Indian society continues. With universal adult suffrage adopted as part of the Constitution of the Republic in 1950, the general populace has gradually come to realize the power of their franchise. This has led to a political awareness that differs from the political movement to end colonial rule. The Constitution also put in place a program for the uplift of the depressed sections of society by way of quotas and reservations for certain groups in employment, education, and so on. This affirmative action program, according to the Constitution, was originally meant for certain exceptionally disadvantaged groups and was to be in place for 10 years, which was considered an adequate length of time to bring them into the mainstream. It has subsequently been expanded to cover more groups, and has also been extended from time to time—almost indefinitely. There have been attempts by several communities to get into these special categories that get preferential treatment, prompting some social commentators to refer to the phenomenon as "de-sanskritisation." These developments have led to a much more acute desire for equality, social as well as economic, on the part of large sections of society. It has also resulted in the emergence of several political formations whose ideology is essentially based on what is referred to as "social justice." The entire system is thus embroiled in an intense and broad-based struggle with multiple stakeholders and contestants who are forever increasing in numbers and hence resulting in the formation of new groups.

Yet another struggle is at the religious and cultural levels, broadly coinciding with the resurgence of strong religious beliefs elsewhere in the world (e.g., Islam, Christianity, etc). Also in India there has been a resurgence of some strong beliefs in Hinduism, once described as a very broad-based, tolerant, and resilient faith (Basham, 1954/1967, p. 347). In Nehru's words, *"Hinduism as a faith, is vague, amorphous, many sided, all things to all men. It is hardly possible to define it, or indeed to say definitely whether it is a religion or not, in the usual sense of the word. In its present form, and even in the past, it embraces many beliefs and practices, from the highest to the lowest, often opposed to or contradicting each other. Its essential spirit seems to be to live and let live" (Nehru, 1985, p. 75).* Being so amorphous, Hinduism allows itself to varying and differing interpretations. Some political groupings have chosen Hinduism as a platform that they feel would help them attain political power. Coinciding with religious resurgence elsewhere in the world, as suggested by changes in Iran, Bosnia- Herzegovina, and the United States, it has also become an important and potentially contentious social and political issue in recent times.

Liberalization and restructuring of the economy has also been a major influence in recent years with particular emphasis on business and industry in India. India had been more or less a centrally planned economic system for almost four decades since its independence in 1947. Though there was a fairly well-developed and strong private sector, the overall economy was controlled and regulated by the government. Though some initial and tentative steps toward easing of controls were taken in the mid-1980s, a major exercise in restructuring and liberalization of the economy was undertaken from 1991 onward. Far-reaching changes in the economic environment have taken place in the last few years. Globalization is becoming an often-used expression. It is significant that broad economic policies have continued without any serious disturbance despite frequent changes in the government with political parties of different ideologies being in power.

Another feature of Indian society in the recent past has been the growth of materialism. In some ways it is also linked with economic liberalization and restructuring, and the information explosion resulting from the increasing spread of electronic mass media, particularly television. The rise of materialism coupled with a desire to get rich quickly has blurred the distinction between ends and means, resulting in fairly large-scale and deep-seated corruption. It has not been confined only to the lower levels of government officials but has also spread to almost the entire political system (Walsh, 1996).

The disillusionment with corruption in high places is somewhat counterbalanced by the judiciary, which has, over the last few years, become quite proactive. India has the fairly standard system of the three organs of the state—the legislature, the executive, and the judiciary—each being independent of one another as a system of checks and balances. The judiciary, for most of the time, had been a conservative, reactive, and sedate upholder of the law and interpreter of the statutes and the Constitution. Over the last few years, with the general populace losing confidence in the executive, particularly the bureaucracy, and becoming clearly disenchanted with the political class, the judiciary seems to have taken on its role much more actively. "Public interest litigation" in which concerned citizens file suits in court on matters of public and social interest, although they may not be affected by it individually, has become quite common. In some major and sensitive cases, the courts monitor the progress of investigations by decreeing that the investigating agencies report to them periodically, at specified intervals.

A major change is also under way concerning the political governance in the country. For almost 35 years since independence, the ruling party at the central government and in most state governments was the Indian National Congress, which had also been at the forefront of the independence movement. Some of the states had been governed by non-Congress parties for varying durations, and there were two short-lived attempts at a non-Congress government at the center. In the last 5 to 7 years however, a majority of states have voted non-Congress parties to power, and there is currently a coalition of 13 non-Congress parties in power at the center. Another distinguishing feature is that a number of parties in power in the states are regional in character, several confined solely to their respective states. Some of these regional parties also play significant roles in the coalition government at the center. The era of strong national parties and single-party governments at the center and in the states seems to be giving way to a system of strong regional parties that work together for mutual benefit at the national level. The political governance system thus seems to be moving from a unitary to a truly federal one.

All of the aforementioned developments are taking place against a general backdrop of increasing urbanization, gradual breakdown of the traditional rigidities of the caste system particularly in urban areas, increasing spread of literacy and education,[3] and above all, rising levels of awareness and expectations. The situation in India therefore appears to be one of "sharing of environment and ethos by communities and of their vibrant participation in political and economic processes and ritual roles [and] a sense of harmony ... in spite of conflicts and contradictions" (Singh, 1992, pp. 100–101). This situation suggests that India is likely to score high on the GLOBE societal collectivism dimension.

One of the leading social commentators, reviewing the developments in India as it approached the completion of 50 years of independence, described India to be a "major

---

[3]"Nationwide, literacy is 52 percent, compared with 24 percent three decades ago. More than a third of the country's lower-caste people were literate in 1991, up from 10 percent in 1961" (Spaeth, 1996, p. 44).

socio-historical entity representing one idea of one civil society that is composed of a small set of closely interrelated attributes. One large unity composed of diverse yet co-terminating pluralities" (Kothari, 1997, p. 7). He identified the following three major forces that have strongly influenced India over time and whose interactions have got "deeper and sharper [as] the Indian cultural landscape took a more political thrust":

> (i) a hierarchical social order through which infinite ambiguities have been at once tolerated and regulated, (ii) a multi-cultural framework of governance which has restrained hegemonical and "majoritarian" tendencies, and (iii) a highly flexible ethical code through which constant and continuing contradictions, clash of personalities, major paradoxes in elite behavior as well as instances of humiliation, acrimony and hypocritical behavior in the conduct of public affairs are managed. (Kothari, 1997, p. 7)

GLOBE Dimensions of Societal Culture

Given this kind of a background in society and culture, how may India be expected to show up on the core GLOBE dimensions of societal culture? This is a tricky question given the diversity and complexity of Indian culture and the transition it seems to be going through. Nonetheless some assessments follow. Collectivism, Humane Orientation, and Power Distance can be expected to be relatively high. Gender Egalitarianism is likely to be low because India continues to be a male-dominated society, like many others in spite of all sorts of laws and reforms that have been initiated from time to time. A high tolerance for uncertainty can be expected; hence low values of Uncertainty Avoidance. On similar lines, one may expect high Future Orientation. Both of these are based on the general long-term and even "hereafter" approach that is not too uncommon. Performance Orientation is more difficult to comment on and perhaps an expectation of moderate Performance Orientation is the most reasonable. This is in some way influenced by the teachings of what has been called "the most famous ethical text of ancient India, the Bhagvad Gita." The essence of the teachings "is summed up in the maxim 'your business is with the deed, and not the result.'" The general philosophy is that:

> In every circumstances there are actions which are intrinsically right (and) the right course must be chosen according to the circumstances, without any considerations of personal interest or sentiment. ... The inspiration of the Bhagvad Gita has been widely felt in India from the time of the Guptas to the present day, and it has been commended by Christians and Muslims, as well as by Hindus, whose most influential scripture it is. (Basham, 1954/1967, pp. 344–345)

It enjoins people to do their duty without thinking about or expecting the outcome or results.

2. LEADERSHIP IN INDIA

Leadership is a very popular issue in India. It is, or at least leaders are, a very common topic of discussion among people from all sections of Indian society. Whereas discussions about political leadership are possibly the most common, often with a certain amount of disdain, cynicism, and even disgust, leaders in other areas such as the captain of the Indian cricket team, and owners, founders, chief executives of leading business houses, are also discussed often. The importance of leadership is also attested to by the fact that statues of a variety of leaders—political, social, and religious—are erected all over, from big cities to small towns. A large number of public-service institutions such as hospitals, schools, colleges, and airports are named after leaders. Portraits of historical and religious leaders are often voluntarily displayed in public places such as shops, cafes, and offices.

India has obviously produced a large number and a wide variety of leaders over the centuries, and several of them have been very popular. The range of effective leadership can be illustrated by four examples, those of Chandragupta Maurya, Ashoka, Akbar, and Gandhi. Chandragupta Maurya ruled for 24 years around 320 BC and has been described as the chief architect of the greatest of India's ancient empires (Basham, 1954/1967). He was a *warrior-king* who consolidated several smaller states into one large kingdom. He was the beneficiary of the advice from Chanakya (also known as Kautilya) who is believed to be the author of *Arthasastra,* a treatise on statecraft and governance. Chandragupta therefore was also very skillful at political manipulation. Ashoka, whose reign began around 269 BC, ruled as a tyrant for the first 8 years, which culminated in the conquest of Kalinga in which more than 100,000 people were believed to have been killed and over 150,000 captured. Ashoka then had a change of heart and became a pacifist. This is found in many of his "own inscriptions which are the oldest surviving Indian written documents of any historical significance … [consisting] of a series of edicts engraved in a very similar form on rocks and pillars at widely scattered points all over India" (Basham, 1954/1967, p. 53). These show Ashoka to be a benevolent king who introduced humanity in to his internal administration and abandoned aggressive warfare in his dealings with other states. He also strongly supported the doctrine of *ahimsa,* meaning nonviolence and noninjury to humans as well as animals, which was used very effectively centuries later by Gandhi in the Indian struggle for independence from the British rule. After his first 8 years, Ashoka became a prime example of a *philosopher-king,* an example that in a way was later repeated in modern India when Dr. S. Radhakrishnan, a scholar and professor of philosophy, was elected as the president of India in 1962.

The third example of historically effective leadership is that of Akbar (1555–1606), who was one of the Mughal Emperors. He seemed to have understood the complexity of Indian society and polity, and realized that tolerance of differences in religion, language, social customs, and so forth, was essential for the empire to survive. He abolished all preferences and discriminations based on religion, appointing people to high state offices with disregard to their religious beliefs, and encouraged intercommunal marriages by setting an example himself. He even tried to propagate a new integrative religion, *Din-e-Illahi,* which attempted to combine the best of all existing religions in India at that time. Akbar could thus be considered an *enlightened pragmatic* ruler.

The last example is that of Gandhi, who symbolized a unique style of leadership that converted materialistic weaknesses into spiritual and political strengths. Starting his professional life as a barrister, trained in Britain, and evolving into something like a self-sacrificing saint, Mohandas Karamchand Gandhi[4] was without doubt the most important leader of the 20th century who shaped the destiny of modern India. He is referred to as the "Father of the Nation" due to his signal contribution to the Indian freedom movement against the British rule. His approach consisting of nonviolent struggle and civil disobedience, which had its beginnings during his stay in South Africa, had a profound impact on the course of the Indian freedom struggle. His concept of *Satyagraha* (literal translation meaning "insistence on truth") has found a permanent place in the industrial relations scenario in India as a common

---

[4]Popularly almost universally called Mahatma Gandhi, *Mahatma* meaning the great soul.

method of protest by unions and dissatisfied employees. It often takes the form of the employees sitting down and refusing to move unless their demands are met or satisfactory negotiations are concluded. Gandhi's statues are found in almost all cities and towns, roads and public buildings are often named after him, his birthday is observed as a national holiday, and his philosophy and teachings are invoked on numerous public occasions, though very little of it is followed in practice. It is not easy to label Gandhi's leadership style but *charismatic, inspirational, visionary,* and *value based* come closest to capturing the essence of his impact on the multitude of his followers.

Other important leaders of the 20th century were all those who contributed to the freedom struggle. Although there is almost a pantheon of these, two stand out: Jawaharlal Nehru and Vallabhbhai Patel. Nehru was the prime minister of the country for the first 17 years of its independent existence, until his death in 1963. He is credited with creating the industrial and technical infrastructure that India today has in terms of basic industries, though his economic policies of a planned economy have become a matter of debate over the last few years. Vallabhbhai Patel, often referred to as the Iron Man of India, was the minister for home affairs in the government of independent India. He was reputed to be a very able and strong administrator. He is credited with bringing about the merger of all the "princely" states with the Union of India, thus making the geographic expanse of India into a single political entity. Though both Nehru and Patel were extremely close to Gandhi, it is believed that Gandhi chose Nehru as his successor. It is widely speculated that independent India may have evolved into a very different kind of country had the practical and action-oriented administrator, Patel, been chosen by Gandhi instead of the romantic intellectual and visionary, Nehru, with his belief in Fabian socialism.[5]

It is interesting, as well as curious, that in spite of such widespread interest in leaders, rigorous academic research studies have been lacking. A review of research by Sinha (1994) identified two broad streams of leadership studies. One of these streams dealt with the personal characteristics and traits, distinguishing leaders from nonleaders, and did not yield any theoretical formulation. The other dealt directly with effective leadership styles that reflected a mixture of concern for task, for turbulent environment, and for the cultural needs and values. Culturally specific phenomena such as personalized and dependency relationship, power distance, care, consideration, and familial attachment were all found to affect leadership practices.

Whereas there is a dearth of rigorous research-based writing, there is a plethora of writing on leadership in the popular press. Political leadership is of course the most common topic for such writings. The writings cover a wide spectrum—from profiles and lives of political leaders, to serious conceptual issues such as the implications of the waning of charisma for democratic politics (Beteille, 1996). There is also a lot written on and about business, religious, and social leaders. Most of the writing on religious and social leaders is done by their followers, sects, or cults, but business leaders are written about by a wide cross-section of people (e.g., Karkaria, 1992; Lomax, 1986; Piramal, 1996). The business press also often writes about various aspects of leadership such as leadership training (Jayakar & Parthasarathy, 1996), and requirement of leadership for the emerging business environment (Jayakar, 1996).

Political leadership in India has become highly discredited over the last few years. Expedience, self-serving actions, use of caste, community, corruption, and religion for political

[5]A tremendous amount of writing is available on and by Gandhi, and also about Nehru albeit to a somewhat lesser extent. Two representative references about Patel are Shankar (1974) and Gandhi (1990).

and vote-gathering purposes, all are commonplace. It has been described as "a brazen-faced game of power, competitive in all its pejorative connotations … [with] commercialization and criminalization of politics and its caste and class based in-breeding [leading to] manipulation of mass psyche, blatant communalization and misdirection on the basis of narrow, partisan identities" (Kabra, 1994, p. 285). There is a general disenchantment with political leaders and a hankering for what it was like in the past. "We had wonderful leaders, people who had sacrificed everything for their country" recalls P. N. Bhagwati, who was chief justice of the Supreme Court in the mid-1980s (*Time,* 1996, p. 36).

Leadership of business organizations is however somewhat different. There are big business houses whose founders, and even some of their successors, are often looked up to with admiration, adulation, and respect. The House of Tatas is one such example whose founder Jamsetji Nusserwanji Tata, and later his successor JRD Tata, have both been admired (Fyzee, 1991; Harris, 1958). The business press writes about leaders, leadership, and related issues quite frequently. A recent feature titled "How to Use the New Leadership to Run Your Company" in one of the business magazines, based on interviews with leaders from some prominent business organizations, proposed five "leadership qualities and behaviors that the CEO of the futurcorp must demonstrate." These were leading by vision, by inspiration, by influence, by empowerment, and by expertise. The feature concluded that currently the situation in India is one whereby a business leader needed to "inspire highly-empowered employees to greater heights. … Set organizational goals more audacious than ever thought possible. … Lead his people to fulfilling those ambitions by convincing them of the need for doing so. Greatness, not efficiency, is his guiding passion" (Jayakar, 1996, p. 82). Extracts from some of the interviews are given in Appendix B.

3. METHODOLOGY OF GLOBE RESEARCH IN INDIA

The GLOBE research in India consisted of focus groups, interviews, media analysis, literature review, participant and unobtrusive observation, and questionnaire-based data collection. Three focus groups were conducted, two in India, one in the United States. Of the two in India, one was carried out with nine managers from the Indian subsidiary of an American company. This company was very close to the private sector, the free-market end of the continuum of Indian economy. All of the nine participants worked at a manufacturing plant located in western India. The second focus group in India had eight participants; all were managers of a very large bank owned and operated by the government. This bank came very close to the public sector–controlled economy end of the Indian economy. Although the bank operated all over the country and its managers could be located anywhere, participants in the focus group had only been situated in one of the states in western India. The work experience of the participants in these two focus groups ranged from 8 to 32 years with a mean of 18.26 years, and they belonged to different levels of middle management. Participants in both the focus groups in India were given a preparatory assignment prior to the focus group. The assignment is shown in Appendix C.

The focus group conducted in the United States had nine participants, all of whom had work experience in India ranging from 1 to 8 years with a mean of 3.2 years. All of the participants were engaged in graduate studies in the United States at the time of the focus group. Four participants had worked in public-sector organizations, four in the government, and one in a private-sector firm.[6]

---

[6]The focus group in the United States was conducted by Rabi Bhagat.

Two types of interviews were conducted. Semistructured interviews were carried out with 15 managers (8 from the manufacturing plant and 7 from the bank) who had participated in the two focus groups in India. These interviewees, though belonging to different states, had spent a major portion, if not all, of their working lives in the same state in western India. The duration of these interviews ranged from 45 minutes to 1½ hours. These interviews were semistructured in the sense that though the interviewer had a list of questions to be asked, these were only possible and guiding questions, the later ones being open-ended questions. The interviews were thus essentially free-flowing in which the interviewees were actually encouraged to express themselves freely. Some of the guiding questions used in the interviews are given in Appendix D.

Interviews in the second set were almost completely unstructured and free-form. These were conducted with three middle managers from a financial services firm. This firm had a network of offices and branches all over the country. All three interviewees worked at the corporate office and their work experience ranged from 3 to 8 years. One of the three was a woman. The interviewees belonged to different parts of the country; one was from a western state, one from a state in the northwest of India, and one from the south. The duration of these interviews varied from 1½ to 2½ hours. The interviews began with a brief description of the project and the interviewees were asked to describe their perception and understanding of leadership. Some of the opening comments by the interviewer were as follows:

> What, in your opinion, is leadership? What is a leader? What makes a good leader? What do you think are different types of leaders? Why are some good, why are some not so good? ... It is a free-flowing thing—trying to capture your concept and understanding of leadership in all its essence, in all its diversions, in all its components. ... Please give me your spontaneous views— but in as much detail as possible.

After the opening remarks, the interviewees expressed themselves as unhindered and the interviewer did not interfere except either to request clarification, or elaboration, or to ask a question when the interviewee seemed to come to the end of the description of an idea, an incident, or a concept. The three interviews were audiotaped and were subsequently transcribed. The transcriptions were content analyzed and the conclusions were shared with the interviewees in a follow-up discussion. The interviewees were asked for their reactions to the results of the content analysis of the transcripts. These discussions lasted for about half an hour with each interviewee. The interviewees agreed with most of the findings and did not suggest any significant changes in what had been inferred from the analysis as their view of leadership.

Media analysis was done by reviewing the contents of two daily newspapers, one general *(The Times of India)* and one business *(The Economic Times)* for two periods of two weeks each, with a gap of one month in between; and two news magazines, one general *(India Today)* and one business *(Business India),* two issues of each, with a gap of 1 month in between. The circulation figures for these four publications are given in the accompanying Table 27.1. *The Times of India* had the highest circulation among all the daily newspapers, and *The Economic Times* had the highest circulation among all the business, economic, and financial newspapers.

All reports that had anything to do with or referred even parenthetically to leadership were marked and extracted for analysis. These were then content analyzed with the objective of developing an understanding of leadership as it is viewed by society. Obviously this emergent view of leadership in society was to some extent influenced by the editorial slant of these four publications.

TABLE 27.1
Newspaper Circulation Rates

Newspaper	Circulation
The Times of India	1,074,000
The Economic Times	372,000
India Today	407,000
Business India	97,572

Note. From Audit Bureau of Circulations, New Delhi (July to December 1996).

Content analyses of the interviews and media reports were done by a research associate following guidelines contained within GLOBE documents authored by Agar (n.d.) and Thomas (n.d.). Findings of the analyses by the research associate were reviewed and cross-checked by the author. Participant and unobtrusive observations were made by some of the researchers involved in the project, and three other individuals who were considered informed and knowledgeable. These participants responded to a pool of items that could be observed by people who were part of the society.

The quantitative data were collected from a total of 214 middle-managerial respondents belonging to 10 organizations in two industries, financial services and food processing, with 113 and 101 respondents respectively. (Brief notes on these two industries are in Appendices E and F). There were five organizations in each industry. Six of the organizations were in the private sector and four were in the public sector. Seven were located in the western part of the country, two in the north, and one in the south. The number of respondents per organization varied from 10 to 44. Woman accounted for 30 out of the total 214 respondents. The average age of the respondents was 38.36 years, ranging from 21 to 63 years.

4. RESULTS

The results of the qualitative analyses are presented first, followed by those of the quantitative data.

Qualitative Analysis

Focus Group and Semistructured Interviews

All participants in the focus groups and all the interviewees almost unanimously saw leadership and management to be different. A large majority felt that leadership was a broader and somewhat "higher level" function than that of management.

The most common descriptions of *leadership* included having a vision, and a clear and broad direction and goal or objective. Leaders were expected to carry people with them, inspire individuals, and get them to do near impossible things. Effective communications and risk taking were considered important components of leadership. Leaders were also described as "knowing the pulse of the people," "finding out how people's minds tick and making it happen that way," having an intuitive understanding of people, caring—almost like a parent or "a king in the old days," being "natural," courageous, and innovative. They were also expected to develop the trust and loyalty of the followers and command their respect without having to ask for it, to set an example through their behaviors and actions, and to practice what they preached. Demonstrated capacity to solve problems, being high on integrity, ability to get an active consensus from a core group, and maintaining a network of contacts and connections were some of the other characteristics of outstanding leaders.

Most participants considered political leaders to be different from business leaders. Political leaders were considered to be more self-serving, clever, and exploitative, whereas business leaders were normally considered to be visionaries and charismatic, particularly within the context of their business organizations. Some truly exceptional business leaders were felt to have transcended the boundaries of their organizations and become leaders in society at large.

The definitions of leadership that emerged were "steering a group of people to contribute willingly towards a vision" and the "ability to get people to work willingly and enthusiastically towards one's own and organizational goals and priorities." A minority definition was "getting the job done through people." This rather small proportion of respondents felt that leadership was one of the components of management and that this component was confined to people or the human element of management. They, unlike the majority, thought leadership to be a narrower function than management.

Outstanding Leadership.   When asked to cite critical incidents to illustrate outstanding leadership, participants referred to unusual and almost dramatic behaviors such as Gandhi going on a fast to stop communal riots during India's partition and independence in 1947, and the chief executive of an organization making a decision, which he was apparently not authorized to make, publicly and on the spur of the moment, and sticking to it later. Outstanding leaders were thus expected to do things that were unusual, path breaking, and considered worthy, noble, innovative; and having done such things, were expected to stand by them and carry them through. Inspiring people, and being (a) a change agent and challenging the status quo, and (b) a visionary, were considered integral to being an outstanding leader. Perseverance, dedication, charisma, empathy, valuing people as individuals and as human beings and not only as followers or employees, capacity to spot the right people, high personal output, and going beyond the normal, were other characteristics of outstanding leaders. Courage, integrity, and self-confidence were considered to be the basic requirements for outstanding leadership.

Actions of leaders which significantly increased the motivation and commitment of the participants and made them "go above and beyond the call of duty" included (a) giving recognition for a job well done and for doing something that was not in the normal range of their responsibilities, (b) providing a sense of achievement to followers, (c) encouraging new, unusual initiatives, (d) reposing faith and confidence in followers, and giving them freedom, (e) involving followers in areas of work not directly related to them, and (f) taking personal care of the well-being of followers.

Leadership Style.   There were two broad conclusions. One, outstanding leaders have to be flexible in their behaviors and have to display a complex mixture of leadership styles depending on the situations they face. Two, there appeared to be general support and preference for *proactive, morally principled and ideological,* and *bold and assertive* styles of leadership as compared to reactive, pragmatic, and instrumental, and quiet and nurturing styles, respectively. Some participants felt that although expediency was acceptable, it had to be confined within certain limits saying "though achieving the end is what a leader is judged on, means are also important." An overwhelming majority, however, maintained that ideological and moral commitment is essential for outstanding leadership. The greatest flexibility appeared to be expected *and* accepted on the bold/assertive and quiet/nurturing dimensions.

Obstacles and Constraints Faced by Outstanding Leaders.   Two broad obstacles mentioned by respondents related to people (followers) not wanting to take responsibility, and communication problems and barriers. Leaders dealt with these by setting a personal example, and by clarifying the message and objective. Most respondents, however, felt that obstacles and constraints, though ubiquitous, do not really affect an outstanding leader. A common refrain was that obstacles and constraints can always be overcome if the leader is on high moral ground. One of the respondents said, "It is the mind-set which is more important." Another way to deal with obstacles and constraints was to "change people's perceptions of the constraints and obstacles, and to modify people's limits of compromise."

Role Models and Status.   Leaders are expected to be role models of values such as righteousness, dynamism, and innovation. Leadership is considered as not only desirable but necessary and even admirable. Leaders usually have high status and are generally looked up to and respected.

However, not all individuals in positions of authority are considered to be leaders in the real or strict sense. Current political leaders are an interesting example. They are specifically referred to as "political" leaders because of their present positions or because they have made political activity or politics as their profession. They also have a somewhat high status and are given importance because they happen to be part of the political establishment and can be instrumental in getting things done in a society such as India where there is considerable political meddling in almost all walks of life.

However, they are generally not considered to be good role models and do not evoke real respect and admiration. Interestingly, out of the 19 people mentioned as examples of outstanding leadership during the focus groups and interviews, only 4 were political leaders. Three of these four belonged to an earlier generation that was involved in India's freedom struggle in the 1940s, and one was India's prime minister from the early 1970s to mid-1980s. The latter died in 1984 and, therefore, may not really qualify as a contemporary political leader. Contemporary political leadership, thus, occupies a somewhat enigmatic position in Indian society—more like a necessary evil.

The remaining individuals mentioned as examples of outstanding leaders included 10 business and industry leaders, 3 social workers (including 2 environmentalists), 1 army general, and 1 spiritual-cum-religious leader. The complete list of these 19 individuals is in Appendix G. Most of these 19 are very well known although a couple of names are less familiar. These were senior managers in the organizations for which some of the participants worked.

The attributes of a normally effective manager, an above-average manager, and an outstanding leader, as listed by the participants in the two focus groups conducted in India, are given in Table 27.2.

In addition to what is mentioned in Appendix C, participants from both of the focus groups in India were asked to choose a country other than India, and compare the characteristics of managers in that country with those of managers in India. Participants in both the focus groups chose the United States for this comparison. The results of this are contained in Table 27.3.

TABLE 27.2
Findings of Focus Groups Conducted in India

Normally Effective Manager	Above-Average Manager	Outstanding Manager in (addition to "above average" manager)
Getting things done on time	Getting things done on time, with fewer resources	Inspiring people to unusual dedication and strong commitment
Carry out given work Maintenance function, motivates people	Demanding from his or her peoples, Inspires people; hard task master, if situation demands	Visionary, Future oriented Imaginative, creative, innovative; always works with and leads the team
Uses power and fear	Will carve out little bit extra work; over & above given work	Inspires confidence, not only below but also above the line/hierarchy
Just about manages to do what is set out for him or her	Creative, above maintenance	Looks for new opportunities, untrodden paths
Goal set by the organization is the ultimate, nothing beyond that	Creates atmosphere to make work itself motivating	Charismatic
Routine worker-type	Uses love and willingness	Good communicator
Generally less often, to lesser extent the characteristics of above-average manager	Thinks beyond his or her area of immediate responsibility	Vision more expanded, going beyond the commonly under stood boundary of organizations, society, etc.
	Attaches a lot of value to work, also to people	Getting people to do something that most others have not been able to do
	Greater delegation, selective monitoring	Rises to the occasion
	Gets involved in things outside the work environment	Looks at things in totality, macro view, overall picture
	Flexibility of behaviors	Quick grasping power
	Concerned about development of his or her people	Pushing boundaries beyond what is considered possible
		Practices what he or she preaches
		Courage to take larger or greater risk
		Fast response
		Also builds the team
		Translating vision into mission
		Trust of followers
		Motivator
		Empathy
		Carrying people with him or her
		Human element (humane)
		Deductive, decisive
		Conceptual abilities

TABLE 27.3
Comparison of Indian and American Managers in Focus Groups Conducted in India

Indian Managers	American Managers
• Somewhat lackadaisical and indifferent	• Task oriented
• More relationship oriented	• Impersonal
• Somewhat knowledgeable in several areas/fields	• Tend to be specialized but only in one area
• Long-term time horizon	• Short-term time horizon (here and now, at the most couple of years)
• Believe verbal statements	• Don't believe in verbal statements; require documentary proof
• More trusting	• Less trusting
• Emotion oriented	• Fact oriented
• Efforts oriented	• Result oriented
• Less demanding	• More demanding
• Conservative, cautious	• Generally less conservative
• Low risk taking	• Higher risk taking
• "Hurting others is not good"	• "Does not matter if others are hurt"
• Greater human touch (humane)	• Materialistic, cold
• Formal	• Informal
	• Better equipped in terms of equipment & facilities
	• Better time managers

Media Analysis

The summarized findings of the media analysis are shown in Table 27.4. The characteristic most frequently mentioned in the context of leadership and leaders is "change," followed by a somewhat distant second, "action." The rankings of these two are identical in both time periods, indicating consistency across time periods. Characteristics other than change and action, which appeared consistently among the top 10 in both periods, were control, direction, communication, culture, and charisma. Some statements illustrative of these characteristics that appeared in media reports are given in Appendix H.

Leaders, according to media analysis, therefore are above all expected to be harbingers of change, and action oriented. They should be able to exercise control and provide direction. The ability to communicate effectively is also an important requirement. An interest in and a concern for cultural values is also useful for effective leadership. Though charisma was among the top 10 in both time periods, its relatively low ranking is worth noting. A possible and partial explanation may be that a large majority of media reports pertained to political leadership and the low ranking of charisma may be a reflection of the low esteem of the current political leadership in society. The even lower ranking of "vision," which overall ranked 15, is also worth noting. It was ranked 17 and 11 in the two time periods. The explanation for this also could be similar to that for charisma.

Unstructured Interviews

The results of the content analysis of unstructured interviews are shown in Table 27.5. In this case the top two characteristics of leaders are communication skills and vision, followed by direction, action, change orientation, and charisma. Some illustrative statements made by the interviewees about these characteristics are given in Appendix I.

TABLE 27.4
Results of Media Analysis

Characteristics of Leadership and Leaders	Total			First Period			Second Period		
	Rank	Freq.	%	Rank	Freq.	%	Rank	Freq.	%
Change	1	103	27.76	1	46	27.06	1	57	28.36
Action	2	52	14.29	2	19	11.18	2	34	16.92
Control	3	24	6.47	3	16	9.41	5	8	3.98
Direction	4	22	5.93	4	15	8.82	7	7	3.48
Communication	5	19	5.12	9	7	4.12	3	12	5.97
Culture	6	18	4.85	10	6	3.53	3	12	5.97
Charisma	7	17	4.59	6	9	5.29	5	8	3.98
Objective	8	13	3.50	6	9	5.29	11	4	1.99
Energetic	9	11	2.96	8	8	4.71	15	3	1.49
Systematic	9	11	2.96	5	11	6.47	–	–	–
Image	11	9	2.43	12	3	1.76	8	6	2.99
Strategy	12	6	1.62	–	0	–	8	6	2.99
Caste	12	6	1.62	–	0	–	8	6	2.99
Autocratic	12	6	1.62	12	3	1.76	15	3	1.49
Commitment	15	5	1.35	11	4	2.35	23	1	0.50
Aggression	15	5	1.35	15	2	1.18	15	3	1.49
Role Model	15	5	1.35	17	1	0.59	11	4	1.99
Vision	15	5	1.35	17	1	0.59	11	4	1.99
Knowledge	19	4	1.08	17	1	0.59	15	3	1.49
Survival	19	4	1.08	12	3	1.76	23	1	0.50
Facilitate	19	4	1.08	–	2	–	11	4	1.99
Confident	19	4	1.08	15	1	1.18	20	2	1.00
Shrewd	23	3	0.81	17	–	0.59	20	2	1.00
Manipulative	23	3	0.81	–	–	–	15	3	1.49
Corruption	23	2	0.54	–	–	–	20	2	1.00
Ambition	26	1	0.27	–	–	–	23	1	0.50
Glamour	27	1	0.27	–	–	–	23	1	0.50
Optimistic	27	1	0.27	–	–	–	23	1	0.50
Accusation	27	1	0.27	–	–	–	23	1	0.50
Competition	27	1	0.27	–	–	–	23	1	0.50
Accommodate	27	1	0.27	–	–	–	23	1	0.50
Avoidance	27	1	0.27	17	1	0.59	–	–	–
Democratic	27	1	0.27	17	1	0.59	–	–	–
Responsibility	27	1	0.27	17	1	0.59	–	–	–
Total		371	100.3		170	10.00		201	100.4

Though the rankings of the media analysis and unstructured interviews do exhibit a general and overall similarity, the differences in the ranking of specific characteristics may indicate a subtle yet important difference. Unstructured interviews were conducted with middle managers of a business organization and the importance given by them with regard to communication, vision, and direction possibly reflects a view about business leadership, whereas the media reports may reflect a general view somewhat more focused on political and social leadership.

TABLE 27.5
Content Analysis of Unstructured Interviews

Characteristics of Leaders	Rank	Frequency	Percent
Communication Skills	1	12	16.00
Vision	2	9	12.00
Direction	3	6	8.00
Action	3	6	8.00
Change Orientation	3	6	8.00
Charisma	3	6	8.00
Understanding	3	6	8.00
Responsibility	8	4	5.33
Knowledge	9	3	4.00
Aggression	10	3	4.00
Strategy	11	2	2.67
Autocratic	11	2	2.67
Energy	13	1	1.33
Optimistic	13	1	1.33
Cultured	13	1	1.33
Dynamic	13	1	1.33
Systematic	13	1	1.33
Value-Driven	13	1	1.33
Entrepreneurial	13	1	1.33
Egoistical	13	1	1.33
Delegative	13	1	1.33
Broad-minded	13	1	1.33
Total		75	100

Summary of Qualitative Results

Combining the results of all the qualitative data, six characteristics seem to be most strongly associated with effective leadership in India. Communication and direction are the most important followed by vision, action orientation, charisma, and change.

Participant and Unobtrusive Observation

A summary of participant and unobtrusive observations pertaining to the core GLOBE dimensions of societal culture is given next.

Performance Orientation.   Most organizations of a medium to large size have formal performance appraisal systems in place. It is, however, not uncommon for evaluators to avoid giving poor performance ratings. Promotions are often based on a combination of performance rating, seniority, and suitability. Society as a whole does recognize and respect individual achievement. Several schools recognize scholastic performance through rewards. Universities usually award medals to top-performing graduates. The government also confers awards for achieving excellence in various fields including sports. Admissions to leading undergraduate colleges are almost always based on the academic performance at the high school level. Entrepreneurship, traditionally confined to certain community groups, has in the past few years started becoming more widespread; and entrepreneurs have started attracting increasing social recognition.

Future Orientation.   Historically and traditionally, Indian society has emphasized the "hereafter" in preference to the "here and now," and therefore has been generally future oriented. The government also encourages future orientation by providing tax breaks on savings. There is no state-funded social security system, but employers are required by law to contribute to what is called a provident fund to provide postretirement benefits for employees. Interest paid on housing loans is eligible for tax benefits. The concept of providing for the "hereafter" at times extends to even providing for after death, with some people engaging in actions, ceremonies, and rituals that they hope will improve their lot in their next lives following the doctrine of *karma*. These sometimes take the form of contributions to charitable and religious activities and institutions.

Gender Egalitarianism.   India's society continues to be male-dominated in spite of having had a very strong woman prime minister (who was sometimes described as "the only *man* in the cabinet"), who had one of the longest tenures in that position. The number of women in the higher echelons of all professions is still minuscule. A large majority of women continue to be homemakers and are expected to be so, in spite of making substantial contributions to the income-generating activities of the family such as agriculture in rural areas. In urban areas where more women work outside their homes, caring professions such as nursing and teaching are considered more appropriate for women. There are no professions that women are legally prevented from entering. India has women working as commercial pilots and as officers in the Army, for example. Even when they work as professionals outside the home, responsibility for housework and childrearing continues to rest almost solely with women.

A large majority of national and social heroes are men. The literacy rate for women is lower than that for men. Traditionally it was considered preferable and sometimes even necessary for a woman to bear male children for two reasons, dowry and continuing the family lineage; and having female children was often considered undesirable. This situation continues in some sections of society even today, though dowry is forbidden by law. Polygamy is illegal except for some religious groups under certain conditions. Women were excluded from entering some temples and from priesthood until very recently but legal action has abolished these restrictions. There has been a substantial amount of legislation to reduce gender differentiation, including the reservation of 33% of elected positions in the *panchayats* (village councils) for women.

Humane Orientation.   Accidents at work are required to be investigated and reported to designated authorities. There are specific provisions in law for compensation for injuries arising in the workplace. There is a law against begging but its implementation is very slack. There *are* a few institutions, generally religious, that provide food for the homeless and the poor. Adult and child prisoners are kept in separate facilities. There are special schools for handicapped people, but not all those with handicaps can take advantage of them. Organizations are encouraged by the government to employ handicapped people. Cases of brutality and torture by the police do happen but they also create uproar. The preferred mode of settling personal disputes is conciliation or arbitration, as opposed to involving the police, partly due to their reputation for not helping. Whenever an individual suffers a personal or family tragedy, neighbors, friends, and acquaintances always offer and do provide help. Being altruistic and charitable is also considered to help in improving one's lot after life, and thus overlaps with future orientation.

Power Distance. Indian society is quite structured and stratified. Two major contributors to this are the centuries-old caste system and almost 200 years of British rule. The Indian Civil Service, which the British used as a major instrument of governance, and an Indianized version of which continues even today, was a very hierarchical and formal structure, and has had a widespread impact on Indian organizations. Work titles are often displayed on doors. Offices, office spaces, and privileges at work tend to reflect one's status in the organization. Eating places for workers and managers are often different. Social rights and privileges vary with one's status and are fairly clearly understood. There are "powerful" families in every village, town, and city, and their power is generally accepted by most other residents. Certain groups or classes of people are considered to be influential and they evoke respect from others. Wealthier families tend to have full-time domestic help, often referred to as servants. Families of political leaders often come to be considered to have higher status.

Collective Orientation. The family continues to be one of the basic units of Indian society. Children are trained to first depend on, and subsequently support, the family. The concept of "joint" or "extended" family where more than two generations live as part of one household, which weakened for some time, seems to have acquired a new lease on life particularly in urban areas. With an increasing number of women in cities working outside the home, grandparents are now often considered a welcome resource for the child care that they provide because it is not easily available otherwise. Unmarried adults usually live with parents, and the "joint family" arrangement often continues even after the children get married. In some major cities, it also happens as an economic necessity as affordable housing is often hard to find. In such joint households, a "common kitchen" is often a standard feature where meals for everyone are cooked and eaten together. When friends and colleagues at work go out to eat, dishes are invariably shared. It is quite common for older members of the family to arrange marriages for younger members, even when the latter are professionally and economically independent. Help of family members and friends is often sought, and provided, in dealing with personal problems and crises.

Uncertainty Avoidance. Attempts to reduce the unpredictability of future events are quite common. There are specified age limits for voting and for holding public offices, and there is a minimum age for marriage. Social customs and norms especially for major life events such as birth, marriage, and death are quite well established and are widely followed, though these vary depending on religious and social grouping. There is great stress on good performance at school particularly among children of middle-class parents, at times resulting in too much pressure on the children. Religious beliefs and practices arising out of them are a major source of attempts to reduce uncertainty of the future.

Culture-Specific Manifestations of Indian Culture

Given the diversity and complexity of society and culture in India, it is not easy to find manifestations of "Indian" culture that are (a) common to the entire country without exception and (b) unique to the country insofar as these are not found in other countries. A few characteristics, however, do stand out, though they are also found in several other countries whose societies may be termed as traditional and collectivist. Some of these are briefly described next.

Rituals and Ceremonies.   Rituals, ceremonies, and other similar practices are quite common in almost all walks of life. Initiation of major activities, such as starting a new business, opening a new plant, date of marriage, and even swearing-in of cabinets, are often scheduled around what are considered to be auspicious dates and times. There is a widespread interest in astrology. Astrologers are often consulted not only to reveal what the future holds, but also to determine the appropriate date and time to undertake important activities.

Concept of Time.   There is a kind of ambivalence about time and punctuality. Whereas a number of official and business activities do occur in a preset, though somewhat flexible time frame, social activities and functions are often delayed. This ambivalence was attributed by a Western observer to language when he discovered that the word for yesterday and tomorrow in some Indian languages was the same (*kal*), and therefore it did not make a difference if a meeting was held yesterday or tomorrow, for example. It was, however, explained to this observer that whereas one particular day might be critical in a finite and limited concept of time, it was not so in an unending continuum of time, which goes on even before and after one's present life. This was a possible reason as to why the need for two different separate words for yesterday and tomorrow was not felt. This is in some ways similar to the different concepts of time mentioned by Edward Hall (1976).

Family-Controlled and -Managed Business Organizations.   Some of the largest business organizations in India are controlled by the families of their founders. The families control the management of these companies even though they own only a minority of common stock. Some of the current prominent business families are the Tatas, Birlas, Ambanis, Mahindras, and Shrirams. Such companies, or groups of companies, are usually headed by a member of the family, often a son or grandson of the founder. Key positions in management are often held by members of the "extended" family, which might include relatives by marriage, or by close friends and confidants. A dilution of management control to professional managers, who are not connected to the family, happens with generational changes and often becomes substantial by the third generation after the founder.

Deference to Age and Status.   In keeping with the traditional nature of the society and in spite of being in transition, people of higher age and status are still often treated with respect and deference. Seniority continues to have value in almost all types of organizations. It is common for seniors to be addressed formally by their last name. Honorifics such as Mr., Mrs., Sir, and Madam, and their equivalents in Indian languages are widely used.

Quantitative Analyses

The results comparing India with other cultures are presented first, followed by somewhat detailed results of confirmatory and exploratory factor analyses of leadership items.

Societal Culture "As Is" and "Should Be"

Table 27.6 contains India's average scores for societal culture "As Is" and societal culture "Should Be" based on the nine core GLOBE dimensions of societal culture. The table also shows the ranking of India for each of the dimensions when compared against the other 61 countries that participated in Phase 2 of the GLOBE Research Program. Countries scoring the highest and the lowest on each dimension are also identified along with their average scores.

TABLE 27.6
Societal Culture "As Is" and "Should Be"

Societal Culture "As Is"	India (Rank)	Highest (Country)	Lowest (Country)
Assertiveness	3.73 (53)	4.80 (Albania)	3.38 (Sweden)
Institutional Collectivism (Collectivism I)	4.38 (25)	5.22 (Sweden)	3.25 (Greece)
In-Group Collectivism (Collectivism II)	5.92 (4)	6.36 (Philippines)	3.53 (Denmark)
Future Orientation	4.19 (15)	5.07 (Singapore)	2.88 (Russia)
Gender Egalitarianism	2.90 (55)	4.08 (Hungary)	2.50 (South Korea)
Humane Orientation	4.57 (9)	5.23 (Zambia)	3.18 (Germany)
Performance Orientation	4.25 (23)	4.94 (Switzerland)	3.20 (Greece)
Power Distance	5.47 (16)	5.80 (Morocco)	3.89 (Denmark)
Uncertainty Avoidance	4.15 (29)	5.37 (Switzerland)	2.88 (Russia)

Societal Culture "Should Be"	India (Rank)	Highest (Country)	Lowest (Country)
Assertiveness	4.76 (7)	5.56 (Japan)	2.66 (Turkey)
Institutional Collectivism (Collectivism I)	4.71 (32)	5.65 (El Salvador)	3.83 (Georgia)
In-Group Collectivism (Collectivism II)	5.32 (50)	6.52 (El Salvador)	4.94 (Switzerland)
Future Orientation	5.60 (29)	6.20 (Thailand)	4.33 (Denmark)
Gender Egalitarianism	4.51 (36)	5.17 (England)	3.18 (Egypt)
Humane Orientation	5.28 (44)	6.09 (Nigeria)	4.49 (New Zealand)
Performance Orientation	6.05 (26)	6.58 (El Salvador)	4.92 (S.Africa Black Sample)
Power Distance	2.64 (38)	3.65 (S.Africa Black Sample)	2.04 (Colombia)
Uncertainty Avoidance	4.73 (29)	5.61 (Thailand)	3.16 (Switzerland)

The highest rankings obtained by India for Society "As Is" are on In-Group Collectivism, Humane Orientation, Future Orientation, and Power Distance. This is as would be expected from the description of the evolution of Indian culture in an earlier section of this chapter. The contradiction in Indian society has been described as follows: *"The conflict is between two approaches to the problem of social organization, which are diametrically opposed to each other: the old Hindu conception of the group being the basic unit of organization, and the excessive individualism of the west, emphasizing the individual above the group" (Nehru, 1985, p. 246).*

The scores for India are quite high among all of the participating countries on all dimensions except Gender Egalitarianism and Assertiveness. The score for Uncertainty Avoidance is somewhat different from the expectation of a lower value as mentioned in an earlier section. The relatively low score on Gender Egalitarianism indicates a greater emphasis on the male role, as expected. High scores on In-Group Collectivism and Power Distance are also in keeping with expectations. The relatively high score on Performance Orientation is somewhat surprising because only a moderate Performance Orientation was expected. This might be due to the increasing focus on material success and may also be a reflection of the recent changes in the economic policy and environment, which have consciously encouraged competition.

The most significant finding following a comparison of the "As Is" scores of India with the "Should Be" scores is that for Power Distance. A strong preference for the reduction of Power Distance is indicated. This is in keeping with the earlier conclusion that political equality experienced since independence has increased the desire for social equality, and that a struggle for altering broad power relations in the society at large is currently in existence. Another dimension for which a preference for lowering, though marginal, has been expressed is In-Group Collectivism. The focus on materialism is possibly also causing an increase in individualism in society, particularly among the managerial class, which experiences competition every day, particularly at work. There appears to be a clear preference for a higher level of Performance Orientation, Future Orientation, Gender Egalitarianism, and Assertiveness. The preferred increases in Humane Orientation and Uncertainty Avoidance are not as high as those in the former four dimensions. The least increase preferred is in Institutional Collectivism. Though India is a traditional, conservative, and male-dominated society in a number of ways, respondents' preference for equal emphasis for male and female roles is an indicator of the depth of the change which society is going through on the gender issue.[7]

Leadership

India's average scores and rankings based on the 21 first-order leadership scales used in the GLOBE research program are in Table 27.7, which also shows the countries scoring the highest and the lowest on these scales.

Among intercountry rankings, the highest rankings for India are for charismatic (self-sacrificial), face saver, self-centered (9 each), and malevolent (2). It is, however, important to note that these are the scales getting the highest ranking for India in the *intercountry comparisons*, and that these are *not* the scales that got the highest ranking among different scales *within India.*

The five highest ranking scales *within* India are charismatic (visionary), integrity, administratively competent, performance orientation, and charismatic (inspirational), in that order. These are followed by decisive, team integrator, and diplomatic. Malevolent, self-centered, nonparticipative, autocratic, and face saver are the five lowest ranking scales *within* India.

---

[7]This assumes even greater significance as only 14% of the sample were women.

TABLE 27.7
First-Order Leadership Dimensions

Attribute	India (Rank)	Highest (Country)	Lowest (Country)
Administratively Competent	5.98 (20)	6.42 (Iran)	4.53 (France)
Autocratic	3.10 (12)	3.86 (Russia)	1.89 (Canada)
Autonomous	3.85 (32)	6.05 (Argentina)	2.27 (Brazil)
Charismatic (Inspirational)	5.93 (42)	6.63 (Ecuador)	5.04 (Qatar)
Charismatic (Self-Sacrificial)	5.45 (9)	5.99 (Ecuador)	3.98 (France)
Charismatic (Visionary)	6.02 (40)	6.50 (Ecuador)	4.62 (Qatar)
Collaborative Team Oriented	5.51 (31)	6.09 (Brazil)	4.42 (Qatar)
Conflict Inducer	4.24 (18)	5.01 (Taiwan)	3.09 (Denmark)
Decisive	5.83 (33)	6.37 (Philippines)	3.62 (Qatar)
Diplomatic	5.70 (12)	6.05 (Argentina)	4.49 (Qatar)
Face Saver	3.57 (9)	4.63 (Albania)	2.05 (Finland)
Humane	5.17 (12)	5.68 (Georgia)	2.23 (Argentina)
Integrity	5.99 (42)	6.79 (Ecuador)	4.72 (Argentina)
Malevolent	2.35 (2)	2.67 (S-Africa Black Sample)	1.33 (Brazil)
Modesty	5.33 (14)	5.86 (Iran)	4.14 (Kazakhstan)
Nonparticipative	2.93 (17)	3.61 (Albania)	1.86 (France)
Performance Orientation	5.96 (41)	6.64 (Ecuador)	4.51 (Qatar)
Procedural	4.1 (23)	5.12 (Albania)	2.82 (Denmark)
Self-Centered	2.63 (9)	6.2 (Albania)	1.55 (Finland)
Status Conscious	4.18 (36)	5.93 (Kuwait)	3.00 (Argentina)
Team Integrator	5.83 (37)	6.43 (Brazil)	4.1 (Qatar)

India was among the countries that scored quite high on the latter scales. The high inter-country ranking of India on these scales can be understood in the context of Indians having "developed 'encompassing systems' (Dumont, 1970) through which contradictions between thoughts and

TABLE 27.8
Second-Order Leadership Dimensions

Attribute	India (Rank)	Highest (Country)	Lowest (Country)
Autonomous	3.85	4.63	2.27
	(32)	(Russia)	(Brazil)
Charismatic	5.85	6.46	4.51
	(36)	(Ecuador)	(Qatar)
Humane	5.26	5.75	3.82
	(9)	(Iran)	(France)
Participative	4.99	6.09	4.5
	(48)	(Canada)	(Albania)
Self-Protective	3.77	4.62	2.55
	(15)	(Albania)	(Finland)
Team Oriented	5.72	6.21	4.74
	(41)	(Ecuador)	(Qatar)

actions, instead of leading to dissonance and confrontation, are *balanced, accommodated, integrated,* or *allowed to coexist* (Marriott, 1976)" (Sinha, 1997, p. 61, emphasis in original). Being self-centered also has roots in the importance assigned to understanding oneself in some of the traditional belief systems in India. Introspection is often valued as an important activity even to process external experiences. Roland's (1988) observation that Indians can keep important secrets in a much more guarded manner and for longer durations than Americans, even in therapeutic situations, may also be considered as an indicator of being self-absorbed. Face saving acquires importance due to the high sensitivity of Indians to context their thoughts and practices (Ramanujan, 1989). Triandis and Bhawuk (1997) claim even lying to be acceptable in collectivist cultures when it serves the purpose of saving face. The preference for autocratic leadership can possibly be traced to the long history of benevolent, autocratic monarchs. The rankings following the five highest, those of decisive, team integrator, diplomatic, collaborative (team oriented), charismatic (self-sacrificial), modesty, and humane, appear to fit the expectations from the description of Indian leadership given earlier. It is also worth noting that the average scores for India are placed in the top half of all the participating countries for 13 of the 21 scales. These 13 scales are administratively competent, autocratic, charismatic (self-sacrificial), collaborative (team oriented), conflict-inducer, diplomatic, face saver, humane, malevolent, modesty, nonparticipative, procedural, and self-centered. This gives a general idea of the comparative perception of the attributes for effective leadership in India.

Second-Order Leadership Dimensions

India's average scores and rankings on the six second-order leadership dimensions of the GLOBE Research Project are in Table 27.8. The countries scoring the highest and the lowest on these dimensions are also shown.

In the *intercountry comparison,* India's highest rankings are on the humane (9) and self-protective (15) dimensions. In a comparison of the dimensions *within India,* charismatic scores the highest (5.85), followed by team oriented (5.72), and humane (5.26). Participative (4.99) is the middle dimension, whereas self-protective (3.77) and autonomous (3.85) are the lowest two dimensions.

TABLE 27.9
Confirmatory Factor Analysis of Leadership Scales Goodness-of-Fit Indicators

Statistics	First-Order CFA (16 Scales Structure Acc. to Pilot Study 2)	Second-Order CFA Modified Factor Structure 14 Scales	16 Scales Could Load on Different Factors
	Column 1	Column 2	Column 3
Chi Square	2454.94	313.97	30.11
Df	510	70	58
P	0.00	0.00	0.99
Number of items	36	14	16
CFI	0.62	0.91	1.00
GFI	0.62	0.84	0.98
AGFI	0.48	0.77	0.96
PGFI	0.45	0.56	0.42
NFI	0.58	0.88	0.99
NNFI	0.51	0.88	1.02
PNFI	0.44	0.68	0.48
RMSEA	0.13	0.12	0.00
RMSR	0.19	0.10	0.02
Sig Load	1 ns	1 ns	3 ns

Note.   CFI = comparative fit index; GFI = goodness of fit index; AGFI = adjusted goodness-of-fit index; NFI = normed fit index; PGFI = parsimony goodness-of-fit index; NNFI = non-normed fit index; PNFI = parsimony normed fit index; RMSR = root mean square residual; RMSEA = root mean square error of approximation.

Factor Analysis of Leadership Items

Though the leadership instrument contained 112 items, only 76 items were used for the factor analyses reported next. The remaining items were not included for the following two reasons:

- Previous work with these items in the two pilot studies of GLOBE indicated that these were universally endorsed as being indicators of effective leadership, and failed to load on the previously developed GLOBE scales. These items were thus referred to as the "universals."
- Using 76 items with 214 observations provided an adequate item–observations ratio for performing factor analysis.

Confirmatory Factor Analyses.   A confirmatory factor analysis (CFA) of the 76 items was attempted to determine if the data were best represented by the 16-factor solution of the GLOBE Pilot Study 2.[8] The 76 items were aggregated into 36 parcels, which is a common practice in structural equation modeling (Bernstein & Teng, 1989; Kishton & Widaman, 1994; Takahashi & Nasser, 1996). The rules employed for aggregation were: (a) Each factor should contain at least 2 parcels and at most three parcels, and (b) only items that were highly correlated were combined so that to the extent possible only items with common variance were aggregated. The results of this and subsequent CFAs are presented in Table 27.9.

---

[8]The CFA was done with reference to the analysis and findings of GLOBE Pilot Study 2 because that was the final step in developing the GLOBE instruments. Please see House et al. (2004) for a description of the process of developing the GLOBE instruments.

TABLE 27.10

Confirmatory Factor Analysis for Second-Order Factor Structure of Leadership Scales

Characteristic	Second-Order Factors				
	Factor 1	Factor 2	Factor 3	Factor 4	Factor 5
Visionary	0.90*				
Performance Orientation	0.89*				
Inspirational	0.88*				
Decisive	0.85*				
Diplomatic	0.84*				0.05
Integrity	0.52*		0.34*		
Collective		0.89*			
Procedural		0.83*			
Bureaucratic		0.59*			
Calm			0.89*		
Humane Orientation			0.67*		
Individualism				0.89*	
Autocratic					0.89*
Status-Conscious					0.54*

Note. Five second-order factors, 14 scales of Pilot Study 2, India data. Factor labels: 1 = Charismatic and Action-Oriented Leadership; 2 = Bureaucratic Leadership; 3 = Humane Leadership; 4 = Individualistic Leadership; 5 = Autocratic Leadership.
*$p < 0.05$.

From column 1 of Table 27.9 it is seen that the 16-factor model indicated a poor data–model fit. None of the indices meet the generally accepted criterion levels for fit (Tabachnik & Fidell, 1996). However, this result was not entirely unexpected. Attempting to capture 16 latent variables through 36 parcels is expected to be unwieldy due to the high levels of random error in the items (parcels) (Bagozzi & Heatherton, 1994), further exacerbated by the covariations among the 16 latent variable themselves. Subsequently, to overcome the problems associated with the partially disaggregated approach explained earlier, a second-order CFA of the 16 scales identified in the Pilot Study 2 was attempted with the Indian data, to examine the stability of the five-factor structure that emerged in Pilot Study 2. A 16×16 correlation matrix was analyzed using maximum likelihood estimation. The CFA did not converge due to problems of multicollinearity particularly with the self-centered and face-saving dimensions. Because these two dimensions were contaminating the entire data set, they were eliminated and the resulting 14×14 correlation matrix was analyzed. The results showed a remarkable improvement in fit indices (chi-square = 313.965, $p < .00$, CFI = 0.905, GFI = 0.844, AGFI = 0.766, RMSEA = 0.123—column 2 of Table 27.9). All factor loadings, as shown in Table 27.10, were significant except for the loading of the diplomatic dimension on Factor 5. Also, the pattern of factor loadings closely matched the factor loadings obtained in Pilot Study 2, which are shown in Table 27.11.

Although the fit indices improved substantially, they did not reach acceptable levels. However, this is to be expected. Given that the items theoretically classified under their respective content domains did not empirically load correspondingly in the Indian sample, the second-order CFA displayed problems of multicollinearity that worked to reduce the overall data–model fit. Though it would have been ideal to do a second-order CFA of the 18-scale Indian model with a second sample from India, it could not be done because a

TABLE 27.11
Confirmatory Factor Analysis for Second-Order Factors Structure of Leadership Scales

Characteristic	Second-Order Factors				
	Factor 1	*Factor 2*	*Factor 3*	*Factor 4*	*Factor 5*
Decisive	0.83[*]				
Visionary	0.80[*]		0.23[*]		
Performance Orientation	0.67[*]				
Inspirational	0.62[*]		−0.20[*]		
Diplomatic	0.62[*]				0.22[*]
Integrity	0.46[*]		0.51[*]		
Face Saving	−0.34[*]				
Self-Centered	−0.64[*]	0.11		0.76[*]	
Collective		0.90[*]			
Procedural		0.77[*]			
Bureaucratic		0.56[*]			
Status-Conscious		0.29[*]			0.40[*]
Calm			0.83[*]		
Humane Orientation			0.80[*]		
Individualism				0.57[*]	
Autocratic					1.00[*]

Note.   Pilot Study 2 data. Factor labels: 1 = Charismatic and Action-Oriented Leadership; 2 = Bureaucratic
Leadership; 3 = Humane Leadership; 4 = Individualistic Leadership; 5 = Autocratic Leadership.
[*]$p < 0.05$.

second sample was not available. However, some preliminary modifications were attempted
that helped in increasing the overall data–model fit. The modifications effected were the
following:

- Face-saving dimension was allowed to load on Factor 5.
- Humane orientation was allowed to load on Factor 2.
- Bureaucratic dimension was allowed to load on Factor 5.
- Self-centered dimension was allowed to load on Factor 5.
- Procedural dimension was allowed to load on Factor 1.

The fit indices of this CFA are in column 3 of Table 27.9 and the resultant factor loadings are
in Table 27.12.

With these modifications the data–model fit improved further and even the chi-square value
was nonsignificant, indicating a good fit. Some possible explanations for the results are:

- The self-centered dimension has been problematic in all the analyses performed on the
Indian sample, indicating a multicollinearity problem. It loaded significantly on both Factors
1 and 5, whereas theoretically it should have loaded on Factor 4. This could mean that in the
Indian context, self-centeredness is more strongly positively associated with autocratic
leader behaviors and strongly negatively associated with charismatic leader behaviors.

TABLE 27.12

Confirmatory Factor Analysis for Second-Order Factors Structure of Leadership Scales

Characteristic	Second-Order Factors				
	Factor 1	Factor 2	Factor 3	Factor 4	Factor 5
Performance Orientation	0.98*	−0.15*			
Inspirational	0.89*			0.20*	−0.18*
Decisive	0.85*				
Visionary	0.77*	0.19*			
Collective	0.64*	0.34*			
Procedural	0.58*	0.01	0.28*		
Integrity	0.51*		0.38*		
Diplomatic	0.41*		0.49*		
Face Saving	−0.13				0.78*
Self-Centered	−0.57*				0.86*
Humane Orientation		0.90*			
Bureaucratic		0.46*		−0.27*	0.68*
Status-Conscious		0.14			0.49$_*$
Calm			0.89*		
Autocratic			−0.28*		0.79*
Individualism				0.89*	

Note. Five second-order factors, 16 scales of Pilot Study 2, Indian data. Scales allowed to load on other than original factors. Factor labels: 1 = Charismatic and Action-Oriented Leadership; 2 = Bureaucratic Leadership; 3 = Humane Leadership; 4 = Individualistic Leadership; 5 = Autocratic Leadership.
*$p < 0.05$.

- The face-saving dimension, which in Pilot Study 2 had a negative loading on Factor 1, displayed a high positive loading on Factor 5 in the Indian sample. Again face saving is highly related to autocratic leadership styles.
- The higher loading of the bureaucratic dimension on the autocratic factor (Factor 5), than on the bureaucratic factor (Factor 2) itself, and the high loading of the humane orientation on the bureaucratic factor are somewhat surprising. Although these results are not easily explainable, it is possible that some of the bureaucratic items covary with autocratic items and some with humane orientation. This could be an interesting pointer to the way bureaucracies work in India. Certain features where the top management forces all important decisions on the lower levels, may be perceived to be autocratic, while at the same time a degree of fairness on issues such as promotions, salaries, perks, and welfare, which the system ensures, may be perceived to be facets of an humane orientation.
- Another surprising finding was that the procedural dimension did not load on the bureaucratic factor (Factor 2). It instead showed significant loadings on Factors 1 and 3. This is probably more due to problems of multicollinearity in the data than to substantive reasons.
- All other dimensions loaded on the theoretically specified factors.

Individual CFAs of the 16 Scales. Individual CFAs of the 16 scales were done to confirm the unidimensionality of each of them. CFA of one factor (Humane Orientation) could not be carried out due to underidentification (two-item scale). The results are presented in Table 27.13.

TABLE 27.13

Confirmatory Factor Analysis of Individual Leadership Scales (Pilot Study 2)

Statistics	Perf. Oriented	Autocratic	Calm	Charismatic	Inspirational	Collective	Decisive	Diplomatic	Face-saver	Visionary	Integrity	Bureaucratic	Procedural	Individualism	Self-centered
Ch^2	0.42	4.54	0.082	4.81	0.97	1.72	0.082	0.48	6.03	18.88	0.014	1.07	0.0038	0.079	0.28
Df	1	6	1	1	8	6	2	3	1	20	1	2	1	1	2
P	0.52	0.60	0.77	0.03	1.00	0.94	0.96	0.92	0.014	0.53	0.91	0.787	0.95	0.78	0.87
# Items	3	6	4	3	8	6	4	5	3	9	4	5	4	4	4
CFI	1.00	1.00	1.00	0.86	1.00	1.00	1.00	1.00	0.45	1.00	1.00	1.00	1.00	1.00	1.00
GFI	1.00	0.99	1.00	0.99	1.00	1.00	1.00	1.00	0.98	0.98	1.00	1.00	1.00	1.00	1.00
AGFI	0.99	0.98	1.00	0.92	1.00	0.99	1.00	1.00	0.90	0.96	1.00	0.99	1.00	1.00	1.00
PGFI	0.17	0.28	0.10	0.16	0.22	0.29	0.20	0.20	0.16	0.44	0.10	0.20	0.10	0.10	0.20
NFI	1.00	0.97	1.00	0.84	1.00	0.99	1.00	1.00	0.50	0.97	1.00	0.99	1.00	1.00	1.00
NNFI	1.01	1.03	1.03	0.58	1.07	1.04	1.04	1.06	-0.65	1.00	1.02	1.06	1.02	1.07	1.09
PNFI	0.33	0.39	0.17	0.28	0.29	0.40	0.33	0.30	0.17	0.54	0.17	0.30	0.17	0.17	0.33
RMSEA	0.00	0.00	0.00	0.13	0.00	0.00	0.00	0.00	0.15	0.00	0.00	0.00	0.00	0.00	0.00
RMSR	0.010	0.023	0.003	0.054	0.008	0.015	0.004	0.008	0.064	0.028	0.001	0.001	0.001	0.005	0.008
Sig Load	All	All	All	All	All	All	All	All	1 ns	All	All	1 ns	All	3 ns	All

Note. Indian data. CFI = comparative fit index. GFI = goodness-of-fit index. AGFI = adjusted goodness-of-fit index. PGFI = parsimony goodness-of-fit index. NFI = normed fit index. NNFI = non-normed fit index. PNFI = parsimony normed fit index. RMSR = root mean square residual. RMSEA = root mean square error of approximation.

TABLE 27.14

Leadership Scales Based on Indian Data Principal Components Analysis (Varimax Rotation)

Scales	No. of Items	% Var. Explained	Alpha
Integrity	11	26.4	0.91
Charismatic	7	7.0	0.88
Performance Oriented	7	4.8	0.88
Collective	6	4.2	0.83
Organized	4	3.7	0.80
Entrepreneurial	3	2.7	0.60
Self-starter	4	2.5	0.79
Autocratic	5	2.5	0.71
Consultative	4	2.3	0.74
Visionary	4	2.2	0.66
Problem Solver	2	2.1	0.69
Evasive	2	2.0	0.55
Individualistic	4	2.0	0.62
Bureaucratic	2	1.8	0.55
Elitist	1	1.7	–
Dictatorial	1	1.6	–
Inspirational	2	1.5	0.45
Worldly	1	1.3	–
Total		72.3	

It is seen from Table 27.13 that all scales except face saving and charismatic demonstrate adequate fit indices indicating unidimensionality. The problems with the face-saving scale have already been discussed. In addition, the face-saving items indicate very low interitem correlations (from 0.08 to 0.17), which explains poor unidimensionality. The case is the same with the charismatic dimension, the items of which had inter-item correlations ranging from .19 to .26. Unidimensionality was replicated for the remaining 13 scales.

Exploratory Factor Analysis.   Because the 16-factor Pilot Study 2 model did not seem to fit the Indian data very well, an exploratory factor analysis of the 76 leadership items was conducted. An initial principal components analysis yielded 19 factors. Because 4 four of these 19 factors consisted of only one item each, a 16-factor solution was extracted and rotated using the varimax criterion, to compare it with the results of Pilot Study 2. The factors that emerged were significantly different from the results of Pilot Study 2 and were not interpretable under the original 16-factor classification of Pilot Study 2. The 16-factor solution was therefore abandoned for the Indian sample.

The 19-factor solution resulted in many of the factors of Pilot Study 2 being duplicated, though the pattern of loadings and the factor structure differed significantly. One factor (worldly, number 18), which had only one item (effective bargainer), was eliminated as it also loaded highly (.7633) on Factor 2. It was decided to retain this item under Factor 2 because it was interpretable. Table 27.14 presents the resulting 18 scales, along with the number of items in each scale, Cronbach's alpha coefficients, and percentage of variance explained by each of the scales.

Two scales that emerged from the Indian data and that do not correspondingly appear in the results of Pilot Study 2 are worldly and elitist. This is probably because respondents in the Indian sample did not see any of the other characteristics in the leadership scales to covary with worldly and elitist resulting in these emerging as two distinct scales. Calm, which appears as a scale in Pilot Study 2, does not show up in the Indian data. This is probably because the calm factor contains items such as self-effacing, which may not have been fully and completely understood by some of the respondents. Self-effacing is not a very commonly used expression in India.

Respondents in the Indian sample do not seem to have been able to clearly distinguish between the items indicating autocratic and dictatorial natures. Items indicating individualism and self-centeredness have merged, which is not unexpected. Similarly, items from the original procedural dimension have merged with the organized and bureaucratic scales respectively, which again is not surprising.

The first scale in Pilot Study 2 seemed to clearly indicate performance orientation, whereas in the Indian data the first factor with 11 items loading on it points to items indicating a collective orientation, integrity, and diplomacy. It is a tentative pointer that there was reasonable consensus in the Indian sample over the characteristics that contribute to a person being an effective leader. This is consistent with the overall impression that whereas Western managers emphasize greater task orientation, Indian managers are more relationship oriented. Findings of the two focus groups conducted in India, given in Table 27.3, also confirm this.

In conclusion, the leadership scales that emerged from the Indian data seem to generally agree with the scales that emerged in Pilot Study 2. The relative importance of the factors as seen from the order of emergence and the pattern of loadings are somewhat different, possibly due to differing perceptions of the characteristics of effective leaders.

Second-Order Exploratory Factor Analysis of Indian Data. The 18 scales that emerged from the exploratory factor analysis of Indian data were subjected to a principal components factor analysis with a varimax rotation. A total of three factors accounting for 58.7% of the variance emerged. The factor loadings for the rotated factor solution, along with the variance explained by each factor, are presented in Table 27.15.

The three factors were labeled as "charismatic and action-oriented leadership," "autocratic leadership," and "bureaucratic leadership," generally in keeping with the labels used in the second-order exploratory factor analysis in Pilot Study 2. The Indian data did not yield the remaining two second-order factors of Pilot Study 2, namely, humane leadership and individualist leadership.

A word of caution is necessary here about the within-society factor analysis of the data reported earlier. As discussed in Hanges and Dickson (2004), the GLOBE scales were designed to measure organizational or societal-level variability. The scales were never intended to meaningfully differentiate among individuals within a particular society. However, even though the scales were not constructed to provide such information, it may be interesting to assess whether similar factors differentiate individuals within a society. It should be noted, however, that we expect that the loadings of the GLOBE scale's items on within society factors should be lower than reported in Hanges and Dickson (i.e., because of the within-society restriction of the GLOBE scales true-score variability, which was based on between-society differences). Furthermore, one should not interpret these within society factor analyses as replications of the GLOBE factor structure. This analysis is intended as an exploration of the themes captured by GLOBE in a new domain (i.e., individual differences within a society). Finally, the absence of a GLOBE factor within a society should not be automatically interpreted as the factor being irrelevant to the people in that country. Rather, a factor may fail to emerge within a society even when that theme is extremely critical because

TABLE 27.15
Second-Order Factor Structure of 18 Leadership Scales—Exploratory Factor Analysis

Leadership Characteristics	Second-Order Factors		
	Factor 1	Factor 2	Factor 3
Integrity	0.89		
Organized	0.84		
Action Orientation	0.83		
Self-Starter	0.81		
Charismatic	0.75		
Collective	0.73		
Problem Solver	0.72		
Visionary	0.67		
Entrepreneurial	0.67		
Inspirational	0.56		
Worldly	0.54		
Autocratic		0.82	
Dictatorial		0.87	
Individualistic		0.58	
Evasive		0.53	
Consultative		−0.59	
Bureaucratic			0.79
Elitist			0.52
Eigen Value	7.02	2.52	1.02
% Var. Exp.	39.0	14.0	5.7

Note.   Factor labels: Factor 1: Charismatic and Action-Oriented Leadership; Factor 2: Autocratic Leadership; Factor 3: Bureaucratic Leadership.

there was no variability in how the individuals from a single society rated the items (e.g., they all rated the items a 7). Factor analysis requires variability and so a factor could fail to emerge because it is extremely critical or completely irrelevant to the people within a society.

Summary of Analyses of Leadership Data

Various analyses of the leadership data indicate that:

- The results obtained from the Indian data are generally similar but not identical to those obtained in Pilot Study 2.
- The leadership scales seem to exhibit satisfactory psychometric properties with the Indian data.
- Relationship orientation seems to be a more important characteristic of effective leaders in India than performance or task orientation.
- At the aggregate level, the most effective leadership styles in India seem to be charismatic and action oriented, autocratic, and bureaucratic.

The most effective leadership style in India would thus combine integrity, being organized, an action orientation, being a self-starter, charisma, and a collective orientation; with being a problem solver, a visionary, entrepreneurial, and inspirational, in that order. This would be a tall order for any one person to fulfill but is not really surprising given that "two sets of values—vertical collectivism and individualism—coexist in Indian organizations" (Sinha, 1997, p. 60). It is possibly the existence of such seemingly mutually contradictory sets of values that makes such a comprehensive set of demands for being an effective leader in Indian organizations.

5. DISCUSSION

The findings of both qualitative and quantitative analyses are in general agreement on the importance of action orientation and charisma, and these can therefore be considered to be the most important characteristics for effective leadership in India. Four characteristics, communication, direction, vision, and change orientation, which the qualitative analyses found to be important, did not attain the same level of importance as in the quantitative analyses. Similarly, being bureaucratic, autocratic, and collectivistic, which emerged as important in the quantitative analysis, were not as prominent in the qualitative analysis. In part this could be a function of the two methodologies, qualitative and quantitative. It may also be a reflection of the complexity of India, which has been described as "a land famous for extremes" (Walsh, 1996, p. 30).

Collectivism and humane orientation continue to be the most important characteristics of Indian culture. This is in keeping with earlier findings (Triandis et al., 1986). Society appears to be in a period of major transition toward power equalization. At the same time there is an increasing preference for individualism.

Taking an overall view, two distinct though interrelated characteristics of Indian society seem to stand out. One is that Indian culture is ancient yet continuously living and evolving. The second is the great complexity and diversity of Indian society and culture. These two characteristics, in combination with other features of Indian society, do demand unique attributes, abilities, and behaviors of leaders in India. This may require a high tolerance for ambiguity, and the ability to balance a diverse set of factors not at the lowest but at a rather high common denominator. A phrase often used in India, "unity in diversity," does seem to capture some of this special requirement but not all of it.

Practical Implications for Foreign Managers Working in India or Dealing With Indian Managers

It is therefore important for managers and leaders from other cultures who have to, or plan to, work with organizations in India, to be prepared to deal with a wide range of organizational and leadership practices. Given the size, diversity, and complexity of the country and society, and variations within them, it is not possible to provide a list of "do's and don'ts." The interaction, and more often mere coexistence, of collectivist and individualist values; and the adoption, by many Indian organizations, of the formal systems of management in a *vertical collectivist* culture (Sinha, 1997), often creates an unpredictable situation. The experience of a foreign national visiting India on work is likely to go through three phases of surprise. First is the surprise, and often shock in the first instance, being at how things work, or more often don't work, and how different they appear to be from what the visitor is used to in his or her culture. As the visitor becomes somewhat knowledgeable about the situation, the cause of surprise is likely to be the similarity to a number of practices in their own culture. This is because the range of phenomena in Indian culture is so broad that almost every visitor finds something that is familiar. The surprise in the third stage comes when one discovers that although the practices seem similar, their basic causes or driving forces are quite different. The quest thus continues, leading to a deeper and richer understanding of and appreciation for the country and its culture. Reaching this stage obviously requires time and therefore a strong recommendation for any foreign manager working in India is to have a lot of patience. The resultant prescription for dealing with India, and also for any other foreign culture, is to *expect* differences, to *accept* differences, and also to *respect* differences, without overlooking similarities.

Limitations and Suggestions for Future Research

Any attempt at capturing the totality of societal and organizational culture, and leadership practices in a country such as India with a sample of 214 respondents from 10 organizations in two industries, has obvious limitations even if it is complemented by a number of qualitative research methods. A much larger sample would be required for any attempt at randomization and representativeness. It would also be very useful to match subsamples based on factors such as regions, industries, languages, religions, ownership especially private and public sectors, and size.

Other limitations arise out of embeddedness and pervasiveness of culture. A person researching his or her own culture has the potential for experimenter bias, which is perhaps best captured by the saying "fish will be the last to discover water." The influence that Western perceptions and characterizations of India have had on the self-perceptions of Indians themselves compounds these complications (Sen, 1997). Formal management education in India, introduced in the early 1960s, has certainly had an impact on organizational and management practices in the country, some of which must obviously have been reflected in the responses of participants in various aspects of GLOBE research in India.

Complexity of society also creates limitations of its own. For example, the media analysis in this study was restricted to the English-language press. It would obviously have been revealing to also analyze press reports of some of the Indian languages. The multiplicity of languages (12 different language families, 15 "official" languages recognized by the Constitution of the country, and 24 different mutually unintelligible scripts) makes it a major endeavor in itself. It is these features of India that make it an almost ideal setting for a full-blown GLOBE project of its own.

ACKNOWLEDGMENTS

Leena Bhandari was involved in several aspects of the GLOBE Project in India. Her contributions to the collection and analysis of both quantitative and qualitative data for Phase 2 of the project and the literature review are especially acknowledged. E. Sendil Kumar contributed significantly to the analysis of leadership data, particularly the confirmatory and exploratory factor analyses. His contribution is gratefully acknowledged. This chapter, and indeed this book, would not have been possible without the unstinted cooperation of my secretary, Sugatha Nair. Her assistance has been invaluable, and I am grateful to her.

REFERENCES

Agar, M. (n.d.). *Qualitative research manual, I and II.* GLOBE Research Project.
Bagozzi, R. P., & Heatherton, J. F. (1994). A general approach to representing multifaceted personality constructs: Application state self-esteem. *Structural Equation Modeling, 1,* 35–67.

Basham, A. L. (1967). *The wonder that was India*. Delhi, India: Rupa/Fontana Books. (Original work published 1954)

Bernstein, H., & Teng, G. (1989). Factoring items and factoring scales are different: Spurious evidence for multidimensionality due to item categorization. *Psychological Bulletin, 105,* 467–477.

Beteille, A. (1996, April 29). Waning of charisma: Implications for democratic politics. *The Times of India* (Ahmedabad edition), p. 8.

Bose, N. K. (1967). *Culture and society in India*. Bombay, India: Asia.

de Boer, K., & Pandey, A. (1997). India's sleeping giant: Food. *The McKinsey Quarterly, 1,* 82–96.

Dumont, L. (1970). *Homo hierarchicus*. Chicago: University of Chicago Press.

Food and Agriculture, Integrated Development Action. (1997). New Delhi: Confederation of Indian Industry (CII).

Fyzee, M. (1991). *Aircraft and engine perfect: The story of JRD Tata who opened up the skies for his country*. New Delhi, India: Tata McGraw-Hill.

Gadgil, M., & Guha, R. (1992). *This fissured land: An ecological history of India*. Delhi, India: Oxford University Press.

Gandhi, R. (1990). *Patel: A life*. Ahmedabad, India: Navajivan.

Gelli, R. (1996). Banking services after 90's: Some sweeping changes. *Saket Industrial Digest* (First Anniversary Issue), pp. 145–147.

Hall, E. T. (1976). *Beyond culture*. Garden City, NY: Doubleday.

Hanges, P. J., & Dickson, M. W. (2004). *The development and validation of scales to measure societal and organizational culture*. In R. J. House, P. J. Hanges, M. Javidan, P. J. Dorfman, V. Gupta, V., & GLOBE Associates (Eds.), *Culture, leadership, and organizations: The GLOBE study of 62 societies* (pp. 122–151). Thousand Oaks, CA: Sage.

Harris, F. R. (1958). *Jamsetji Nusserwanji Tata: A chronicle of his life* (2nd ed.). Bombay, India: Blackie & Son.

Hofstede, G. (1980). *Culture's consequences: International differences in work-related values*. Beverly Hills, CA: Sage.

House, R. J., Hanges, P. J., Javidan, M., Dorfman, P. W., Gupta, V., & GLOBE Associates. (2004). *Cultures, leadership, and organizations: The GLOBE study of 62 societies*. Thousand Oaks, CA: Sage.

Jayakar, R. (1996, March 22–April 6). How do you use the new leadership to run your company? *Business Today,* pp. 80–89.

Jayakar, R., & Parthasarathy, R. (1996, January 7–21). How to train for leadership. *Business Today,* pp. 198–203.

Kabra, K. N. (1994). Leadership and development: Some reflections in the Indian context. *Indian Journal of Public Administration, VXL*(3), 279–286.

Karkaria, B. J. (1992). *Dare to dream: The life of Rai Bahadur Mohan Singh Oberoi*. New Delhi, India: Viking Penguin.

Kishton, J. M., & Widaman, K. F. (1994). Unidimensional versus domain representative parcelling of questionnaire items: An empirical example. *Educational and Psychological Measurement, 54,* 757–765.

Kothari, R. (1997, July 28). India: The growing confidence of the poor. *The Times of India* (Ahmedabad edition), p. 7.

Lomax, D. (1986). *The money makers*. London: BBC Publications.

Marriott, K. (1976). Hindu transactions: Diversity without dualism. In B. Kapferer (Ed.), *Transactions and meaning: Directions in anthropology of exchange and symbolic behaviour*. Philadelphia: ISHI

Nehru, J. (1985). *The discovery of India* (Centenary ed.). Delhi, India: Oxford University Press. (Original work published 1946)

Parekh, H. T. (1975). Indian capital market: Past, present, and future. *The Journal of the Indian Institute of Bankers, 46*(1), 36–44.

Piramal, G. (1996). *A view of the Maharajas*. New Delhi, India: Viking.

Ramanujan, A. K. (1989). Is there an Indian way of thinking? An informal essay. *Contributions to Indian Sociology, 25,* 41–58.

Risely, H. T. (1981). *Tribes and castes of Bengal.* Calcutta, India: Firma KLM. (Original work published 1891)

Roland, A. (1988). *In search of self in India and Japan: Towards a cross-cultural psychology.* Princeton, NJ: Princeton University Press.

Sen, A. (1997). Indian traditions and the Western imagination. *Daedalus: Journal of the American Academy of Arts and Sciences, Spring,* 1–25.

Shankar, V. (1974). *My reminiscences of Sardar Patel.* Delhi, India: Macmillan.

Singh, K. S. (1992). *People of India: An introduction* (National Series Vol. 1). Calcutta: Anthropological Survey of India.

Sinha, J. B. P. (1994). Major trends in research on leadership and power. *Indian Psychological Abstracts, 1*(2) 385–414.

Sinha, J. B. P. (1997). A cultural perspective on organizational behaviour in India. In C. P. Earley & M. Erez (Eds.), *New perspectives on international industrial/organizational psychology* (pp. 53–74). San Francisco: New Lexington Press.

Spaeth, A. (1996, March 25). Society. *Time,* pp. 43–44.

Srinivas, M. N. (1966). *Social change in modern India.* Berkeley: University of California Press.

Tabachnik, B. G., & Fidell, L. S. (1996). *Using multivariate statistics* (3rd ed.). New York: HarperCollins.

Takahashi, T., & Nasser, F. (1996, April). *The impact of using item parcels on ad hoc goodness of fit indices in confirmatory factor analysis: An empirical example.* Paper presented at the annual meeting of the American Educational Research Association, New York.

The gravy train (1997, July 7). *Business World,* pp. 18–25.

Thomas, J. (n.d.). *The effective leader as portrayed in the US popular media.* GLOBE Research Project.

Time. (1996, March 25).

Triandis, H. C., & Bhawuk, D. P. S. (1997). In C. P. Earley & M. Erez (Eds.), *New perspectives on international industrial/organizational psychology* (pp. 13–52). San Francisco: New Lexington Press.

Triandis, H. C., Bontempo, R., Betancourt, H., Bond, M., Leung, K., Brenes, A., et al. (1986). The measurement of the etic aspects of individualism and collectivism across cultures [Special issue]. *Australian Journal of Psychology, 38,* 57–267.

Walsh, J. (1996, March 25). India. *Time,* pp. 29–34.

Appendix A

Basic Information on India

India is located in the continent of South Asia, between the Arabian Sea and the Bay of Bengal. It shares borders with Bangladesh, Bhutan, China, Myanmar (Burma), Nepal, and Pakistan. Its total area is 3.3 million square kilometers, and it has a coast line of almost 7,000 kms. It has a variety of climate zones from tropical monsoon in the south, to temperate in the north, to cold in the Himalayas. The terrain also varies from upland plain (the Deccan Plateau) in the south, to flat and rolling plains along the Ganges, to desert in the west, and mountains in the north. It has the fourth-largest coal reserves in the world, and a number of other mineral deposits.

It is the second most populous country in the world with the latest estimates of population exceeding 1 billion. The economy is a mixture of traditional village farming and handicrafts on one end, to modern agriculture, a wide range of modern industries, and a multitude of services on the other. It has emerged as one of the world's leading exporters of computer software in the last decade. Other industries include textiles, chemicals, food processing, steel, transportation equipment, cement, mining, petroleum, machinery, and machine tools. The World Bank estimated the gross domestic product (GDP) in 1995 to be U.S.$329.9 billion. Local estimates however placed the GDP for 1995–1996 at Rupees 9.85,787 crores (equivalent of U.S.$281.65 billion, @U.S.$1 = Rs.35[1]) showing an increase of 14.5% over the similar estimates for the previous year. Per capita income for 1995–1996 was estimated at Rupees 9,321, with an increase of 12.54% over the previous year.

SOURCES

India: A reference. (1996). New Delhi: Government of India, Publications Division.
National Accounts Statistics. (1997). New Delhi: Government of India, Central Statistical Organization, Department of Statistics, Ministry of Planning and Programme Implementation.
Trends in developing economies. (1996). Washington, DC: The World Bank.

---

[1]This was the exchange rate in 1998. In 2003, it was U.S.$1 = Rs.46.82. This also applies to figures in Appendixes F and G.

Appendix B

Quotations From Prominent Business Leaders of India

Sanjay Lalbhai, Managing Director, Arvind Mills, describes today's leader as follows:

> The new leader has a well balanced intellect, mind and multi-disciplinary (holistic) perspective. He listens more and speaks less, observes more and concludes less, uses "we" more than "I," and says "let's go" more often than "go." He takes more than his share of blame and less than his share of credit. He's open and yet decisive, focuses on human processes rather than only on end results, and is more of a coach and less of a boss (Jayakar, 1996, p. 80).

And according to Maitreya Doshi, Managing Director, Premier Automobiles *"The self-confidence to share power with others in the organization is crucial for the leader" (Jayakar, 1996, p. 82).*

Leading by Vision

On leading by vision, S. D. Kulkarni, Managing Director, Larsen, & Tubro, said: *"The CEO has to influence and direct, through a vision, how the organization wants to position itself, and what it wants to do" (Jayakar, 1996, p. 83).*

And according to Adi Godrej, CEO, Godrej Group, *"A leader needs to formulate and understand his company's strategy, take a major part in building it, ensure that it secures the commitment of everyone in the organization, and then devote a lot of energy and time in ensuring that it is carried through" (Jayakar, 1996, p. 83).*

Leading by Inspiration

On leading by inspiration, N. Sankar, Managing Director, Champlast Sanmar, said: *"The new leader has to be first among equals" (Jayakar, 1996, p. 84).*

And according to Suresh Krishna, CEO, Sundaram Fasteners, *"A leader needs not just far-sighted vision, but also commitment to his beliefs, and, above all, commitment to his people" (Jayakar, 1996, p. 84).*

Leading by Influence

On leading by influence, Arun Maira, Vice President, Arthur D. Little, said: *"The CEO-as-leader will have to influence the performance of the network that his company is becoming, without exercising line authority over every part of the network" (Jayakar, 1996, p. 80).*

Leading by Empowerment

On leading by empowerment, Anand Mahindra, Deputy Managing Director, Mahindra and Mahindra, said: *"The leader has to spend a lot of time on selecting appropriate people, and on designing processes to get the best performance and behavior"* (Jayakar, 1996, p. 86).

Leading by Expertise

On leading by expertise, Ajay Piramal, CEO, Piramal Group, said: *"The main challenge for the new leader is to convert managers into entrepreneurs" (Jayakar, 1996, p. 88).* And later, *"Dhirubhai Ambani, Chairman of the Reliance Group is a hero in the eyes of his company's employees ... precisely because of his demonstrated—and disseminated—competence of financing and finishing mega projects on global scales" (Jayakar, 1996, p. 88).*

Appendix C

Focus Group Exercise
Participant Assignment

This assignment should take about 45 minutes.

To begin with think of a person whom you know, or have observed several times, and whom you judge to be an *outstanding leader.* If you do not know such an individual personally, select a prominent leader about whom you have read or one whom you have observed in the media, and whom you judge to be an outstanding leader.

Now visualize an important incident in which the leader has interacted with one or more of her or his subordinates or followers. Spend about 3 minutes recalling the incident in detail, and visualizing the behavior of both the leader and the subordinates/followers.

1. Please write a short story about the incident using the following questions as guides. Devote one or two paragraphs to each of the following questions. The total story should take no more than about 15 minutes.

   What were the background circumstances that led up to the event?
   Who were the people involved? What were their formal positions, relationships to each other?
   What was said during the incident? Did the leader do anything that was particularly effective? Ineffective? Please describe.
   What feelings were experienced by each party?
   What was the outcome? Was it a successful incident? Did the leader achieve his or her objective?

Now think of a person whom you know, or have observed several times, and whom you judge to be a *competent manager but not an outstanding leader.* Visualize an important incident in which the manager has interacted with one or more of her or his subordinates or followers. Spend about 3 minutes recalling the incident in detail, and visualizing the behavior of both the manager and the subordinates/followers.

1. Now write another short story in which you address the same questions mentioned above.
2. Now please develop a list of attributes (skills, abilities, personality traits, values, behaviors) that you believe distinguish outstanding leaders from competent managers in general.

Please send both the short stories and the list of attributes to:
Professor J. S. Chhokar
Indian Institute of Management
Vastrapur
Ahmedabad—380 015
Thank you.

Appendix D

Guiding Questions for Semistructured Interviews

- What is your understanding or personal definition of leadership?
- Is there a difference between a competent manager and an outstanding leader? If yes, what is it? Please elaborate.
- What is your perception of the opposite of outstanding leadership? Can you think of someone who is or was in positions of leadership but does or did not exercise outstanding leadership? What kind of, and what specific behaviors does or did this person engage in?
- Please describe a critical incident that illustrates outstanding leadership.
- Did the leader face any obstacles in the incident just described by you? If yes, what were these and how did the leader get over them?
- Can you name two or three people whom you think were or are outstanding leaders, preferably well-known individuals?
- What makes these people outstanding leaders? Are there some characteristics, qualities, behaviors of these people that (a) are common among them, and (b) differentiate them from other people?
- Can you think of something that a leader did that resulted in your strong acceptance or support of that leader, or resulted in significantly increased motivation or effort on your part in the interest of the leader's vision, objective, or mission?

Appendix E

Financial Services Industry

Money lending was a recognized activity in India even in ancient times. Somewhat formal financial activity also had an early beginning. Exchange and trading of shares (stock) began in Bombay in 1870 and the Native Share and Stock Brokers' Association was established in 1875. This association subsequently evolved into the Bombay Stock Exchange (Parekh, 1975). By the early 1940s, stock exchanges had been set up in most large cities. After independence in 1947, there was greater institutionalization of the finance function and the financial services industry came under increasing government control. The Reserve Bank was nationalized in 1949. Several financial institutions were set up by the government, the prominent ones being the Industrial Finance Corporation of India (IFCI) in 1948, State Financial Corporations in various states during 1952 and 1953, the Industrial Credit and Investment Corporation of India (ICICI) in 1955, and the Industrial Development Bank of India (IDBI) in 1964. There was also a gradual growth of the capital market in India. The setting up of the Unit Trust of India (UTI), a mutual fund, in 1964 brought the savings of small investors into the capital market. Nationalization of banks and life insurance in 1969 strengthened government control within the industry. The Indian banking sector in 1995 consisted of 280 scheduled commercial banks (including 27 public-sector banks and 24 foreign banks) and 2 nonscheduled commercial banks spread over 62,000 branches. The deposits of public-sector, private-sector, and foreign banks in 1995 were Rs.3,10,456 crore, Rs.26,106 crore, and Rs.28,350 crore (U.S.$88,700 million, U.S.$7,459 million, and U.S.$8,100 million)[1] respectively. The respective advances were Rs.1,84,361 crore, Rs.15,159 crore and Rs.16,761 crore (U.S.$52,675 million, U.S.$4,331 million, and U.S.$4,789 million) (Gelli, 1996).

The financial services sector has undergone major changes with economic restructuring and liberation, which has acquired a lot of momentum since 1991. Although the pace of change has certainly accelerated since 1991, gradual changes had been taking place even before that. The 1980s, for example, saw the introduction of new services such as leasing, venture capital, factoring, and specialized merchant banking. Several new institutions such as the Security and Exchange Board of India (SEBI), Credit Rating and Information Service of India Limited (CRISIL), and Stock Holding Corporation of India Limited (SHCIL) also came into being. New financial instruments, such as cumulative convertible preference shares (CCPSs), zero coupon bonds (ZCBs), commercial paper (CP), and warrants, added variety to the financial services industry.

Subsequent to the advent of liberalization, the industry has changed and continues to change rapidly. Currently, there is no control on the pricing of securities; a regulatory agency, the Controller of Capital Issues, has actually been closed down with some, but only some, of its functions being transferred to SEBI; the rupee has been made partially convertible; private

---

[1]This was the exchange rate in 1998. In 2003, it was U.S.$1 = Rs.46.82. This also applies to figures in Appendixes F and G.

and foreign mutual funds have been allowed to operate. This period of rapid change and deregulation has also seen some instances where almost the entire financial system has been abused by individuals for personal, unlawful gain. These aberrations seem to appear from time to time but so far have not caused serious, nonrepairable damage to the system.

The financial services industry in India is currently, and has been for the last few years, very dynamic and competitive. The competition is quite fierce with a number of new and aggressive firms being set up and heavy investments in the Indian market by foreign institutional investors (FIIs). The involvement of foreign financial services companies has also had a strong impact on the industry, further increasing intensity of the competition.

Appendix F

Food Processing Industry

Whereas food-processing *activity* has been in India since times immemorial as an essential part of human existence, the development of the food-processing *industry* has been described as "diminutive." "India is an agricultural giant, but a foods pygmy" ("The Gravy Train," 1997). The combined turnover of the country's 10 largest food companies is U.S.$2 billion (Rs.7,200 crore),[1] about one 10th of what Nestlé's European operations achieve (de Boer & Pandey, 1997). Even then food production and processing accounted for 26% of India's GDP, and for over 60% of employment ("The Gravy Train," 1997).

The primary reason for the industry not having developed to anywhere near its potential seems to be the preponderance of the small-scale and unorganized sectors within the industry. Several value-added food items, ice creams, for example, were until recently "reserved" for the small-scale industries (SSI) sector with the result that economies of scale and the required levels of investment could not be achieved. According to a recent estimate "two thirds of the industry is accounted for by small-scale units and unorganized sectors, which together account for half the total value of foods produced" ("The Gravy Train," 1997, p. 21). The very close interlinkages between agriculture and food processing also make the latter quite a sensitive political issue because any changes in the food-processing industry have a significant impact on, and consequences for, agriculture. "Low yields, combined with excessive number of intermediaries in the procurement chain, the waste, and the loss of value, lock India's food chain in a vicious cycle of low investment, low skill, low yield, low efficiency, and low added value" (de Boer & Pandey, 1997, p. 92).

The government seems to have recognized the need and potential to develop this industry in the mid-1980s when a separate Ministry of Food Processing was set up at the central (federal) government. With progressive restructuring of the Indian economy, which began slowly in the mid-1980s and has become the cornerstone of all economic policy since 1991:

> The government's focus has recently turned to encouraging the role of agriculture in India's development. In consequence it is actively reforming both food legislation and the taxation structure.... There now seems to be increasing recognition that developing the food industry is crucial to raising agricultural productivity and achieving rural prosperity. As a result, large-scale investment is being more actively encouraged. (de Boer & Pandey, 1997, pp. 92–93)

The industry is thus undergoing a major transition with a certain amount of consolidation taking place and larger companies getting more actively involved, the government trying to play a facilitative and enabling rather than a controlling role, and a number of multinational companies entering the industry. As a consequence of increasing population and prosperity, the overall market for value-added foods is expected to treble from the current level of U.S.$21.4 billion (Rs.74,900 crore) to U.S.$62.5 billion (Rs.2,18,750 crore) by the year 2005 (Food and Agriculture, Integrated Development Action, 1997).

---

[1]This was the exchange rate in 1998. In 2003, it was U.S.$1 = Rs.46.82.

Appendix G

Outstanding Leaders Mentioned During Focus Groups and Semistructured Interviews

Political:

Mahatma Gandhi
Jawaharlal Nehru
Subhaschandra Bose
Indira Gandhi

Social Workers:

Ela Bhat
Medha Patkar
Sunderlal Bahuguna

Military:

Field Marshal Sam Manekshaw

Spiritual-Religious:

Swami Vivekananda

Business:

JRD Tata
Jamsetji Nusserwanji Tata
Rusi Mody
RK Talwar
DN Ghose
GD Birla
Aditya Birla
Ashwin Nagarwadia
Dhirubhai Ambani
Rahul Bajaj

Appendix H

Illustrative Statements from Media Analysis

Change

- India is going through a major transition in all spheres: economic, social, and political. By and large the political structure follows the contours of the social power structure. Sections of society that have been excluded from positions of power have become politically conscious. Parties like the Janata Dal, the Samajwadi Party, and the Bahujan Samaj Party directly reflect their aspirations. But all of the other parties are also fielding increasing numbers from these social groups.
- *Change is a two-sided coin. It can fire up imaginations and churn up the juices in an organization. Equally, it can induce fear and a spell of uncertainty. One change that produces a feeling akin to dread is a change in a company's ownership or top management. Both are inevitable in this liberalized world. Mergers and acquisitions are going to increase in number, as industrial houses restructure their business portfolios. In the performance-oriented culture that multinationals are now brining in, chief executives have to deliver or suffer the ignominy of being turfed out.*
- *"We need a pragmatic approach and should change with the times in our own self interest,"* he said.

Action

- As a nation, *"we have to reinvigorate our efforts to eliminate social and economic injustice and this involves the task of immense magnitude in which all of us have to participate actively. Purposive action is the need of the hour."* The President advised.
- Action against ministers who are continuing to campaign against party candidates, despite repeated warnings by the state leadership, also appears imminent. The suspension of the MLAs is being seen here as the final warning to them.

Charisma

- For ultimately those leaders who have shown vote catching magic, the ability to form governments and forge ruling alliances, are likely to tap their personal power bases, caste discrimination and personal charisma in order to emerge as India's new king makers.
- Amid the flock of Hindutva hawks, Vajpayee is the moderate voice and the BJP's star campaigner. His considerable charisma apart, he lends a liberal touch to the party's image and, therefore, is the BJP's best bet to attract a significant chunk of the undecided voters.

Control

- Rao had assumed control at a crucial period, headed a minority government and successfully piloted the affairs of the country for the full term.

Culture

- The BJP is committed to the concept of one nation, one people, one culture, and asserts that its nationalist vision is defined by the nation's ancient cultural heritage.

Direction

- Though issues such as corruption, casteism, communalism, stability and price-rise are likely to figure prominently in the campaigning by both of the main parties, the BJP, a senior party leader said, would concentrate its energies on giving a new direction to society, its "clean" rule and "splendid" record in implementing its poll promises in the state.

Communication

- When Indira Gandhi found herself up against a powerful syndicate, she broke loose by communicating directly with the people and went on to exercise complete control over the party apparatus.
- Vajpayee's greatest appeal is his oratorical skills, which he uses to a telling effect. His style is that of an accomplished stage actor—his speeches punctuated with pregnant pauses, voice high pitched one moment, and down to a whisper the next, as if he were sharing a secret with the crowd.

Appendix I

Illustrative Statements From Unstructured Interviews

"Communications … the ability to communicate … is also very important in leaders … of course."

"He should be able to communicate effectively. And in communication, I think one of the major skills in communications is listening…. So if you are not a good listener, you cannot be a good communicator because one way communication is no communication, you're just talking. So, that is the third thing that comes out of this … [not clear] … decision making, being able to communicate that, decisions and all … those things … those are important."

"Communication skills … here I mean not the … the way he talks … that kind of … thing … his ability to … make … people understand … what exactly he wants to communicate basically … actually … there should not be any kind of gaps like…. It is not necessary to have language skills and all …"

"He should be good at communication, whatever is that vision … that he is going to see, he should be able to communicate it … and he has to be articulate because … that vision that he is seeing, he should be able to put it in the way that … would inspire people to follow and make them also see the same thing."

"Either he makes the vision evolve or he communicates it in such a way that … [pause] … they are sold on it you know, that they can identify themselves … with the same … a'h … vision or the mission he has."

"I would say a very important quality of leadership would be that you should be able to see much beyond … (pause) … because that is how you are going to lead. And the perspective should be not only that much beyond but a holistic … larger perspective of everything."

"He has got a clear vision, direction … he is very knowledgeable … very influential in the industry and as a person he has got some kind of clear-cut vision."

SUB-SAHARAN AFRICA CLUSTER

The Sub-Saharan Africa Cluster in the GLOBE Research Program consisted of Namibia, Nigeria, South Africa (Black sample), Zambia, and Zimbabwe. Some characteristics of this cluster are included in the chapter of South Africa which provides also some information on the black population of South Africa.

The only societal culture dimension on which the Sub-Saharan Africa cluster was amongst the high scores is Humane Orientation. Its scores on all the remaining eight dimensions of societal culture viz. Assertiveness, Future Orientation, Gender Egalitarianism, In-Group Collectivism, Institutional Collectivism, Performance Orientation, Power Distance, and Uncertainty Avoidance were in the mid range. It was not in the low score range in any of the societal culture dimensions.

The Sub-Saharan Africa cluster viewed Charismatic/Value Based, Team Orientated, and Participative leadership as positive contributors to outstanding leadership. Humane Oriented leadership is also seen as a high contributor to outstanding leadership. Autonomous leadership and Self Protective leadership were seen as slightly impeding affective leadership.

Countries in this cluster share a common heritage of colonization and suppression through slavery. This common experience has resulted in a deep sense of sharing the common faith of suffering and the region is therefore characterized by norms of reciprocity, suppression of self-interest, the virtue of symbiosis and human interdependence (Mangaliso, 2001).

REFERENCES

House, R. J., Hanges, P. J., Javidan, M., Dorfman, P. W., Gupta, V., & GLOBE Associates (2004). *Culture, leadership, and organizations: The GLOBE study of 62 societies.* Thousand Oaks, CA: Sage Publications, Inc.
Mangaliso, M. P. (2001). Building competitive advantage from Ubuntu: Management lessons from South Africa. *Academy of Management Executive, 15(3),* 23–33.

28

▼▼▼▼▼▼▼

Culture and Leadership in 25 Societies: Integration, Conclusions, and Future Directions

Felix C. Brodbeck
Aston University, Birmingham, England

Jagdeep S. Chhokar
Indian Institute of Management, Ahmedabad, India

Robert J. House
University of Pennsylvania, USA

The GLOBE (Global Leadership and Organizational Behavior Effectiveness) Research Program is a worldwide organization of some 170 scholars from about 60 nations who investigate the cross-cultural forces relevant to effective leadership and organizational practices. Approximately 17,300 middle managers from 950 organizations in 61 countries participated in the first two phases of the GLOBE program.

In his foreword to the previous volume of GLOBE studies (House et al., 2004), Harry Triandis calls GLOBE "the Manhattan Project of the study of the relationship of culture to conceptions of leadership" (p. xv). Others see it "as the most ambitious study of leadership" (Morrison, 2000) and "perhaps the most large-scale international management research project that has ever been undertaken" (Leung, Foreword, this volume, p. xiii). Not only has its unique magnitude and scope been acknowledged in management research, but so too have the contributions it has made to the field of applied social sciences. For these, GLOBE was awarded the Scot E. Meyers Award for Applied Research in the Workplace, 2005, from the U.S. American Society of Industrial and Organizational Psychology (SIOP).

GLOBE is a multiphase project. In the first two phases (Phase 3 is currently under way) quantitative instruments were developed and used to measure various aspects of the 61 countries studied. Emphasis was laid on the development of reliable and valid instruments for cross-cultural measurement and on the validation of a cross-level and cross-cultural theory of the relationships between culture, and societal, organizational, and leadership effectiveness. These two phases are described in the first GLOBE volume (House et al., 2004) in which a *culture-general* approach is taken by emphasizing quantitative methods and comparisons between industries, countries, and cultural clusters. The objective was to provide a description of the relative rankings of 61 countries with respect to reported leadership effectiveness, of societal cultural attributes, and their effect on organizational processes in the context of each of 61 countries.

During the first two phases of GLOBE there was also an emphasis on *culture-specific* approaches by using an array of qualitative methods with the aim to provide a rich ethnographic description of societal culture, organizational processes, and managerial leadership in the context of particular countries.

The present GLOBE volume is devoted to combining both the culture-general and the culture-specific approaches. It addresses the criticism of culture-general research, with high levels of abstraction and its neglect of subtle, but important local variations and nuances (Morris, Leung, Ames, & Lickel, 1999), by augmenting culture-general constructs and frameworks with the richness of culturally contingent concepts and findings (Yang, 2000). The collection of 25 country chapters presented here with their culture-specific findings and insights give the "culture general skeleton flesh and blood" as Kwok Leung has formulated it.

What is meant by this, we could not say better than he did in his foreword to our book: "Combining qualitative and quantitative results, and drawing on the extant cultural knowledge and indigenous research on leadership, each of the 25 country-specific chapters describes how leadership is conceptualized and enacted in its cultural milieu, and explores how *emic* dynamics are related to the *etic* constructs and frameworks derived from the GLOBE project. It is exactly this type of synergistic integration of culture-general and culture-specific knowledge that is able to address the respective deficiencies of pan-cultural and indigenous research." No wonder, that Kwok Leung in the foreword to this volume asserts that GLOBE will "go down in the history of management research as a hallmark for diversity, inclusiveness, richness, and multilateralism."

This second GLOBE book is a product of collective efforts of about 60 scholars from the 25 countries it includes. Most of them have also participated in the overall GLOBE project from its beginnings in the mid-1990s as Country Co-Investigators (CCIs). They thus have firsthand experience with the GLOBE data collection process and with the manifold discussions among GLOBE CCIs about how to best use the developed methods and concepts and about how to interpret the results found in Phases 1 and 2 of the GLOBE research program (House et al., 2004).

In preparing their country chapters, authors worked from a master template that is described in the introduction chapter of this book. The overall task was to link the quantitative and comparative results obtained during the GLOBE Phases 1 and 2 with the results from the country-specific data that the authors have gathered and analyzed themselves consisting of country-specific literature reviews, one-to-one interviews with managers, focus group interviews, media analyses, unobtrusive measures, and participant observation. The culture-specific qualitative research has been also directed toward triangulating the quantitative findings. Such triangulation can reveal corroboration of some of the quantitative findings and contradictions to these findings. Where contradictions were found the investigators were encouraged to dig further to yield meaningful interpretations. The overall purpose of the master template was to give guidance for making chapters similar in scope and structure, but also to provide for the freedom to explore and further investigate country-specific characteristics and findings about culture, organization, and leadership.

Each chapter draft has been reviewed several times. In a first round, two or three management and social science scholars reviewed each chapter draft. They originated from or had lived sufficiently long in the country described in the chapter they reviewed. This was done to increase the culture-specific reliability and validity of each chapter's content. In the second round of reviews, which was conducted by the editors of this book, chapter authors were supported in relating their culture-specific findings and interpretations to the culture-general GLOBE concepts and measures. This way, proper use of concepts and methods was ensured. Furthermore, the draft to this conclusion chapter has been sent out to all chapter authors for reviewing and their comments were taken into account. In some cases, the interpretations of findings required further discussions and the present collection of chapters reflects how these were resolved or were further developed into intriguing questions when resolution could not be achieved.

Each of the 25 country chapters discloses the unique aspects of the country and presents numerous insights about the society, organization, and leadership in the culture studied. The volume is filled with a wide variety of country-specific findings and interpretations. It offers answers for many country-specific questions of interest for those who live in the respective country, for those who intend to live and work there, and for those who want to know more about a country's societal and organizational culture and leadership.

We now turn to an integrative view to point out particularly interesting findings, to identify commonalities among culture-specific findings, and to discuss intriguing theoretical and methodological issues. We derive questions for future research and practical implications, from which researchers, students, and practitioners can benefit.

In the first part of this chapter, we address issues about societal culture. In the second part, we describe leadership and the link between culture and leadership from a between-country perspective and from multiple within-country perspectives.

1. SOCIETAL CULTURE

For Project GLOBE culture is defined as, "shared motives, values, beliefs, identities, and interpretations or meanings of significant events that result from common experiences of members of collectives that are transmitted across generations" (House et al., 2004, p. 15). For the culture-general purposes of GLOBE, culture has been operationalized by the use of indicators reflecting cultural manifestations of the commonality (agreement) among members of collectives with respect to the psychological attributes described in the aforementioned definition of culture, and with respect to observed and reported practices of entities such as families, schools, work organizations, economic systems, legal systems, and political institutions. The objective is to compare a large sample of societies on dimensions of culture that are cross-culturally valid.

Results from such a culture-general approach can be also useful for a culture-specific analysis of societies by positioning societies within a sample of relevant others. For this, it is important that the definition of culture also addresses culture-specific aspects. As Triandis (2004) points out, GLOBE defines culture in accord with anthropologists' definitions; for example, Redfield (1948) defines culture as "shared understandings made manifest in act and artifact"(p. vii). The GLOBE dimensions of cultural *practices* represent perceptions of *acts* or of "the way things are done in a culture," and the GLOBE dimensions of cultural *values* are human made *artifacts* in the sense of judgments about "the way things should be done." As part of GLOBE, culture was measured on the basis of both the cultural-practices and the cultural-values perspectives, which have not been investigated separately *and* simultaneously in previous cross-cultural research.

Cultural Practices and Cultural Values

The nine core cultural dimensions identified by GLOBE (Assertiveness, Future Orientation, Gender Egalitarianism, In-Group Collectivism, Humane Orientation, Institutional Collectivism, Uncertainty Avoidance, Performance Orientation, Power Distance) consist of items that incorporate the previously described entities and events (for definitions, see the introduction chapter of this book; for detailed coverage of each dimension, see House et al., 2004). Furthermore, they address two distinct kinds of cultural manifestations: modal practices and modal values.

Modal practices within a country are measured by the responses of middle managers to questionnaire items concerning "What is" or "What are" common behaviors, institutional practices, proscriptions, and prescriptions in their society (termed "As Is" dimensions). Modal values are measured by questionnaire items concerning judgments about "What should be" common behaviors, institutional practices, proscriptions and prescriptions (termed "Should Be" dimensions). Both sets of GLOBE measures have been validated (e.g., by establishing convergent and discriminant validity) on the country level of analysis with different sets of data from outside GLOBE (Gupta, De Luque, & House, 2004) and with societal-value data from prior cross-cultural studies (Hanges & Dickson, 2004; Hanges & Dickson, 2006).

There have been long discussions among GLOBE researchers about the meaning of disparities between societal cultural practices and values scores on the GLOBE dimensions within countries. Various views on this issue are presented in the country chapters of the present volume. We think that it is premature to seek closure to this debate and therefore present one hypothesis that aligns well with the empirical data from GLOBE. We termed it the *deprivation hypothesis.*

On an individual level of analysis (the level that the GLOBE measures tap to make inferences about societal and organizational culture) the disparity between perceptions of practices and value judgments can be interpreted as deprivation. That is, when respondents perceive practices as less or more dominant in their society or organization than they think they should be, or perceive them as inappropriate, there will be a disparity between their reports of practices and values. On a society or organizational level of analysis, their common perceptions of a disparity between practices and values imply the people's sympathy with respectively higher or lower levels of cultural values than practices. Empirical evidence for the deprivation hypothesis is presented in a later section of this chapter together with a discussion about how deprivation can result in cultural change and which factors and psychological processes are likely to be involved.

Culture Clusters

The authors of the country chapters also reflected on the relative positioning of their country's practices and values scores and they triangulated these results within the context of the qualitative results they obtained about their country's societal culture, organizations, and leadership. Furthermore, in many cases chapter authors compared their country's scores and further qualitative evidence to relevant other countries or to meaningful groups of countries. One particularly meaningful subset of reference countries are those that are positioned in the same cultural region or cluster of countries. For an example, in the chapter about Singapore, this society's scores are compared to the scores of other Confucian Asian countries (China, Hong Kong, Japan, South Korea, Taiwan). These have been identified by GLOBE to belong to the same cultural cluster as Singapore.

TABLE 28.1
The Ten GLOBE Cultural Clusters of 61 Countries

Anglo Cultures	Latin Europe	Nordic Europe	Germanic Europe	Southern Asia
Australia	**France**	**Finland**	**Austria**	**India**
England	**Portugal**	**Sweden**	**Germany**	Indonesia
Ireland	**Spain**	Denmark	(Former West & East)	Iran
New Zealand	Israel		**Netherlands**	Malaysia
South Africa	Italy		**Switzerland**	Philippines
(White Sample)	Switzerland		(German speaking)	Thailand
	(French			
USA	speaking)			
Canada				
Eastern Europe	**Latin America**	**Sub-Sahara Africa**	**Middle East/Arab**	**Confucian Asia**
Greece	**Argentina**	South Africa	**Turkey**	**China**
Russia	**Colombia**	(Black Sample)	Egypt	**Hong Kong**
Albania	**Mexico**	Namibia	Kuwait	**Singapore**
Georgia	Bolivia	Nigeria	Morocco	Japan
Hungary	Brazil	Zambia	Qatar	South Korea
Kazakhstan	Costa Rica	Zimbabwe		Taiwan
Poland	Ecuador			
Slovenia	El Salvador			
	Guatemala			
	Venezuela			

Note. Countries named in bold letters are covered by a chapter in this volume.

On the basis of the data on cultural practices and values from 61 countries, GLOBE has identified altogether 10 cultural clusters around the world (see Table 28.1) that correspond highly with previously published attempts to identify distinguishable cultural regions (Gupta & Hanges, 2004). Countries from the same cluster share characteristics such as geographic proximity and climate zone, mass migration and ethnic social capital, and religious and linguistic roots. For example, countries within the Germanic cluster (Germany–former East and West, Switzerland–German speaking, Austria, the Netherlands) share a geographic region (central Europe), are similar in climate, and have common linguistic, religious, and geopolitical roots in history. Each of the Germanic countries is covered by a chapter in this book and in each chapter (from a country-specific perspective) the respective underlying historical and cultural developments are reflected so that the reasons why they have highly similar profiles, and also where and why there are subtle differences on the GLOBE dimensions between these countries, become apparent. For another example, countries from the Anglo cluster (England, Ireland, United States, Canada–English speaking, New Zealand, Australia, South Africa–White sample) span across various continents with different climatic zones, however, colonization and mass migration formed the basis for common linguistic and religious roots and for similarity in ethnic social capital.

Although different levels of economic development can moderate cultural differences between countries, the characteristics of the societal cultural background shape the people's fundamental attitudes, beliefs, values, and behaviors to an extent that accounts for a large proportion of the prevailing differences between societies and cultural regions (Gupta et al., 2004).

We used the 10 cultural clusters identified by GLOBE to structure the presentation of country chapters in this book. This is meant to be helpful for the reader who wants to compare countries from the same and different cultural regions, for example, in order to identify subtle differences between countries of the same cluster or to identify interesting overlap between countries from different cultural clusters. This helps to understand cultural similarities and differences between countries and cultural regions better and to become aware of the impact the sometimes subtle differences in societal culture and leadership concepts can have on the effectiveness of cross-cultural encounters at work. We are convinced that the 10 clusters identified by GLOBE serve as a useful framework for managing complexities of multicultural operations.[1]

In Figures A1 to A9 (see Appendix A) the 10 cultural clusters are used to group the 25 countries covered in this book (plus one further entry, because Germany is represented by two samples, one for former East and one for former West Germany) together with the remaining 35 GLOBE countries that are also covered in the wider GLOBE study. Figures A1 to A9 show the relative positioning of countries and country clusters with respect to the GLOBE dimensions of societal cultural practices ("As Is") and values ("Should Be"). In the following subsections, we give examples of how country comparisons within and across cultural clusters, in combination with selected information from the country chapters in this book, can be a useful tool to improve our understanding of a country's societal culture and development.

Cluster-Typical and Boundary-Spanning Societies

Certain societies can be seen as more or less typical for a particular cultural cluster. Some societies' characteristics are highly prototypical for the country cluster they are member of. For example, the United States and England are positioned well in the middle of the Anglo cluster for most of the nine GLOBE dimensions (see Figures in Appendix A1 to A9); the same holds true for Germany-West or Austria within the Germanic cluster or for Argentina and Colombia for the Latin America cluster. There are also countries that are positioned at the boundaries of culture clusters with respect to several GLOBE dimensions. For example, the Netherlands', which is in the Germanic cluster, societal characteristics overlap with characteristics of societies from the Nordic European cluster, notably for Power Distance, In-Group Collectivism, Institutional Collectivism, and Gender Egalitarianism (see Figures A2, A3, A4, and A8). In some characteristics, the Netherlands also fits to the Anglo cluster, notably for Uncertainty Avoidance (see Figure A1). Gupta and Hanges (2004) present evidence that the Nordic and the Germanic cultural clusters overlap considerably, due to common cultural roots and geographical proximity.

Societies that are at the boundaries of cultural clusters may share several characteristics with countries from several cultural clusters also for reasons other than geographic proximity. For example, in the chapter about Singapore, GLOBE societal culture scores from countries that also belong to the cultural cluster of Confucian Asia (China, Hong Kong, Japan, South Korea, and Taiwan) are compared to the respective scores for Singapore. The profile of Singaporean GLOBE scores often align with the average profile of the Confucian Asia

---

[1] Note that some aspects of culture and leadership in the 10 cultural clusters are also described in various chapters in the book edited by House et al. (2004). A special Issue of the *Journal of World Business* (Vol. 37, 2002) is devoted to describing culture and leadership in 6 of the 10 GLOBE cultural clusters (Germanic Europe, Anglo, Latin Europe, Eastern Europe, Middle East, and Southern Asia).

cluster, but also with the profiles of other countries (e.g., Japan) and country clusters (e.g., Anglo). Specifically, in Figure A1 it can be seen that Singapore scores about as high on Uncertainty Avoidance practices as other Nordic and Germanic countries. When comparing Singapore to the countries from the Confucian Asian cluster it can be seen in Figure A1 that Singapore's scores differ from the average profile in this cluster. Moreover, Singapore shows a marked downward trend from high practices to low values in Uncertainty Avoidance. Only Hong Kong shows the same downward trend, which, however, is much less in magnitude. All other countries from the Confucian Asian cluster show lower practices than values in Uncertainty Avoidance, indicating a different developmental trend for their societies. Other examples where Singapore deviates from its cultural cluster's profile are Assertiveness (Singapore's scores and trend resemble more the profile of the Anglo cluster; see Figure A7) and Gender Egalitarianism (scores and trend resemble more the profiles of the Anglo and the Nordic European cluster; see Figure A8). As has been discussed in the chapter about Singapore, these findings align with the results from the historical and ethnographic analyses. The authors conclude that Singapore blends Chinese, Malay, and English cultural elements as a result of colonialism (from the UK), emigration (from China and Malaysia), and openness to managerial and business practices from Western cultures (e.g., UK, United States) and also from modern Asian cultures (e.g., Japan).

From a practitioners' point of view, establishing subsidiaries in boundary-spanning societies such as Singapore or the Netherlands can help multinational companies to gain easier access to the necessary cultural know-how and experiences before they establish subsidiaries in countries that belong to the same cultural cluster but are more foreign to them. For example, the GLOBE data indicate that from the perspective of a company based in the Anglo cluster, the countries from the Confucian Asian cluster should be approached via Singapore and countries from the Germanic or Nordic European clusters via the Netherlands.

Subcultures Within Societies

The question of whether the GLOBE sample represents the societies well enough has been raised by cross-cultural scholars (e.g., Triandis, 2004). What is meant is that subcultures in societies, especially of large and culturally heterogeneous countries (e.g. China, India, or the United States) may not be adequately represented by GLOBE because samples were not systematically drawn to cover different subcultures. This is true and future research needs to address this issue, especially for the larger countries just mentioned. However, some systematic sampling that accounts for the existence of subcultures was performed in several societies covered by GLOBE. The German sample systematically represents regions from former East Germany and former West Germany. These two regions were separated after World War II into two different nations each belonging to a different political and economical system. West Germany was embedded in the Western economic system and the NATO military alliance. East Germany was embedded in the communist economic system and the Warsaw Pact for about 40 years until Germany was reunited in 1990 (for details, see the German chapter). Switzerland is also represented with two samples: One sample was drawn from the German-speaking part, which is covered by the Swiss chapter in this volume. Another sample was drawn from the French-speaking part of Switzerland. Although not covered by a chapter in this book, its data contributed to the overall GLOBE results that are covered in the figures of this chapter (see Appendixes A and B).

In Figures A1 to A9, one can see that on most GLOBE dimensions, East and West Germany score highly similar. Overall, the data support the view that both parts of Germany are very close to each other culturally and are centrally positioned within the Germanic cultural cluster. Only subtle differences exist between these regions, some of which point toward the legacy of the "iron curtain" that separated the Eastern communist from the Western capitalist systems. In contrast, the cultural practices and values in French-versus German-speaking Switzerland differ so much that the respective subcultures were positioned in different cultural clusters. French-speaking Switzerland shares more characteristics with countries from the Latin European cluster than with countries from the Germanic clusters— the opposite is true for German-speaking Switzerland.

Thus, GLOBE not only presents evidence for subcultures within countries to exist, its results also underline the fact that subcultures within the same country may be positioned in different cultural clusters with considerable differences in their societal cultural profile. Furthermore, all chapter authors took great care in specifying the cultural group from which they selected the respondents. For example, in the chapter about England it is described clearly that its content is representative of the English, but not necessarily of the Welsh, the Scottish, or the Northern Irish within the United Kingdom. The major cultural divides within countries are also acknowledged in each chapter.

Different "Species" of Collectivistic Societies

The constructs of collectivism and individualism have attained the status of paradigm in cross-cultural psychology (Segall & Kagitçibasi, 1997). In the last 25 years, more than 1,400 articles and numerous books have been published on these dimensions (for a review, see Gelfand, Bhawuk, Nishii, & Bechthod, 2004). Triandis (1994) pointed out that collectivistic and individualistic cultures, on the one hand, can be specified by some common defining attributes, but on the other hand, they differ on additional culturally specific elements of the constructs. He therefore suggested that the construct should be polythetically defined as in other sciences, for example, in zoology: The defining features of the category "bird" are wings and feathers, but distinguishing between different species of birds requires consideration of some further combinations of attributes (e.g., yellow beak, carnivorous). Analogously, for distinguishing between the cultures of societies, the simple dichotomy of collectivism versus individualism is not sufficient. Further theoretical and empirical refinement is necessary.

GLOBE established the distinction between In-Group Collectivism and Institutional Collectivism. In-Group Collectivism is the degree to which individuals express pride, loyalty, and cohesiveness in their organizations, families, circle of close friends, or other such small groups. Institutional Collectivism is the degree to which institutional practices encourage and reward collective distribution of resources and collective action. The latter scale measures an aspect of collectivism that differs from those published in the literature. Gelfand et al. (2004) note that "Institutional Collectivism seems to be part of a cultural syndrome wherein such cultures are future focused and performance oriented yet [they] seek to accomplish such orientations through practices that emphasize being concerned about others, and not being assertive or power domineering" (p. 476). More detailed descriptions of these two dimensions and manifold empirical data about the scales' interrelations with established measures of collectivism are given in Gelfand et al.

For the purposes of this chapter, we focus on the culturally specific descriptions made in the country chapters in order to reflect the variety of meanings the culture-general GLOBE constructs imply when seen from a within-country perspective. Furthermore, by taking multiple GLOBE dimensions into account, we explore "further combinations of attributes" that are helpful in distinguishing between different "species" of collectivistic societies.

From inspection of Figures A3 and A4 it can be seen that the GLOBE societies and country clusters differ substantially in their positioning on In-Group Collectivism and Institutional Collectivism practices and values. Let us first take a bird's-eye view by looking at the country clusters.

For In-Group Collectivism (Figure A3) the Nordic, Anglo, and Germanic countries (which are typically seen as individualistic societies) and the Latin European countries display medium levels in cultural practices (exceptions are Portugal, Spain, and Ireland with somewhat higher levels). The countries in these clusters aspire for significantly higher levels of In-Group Collectivism values ("Should Be"). The countries from the Latin America cluster show high practices ("As Is") scores and all but one aspire to even higher levels in respective values ("Should Be"). In contrast, the countries from the remaining clusters (Eastern Europe, Middle East, Confucian Asia, Southern Asia, Sub-Sahara Africa), most of which are positioned on high levels of In-Group Collectivism practices, show high variance in how the In-Group Collectivism values deviate from the respective practices. Note that the range of values scores overlaps strongly with the range of practices scores (see Figure A3). This variance calls for closer inspection of individual countries.

Before we do this, let us take another bird's-eye view on Institutional Collectivism (Figure A4), which shows a picture different from the aforementioned. Most country clusters display medium levels on Institutional Collectivism practices while aspiring for higher levels in values. One exception is the Nordic Europe cluster, where Institutional Collectivism practices are seen to be rather high and the desired values are positioned much lower. A similar trend, but less in magnitude and more around the midpoint, is apparent for the Anglo cluster. Interestingly, the countries from the Confucian and Southern Asian clusters, which traditionally are seen as prototypes of collectivistic societies, score only medium on Institutional Collectivism practices (with only one exception in the Confucian Asia cluster), and the countries of the Confucian Asian cluster display a pattern of sometimes higher and sometimes lower levels of value scores (see Figure A4).

We now explore culturally specific "combinations of attributes" for some selected societies—China, India, Turkey, and Sweden—in order to distinguish between different "species" of collectivistic societies.

China.   Positioned in the Confucian Asia cluster, China is traditionally seen as a typical example for a collectivistic society. The disparity between high levels of In-Group Collectivism (Figure A3) and only medium levels of Institutional Collectivism (Figure A4) finds an explanation in what the chapter authors write about the kind of collectivism that is endorsed in the Chinese culture. Chinese people live within networks of *guanxi* (relationships or ties) and are very careful with *renqing* (emotional reactions to other people) and *mianzi* (face). Moreover, they prefer governance by ethics (*li zhi*) over governance by law (*fa zhi*). The reliance on people rather than on law naturally promotes the practice of *guanxi,* because the social context of individuals (rather than institutional authority) defines what is permissible in a given context. This explains why In-Group Collectivism is more strongly endorsed in China than Institutional Collectivism. Thus, the two GLOBE dimensions help us to represent a specific "combination of attributes" that identifies the specific nature of China's collectivism in more detail.

There is another interesting "combination of attributes" to explore. Within the Confucian Asia cluster, China shows the strongest downward trend from high levels of In-Group Collectivism to medium levels of respective values (the disparity is even stronger than for Hong Kong; China starts at a considerably higher practice level than Hong Kong does). The chapter authors argue that this is the result of the dramatic changes taking place in China, especially within the business context. China's collectivistic orientation is being challenged by the import of Western-style management principles and market economy–oriented values. The chapter authors speak of "a growing spirit of 'Chinese-style' individualism" and give examples of respective developments in the Chinese society in their chapter.

India. The In-Group Collectivism scores reported for India (Southern Asia cluster) are similar to the scores reported for China. As is described in the chapter about India, its form of collectivism is primarily based on the family, which continues to be one of the basic units of Indian society. This explains, in a somewhat different way from the case of China, why the In-Group Collectivism score for India is higher than its Institutional Collectivism score. Furthermore, India's downward trend from high In-Group Collectivism practices to medium values is about as strong as for China. This trend provides an explanation that is similar to the reasons given for China: For India the focus on materialism is said to cause an increase in individualism in society, particularly among the managerial class, which experiences competition every day at work.

Turkey. Turkey (Middle East cluster) is also positioned in the high bands of In-Group Collectivism practices. It ranks fifth highest on practices in the total GLOBE sample. Its respective In-Group Collectivism cultural values score is very much on the same level as the respective cultural-practices score. Thus, there seems to be no societal cultural reflection of an influx of materialistic and individualistic practices and values into the Turkish society. For Turkey (similar to India) the family stands at the center of life in society, which is also endorsed by the Turkish interpretations of the Islam religion, and people have a high trust of family members (note that most organizations in Turkey are family owned). Furthermore, ties between people in Turkey are also established by belonging to the same region (i.e., born and raised with family roots there), and more generally, the people have a strong commitment to their relationships in social networks (similar to China). All this together explains Turkey's higher levels of In-Group Collectivism practices as compared to Institutional Collectivism practices.

Aside from no apparent differences between high levels of In-Group Collectivism (which sets Turkey's collectivism apart from China's and India's) there is a strong upward difference towards Institutional Collectivism, from medium levels of cultural practices to high levels in the respective cultural values. The chapter authors explain the medium level of Institutional Collectivism practice by the marked distrust of the Turkish people in institutions and "others" within and outside their society (apart from family and regional bonds), which they trace to the long history of multiple invasions of the region. Despite considerably higher Institutional Collectivism values than practices (which may indicate developments toward more state control over collective goods and individual risks), Turkey's other cultural characteristics do not align with the cultural syndrome related to high Institutional Collectivism that was described previously (cf. Gelfand et al., 2004). In contrast, the levels of Power Distance (Figure A2) and Assertiveness (Figure A7) are comparatively high and the levels of Future Orientation (see Figure A5) and Performance Orientation (Figure A6) are comparatively low. Overall these results for Turkey suggest that the Turkish blend of collectivism continues to be mainly based on In-Group Collectivism (pride, loyalty, and cohesiveness within organizations, families, circles of close friends, and other small groups). An actual cultural change toward higher levels of Institutional Collectivism practices (institutional practices that encourage and reward collective distribution of resources and collective action) appears difficult to achieve.

Sweden. It seems to be a paradoxical finding, but Sweden's traditionally individualistic society (it scores second lowest on In-Group Collectivism cultural practices; see Figure A3) displays the highest score of all GLOBE countries for Institutional Collectivism cultural practices (see Figure A4). As the chapter authors point out, in Sweden individual independence and strength is stressed, which is expressed as a tendency to be left alone or the desire "not to be beholden to anyone." The word *ensamhet* (solitude) has a positive connotation. It suggests inner peace, independence, and personal strength. Swedish children are encouraged to become independent from their family at an early stage. The character *Pippi Longstocking* (*Pippi Långstrump*), created by the Swedish author Astrid Lindgren, symbolizes the "mature" Swedish child. Being able to take care of oneself, independent of a family, as Pippi always does, is regarded as something positive. The family context as a basis for life-long social bonding does not seem to play a significant role in Swedish society.

That Sweden is a prototypical "species" of the cultural syndrome of Institutional Collectivism is apparent in its comparatively low practices scores for Power Distance (Figure A2) and Assertiveness (Figure A7), and its high levels of Future Orientation (see Figure A5). Furthermore, it is apparent in some peculiarities of the Swedish society. According to the chapter authors' descriptions, a very high proportion (87%) of employees are unionized compared to 34% in the UK, 24% in Japan, and 9% in France, Sweden's tax rates are extremely high compared to other countries and taxation is used to enable state and local governments to assume extensive responsibility for many collective services such as education, the labor market, industrial policies, care of the sick and elderly, pensions and other types of social insurance, and environmental protection. The Swedish enjoy unique collective rights, for example, the Right of Public Access (*Allemansrätten;* "Every Man's Right"), which makes the individual landowner's interests subordinate to collective interests by granting every individual the right to access other people's property (to pick wildflowers, mushrooms, berries; to bathe in and travel by boat on other people's water). All these indicate clearly that collective goods in Sweden, and the people's access to them, are well protected and maintained by their institutions.

We concur with the Swedish chapter authors who develop a plausible explanation, on the basis of their within-country analyses, for the contradiction between the GLOBE results and Hofstede's (1980) assertion that Sweden is clearly an individualistic culture. Hofstede did not distinguish between In-Group Collectivism (what Hofstede's Individualism-Collectivism dimension mainly measures)[2] and the form of Collectivism which is based on a whole society. The distinction between In-Group and Institutional Collectivism is obviously important for better specification of the Swedish type of collectivism. And it appears helpful for characterizing "individualistic" societies, which rank highly on the Institutionalized Collectivism dimension (further examples are Norway, Denmark, or New Zealand), as well as for distinguishing between the different blends of "collectivism" shown in societies such as China, India, and Turkey.

For distinguishing between the cultures of societies and for characterizing cultures from a culture-specific perspective, the simple dichotomy of collectivism versus individualism is not sufficient. On the one hand, the previously described findings provide a further theoretical and empirical refinement of concepts for cross-cultural measurement as was suggested by

---

[2]As was shown by Gelfand et al. (2004), based on between-country analyses, Hofstede's Individualism scale corresponds mainly with GLOBE's In-Group Collectivism practices scale ($r = -.83$, $p < .05$), and it is nearly unrelated to the Institutional Collectivism practices scale ($r = .15$, ns).

Triandis (1994). On the other hand, the findings serve as an example for how results from culture-specific (within-country) and culture-general (between-country) analyses can corroborate into new insights.

Implications for the Evolution of Culture

One major question in cross-cultural research is, "how do different cultures evolve?" Numerous cross-cultural scholars have posited that cultural species or syndromes develop as adaptations to the ecological context (e.g., Berry, Poortinga, Segall, & Dasen, 1992; for alternative views, see Cohen, 2001). Existing cultures can thus be seen as viable solutions to a certain set of problems in their history that derive from the respective ecological context within which they have developed. For an example, Barry, Bacon, and Child (1959) illustrated in a classic study that cultural individualism, which supports self-reliance and freedom, is crucial for the survival in hunting-and-gathering ecologies, whereas in agricultural ecologies, societal collectivism, which endorses conformity and obedience, is crucial for survival. And as societies move toward industrialization, Triandis (1994) further argued, there is a shift toward an emphasis on individualism.

From principles of biological evolution, however, we know that shifts "backward" in the developmental history are extremely unlikely. Similarly, sustained survival of a culture is less about solving yesterday's problems than about solving today's problems and those in the future. Thus, it is important for societies to recognize the relevant ecological factors of the present and anticipate those in the future in order to adapt to them successfully.

Considering the preceding discussion, the GLOBE findings about the cultural syndrome around Institutional Collectivism can help us to better understand different "species" of collectivism and how they are developing. For example, societies like Sweden, which show high levels of Institutional Collectivism, seem to have found a formula for combining the fulfillment of individualized needs with collective economic prosperity and social welfare. Interestingly, in Sweden at the end of the 20th century, the In-Group Collectivism seems much more desirable than the Institutional Collectivism the Swedish society had managed creating, whereas in China, a clear trend toward more individualism in general is apparent. In-Group Collectivism and Institutional Collectivism are both desired to be less important in China. It appears that the Chinese culture responds to its problems of industrialization by a trend toward individualism whereas the Swedish society seems to adapt to a postindustrialization environment by a trend toward In-Group collectivism. Note that from a western point of view, the Chinese societal cultural development may be seen as a "backward trend," however, viewed from China's perspective with its long history of collectivism and its shorter history of communism, it is not.

Summary

In the first part of this chapter we have described how the GLOBE practices and values measures of societal culture, in combination with qualitative and ethnographic descriptions of individual societies, can help to improve our understanding about what the similarities and differences in societal cultures actually mean, about how they come to be, and how we can identify societal changes that are likely to happen in the future.

Obviously, a much more detailed account of each of the culture-specific issues mentioned earlier, and many more, are discussed in the individual country chapters presented in this volume. It is neither possible nor necessary to include all of them here.

In the next part, we combine the GLOBE findings about societal culture and leadership from a culture-general perspective with the findings from the culture-specific analyses about culture and leadership undertaken in each of the 25 country chapters of this book.

2. LEADERSHIP ACROSS AND WITHIN CULTURES

For GLOBE the focus is on *organizational leadership*—not leadership in general or leadership in other domains, such as political, military, or religious leadership. GLOBE defines organizational leadership as "the ability of an individual to influence, motivate, and enable others to contribute toward the effectiveness and success of the organizations of which they are members" (House & Javidan, 2004, p. 15).

Because one of the major research questions of GLOBE is to estimate the extent to which societal and organizational culture influence the cognitions people hold about the nature of effective leadership, the concept of *implicit leadership* theory (ILT; Lord & Maher, 1991) is used. ILT focuses on individual-level differences in cognitions about which leadership attributes such as personal characteristics, attitudes, and behaviors contribute to or impede effective leadership. Such leadership *prototypes* (also referred to as schemas, cognitive categories, or mental models in the social-psychological literature) are assumed to affect the extent that an individual accepts and responds to others as leaders (Lord & Maher, 1991).

Culturally Endorsed Implicit Leadership Theory (CLT)

GLOBE extended ILT to a culture-level theory that explains how culture influences leadership by focusing on cognitions about effective leaders that are shared by members of an organization or society. On the basis of the GLOBE data, Hanges and Dickson (2004) provide convincing evidence for agreement in the people's cognitions about leadership within cultural groups, which validates the aggregation of individual ratings to the organizational and societal level of analysis. Dorfman, Hanges, and Brodbeck (2004) refer to the shared cultural-level analogue of individual ILT as *culturally endorsed implicit leadership theory (CLT)* and describe universal as well as culture-contingent dimensions of CLTs and how these are endorsed within the GLOBE countries and cultural clusters.

In the current volume, a further step forward is taken by combining the culture-specific and culture-general analyses about leadership prototypes in order to describe particular "species" and "combinations of attributes" of leadership prototypes that are endorsed in the 25 societies covered in this book.

How Leadership Prototypes Link to the Cultural Context

The GLOBE hypotheses about relationships between societal culture and leadership CLTs are derived on several grounds. Culture (on societal and organizational levels) can be seen to define a set of acceptable and unacceptable behaviors and values. Through socialization and acculturation, on the one hand, individuals develop a set of expectations about what constitutes effective leadership (leadership prototypes), and on the other hand, individuals learn to conform to respective cultural norms when they act as leaders themselves. Over time, certain individuals become particularly skilled at acceptable behaviors; for example, successful managers are particularly well socialized and acculturated. On the basis of predictions from ILT, those individuals who display leadership attributes that are more in line with the culturally accepted CLTs have a higher likelihood to be accepted and responded to as a leader by followers of the same cultural group. Thus, from the perspective of cross-cultural transitions, successful adaptation to a particular cultural environment can be dysfunctional when managers are placed in a different cultural environment (e.g., via expatriation) within which the culturally endorsed leadership concepts are different from those endorsed in their home culture.

Leadership Effectiveness in Cultural Context

Our culturally endorsed theory of leadership predicts that leader behaviors that are accepted and effective within a collective are the attributes and behaviors that most clearly fit within the parameters of the cultural forces surrounding the leader (House, Wright, & Aditya, 1997). However, it is arguable whether leaders need to fully match their behaviors and values to cultural expectations to be effective. Leader behavior that deviates slightly from dominant cultural values can encourage innovation and performance improvement. Thus, nontraditional and unexpected leadership attributes, especially when they are in line with espoused values that indicate developmental trends within a society or organization (i.e. "Zeitgeist" for culture change), can also have higher acceptance and stronger positive response on part of the followers. These propositions are in line with Hollander's *social exchange theory* (1958, 1980), which suggests that innovation from leaders is not only accepted but expected.

It is also possible that certain leadership attributes are universally accepted and considered effective worldwide, regardless of the specific cultural values espoused in a particular collective.

With these theoretical considerations in mind, the GLOBE researchers operationalized and empirically explored CLT prototypes in the way described in the following subsection, which has been used in all 25 country chapters presented in this book.

Measurement of CLTs

For the culture-general purposes of GLOBE, leadership prototypes have been operationalized by the use of indicators reflecting individual ILTs. The GLOBE respondents were instructed to think of people in their organization or industry who are exceptionally skilled at motivating, influencing, or enabling them, others, or groups to contribute to the success of the organization or task. Managers responded to 112 questionnaire items, each containing behaviors or characteristics that describe leaders with a short definition for clarifying what is meant (e.g., Item 2-16: Trustworthy—Deserves trust, can be believed and relied upon to keep his/her word) and rated them on a 7-point Likert-type scale (1 = greatly inhibits; 2 = somewhat inhibits; 3 = slightly inhibits a person from being an outstanding leader; 4 = has no impact; 5 = contributes slightly; 6 = contributes somewhat; 7 = contributes greatly to a person being an outstanding leader).

Hanges and Dickson (2004, 2006) describe how these 112 leadership attributes were statistically grouped into 21 first-order factors (termed *primary leadership dimensions*) and consolidated into 6 second-order factors referred to as *global leadership dimensions*. Justification for the term *global* is based on the use of several techniques that provide evidence that the final composition of factor attributes are comparable across all GLOBE countries:

1. In order to avoid ethnocentrism in item selection, GLOBE colleagues from around the world participated to generate the original item pool of about 735 attributes.
2. In order to assure common understanding of items and reliability in dimensional categorization, Q-sorting was undertaken involving colleagues from around the world.
3. In order to make sure that item wordings and meanings are not distorted or culturally unacceptable, independent translation and back- translation was performed and item

reports were written for each country, indicating potential difficulties—for example, in Germany, the word *Leader* could not be directly translated into "Führer" because of the negative connotation of this word since the Holocaust.

4. Only those items that "survived" the aforementioned procedures were used in the GLOBE questionnaire.

5. Based on two independent country samples, multilevel exploratory and confirmatory factor analyses were undertaken to derive leadership dimensions that differentiate between the GLOBE societal cultures regarding attributes that are perceived by more than 17,000 managers from about 950 organizations in 61 societies to influence effective leadership.

The resulting *global* CLT leadership dimensions are labeled and defined as follows (see also Table 28.2):

1. *Charismatic/Value Based leadership:* reflects the ability to inspire, to motivate, and to expect high performance outcomes from others based on firmly held core values. It includes six subscales labeled visionary, inspirational, self-sacrificial, integrity, decisive, and performance oriented.

2. *Team Oriented leadership:* reflects effective team building and implementation of a common purpose or goal among team members. It includes five subscales labeled team collaborative, team integrator, diplomatic, malevolent (reverse scored), and administratively competent.

3. *Participative leadership:* reflects the degree to which managers involve others in making and implementing decisions. It includes two subscales labeled autocratic (reverse scored) and participative.

4. *Humane Oriented leadership:* reflects supportive and considerate leadership but also includes compassion and generosity. It includes two subscales labeled humane orientation and modesty.

5. *Autonomous leadership:* refers to independent and individualistic leadership. This is a newly defined leadership dimension that has not previously appeared in the literature. It includes a single subscale labeled autonomous.

6. *Self-Protective leadership:* focuses on ensuring the safety and security of the individual. This leadership dimension includes five subscales labeled self-centered, status-conscious, conflict inducer, face saving, and procedural.

The six global leadership dimensions are summary indices of the characteristics, skills, and abilities culturally perceived to contribute to, or inhibit effective leadership.

Universal Dimensions of Leadership

The GLOBE team hypothesized and empirically demonstrated that members of different cultures share a common frame of reference regarding effective leadership (House et al., 2004). Dorfman et al. (2004) determined the extent to which specific leadership attributes and behaviors are universally endorsed as contributing to effective leadership, in contrast to those that are culturally contingent. Most leadership attributes from the Charismatic/Value Based and Team Oriented leadership dimensions were universally seen as positive. We first take a bird's-eye view on how the 25 societies described in this volume are distributed on these two universal dimensions of leadership.

TABLE 28.2
GLOBE Leadership Dimensions, Scales, and Items

Global Dimensions First-Order Factors	Questionnaire Items (Definitions omitted)
Charismatic/Value Based	
Visionary	Visionary, foresight, anticipatory, prepared, intellectually stimulating, future oriented, plans ahead, inspirational.
Inspirational	Enthusiastic, positive, encouraging, morale booster, motive arouser, confidence builder, dynamic, motivational.
Self- Sacrificial	Risk taker, self-sacrificial, convincing.
Integrity	Honest, sincere, just, trustworthy.
Decisive	Willful, decisive, logical, intuitive.
Performance Oriented	Improvement, excellence, and performance oriented.
Team Oriented	
Team Collaborative	Group oriented, collaborative, loyal, consultative, mediator, fraternal.
Team Integrator	Clear, integrator, subdued, informed, communicative, coordinator, team builder.
Diplomatic	Diplomatic, worldly, win/win problem solver, effective bargainer.
Malevolent (reversed)	Irritable, vindictive, egoistic, noncooperative, cynical, hostile, dishonest, nondependable, intelligent.
Administrative competent	Orderly, administratively skilled, organized, good administrator.
Participative	
Autocratic (reversed)	Autocratic, dictatorial, bossy, elitist, ruler, domineering.
Participative	Nonindividual, egalitarian, nonmicromanager, delegating.
Humane Orientation	
Humane Orientation	Generous, compassionate.
Modesty	Modest, self-effacing, patient.
Autonomous	Individualistic, independent, autonomous, unique.
Self-Protective	
Self-Centered	Self-interested, nonparticipative, loner, asocial.
Status-Conscious	Status-conscious, class-conscious.
Conflict Inducer	Intragroup competitor, secretive, normative.
Face Saving	Indirect, avoids negatives, evasive.
Procedural	Ritualistic, formal, habitual, cautious, procedural.

Charismatic/Value Based Leadership.   In Figure B1 (see Appendix B), the country scores for Charismatic/Value Based leadership are plotted and grouped according to the 10 GLOBE country clusters. It can be seen that with very few exceptions, the country scores range between 5.5 and 6.5 on the 7-point scale and the median is 5.9. From the overall distribution (even the outlier scores are above the mid-point of the scale) it is evident that Charismatic/Value Based leadership is positively endorsed in all GLOBE countries and cultural clusters.

Figure B1 (Appendix B) also shows statistically derived "bands" (gray shaded) of country scores (Hanges, Dickson, & Sipe, 2004). The scores of countries within the same band are statistically not significantly different from each other. For example, applying the banding procedure to the country distribution for Charismatic/Value Based leadership shows that France is an outlier (due to response bias; see Hanges, 2004). Furthermore, it can be seen that Singapore (Confucian Asian cluster) is positioned in a higher band of Charismatic/Value Based leadership than the other Confucian Asian cluster countries, and it is positioned in the same band as most of the countries in the Nordic and German clusters.

Team Oriented Leadership.   Figure B2 depicts the results for Team Oriented leadership, which was identified to be the second universally endorsed leadership dimension. This time, and again with very few exceptions, the country scores range between 5.5 and 6.3 (median = 5.8), which speaks for a generally positive endorsement of Team Oriented leadership in all GLOBE countries and country clusters. Overall, the country scores for Team Oriented leadership are slightly lower than for Charismatic/Value Based leadership. However, the least variability among culture clusters was found for the Team Oriented and not for the Charismatic/Value Based leadership dimension (Dorfman et al., 2004), although the range of the latter dimension is likely subject to restriction of range due to the scores being nearer to the end of the scale. Thus, Team Orientation seems to be a leadership principle that very much unites managers' culturally endorsed cognitions about the nature of effective leadership in societies and cultural clusters around the world.

Links Between Culture and Leadership

Despite the culture-general evidence for the universal endorsement of most of the Charismatic/Value Based and Team Oriented leadership items (Dorfman et al., 2004), applying the banding procedure described previously shows that there are significant differences between societies and cultural clusters in how strongly each of these leadership dimensions is endorsed. Furthermore, based on the total sample of countries, GLOBE has presented empirical evidence according to which there are significant links between these leadership dimensions and societal cultural and organizational cultural dimensions (Dorfman et al., 2004, Table 21.10, p. 699 ff).

As hypothesized by GLOBE researchers, regression analyses revealed that the most important predictor of the Charismatic/Value Based leadership dimension is the Performance Orientation cultural dimension. Societies and organizations that value excellence, superior performance, performance improvement, and innovation will likely seek leaders who exemplify Charismatic/Value-Based qualities. Team Oriented leadership was best predicted by cultural values of In-Group Collectivism and Humane Orientation and was negatively related to Assertiveness cultural values and practices. Unexpectedly, a positive relationship between Team Oriented leadership and Uncertainty Avoidance emerged. The more a society or organization values the reduction of uncertainty, the more team orientation is reported to contribute to effective leadership.

The remaining four leadership dimensions introduced earlier are all culturally contingent. There is high variability between country scores and sometimes even obvious disagreement between managers from different cultures about whether the respective leadership characteristics inhibit or contribute to outstanding leadership. In the next section, we therefore summarize the findings for Participative, Autonomous, Humane, and Self-Protective leadership (see

Figures B3 to B6). It can be seen that different "species" of leadership prototypes emerged for each leadership dimension depending on which societies and cultural clusters were examined. Together with the previously described evidence, this also leaves the possibility that there exist different "species" or "combinations of attributes" for Charismatic/Value Based and Team Oriented leadership prototypes. These are explored in the section after the next.

Culturally Endorsed Dimensions of Leadership

According to the scatter plots in Figures B3 to B6, the medians of the four remaining leadership dimensions are positioned considerably lower than the medians for the aforementioned two universal leadership dimensions. Furthermore, the distributions of country scores show considerable variation among countries and country clusters for the culturally contingent leadership dimensions. This means that they are particularly sensitive to societal cultural differences, and thus can add significantly to our understanding of the peculiarities of leadership prototypes endorsed in particular societies.

For each dimension, we describe the distributional characteristics of country scores across cultural clusters and we highlight country-specific data and interpretations provided within the country chapters in order to enrich our understanding about the leadership prototypes endorsed in particular societies. This is done separately for each leadership dimension, so that we can also develop a better understanding about how GLOBE dimension are contextualized within particular societies and what the respective manifestations are.

Participative Leadership. Participative leadership (median = 5.3, range: 4.5–6.1) is reported to contribute to outstanding leadership for all societies and culture clusters studied. However, considerable variation exists among countries and clusters (see Figure B3). From GLOBE's culture-general analyses, we know that Participative leadership positively relates to societal and organizational cultural values of Humane Orientation, Performance Orientation, and Gender Egalitarianism, and negatively to Uncertainty Avoidance (Dorfman et al., 2004). From inspection of Figure B3, it can be seen that the Nordic Europe, Germanic Europe, and most of the Anglo countries as well as some individual countries, notably France, Argentina, and Greece, are particularly attuned to Participative leadership. Most of the countries from Latin Europe, Latin America, Eastern Europe, Middle East, Confucian Asia, Southern Asia, and Sub-Saharan African clusters only slightly endorse this leadership dimension positively.

Interestingly, several countries that score particularly high on participative leadership are from different cultural clusters: Finland (Nordic), France (Latin European), Austria, Switzerland and West Germany (Germanic), United States (Anglo), Argentina (Latin American), and Greece (East European). From the respective country chapters, it emerged that different "species" of Participative leadership are endorsed in these societies.

In the Finnish and the Argentine chapters, Participative leadership is mentioned only a few times. Managers from Finland are portrayed to lead not by giving orders, but by motivating, setting an example to subordinates, and allowing for participation in decision making, which aligns with Finland's low scores on Assertiveness societal cultural practices and values. In Argentina, it is the nonparticipative leadership style the authors focus on, which is described as most suspicious of being "in the service of [a leader's] own greed." Whereas in Finland, Participative leadership is seen as one of several leadership characteristics that positively define effective leadership, which is in opposition to directive leadership, in Argentina, the authors solely focus attributes of *non*participative leadership as strongly rejected by managers.

In the French chapter, participation is among the most often used and cited terms to describe leadership. Principles of participation seem to be much more important for leadership in France and for the French societal culture in general than in most other countries. On the one hand, Participative leadership serves as a counterpart to a narcissistic leadership style apparent among French managers (Lebel, 1985). This leadership style appears to trace back to the pre-Revolutionary period in France (before 1789) where elegance, grandeur, elitist, and aristocratic values were endorsed. On the other hand, Participative leadership is described to help maintain the "one person, one vote" principle (rooted in the principle of egalitarianism in France's post-Revolutionary period) and to oppose the principle of weighting people's votes on the basis of accumulated power and capital (which apparently stems from the pre-Revolutionary period). The French chapter authors conclude that French managers seem to not espouse a consistent principle of participation, but to consistently reject nonparticipative leadership behavior.

In contrast, in Austria, as well as in German-speaking Switzerland and in Germany, participation is described to be a well-established societal cultural practice, represented in legal principles such as the social partnership model. This is also mirrored in the cultures of Austrian organizations, represented through the legal principles of codetermination, which is also endorsed in Germany. Thus, rather than being used as an "opposing" principle (e.g., against directive, autocratic, or elitist leadership), for Austrian and other Germanic societies, participation and Participative leadership are positively defined cultural practices and values manifest in various societal and organizational institutions.

Additional empirical evidence from behavioral field experiments (along the lines of the Vroom & Yetton model of participation) presented by Reber, Jago, Aucr-Rizzi, and Szabo (2000) positions Austria as significantly higher in participative decision making at work (similar to Germany and Switzerland; Brodbeck et al., 2000; Szabo, Reber, Weibler, Brodbeck, & Wunderer, 2001) than Finland, France, the Czech Republic, Poland, Turkey, and the United States. Furthermore, Austrian as well as German managers are portrayed to use participation to bring more information and different perspectives to bear on the task. Even more interesting, the Austrian managers respond to and resolve conflict among subordinates by becoming *more* participative. In contrast, managers in France, Finland, the United States, Poland, and the Czech Republic tend to display more autocratic leadership behaviors when conflict occurs.

The U.S. chapter authors portray Participative leadership to be not part of the traditionally U.S. American prototype of a "heroic" leader. However, it seems to be on the rise. On the one hand, the U.S.-based leadership literature diagnoses a need for Participative leadership in accord with a need for process-oriented, collaborative, systemic, and "global" leadership. On the other hand, on the basis of the quantitative and qualitative GLOBE findings, the chapter authors conclude that Participative leadership is positively connoted and associated with treating others as equals, being highly informal, tapping into the inner passions of the people, and being not preoccupied with oneself. In the United States, the nature of Participative leadership is described as being part of a set of personal characteristics. Outstanding contemporary leaders should have Participative leadership as well as Charismatic and Humane Oriented characteristics.

For the Greeks, who are portrayed by the country chapter author as natural participators and compulsive egalitarians, the management is characterized to a large extent by formal relationships, which, however, are usually not approved of and are often questioned by the people. What is meant by contemporary Participative leadership in Greece seems to focus mainly around certain communication behaviors, which the chapter authors describe as "listening to suggestions and inviting comments from employees."

In summary, from the described multiple country-specific accounts of Participative leadership, we can derive at least four different "species" that describe how Participative leadership manifests itself and is rooted in different societal cultural practices and values: (a) as an opposition to nonparticipative, autocratic, or directive leadership (e.g., Finland, Argentina, France); (b) as a legal principle to organize interactions at work between labor and capital (or management) manifest in societal and organizational cultural practices and values (e.g., Austria and other Germanic countries); (c) as a set of personal characteristics in modern North American leadership conduct that surface, for example, in treating others as equals, being informal and not preoccupied with oneself (e.g., United States); and (d) as a set of communication behaviors like listening and inviting suggestions from others that aligns with societal cultural resentment against formal rules and a preference for open exchange (e.g., Greece).

From a purely culture-general perspective, these different "species" of Participative leadership would not have surfaced because all described societies score in the same high band of the GLOBE scale of Participative leadership (see Figure B3).

Humane Oriented Leadership.   Humane Oriented leadership (median = 4.9, range: 3.8–5.8; see Figure B4) was reported among cultures and clusters to contribute to effective leadership in varying degrees or to have no impact. From GLOBE culture-general analyses (Dorfman et al., 2004), we know that the most important predictor of Humane Oriented leadership are Humane Orientation societal and organizational cultural values such as concern, sensitivity, friendship, tolerance, and support for others. According to Figure B4, higher scores are found for the Anglo, Confucian Asian, Southern Asian, and Sub-Saharan Africa clusters. Lower scores are reported for most of the Nordic, Germanic, and Latin European countries. France as an outlier is positioned below the midpoint of the scale. The scores reported for countries from the Middle East and East European clusters vary considerably on this dimension. Again, different "species" of Humane Oriented leadership emerged from the further information presented in country chapters.

In the chapter about Ireland, which is one of the prototypical representatives of the Anglo cultural cluster, the authors diagnose a match between comparatively high levels on Humane Oriented leadership (explained on the basis of societal values for nonassertiveness and indirectness in interpersonal communication) and Humane Orientation societal cultural practices (explained by strong Christian and Catholic heritage and the small size of the country) in their society. These translate into the expectation that Irish leaders should behave in a humane, modest way and not flaunt their authority. In the other countries from the Anglo cluster, a pattern similar to the Irish is found (although levels of societal cultural Humane Orientation practices are somewhat lower) in that Humane Oriented leadership focuses mainly around issues of interpersonal behavior.

For the United States, Humane Orientation societal cultural values and practices translates into friendly, open, and generous interpersonal behavior, compassionate in times of crisis, which is mirrored by the quantitative and qualitative findings for Humane Oriented leadership indicating that leaders should appreciate and respect the inherent humanity and dignity of the people they work with, communicate with a wide range of different people, and actively encourage them to express their different points of view, beliefs, and values. For Australia, an enigma is presented, in that the media analysis suggests on the one side, in line with the quantitative GLOBE results about high Humane Oriented leadership, that leaders are expected to show modesty, equanimity, egalitarianism, and a lack of pomposity. This is also in line with low–Power Distance societal cultural practices—the lowest among all Anglo countries. On the other side, media analysis also suggests that Australian leaders can become more aggressive and face-saving in confrontational and crisis situations. In New Zealand, an egalitarian approach is seen to be an important part of Humane Oriented leadership, but coupled with clear and direct communication. Finally, for South Africa–White sample, which is also part of the Anglo cluster, the high GLOBE score on Humane Oriented leadership is supported by similar results from media analysis. However, South Africa seems to differ from other countries of the Anglo cluster by showing very low levels of Humane Orientation societal cultural practices (see Figure A9), which compare to the low levels shown by Germanic countries, including the Netherlands, which had colonial influence on South Africa's population in the past.

In Confucian Asian countries, such as China and Singapore, the strong endorsement of Humane Orientated leadership has somewhat different behavioral consequences and it is based on different societal cultural roots than in Anglo countries. In China, where Humane Orientation societal cultural practices are comparatively high, being a humane leader means to align with Confucian principles of moderation and human-heartedness, which is closely related to *ren* (being benevolent, kind). Thus, people in general and leaders in particular are expected to be kind to others and to maintain a harmonious environment with a strong sense of *renqing* (i.e., implicit set of rules that involves reciprocation in the form of money, goods, information, status, service, and affection). China's high score on Humane Orientated leadership is also supported by results from interview and media analyses.

For Singapore, the chapter authors diagnose low Humane Orientation societal cultural practices, which they see as a consequence of the high degree of control on individual behaviors and many rules adopted from British colonization (e.g., punishment with a cane) that remain unchanged until today. The high scores on Humane Orientated leadership are seen as a consequence of Confucian principles. However, the Confucian principles for leadership endorsed in Singapore seem to be contextualized within Institutional Collectivism practices (e.g., Singapore managers are more willing to make self-sacrifice for their *society*) in addition to In-Group Collectivism cultural practices, as is the case for China, where leaders are expected to behave according to the principle that organizational members are seen as "family" members and treated accordingly.

For India, both scores, for Humane Orientation societal cultural practices and for Humane Oriented leadership, are positioned very high among the GLOBE countries. As put forward by the Indian chapter author, ample proof can be cited for the most striking feature of ancient India's civilization being its humanity. For just one example from India's recent history, the traditional doctrine of *ahimsa,* nonviolence and noninjury to humans as well as animals, was used effectively by Gandhi in the Indian struggle for independence from British rule. India's humanity is primarily rooted in family bonds (high In-Group Collectivism), but is contemporarily challenged by a considerable influx of Western-style individualism. For leaders, the expectation with respect to Humane Orientated leadership is to repose faith and confidence in followers, give them freedom, and take personal care of their well-being. The latter seems to match to some extent with Confucian principles endorsed in China, however, it is rooted in a different philosophical tradition in India. Finally, and different from the course taken by Singapore, which has maintained principles of human conduct from British colonization, in India, traditional humane principles in society and contemporary leadership prototypes seem to be more strongly aligned with each other.

From these multiple culture-specific accounts of how differently humane orientation is rooted and manifests itself in different societies, we can again derive several different "species" of Humane Oriented leadership: (a) as a set of values and behaviors that espouse equanimity, egalitarianism, and not flaunting one's own status as a leader (evident in several Anglo countries); (b) as friendly, open, and generous interpersonal conduct; in times of crisis direct and clear (in New Zealand), compassionate (in the United States) or aggressive (in Australia); (c) as a Confucian principle of moderation and maintaining harmonious social relationships (China, partly in Singapore); or (d) as a traditional principle of humanity reposing faith and confidence in followers, giving them freedom, and taking personal care of their well-being (India).

How does it come about that in some societies Humane Oriented leadership is reported to be more or less unrelated to outstanding leadership? This is the case in Finland, Germany, Russia, and France from the chapters included in this book (see Figure B4).

For Finland, despite the fact that according to the Finnish Tourist Board (see chap. 4, this volume), foreigners find Finnish people friendly and ready to help, despite a medium to high score on Humane Orientation cultural practices (encouraging fairness, altruism, caring and kindness to others), and despite a low score on Assertiveness societal cultural practices, Humane Oriented leadership is perceived to not relate to effective leadership in Finland. Inspection of the results from interviews and media analysis reveals that the humane principles of leadership endorsed in Finland are somewhat different from what is measured by the respective GLOBE leadership scale. Among the top-ranked attributes of outstanding leaders in Finland are "developing others" (i.e., the leader involves subordinates and helps develop their self-esteem), "being sensitive" (i.e., leaders show their feelings), and a "good listener" (i.e., leaders know and notice their subordinates needs). Compared to these leadership attributes, which obviously promote Humane Orientation at work, the leadership attributes measured by the GLOBE Humane Oriented leadership scale (i.e., being generous, compassionate, modest, self-effacing, and patient; see Table 28.2) tap aspects that only partially overlap with the behaviors described for Finland. The Humane Oriented leadership attributes measured by GLOBE match particularly well with the forms of friendly, open, and generous interpersonal conduct, which is endorsed in countries from the Anglo cluster.

Further evidence from Germany, Russia, and France strengthens the case for different cultural "species" of Humane Orientated leadership. In Germany, the reason why Humane Oriented leadership is reported as only marginally related to effective leadership is different from Finland. For Germany, the chapter authors argue that the low levels of Humane Orientation societal cultural practices and values are in line with the high Assertiveness cultural practices endorsed in Germany. This consists of getting the task done, minimizing errors, and achieving high-quality standards being more important at work than being friendly, generous, modest, and patient. Furthermore, the authors describe that the German approach in Humane Orientation cultural practices is manifest in institutionalized societal caring for people, rather than in interpersonal relations between people. Driven by a strong tendency to avoid uncertainty in people's lives, very elaborate and costly social systems have been developed by the state in order to take care of people and to reduce risks to individuals. Here the underlying societal cultural values are mirrored by how the relationships between employees and leaders are organized. As was pointed out earlier, the labor–capital relations in several countries of the Germanic cluster are based on principles of codetermination and participation, which are institutionalized by law in society and in organizations, which is also the case for Germany. Accordingly, it appears that leadership in Germany is more institutionalized, and thus also more depersonalized, than in many other countries. This leaves less room for Humane Oriented leadership with respect to interpersonal behavior (as it was measured by GLOBE) to impact on perceived leadership effectiveness.

In Russia, Humane Orientation and modesty in leadership conduct are reported to be neutral to perceptions of outstanding leadership. This corresponds also to the findings from media analyses, according to which an outstanding Russian leader should have a good image, linked to success, competencies, and social and professional recognition. These serve to facilitate the ability to attract people, settle disputes, bring about change in organizations, and control the situation. Russian leaders also are reported to display strong action orientation such as being nonhesitant, a real fighter, hard-working, restless, enduring, and self-sacrificial. Characteristics of interpersonal relationships at work between leaders and followers or peers are rarely mentioned in the chapter about Russia. There seem to be neither societal cultural norms nor leadership principles that prescribe kindness, compassion, being generous, modest, or patient in interpersonal behavior at work. Humane Oriented leadership is portrayed to be irrelevant to the concept of effective leadership *in Russia.*

For France, the chapter authors report, that Humane Oriented leadership is perceived to actually inhibit outstanding leadership because it can affect a leader's credibility. The authors' explanation of how this comes about is in brief: (a) In France managers have a low tolerance for mistakes at work, and thus are likely to come across as task oriented rather than people oriented (similar to German managers); (b) the focus is on events that materialize and the role of the leader as the main actor is downplayed in favor of a "whole systems" view; and (c) leaders are key actors in public and as such are expected to be rational, intellectual, objective, and concerned about the "whole system" rather than concerned about individuals. Being more concerned about individuals can result in suspicions about their credibility. The French also diagnose that a leader's "neutrality" is an important culture-specific trait. Leaders are expected to be very well educated, operate discreetly, and be strong in serving their company and country. The French view of an outstanding leader as being "objective," "neutral," and concerned about the "whole system" shares some characteristics with the institutionalized and depersonalized leadership concept held in Germany.

In summary, we have identified two reasons why Humane Oriented leadership is perceived to be unrelated or even an inhibitor to outstanding leadership in certain societies: (a) Characteristics other then the ones measured by GLOBE seem more relevant for humane orientation (as in Finland); and (b) a preference for depersonalized and institutionalized forms of leadership prevails in a society, which make certain characteristics of Humane Orientated leadership (at least those interpersonal facets that were measured by GLOBE) appear as obsolete to the responding managers (e.g., Russia, Germany) or even as dysfunctional (e.g., France).

Autonomous Leadership.   For Autonomous leadership (median = 3.9, range: 2.3–4.7) the highest variation among cultures and culture clusters is apparent (see Figure A5). The GLOBE culture-general analysis (Dorfman et al., 2004) demonstrates that Autonomous leadership is negatively related to Institutional Collectivism values at both societal and organizational levels of analysis.

Between societies and culture clusters, there exists a marked disparity about whether Autonomous leadership inhibits or contributes to effective leadership. Some individual countries from different cultural clusters are positioned more clearly in the range where Autonomous leadership is perceived to contribute to effective leadership (e.g., Austria, Argentina, Russia, Hong Kong), whereas other countries (e.g., the Netherlands, Colombia) or several countries that are part of the same cultural cluster (e.g., Spain, Portugal, France from the Latin European cluster) are positioned below the midpoint of the scale where Autonomous leadership is perceived to inhibit effective leadership.

A comparison of two cultural clusters, the Germanic and the Anglo clusters, which are particularly distinct from each other on the Autonomous leadership dimension (see Figure B5), can shed some light on why there is disparity about the role of Autonomous leadership being perceived as a contributor or inhibitor to effective leadership: In most country chapters of the Germanic cluster, Autonomous leadership is explicitly discussed in relation to effective leadership behavior, whereas in the chapters about Anglo countries autonomy is mainly seen as a societal cultural value or an individual right and seldom referred to as a leadership attribute relevant for effective leadership.

In the chapter about Germany East and West, autonomy on both the leader's and the followers' sides is reported to have positive implications for effective leadership, because it relates to principles of participation by which autonomous and technically competent leaders and followers negotiate their contributions to performing the tasks at hand to the highest possible standards. The latter is also addressed in the Austrian chapter, although not directly referred to as "Autonomous leadership," but rather as "long leash" leadership, which means giving the employees space to come up with their own ideas and solutions, and thus, to actively participate at work. As for Germany, the Austrian "long leash" blend of Autonomous leadership seems to also tie into principles of participation (see earlier discussion on Participative leadership).

The German-speaking Swiss are reported to generally respect autonomy and freedom in their society. From within-country factor analysis, the authors infer that leaders who display Autonomous leadership characteristics may be seen as "bossy." This can explain why leaders from the neighbor Germany, when they are working in Switzerland, are sometimes perceived as "too bossy." Due to their cultural background, leaders from Germany tend to be less subtle in displaying Autonomous leadership behaviors (this is discussed in more detail in the German chapter). Furthermore, on reinspection of the factor analytical results presented in the Swiss chapter, we found that autonomous leadership is also positively related to what they term the "Great Leader," who is described as inspirational, decisive, and performance oriented (among other attributes). This is in line with the culture-general findings for Switzerland, showing that in relation to other countries (see Figure B5), the Swiss managers seem to tolerate autonomous leadership to at least some degree, although not as strongly as managers from Germany and other Germanic countries do.

For the Netherlands, which displays the lowest scores on Autonomous leadership among all Germanic countries (below the scale's midpoint and significantly lower than the other Germanic countries; see Figure B5), the chapter authors report that although a high degree of individual autonomy with an emphasis on self-reliance is positively endorsed in the Dutch society, Autonomous leadership is perceived to relate strongly to the negatively connoted attributes of self-centeredness and autocratic leadership that are part of the Self-Protective leadership dimension discussed later. The findings for the Netherlands align more with what is described about Humane Oriented leadership for Anglo countries; namely, leaders should not flaunt their authority and should behave in an egalitarian way. This is in contrast to the other Germanic manifestations of Autonomous leadership.

Similar to what is described for the Netherlands, the U.S. chapter authors note that the high individualism in society does not automatically translate into a preference for Autonomous leadership. And for New Zealand, Autonomous leadership is described to relate to negatively perceived self-promoting leadership, which includes elements of self-centered and directive leadership (which are part of Self-Protective leadership, discussed later).

The finding that Autonomous leadership is rejected in the Netherlands for reasons similar to those in the United States and other Anglo countries provides further evidence for the

Netherlands to be seen as a "boundary-spanning" society between the Anglo and Germanic cultural clusters.

In summary, depending on how Autonomous leadership is connoted and manifested within a society, there seems to be something to gain and something to lose with respect to leadership effectiveness. In Germanic cultures (except for the Netherlands) where the task-oriented aspects of autonomy at work are important, Autonomous leadership is seen as a promoter of independent thought and action that is likely to result in high performance quality. In Anglo cultures and the Netherlands, people-oriented aspects of autonomy are more generally endorsed, Autonomous leadership is more likely to be seen as an inhibitor to effective leadership due to an overlap with self-centered, autocratic, and directive leadership attributes.

An addendum for France needs to be made with respect to the concept of autonomy. It seems to be embedded in the same societal cultural practices and values with the same negative consequences as was described for Humane Oriented leadership. In France, Autonomous leadership is reported to be an inhibitor of effective leadership. Leaders are expected to adjust to the constraints imposed by the government, the social milieu, and regional peculiarities. If they are seen to act autonomously, as individuals or loners, who try to achieve the goals on their own with low Participation, they appear to work against the "whole system," and thus are subject to suspicions, thereby losing credibility.

Self-Protective Leadership. For Self-Protective leadership (median = 3.5: range: 2.5–4.7), which is mainly perceived as an inhibitor or neutral to effective leadership, there is also considerable variation among cultures and culture clusters. From GLOBE's culture-general analysis (Dorfman et al., 2004) we know that Self-Protective leadership positively relates to Power Distance and Uncertainty Avoidance societal and organizational cultural values. In Figure B6 a clear trend is visible: For Nordic, Germanic, Anglo, and Latin European cultural clusters, Self- Protective leadership is reported to be a clear inhibitor of effective leadership (note their ascending scores). In contrast, for Latin American, East European, Middle East, Confucian Asia, Southern Asia, and Sub-Saharan African clusters, higher scores are shown, most of which are in the region of "no impact" or even "slightly contributing" to effective leadership.

Not very much other than rejection for Self-Protective leadership is diagnosed for all Nordic, Germanic, Anglo, and several Latin European societies. Throughout the respective chapters, it is reported to inhibit outstanding leadership and to relate to a variety of other maladaptive leadership attributes such as high power orientation.

For Turkey, the chapter authors report Self-Protective leadership to impede effective leadership, but it also links with the status consciousness, which is positively connoted in Turkey. For Russia, Self-Protective leadership is reported to overall impede effective leadership, though it is linked to the concepts of status consciousness and conflict-inducing behaviors, which are both positively connoted in Russia.

For Mexico, where the country score for Self-Protective leadership comes very close to the "no impact" midpoint of the scale, the chapter authors report positively connoted paternalistic attitudes combined with dominance orientation (Assertiveness) and a tendency to accept high levels of Power Distance, which all nurture acceptance of or at least negligence toward Self-Protective leadership. It is therefore not surprising that for Mexico some positive endorsement of Self-Protective leadership is manifest for two attributes, status consciousness and procedural, which are seen to slightly contribute to effective leadership.

With the exception of Singapore, in Middle East, Confucian Asian, Southern Asian, and Sub-Saharan African countries, the scores for Self- Protective leadership cross the scale's midpoint toward contributing to effective leadership. Unfortunately, none of the countries that are positioned well above the midpoint of the scale provided a country chapter for this volume. So we can't learn more from these countries about how concepts of Self-Protective leadership link positively to societal culture practices, values, and leadership effectiveness.

However, from the chapters assembled in this volume we can learn more about what Self-Protective leadership means within their respective cultural contexts when we delineate the dimension into its scales; *face saving* on the one side, with attributes such as indirect, avoids negatives, and evasive (see Table 28.2), and *hierarchic or paternalistic* leadership on the other side, manifest in status-conscious, conflict-inducing, or procedural leadership behaviors and attributes such as status and class consciousness, intragroup competitor, secretive, normative, ritualistic, formal, habitual, cautious, and procedural (see Table 28.2).

Face-Saving Leadership.   Other researchers have speculated that the relative tolerance for Self-Protective leadership in Asian cultures may be due to the concept of face saving to reflect group-protective rather than self-protective motives, and therefore would be viewed more positively in these more collectivistic societies (e.g., Dorfman et al., 2004). Proponents of the "face saving" hypothesis claim that even lying is acceptable in collectivist cultures when it serves the purpose of saving face (e.g., Triandis & Bhawuk, 1997).

We think that how face saving is connoted in relation to leadership within societies is a matter of what is prescribed by the societal cultural practices and values for answering the question of whose "face" is to be primarily protected by leaders, their own, the face of other individuals, or the face of a whole group or collective. It is plausible to assume that in collectivistic societies, it is the face of the group or collective that should be primarily protected, but not at the neglect of group members as individuals.

In a first step, we investigated the assumption that face-saving leadership is viewed more positively in collectivistic as compared to individualistic societies on the basis of culture-specific descriptions from selected country chapters in this book. For China, the Self-Protective leadership score is slightly below the midpoint of the scale and the chapter authors conclude that it has no impact on effective leadership. From closer inspection, it is evident that face-saving leadership behavior is seen as neutral or inhibiting effective leadership in China. Interestingly, a stronger tolerance for Self-Protective leadership is manifest in the positive endorsement of status consciousness and conflict-inducing behaviors, which speaks to hierarchical or paternalistic concepts of leadership rather than to face-saving leadership. The Indian chapter author underlines the fact that "face saving" is among the five lowest ranking subscales *within* India, perceived to inhibit effective leadership. He explains the relatively high rank on "face-saving" leadership (Rank 9) India holds among all GLOBE countries on the basis of its importance for social sensitivity and contextualizing one's thoughts and practices within relevant social contexts. Interestingly, similar to China, status-conscious, conflict-inducing, and procedural leadership are more positively endorsed (all above the scale midpoint) than face-saving leadership, which also speaks for a stronger endorsement of hierarchical or paternalistic leadership than for face-saving leadership in India. In Singapore, face-saving behavior is negatively endorsed and Self-Protective leadership scores significantly lower than in other Confucian Asian countries. The chapter authors argue that this is likely to be a consequence of Western (individualistic) cultural influences.

In the second step, we undertook a more systematic review of all GLOBE countries with the following results: First, with the exception of Albania (4.63), Taiwan (4.53), and Iran (4.03), in all GLOBE countries face-saving leadership behaviors are *negatively* connoted. Second, from correlation analyses of cultural practices a pattern emerged that supports the view that face-saving leadership correlates positively with In- Group Collectivism ($r = .60$,

$p < .01$, $N = 61$). No particular distinction emerged for Asian cultures compared to other cultures with an In- Group collectivistic profile, such as Latin America, Eastern Europe, or the Middle East.

The societal cultural divide between individualistic and collectivistic societies is apparent for face-saving leadership, is restricted in its relevance, in that it predicts the degree to which face-saving leadership behavior is seen as *neutral or rejected* within societies. The divide does not predict the degree to which face-saving leadership is *accepted* or *rejected*. Second, the divide extends across all In-Group Collectivistic societies, no matter whether they are from Asian clusters or not. This speaks against the assumption that face-saving behaviors are particularly important for being perceived as an effective leader in collectivistic societies or in Asian countries in particular. It rather seems to not promote or to nurture effective leadership in nearly all Globe countries.

Hierarchic-Paternalistic Leadership.   Another dimension that divides collectivistic and individualistic cultures seems more important to effective leadership. We termed it *Hierarchic-Paternalistic Leadership,* which taps the components of Self-Protective leadership that do not directly connote face-saving behavior. To the extent that Self-Protective leadership reflects status-conscious, conflict-inducing, or procedural behaviors (see Table 28.2) it is perceived *positively* in In-Group collectivistic societies and *negatively* in individualistic societies. In order to underpin these observations with broader empirical data, we undertook a systematic post hoc review of all chapters on the respective subscales with the following findings: Status consciousness, conflict inducer, and procedural behaviors are mostly *positively* endorsed in countries from Eastern Europe (including East Germany!), Middle East, Confucian Asia (excluding Singapore!), Southern Asia, and Sub-Saharan Africa. In contrast, the same leadership behaviors are perceived to *inhibit* outstanding leadership in countries from the Nordic European, Germanic (excluding East Germany!) and Anglo (including Singapore!) clusters. For Latin America and Latin Europe, results are mixed with a trend toward positive endorsement. The divide translates into correlations between In-Group Collectivism practices and the leadership subscales- status conscious ($r = .60$, $p < .01$, $N = 61$), conflict-inducing ($r = .62$, $p < .01$, $N = 61$), and procedural behaviors ($r = .65$, $p < .01$, $N = 61$).

For these hierarchic-paternalistic leadership attributes, the cultural divide is similar in magnitude to the cultural divide reported for face-saving leadership. However, the theoretically important difference is that it cuts across the respective scale's midpoints, which partitions societies in which the respective leadership behaviors are perceived as either inhibiting or contributing to outstanding leadership. Thus, it is of particular relevance to the leadership context.

In summary, we conclude that along the In-Group Collectivism–Individualism dimension there are two different cultural divides, one for "face saving" and another one for "hierarchic-paternalistic" leadership. They differ in that face-saving leadership is perceived as neutral or inhibiting outstanding leadership among nearly all GLOBE countries, whereas hierarchic-paternalistic leadership is perceived as either contributing to effective leadership in In-Group Collectivistic societies or inhibiting effective leadership in individualistic societies.[3]

---

[3]Participative leadership, which is perceived to contribute slightly or more to outstanding leadership among all GLOBE countries, can be seen as the opposite end to both face-saving and hierarchic-paternalistic leadership. On the country level, it correlates highly negatively with face-saving leadership ($r = -.74$, $p < .01$, $N = 61$), and with each of the elements of "hierarchic-paternalistic" leadership: status-conscious ($r = -.46$, $p < .01$, $N = 61$), conflict inducing ($r = -.73$, $p < .01$, $N = 61$), and procedural leadership ($r = -.59$, $p < .01$, $N = 61$).

Cultural Variations in CLT Profiles

From GLOBE, the answer to the common question that permeates the cross-cultural management literature, "does culture influence leadership?" is a clear "Yes." The GLOBE findings indicate that although there are commonalities across societies, culture influences leadership in a number of ways. As was described earlier, not only do societies and cultural clusters vary considerably on the CLT dimensions of Humane Oriented, Participative, Autonomous, and Self-Protective leadership, they also show a variety of culture-specific leadership concepts by which particular "species" of CLT dimensions become manifest.

Dorfman et al. (2004) note that the findings about the GLOBE leadership dimensions present an enigma; they highlight commonalities among cultures by illustrating their universal endorsement of some leadership attributes and global CLT leadership dimensions while simultaneously highlighting meaningful differences indicated in the findings of cultural specificity for certain leadership attributes and CLT dimensions.

It appears that herein the cultural-general approach described in the first GLOBE book (House et al., 2004) has reached a limit that calls for culture-specific analyses of multiple countries and cultural clusters. Therefore, in the current GLOBE volume, both approaches were combined.

In earlier parts of this chapter, we have discussed culture-specific in combination with culture-general findings about societal cultural practices and values and about the four culturally contingent leadership dimensions. Understandably, we can't discuss (or even just acknowledge) *all* culture-specific findings that are presented in the individual country chapters. They can give you a much more detailed account of culture-specific leadership phenomena accompanied by ample and rich examples.

For the readers' convenience, we have undertaken a systematic review of all chapters resulting in summary descriptions of country- specific CLT profiles, which we combined with qualitative findings about leadership reported in the respective chapters (see Table 28.3).

In Table 28.3, also a closer look can be taken at how the "universal" Charismatic/Value Based and Team Oriented leadership dimensions combine with the other four CLT dimensions within each of the 25 societies. We summarized the most prominent country-specific "combinations of attributes" of CLT prototypes (see Figures B1 to B6), grouped them according to the 10 cultural clusters identified by GLOBE, and highlight the differences and commonalities of countries from the same cluster and what distinguishes the latter from other clusters. Our assessments are underpinned by culture-specific examples of leadership attributes, which featured prominently within the country chapters.

The descriptions of CLT profiles of the countries and country clusters in Table 28.3 are necessarily incomplete. The purpose of the summary descriptions was not to substitute the country chapters; instead the purpose was to highlight culture-specific aspects of CLT profiles by demonstrating the extent to which the perception and enactment of leadership is culture bound and can vary between cultures within and between cultural clusters.

From the descriptions in Table 28.3 and from the country scores depicted in Figures B1 to B6, it is apparent that the leadership data reported for France and for countries from the Middle East cluster are most distinct from the rest of the GLOBE countries. We therefore explore potential reasons for these findings and their implications for the study of cross-cultural leadership.

A Note About the French CLT Profile.   The French chapter authors provide some back ground information that is helpful to interpret their county's CLT profile summarized in

GLOBE Country Cluster	Countries Described in a Chapter in this Volume	Commonalities	Differences
Nordic European Cluster *Finland, Sweden, Denmark* A blend of high Charismatic/Value Based and high Team Oriented leadership is endorsed with considerable elements of Participative leadership, thereby tolerating Autonomous leadership and strongly rejecting Self-Protective leadership.	***Finland.*** Effective leaders are portrayed to be not only inspirational figureheads in the forefront who energize an organization (Charismatic/Value Based) but also to instill a creative work climate, collaborate with subordinates, to be unusually communicative (Team Oriented and Participative), and to actively help employees develop (Humane Orientated leadership). Self-Protective leadership is most strongly rejected. ***Sweden.*** Effective leaders are perceived to be not only Charismatic/Value Based (especially visible, inspirational, visionary, performance oriented, decisive, with integrity) and Team Oriented (especially egalitarian, team integrative, and collaborative) with a strong belief in the power of teams, but also Participative by allowing and asking for individual autonomy and involvement. They are accepted as rational and pragmatic leaders who don't display procedural, conflict-inducing, administrative, or status-conscious behaviors.	What is common to Finland and Sweden and sets them apart from other countries in the GLOBE study is that Charismatic/Value Based and Team Oriented leadership combine with a very strong dislike for Self-Protective and Nonparticipative leadership.	Finland and Sweden seem to differ particularly on how Humane Oriented leadership is enacted: In Finland, it is enacted by personal sensitivity and developmental support. In Sweden, it is enacted by egalitarian approaches that grant individual autonomy.
Germanic Cluster *Austria, Germany East/West, Switzerland (German-speaking), the Netherlands*	***Austria.*** Effective leaders are perceived as high on Participative leadership (especially in decision making, responding to conflict, following the institutionalized systems of social partnership and codetermination) and high on Charismatic/Value Based leadership	What is common to the Germanic countries and sets them apart from other countries in the GLOBE study is that Participation is a key principle that combines with Charismatic/Value Based and	How Participative leadership is achieved in Germanic countries differs notably: Austrians have institutionalized participation but basically trust a *(Continued)*

1051

TABLE 28.3 (Continued)

GLOBE Country Cluster	Countries Described in a Chapter in this Volume	Commonalities	Differences
Participative leadership is very positively endorsed—highest among all 10 country clusters. It is seen to be as important as Charismatic/Value Based leadership and even somewhat more important than Team Oriented leadership. Autonomous leadership is often viewed in a positive manner (an exception is the Netherlands) and Self-Protective leadership is commonly viewed more negatively than in most other country clusters.	(especially visionary with high integrity, "a person with handshake qualities," decisive). Team Orientated leadership is less strongly endorsed. Leaders are expected to be oriented toward consensus and long-term benefits for all by placing a focus on communication ("talking brings people together") with a concept of team working that also allows for autonomy at work ("long leash" supervision). **Germany.** Participative leadership is a key principle (less so in East Germany) combined with tolerance for Autonomy, whereas Self-Protected leadership is strongly rejected (less so in East Germany). The CLTs of East and West Germans strongly overlap in Charismatic/Value Based leadership (especially visionary, performance oriented, inspirational) in combination with Team Orientation (especially administrative competence and team integrative behaviors), technical competency, and a clear task focus. Humane Orientation is only weakly endorsed. Instead leadership is institutionalized and depersonalized and the impact of the leader as a person is downplayed. **Switzerland (German-speaking).** For a Swiss leader, Participative leadership is a key principle alongside low Assertiveness. Second most important is Charismatic/Value	Team Oriented leadership. "Heroic" leaders are not accepted. Further insights about societal culture and leadership in the Germanic country cluster are described by Szabo et al. (2002). (See also Weibler et al., 2000.)	leader with "handshake qualities" and "long leash" supervision who brings people together. Germans institutionalized participation and leadership thereby downplaying the leader as a person. The Swiss work from consensus principles and dislike leaders who try to position themselves in the center of attention. The Dutch work from principles of consultation and integration ("polder model") and don't welcome a strong "single-person" leadership style.

(Continued)

TABLE 28.3 (Continued)

GLOBE Country Cluster	Countries Described in a Chapter in this Volume	Commonalities	Differences
	Based leadership (especially integrity, visionary, inspirational, self-sacrificial, performance orientation, decisive) combined with Team and Humane Oriented forms of leadership (especially diplomatic, administratively competent, team integrator, collaborative, modest). Leaders should avoid placing themselves in the center of attention.		
	Netherlands. Effective leaders are perceived to combine Charismatic/Value Based (especially inspirational, visionary, achievement oriented, innovative, trustworthy), Team Oriented (especially good communicator and team player), and Participative leadership with consultation, consensus seeking, integrating different opinions ("polder model"), flexibility, and the willingness to share power. A strong, single-person type of leadership is not welcomed, which also aligns with Autonomous leadership to be seen as an inhibitor of effective leadership.		
Anglo Cluster *Australia, England, Ireland, New Zealand, South Africa (White sample), United States, Canada (English-speaking)*	*Australia.* Effective leaders are perceived as being predominantly achievement orientated, visionary, inspirational, decisive (Charismatic/Value Based) with high egalitarian standards, so that they can always be seen as team and humane oriented ("one of the boys," "a mate"). Leaders who are seen to overperform,	What is common to the Anglo countries and sets them apart from other countries in the GLOBE study is the paramount role of Charismatic/Value Based leadership, followed by Team Oriented and Participative leadership.	How Anglo leaders are expected to achieve charismatic, person, and team oriented leadership differs notably: In England, leaders are expected to earn their followers' loyalty

(Continued)

TABLE 28.3 (Continued)

GLOBE Country Cluster	Countries Described in a Chapter in this Volume	Commonalities	Differences
Charismatic/Value Based leadership is strongly endorsed (highest of all clusters), combined with Team Oriented leadership (less in New Zealand) and elements of Participative leadership, which is enacted in a Humane Oriented manner. Self-Protective behaviors are viewed negatively.	being arrogant or status-conscious (Self-Protective leadership) are likely to find themselves in the position of the "tall poppy" —ready to be cut down. *England.* Effective leaders in England are perceived as decisive, inspirational, visionary, performance oriented, with high integrity (Charismatic/Value Based) and diplomacy. They don't rely on the followers' loyalty but rather earn it with a consultative and informed approach (Team and Humane Oriented leadership), while being dependable and honest. Merchant adventurers (self-centered, individualistic, intelligent, egotistic, nonegalitarian, ruthless, cunning) are described as an antiprototype of leadership who sometimes emerge as successful self-made millionaires. *Ireland.* Charismatic/Value Based leadership (especially vision, performance orientated, future focused, self-sacrificing in the interest of their organization) is strongly endorsed. Effective leaders have a "helicopter view" and inspire followers by getting them "to buy into their vision," achieved by integrity, trust, loyalty, and consensual decision making, not flaunting their authority (Participative and Team Orientated leadership), which can sometimes translate into	In all Anglo countries, a *person-oriented* leadership concept is endorsed wherein leaders are expected to deliver the desired results by operating as part of "teams" or "clans" rather than as part of "bureaucracies" or "institutions" (as, for example, in Germany or France). Further insights about societal culture and leadership in the Anglo country cluster are presented by Ashkanasy, Trevor-Roberts, and Earnshaw (2002).	with a consultative and informed approach. In Ireland, leaders should not flaunt their authority and inspire followers to buy into their vision with integrity, loyalty, and consensual decision making. In Australia, leaders need to be seen as "one of the boys," to have high egalitarian standards, and to not stick out as overperforming or arrogant (a "tall poppy"). In New Zealand, "tall poppies" are also cut down. However, apart from being in line with the "Kiwi"-culture archetype (flexible and pragmatic), a strong autocratic leader seems preferable to a sensitive facilitator. Among the White population of South Africa, leaders are expected to be strong and direct, fair and firm, but there also seems to be the hope that business leaders establish more democracy and principles of empowerment. In the United States, the image of the "heroic" leader who promotes team spirit and who cares about people seems to develop toward Participative leadership.

(Continued)

1054

TABLE 28.3 (Continued)

GLOBE Country Cluster	Countries Described in a Chapter in this Volume	Commonalities	Differences
	remaining in the background and influencing through networking and clientelist relations. Leaders should behave in a kind and modest way (Humane Oriented). The chapter authors note that business leaders have not yet earned a place in public memory, which is focused on an ideal of leadership centered on the patriot-hero and liberator. *New Zealand*. Paramount for a leader is performance orientation, taking action, and delivering results. They should also enthuse and inspire followers via personal commitment, perseverance, and example, all balanced by a modest, self-deprecating (Humane Orientation) "one of the boys" attitude combined with a strong egalitarian emphasis—"tall poppies" are also cut down. Flexible rule application (lack of red tape), and a good understanding of the "clan" rather than the "bureaucracy" approach to management (Team Orientation, Participation) helps leaders to be accepted. The "Kiwi"-culture archetype is practical—"can fix anything with a piece of No. 8 fencing wire"—with a dislike for autocratic leaders. However, the chapter author notes that "respect for the dictator is lurking," because the country's pioneering background seems to make a strong autocrat preferable to a sensitive facilitator.		

(Continued)

TABLE 28.3 (Continued)

GLOBE Country Cluster	Countries Described in a Chapter in this Volume	Commonalities	Differences
	South Africa–White sample. Effective leaders are perceived to take risks, to be trustworthy, persistent, and motivating, who can inspire others to willingly follow a vision (Charismatic/Value Based), who show strong and direct, fair and firm, but also democratic, empowering, and authority-delegating leadership (Participative). Tendencies toward bureaucratic leadership are tolerated. Effective leaders make followers more self-confident and to believe in themselves, their abilities, and their worth (Humane Oriented).		
	United States. Charismatic/Value Based leadership (especially inspire, stand up, focus efforts, strive for excellence, seek change, and act quickly) is most strongly espoused. Effective leaders are often seen as a "hero" but should also be Participative (egalitarian, informal, open to suggestions, delegates, engages followers), Team Oriented (e.g., promote team spirit), and Humane Oriented (open, friendly, respecting the dignity of each person, help others grow, mentor them). Finally, outstanding leaders are expected to understand their own personal strengths, liabilities, and vulnerabilities and to not take themselves overly seriously (low on Self-Protection).		
Latin Europe Cluster *France, Portugal, Spain, Italy, Switzerland (French-speaking), Israel*	**France.** Participative leadership is most strongly endorsed and Self-Protective Leadership is strongly rejected. Charismatic/Value Based and Team Oriented leadership contribute to outstanding	It is difficult to identify a theme for effective leadership that unifies the three Latin European countries described.	The French refrain from the high endorsement of Team Oriented leadership that is dominant among Latin European countries. Instead,

(Continued)

TABLE 28.3 (Continued)

GLOBE Country Cluster	Countries Described in a Chapter in this Volume	Commonalities	Differences
In this cluster, there is large between-country variation on all CLT dimensions (in part due to the distinct positioning of France). An effective leader is expected to show Team Oriented leadership with elements of Charismatic/Value Based leadership (except for France, where Participative leadership is most strongly endorsed). Autonomous leadership is seen as neutral or rejected and Humane Oriented leadership does not seem to play a particularly important role (in France it is even seen to inhibit effective leadership). Self-Protective leadership is overall not endorsed.	leadership (although France ranks lowest on these among all GLOBE countries) whereas Autonomous and Humane Oriented leadership inhibit it. When the leaders' actions are interpreted as personal considerations rather than serving "the whole" their credibility suffers. Furthermore, intellectualism, planning, and abstraction skills are noted to be important for an outstanding leader. The chapter authors suggest that an effective leader in France also needs to act "according to French standards" and that the quantitative part of the GLOBE study may not have properly picked up the peculiarities of leadership in France (see further discussion in the text). ***Portugal.*** Effective leaders are perceived to be primarily Team Oriented (affiliation motives are stronger than power motives, interpersonal skill, persuasion skill, fairness, consideration). Charismatic/Value Based (especially visionary, imaginative, courageous, hard-working, honest) and Participative leadership (especially contactable, communicative, democratic) are also positively endorsed, but secondary to Team Orientation. Humane Oriented leadership (especially friendliness, tolerance, generous, gentle) is positively endorsed. Also helpful are diagnostic and technical skills, as well as a talent for improvisation ("Muddling through"). The chapter authors note that a suspicion toward power still lingers over the collective memory of the Portuguese people.	Between-country variance is considerably high (see column on the right). Further insights about societal culture and leadership in the Latin European country cluster are presented by Jesuíno (2002).	among Latin European countries they show the strongest endorsement of Participative leadership. The least endorsement of Humane Oriented leadership among all GLOBE countries is shown in France. Team Oriented leadership is most pronounced in Spain and Portugal. Both also endorse "improvisation" as an attribute of effective leadership, although slightly different in connotation: "efficient, flexible, and pragmatic" in Spain and "muddling through" in Portugal. Finally, similar to most Latin American countries, the Spanish seem to tolerate Self-Protective leadership to a higher extent than most countries from the Latin European cluster including Portugal and France.

(Continued)

TABLE 28.3 (Continued)

GLOBE Country Cluster	Countries Described in a Chapter in this Volume	Commonalities	Differences
	Spain. An effective leader in Spain is perceived to be high on Team Oriented (especially collaborative) and Charismatic/Value Based leadership (especially performance oriented, inspirational, decisive, visionary, integrity), with elements of Participative and Humane Oriented leadership. Autonomous and Self-Protective leadership are perceived as inhibitors to outstanding leadership, although the relative tolerance for Self-Protective behavior is significantly higher than in other Latin European countries. Spanish leaders should also be efficient, pragmatic, flexible, and master the dichotomy of being "soft and nurturing" while being "strong and self-confident."		
Latin America Cluster *Argentina, Colombia, Mexico, Bolivia, Brazil, Costa Rica, Ecuador, El Salvador; Guatemala, and Venezuela* On the basis of all listed countries from the Latin American cluster, leaders are expected to practice Charismatic/Value Based and Team Oriented leadership, while being lenient to Self-Protective	***Argentina.*** Charismatic/Value Based, Team Oriented, and Participative leadership are endorsed equally strongly. Autonomous leadership is endorsed comparatively highly and some elements of Self-Protective leadership (especially status-oriented and conflict-inducing behavior) are positively endorsed. The chapter authors note that people in Argentina identify with individual leaders and not with their programs, but that "to govern" and "to rule as a strong man" are never far apart. A leader's vision can fascinate followers despite them knowing that many leaders may be manipulative. Skepticism prevails among Argentinean	What is common to the three Latin American countries described and sets them apart from other countries in the GLOBE study is the endorsement of Team Oriented and Charismatic/Value Based leadership in combination with a relatively high tolerance for Self-Protective leadership. Status consciousness and conflict-inducing behaviors seem accepted leadership attributes. In all three countries, people seem to	Some marked differences are also apparent: In Argentina, comparatively high leader autonomy is tolerated and a "strong man ruling" seems to be no surprise. In contrast, in Colombia, leader autonomy is not accepted. Instead leaders are expected to be accessible, nonautocratic, and to work well with people. In Mexico, leaders are expected to treat followers "as part of the extended family,"

(Continued)

TABLE 28.3 (Continued)

GLOBE Country Cluster	Countries Described in a Chapter in this Volume	Commonalities	Differences
leadership. Humane Oriented and Participative leadership are positively endorsed, however, with high between-country variation for the latter and low variation for the former. Autonomous leadership is perceived negatively (e.g., in Colombia), neutrally (e.g., in Mexico), or positively (e.g., in Argentina).	respondents who find true Charismatic/Value Based leadership unlikely to exist in their society. *Colombia.* Charismatic/Value Based (especially performance, future and performance orientation, vision, integrity, decisive) and Team Oriented leadership (especially team integrator, administratively competent, diplomatic) combine with flexibility, creativity, and a long-term vision for innovation. Humane Oriented (in the sense of "has a way with people," "works well with people," modesty) and Participative leadership (especially nonelitist and nonautocratic) are positively endorsed. Autonomous leadership is seen as impeding outstanding leadership, but some acceptance of Self-Protective leadership (i.e., conflict inducer and status consciousness) is evident. *Mexico.* Charismatic/Value Based leadership with a high emphasis on performance orientation, a machismo image, and Team Oriented leadership (emphasizing personal networks, which are trusted more than costs and profits) are the major contributors to effective leadership. Humane Oriented leaders appear paternalistic, but show sensitivity to the dignity and worth of individuals by being simpatico. This somewhat contributes to effective leadership	identify with individual leaders who operate within paternalistic social structures.	to be machismo and simpatico, but also performance oriented.

(Continued)

TABLE 28.3 (Continued)

GLOBE Country Cluster	Countries Described in a Chapter in this Volume	Commonalities	Differences
	as well as several elements of Self-Protective leadership such as status consciousness and procedural. Participative leadership is seen as near to neutral but Autonomous leadership is seen as less desirable. Strong paternalistic attitudes in Mexico contribute to employees' expectations to be treated "as part of the extended family."		
Eastern Europe Cluster *Greece, Russia, Albania, Georgia, Hungary, Kazakhstan, Poland, Slovenia* An exemplar of effective leadership typical for that cluster would be one who combines Team Oriented with Charismatic/Value Based leadership, displays comparatively high levels of Autonomous leadership, and is not reluctant to engage in Self-Protective behaviors. There is considerable variation between countries from that cluster on Participative leadership (from slight positive to strong positive endorsement) and for Humane Oriented leadership (from neutral to positive endorsement).	*Greece.* For an effective leader, Team Oriented (especially collaborative, administratively competent, diplomatic, and decisive) combines with Charismatic/Value Based leadership (especially visionary, inspirational, integrity, self-sacrificial). The also positively endorsed Participative leadership approach defines a set of communication behaviors (e.g., listening, inviting suggestions, open exchange of opinion) that align with resentment against formal rules and a preference for open exchange apparent in Greek society. Humane Orientated leadership is positively endorsed (here the authors note that personal connections with peers and subordinates speed up operations). Status consciousness, self-centeredness (Self-Protective leadership), and autonomous leadership behaviors, which seem to service a leader's "ego," appear tolerated in Greek society. In contrast, nonparticipative and autocratic leadership behaviors are strongly rejected.	For the exception of the common endorsement of Self-Protective leadership attributes (high status consciousness), the CLTs endorsed in Russia and Greece, representing the Eastern Europe cluster in our volume, couldn't be more different from each other. Further insights about societal culture and leadership in the Eastern Europe country cluster are presented by Bakacsi, Sandor, Andras, and Victor (2002).	Greece and Russia are positioned on opposite ends of the distribution of country scores in the Eastern European cluster for nearly all CLT dimensions (see Figures B1 to B7).

(Continued)

TABLE 28.3 (Continued)

GLOBE Country Cluster	Countries Described in a Chapter in this Volume	Commonalities	Differences
	Russia. For effective leaders in Russia, Autonomous leadership (especially individualistic, independent, and unique) is paramount. It is linked to "action-oriented" leadership, also strongly endorsed in Russia (i.e., act with no hesitation, real fighter, hard-working, enduring, self-sacrificial) and is as strongly endorsed as are Charismatic/Value Based (especially visionary, decisive, inspirational) and Team Oriented leadership behaviors. The latter mainly means to be administratively competent and collaborative oriented. Autocratic leadership behaviors seem to be tolerated. What matters are a good "image" (it is linked to success, competency, professional and social recognition) and acting as a "facilitator" (i.e., attract people, settles disputes, controlling the situation), which seems to be the Russian manifestation of Participative leadership. Humane Orientation is seen as neutral to effective leadership whereas status consciousness and conflict-inducing behaviors (Self-Protective leadership) are positively endorsed.		
Middle East Cluster *Turkey, Egypt, Kuwait, Morocco, and Qatar* There is considerable between-country variation, especially for	**Turkey.** Effective leaders in Turkey should display high Team Oriented (especially team integrator, administratively competent, diplomatic) and Charismatic/Value Based leadership (especially decisive, visionary, integrity, inspirational), which set Turkey apart from most other Middle East countries.	See text for further discussion of Turkey and countries from the Middle East cluster.	

(Continued)

TABLE 28.3 (Continued)

GLOBE Country Cluster	Countries Described in a Chapter in this Volume	Commonalities	Differences
Charismatic/Value Based and Team Oriented leadership, overall viewed as contributing to effective leadership. Humane Oriented leadership is perceived as contributing or neutral, Autonomous leadership as contributing, neutral, or inhibiting, and Self-Protective leadership as neutral or inhibiting to effective leadership. Medium endorsement of Participative leadership seems to be common among all Middle East countries.	An emphasis on Participative leadership that is open to feedback and criticism, and accepting of one's own mistakes, and Humane Oriented leadership is visible. Although, the Turkish blend of the latter seems paternalistic because leaders are expected to create a family-like atmosphere, be concerned and interfere with private problems of followers, and attend their social events such as wedding ceremonies of their children. Autonomous leadership is tolerated. Several aspects of Self-Protective leadership are positively endorsed (status consciousness) or neutral (conflict inducer, procedural) to effective leadership.		
Confucian Asia Cluster *China, Hong Kong, Singapore, Japan, South Korea, Taiwan* Charismatic/Value Based and Team Oriented leadership are most strongly endorsed among the societies of this region. However, the levels on these two dimensions are lower than for most other country clusters. Humane Oriented leadership is positively endorsed with levels that are similar to the Anglo	**China.** For an effective leader in China, the qualities of Team Oriented leadership (especially administrative skill, integrator, collaborative), Charismatic/Value Based (especially integrity, inspirational, visionary), and Humane Oriented leadership should combine. The Chinese way of Humane Oriented leadership aligns with Confucian principles of moderation and humane heartedness, or *ren*, which means to be benevolent and kind, and maintaining harmony by *renqing*, meaning reciprocation. Participative leadership, which is slightly positive endorsed, seems to be manifest in a particular Chinese way: Apart from showing modesty, leaders should be open to new information and well	What is common to the three countries from the Confucian Asia cluster described here and sets them apart from other countries in the GLOBE study is their Confucian blend of Team Oriented leadership, manifest in the endorsement of mainly collaborative and administrative competencies, and Humane Oriented leadership, manifest in moderation and human-heartedness.	In China and Hong Kong, the common Confucian themes in the Asia cluster are complemented by the acceptance of conflict-inducing behaviors and status consciousness, which speaks to a traditional hierarchic-paternalistic leadership concept: Leaders nurture, consider, and show sympathy in exchange for the followers' unquestioned loyalty, dedication, and compliance. This traditional view of leadership seems less pronounced in Singapore,

(Continued)

TABLE 28.3 (Continued)

GLOBE Country Cluster	Countries Described in a Chapter in this Volume	Commonalities	Differences
cluster. Participative leadership is somewhat positively endorsed, but ranks significantly lower than in Nordic, Germanic, Anglo, Latin European, and Latin American countries. Self-Protective leadership, although seen as neutral or as inhibiting outstanding leadership, ranks among the highest within all country clusters alongside Southern Asia and Middle East.	"networked" (*guanxi*) thereby constantly trying to improve themselves. This system assures input from all relevant sources, but in a different way than the egalitarian-democratic principles of participation enacted in individualistic cultural clusters do, which are based on an individualistic concept of the "Self." The Confucian concept of the "Self" is collective in nature, and thus, when leaders are well networked and therefore develop themselves, the collective as a whole can profit. Self-Protective leadership in the form of face-saving and procedural behaviors is seen as neutral, as is Autonomous leadership, but in the form of status-conscious and conflict-inducing behaviors it is seen as contributing to outstanding leadership. ***Hong Kong.*** Team Oriented (especially collaborative, administrative skill, diplomatic) and Charismatic/Value Based leadership (especially inspirational, visionary, performance oriented, delivering results) are major contributors to effective leadership. Humane Oriented and Participative leadership matter to some extent. True empowerment, however, is not accepted. In line with Confucian values, leaders should be respected, obeyed, and not questioned, resulting in a predominantly autocratic conduct of leadership. This would explain the positive acceptance of Self-Protective leadership		where a more democratic approach to leadership emerged, manifest in the highest levels of participation within Confucian and Southern Asia, which signals source acceptance of empowerment principles.

(*Continued*)

TABLE 28.3 (Continued)

GLOBE Country Cluster	Countries Described in a Chapter in this Volume	Commonalities	Differences
	attributes such as status consciousness and conflict-inducing behaviors. Autonomous leadership, in the sense of entrepreneurial spirit, cool-mindedness, calm, individualistic at work–collectivistic with family and friends, is perceived positively. This view of Autonomous leadership sets Hong Kong apart not only from all Confucian Asian but also from all Anglo countries—despite its colonial past and economic development up until 1996, which were shaped by representatives of the Anglo culture.		
	Singapore. Effective leadership is linked with Charismatic/Value Based (especially performance oriented, visionary, integrity) and Team Oriented attributes (especially collaborative, administrative skilled, diplomatic). The Charismatic/Value Based and the Participative leadership scores are in a significantly higher band than those from all other Confucian countries (see Figures 1B and 3B). The relatively high endorsement of Humane Oriented leadership aligns partially with Confucian principles of moderation and maintaining harmonious social relationships.		
Southern Asia Cluster *India, Indonesia, Iran, Malaysia, the Philippines, Thailand*	*India.* For effective leadership Charismatic/Value Based (especially inspirational, integrity, performance orientation, visionary, decisive) and Team Oriented leadership	India positions very much near the median of the distribution of all countries from the Southern Asia Cluster, except for a lower	

(Continued)

TABLE 28.3 (Continued)

GLOBE Country Cluster	Countries Described in a Chapter in this Volume	Commonalities	Differences
In the countries from this cluster, Charismatic/Value Based and Team Oriented leadership are perceived to be contributing most to effective leadership. Participative leadership is viewed positively, as is Humane Oriented leadership, on which the Southern Asian cluster ranks highest among all country clusters. Autonomous leadership is reported to be neutral as is Self-Protective leadership, on which the Southern Asian cluster also ranks highest (alongside Confucian Asia and the Middle East) among all country clusters.	(especially administratively competent, team integrator, collaborative), are most strongly endorsed. Humane Oriented leadership is seen to be next most important. India is positioned among the highest ranking countries on this dimension. Participative leadership is viewed somewhat positively and Autonomous leadership is reported to slightly inhibit outstanding leadership. For Self-Protective leadership, attributes of face saving and self-centeredness are negatively endorsed, but conflict-inducing behaviors and status-conscious are tolerated, with a slight positive endorsement. Overall, relationship orientation seems to be a particularly important characteristic of outstanding leaders in India, which is positively accepted when it combines with charismatic and action-oriented behaviors, but also tolerated when it combines with paternalistic and bureaucratic behaviors.	level of Team Oriented leadership. The country chapter on India may therefore give a good first glimpse into basic concepts of societal culture and leadership behaviors in the Southern Asian region.	
Sub-Sahara Africa Cluster *South Africa (Black sample), Namibia, Nigeria, Zambia, Zimbabwe* Charismatic/Value Based, Team Oriented, and Participative leadership are viewed as contributors to effective	***South Africa (Black sample).*** As is described by the South African chapter authors, they have gathered quantitative data about South Africa's black population in a somewhat different way than was prescribed by GLOBE. Therefore, we cannot report on the endorsement of CLT leadership dimensions. Instead, we cite here some examples from the authors' qualitative findings where South Africa's white and black samples were directly compared: *Blacks are*		

(Continued)

TABLE 28.3 (Continued)

GLOBE Country Cluster	Countries Described in a Chapter in this Volume	Commonalities	Differences
leadership. Humane Oriented leadership is most highly endorsed in comparison to all other country clusters. The Autonomous and Self-Protective CLT dimensions are seen as slightly impeding effective leadership.	*not as results driven as whites," "Blacks focus on people instead of skills," "Whites are more task focused than people oriented," "Blacks divide/share responsibility in order to protect the non performer," "Blacks emphasize the team above the individual."* On the basis of these and further qualitative and quantitative findings, the chapter authors portray a cultural divide between South Africa's Black and White populations in terms of what constitutes effective leadership: for the White sample a euro-centric performance and individualism oriented leadership style is portrayed, which is also reflected in the respective GLOBE data, whereas among the Black sample a people and collectivism oriented leadership style is preferred.		

Table 28.3. The state and regional governments in France are intimately related to how business is done, as are other factors such as type of industry or a firm's size (e.g., human relations are particularly important in smaller, family-based firms). For leaders it is thus essential to adapt to the peculiarities in the regional, economical, and social milieus in which they operate. If these factors are indeed more strongly shaping the business and leadership culture in France than in most other GLOBE countries, as is argued by the French chapter authors, it is highly relevant for our discussion of "species" of French leadership prototypes.

When leadership cultures differ strongly due to governmental, industry, regional, and social factors, flexible modification of leadership styles and techniques for handling management–employee relations are required, especially when managers are likely to transfer from one milieu to another several times during their career. This may be the reason for why the French leadership prototype is the most different from all GLOBE countries. The many rule systems and social milieus to which French leaders need to adapt may require a whole variety of different leadership styles and attributes. When these are statistically aggregated to the country level of analysis, the resulting country score may to some extent represent an "artificial" statistical aggregate of many heterogeneous mental representations of leadership, rather than a shared concept of leadership about which there is sufficient consensus across the whole society to warrant the use of statistical aggregation techniques (for a detailed discussion of how culture analysis can account for such phenomena, see Atran, Medin, & Ross, 2005).[4]

A Note About the CLT Profiles in the Middle East Cluster.   Dorfman et al. (2004) diagnose a number of striking differences between the Middle East cluster and the other GLOBE country clusters. They also note that almost all Middle East CLT dimension scores rank at the low end of the continuum when compared to other country clusters, with the exception of Self-Protective leadership where scores are relatively high. Thus, the possibility of response biases affecting the findings has to be taken into account (Hanges, 2004). However, only two of the five Middle East countries were identified as having strong response biases on GLOBE scales (75% for Morocco, 44% for Qatar; Hanges, 2004, p. 749).

One could speculate that in countries of the Middle East and Arab world less leadership is required from their leaders as compared to other countries, but this seems unlikely. Alternatively, as is described in the Turkish chapter and for Middle East countries (Bakacsi, Sandor, Andras, & Victor, 2002), leaders may be predominantly perceived within the social context they are part of (i.e., in relation to others) rather than as an individual with a particular set of attributes, which relates to In-Group collectivistic values. Another explanation is that some of the critical leadership attributes for this cluster were not part of the GLOBE attribute list (a similar point was made for the French country chapter). In a separate study, after having established confirmatory factor analytical evidence that the six GLOBE CLT dimensions hold up in this region, Dastmalchian, Javidan, and Alam (2001) identified additional leadership attributes that point to a culture-unique traditional leadership profile (i.e., familial, humble, faithful, self-protective, and considerate leadership). These leadership attributes underline the notion that the pervasive influence of the Islamic religion is a key to understanding the Middle East or Arab world. For a more in-depth discussion of societal culture and leadership

---

[4]Our considerations gain credibility in the light of two further findings for France. First, for the exception of Participative Leadership, all other country scores for France are at the lower end of the CLT scales. Second, when accounting for cultural response bias (Hanges, 2004, p. 749) it was found that 72% of the French GLOBE scales scores were biased and thus identified as outliers. This is the second-highest outlier rate among the 61 GLOBE countries (Morocco ranks first with 78%).

in the Middle East/Arab regions, see Kabasakal and Bodur (2002). Further examples of leadership attributes not measured as part of GLOBE, which emerged in other countries as well, are discussed later in this section.

Further Issues

Some further issues emerged from the combined culture-specific and culture-general assessment of culture and leadership in the country chapters.

Mixed Leadership Types.   Leadership prototypes are seldom found in purity. For example, for Germany, it is reported that some attributes of the disliked oppressive leader (loner, asocial) resemble attributes of the more positively perceived autonomous leader (independent, unique). Due to the overlap with Autonomous leadership, oppressive leadership behavior may be tolerated to some extent. In social reality, there is always uncertainty, incomplete information, and ambiguity, which allow substantial latitude for the formation of impressions about people in general and leaders in particular. Therefore, there can be variance in individual perception of leaders. For example, Autonomous leadership can also lead to an unjustified perception of leader weakness or lack of knowledge concerning the work of the followers when it is misperceived as an oppressive leadership style. Similar examples can be cited for all possible combinations of CLT dimensions.

Boundary-Spanning Societies and Subcultures in Leadership.   In the first part of this chapter, so-called "boundary-spanning" societies were identified, which combine societal cultural practices and values from two or more cultural clusters, for example, the Netherlands (Anglo, German, and Nordic) and Singapore (Anglo, Confucian Asian, and Southern Asian). On the basis of their Leadership CLT dimensions, these countries emerged again as boundary spanners, in that the leadership CLTs found comprise a respective mix of characteristics. Similarly, the same subcultures of one country that were distinguishable on the basis of societal cultural practices and values emerged again as distinct from each other on the basis of their CLTs. Examples are French- versus German-speaking Switzerland, and East versus West Germany. East and West Germany are overall very similar in societal culture. However they differ considerably on Power Distance societal practices, which are higher in East Germany. In the same way, they differ on Self-Protective leadership, which is related to Power Distance across all GLOBE countries.

These findings can be taken as a further support of the overall proposition made by GLOBE that culture shapes leadership perceptions.

Leaders as Managers and in Other Roles

In several country chapters, the issue of whether there is a difference between leaders and managers, and which characteristics distinguish between the two, has been described as a result of qualitative analyses, such as interviews and focus group discussions. In all those chapters, a difference between leaders and managers is reported to have emerged. The overall gist across all chapters is that leaders try to do the right thing, are good with people, and are change agents. Managers try to do things right, are good with tasks, and keep the system running. Still, there is ample cultural variation in what the specific attributes, connotations, and prescriptions for leaders are.

For China, it was pointed out that generally their leaders are also Party members and are expected to enact their leadership role in accordance with the political prescriptions. For example, the leaders who participated in the focus group interviews conducted in China were all Party members, some of them in leading positions. A similar point was made for leaders in the former East Germany before its reunification with West Germany in 1990. In East Germany before 1990, leading positions were preferably given to Party members and it was expected that they educate and develop followers according to the doctrines of the Socialist Party.

From these observations it appears that, over and above societal cultural factors, the characteristics of the leadership CLTs also depend on the roles within which organizational leadership is usually practiced within a society.

Leadership Attributes That Emerged Within Country Chapters. As described earlier, all effort was undertaken to ensure that the array of leadership attributes sampled as part of the GLOBE study is as broad as possible and derives from the sample of countries studied (cf. House et al., 2004). We did not expect to have captured them all and we are pleased with the fact that many leadership attributes and themes emerged from the country chapters that were not in the plans of GLOBE.

On the basis of within-country factor and cluster analyses of the GLOBE item pool and from the qualitative studies, some unexpected leadership attributes and themes emerged.

In Germany and New Zealand, *technical skills,* in the sense of mastering the nonmanagerial components of a particular job, emerged as an attribute of effective leadership. In France and Germany, *being well educated,* in the sense of a broad knowledge base and good abstraction skills, was identified as an important leadership attribute. A *good sense of humor* was perceived to be important for being an effective leader, for example, in China and Hong Kong. In the Finnish chapter, *clear,* in the sense of being explicit about rules, values, and policies in the company, and *being sensitive,* that is, the leaders show their feelings, were pointed out as important leadership characteristics.

More leadership attributes that were not anticipated by GLOBE researchers in Phases 1 and 2 can be found in the country chapters, often as part of a discussion about the societal cultural context in which they are embedded.

Summary

CLT profiles based on the combination of the six GLOBE leadership dimensions are useful for portraying commonalities *and* differences in leadership perceptions across a variety of countries and culture clusters. However, the CLT profiles do not tell us the whole story. In several instances, we identified a variety of "species" that represent different culture-specific connotations and enactments of Humane Oriented, Participative, Autonomous and Self-Protective leadership. We also identified certain "combinations of attributes" manifest in the overall CLT profile, which help us to better understand the different culture-specific connotations and enactments of Charismatic/Value Based and Team Oriented leadership in each country. Finally, several leadership themes and attributes emerged not reported in the first GLOBE volume (House et al., 2004).

Overall, these findings demonstrate the importance of doing both quantitative and qualitative research with respect to the study of cultures and leadership. They also suggest that we should expect considerable variability in how managerial leadership is perceived, understood, and enacted in different societies.

We find it remarkable how similar, for example, Austria, Germany, and Switzerland score on the CLT dimensions when viewed from a culture- general perspective. But when analyzed in more depth from a culture-specific perspective, differences emerge in how leadership is embedded within different systems of cultural practices and values, how leadership is thus perceived differently, and which different prescriptions for the enactment of leadership follow from that. Still, when the CLT profile of the Germanic cluster is compared to other countries or cultural clusters, the commonalities are clearly visible and they make the Germanic cultural region distinct from other cultural regions and countries. Analogously this holds true for each of the other cultural clusters and groups of countries analyzed.

We realize that not only is there considerable variability among cultural regions and societies, there is also variability among subcultures and individuals within each society. However, given that countries as well as country clusters vary significantly in leadership CLTs, this implies that differences among individuals within cultures do not overwhelm country and cluster differences and that we are justified in thinking of societies and clusters as viable entities that reveal interesting leadership CLTs across the world.

3. LIMITATIONS AND DIRECTIONS FOR FUTURE RESEARCH

The GLOBE researchers have made some deliberate decisions that set clear limitations on the samples and methods used within each country.

For good reasons (see House et al., 2004) only leadership *in organizations* was studied, and only *middle managers* were sampled from only *two to three* identical *industries* per country. Clearly this does not constitute a fully representative sample, though it does help considerably in comparisons across countries. Across these three industries, GLOBE results for societal culture and leadership (Dorfman et al., 2004; Gupta et al., 2004; Hanges et al., 2004; House et al., 2004) and even for organizational culture (Brodbeck, Hanges, Dickson, Gupta, & Dorfman, 2004) are very consistent, although there are considerable differences in technology, environment, methods of management, and government control. As a consequence, it is likely that our findings concerning culturally generalizable CLT dimensions are truly generalizable across a much wider array of industries. On the basis of these data, construct validation on the country level of analysis was established by triangulating all GLOBE scales with a whole variety of external data sources. The results increase our confidence in the GLOBE scales to provide us with a good basis to start with (House et al., 2004).

The limitations of the GLOBE study that focus on the quantitative culture-general part of the GLOBE project have been discussed elsewhere (House et al., 2004). Here we focus on those limitations that result from or directly affect the combined culture-general and culture-specific approach taken in this volume.

In order to combine the two approaches, CCIs from all 61 countries from the original GLOBE sample were asked to conduct an array of qualitative data analyses within their country by nonobtrusive measurement of observable cultural indicators. The individual country chapters included in this volume account for a little less than half of these countries. Of the 10 major regions of the world that were identified in Phase 2 of GLOBE, 7 are represented in this volume by at least two countries and two further clusters are represented by one country. However, not all country chapters conducted the full set of qualitative analyses specified for reasons unique to their own environment and access to relevant data.

Another limitation may be seen in the argument that the CCIs who research their own culture have a bias-potential that is perhaps best captured in the saying "fish will be the last to discover water." This, however, is offset by the benefit of the multiple standard instruments and methods used in GLOBE Phase 2 (House et al., 2004) that helped to establish objectivity. Furthermore, working from a within-country perspective permits a deeper interpretation of the quantitative and qualitative findings. For being able to sensibly interpret culture-specific data, firsthand knowledge and experience with the cultural context is necessary and helpful.

For an example, the Dutch chapter authors notice that some culture-specific features of their culture are hard to describe so that people from different cultural context would know what it means. The Dutch word *gezelligheid* is a very common term in the Netherlands, which can be defined as a cozy, pleasant, rather "intimate" social climate within a group. But if you have not experienced it, it is difficult to understand what it really means. Our German coeditor, however, felt that he we have an idea of what it meant, because in Germany, the term *Geselligkeit* refers to a similar social phenomenon (note that the Dutch and the German words are very similar to each other). Still we doubt whether the Dutch authors would agree if we were to imply that the Dutch and the German terms mean *exactly* the same. Moreover, we even doubt that there would be complete agreement among a group of Dutch people that *gezelligheid* means exactly the same to each one of them. The point we are trying to make is that for creating agreement about what is meant by a term or concept, we need to make abstractions, which means to subtract idiosyncrasies of individual understanding (when agreement about a term between individuals needs to be established) or to subtract idiosyncrasies of a particular societal cultural understanding (when agreement about a term between societies needs to be established). This abstraction–concretion dilemma is at the very heart of combining culture-general with culture-specific research.

With the double strategy taken by GLOBE, the quantitative culture-general approach resulting in validated measures (House et al., 2004) combined with the qualitative culture-specific approach taken by 25 GLOBE countries, we hope we have contributed to the cross-cultural study of leadership, in the form of developing meaningful abstract concepts about societal culture and leadership for comparing societies, in combination with the multiethnic study of leadership, in the form of meaningful idiosyncratic concepts within societies that relate to the aforementioned in a comprehensible way.

Perceived Leadership and Its Effects "In Situ"

By focusing on CLTs, GLOBE has implicitly reaffirmed the critical role of "leadership in the eye of the beholders." From theory and empirical research about ILTs, we know that perceived effective leadership is likely to fit the implicit leadership concepts held by followers. And leadership is most effective when the fit between attributes of a leader and the followers' leadership concepts is high. Followers are more motivated and committed when their leadership expectations are met and misunderstandings and reluctance against influence attempts are less likely (cf. Lord & Maher, 1991).

Accordingly, GLOBE researchers predict that the societal cultural distance is relevant for the leadership concepts endorsed in societies, and differences in CLT profiles matter for leadership effectiveness across cultural boundaries. The higher the fit the more effective cross-cultural leadership attempts would be. This proposition is currently being tested on an organizational level of analysis as part of GLOBE Phase 3. Further research is needed at the individual level of analysis, for example, by experimentally investigating the hypothesized link between the degree of fit between culturally endorsed leadership concepts and the behavioral consequences on part of followers, peers, and superiors of target leaders.

A related point was made in the country chapter on Austria, where it is argued that the particular work context *"in situ"* within which leadership takes place should also be taken into account. This was done by Smith et al. (2002) in which middle managers from 47 countries reported how they handled eight specific situations at work. Results from a subsample of the GLOBE study have been shown to strongly relate to earlier findings reported by Smith (1997; cf. Brodbeck et al., 2000). Thus, there seems to be not only an occasion for further research but also a common basis from which to work.

Considering Cultural Change

In several country chapters, the point was made that due to dramatic changes during the sampling of the GLOBE data, some distortions of the findings are likely. Argentina, for example, underwent a deep economic crisis during the mid-1990s. This may have affected the managers' responses to the cultural practices and cultural values. Respondents may have shifted their values toward more value idealization. They also may have changed their leadership perceptions such that they found true Charismatic/Value Based leadership unlikely to exist in their society. Observations like these cast doubt on the stability of the GLOBE findings for countries that underwent considerable change during the data-gathering phase. However, there is considerable corroboration between the Phase 2 quantitative findings and the findings reported in this book.

Some precautions against the described problem were taken. For example, the quantitative GLOBE data were linked to historical, economical, and cultural developments described within each country chapter, and for the across-countries analyses, external data sources, which cover a time span of up to 50 years, were used to triangulate the GLOBE scales. These precautions, however, do not fully solve the problems a changing environment imposes on the analysis of culture and leadership prototypes.

Another way of going about the problems imposed by environmental changes is by focusing on the particular cultural and leadership dimensions where skepticism is permissible within a particular society. The Portuguese chapter authors, for example, express skepticism about the viability of the high endorsement of Team Oriented and Participative leadership. This is due to the 1996 political environment in which the Portuguese were striving for a drastic change from an autocratic orientation toward more dialogue and team spirit at work. The authors see the high endorsement of the Charismatic/Value Based and Team Oriented leadership concepts to be more temporary rather than a valid cultural pattern.

Similar discussions, each resulting in different conclusions depending on the country-specific circumstances, are described for New Zealand, where data collection took place following one of the most significant periods of economic and social restructuring, for Germany with respect to various pos-reunification consequences (after 1990), for Hong Kong's high future orientation, which is seen as a consequence of the "handing over" to China in 1996, for Spain with respect to the 40 years of Franco dictatorship, or for Austria, in which a change of the political landscape was diagnosed during the time of data sampling (for details, see the respective chapters).

We also believe that cultural changes occur slowly over long periods of time in the range of 50 or more years. For example, East Germany was found in Phase 2 of GLOBE to be more similar to West Germany than to other Soviet-dominated countries, despite the fact that East Germans lived under communist doctrines for about 40 years since the end of World War II.

There is no question about GLOBE currently being a basically cross-sectional study, for which the problems of controlling the impact of context factors, changing conditions, and establishing empirical evidence for making causal inferences remain valid. Future research should therefore investigate the relationships between societal and organizational culture and leadership effectiveness longitudinally. The methods developed and the insights reported in the previous volume (House et al., 2004) and in the current volume provide a basis from which to start.

The Convergence Hypothesis.   One particularly intriguing proposition in the cross-cultural management literature is that modern industrialization and globalization will lead to worldwide cultural convergence so that effective and ineffective global management practices will inevitably surface (*convergence hypothesis;* cf. Dorfman et al., 2004). In some of our chapters, an influx of Western societal cultural values and leadership approaches in other cultural regions have been diagnosed, for example, in China, India, and Singapore, which seem to support the aforementioned proposition, if one is prepared to accept convergence toward Western values as a global trend. However, in other societies, this has not been the case, although political developments may make us expect it. For example, Turkey has been and will continue to negotiate with the European Community to become a full member. According to the GLOBE data, however, no marked influx of Western societal cultural values and leadership concepts into the Turkish society are currently apparent.

The United States is described to even move away from the Charismatic/Value Based "heroic" leadership prototype, which from a Western point of view appears as a likely focus for global convergence. The U.S. chapter authors diagnose a shift toward more Participative leadership, which is currently endorsed in Nordic and Germanic countries, as well as in France, Argentina, and Greece. Thus, change in leadership prototypes around the world seems to happen. However, it appears to go in various directions rather then to converge into one focus.

Overall, the GLOBE results present us with an enigma. On the one side, they speak to the universal endorsement of certain leadership characteristics (Charismatic/Value Based and Team Oriented leadership). On the other side, GLOBE provides equally strong evidence for the existence of culture-specific "species" or "combinations of attributes" of leadership concepts held within individual countries and cultural regions. Thus, it remains to be seen, via longitudinal studies, whether there is cultural convergence or divergence apparent in the modern world.

Based on the notion that the values and beliefs of people in various societies are fundamentally stable in nature, put forward by historians and social psychologists (e.g. Inkeles, 1981; Smith & Bond, 1993), the more leadership prototypes are shown to be culturally endorsed, the less likely they are to converge worldwide. Thus, with an eye on the possibility of future GLOBE phases with a longitudinal design, the convergence hypothesis can be reformulated into the following questions: "Which leadership dimensions are likely to converge and which are not?" and "Which dimensions converge more quickly than others?" We think that the universal and culturally contingent leadership dimensions identified by GLOBE provide us with a useful tool for answering these questions. Dimensions that change very slowly might be referred to as core leadership dimensions. And those dimensions that change more rapidly might be referred to as peripheral leadership dimensions. For any particular society, knowledge of both is necessary for a comprehensive understanding of that culture and the leadership practiced within it.

The Deprivation Hypothesis.   Earlier in this chapter, the deprivation hypothesis was introduced as an explanation for disparities between societal cultural practices and values scores. The disparity is based on respondents who perceive societal cultural practices as less or more dominant in their society or organization than they think they should be, or perceive them as inappropriate. On a society or organizational level of analysis, the respondents' common perceptions of a disparity between practices and values imply their sympathy with respectively higher or lower levels of cultural values than practices.

The deprivation hypothesis receives support from the GLOBE data. Whereas the standard cross-cultural literature assumed that societal cultural practices and values are positively correlated on the country level of analysis (Triandis, 2004), the GLOBE data show that they are mostly negatively related. For seven out of the nine GLOBE dimensions, the country-level practices dimensions are significantly negatively correlated with their values counterparts: Uncertainty Avoidance ($r = -.62$, $p < .05$), Institutional Collectivism ($r = -.61$, $p < .05$), Power Distance ($r = -.43$, $p < .05$), Future Orientation ($r = -.38$, $p < .05$), Humane Orientation ($r = -.32$, $p < .05$), Performance Orientation ($r = -.28$, $p < .05$), and Assertiveness ($r = -.26$, $p < .05$). The two exceptions are In-Group Collectivism ($r = +.21$, $p < .10$) and Gender Egalitarianism ($r = +.32$, $p < .05$). It appears that higher scores on practices dimensions are mostly associated with lower scores on respective values dimensions and vice versa.[5]

The deprivation hypothesis does not suffice to explain or predict actual cultural change because the behavioral consequences of deprivation are not specified. Cognitive dissonance theory (Festinger, 1957) can assist us in deriving assumptions about the likelihood of actual cultural change. On an individual level, disparity between perceptions of practices and values can be seen as evidence of *cognitive dissonance* in the respondents' minds (i.e., two or more cognitions about a target oppose each other). Cognitive dissonance creates a tension that needs to be resolved, which according to Festinger (1957) results in a drive toward establishing consonance among related cognitions. Cognitive consonance can be achieved by two distinct processes:

First, cognitive consonance can be brought about by actual behavior change, which is intended to result in an alignment of the current practices ("As Is") with the desired values ("Should Be") into future practices. However, most people (often correctly) assume that change in individual behavior is unlikely to result in culture change. So they don't even try. However, if changes in cultural practices in the desired direction appear (likely) to happen for most people in a society, actual changes in individual behavior are more likely. We think that an important factor that improves the deprivation hypothesis's predictive power for cultural change is whether people believe that cultural change is possible or is already ongoing ("Zeitgeist"). Under these conditions people are more likely to respond positively to changes toward the cultural values they desire by respective behavior changes.

Second, cognitive consonance can also be established by changing the relevant cognitions without changing behavior. That is, the differences in perceptions of "what is" and "what should be" on an individual level may represent the *result* of previous attempts to reduce cognitive dissonance without (expected) behavior change. A restructuring of individual cognitions

---

[5]For some cultural dimensions, virtually all cultures studied by GLOBE desire less (Power Distance, Figure A2 in Appendix A) or more (Future Orientation, Figure A5; Performance Orientation, see Figure A6) than they have now. For these dimensions, the negative-country level correlations between practices and respective values are based on a specific distributional pattern. Those countries who have lower scores on worldwide positively connoted dimensions (Performance Orientation, Future Orientation) desire more of an increase than those who have higher scores, and those countries who have higher scores on a worldwide negatively connoted dimension (Power Distance) desire more of a decrease than those who have lower scores. Thus, the negative correlations for these dimensions do not imply that countries who are high on, for example, Performance Orientation want to be less performance oriented or countries who are low on Power Distance do want to have more. On other dimensions this may be the case.

about the culture one lives in is particularly likely when changes in the cultural practices in the desired direction seem unlikely or impossible to happen from the perspectives of most of the respondents.

For example, let us assume that the societal cultural practices of high Uncertainty Avoidance in a culture are perceived to be rather high but the people do not like certain implications that come with these high levels of Uncertainty Avoidance (e.g., people dislike the restrictions and limitations imposed on them by high–Uncertainty Avoidance practices). If respective changes in the cultural practices seem unlikely to happen from the people's point of view, the behavioral routes for reducing cognitive dissonance by alignment of cultural practices with values appear blocked. As a consequence, people change their cognitions in order to reduce cognitive dissonance; more specifically, the perceptions of negatively connoted cultural practices are exaggerated (in this example, toward higher levels of Uncertainty Avoidance practices), because this makes them more consonant with the negative connotations people hold about them (i.e., current levels appear "too high"), and the judgments about cultural values are exaggerated to the opposite end of where the practices are seen, because this makes them more consonant with the people's negative connotations about the current cultural practices. Both processes taken together augment the difference between the perception of cultural-practices and -values scores. Thus, when marked differences between cultural-practices and -values scores are evident, this can also be taken as an indicator of *practical skepticism* (i.e., exaggerated negative perceptions of "what is") paired with *value idealism* (i.e., exaggerated positive perceptions of "what should be").

The two explanations of what the disparity between practices and values scores indicate for the development of societal or organizational culture do not necessarily contradict each other. The people's readiness for change toward the desired values, on the one side, and the people's sympathy for the desired values paired with skepticism about real change, on the other side, at least point in the same direction, namely toward the level of the desired values. Whether the espoused values in a society will be enacted in the future depends on whether the people feel that the change in the desired direction is realistic or not.

In the GLOBE program, we have not yet measured the extent to which people perceive change toward desired values to be realistic in their society. Thus, the predictive power of the described theory needs to be tested in future research. However, judgments about whether future change in certain cultural aspects in a society (or organization) is likely or not can be derived from the culture-specific evidence discussed in country chapters.

For an example, in several countries people show considerable disparity between their responses to comparatively high practices and comparatively low values levels of Uncertainty Avoidance (e.g., Sweden, Germany, Switzerland–German speaking, and Singapore).

Based on the qualitative findings about their respective country, the chapter authors give different answers to the question of whether future change is likely or not. In Sweden, Uncertainty Avoidance practices are rated lower than Uncertainty Avoidance values. This may suggest a movement toward the reduction of Uncertainty Avoidance practices. The same disparity is reported by the German respondents. However, the authors of the German chapter are more skeptical about their society's future development in that respect. They argue that high Uncertainty Avoidance is so deeply rooted in German society and history (e.g., via people's beliefs, institutional and organizational practices, economic and legal systems) that it is rather difficult to change. For Singapore, which scores highest among Asian societies for Uncertainty Avoidance cultural practices, well within the region of the high levels of Nordic and Germanic societies, the authors make the point that current governmental policy is actively encouraging people to overcome their "fear of failure" by supporting them to learn successful entrepreneurship at home and abroad, which in the authors' view makes true change of the society toward less Uncertainty Avoidance more likely.

For another example, again with Singapore, we can ask the question of whether the high Humane Oriented leadership score (see Figure B4) can be taken as an indicator of a Confucianism-based force that drives the disparity between very low Humane Orientation cultural practices and very high respective values in Singapore (see Figure A9) toward more Humane Orientation cultural practices in the future. The answer is: It depends on how the current cultural trends are interpreted by most of the people in Singapore. The disparity between Humane Orientation cultural practices and values may well be the expression of *practical skepticism,* because the people believe that the strict governmental regime is unlikely to change with respect to Humane Orientation, paired with high *value idealism,* because people overly adore Confucian principles of humane conduct and project them into their concepts of effective leadership. A similar example can be derived from the situation in South Africa: It shows the highest score of Humane Oriented leadership among all Anglo countries and the lowest score on Humane Oriented cultural practices. Again, this may reflect a practical skepticism paired with value idealism, which expresses the people's hope in their business leaders to create a better and more humane society (see the very high scores on Humane Oriented leadership for South Africa in Figure B4).

The GLOBE data from quantitative and qualitative analyses show in the instances, where disparities between cultural practices and desired values were found, that cultural values rather than cultural practices more strongly predicted what is perceived to be effective leadership. For a similar point, see Dorfman et al. (2004). In the case of disparity between cultural practices and values, it seems that the leaders are valued for representing the desired societal cultural values, perhaps in compensation for the low emphasis placed on the respective cultural practices. This seems to express the people's hope that their leaders can help to implement desired cultural change.

Cultural Diversity Within Societies

Culture not only changes in time, it also disperses geographically via emigration and multicultural coexistence. We have described previously, that one shortcoming of GLOBE is that cultural subgroups within countries were not systematically taken into account. And despite the great care taken by chapter authors for describing the dominant culture and various subcultures in their society, some limitations still remain.

For example, as is noted in the English chapter, in Britain a mixture of different cultures coexists in different ways, (a) as geographically bound societal entities, for example, Scotland, Wales, and England, and (b) as ethnic cultures that overlay the English, Scottish, or Welsh cultures, for example, Jewish, Quaker, Islamic, and other religious-based cultures, and Chinese, African, Indian, and Pakistani and other ethnic-based cultures. Not only in the United Kingdom, but also in many other countries such as Singapore, United States, Mexico, Turkey, or Germany, the influx of populations from other parts of the world has created a diversity of subcultures. Their values more or less fuse with those of the dominant culture and create nuances in business style and practice. These nuances are not represented within the GLOBE data. Instead, a perhaps naive approach was taken, such that the dominant culture within each country was measured. However, this shortcoming in the GLOBE database does not need to remain a permanent one. We see no particular difficulties in using the measures and methods presented in this and the previous GLOBE volume for a more fine-grained study of the various subcultures within different countries.

Measuring Leadership in Various Subgroups and Contexts

The middle managers who participated in the GLOBE study are a particular subgroup in society that may have different views than other groups from the same society have. For example, in Austria and Ireland, it was tested with the GLOBE scales whether managers and students from the same society converge in their views more strongly than Irish and Austrian students on the one side, and Irish and Austrian managers, on the other side (Keating, Martin, & Szabo, 2002). Although several differences between the groups were identified—obviously they differ in age or work experience—the cultural practices and values of both groups differentiated the two cultures significantly. This is only one study and it is based on only two countries and two subgroups within each. Further studies are necessary to validate the GLOBE country-level findings in this respect on the basis of different and more representative samples of respondents and countries.

There is also a great deal to learn about gender differences across cultures. On the basis of the GLOBE sample, Emrich, Denmark, and den Hartog (2004) demonstrated statistically significant, but not substantial, gender differences for four of the six leadership dimensions (the variances accounted for are very low; they range from 0.2% to 0.9%). Female managers rated Charismatic/Value Based, Participative, and Team Oriented leadership higher as contributing to effective leadership than the male managers did, who in return rated Self-Protective leadership as more inhibiting to effective leadership than female managers did.

Furthermore, gender differences were more apparent in certain cultures than in others. For example, gender differences on Team Oriented leadership were much smaller in the United States than in Hong Kong. Further empirical evidence shows that male and female managers rate CLT dimensions more similarly the more Gender Egalitarian their societies is reported to be (see the dissertation from Paris, 2003, which gives a more complete exploration of gender differences in the GLOBE sample).

There are further issues with respect to subgroup effects. For some countries although the distribution of gender was noted to be representative for the respective country and industries, the resulting numbers as part of the country sample drawn seem rather low with respect to considerations of statistical power. For example, in Spain, 12% from a total of $N = 173$ participants were female, which sums up to about only 20 respondents from the female managerial population in Spain.

Other issues related to subgroups of respondents are more conceptual in nature. The GLOBE sample relies on middle managers as informants. Thus, it does not represent the perceptions of nonmanagerial staff. If one agrees that leadership is "in the eye of the beholder," which is a central focus of the CLTs measured by GLOBE, then more research is necessary to also learn about the values, beliefs, and expectations of those who are not in leadership positions.

In order to get a more balanced view across the various job levels in organizations with leadership functions, it is necessary to also include lower and higher levels of management. Some chapter authors took the managerial level explicitly into account. For example, in Portugal, the expectations about leadership behavior were shown to vary depending on which managerial level (top, middle, lower) is concerned. The U.S. chapter authors suggest that their finding of a relatively high endorsement of Participative leadership may be due to the choice of middle managers as respondents, whose particular role as managers "in the middle" of their organizational environment necessitates that they be participative and sensitive to others' needs. Thus, not only the results for the United States may differ to some extent when other managerial levels are investigated. Again, we think the GLOBE scales provide the tools to test this and related propositions.

In the chapter about Turkey, it is noted that few or none of the responding managers worked in small or publicly owned organizations, which is in line with the characteristics of most of the organizations in the overall GLOBE sample. However, for Turkey it may have distorted the picture to some extent, because most of their organizations are family-owned small businesses.

The effects the three industries measured (telecommunication service providers, food processing, and financial service providers) may have were explicitly taken into account by GLOBE. In most chapters where results were compared across industries, no marked differences were found. This is in line with the GLOBE results reported by Brodbeck et al. (2004) according to which industry main effects on organizational culture are low (Eta^2 range from .00 to.11) when compared to the much higher effects of societal culture (Eta^2 range from .21 to .47). However, Brodbeck et al. also report interaction effects of medium magnitude (Eta^2 range from .06 to .42), indicating that there can be marked differences in organizational culture between industries *within* particular societies, depending on which legislation or economic dynamics are in effect for individual industries and not for others. Against the background of these findings, the issue of not having sampled industries that are of particular importance for an individual country, such as in Finland, the paper and metal industries, is noteworthy.

Two issues are of particular relevance to further developing the concept of leadership that has been used by GLOBE.

The U.S. chapter authors argue that the research methodology of the GLOBE leadership questionnaire invited an *a priori* definition of leadership as something that an individual does. Indeed, as was described previously, their chapter displays a preference for a trait-based bias of leadership as well as an influence model of leadership, potentially preventing other perhaps more collective notions of leadership to emerge. We think that the GLOBE leadership concept and the methods used may have been somewhat biased in favor of a trait-based and personalized understanding of the leadership process. However, it appears from several country chapters that the bias did not affect the understanding and descriptions of culture-specific leadership concepts that differ from a trait-based understanding. In many country reports, leadership is described to reside more within organizations or institutions rather than in an individual, such as in France or Germany, or in a person with a collective Self, which makes her an intimate part of a group or collective, such as in China or India, or the person as a leader is downplayed and not seen as something special, such as in the Netherlands, Finland, or Switzerland.

The authors of the chapter on Spain make the point that the way the GLOBE research was carried out may have led to the expression of overly enthusiastic views about charismatic leaders that contrasts the skepticism history would suggest. "Throughout history, charismatic political leaders in Europe and Mediterranean countries have been a source of initially stable governments, which later promoted a long series of bloody, criminal, or belligerent actions. It has been the case, in this century, of Bin Laden, Franco, Gadafi, Hassan II, Hitler, Milosevic, Mussolini, Stalin, and Yeltsin. Each of these leaderships combined visionary as well as inspirational perspectives" (adopted from the Spanish chapter). The authors continue by saying that "the historical reality should at least temper the enthusiasm of some foreign observers who highlight the short-term advantages of charismatic leadership without paying to much attention to the disastrous long-term consequences."

Questions for Future Research

From the results and limitations described in the preceding sections, many questions for future research can be derived. We close this section by summarizing some of them that seem particularly pertinent and compelling.

The GLOBE data generated to date do not allow stringent predictions about actual leadership behavior in organizations and cross-cultural situations. This requires further *in situ* investigations of how particular cultural backgrounds influence leadership behavior and effectiveness within and across cultural boundaries. The latter would translate into the following research question: If the CLT profiles of the hosting cultures are not enacted by the leader or expatriate, will the leader be less accepted, less effective? In accord with this question, it is worth investigating whether and to what extent the behaviors of existing leaders typically reflect the leadership profiles endorsed in their home culture.

Also, not very much is known about the psychological, social-psychological, and sociological mechanisms by which leadership prototypes, and their respective behavioral consequences are linked to societal cultural and organizational cultural practices and values. In that respect, the previously described theory that uses principles of cognitive dissonance theory to predict how differences between perceived practices and values translate into change on the individual, the organizational, and the societal level, deserves some attention.

More focused on the leadership process are the two further questions raised by House, Wright and Aditya (1997): Does leader behavior that deviates slightly from dominant cultural practices and/or values encourage innovation and performance improvement—as such behaviors are nontraditional and unexpected? Are leader behaviors that may be universally accepted also more effective, within and across cultural contexts?

The limited scope of GLOBE with respect to cultural subgroups within societies, but also with respect to the degree of variability within societies, or the density or looseness of cultural prescriptions, may be turned into research questions like these: Are CLT leadership dimensions more rigidly set for homogeneous societies, such as Japan, than for culturally diverse societies, such as the United States? (Dorfman, 2004; Dorfman et al., 2004).

Furthermore, with increasing globalization it is likely that leadership prototypes derive from experiences made in more than one culture? Would cross-cultural experience be reflected in "blended" leadership prototypes? How can these be measured? Are culturally endorsed blends of leadership prototypes also reflected in respective leadership behaviors? Would these be more effective in respective cross-cultural leadership contexts?

Another direction for future research is the assessment of the magnitude and speed with which perceptions of cultural practices and values, including managerial and leadership practices, change and the degree to which between-country differences remain stable or vary over time, which requires longitudinal approaches. Such admittedly very time-intensive and costly projects could help us to answer many important questions, like the validity of the culture convergence hypotheses. Such projects could also help to estimate the accuracy of cross-cultural data more generally, for example, with respect to the question of whether and how quickly the data become outdated or obsolete. In that respect, an interesting point was made in the country chapter from Singapore: After portraying Singapore as a society that can change rapidly, the question was raised of whether investigating culture as a dependent variable could be helpful to identify the relative importance of culture shaping factors in societies, such as technological change, modernization, or governmental policy.

4. PRACTICAL IMPLICATIONS

Multinational and domestic organizations are becoming more and more culturally diverse, as is their customer base, which tends to spread around the whole world. Alongside these effects of globalization, there is a growing need for managers in organizations who can effectively work in different cultural environments and in multicultural settings (Dorfman et al., 2004). It is known that organizations that proactively take part in the globalization process increase the number of their expatriate managerial staff throughout the world (Cullen, 2002).

More generally, worldwide immigration during the past century up to today has resulted in hundreds of millions of people with different cultural background who work and live in close regional proximity. This trend is particularly apparent in the metropolitan regions in which soon 50% of the world population will be living and working. Another sphere where different cultures encounter is the Internet (World Wide Web), which provides for an environment of its own, within which people from anywhere in the world can interact and work together anytime.

Despite the increase of multicultural diversity in many people's immediate social environment and in a fast-growing virtual environment, it is unlikely that the major societal cultures in the world converge into an amalgam of a global cultural standard. Some authors perceive it to be more likely that cultural differences among societies will be exacerbated as they adapt to modernization while simultaneously striving to preserve their cultural heritage and social identity (cf. Dorfman et al., 2004). As has been described previously, the GLOBE findings (House et al., 2004) and other cross-cultural studies (e.g. Smith, 1997, Smith et al., 2002) suggest that the fundamentally stable nature of the values and beliefs of people in different cultural regions is likely to remain stable. If the multicultural world doesn't change into a monocultural one, it is time for us to change and to become more aware of the cultural backgrounds of people different from us.

This volume of 25 country chapters provides the basis for developing a comprehensive understanding of the cultural practices, values, and behaviors that are associated with effective leadership in a variety of societies from all major cultural regions in the world. This should be of interest not only to managers who want to develop their awareness of the critical aspects of effective leadership in different cultures, but also to everyone who is interested in developing a better understanding of the different cultural backgrounds that shape the way other people feel, think, and act at work and in other contexts.

Before we discuss how the GLOBE results can be used to inform managers and everyone about cultural practices and values that are more or less foreign to them, two general notes about interpersonal and cross-cultural encounter need to be made:

First, anyone who works with others—from a different culture or not—should try to gain a deeper understanding of the other person's implicit and explicit theories about working together, leadership, and followership, *and* of his or her own respective concepts. By reflecting on *both,* the similarities and differences come into focus and can be reflected on.

Second, as was lucidly described in the U.S. chapter of this volume, one should "continuously and repeatedly assess, hypothesize, and act (AHA principle) when entering and working in a new cultural environment. As Germanic cultures tend to say, 'the devil is in the detail' (in the United States, it is said at times that 'God is in the detail'). Whatever the case may be, things are not always what they appear to be and often seemingly clear similarities in expected leader behaviors may lead to the greatest misunderstandings and/or conflicts."

In each of the 25 country chapters, many examples and rich descriptions are given about how the working relationships and leadership processes in organizations are shaped by the cultural practices and values. Most chapters devote a whole section to recommendations about what foreign and domestic managers should keep in mind when acting as a leader in the respective societal contexts. Apart from the solid empirical data these descriptions and recommendations are based on, additional credibility derives from the fact that the chapters were written by GLOBE CCIs who grew up or have spent a considerable amount of time working and living in the country they write about.

At first glance, some of the examples and recommendations given may appear somewhat strange or incomprehensible to the reader. This is actually the best starting point to ask the important "Why" questions and to discover more about the underlying "logic" a culture works from. Note that we seem to intuitively use the logic of the culture we grew up with, similar to how we learned our primary language. However, remember how many "Why" questions children ask once they know the primitive basics. Asking them and trying to answer them, for example, by using the AHA principle, is an effective way to develop your understanding of a culture—be it your own or a different one.

The culture-general results from GLOBE provide empirically well-grounded information about any combination of target countries from the 61 societies studied. A set of cross-culturally validated measurement tools is also provided: altogether nine dimensions, each for cultural practices and cultural values, each for societal cultures and organizational cultures, plus six global leadership dimensions, which consist of 21 subdimensions and altogether 112 item descriptions, carefully defined in their meaning. These results and tools can be used to develop the content of cross-cultural training and coaching exercises, as well as diagnostic tools and training exercises that mimic situations of cultural overlap.

Cultural overlap is known to evoke critical situations, where ambiguities and inconsistencies prevail to each of the parties involved. This is likely to result in dysfunctional work behavior. Critical situations emerge when members of different cultures interact, because they hold different reference frames and approach the situation with their own culture-specific perspective. The GLOBE data can be used to identify those dimensions that most likely contribute to the emergence of critical situations between parties from certain target cultures and to develop training situations accordingly.

In addition to that, the findings from the culture-specific analyses in each chapter help to specify, for example, which concept and which ambiguous signal or misunderstanding should be addressed when developing cross-cultural training and coaching situations and how to tailor them to leader–follower relationships involving delegation, consultation, and normal, everyday decision making. Each chapter provides rich and valuable information regarding effective leadership actions that match or mismatch cultural norms.

When cultures differ in their practices and values, expatriates' preparation and adjustment is generally necessary. It is more difficult, and thus takes more time, effort, and preparation, to adjust to another culture if the cultural differences are large and manifold because it implies that a higher amount of cognitive and behavioral restructuring is necessary. The combination of culture-general and culture-specific reflections in each country chapter, and the integrated summaries and overviews described in this chapter, can inform senior management and international HR staff about the critical issue of *how much* prior training, coaching, and actual experience in a particular host country is necessary to ensure effective leadership.

Furthermore, the comparative analysis of societal culture practices and values, graphically displayed in Figures A1 to A9 (Appendix A), informs about the direction and the likelihood of cultural change in particular countries and regions.

The positioning of individual countries within cultural clusters can also help to identify to what extent and in which respects a target country can be seen as a typical or an atypical representative of the cultural region it is a member of, in terms of cultural values and practices (see Figures A1 to A9) and in terms of leadership profiles (see Figures B1 to B6). Furthermore, several boundary-spanning societies, which share cultural elements or elements of leadership prototypes with two or more cultural clusters, have been identified. They may serve as cultural transition points through which a whole cultural region can be more safely explored.

One final note on the conventional wisdom that cultural distance is dysfunctional and often leads to failure of cross-border collaboration, joint ventures, or mergers. We think cultural distance is not dysfunctional per se. It rather should be seen as an opportunity to discover cultural practices elsewhere, which can be helpful to solve problems at home and vice versa. It has to be acknowledged, though, that it is difficult to understand how foreign practices function without knowing more about the context within which they operate. In the multiple within-country perspective of the country chapters, the attempt is to display each culture's "logic" of functioning and the deeper meaning of what the abstract GLOBE concepts mean once they are embedded within the respective cultures. The country chapter authors undertook great efforts to carefully explain what the meanings behind the abstract GLOBE concepts within their society are, how the cultural practices and values have developed throughout history, how they relate to effective leadership, and what future developments are likely to occur. We are therefore convinced that the content of this volume facilitates the discovery of cultural and leadership practices in other cultures that may be helpful to solve problems at home and elsewhere.

REFERENCES

Ashkanasy, N. M., Trevor-Roberts, E., & Earnshaw, L. (2002). The Anglo cluster: Legacy of the British Empire. *Journal of World Business, 37,* 28–39.

Atran, S., Medin, D. L., & Ross, N. O. (2005). The cultural mind: Environmental decision making and cultural modeling within and across populations. *Psychological Review, 112,* 744–776.

Bakacsi, G., Sandor, T., Andras, K., & Victor, I. (2002). Eastern European cluster: Tradition and transition. *Journal of World Business, 37,* 69–80.

Barry, H., III, Bacon, M. K., & Child, I. L. (1959). A cross-cultural survey of sex differences in socialization. *Journal of Abnormal and Social Psychology, 55,* 327–332.

Berry, J. W., Poortinga, Y. H., Segall, M. H., & Dasen, P. R. (1992). *Cross-cultural psychology: Research and applications.* New York: Cambridge University Press.

Berry, J. W., Segall, M. H., & Kagitçibasi, C. (1997). *Handbook of cross-cultural psychology.* Needham, MA: Allyn & Bacon.

Brodbeck, F. C., Frese, M., & 40 coauthors (2000). Cultural variation of leadership prototypes across 22 European countries. *Journal of Occupational and Organizational Psychology, 73,* 1–29.

Brodbeck, F. C., Hanges, P. J., Dickson., M. W., Gupta, V., & Dorfman, P. W. (2004). Comparative influence of industry and societal culture on organizational cultural practices. In R. J. House, P. J. Hanges, M. Javidan, P. Dorfman, & V. Gupta (Eds.), *Leadership, culture, and organizations: The GLOBE study of 62 societies* (pp. 654–668). Thousand Oaks, CA: Sage.

Cohen, D. (2001). Cultural variation: Considerations and implications. *Psychological Bulletin, 127,* 451–471.

Cullen, J. B. (2002). *Multinational management: A strategic approach* (2nd ed.). Cincinnati, OH: South-Western Thomson Learning.

Dastmalchian, A., Javidan, M., & Alam, K. (2001). Effective leadership and culture in Iran: An empirical study. *Applied Psychology: An International Review, 50*(4), 532–551.

Dorfman, P. (2004). International and cross-cultural leadership research. In B. J. Punnett & O. Shenkar (Eds.), *Handbook for international research* (2nd ed, pp. 265–355). Ann Arbor: University of Michigan Press.

Dorfman, P. W., Hanges, P. J., & Brodbeck, F. C. (2004). Leadership and cultural variation: The identification of culturally endorsed leadership profiles. In R. J. House, P. J. Hanges, M. Javidan, P. Dorfman, & V. Gupta (Eds.), *Leadership, culture, and organizations: The GLOBE study of 62 societies* (pp. 669–720). Thousand Oaks, CA: Sage.

Emrich, C. G., Denmark, F. L., & den Hartog, D. N. (2004). Cross cultural differences in Gender Egalitarianism: Implications for societies, organizations and leaders. In R. J. House, P. J. Hanges, M. Javidan, P. Dorfman, & V. Gupta (Eds.), *Leadership, culture, and organizations: The GLOBE study of 62 societies* (pp. 343–394). Thousand Oaks, CA: Sage.

Festinger, L. (1957). *A theory of cognitive dissonance.* New York: Harper & Row.

Gelfand, M. J., Bhawuk, D. P. S., Nishii, L. H., & Bechthold, D. J. (2004). Individualism Collectivism. In R. J. House, P. J. Hanges, M. Javidan, P. Dorfman, & V. Gupta (Eds.), *Leadership, culture, and organizations: The GLOBE study of 62 societies* (pp. 437–512). Thousand Oaks, CA: Sage.

Gupta, V., De Luque, M. S., & House, R. J. (2004). Multisource construct validity of GLOBE scales. In R. J. House, P. J. Hanges, M. Javidan, P. Dorfman, & V. Gupta (Eds.), *Leadership, culture, and organizations: The GLOBE study of 62 societies* (pp. 152–177). Thousand Oaks, CA: Sage.

Gupta, V., & Hanges, P. J. (2004). Regional and climate clustering of societal cultures. In R. J. House, P. J. Hanges, M. Javidan, P. Dorfman, & V. Gupta (Eds.), *Leadership, culture, and organizations: The GLOBE study of 62 societies* (pp. 178–218). Thousand Oaks, CA: Sage.

Hanges, P. J. (2004). Appendix B: Response bias correction procedure used in GLOBE. In R. J. House, P. J. Hanges, M. Javidan, P. Dorfman, & V. Gupta (Eds.), *Leadership, culture, and organizations: The GLOBE study of 62 societies* (pp. 737–752). Thousand Oaks, CA: Sage.

Hanges, P. J., & Dickson, M. W. (2004). The development and validation of the GLOBE culture and leadership scales. In R. J. House, P. J. Hanges, M. Javidan, P. Dorfman, & V. Gupta (Eds.), *Leadership, culture, and organizations: The GLOBE study of 62 societies* (pp. 122–151). Thousand Oaks, CA: Sage.

Hanges, P. J., & Dickson, M. W. (2006). Agitation over aggregation: Clarifying the development of and the nature of the GLOBE scales. *Leadership Quarterly, 17,* 522–536.

Hanges, P. J., Dickson, M. W., & Sipe, M. T. (2004). Rationale for GLOBE statistical analyses: Societal rankings and test of hypotheses. In R. J. House, P. J. Hanges, M. Javidan, P. Dorfman, & V. Gupta (Eds.), *Leadership, culture, and organizations: The GLOBE study of 62 societies* (pp. 219–234). Thousand Oaks, CA: Sage.

Hofstede, G. (1980). *Cultures' consequences: International differences in work-related values.* London: Sage.

Hollander, E. P. (1958). Conformity, status, and idiosyncrasy credit. *Psychological Review, 65,* 117–127.

Hollander, E. P. (1980). Leadership and social exchange processes. In K. J. Gergen, M.S. Greenberg, & R. H. Willis (Eds.), *Social exchange: Advances in theory and research* (pp. 343–354). New York: Plenum.

House, R. J., Hanges, P. J., Javidan, M., Dorfman, P. W., Gupta, V., & Globe Associates. (2004). *Culture, leadership, and organizations: The GLOBE study of 62 societies.* Thousand Oaks, CA: Sage.

House, R. J., & Javidan, M. (2004). Overview of GLOBE. In R. J. House, P. J. Hanges, M. Javidan, P. Dorfman, & V. Gupta (Eds.), *Leadership, culture, and organizations: The GLOBE study of 62 societies* (pp. 9–28). Thousand Oaks, CA: Sage.

House, R. J., Wright, N. S., & Aditya, R. N. (1997). Cross-cultural research on organizational leadership: A critical analysis and a proposed theory. In P. C. Earley & M. Erez (Eds.), *New perspectives in international industrial/organizational psychology* (pp. 535–625). San Francisco: New Lexington Press.

Inkeles, A. (1981). Convergence and divergence in industrial societies. In M. O. Attir, B. Holzner, & Z. Suda (Eds.), *Directions of change: Modernization theory, research and realities* (pp. 3–38). Boulder, CO: Westview.

Jesuino, J. C. (2002) Latin Europe cluster: From south to north. *Journal of World Business, 37,* 81–89.

Kabasakal, H., & Bodur, M. (2002). Arabic cluster: A bridge between East and West. *Journal of World Business, 37,* 40–54.

Keating, M. A., Martin, G. S., & Szabo, E. (2002). Do managers and students share the same perceptions of societal culture? *International Journal of Intercultural Relations, 26*(6), 633–652.

Lebel, P. (1985). *Le triangle du management* [The management triangle]. Paris: Editions d'Organization.

Lord, R. G., & Maher, K. J. (1991). *Leadership and information processing: Linking perceptions and performance* (Vol. 1). Cambridge, MA: Unwin Hyman.

Meindl, J. R., Ehrlich, S. B., & Dukerich, J. M. (1985). The romance of leadership. *Administrative Science Quarterly, 30,* 78–102.

Morris, M. W., Leung, K., Ames, D., & Lickel, B. (1999). Incorporating perspectives from inside and outside: Synergy between *emic* and *etic* research on culture and justice. *Academy of Management Review, 24,* 781–796.

Morrison, A. J. (2000). Developing a global leadership model. *Human Resource Management Journal, 39*(2&3), 117–158.

Paris, L. (2003). *The effect of gender and culture on implicit leadership theories: A cross-cultural study.* Unpublished doctoral dissertation, New Mexico State University, Las Cruces.

Reber, G., Jago, A. G., Auer-Rizzi, W., & Szabo, E. (2000). Führungsstile in sieben Ländern Europas— Ein interkultureller Vergleich [Leadership styles in seven European countries—A cross-cultural comparison]. In E. Regnet & L. M. Hofmann (Eds.), *Personalmanagement in Europa* (pp. 154–173). Göttingen, Germany: Verlag für Angewandte Psychologie.

Redfield, R. (1948). Introduction. In B. Malinowski, *Magic, science and religion* (pp. ii–viii). Boston: Beacon Press.

Segall, M. H., & Kagitçibasi, C. (1997). Introduction. In J. W. Berry, M. H. Segall, & K. Kagiçibasi (Eds.), *Handbook of cross-cultural psychology* (pp. xxv–xxxv). Needham, MA: Allyn & Bacon.

Smith, P. B. (1997). Leadership in Europe: Euro-management or the footprint of history? *European Journal of Work and Organizational Psychology, 6,* 375–386.

Smith, P. B., & Bond, M. H. (1993). *Social psychology across cultures: Analysis and perspectives.* London: Harvester Wheatsheaf.

Smith, P. B., Peterson, M. F., Schwartz, S. H., & 43 other coauthors (2002). Cultural values, sources of guidance and their relevance to managerial behavior: A 47 nation study. *Journal of Cross-Cultural Psychology, 33*(2), 188–208.

Szabo, E., Brodbeck, F. C., den Hartog, D., Reber, G., Weibler, J., & Wunderer, R. (2002). The Germanic Europe cluster: Where employees have a voice. *Journal of World Business, 37*(1), 55–68.

Szabo, E., Reber, G., Weibler, J., Brodbeck, F., & Wunderer, R. (2001). Values and behavior orientation in leadership studies: Reflections based on findings in three German-speaking countries. *Leadership Quarterly, 12*(2), 219–244.

Triandis, H. C. (1994). *Culture and social behavior.* New York: McGraw-Hill.

Triandis, H. C. (2004). Foreword. In R. J. House, P. J. Hanges, M. Javidan, P. Dorfman, & V. Gupta (Eds.), *Leadership, culture, and organizations: The GLOBE study of 62 societies* (pp. xv–xix). Thousand Oaks, CA: Sage.

Triandis, H. C., & Bhawuk, D. P. S. (1997). Culture theory and the meaning of relatedness. In P. C. Earley & M. Erez (Eds.), *New perspectives in international/organizational psychology* (pp. 13–52). New York: New Lexington Free Press.

Weibler, J., Brodbeck, F. C., Szabo, E., Reber, G., Wunderer, R., & Moosmann, O. (2000). Führung in kulturverwandten Regionen: Gemeinsamkeiten und Unterschiede bei Führungsidealen in Deutschland, Österreich und der Schweiz [Leadership in culturally related regions: Communalities and differences of leadership concepts in Germany, Austria and Switzerland]. *Die Betriebswirtschaft (DBW), 60,* 588–606.

Yang, K. S. (2000). Mono-cultural and cross-cultural indigenous approaches: The royal road to the development of a balanced global psychology. *Asian Journal of Social Psychology, 4,* 241–263.

APPENDIX A: Societal Culture "As Is" and "Should Be" in 25/61 Globe Countries

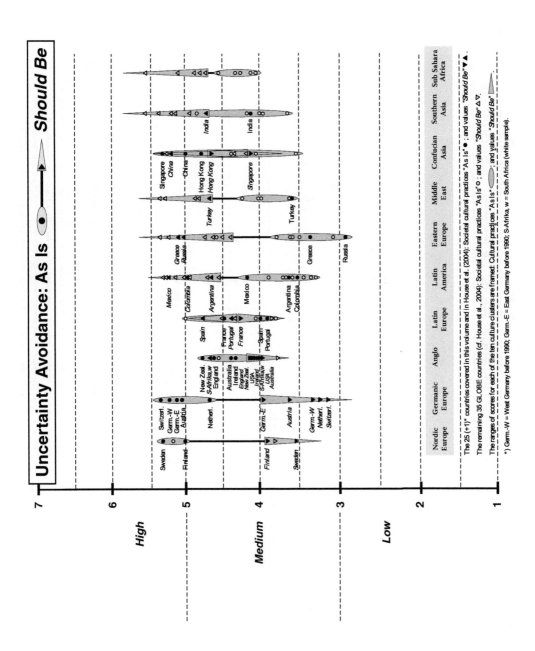

Figure A1. GLOBE dimension of societal culture practices ("As Is") and values ("Should Be")— Uncertainty Avoidance.

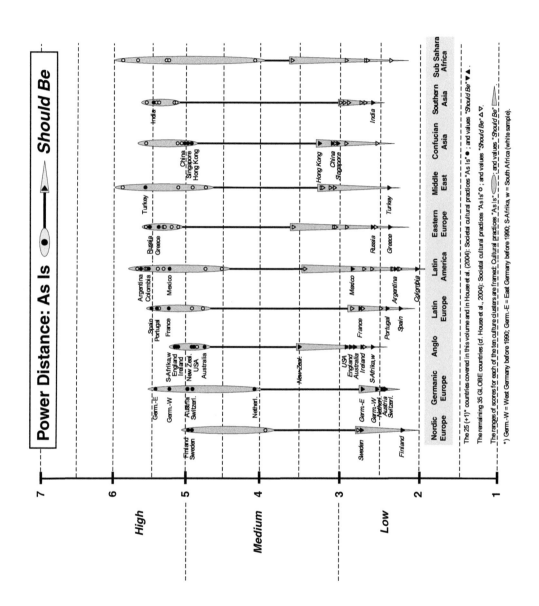

Figure A2. GLOBE dimension of societal culture practices ("As Is") and values ("Should Be")—
Power Distance.

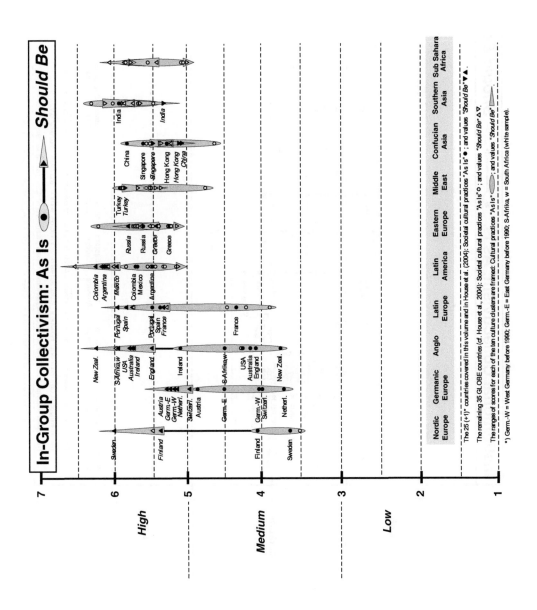

Figure A3.   GLOBE dimension of societal culture practices ("As Is") and values ("Should Be")—In-Group Collectivism.

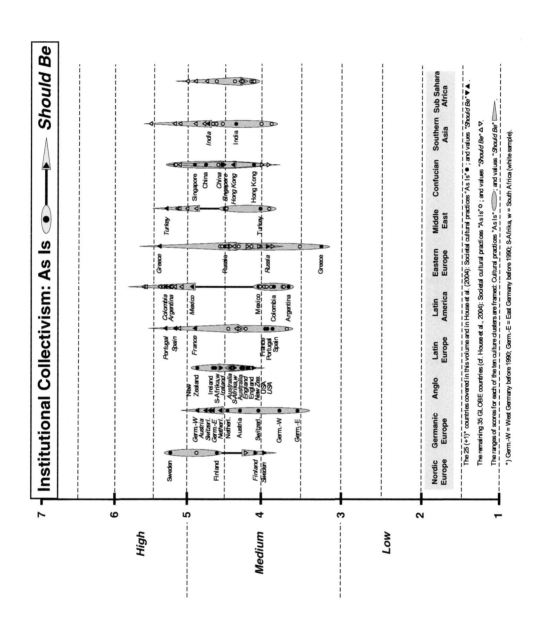

Figure A4. GLOBE dimension of societal culture practices ("As Is") and values ("Should Be")—
Institutional Collectivism.

1088

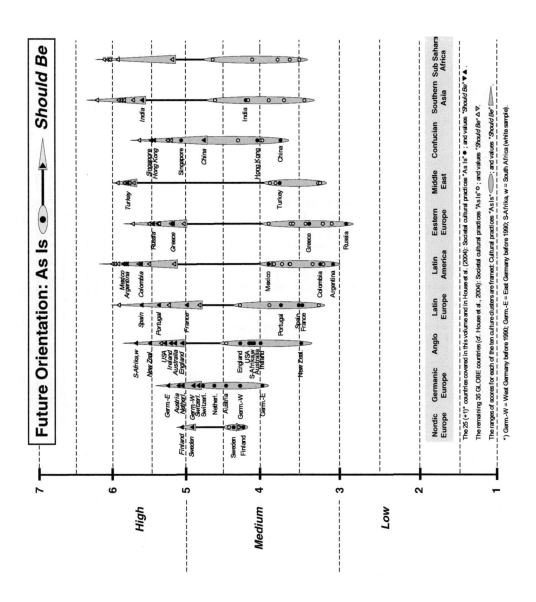

Figure A5.   GLOBE dimension of societal culture practices ("As Is") and values ("Should Be")—
Institutional Collectivism.

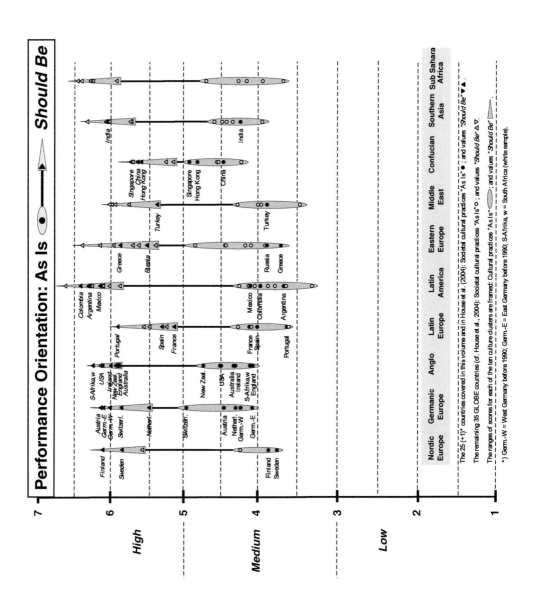

Figure A6. GLOBE dimension of societal culture practices ("As Is") and values ("Should Be")—Performance Orientation.

1090

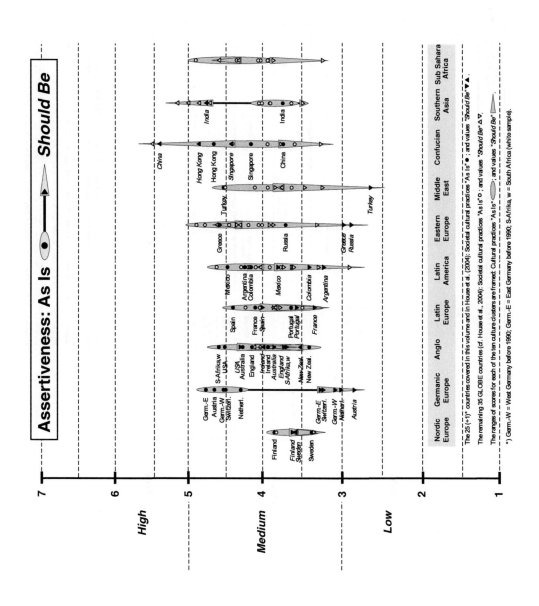

Figure A7. GLOBE dimension of societal culture practices ("As Is") and values ("Should Be")—
Assertiveness.

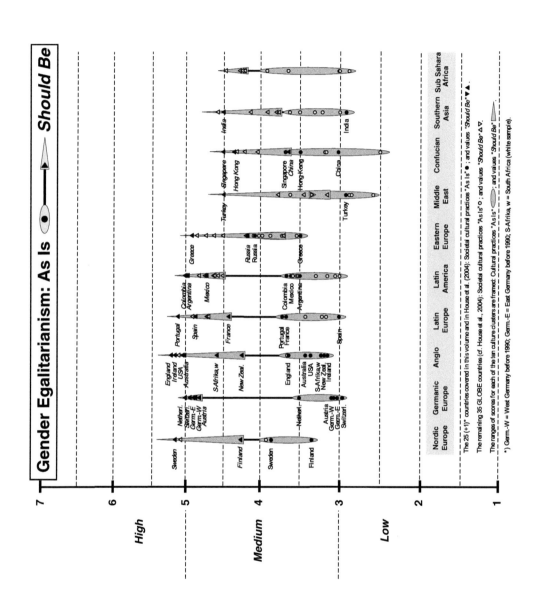

Figure A8.   GLOBE dimension of societal culture practices ("As Is") and values ("Should Be")—
Gender Egalitarianism.

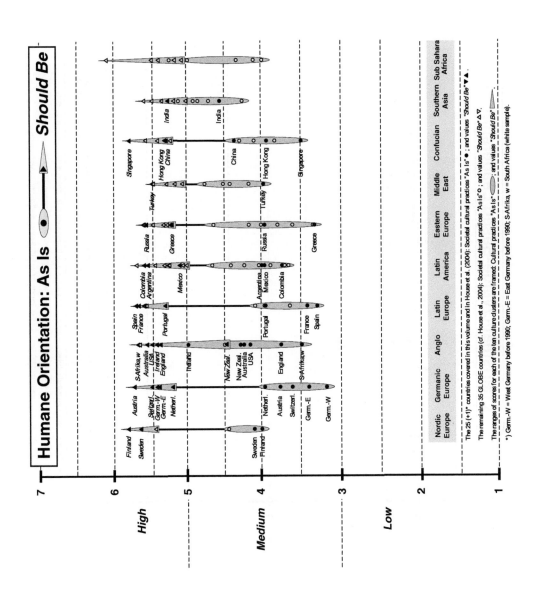

Figure A9.   GLOBE dimension of societal culture practices ("As Is") and values ("Should Be")—
Humane Orientation.

1093

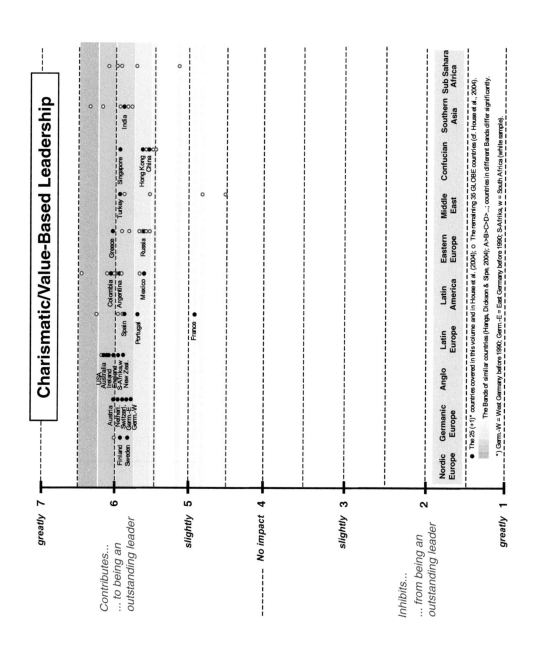

Figure B1.   Global leadership dimension—Charismatic/Value-Based Leadership.

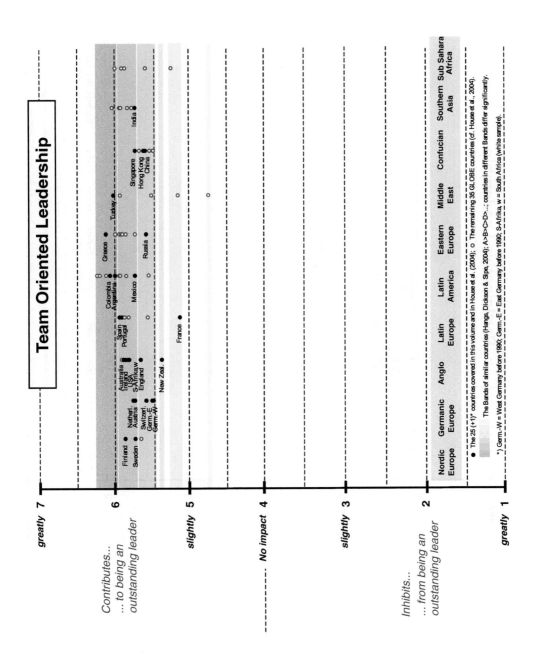

Figure B2.   Global leadership dimension—Team Oriented Leadership.

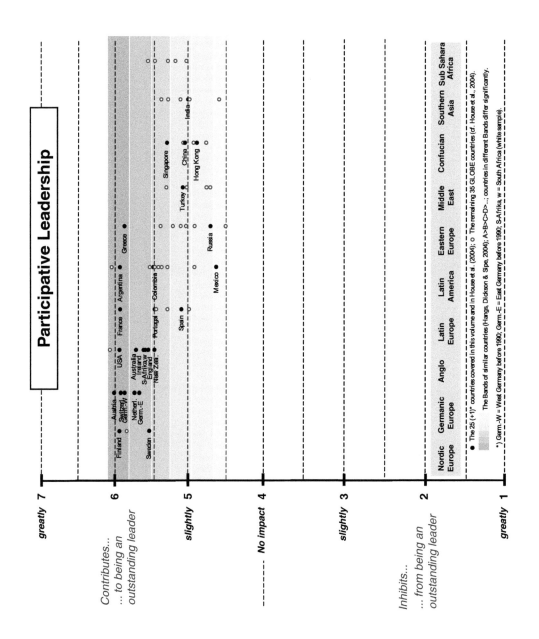

Figure B3.   Global leadership dimension—Participative Leadership.

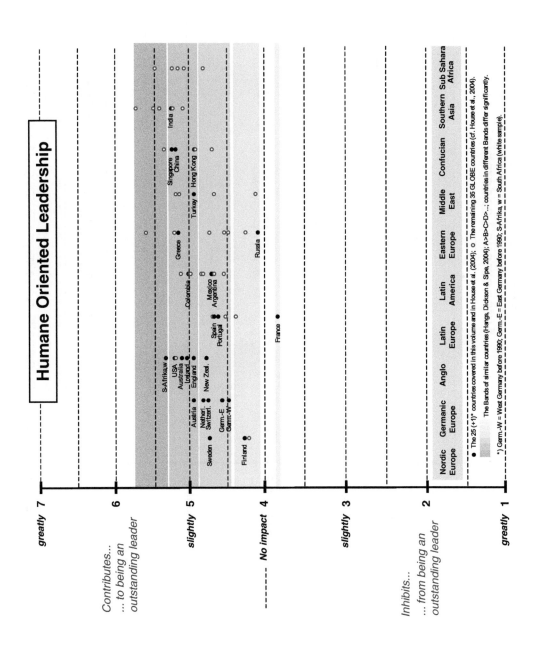

Figure B4.   Global leadership dimension—Humane Oriented Leadership.

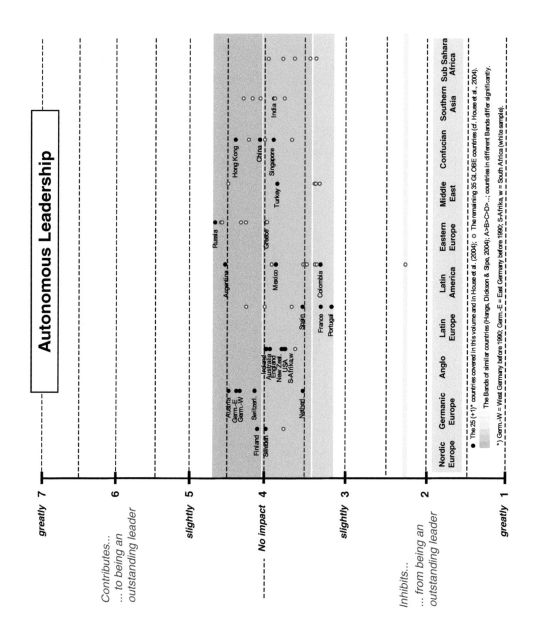

Figure B5.   Global leadership dimension—Autonomous Leadership.

1098

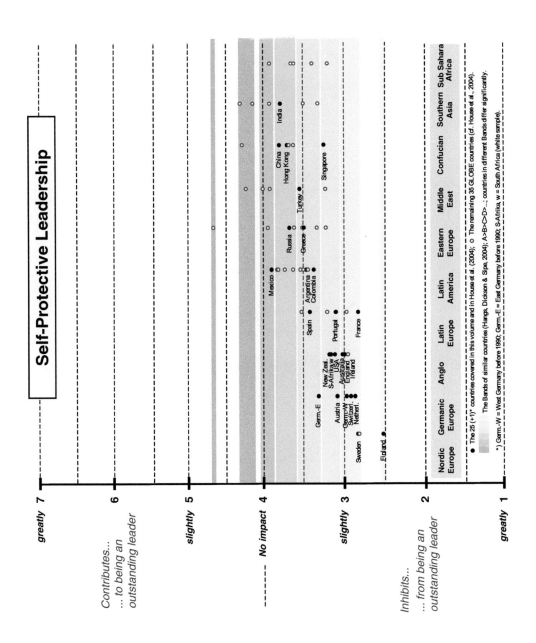

Figure B6.   Global leadership dimension—Self-Protected Leadership.

Author Index

Subject Index

Dan wei (organizations), 893
Davin, Dan, 406
Débrouillard, 566
Decision making, Austrian leaders and, 136–137
Decisive leadership, 526
  Australia, 314
  Austria, 135
  Finland, 95, 98
  Turkey, 867
  United States, *517, 521, 523*
De Gaulle, Charles, 548
de Klerk, F. W., 438
de la Madrid, Miguel, 729
Democracy
  Austria, 123
  Classical Greece, 769
  Russia, 815
  Switzerland, 256
Democratic relations, Austrian leadership and, 136
Denominational segregation, 221
Deprivation hypothesis, 1028, 1076–1078
Deregulation
  Australia banking system and, 326, 327
  in England, 338
"De-sanskritisation," 976
Desarrollismo (developmentalism), 661
Deutsche Demokratische Republick. *See* East
    Germany
Deutsche Nation (German Nation), 149
Deutschland (German Nation), 149
de Valera, Eamon, 363, 377, 382
Diamond industry, 436
Diário de Noticias (Portuguese newspaper),
    606, 607
Diário Económico (Portuguese newspaper), 606
Dias, Bartholomew, 435
Diaz, Porfirio, 727–728
Dickson, Marcus, 6
Dictators
  New Zealand, 423
  Portugal, 591
Diefthintis (director), 789
Die Zeit (German newspaper), 157, 158
Din-e-Illahi, 979
Dingaan, 436
Diplomatic leadership
  Greece, 793
  Ireland, 389
  United States, *518, 521, 523*
Directive leadership, in Mexico, 736, 737, 758
Dirigente (leader), 645
Disabled persons

  in Colombia, 700–701
  Swedish attitudes toward, 45–46
Discrimination. *See* Racism
Diutischin liute (German people), 149
Diversity, U.S. society and, 480
Divorce
  Argentina, 669
  Australia, 307–308
Doctrine of the mean, 879
"Dole bludgers," 316
Dominion (New Zealand newspaper), 414
Dong Zhongsu, 878
Dorfman, Peter W., 6
Douglas, Roger, 401
Downsizing, in the United States, 506–507
Dowry, 990
Drake, Sir Francis, 342
DTZ Zadelfhoff, 234
Dueño/owner icon, 676, 677
Dufour, Henri, 279
Dunant, Henri, 280
Dünya (Turkish newspaper), 839
Durchwurstein (muddling through), 144
Dutch East India Company, 435
Dynamism, English leadership and, 342, 347

E

Eanes, António Ramalho, 587, 608
Eastern Europe cluster, 765
  leadership profiles, *1062–1063*
East Germany
  anxiety and, 166
  creation of, 153
  cultural change and, 1075
  East *vs.* West polarization and, 201
  economic system, 199
  GLOBE Research Project
    media analysis, 157, 202
    questionnaire sample size and characteris-
      tics, 155–157
  issues of sampling, 1031, 1032
  leadership
    charismatic, 177
    Communist Party membership and, 1071
    comparative analysis of leadership
      scores, 213
    comparative studies in, 170
    factor analysis results, 204–212
    first-order dimension, 173–175
    the Humble Collaborator, 177–178
    individualistic, 178

T - #0171 - 230425 - C0 - 254/178/55 - PB - 9780367866662 - Gloss Lamination